-5

PSYCHOLOGY

SECOND EDITION

Carole Wade

COLLEGE OF MARIN

Carol Tavris

HarperCollinsPublishers

A list of text, table, and illustration credits appears as a ''Credits'' section at the back of this book and is hereby made part of this copyright page.

Sponsoring Editor/Laura Pearson
Development Editor/Marian Wassner
Project Editor/Donna DeBenedictis
Art Direction/Teresa Delgado
Text Design/Delgado Design
Cover Coordinator/Mary Archondes
Cover Design/Saul Bass
Photo Research/Inge King
Production Manager/Jeanie Berke
Production Assistant/Beth Maglione

Psychology, Second Edition

Copyright © 1990 by HarperCollins*Publishers* Inc.

Library of Congress Cataloging-in-Publication Data
Wade, Carole.
    Psychology / Carole Wade, Carol Tavris.—2nd ed.
      p.   cm.
    Includes bibliographical references.
    ISBN 0-06-046869-6
    1. Psychology.   I. Tavris, Carol.   II. Title.
BF121.W27   1989
150—dc20   89-39148
                                                         CIP

91 92 9 8 7 6 5 4

Contents at a Glance

CONTENTS

CHAPTER *2*

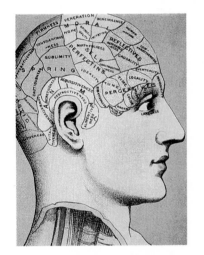

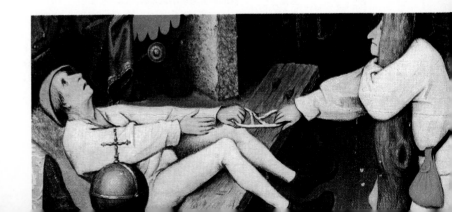

PART TWO
THE BIOLOGICAL BASES OF BEHAVIOR 77

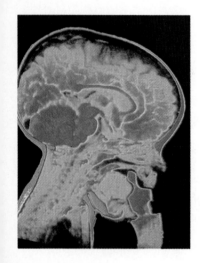

CHAPTER **5**

SENSATION AND PERCEPTION 155

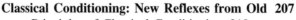

PART THREE
LEARNING, THINKING, AND FEELING 203

CHAPTER 8

COGNITION II: THOUGHT AND LANGUAGE 281

CHAPTER 9

EMOTION 312

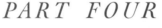

PART FOUR
DEVELOPMENT OF THE INDIVIDUAL 383

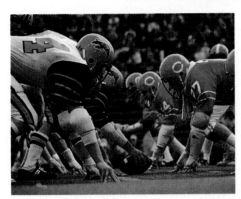

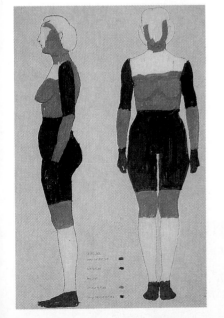

CHAPTER *12*

MEASURING AND EXPLAINING HUMAN DIVERSITY 419

PART FIVE
HEALTH AND DISORDER 535

CHAPTER *17*

PART SIX
SOCIAL INTERACTIONS 649

CHAPTER *18*

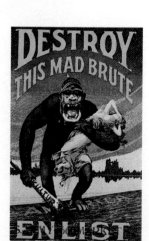

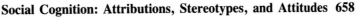

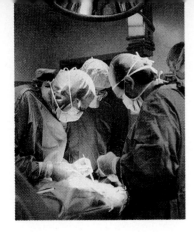

EPILOGUE:

TAKING PSYCHOLOGY WITH YOU 692

APPENDIX:

STATISTICAL METHODS

To the Instructor

It's an exciting but difficult time to be a psychologist. The field is exploding in all directions at once; the controversy between research and clinical practice is growing; and applications of psychological research are affecting virtually all aspects of our lives. Yet we are also witnessing the rise of cults, beliefs, and philosophies that have a quasi-scientific veneer and that pose a serious challenge to scientific psychology. It is getting harder and harder for the public to distinguish reputable psychological work from what R. D. Rosen (1977) calls "psychobabble."

So it is an exciting but difficult time to teach an "introduction" to psychology. What, exactly, should be introduced? Certainly not every nook and cranny of this complex field, or students would be exhausted by the third week. Indeed, students have often told us that psychology seems to them an accumulation of facts—fascinating facts, perhaps, but ones that add up only to a collection of bits and pieces. They have a point. If anything, the "bits-and-piecesness" of contemporary psychology, in the continuing absence of a unifying paradigm, has become more of a problem.

We wrote this book because we felt we could offer students something more than discrete findings and theories. Psychology is more than a body of knowledge; it's a way of approaching and analyzing the world. Indeed, it's a way of asking questions about everything from the smallest curiosities to the largest matters of life and death. Our science is one of the few to combine skepticism and rationality with compassion and caring. We set out to write a book that would not only convey the content of psychology, but would also get students to think about and use what they had learned. We wanted to show them what it is like to *think* like a psychologist.

CRITICAL AND CREATIVE THINKING

Our approach is based on critical thinking, an important movement in educational reform. Its aim is to move students beyond the common view that knowledge is something to be ingested, digested, and regurgitated. By the time they finish this book, readers should understand that to "do" psychology, one must be imbued, paradoxically, with both intellectual cautiousness and an open mind. They should appreciate that knowledge is advanced when people resist leaping to conclusions on the basis of personal experience alone (so tempting in psychological matters!), when they apply rigorous standards of evidence, and when they listen to other views.

In this edition, we have clarified what we mean by critical thinking and sharpened our approach to using it. For instance, we realized it was important to emphasize that by *critical thinking* we do not simply mean *negative thinking*. Many students use the word "critical" in a negative, debunking sense (as in "she was critical of that movie"). Sometimes, of course, thinking critically does require skepticism and debunking. But it also involves the ability to generate ideas, think of their implications, be creative with explanations, and ask imaginative questions. It means breaking out of preconceived categories. It means being open-minded (although not so open-minded, as the philosopher Jacob Needleman observes in Chapter 1, "that your brains fall out"). All these skills are *positive* aspects of critical thinking that we emphasize. We have added, in the first chapter, a full discussion of critical and creative thinking—what it is (and isn't), the guidelines for achieving it, and the reasons it is particularly relevant to the study of psychology (see pages 31–36). A pictorial essay (on pages 40–41) further illustrates the guidelines discussed.

In response to suggestions from users of the first edition, who wanted us to indicate to students where critical thinking occurs in the text, we have included some "signposts." These signposts, found in color type in the margins, raise questions drawn from the accompanying discussion. We wish to emphasize that they are *not*, in themselves, illustrations of critical thinking, although they raise, we hope, good questions. Rather, they point to some (though by no means all) of the critical thinking analyses or issues in the text. They are meant to invite the reader into the discussion.

Other aspects of our approach to critical and creative thinking include:

- A special feature in each chapter entitled **Think About It,** which presents psychological, social, or philosophical issues that have no easy answers. These essays raise provocative questions and invite the student to ponder them. (Some instructors require students to choose one or more of these for term papers.) Do our senses limit our knowledge of "reality"? Where in the brain does the "self" reside? What is "sexuality"? Do animals think? Are wars inevitable?
- The use of occasional *photographic* "think about its." Our photo selections are designed not only to illustrate points in the text, but to highlight contro-

versies and raise questions. Do Americans really like children? Why does the stress of an administrator get more attention than the stress of a factory worker? What, exactly, does "personality" consist of, and is it even consistent? Which psychological disorders, if any, should be cause for "diminished responsibility" for one's actions?

- The inclusion of methods—how the evidence was gathered and evaluated—in discussions of findings throughout the text. When we report a finding, we also ask: How should this research be evaluated? Was the study designed well? What is the finding's larger significance? (For example, a study finds that "men are more than twice as likely as women to fear attachment." Interesting—until we consider that the numbers in question are 18 percent of the men to 8 percent of the women.) Likewise, we ask: Does controlled research really find that "bonding" is essential to infant development? What do the data really show about the nature-nurture debate in intelligence and personality?

Ultimately, critical and creative thinking is a matter of style, integral to the presentation of material. We believe it is important to weave critical thinking into the text itself, instead of simply providing "thought questions" or exercises. We apply it to concepts that many students approach uncritically, such as astrology, "premenstrual syndrome," and the "instinctive" nature of love and desire. But we also apply it to some assumptions that *psychologists* have accepted unquestioningly, including stages in adult development, the decisive importance of childhood to later life, and the hierarchical nature of motives. By probing beneath assumptions and presenting the most recent evidence available, we hope to convey the excitement and challenge of psychological research and theory.

APPLICATIONS: TAKING PSYCHOLOGY WITH YOU

The principles and findings of psychology can be applied to individuals and to groups, institutions, and society as a whole. We cover such applications not only in the main body of the text but also in a discussion at the end of each chapter called **Taking Psychology with You.** Drawing on research reported in the chapter, the section tackles topics of practical concern, such as coping with the stresses of life, helping a friend who is suicidal, managing anger, rearing children, improving memory (and appreciating forgetfulness!), and resisting friendly and not-so-friendly tactics of persuasion. Some of the discussions are about "taking critical thinking with you," as in Chapter 11 (how not to fall victim to the Barnum Effect) and in Chapter 12 (how not to misinterpret the normal occurrence of astonishing coincidences).

The final "Taking Psychology with You" feature is the **Epilogue,** which represents a unique effort to show

readers that the vast number of seemingly disparate studies and points of view they have just read about *are* related. The epilogue contains two real-life problems that most students can be expected to encounter (if they haven't already): the end of a love relationship and difficulties at work. For each situation, we show how many of the topics *throughout* the book can be applied to understanding and coping with it; readers learn that solving a real problem requires more than finding the "right" study from the "right" school of psychology. Many instructors have told us that they find this epilogue a useful way to help students integrate some of the diverse approaches of contemporary psychology. Asking students to come up with research findings that might apply to other "problems in living" makes for a good term-paper assignment as well.

INVOLVING THE STUDENT

One of the sturdiest findings about learning is that it requires the active encoding of material. Three features in particular encourage students' active involvement and provide pedagogical support:

- A separate handbook called *Learning to Think Critically: A Handbook to Accompany* **Psychology, Second Edition.** This handbook, free to all students whose instructors order it, illustrates how critical and creative thinking skills and psychological research can be applied to beliefs about love, intimacy, attraction, and commitment. Some instructors assign this booklet to teach critical thinking skills, either at the beginning of the course or along with Chapter 8, on thought and problem solving. Others assign it in tandem with Chapter 18, on social psychology, focusing on the research content of the handbook.
- **Quick Quizzes** are periodic self-tests that encourage students to check their own progress, and to go back and review if necessary. Mindful of the common tendency to skip quizzes or to peek at the answers, we have used various formats and have included entertaining examples in order to motivate students to test themselves. These quizzes do more than just test for memorization of definitions; they tell students whether they comprehend the issues. We think they will be useful to students of all abilities.
- A **running glossary** defines boldfaced technical terms on the pages where they occur (or on the facing page) for handy reference and study. All entries can also be found in a cumulative glossary at the back of the book.

Other special features include chapter outlines, lists of key words, and chapter summaries in numbered paragraph form.

ON INTEGRATING GENDER AND CULTURE INTO MAINSTREAM PSYCHOLOGY

We used to joke with other instructors that for too long psychology was the study of the white male sophomore . . . rat. There was a pervasive feeling throughout our discipline that "hard, scientific" psychology did not trouble itself with "soft, unscientific" matters such as gender, age, and culture. If a Japanese woman or a black American man or a white Canadian woman did not respond to an experiment the way a typical young white male American sophomore did, then they were ignored.

Two important developments have forced psychology to recognize that universal principles of behavior cannot always be deduced from a narrow sample of humanity. One is the growing diversity of college students themselves, many of whom now include older adults (who are often amused at the "findings" based on 19-year-olds) and people of every ethnicity (who are often baffled by "findings" based solely on Anglo-Americans). A second comes from the increasing number of scientific studies showing that culture is not merely a superficial gloss on human behavior, but a profound influence that affects virtually all aspects of human behavior and possibly human physiology as well. That is why the Western bias in psychology has undermined the *scientific* generality of its research. Across the country, "curriculum integration" projects are being designed to help instructors incorporate the results of this wave of research into their courses.

Research in gender and culture has not only provided specific findings on gender or cultural differences (and, less often, similarities). It has also provided *new perspectives* and *new questions* in traditional areas of inquiry. For example, why have most chapters on "motivation" focused mainly on the traditional male domain of *achievement* motivation? Research in gender studies has highlighted the importance of other key motives for everyone—affiliation, love, curiosity, understanding, intrinsic satisfactions. Similarly, most Western approaches to stress emphasize "fighting back" and "being in control." Research on Eastern approaches, however, forces us to reconsider these notions that are so basic to our concept of mental health.

We believe that the relevant studies and the larger perspectives on gender and culture should be raised *where they occur in the text,* not relegated to a separate chapter. Are there sex differences in the brain? That controversial issue belongs in the brain chapter. Do women and men differ in the meanings and motives they attach to love and sex? This topic belongs in the motivation chapter. Do men and women express emotion differently? That question belongs in the emotion chapter.

Likewise, not all cultures regard the "self" or the "individual" as Westerners do or place the same priority on competition. What are the consequences for personality theories? Cultures differ in the display rules of emotion. What, if anything, does that tell us about the universality of emotional experience? People are supposed to have a biologically built-in need for "closure," especially for unfinished tasks. So how come the Hopi could leave their houses half-built and go on to other tasks? The answers to these and other questions illuminate our understanding of human behavior.

We wish to emphasize that we have not written an anthropology text or a women's studies book. We have written a psychology text: one that, we hope, will expand a student's vision and understanding of the many and varied influences on the human being; one that, we hope, acknowledges that a scientific psychology must be the study of all human beings.

WHAT'S NEW?

In addition to the sharpened focus on critical and creative thinking, this edition includes significant changes in content and appearance.

- **A Closer Look at . . ."** In recognition of the growing number of specialty areas in psychology, we have included, in certain chapters, a feature that focuses on the research of emerging subdisciplines, such as neuropsychology (Chapter 3), human factors (Chapter 5), industrial/organizational psychology (Chapter 10), gerontology (Chapter 14), psychoneuroimmunology (Chapter 15), and forensic psychology (Chapter 16).
- **Art and Design.** An expanded art and photo program provides exciting visual support to the text discussion. A brand-new design, in full four color, enlivens and clarifies the text.
- **Supplements.** A fully revised, enlarged, and improved program of supplements, including the Coast Videos and new interactive software, accompanies the text (see "Supplements" below).
- **Revised content and updated research throughout.** Some highlights are:

Chapter 1 (introduction) contains a new section on thinking critically and creatively about psychology; and elevates the *sociocultural* perspective to one of the five major levels of explanation that psychology considers.

Chapter 3 (brain and nervous system) contains an expanded discussion of neurotransmitters, with a new table on the known and suspected effects of the major ones; and a revised section on localization of function offers a resolution of the "localized versus distributed" debate that has raged in psychology for decades.

Chapter 4 (biological rhythms and states of consciousness) contains expanded and updated discussions of subconscious and nonconscious processing and of dream theories; new cross-cultural research on the effects of marijuana; and an expanded critical discussion of age- and past-life regression theories.

Chapter 8 (thought and language) contains new research on numerical abilities of animals; a new approach to measuring creativity; recent research on language learning in nonhuman primates; and new cross-cultural research on how language may influence the acquisition of mathematical skills.

Chapter 9 (emotion) reviews the latest work in this burgeoning new field, including an expanded discussion of new theories of "basic emotions," as measured in different ways; recent work on the physiology of emotions (especially brain and facial-expression studies); and promising new cognitive research on the origins of differences in emotional *range* and emotional *intensity*.

Chapter 12 (testing, individual differences) has been reorganized to make this technical and conceptually difficult topic easier to comprehend. We describe and critically discuss the most recent twin research on the heritability of personality and intelligence; review new research on the genetic basis of social inhibition—and how genes interact with environmental influences on temperament; and help students critically appraise claims that personality, intelligence, and talent are "all in the genes."

Chapter 13 (child development) includes new research on stages in the development of *empathy;* cross-cultural modifications, as well as psychological ones, of Piaget; and exciting new research showing that the great majority of children of alcoholics and abusers are not doomed to repeat their parents' problems.

Chapter 15 (health, stress, and coping) has been completely rewritten as a result of sweeping changes in the field. We now include more on health habits and practices; critically review and reject popular ideas that have not held up (e.g., Type A and hardiness); report new research findings that contradict old wisdom (e.g., the benefits of illusion); and, most important, analyze the complex relationship between personality and disease.

Chapter 16 (abnormal) reports the controversial research suggesting that clinical psychologists are no better than nonprofessionals at predicting abnormal behavior (such as "dangerousness"); evaluates the "politics of diagnosis" in the new *DSM-III-R* categories; and reviews the latest work on possible genetic markers in schizophrenia and manic depression.

Chapter 17 (psychotherapy) contains an expanded section on family therapy and the new diagnostic and descriptive tool of the genogram; adds "Cuento [folktale] therapy" to illustrate a cross-cultural therapeutic method; and has an entirely new section on rehabilitation psychology and community psychology.

SUPPLEMENTS PACKAGE

Psychology, Second Edition, is supported by a new and complete teaching and learning package that includes the following supplements.

PRINT SUPPLEMENTS AND TRANSPARENCIES

Instructor's Resource Manual.   Written by Sarah Rundle, formerly of the University of California, Dominguez Hills, this manual contains a wealth of teaching aids for each chapter: learning objectives, activities, lecture modules, and writing and thinking exercises, all keyed to chapter outlines. In addition, the manual includes general teaching strategies, guided lab experiments, student worksheets, and "Teacher-to-Teacher," a section that highlights typical problem areas for students, offers suggestions for teaching those areas, and includes an integrated class plan incorporating many of the text's supplements. A special media section, prepared by Eva Conrad of San Bernardino Valley College, features original essays, abstracts, and an evaluative film guide.

Student Resource Manual.   Written by Judith Sugar of Colorado State University, Frank Calabrese of the Community College of Philadelphia, and Jeanette Cleveland and Kevin Murphy of Colorado State University, this highly acclaimed manual has been extensively updated to reflect the new coverage in the second edition. It includes learning objectives, annotated chapter outlines, a glossary of key terms, critical thinking questions corresponding to concepts in the text, and self-tests with answers.

Test Bank.   Three thousand test items are featured in this all-new, class-tested supplement written by Grace Galliano of Kennesaw State College. Reviewed by content and testing experts, it offers questions that test conceptual knowledge and are referenced by learning objectives, cognitive type, and difficulty level. Also new to this edition, "scenario" questions tell stories and then ask students to respond to questions by synthesizing concepts from the text. A set of 25 preselected items from each chapter is also provided for use as review quiz.

Transparencies.   Two sets are available to provide visual support for classroom lectures and discussion: a set of 102 full-color acetates accompanied by a *User's Guide;* and a new set of 25 acetates tied directly to the art program in the second edition. This new set is also available as full-color slides.

SOFTWARE SUPPLEMENTS

Harper Test.   The *Test Bank* is available on a computerized test-generation system that allows professors to create fully customized tests. It can be obtained in Apple, Macintosh, and IBM versions.

Instructor's Resource Manual Diskette.   This computerized version of the *Instructor's Resource Manual* runs on any compatible IBM word-processor program.

START.   Available through CONDUIT, this interactive program takes students through experiments in reaction time, memory, and learning. Apple and IBM versions are available.

THE BRAIN.   Developed by James Witherspoon, this program simulates physiological experiments demonstrating such sensory and motor functions as how the brain responds electrically to visual images and sound, and how blood flow in the brain changes with movement. It is available for IBM computers.

JOURNEY. You can take students through a concept-building tour of the psychology experiment, the nervous system, learning, development, and psychological assessment with this new program developed by Intentional Educations. Each module is self-contained and comes complete with step-by-step pedagogy. Students may randomly access any of the program's functions: tutorial, simulation, experiment, review sections, and dictionary. This program is available for IBM and Macintosh users.

MEDIA SUPPLEMENTS

Coast Videos. The award-winning production team at Coast Telecourses has developed a unique set of programs that uses interviews with experts, experiments, and dramatizations to bring major topics and new controversies in psychology to life. An accompanying *Faculty Guide* describes each program and offers suggestions for using the videos in the classroom.

Video Briefs. A unique collection of edited video modules, each 5–10 minutes in length, has been excerpted from the Coast Video series to complement the text. Available on two ½-inch videocassettes and accompanied by a *Faculty Guide,* these "briefs" provide instructors with provocative audiovisual lecture launchers.

"The Mind." This highly acclaimed seven-part PBS series was produced as a counterpart to "The Brain" series. Keyed directly to the main text, the programs are fully described in the *Instructor's Resource Manual.*

Film and Video Rentals. Indiana University's psychology archives include over 350 films and videos that are available for free five-day rentals.

THE INTEGRATOR

You'll learn how to integrate all of these supplements with *The Integrator,* a carefully developed cross-referencing guide. Providing a complete index of all the software, media, and print materials, this guide offers teaching techniques for a multimedia presentation of every chapter of *Psychology,* Second Edition.

ACKNOWLEDGMENTS

Like any other cooperative effort, writing a textbook requires a support team. The following reviewers and consultants made many valuable suggestions during the development of the first and second editions of *Psychology,* and we are grateful for their contributions.

Benton E. Allen
Mt. San Antonio College
Susan M. Andersen
University of California, Santa Barbara
Lynn R. Anderson
Wayne State University
Emir Andrews
Memorial University of Newfoundland

Patricia Barker
Schenectady County Community College
Ronald K. Barrett
Loyola Marymount University
Allan Basbaum
University of California, San Francisco
Bill E. Beckwith
University of North Dakota
David F. Berger
SUNY at Cortland
Michael Bergmire
Jefferson College
Philip J. Bersh
Temple University
Laura L. Bowman
Kent State University
John R. Braun
University of Bridgeport
Sharon S. Brehm
University of Kansas
Robert C. Brown, Jr.
Georgia State University
Sylvester Briggs
Kent State University
Peter R. Burzynski
Vincennes University
Jean Caplan
Concordia University
Bernardo J. Carducci
Indiana University Southeast
Paul Chance
Contributing Editor, Psychology Today
Samuel Clement
Marianopolis College
Eva Conrad
San Bernardino Valley College
Richard L. Cook
University of Colorado
Wendi Cross
Ohio University
Robert M. Davis
Purdue University School of Science, IUPUI
Michael William Decker
University of California, Irvine
Geri Anne Dino
Frostburg State University
Ronald Finke
SUNY at Stony Brook
John H. Flowers
University of Nebraska–Lincoln
William F. Ford
Bucks County Community College
Donald G. Forgays
University of Vermont
Mary Gauvain
Oregon State University

Margaret Gittis
Youngstown State University

Carlos Goldberg
Indiana University–Purdue University at Indianapolis

Carol Grams
Orange Coast College

Richard A. Griggs
University of Florida

Neil Helgeson
The University of Texas at San Antonio

John E. Hesson
Metropolitan State College

John P. Hostetler
Albion College

John Hunsley
University of Ottawa

Timothy P. Johnston
University of North Carolina at Greensboro

Chadwick Karr
Portland State University

Yoshito Kawahara
San Diego Mesa College

Geoffrey Keppel
University of California, Berkeley

Harold O. Kiess
Framingham State College

Gary King
Rose State College

Jack Kirschenbaum
Fullerton College

Donald Kline
University of Calgary

Stephen M. Kosslyn
Harvard University

George S. Larimer
West Liberty State College

S. David Leonard
University of Georgia

Herbert Leff
University of Vermont

R. Martin Lobdell
Pierce College

Nina Lott
National University

Marc Marschark
University of North Carolina at Greensboro

Monique Martin
Champlain Regional College

Debra Moehle McCallum
University of Alabama at Birmingham

D. F. McCoy
University of Kentucky

C. Sue McCullough
Texas Woman's University

Elizabeth McDonel
University of Alabama

Susanne Wicks McKenzie
Dawson College

Mark B. McKinley
Lorain County Community College

Ronald K. McLaughlin
Juniata College

Frances K. McSweeney
Washington State University

Mary Jo Meadow
Mankato State University

Laura J. Metallo
Five Towns College

Maribel Montgomery
Linn-Benton Community College

Douglas G. Mook
University of Virginia

T. Mark Morey
SUNY College at Oswego

James S. Nairne
University of Texas at Arlington

Douglas Navarick
California State University, Fullerton

Robert A. Neimeyer
Memphis State University

Nora Newcombe
Temple University

David Page
Nazareth College

M. Carr Payne, Jr.
Georgia Institute of Technology

Dan G. Perkins
Richland College

Gregory Pezzetti
Rancho Santiago Community College

Wayne Poniewaz
University of Arkansas, Monticello

Paula M. Popovich
Ohio University

Reginald L. Razzi
Upsala College

Joe Rubinstein
Purdue University

H. R. Schiffman
Rutgers University

David A. Schroeder
University of Arkansas

Marvin Schwartz
University of Cincinnati

Shelley Schwartz
Vanier College

Joyce Segreto
Youngstown State University

Kimron Shapiro
University of Calgary

Phillip Shaver
SUNY at Buffalo

Susan A. Shodahl
San Bernardino Valley College
Art Skibbe
Appalachian State University
William P. Smotherman
SUNY at Binghamton
Samuel Snyder
North Carolina State University
A. Stirling
John Abbott College
Milton E. Strauss
Johns Hopkins University
Judith Sugar
Colorado State University
Shelley E. Taylor
University of California, Los Angeles
Barbara Turpin
Southwest Missouri State University
Ronald J. Venhorst
Kean College of New Jersey
Wayne A. Viney
Colorado State University
Benjamin Wallace
Cleveland State University
Charles R. Walsmith
Bellevue Community College
Thomas J. Weatherly
DeKalb College–Central Campus
Gary L. Wells
University of Alberta
Warner Wilson
Wright State University

Our editorial and production team at Harper & Row was superb, and we are enormously grateful to these talented people for their hard work, commitment to quality, and patience. In particular, we thank Marian Wassner for her meticulous editing and unflagging energy and support; Laura Pearson, for brilliantly coordinating all the elements of the book with its ancillaries; Anne Harvey, for expertly organizing and implementing the marketing plan; Steve Eisen, for his excellent work commissioning and supervising the supplementary materials; and Jinny Joyner, for careful manuscript editing. Donna DeBenedictis, our project editor, has now survived two editions of this book, inspiring us to meet deadlines with such charm and humor that we always felt appreciated rather than pressured. Under Teresa Delgado's direction, the book now has a stunning new design that weaves the many elements together with clarity and elegance. Inge King, our photo researcher, assembled a magnificent assortment of pictures for the book, never complaining when we kept saying, "Couldn't you find one like this . . .?" And, with a watchful eye on everything, Editor in Chief Judith Rothman kept our spirits up whenever they flagged, thanks to her confidence in us and in this book. We also thank two student researchers, Philippe Ballaire and Kerry Sandler, for their assistance.

Words fail us in thanking Saul Bass for the cover design. His stunning illustration, which builds on and expands the image of the first edition, conveys the creativity and critical thinking that represent art and psychology at their best. Our appreciation also goes to Art Goodman and the rest of the fine staff at Saul Bass/Herb Yager and Associates.

Most of all, we thank Howard Williams and Ronan O'Casey, who sustain us with love, humor, and strong coffee.

We have enjoyed writing this book, and we hope you will enjoy reading and using it. Your questions, comments, and reactions on the first edition allowed us to make many improvements this time around. Please let us hear from you.

Carole Wade
Carol Tavris

To the Student

If you are reading this introduction, you are starting your introductory psychology course on the right foot. It is always a good idea to get a general picture of what you are about to read before charging forward, just as it is best to find out what California looks like before moving there from Cleveland or Kennebunkport.

Our goal in writing this book is to guide you to *think critically* and imaginatively about what you read, and to *apply* what you learn to your own life and the real world. We ourselves have never gotten over our initial excitement about psychology, and we have done everything we can think of to make the field as absorbing for you as it is for us. However, what you bring to this book is as important as what we have written. This text will remain only a collection of pages with ink on them unless you choose to interact with its content. The more actively you are involved in your own learning, the more successful the book and your course will be, and the more enjoyable, too.

In our years of teaching, we have found that certain study strategies can vastly improve learning, and so we offer the following suggestions. Do not read the text in the same way as you might a novel, taking in large chunks at a sitting. To get the most from your studying, we recommend that you read only a part of each chapter at a time. And instead of simply reading silently, try to *restate* what you have read in your own words at the end of each major section. Some people find it helpful to write down main points on a piece of paper or on index cards. Others prefer to recite main points aloud to someone else or to themselves (which may require some privacy!). Do not count on getting by with just one reading of a chapter. Most people need to go through the material at least twice, and then review the main points several times before an exam.

Individuals often develop their own unique strategies for studying, and we don't want to discourage you from doing so. Whatever approach you use, though, it should involve an active response to the material. Here are some hints for enhancing your learning:

- A good first step is to read the chapter title and outline to get an idea of what's in store. Browse through the chapter, looking at the pictures and reading the headings.
- Every chapter contains several *Quick Quizzes* that permit you to test your understanding and retention of what you have just read and your ability to *apply* the material to examples. (Do not let the word "quiz" give you a sinking feeling. These quizzes are for your practical use and, we hope, for your enjoyment.) When you can't answer a ques-

tion, do not go on to the next section; pause right then and there, review what you've read, and then try again.
- Every important new term is printed in **boldface** and is defined in the margin of the page on which it appears or on the facing page. The marginal glossary permits you to find all key terms and concepts easily, and will help you when you study for an exam. A full glossary also appears at the end of the book.
- "Critical thinking signposts," found in color type in the margins, indicate where critical thinking analyses or issues appear in the text.
- When you have finished a chapter, read the summary. Some students tell us they find it useful to write down their own summary first, then compare it with the book's. Reading over the summary right before a test can also be helpful.
- Use the *Key Words* list at the end of each chapter as a checklist. Try to define and discuss each term in the list to see how well you understand and remember it. If you need to review a term, a page number is given to tell you where it is first mentioned in the chapter.

There are some other features of this book that you should know about. In each chapter, a *Think About It* box poses a provocative question that has no easy answer. We hope you will have as much fun pondering these questions as we did writing about them. Another box, called *A Closer Look at . . .*, examines various research specialties within psychology in depth. At the end of each chapter, a feature called *Taking Psychology with You* draws on research to suggest ways you can apply what you have learned to everyday problems and concerns, such as living with stress, coping with life's transitions, and getting a better night's sleep, and to more serious ones, such as coping with life's "crises" or helping a suicidal friend.

You will notice that discussions of studies and theories are followed by one or more *citations* in parentheses. A citation tells the reader where the original research report or theoretical work was published. It consists of the author's name and the date of publication (for example, [Smith, 1984]). The full reference, with the name of the article or book and other information, can be found in a *bibliography* at the end of the book. Students often find citations useful, especially for locating material for term projects and reports.

At the back of the book you will also find an *author index* and a *subject index*. The author index lists the name of every author cited in the book and the pages where the person's work is discussed. If you want to review a study by someone named Snodgrass, but you can't recall where it was covered, look under ''Snodgrass'' in the author index. The subject index provides a listing of all the major topics mentioned in the book. If you want to review material on, say, depression, you can look up ''depression'' in the subject index.

Most psychology books stop abruptly with the last chapter, leaving the reader with the impression that early lessons have little to do with later ones. At the end of this book, you will find an *Epilogue* that shows you how you can integrate and use the findings and theories you have read about to understand events, make wise decisions, and cope with life's inevitable challenges and changes. We consider the epilogue to be important because it suggests how you can carry psychology out of your classroom and into the ''real world.''

We also recommend an important supplement that is available to help you study and expand upon the material in this book. The *Student Resource Manual* contains review material, self-tests, and exercises that show you how to apply the concepts in the book.

We have done our utmost to convey our own enthusiasm about psychology, but in the end, it is your efforts as much as ours that will determine whether you find psychology to be exciting or boring, and whether the field will matter in your own life. We welcome your ideas and reactions so that we will know what works for you and what doesn't. In the meantime, welcome to psychology!

Carole Wade
Carol Tavris

PSYCHOLOGY

P A R T

O N E

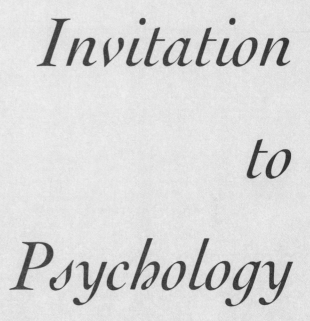

An
Invitation
to
Psychology

CHAPTER 1

What Is Psychology?

The purpose of psychology is to give us a completely different idea of the things we know best.

PAUL VALÉRY

Anne Frank (1929–1945)

*I*n 1945, a 15-year-old Jewish girl named Anne Frank died of typhus at Bergen-Belsen, a notorious Nazi death camp. She had spent the previous two years with her parents, her sister, and four others in a cramped apartment in Amsterdam, hiding from German troops occupying Holland. Unable to go outside, the group depended entirely on Christian friends for food and other necessities. Anne, who was a gifted writer and astute observer, recorded in her diary the fears, frustrations, and inevitable clashes of people forced to live 24 hours a day in close proximity. Yet she never despaired or lost her sense of wonder at life's joys. With humor and grace, she described the pleasure of family celebrations, the thrill of first love, the excitement of growing up. Shortly before the Gestapo discovered the hideout, Anne wrote, "It's really a wonder that I haven't dropped all my ideals, because they seem so absurd and impossible to carry out. Yet I keep them, because in spite of everything I still believe that people are really good at heart. I simply can't build up my hopes on a foundation consisting of confusion, misery, and death."

Many years later, and thousands of miles away, Charles "Tex" Watson grew up, apparently uneventfully, in a small American town. A handsome boy, Charles attended church, earned high grades, and competed successfully in football, basketball, and track. During his junior year in high school his fellow students named him the outstanding member of his class. Then, a few years after leaving home for college, Watson fell in with the Charles Manson cult. Manson was a charismatic figure who convinced his followers that he was divinely chosen to lead them and demanded their blind obedience. In 1969, on Manson's orders, the cult savagely slaughtered seven innocent people in Los Angeles. Tex Watson, the young man who had earlier seemed so full of promise, cold-bloodedly carved his initials on the chest of one of the victims.

Why did Anne Frank, living in the constant shadow of death, retain her love of humanity? Why did Tex Watson, with everything to live for, turn to brutal acts of violence? How can we explain why some people are overwhelmed by petty problems, while others, faced with real difficulties, remain mentally healthy? What principles can help us understand why some human beings are confident players in the game of life, while others angrily reject its rules?

If you have ever asked yourself such questions, welcome to the world of psychology. You are about to explore a discipline that studies human behavior, with all its complexities and contradictions. Psychologists take as their subject the entire spectrum of brave and cowardly, wise and silly, intelligent and stupid, beautiful and brutish things that human beings do. Their aim: to examine and explain how human beings—and animals, too—learn, remember, solve problems, perceive, feel, and interact with others.

Many people, when they hear the word *psychology*, think of mental disorder and abnormal behavior. But psychologists do not confine their attention to extremes of behavior. They are just as likely to focus on commonplace experiences—experiences as universal and ordinary as rearing children, remembering a shopping list, daydreaming, and even gossiping. Most of us, after all, are neither saints nor sinners but a curious combination of both positive and negative qualities. Psychology, in short, is not only about martyrs and murderers; it is also about *you*.

A Matter of Definition

Psychology, as one psychologist has noted, has a way of outgrowing its formal definitions (Tyler, 1981). At the start of this century, most psychologists considered psychology to be the study of mental life, the mind, or consciousness. Within a few years, however, such definitions came under attack as vague and unscientific. As we shall see, between the 1920s and the 1950s many psychologists preferred to define their discipline as the study of behavior, because what people do—unlike what they think or feel—can be directly observed and measured. But this definition also came under attack. To those who still wanted to study thinking, dreaming, and all the other fascinating things that go on between people's ears, confining psychology to behavior made no more sense than confining literature to short stories or history to a description of military battles.

Today, most psychologists are willing to make room for both behavior and mind in the formal definition of psychology. In this book we, too, take a broad approach. We define **psychology** as *the scientific study of behavior and mental processes and how they are affected by an organism's physical state, mental state, and external environment.*

We realize that this brief definition of psychology is a little like defining a car as ''a vehicle for transporting people from one place to another.'' Such a definition is accurate as far as it goes, but it doesn't tell you what a car looks like, how cars differ from trains and buses, how Fords differ from Ferraris, or how a carburetor works. Similarly, to get a good, clear picture of what psychology is, you need to have more information—about its methods, its findings, its ways of interpreting data. Your course and the rest of this textbook will give you this information. We can begin with psychology's main goals.

Psychology's main goals

Psychology's goals are straightforward: to (1) *describe*, (2) *understand*, (3) *predict*, and (4) *control* or *modify* behavior and mental processes. There is a logical order to these goals: We must be able to describe behavior or mental processes accurately before we can understand them; understand them before we can make predictions with confidence; and make reliable predictions before we can attempt any changes.

In a sense, every human being is an amateur psychologist. Everyone wants to describe, understand, predict, and control behavior and mental processes, both their own and those of other people. Suppose your best friend has just nagged you for the 345th time about your tendency to subsist solely on pizza, potato chips, and soda pop. You might describe the behavior (''Frieda is always on my back about the way I eat''); attempt to understand its cause (''She's a health nut''); make a prediction about the future (''If I don't do something, I'm going to be nagged for the rest of my life''); and try to bring about a change (''I'll eat wheat germ and drink carrot juice once a week, and maybe that will buy me some peace'').

But if psychologists' goals are the same as everyone else's, what makes psychology a special discipline? The answer is that most people form opinions about human behavior and experience in a casual way. Most psychologists, in contrast,

psychology *The scientific study of behavior and mental processes and how they are affected by an organism's physical state, mental state, and external environment. The term is often represented by Ψ, the Greek letter psi (usually pronounced SY).*

follow rigorous and systematic procedures, to be described in the next chapter. They resist reaching for conclusions until they have evidence that can be checked and verified by others. They test their ideas. For example, do lie detector machines work? A nonpsychologist might base an opinion on conjecture, media accounts, or the claims of professional lie detector interpreters. Psychologists, however, have studied the question by comparing the results of lie detector tests taken by people already known by the researcher to be guilty or innocent of a crime. Lie detectors, it turns out, are highly inaccurate: Many innocent people fail the test, and many guilty people pass with flying colors (Kleinmuntz & Szucko, 1984).

There has sometimes been heated, even bitter debate among both psychologists and nonpsychologists about psychology's fourth goal, the control or modification of behavior and mental processes. When psychologists talk about control, they are thinking about improving education and child rearing, increasing work productivity, reducing crime, teaching social skills, helping people get rid of unwanted habits, and making other useful contributions to society. However, some people worry that governments or ambitious individuals will use the control techniques of psychology to set themselves up as Big Brother and manipulate the population.

Defenders of behavioral control point out that psychologists did not invent the idea. In fact, all of us control others, and in turn are controlled by others, each and every day. The last time you tried to attract someone's romantic interest, get a child to do something he or she didn't want to, or win an argument, *you* were attempting to exert behavioral control. Even people who consider themselves easygoing, live-and-let-live types control others, whether intentionally or not—by their actions, their responses, their facial expressions, and even their silences.

The findings of any science can be used in ways that help or hurt people, depending on the political decisions made by society. Psychologists who include control as a goal believe that psychological findings and principles, if used wisely, can contribute to human welfare and happiness. We exert control anyway, they say. We might as well know what we are doing.

QUICK ▪ QUIZ

Pause now to be sure you understand psychology's goals. Below are four statements that a psychologist might make. Name the goal that is met by each statement: description, understanding, prediction, or control.

1. Children begin to combine words at about age 2.
2. You can overcome your fear of snakes by gradually exposing yourself to pictures of snakes and eventually to real snakes.
3. The more meaningful a paragraph is, the better it will be remembered.
4. One reason men are slightly better on the average than women in mathematical problem solving is that men have taken more math courses.

Answers:

1. description   2. control   3. prediction   4. understanding

(*Note:* This self-test does not ask you to parrot back a memorized list of psychology's goals but rather to recognize an example of each. If you can do this, you have not only memorized, you have also understood. If you had difficulty, we recommend that you reread the preceding section.)

People sometimes think that psychology is ''only common sense.'' But common sense does not tell us why some people dress up in funny outfits, risk their lives to climb a rock, or, like singer Karen Carpenter, intentionally starve themselves to death.

Psychology and common sense

Psychology is a popular topic, and much of its vocabulary has crept into everyday speech. If someone says that Annette ''unconsciously'' hates her father or that Frank was ''conditioned'' to be moody by his unhappy childhood, that person is speaking the language of psychology.

Because many psychological terms are familiar, people sometimes think that psychology is nothing but common sense. The wisdom of the ages, they say, already tells us why people act as they do, so who needs data? And indeed, psychological research sometimes does confirm what many people already believe. Usually, however, the obviousness of a finding is only an illusion. Armed with the wisdom of hindsight, people maintain that they ''knew it all along,'' when in fact they did not.

Consider this demonstration: An instructor tells an introductory psychology class that ''according to research, couples whose careers require them to live apart are more likely to divorce than other couples.'' Most students will claim they are not surprised. After all, as everyone knows, ''out of sight, out of mind.'' Then, in another class, the instructor changes the report: ''According to research, couples whose careers require them to live apart are less likely to divorce than other couples.'' This ''finding'' is exactly the reverse of the first one, but again, most students will claim they expected it. After all, as everyone knows, ''absence makes the heart grow fonder.'' Both results, once they are ''known,'' seem intuitively obvious, whether true or not (Myers, 1980; Wood, 1984).

Familiar sayings can be used to support opposing results because ''common sense'' is actually full of contradictions. Moreover, common sense oversimplifies. A psychologist would want to determine the *conditions* under which absence does or does not make the heart grow fonder. For example, one important factor is the degree of emotional attachment felt by a couple before a separation; absence often intensifies a bright flame but extinguishes a weak one (S. Brehm, 1985).

Despite the illusion of obviousness, psychological research also yields frequent surprises. For example, according to popular belief, ''the child is father to the man'' (or mother to the woman, as the case may be); that is, early experiences determine how a person ''turns out,'' for better or for worse. But actually, although childhood certainly influences adulthood, a human being is never a finished product. As we will see in Chapters 13 and 14, many abilities, behaviors, and personality traits can change throughout life in response to new situations. Even children traumatized by abuse, neglect, or war can become happy, secure adults if their circumstances improve (Rathbun, DiVirgilio, & Waldfogel, 1958; Thomas & Chess, 1984).

This, of course, is good news. Sometimes, though, psychological research tells us things we may not *want* to know. For example, studies show that most people are willing to inflict physical harm on another person if they are told to do so by an authority figure. They are likely to suffer terrible emotional stress because of their actions, but they obey anyway (Milgram, 1963, 1974). This is a disturbing finding, with important political and moral implications. To take another example: Despite all the warnings against judging a book by its cover, most people do exactly that. Research shows that good-looking individuals are more likely than others to attract dates and get jobs. Attractive people even receive shorter jail sentences for crimes (Berscheid, 1985). This is sobering stuff for a society that considers itself to be democratic and egalitarian.

Psychology, then, may or may not confirm what you already believe about human nature. We want to emphasize, though, that findings do not *have* to be surprising to be scientifically important. Psychologists may enjoy announcing results that startle people, but they also seek to extend and deepen understanding of generally accepted facts. After all, long before the laws of gravity were discovered, people knew that an apple would fall to the ground if dropped from a tree. But it took Isaac Newton to discover the principles that explain why the apple falls and why it travels at a particular speed. Psychologists, too, seek to deepen understanding of an already familiar world.

*Sir Isaac Newton
(1642–1727)*

Psychology's relatives

Psychology belongs to a family of disciplines known as the social (or sometimes the behavioral) sciences. All of these sciences encourage us to analyze human problems objectively and to search for reliable patterns in behavior. All teach us to appreciate both the similarities and the differences among individuals and groups. But there are some important differences in emphasis.

Sociology is the study of groups and institutions within society, such as the family, religious institutions, the workplace, and social cliques. In general, sociologists pay less attention than psychologists do to personality and individual differ-

sociology *The study of the organization, development, and institutions of human society.*

ences. However, one specialty, social psychology, falls on the border between psychology and sociology; it focuses on how social groups and situations affect an individual's behavior.

Anthropology is concerned with the physical and cultural origins and development of the human race. Anthropologists typically focus on an entire society. Because it is difficult to study complex civilizations, they tend to concentrate on nontechnological societies. In contrast, most psychologists study behavior only in their own societies; they take specific behaviors or mental processes as the topic for analysis, rather than the entire society. However, some psychologists do investigate psychological issues cross-culturally, examining both differences and similarities among cultures.

Two other disciplines are often counted as social sciences. *Economics* is the study of how people produce, distribute, and consume goods and services. *Political science* is the study of political behavior and the establishment and conduct of government. Each of these two sciences bites off just a piece of the behavioral pie; in contrast, psychology, sociology, and anthropology search for general principles of human nature.

Of all the social sciences, psychology relies most heavily on laboratory experiments and observations. At the same time it is the most personal of the social sciences, focusing more than the others on the individual and his or her well-being. Psychology also makes more use of biological information than the other disciplines do (except for physical anthropology, which is concerned with the physical evolution of the species). In fact, some psychologists classify psychology with the biological and life sciences rather than the social sciences. **Biology** is concerned with the structure and functioning of all living things, from trees to turtles. When psychologists do biological research, however, it is only for the light their findings may shed on behavior or mental activities.

Psychology has one other sister science: **psychiatry**. Psychiatry is the medical specialty concerned with mental disorders, maladjustment, and abnormal behavior. Psychiatrists are medical doctors who have had three or four years of general medical training, a yearlong internship in general medicine, and a three-year residency in psychiatry. Not much psychology is taught in medical school, but during the residency period a psychiatrist learns to diagnose and treat psychiatric patients under the supervision of a more experienced physician. Some psychiatrists go on to do research on mental problems rather than work with patients.

As we will see later in this chapter, *clinical psychologists* also treat patients, but they have an advanced degree in psychology rather than a medical degree. Although there are many similarities in what psychiatrists and clinical psychologists do, there are also important differences. Psychiatrists are more likely than psychologists to treat severe mental disorders. They tend to be more medically oriented because they have been trained to diagnose physical problems that can cause mental ones. Most important, psychiatrists can write prescriptions and thus far psychologists cannot. This fact can affect their approach to emotional problems. For example, if a patient is depressed, a psychiatrist will often prescribe an antidepressant drug in addition to other kinds of treatment. A psychologist is more likely to take a purely psychological approach, such as helping the person to think differently about his or her problems or encouraging behavior that raises self-esteem.

Most of the findings in this book come from research done by psychologists, but we will occasionally refer to findings from other fields. When scholars and scientists cultivate only their own gardens, they may miss ways to improve their intellectual harvest. Now and then it is a good idea to glance over to see what is happening in someone else's yard.

anthropology *The study of the physical, social, and cultural origins and development of the human race.*
biology *The study of the evolution, structure, and functioning of living organisms.*
psychiatry *The medical study, diagnosis, treatment, and prevention of mental disorders.*

QUICK QUIZ

Do you have the distinctions among the various fields straight? Try to match each topic on the left with a discipline on the right.

1. How the structure of a bureaucracy affects job satisfaction ℯ
2. Sexual customs among the Turu tribe of Africa ℯ
3. The molecular structure of bodily cells ♭
4. Tranquilizers in the treatment of depression ∞
5. The effects of anxiety on IQ scores ♉

a. psychiatry
b. biology
c. anthropology
d. psychology
e. sociology

Answers:

1. e 2. c 3. b 4. a 5. d

Psychology's Past: From the Armchair to the Laboratory

Men and women have always speculated about what makes people tick. And most of the great thinkers of history, from Aristotle to Zoroaster, raised questions that today would be called psychological. Philosophers, physicians, historians, and political theorists all wanted to know how people take in information through their senses, use information to solve problems, become motivated to act in a particular way, and undergo emotional or mood changes. But unlike modern psychologists, most of these scholars did not rely heavily on **empirical** evidence—evidence gathered by careful observation, experimentation, and measurement. Their observations were often simply anecdotes or descriptions of individual cases.

This does not mean that the forerunners of modern psychology were always wrong. Often they were right. Hippocrates, the ancient Greek known as the father of modern medicine, observed patients with head injuries and inferred that the brain must be the ultimate source of "our pleasures, joys, laughter, and jests as well as our sorrows, pains, griefs, and tears." And so it is.

But without empirical methods, the forerunners of psychology also committed some terrible blunders. Even Aristotle, one of the first great philosophers to advocate the use of empirical methods, did not always use them himself. He thought that the brain could not possibly be responsible for sensation since the brain itself feels no pain, and he concluded that the brain was simply a radiator for cooling the blood. Aristotle was absolutely right about the brain being insensitive. But he was wrong about the brain being a radiator, and about many other things. (For example, he believed that small people have poor memories!)

A good example of how prescientific psychology could lead down a blind alley comes from the seventeenth century. At that time, when physics and physiology were still young sciences, scholars were puzzled about how living things could move about. The great French mathematician and philosopher René Descartes [Day-CART] suggested that animals could be thought of as machines. Descartes concocted a complicated theory of motion that compared muscles and tendons to engines and springs (Jaynes, 1973b). But he could not quite bring himself to call his own species a mere mechanical contraption. Human beings, he decided, possessed

empirical *Relying on or derived from observation, experimentation, or measurement.*

a mind, or immortal soul, which for him was the same thing. According to Descartes, this mind/soul squeezed the pineal [pie-NEE-ul] gland, a small blob of tissue in the center of the brain, this way and that. The pineal gland, the bridge between the soul and the body, in turn caused "animal spirits" (brain fluids) to flow down nerves, which Descartes believed were hollow tubes leading to muscles. When brain fluid entered a muscle it made it billow out like a balloon, resulting in the movement of a limb. Most of these ideas were based on pure speculation.

It is always tempting to ridicule the outmoded ideas of the past, as the psychologists of the future may do someday when they look back at *us*. We should keep in mind that even without scientific methods, the great thinkers of history often had insights and made observations that led to later advances. For example, although many of his theories were disproved, Descartes made important contributions to modern psychological thinking. He argued that stimulating a sense organ caused a signal of some sort to travel to the brain, which then *reflected* the signal back to the muscles. Thus was born the concept of a *reflex*. Descartes' description of reflexes was not quite correct, but his work led to the idea that the actions of living things are determined by *stimuli*, or physical changes in the environment. Three centuries later, this "stimulus-response" model came to dominate much of American psychology. More generally, by rejecting the then common belief that human behavior is governed by unknowable forces, by openly doubting conventional wisdom, and by searching for physical explanations of behavior, Descartes helped promote scientific attitudes.

Still, until the nineteenth century, psychology was pretty much a hit-or-miss sort of business. It was not recognized as a separate field of study, and there were few formal rules on how it was to be conducted.

The birth of modern psychology

People love to date the beginning of things. They celebrate not only their own birthdays but also those of their marriages, their countries, their clubs, their schools. Psychologists are no different. They have decided, by common agreement, that psychology as a formal science was born in the year 1879, with the establishment of the first official psychological laboratory in Leipzig, Germany.

The "father" of psychology, it is generally agreed, was a German named Wilhelm Wundt [VILL-helm Voont] (1832–1920). Wundt was trained in medicine and philosophy. Over some 60-odd years he turned out volume after volume on psychology, physiology, natural history, ethics, and logic. What most people remember about Wundt, however, is that he was the first person to announce (in 1873) that he intended to make psychology a science.

Actually, psychology had many fathers, and several mothers too. Various philosophers, especially in England, had paved the way by arguing that all knowledge must be based on sensory experience and not on speculation or pure reasoning. A number of individuals, in both Europe and North America, were already doing some psychological research and teaching some psychological topics when Wundt set up his laboratory. The Leipzig laboratory, however, was the first to be formally established and to have its results published in a scholarly journal. Although it started out as just a few rooms in an old building, it soon became the "place to go" for anyone who wanted to become a psychologist. Many of America's first psychologists got their training there (Mueller, 1979).

Researchers in Wundt's laboratory did not study the entire gamut of topics that today's psychologists do. Most concentrated on sensation, perception, reaction

This sketch by René Descartes shows his concept of reflex action. Energy from the fire (A) travels to a cavity in the brain (F) and is reflected back to a muscle that moves the foot (B). Descartes failed to distinguish pathways that carry signals to the brain from those that carry signals away, and he thought movement occurred when "animal spirits" flowed down hollow nerves. However, his basic notion, that behavior occurs in response to physical events in the environment, had a strong influence on later stimulus-response psychology.

Wilhelm Wundt (1832–1920), on the right, with co-workers.

times, imagery, and attention, and avoided learning, personality, and abnormal behavior (Boring, 1950). Wundt himself doubted that higher mental processes, such as abstract thinking, could be studied experimentally. He thought such topics were better understood by studying culture and natural history.

One of Wundt's favorite research methods was called trained introspection. **Introspection** involved the careful observation and analysis by specially trained people of their own mental experiences, under controlled conditions. Looking inward wasn't as easy as it sounds. Wundt's introspectors had to make 10,000 practice observations before they were allowed to participate in an actual study. Once trained, they might take as long as 20 minutes to report their inner experiences during a 1.5-second experiment (Lieberman, 1979). Wundt hoped trained introspection would yield reliable, verifiable results. Ironically, however, although Wundt made his mark on history by declaring psychology to be an objective science, introspection was soon abandoned by other psychologists because it wasn't objective enough.

Two early psychologies

Wundt's ideas were popularized in America in somewhat modified form by one of his students, E. B. Titchener. Titchener's brand of psychology became known as **structuralism**. Structuralists hoped to analyze sensations, images, and feelings into their most basic elements, much as a chemist might analyze water into hydrogen and oxygen atoms. For example, a person might listen to a metronome clicking and report exactly what he or she heard. Most people said they perceived a pattern (such as, CLICK click click CLICK click click), even though the clicks of a metronome are actually all the same. Or a person might be asked to break down all the different components of taste when biting into an orange (sweet, tart, wet, etc.).

But structuralism soon went the way of the dinosaur. After you have discovered the building blocks of a particular sensation or image and how they link up, then what? Years after structuralism's demise, Wolfgang Köhler (1959/1978) recalled how he and his colleagues had responded to it as students: "What had disturbed us was . . . the implication that human life, apparently so colorful and so intensely dynamic, is actually a frightful bore."

The structuralists' reliance on introspection also got them into hot water. To see why, imagine that you are a structuralist who wants to know what goes on in people's heads when they hear the word *triangle*. You round up some trained introspectors, say *triangle*, and ask them about their mental experience. Most of your respondents report a visual image of a form with three sides and three corners. Elbert, however, reports a flashing red form with equal angles, and Endora insists she saw a revolving colorless form with one angle larger than the other two. Which attributes of *triangle* would you conclude were basic? This is exactly what happened in structuralist studies; people disagreed. Some even claimed they could think about a triangle without forming any visual image at all (Boring, 1953).

Another early school of psychology was called **functionalism**. One of its leaders was William James (1842–1910), an American philosopher and psychologist who argued that searching for building blocks of experience was a waste of time, because the brain, and thus the mind, is constantly changing. Permanent and fixed ideas—of triangles or anything else—do not appear periodically before the "footlights of consciousness" and are as fictional as the jack of spades.

Where the structuralists simply asked *what* happens when an organism does something, the functionalists asked *how* and *why*. Their focus on the *function*, or

introspection *A form of self-observation in which individuals examine and report the contents of their own consciousness.*

structuralism *An early approach to psychology that stressed analysis of immediate experience into basic elements.*

functionalism *An early approach to psychology that stressed the function or purpose of behavior and consciousness.*

purpose, of behavior was inspired in part by the evolutionary theories of British naturalist Charles Darwin (1809–1882). According to Darwin, a biologist's job is not merely to describe, say, the brilliant plumage of the peacock or the drab markings of a lizard but also to figure out how these attributes enhance survival. (Do they help the animal attract a mate? Hide from its enemies?) Similarly, the functionalists wanted to know how various behaviors help a person (or animal) adapt to the environment. They looked for underlying causes and practical consequences of specific behaviors and mental strategies. Unlike the structuralists, they felt free to pick and choose among many methods and to broaden the field of psychology to include the study of children, animals, religious experiences, and what James called the "stream of consciousness."

As a distinct school of psychology, functionalism had a rather short life. It seems to have lacked the sort of precise theory or program of research that inspires passion and wins recruits. Also, it endorsed the study of consciousness just as that concept was about to fall out of favor. However, the functionalists' emphasis on the causes and consequences of behavior was to set the course of modern psychology.

William James (1842–1910)

QUICK ■ QUIZ

Check your memory of the preceding section by choosing the correct response from the pair in parentheses.

1. Psychology has been a science for about (2000/100) years.
2. The forerunners of modern psychology depended heavily on (casual observation/empirical methods).
3. Credit for founding modern psychology is generally given to (William James/Wilhelm Wundt).
4. Early psychologists who emphasized how behavior helps an organism adapt to its environment were known as (structuralists/functionalists).
5. Introspection was rejected as a research method because it was too (subjective/time consuming).

Answers:

1. 100 2. casual observation 3. Wilhelm Wundt 4. functionalists 5. subjective

Psychology's Present: Behavior, Mind, and Body

During the first half of this century, several psychological movements contended for a place in the sun, some briefly, others more successfully. Today, five major points of view predominate. We know that remembering a bunch of abstract theories can be as frustrating as trying to hold water in a sieve. We think you will remember these theories better if you can apply them to a concrete issue. The issue we have chosen, out of many possible ones, is violence. Violence takes many different forms: spouse and child abuse, street crime, political terrorism, mass murder, war. Armchair speculation has done little to eliminate it, but psychological theories and research can increase our understanding of why it occurs and point to some possible

The astonishing diversity of human behavior is vividly captured in Pieter Brueghel's depiction of Dutch proverbs, rhymes, and folk sayings. Psychologists approach the many facets of human behavior from five major perspectives.

solutions. We will use the issue of violence to illustrate the perspectives taken by the five major approaches in psychology.

The behavioral perspective

In 1913, a psychologist named John B. Watson (1878–1958) published a paper that rocked the still-young science of psychology. In "Psychology as the Behaviorist Views It," Watson argued that if psychology were ever to be as objective as physics, chemistry, and biology, it would have to give up its preoccupation with the mind and consciousness. Psychologists, he said, should throw out introspection as a method of research and reject terms like *mental state*, *mind*, or *emotion* in explanations of behavior. They should stick to what they can observe and measure directly: acts and events actually taking place in the environment. In short, they should give up mentalism for **behaviorism**. A behaviorist would not study pain by asking people what a pinprick felt like. A behaviorist would simply observe what happened if you stuck someone's finger with a pin—tears, withdrawal of the hand, or whatever.

Watson wrote approvingly of studies by the Russian physiologist Ivan Pavlov (1849–1936). Pavlov had shown that many kinds of automatic or involuntary be-

behaviorism *An approach to psychology that emphasizes the study of objectively observable behavior rather than inner mental experiences. Behaviorists stress the role of the environment as a determinant of human and animal behavior.*

havior, such as salivating at the sight of food, were simply learned responses to specific changes, or stimuli, in the environment. Like Pavlov, Watson believed that certain basic laws of learning could explain the behavior of both human beings and animals. Later, another behaviorist, B. F. Skinner (1904–   ), extended this approach, with important modifications, to voluntary acts, such as turning on a light switch, riding a bike, or getting dressed. Skinner showed that the consequences of an act affect the probability of its occurring again (see Chapter 6).

Behaviorists have sometimes been accused of denying that ideas and thoughts exist—of believing ''that human beings do not think or ponder or worry, but instead only *think* that they do'' (C. Sherif, 1979). This is not correct. In everyday conversation, behaviorists are as likely as anyone else to say that they think or feel this or that. They realize that they are conscious! A Watsonian behaviorist would argue that thoughts, emotions, and visual images are not the proper subject matter of a science. However, as we will see in Chapter 6, Skinner believes that private events can be studied, so long as they are treated as a form of behavior. Verbal reports can be used as imperfect clues to these events. What we should *not* do, according to Skinner and other behaviorists, is use mental events to *explain* behavior. For behaviorists, the prediction and control of behavior depend on specifying the environmental conditions that maintain it. Thus behaviorists have traditionally viewed discussions of ''the mind'' with suspicion.

When it was first presented, behaviorism excited not only psychologists but also sociologists and political scientists. Here, at last, was a way for the social sciences to be hardheaded and earn the respect of a skeptical world. In many ways stimulus-response or ''S-R'' psychology, as it was informally called, narrowed the scope of psychology. But in other ways it broadened it, for it permitted the study of animals, infants, and mentally disturbed persons, groups that could not be studied at all through introspection. Behaviorism soon became the predominant American school of experimental psychology and remained so until the early 1960s (E. R. Hilgard, 1980).

John B. Watson (1878–1958)

For behavioral psychologists, human behavior, even such an ordinary event as an intimate conversation between friends, is explainable largely in terms of its environmental consequences. One such consequence is the rewarding attention we get from others.

Today, behaviorism continues to be a potent force in psychology, but in modified form. Many psychologists combine elements of classic behaviorism with approaches that allow the study of thinking and consciousness. Instead of focusing on discrete stimuli, they look at general ways in which the environment affects behavior. They also consider people's expectations, anticipations, and interpretations of the environment. One outgrowth of behaviorism, **social learning theory**, has been used to show how people acquire new behaviors by observing and imitating others.

What can behavioral approaches tell us about violence and aggression? Behaviorists do not probe the inner lives or motives of violent people. Instead, behaviorally oriented research identifies the sorts of situations that promote violence and the kinds of payoffs it earns for its perpetrators. For example, studies find that aggressiveness in children increases when a teacher unwittingly rewards it with attention (Serbin & O'Leary, 1975). Violent behavior can be reduced or eliminated by withdrawing rewards for it and by rewarding cooperative, friendly behavior instead (Fixsen et al., 1978). Laboratory studies have shown that some children also learn to be aggressive by imitating the aggressive behavior of others, including behavior depicted on television and in movies (Bandura, 1973; Eron, 1980).

Because of its practical applications, the behavioral approach has touched many lives. Behavioral techniques have helped people eliminate unreasonable fears, quit smoking, lose weight, toilet train infants, and acquire better study habits. In addition, behavioral research has given psychology some of its most reliable findings. Behaviorism's insistence on precision and objectivity has done much to make psychology a science.

The psychoanalytic perspective

The year was 1900. In Vienna, an obscure physician published a book called *The Interpretation of Dreams*. The book was not what you would call an overnight sensation: Over the next eight years the publisher managed to sell only 600 copies. Who could possibly have known that the author's ideas would influence psychology, medicine, philosophy, literature, and art?

That author was Sigmund Freud (1856–1939), whose name today is as much a household word as Einstein's. A neurologist by training, Freud originally hoped for a career as a medical researcher, but research did not pay well and family responsibilities forced him to go into private practice as a physician. Freud was a good listener. As he listened to his patients' reports of depression, nervousness, and obsessive habits, he became convinced that many of their symptoms had mental, not bodily, causes. Their distress was due, he concluded, to conflicts, memories, and emotional traumas that often went back to early childhood. Freud's ideas grew into a broad theory of personality. Both his theory and his methods of treating people with emotional problems became known as **psychoanalysis**.

Freud argued that our most important impulses and motives are sexual and aggressive in nature. Because these primitive urges are threatening, we push them out of consciousness, deep into our *unconscious* minds. We are not aware of them as we go blithely about our daily business. Yet they do make themselves known, in hundreds of small ways. Freud (1905a) wrote, "No mortal can keep a secret. If the lips are silent, he chatters with his fingertips; betrayal oozes out of him at every pore." Unconscious thoughts find expression in dreams, slips of the tongue, apparent accidents, even jokes. Virtually all behavior is meaningful, no matter how trivial it may seem. But whereas a behaviorist is concerned with observable acts, a psychoanalyst tries to dig below the surface of a person's behavior to uncover the

Sigmund Freud (1856–1939), with his daughter Anna, who later also became a psychoanalyst.

social learning theory *The theory that human social behavior is learned through observation and imitation of others and is maintained by positive consequences.*

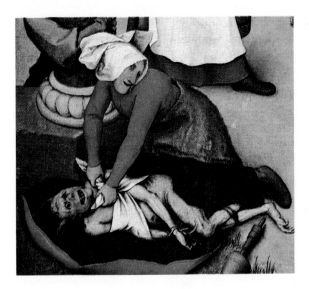

For psychoanalysts, behavior is explained primarily by unconscious needs and motives. Everyone, in this view, struggles to control instinctive "demons" of aggression and sexuality that threaten to disrupt civilization.

roots of personality. Whereas a behaviorist emphasizes the external environment, the psychoanalyst emphasizes processes that go on within the individual. In effect, the psychoanalyst is an archeologist of the mind.

Freud viewed aggression as a basic human instinct, lodged in the unconscious part of the mind. The duty of society, he said, is to get people to channel their aggressive energy into productive, socially useful activities. A Freudian might say that the corner butcher, a world-famous surgeon, and an Olympic athlete are all channeling their aggressive energy in healthy directions. Aggressive energy that is not channeled into productive activity is released in violent actions, such as murder and war.

The greatest impact of psychoanalysis has been felt in the study and treatment of abnormal behavior. Most psychoanalysts have not had much to say about normal learning, thinking, or perceiving. And even in the treatment of abnormal behavior, psychoanalysis does not have the prominence it once did; it now competes with many different approaches (see Chapter 17). Critics have faulted psychoanalysts for basing their conclusions on a limited number of patients in therapy, and they have found psychoanalytic claims, such as that human aggressiveness is instinctive, difficult to verify scientifically. Critics have also noted that psychoanalytic theory blames an individual's distress almost entirely on the person's own complexes and hang-ups, ignoring possible political and social explanations. Most clinical psychologists, however, believe that psychoanalysis has increased understanding of the ways in which people unconsciously protect themselves from anxiety and emotional conflict. And by making us aware that we are not always the best judges of our own motives and behavior, psychoanalysis has made a lasting contribution to psychology and human understanding.

The cognitive perspective

For decades, behaviorism and psychoanalysis ruled in psychology, with the first governing most research and the second guiding most psychotherapy. Then, in the 1950s, changes began to occur. The gloomy outlook of the psychoanalysts gave way to a more balanced view of human nature. At the same time, the mind reemerged as a respectable topic of scientific study.

psychoanalysis *An approach to psychology that emphasizes unconscious motives and conflicts. It encompasses both a theory of personality and a method of psychotherapy.*

Not that the mind was ever entirely absent. Even John Watson was forced to talk about internal stimuli and responses (things that happen inside a person that are not directly observable). The study of mental processes was also kept alive by a movement called **Gestalt psychology**, which began in Germany in 1912 and flourished in the 1920s and 1930s. In German, *gestalt* means "pattern" or "configuration." Gestalt psychologists studied how people interpret sensory information in order to acquire knowledge (see Chapter 5).

In America, however, mental processes remained more or less in the academic doghouse until the 1950s. The reaction to both Freudian pessimism and behavioristic "mindlessness" emerged initially in the form of a "third force" in psychology, called **humanistic psychology** (or **humanism**). One founder of this approach, Abraham Maslow (1908–1970), noted that Freud had based his ideas largely on contacts with unhappy people who were plagued by hostility, fear, and depression. Although Freud reportedly once said that the meaning of life was to be found in work and love, rarely did he discuss joy, compassion, and the nobler aspects of human nature. Behaviorists, too, ignored human hopes and aspirations, though for different reasons. Maslow (1971) wrote, "When you select out for careful study very fine and healthy people, strong people, creative people, saintly people, sagacious people . . . then you get a very different view of mankind. You are asking how tall can people grow, what can a human being become?"

Humanists differed from other psychologists in emphasizing free will. Human behavior, they said, is not completely determined by either the immediate environment or past experiences; we are able to make choices and control our destinies. Nor did humanists give high priority to discovering general laws of behavior. Their mission was to help people express themselves creatively, understand themselves, and achieve their full human potential. Because of these goals, critics accused humanism of being vague and unscientific, of being more a philosophy of life than a psychology. And indeed, humanism never did translate into a broad program of empirical research; its impact was primarily on personality theory (Chapter 11) and psychotherapy (Chapter 17). However, humanists did succeed in directing psychology's attention to the study of human thoughts, values, and purposes.

Other influences also helped usher the mind back into psychology. For example, the development of the computer encouraged scientists to study problem solving, informational "feedback," and other mental processes. The result was the rise of **cognitive psychology**. (The word *cognitive* comes from the Latin for "to know.") Cognitive psychologists study how we attend, perceive, think, remember, solve problems, and arrive at beliefs. They argue that we cannot understand much about how people use language, acquire moral codes, experience emotions, or behave in social groups unless we know what is going on in their heads. However, cognitive researchers have not returned to the structuralists' heavy dependence on introspection; instead, they have developed new ways to infer mental processes from observable behavior.

Cognitive psychology does not yet have a unifying theory, and unlike the other "brands" of psychology discussed so far, it lacks an acknowledged spokesperson. It is also less concerned than the other approaches with fundamental philosophical issues, such as free will versus determinism or the goodness or badness of human nature. Yet hardly a topic in psychology has remained unaffected by the cognitive perspective (E. R. Hilgard, 1980). Cognitive researchers have studied how people explain their own behavior, understand a sentence, solve intellectual problems, reason, form opinions, and remember events. They have busily rushed into areas of study where behaviorists once feared to tread: sleeping, dreaming, hypnosis, and drug-induced states of consciousness.

Gestalt [geh-SHTALT] psychology *An approach to psychology that emphasizes the perception, learning, and mental manipulation of whole units rather than their analysis into parts. From the German word for "pattern" or "form."*

humanistic psychology (humanism) *An approach to psychology that emphasizes personal growth and the achievement of human potential more than the scientific understanding, prediction, and control of behavior.*

cognitive psychology *An approach to psychology that emphasizes mental processes in perception, memory, language, problem solving, and other areas of behavior.*

Cognitive psychologists emphasize perceptions, thought processes, and how people explain events. When a problem arises, a person's behavior will depend in part on whether he or she interprets it as a challenge or "cries over spilt milk."

How does a cognitive psychologist analyze violence? Cognitive research has shown that our actions are influenced by how we perceive reality and the intentions of others (Averill, 1982; Beck & Emery, 1985). People who are quick to become violent often assume that others are insulting them. If someone does something they dislike, they attribute the action to meanness and malice. They see provocation everywhere. They accept negative stereotypes about those who are different from themselves, and they divide the world up into "us" and "them." In contrast, nonviolent people are able to take another person's perspective. If someone does something they dislike, they are apt to say, "He had a bad day" instead of "He's a rotten person." They avoid blowing disputes out of proportion. They can generate alternative ways of solving disagreements. Thus, in the cognitive view, the solution to violence (and to other human problems as well) is to change destructive and distorted thinking patterns.

Like every other approach to psychology, the cognitive perspective has its critics. Some consider its explanations of behavior too mentalistic. They complain that choosing between competing cognitive explanations is often difficult. However, the cognitive approach is one of the strongest forces today in psychology, and its findings have made psychology a more complete science.

The physiological perspective

The physiological approach to psychology has been an important one from the very beginning. Psychologists have always known that to understand the mind they must study the nervous system. In fact, Wilhelm Wundt's best-known work was called *Principles of Physiological Psychology*, and for good reason: He and most other early researchers expected their science to rest on a firm foundation of anatomy and biology.

The basic idea behind **physiological psychology** is that all actions, feelings, and thoughts are associated with bodily events. Electrical impulses shoot along the intricate pathways of the nervous system. Hormones course through the bloodstream, signaling body organs to slow down or speed up. Special chemical substances flow across the tiny gaps that separate one brain cell from another. Physio-

physiological psychology
An approach to psychology that emphasizes bodily events and changes associated with feelings, actions, and thoughts.

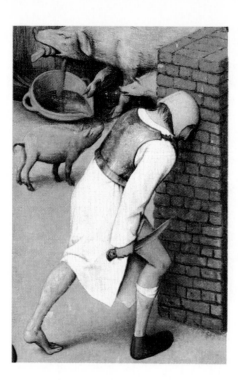

Some people literally bang their heads against a wall. Physiological psychologists look for the causes of such abnormal behavior, and of normal actions as well, in brain circuits and bodily processes.

logical psychologists want to know how these bodily events interact with events in the external environment to produce perceptions, memories, and behavior. Many physiological researchers hope that their discoveries, along with those of biochemists and other scientists, will help solve some of the mysteries of mental problems.

Some of that research might help us understand certain types of violence. Experiments with animals show that stimulation of particular brain areas tends to produce behavior associated with rage. Stimulation of other areas produces calm, placid behavior. Some cases of sudden, unprovoked violence by human beings may be traceable to brain tumors, injuries, and diseases or to more subtle neurological disorders (Lewis, 1981; Moyer, 1983).

In the past few decades, new techniques have made it possible to explore areas of an organism's "inner space" where no one has ventured before (see Chapter 3). As we will see, the results can tempt people to reduce complex psychological issues to the actions of hormones, nerve cells, genes, and enzymes, and to ignore important psychological and social factors. But the physiological approach has a useful message for us all: We cannot know ourselves if we do not know our bodies. That is why physiological discoveries are found in many sections of this book.

The sociocultural perspective

Most psychologists (with the exception of the behaviorists) study forces within the individual—biological, cognitive, or motivational—that affect a person's behavior. During the 1930s and 1940s, some psychologists began to question this **intrapsychic** (within the person) focus. They wanted to know how dictators like Adolf Hitler could persuade people to commit the kinds of atrocities that led to the deaths of Anne Frank and millions of others. They wondered why apparently nice people often hold hateful racial or ethnic stereotypes and whether such attitudes could be changed. They asked how cultural values and political systems affect everyday

intrapsychic *Within the mind or self.*

experience. We call the view that emerged from these questions the **sociocultural perspective**.

Researchers working from this perspective have shown that most people (including psychologists) tend to overlook how the social context shapes nearly everything we do—how we perceive the world, express joy, manage our households, rear our children. Most of us overestimate the contribution of personality traits to our own behavior and the behavior of others and underestimate the influence of the particular historical, cultural, and social situation in which we happen to find ourselves. We are like fish who, having always lived in water, are unaware of its existence. We assign blame and give credit, without noticing that context, rather than personality, determined an outcome.

Psychologists who emphasize the ''socio'' side of the sociocultural perspective examine influences on behavior within a culture or situation. For example, they might study how access to job opportunities affects people's goals and ambitions (Chapter 10), how gender roles influence the expression of emotion (Chapter 9), or how groups affect attitudes (Chapter 18). Psychologists who emphasize the ''cultural'' side of the perspective study how differences among cultures affect behavior. They might look at how cultural expectations about children's family responsibilities affect moral development (Chapter 13) or how Eastern versus Western attitudes toward personal control affect the experience of stress (Chapter 15).

In the sociocultural view, the answer to violence and cruelty does not reside in instincts, brain circuits, or personal dispositions, but in social and cultural rules about when to aggress and against whom. When groups or societies are small and closeknit, and when individuals must cooperate to survive, people tend to fear aggression. Eskimos, for example, often regard the mildest protest, the slightest raised tone, the merest hint of a frown, as a serious threat. Eskimos consider anger to be dangerous and intolerable, appropriate only for babies, the insane, the sick— and *kaplunas*, white people (Jean Briggs, 1970). In contrast, societies that value competition or power often foster aggression, both within the society and against outsiders. (Consider our own culture's fondness for Rambo movies, boxing matches, and hostile corporate takeovers.) To reduce violence, then, there must be social change, not merely personal change.

The sociocultural perspective can lead to glib generalizations about ethnic groups, nations, and cultures. But because human beings are social animals, this

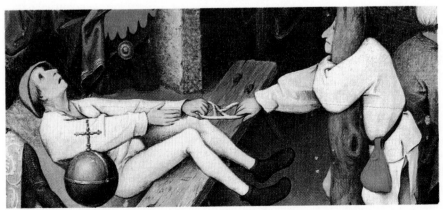

For psychologists who take a sociocultural perspective, human behavior depends on many outside influences, ranging from the immediate situation to the larger culture. They might ask why relationships in some societies are a tug of war, whereas those in other societies are more cooperative.

sociocultural perspective
An approach to psychology that emphasizes social and cultural influences on behavior.

perspective can also expand our ability to understand and predict human behavior. We will be examining the influence of society and culture in Chapter 18 and in our discussions of perception, emotion, child development, and many other topics.

A note on psychology's multiple personalities

The differences among the various schools of psychology are very real; they have produced passionate arguments, and sometimes stony silences, among their defenders. But not all psychologists feel they must swear allegiance to one approach or the other. Many, if not most, are *eclectic*, using what they believe to be the best features of diverse theories and schools of thought. Further, most psychologists agree on certain broad guidelines about what is and what is not acceptable in their discipline. Most believe in gathering empirical evidence instead of arriving at conclusions through reasoning alone. Nearly all reject supernatural explanations of

Think About It

Sense and Nonsense About Human Experience

You have probably heard that human beings are different from other animals because we have language, use tools, or can think. But to communications psychologist George Gerbner (1988), we are unique because we tell stories—and live by the stories we tell. All of us need to explain ourselves and the workings of the world around us. We are constantly constructing stories that will make sense of confusing, surprising, or unfair events. Which stories are right? Marriages have broken up and wars have been waged over that question.

Psychology and other sciences offer certain kinds of stories about human behavior; they are called "theories." But psychology has plenty of nonscientific competitors. Are you having romantic problems? An astrologer may advise you to choose an Aries instead of an Aquarian as your next love. Are you unable to make decisions? A "channeler" will put you in touch with a 5000-year-old equivalent of Dear Abby. Are you fighting the battle of the bulge? An expert in "past lives regression" will explain that the problem is not in your unhappy childhood but in your unhappy previous life; perhaps in the fourteenth century you were a pudgy peasant.

Nonscientific approaches to human experience

share psychology's basic goals of describing, explaining, predicting, and modifying behavior. Moreover, by analyzing personality and dispensing advice, many of their practitioners operate in effect as unlicensed psychological counselors. You hear about their famous clients all the time—movie stars, rock singers, Wall Street brokers, even politicians. During former President Reagan's term of office, Nancy Reagan sought the advice and consent of an astrologer before permitting White House staffers to set her husband's schedule.

When deciding which stories about human behavior to believe, it helps to distinguish two questions that are often confused: *Does it work?* and *Is it true?* Many stories "work" for people; that is, they help people feel better, provide entertainment, reassure people that they are normal, or simplify a complicated world. But for a story, theory, or system to be *true*, or valid, it must consistently explain or predict behavior or events with better than chance accuracy.

Throughout history, people have turned to religion for answers to ultimate questions of life and death, spirituality, and meaning. Religious explanations are for the most part impossible to test for accuracy; they are a matter of faith. But other nonsci-

events—evil spirits, psychic forces, miracles, and so forth. This insistence on rigorous standards of proof sets psychology apart from other, nonscientific explanations of human experience (see ''Think About It'').

Some psychologists hope that in time they will be able to resolve their differences and settle on a single *paradigm*—a guiding model or theory—that will define what psychologists should study and how they should study it. They hope that such a paradigm will do for psychology what the laws of motion did for physics and evolutionary theory did for biology. Given the complexity of their subject matter, however, a unifying paradigm may be as elusive as the Holy Grail. Even as psychologists yearn for unity, individual researchers are heading off in different directions. While some seek the answers to psychological problems by studying biology, others are tracing psychological problems to social pathology—to poverty, unemployment, racism, sexism, ageism, and urban crowding (Albee, 1982). While some want to bring psychology back to its philosophical roots, others are investing their energy in computer simulations and space-age technology. Grand theories have

entific systems of belief are testable in principle, although their followers often ignore the basic rules of evidence. One such rule is that you have to make predictions in advance of, not after, the fact. For example, you don't get to observe an earthquake and *then* argue that the planets predicted it.

When you look closely, you find that nonscientific or pseudoscientific predictions are rarely correct *in advance*. For example, in a review of many studies, Geoffrey Dean (1986, 1986/87) found that predictions made by highly trained astrologers have only chance-level accuracy. Their occasional on-target predictions are the result of shrewd guesses (''Mideast tensions will continue''), vagueness (''A tragedy will hit the country this spring''), or inside information (''Starlet A will marry director B''). And astrologers are no better at describing individuals' personalities based on their birth charts; they do *worse* than they would simply by guessing. Dean concludes that astrology is ''psychological chewing gum, satisfying but ultimately without real substance.''

Even when people know about a system's inadequacies, they may ignore them, out of a need to believe. The task of the skeptical person is to separate faith from evidence. The Amazing Randi, a magician who devotes his time to debunking pseudoscientific claims, once sent a birth chart to a noted astrologer for analysis. The astrologer, thinking the chart was Randi's own, sent back a glowing description of a virtuous, steadfast fellow. In fact, the chart was based on the birthdate, birth hour, and birthplace of a convicted and hanged rapist.

In this chapter and others, you will learn that psychology tells more than one ''story.'' A Freudian's explanation of your personality will not be the same as a cognitive psychologist's, and neither ''story'' will be the same as a behaviorist's. In later chapters, we will be offering you ways to think critically about various psychological approaches as well as about those of psychology's nonscientific competitors.

In the meantime, ask yourself what else you need to know to evaluate a theory besides the fact that it is coherent and appealing, and you want it to be true. What is the harm in accepting an explanation of human behavior that has no evidence to support it? Why does it matter whether we attribute our fates to the alignment of heavenly bodies, past lives, spirit guides, ''psychic energy,'' or our own decisions and actions? Think about it.

been replaced by more specific ones that address particular kinds of questions. Human behavior does not seem to lend itself to simple, all-encompassing theories. It is like a giant mosaic made up of many fragments, so complicated that no single approach can take in the whole picture. Put all the approaches together, though, and the result is a rich, multicolored, absorbing psychological portrait.

QUICK ∎ QUIZ

Anxiety is a common problem. Match each possible explanation on the left with a psychological perspective on the right.

1. Anxious people often think about the future *e* in distorted ways.
2. Anxiety is due to forbidden, unconscious *b* desires.
3. Anxiety symptoms often bring hidden re- *a* wards, such as being excused from exams.
4. Excessive anxiety can be caused by a *d* chemical imbalance.
5. America's emphasis on competition and success promotes worry and anxiety. *c*

a. behavioral
b. psychoanalytic
c. sociocultural
d. physiological
e. cognitive

Answers:
1. e 2. b 3. a 4. d 5. c

What Psychologists Do

Now you know the main viewpoints that guide psychologists in their work. But what do psychologists actually do between breakfast and dinner?

When most people hear the word *psychologist* they probably imagine a therapist listening intently while a client, perhaps stretched out comfortably on a couch, pours forth his or her troubles. Many psychologists do fit this image (though chairs are more common than couches these days), but others do not.

According to the last count, more than 102,000 people in the United States work in psychology (Stapp, Tucker, & Vandenbos, 1985). About two-thirds of them have doctorates; most of the rest have master's degrees. Their activities generally fall into three categories: (1) research, (2) education, and (3) health or mental health services (sometimes referred to as psychological "practice"). Figure 1.1 shows primary employment settings of both doctoral- and master's-level psychologists. Most psychologists, though, wear more than one professional hat. Dr. Rock might spend half the day doing research in a university laboratory and the other half teaching courses. Dr. Roll might see patients in a mental health clinic three days a week and do research on the causes of depression the other two.

Psychological research

Psychological researchers work for universities and colleges, the government, the military, schools, and business. Some, seeking knowledge for its own sake, work in

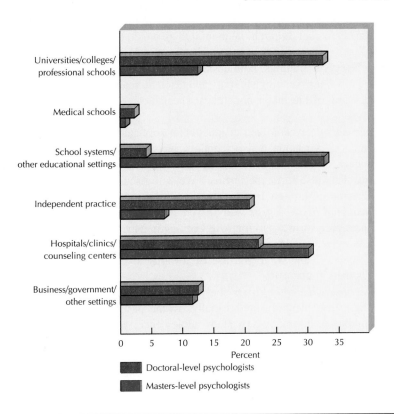

FIGURE 1.1

Where psychologists work
This graph shows the primary employment settings of doctoral- and masters-level psychologists. (The percentages do not quite total 100 because of rounding and because a few persons surveyed failed to specify a setting.) As the text notes, many psychologists work in more than one setting. (Based on Stapp, Tucker, & VandenBos, 1985.)

basic psychology, or "pure" research. Others, concerned with the practical uses of knowledge, work in **applied psychology**. A psychologist doing basic research might ask, How do children, adolescents, and adults differ in their approach to moral issues such as honesty? An applied psychologist might ask, instead, How can knowledge about moral development be used to prevent juvenile delinquency? A psychologist in basic science might ask, Can a nonhuman primate, such as a chimpanzee or a gorilla, learn to use sign language? An applied psychologist might ask, Can techniques used to teach language to a chimpanzee be used to help retarded or disturbed children who do not speak?

At one time, the "pure" approach had more prestige among psychologists than the applied approach (C. W. Sherif, 1979). This began to change during World War II, when the U.S. government encouraged psychologists to apply their findings to the training, education, and health care problems facing the country. Many well-known psychologists answered the call. Since then, applied psychologists have made important contributions in such areas as health, education, marketing, management, consumer behavior, industrial design, personnel selection, and urban planning. Most psychologists now recognize that basic and applied psychology are equally important. Although basic psychology can sometimes lead to useful discoveries by accident, such accidents cannot be depended on. On the other hand, insisting that psychological research always be relevant is like trying to grow flowers by concentrating only on the blossoms and ignoring the roots (E. L. Walker, 1970).

basic psychology *The study of psychological issues in order to seek knowledge for its own sake rather than for its practical application.*
applied psychology *The study of psychological issues that have direct practical significance and the application of psychological findings.*

Basic research is root research. Without it there would be little scientific knowledge to apply.

Psychologists' findings, both basic and applied, fill this book, so you can get a good idea of *what* psychologists study and teach by scanning the Table of Contents. Here are a few of the major nonclinical specialties:

Experimental psychologists conduct laboratory studies of learning, motivation, emotion, sensation and perception, physiology, human performance, and cognition. (Don't be misled by the term *experimental*, though; other researchers also run experiments.) We will discuss many of their findings in Chapters 3 through 10.

Educational psychologists study psychological principles that explain learning and search for ways to improve learning in educational systems. Their interests range from the application of findings on memory and thinking (see Chapters 7 and 8) to the use of rewards to encourage achievement (see Chapters 6 and 10).

Developmental psychologists study how people change and grow over time, physically, mentally, and socially. In the past their focus was mainly on childhood, but many now study adolescence, young adulthood, the middle years, or old age. We will take a close look at their findings in Chapters 13 and 14.

Industrial/organizational psychologists study behavior in the workplace. They are concerned with group decision making, employee morale, work motivation, productivity, job stress, personnel selection, marketing strategies, equipment design, and many other issues. We will discuss their findings at several points in this book, but especially in Chapter 10.

Psychometric psychologists design and evaluate tests of mental abilities, aptitudes, interests, and personality. Nearly all of us have had first-hand experience with one or more of these tests—in school, at work, or in the military. We will discuss test construction and the controversies that surround testing in Chapter 12.

Social psychologists study how groups, institutions, and the social context influence individuals and vice versa. Among their interests are conformity, obedience, competition, cooperation, leadership styles, and prejudice. We will take up these topics in Chapter 18.

The practice of psychology

Over half of new psychology doctorates now go to practitioners (Howard et al., 1986). Practitioners work in general hospitals, mental hospitals, clinics, schools, counseling centers, and private practice. Their object is to understand and improve physical and mental health. Some are *counseling psychologists*, who help people deal with problems of everyday life, such as test anxiety or low job motivation. Others are *school psychologists*, who work with parents, teachers, and students to enhance students' performance and emotional development. The majority, though, are *clinical psychologists*, who diagnose, treat, and study mental or emotional problems and disabilities. Clinicians are trained to do **psychotherapy** with highly disturbed people as well as with those who are simply troubled or unhappy or who want to learn to handle their problems better.

In most states, a license to practice clinical psychology requires a doctorate. Most clinicians have a Ph.D., some have an Ed.D. (doctorate in education), and a

psychotherapy *The treatment of mental disorders, emotional problems, and personality difficulties.*

Psychologists may be researchers and/or practitioners. In the photograph on the left, Patricia Goldman-Rakic (center) and her colleagues use newly developed technology to study the brain mechanisms underlying mental processes. In the photograph on the right, a clinical psychologist helps a client cope with an emotional problem.

smaller number have a relatively new degree called a Psy.D. (doctorate in psychology, pronounced "sy-dee"). Whichever degree they earn, clinical psychologists typically do four or five years of graduate work in psychology, plus a year's internship under the direction of a practicing psychologist. In clinical programs, the Ph.D. and Ed.D. are designed to prepare a person both as a scientist and clinical practitioner; they require completion of a dissertation, a major scholarly work (usually involving research) that contributes to knowledge in the field. The Psy.D. focuses on professional practice and does not usually require a dissertation. However, it does require the student to complete a research study, theoretical paper, literature review, or some other scholarly project.

Psychologists and psychiatrists are not the only professionals who do mental health work; so do marriage, family, and child counselors, school counselors, and social workers. Licensing requirements for these professions vary somewhat from state to state but usually include a master's degree in psychology or social work and one or two years of supervised experience. Counselors ordinarily treat general problems in adjustment and not serious mental disturbance.

Nonprofessionals often confuse the terms *clinical psychologist*, *psychotherapist*, and *psychoanalyst*. Anyone who does psychotherapy is a psychotherapist; and in most states almost anyone can say that he or she is a "therapist" of one sort or another, so checking credentials is important. A psychoanalyst is a person who practices one form of therapy, psychoanalysis. To call yourself a psychoanalyst, you must get specialized training at a recognized psychoanalytic institute, and must usually undergo extensive personal psychoanalysis yourself. Psychiatrists are more likely to have had psychoanalytic training than are psychologists.

Psychology in the community

In the past few decades psychology has probably expanded faster than any other field, in terms of scholars, publications, and specialties. The American Psychological Association, psychology's largest professional organization, now has 45 divisions. Some of these divisions represent the major fields described in this chapter, such as developmental or physiological psychology; others represent special research or clinical interests, such as the psychology of women, sports psychology, environmental psychology, and the psychological study of gay and lesbian issues. Look around your community and you are apt to find psychologists. Besides doing

Psychologists work in many settings, from classrooms to courtrooms. This woman is a prison psychologist.

research, teaching, and treating patients, they advise commissions on how pollution and noise affect mental health. They educate judges and juries about the reliability of eyewitness testimony. They assist the police in emergencies involving hostages or disturbed persons. They conduct public opinion surveys. They run suicide prevention "hot lines." They consult with zoos on the care and training of animals. They help coaches improve the athletic performance of their teams. And on and on.

No wonder people are a little fuzzy about what a psychologist is. George Miller has related what happens when he tells people his profession:

> Some people say: "So you're a psychologist. I think my wife's calling," and off they go. Then there's the opposite reaction: "So you're a psychologist. Well I'm something of a psychologist myself," and they describe how they trained their dog to bring in the newspaper. Other people ask about their children's test scores, and still others want me to interpret their dreams. All I can say is: "I'm not that kind of psychologist!" (in J. Miller, 1983, pp. 15–16)

QUICK ■ QUIZ

Let's try a game of "What's My Line?" Which kinds of psychologist are most likely to have the following job descriptions?

1. Studies emotional development during childhood. *developmental*
2. Does laboratory studies of visual perception in animals. *experimental*
3. Treats eating disorders in a mental health clinic. *clinical*
4. Consults with industry on marketing strategies. *industrial*

Answers:

1. developmental 2. experimental 3. clinical 4. industrial/organizational

Thinking Critically and Creatively About Psychology

These days, most people know that you have to exercise the body to keep it in shape. But they assume that thinking doesn't take any effort at all, and certainly no practice. You just do it, like breathing. But thinking does need practice. All around us we can see examples of flabby thinking, lazy thinking, emotional thinking, and nonthinking. Sometimes people justify their mental laziness by proudly telling you they are ''open-minded.'' ''It's good to be open-minded,'' replies philosopher Jacob Needleman, ''but not so open that your brains fall out.''

We believe that one of the greatest benefits of studying psychology is that you learn not only how the brain works in general but how to use yours in particular—by thinking critically. **Critical thinking** is the ability and willingness to assess claims and make objective judgments on the basis of well-supported reasons. It is the ability to look for flaws in arguments and resist claims that have no supporting evidence. *Critical thinking, however, is not merely negative thinking.* It also fosters the ability to be *creative and constructive*—to generate possible explanations for findings, think of implications, and apply new knowledge to a broad range of social and personal problems. You can't really separate critical thinking from creative thinking, for it is only when you question *what is* that you can begin to imagine *what can be*.

Here is an example of what we mean. Many people, when faced with a setback to their expectations, narrow their horizons instead of expanding them. We know a fellow named Victor whose entire dream in life was to be a veterinarian. Victor's love of animals was legendary: At 3, he wouldn't let you kill a bug in his presence. But Victor wasn't admitted to any of the veterinary schools he applied to, and his reaction was panic and despair: ''My whole life is ruined!'' At first, Victor was not thinking critically; he had divided his possibilities into only two alternatives: become a veterinarian, or nothing. But by examining this assumption and by *thinking creatively* about all the possible occupations that would make use of his love of animals, Victor realized his choices were endless: pet-shop owner, Hollywood ''pet therapist,'' trainer at Sea World, designer of humane zoos, organizer for an endangered-species group, ecologist, wildlife photographer. . . .

Does critical thinking sound hard? It's not, really, once you get into the proper spirit and pick up a few skills. Researchers find that people don't usually use such skills until their mid-twenties or until they have had many years of higher education—if then (Kitchener & King, 1989; Schmidt, 1985; Welfel & Davison, 1986). That does not mean, however, that people *can't* think critically. Even young children often do so, though they may not get much credit for it. We know one fourth-grader, who, when told that ancient Greece was the ''cradle of democracy,'' replied, ''But what about the women and slaves, who couldn't vote and had no rights? Was Greece a democracy for them?'' That's critical thinking. And it is also creative thinking, for once you question the basic assumption that Greece was a democracy for everyone, you can begin to imagine other interpretations of Greek civilization at that time.

However, we do agree with the growing number of educators, philosophers, and psychologists who believe that the American educational system shortchanges students by not encouraging them to think critically and creatively. Too often, say these critics, both teachers and students view the mind as a bin for storing ''the right answers'' or a sponge for ''soaking up knowledge.'' The mind is neither a bin nor a sponge. Remembering, thinking, and understanding are all active processes. They

critical thinking *The ability and willingness to assess claims and make objective judgments on the basis of well-supported reasons.*

require judgment, choice, and the weighing of evidence. Unfortunately, children who challenge prevailing opinion at home or in school are often called ''rebellious'' rather than ''involved.'' As a result, say the critics, many high school and college graduates cannot formulate a rational argument or see through misleading advertisements and propaganda that play on emotions. They do not know how to go about deciding whether to have children, make an investment, or support a political proposal. They do not know how to come up with imaginative solutions to their problems. In short, they cannot use their heads.

Critical thinking involves a set of skills that you can apply to any subject you study or problem you encounter. But it is particularly relevant to psychology, for three reasons. First, the field itself includes the study of thinking, problem solving, creativity, curiosity, and other components of this process, and by its very nature fosters critical and creative thinking. In one recent study, graduate students in psychology substantially improved in their ability to reason about the events of everyday life. In contrast, graduate students in chemistry showed no improvement (Lehman, Lempert, & Nisbett, 1988). Second, the field of psychology generates many competing findings on topics of immediate personal and social relevance, and people need to be able to evaluate these findings and their implications. Third, the public's appetite for psychological information has created a huge market for what R. D. Rosen (1977) calls ''psychobabble'': pseudoscience and quackery that use a veneer of psychological language. Critical thinking can help you separate psychology from psychobabble.

In part, learning to think critically means following the rules of logic. But there are also some general guidelines involved (Ennis, 1985; Paul, 1984; Ruggiero, 1988). Here are eight of the essential ones:

1. *Ask questions; be willing to wonder.* What is the one kind of question that most exasperates parents of young children? ''Why is the sky blue, Mommy?'' ''Why doesn't the plane fall?'' ''Why don't pigs have wings?'' Unfortunately, as children grow up, they tend to stop asking ''why'' questions. (Why do you think this is?)

''The trigger mechanism for creative thinking is the disposition to be curious, to wonder, to inquire,'' writes Vincent Ruggiero (1988). ''Asking 'What's wrong here?' and/or 'Why is this the way it is, and how did it come to be that way?' leads to the identification of problems and challenges.'' Some occupations actually teach their trainees to think this way. Industrial engineers are taught to walk through a company and question everything, even procedures that have been used for years. Other occupations prefer to give trainees ''received wisdom'' and discourage criticism.

2. *Define the problem.* Once you've raised the question, the next step is to identify the issues in clear and concrete terms. ''What makes people happy?'' is a fine question for midnight reveries, but it will not lead to answers unless you have specified what you mean by ''happy.'' One psychologist defined a ''happy marriage'' as one that had lasted ten years and produced two children (Toman, 1976). Would you agree with that definition?

The wrong formulation of a question can produce misleading or incomplete answers. The question ''How does hypnosis improve memory for events?'' assumes that hypnosis always improves memory. But putting the matter another way— ''How does hypnosis *affect* memory?''—allows for other possibilities. (As you will learn, hypnosis can also increase memory *errors*, and some hypnotized people will even cheerfully make up details of an event that never happened.)

3. *Examine the evidence.* Have you ever heard someone in the heat of argument exclaim, ''I just know it's true, no matter what you say'' or ''That's my opinion; nothing's going to change it'' or ''If you don't understand my position, I can't explain it''? Have you ever said such things yourself? Accepting a conclusion without evidence, or expecting others to do so, is a sure sign of uncritical thinking (or of no thinking at all). It implies that all opinions are equal, and they are not. A critical thinker asks, *What evidence supports or refutes this argument and its opposition? How reliable is the evidence?* If it is not possible to check the reliability of the evidence, the critical thinker considers whether its source has been reliable in the past.

Some well-known popular beliefs have been widely accepted on the basis of (a) poor evidence or even (b) no evidence. For example, many people believe that it is psychologically and physically healthy to ''ventilate'' their anger at the first person, pet, or piece of furniture that gets in their way. Actually, years of research in many different fields suggest that sometimes expressing anger is beneficial, but more often it is not. Often it makes the angry person angrier, makes the target of the anger angry back, lowers everybody's self-esteem, and fosters hostility and aggression (see Chapter 9). Yet the belief persists, despite the lack of evidence to support it. Can you think of some reasons why this might be so?

4. *Analyze assumptions and biases.* Critical thinkers evaluate the assumptions and biases that lie behind arguments—beliefs that are taken for granted and biases about how the world works. They ask how these assumptions and biases influence claims and conclusions in the books they read, the political speeches they hear, the news programs they watch, and the ads that bombard them every day. Here is a real example: The manufacturer of a popular pain reliever advertises that hospitals prefer its product over all others. The natural assumption—the one the advertiser wants you to make—is that this product is better than all others. Actually, hospitals prefer it because it is cheaper than its competitors.

Critical thinkers also are aware of their own assumptions and are willing to question them. For example, many people are biased in favor of their parents' ways of doing things. When faced with difficult problems, they usually reach for familiar solutions, saying, ''If my dad did it this way, that's the way I'll do it,'' or ''I was brought up to believe that the best way to discipline children is to beat them.'' But critical thinking requires us to examine our biases when the evidence contradicts them.

All of us, of course, carry around a headful of assumptions about how the world works: Do people have free will or are they constrained by biology and upbringing? Is socialism or capitalism the solution to poverty? If we don't make our assumptions explicit, our ability to interpret evidence objectively can be seriously impaired.

5. *Avoid emotional reasoning: ''If I feel this way, it must be true.''* Emotion has a place in critical thinking. Without it, logic and reason can lead to misguided or destructive decisions and actions. Indeed, some of the most cold-blooded monsters of human history have been bright, even brilliant, thinkers. But when ''gut feelings'' replace clear thinking, the results are equally dangerous. ''Persecutions and wars and lynchings,'' observes Edward de Bono (1985), ''are all a result of gut feeling.''

Because our feelings seem so right, it is hard to understand that people with opposing viewpoints feel just as strongly. But they do, which means that feelings alone are not a reliable guide to the truth. As you begin this book, you may hold strong, passionate beliefs about child rearing, drugs, astrology, ideal body weight, the origins of intelligence, the nature of ''mental illness,'' men and women, whites and blacks, Americans and Japanese, heterosexuals and homosexuals. Try to set these feelings aside so they won't interfere with your consideration of evidence bearing on such issues. Keep in mind the words of English poet and essayist Alexander Pope: ''What reason weaves, by passion is undone.''

It's fine to be an optimist, but critical thinkers also try to separate truth from fiction. (Reprinted by permission of UFS, Inc.)

6. *Don't oversimplify.* A critical thinker looks beyond the obvious, resists easy generalizations, and rejects either/or thinking. For example, when life serves up a miserable situation, should you deny your problems (''Everything's fine; let's go to the movies'') or face them head-on? Either answer oversimplifies. As we will see in Chapter 15, sometimes denial can keep people from solving their problems, but sometimes it helps them get through painful situations that can't be changed.

Often in an argument you will hear someone generalize from one tiny bit of evidence to the whole world. An example is arguing by anecdote: One crime committed by a paroled ex-convict means the whole parole program is bad; one friend of yours who hates his or her school means that everybody who goes there hates it. Anecdotal generalizations are the source of stereotyping as well: One dishonest welfare mother means they are all dishonest; one bad experience with a New Yorker means that all New Yorkers are difficult. A critical thinker wants more evidence than one or two stories before drawing generalizations. The same applies to thinking about one's own life. For example, many people generalize from one negative event to a whole pattern of defeat, creating no end of misery: ''I did poorly on this test, and now I'll never get through college or have a job or kids or anything.''

7. *Consider other interpretations.* A critical thinker creatively formulates hypotheses that offer reasonable explanations of characteristics, behavior, and events. The ultimate goal is to find an explanation that accounts for the most evidence with the fewest assumptions. But critical thinkers are careful not to shut out alternative explanations too soon. They generate as many interpretations of the evidence as possible before settling on the most likely one.

A recent study of Swedish couples, for instance, found that those who lived together before marriage were 80 percent more likely to separate or divorce than those who had lived apart (Bennett, Blanc, & Bloom, 1988). *Time* magazine promptly concluded that ''premarital cohabitation may be hazardous to your marriage,'' and Dear Abby advised a reader that if she wanted her forthcoming marriage to last she shouldn't cohabit beforehand. But there is another plausible conclusion: that people who cohabit before marriage are less committed to the institution of marriage and therefore more inclined to leave an unhappy marriage. This was the interpretation the researchers themselves favored.

8. *Tolerate uncertainty.* Ultimately, learning to think critically teaches us one of the hardest lessons of life: how to live with uncertainty. As we have seen, it is important to examine the evidence before drawing conclusions. But we all encounter situations in which there is little or no evidence on which to base any conclusions. Sometimes the evidence merely allows us to draw tentative conclusions. And sometimes, exasperatingly, the evidence seems good enough to permit strong and sturdy conclusions . . . until new evidence throws our beliefs into disarray. Critical thinkers are willing to accept this state of uncertainty. They are not afraid to say, ''I don't know'' or ''I'm not sure.'' This admission is not an evasion but a spur to further creative inquiry.

The desire for certainty often makes people uncomfortable when they go to experts for ''the'' answer and the expert cannot give it to them. Some patients demand of their doctors, ''What do you mean you don't know what's wrong with me? Find out and fix it!'' Some students demand of their professors, ''What do you mean it's a controversial issue? Just tell me the answer!'' Many Americans, after nearly 30 years, are still demanding answers to the mystery of the assassination of President John F. Kennedy and have trouble accepting the fact that we may never know *for sure* who killed him and why.

The need to accept a certain amount of uncertainty does not mean that we must live without beliefs and convictions. ''The fact that today's knowledge may be overturned or at least revised tomorrow,'' says Ruggiero (1988), ''could lead us to the kind of skepticism that refuses to embrace any idea. That would be foolish because, in the practical sense, it is impossible to build a life on that view. Besides, it is not the embracing of an idea that causes problems—it is the refusal to relax that embrace when good sense dictates doing so. It is enough to form convictions with care and carry them lightly, being willing to reconsider them whenever new evidence calls them into question.''

Like the man who was delighted to learn he had been speaking prose all his life, many people already know some of these basic guidelines of critical and creative thinking. They do it, we might say, without thinking about it. Our aim is to make the guidelines more explicit and help you to shape up your mental muscles. In the remaining chapters, you will have many opportunities to apply this skill, both to psychological theories and to everyday life. From time to time, in the margins of the text, we will draw your attention to discussions in which critical and creative thinking is particularly important. (Feel free to find others!) For a preview of some of the issues to be discussed, see the photographs on pp. 40–41.

Keep in mind, though, that critical thinking is as much an attitude as it is a skill. We are probably all much less open-minded than we think. We take comfort from believing that only *other* people are biased or need to think more clearly. Critical thinking requires a willingness to submit even your most cherished beliefs to honest analysis. That is why intelligent people are not always critical thinkers. Clever debaters can learn to poke holes in the arguments of others, while twisting facts or conveniently ignoring arguments that might contradict their own position. But true critical thinking, according to philosopher Richard W. Paul (1984), is ''fair-mindedness brought into the heart of everyday life.''

Critical thinking is not for people who want psychology to give them final answers and simple solutions. Psychological facts do not simply pile up like a collection of postage stamps or trading cards. As new facts are added to our store of knowledge, others are discarded. Existing facts are continually being reorganized, reinterpreted, and assigned new meanings.

Some philosophers of science actually argue that all scientific theories *must* eventually fail. As knowledge grows, so does ignorance, for the more we know, the more questions we think to ask (Kuhn, 1981). As findings accumulate, existing theories become strained. Eventually they cannot explain all the evidence, no matter how they are stretched. It is like trying to fit a queen-sized sheet on a king-sized bed. When you tuck the sheet in at the head of the bed, it is too short at the bottom; when you tuck it in at the bottom, it is too short at the top. Eventually you have to get a new sheet or a new bed. Similarly, the scientist eventually is forced to show that new findings are wrong or get a new theory.

Does all this mean that there is no such thing as scientific progress? Not at all. After each failure, a new and better theory arises from the ashes of the previous one, explaining more facts, solving more puzzles. This can be frustrating for those who want psychology and other sciences to hand them some absolute truths. But it is exciting for those who love the pursuit of understanding as much as the collection of ''facts.'' As neuroscientist John C. Eccles (1981) recalled, his training taught him to ''rejoice in the refutation of a cherished hypothesis, because that, too, is a scientific achievement and because much has been learned by the refutation.''

If you are ready to share in the excitement of studying psychology—if you, like Eccles, love a mystery—then you are ready to read on.

Taking Psychology with You

What Psychology Can Do for You— And What It Can't

If you intend to become a psychologist or mental health professional, you have an obvious reason for taking a course in introductory psychology. But psychology can contribute to your life in many ways whether you plan to work in the field or not. Here are a few things psychology can do for you:

1. *Make you a more informed person.* One purpose of education is to acquaint people with their cultural heritage and with humankind's achievements in literature, the humanities, and science. In contemporary society, being a well-informed person requires knowing something about psychology. One psychologist has written, ''What geology was to the early nineteenth century, biology to the late nineteenth century, and physics to the first half of the twentieth century, so psychology is . . . [to] . . . the latter half of the twentieth century, its central major science'' (Jaynes, 1973a). Geologists, biologists, and physicists might not agree, but certainly psychology plays a large role in our culture.

2. *Satisfy your curiosity about human nature.* When the Greek philosopher Socrates admonished his fellow human beings to ''know thyself,'' he was only telling them to do what they wanted to do anyway. The topic that seems to fascinate human beings most is human beings. Psychology, along with the other social sciences, literature, history, and philosophy, can contribute to a better understanding of yourself and others.

3. *Help you increase control over your life.* Throughout this book we will be suggesting ways in which you can apply the findings of psychology to your own life. Psychology cannot solve all your problems, but it does offer techniques that may help you handle your emotions, improve your memory, and eliminate unwanted habits. It can also foster an attitude of objectivity that is useful for analyzing your behavior and your relationships with others.

4. *Help you on the job.* Some people reading this book will probably go on to become psychologists. Others will find a bachelor's degree in the field useful for getting a job in a helping profession, for example, as

a welfare caseworker or job rehabilitation counselor. People with a bachelor's degree in psychology also teach the subject in high schools. Still other readers, whether they earn a psychology degree or not, will go on to jobs (or already have jobs) in which psychological insights are useful. Anyone who works as a nurse, doctor, social worker, member of the clergy, police officer, or teacher can put psychology to work on the job. People who have lots of contact with others—waiters, flight attendants, bank tellers, receptionists—can make psychology work for them. Finally, psychology can be useful to those whose jobs require them to predict people's attitudes and behavior—for example, salespeople, labor negotiators, politicians, advertising copywriters, merchandise buyers, personnel managers, product designers, market researchers, magicians. . . .

5. *Give you insights into political and social issues.* Examine the front page of any newspaper: Most of the stories you find there are likely to raise questions studied by psychologists. Crime, drug abuse, discrimination, and war are not only social issues but psychological ones. Psychologists argue among themselves about whether they should use the results of their research to advocate specific public policies on such issues (see R. C. Atkinson, 1977; Sperry, 1977). Most agree, though, that reliable information, scientifically arrived at, can help society achieve its political and social aims whether or not scientists help determine those aims. Psychological knowledge alone cannot solve the complex political, social, and ethical problems that fill the news, but it can help you make informed judgments about them. Knowing, for example, that involuntary crowding often leads to stress and abnormal behavior may affect your views on conditions in schools and prisons. Knowing that being sexually harassed lowers a person's self-esteem and sense of control may influence your views on antiharassment legislation.

As you can see, we are optimistic about psychology's role in the world. But we want to caution you that sometimes people expect things from psychology that it cannot deliver; for example:

1. *It can't tell you the meaning of life.* Some people follow individual psychologists the way others follow religious leaders and gurus, hoping for enlightenment (Albee, 1977). There is no such thing, however, as instant wisdom. A personal philosophy about the purpose of life requires not only the acquisition of knowledge but also reflection and a willingness to learn from life's experiences.

2. *It won't relieve you of personal responsibility for your actions.* It is one thing to understand the origins of offensive or antisocial behavior and another thing to *excuse* it. Knowing that your short temper is a result, in part, of your unhappy childhood doesn't give you a green light to yell at your neighbors. Nor does scientific neutrality mean that *society* must be legally or morally neutral. A better understanding of the psychological origins of child beating may help us reduce child abuse and treat offenders, but we can still hold child beaters accountable for their behavior.

3. *It doesn't provide simple answers to complex psychological questions.* You have already found out in this chapter that psychologists (like other scientists) often disagree among themselves. By the time you finish this book, you will have discovered that there is controversy even about some very basic issues, such as the causes of mental disturbance and the existence of stable personality traits.

To say that psychology has limitations, however, is not to underestimate its contributions to our lives. In a presidential address to the American Psychological Association, George Miller (1969) called on his colleagues to "give psychology away." It was time, he said, for them to emerge from their laboratories and make an impact on the world around them. They should not assume the role of experts jealously guarding their professional secrets. "Psychological facts," he said, "should be passed out freely to all who need and can use them." Ever since, critics have complained that psychologists don't know enough to "give it away." Some say that too much of psychology is common sense, and others make the opposite claim—that human behavior is infinitely mysterious, so psychologists might as well pack up their laboratories and go home. We don't agree. Behavioral scientists know the questions they raise are difficult—harder than those tackled by such "hard" sciences as physics and chemistry (Diamond, 1987). You can't put an attitude, emotion, or thought in a test tube or measure it with calipers. But that doesn't mean human behavior is beyond understanding. Even love is yielding its secrets.

At the end of each chapter, starting with the next one, you will have the opportunity to decide whether psychology does, in fact, have something to give away. The "Taking Psychology with You" section will suggest ways to apply psychological findings to your own life—in your relationships, on the job, or at school. We hope this information helps you understand, predict, and control events in your own personal world.

KEY WORDS

Use this list of key words to check your understanding of terms in this chapter. If you have trouble defining a word, you can find it on the page number given.

psychology 7	Ivan Pavlov 16
sociology 10	B. F. Skinner 17
anthropology 11	social learning theory 18
biology 11	Sigmund Freud 18
psychiatry 11	psychoanalysis 18
empirical 12	Gestalt psychology 20
Wilhelm Wundt 13	Abraham Maslow 20
introspection 14	humanistic psychology 20
structuralism 14	cognitive psychology 20
functionalism 14	physiological psychology 21
William James 14	intrapsychic 22
Charles Darwin 15	sociocultural perspective 23
John B. Watson 16	paradigm 25
behaviorism 16	applied versus basic psychology 27

SUMMARY

1. Psychology is the study of behavior and mental processes and how they are affected by an organism's external and internal environment. Its goals are to describe, understand, predict, and control behavior and mental processes, using rigorous and systematic procedures. There is some controversy over the goal of control.

2. Psychological findings sometimes confirm, but often contradict, ''common sense.'' When psychological results do seem obvious, it is often because people overestimate the ability they might have had to predict the outcome of a study. In any case, a result does not have to be surprising to be scientifically important.

3. Psychology has links with other social sciences, with biology, and with psychiatry, but there are important differences in emphasis.

4. Until the late 1800s, psychology was not a science. A lack of empirical evidence often led to serious errors in the description and explanation of behavior. But psychology's forerunners also made valid observations and had useful insights. Descartes is a good example.

5. The official founder of scientific psychology was Wilhelm Wundt, whose work led to an approach called *structuralism*. Structuralism emphasized the analysis of immediate experience into basic elements. It was soon abandoned because of its reliance on introspection. Another early approach, *functionalism*, emphasized the purpose of behavior. It did not last long either, but it greatly affected the course of psychology.

6. Five points of view predominate today in psychology. The *behavioral perspective* emphasizes the study of observable behavior and rejects mentalistic explanations. The *psychoanalytic perspective* emphasizes unconscious motives and desires, especially sexual and aggressive ones. The *cognitive perspective* emphasizes mental processes in perception, problem solving, belief formation, and other human activities. The *physiological perspective* emphasizes bodily events associated with actions, thoughts, and feelings. The *sociocultural perspective* emphasizes how social and cultural rules, values, and expectations affect individual beliefs and behavior. Each of these approaches has made an important contribution to psychology, and each also has its critics. Many, if not most, psychologists draw on more than one ''school'' of psychology.

7. Psychologists teach, do research, and provide mental health services. Applied psychologists are concerned with the practical uses of psychological knowledge. Basic psychologists are concerned with knowledge for its own sake. Psychological specialties include, among others, experimental, educational, developmental, industrial/organizational, psychometric, social, counseling, school, and clinical psychology.

8. One of the greatest benefits of studying psychology is the development of *critical thinking* skills and attitudes. The critical thinker is curious and asks questions; defines problems clearly and accurately; examines the evidence; analyzes assumptions and biases; avoids emotional reasoning; avoids oversimplification; considers alternative interpretations; and tolerates uncertainty. Critical thinking is not for those who want psychology to give them final answers and simple solutions, but it can open up exciting paths in the pursuit of understanding.

What's Ahead: Thinking Critically About Psychology

In the pages ahead, we will apply the eight guidelines to critical thinking discussed in Chapter 1 to a variety of psychological topics.

2. Define the problem. *People talk about "intelligence" all the time, but what is it exactly? Does the musical genius of a world-class violinist like Anne-Sophie Mutter count as a kind of intelligence? Is intelligence confined to what IQ tests measure, or does it also include other kinds of wisdom, knowledge, and "smarts"? We will be taking up these issues in Chapter 12. (© Crickmay/Daily Telegraph/International Stock Photo)*

1. Ask questions; be willing to wonder. *The sight of this Chinese man standing alone against awesome military might inspired millions of people around the world. What gives some people the courage to risk their lives for their beliefs? Why, in contrast, do so many people "go along with the crowd" and mindlessly obey authority? Social psychologists have probed these questions in depth, as we will see in Chapter 18. (© Stuart Franklin/Magnum)*

3. Examine the evidence. *Amazed onlookers watch as illusionists Siegfried & Roy demonstrate "levitation" on a Las Vegas street corner. Illusionists take advantage of the fact that people are willing to trust the evidence of their own eyes, even when such evidence is misleading, as discussed in Chapter 5. (© Chris Callis)*

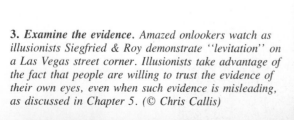

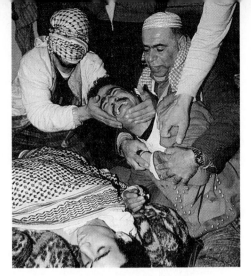

4. Analyze assumptions and biases. *Cultural and personal biases lead many people to believe that men are ''naturally'' less expressive emotionally than women. But which men, which cultures, and which emotions? This Palestinian man, grieving over his dead son, does not fit Western stereotypes. As we will see in Chapter 9, cultural display rules have a powerful influence on when, how, and to whom we express our feelings. (© Tannenbaum/Sygma)*

5. Avoid emotional reasoning. *Chances are that this photograph inspires an emotional reaction in you. Passionate feelings about controversial issues like abortion can keep us from considering other viewpoints. The resolution of differences requires that we move beyond emotional reasoning (''I feel this way strongly, so I must be right'') and think dialectically, weighing point and counterpoint, as discussed in Chapter 8. (© Dennis Brack 1989/ Black Star)*

6. Don't oversimplify. *Is the left side of the brain entirely analytic, rational, and sensible? Is the right side always intuitive, emotional, and spontaneous? As we will see in Chapter 3, the two hemispheres of the brain do have some specialized ''talents,'' but it's easy to exaggerate the differences. (Courtesy of Natural Nectar Corporation)*

7. Consider other interpretations. *Like this underwater researcher, some people are high achievers in their work. One explanation attributes their attainments mainly to personal ambition and drive (''She's really motivated''). An alternative explanation, supported by new evidence, emphasizes the importance of work settings and conditions in fostering good morale and pride of accomplishment, as we will see in Chapter 10. (© David R. Austen/Stock, Boston)*

8. Tolerate uncertainty. *Some questions have no easy answers, and may even be unanswerable in principle. For example: What are the origins of sexual orientation? Many theories have been offered, but no single explanation can account for the many variations of homosexuality or of heterosexuality, as we will see in Chapter 10. (© Jim Anderson 1983/Woodfin Camp & Assoc.)*

CHAPTER 2

How Psychologists Know What They Know

*E*very culture has its theories about dreams. In some, dreams are thought to occur when the spirit leaves the body to wander the world or speak to the gods. In the Bible, dreams provided revelations: It was while dreaming, for example, that Joseph learned there was to be a famine in Egypt. A Chinese Taoist of the third century B.C. pondered the possible reality of the dream world. He told of dreaming that he was a butterfly merrily flitting about. "Suddenly I woke up and I was indeed Chuang Tzu. Did Chuang Tzu dream he was a butterfly, or did the butterfly dream he was Chuang Tzu?"

Until recently, dreams seemed beyond the reach of science. No one knew much about them, not even how common they were or how long they lasted. Introspection led to a dead end. Some people claimed they dreamed each night, others that they never dreamed. Some said their dreams went on for hours, but others subscribed to a popular belief that all dreams were compressed into a second or two. No one could be sure which subjective reports were accurate. How was anyone to study dreams objectively?

In the 1950s, a breakthrough occurred: Psychologists and other scientists learned to use technology to probe the world of slumber. They drew on the invention, two decades earlier, of the electroencephalograph, a machine that uses small, circular electrodes placed on the scalp to measure the brain's electrical activity (see Chapter 3). Volunteers spent their nights sleeping in laboratories while scientists observed them and measured changes in their "brain wave" patterns. Recordings of muscle tension, breathing, and other physiological responses were also made.

In 1953, a student in a sleep laboratory where infants were being studied noticed that the babies' eyes often darted around beneath their lids as they slept. It was the sort of unplanned observation that can set off a chain reaction in science. Researchers soon discovered that adults' eyes did the same thing every hour and a half or so, for periods lasting from a few minutes to as long as an hour and averaging about 20 minutes in length. Whenever eye movements began, the pattern of electrical activity from the sleeper's brain changed to resemble that of alert wakefulness. What's more, when volunteers were awakened during periods of rapid eye movement (REM), they usually reported dreaming, while at other times they usually did not.

Old questions soon found new answers. Researchers learned that *everyone* dreams. (There has been only one apparent exception, an Israeli man with shrapnel embedded in his brain.) People who claim they never dream do recall dreams if awakened during REM sleep. In fact, they are just as likely to dream as other people (Goodenough et al., 1959). Also, dreams are *not* compressed into an instant. When volunteers are awakened 5 minutes after REM starts, they report shorter dreams than when they are awakened after 15 minutes (Dement & Kleitman, 1957). Other findings suggest that the events in dreams take just as long as they seem to. If you dream that you are singing all the verses to "A Hundred Bottles of Beer on the Wall," your dream probably lasts as long as it takes to sing the song. Most dreams take several minutes, and some may last half an hour.

Sleeping and dreaming are discussed more fully in Chapter 4. We have touched on the topic here to illustrate why research methods, the focus of this chapter, are so

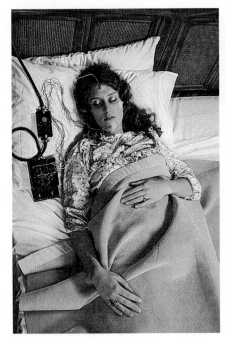

Innovative research methods have enabled psychologists to study many questions that once seemed unanswerable. Here, a volunteer in a sleep experiment slumbers while researchers measure her brain and muscle activity. If awakened during periods of rapid eye movement, she is likely to report that she has been dreaming.

important to psychologists. *These methods are the tools of the psychologist's trade.* They allow researchers to separate the kernel of truth from the chaff of unfounded belief. Sometimes, as in the case of dreaming, an innovative or clever method even reveals answers to questions that previously seemed impossible to study.

Science Versus Pseudoscience

Perhaps you are saying to yourself, "Okay, psychologists have to know about research methods. But what can knowing about them do for me (besides help me pass this course)? Why not just get to the findings?" In this section, we will give you two answers. Then we will look at the assumptions and procedures that you need to know about if you are to distinguish good science from bad.

Why study methodology?

A psychologist has published a paper in which she states that all of the abusive parents in a sample from a large midwestern city were mistreated as children. Does this mean that any child who is abused will grow up to become an abusive parent?

One reason to study methodology is that it can help you identify fallacies in your own or other people's thinking. Good methods are the psychologist's weapons against mental errors, but they can be used by nonpsychologists as well. Consider the tendency we all have to look for evidence that supports our ideas and to ignore evidence that doesn't. Sometimes this can have profound personal consequences. Adults who were abused early in life are often afraid to have children of their own because they think their experience has ruined them as parents. Social workers, judges, and other professionals sometimes make the same assumption: One judge denied a woman custody of her children solely because she had been abused as a

TABLE 2.1
EXAMINING THE EVIDENCE

Is an abused child likely to become an abusive parent? People often base their answer solely on confirming cases, represented by the upper left-hand cell of this table. Psychological researchers consider all four types of evidence in the table.

Abused as a child?

		Yes	No
Abusive as a parent?	**Yes**	Abused children who become abusive parents	Nonabused children who become abusive parents
	No	Abused children who do not become abusive parents	Nonabused children who do not become abusive parents

child, although the woman had never harmed her children. People who think that abusiveness inevitably passes from one generation to another are considering only confirming cases—abused children who become abusive adults. They disregard those who have suffered abuse but do not mistreat their children. A psychologist would consider both groups, as well as people who were not abused as children and then grew up to be—or not to be—abusive parents (see Table 2.1). As we will see in Chapter 13, when you take all the data into account, you find that although being abused is certainly a risk factor for becoming an abusive parent, most abused children do *not* grow up to mistreat their own offspring (Kaufman & Zigler, 1987).

Many other mental stumbling blocks interfere with the ability to describe, understand, and predict behavior accurately. You will find further examples in "Taking Psychology with You" at the end of this chapter.

A second reason for studying methodology is to become a more critical consumer of psychological findings. Psychology can be useful to you in many ways, but you should not accept every reported finding uncritically. You are constantly being bombarded with conflicting claims about matters that can affect your life—claims about how you should break bad habits, rear your children, dress for success, settle marital disputes, overcome shyness, reduce stress. Not all studies on such matters are created equal, and some advice from self-styled "experts" is based on no research at all. As psychologists, we hope that when you hear and read about psychological issues, you will consider how the information was obtained and how the conclusions were reached.

What makes research scientific?

When we refer to psychologists as scientists, we do not mean that they work with complicated gadgets and machines; many classic studies have been done with no more than paper and pencil. Nor do we mean that they wear white lab coats and carry clipboards, though some psychologists do. Scientific psychology has more to do with attitudes and procedures than with apparatus. It shares with other sciences the assumption that *the universe is an orderly place that operates according to certain general laws.* It assumes that these laws can be learned by systematically collecting evidence and testing ideas.

Philosophers have written many fat books on the features that distinguish science from other ways of knowing. We can't go into all these features, but here are a few key characteristics of the ideal scientist:

1. *Skepticism.* Scientists do not accept ideas on faith or authority; their motto is "Show me!" Some of the greatest scientific breakthroughs have been made by those who dared to doubt what everyone else assumed to be true: that the sun revolves around the earth, that illness can be cured by applying leeches to the skin, that madness is a sign of demonic possession. In the everyday world of the researcher, skepticism means accepting conclusions, both new and old, with caution. Caution, however, must be balanced by an openness to new ideas and evidence. Otherwise, the scientist may wind up as shortsighted as the famous physicist Lord Kelvin, who at the end of the nineteenth century declared confidently that "radio has no future," that "X-rays will prove to be a hoax," and that "heavier-than-air flying machines are impossible."

2. *Reliance on empirical evidence.* Unlike plays and poems, scientific theories and hypotheses are not judged by how artistically pleasing or entertaining they are. When an idea is first proposed, it may generate excitement simply because it is plausible, imaginative, or appealing. But no matter how true or right it seems, eventually it must be backed by evidence if it is to be taken seriously. This evidence must be *empirical,* that is, based on careful observation or experimentation. A collection of personal accounts or anecdotes will not do. Consider the plausible notion that *infantile autism,* a profound mental disorder that first appears in early childhood, is caused when a child is rejected by an emotionally cold mother (Bettelheim, 1967). Some clinicians once accepted this idea, which was based on therapists' personal observations of a limited number of cases. But they were wrong. When researchers carefully observed parents of autistic children and gave them standard personality tests, they found them to be no different on average than parents of normal children (DeMyer, 1975; Wolff & Morris, 1971). Today there is general agreement that autism stems from a neurological problem.

3. *Precision.* Most research starts out with a **hypothesis**, a statement that attempts to describe or explain behavior. Initially, the hypothesis may be stated in very general terms, as in "Anxiety increases sociability." But before any research can be done, the hypothesis must be put into more specific terms; for example, "People who are anxious about a threatening situation tend to seek out others who face the same threat." Some hypotheses are derived from a general **theory**, or organized system of assumptions and principles that purports to explain certain phenomena and how they are related. Others are suggested by a previous finding or by casual observation.

A hypothesis leads to explicit predictions about what will happen in a particular situation. In a prediction, vague terms such as *anxiety* or *physical danger* are given **operational definitions** that specify how they are to be observed and measured. For example, *anxiety* might be defined as a score on an anxiety questionnaire and *physical danger* as the threat of an electric shock. The prediction might be, "If you raise people's anxiety scores by telling them they are going to receive electric shocks, and then give them the choice of waiting alone or with others in the same situation, they will be more likely to choose to wait with others than they would if they were not anxious." The prediction is then tested, according to certain procedures.

In contrast, pseudoscientists—people who pretend to be scientific—often hide behind vague and empty statements and predictions that are nearly meaningless. If

hypothesis *A statement that attempts to predict or account for a set of phenomena. Scientific hypotheses specify relationships among events or variables and are supported or disconfirmed by empirical investigation.*
theory *An organized system of assumptions and principles that purports to explain a specified set of phenomena and their interrelationships.*
operational definition *A precise definition of a term in a hypothesis that specifies how it is to be observed and measured.*

your astrological forecast tells you that "today will be a good time to take care of unfinished tasks," what have you learned? Isn't every day a good one for crossing things off your list?

4. *Openness.* Scientists must be willing to tell others where they got their ideas, how they tested them, and what the results were. They must do this clearly so that other scientists can repeat, or **replicate**, their studies to verify the findings. Secrets do not advance scientific knowledge.

5. *Willingness to make "risky predictions."* A scientist must state ideas in such a way that they can be *refuted,* or disproved by counterevidence. That doesn't mean the ideas *will* be disproved, only that they *could* be if certain kinds of facts were discovered. A researcher who will not stick his or her neck out and risk *disconfirmation* is not a true scientist. A willingness to make risky predictions forces scientists to take negative evidence seriously.

This last characteristic is a little tricky, so let's take an example. Most psychologists view **parapsychology**, the study of extrasensory perception (ESP) and other "psychic" phenomena, as a pseudoscience. One objection, among many, is that parapsychologists often refuse to make risky predictions. If someone who claims to have ESP does better than chance at guessing a series of symbols on hidden cards, parapsychologists exclaim, "Aha, ESP at work!" But if the person performs only at chance levels, they say that the person had a bad day or that the "vibes" were bad. If the person does worse than chance, they say ESP was working, but in the opposite direction! The official policy of the *Journal of Parapsychology* is to reject any negative findings for publication, which means there is no way to disprove parapsychological notions (Radner & Radner, 1982).

Some critics of psychoanalysis find it guilty of the same thing. If a person recalls some conflict in childhood that psychoanalysts think is universal, the psychoanalysts say, "Aha, evidence for our theory!" If a person can't recall such a conflict, the psychoanalysts say it must have been repressed (forced into the unconscious mind so that it can't be remembered). Thus there is no evidence that can count against the theory. *Any theory that cannot in principle be refuted is unscientific.*

Do psychologists and other scientists always live up to the lofty standards expected of them? Of course not. Like everyone else they are human. They may put too much trust in their personal experiences. They may deceive themselves. They may permit ambition to interfere with openness. They may fail to put their theories fully to the test: It is always easier to be skeptical about someone else's ideas than about your own pet theory. In one study of eminent space scientists, every one of the 42 researchers interviewed thought the stereotype of the emotionally neutral scientist was naive (Mitroff, 1974). Even Albert Einstein sometimes resisted data that might have disconfirmed his own ideas.

Commitment to one's theories is not a bad thing. Passion is the fuel of progress. It motivates researchers to think boldly, defend unpopular ideas, and do the exhaustive testing that is often required. But passion can also cloud objectivity and in a few sad cases has even led to fraud (Roman, 1988; Stewart & Feder, 1987). That is why science must be a *communal affair.* Scientists are expected to share their evidence and procedures with others. They must persuade skeptical colleagues that their position is well supported. The scientific community—in our case, the psychological community—acts as a jury, scrutinizing and sifting the evidence, approving some viewpoints and relegating others to the scientific scrap heap. This public process gives science a built-in system of checks and balances and makes it self-correcting. Individuals are not always objective or even rational, but science forces them to justify their claims.

replicate *To duplicate or repeat.*

parapsychology *The study of phenomena, such as extrasensory perception, that do not appear explainable by known natural laws.*

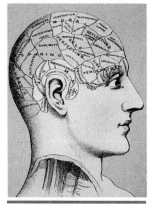

FIGURE 2.1

A wrong-headed theory
Nineteenth-century phrenologists thought that different parts of the brain accounted for specific traits of character and personality, and that these traits could be "read" from bumps on the skull. Like many pseudoscientific theories before and since, phrenology was wildly popular— and nonsense.

QUICK QUIZ

Test your understanding of science by identifying which of its rules each of the following historical figures violated.

1. The great Isaac Newton (1642–1727) discovered the basic laws of motion and invented calculus. But he also had a secret side. For years he experimented with alchemy, trying to turn base metals into gold and concoct special potions that would give him occult powers. He never told his colleagues what he was doing. *openness*

2. Alfred Russel Wallace (1823–1913) hit upon the theory of evolution at about the same time that Charles Darwin did. Later he became fascinated by attempts to communicate with the dead. To prove that communication with spirits was possible, he had professional mediums conduct séances. He trusted these mediums and was persuaded by their demonstrations.

3. Joseph Gall (1758–1828) was an Austrian physician who thought character was revealed by the bumps on a person's skull. He reported that he had examined many thieves who had large bumps above the ears. Gall also found people with "stealing bumps" who were not thieves. In such cases, he explained, a bump for "religiosity" or some other admirable trait held the person's thieving impulses in check (see Figure 2.1).

Answers:

1. Newton violated the requirement of openness. 2. Wallace was gullible rather than skeptical. 3. Gall failed to make risky predictions; his theory was impossible to refute by counterevidence because he could explain anything away by referring to one or another "bump."

Ferreting Out the Facts: Descriptive Studies

Psychologists use several different methods in their research, depending on the kinds of questions they want to answer. These methods are not mutually exclusive. Just as a police detective may use a magnifying glass *and* a fingerprint duster *and* interviews of suspects to figure out "who done it," psychological "sleuths" may draw on different techniques at different stages of an ongoing investigation.

Many psychological methods are **descriptive** in nature. That is, they allow a researcher to describe behavior but not to explain its causes. Some descriptive methods are used primarily by clinicians to describe the behavior of individuals. Others are used primarily by researchers to compare groups of people and arrive at generalizations about human behavior. Certain methods can be used in either way. In this section we will discuss the most common descriptive methods. (Suggestion: As you read, list each method's advantages and disadvantages on a piece of paper. When you finish this and the next two sections, check your list against the one in Table 2.2 on p. 63.)

descriptive methods
Methods that yield descriptions of behavior but not causal explanations.
case history (case study) *A detailed description of a particular individual under study or treatment.*

Case histories

A **case history** (or **case study**) is a detailed description of a particular individual. It may be based on careful observation or formal psychological testing. It may include information about the person's childhood, dreams, fantasies, experiences, relationships, and hopes—anything that will increase insight into the person's behavior. Case histories are most commonly used by clinicians, but they are occasionally used by academic researchers as well. They are especially valuable in the investigation of a new topic. Many early language researchers started out by keeping detailed diaries on the language development of their own children. A case history can be a rich source of hypotheses for future research.

Case histories illustrate psychological principles in a way that abstract generalizations and cold statistics never can, which is why we have peppered this book with them. They also produce a more detailed picture of an individual than other methods do. Often, however, case histories depend on people's memories of the past, and such memories may be both selective and inaccurate. Moreover, because case histories focus on individuals, they have severe drawbacks that limit their usefulness for psychologists who want to generalize about human behavior. The person who is the subject of a case history may be unlike most other people, or even those of the same economic class or age group. Moreover, it is often hard to know how to choose one interpretation of a case over another.

Still, case histories can be enlightening when practical or ethical considerations prevent information from being gathered in other ways. Let's take an example. Many psychologists believe that a "critical period" for language learning occurs between late infancy and puberty (Lenneberg, 1967). They argue that a child who fails to learn a language will be unable to catch up completely later on, no matter how much special tutoring the person gets. How can psychologists test this hypothesis? Obviously, they cannot put children in solitary confinement until adolescence and then suddenly expose them to language. However, they can study the tragic cases of children who were abandoned or isolated by their parents and were therefore prevented from acquiring language until they were rescued, sometimes after many years of solitude. These "experiments of nature" often leave many questions unanswered: How long was the child alone? At what age was the child isolated or abandoned? Was the child born mentally retarded? Did the child have a chance to learn any language before the ordeal began? But they can also provide valuable information.

In 1970, social workers discovered a 13-year-old girl whose parents had locked her up in one small room since age 1½. During the day they usually strapped her in a child's potty seat. At night they confined her to a straitjacketlike sleeping bag. The mother, a battered wife who lived in terror of her husband, barely cared for the child. The father barked and growled at the little girl like a dog and physically abused her. There was no television or radio in the home, and no one spoke a word to the child. If she made the slightest sound, her father beat her with a large piece of wood.

Genie, as researchers later called her, hardly seemed human when she was finally set free from her terrifying prison. She did not know how to chew or stand erect and she was not toilet trained. She slobbered uncontrollably, masturbated in public, and spit on anything that was handy, including herself and other people. When she was first observed by psychologists, her only sounds were high-pitched whimpers. She understood only a few words, probably learned shortly after her release.

Yet Genie was alert and curious. Placed in a hospital rehabilitation center and then a foster home, she made rapid progress. She developed physically, learned some basic rules of social conduct, and established relationships with others. Gradually she began to use words and understand short sentences. Eventually she was able to use language to convey her needs, describe her moods, and even lie. How-

This picture was drawn by Genie, the adolescent girl described in the text, who endured years of isolation and mistreatment. It shows one of Genie's favorite pastimes: listening to researcher Susan Curtiss play classical music on the piano. Genie's drawings were used along with other case material to study her mental and social development.

ever, her grammar and pronunciation of words remained abnormal even after several years. Susan Curtiss (1977) studied Genie's language development as part of her doctoral work and concluded that Genie's case supported the "critical period" hypothesis.

Ironically, then, the unusual and even bizarre circumstances of one person's life can shed light on a general question about human nature. Most case histories, however, are *sources* rather than *tests* of hypotheses.

Naturalistic observation

The primary purpose of **naturalistic observation** is to describe behavior as it occurs in the natural environment. Ethologists (scientists who study animal behavior), like Jane Goodall and the late Dian Fossey, use this method to study apes and other animals. Psychologists use naturalistic observation wherever people happen to be—at home, on playgrounds, in schoolrooms and offices. Most researchers find naturalistic observation more acceptable than the case history method because it usually involves many **subjects**. Often it is the first step in a program of research. You need a good description of behavior before you can explain it.

In one study using naturalistic observation, a social psychologist and his students ventured into a common human habitat—bars. They wanted to know whether people who drink in bars consume more alcohol when they are in groups than when they are alone. They visited all 32 pubs in a middle-sized city, ordered beers, and proceeded to record on napkins and pieces of newspaper how much the other patrons imbibed. They found that drinkers in groups consumed more than individuals who were by themselves. Those in groups didn't drink any faster; they just lingered in the bar longer (Sommer, 1977).

Note that the student researchers in this study did not rely on their impressions or memories of how much people drank. In observational studies, it is important to *count, rate,* or *measure* behavior. This procedure helps to minimize the tendency of most observers to notice only what they expect or want to see. Careful record keeping ensures accuracy and allows different observers to cross-check their obser-

naturalistic observation
The observation of subjects in their natural environment.
subjects *Animals or human beings used in research.*

These people are simply taking a lunch break and enjoying the sun, but a researcher using naturalistic observation could raise many questions about their behavior. How far apart do strangers sit as opposed to acquaintances? Who looks at whom, and for how long? Who talks or interrupts more often, men or women? (See if you can come up with some further research questions of your own.)

vations. Cross-checking is necessary to make sure the observations are reliable, or consistent, from person to person.

Note, too, that the researchers took pains to avoid being obvious about what they were doing. If they had marched in with video cameras and announced that they were psychology students, people might not have behaved naturally. In other studies, researchers have concealed themselves entirely. When such precautions are taken, naturalistic observation gives us a glimpse of subjects as they really are. However, it does *not* tell us what caused their behavior. For example, the barroom results do not necessarily mean that being in a group makes people drink a lot. People may join a group because they are already interested in drinking and find it more comfortable to hang around the bar if they are with others.

Laboratory observation

In **laboratory observation**, the researcher's observations take place in a setting determined by the researcher, usually a laboratory. The researcher attempts to re-create a situation that ordinarily takes place in the natural environment. In the laboratory, the psychologist has more control over what is going on. He or she can use sophisticated equipment (as in the sleep studies), control how many people are observed at once, get a clear line of vision while observing, and so forth.

Suppose you want to know how infants of different ages respond when left in the company of a stranger. You could go to a nursery school to observe infants, but most of the children would probably already be toddlers and would already know the nursery school personnel. You could sit around in a playground, but it would be a long time before you would find a parent leaving an infant alone. You could visit private homes, but that might be slow and inconvenient.

One solution is to have parents and their infants come to your laboratory, observe them together for a while through a one-way window, then have a stranger enter the room and, a few minutes later, have the parent leave. You could record signs of distress, interactions with the stranger, and other behavior. Laboratory observations like these have shown that very young infants carry on cheerfully with whatever they are doing when the parent leaves. However, by the age of about 8 months they often burst into tears or show other signs of what child psychologists call *separation anxiety* (Ainsworth, 1979).

laboratory observation *The observation of subjects in a research laboratory.*

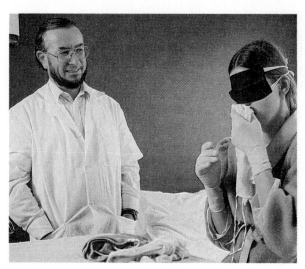 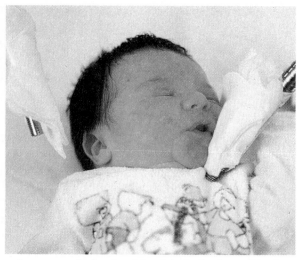

Can mothers and infants recognize one another's odors? It might be hard to tell in the natural environment, with its many distractions and scents—for example, the background fragrance of dinner cooking. But in the laboratory, researchers have better control over the factors they are investigating. Using laboratory methods, French ethologist Hubert Montagner (1985) has shown that infants as young as three days are calmer when they get a whiff of gauze worn by their mothers than when they smell gauze worn by other women. Moreover, by then mothers can distinguish their own baby's shirt from the shirts of other newborns on the basis of smell alone.

Probably the most highly publicized laboratory observations of all time were by physician William Masters and his co-worker, Virginia Johnson, during the 1950s. Masters and Johnson wanted to study the physiology of sexual arousal—changes in heart rate, blood pressure, blood vessel engorgement, and so forth. People in the throes of passion are not good observers of subtle physiological changes. Even if they were, many changes would simply not be visible to them. Collecting physiological data, therefore, requires the use of special measuring and recording devices. For this reason, Masters and Johnson (1966) recruited volunteers to masturbate and have intercourse in a laboratory at Washington University. In a few short years they were able to learn more about the physiology of sex than had ever been known before.

Like naturalistic observation, laboratory observation is more useful for describing than explaining behavior. For example, sleep studies show that rapid eye movements are associated with dreaming. But why? Many researchers believe that a sleeping person "watches" the events in a dream as one would watch a movie screen. But then, what does a newborn baby watch? Could it be only a coincidence that dreams and eye movements occur at the same time? Another shortcoming of this method is that behavior in the laboratory may differ from behavior in the normal environment. As we will see, this is also a problem in experiments.

Surveys

surveys *Questionnaires and interviews that ask people directly about their experiences, attitudes, or opinions.*

A quick way to get information about people is to ask them for it. Questionnaires and interviews that ask people directly about their experiences, attitudes, or opinions are called **surveys**. Surveys have been done on many topics, from consumer preferences to sexual preferences. Most people are familiar with surveys in the form of national opinion polls, such as the Gallup poll.

Surveys produce bushels of data, but they are not easy to do well. The biggest hurdle is getting a **sample** that is **representative** of the larger **population** that the researcher wishes to describe. Suppose you want to know what college freshmen think about the draft. You can't question every college freshman in the United States; you must choose a sample of 50 or 100 or 1000. Special selection procedures can be used to ensure that this sample will be representative, that is, that it will contain the same proportion of women, men, blacks, whites, poor people, rich people, Catholics, Jews, and so forth, as the general population of college freshmen. The sample's size is less critical than its representativeness; a small but representative sample may yield extremely accurate results. In contrast, surveys and polls that fail to use proper sampling methods may yield questionable results. A newspaper that asks its readers to vote yes or no by telephone on a controversial question is hardly conducting a scientific poll. Only those who feel very strongly about an issue (*and* read the newspaper) are likely to call in, and those who feel strongly may be likely to take a particular side. A psychologist or statistician would say that the poll suffers from **volunteer bias**: Those who volunteer to take part probably differ from those who stay silent.

Similarly, many magazines—*Redbook, Cosmopolitan, Playboy, Psychology Today, The Ladies' Home Journal*—have done surveys on the sexual habits of their readers. The readers who respond to these surveys may be more (or possibly less) sexually active, on the average, than those who do not respond. In addition, people who read magazines regularly tend to be younger, more educated, and more affluent than the American population as a whole, and these characteristics may affect the results. When you read a survey, always ask, "What sorts of people participated?" Volunteer bias and a nonrepresentative sample do not necessarily mean that a survey is worthless or uninteresting, but they do mean that the results may not hold for other groups. (Volunteer bias can be a problem in any kind of study. Masters and Johnson have been criticized for using laboratory observations of volunteers to generalize about the population as a whole.)

A final problem with surveys is that people sometimes lie. This is especially likely when the survey is about a touchy topic ("What? Me do that? Never!"). The likelihood of lying is reduced when respondents are guaranteed anonymity. There are some ways to check for lying—for example, by asking the same question several times in different ways—but not all surveys use these techniques. Moreover, even when people do not intentionally lie, they may misremember. Still, if surveys are conducted carefully and interpreted with caution they can be very informative.

Tests

Psychological tests, like surveys, often require people to answer a series of written or oral questions, but they tend to elicit information less directly than surveys do. Answers are often totaled to yield a single numerical score, or a set of scores, that reveals something about the person. There are tests to measure personality traits, emotional states, aptitudes, interests, abilities, and values. They are used in educational and job settings and in clinical work to evaluate individuals, promote self-understanding, or evaluate treatments and programs, and in scientific research to draw generalizations about groups. Some tests measure beliefs, feelings, or behaviors of which an individual is aware. Others are designed to tap unconscious feelings or motives. Psychological tests are an improvement over simple self-evaluation because many people have a distorted view of their own abilities and traits (see "Think About It").

Your favorite magazine has just published a sensational survey of its female readers called "The Sex Life of the American Wife." The survey reports that "Eighty-seven percent of all wives like to make love in rubber boots." Is this claim justified? What would be a more accurate title for the survey?

sample *A group of subjects selected from a population for study in order to estimate characteristics of the population.*

representative sample *A sample that matches the population in question on important characteristics such as age and sex.*

population *The entire set of individuals from which a sample is drawn.*

volunteer bias *A shortcoming of findings derived from a sample of volunteers instead of a representative sample.*

psychological tests *Procedures used to measure personality traits, emotional states, aptitudes, interests, abilities, and values.*

Think About It

Are You Better Than Average?

Many people form their beliefs about human nature by studying a sample of one—themselves. Or perhaps they expand the sample just a bit to include their best friend, worst enemy, and the neighborhood grocer. They assume that their opinions, values, and attitudes, or those of people they happen to know, are typical of "most people." Often, this is a delusion.

However, when it comes to socially desirable character traits and abilities, people tend to make a different error. Instead of seeing themselves as typical, they think they are *better* than average, even when they are not. For example, what percentage of your fellow students do you think are more honest than you? More attractive? More considerate? More knowledgeable about politics? When presented with questions like these, most people say that only a small percentage of people outshine them. On the average, in other words, people think they are better than average. In one study of 829,000 high school seniors who took the College Boards, not one student thought that he or she was below average in the ability to get along with others. A majority thought they were in the top 10 percent, and a quarter said they were in the top 1 percent (Myers, 1980).

Now, not everyone can be better than average; it's a statistical impossibility. Some people must be deceiving themselves. At times, this deception may mask underlying insecurities and self-doubts. That is not necessarily a bad thing; a "positive self-bias" can bolster self-confidence and ward off depression. But it can also interfere with a person's objectivity

and ability to make sound decisions (Myers & Ridl, 1979; Wood, 1984). For example, if you mistakenly think you are healthier than average, you may not get needed vaccinations against disease.

Because of the "better than average" phenomenon, psychologists are cautious about trusting people's self-reports concerning their own personality traits and abilities. A psychologist who wanted to know how many people are especially helpful to others would not simply ask people to judge their own helpfulness. He or she would use a more objective method, either observational or experimental. Objective methods also force the *researcher* to be objective, for even psychologists who know about biases are not immune. Objective methods require researchers who think their opinions, ideas, and conclusions are better than average to prove it.

How susceptible are you to believing you are better than average when you are not? As you read the preceding paragraphs, did you find yourself insisting that you were not one of those overly prideful people who exaggerate their strengths, that you were better than average in this regard? Perhaps you were demonstrating the phenomenon! On the other hand, most people actually are better than average in some way or other; the trick is to know when your perceptions of your strengths are valid. The solution to pride is not false modesty. As two writers on this topic point out (Myers & Ridl, 1979), "False modesty can actually lead to an ironic pride in one's better-than-average humility." Think about it.

---

valid test *A test that measures what it sets out to measure.*

reliable test *A test that yields consistent results from one time and place to another.*

Test construction, administration, and interpretation require specialized training. It is extremely difficult to construct a test that is **valid** (measures what it sets out to measure) and **reliable** (yields the same results from one time and place to the next). A test that purports to measure creativity is not valid if it actually measures verbal sophistication. A vocational interest test is not reliable if it tells Tom he would make a wonderful engineer but a poor journalist, and then gives different results when Tom takes the test again a week later. The "psychological tests" frequently found in magazines and Sunday supplements often are not constructed scientifically. They are simply lists of questions that someone thought sounded good.

QUICK ▪ QUIZ

Which descriptive method would be most appropriate for studying each of the following topics? Why? (P.S.: We did not make up these topics. Each has been the focus of research.)

1. Ways in which the playground games of boys differ from those of girls *b*
2. Changes in attitudes toward nuclear disarmament after a television movie about nuclear holocaust *d*
3. The mathematical skills of U.S. children compared with those of Japanese children *e*
4. Physiological changes that occur when people watch violent movies *c*
5. The psychosexual development of a male infant who was reared as a female after his penis was accidentally burned off during a supposedly routine circumcision involving electrocauterization *a*

a. case study
b. naturalistic observation
c. laboratory observation
d. survey
e. test

Answers:

1. b 2. d 3. e 4. c 5. a

Looking for Relationships: Correlational Studies

In descriptive research, psychologists often want to know whether two or more phenomena are related, and if so, how strongly. To find out, they do **correlational studies**. If a researcher surveyed college students to find out how many hours a week they spent watching television, the study would not be correlational. If the researcher went on to look for a relationship between hours in front of the television and grade point average, then it would be.

The word **correlation** is often used as a synonym for "relationship." Technically, however, a correlation is a numerical measure of the *strength* of the relationship between two or more things. The "things" may be events, scores, or anything else that can be recorded and tallied. In psychological studies, such things are called **variables** because they can vary in quantifiable ways. Height, weight, age, income, IQ scores, number of items recalled on a memory test, number of smiles in a given time period—anything that can be measured, rated, or scored can serve as a variable.

Correlations always occur between *sets* of observations. Sometimes the sets come from one individual. Suppose you measured both a person's temperature and the person's alertness several times during the day. To check for a relationship between temperature and alertness, you would need several measurements, or values, for each variable. Of course, your results would hold only for that individual. In research, sets of correlated observations usually come from many individuals or are used to compare groups of people. For example, in research on the origins of intelligence, psychologists look for a relationship between the IQ scores of parents

correlational study *A descriptive study that looks for a consistent relationship between two phenomena.*
correlation *A measure of how strongly two or more variables are related to each other.*
variables *Characteristics of behavior or experience that can be measured or described by a numeric scale. Variables are manipulated and assessed in scientific studies.*

and children. To do this, they must gather scores from a *set* of parents and a *set* of their children. You cannot compute a correlation if you only know the IQs of one particular parent-child pair. To say that a relationship exists, you need more than one pair of values to compare.

A **positive correlation** means that high values of one variable are associated with high values of the other, and that low values of one variable are associated with low values of the other. It is easy to think of variables that are positively correlated: height and weight, IQ scores and school grades, and hemline lengths and stock market prices (or so they say; we're not so sure about this last one). Rarely is a correlation perfect, though. Some tall people weigh less than some short ones; some people with average IQs are superstars in the classroom; and sometimes stock prices rise when hemlines fall. Figure 2.2(a) shows a positive but not perfect relationship between educational level and annual income.

A **negative correlation** means that high values of one variable are associated with *low* values of the other [see Figure 2.2(b)]. In the automobile business, the older the car, the lower the price, except for antiques and models favored by collectors. As for human beings, in general the older adults are, the fewer miles they can run and the fewer hairs they have on their heads. See if you can think of some other variables that are negatively correlated. Remember, though, a negative correlation indicates that a certain kind of relationship exists. If there is *no* relationship between two variables, we say they are *uncorrelated*. Freckles and IQ scores are uncorrelated.

The statistic used to express a correlation is called the **coefficient of correlation**. A perfect positive correlation has a coefficient of +1.00. Suppose you weighed ten people and listed them in order, from lightest to heaviest. Then suppose you measured their heights and listed them in order, from shortest to tallest. If the names on the two lists were in the identical order, the correlation between weight and height would be +1.00. A perfect negative correlation would have a coefficient of −1.00. When there is no association between two variables, the coefficient is zero or close to zero. If you hear that the correlation between two things is +.80, it means that they are very strongly related. If you hear that the correlation is −.80, the relationship is just as strong, though negative.

Correlations allow researchers, using statistical techniques, to make general predictions about a variable if they know how it is related to another one. But because correlations are rarely perfect, predictions about a particular *individual* may be inaccurate. If you know that a person is well educated, you might predict, in the absence of any other information, that the person is fairly well off, because education and income are positively correlated. You would not be able to say exactly how much the person earned, but you would probably guess that it was relatively high. You could be wrong, though. Some people with doctorates earn low salaries, and some people with only a grade school education make fortunes.

Correlational studies in the social sciences are common and are often reported in the news. But beware—they can be misleading. The important thing to remember is that *a correlation does not show causation*. It is easy to assume that if A predicts B, A must be causing B—that is, making B happen—but that is not necessarily so. The number of storks nesting in certain French villages is reportedly correlated (positively) with the number of human births in those villages. In other words, knowing when the storks nest allows one to predict when more births than usual will occur. But clearly that doesn't mean that storks bring babies or that babies attract storks. Human births seem to be somewhat more frequent at certain times of the year (you might want to speculate on the reasons), and the peaks just happen to coincide with the storks' nesting periods.

positive correlation *An association between increases in one variable and increases in another.*

negative correlation *An association between increases in one variable and decreases in another.*

coefficient of correlation *A measure of correlation that ranges in value from −1.00 to +1.00.*

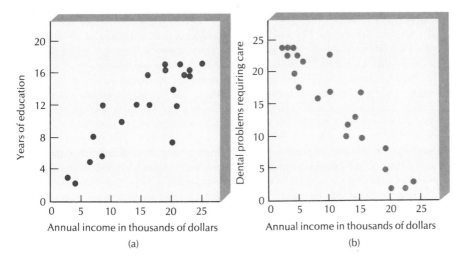

FIGURE 2.2

Correlations
Graph (a) shows a positive (though not perfect) correlation between education and income in a group of 20 men. Each dot represents a man. You can find each man's educational level by drawing a horizontal line from his dot to the vertical axis. You can find his income by drawing a vertical line from his dot to the horizontal axis. Graph (b) shows a negative correlation between average income and the incidence of dental disease for groups of 100 families. Each dot represents one group. In general, the higher the income, the fewer the dental problems. (From Wright, 1976.)

The stork example may seem obvious, but in other cases, unwarranted conclusions about causation are more tempting. For example, there is a significant correlation between circulation rates of adult magazines like *Penthouse* and *Playboy* and rates of reported rape (Scott & Schwalm, 1988). States like Alaska and Nevada, with high rape rates, tend to have high sales of such magazines. States like Maine and West Virginia, with low rape rates, tend to have low sales. Does this mean that the reading of adult magazines promotes rape? It is possible, but such a conclusion would be unwarranted. In areas with high rape rates, people who are already prone to rape may be especially likely to buy erotic magazines. Or a third factor, such as attitudes toward women, may affect both magazine sales and rape statistics (though the study that established the correlation did control for several such possibilities). Moreover, there is some evidence that sexually permissive areas of the country are more likely than nonpermissive areas to have accurate rape reporting procedures.

The moral of the story: When two variables are associated, one may or may not be causing the other.

QUICK ▪ QUIZ

Are you clear about correlations? Find out now by identifying each of the following as either a positive or a negative correlation. Then further test your understanding by generating two or three possible explanations for each finding.

1. The higher a child's IQ, the less physical force her mother is likely to use in disciplining her.
2. The higher a male monkey's level of the hormone testosterone, the more aggressive he is likely to be.
3. After a certain age, the older people are, the less frequently they tend to have sexual intercourse.
4. The hotter the weather, the more crimes against persons (such as muggings) tend to occur.

Answers:
1. Negative correlation. Physical force may impair a child's intellectual growth; brighter children may elicit less physical discipline from their parents; brighter mothers may have brighter children and may also tend to use less physical force.
2. Positive correlation. The hormone might cause aggressiveness or acting aggressively might stimulate hormone production. **3.** Negative correlation. Older people may have less interest in sex than younger people; older people may have less energy for sex; older people may think they are supposed to have less interest in sex and behave accordingly; older people may have trouble finding sexual partners. **4.** Positive correlation. Hot temperatures may make people edgy and cause them to commit crimes; potential victims may be more plentiful in warm weather because more people go out at night and stroll outside; criminals may find it more comfortable to be out committing their crimes in warm weather than in cold. (Note: Our explanations are not the only ones possible.)

Everyone knows that alcohol and the operation of heavy machinery don't mix—but what about the effects of nicotine on such work? What sort of experiment might answer that question?

experiment *A controlled test of a hypothesis in which the researcher manipulates one variable to discover its effect on another.*
independent variable *A variable that an experimenter manipulates.*
dependent variable *A variable that an experimenter predicts will be affected by manipulations of the independent variable.*

Hunting for Causes: The Experiment

Descriptive studies often lead researchers to propose explanations of behavior, but to actually track down the causes of behavior, psychologists rely on the experimental method. An **experiment** allows the researcher to *control* the situation being studied. Instead of being a passive recorder of what is going on, the researcher actively does something that he or she thinks will affect the subjects' behavior.

Variables

Suppose you come across reports that cigarette smoking improves performance on simple reaction time tasks. You do not question these findings, but you have a hunch that the nicotine in cigarettes may have the opposite effect on more complex or demanding kinds of behavior, such as driving. You know that on the average, smokers have more vehicular accidents than nonsmokers (DiFranza et al., 1986). But this relationship doesn't prove that smoking *causes* accidents. Perhaps smokers are simply greater risk takers than nonsmokers, be the risk lung cancer or trying to beat a red light. Or perhaps the distraction of falling cigarette ashes or of fumbling for matches explains the relationship, rather than smoking itself. So you decide to do an experiment. In a laboratory, you ask smokers to ''drive'' on a Monte Carlo-type road, using a computerized driving simulator equipped with a stick shift and a gas pedal. The object is to maximize distance by driving as fast as possible while avoiding rear-end collisions. (This task is similar to a video game called Turbo.) At your request, some of the subjects smoke a cigarette immediately before climbing into the driver's seat. Others do not. You are interested in comparing how many collisions the two groups have. (The basic design of this experiment is portrayed in Figure 2.3. You may want to refer to the figure from time to time as you read the next few pages.)

The aspect of an experimental situation manipulated or varied by the researcher is known as the **independent variable**. The reaction of the subjects—the behavior that the researcher tries to predict—is called the **dependent variable**. Every experiment has at least one independent and one dependent variable. In our example, the

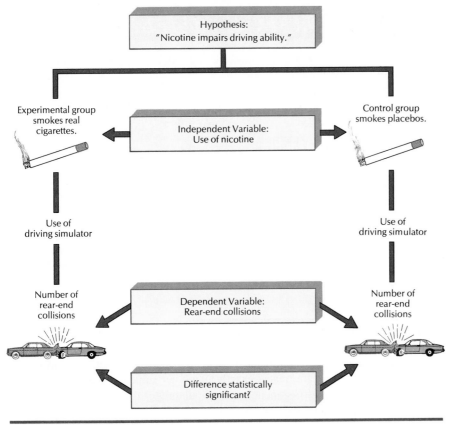

FIGURE 2.3

Do smoking and driving mix?

The text suggests an experiment to test the hypothesis that the nicotine in cigarettes impairs driving skills. The independent variable is use or nonuse of nicotine. The dependent variable is the number of rear-end collisions while operating a driving simulator. (A similar study, using more complex procedures, was reported by Spilich, 1987.)

independent variable is the level of nicotine use: one cigarette versus none. The dependent variable is the number of rear-end collisions.

Ideally, everything about the experimental situation *except* the independent variable is held constant, that is, kept the same for all subjects. You would not have some people use a stick shift and others an automatic, unless shift type were an independent variable. Similarly, you would not have some people go through the experiment alone and others perform in front of an audience. Holding everything but the independent variable constant ensures that whatever happens is due to the researcher's manipulation and nothing else.

Understandably, students often have trouble keeping independent and dependent variables straight. You might think of it this way: The value of the dependent variable *depends* on the value of the independent variable. When psychologist Smith sets up an experiment, she thinks, ''If I do (such and such), the subjects in my study will do (such and such).'' The first ''such and such'' represents the independent variable, the second the dependent variable. Most variables may be either independent or dependent, depending on what the experimenter is manipulating and trying to predict.

QUICK⌐QUIZ

Name the independent and dependent variables in studies designed to answer the following questions:

1. Whether sleeping after learning a poem improves memory for the poem
2. Whether the presence of other people affects a person's willingness to help someone in distress
3. Whether people get agitated from listening to rock and roll

Answers:

1. Opportunity to sleep after learning is the independent variable; memory for the poem is the dependent variable. 2. The presence or absence of other people is the independent variable; willingness to help others is the dependent variable. 3. Exposure to rock and roll is the independent variable; agitation is the dependent variable.

Experimental and control groups

You've developed a new form of therapy that you believe cures anxiety: Sixty-three percent of the people who go through your program improve. Why shouldn't you rush out to open an Anxiety Clinic?

Experiments usually require both an experimental group and a **control group**. People in the control group are treated exactly like other subjects except that they are not exposed to the same ''treatment'' or manipulation of the independent variable. Without a control group, you can't be sure the subjects' behavior would not have occurred anyway, even without your manipulation.

In the nicotine experiment, the subjects who smoke before driving make up the experimental group, and those who refrain from smoking make up the control group. We want these two groups to be roughly the same in terms of average driving skill. It wouldn't do to start out with a bunch of reckless roadrunners in the experimental group and a bunch of tired tortoises in the control group. We probably also want the groups to resemble each other in average intelligence, education, smoking history, and other characteristics. To accomplish this, we can use **random assignment** to place people in the groups. We might randomly give each person in the study a number, then put all those with even numbers in the experimental group and all those with odd numbers in the control group. At the beginning of the study, each subject will have the same probability as any other subject of being assigned to a given group. If we have enough subjects in our study, individual differences among them are likely to be roughly balanced in the two groups. However, for some characteristics, such as sex, we may decide not to depend on random assignment. Instead, we may deliberately assign an equal number of people from each category (e.g., male and female) to each group.

control group *A comparison group of subjects who are not exposed to the same ''treatment'' or manipulation of the independent variable as experimental subjects are.*

random assignment *A procedure for assigning people to experimental and control groups in which each individual has the same probability as any other of being assigned to a given group.*

Sometimes researchers use several different experimental and control groups. For example, in our nicotine study, we might want to examine the effects of different levels of nicotine by having smokers abstain for zero, one, two, three, or four hours before ''driving,'' and by including a group of nonsmokers as well. For now, however, let's focus just on experimental subjects who smoked cigarettes right before ''driving'' and control subjects who did not.

We now have two groups. We also have a problem. In order to smoke, the experimental subjects must light up and inhale. Those acts might set off certain expectations—of feeling relaxed, getting nervous, feeling confident, or whatever.

These expectations, in turn, might affect driving performance. It would be better to have the control group do everything the experimental group does *except* use nicotine. Therefore, let's change the experimental design a bit. Instead of having the control subjects simply refrain from smoking, we will give them a **placebo**, or fake treatment. Placebos, which are used frequently in drug research, often take the form of pills or injections. Assume that it's possible in the nicotine study to use phony cigarettes that taste and smell like the real thing but contain no active ingredients. Our control subjects will not know their cigarettes are fake and will have no way of distinguishing them from real ones. Now if they have substantially fewer collisions than the experimental group, we will feel safe in concluding that nicotine increases the probability of an auto accident. (Placebos, by the way, sometimes produce effects that are as strong or nearly as strong as those of a real treatment. Phony alcohol may make people feel high and phony injections may eliminate pain. These placebo effects, though well known, are a puzzle awaiting scientific solution.)

Experimenter effects

Because expectations can influence the results of a study, subjects should not know whether they are in an experimental or control group. When this is so (as it usually is), the experiment is said to be a **single-blind study**. But subjects are not the only ones who bring expectations to the laboratory; so do researchers. Their expectations (and hopes for a reportable result) may cause them inadvertently to influence participants' responses through facial expressions, posture, tone of voice, or some other cue.

Several years ago, Robert Rosenthal demonstrated how powerful such **experimenter effects** can be. He had students teach rats to run a maze. Half the students were told their rats had been bred to be ''maze bright,'' half that their rats had been bred to be ''maze dull.'' In reality, there were no genetic differences between the two groups of rats. During the course of the experiment, the supposedly brainy rats actually did learn the maze more quickly! If an experimenter's expectations can affect a rodent's behavior, reasoned Rosenthal, surely they can affect a human being's. He went on to demonstrate this in many other studies (R. Rosenthal, 1966, 1968).

Unfortunately, the cues an experimenter may give subjects can be as subtle as the smile on the Mona Lisa. In fact, the cue may *be* a smile. In one of his studies, Rosenthal found that male researchers were far more likely to smile at female subjects than at males. Since one smile tends to invite another, such behavior on the part of the experimenter could easily ruin a study on friendliness or cooperation. ''It may be a heartening finding to know that chivalry is not dead,'' noted Rosenthal, ''but as far as methodology is concerned it is a disconcerting finding.''

One solution to the problem of experimenter effects is to do a **double-blind study**. In such a study, the person running the experiment (the one having actual contact with the subjects) does not know which subjects are in which groups until the data have been gathered. Double-blind procedures are common in drug research. Different doses of a drug are coded in some way, and the person administering the drug is kept in the dark about the code's meaning until after the experiment. To run the nicotine study in a double-blind fashion, we would keep the person dispensing the cigarettes from knowing which ones were real and which were placebos. In psychological research, double-blind studies are often more difficult to design than those that are merely single-blind. The goal, however, is always to control everything possible in an experiment.

placebo *An inactive substance or fake treatment used as a control in an experiment or given by a medical practitioner to a patient.*

single-blind study *An experiment in which subjects do not know whether they are in an experimental or control group.*

experimenter effects *Unintended changes in subjects' behavior due to cues inadvertently given by the experimenter.*

double-blind study *An experiment in which neither the subjects nor the researchers know which subjects are in the control group(s) and which in the experimental group(s) until after the results are tallied.*

QUICK ▪ QUIZ

Can you say what's wrong with these two studies?

1. A kidney specialist and a psychiatrist treated mentally disordered patients by filtering their blood through a dialysis machine (normally used with kidney patients). They reported several cases of dramatic improvement, which they attributed to the removal of an unknown toxin (Wagemaker & Cade, 1978).
2. A sex researcher surveyed women on their feelings about men and love. She sent out 100,000 lengthy questionnaires to various women's groups and got back 4,500 replies (a 4.5 percent return). On the basis of these replies, she reported that 84 percent of women are dissatisfied with their relationships, 98 percent want more communication, and 70 percent of those married five years or more are having extramarital affairs (Hite, 1987).

Answers:

1. The dialysis study had no control group and was not done double-blind. Patients' expectations that the fancy "blood-cleansing" equipment would wash their madness out of them might have influenced the results, and so might the researchers' expectations. Later studies, using double-blind procedures, assigned control subjects to fake dialysis. Their blood was circulated through the machine but was not actually filtered. Little improvement occurred in either the experimental or the control condition, and improvement was no more likely during real treatment than during fake treatment (Carpenter et al., 1983). 2. Because of the way the sample was recruited and the low return rate, the findings may be flawed by volunteer bias. Although the study produced thought-provoking information on the feelings of many women, figures and percentages are not necessarily valid for the general population.

Evaluating the Findings:
Why Psychologists Use Statistics

If you are a psychologist who has just done an observational study, a survey, or an experiment, your work has only just begun. Once you have some results in hand, you must do three things with them: (1) describe them, (2) assess how meaningful they are, and (3) figure out how to explain them.

Descriptive statistics: Finding out what's so

Let's say that 30 people in the nicotine experiment smoked real cigarettes and 30 smoked placebos. We have recorded the number of collisions each person had on the driving simulator. Now we have 60 numbers. What can we do with them?

The first thing we must do is summarize the data. The world does not want to hear how many collisions each person had. It wants to know what happened in the "nicotine group" as a whole, compared to what happened in the control group. To provide this information, we need numbers that sum up our data. Such numbers are known as **descriptive statistics**. They are often depicted in graphs and charts.

descriptive statistics *Statistics that organize and summarize research data.*

	TABLE 2.2	
	RESEARCH METHODS IN PSYCHOLOGY: THEIR ADVANTAGES AND DISADVANTAGES	
Method	**Advantages**	**Disadvantages**
Case history	Good source of hypotheses. Provides in-depth information on individuals. "Experiments of nature" shed light on situations/problems that are unethical or impractical to study in other ways.	Individual may not be representative or typical. Difficult to know which subjective interpretation is best.
Naturalistic observation	Allows description of behavior as it occurs in the natural environment. Often useful in first stages of research program.	Allows researcher little or no control of the situation. Observations may be biased. Does not allow firm conclusions on cause and effect.
Laboratory observation	Allows more control than naturalistic observation. Allows use of sophisticated equipment.	Allows researcher only limited control of the situation. Observations may be biased. Does not allow firm conclusions on cause and effect. Behavior in the laboratory may differ from behavior in the natural environment.
Survey	Provides large amount of information on large numbers of people.	If sample is nonrepresentative or biased, it may be impossible to generalize from the results. Responses may be inaccurate or untrue.
Tests	Yield information on personality traits, emotional states, aptitudes, abilities.	Difficult to construct tests that are valid and reliable.
Correlational study	Shows whether two or more variables are related.	Does not permit identification of cause and effect.
Experiment	Allows researcher to control the situation. Permits researcher to identify cause and effect.	Situation is artificial and results may not generalize well to the real world. Sometimes difficult to avoid experimenter effects.

A good way to summarize the data is to compute group averages. The most commonly used type of average is the **arithmetic mean**. (For two other types, see the Appendix.) We can compute a mean for the nicotine group simply by adding up all 30 numbers and dividing by 30. We can do the same for the control group. Now our 60 numbers have been boiled down to 2. For the sake of our example, we will assume that the nicotine group had an average of 10 collisions, while the control group's average was only 7.

It is easy to be misled by the term *average*. It does *not* necessarily mean "typical." It could be that no one in our nicotine group actually had 10 collisions. Remember, the mean merely summarizes a mass of data. Perhaps half the people in the nicotine group were motoring maniacs and had 15 collisions, while the others were more cautious and had only 5. Perhaps almost all the subjects had 9, 10, or 11 collisions. Perhaps accidents were evenly distributed between zero and 15. The mean does not tell you about the variation in subjects' responses; there are other statistics for that. One, the **range**, gives the difference between the lowest and

arithmetic mean *An average that is calculated by adding up a set of quantities and dividing the sum by the total number of quantities in the set.*

range *A measure of the spread of scores, calculated by subtracting the lowest score from the highest score.*

FIGURE 2.4

Averages can be misleading
The statistical mean does not always give a clear picture of events. It is also important to know how much events deviate from the mean and how they are distributed.

FIGURE 2.5

Same mean, different variances
In both distributions of scores the mean is 5, but in (a) the scores are clustered around the mean, whereas in (b) they are widely dispersed. (From Wright, 1976.)

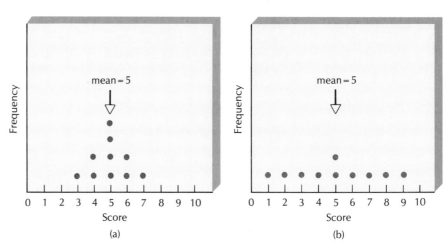

highest scores in a distribution of scores. If the lowest number of collisions in the nicotine group was 5 and the highest was 15, the range would be 10. Another, the **variance**, is more informative. Basically, the variance is a number that tells you how clustered or spread out the individual scores are around the mean (see Figures 2.4 and 2.5). Knowing about variance can help you understand certain passionate debates in psychology. The concept of variance has been important, for example, in arguments over the meaning of group differences in IQ (see Chapter 12). But when research is reported in the mass media, the public usually hears only about the mean.

There are other kinds of descriptive statistics as well, including the coefficient of correlation, which we covered earlier. Descriptive statistics are discussed in greater detail in the Appendix.

Inferential statistics: Asking "so what?"

At this point in our nicotine study, we have one group with an average of 10 collisions and another with an average of 7. Should we break out the champagne? Try to get on TV? Call our mothers?

Better hold off. Descriptive statistics do not tell us whether the outcome is anything to write home about. Perhaps if one group had an average of 15 and the other an average of 1 we could get excited. But rarely does a psychological study produce what one of our colleagues calls an ''interocular'' effect—one that hits you between the eyes. In most cases there is a possibility that the difference between the two groups was due simply to chance. Perhaps the people in the nicotine group just happened to be a little more accident-prone during the study, and their behavior had nothing to do with smoking. It would be surprising if the two groups had *exactly* the

variance *A measure of the dispersion of scores around the mean.*

same number of collisions; we would expect *some* difference just by chance.

To find out how significant the data are, the psychologist uses **inferential statistics**. They permit a researcher to draw *inferences* (conclusions based on evidence) about the findings. There are many inferential statistics to choose from, depending on the kind of study and what the researcher wants to know. Like descriptive statistics, they involve the application of mathematical formulas to the data. (See Appendix.)

Inferential statistics do not merely describe or summarize the data. *They tell the researcher how likely it is that the result of the study occurred by chance.* More precisely, they reveal the probability of obtaining an effect as large as (or larger than) the one observed, if manipulating the independent variable actually has no reliable effect on the behavior in question. It is impossible to rule out chance entirely. However, if the likelihood of the result occurring by chance is extremely low, we say the result is **statistically significant**. This means that the probability that the difference is "real" is overwhelming—not certain, mind you, but overwhelming. By convention, psychologists consider a result significant if it would be expected by chance 5 or fewer times in 100 repetitions of the study. (Another way of saying this is that the result is significant at the .05, or "point oh five," level.)

Inferential statistics are necessary because a result that seems unlikely may not be. For example, how probable do you think it is that in a room of 25 people, at least two have the same birthday? Most people think it is very unlikely, but in fact, the odds are better than even. Even if there are only 10 people in the room, the chances are 1 in 9. Among the U.S. presidents, two had the same birthday (Warren Harding and James Polk) and three died on the fourth of July (John Adams, the second president; Thomas Jefferson, the third; and James Monroe, the fifth). Surprising? No. Such "coincidences" are not statistically striking at all.

With inferential statistics, we can find out if an experimental result is truly a rare event. In our study (as summarized in Figure 2.3), they would tell us how likely it is that the difference between the nicotine group and the placebo group occurred by chance. If the difference could be expected to occur by chance in 6 out of 100 studies, we would have to say that the results failed to support the hypothesis. That is, we would be forced to conclude that the difference we obtained might well have occurred merely by chance. You can see that psychologists refuse to be impressed by just any old result.

QUICK ▪ QUIZ

Check your understanding of the descriptive/inferential distinction by placing a check in the appropriate column for each phrase:

	Descriptive statistics	Inferential statistics
1. Summarize the data	✓	
2. Give likelihood of data occurring by chance		✓
3. Include the mean	✓	
4. Give measure of statistical significance		✓
5. Tell you whether to call your mother		✓

Answers:

1. descriptive 2. inferential 3. descriptive 4. inferential 5. inferential

inferential statistics *Statistical tests that allow researchers to assess how likely it is that their results occurred merely by chance.*
statistically significant *Term used to refer to a result that is extremely unlikely to have occurred by chance.*

From the laboratory to the real world: Interpreting the findings

The last step in a study is to figure out what the findings mean. Trying to understand behavior from uninterpreted findings is like trying to become fluent in Swahili by reading a Swahili-English dictionary. Just as you need the grammar of Swahili to tell you how the words fit together, the psychologist needs hypotheses and theories to explain how the facts that emerge from research fit together.

Sometimes it is hard to choose between competing explanations. Does nicotine disrupt driving by impairing coordination? By increasing a driver's vulnerability to distraction? By interfering with the processing of information? By clouding judgment or distorting the perception of danger? In general, the best explanation is the one that accounts for the greatest number of findings and makes the most accurate predictions about new findings. In interpreting any particular study, we must be careful not to go too far beyond the facts. There may be several explanations that fit the facts equally well, which means that more research is needed to determine the best explanation.

A major difficulty in interpreting laboratory experiments is that the conclusions may not generalize well to the real world. The laboratory, furnished as it is with special equipment, one-way windows, and researchers, is a very special kind of setting, one that may call forth certain kinds of behavior rarely seen elsewhere (C. Sherif, 1979). The psychologist confronts a dilemma: The more control he or she exercises over the situation, the more unlike real life it may be.

For this reason, many psychologists are calling for more field research, or careful study of behavior in natural settings. Some are also pointing out the need for more consideration of cultural and social influences on behavior, which are difficult to manipulate in the laboratory. Different methods tend to be appropriate for different questions (see Table 2.3). However, there is growing agreement that different methods can also complement each other. That is, one method can be used to confirm, disconfirm, or extend the results obtained with another. If the findings of studies using various methods converge, there is greater reason to be confident about them (Scarr, 1983). On the other hand, if they conflict, researchers will know they must modify their hypotheses or do more research.

Laboratory and field studies are both important in psychological research. An industrial/organizational psychologist might be interested in doing a field study to investigate the management style of the man who is pointing. Instead of staying in an office, this man "manages by wandering around," moving from one production group to another during the day. How might this technique affect employee morale and productivity?

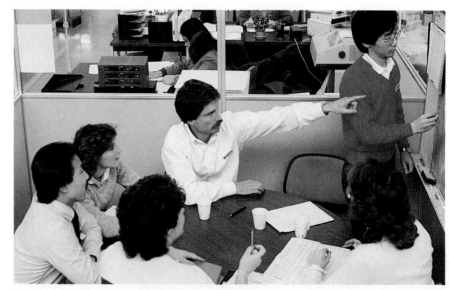

TABLE 2.3
PSYCHOLOGICAL RESEARCH METHODS CONTRASTED

Psychologists may use different methods to answer different questions about a topic. To illustrate, this table shows some ways in which the methods described in this chapter can be used to study different questions about aggression. The methods listed are not necessarily mutually exclusive. That is, sometimes two or more methods can be used to investigate the same question. As discussed in the text, findings based on one method may extend, support, or disconfirm findings based on another.

Method	**Purpose**	**Example**
Case study	To understand the development of aggressive behavior in a particular individual; to formulate research hypotheses about the origins of aggressiveness.	Developmental history of mass killer Tex Watson.
Naturalistic observation	To describe the nature of aggressive acts in early childhood.	Observation, tally, and description of hitting, kicking, etc. during free-play periods in a preschool.
Laboratory observation	To find out if aggressiveness in pairs of same-sex and opposite-sex children differs in frequency or intensity.	Observation through a one-way window of same-sex and opposite-sex pairs of preschoolers. Pairs must negotiate who gets to play with an attractive toy that has been promised to each child.
Survey	To find out how common domestic violence is in the United States.	Questionnaire asking anonymous respondents (in a sample representative of the U.S. population) about the occurrence of slapping, hitting, etc. in their homes.
Tests	To compare the personality traits of aggressive and nonaggressive persons.	Administration of personality tests to violent and nonviolent prisoners.
Correlational study	To examine the relationship between aggressiveness and television viewing.	Administration to college students of a paper-and-pencil test of aggressiveness and a questionnaire on number of hours spent watching TV weekly; computation of correlation coefficient.
Experiment	To find out whether high air temperatures elicit aggressive behavior.	Arrangement for individuals to "shock" a "learner" (actually a confederate of the experimenter) while seated in a room heated to either 72°F or 85°F.

As an example, consider research on aging. When psychologists compare the mental test scores of young and old people, they usually find that younger people outscore older ones. This type of research, in which groups are compared at a given time, is called **cross-sectional**. Other researchers, however, have used **longitudinal** studies to investigate mental abilities across the life span. In a longitudinal study, people are followed over a period of time and reassessed at periodic intervals. In contrast to cross-sectional studies, longitudinal studies find that as people age they often continue to perform as well as they ever did on many types of mental tests. A general decline in ability does not usually occur until the seventh or eighth decade of life (Baltes, Dittman-Kohli, & Dixon, 1984). Why do results from the two types of studies conflict? Apparently, cross-sectional studies measure generational differences; younger generations tend to outperform older ones, perhaps because they are better educated or more familiar with the types of items used on the tests. Without

cross-sectional study *A study in which groups of subjects of different ages are compared at a given time.*

longitudinal study *A study in which subjects are followed and periodically reassessed over a period of time.*

longitudinal studies, we might falsely conclude that mental ability inevitably declines with age.

Another problem in interpreting research results is that *statistical significance does not always imply real-world importance*. A result may be reliable (consistent), and therefore statistically significant, but at the same time small and of little consequence in everyday life. Psychologists are now using an important new technique called *meta-analysis* to find out when this is so. Meta-analysis statistically combines the results from many studies, instead of assessing each study's results separately. It tells the researcher how much of the variation in scores across all the studies examined can be explained by a particular variable. Meta-analysis has turned up some surprises. For example, "well-established" sex differences in verbal ability, spatial-visual ability, aggressiveness, and suggestibility, though usually reliable, turn out to be quite small (see Chapter 3). In most cases, gender accounts for only 1 to 5 percent of the variance in scores, and verbal differences have declined over the years to the vanishing point (Eagly & Carli, 1981; Feingold, 1988; Hyde, 1981, 1984; Hyde, Fennema, & Lamon, in preparation; Hyde & Linn, 1988). In plain English, this means that a person's gender is a poor clue to the person's behavior in these four areas (see Figure 2.6).

Finally, one must not generalize beyond the type of subjects studied. We saw earlier that in surveys the sample of subjects must be representative of the population that the researcher is interested in. The same holds for other types of studies, including experiments. Historically, many experiments in psychology have been done only with white, middle-class, male college students. Findings from such studies may not apply to nonwhites, low-income people, females, or nonstudents.

By the way, a nicotine study similar to our hypothetical example, but with somewhat different and more complicated procedures, was actually done by George J. Spilich (1987). Smokers who lit up before driving got a little farther on the "road" but also had significantly more rear-end collisions on average (10.7) than temporarily abstaining smokers (5.2) or nonsmokers (3.1). Whether these findings will have any impact on car insurance rates remains to be seen. However, they have

A study reports that women are "significantly" better than men at tongue twisters. On closer examination, you find that women are "better" by an average of three seconds. Does this finding make any difference in real life?

FIGURE 2.6

Is this a meaningful difference?

Group differences that are statistically significant are not always useful for predicting behavior. For example, seventh-grade boys do better on the average than seventh-grade girls on the mathematics section of the Scholastic Aptitude Test. But as this graph shows, the difference, although reliable, is tiny, and male and female scores greatly overlap. Thus, it is impossible to predict with any confidence whether a particular boy will outperform a particular girl. (From Sapolsky, 1987, based on data from Benbow & Stanley, 1983.)

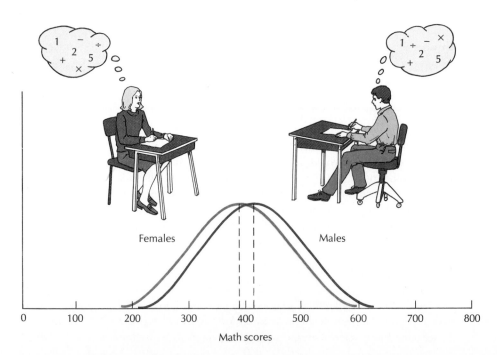

already had one effect: After reading of this research, the head of Federal Express banned smoking on the job for all of the company's 12,000 drivers (Spilich, 1988, personal communication).

Keeping the Enterprise Ethical

Scientists sometimes have an image problem. Their insistence that nothing be taken for granted and their tendency to turn answers into questions is sometimes seen as threatening. Fear of science has found expression in hundreds of ''mad scientist'' books and films, from Mary Shelley's *Frankenstein* to Anthony Burgess's *A Clockwork Orange*. Psychologists, who generally view themselves as nice people, tend to dismiss such fears as irrational. But it is true that the control exercised by scientists in their laboratories can be abused. The world learned that lesson at the Nuremberg trials in 1945, when 20 Nazi doctors were convicted of conducting shockingly sadistic experiments on concentration camp inmates, all in the name of science.

The American Psychological Association (APA) recognizes the need for ethical guidelines and has a formal code that all members must follow, both in clinical practice and in psychological research. Federal regulations also govern scientific research. But there are some ethical problems that have no easy solutions. Even the most seemingly harmless study may have an unintended impact on the participants' lives.

For example, in one large study of dating couples, boyfriends and girlfriends separately answered questions about their involvement in the relationship, the balance of power in the relationship, their goals, and their problems. In a follow-up questionnaire a year later, subjects were also asked whether the study itself had affected their relationships. Almost half of the respondents said yes (perhaps an underestimate, since some romantic souls probably hated to admit it). They reported that filling out the questionnaire made them think about issues they had previously ignored or avoided and stimulated franker discussions with their partners. In most cases, self-examination and increased communication resulted in stronger commitment or an improved relationship, but sometimes it led to conflict or seemed to hasten a breakup. ''Attending your sessions affected me very much in regard to my feelings toward him,'' said one young woman. ''I realized just how competitive our relationship was and how serious my resentment was of him. I can actually mark the shift in our relationship during the third session'' (Rubin & Mitchell, 1976).

The APA code of ethics calls on psychologists to respect the dignity and welfare of their subjects. It states that human subjects must voluntarily consent to participate in a study and must know enough about it to make an intelligent decision, a doctrine known as ''informed consent.'' Once a study begins, a subject must be free to withdraw from it at any time. Moreover, in most colleges and universities, an ethics committee oversees all proposed research. Most issues that arise are not very controversial, but two issues continue to be hotly debated: the use of animals and the practice of deception.

Should animals be used in research?

Animals are used in about 7 or 8 percent of psychological studies. Ninety-five percent of the animals are rodents (American Psychological Association, 1984). Psychologists are especially partial to the Norwegian white rat, which is bred specifically for research purposes and is relatively cheap and healthy. But they also occasionally use pigeons, cats, monkeys, apes, and other species. Most studies involve no harm or discomfort to the animals—for example, observations of dogs' mating habits. Others have involved physical or psychological harm, such as experiments in which infant monkeys are reared apart from their mothers and as a consequence develop abnormal behavior. Some studies require the animal's death, as, for example, when rats brought up in deprived or enriched environments are sacrificed so that their brains can be examined for any effects.

Some psychologists who study animals are interested in comparing different species or hope to learn more about a particular species. Their work generally falls into the area of basic science, but often there are practical benefits. Understanding the behavior of a gull may help animal workers when an oil spill or an unusual weather condition threatens gulls' survival. Understanding how pandas conduct their courtship rituals can help zoos breed pandas in captivity and save them from extinction. Using behavioral principles, farmers have been able to reduce crop destruction by birds and deer without resorting to their traditional method— shooting the animals.

Other psychologists who use animals are primarily interested in principles that apply to both animals and people. Many animals have biological systems or behavioral patterns similar to those of human beings. In many cases, using animals gives the researcher more control over variables than would otherwise be possible. In others, practical or ethical considerations prevent the use of human beings. These studies have led to many improvements in human health and well-being. Findings have helped psychologists develop methods for treating enuresis (bed-wetting) and fecal incontinence (loss of bowel control); improve classroom learning; teach retarded children to communicate; develop a device to correct curvature of the spine; devise behavioral therapies for treating emotional problems and substance abuse; combat life-threatening malnutrition caused by chronic vomiting in infants; rehabilitate patients with neuromuscular disorders; teach people to control stress-related symptoms such as high blood pressure and headaches; treat suicidal depression; develop better ways to reduce chronic, crippling pain; train animal companions for the disabled; and understand the mechanisms underlying memory loss and senility— to name only a few benefits (N. Miller, 1985). Many such breakthroughs have been the unforeseen result of basic laboratory studies using animals (Feeney, 1987).

Animals are often used to study the biological bases of emotion and motivation. Here, electrical stimulation of certain brain areas, delivered by remote control, has produced rage in two previously peaceful monkeys.

Nonetheless, in recent years, animal research has provoked an emotional controversy. Most criticism has centered on the medical use of animals. (Animals are routinely used in drug testing and the development of surgical procedures and have made possible such breakthroughs as bypass surgery, pacemakers, heart transplants, and polio vaccines. But they are also used to test commercial products, such as eye makeup.) Psychologists have also come under fire. A few years ago, a Maryland psychologist studying the nervous system was convicted of cruelty to animals after he cut the nerve fibers controlling limb sensation in 17 monkeys. The purpose of his research was to find ways to restore the use of crippled limbs in stroke victims. The charges alleged abusive treatment of the animals. The psychologist's conviction was eventually reversed on appeal, but in the meantime the government had withdrawn its funding of the project.

One animal rights group calls psychological research with animals "an American holocaust" and wants an immediate halt to all animal studies. Few psychologists would support such an extreme view, but many are concerned about the treatment of laboratory animals and the conditions under which they are caught and shipped to the United States, and they have called on the American Psychological Association to police its members more carefully. The APA ethical code has always contained provisions covering the humane treatment of animals, and in 1985, more comprehensive guidelines were issued by a special APA committee. However, the APA is concerned about proposals to ban or greatly reduce animal research. In most psychological research using animals, alternate methods are not feasible. For example, brain research would virtually halt if animals could not be used. The APA feels that protective legislation for animals is desirable but must not jeopardize productive research that reduces human suffering and improves human welfare.

Should psychologists lie to their subjects?

Another emotional issue has to do with human subjects. Unlike a laboratory rat, human beings may be able to figure out what a study is all about. In many cases, this knowledge can affect their behavior and wreck the research. If you realize that a study is about altruism, the willingness to help others, you may try to outdo Mother Teresa as a Good Samaritan. If you guess that the study is about verbal ability, you may become as talkative as a sportscaster at the Super Bowl.

The obvious way around this problem is to disguise the purpose of the study or, to put it more bluntly, to lie. Deception is common in psychological research, especially in social psychology. By the early 1970s about 40 percent of all research in social psychology used deception (Hunt, 1982). Such research has borne bountiful fruit, as we will see again and again in later chapters. But sometimes it has also caused anxiety or embarrassment for the subjects.

One study that sparked a bonfire of criticism was reported by Stanley Milgram in 1963. Milgram's subjects were told to administer progressively stronger electric shocks to another person by pulling a series of levers on a "shock generator machine." The levers had labels ranging from "Slight Shock" to "Danger: Severe Shock," with two levers at the very end simply marked "XXX." The person to be shocked was a stranger and had never provoked the subject in any way. Actually, this person was in league with the researcher and the "shock" was never delivered, but the subjects didn't know that. They had been told that the purpose of the study was to investigate how punishment affects memory, with the subject acting as "teacher" and the other person acting as "learner." The real purpose was to find out whether people will obey an authority figure who orders them to violate their own ethical code.

Milgram's experiment is one of the best-known studies in psychology, and we will discuss it in greater detail in Chapter 18. Right now, we will simply tell you that a whopping 65 percent of the subjects (all male in the initial study) went all the way, eventually pulling the last lever (XXX). But their obedience cost them emotional pain. Many, said Milgram, were observed to "sweat, tremble, stutter, bite their lips, groan, and dig their fingernails into their flesh," and these "were characteristic rather than exceptional responses to the experiment." After the experiment, subjects were interviewed and told the true purpose of the study. Procedures were taken "to assure that the subject would leave the laboratory in a state of well-being." The subject met his supposed victim, and "an effort was made to reduce any tensions that arose as a result of the experiment."

A rising tide of concern about the morality of deception and its possibly harmful effects on subjects eventually led to a tightening of controls. Although deception is still widely used, it is now done more cautiously. According to the APA ethical guidelines, before using deception a researcher must determine whether it is justified by the study's potential scientific, educational, or applied value and must explore possible alternatives that do not require deception. The investigator must protect subjects from physical and mental discomfort or harm, and if any risk exists, must tell them. Many studies conducted a decade or two ago probably could not be done today. Milgram's study, which won the American Association for the Advancement of Science award for social-psychological research in 1964, is one of them.

Critics of deception feel that procedures with the potential for causing emotional harm are still too widespread. They cite reports of subjects who were disillusioned or felt ashamed after they learned some unpleasant truths about themselves in a psychological study. They claim that "debriefing"—telling the subject about the study's true purpose after it is all over—does not always help. These critics, including some psychologists, argue that deception deprives subjects of free choice and treats them as mere pawns in the research game. They also worry that the use of deception may undermine psychology's credibility with the public and contribute to lowered standards of integrity (Baumrind, 1985; R. Goldstein, 1981).

Psychologists who defend deception say that in practice the risks to subjects have been minor. The few follow-up surveys that have been done generally support this claim. Most people, looking back on their participation in deceptive research, say they think the stress was justified by the knowledge gained. Even those in Milgram's study felt that way. Eighty-four percent of them said later they were glad they had participated, and only 1.3 percent expressed regret; the rest were neutral (Milgram, 1974). Defenders of deception also point out that many kinds of information cannot be obtained without it (Baron, 1981).

The continuing debates over animal research and deception show that research methods can arouse as much controversy as findings do. Controversy exists not only about ethics but also about what particular methods can and cannot reveal. Methods are the very heart of science, so it is not surprising that psychologists spend considerable time discussing and debating their procedures for collecting, evaluating, and presenting data.

We hope that as you read the following chapters, you will resist the temptation to skip descriptions of how studies were done and to attend only to the results. We know that the mere mention of numbers and procedures starts some people nodding and yawning. But remember, a bad study, even if it is repeated a hundred times, can tell us nothing. If the assumptions and methods of a study are faulty, so are the results and the conclusions based on them. Ultimately, what we know about human behavior is inseparable from how we know it.

Taking Psychology with You

"Intuitive Statistics": Avoiding the Pitfalls

Everyone uses intuition and hunches to generate hypotheses about human behavior. Scientists are required to confirm their hypotheses through careful research and rigorous statistical analysis. In daily life, though, people usually test their ideas through casual observation and the use of "intuitive statistics," notions about probabilities that may or may not be correct. These unscientific methods often work well but can sometimes lead to errors. You can take Chapter 2 with you by watching out for common statistical mistakes in your own thinking.

For example, you have learned how misleading it can be to "accentuate the positive and eliminate the negative" by ignoring nonoccurrences of some phenomenon (see p. 45). Sherlock Holmes, the legendary detective, was aware of the value of nonoccurrences. In one episode he invited a police inspector to consider "the curious incident of the dog in the nighttime." The inspector protested that the dog did nothing in the nighttime. Holmes replied that *that* was the curious incident: The dog's silence proved that the intruder in the mystery was someone well known to the dog (Ross, 1977). Like Sherlock Holmes, we all need to be aware of what nonoccurrences can tell us. The next time you read about a furloughed prisoner who commits a crime, ask yourself how many furloughed prisoners don't commit crimes. (By and large, furlough programs have been successful, which is why many states have adopted them.)

Other "intuitive statistics" can also trap us in false conclusions. For example, how would you answer the following questions?

1. If black has won four times in a row at the roulette wheel, would you be inclined to bet next on red or on black?

2. Where are you more worried about safety, in a car or plane?

3. If your psychology instructor has a friend who is a professor and that person is rather shy, is slight of stature, and likes to write poetry, is the friend's field more likely to be Chinese studies or psychology?

When given the first question, many people feel that it is red's "turn" to win. Yet black and red are equally likely to win on the fifth play, just as they were on the first four (assuming that the wheel is fair). How could the probabilities change from one play to the other? A roulette wheel has no memory. The same is true for tossing coins. If you get four heads, the chance of a head on the fifth toss is still .50. The probability of a head or tail does not change from toss to toss, though over the long run (if the coin is fair), there will be a balance of heads and tails. But many people fail to realize this. They succumb to the Gambler's Fallacy, the belief that a "run" of one event alters the chances of that event occurring again. The Gambler's Fallacy is common outside the casino. Many people think that parents with three girls are "due" for a boy, but the odds are the same as they always were (50 percent for most people; more or less than 50 percent when the man happens to produce a larger-than-average supply of male-producing or female-producing sperm).

What about the second question? You may already know that airplanes are actually safer than cars. On the average, about 130 auto deaths occur daily in the United States, far more than occur in plane crashes, even controlling for number of passenger miles traveled. Over a lifetime average of 50,000 car trips, the probability of being killed in an accident is one in 100, and the probability of being seriously injured is one in three (Slovic, Fishhoff, & Lichtenstein, 1978). Yet despite such statistics, most of us still feel safer in cars, because we overestimate the probability of an event when examples are readily available (Tversky & Kahneman, 1973). We can all recall specific airplane disasters; they make headlines because so many people die at once. A single vivid plane crash lingers longer in memory than the hundreds of auto accidents regularly reported in the local newspaper. Thus airplane fatalities *seem* more likely.

Finally, on the third question, many people predict that the instructor's friend is in Chinese studies (Ross, 1977). But this is unlikely, since there are very few professors of Chinese studies in the United States and there are thousands of professors of psychology. Also, a psychology instructor is likely to have more friends in psychology than in Chinese studies. People go astray on this question because they are influenced by their stereotypes about people and ignore statistical probabilities.

We have led you through this little exercise to show you how intuitions can be clouded by biases and fallacies despite people's best efforts to be rational. The scientific approach is the psychologist's way of avoiding such pitfalls.

KEY WORDS

hypothesis 46
theory 46
operational definition 46
replicate 47
"risky predictions" 47
parapsychology 47
descriptive methods 48
case history 48
naturalistic observation 50
subjects 50
laboratory observation 51
surveys 52
sample 53
representative sample 53
population 53
volunteer bias 53
psychological tests 53
valid test 54
reliable test 54
correlational study 55
correlation 55
variables 55

positive correlation 56
negative correlation 56
coefficient of correlation 56
experiment 58
independent variable 58
dependent variable 58
control group 60
random assignment 60
placebo 60
single-blind study 60
experimenter effects 60
double-blind study 60
descriptive statistics 62
arithmetic mean 63
range 63
variance 64
inferential statistics 65
statistically significant 65
cross-sectional study 67
longitudinal study 67
meta-analysis 68

SUMMARY

1. Research methods are the tools of the research psychologist's trade. A knowledge of methodology can also benefit nonpsychologists, by alerting them to errors in thinking and making them astute consumers of psychological findings.

2. The ideal scientist is open-minded but skeptical of claims that rest solely on faith or authority; relies on empirical evidence; states hypotheses and predictions precisely; is open about his or her work; and is willing to make "risky predictions." The fact that science is a public process makes it self-correcting.

3. Descriptive methods allow researchers to describe behavior but not to explain its causes. Some descriptive methods are used by both clinicians and researchers.

4. *Case histories* are detailed descriptions of particular individuals. They are most commonly used by clinicians but are occasionally gathered by academic researchers. Unusual cases sometimes shed light on general questions about behavior. But case histories are typically sources rather than tests of hypotheses because the person under study may not be representative of people in general.

5. *Naturalistic observation* is used to obtain descriptions of how subjects behave in their natural environment. It is often the first step in a research program.

6. *Laboratory observation* allows more controlled observation and the use of special equipment.

7. *Surveys* are questionnaires or interviews that ask people directly about their experiences, attitudes, and opinions. Precautions must be taken to obtain a *sample* that is *representative* of the *population* in question.

8. *Psychological tests* measure personality traits, emotional states, aptitudes, interests, abilities, and values. A good test must be valid (measure what it sets out to measure) and reliable (yield consistent results).

9. In descriptive research, studies that look for a relationship between two or more phenomena are known as *correlational*. A *correlation* is a measure of the strength of the relationship between variables. Correlations may be positive or negative. A correlation does *not* necessarily show causation.

10. *Experiments* are used to track down the causes of behavior. They allow the researcher to control the situation, manipulate an *independent variable,* and assess the effects of the manipulation on a *dependent variable. Random assignment* is usually used to place people in experimental and control groups. In some studies, control subjects receive *placebos.* Precautions, such as *single-blind* and *double-blind* procedures, must be taken to prevent the expectations of the subjects or the experimenter from affecting the results.

11. Psychologists use *descriptive statistics,* such as the *mean, range,* and *variance,* to summarize their data. They use *inferential statistics* to find out how likely it is that the results of a study occurred merely by chance. The results are *statistically significant* if this likelihood is very low.

12. In interpreting findings, care must be taken to avoid going too far beyond the facts, overgeneralizing, or exaggerating the real-world significance of the findings. It is often useful to use one method to confirm, disconfirm, or extend results obtained by another. For example, the results of *cross-sectional* and *longitudinal* studies can be compared.

13. The fact that psychological research methods can affect subjects in unintended ways raises certain ethical problems. Two particularly controversial issues are the use of animals in research and the use of deception in studies of human subjects.

P A R T

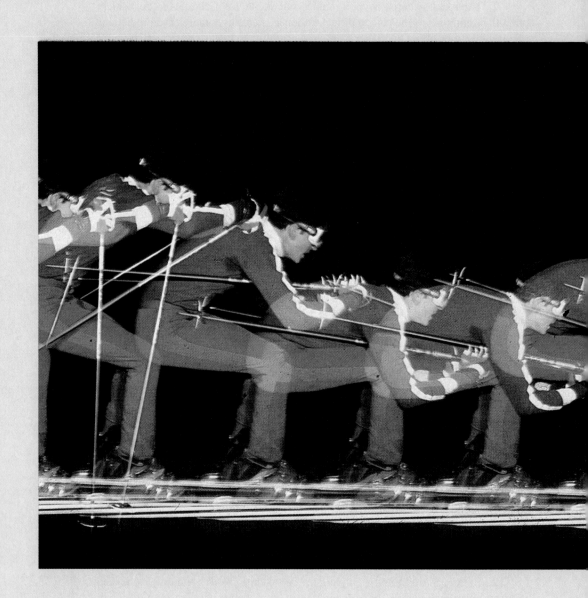

T W O

The Biological Bases of Behavior

CHAPTER 3

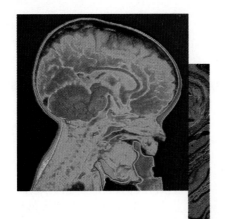

The Brain and the Nervous System

The brain—is wider than the Sky—
For—put them side by side—
The one the other will contain
With ease—and You—beside.

EMILY DICKINSON

*D*r. P., a cultured and charming musician of great repute, had a problem. Though his vision was sharp, he no longer recognized people or objects. Like the old cartoon character Mr. Magoo, he would pat the heads of water hydrants and parking meters, thinking them to be children, or chat with pieces of furniture and wonder why they wouldn't reply. He could spot a pin on the floor but did not know his own face in the mirror. He defined an object presented to him as "a convoluted red form with a linear green attachment" but had no idea it was a rose until he smelled it. Neurologist Oliver Sacks (1985), who examined Dr. P., recalls that while Dr. P. was looking around for his hat, "He reached out his hand and took hold of his wife's head, tried to lift it off, to put it on. He had apparently mistaken his wife for a hat!"

The problem, as you may have guessed, was damage in the part of the brain that controls visualization, due perhaps to a tumor or disease. This damage prevented Dr. P. from recognizing things, remembering the past visually, or even dreaming in visual images. As Sacks notes, the man who mistook his wife for a hat was stranded in "a world of lifeless abstractions."

Cases of brain damage, like Dr. P.'s, show us clearly that the brain is the bedrock of behavior. **Neuropsychologists**, along with other **neuroscientists**, explore that bedrock, searching for the basis of behavior in the structure, biochemistry, and circuitry of the brain and the rest of the nervous system. Among their many interests are the biological foundations of consciousness (Chapter 4), perception (Chapter 5), memory (Chapter 7), emotion (Chapter 9), intelligence (Chapter 12), and stress (Chapter 15). We will discuss their findings at many places in this book. In this chapter, we will review some basic concepts and describe the structure of the brain and the rest of the nervous system.

At this moment your own brain, assisted by other parts of your nervous system, is taking in these words. Whether you are excited or bored, your brain is registering a reaction. As you continue reading, your brain will (we hope) store away much of the information in this chapter for future use. Later on your brain may enable you to smell a flower, climb the stairs, greet a friend, solve a personal problem, or laugh at a joke. But the brain's most startling accomplishment is its knowledge that it is doing all these things. This self-awareness makes the study of the brain different from the study of anything else in the universe. The scientist uses the cells, chemicals, and circuitry of his or her own brain to understand the cells, chemicals, and circuitry of the brain.

Because the brain is the guardian of personal experience and memory, it is the site of self-identity. In this age of medical miracles, you can survive the loss of your kidneys, your liver, or even your heart. These and other body parts can be replaced by artificial devices or organs from human donors. But who would want to receive an entire transplanted brain? Lose your own, particular, unique brain, and you lose your life in every meaningful sense of the word. That is why an absence of brain

neuropsychology *The field of psychology that studies the neural and biochemical bases of behavior and mental processes.*

neuroscience *An interdisciplinary field of study concerned with the structure, function, development, and biochemistry of the nervous system.*

80

activity has come to be accepted by most medical practitioners as evidence of death, even when the heart, lungs, and other organs can be kept going artificially.

No wonder William Shakespeare once called the brain ''the soul's frail dwelling house.'' Actually, though, the brain is more like one room in a house filled with many rooms and passageways. The ''house'' is the nervous system as a whole. Before we can understand the windows, walls, and furniture of that house, we need to examine the overall floor plan.

The Nervous System: A Basic Blueprint

The purpose of a nervous system is to gather information, produce responses to stimuli, and coordinate the workings of different cells. Even the lowly jellyfish and the humble worm have the beginnings of a nervous system. In very simple organisms, which do little more than move, eat, and eliminate wastes, the ''system'' may be no more than one or two nerve cells. In human beings, who do such complex things as dance, cook, and take psychology courses, the nervous system contains billions of cells. The system is divided into two main parts: the **central nervous system (CNS)** and the **peripheral nervous system (PNS)** (see Figure 3.1).

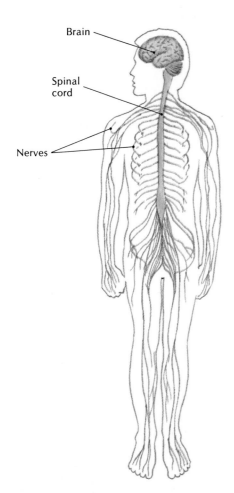

Brain

Spinal cord

Nerves

FIGURE 3.1

The central and peripheral nervous systems

The central nervous system, shown here in gold, consists of the brain and spinal cord. The peripheral nervous system, shown in purple, consists of 43 pairs of nerves that transmit information to and from the central nervous system. Twelve pairs of cranial nerves in the head enter the brain directly. Thirty-one pairs of spinal nerves enter the spinal cord at the spaces between the vertebrae (bones) of the spine.

---

central nervous system
The portion of the nervous system consisting of the brain and spinal cord.
peripheral nervous system
All portions of the nervous system outside the brain and spinal cord. Includes sensory and motor nerves.

The central nervous system

The central nervous system processes, interprets, and stores incoming sensory information—information about tastes, sounds, smells, color, pressure on the skin, the state of internal organs, and so forth. It also sends out orders destined for muscles, glands, and body organs. The central nervous system has two parts: the brain and the spinal cord. We will consider the brain in some detail a little later.

The **spinal cord** is actually an extension of the brain. It runs from the base of the brain down the center of the back, protected by a column of bones. The cord acts as a sort of bridge between the brain and the parts of the body below the neck. But the spinal cord is not merely a bridge. It also produces some behaviors on its own, without any help from the brain. These behaviors, called spinal **reflexes**, are automatic, requiring no conscious effort. For example, if you accidentally touch a hot iron, you will immediately pull your hand away, even before the brain has had a chance to register what has happened. Nerve impulses bring a message to the spinal cord (HOT!), and the spinal cord immediately sends out a command via other nerve impulses, telling muscles in your arm to contract and pull your hand away from the iron. (Reflexes above the neck, such as sneezing and blinking, involve the lower part of the brain rather than the spinal cord.)

The neural circuitry underlying a reflex is called a **reflex arc**. In the case of some reflexes, such as the jerking of a knee when it is tapped, the reflex arc is extremely simple (see Figure 3.2). In other cases, it is quite complex. For example, if you step on a piece of glass, you will reflexively withdraw your foot and at the same time shift your weight in subtle ways to maintain your balance. Such adjustments require the coordination of many neural messages entering and exiting from the spinal cord.

The neural circuits underlying many spinal reflexes are linked to other neural pathways that run up and down the spinal cord, to and from the brain. Because of

spinal cord *Collection of neurons and supportive tissue running from the base of the brain through the spinal column.*

reflex *Automatic response to a stimulus.*

reflex arc *The neural circuitry underlying a reflex.*

FIGURE 3.2

A simple reflex arc
In the knee-jerk (patellar) reflex, a tap on the patellar tendon of the knee causes a sensory impulse to travel to the spinal cord. A motor impulse then travels back to a muscle, causing it to contract, and the leg involuntarily extends at the knee. Many reflexes have a circuitry that is more complex than that of the knee-jerk reflex.

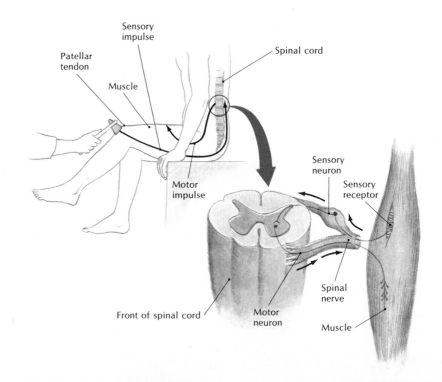

these connections, reflexes, although not requiring conscious awareness, can sometimes be influenced by thoughts and emotions. An example is erection in men, a spinal reflex that can be inhibited by anxiety or distracting thoughts, and initiated by erotic thoughts. Further, some reflexes can be brought under conscious control. If you concentrate, you may be able to keep your knee from jerking when it is tapped. Similarly, most men can learn to voluntarily control ejaculation, also a spinal reflex.

The peripheral nervous system

The peripheral (meaning "outlying") nervous system handles the central nervous system's input and output. It contains all portions of the nervous system outside the brain and spinal cord, right down to nerves in the tips of the fingers and toes. Science fiction writers love to write stories about disembodied but functioning brains. In reality, a brain that could not get information about the world by means of a body equipped with a peripheral nervous system would have nothing to think about. It would be as worthless as a radio without a receiver. **Sensory nerves** in the peripheral nervous system carry messages from special receptors in the skin, muscles, and other internal and external sense organs to the spinal cord, which sends them along to the brain. These nerves put us in touch with both the outside world and the activities of our own bodies. **Motor** (motion-producing) **nerves** carry orders from the central nervous system to muscles, glands, and internal organs. They enable us to move our bodies, and they cause glands to contract and secrete various substances, including chemical messengers called *hormones*.

The peripheral nervous system is further divided into two parts: the **somatic nervous system** and the **autonomic nervous system**. The somatic (bodily) nervous system, sometimes called the *skeletal nervous system*, controls the skeletal muscles of the body and permits voluntary action. When you turn off a light or write your name, your somatic system is active. The autonomic (self-governing) nervous system regulates blood vessels, glands, and internal (visceral) organs like the bladder, stomach, and heart. When you happen upon the secret object of your desire and your heart starts to pound, your hands get sweaty, and your cheeks feel hot, you can blame your autonomic nervous system.

The autonomic nervous system works more or less automatically, without a person's conscious control. We say "more or less" because some people may be able to heighten or suppress certain autonomic responses intentionally. In India some yogis reportedly can slow their heartbeat and metabolism (energy consumption) so dramatically that they can survive in a sealed booth long after most of us would have suffocated. And in the 1960s and 1970s, Neal Miller (1978) and his colleagues showed that you don't have to be a yogi to control internal, or visceral, responses. Ordinary people can do it too, using a technique called **biofeedback**. Biofeedback involves the use of monitoring devices to track the bodily process in question and signal a person whenever he or she makes the desired response. Typically a light goes on or a tone sounds each time the response occurs. Instructions may include specific methods for producing the response, or the person may simply be told to try to increase the frequency of the signal.

There is little question that biofeedback can help people control *voluntary* responses. For example, in one application it has helped teenagers with scoliosis (curvature of the spine) alter their posture and overcome their disorder (Dworkin & Dworkin, 1988). Many researchers also report that some people can learn to control *autonomic* responses, such as blood pressure, blood flow, heart rate, and skin tem-

sensory nerves *Nerves in the peripheral nervous system that carry sensory messages toward the central nervous system.*

motor nerves *Nerves in the peripheral nervous system that carry messages from the central nervous system to muscles, glands, and internal organs.*

somatic nervous system *Subdivision of the peripheral nervous system that controls skeletal muscles. Also called skeletal nervous system.*

autonomic nervous system *Subdivision of the peripheral nervous system that regulates the internal organs and glands.*

biofeedback *Technique for controlling bodily functions by attending to an instrument that monitors the function and signals changes in it.*

Some patients with spinal cord injuries lose consciousness when sitting upright because their blood pressure plunges. Here, Neal Miller, a pioneer in biofeedback research, trains a patient to control her blood pressure at will so that she can lead a fuller life.

perature. Some clinicians are using biofeedback training to treat high blood pressure, asthma, and migraine headaches (although there is great controversy about success rates). It is not clear, however, whether the control that occurs over autonomic responses is direct or indirect. When people learn to raise or lower their heart rate, for example, are they doing so directly, or are they producing the response indirectly by using chest (skeletal) muscles to speed up or slow down their breathing, which in turn affects heart rate?

In early experiments on this issue, Miller and his colleagues taught rats to alter their heart rates by rewarding the animals whenever their rates changed in the desired direction (N. Miller, 1969). To prevent the rats from using chest or other skeletal muscles, the researchers paralyzed them with the drug curare. But exhaustive research since then has failed to replicate these and other visceral learning results in animals (Dworkin & Miller, 1986). Today, we still do not have an explanation for the autonomic effects of biofeedback.

There is one more important nervous system division you should know about. The autonomic nervous system is itself divided into two parts: the **sympathetic** and **parasympathetic nervous systems**. These two parts work together but in opposing ways to adjust the body to changing circumstances (see Figure 3.3). To simplify a bit, the sympathetic system acts like the accelerator of a car, mobilizing the body for action and an output of energy. It makes you blush and sweat, and it pushes up your heart rate and blood pressure. The parasympathetic system is more like a brake. It

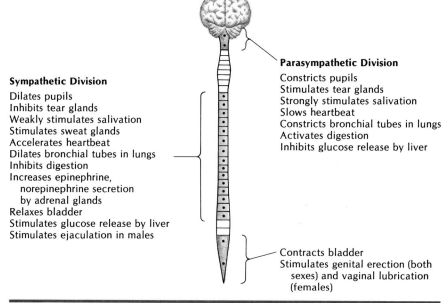

Sympathetic Division
Dilates pupils
Inhibits tear glands
Weakly stimulates salivation
Stimulates sweat glands
Accelerates heartbeat
Dilates bronchial tubes in lungs
Inhibits digestion
Increases epinephrine,
    norepinephrine secretion
    by adrenal glands
Relaxes bladder
Stimulates glucose release by liver
Stimulates ejaculation in males

Parasympathetic Division
Constricts pupils
Stimulates tear glands
Strongly stimulates salivation
Slows heartbeat
Constricts bronchial tubes in lungs
Activates digestion
Inhibits glucose release by liver

Contracts bladder
Stimulates genital erection (both
    sexes) and vaginal lubrication
    (females)

FIGURE 3.3

The autonomic nervous system
The two divisions of the autonomic nervous system have different functions. In general, the sympathetic division prepares the body for an expenditure of energy, and the parasympathetic division restores and conserves energy. But this does not mean that sympathetic impulses always stimulate an organ or that parasympathetic ones always inhibit an organ. The effects depend on the particular organ. For example, sympathetic impulses stimulate sweating and adrenal secretions but inhibit tearing of the eye and digestion. Sympathetic nerve fibers exit from areas of the spinal cord shown in yellow in this illustration. Parasympathetic nerve fibers exit from the base of the brain and from areas of the spinal cord shown in purple.

doesn't stop the body, but it does tend to slow things down or keep them running smoothly. It conserves energy and helps the body store it. If you have to jump out of the way of a preoccupied motorcyclist, sympathetic nerves increase your heart rate. Afterwards, parasympathetic nerves slow it down again and keep its rhythm regular. Both systems are involved in emotion and stress.

QUICK ■ QUIZ

Speaking of stress, you may be feeling a bit overwhelmed by the many terms introduced in the last few paragraphs. Pause now to test your memory by mentally filling in the missing parts of the nervous system "house."

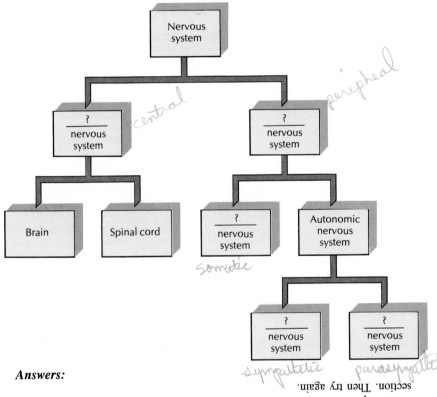

Answers:

Check your answers against Figure 3.4. If you had any difficulty, or if you could label the parts but could not remember what they do, review the preceding section. Then try again.

Communication in the Nervous System: The Nuts and Bolts

The blueprint of the nervous system just given provides a general idea of its structure. When we examine the nervous system more closely, we discover that it is made up in large part of **neurons**, or nerve cells. Neurons are held in place by **glial cells** (from the Greek for "glue"), which also provide them with nutrients, insulate them, and remove cellular "debris" when they die.

sympathetic nervous system *Subdivision of the autonomic nervous system that mobilizes bodily resources and increases the output of energy during emotion and stress.*

parasympathetic nervous system *Subdivision of the autonomic nervous system that operates during relaxed states and conserves energy.*

neuron *Cell that conducts electrochemical signals; basic unit of the nervous system. Also called a* nerve cell.

glial cells *Cells that hold neurons in place and provide them with nutrients.*

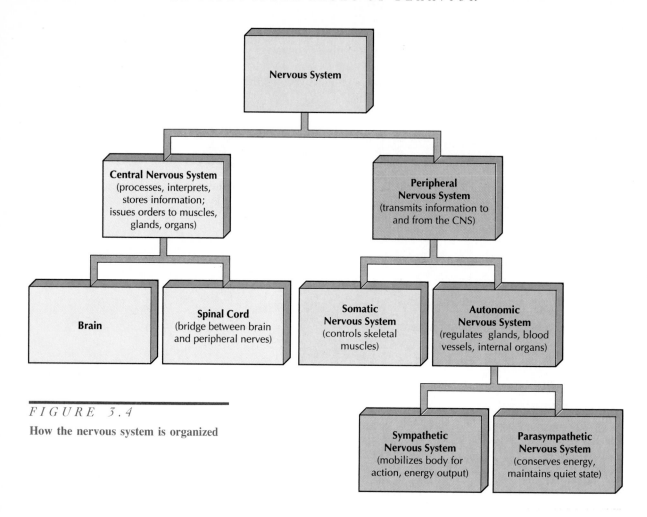

FIGURE 3.4

How the nervous system is organized

Neurons are communication specialists. They transmit information to, from, or inside of the central nervous system, and are often called the building blocks of the nervous system. They do not look much like blocks, though. They are more like snowflakes, exquisitely delicate, differing from each other greatly in size and shape (see Figure 3.5). No one is sure how many neurons the brain contains, but a typical estimate is 100 billion, about the same number as there are stars in our galaxy, and some estimates go as high as a *trillion*. All these neurons are busy most of the time. If that doesn't impress you, consider this: Since we seem to be born with virtually all of the brain neurons we will ever have, the human embryo must gain neurons at the average rate of more than 250,000 a *minute* (Cowan, 1979).

The structure of the neuron

As you can see in Figure 3.6, a neuron has three main parts: a **cell body**, **dendrites**, and an **axon**. The *cell body* is shaped roughly like a sphere or a pyramid. It contains the biochemical machinery for keeping the neuron alive. It also determines whether the neuron should "fire," that is, transmit a message to other neurons. The *dendrites* of a neuron look like the branches of a tree. They act like antennas, receiving messages from other nerve cells and transmitting them toward the cell body. The *axon* is like the tree's trunk, though more slender. It transmits messages away from

cell body *The part of the neuron that keeps it alive and determines whether it will fire.*

dendrites *Branches on a neuron that receive information from other neurons and transmit it toward the cell body.*

axon *Extending fiber of a neuron that conducts impulses away from the cell body and transmits them to other neurons.*

nerve *A bundle of nerve fibers (axons) in the peripheral nervous system.*

myelin sheath *Fatty insulating sheath surrounding many axons.*

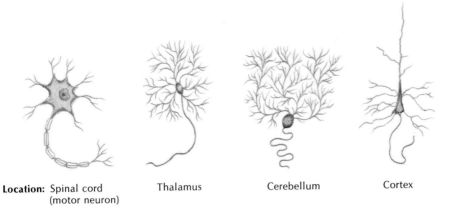

Location: Spinal cord (motor neuron)   Thalamus   Cerebellum   Cortex

the cell body to other cells. Axons have branches at their tips, but these branches are usually less numerous than dendrites. Dendrites and axons give each neuron a double role: As one researcher puts it, a neuron is first a catcher, then a batter (Gazzaniga, 1988).

In adult human beings, axons vary from only a tenth of a millimeter to a few feet in length. The large ones, of course, are found outside the brain. In the peripheral nervous system, the axons of individual cells collect in bundles called **nerves** (not to be confused with nerve *cells*). The human body has 43 pairs of peripheral nerves, one nerve from each pair on the left side of the body and the other on the right. Most of these nerves enter or leave the spinal cord, but the 12 pairs that are in the head go directly to and from the brain. (The central nervous system also contains bundles of neuron fibers, but they are called *tracts*.)

Most axons are insulated by a layer of fat cells called the **myelin sheath**. A major purpose of this covering is to prevent signals from adjacent cells from interfering with each other. The myelin sheath is divided into segments that make the

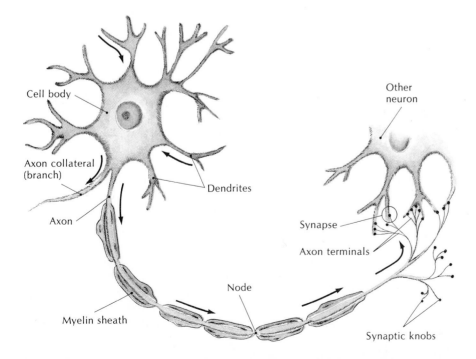

Cell body

Other neuron

Axon collateral (branch)

Dendrites

Axon

Synapse

Axon terminals

Node

Myelin sheath

Synaptic knobs

FIGURE 3.6

Structure of a neuron
Incoming neural impulses are received by the dendrites of a neuron and transmitted to the cell body. Outgoing signals pass along the axon to terminal branches. The arrows show the direction in which impulses travel.

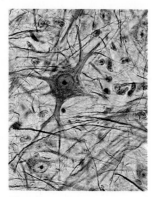

This photograph, taken through a microscope, reveals the delicate fibers of a human motor neuron.

axon look a little like a string of link sausages. When a neural impulse travels down the axon, it "hops" from one break in the "string" to another, making direct contact with the nerve cell. This action allows the impulse to travel faster than it could if it had to move along the entire axon. The thicker the myelin sheath, the faster the impulse. Nerve impulses travel more slowly in babies than in older children and adults because babies' myelin sheaths have not fully developed.

How neurons communicate

Neurons do not form a continuous chain, with one neuron touching another. If they did, the number of connections would be inadequate for the amount of information the nervous system must handle. Instead, individual neurons are separated by tiny gaps called **synapses** (see Figure 3.6). Most synapses are located where the axon of one neuron almost meets the dendrites or cell body of another. Synaptic gaps, 500 times thinner than the finest hair, leave enough space for each neuron to communicate with hundreds and even thousands of other cells. As a result, the number of communication links among neurons is in the trillions or perhaps even the quadrillions.

Though we seem to be born with all the neurons we will ever have, many synapses have not yet formed at birth. Axons and dendrites continue to grow as a result of both physical maturation and experience with the world. Tiny projections on dendrites called *spines* increase both in size and in number. How new circuits form, however, is not yet clear. According to one theory, neural circuits necessary for survival are in place at birth; but after birth, other neurons, involved in complex behavior, continue to grow, their dendrites and axons forming synaptic connections in a random fashion. Experience causes some of these synaptic connections to become active, and they survive. Other, "unused" synaptic connections wither away because cells or their branches die (Hirsch & Jacobson, 1975). Whether this particular theory is correct or not, it is clear that the brain is a dynamically changing structure. Indeed, the enlargement of neurons because of experience appears to continue throughout life (Connor & Diamond, 1982).

Neurons speak to one another—or in some cases to muscles or glands—in an electrical and chemical language. A wave of electrical voltage travels down a nerve cell's axon somewhat as fire travels along the fuse of a firecracker (Stevens, 1979). When it reaches the buttonlike tip (synaptic knob) at the end of a branch on the axon, it must get its message across the synapse to another cell. At this point, tiny chambers, or **synaptic vesicles**, in the axon's tip open and release a few thousand molecules of a chemical substance called a **neurotransmitter** (or *transmitter* for short). Like a ferry captain carrying a message from one island to another, the neurotransmitter travels across the gap (see Figure 3.7).

Once across the synapse, the transmitter molecules fit into slots (receptors) on the receiving neuron much as a key fits into a lock. The result is that changes occur in the membrane, or wall, of the receiving cell. (The physics of this process involves a change in electrical potential caused by the flow of sodium and potassium ions across the membrane of the neuron.) Sometimes the transmitter acts to trigger or excite an electrical impulse. Sometimes it acts to inhibit or prevent an impulse from occurring. What the neuron actually does depends on the combined influence of all the neurons that are "talking" to it. Thousands of messages, both excitatory and inhibitory, may be coming into the cell. Essentially the neuron must average them. But how it does this, and how it "decides" whether or not to fire, is still a puzzle.

synapse *Microscopic gap between neurons at which transmission of nerve impulses occurs.*

synaptic vesicles *Chambers at the tip of an axon that contain neurotransmitter molecules.*

neurotransmitter *Chemical substance that is released by a transmitting neuron at the synapse and alters the activity of a receiving neuron.*

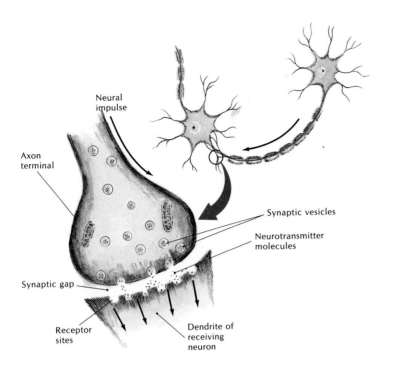

Neural impulse

Axon terminal

Synaptic vesicles

Neurotransmitter molecules

Synaptic gap

Receptor sites

Dendrite of receiving neuron

FIGURE 3.7

Neurotransmitter crossing a synapse
Neurotransmitter molecules are released into the synaptic gap between two neurons from vesicles (chambers) in the transmitting neuron's axon terminal. After crossing the gap, the molecules bind to receptor sites on the receiving neuron. As a result, the electrical state of the receiving neuron changes and it becomes either more or less likely to fire an impulse, depending on the type of transmitter substance. A neuron may have synaptic connections with hundreds or even thousands of other neurons.

The message that reaches a final destination depends on how frequently particular neurons are firing, how many are firing, what types are firing, and where they are located. It does not depend on how strongly individual neurons are firing because a neuron always fires in an *all or none* fashion. That is, the neuron's axon either does fire or doesn't fire, but if it does, it gives the impulse everything it's got.

Chemical messengers in the nervous system

It takes a lot of nerve to make up the nervous system "house," but that house would remain dark and lifeless without certain chemicals that convey messages from place to place within it. These chemicals fall into two classes: neurotransmitters, which we have already mentioned, and hormones.

Neurotransmitters: Versatile couriers. As we have seen, neurotransmitters make it possible for one neuron to excite or inhibit another. Dozens of substances are known or suspected to be transmitters, and the number keeps growing. Neurotransmitters exist not only in the brain but also in the spinal cord, the peripheral nerves, and certain glands. Every year more is learned about the critical role these substances play in mood, memory, and psychological well-being. It has become increasingly clear that abnormalities in neurotransmitter production or use can contribute to mental disorders. In Chapter 16 we will see that imbalances in the neurotransmitters *dopamine* and *serotonin* may underlie such severe mental disturbances as schizophrenia and depression. An overabundance of serotonin may contribute to childhood autism, a disorder characterized by self-stimulation, social unresponsiveness, and language deficits (Yuwiler, Geller, & Ritvo, 1985). And a deficiency in the neurotransmitter *acetylcholine* has been implicated in Alzheimer's disease, a devastating condition most common in the elderly. Alzheimer's causes memory loss, personality changes, and eventual disintegration of all physical and mental abilities.

A Closer Look at Neuropsychology

The Biology of Pleasure

Like other psychologists, neuropsychologists want to explain the miseries of human life—stress, mental confusion, pain, disease. But they also hope to explain the joys of human life—the satisfaction of eating a bowl of chocolate ice cream, the comfort in the arms of a lover, the euphoria of a good laugh. They search for the sources of pleasure in the cells and circuits, enzymes, and electric signals of the nervous system.

Some early clues to the neural basis of pleasure were uncovered by James Olds and Peter Milner, who established the existence of specific "pleasure centers" in the area of the brain known as the limbic system (see page 100 of the text). They discovered that a rat could be trained to press a lever on the side of its cage to get its limbic system buzzed with electricity delivered through tiny electrodes (Olds, 1975; Olds & Milner, 1954). Some rats would press the bar thousands of times an hour, for 15 or 20 hours at a time, until they collapsed from exhaustion. When they revived, it was right back to the bar. The little hedonists couldn't be lured away by water, food, or even the provocative gestures of an attractive rat of the opposite sex. You may be either relieved or disappointed to know that human beings do not act like rats in this regard. Patients who have volunteered to have their pleasure centers stimulated as a treatment for depression say the experience is generally "pleasant" (Sem-Jacobsen, 1959). But the earth doesn't move, and electrical "self-stimulation"

cannot cure depression or provide an electrical "high" for thrill-seekers.

In recent years the search for the neuropsychology of pleasure has shifted from specific neural circuits to the widespread action of endorphins, the nervous system's opiatelike chemicals. The limbic system contains some of the highest concentrations of endorphins and endorphin receptors in the brain. Endorphins, it seems, not only relieve pain but also produce pleasure.

In one study, neuroscientist Avram Goldstein (1980) asked students to name personal experiences that gave them an emotional thrill. Nearly all mentioned listening to a musical passage, and many reported feeling a "tingling" sensation during such experiences. Using a double-blind procedure (see Chapter 2), Goldstein then had some of the "tinglers" listen to their favorite music before and after receiving either a placebo or an injection of naloxone, a chemical that blocks the effects of endorphins. In some people, whether their tastes ran to rock or Rachmaninoff, naloxone reduced the frequency and intensity of tingles. The implication: Endorphins may mediate musical enjoyment.

Other research, using animals, has demonstrated a link between endorphins and the pleasures of social contact. In one series of studies, Jaak Panksepp and his colleagues (1980) gave low doses of morphine or endorphins to young puppies, guinea pigs, and chicks. After the injections, the animals

---

One group of recently discovered neurotransmitters is known as *endogenous opioid peptides*, or more popularly as **endorphins** (Davis, 1984; Snyder, 1980). These opiate-like substances fall into three classes that differ somewhat in chemical structure and distribution in the nervous system: endorphins proper, enkephalins, and dynorphins. They have effects similar to those of such natural opiates as heroin and morphine; that is, they reduce pain and promote pleasure. (For more on the role of endorphins in pleasure, see "A Closer Look at Neuropsychology.")

Endorphin levels seem to shoot up when an animal or person is either afraid or under stress. This is no accident; by making pain controllable in such situations, endorphins give a species an evolutionary advantage (Levinthal, 1988). When an organism is threatened, it needs to do something fast—fight, flee, or cope. Pain, however, can interfere with action: If a mouse pauses to lick a wounded paw it may become a cat's dinner; if a soldier is overcome by his injury, he may never manage

endorphins [en-DOR-fins]
Neurotransmitters that are similar in structure and action to opiates; involved in pain reduction, pleasure, and memory. (Technically known as endogenous opioid peptides.)

cried much less than usual when separated from their mothers. (In all other respects they behaved normally, and they did not appear sedated.) The injections seemed to provide a biochemical replacement for the mother, or more specifically, for the endorphin surge presumed to occur during contact with her. Conversely, when young guinea pigs and chicks received a chemical that *blocks* the effects of opiates, crying increased. These findings suggest that an endorphin-stimulated euphoria may be a child's initial motive for seeking affection and social comfort. In effect, a child attached to his or her parent is a child addicted to love.

What would happen if a child's endorphin system failed to function normally? Some years ago, Panksepp (1979) and James Kalat (1978) independently suggested that the result could be childhood autism. Autism is characterized by self-stimulation (for instance, rocking and twirling) and a lack of social responsiveness. Autistic children usually do not speak, establish eye contact, or respond to other people. They do not seem to like being touched or held, and unlike normal children, they do not go through a stage of clinging to their parents. Often they appear to be insensitive to pain, and some seriously hurt themselves by banging their heads against walls, biting their fingers, or poking themselves with sharp objects. Some of these behaviors are also characteristic of adult opiate addicts. Perhaps, then, childhood autism results from an overactivity of the opioid system. If a child already has an oversupply of endorphins, he or she has no biochemical need to seek the comfort of a close relationship.

There is some research to support this theory. For example, one Swedish study found that half the autistic children examined had abnormally high endorphin levels in their cerebrospinal fluid (Gillberg, Terenius, & Lönnerholm, 1985). And there is evidence that opioid blockers may reduce certain autistic behaviors, such as self-injury and the avoidance of being hugged, in at least some children (Campbell et al., 1988; Herman et al., 1987; Herman et al., 1989). But endorphins are just one clue to the origins of autism. The condition also has been linked to cellular abnormalities in the cerebral cortex and cerebellum, immune system abnormalities, and (as mentioned in the text) high levels of the neurotransmitter serotonin.

Future research is likely to tell us more about the neurochemistry of love, attachment, and other pleasures. But keep in mind that research findings in this area are still preliminary, and conclusions are speculative. Also, the effects of endorphins are subtle. Most important, happiness is more than a matter of chemistry. Even if we could monitor every cell and circuit of the brain, we still would want to understand the circumstances, thoughts, and social rules that determine whether we are gripped by hatred, consumed by grief, lifted by love, or transported by joy.

to get off the battlefield. Of course, as we all know, the body's built-in system of counteracting pain is only partly successful, especially when painful stimulation is prolonged. Researchers are now searching for ways to stimulate endorphin production or administer endorphins directly in order to alleviate pain. Some techniques may already exist. For example, there is some evidence that acupuncture eases pain in part by causing endorphin levels to rise (Mayer et al., 1976).

The study of neurotransmitters is complicated by the fact that each one plays multiple roles (see Table 3.1). The effect of a given substance depends on the location of the neurons it serves and whether it excites or inhibits those neurons. Moreover, the functions of different substances often overlap. For example, both dopamine and serotonin seem to influence mood. Still, many researchers believe that unlocking the mysteries of these magic molecules will set off a revolution in our understanding of both mind and body, and may even help us improve their function-

TABLE 3.1
MAGIC MOLECULES

These are some of the better understood neurotransmitters and some of their known or suspected effects.

Acetylcholine (uh-seet-ul-COE-leen)	Involved in muscle action, cognitive functioning, memory, emotion. Deficit associated with Alzheimer's disease.
Norepinephrine (nor-ep-uh-NEF-rin)	Increases heart rate and slows intestinal activity during stress. Involved in learning, memory, wakefulness, emotion. Abnormal levels associated with mania and depression.
Serotonin (sair-uh-TOE-nin)	Linked to sleep, appetite, heightened sensory states, pain suppression, emotion. Deficit associated with severe depression.
Dopamine (DOE-puh-meen)	Involved in voluntary movement, learning, memory, emotion. Deficit associated with Parkinson's disease. Abnormally high level linked by some researchers to schizophrenia.
GABA (gamma amino butyric acid)	The major inhibitory neurotransmitter in the brain. Abnormal GABA activity implicated in sleep and eating disorders and in various convulsive disorders. Some studies suggest an inability to use GABA underlies Huntington's disease.
Endorphins (en-DOR-fins)	Involved in pain suppression, appetite, blood pressure, mood, perception of pleasure, learning, memory.

ing. During the past few years, surgeons in several countries have experimentally grafted dopamine-producing brain and adrenal gland tissue from miscarried fetuses into the brains of people suffering from Parkinson's disease, a disorder associated with a deficiency of dopamine (Allen, 1987; Madrazo et al., 1988). Although it is unclear whether these grafts actually survive, there have been some reports of a reduction in such symptoms as muscular tremors and rigidity. In other research, when rats suffering alcohol-induced memory problems have received grafts of fetal rat brain tissue rich in acetylcholine, their memories have improved (Arendt et al., 1988.) However, at present, brain tissue transplants in human beings are considered highly risky, and the long-term results are in doubt.

Are neurotransmitters the key to new treatments for medical and psychological disorders? Or are the interactions among the different substances so complex that tinkering with them will prove dangerous? While scientists try to answer such questions, many of us are already doing things that affect our own neurotransmitters, usually without knowing it. Various drugs used recreationally or for medical purposes either block or enhance the effects of particular neurotransmitters (see Chapter 4). Even ordinary foods can influence the availability of neurotransmitters in the brain, as we discuss in "Taking Psychology with You" at the end of this chapter.

Hormones: Long-distance messengers. **Hormones** are chemical substances that are produced in one part of the body but affect another. They originate primarily in **endocrine glands**, which deposit them directly into the bloodstream (see

hormones *Chemical substances that are secreted by organs called* glands *and affect the functioning of other organs.*

endocrine glands *Internal organs that produce hormones and release them into the bloodstream.*

Figure 3.8). The bloodstream then carries them to organs and cells that may be far from their point of origin. Some endocrine glands are activated by nervous system impulses. Conversely, hormones affect the way the nervous system functions.

Hormones have dozens of jobs, from promoting bodily growth to aiding digestion to regulating metabolism. In this book, we will be particularly interested in three types of hormones. The first is *insulin*, which is produced by the *pancreas*, plays a role in the body's use of glucose (a sugar), and affects appetite (see Chapter 10). The second type includes substances produced by the *adrenal glands*, which are perched right above the kidneys. The adrenal glands are involved in emotion and responses to stress. Each gland is composed of an outer layer, or *cortex*, and an inner core, or *medulla*. The outer part produces *cortisol*, which increases blood-sugar levels and enhances energy. The inner part produces *epinephrine* (adrenaline) and *norepinephrine* (noradrenaline). When these hormones are released in your body, they activate the sympathetic nervous system, which in turn prepares you for action.

The other hormones that will especially concern us are the sex hormones. They are secreted by tissue located within the gonads—testes in men, ovaries in women. There are three main types of sex hormones. All three occur in both sexes, but in differing amounts. **Androgens** (the most important of which is *testosterone*) are masculinizing hormones produced mainly in the testes but also in the ovaries and adrenal cortex. Androgens produce the physical changes males experience at puberty, cause pubic and underarm hair to develop in females, and appear to influence sexual arousal in both sexes. **Estrogens** are feminizing hormones produced primarily in the ovaries but also in the testes and adrenal cortex. They produce the physical changes females experience at puberty and influence the course of the menstrual cycle. **Progesterone** is a hormone that contributes to the growth and maintenance of

androgens *Masculinizing hormones.*
estrogens *Feminizing hormones.*
progesterone *Hormone essential in the maintenance of pregnancy.*

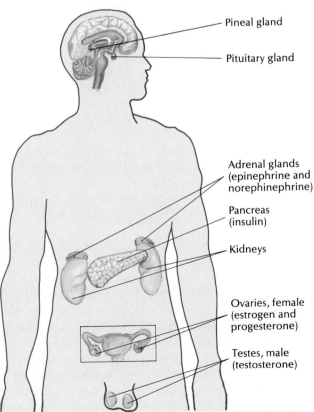

Pineal gland

Pituitary gland

Adrenal glands
(epinephrine and
norephinephrine)

Pancreas
(insulin)

Kidneys

Ovaries, female
(estrogen and
progesterone)

Testes, male
(testosterone)

FIGURE 3.8

Some endocrine glands
This figure shows those parts of the endocrine system that are discussed in this book because of their particular interest to psychologists. The hormones named in the diagram have various known or suspected effects on behavior or emotion.

the uterine lining in preparation for the implantation of a fertilized egg. It is produced mainly in the ovaries, but small amounts are also produced in the testes and adrenal cortex. In the next chapter, we will examine the possibility that fluctuating sex hormones affect mood and behavior.

Note that although we have discussed neurotransmitters and hormones as separate substances, they are not always chemically distinct. The two classifications are like clubs that admit some of the same members. A particular chemical may belong to more than one classification depending on where it is located and what function it is performing. For example, epinephrine and norepinephrine, which are adrenal hormones, also appear to function as neurotransmitters in the brain. Nature has been efficient, giving various substances different tasks to perform.

QUICK ■ QUIZ

Each definition is followed by a pair of words. Which word best fits the definition?

1. Basic building blocks of the nervous system *(nerves/neurons)*
2. Cell parts that receive nervous system impulses *(axons/dendrites)*
3. Gap between neurons *(synapse/myelin sheath)*
4. Opiate-like substance in the brain *(dopamine/endorphin)*
5. Chemicals that make it possible for neurons to communicate *(neurotransmitters/hormones)*
6. Hormone closely associated with emotional excitement *(epinephrine/estrogen)*

Answers:

1. neurons 2. dendrites 3. synapse 4. endorphin 5. neurotransmitters 6. epinephrine

The Brain: Organ of the Mind

A disembodied brain is not very exciting to look at. Stored in a formaldehyde-filled container, it is merely a putty-colored, wrinkled glob of tissue that looks a little like a walnut whose growth has gotten out of hand. It takes an act of imagination to envision this modest-looking organ writing *Hamlet*, discovering radium, painting *The Last Supper*, or inventing French cuisine. Obviously, you can't judge a book, or a brain, by its cover.

The sources of human brain power

What is it that makes the human brain so much more powerful than any other animal's? One answer that might occur to you is size. Human brains are larger and heavier than those of our primate cousins, the monkeys and apes. Big brains, however, do not necessarily mean big intellects. Elephants, dolphins, and whales all have much larger brains than ours, and none of them has come up with algebra or the theory of evolution. Within our species, brain size is important only when a person is born with an abnormally tiny brain, which causes severe retardation. The heaviest human brain ever measured belonged to someone with an abnormally low IQ (Davis, 1984).

A better predictor of a species' intelligence than simple brain size is the ratio of brain weight to body weight. An elephant has a huge brain, but it accounts for only .2 percent of that animal's total body weight. Our brain is larger *for our size* than that of most other animals. Therefore we don't have to use an enormous proportion of our brains just to move our bodies around. We have plenty of brain cells left over for more important things, like planning a trip to Hawaii or composing a love poem. However, even brain-body ratio isn't the whole answer. A sparrow's brain weighs more in proportion to its body than ours does, yet it is still a bird brain.

The thing that really sets the human brain apart is the sheer complexity of its wiring. This complexity far exceeds that of any computer in existence. Much of the brain's most complicated wiring is packed into its enormous cauliflowerlike cap. This brain structure, the *cerebrum*, reaches its greatest development in our species. It is where the higher forms of thinking go on. Compared to many other creatures we may be ungainly, feeble, and thin-skinned, but our well-developed cerebrum enables us to overcome these limitations and creatively control our environment, for better or for worse.

Differences in brain structure, then, can explain species differences. Are there also brain structure differences that explain intellectual variations among people? So far, no one has identified an anatomical basis for superior intellect. In the most recent effort, a group of neuroanatomists looked at four tiny pieces of Albert Einstein's brain (Diamond et al., 1985). In one area, they found more glial cells per neuron than in control brains from 11 nongeniuses. Perhaps this means that Einstein used that section of his brain more than other people do, and so the neurons needed more nutrients. (Glial cells can multiply.) But there are problems with this conclusion. For example, an increased proportion of glial cells relative to neurons may be related to aging, and Einstein was 76 when he died. Based on our present understanding of the brain, it seems unlikely that genius can be traced to the gross anatomy of the brain. It's more probable that individual differences in intelligence are related to differences in the wiring of neural circuits, the amount or efficiency of neurotransmitters, or metabolism rates (Gazzaniga, 1988). Even if such differences are confirmed, however, scientists will have to establish whether they are present from birth or develop as the result of experience.

Eavesdropping on the brain

Psychologists are generally more interested in studying what happens in living brains than in examining dead ones. You may be wondering how this can be accomplished, since the brain is encased in a thick protective vault of bone. One approach is to study patients who have had a part of the brain damaged or removed because of disease or injury. Another is to purposely damage or remove sections of brain in animals, then observe the effects.

The brain can also be probed by using devices called **electrodes**. Some electrodes are coin-shaped and are simply pasted or taped on the scalp. They detect the electrical activity of millions of neurons in particular regions of the brain and are widely used in research and medical diagnosis. The electrodes are connected by wires to a machine that translates the electrical energy from the brain into wavy lines on a moving piece of paper or visual patterns on a screen. That is why we refer to electrical patterns in the brain as ''brain waves.'' Different wave patterns are associated with sleep, relaxation, and mental concentration (see Chapter 4).

electrodes *Devices used to apply electric current to tissue or detect neural activity.*

A brain wave recording is called an **electroencephalogram (EEG)**. A standard EEG is useful, but not very precise, because it reflects the firing of many cells at once. "Listening" to the brain with an EEG machine is like standing outside a sports stadium—you know when something is happening, but you can't be sure what it is or who is doing it. But fortunately, computer technology can be combined with EEG technology to get a clearer picture of brain activity patterns associated with specific events and mental processes. To analyze such patterns, or **evoked potentials**, researchers use a computer to extract all the background "noise" being produced by the brain, leaving only the pattern of electrical response to the event.

For even more specific information, researchers use needle electrodes. These are very thin wires or hollow glass tubes that can be inserted into the brain, either directly or through tiny holes in the skull. Only the skull needs to be anesthetized; the brain itself, which processes all bodily sensation and feeling, feels nothing when touched. Therefore a human patient or an animal can be awake and not feel pain during the procedure. Needle electrodes can be used both to record electrical activity from the brain and to stimulate the brain with a weak electrical current. Stimulating a given area often results in a particular sensation or movement. *Microelectrodes* are so fine that they can be inserted into single cells (see Figure 3.9).

During the past few years, even more amazing doors to the brain have opened. Researchers can now get a clear visual image of the inside of the body, in living color, without so much as lifting a scalpel. One method, the **PET scan (positron-emission tomography)**, goes beyond anatomy to record biochemical changes in the brain as they are happening. It takes advantage of the fact that nerve cells convert glucose, a sugar, into energy. A researcher can inject a patient with a glucoselike substance that contains a harmless radioactive element. This substance travels to brain areas that are particularly active and are consuming glucose rapidly. The substance emits radiation, which is a telltale sign of activity, like cookie crumbs on a child's face. The radiation is detected by a scanning device, and the result is a computer-processed picture of biochemical activity on a display screen, with different colors indicating different levels of activity. Although PET scans are designed to diagnose physical abnormalities, they can be used to find out which parts of the brain are active during particular activities and emotions. These pictures can tell us what happens in the brain when a person hears a song, feels angry, or shifts attention from one task to another. Already they have yielded some evidence that certain brain areas in people with emotional disorders are abnormally quiet or active.

Another technique, **magnetic resonance imaging (MRI)**, allows the exploration of "inner space" without injecting chemicals, and produces some of the most accurate images yet of living body and brain tissue. Powerful magnetic fields and various radio frequencies are used to produce vibrations in the nuclei of atoms making up body organs. These vibrations are picked up as signals by special receivers. A computer then analyzes the signals, taking into account their strength and

electroencephalogram (EEG) *A recording of neural activity detected by electrodes.*

evoked potentials *Patterns of brain activity produced in response to specific events.*

PET scan (positron-emission tomography) *A method for analyzing biochemical activity in the brain, using injections of a glucoselike substance containing a radioactive element.*

Magnetic resonance imaging (MRI) *A method for studying body and brain tissue, using magnetic fields and special radio receivers.*

brain stem *Part of the brain at the top of the spinal cord; responsible for automatic functions such as heartbeat and respiration.*

reticular activating system (RAS) *Dense network of neurons found in the core of the brain stem; arouses the cortex and screens incoming information.*

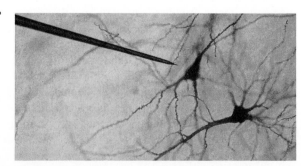

FIGURE 3.9

Recording from a single neuron
A microelectrode is used to record the electrical impulses generated by a single cell in the brain of a monkey.

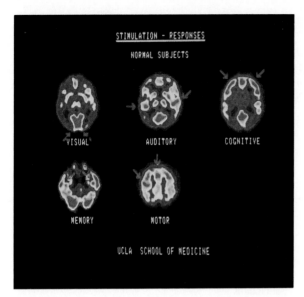

These PET scans show rates of metabolic activity in the brain during various tasks. Red indicates areas of highest activity; violet, areas of lowest activity. The arrows point to regions that are maximally active when people are asked to look at a complicated visual scene (top left), listen to a sound (top center), perform a mental task (top right), recall aspects of stories heard previously (bottom left), or move the right hand (bottom center).

duration, and converts them into a high-contrast picture. Like the PET scan, MRI is used both for diagnosing disease and studying normal brain activity, and is yielding new insights into the workings of the brain.

A Quick Tour of the Brain

Neurosurgeon Joseph Bogen (1978) once suggested that a 30-story replica of the brain be built so that people could learn about brain anatomy the way they learn about a neighborhood—by strolling through it. No one has followed up on that suggestion, so we must make do with an imaginary tour. Pretend, then, that you have shrunk to microscopic size and that you are wending your way through the "soul's frail dwelling house." That house is commonly thought of as having three main sections: the *hindbrain*, *midbrain*, and *forebrain* (see Table 3.2). The more reflexive or automatic a behavior is, the more likely it is to be controlled by areas in the hindbrain and midbrain. The more complex a behavior, the likelier it is to involve the forebrain. Major structures of the brain are shown in Figure 3.10.

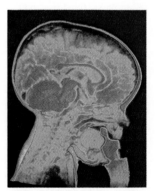

This magnetic resonance image shows a child's brain—and the bottle given to him to quiet him during the seven minutes it took to obtain the image.

The hindbrain: Vital functions

Our guided tour begins at the base of the skull, with the **brain stem**, which began to evolve some 500 million years ago in segmented worms. The brain stem looks like a stalk rising out of the spinal cord. Pathways to and from upper areas of the brain pass through its two main structures, the *medulla* and the *pons*. The pons is involved in (among other things) sleeping, waking, and dreaming. The medulla is responsible for prewired functions that do not have to be consciously willed, such as breathing and heart rate. Hanging has long been used as a method of execution because when it breaks the neck, nervous pathways from the medulla are severed, stopping respiration (Bailey, 1975).

Another important structure, extending from the core of the brain stem into the midbrain and forebrain, is the **reticular activating system (RAS)**. This dense network of neurons, which has connections with many higher areas of the brain,

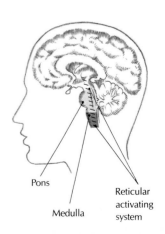

Pons

Medulla

Reticular activating system

TABLE 3.2
MAJOR SUBDIVISIONS OF THE HUMAN BRAIN

The brain has three major sections: the hindbrain, midbrain, and forebrain. The sub-structures listed in this table are described on subsequent pages. (The brain stem, not listed here, includes the medulla and pons.)

Hindbrain	medulla
	pons
	reticular activating system (extends into midbrain)
	cerebellum
Midbrain	tracts to and from upper portions of brain
	centers (nuclei) that receive sensory and motor information
Forebrain	cerebral cortex
	cerebrum
	corpus callosum
	olfactory bulb
	thalamus
	hypothalamus
	pituitary gland
	limbic system

cerebellum *Brain structure that regulates movement and balance.*

cerebrum [suh-REE-brum] *Largest brain structure, comprising the upper part of the forebrain; in charge of most sensory, motor, and cognitive processes in human beings. From the Latin for "brain."*

cerebral hemispheres *The two halves of the cerebrum.*

thalamus *Brain structure that relays sensory messages to the cerebral cortex.*

hypothalamus *Brain structure involved in emotions and drives vital to survival, such as fear, hunger, thirst, and reproduction; regulates the autonomic nervous system.*

pituitary gland *Small endocrine gland at the base of the brain that releases many hormones and regulates other endocrine glands.*

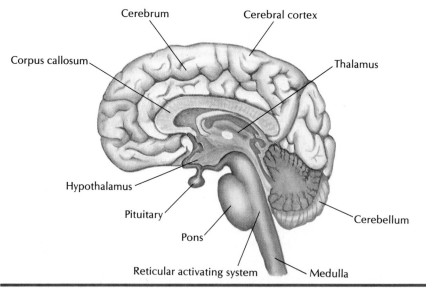

FIGURE 3.10

The human brain

This drawing, a cross section, shows the brain as though it were split in half. The view is of the inside surface of the right half.

screens incoming information. Irrelevant information is filtered out. Important information is passed on to higher centers. The RAS also arouses the higher centers when something happens that demands their attention. The RAS may be referred to as a "lower" part of the brain, but without it we could not be alert, nor perhaps even conscious.

Standing on the brain stem and looking toward the back part of the brain, we see a roundish structure about the size of a small fist, bulging out from the pons. It is the **cerebellum**, or "lesser brain," which contributes to a sense of balance and coordinates the muscles so that movement is smooth and precise. If your cerebellum were damaged, you would probably become clumsy and uncoordinated. You might have trouble using a pencil, threading a needle, or riding a bicycle.

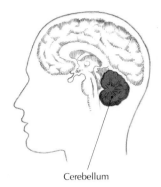

Cerebellum

The midbrain: Important way stations

The midbrain contains neural tracts that run to and from the upper portions of the brain. Various areas of the midbrain perform special functions. For example, one area receives information from the visual system and is involved in eye movements. Some researchers consider the midbrain to be part of the brain stem. In this book, we are not concerned with details about the structure of the midbrain.

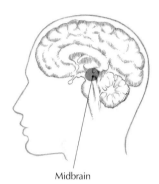

Midbrain

The forebrain: Emotions, memory, and thought

Standing atop the midbrain, we see that the largest part of the brain, the forebrain, is still above us. The uppermost part of the forebrain, the **cerebrum**, is divided into two halves, or **cerebral hemispheres**. In general, the right hemisphere is in charge of the left side of the body, and vice versa. As we will see later, the two sides also have somewhat different talents.

Several structures in the forebrain are invisible from the outside. Half of each structure lies in the right side of the brain and half in the left. One such structure is the **thalamus**, the busy traffic officer of the brain. As sensory messages come into the brain, the thalamus directs them to various higher centers. For example, the sight of a sunset sends signals that the thalamus directs to a vision center. The only sense that completely bypasses the thalamus is the sense of smell, which has its own private switching station, the *olfactory bulb*. The olfactory bulb lies near areas that control emotion. Perhaps that is why particular odors—the smell of fresh laundry, gardenias, a steak sizzling on the grill—often rekindle memories of important experiences in one's life.

Still standing atop the midbrain, we glance toward the front of the brain and notice a tiny, bean-shaped structure right under the thalamus. Appropriately enough, it is called the **hypothalamus** (*hypo* means "under"). The wee size of the hypothalamus is no indicator of its importance. It is involved in powerful drives associated with the survival of both the individual and the species—hunger, thirst, emotion, sex, and reproduction. It regulates body temperature by triggering sweating or shivering. It controls the complex operations of the autonomic nervous system.

Hanging down from the hypothalamus, connected to it by a short stalk, is a cherry-sized structure that is *not* made up of neurons. It is the **pituitary gland**, an endocrine gland. The pituitary is often called the body's "master gland" because it controls many other endocrine glands. The master, though, is really only a supervisor. The true boss is the hypothalamus. The hypothalamus sends chemicals to the

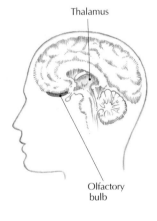

Thalamus

Olfactory bulb

Hypothalamus

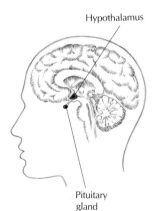

Pituitary gland

FIGURE 3.11

The limbic system
Structures of the limbic system play an important role in memory and emotion.

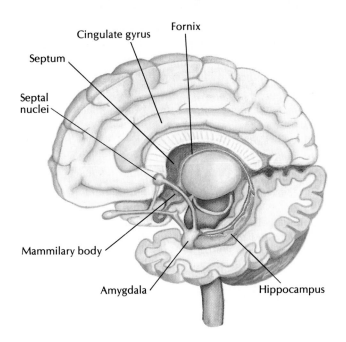

pituitary that tell it when to "talk" to the various endocrine glands. The pituitary, in turn, sends hormonal orders to the glands.

The hypothalamus has many connections to surrounding areas that form a sort of border on the underside of the brain's "cauliflower." Together these areas make up the **limbic system** of the brain (see Figure 3.11). (*Limbic* comes from the Latin for "border." Some brain specialists include the hypothalamus and parts of the thalamus in the limbic system.) The limbic system is heavily involved in emotions we share with other animals, like rage and fear. As we noted in "A Closer Look at Neuropsychology" on page 90, it also contains many "pleasure centers"—areas that, when electrically stimulated, seem to bring pleasure to an animal.

Another important feature of the limbic system is the **hippocampus**, which has a shape that must have reminded someone of a sea horse, for that is what *hippocampus* means. This structure is larger in human beings than in any other species. One of its duties seems to be to compare sensory messages with what the brain has learned to expect about the world. When expectations are met, the hippocampus tells the reticular activating system, the brain's arousal center, to "cool it." It wouldn't do to be highly aroused in response to *everything*. What if neural alarm bells went off every time a car went by, a bird chirped, or you felt your own saliva trickling down the back of your throat?

The hippocampus has also been called the "gateway to memory" because (along with other brain areas) it seems to enable us to store new information for future use. Some of what we know about this ability comes from case histories of people who have suffered brain damage. One man, known to researchers as H. M., was studied for many years by Brenda Milner (Milner, 1970; Milner, Corkin, & Teuber, 1968) and is still being studied today. In 1953, when H. M. was 27, surgeons removed most of his hippocampus, along with part of another limbic structure, the *amygdala*, in a last-ditch effort to relieve his severe, life-threatening epilepsy. After the operation, the young man's seizures were milder and could be controlled by medication. His memory, however, had been affected dramatically.

limbic system *Group of brain areas involved in emotional reactions and motivated behavior.*
hippocampus *Brain structure thought to be involved in the storage of new information in memory.*

Although H. M. continued to recall most events before the operation, especially those that had occurred at least three years before, he could no longer remember new experiences for much longer than 15 minutes. They seemed to vanish like water down the drain. Milner and H. M.'s doctors had to reintroduce themselves every time they saw him. He would read the same issue of a magazine over and over again without realizing it. He could not recall the day of the week, the year, or even his last meal. Today, he will occasionally recall an unusually emotional event, such as the assassination of someone named Kennedy. He has managed to learn some new manual, perceptual, and problem-solving skills, which apparently draw on a different part of the brain than do facts and events. He forgets the training sessions, though. For the most part, history stopped for H. M. on the day of his operation. H. M. says that for him life is like constantly waking from a dream.

Various theories have been proposed to explain the exact nature of H. M.'s memory loss. According to one, H. M. stores new information but cannot retrieve it (Marslen-Wilson & Teuber, 1975). However, this theory does not explain why H. M. *can* retrieve old information stored before the operation. Another possibility is that the damage to H. M.'s hippocampus has weakened the process of *consolidation*, by which new memories become relatively fixed or durable (Rozin, 1976). (We will meet H. M. again, in Chapter 7.)

The thalamus is also involved in storage of new information. It seems to work on the original formation of a memory rather than on its consolidation. Sometimes a vitamin deficiency associated with prolonged alcoholism produces damage in the thalamus if a person lacks a particular enzyme because of a genetic error. The symptoms of this condition, known as Korsakoff's syndrome, are in many ways similar to those suffered by H. M.

The cerebral cortex: The brain's thinking cap

Working our way right up through the top of the brain, we find that the forebrain is covered by a layer of densely packed cells known as the **cerebral cortex**. The cortex is part of the forebrain, but because it is so important we are discussing it separately.

Cell bodies in the cortex, as in many other parts of the brain, are crowded together and produce a grayish tissue; hence the term *gray matter*. In other parts of the brain and nervous system, long, myelin-covered axons prevail, producing *white matter*. The cortex contains almost three-fourths of all the cells in the human brain (Schneider & Tarshis, 1986). In only 1 square *inch* of the cortex there are around 10,000 miles of synaptically connected nerve cells. In the entire cortex there are enough connections to stretch from the earth to the moon and back again, and then back to the moon (Davis, 1984).

Standing atop the cortex, we note that it has many deep crevasses and wrinkles. The folds in the brain's surface enable it to contain its billions of neurons without requiring us to have the heads of giants—heads that would be too big to permit birth. In other mammals the cortex is less crumpled, and in the rat it is quite smooth.

From our vantage point on the brain's surface we can see that deep grooves or fissures divide the cortex into four distinct regions, or lobes (see Figure 3.12):

▪ The *occipital lobes* (from the Latin for "in back of the head") are at the lower back part of the brain. Among other things, they contain the *visual cortex*, where visual signals are processed. Damage to the visual cortex can cause impaired visual recognition or blindness.

cerebral cortex *Thin layer of cells covering the cerebrum; largely responsible for higher functions. Cortex is Latin for "bark" or "rind."*

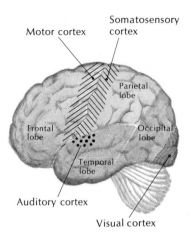

Motor cortex
Somatosensory cortex
Parietal lobe
Frontal lobe
Occipital lobe
Temporal lobe
Auditory cortex
Visual cortex

FIGURE 3.12

Lobes of the cerebrum
Deep fissures divide each cerebral hemisphere of the brain into four lobes associated with different general functions. In this drawing, crosshatched areas show regions specialized for movement and bodily sensation, and dotted areas show regions specialized for vision and hearing.

▪ The *parietal lobes* (from the Latin for "pertaining to walls") are at the top of the brain. They contain the *somatosensory cortex*, which receives information about pressure, pain, touch, and temperature from all over the body. Sensory information tells you what the movable parts of your body are doing at every moment. Without this ability, you would not be able to perform such a simple task as touching your nose with your eyes shut. Different parts of the sensory cortex are associated with different body parts. The areas associated with the hands and the face are disproportionately large since these parts are particularly sensitive.

▪ The *temporal lobes* (from the Latin for "pertaining to the temples") are at the sides of the brain, just above the ears, behind the temples. They are involved in memory, perception, emotion, and language comprehension, and they contain the *auditory cortex*, which processes sounds.

▪ The *frontal lobes*, as their name indicates, are located toward the front of the brain, just under the skull in the area of the forehead. They contain the *motor cortex*, which issues orders to the 600 muscles of the body that produce voluntary movement. They also seem to be responsible for the ability to make plans, think creatively, and take initiative.

The descriptions just given are simplified ones; there is considerable overlap in what the various lobes do. Still, when a surgeon probes these four pairs of lobes with an electrode, different things tend to happen. If current is applied to the somatosensory cortex, in the parietal lobes, the patient may feel tingling in the skin. If the visual cortex, in the occipital lobes, is stimulated, the person may report a flash of light or swirls of color.

But in most areas of the cortex, nothing happens after electrical stimulation. These "silent" areas, which are sometimes called the *association cortex*, appear to be responsible for higher mental processes. The silent areas of the cortex are just beginning to reveal their secrets. Psychologists are particularly interested in new information about the forwardmost part of the frontal lobes, the *prefrontal cortex*. This area barely exists in mice and rats and takes up only 3.5 percent of the cerebral cortex in cats, about 7 percent in dogs, and 17 percent in chimpanzees. In human beings, it accounts for fully 29 percent of the cortex (M. Pines, 1983).

Scientists have long known that the frontal lobes must have something to do with personality. The first clue appeared in 1848, when an accident drove an inch-thick iron rod clear through the head of a young railroad worker named Phineas Gage. The rod (still on display at Harvard University) entered beneath the left eye and exited through the top of the head, destroying much of the front of the brain.

Miraculously, Gage survived. What's more, he retained the ability to speak, think, and remember. But his friends complained that he was ''no longer Gage.'' In a sort of Jekyll and Hyde transformation, Gage changed from a mild-mannered, friendly, efficient worker into a foul-mouthed, ill-tempered, undependable lout who could not hold a steady job or stick to a plan.

Other sorts of damage to the frontal lobes, including tumors and war injuries, show that they are involved in planning, goal setting, and intention, or what is commonly called ''will.'' They govern the ability to do a series of tasks in the proper order and to stop doing them at the proper time. The pioneering Soviet psychologist A. R. Luria (1980) studied many cases in which damage to the frontal lobes disrupted these abilities. One man observed by Luria kept trying to light a match after it was already lit. Another planed a piece of wood in the hospital carpentry shop until it was gone, and then went on to plane the workbench.

Luria gave tumor patients a series of simple tasks to test their ability to follow instructions. In one, the patients had to draw a line of crosses alternating with circles. They would usually start out correctly but then lapse into all crosses or all circles. In another task, patients were supposed to use colored blocks to make a pattern, but instead they placed blocks together impulsively, without developing a strategy. They seemed to lack an ''internal program'' to guide their actions (see Figure 3.13).

Scientists are now starting to map the actual circuitry of the frontal lobes. Their subjects are brain injury patients and monkeys. Their tools are the sophisticated techniques discussed earlier—microelectrodes, injections of radioactive substances, and brain scans. These researchers hope to link specific areas of the frontal lobes with specific mental abilities.

Phineas Gage's skull and a cast of his head, on display at the Harvard Medical School, show the extent of the injury that so dramatically altered his behavior and personality. You can see where the tamping iron penetrated the skull.

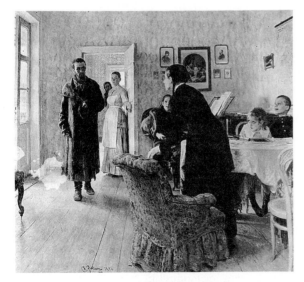

FIGURE 3.13

Frontal lobes and planning *The tracings below the painting show the eye movements of a person with a healthy brain as he examined the painting. Note that he focused primarily on such important details as faces. The other tracings show the eye movements of a person with frontal lobe damage. This person seemed to lack a guiding plan for examining the painting. Such evidence points to the importance of the frontal lobes in initiating and carrying out plans.*

QUICK ■ QUIZ

Match the descriptions on the left with the terms on the right.

1. Filters out irrelevant information
2. The "gateway to memory"
3. Controls autonomic nervous system; involved in drives associated with survival
4. Has two hemispheres
5. Crumpled outer covering of the brain
6. Site of motor cortex; associated with planning, thinking creatively, taking initiative

a. reticular activating system
b. cerebrum
c. hippocampus
d. cerebral cortex
e. frontal lobes
f. hypothalamus

Answers:

1. a 2. c 3. f 4. b 5. d 6. e

The Two Hemispheres of the Brain

We have seen that the cerebrum is divided into two hemispheres that control opposite sides of the body. Though similar in structure, the hemispheres have somewhat separate talents, or areas of specialization. This raises an interesting question: Should the hemispheres be considered equal partners in human functioning, or is one like a senior partner and the other only a junior partner?

Two minds in one skull: Split brains

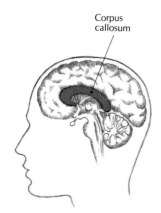

Corpus callosum

In a normal brain, the two hemispheres communicate with one another across a large bundle of nerve fibers called the **corpus callosum**. Whatever happens in one side of the brain is instantly flashed to the other, so behavior is smooth and well coordinated.

What would happen, though, if the communication lines were cut? An early clue occurred in a case history published in 1908. A woman was hospitalized because she repeatedly tried to choke herself with her left hand. She would try with her right hand to pull the left hand away from her throat, but she claimed that the left hand was beyond her control. She also did other destructive things, like throwing pillows around and tearing her sheets, but only with her left hand. A neurologist suspected that the woman's corpus callosum had been damaged so that the two sides of the brain could no longer communicate. When the woman died, an autopsy showed that he was right (Geschwind, in J. Miller, 1983).

This case suggests that the two sides of the brain can experience different emotions. What would happen if they were completely out of touch? Would they think different thoughts and store different memories? In 1953, Ronald E. Myers and Roger W. Sperry took the first step toward answering this question by cutting the corpus callosum in cats. They also cut certain nerves leading from the eyes to the brain. Normally, each eye transmits messages to both sides of the brain. After this procedure, a cat's left eye sent information only to the left hemisphere and its right eye only to the right hemisphere.

At first the cats did not seem to be affected much by this drastic operation. But Myers and Sperry showed that something profound had happened. They trained the

corpus callosum *Bundle of nerve fibers connecting the two cerebral hemispheres.*

cats to perform various tasks with one eye blindfolded. For example, a cat might have to push a panel with a square on it to get food but ignore a panel with a circle. After the task was learned, the researchers switched the blindfold to the cat's other eye and tested the animal again. Now the cats behaved as if they had never learned the trick. Apparently, one side of the brain didn't know what the other side was doing. It was as if the animals had two minds in one body. Later studies confirmed this result with other species, including monkeys (Sperry, 1964).

In all the animal studies, ordinary behavior, such as eating and walking, remained normal. Encouraged by this finding, a team of surgeons led by Joseph Bogen decided in the early 1960s to try cutting the corpus callosum in patients with very severe epilepsy. Epilepsy is a brain dysfunction that has many causes and takes many forms, and that often causes seizures. In some forms, disorganized electrical activity spreads from an injured area to other parts of the brain. Usually, these electrical brainstorms are brief and mild and can be controlled by drugs. In the patients in question, the condition did not respond to drugs and was completely debilitating, even life-threatening. The operation was a last resort. The surgeons reasoned that by cutting the connection between the two halves of the brain they could stop the spread of electrical activity from one hemisphere to the other.

The operation generally proved very successful. Seizures were reduced and sometimes disappeared completely. As an added bonus, these patients gave psychologists a chance to find out what each half of the brain can do when it is quite literally cut off from the other. It was already known that the two hemispheres are not mirror images of one another. In most people, language is largely handled by the left hemisphere: speech production in an area of the left frontal lobe known as *Broca's area*, meaning and language comprehension in an area of the left temporal lobe known as *Wernicke's area*. Therefore, a person who suffers brain damage because of a stroke (a blockage in or rupture of a blood vessel in the brain) is much more likely to have language problems if the damage is in the left side than if it is in the right. How would splitting the brain affect language and other abilities?

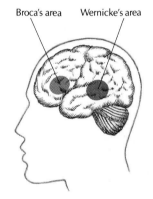

Broca's area   Wernicke's area

In their daily lives, "split-brain" patients did not seem affected by the fact that the two sides of their brains were incommunicado. They could walk, talk, and in general lead normal lives. Apparently connections in the undivided brain stem kept body movements normal. But in a series of ingenious studies, Sperry and his colleagues (and later other researchers as well) showed that perception and memory had been profoundly affected, just as they had been in earlier animal research. In 1981, Sperry received a Nobel Prize for his work.

To understand this research, you must know a little more about how nerves connect the eyes to the brain. (The human patients, unlike Myers and Sperry's cats, did not have these nerves cut.) If you look straight ahead, everything in the left side of the scene before you goes to the right half of your brain, and vice versa. This is true for both eyes (see Figure 3.14).

The basic procedure was to present information only to one or the other side of the subjects' brains. In one early study (Levy, Trevarthen, & Sperry, 1972), the researchers took photographs of different faces, cut them in two, and pasted different halves together (see Figure 3.15). The reconstructed photographs were then presented on slides. The person was told to stare at a dot straight ahead, on the middle of the screen, so that half the image fell to the left of this point and half to the right. Each image was flashed so quickly that there was no time for the person to move his or her eyes. When the subjects were asked to say what they had seen, they named the person in the right part of the image. But when they were asked to *point* with their left hands to the face they had seen, they chose the person in the left side of the image. Further, they claimed they had noticed nothing unusual about the

FIGURE 3.14

Visual pathways
Each hemisphere of the brain receives information about the opposite side of the visual field. For example, if you stare directly at the corner of a room, everything to the left of the juncture is represented in your right cerebral hemisphere and everything to the right is represented in your left cerebral hemisphere. This is so because half the axons in each optic nerve cross over (at the optic chiasma) to the opposite side of the brain. Normally, each hemisphere immediately shares its information with the other one. However, in split-brain patients, severing of the corpus callosum prevents such communication from occurring.

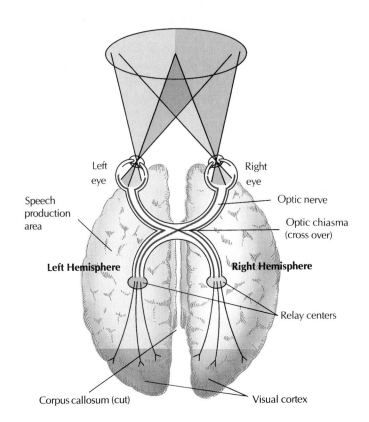

original photograph! Each side of the brain saw a different half image and automatically filled in the missing part. Neither side knew what the other side had seen.

Why did the patients name one side of the picture but point to the other? Speech centers are in the left hemisphere. When the person responded with speech, it was the left side of the brain talking. When the person pointed with the left hand, which is controlled by the right side of the brain, the right brain was giving *its* version of what the person had seen.

In another study, the researchers presented slides of ordinary objects, and then suddenly flashed a slide of a nude woman. Both sides of the brain were amused, but because only the left side has language, the two sides responded a bit differently. When the picture was flashed to her left hemisphere, one woman laughed and identified the picture as a nude. When it was flashed to her right hemisphere, she said nothing but began to chuckle. Asked what she was laughing at, she said, "I don't know . . . nothing . . . oh—that funny machine." The right hemisphere could not describe what it had seen, but it reacted emotionally, just the same (Gazzaniga, 1967).

A question of dominance

Some popular self-improvement programs promise to sharpen up your logical "left brain" and liberate your artistic "right brain." Why do so many people get carried away with the right brain/left brain dichotomy? Does the evidence support their enthusiasm—and their programs?

Since the initial split-brain studies, many others have been carried out. (Several dozen people have undergone the split-brain operation during the past quarter century.) Research on left-right differences has also been done with people whose brains are intact. Electrodes have been used to measure activity in the left and right sides of the brain while subjects perform different tasks (Galin & Ornstein, 1972; Ornstein, 1978). Blood flow to the two hemispheres has been measured during verbal and spatial tasks (Gur et al., 1982). The results confirm that nearly all

FIGURE 5.15

Divided brain, divided view
Split-brain patients were shown composite photographs, then asked to pick out the face they had seen from a series of intact photographs. These patients said they had seen the face that had been on right side of the composite, yet they pointed with their left hands to the face that had been on the left. Because the two hemispheres of the brain could not communicate, the verbal left hemisphere was aware of only the right half of the picture and the relatively mute right hemisphere was aware of only the left half.

right-handed people and a majority of left-handers process language mainly in the left hemisphere. The left side also seems superior to the right in various kinds of logical, sequential tasks, such as solving math problems or understanding technical material. Because of these cognitive abilities, many researchers refer to the left hemisphere as *dominant*. They believe that the left side usually exerts control over the ''minor'' right hemisphere. One well-known split-brain researcher, Michael Gazzaniga (1983), has argued that without help from the left side, the right side's mental skills would probably be ''vastly inferior to the cognitive skills of a chimpanzee.'' He also believes that the left hemisphere is constantly trying to explain actions and emotions generated by brain parts whose workings are nonverbal and outside of conscious awareness.

You can see in split-brain patients how the left brain concocts explanations. In one classic example, a picture of a chicken claw was flashed to a patient's left hemisphere, a picture of a snow scene to his right. The task was to point to a related image for each picture from an array, with a chicken the correct choice for the claw and a shovel for the snow scene. The patient chose the shovel with his left hand and the chicken with his right. When asked to explain why, he responded (with his left hemisphere) that the chicken claw went with the chicken, and the shovel was for cleaning out the chicken shed. The left brain had seen the left hand's response but did not know about the snow scene, so it interpreted the response by using the information it did have (Gazzaniga, 1988). In people with intact brains, says Gazzaniga, the left brain's interpretations account for the sense of a unified, coherent identity. (For more on the brain and self-awareness, see ''Think About It.'')

Think About It

Where Is Your "Self"?

When you say, "I am feeling unhappy," who is the "I" doing the feeling? When you say, "I've decided to have a hot dog instead of a hamburger," who is the "I" doing the choosing? When you say, "My mind is playing tricks on me," who is the "me" watching your mind play those tricks? Who is being tricked? Brainteasers like these have been baffling philosophers for thousands of years. How can the self observe itself? Isn't that a little like a finger pointing at its own tip?

The ancient Egyptians reportedly believed that the "self" in charge of a person's actions and thoughts was a little man, a *homunculus*, residing in the head. Descartes, as we saw in Chapter 1, located the physical site of the mind in the brain's pineal gland. Western religions resolved the problem by teaching that there is an immortal self or soul that exists entirely apart from the mortal brain.

Most modern brain scientists (with a few notable exceptions) consider mind to be a matter of matter; there is no "ghost in the machine." Although they may have personal religious convictions about a soul, most assume that "mind" or "self-awareness" can be explained in physical terms as a product of the cerebral cortex. What is not clear, though, is why damage to the cortex, or even removal of an entire hemisphere, usually leaves a person's sense of self intact.

Nobel Prize-winning biologist Francis Crick (1979) thinks the sense of self is merely a reflection, a kind of byproduct, of some sort of overall control mechanism in the brain. Neurologist Richard Restak (1983) notes that many of our actions and choices seem to occur without direction by a conscious self: "There is not a center in the brain involved in the exercise of will any more than there is a center in the brain of the swan responsible for the beauty and complexity of its flight. Rather, the brains of all creatures are probably organized along the lines of multiple centers and various levels." Similarly, brain researcher Michael Gazzaniga (1985) suggests that the brain is organized as a loose confederation of independent "modules," or mental systems, all working in parallel. Except for one, these modules are nonverbal. The sense of a unified self or consciousness is an illusion that occurs because the one verbal module, the "interpreter" (usually in the left hemisphere), is constantly constructing a theory to explain the actions, moods, and thoughts of the others.

Curiously, such views, which hold that many selves (or modules) rather than just one reside in the same head, come close to those of Eastern spiritual traditions. Buddhism, for example, teaches that the "self" is not a unified "thing" but a collection of thoughts, perceptions, concepts, and feelings that change from moment to moment. The unity and permanence of the self are considered an illusion. Such notions are contrary to what most of us in the West, including psychologists, have always assumed about our "selves."

What do you think about the existence and location of your "self"? And who, by the way, is doing the thinking?

Other researchers, including Sperry (1982), have rushed to the right hemisphere's defense. The right side, they point out, is no dummy. It is superior in problems requiring visual-spatial ability, the ability you use to read a map or follow a dress pattern, and it excels in facial recognition. (Poor Dr. P., at the beginning of this chapter, had damage in the right hemisphere.) It is involved in creating and appreciating art and music. It recognizes nonverbal sounds, such as a dog's barking. The right brain also seems to have some language ability. Typically it can read a word briefly flashed to it and can understand an experimenter's instructions. In a few split-brain patients, language ability has been quite well developed. Research

"It's finally happening, Helen. The hemispheres of my brain are drifting apart."

with other brain-damaged people finds that the right brain actually outperforms the left at understanding familiar idioms and metaphors (such as "turning over a new leaf") (Van Lancker & Kempler, 1987).

Some brain researchers have also credited the right hemisphere with having a unique cognitive style, one that is holistic (sees things as wholes) and intuitive, in contrast to the left hemisphere's more analytic mode. Neuropsychologist Jerre Levy (1983) concludes that the right hemisphere is active, responsive, and highly intelligent. "Could the eons of human evolution have left half of the brain witless?" she asks. "Could a bird whose existence is dependent on flying have evolved only a single wing?"

It has been suggested that our culture treats the right side like a slighted stepchild, formally educating the left side but letting the right side pretty much fend for itself (Buzan, 1976; Edwards, 1986). Robert Ornstein (1977) argues that this left-brain bias is a Western phenomenon. According to Ornstein, the East, with its traditions of meditation, yoga, and nonverbal knowing, favors a more right-brained, intuitive, holistic kind of consciousness. Ornstein suggests that a synthesis of the two approaches might result in a more complete and harmonious experience of reality. However, not all brain researchers agree that a conscious attempt at synthesis is necessary. Popular writers, they observe, have tended to oversimplify and exaggerate hemispheric differences. As Sperry (1982) himself notes, "The left-right dichotomy . . . is an idea with which it is very easy to run wild." Perhaps this is because human beings like to make sense of the world, and one easy way to do that is to divide humanity into opposing categories: liberals versus conservatives, good guys versus bad guys, right-brained types versus left-brained types. This sort of dualistic thinking can lead to the conclusion that all we have to do is fix up one of the categories (e.g., make all those left-brained types a little more intuitive) and the world will be a better place. The two hemispheres *do* have different specialties, but they do not always divide up as one might expect. In most real-life activities, the two hemispheres seem to cooperate naturally as partners, with each making a valuable contribution (Kinsbourne, 1982; J. Levy, 1985).

Some popular self-improvement programs promise to sharpen up your logical "left brain" and liberate your artistic "right brain." Why do so many people get carried away with the right brain/left brain dichotomy? Does the evidence support their enthusiasm—and their programs?

QUICK ▪ QUIZ

Keeping in mind that both sides of the brain are involved in most activities, see if you can identify which side is most closely associated with each of the following:

1. Enjoying a musical recording R
2. Wiggling the left big toe R
3. Giving a speech in class L

4. Balancing a checkbook L
5. Recognizing a long-lost R friend

Answers:

1, 2, and 5 are most closely associated with the right side; 3 and 4, with the left.

Two Stubborn Issues in Brain Research

If you have mastered the definitions and descriptions in this chapter, you are prepared to read press accounts of advances in neuropsychology intelligently. You will soon find that many mysteries remain about how the brain works in memory, thought, and emotion. We end the chapter with two of them.

How specialized are separate brain parts?

Is a piece of information stored in one specific spot or distributed throughout the brain? Researchers have generally assumed that only one answer can be true. Could both be true?

One of the most persistent questions in brain research has been this: Where are specific memories, habits, perceptions, and abilities stored? Most theories assume that different brain parts perform different jobs and store different sorts of information. This concept, known as **localization of function**, goes back at least to Joseph Gall (1758–1828), an Austrian anatomist who thought personality and character traits were reflected in the development of different areas of the brain (see Figure 2.1 in Chapter 2). Objective research eventually showed that Gall's theory of *phrenology* was completely wrong-headed (so to speak) but that his basic notion of specialization had merit. Specific centers for speech production and language comprehension were identified; the motor cortex and the various centers of sensation were located; clinical observations established that brain damage often had different consequences depending on where the damage occurred; and the split-brain studies showed that the two cerebral hemispheres have somewhat different talents. Today we know that even specific nerve cells have their specialties. When you look at diagonal lines, certain cells in your visual cortex fire. When you look at horizontal or vertical ones, different cells fire (see Chapter 5). Further, studies of sea snails suggest that very simple forms of learning are associated with changes in the membranes of particular nerve cells (Alkon, 1984) or with an increase or decrease of transmitter substances released at specific synapses (E. Kandel, 1979; Kandel & Schwartz, 1982).

Because of such findings, localization remains the guiding principle of modern brain theories (Gardner, 1985). However, there is another, minority view. It holds that perceived, learned, or remembered information is *distributed* across large areas of the brain, perhaps even the entire cortex. One of the first to make this argument was Karl Lashley, who many years ago set out to find where specific memories were stored in the rat's brain. His search turned out to be more frustrating than

localization of function
Specialization of particular brain areas for particular functions.

looking for a grain of sugar in a pile of sand. Lashley trained rats to run a complicated maze in order to find food, then destroyed a part of each rat's cortex. Destroying any section of the cortex led to some loss of the behavior, but the size of the area damaged was more important than where the damage was located, and even when Lashley removed over 90 percent of a rat's visual cortex, the animal could still find its way through the maze. After a quarter of a century, Lashley (1950) finally gave up searching for specific memory traces. He jokingly remarked that perhaps "learning just is not possible." More seriously, he concluded that every part of the cortex must somehow influence every other part.

How might the brain function as an integrated whole? According to theorist E. Roy John (1976; John et al., 1986), when we learn that Columbus discovered America or remember that 6 times 8 equals 48, it is not because certain cells fire or because a particular connection among cells is formed. What matters is the *average pattern* of cell activity throughout the brain. This pattern, John believes, has a particular rhythm. Imagine that the billions of cells in the brain are like the members of a gigantic orchestra. Each instrument is making noise in a more or less random way, as when an orchestra is tuning up. When a particular thought or memory occurs, most of the instruments in one section start to play a tune that has a definite rhythm. However, some instruments in other sections do so as well.

Another holistic approach compares brain processes to holography (Pribram, 1971, 1982). Holography is a system of photography in which a three-dimensional image is reproduced by means of light-wave patterns that are recorded on a photographic plate or film (the hologram). Information about any point in the image is distributed throughout the hologram. Thus any given area of the hologram contains the information necessary for producing the entire image. Similarly, some forms of knowledge may be dispersed throughout the brain, just as Karl Lashley thought.

Holistic views run counter to much of what we know about the brain (Squire, 1987). They do not explain why damage to even tiny brain areas can have specific and devastating effects. Nor do they account for decades of research showing that particular functions (visual processing, language production, generation of mental images) are associated with specific brain areas. (In Chapter 7, we will discuss the involvement of various brain areas in memory.) But the notion of localization also has some problems. For example, it cannot account for the remarkable flexibility of the brain (psychologists call it *plasticity*). Sometimes people who cannot recall simple words after a stroke regain normal speech within a matter of months. Similarly, people who cannot move an arm after a head injury may regain use of it after therapy. A few individuals have even survived the removal of an entire cerebral hemisphere without major disabilities! One explanation is that patients who recover from brain damage have learned to use entirely new strategies to accomplish the mental and physical tasks in question. Another possibility, however, is that the brain is, indeed, like a giant orchestra, and the players know one another's music. If one violinist can't make it to the performance, another violinist or perhaps a cellist may be able to fill in.

Well, then, is information in the brain localized or distributed? The best way out of this dilemma may be to recognize that both answers can be true. Neuropsychologist Larry Squire (1986, 1987) observes that any particular perception, habit, or memory includes many bits and pieces of information, often gathered from more than one sense: sounds, images, locations, facts. Specific collections of neurons in the brain may handle specific pieces of information, and many such collections, distributed across wide areas of the brain, may participate in representing an entire event. In other words, the parts of the event are localized; the whole is distributed. This view has the virtue of reconciling apparently opposite positions. However, we

A series of self-portraits by artist Anton Raderscheidt after he suffered a stroke demonstrates the remarkable plasticity of the human brain. The stroke damaged the part of Raderscheidt's brain involved in visual attention. In a painting done two months after the stroke (upper left), the artist omitted half his face, although he could see it perfectly well. A portrait done several months afterward (upper right) was more complete, and one done nine months after the stroke (bottom) showed the entire face and filled the canvas. It is still unclear how healthy parts of the brain take over functions once performed by damaged parts.

still are a long way from knowing how the many aspects of a memory or ability finally link together to form a whole. Nor do we understand yet why some people recover from damage to the brain while others, with similar damage, are permanently disabled.

Are there "his" and "hers" brains?

Perhaps no topic in brain research is as subject to muddy thinking, emotional reasoning, and faulty conclusions as sex differences in the brain. Does the pursuit of small differences obscure a larger question? Specifically what, if anything, can such differences tell us about real-life behavior?

A second stubborn controversy concerns the existence of sex differences in the brain. Efforts to distinguish male from female brains have a long and not always glorious history in psychology. During the nineteenth century, "findings" on male-female brain differences often flip-flopped in a most suspicious manner (Shields, 1975). At first, scientists doing dissection studies reported that women's frontal lobes were smaller than men's, and that their parietal lobes were larger. This presumably explained women's intellectual shortcomings. Then, around the turn of the century, people began (mistakenly) to attribute intellect to the parietal lobes rather than the frontal lobes. Suddenly there were reports that women had *smaller* parietal lobes and larger frontal lobes. You probably won't be surprised to learn that these researchers often knew the sex of the brains they were dissecting.

Since the 1960s, newer theories about male-female brain differences have come and gone just as quickly. A few years ago there was speculation that women were more "right-brained" and men were more "left-brained." It soon became clear, however, that the abilities popularly (and often incorrectly) associated with the two sexes did not fall neatly into one or the other side of the brain. The left side was more verbal (presumably "female"), but it was also more mathematical (presumably "male"). The right side was more emotional ("female"), but it was also more spatially talented ("male").

To evaluate the issue of sex differences, we need to ask two separate questions: Do physical differences actually exist in male and female brains? And if such differences do exist, what do they have to do with behavior?

Let's consider the first question. Various sex differences have been observed in anatomical studies of animal brains, especially in areas related to reproduction. For example, there are sex differences in the levels of various neurotransmitters in rats' brains (McEwen, 1983a). Also, in male rats, the right half of the cerebral cortex is thicker than the left in most areas, while in females the opposite tends to be true, though most of the left-right differences are not significant (Diamond et al., 1983).

Human sex differences, however, have been more elusive. A few years ago, two anthropologists autopsied 14 human brains and reported that one section of the corpus callosum was larger in females than in males (de Lacoste-Utamsing & Holloway, 1982). (The corpus callosum, you will recall, connects the two cerebral hemispheres.) Many writers immediately concluded that in women, the two hemispheres must communicate more efficiently. Men's brains, they decided, are more **lateralized**; that is, men rely more heavily on one or the other side of the brain when performing particular tasks, whereas women are more likely to use both sides. More recent studies, however, using magnetic resonance imaging to study *living* brains, get conflicting results. Some researchers report sex differences (L. Allen et al., 1987), but others can't find any (Bleier, 1987; Bleier, Houston, & Byne, 1986).

Some researchers have tried to study male-female brain differences indirectly, by observing what happens to men and women after a stroke (Inglis & Lawson, 1981; McGlone, 1978). One finding is that left-hemisphere damage is more likely to cause language problems in men than in women. Some people think this means, again, that men's brains are more lateralized. But others draw just the opposite conclusion. They argue that a smaller left-hemisphere area controls language in women then in men, so damage is more likely to "miss" the language area in women (Kimura, 1985; Kimura & Harshman, 1984).

In sum, sex differences in the human brain, which have made headlines in recent years, are not well established. Also, when differences are reported, they tend to be smaller than in animals. This brings us to the second question: If reliable physiological differences do exist, what do they mean? Speculations are as plentiful as ants at a picnic, but the fact is that no one really knows the answer to this question either (Fausto-Sterling, 1985). To answer it, we would need to know how brain organization and chemistry affect human abilities and traits in general, and we don't.

Those who believe that brain differences can explain psychological differences often take the psychological differences for granted, relying on popular stereotypes or obsolete findings rather than recent evidence. As a result, they fail to realize that the behaviors they wish to explain do not exist! For example, several brain research-

lateralization *Specialization of the two cerebral hemispheres for particular psychological operations.*

ers have suggested that brain differences might account for male-female differences in verbal ability. But as we saw in Chapter 2, verbal differences (which used to favor women) no longer exist (Feingold, 1988; Hyde & Linn, 1988). Other differences, most notably mathematical and spatial-visual ones, have been exaggerated. Men do slightly outperform women in math, but only in selected (e.g., gifted) samples, not in the general population (Hyde, Fennema, & Lamon, in preparation). And men excel on the average in only one type of spatial ability, the ability to rotate objects mentally; on other measures, the sexes perform equally (Linn & Petersen, 1985).

It can be tempting to reach for biological explanations for complex behaviors. But when thinking about sex differences in the brain, or about any of the findings discussed in this chapter, two important points need to be kept firmly in mind.

First, brain organization—the proportion of brain cells found in any particular part of the brain—varies considerably from person to person. Therefore, any sweeping generalizations about the brain, whether they are about the left and right hemispheres, localization of function, or sex differences, are bound to be oversimplifications. As Sperry (1982) notes, ''The more we learn . . . the stronger the conclusion becomes that the individuality inherent in our brain networks makes that of fingerprints or facial features gross and simple by comparison.''

Second, different experiences and environments may affect the way brains are organized to do various jobs. A cross-cultural example may make this point clear. The brains of the Japanese may not be lateralized in the same way as the brains of Westerners (including Americans of Japanese descent). There is some evidence that the Japanese process nonverbal human and animal sounds and Japanese instrumental music in the left hemisphere rather than the right, where we would expect them to be processed on the basis of split-brain studies. One possible explanation (a speculation, far from proven) is that because the Japanese language is rich in vowel sounds, and therefore has a musical quality, the left hemisphere learns to process nonverbal sounds (Sibatani, 1980; Tsunoda, 1985). Similarly, different experiences could conceivably result in some organizational differences between men's and women's brains. (We will examine the impact of experience on the brain more closely in Chapters 7 and 12.)

As we have seen in this chapter, the more we know about our physical selves, the better we understand our psychological selves. Yet biological research does not always answer behavioral questions. Physiological findings are most illuminating when they are integrated with what we know about personal perception and cultural experience. Analyzing a human being in terms of physiology alone is like analyzing the Taj Mahal solely in terms of the materials used to build it.

Taking Psychology with You

Food for Thought: Diet and Neurotransmitters

''Vitamin cures impotence!''
''Mineral boosts brainpower!''
''Chocolate chases the blues!''
Claims like these have long given nutritional theories of behavior a bad reputation. In the late 1960s, when Nobel laureate Linus Pauling pro-

posed that some mental illnesses might result from an unusual need for massive doses of particular vitamins, few serious researchers listened. Mainstream medical authorities classed Pauling's "orthomolecular psychiatry" with such infamous cure-alls as snake oil and leeches.

Most mental health professionals today remain skeptical of unorthodox nutritional treatments for mental illness. But they may have to eat at least some of their words. The underlying premise of these treatments, that diet affects the brain and therefore behavior, is getting a second look. Well-publicized claims that sugar or common food additives lead to undesirable behavior remain unproven. However, there is a growing respect for the role that various nutrients might play in mood and performance.

Some of the most exciting work has concerned the role of diet in the synthesis of neurotransmitters, the brain's chemical messengers. Certain nutrients serve as precursors, or building blocks, for particular neurotransmitters. Tryptophan, an amino acid found in protein-rich foods (dairy products, meat, fish, and poultry), is a precursor of the neurotransmitter serotonin. Tyrosine, another amino acid found in proteins, is a precursor of norepinephrine, epinephrine, and dopamine. Choline, a component of the lecithin found in egg yolks, soy products, and liver, is a precursor of acetylcholine.

In the case of tryptophan, the path between the dinner plate and the brain is an indirect one. Tryptophan leads to the production of serotonin, which appears to reduce alertness, promote relaxation, and hasten sleep. Since tryptophan is found in protein, you might think that a high-protein meal would make you drowsy, and carbohydrates (sweets, bread, pasta, potatoes) would leave you relatively alert. Actually, the opposite is true. High-protein foods contain several amino acids, not just tryptophan, and they all compete for a ride on carrier molecules headed for brain cells. Because tryptophan occurs in foods in small quantities, it doesn't stand much of a chance *if* all you eat is protein. It is in the position of a tiny child trying to push aside a crowd of adults for a seat on the subway. Carbohydrates, however, stimulate the production of insulin, and insulin causes all the other amino acids to be drawn out of the bloodstream while having little effect on tryptophan. So carbohydrates increase the odds of tryptophan making it to the brain (Wurtman, 1982).

Paradoxically, then, a high-carbohydrate, no-protein meal should make you relatively calm or lethargic and a high-protein one should promote alertness. Initial studies with human beings support this conclusion (Spring, Chiodo, & Bowen, 1987; Wurtman & Lieberman, 1982-83). It follows that if you have a 10:00 A.M. class, you might do better to include some meat or eggs in your breakfast than to eat only a sweet roll or sugared cereal. On the other hand, if you want a slumber-promoting snack at bedtime, a drink high in carbohydrates, like fruit juice, might be helpful.

Other research suggests that tyrosine may combat depression (Gelenberg et al., 1982-83). Further, choline (in lecithin) may improve memory in people with certain brain disorders that involve acetylcholine deficiencies, such as Alzheimer's disease, though studies so far have been inconclusive (Blass & Weksler, 1983; Corkin et al., 1982). Neurotransmitters cannot be given directly to patients because these substances cannot cross from the bloodstream into the brain. But someday special diets or directly administered precursors of neurotransmitters may actually replace or supplement drugs in the treatment of certain physical and mental conditions.

Keep in mind, though, that research in this area is just beginning. Studies with human beings have shown links between diet and behavior, but they have not conclusively pinned down the neurochemistry. Individuals differ in how they respond to different nutrients. Also, the effects are subtle (many other factors also influence mood and behavior), and some of them depend on the age of the subjects and the time of day a meal is eaten. Alan Gelenberg, a psychiatrist who is studying tyrosine, notes that health food publications tend to exaggerate his findings. "Then some health food stores stock something they call tyrosine—who knows what's in it—and people are writing from all over wanting to know how much they should take" (quoted in Weisburd, 1984). People have also rushed out to buy lecithin preparations, without realizing that those sold in health food stores are too impure to be of much value.

Clearly, nutrients can and do affect the brain and behavior. But these nutrients interact in complex ways. If you don't eat protein, you won't get enough tryptophan, but if you go without carbohydrates, the tryptophan found in protein will be useless. The moral of the story is that if you're looking for brain food, you are most likely to find it in a well-balanced diet.

KEY WORDS

neuropsychology 80
neuroscience 80
central nervous system 81
peripheral nervous system 81
spinal cord 82
reflex 82
reflex arc 82
sensory nerves 83
motor nerves 83
somatic nervous system 83
autonomic nervous system 83
biofeedback 83
sympathetic nervous system 84
parasympathetic nervous system 84
neuron 85
glial cells 85
cell body 86
dendrites 86
axon 86

nerve 87
tract 87
myelin sheath 87
synapse 88
synaptic vesicles 88
neurotransmitter 88
endorphins 90
hormones 92
endocrine glands 92
insulin 93
adrenal glands 93
epinephrine 93
norepinephrine 93
androgens 93
estrogens 93
progesterone 93
electrodes 95
electroencephalogram (EEG) 96
evoked potentials 96

SUMMARY

1. The nervous system is the bedrock of behavior. For purposes of description, it is divided into the *central nervous system* (CNS) and *peripheral nervous system* (PNS). The CNS, which includes the brain and spinal cord, processes, interprets, and stores information and issues orders destined for muscles, glands, and organs. The PNS transmits information to and from the CNS by way of sensory and motor nerves.

2. The peripheral nervous system is made up of the *somatic nervous system*, which controls voluntary actions, and the *autonomic nervous system*, which regulates blood vessels, internal organs, and various glands. The autonomic system usually functions without conscious control. Some people can learn to control their autonomic responses to some degree, using *biofeedback* techniques, but it is not clear whether this control is direct or indirect.

3. The autonomic nervous system is divided into the *sympathetic nervous system*, which mobilizes the body for action, and the *parasympathetic nervous system*, which conserves energy.

4. *Neurons* are the basic units of the nervous system. Each neuron consists of a *cell body*, *dendrites*, and an *axon*. When a wave of electrical voltage reaches the end of an axon, *neurotransmitter* molecules are released into the *synapse*. When these molecules fit into slots, or receptor sites, on the receiving neuron, the receiving neuron becomes either more or less likely to fire. Neurotransmitters play a critical role in mood, memory, and psychological well-being.

5. *Endorphins*, which are special kinds of neurotransmitters, resemble opiates in both structure and function: They reduce pain and promote pleasure. As we saw in ''A Closer Look at Neuropsychology,'' endorphins may be linked to the pleasures of social contact, and an overactive endorphin system may contribute to the social withdrawal characteristic of autism.

6. *Hormone* levels affect, and are affected by, the nervous system. Insulin, adrenal hormones, and sex hormones have been of special interest to psychologists.

7. Human brains are more powerful than those of other species because of their complex circuitry. Researchers study the brain by observing brain-damaged patients, operating on the brains of animals, and using such techniques as electroencephalograms (EEGs), PET scans, and magnetic resonance imaging (MRI).

8. In the *hindbrain*, the *brain stem* controls automatic functions such as heartbeat and breathing. The *reticular activating system* screens incoming information and is responsible for alertness. The *cerebellum* contributes to balance and muscle coordination.

9. In the *forebrain*, the *thalamus* directs sensory messages to appropriate centers. The *hypothalamus* is involved in emotion and in drives associated with survival and controls the autonomic nervous system. The *limbic system* is involved in emotions that we share with other animals and contains many "pleasure centers." The *hippocampus* plays a critical role in memory.

10. The *cerebrum*, the upper part of the forebrain, is made up of two hemispheres. Because the *cerebral cortex*, or outer covering of the cerebrum, is crumpled, it can contain billions of neurons without requiring the brain to be too big for the skull. The occipital, parietal, temporal, and frontal lobes of the cortex have specialized (but partially overlapping) functions. The *association cortex* appears to be responsible for higher mental processes.

11. Split-brain studies of patients whose *corpus callosums* have been cut show that the two cerebral hemispheres have somewhat different "talents." In most people, language is processed mainly in the left hemisphere, which generally appears to be specialized for logical, sequential tasks. The right hemisphere appears to be specialized for visual-spatial tasks, facial recognition, and appreciation of art and music. However, in most mental activities, the two hemispheres cooperate as partners, with each making a valuable contribution.

12. Most brain theories emphasize that different brain parts perform different jobs and store different sorts of information, a concept known as *localization of function*. Some researchers, however, argue that perceived, learned, or remembered information is *distributed* across large areas of the brain and that the brain functions as an integrated whole. Both views may have merit: Specific locations in the brain may handle specific pieces of information, and many such collections, distributed across wide areas of the brain, may participate in representing an entire event.

13. Sex differences have been observed in anatomical studies of animal brains. Sex differences in human brains, however, have been more elusive, and there is controversy about their existence and their meaning. It is unclear how reported brain differences are related to sex differences in human behavior. Several proposals fail to take into account that sex differences in ability have been disappearing, and in the case of verbal ability, no longer exist.

14. Individual brains vary considerably in their organization. Further, different experiences and environments may affect brain development. These points should be kept in mind when interpreting brain findings. Such findings are most illuminating when they are integrated with psychological and cultural ones.

C H A P T E R 4

Body Rhythms and Mental States

Like a bird's life, [consciousness] seems to be made of an alternation of flights and perchings.

WILLIAM JAMES

At one point in Lewis Carroll's *Alice in Wonderland*, the harried heroine has a bewildered discussion with herself: "Dear dear!" she thinks. "How queer everything is today! And yesterday things went on just as usual. I wonder if I've been changed in the night? Let me think: *was* I the same when I got up this morning? I almost think I can remember feeling a little different. But if I'm not the same, the *next* question is, 'Who in the world am I?' Ah, *that's* the great puzzle!" It's no wonder Alice is confused. During her adventures in the topsy-turvy world of Wonderland, she shrinks to within only a few inches of the ground, then shoots up beyond the treetops. The crazy antics of the inhabitants make her smile one moment and shed a literal pool of tears in the next. The ordinary assumptions of the world constantly dissolve in a sea of logical contradictions.

In a way, we all live in a sort of Wonderland. For a third of our lives we reside in a realm where the ordinary rules of logic and experience are suspended: the dream world of sleep. Moreover, throughout the 24-hour day, mood, alertness, efficiency, and **consciousness** (the awareness of oneself and the environment) are in perpetual flux, sometimes shifting as dramatically as Alice's height.

The techniques and concepts described in the previous chapter are being used to learn more about these fluctuations. Starting from the assumption that mental and physical states are as intertwined as sunshine and shadow, psychologists are exploring the links between subjective experience and bodily changes—changes in brain activity, hormone levels, and the action of neurotransmitters. In recent years, they have come to view changing **states of consciousness** as part of the ebb and flow of experience over time, an ebb and flow associated with predictable bodily events. For example, dreaming, traditionally classified as a state of consciousness, is also part of a 90-minute cycle of brain activity. Alternating periods of dreaming and nondreaming during the night occur in a **biological rhythm**.

Studying subjective experience in terms of distinct states is like looking at a snapshot of consciousness. Examining subjective experience in terms of ongoing rhythms is more like watching a motion picture. In this chapter, we will first run the motion picture, to see how functioning and consciousness vary predictably over time. Then we will zoom in on some specific "stills," examining in greater detail what wakefulness, daydreaming, and sleep dreaming are like. Finally, we will turn to ways of "retouching the film" by deliberately altering consciousness.

consciousness *The awareness of the environment and one's own existence, sensations, and thoughts.*

states of consciousness *Distinctive and discrete patterns in the functioning of consciousness, characterized by particular modes of perception, thought, memory, or feeling.*

biological rhythm *A periodic, more or less regular fluctuation in a biological system; may or may not have psychological implications.*

Biological Rhythms: The Tides of Experience

Wouldn't it be nice to know beforehand when you were about to have a bad day or were going to be in top form? People who sell "biorhythm charts" claim you can. According to a theory they cite, whose roots go back a century, 28-day mood cycles, 33-day intellectual cycles, and 23-day physical cycles begin at birth and continue like clockwork throughout life. Half of each cycle is said to be positive and half negative, and the point at which a cycle changes from positive to negative is said to be "critical"—ripe for errors, accidents, and illness. Proponents of this "theory" will tell you that Clark Gable, Harry Truman, and other famous people had heart attacks or died on double or triple critical days. They may also cite "scientific studies" showing that accidents declined after bus drivers or pilots were warned to be particularly careful on critical days.

Can you spot the problems with this "evidence"? One problem is that the anecdotal accounts ignore *negative* data, all the cases of people who have remained perfectly healthy on critical days or died on noncritical ones. As for the "studies," they failed to include safety warnings to subjects who were *not* entering a "critical" period. Without such a control group, all a biorhythm study shows is that warning people to be careful makes them careful. And even on the face of it, the biorhythm theory is implausible: Everything we know about the human body tells us that it is not rigidly regular. Illness, fatigue, stress, and emotional excitement can all affect the way a person functions.

When people have taken the trouble to test the biorhythm theory scientifically, by examining occupational accidents or the performance of sports stars, they have consistently failed to find any support whatsoever for it (Louis, 1978). Yet biorhythm charts are still being marketed. Apparently, one human characteristic that does not fluctuate much is gullibility! On the other hand, it is true that human beings, unlike robots and computers, do not operate in an unvarying way 24 hours a day, 7 days a week, 52 weeks a year. We've got rhythm! In fact, we experience dozens of periodic, more or less regular ups and downs in physiological functioning. Biological "clocks" in our brains govern the waxing and waning of hormone levels, urine volume, body temperature, blood pressure, and even the responsiveness of brain cells to stimulation. These cycles are what scientists mean by biological rhythms, and they fall into three categories:

1. *Circadian rhythms occur approximately every 24 hours*. The best known circadian rhythm is the sleep-wake cycle, but there are hundreds of others that govern physiology and performance.

2. *Ultradian rhythms occur more frequently than once a day; many occur about every 90 minutes*. Stomach contractions, certain hormone levels, appetite for food, oral behavior (smoking, pencil chewing, snacking), susceptibility to visual illusions, performance on verbal and spatial tasks, and alertness all follow roughly a 90-minute schedule when social customs or the three-meal-a-day habit do not intervene (Friedman & Fisher, 1967; Klein & Armitage, 1979; Kripke, 1974; Lavie, 1976). The most frequently studied ultradian rhythm, as we will see, occurs during sleep.

3. *Infradian rhythms occur less frequently than once a day*. The female menstrual cycle, which occurs once every 28 days on the average, is an example.

Many biological rhythms have important health implications. For example, body cells respond to certain drugs on a circadian schedule. Therefore, a drug may be effective and safe at one time of day but ineffective or harmful at another. Some biological rhythms are also associated with mental or emotional changes, which makes them particularly interesting to psychologists. With better understanding of our internal tempos, we may be able to design our days to take the best advantage of our bodies' natural cycles.

Circadian rhythms

Circadian rhythms exist in plants, animals, insects, and human beings. They reflect the adaptation of organisms to the many changes associated with the rotation of the earth on its axis, such as changes in light, air pressure, temperature, and wind. But

People who sell biorhythm charts would have us believe that Clark Gable and James Dean died when they did because their "biorhythms" were in a trough. What facts are these people leaving out?

circadian [sur-CAY-dee-un] rhythm *A biological rhythm with a period (from peak to peak or trough to trough) of about 24 hours. From the Latin* circa, *"about," and* dias, *"a day."*

ultradian [ul-TRAY-dee-un] rhythm *A biological rhythm that occurs more frequently than once a day. From the Latin for "beyond a day."*

infradian [in-FRAY-dee-un] rhythm *A biological rhythm that occurs less frequently than once a day. From the Latin for "below a day."*

A morning glory is only "glorious" in the morning. Animals and human beings also have daily physical and behavioral rhythms.

many circadian rhythms are no longer dependent on external cues, for they are generated from within; in technical terms, they are *endogenous*.

Human circadian rhythms are studied by isolating volunteers from sunlight, clocks, environmental sounds, and other cues to time. Artificial light is kept at a constant level, varied by the researcher, or turned on and off by the volunteers when they retire or awaken. The first research of this kind was done in the 1960s in France and West Germany, and since then hundreds of studies have been reported (Aschoff & Wever, 1981; Moore-Ede, Sulzman, & Fuller, 1984). Some hardy souls have spent weeks or even months alone in caves and salt mines, linked to the outside world by only a one-way phone line and a cable transmitting physiological measurements to the surface. More often, though, volunteers live in specially designed bunkers equipped with record players, comfortable furniture, and temperature controls.

In a typical study, a person sleeps, eats, and works whenever he or she wishes, free of the tyranny of the timepiece. Living on a self-imposed schedule in this way is called *free-running*. Researchers find that when time cues are unavailable, a few individuals settle into a "day" that is shorter than 24 hours—as short as 16 hours in some cases. Others free-run on a cycle that is considerably longer than 24 hours. But for the majority, an average "day" is about 25 hours long. During each successive cycle the person tends to go to sleep a little later and get up a little later (see Figure 4.1). Temperature, blood pressure, and hormone cycles usually follow suit. When these volunteers emerge from their isolation, they think much less time has passed than actually has.

During ordinary living, time cues abound and our bodies adapt to a strict 24-hour schedule. For example, body temperature varies by about 1 degree Fahrenheit during a 24-hour period. For most people, it peaks in the late afternoon and sinks to a low point during the second half of sleep. These peaks and valleys are a good predictor of performance on simple, repetitive perceptual-motor tasks. Thus people tend to do best on nut-and-bolt assembly tests and rifle aiming in the afternoon,

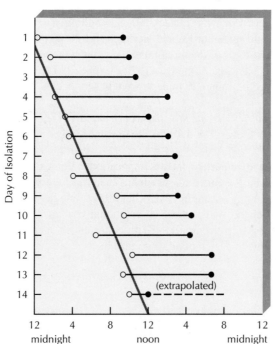

FIGURE 4.1

The days grow longer
This is a chart of sleep periods for a volunteer living in isolation from all time cues. Open circles show when the person went to bed, and solid circles show when the person rose. Like most volunteers living in isolation, this individual tended to retire and awaken later and later as the study wore on—in this case, an average of 49 minutes later each day. The pattern is represented by the diagonal red line. (From Webb & Agnew, 1974.)

when temperature peaks (Colquhoun, 1981). Performance on intellectually more complex tasks depends on which skills are required. Immediate processing of information—for example, detecting a signal on a sonar screen—tends to be done best in the late afternoon or early evening. Verbal reasoning and remembering material for short periods are done best in the morning or at midday (Monk et al., 1983).

Researchers originally thought that one clock or pacemaker, in the hypothalamus of the brain, might directly control the dozens of different human circadian rhythms. It now seems that several self-sustaining but interrelated clocks are ticking away in different parts of the brain. The clocks may be coupled (linked) to each other and possibly also to a "super clock," or overall coordinator, located in a tiny area of the hypothalamus. Normally the various rhythms they govern are synchronized, just as wristwatches can be synchronized. Their peaks may occur at different times, but they occur with the same frequency and in phase with one another; if you know when one rhythm peaks, you can predict when another will. This *internal synchronization* seems to be choreographed by rising and falling levels of various hormones and neurotransmitters (Moore-Ede & Sulzman, 1981). One hormone, melatonin (secreted by the pineal gland), may keep the "super clock" in phase with the light-dark cycle (Reppert et al., 1988). Melatonin treatments were recently used to synchronize the disturbed sleep-wake cycle of a blind man whose problems apparently stemmed from his inability to sense light and dark (Arendt, Aldhous, & Wright, 1988).

When a person's normal routine changes, circadian rhythms may be thrown out of phase with one another. Such *internal desynchronization* often occurs when people take airplane flights across several time zones. Sleep and wake patterns adjust quickly, but temperature and hormone cycles can take several days to return to normal. The resulting "jet lag" affects mental and physical performance. A mini-version of jet lag seems to occur in some people when they have to "spring forward" into daylight savings time, losing an hour from the 24-hour day. They may sleep less well than usual and feel a little tense and out of sorts during the week following the time change. In contrast, "falling back" into standard time, which produces a 25-hour day and time for some extra sleep, does not seem to be a strain (Monk & Aplin, 1980).

Travel is often exhausting, and jet lag can make it worse. Because most people, when freed from the clock, have a natural day that is somewhat longer than 24 hours, jet lag tends to be more noticeable and long-lasting after eastbound travel (which shortens the day) then after westbound (which lengthens it).

Internal desynchronization also occurs when workers must adjust to a new shift. Efficiency drops and the person feels tired and irritable. Sleep disturbances and digestive disorders may occur. Night work itself is usually not the problem: If people consistently work at night and sleep during the day, they can often adapt. However, many swing and night shift assignments are made on a rotating basis, so people's rhythms don't have a chance to resynchronize. Ideally, a rotating work schedule should take into account circadian principles by switching workers forward to a later schedule rather than backward to an earlier one. For example, if the person has been working from midnight to 8:00 A.M., the next shift should be 8:00 A.M. to 4:00 P.M. rather than 4:00 P.M. to midnight. Also, changes should be made as infrequently as possible. A three-week schedule of rotation is better than a one-week schedule (Czeisler, Moore-Ede, & Coleman, 1982).

We want to emphasize that circadian rhythms are not perfectly regular and are easily modified by daily experiences. Body temperature tends to peak in the afternoon, but a hot shower in the morning can push it up, too. Hormones rise and fall in a characteristic pattern, but stress can alter the pattern. Also, circadian rhythms differ from individual to individual: Some people are feeling their oats by ten in the morning; others aren't ready for action until four in the afternoon. Research with animals suggests that such individual differences may be at least partly genetic (Ralph & Menaker, 1988). You may be able to learn about your own personal pulses through careful self-observation.

The rhythms of sleep

The most obvious circadian rhythm governs sleeping and wakefulness. Human beings and most animals go to sleep once every 24 hours. Why is sleep such a profound necessity? Surprisingly, no one really knows.

Why do we sleep? Some researchers believe that sleep provides a "time-out" period for the body to restore depleted reserves of energy, eliminate waste products from muscles, repair cells, or recover abilities lost during the day. The idea that sleep is for physical rest and recuperation accords with common sense and with the undeniable fact that at the end of the day we feel tired and crave sleep. Though most people can function fairly normally after a day or two of sleeplessness, sleep deprivation that lasts for four days or longer is extremely uncomfortable. Laboratory studies of human beings and observations of people participating in "wake-athons" have shown that after several days, sleeplessness often leads to irritability, hallucinations, and delusions (Dement, 1978; Luce & Segal, 1966). In animals, forced sleeplessness eventually leads to death, and the same thing may be true for people. There is a case on record of a man who abruptly began to lose sleep at age 52. After sinking deeper and deeper into an exhausted stupor, he developed a lung infection and died. An autopsy showed he had lost almost all of the large neurons in two areas of the thalamus that have been linked to sleep and hormonal circadian rhythms (Lugaresi et al., 1986). A favorite method of torture during the Spanish Inquisition was the *Tortura insomnia*, sleep deprivation, which was said to drive victims mad and eventually kill them.

Yet, although physical changes do take place during sleep, no one has shown that sleep is actually necessary for them to occur. Wastes are removed from muscles even without sleep; you just have to rest for a few minutes. When people go many days without sleep, they do not then require an equal period of time to "catch up"; one night's rest usually eliminates all symptoms of fatigue (Dement, 1978). In

Whatever your age, sometimes the urge to sleep is irresistible—but no one yet knows why.

ordinary life, the amount of time we sleep does not necessarily correspond to how active we have been during the day; even after a relaxing day on the beach, we usually go to sleep at night as usual. For all these reasons, simple rest or energy restoration cannot be the sole purpose of sleep.

Some writers have suggested that sleep evolved because it conserved energy or involved curling up quietly in a secluded place that provided safety from predators (Meddis, 1977; Webb, 1974). But these hypotheses do not explain why sleep involves a loss (or at least a partial loss) of consciousness. The late Christopher Evans (1984), a British psychologist, noted that losing consciousness actually puts an organism at risk. Muscles that are usually ready to respond to danger relax. Senses that are usually seeking signs of other organisms grow dull. During wakefulness, you might be temporarily distracted by eating, drinking, or mating, but you can interrupt your activity at will and your sensory abilities remain in operation. "The behavior patterns involved in sleep," said Evans, "are glaringly, almost insanely, at odds with common sense."

It may be that sleep serves the brain more than the rest of the body. Only animals with brains or at least an integrated bundle of central nervous system tissue show unmistakable signs of sleep (Evans, 1984). During sleep, most of the brain, far from simply resting, remains quite active. Moreover, brain waves during sleep change in predictable ways, as we are about to see. The biological function of sleep, then, may have something to do with brain function.

The realms of sleep. Sleep is not a continuous, quiet, resting state. Within sleep, there is a briefer, ultradian rhythm. In all mammals, periods of **rapid eye movement**, or **REM**, alternate with periods of few eye movements, or non-REM (NREM). In human beings, a majority of REM periods are associated with dreaming, whether or not the dreams are recalled (Aserinsky & Kleitman, 1955; Dement, 1955; Dement & Kleitman, 1957). As we noted in Chapter 2, these dreams do not occur in an instant but in "real time." Dreams can also occur during non-REM sleep, but they are usually less vivid and more realistic than those during REM sleep.

rapid eye movement (REM) sleep *Sleep periods characterized by eye movement, loss of muscle tone, and dreaming.*

FIGURE 4.2

Brain wave patterns during sleep
Most types of brain waves are present throughout sleep, but different ones predominate at different stages.

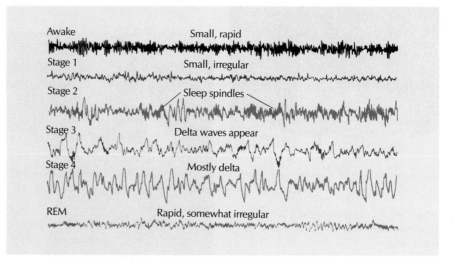

In adults, REM periods occur about every 90 minutes, on the average, or four to six times a night. They account for between a fifth and a quarter of total sleep time. Non-REM periods are themselves divided into shorter, distinct stages. Electroencephalogram (EEG) recordings made in sleep laboratories show that each of these stages is associated with a particular brain wave pattern (see Figure 4.2).

When you first climb into bed, close your eyes, and relax, your brain emits bursts of **alpha waves** in a regular, high-amplitude, low-frequency rhythm of 8 to 12 cycles per second. Alpha is associated with relaxing or not concentrating on anything in particular. Gradually these waves slow down even further and you drift into the Land of Nod, passing through four "realms" or stages, each deeper than the previous one.

1. *Stage 1.* Your brain waves become small and irregular, indicating activity with low voltage and mixed frequencies. You feel yourself drifting on the edge of consciousness, in a state of light sleep. If awakened, you may recall fantasies or a few visual images.

2. *Stage 2.* Your brain emits occasional short bursts of rapid, high-peaking waves called *sleep spindles*. Light sounds or minor noises probably won't disturb you.

3. *Stage 3.* In addition to the waves characteristic of stage 2, your brain occasionally emits very slow waves of about one to three cycles per second, with very high peaks. These **delta waves** are a sure sign that you will be hard to arouse. Your breathing and pulse have slowed down, your temperature has dropped, and your muscles are relaxed.

4. *Stage 4.* Delta waves have now largely taken over, and you are in deep sleep. It will take vigorous shaking or a loud noise to awaken you, and you won't be very happy about it. Oddly enough, though, if you talk or walk in your sleep, this is when you are likely to do so.

This sequence takes about 30 to 45 minutes. Then it reverses, and you progress back up the ladder from stage 4 to 3 to 2 to 1. At that point, about 70 to 90 minutes after the onset of sleep, something peculiar happens. Stage 1 does not turn into drowsy wakefulness, as one might expect. Instead, your brain begins to emit long bursts of very rapid, somewhat irregular waves, similar to those produced during stage 1. Your heart rate increases, your blood pressure rises, and your breathing becomes faster and more irregular. There may be small, convulsive twitches in the

alpha waves *Relatively large, slow brain waves characteristic of relaxed wakefulness.*

delta waves *Slow, regular brain waves characteristic of stage 3 and stage 4 sleep.*

face and fingers. In men, the penis becomes somewhat erect as vascular tissue relaxes and blood fills the genital area faster than it exits. In women, the clitoris enlarges, the vaginal walls become engorged, and vaginal lubrication increases. (These genital reactions have nothing to do with sexy dreams; they occur even if you are dreaming about mowing the lawn or solving a math problem.) At the same time, most of your skeletal muscles go as limp as a rag doll, preventing your aroused brain from producing physical movement and keeping you from acting out your dreams. Though you are supposedly in a ''light'' stage of sleep, you are hard to awaken. You have entered the realm of REM.

Because the brain is extremely active while the body is almost devoid of muscle tone, the REM period has also been called ''paradoxical sleep.'' The more eventful the dream during this period, the more frequent the rapid eye movements. But researchers disagree about whether the eye movements correspond to what is happening in the dream. Some think they are no more related to dream content than are inner ear muscle contractions, which also occur during REM sleep (Kelly, 1981b).

REM and non-REM sleep continue to alternate throughout the night, with the REM periods tending to get longer and closer together as the hours pass (see Figure 4.3). An early REM period may last only a few minutes, whereas a later one may go on for 20 or 30 minutes and sometimes as long as an hour. (That is why people are likely to be dreaming when the alarm goes off in the morning.) In the later part of sleep, stages 3 and 4 become very short or disappear. But the cycles are far from regular. An individual may bounce directly from stage 4 back to stage 2, or go from REM to stage 2 and then back to REM. Also, the time between REM and non-REM is highly variable, differing from person to person and also within a particular individual. In fact, scientists must use sophisticated statistical methods to ''see'' the regularity in the REM and non-REM cycles.

The purpose of REM sleep is still a matter of debate, but clearly it does have a purpose. If you wake people every time they lapse into REM sleep, nothing dramatic will happen. When finally allowed to sleep normally, however, they will spend a much longer time than usual in the REM phase. Electrical brain activity associated with REM may burst through into quiet sleep and even into wakefulness. The subjects seem to be making up for something they were deprived of.

Since cats sleep so much—up to 80 percent of the time!—it's easy to catch them in the various stages of slumber. A cat in NREM sleep (top) remains upright, but during REM sleep (bottom) its muscles go limp and it flops onto its side.

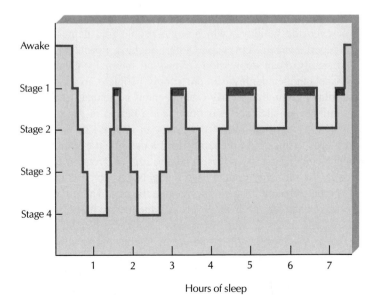

Hours of sleep

FIGURE 4.3

The changing rhythms of sleep

This graph shows the pattern of a typical night's sleep for a young adult. Time spent in REM sleep is represented by the colored bars. REM periods tend to lengthen as the night goes on. In contrast, stages 3 and 4, which dominate non-REM sleep early in the night, may disappear as morning approaches. (From Kelly, 1981a.)

QUICK ■ QUIZ

Match each term with the appropriate phrase.

1. REM periods
2. alpha
3. stage 4 sleep
4. stage 1 sleep

a. delta waves and talking in sleep
b. irregular brain waves and light sleep
c. relaxed but awake
d. active brain but inactive muscles

Answers:

1. d 2. c 3. a 4. b

The menstrual cycle and other long-term rhythms

According to Ecclesiastes, "To every thing there is a season, and a time for every purpose under heaven." Modern science agrees: Long-term (infradian) cycles have been observed in everything from the threshold for tooth pain to mortality and conception rates. In some cases of severe depression, symptoms occur every winter, when periods of daylight are short, and clear up every spring, as daylight increases. This pattern, dubbed "seasonal affective disorder" (SAD), seems to disappear in some people when they spend time each day sitting in front of extremely bright fluorescent lights (N. Rosenthal et al., 1985).

Some researchers think the winter doldrums are related to fluctuations in *melatonin,* the hormone secreted by the pineal gland. Animal studies suggest that information about light and dark travels from the eyes along a neural pathway leading through the hypothalamus and on to the pineal gland. In most people, melatonin peaks during the night and falls with the approach of day; in many winter depressives, the cycle seems to begin and end later than normally (Lewy et al., 1987). But it is hard to prove that human long-term cycles are endogenous. The winter blues could also be caused by the mental association of short days with cold weather, inactivity, or even the holidays, which some people find depressing. Similarly, some people report *summer* depression (Wehr, Sack, & Rosenthal, 1987), but this does not necessarily mean depression follows an internally generated biological rhythm. Perhaps summer depressives are simply people who can't take the heat.

One infradian rhythm that clearly *is* endogenous is the menstrual cycle. Several hormones in human females ebb and flow over a period of roughly 28 days, the lunar month. During the first half of the cycle, an increase in estrogen causes the lining of the uterus to thicken in preparation for a possible pregnancy. At midcycle, ovulation occurs and the ovaries release a mature egg, or ovum. After ovulation, the ovarian follicle, or sac, that contained the egg begins to produce progesterone, which helps prepare the uterine lining to receive the egg. Then, if conception does not occur, estrogen and progesterone levels fall, the uterine lining sloughs off as the menstrual flow, and the cycle is ready to repeat itself. For psychologists, the interesting question is whether or not emotional or intellectual changes are correlated with the physical ones. Folklore and tradition say that menstruating women are emotionally unstable. Doctors and counselors, who are sometimes influenced more by folklore and tradition than they care to admit, have often agreed.

Recently, a cluster of symptoms associated with the days preceding menstruation—including fatigue, backache, headache, tension, depression, and mood swings—has come to be thought of as an ''illness'' and has been given a label, premenstrual syndrome (PMS). Some popular books refer to ''millions'' of sufferers or assert that ''most'' women have PMS, though there are no statistics to back up such claims. Proposed explanations of the syndrome include progesterone deficiency, estrogen/progesterone imbalance, water retention, and a fall in the level of endorphins (the brain's natural opiates), but there is no general agreement about causes, and no one has established that women reporting PMS differ hormonally from other women (Hopson & Rosenfeld, 1984). Nor is there convincing evidence as yet that any particular treatment works better than a placebo, though there have been many anecdotes and testimonials.

Discussions of ''PMS'' often fail to distinguish physical from emotional symptoms, and this distinction is critical in evaluating the phenomenon. It is well established that menstrual and premenstrual cramps, water retention, and other physical symptoms usually have a physical basis and respond to medical treatment; there is no controversy there. But there is reason to question the reality of *emotional* symptoms, even though many women insist that they have them. Self-reports can be a poor guide to reality, no matter how valid they feel to the person doing the reporting. For one thing, a woman might easily attribute a blue mood before menstruation to her impending period, although at other times of the month she would blame a grouchy professor, a disappointing date, or a stressful day. Or she may notice that she feels depressed or irritable when these moods happen to occur premenstrually, but overlook times when these moods are *absent* premenstrually, and wrongly conclude that she ''typically'' gets moody before her periods.

Most important, a woman's perceptions of her own emotional ups and downs can be influenced by expectations and menstrual myths (Parlee, 1973). To get around this problem, several psychologists have polled women (and sometimes men) about their psychological and physical well-being *without revealing the true purpose of the study*. Using a double-blind procedure, some researchers have had people report symptoms for a single day and have then gone back to see what phase of the cycle the women were in. Others have had subjects keep daily records over an extended period of time. In either case, guess what they have found? Overall, women do *not* report more emotional symptoms or fluctuations than men do. What's more, the relationship between cycle stage and symptoms turns out to be weak or nonexistent (Alagna & Hamilton, 1986; Burke, Burnett, & Levenstein, 1978; Englander-Golden, Whitmore, & Dienstbier, 1978; Parlee, 1982; Slade, 1984; Vila & Beech, 1980). At the conclusion of one recent study, women *recalled* their moods as having been more unpleasant before and during menstruation, but their own daily reports failed to bear them out (McFarlane, Martin, & Williams, 1988). Results like these, reported many times over the past decade, are unknown to most of the public and have been ignored by many doctors and clinicians.

Of course, men also have their emotional ups and downs. Is there a hormone-mood link in men? Testosterone, an important androgen (masculinizing hormone), fluctuates daily in all men. It also seems to follow a longer cycle in some, the length of the cycle varying from one man to another (Doering et al., 1974). So far, there is only weak or conflicting evidence for a connection between mood and testosterone or other androgens in males. In one study, which measured daily mood and hormone changes in young men for a month, high testosterone levels predicted high hostility for some men, but low hostility for others (Doering et al., 1974). In another study, testosterone rose in men who were feeling elated after winning a $100 prize in a tennis match (Mazur & Lamb, 1980), but in a third study, teenagers with

Many women believe they are more irritable premenstrually. Then why do their own daily reports fail to bear them out? And why do men report as many mood changes as women do over the span of a month?

characteristically high testosterone levels had a tendency to feel sad (Susman et al., 1987). Perhaps further research will clarify these results. However, to date, far more attention has been paid to hormones and moods in women, perhaps because each month women have a visible reminder of hormonal changes, while men do not.

In any case, few people of either sex are likely to undergo dramatic personality changes because of their hormones. Hormonal *abnormalities* may produce psychological symptoms, just as a brain tumor might. Stress can also lead to physical or emotional symptoms: In one study, full-time homemakers with young children reported the most severe "PMS" (Sanders et al., 1983). And in women, unusually severe premenstrual pain or discomfort may affect mood. But for most people, the relationships between body rhythms and mental states are subtle and varied. An increased state of arousal or sensitivity may contribute to nervousness and restlessness—or to creative energy and vitality. The impact of any bodily change, whether it is circadian, ultradian, or infradian, depends on how we interpret it and how we choose to respond to it.

Ordinary States of Consciousness

Capturing any one state of consciousness in words can be as frustrating as trying to catch a mote of dust as it drifts by on a sunbeam. Consciousness is constantly changing, with one "state" melting seamlessly into another. As William James (1890/1950) noted long ago, "Consciousness . . . does not appear to itself chopped up in bits. . . . A 'river' or a 'stream' are the metaphors by which it is most naturally described." We turn now to phases of the stream: alert wakefulness, daydreaming, and sleep dreaming.

Alert wakefulness

Much of this book is about the conscious perceptions, thoughts, and emotions of alert wakefulness. Awareness of the here and now, and also our own thoughts, memories, and goals, enables us to make decisions, carry out plans, and interpret the world and our own behavior with a flexibility that exceeds that of any other species.

As we will see in the next chapter, during alert wakefulness we focus our attention on specific things and events, filtering out whatever is irrelevant so that we can respond appropriately. Under normal conditions, we seem able to focus on only one source, or channel, of information at a time. Similarly, it is difficult to perform more than one complex task at a time. But it is not impossible. With proper training, people can learn to perform simultaneously such complex tasks as reading and taking dictation (Hirst, Neisser, & Spelke, 1978).

Conscious processing is only one small part of what goes on in our heads during ordinary wakefulness. Many physical and mental processes occur outside of the focus of awareness, without any intention on our part; like ol' man river, they just keep rolling along. Freud spoke of *unconscious* thoughts, feelings, and desires that we purposely repress because they are too painful to confront. Two other categories of mental processing also lie outside of immediate awareness, but they have nothing to do with the repression of emotionally threatening material.

Subconscious processes are ones that can be brought into consciousness when necessary. They allow us to handle more information and perform more complex tasks than if we depended entirely on conscious processing, because they can occur

subconscious process *A mental process occurring outside of conscious awareness but accessible to consciousness when necessary.*

Usually we focus on only one source of information at a time. But fortunately for this dad, it is sometimes possible to divide attention by doing two tasks simultaneously or switching rapidly back and forth between them.

in parallel (Kahneman & Treisman, 1984). Consider all the automatic routines that we perform "without thinking," though they might once have required careful, conscious attention: typing, driving a car, decoding the letters in a word in order to read it. Consider, too, our subconscious processing of incoming sensory information, such as the ticking of a clock or the hum of a refrigerator's motor.

Nonconscious processes include processes that remain outside of awareness but which nonetheless affect behavior. Many of these are biological: the body's regulation of hormone production, blood pressure, heart rate, and so forth. But some researchers believe that certain "higher" mental processes also go on entirely out of awareness, although we might think we are consciously controlling them. In one fascinating study, physiologist Benjamin Libet (1985) told volunteers to flex a wrist or finger whenever they felt like doing so. As soon as the urge to flex occurred, the person noted the position of a dot revolving on a clocklike screen. Electrodes monitored changes in brain activity occurring immediately before the volunteers' muscular movements, changes known as "readiness potentials." Libet found that readiness potentials occurred about half a second before muscle movement, but conscious awareness of an intention to move the muscle (as inferred from reports of dot position) occurred about three-tenths of a second *after* that. In other words, the brain seemed to be initiating action before the person was aware of it.

Libet draws an analogy between these results and what happens when a sprinter hears a starting gun. The sprinter will take off in less than a tenth of a second after the gun fires, yet that is too short a time to consciously perceive the sound. According to Libet, the runner must be responding unconsciously; then, after the sound enters awareness, the mind "corrects" the sequence, so the person thinks he or she heard the sound before actually moving. Libet's results are in agreement with current speculations about nonconscious processing in the brain (see Chapters 3 and 5).

You can see that alert wakefulness is not a simple matter of conscious functioning. Even ordinary awareness may be more complex or fragmented than is commonly believed. As one researcher notes,

> If you consider your thoughts as you listen to a speaker, you will realize how many streams of self-talk go on at once. Even if you are quite attentive, you will find yourself carrying on several interior conversations: "How long is he going to talk? Where will I eat lunch? Who is that weird person in the next row?" You have short-range plans, long-

nonconscious process *A mental process occurring outside of and not available to conscious awareness.*

range plans, accidental intrusions that drift in and out of awareness.
[E. R. Hilgard, 1978, p. 49]

Perhaps, then, we should talk about parallel *streams* of consciousness, rather than just one stream.

Daydreaming

During alert wakefulness, the contents of consciousness are relatively organized, meaningful, clear, and real. Often, though, less coherent thoughts, images, and sensations gain the stage, and we lapse into daydreaming. Most daydreams focus on current concerns and challenges, especially those we feel emotional about, like relationships or life goals (Klinger, 1987). Daydreams also review past events (''What should I have done?'') or allow us to indulge in fantasies about sex, sudden wealth, and other sources of pleasure.

It's natural to daydream.

    Almost all adults daydream. These reveries, which so often interfere with concentration, follow a 90-minute (ultradian) cycle. In one study of daydreaming, college students spent ten hours in a comfortable but bare room, without clocks, books, or other distractions (Kripke & Sonnenschein, 1978). Every five minutes they wrote down what they had been thinking during the preceding interval. Electrodes monitored their brain waves and eye movements. Several days later the students returned to the laboratory and rated each thought according to how dreamlike it was. Daytime flights of fantasy, unlike sleeping dreams, were associated with reduced eye movement and a high level of alpha activity. At the peak of each cycle, thoughts and images were likely to be emotional or even bizarre; for example: ''I was just hearing a Beethoven symphony in my head with my eyes closed, then I got images of a muscular, hairy, male body with a strong feeling of sexual potency.'' At the trough of a cycle, thoughts were more likely to concern the present situation, personal problems, or future plans: ''What's the last hour of this going to be like? Wondering how fast the output can be scored. Various thoughts about what I have seen of the VA hospital. Very tired, wiggling my feet to stay awake'' (Lavie & Kripke, 1975).

    In daily life, of course, the rhythm of daydreaming can be affected by what you are doing and where you are. Daydreaming is especially likely to occur when you are alone, waiting to fall asleep, riding on a bus or train, or doing some routine or boring activity.

    In our work-oriented culture, we often dismiss daydreaming as a waste of time. It is true that some people daydream more than they would like, perhaps because they are frustrated with or bored by real life. It is also true that depressed people may dwell on their problems in daydreams, making themselves even more miserable. But for most of us, daydreaming is a natural, and in fact desirable, consequence of the ongoing activity of the brain (Singer, 1976; Klinger, 1987). Daydreams exercise our creativity, entertain us when life gets boring, and keep our spirits up by providing a brief vacation from the burdens of reality. They are the escape clauses in our life sentences.

Sleep dreaming

In sleep dreaming, as in daydreaming, the focus of attention is inward, though sometimes an external event such as the ringing of an alarm clock can influence the dream. Ordinarily, you have no background awareness of where you are or of your own body. Some people, however, report dreams in which they know they are dreaming and they feel as though they are conscious. These *lucid dreams* seem to involve a split in consciousness known as **dissociation**. During the dream, consciousness seems to divide into a dreaming part and an observing part. Some people have learned, with training, to produce lucid dreams at will and control the action in them, much as a scriptwriter decides what will happen in a movie (Garfield, 1974; LaBerge, 1986). Controlling one's dreams may offer a way of using them to solve problems or enhance creativity.

While a dream is in progress, it may be vivid or vague, terrifying or peaceful, colorful or bland. It may also seem to make perfect sense—until you wake up. Then it is often recalled as illogical and bizarre. The flow of a dream is usually not as smooth as the flow of waking consciousness; events occur without transitions. REM dreams, which are usually more vivid than non-REM dreams, are often reported as adventures or stories. Non-REM dreams tend to be described as vague, fragmentary, unemotional, and commonplace.

Shakespeare's Hamlet yearned "to sleep, perchance to dream." In fact, there is no "perchance" about it, for we all dream every night. Why? Why doesn't the brain just *rest,* switching off all thoughts and images and launching us into a coma? Why, instead, do we spend our nights flying through the air, battling monsters, or flirting with an old flame in the fantasy world of our dreams?

The psychoanalytic explanation.   One of the first psychologists to take dreams seriously was Sigmund Freud, the founder of psychoanalysis. After analyzing many dreams, including some of his own, Freud concluded that our nighttime fantasies provide a "royal road to the unconscious." In dreams we are able to gratify forbidden or unrealistic wishes and desires, usually sexual, that have been forced into the unconscious part of the mind. If we did not dream, energy invested in these wishes and desires would build up to intolerable levels, threatening our very sanity.

Freud's view was that no matter how absurd a dream may seem, it has meaning and logic. But if a dream's theme arouses anxiety, the rational part of the mind must disguise and distort it. Otherwise the dream would wake the dreamer up, intruding into consciousness. In dreams, therefore, one person may be represented by another—for example, a father by a brother—or even by several different characters. Similarly, thoughts and objects are translated into symbolic images. A penis may be disguised as a snake, umbrella, dagger, or other elongated object; a vagina, as a tunnel, entranceway, or cave; and the human body, as a house.

To understand a dream, Freud said, we must distinguish its *manifest* content, the aspects of it that we consciously experience during sleep and may remember upon wakening, from its *latent* or hidden content, the unconscious wishes and thoughts being expressed symbolically. Freud warned against the simpleminded translation of symbols, however. Each dream had to be analyzed in the context of the dreamer's waking life as well as the person's associations to the dream's contents. Not everything in a dream is symbolic. Sometimes, Freud cautioned, "a cigar is only a cigar."

Most psychologists today accept Freud's notion that dreams are more than incoherent ramblings of the mind, but many quarrel with his interpretations. His critics point out that there are no clear rules for interpreting the latent content of dreams and no objective way to know whether a particular interpretation is correct. Many modern psychologists believe that most dreams reflect not deep-seated or infantile wishes but the ongoing emotional preoccupations of waking life—concern over relationships, work, sex, or health (Webb & Cartwright, 1978).

dissociation *Separation of consciousness into distinct parts.*

A Maiden's Dream, *by Lorenzo Lotto (1480–1530), evokes the mysterious imagery of dream life.*

Dreams as information processing. A very different approach to dreams views them as opportunities to sort through and process information. Earlier, we raised the question of why sleep occurs. According to Christopher Evans (1984), the answer is mental housekeeping. The brain, said Evans, must shut out sensory input so that it can assimilate new data and update what has already been stored. It divides new information into "wanted" and "unwanted" categories, makes new associations, and revises old "programs" (to use a computer analogy) in light of the day's experience. The data it works on include not only recent events but also ideas, obsessions, worries, wishes, and thoughts about the past. What we recall as dreams are really only brief snippets from an ongoing process of sorting, scanning, and sifting that occurs during REM sleep and possibly throughout the night. Because they give us only a glimpse of the night's mental activity, they naturally seem odd and nonsensical when recalled.

A somewhat similar idea has been proposed by Francis Crick, co-discoverer of the structure of DNA, and his colleague, Graeme Mitchison. Crick and Mitchison (1983) argue that during REM periods, the brain jettisons mental garbage—information it doesn't need, undesirable ways of behaving, accidental connections in the brain. In short, we dream in order to forget. Crick and Mitchison speculate that random firing from the brain stem sets off the undesirable connections that have overloaded the cortex, including fantasies, obsessions, and hallucinations, thereby defusing them. The subjective result of this firing is a dream. In this view, there is no reason to search through the garbage for tidbits of meaning. In fact, trying to remember dreams defeats their purpose and could even lead to mental disorders—an idea guaranteed to anger psychoanalysts!

Information-processing approaches to dreaming, unlike Freud's, might explain why REM sleep occurs in fetuses, babies, and animals as well as in adult human beings. They, too, need to "sort things out." Newborns, in fact, spend about 50 percent of their sleeping hours in REM sleep, versus only 20 percent for adults. Since everything that is happening to them is new, perhaps they have more writing and revising of "programs" to do. However, like Freud's theory, both Evans's theory and Crick and Mitchison's are difficult to test.

The activation-synthesis theory. Most theories of dreaming are vague about physiology, if they mention it at all. An exception is the activation-synthesis theory, proposed by Allan Hobson and Robert McCarley (1977; Hobson, 1988; McCarley & Hoffman, 1981). In this theory, dreams are not, in Shakespeare's words, "children of an idle brain." Rather, they are the result of neurons firing spontaneously in the lower part of the brain, specifically in the pons. These neurons control eye movement, gaze, balance, and posture, and send messages to distant areas of the cortex responsible during wakefulness for voluntary action. Such sleeptime signals have no psychological significance in themselves, but the cortex tries to make sense of them by *synthesizing*, or combining, them with existing knowledge and memories to produce some sort of coherent interpretation. For example, when neurons fire in the part of the brain that handles balance, the cortex may generate a dream about falling. When signals occur that would ordinarily produce running, the cortex may manufacture a dream about being chased. Since the signals themselves lack coherence, the interpretation—the dream—is also likely to be incoherent and confusing. And since cortical neurons that control storage of new memories are turned off during sleep, we typically forget our dreams upon waking.

Hobson (1988) also suggests an explanation for why REM sleep and dreaming do not occur continuously through the night. Giant cells found in the reticular activating system of the pons, sensitive to the neurotransmitter acetylcholine, appear to turn on REM sleep. They then proceed to fire in unrestrained bursts, like a machine gun. Eventually, though, the magazine is emptied. "If synapses are like cartridges," writes Hobson, "it may be that is why REM sleep ends; no more synaptic ammunition." Only when the neurons "reload" can firing, and REM sleep, resume. In support of this idea, Hobson notes that when sleeping volunteers are injected with drugs that stimulate acetylcholine, REM sleep and dreaming increase. When they are injected with a drug that negates the effects of acetylcholine, REM sleep and dreaming decrease (Gillin et al., 1985).

Wishes, according to Hobson and McCarley, do not cause dreams; brainstem mechanisms do. But that doesn't mean dreams are meaningless. According to Hobson (1988), the brain "is so inexorably bent upon the quest for meaning that it attributes and even creates meaning when there is little or none to be found in the data it is asked to process." By studying these attributed meanings, you can learn about your unique perceptions, conflicts, and concerns—not by digging below the surface of the dream, as Freud would, but by examining the surface itself. Or you can simply relax and enjoy the nightly entertainment that dreams provide.

At present, the activation-synthesis model is the most completely developed modern approach to dreaming. However, not all physiological psychologists agree with Hobson and McCarley's evidence (Vogel, 1978). Even Hobson admits that the physiological data are stronger on activation than on synthesis. Much remains to be learned about the purpose of dreaming and of sleep itself.

QUICK ▪ QUIZ

A dreamer imagines himself as a tiny infant crawling through a long, dark tunnel looking for something he has lost. Which theory of dreams would be most receptive to each of the following explanations?

1. The dreamer has recently misplaced several things and is worried that he is developing memory problems.
2. While the dreamer was sleeping, neurons in his pons that would ordinarily stimulate leg muscle movement discharged.
3. The dreamer has repressed an early sexual attraction to his mother; the tunnel symbolizes her vagina.

Answers:

1. Evans's information-processing theory (the dreamer is processing information about recent experience)   2. Hobson and McCarley's activation-synthesis theory   3. Freudian psychoanalytic theory

---

Altered States of Consciousness

Up to this point we have examined only ordinary states of consciousness that everyone experiences. Are there other states we can enter if we learn how to unlock the right doors? William James (1902/1936), who was fascinated by alterations in consciousness, thought so. After inhaling nitrous oxide, sometimes called "laughing gas," he wrote, "Our normal waking consciousness, rational consciousness as we call it, is but one special type of consciousness, whilst all about it, parted from it by the filmiest of screens, there lie potential forms of consciousness entirely different."

James believed that psychologists should study these other forms of consciousness, but for half a century few took his words seriously. Consciousness was out of favor as a topic of scientific concern. Then, during the 1960s, attitudes changed. During that decade of political and social upheaval, millions of people began to explore techniques for deliberately producing **altered** or **alternate states of consciousness**. (Some people use the term *alternate* for *any* state other than alert wakefulness, including sleep. Others use *alternate* in place of *altered* for deliberately produced states because it seems more morally neutral. Here we use the terms interchangeably.) As we note in "Think About It," some writers felt that altering consciousness could enhance creativity and deepen insight. Psychologists, who for their own reasons were rediscovering consciousness (see Chapter 1), took an interest in methods of changing it, and the "filmy screen" described by James finally began to lift.

One method of altering consciousness, **meditation**, uses various techniques to focus the mind and eliminate distracting thoughts. The goal is an immediate and alert awareness of the here and now, without the intrusion of mental concepts and symbols. In many religious traditions, meditation is an important spiritual practice. Western researchers, however, have been more interested in its ability to relieve stress (see Chapter 15). Studies of alterations in consciousness have centered instead on two other topics, drugs and hypnosis.

altered (alternate) state of consciousness *A deliberately produced state of consciousness that differs from ordinary wakefulness or sleep.*

meditation *A practice aimed at focusing consciousness and eliminating all distracting thoughts.*

Think About It

Does Consciousness Need Altering?

▪ In Jerusalem, hundreds of male Hasidic Jews celebrate the completion of the annual reading of the holy Torah by dancing in the streets. Though it is warm and the men are dressed in long black coats, they go on for hours, never tiring. For them, dancing is not a diversion; it is a path to religious ecstasy.

▪ In South Dakota, several Sioux Indians sit naked in the darkness of the sweat lodge, a circular hut covered with hides and blankets. A medicine man offers prayers and leads chants. Then he throws water on a pit of red-hot rocks, and an enormous wave of heat envelops the participants. The heat is so crushing that they must concentrate all their thoughts on coping with it. Their reward will be euphoria, the transcendence of pain, and according to Sioux belief, possible connection with the Great Spirit of the Universe.

▪ Deep in the Amazon jungle, a young man is training to be a *shaman*. For weeks he has starved himself. Now he enters a trance, aided by a whiff of hallucinogenic snuff made from the bark of the *Virola* tree. As a full shaman the young man will be expected to enter trances regularly to communicate with animals, spirits, and supernatural forces.

These three rituals, seemingly quite different, are all aimed at release from the confines of ordinary consciousness. Cultures around the world have devised such practices, often as part of their religions. In India, a *sadhu* (Hindu holy man) uses yoga to achieve a state of sublime detachment that makes him insensitive to pain as he calmly lies on a bed of sharp cactus spines. The Maulavis of Turkey, the "whirling dervishes," use spinning dances to accomplish much the same thing. As Muslims, they dance mainly to unite their souls with Allah, but

their trances also enable them to show their faith by fearlessly piercing their cheeks or touching burning coals. Hinduism, Sufiism, and Buddhism, and some forms of Judaism and Christianity, all use meditation as a way of achieving emotional detachment, a direct experience of the moment, and transcendence of the self—a state of spiritual enlightenment known in Eastern cultures as *satori*, *nirvana*, *kensho*, or *samadhi*.

Because attempts to alter consciousness appear to be universal, some writers have suggested that they reflect a basic human need. In *The Natural Mind* (1972/1986), physician Andrew Weil argued that this need might be a biological one that enables us to shift to a more intuitive, creative mode. Children, he says, are trying to alter consciousness when they purposely hyperventilate or when, like the dervishes, they whirl around and around. Adults in our culture, having learned that such behavior is silly or inappropriate, resort to alcohol and other recreational drugs for the same reason. However, the fact that all or most societies have ways of altering consciousness does not mean that every method of doing so is beneficial or desirable. Further, cultures and individuals may have different motives for trying to disrupt everyday ways of perceiving and thinking.

Is there actually a basic need to go beyond the ordinary states of wakefulness and sleep? Are people looking for a natural high when they schuss down the ski slope, push themselves to their physical limits in the Boston Marathon, or (much more commonly) make love? In our culture, when is the search for an altered state a sign of creativity and growth, and when is it a sign of boredom and escapism? What do you think?

Consciousness-altering drugs

Perhaps the fastest, though also the riskiest, way to alter consciousness is to use a **psychoactive drug** to alter the body's biochemistry. A drug is psychoactive if it can influence perception, mood, thinking, memory, or behavior. Nearly every human society has discovered at least one such substance, natural or artificial, and has used

psychoactive drug *A drug capable of influencing perception, mood, cognition, or behavior.*

All cultures seem to find ways to alter ordinary consciousness. The Maulavis of Turkey (left), the famous "whirling dervishes," spin in an energetic but controlled manner in order to achieve religious rapture and unite their souls with Allah. In many cultures, people learn to meditate (right) as a way to quiet the mind, experience immediate reality, and achieve spiritual enlightenment.

it in rituals or recreationally. Some animals, too, know how to get chemically high. Baboons ingest tobacco, elephants love the alcohol in fermented fruit, and reindeer and rabbits eat intoxicating mushrooms (Siegal, 1983).

In our society, where the "drugs of choice" are caffeine, tobacco, and ethyl alcohol, the use of drugs, especially illicit ones, is an emotionally charged issue. Drug dependence, whether psychological or physical, can lead to social problems and personal tragedy. Many drugs, if used frequently or excessively, can damage body organs, interfere with the ability to work or study, and turn careful drivers into dangerous ones. (Dependence and addiction are discussed further in Chapter 16.)

Because drugs are so controversial, people tend to lump them all together, overlooking the fact that two substances labeled "drugs" may be totally unalike chemically and may have vastly different effects on the nervous system. In public discussion, extremely potent drugs are sometimes confused with others that have only subtle effects or are safe in moderate amounts. (Even the most innocuous substances can be harmful if used in excess. Imagine the effect, for example, of ingesting a large quantity of common table salt.) People may also fail to recognize that light use can have different consequences than heavy use. A recent longitudinal study of teenagers using various drugs found that heavy use of hard drugs interfered with nearly every aspect of a teenager's life, from relationships to schoolwork. But using a drug only once a month or less (especially marijuana or hashish) seemed to have little effect on the social or personal adjustment of most teenagers (Newcomb & Bentler, 1988, 1989). Of course, this finding does not mean that drugs are good for you. Moreover, because of emotional and personal problems, some young people who intend to use drugs only occasionally wind up using them excessively. Light use does not inevitably lead to heavy use, however, and we need to distinguish the two in assessing the physical and psychological effects of drugs.

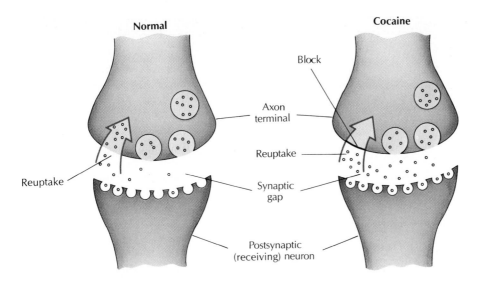

FIGURE 4.4

Cocaine's effect on the brain
Cocaine blocks the ability of brain cells to reabsorb the neurotransmitters dopamine and norepinephrine, so levels of these substances in the brain rise. The result is overstimulation of certain brain circuits and a brief euphoric ''high.'' Then, when the drug wears off, a depletion of dopamine may cause the user to ''crash'' and become sleepy and depressed.

Physical effects. Many psychoactive drugs are prescribed legally in the treatment of physical and mental disorders. There are also dozens of illegal drugs in the United States. Psychoactive drugs work primarily by acting on brain neurotransmitters, the substances that enable messages to pass from one nerve cell to another (see Chapter 3). Some cause more or fewer neurotransmitter molecules to be released at a synapse. Others prevent the reabsorption (''reuptake'') of a neurotransmitter after its release. Still others block the effects of a neurotransmitter on a receiving nerve cell. Figure 4.4 shows how cocaine increases the amount of norepinephrine and dopamine in the brain by blocking the reabsorption of these substances. Animal studies suggest that repeated use of certain drugs, including ''designer drugs'' (potent synthetic chemicals that are easy to concoct and modify), causes permanent brain damage. For example, ''Ecstasy'' (MDMA) seems to permanently damage cells that produce serotonin (Ricaurte et al., 1988).

Most drugs can be classified as stimulants, depressants, opiates, or psychedelics, depending on their effects on the central nervous system and their impact on behavior and mood (see Table 4.1). (Antipsychotic drugs, which are used to treat certain mental disorders, are covered separately in Chapter 17.)

1. Stimulants, such as cocaine, amphetamines (''uppers''), and the nicotine in tobacco, speed up activity in the central nervous system. In moderate amounts, they tend to produce feelings of excitement, confidence, and well-being or even euphoria. In large amounts, they make a person anxious, jittery, and hyperalert, and interfere with sleep. In very large doses, they may cause convulsions, heart failure, and death.

Amphetamines are synthetic drugs usually taken in pill form. Cocaine (''coke'') is a natural drug, derived from the leaves of the coca plant. (It has nothing to do with chocolate, which comes from the cacao bean.) Rural workers in Bolivia

stimulants *Drugs that speed up activity in the central nervous system.*

TABLE 4.1
SOME PSYCHOACTIVE DRUGS AND THEIR EFFECTS

	Type of Drug	Common Effects	Results of Abuse/Addiction
Amphetamines	Stimulant	Wakefulness, alertness, raised metabolism, elevated mood	Nervousness, headaches, loss of appetite, high blood pressure, delusions, psychosis, convulsions, death
Cocaine	Stimulant	Euphoria, excitation, boost of energy, suppressed appetite	Excitability, sleeplessness, sweating, paranoia, anxiety, depression, heart damage, injury to nose if sniffed
Tobacco (nicotine)	Stimulant	Varies, from alertness to calmness, depending on mental set and setting; decreases appetite for carbohydrates	Nicotine: heart disease, high blood pressure, impaired circulation Tars: lung cancer, emphysema, mouth and throat cancer, many other health risks
Caffeine	Stimulant	Wakefulness, alertness, shortened reaction time	Restlessness, insomnia, muscle tension, heartbeat irregularities, high blood pressure
Alcohol (1–2 drinks)	Depressant	Depends on setting, mental set; tends to act like stimulant because it reduces inhibitions, anxiety	
Alcohol (several/ many drinks)	Depressant	Slowed reaction time, tension, depression, reduced ability to store new memories or retrieve old ones, poor coordination	Blackouts, cirrhosis, organic damage, mental and neurological impairment, psychosis, possibly death
Tranquilizers (e.g., Valium); Barbiturates (e.g., phenobarbital)	Depressant	Reduced anxiety and tension, sedation	Increased dosage needed for effects; impaired motor and sensory functions, impaired permanent storage of new information, withdrawal symptoms; possibly convulsions, coma, death (especially when taken with other drugs)
Opium, heroin, morphine	Opiate	Euphoria, relief of pain	Loss of appetite, nausea, constipation, coma, withdrawal symptoms, convulsions, possibly death
LSD, psilocybin, mescaline	Psychedelic	Exhilaration, visions and hallucinations, insightful experiences	Psychosis, paranoia, panic reactions
Marijuana	Mild psychedelic (classification controversial)	Relaxation, euphoria, increased appetite, reduced ability to store new memories, other effects depending on mental set and setting	Throat and lung irritation, lung damage (if smoked), impaired immunity; long-term effects not well established

and Peru chew coca leaf every day, without apparent ill effects. In this country, the drug is usually inhaled (''snorted''), injected, or smoked (in the highly refined form known as ''crack''). These methods give the drug a more immediate, powerful, and dangerous effect. Amphetamines and cocaine make users feel peppy but do not actually increase energy reserves. Fatigue, irritability, and depression may occur when the effects of the drugs wear off.

2. Depressants, such as alcohol, tranquilizers, and barbiturates, slow down activity in the central nervous system. Also known as *sedatives* or *hypnotics*, they usually make you feel calm or drowsy, and may reduce anxiety, guilt, tension, and inhibitions. In large amounts, they may produce insensitivity to pain and other sensations. In very large doses, they may, like stimulants, cause convulsions and death. Use of depressants often leads to **tolerance**: As time goes by, more and more of the drug is needed to get the same effect. When habitual users stop taking the drug, they may suffer severe **withdrawal symptoms**, such as nausea, vomiting, abdominal cramps, and muscle spasms. Tolerance and withdrawal are often assumed to be purely physiological in nature, but in Chapter 6 we will see that learning may play an important role.

People are often surprised to learn that alcohol is a central nervous system depressant. In small amounts, alcohol often affects behavior much as a stimulant would because it first suppresses nerve cell activity in parts of the brain that normally inhibit behavior. Behavior that might ordinarily be checked, such as loud laughter and clowning around, is disinhibited. Like barbiturates and opiates, alcohol can be used as an anesthetic, and if you drink enough, you will eventually pass out. Extremely large amounts of alcohol can kill, by inhibiting the nerve cells in the brain centers that control breathing and heartbeat. That is how one New Jersey college student died recently, after consuming large amounts of alcohol during a night of partying.

Drinking, unlike illicit drug use, is a socially accepted custom in our culture. An estimated 70 to 100 million Americans imbibe socially. In a recent survey, 37.5 percent of high school seniors said they had consumed five or more drinks at one sitting during the past two weeks, and 66 percent said they had used alcohol during the past month (Johnston, O'Malley, & Bachman, 1988). In plays, films, and television shows, heavy drinking is often portrayed as funny or glamorous. As one movie reviewer pointed out, "for large segments of the audience, [alcohol retains] associations with macho behavior, colorful individualism, antiestablishment rebellion, or artistic expression" (Ebert, 1984).

Because of alcohol's effect on judgment, drinkers often are unable to gauge their own competence. Even moderate amounts of alcohol can affect perception, response time, coordination, and balance, despite the drinker's own impression of unchanged or even improved performance (Poley, Lea, & Vibe, 1979). Liquor also affects memory, possibly by interfering with the work of the neurotransmitter serotonin. Information stored before a drinking session remains intact but is retrieved more slowly (Stempel, Beckwith, & Petros, 1986). The ability to store new memories for later use also suffers, even after two or three drinks (Parker, Birnbaum, & Noble, 1976). Consuming small amounts does not seem to affect *sober* mental performance, but even occasional heavy drinking impairs later abstract thought. In other words, a Saturday night binge is more dangerous than a daily drink.

3. Opiates include opium, derived from the opium poppy; morphine, a derivative of opium; heroin, a derivative of morphine; and certain synthetic drugs, such as methadone. All these drugs relieve pain, mimicking the action of endorphins, and most have a powerful effect on the emotions. When injected, they may produce a sudden feeling of euphoria, called a "rush." There may be a decrease in anxiety and a decrease in motivation, although the effects vary. When habitual users stop taking an opiate, they may suffer serious withdrawal symptoms.

4. Psychedelic drugs include substances that alter consciousness by producing hallucinations, changing thought processes, or disrupting the normal perception of

depressants *Drugs that slow down activity in the central nervous system.*

tolerance *Increased resistance to a drug's effects with continued use; as tolerance develops, larger doses are required to produce effects once brought on by smaller ones.*

withdrawal symptoms *Physical and psychological symptoms that occur when someone addicted to a drug stops taking it.*

opiates *Drugs, derived from the opium poppy, that relieve pain and commonly produce euphoria.*

psychedelic drugs *Consciousness-altering drugs that produce hallucinations, change thought processes, or disrupt the normal perception of time and space.*

time and space. Some, such as lysergic acid diethylamide (LSD), are made in the laboratory. Others, such as mescaline (from the peyote cactus) and psilocybin (from various species of mushrooms), are natural. Unlike the hallucinations characteristic of some mental disturbances, which are typically sounds and voices, the hallucinations produced by psychedelics are usually visual (Schneider & Tarshis, 1986). Emotional reactions to psychedelics vary from person to person, and from one time to another for a particular individual. A "trip" may be mildly pleasant or unpleasant, a mystical revelation, or a nightmare.

What about marijuana ("pot," "grass"), probably the most widely used illicit drug in the United States? Marijuana is smoked or, less commonly, is eaten in foods like brownies or cookies. Some researchers classify it as a mild psychedelic. Others feel that both in its chemical makeup and in its psychological effects, marijuana falls outside the major classifications. We know that the major active ingredient in marijuana is tetrahydrocannabinol (THC), derived from the hemp plant, *Cannabis sativa*. But little is known about how THC acts on the nervous system. In some respects, it appears to be a mild stimulant, increasing heart rate and making tastes, sounds, and colors seem more intense. But users report both mild euphoria and relaxation, or even sleepiness. Time often seems to go by slowly.

In moderate doses, marijuana can interfere with the transfer of information to long-term memory, a trait it shares with alcohol. In large doses it can cause hallucinations and a sense of unreality. Some studies also find that the drug impairs coordination, visual perception, and reaction times, though it is not clear how long these effects last. That is what we know. Surprisingly (since marijuana use is so widespread) there is still plenty that we don't know. There have been few long-term studies of the drug, and few facts about it are well established (see Gallagher, 1988).

Existing work on marijuana raises as many questions as it answers. For example, in the 1970s, an interdisciplinary research team studied a group of working-class

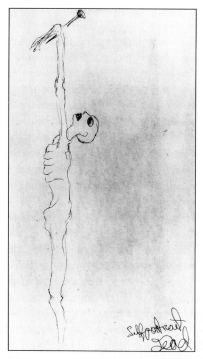
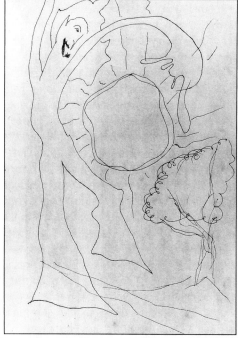

An LSD "trip" may be a ticket to agony or ecstasy. Both of these drawings were done while under the influence of the drug.

Costa Rican men who had smoked an average of almost 10 marijuana cigarettes daily for 17 years. They found no significant physical or psychological differences between these men and a matched group of nonusers. Recently, another team restudied some of the same men. Based on the same tests that were used before, there was no evidence of deterioration in the marijuana users, although the men had now been smoking for 30 years on the average. On three *new* tests, of sustained attention, organizing skills, and short-term memory, the users did do worse than the control subjects, but the differences were subtle (Page, Fletcher, & True, 1988).

Are you more impressed by these men's normal performance on the old tests or by their somewhat inferior performance on the new tests? Those who are worried about marijuana's effects emphasize the latter. In the United States, they point out, even slight impairment of performance might be troublesome since many of us hold jobs requiring mental exertion and alertness. Others, however, note that very few Americans smoke 10 joints a day for 30 years. Also, the marijuana used by Costa Ricans is far more potent than the varieties available in the United States. Moreover, the effects that were observed in Costa Rica could have been due to recent smoking rather than truly long-term mental deficits. The subjects were asked to abstain from smoking for two days before being tested, but it can take days or even weeks for the body to rid itself of THC.

Heavy, prolonged use of marijuana does pose physical dangers (see Table 4.1). Even mild use can cause lung damage when the drug is smoked (Bloom et al., 1987; Wu et al., 1988). However, we cannot yet draw any firm conclusions about psychological consequences, and again, we must be careful not to confuse light or mild use with heavy use. Marijuana is clearly milder in its effects than alcohol, and many researchers doubt that occasional use poses psychological problems for most people (Zinberg, 1984).

Beyond physiology: The psychology of drug effects. People often talk about the effects of a drug as if they were automatic, the inevitable result of the drug's chemistry ("I couldn't help being an obnoxious slob; the booze made me do it"). But as we noted in Chapter 3, trying to understand behavior solely in terms of physiology almost always leads to oversimplification. If we want to understand drugs, we must know more than their chemical properties. Drug responses depend on a person's physical condition, experience with the drug, mental set, and environmental setting.

One person takes a drink and flies into a rage. Another has a drink and "mellows out." What qualities of the user rather than the drug might account for this difference?

▪ *Physical condition* includes body weight, individual tolerance for the drug, and initial state of arousal. A drug may have a different effect after a tiring day than after a rousing quarrel. It may also affect a person differently at one time of the day than another because of the body's circadian rhythms.

▪ *Experience with the drug* refers to the number of times it has been used and the levels of past usage. Trying a drug for the first time—a cigarette, an alcoholic drink, a stimulant—is likely to be neutral or unpleasant. These reactions often change once a person has become familiar with the drug's effects.

▪ *Mental set* refers to expectations about the drug's effects, the reasons for taking the drug, and the presence or absence of a desire to justify some behavior by being "under the influence." For example, some people drink to become more sociable, friendly, or seductive; others drink solely to have an excuse for violence (Gelles, 1979). Because so many crimes of violence are committed when the participants have been drinking, and because so many marital quarrels accompany drinking, alcohol is often assumed to "release" anger and aggression. However, the real source of aggression is not in the alcohol but in the mind of the drinker. The link between alcohol and aggression disappears when people believe they will be held responsible for their actions while drunk (Critchlow, 1983).

People's expectations of how a drug will affect them play a part in how they respond to it. Several studies have identified a ''think-drink'' effect by comparing people who are *actually* drinking liquor (vodka and tonic) with those who *think* they are drinking liquor but are actually getting only tonic and lime juice. (Vodka has a subtle taste, and most people cannot tell the real and phony drinks apart.) Men behave more belligerently when they think they are drinking vodka than when they think they are drinking plain tonic water, regardless of the actual content of the drinks. Both sexes report feeling sexually aroused when they think they are drinking vodka, whether they actually get vodka or not (Abrams & Wilson, 1983; Marlatt & Rohsenow, 1980, 1981).

Alcoholics, too, are influenced by mental set. Alcoholics who have a couple of tonics, thinking they are drinking vodka, develop a ''craving'' for more liquor. A researcher reported the case of an alcoholic who sometimes could drink a dozen whiskeys without a sign of inebriation. At other times he staggered around and became antagonistic after two drinks. His reactions depended on his mood before drinking, which in turn depended on how he was getting along with the people who mattered to him (Rioch, 1975). Expectations and prior mood probably play a role in all psychological drug reactions, including those to coffee and cigarettes.

▪ *Environmental setting* greatly affects an individual's response to a drug. Setting is the reason that a person can have one glass of wine at home alone and fall asleep, but have three glasses of wine at a wedding party and feel full of pep. It is the reason that a person might feel happy and ''high'' drinking with good friends but fearful and nervous drinking with strangers. In one study of reactions to alcohol, researchers found that most of the drinkers became depressed, angry, confused, and unfriendly. Then it dawned on them that *anyone* might become depressed, angry, confused, and unfriendly if asked to drink bourbon at 9:00 A.M. in a bleak hospital room—the setting for the experiment (Warren & Raynes, 1972).

Now, none of this means that alcohol and other drugs are merely placebos (see Chapter 2). Drugs do have physiological effects, many of them quite powerful. However, people must learn from their culture how to interpret these effects and

Expectations about a drug's effects, the motives for using it, and the setting in which it is used all contribute to a person's reactions to the drug.

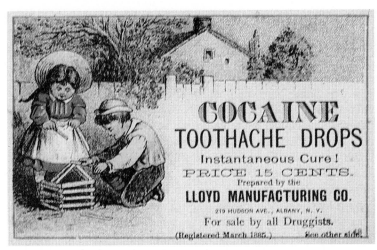

Before its sale was banned in the 1920s, cocaine was widely touted as a cure for everything from toothaches to timidity. The drug found its way into teas, tonics, throat lozenges, and even soft drinks (including, briefly, Coca-Cola, which derived its name from the coca plant). Ingesting it had a less powerful effect than sniffing, injecting, or smoking it, as is done today. However, as cocaine use became associated in the popular mind with criminality and as concerns about abuse grew, public opinion turned against it.

how to behave when they occur. Most Americans start their day with a cup of coffee because it increases alertness. (Textbook authors could not survive without it.) But when coffee was first introduced in Europe, there were protests against it. Women said it made their husbands impotent and inconsiderate—and maybe it did. Conversely, in the nineteenth century Americans looked on marijuana as a mild sedative with no ''mind-altering'' properties. They didn't expect it to give them a high, and it didn't; it merely put them to sleep (Weil, 1972/1986). Today's marijuana, of course, is more potent. But in addition, motives for using it have changed. Young users are often rejecting conventional adult roles and social institutions (D. Kandel, 1984), and that may affect their reactions.

Unfortunately, many people in our society learn drug reactions that include substance abuse and social abusiveness. William James (1902/1936) noted that alcohol awakens faculties ''usually crushed to earth by the cold facts and dry criticisms of the sober hour. Sobriety diminishes, discriminates, and says no; drunkenness expands, unites, and says yes.'' It is one of life's tragedies, he concluded, that so many experience this state ''only in the fleeting earlier phases of what in its totality is so degrading a poisoning.''

QUICK ■ QUIZ

See if you can name the following:

1. An illegal stimulant
2. Two drugs that interfere with the formation of new long-term memories
3. Three types of depressant drugs
4. A legal ''recreational'' drug that acts as a depressant on the nervous system
5. Four factors that influence a person's psychological reactions to a drug

Answers:

1. cocaine   2. marijuana and alcohol   3. barbiturates, opiates, and alcohol   4. alcohol   5. the person's physical condition, prior experience with the drug, mental set, and the environmental setting

Hypnosis

Many years ago a low-budget film showed an innocent young man being hypnotized against his will by a diabolical scientist and forced to commit several murders, none of which he recalled in the waking state. It made a good story, in a B-movie sort of way, but gave a misleading impression of hypnosis. There is no evidence that people can be hypnotized against their will or forced to do things they would never otherwise consider. An individual must *choose* to turn initiative over to the hypnotist and cooperate with the hypnotist's suggestions. (Sometimes, in *self-hypnosis*, the hypnotist is oneself.) However, like drugs, hypnosis can be used to justify letting go of inhibitions. ("I know this looks silly, but after all, I'm hypnotized.") Hypnotized people may also do unusual things if they accept a suggestion that they are in an appropriate situation for doing so. They may take off their clothes if they are convinced they are in the shower or attack someone they are led to believe has killed one of their friends.

Hypnosis is usually defined as a heightened state of suggestibility or responsiveness. It is *not* sleep; brain waves during hypnosis are similar to those of ordinary wakefulness. To induce hypnosis, the hypnotist typically suggests that the person being hypnotized feels relaxed, is getting sleepy, and feels the eyelids getting heavier and heavier. In a singsong or monotonous voice, the hypnotist assures the subject that he or she is sinking "deeper and deeper," without actually falling asleep. Another way to induce hypnosis is to have the person concentrate on a certain color or small object. Some people can be hypnotized by suggestions that they feel particularly strong or alert, or even while they are doing something active, such as riding a bicycle (Bányai & Hilgard, 1976).

People who have been hypnotized report that the focus of attention turns outward, toward the hypnotist's voice. The experience is sometimes likened to total absorption in a good book, a play, or a favorite piece of music. People who can easily become absorbed in such activities, who can suspend ordinary reality and become involved in the world of imagination, make good hypnotic subjects (S. Allen, 1985; J.R. Hilgard, 1979). Not surprisingly, children are in general more easily hypnotized than adults, who often have learned to be wary of fantasy and are unwilling to suspend ordinary perceptions of reality. However, most people are at least somewhat susceptible to hypnotic suggestions.

Hypnotized individuals typically say they feel passive and prone to carry out the hypnotist's suggestions uncritically, even when those suggestions involve some distortion of reality. The person may feel that only the here and now exists; the flow of time slows down or goes unnoticed (though at the hypnotist's suggestion, it may also speed up). There may be a sensation of floating or sinking, and actions may seem to require less effort than normally. The person almost always remains fully aware of what is going on and remembers the experience later, unless explicitly instructed to forget it. (Even then, the memory can be restored by a prearranged signal.)

Because hypnotic suggestions may affect perception, memory, or motivation, hypnosis has many applications in both medicine and psychology. It has been used effectively to treat headaches; anesthetize people undergoing dental work, surgery, or childbirth; eliminate unwanted habits such as smoking or nail biting; improve study skills; and even pump up the confidence of athletes. Under hypnosis, some people can actually control the flow of blood to various parts of their body. Increasing the blood flow hastens the healing of burn wounds. Constricting the flow to cysts, warts, and other growths may help shrink them (Moore & Kaplan, 1983).

Psychologists have done extensive research on pain reduction under hypnosis. In a typical experiment, a hypnotized volunteer places an arm in ice water for

hypnosis *A condition in which attention is focused and a person is extremely responsive to suggestion.*

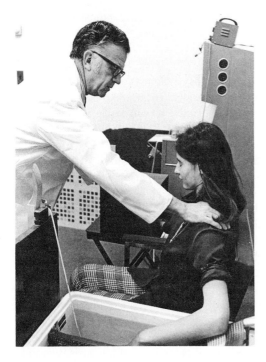

FIGURE 4.5

How much does it hurt?
Ernest Hilgard has conducted many experiments on hypnosis and pain. Ordinarily, a person whose arm is immersed in ice water feels intense pain. But Hilgard has found that if hypnotized people are told the pain will be minimal, they report little or no discomfort, and, like the young woman shown here, seem unperturbed.

several seconds, then rates the pain. Normally, this is an excruciating experience. But when subjects are told that they will feel no pain, they report little or none, nor do they show any obvious signs of distress, such as groaning or grimacing (see Figure 4.5). After the hypnotic session ends, they continue to deny that their arms hurt (Hilgard & Hilgard, 1975).

We know, then, that hypnosis "works." But why? Some psychologists see hypnosis as a true altered state of consciousness, subjectively and objectively different from ordinary wakefulness. Skeptics, though, think there may be less to hypnosis than meets the eye.

Hypnosis as an altered state. Although hypnotized subjects can sometimes control "automatic" body functions like blood flow, hypnosis as a state has not been linked with predictable changes in brain waves, eye movements, skin resistance, or other physiological responses. But Ernest Hilgard, who has studied hypnosis for many years, argues that such responses are not critical for concluding that hypnosis is different from ordinary waking consciousness. After all, he notes, scientists readily accepted the reality of dreams and the existence of sleep as a separate state before anyone knew about rapid eye movements or EEG patterns.

Hilgard's own belief is that hypnosis is an altered state that involves *dissociation*, the split in consciousness we mentioned earlier (E.R. Hilgard, 1977, 1978). In dissociation, one part of the mind operates independently from another. In many hypnotized persons, says Hilgard, only one of the parts goes along with the hypnotic suggestion. The other part is like a *hidden observer*, watching but not participating. Unless given special instructions, the hypnotized person remains unaware of the observer.

Hilgard and his colleagues have attempted to question the "hidden observer" directly. For example, using the ice water procedure, they tell hypnotized subjects that although they will feel no pain, the nonsubmerged hand will be able to signal the level of any hidden pain by pressing a key. In this situation, many people say they feel little or no pain while at the same time their free hand is busily pressing one of the keys. After coming ''out'' of hypnosis these people continue to insist that they were pain-free—unless the hypnotist suggests that the ''hidden observer'' will be able to issue a separate report.

> *Hypnosis as goal-directed fantasy.*   Other psychologists doubt that hypnosis is a true altered state. Theodore Barber, who considers hypnosis to be simply goal-directed fantasy, argues that there is no truly objective way to verify that the hypnotized person is in a separate state (Barber, 1970, 1979; Barber & Wilson, 1977). In fact, says Barber, the notion of a hypnotic state is circular; that is, the explanation of it restates the problem. How do we know that a person is hypnotized? Because he or she obeys the hypnotist's suggestions. And why does the person obey those suggestions? Because the person is hypnotized!

Barber and more recently Nicholas Spanos (1986) argue that all the apparently astounding things that people do while ''under'' hypnosis can also be done in the waking state, *if* people are sufficiently motivated and *if* they believe they can succeed. For example, when the stage hypnotist has a hypnotized person stretch out rigid as a plank between two chairs, with the head on the back of one chair and ankles on the back of another, nothing special is actually occurring. Most unhypnotized people can do the same thing—they only think they can't. Barber and Spanos do not deny that hypnotic suggestion leads to feats of great strength, pain reduction, hallucinations, or the disappearance of warts. However, they cite impressive evidence that suggestion alone, without the special procedures of hypnosis, can produce the same results.

Under hypnosis, a person will cheerfully describe the chocolate cake at her fourth birthday or remember a former life as a 12th-century French peasant. As it turns out, lemon cake was served at that birthday, and she can't speak 12th-century French. What are some possible explanations of these vivid ''memories''?

What about the frequent claim that under hypnosis, almost anyone can relive his or her fourth birthday or a childhood trauma? Stage hypnotists, ''past-lives channelers,'' and even some psychotherapists have reported dramatic ''childlike'' performances by people who have been ''age-regressed,'' either to earlier years or earlier centuries. They use this apparent ''evidence'' of their eyes to argue that people literally revert to an earlier mode of psychological functioning. But is it true?

Michael Nash (1987) has reviewed 60 years of scientific studies on this question. When people are regressed to infancy, do their brain wave patterns become infantile? Do childlike reflexes return? Do outgrown emotional disorders reappear? The answer, Nash finds, is clearly no. What about thinking? Do age-regressed people reason as children do or show child-sized IQs? No; their mental and moral performance, says Nash, remains ''essentially adult in nature.'' What about enhanced recall of childhood events? Once again, the answer is negative. Hypnosis does *not* reliably improve memory for early experiences, even though hypnotized people often swear it does. In one of Nash's own studies, hypnotized individuals tried to recall what their favorite ''transitional objects'' were at age 3 (teddy bears, blankets, and the like). Only 23 percent were accurate, compared to 70 percent of a nonhypnotized control group! (Mothers independently verified the accuracy of this memory.)

Of course, Nash says, people do undergo dramatic changes in behavior and subjective experience when they are hypnotically regressed—they may use baby talk or report that they feel 4 again. But the reason is not that they *are* 4, simply that they are willing to play the role. They will do the same when they are hypnotically *progressed* ahead—say, to age 70 or 80—or regressed to ''past lives.'' Their belief that they are 7 or 70 or 7000 may be sincere and convincing, but it is all in their minds.

Even under the best of circumstances, people find it hard to distinguish an authentic memory from their inferences about what must have happened at the time

Amazing, right? Or maybe not. Although the chair trick is a staple of the stage hypnotist's repertoire, most unhypnotized people can do it, too. The only way to find out if hypnosis produces unique results is to do controlled research—with control groups.

(see Chapter 7). Under hypnosis, the natural tendency to confuse fact and speculation is increased both by a desire to please the hypnotist and by the fact that hypnosis encourages fantasy and vivid imagery. Consider what happens when hypnosis is used to jog the memories of crime victims and trial witnesses. In some cases, it leads to a happy ending. After the 1976 kidnapping of a busload of schoolchildren in Chowchilla, California, the bus driver was hypnotized and was able to recall all but one of the license plate numbers on the kidnappers' car. That clue provided a breakthrough in the case. But in other cases, hypnotized witnesses have been wrong. Research finds that although hypnosis does sometimes boost the amount of information recalled, it also increases errors, perhaps because hypnotized people are more willing than nonhypnotized people to guess, or because they mistake vividly imagined possibilities for actual memories (Dinges et al., 1987; Dywan & Bowers, 1983). Because pseudomemories and errors are so common in hypnotically induced recall, both the American Psychological Association and the American Medical Association are on record as opposing the use of "hypnotically refreshed" testimony in court.

Hypnosis as role playing. But, you say, hypnosis *looks* like an altered state: There's the fixed gaze and the slumped posture. However, hypnosis does not have to involve these bodily reactions. When it does, it may be because most people have acquired an idea of how a hypnotized person is *supposed* to behave from films or nightclub acts. Indeed, Theodore Sarbin and his colleagues believe that role playing is the very essence of hypnosis (Coe & Sarbin, 1977; Sarbin & Coe, 1972).

In this view, the hypnotized person is playing the part of a hypnotized person, a part that has analogies in ordinary life, where we willingly submit to the suggestions of parents, teachers, doctors, therapists, and television commercials. The person is not merely faking or playacting. The role of hypnotized person, like many social roles, is so engrossing and involving that actions occur without conscious intent.

Sometimes objective tests can penetrate the role. Imagine that a person has been given a hypnotic suggestion to become deaf until she receives a tap on the shoulder. The suggestion seems to work; even the crash of cymbals behind her back fails to get her attention or startle her. But then the researcher has the subject participate in a procedure called *delayed auditory feedback*. As she reads a paragraph aloud, her words are recorded and played back to her through earphones with half a second delay. People with normal hearing respond to delayed auditory feedback with stuttering, slurring, and hesitation. They speak more loudly than usual and mispronounce words. (The same thing can happen when a bad long-distance telephone connection produces an echo of your own voice.) Studies have shown that the hypnotized subject, though apparently deaf to her own voice, will respond in exactly the same way as would a hearing person (Barber, 1979). Therefore, she must be able to hear.

Where does this leave us? Each piece of evidence allows alternative interpretations. For example, the person hypnotized to be deaf may not be role playing after all; one part of her consciousness may in fact be deaf, while another, the "hidden observer," can hear and respond normally to the delayed auditory feedback test. Also, some researchers believe that in certain situations, the behavior of hypnotized people is subtly different from that of people who are only role playing (E.R. Hilgard, 1978; Orne, 1979; Spiegel, 1986). Whatever hypnosis is, though, there is no denying its potential as a medical and psychological tool. By studying it, psychologists can learn much about human suggestibility, the power of imagination, and the way we perceive and remember.

QUICK ▪ QUIZ

True or false:

1. Most people are at least somewhat susceptible to hypnotic suggestions.
2. According to Hilgard's theory, hypnosis is a state of dissociation involving a "hidden observer."
3. Hypnosis gives us special powers we do not ordinarily have.
4. Hypnosis reduces errors in memory.
5. Experiments using delayed auditory feedback show that people hypnotized to be deaf cannot hear anything.

Answers:
1. T   2. T   3. F   4. F   5. F

As we have seen in this chapter, changes in consciousness, however they are initiated, allow us to explore how our expectations and explanations of behavior affect what we do and how we feel. States of consciousness are interesting in and of themselves. But under scientific scrutiny, hypnosis, drug-induced states, dreams, and biological rhythms—phenomena once thought beyond the pale of science—can also deepen our understanding of the intimate relationship between body and mind.

Taking Psychology with You

How to Get a Good Night's Sleep

You hop into bed, turn out the lights, close your eyes, and wait for slumber. An hour later, you're still waiting. Finally you drop off, but at 3:00 A.M., to your chagrin, you're awake again. By the time the rooster crows, you have put in a hard day's night.

Insomnia affects most people at one time or another, and many people most of the time. In search of relief, Americans spend hundreds of millions of dollars each year on sleeping aids. Their money is not well spent. Over-the-counter pills are almost worthless for inducing sleep, and prescription drugs such as barbiturates can actually make matters worse. Barbiturates suppress REM sleep, a result that eventually causes wakefulness. They also suppress stages 3 and 4, the deeper stages of sleep.

Any effectiveness barbiturates do have usually disappears within a few days. Other sleep medications, known as benzodiazepines, lead to tolerance more slowly, but they produce a breakdown product that stays in the body during the day and causes diminished alertness and hand-eye coordination problems (Kelly, 1981a). Says one well-known sleep researcher, "Let me put a person on sleeping pills for a month, and I'll guarantee broken sleep" (Webb, quoted in Goleman, 1982).

Studies of sleep suggest that there are better alternatives. Here are some basic principles:

▪ *Be sure you actually have a sleep problem.* Many people only think they don't sleep well. In one study, 55 people reporting to a sleep clinic for help were observed for several nights in the laboratory. Forty-two took less than 30 minutes to fall asleep. Only 30 got less than six and a half hours of sleep per night. Only 26 were awake more than 30 minutes total during the night (Carskadon, Mitler, & Dement, 1974).

The amount of time spent sleeping is not a good criterion of insomnia anyway. If you sleep only five hours a night and feel fine during the day, you don't have a problem. Some apparently healthy people can get by on only three or four hours. As people age, they typically sleep less and more lightly, and often break up sleep into nighttime snoozing and an afternoon nap.

▪ *Get a correct diagnosis of the sleep problem.* Disruption of sleep can result from psychological disturbances, such as severe depression. It can also result from physical disorders. In *sleep apnea*, breathing periodically stops for a few moments, causing the person to choke and gasp. This can happen hundreds of times a night, often without the person knowing it, and may lead to high blood pressure or irregular heartbeat. There are several causes of sleep apnea, from blockage of air passages to failure of the brain to control respiration correctly. A person with apnea needs medical evaluation. In *narcolepsy*, another serious disorder, an individual is subject to irresistible and unpredictable daytime attacks of sleepiness lasting from 5 to 30 minutes. Narcoleptics often lapse immediately into REM sleep, even during the briefest naps. Some researchers think that as many as a quarter million Americans may suffer from this condition, most without knowing it. Friends and relatives may give them little support, thinking they are merely lazy. Narcolepsy may result from problems in the metabolism or release of various neurotransmitters (Mefford et al., 1983).

▪ *Avoid excessive use of alcohol or other drugs.* Many drugs interfere with normal slumber. Alcohol suppresses REM sleep and tranquilizers like Valium and Librium reduce stage 4 sleep. Coffee, tea, cola, and chocolate all contain caffeine, which is a stimulant.

▪ *Go with the flow.* Insomnia can occur when people fight their own natural circadian rhythms, forcing themselves to sleep when they are feeling frisky or to get up when they are still groggy. You probably already know whether you're a lark (early to bed, early to rise) or an owl (late to bed, late to rise). Work and study schedules may not allow you to follow your rhythms exactly, but try not to ignore them completely. Once you find your natural sleep time, try to stick with it.

▪ *Don't associate the bedroom with wakefulness.* When environmental cues are repeatedly associated with some behavior, they can come to trigger the behavior (Bootzin, 1973). (This phenomenon, known technically as *stimulus control*, is explained in Chapter 6.) If you don't want your bedroom to trigger wakefulness, avoid reading, studying, and watching TV there. Also avoid lying awake for hours waiting for sleep, since your frustration will cause arousal that can be associated with the bedroom. If you can't sleep, get up and do something else, preferably something dull, in a different room. When you feel drowsy, try sleeping again. If necessary, repeat the process until you fall asleep easily.

▪ *Take care of your health.* This may sound like a grandmother's advice, but good health habits are probably important for good sleep. Nutrition is one area to watch. As we saw in Chapter 3, the amino acid *tryptophan* promotes the onset of sleep, and there may be other dietary influences on alertness and relaxation. Exercise during the day also seems to enhance sleep, but it should be avoided right before bedtime, since in the short term it heightens alertness.

Finally, since much if not most insomnia is related to anxiety and stress, it makes sense to get to the source of your problems. You can't expect to sleep well with adrenaline pouring through your bloodstream and worries crowding your mind. In an evolutionary sense, sleeplessness is an adaptive response to danger and threat. As Woody Allen once said, "The lamb and the lion shall lie down together, but the lamb will not be very sleepy." When your anxieties decrease, so may your sleepless nights.

KEY WORDS

consciousness 120
states of consciousness 120

biological rhythm 120
circadian rhythm 121

SUMMARY

1. *Consciousness* is the awareness of oneself and the environment. *States of consciousness* are associated with characteristic patterns of psychological and physical functioning. Changes in these states are associated with *biological rhythms*, periodic, more or less regular fluctuations in biological systems. *Circadian* fluctuations occur about once a day, as in the sleep-wake cycle. *Ultradian* fluctuations occur more frequently, often in a 90-minute cycle. *Infradian* fluctuations occur less often than once a day.

2. Alertness and performance on various tasks follow a circadian rhythm. When a person's normal routine changes, circadian rhythms may be *desynchronized*, that is, thrown out of phase with one another. Volunteers who live in isolation from all time cues usually live a ''day'' of about 25 hours.

3. Theorists do not agree on the biological functions of sleep. Sleep is not a continuous quiet, resting state. Periods of *rapid eye movement*, or *REM*, alternate with non-REM sleep in an ultradian rhythm. REM periods are associated with dreaming. For descriptive purposes, non-REM sleep is divided into four stages associated with certain brain wave patterns. During REM sleep, the brain is active and there are other signs of arousal, yet the skeletal muscles are limp; thus REM sleep has also been called ''paradoxical sleep.''

4. Infradian rhythms of many types have been observed, including seasonal fluctuations in vulnerability to depression. However, it is hard to prove that they are endogenous—that is, that they originate within the body and are not due to social or cultural conventions or other external factors.

5. One infradian rhythm that is endogenous is the menstrual cycle, during which various hormones rise and fall predictably. Physical symptoms are associated with the cycle in many women and usually have a biological cause. Emotional symptoms, however, although frequently reported by women, are not well established and tend to fade or disappear in well-controlled (blind) studies. Expectations and subjective interpretations of bodily changes can affect reports of changes in emotion and mood. Few people of either sex are likely to undergo dramatic monthly mood swings or personality changes because of hormones.

6. Ordinary states of consciousness include alert wakefulness, daydreaming, and sleep dreaming. In alert wakefulness, we focus on specific things and events, filtering out whatever is irrelevant. However, a great deal of *subconscious* and *nonconscious* processing also occurs during wakefulness, affecting our behavior. In daydreaming, attention turns to private thoughts, images, and fantasies. Daydreaming may be a natural consequence of the ongoing activity of the brain. Daydream intensity fluctuates in an ultradian rhythm.

7. Sleep dreaming is a state of consciousness that everyone experiences every night. The *psychoanalytic explanation* of dreams is that they allow us to gratify forbidden or unrealistic wishes and desires that have been forced into the unconscious part of the mind. Thoughts and objects may be disguised as symbolic images that provide clues to the dream's meaning. Most psychologists today accept the notion that dreams are more than incoherent ramblings of the mind, but many quarrel with specific psychoanalytic interpretations.

8. A second approach to dreams emphasizes their information-processing function. According to Christopher Evans, sleep gives the brain an opportunity to scan and sort through new data, and dreams are snippets from an ongoing process of mental housekeeping that is otherwise inaccessible to consciousness. A similar idea, advanced by Francis Crick and Graeme Mitchison, holds that during REM periods the brain jettisons mental "garbage."

9. The *activation-synthesis theory* of dreaming, proposed by Allan Hobson and Robert McCarley, holds that dreams occur when the cortex tries to make sense of spontaneous neural firing initiated in the pons. The resulting interpretation is a dream. Dreams do not disguise unconscious wishes, but they can reveal a person's perceptions, conflicts, and concerns. At present, activation-synthesis is the most completely developed and most biologically based modern dream theory.

10. In all cultures, people have found ways to produce *altered* or *alternate* states of consciousness. For example, *psychoactive drugs* alter the body's biochemistry, primarily by acting on brain neurotransmitters. Most drugs can be classified as *stimulants, depressants, opiates*, or *psychedelics*, depending on their central nervous system effects and their impact on behavior and mood. The effects of a drug cannot be explained solely in terms of its chemical properties. They are also influenced by the user's physical condition, prior experience with the drug, and mental set and the environmental setting.

11. *Hypnosis* is a heightened state of suggestibility or responsiveness. Some researchers consider it to be an altered state that involves *dissociation*, or a split in consciousness. Others regard it as goal-directed fantasy or as a form of role playing in which the role is so engrossing that actions occur without conscious intent. Whatever it is, it has valuable uses in both medicine and psychology. Like drug-induced states, dreams, and biological rhythms, it sheds light on the relationship between body and mind.

CHAPTER 5

Sensation and Perception

Minds that have nothing to confer
Find little to perceive.

WILLIAM WORDSWORTH

*S*ince the age of 10 months, S. B. had been blind. An infection had damaged his corneas, the transparent membranes on the front surfaces of the eyes. A cheerful and independent man, S. B. adjusted well to his disability; he married, supported himself, and led an active life. But through the years he continued to dream of regaining his sight.

At last, when S. B. was 52, a doctor successfully performed corneal transplant surgery. Almost as soon as the bandages were removed, S. B. was able to identify common objects and even letters of the alphabet. But there were also some strange gaps in S. B.'s visual world. Though his eyes now functioned well, he seemed blind to objects or parts of objects that he had not previously touched. He could not read facial expressions or recognize pictures of scenery. Although his visual abilities gradually improved, his perception of the world months after surgery remained limited and distorted by his previous sensory experiences. For example, when asked to draw a bus, he produced the sketch in the margin—leaving out the front end, which he had never felt with his hands. In many ways S. B. continued to lead the life of a blind man until his death the year following the operation (Gregory & Wallace, 1963).

S. B.'s story is an unusual one, but it contains lessons that apply to us all. Like S. B., we depend on our senses for our everyday understanding of physical reality. Also like S. B., we have only a partial perception of that reality. Even with normal eyesight, we are blind to all but a tiny portion of the electromagnetic energy waves around us. Even with normal hearing, we are deaf to most of the pressure waves that fill the air. Yet despite these limitations, our senses are also astonishingly complex and sensitive.

In this chapter, you will learn how your sense organs take in information from the environment and how your brain uses that information to construct a reliable model of the world. The boundary between these two processes is not hard and fast, but psychologists traditionally distinguish one from the other by using different labels: sensation and perception.

Sensation is the detection or awareness of changes in physical energy caused by environmental or internal events. The cells that detect such changes are called **sense receptors** and are located in the **sense organs**—the eyes, ears, tongue, nose, skin, and internal body tissues. The receptors for smell, pressure, pain, and temperature are structural extensions (dendrites) of sensory neurons. The receptors for vision, hearing, and taste are distinct cells separated from sensory neurons by synapses. The sensory processes made possible by these sense receptors produce an immediate awareness of sound, color, form, and other basic building blocks of consciousness. They tell us what is happening, both inside our bodies and in the world beyond our own skins.

Without sensation, we would have nothing to laugh, cry, or think about. Yet sensation is essentially the handmaiden of perception. **Perception** is the process by which sensory impulses are organized and interpreted. Perception tells us where one object begins and another ends. It assembles the building blocks of sensory experience into meaningful patterns. The sense of vision produces a two-dimensional image on the back of the eye, but we *perceive* the world in three dimensions. The

sensation *The detection or direct experience of physical energy in the external or internal environment due to stimulation of receptors in the sense organs.*

sense receptors *Specialized cells that convert physical energy in the environment into electrical energy that can be transmitted as nerve impulses to the brain.*

sense organs *Parts of the body that contain the sense receptors.*

perception *The process by which the brain organizes and interprets sensory information.*

sense of hearing brings us the sound of a C, an E, and a G played simultaneously on the piano, but we *perceive* a C-major chord.

Look at the drawing of the cube in the margin. If you stare at the cube, it will flip-flop in front of your eyes. The surface that is on the outside and front will suddenly be on the inside and back, or vice versa. You *sense* only some black lines on a field of white. However, because your brain can interpret the sensory image in alternate ways, you *perceive* two different cubes. The ambiguity is not in the picture but in the eye (actually, the brain) of the beholder. Something similar happens when certain speech sounds are repeated. Say the word "say" over and over again. "Say" will soon become "ace," and then, after a while, "ace" will shift back to "say." The sound signal does not change, only your perception of it.

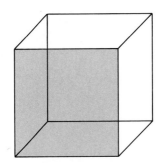

Psychologists study sensation and perception because together they are the foundation of learning, thinking, and acting. Much of the research in this area is of the "pure," or basic, sort. But knowledge about sensation and perception is often put to practical use, for example, in the design of color television sets, hearing aids, and robots that "see," "hear," and "feel," and in the training of flight controllers, astronauts, and others who must make important decisions based on what they sense and perceive.

Our Sensational Senses

At some point you learned that there are five senses corresponding to five sense organs: vision (eyes), hearing (ears), taste (tongue), touch (skin), and smell (nose). The senses have been categorized this way at least since Aristotle's time. There are, however, more than five senses, though scientists disagree about the exact number. The skin, which is the organ of touch or pressure, also senses heat, cold, and pain, not to mention itching and tickling. The ear, which is the organ of hearing, also contains receptors that account for a sense of balance. The internal muscles contain receptors responsible for a sense of bodily movement.

All of our senses evolved for the same purpose: to help us survive. Even pain, which causes so much human misery, is indispensable, for it alerts us to illness and injury. In rare cases, people have been born without a sense of pain. Though free of the hurts and aches that plague the rest of us, they lead difficult lives, for they burn, bruise, and cut themselves more than other people do. One young woman developed inflamed joints because she failed to shift her weight while standing or to turn over in her sleep, acts that people with normal pain sensation perform automatically. At the age of only 29 she died from massive infections, due in part to skin and bone injuries (Melzack, 1973).

Sensory experiences contribute immeasurably to the quality of life, even when they are not directly helping us survive. They entertain us, amuse us, inspire us. If we really pay attention to our senses, said poet William Wordsworth, we can "see into the life of things" and hear "the still, sad music of humanity."

Sensation begins with the sense receptors. When receptors detect an appropriate stimulus—light, mechanical pressure, or chemical molecules—they convert its energy into electrical impulses that travel along nerves to the brain. This conversion of one form of energy into another is known as **transduction**. Sense receptors are biological transducers. Radio receivers, which convert radio waves into sound waves, are mechanical transducers, as are Geiger counters, television sets, and electronic eyes.

Sense receptors are like military scouts who scan the terrain for signs of activity and relay a message when they detect something. These scouts cannot make many

transduction *The conversion of one form of energy to another. Sensory receptors are biological transducers.*

People can often use one sense to overcome a deficiency in another. The Braille system, which uses embossed dots to represent letters, numerals, and punctuation marks, enables millions of blind people to read by means of touch. The system was originally developed in the early nineteenth century by French educator Louis Braille, who was himself blind.

decisions on their own. They must transmit what they learn to field officers—sensory neurons in the peripheral nervous system. The field officers in turn must report to generals at a command center—the cells of the brain. The generals are responsible for analyzing the reports, combining information brought in by different scouts, and deciding what it all means.

The riddle of separate sensations

We now come to a critical question. The various field officers in the sensory system all use exactly the same form of communication, a neural impulse. It is as if they must all send their messages on a tom-tom and can only go "boom." How, then, are we able to experience so many different sensations?

The answer is that the nervous system *encodes* the messages. There are two basic kinds of code (Schneider & Tarshis, 1986). One is *anatomical*; it was first described in 1826 by Johannes Müller, who proposed a theory called the **doctrine of specific nerve energies**. The central idea of the theory is that the nature of a sensory experience depends on which nerve is stimulated. Although some of the physiological assumptions of the theory have been proven wrong, this fundamental concept is generally correct. Different receptors stimulate different nerve pathways, and these in turn lead to different parts of the brain. Signals from the eye cause impulses to travel along the optic nerve to the visual cortex. Signals from the ear cause impulses to travel along the auditory nerve to the auditory cortex. Light and sound waves produce different sensations because they result in the stimulation of different nerves and different brain parts.

The doctrine of specific nerve energies implies that what we know about the world ultimately reduces to what we know about the state of our own nervous system. Therefore, if sound waves could stimulate nerves that end in the visual part of the brain, we would "see" sound. In fact, a similar sort of crossover does occur when you press lightly on the lid of a closed eye and "see" a flash of light. The pressure apparently produces an impulse that travels up the optic nerve to the visual area of the brain. Some people also claim to experience a more dramatic type of crossover, called *synesthesia* (L. Marks, 1975). Typically, these individuals say that sounds or tastes cause them to see colors or images. A few have even reported feeling colors through their fingertips. Most psychologists, though, remain skeptical about such claims, which are not supported by controlled studies.

Our ability to distinguish visual from auditory signals can be accounted for by anatomical encoding. However, it has proven more difficult to link the different skin senses to distinct nerve pathways. The doctrine of specific nerve energies also fails to explain variations of experience within a particular sense—the sight of pink versus red, the sound of a piccolo versus the sound of a tuba, or the feel of a pinprick versus the feel of a kiss. An additional kind of code is therefore necessary to account for the riddle of separate sensations.

This second kind of code has been called *functional*, as opposed to anatomical (Schneider & Tarshis, 1986). Functional codes rely on the fact that particular receptors and neurons fire, or are inhibited from firing, only in the presence of certain sorts of stimuli. At any particular time, then, some cells in the nervous system are firing and some are not. Information about *which* cells are firing, *how many* cells are firing, and the *rate* at which cells are firing constitutes a functional code.

Functional encoding may occur all along a sensory route, starting in the sense organs and ending in the brain. There is still controversy, however, about how functional encoding eventually yields an overall perception of an object. For exam-

doctrine of specific nerve energies *The theory that we experience different sense modalities because signals received by different sense organs stimulate different nerve pathways, which terminate in different areas of the brain.*

ple, most current theories of vision assume that as impulses travel from the eye to lower brain centers and on to higher ones, individual nerve cells abstract more and more information about the visual image. How do they do this? Recall from Chapter 3 that as various neurons converge at a synapse, their overall *pattern* of firing determines whether the neuron on the other side of the synapse is excited or inhibited. The firing (or inhibition) of that neuron, then, actually conveys information to the *next* neuron along the sensory route about what was happening in many other cells. Eventually a single ''hypercomplex'' cell in the cortex of the brain may receive information that was originally contained in the firing of thousands of receptors. However, many researchers believe that the final perception of a stimulus depends not on the firing of a single hypercomplex cell but on the simultaneous activation of various cells in different parts of the brain (E. Kandel, 1981).

Measuring the senses

Just how sensitive are our senses? The answer comes from researchers in the field of **psychophysics**, which is concerned with the relationship between physical properties of stimuli and our psychological experience of them. Drawing on principles from both physics and psychology, these researchers measure how the strength or intensity of a stimulus affects the strength of sensation in an observer.

Absolute thresholds.   One way to find out how sensitive the senses are is to present people with a series of weak stimuli, or signals, and ask them to report which ones they can detect. The smallest amount of energy that a person can detect reliably is known as the **absolute threshold**. The word *absolute* is a bit misleading. People detect borderline signals on some occasions and miss them on others. For various reasons, psychologists have decided that ''reliable'' detection occurs when an individual can detect a stimulus 50 percent of the time.

If you were having your absolute threshold for brightness measured, you would be asked to sit in a dark room and look at a wall or screen. You would then be shown flashes of light varying in brightness. Your task would be to say whether you noticed a flash. Sometimes you would miss seeing a flash, even though you had noticed one of equal brightness on other trials. Other times you would have a ''false alarm,'' thinking that you saw a flash when there was none. Such errors seem to occur in part because of random firing of cells in the nervous system, which produces something like the background noise in a stereo system.

By studying absolute thresholds, psychologists have found that our senses are very sharp indeed (see Table 5.1). Our vision is particularly acute. Even our sense of smell, which seems crude compared to a bloodhound's, is quite good. People can actually smell some substances before they can be detected by odor-sensitive machines, which is why human beings are often used to detect odors in chemical plants and laboratories.

However, our senses are tuned in to only a narrow band of physical energies. For example, as mentioned earlier, we are sensitive visually to only a tiny fraction of all electromagnetic energy (see Figure 5.1). Other species can pick up various sorts of signals that we cannot. Dogs can detect high-frequency sound waves that are beyond our range, as you know if you have ever called your pooch with a ''silent'' doggie whistle. Bats and porpoises can hear sounds two octaves beyond our range. Bees can see ultraviolet rays, and snakes can see tiny changes in temperature. As we discuss in ''Think About It'' on page 161, sensory differences among species raise some intriguing questions about the nature of ''reality.''

psychophysics *The area of psychology concerned with the relationship between physical properties of stimuli and sensory experience.*
absolute threshold *The smallest quantity of physical energy that can be reliably detected by an observer.*

TABLE 5.1
OUR SENSITIVE SENSES

We do not detect all the energy changes around us, but our senses are more sensitive than many people realize. Here are some average absolute thresholds for detecting various types of stimuli.

Sense Modality	Sensitivity
Vision	A candle flame seen from 30 miles on a clear, dark night.
Hearing	The ticking of a watch from 20 feet away in a very quiet place.
Taste	One teaspoon of sugar in 2 gallons of water.
Smell	One drop of perfume diffused through a three-room apartment.
Touch	The wing of a bee falling on your cheek from a height of 1 centimeter.

SOURCE: Galanter, 1962, p. 97.

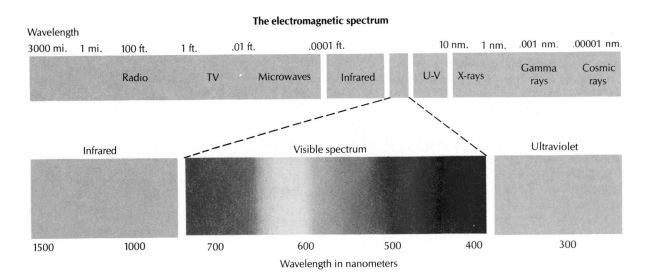

The electromagnetic spectrum

FIGURE 5.1

The visible spectrum of electromagnetic energy
Our visual system detects only a small fraction of the electromagnetic energy around us.

---

signal detectability theory
A psychophysical theory that divides the detection of a sensory signal into a sensory process and a decision process.

The theory of signal detectability. Despite its usefulness, the procedure for measuring absolute thresholds has a serious limitation: Measurements are affected by an observer's tendency to respond, "Yes, I noticed a signal" or "No, I didn't notice anything," when the person is uncertain. When required to make a decision, some people seem to be habitual yea sayers, willing to gamble that the signal was really there. Others are habitual nay sayers, cautious and conservative. Moreover, motives and expectations influence how a person responds. For example, if the observer wants to impress the experimenter, he or she may lean toward a positive response.

Fortunately, this problem of *response bias* is not insurmountable. According to the **theory of signal detectability**, an observer's response in a detection task can be divided into a *sensory process*, which depends on the intensity of the stimulus, and a *decision process*, which is influenced by the observer's response bias. There is a procedure to separate these two components. On some trials ("catch trials"), no stimulus is presented. On others, a weak stimulus is presented. Yea sayers will have more "hits" than nay sayers when a weak stimulus is presented, but they will also have more "false alarms" when no stimulus is presented. As the number of catch

Think About It

In Search of the Real World

Three baseball umpires were arguing about how to distinguish balls from strikes. The first said, "I calls 'em as I sees 'em." The second said, "I calls 'em as they is." The third, obviously feeling superior to the others, said, "They ain't nothin' until I calls 'em!"

This old story raises an issue pondered by philosophers through the ages: Is reality "out there" in the environment or "in here" in a person's mind? Suppose a tree falls in the forest and there is no one around to hear the crash. Is there a noise? *Objectivists* say yes. They believe in the objective reality of a material world that exists completely apart from the perceiver. *Solipsists* (from the Latin words for "alone" and "self") say no. They claim that reality exists solely in the mind of the perceiver. For a solipsist, even the tree has no independent reality. Psychologists usually take the middle ground in this debate. They accept that there is a physical reality, that a falling tree disturbs air molecules and produces pressure waves. But they also note that hearing, like all sensations, is a subjective experience, and so *noise* cannot be said to occur unless someone experiences it.

Since sensation is a subjective experience, our ideas about reality must be affected by our sensory abilities and limitations. That is, things appear to us as they do not only because of *their* nature but because of *ours*. If the entire human race were totally deaf, we might still talk about pressure waves, but we would have no concept of sound. Similarly, if we were all totally color-blind, we might still talk about the wavelengths of light, but we would have no concept of color.

The human way of sensing and perceiving the world is certainly not the only way. Because different species have different needs, their bodies are at-tuned to different aspects of physical reality. Bees are blind to red, but they can see ultraviolet light, which merely gives human beings a sunburn. Since different parts of flowers reflect ultraviolet light at different rates, flowers that appear to us to be a single color must look patterned to a bee. Neither our perception nor the bee's is more "correct."

Some animal sensory systems seem to have no equivalent at all in human beings. Snakes have an organ, in a pit on the head, that detects infrared rays. This organ permits them to sense heat given off by the bodies of their prey. The slightest change in temperature sends a message racing to the snake's brain. There the message is combined with information from the eyes, so that the snake actually sees an infrared pattern—and locates its prey with deadly accuracy even in the dark (Newman & Hartline, 1982). The sensory abilities of other animals, too, seem like something out of a science fiction story. For example, some fish apparently sense distortions of electrical fields through special receptors on the surface of their bodies (Kalmijn, 1982).

Our sensory windows on the world, then, are partly shuttered. But we can use reason, deduction, and technology to pry open those shutters. Ordinary perception tells us that the sun circles the earth, but the great astronomer Copernicus was able to figure out nearly five centuries ago that the opposite is true. Ordinary perception will never let us see ultraviolet and infrared rays directly (unless genetic engineering or evolution drastically changes the kind of organism we are), but we know they are there, and we can measure them.

If science can enable us to overturn the everyday evidence of our senses, who knows what surprises about "reality" are still in store for us? Think about it.

---

trials increases, people in general will become more likely to say "nay." All this information can be used in a complex mathematical formula that yields separate estimates of a person's response bias and sensory capacity. The individual's true sensitivity to a signal of any particular intensity can then be predicted.

The old method of measuring absolute thresholds assumed that there was a single threshold for any given individual, determined entirely by the stimulus. The newer approach of signal detectability theory assumes that the ''threshold'' depends on a decision actively made by the observer. Signal detectability theory has many real-world applications, from screening applicants for jobs requiring keen hearing to training air traffic controllers, whose decisions about the presence or absence of a blip on a radar screen may mean the difference between life and death.

Difference thresholds. Psychologists also study sensory sensitivity by having people compare two stimuli and judge whether they are the same or different. A subject might be asked to compare the weight of two blocks, the brightness of two light bulbs, or the saltiness of two liquids. The smallest difference in stimulation that a person can detect reliably (again, half of the time) is called the **difference threshold** or *just-noticeable-difference (j.n.d.)*. When you compare two stimuli, A and B, the difference threshold will depend on the intensity or size of A. The larger or more intense A is, the greater the change must be before you can detect a difference. If you are comparing the weights of two pebbles, you might be able to detect a difference of only a fraction of an ounce, but not if you are comparing two massive boulders.

According to **Weber's Law**, when a person compares two stimuli, the size of the change necessary to produce a just-noticeable-difference is a constant proportion of the original stimulus. Consider those pebbles and boulders again. Assume, for the sake of argument, that one pebble weighs 5 ounces, and you can just detect the difference between the two pebbles when the second one weighs $\frac{1}{10}$ of an ounce more ($\frac{1}{50}$ of 5 ounces). Assume, too, that the first massive boulder weighs 100 pounds. How much must the second boulder weigh in order for you to tell the difference? The answer is 102 pounds—an addition of $\frac{1}{50}$ of 100 pounds, or 2 pounds. In both cases, the *proportion* of change necessary to produce the just-noticeable-difference is the same. Weber's Law applies to stimuli in the midrange of many dimensions, from weight to smell. The value of the proportion depends on which dimension is being measured (see Table 5.2).

difference threshold *The smallest difference in stimulation that can be reliably detected by an observer when two stimuli are compared. Also called* just-noticeable-difference (j.n.d.).

Weber's Law *Law of psychophysics stating that the change necessary to produce a just-noticeable-difference is a constant proportion of the original stimulus.*

TABLE 5.2
WEBER'S LAW

When you are trying to detect a change in some stimulus, the larger it is, the larger the change must be for you to notice it. According to Weber's Law, the ''just-noticeable-difference'' is a constant proportion of the original stimulus and can be expressed as a fraction. Below are the proportions for various sensory dimensions. Notice that a change in loudness can be detected when the change is equivalent to one-tenth of the original stimulus. In contrast, a change in the brightness of light can be detected when the change is equivalent to only one-sixtieth of the original stimulus. Weber's Law tends to break down when stimulation is very weak or very strong.

Dimension	Ratio
Brightness (white light)	$\frac{1}{60}$
Weight (lifted weights)	$\frac{1}{50}$
Pain (heat on skin)	$\frac{1}{30}$
Hearing (moderately loud tone, middle pitch)	$\frac{1}{10}$
Pressure (on skin)	$\frac{1}{7}$
Smell (raw rubber)	$\frac{1}{4}$
Taste (table salt)	$\frac{1}{3}$

SOURCE: F. A. Geldard, *Fundamentals of Psychology.* New York: Wiley, 1962, p. 93. Copyright © 1962 by John Wiley & Sons, Inc. All rights reserved.

QUICK ▪ QUIZ

1. The Pep-up soft-drink company asks if you can tell which is sweeter, its product or the competition's. The company is measuring a(n) _____ threshold.
2. Even on the clearest night, some stars cannot be seen by the naked eye because they are below the viewer's _____ threshold.
3. According to signal detectability theory, performance on a detection task depends on both a sensory process and a _____ process.
4. Mark is asked to judge whether two bars differ in length. When one bar is 10 millimeters long, the just-noticeable-difference is 1 millimeter: The second bar must be 11 millimeters before a difference is detected. Now another pair of bars is presented. If the first bar is 20 millimeters long, what will the just-noticeable-difference be?

Answers:

1. difference 2. absolute 3. decision 4. 2 millimeters (The j.n.d. is a constant proportion of the first stimulus, in this case 1/10.)

Sensory adaptation

Variety is not only the spice of life; it is the essence of sensation. Our senses are designed to respond to change and contrast in the environment (see Figure 5.2). When a stimulus is unchanging or repetitious, sensation fades or disappears. Receptors get ''tired'' and temporarily stop responding, or nerve cells higher up in the

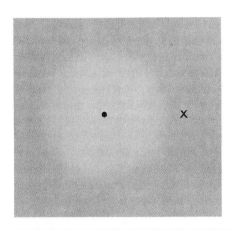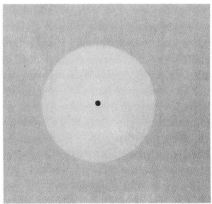

FIGURE 5.2

Now you see it, now you don't

Sensation depends on change and contrast in the environment. Hold your hand over one eye and stare steadily at the dot in the middle of the circle on the right. You should have no trouble maintaining an image of the circle. However, if you do the same with the circle on the left, the image will fade. The gradual change from light to dark does not provide enough contrast to keep the visual receptors in your eye firing at a steady rate. The circle only reappears if you close and reopen your eye or if you shift your gaze to the X.

The effects of sensory deprivation depend on the circumstances. Choosing to spend an hour in a solitary "flotation tank" is one thing; being imprisoned in a dark cell, alone, is another.

You're in a dark room, isolated from sight, sound, smell, and taste. Will you hallucinate and beg to be released, or will you find the experience restful and soothing? What might affect your reaction?

sensory system temporarily switch off. The resulting decline in sensory responsiveness is called **sensory adaptation**. You know that adaptation has occurred when you can no longer smell a gas leak that you noticed when you first entered the kitchen.

We never completely adapt to extremely intense stimuli—a terrible toothache, the odor of ammonia, the heat of the desert sun. We rarely adapt completely to visual stimuli, either; eye movements, both voluntary and involuntary, cause the location of an object's image on the back of the eye to keep changing, so that visual receptors don't have a chance to "fatigue." But in the laboratory, researchers can stabilize the image of a simple pattern, such as a line, at a particular point on the back of a person's eye. They use an ingenious device consisting of a tiny projector mounted on a contact lens. Though the eyeball moves, the image of the object stays focused on the same receptors. After a few minutes, the image fades and disappears; the subject becomes temporarily blind to it.

What happens when our senses adapt to *most* incoming stimuli? In early **sensory deprivation** experiments researchers used special equipment to isolate male volunteers from all patterned sight and sound. Vision was restricted by a translucent visor; hearing by a U-shaped pillow and noise from an air conditioner and fan; and touch by cotton gloves and cardboard cuffs. The volunteers took brief breaks to eat and use the bathroom, but otherwise they simply lay in bed, doing nothing. The results were dramatic (Heron, 1957). Within a few hours, many of the men felt edgy. Some were so disoriented that they quit the study the first day. Those who stayed longer became confused, restless, and grouchy. Many reported hallucinations—at first simple images, then more bizarre visions. One man saw a squadron of marching squirrels, another a procession of marching eyeglasses. Few subjects were willing to remain in the study for more than a few days.

These findings made headlines, of course. But the initial conclusion that sensory deprivation is unpleasant or even dangerous turned out to be an oversimplification (Suedfeld, 1975). In many of the studies, the experimental procedures themselves probably aroused anxiety: They included the presence of "panic buttons," "release from legal liability" forms, and inadequate orientation sessions. Later research, using better methods, showed that hallucinations are rarer and less dramatic than at first thought. Many people enjoy time-limited periods of deprivation, and some perceptual and intellectual abilities actually improve. Like any human experience, the response to sensory deprivation is affected by a person's expectations and interpretations of what is happening. Reduced sensation can be scary if you are locked in a room for an indefinite period, but relaxing if you have retreated to that room on your own for a little time out.

Still, it is clear that the human brain requires a certain amount of sensory stimulation during daily life to function normally. This need may help explain why people who live alone often keep the radio or television set running continuously and why prolonged solitary confinement can be an effective form of torture.

Sensory overload

If too little stimulation can be bad for you, so can too much. Excessive stimulation can lead to fatigue and mental confusion. If you have ever come home from a crowded department store or a noisy sports event nervous, exhausted, and with a splitting headache, you know firsthand about sensory overload.

When people find themselves in a noisy, crowded situation, they can resist overload by blocking out unimportant sights and sounds and focusing only on those

sensory adaptation *The reduction or disappearance of sensory responsiveness that occurs when stimulation is unchanging or repetitious.*
sensory deprivation *Absence of normal levels of sensory stimulation.*

they find interesting or useful. Psychologists have dubbed this the ''cocktail party phenomenon,'' because at a cocktail party a person typically attends to just one conversation, ignoring other voices, the clink of ice cubes, music, and raucous laughter. The competing sounds all enter the nervous system, enabling the person to pick up anything important—even the person's own name, spoken by someone several yards away. Unimportant sounds, though, are not fully processed by the brain. The capacity for **selective attention** shows that the brain is not forced to respond to everything the sense receptors send its way. The ''generals'' in the brain can choose which ''field officers'' get past the command center's gates. Those that don't seem to have anything important to say are turned back.

QUICK ■ QUIZ

For each everyday experience given below, indicate whether it is an example of sensory deprivation, sensory adaptation, or selective attention.

1. You jump into a cold swimming pool, but moments later the water no longer seems so cold.
2. Immobilized in a hospital bed, with no TV or radio in your room, you feel edgy and disoriented.
3. During a break from your job in a restaurant you decide to read. For 20 minutes, you fail to notice the clattering of dishes or orders being called out to the cook.

Answers:
1. sensory adaptation 2. sensory deprivation 3. selective attention

Vision

Vision is the most frequently studied of all the senses, and with good reason. More information about the external world comes to us through our eyes than through any other sense organ. Because we are most active in the daytime, we are ''wired'' to take advantage of the sun's illumination. Animals that are active at night tend to rely more heavily on hearing.

What we see

The stimulus for vision is light; even cats and other animals famous for their ability to get around in the dark need *some* light to see. Visible light may come from the sun or other stars or from light bulbs. It is also reflected off of objects. Light travels in the form of waves, and the way we see the world—our sensory experience—is affected by the characteristics of these waves:

   1. **Hue**, the dimension of visual experience specified by the various names of colors (red, blue, and so forth), is related to the wavelength of light—that is, to the distance between the crests of a wave. Shorter waves tend to be seen as violet and blue, and longer ones tend to be seen as orange and red. (We say ''tend to'' because other factors also affect color perception, as we will explain later.) The sun pro-

selective attention *The focusing of attention on selected aspects of the environment and blocking out of others.*
hue *The dimension of visual experience specified by the various color names and related to the wavelength of light.*

duces white light, a mixture of all the visible wavelengths. Sometimes, though, drops of moisture in the air act like a prism. They separate the sun's white light into the colors of the visible spectrum, and we are treated to a rainbow.

2. Brightness is the dimension of visual experience related to the amount, or intensity, of the light that an object emits or reflects. Intensity corresponds to the amplitude (maximum height) of the wave. Generally speaking, the more light an object reflects, the brighter it appears. Brightness is also affected by wavelength: Yellows appear brighter than reds and blues when physical intensities are actually equal. (For this reason, many fire departments have switched from red engines to yellow ones.)

3. Saturation (colorfulness) is the dimension of visual experience related to the **complexity of light**—that is, to how wide or narrow the range of wavelengths is. When light contains only a single wavelength it is said to be "pure," and the resulting color is said to be completely saturated. At the other extreme is white light, which lacks any color and is completely unsaturated. In nature, pure light is extremely rare. Usually we sense a mixture of wavelengths, and we see colors that are duller and paler than completely saturated ones. The wider the range of wavelengths (that is, the more complex the mixture of wavelengths), the less saturated the color.

Note that hue, brightness, and saturation are all *psychological* dimensions of visual experience, whereas wavelength, intensity, and complexity are *physical* properties of the visual stimulus (that is, of light).

Eyeing the world

Light enters the visual system through the eye, a wonderfully complex and delicate structure that is often compared, rather loosely, to a camera. As you read this section, examine Figure 5.3. Notice that the front part of the eye is covered by the transparent *cornea*. The cornea protects the eye and bends incoming light rays toward a *lens* located behind it. A camera lens works by moving closer to or farther from the opening. However, the lens of the eye works by subtly changing its shape, becoming more or less curved to focus light from objects that are close by or far away. The amount of light that gets into the eye is controlled by muscles in the *iris*,

brightness *Lightness or luminance; the dimension of visual experience related to the amount of light emitted from or reflected by an object.*

saturation *Vividness or purity of color; the dimension of visual experience related to the complexity of light waves.*

complexity (of light) *Refers to the number of different wavelengths contained in light from a particular source.*

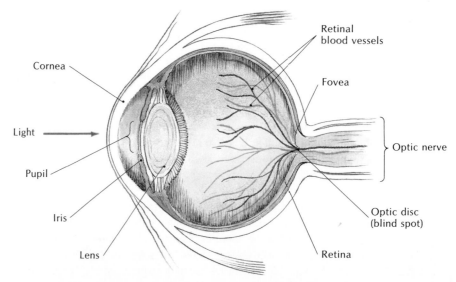

FIGURE 5.3

Major structures of the eye
Light passes through the pupil and lens and is focused on the retina at the back of the eye. The point of sharpest vision is at the fovea.

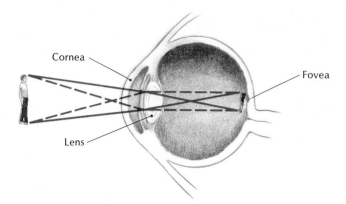

Cornea

Fovea

Lens

FIGURE 5.4

The retinal image
When we look at an object, the light pattern focused on the retina is upside down. René Descartes was probably the first person to demonstrate this fact. He took an ox's eye, cut a piece from the back of it, and replaced the piece with paper. When he held the eye up to the light, he saw an upside-down image of the room on the paper! Retinal images are also mirror-reversed; light from the right side of an object hits the left side of the retina, and vice versa.

the part of the eye that gives it color. The iris surrounds the round opening, or *pupil*, of the eye. When you enter a dim room, the pupil widens, or dilates, to let more light in. When you emerge into bright sunlight, the pupil gets smaller, allowing less light in. You can easily observe these changes by watching your eyes in a mirror as you change the lighting.

The visual receptors are located in the back of the eye, or **retina**. The retina is actually an extension of the brain. In a developing embryo, it forms from tissue that extends out from the brain rather than from tissue that is destined to form other parts of the eye. The lens of the eye focuses light on the retina. As Figure 5.4 shows, the result is an upside-down image (which can actually be seen with an instrument used by eye specialists). Light from the top of the visual field stimulates light-sensitive receptor cells in the bottom part of the retina, and vice versa. The brain interprets this upside-down pattern of stimulation as something that is right side up.

About 120 to 125 million receptors in the retina are long and narrow and are called **rods**. Another 7 or 8 million receptors are cone-shaped and are called, appropriately enough, **cones**. The center of the retina, or *fovea*, contains only cones, clustered densely together. Vision is sharpest at the fovea. From the center to the periphery, the ratio of rods to cones increases, and at the outer edges, there are virtually no cones.

Rods are more sensitive to light than cones are. They enable us to see in dim light or at night. Since they occupy the outer edges of the retina, they also handle side vision. That is why you can sometimes see a star from the corner of your eye although it is invisible when you gaze straight at it. But rods cannot distinguish different wavelengths and therefore are not sensitive to color. That is why it is often hard to distinguish colors clearly in dim light. The cones, on the other hand, are differentially sensitive to specific wavelengths of light and allow us to see colors. However, the cones need plenty of light to respond. They don't help us much when we are trying to find a seat in a darkened movie theater.

Speaking of darkened movie theaters, we have all noticed that it takes some time for our eyes to adjust fully to the darkness. This process of **dark adaptation**, which involves chemical changes in the rods and cones, actually occurs in two phases. The cones adapt quickly, within ten minutes or so, but never become very sensitive to the dim illumination. The rods adapt more slowly, taking twenty minutes or longer, but are ultimately much more sensitive. After the first phase of adaptation, you can see better but not well; after the second phase, your vision is as good as it will get.

Rods and cones are connected by synapses to *bipolar neurons*, which in turn communicate with neurons called **ganglion cells** (see Figure 5.5 on the next page). Usually a single cone communicates (via a bipolar neuron) with a single ganglion

retina *A membrane lining the back of the eyeball's interior that contains the receptors for vision.*
rods *Visual receptors that respond to dim light but are not involved in color vision.*
cones *Visual receptors involved in color vision.*
dark adaptation *A process by which visual receptors become maximally sensitive to dim light.*
ganglion cells *Neurons in the retina of the eye that gather information from receptor cells (by way of intermediate bipolar cells); their axons make up the optic nerve.*

The structures of the retina

For clarity, all cells in this drawing are greatly exaggerated in size. Notice that in order to reach the receptors for vision (the rods and cones), light must pass through the ganglion and bipolar cells as well as the blood vessels that nourish them. Normally we do not see the shadow cast by this network of cells and blood vessels. It always falls on the same place on the retina, and such stabilized images are not sensed (see text). But when an eye doctor shines a moving light into your eye, the treelike shadow of the blood vessels falls on different regions of the retina and you may see it—a rather eerie experience.

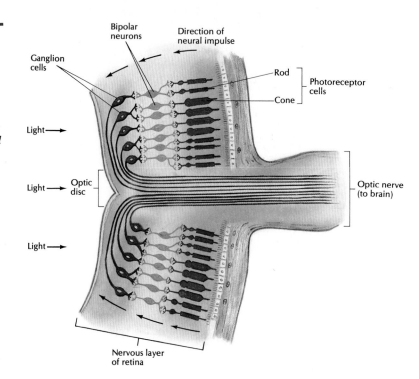

cell; it has a "private line." Rods, in contrast, must communicate via a "party line." That is, whole groups of rods, covering a particular area of the retina, send their messages to a single ganglion cell. (This is an example of the kind of sensory encoding we discussed earlier.)

The axons of the ganglion cells converge to form the *optic nerve*, which carries information out through the back of the eye and on to the brain. Where the optic nerve leaves the eye, at the *optic disc*, there are no rods or cones. The absence of receptors produces a blind spot in the field of vision. Normally we are unaware of the blind spot because (1) the image projected on the spot is hitting a different, "nonblind" spot in the other eye; (2) our eyes move so fast that we can pick up the complete image; and (3) the brain tends to fill in the gap. However, you can find your own blind spot by following the instructions in Figure 5.6.

Why the visual system is not a camera

Because the eye is often compared with a camera, it is easy to assume that the visual world is made up of a mosaic of dots, as in a photograph. But unlike a camera, the visual system is not a passive recorder of the external world. Instead of simply registering spots of light and dark, neurons in the system build up a picture of the world by detecting its meaningful features.

Simple features of the environment, such as spots of light and dark, are coded in the ganglion cells and an area in the thalamus of the brain. In mammals, more complex features are coded in special **feature detector** cells in the visual cortex. This fact was first demonstrated by David Hubel and Torsten Wiesel (1962, 1968), who painstakingly recorded impulses from individual cells in the brains of cats and monkeys. (In 1981, they received a Nobel Prize for their work.) Hubel and Wiesel found that different neurons were sensitive to different patterns projected on a screen in front of the animal's eyes. Most cells responded maximally to moving or

feature detectors *Cells in the visual cortex that are sensitive to specific features of the environment.*

FIGURE 5.6
Find your blind spot
The optic disk of the retina, where the fibers of the optic nerve leave the eye, has no visual receptors and is therefore a blind spot. To find the blind spot in your left eye, close your right eye and look at the magician. Then slowly move the book alternately toward and away from you. The rabbit should disappear when the book is between 9 and 12 inches from your eye.

stationary lines that were oriented in a particular direction and located in a particular part of the visual field. One type of cell might fire most rapidly in response to a horizontal line in the lower right part of the visual field, another to a diagonal line at a certain angle in the upper left part of the visual field. In the real world, such features make up the boundaries and edges of objects.

The image that reaches the brain, then, is not a mosaic of light and dark dots but a combination of lines and angles that the brain somehow integrates into a pattern that makes sense. The process of integration is still not clear to scientists, but progress is being made. Many researchers now think the important visual features of the environment are variations in brightness over broad areas of space rather than edges at a particular point. When researchers present an observer with gratings (series of light and dark bars), some cortical cells respond to a series of many narrow stripes, and others respond to a series of fewer, wider stripes (DeValois & DeValois, 1980). Recent studies also suggest that it is not only the frequency of a cell's firing that contains information but also the pattern or rhythm with which it fires (Richmond et al., 1987). Clearly, the nervous system is extraordinarily "smart," searching for and analyzing separate scraps of sensory information and then putting all the bits and pieces together to construct an overall picture.

How we see colors

For 200 years, psychologists and physiologists have been trying to figure out why we see the world in living color. One approach, the *Young-Helmholtz theory*, or **trichromatic theory**, assumed that there were three mechanisms in the visual system, each especially sensitive to a certain range of wavelengths, and that these interacted in some way to produce all the different color sensations. Another, the **opponent-process theory**, assumed that the visual system treated various pairs of colors as opposing or antagonistic. Modern research suggests that both views are valid, but each explains a different level of processing.

One level of processing occurs in the retina. The retina contains three different types of cones. One type responds maximally to blue (or more precisely, to the band of wavelengths that gives rise to the subjective experience of blue), another to green, and a third to red. The hundreds of colors we see result from the combined activity of these three types of cones.

Total color blindness is usually due to a genetic problem that causes cones of the retina to be absent or malfunctional. The visual world then consists of black, white, and shades of gray. Many animal species are totally color-blind, but the condition is very rare in human beings. Most "color-blind" people are actually *color deficient*. Usually the person is unable to distinguish red and green; the world is painted in shades of blue, yellow, and gray. In rarer instances, a person may be blind to blue and yellow and see only reds, greens, and grays. Color deficiency is

trichromatic theory *A theory that proposes three mechanisms in the visual system, each sensitive to a certain range of wavelengths; their interaction is assumed to produce all the different experiences of hue.*
opponent-process theory (of color) *A theory that assumes that the visual system treats various pairs of colors as opposing or antagonistic.*

FIGURE 5.7

Change of heart
To produce a negative after-image, stare at the black dot in the middle of the heart for at least 20 seconds. Then shift your gaze to a white piece of paper or white wall. You should see an image of a red heart with a blue border.

found in about 8 percent of white men, 5 percent of Asian men, and 3 percent of black and Native-American men (Sekuler & Blake, 1985). Because of the way the condition is inherited, it is very rare in women. Fortunately, color deficiency does not interfere drastically with daily living. A person who is blind to red and green can respond correctly to traffic lights, for instance, because the lights differ in position and brightness as well as hue.

The second stage of color processing occurs in ganglion cells and in neurons in the thalamus of the brain. Some of these cells respond to short wavelengths but are inhibited from firing by long wavelengths, and others show the reverse pattern. Such cells are known as **opponent-process cells** (DeValois, 1960; DeValois & DeValois, 1975; Hurvich & Jameson, 1974). Certain opponent-process cells respond in opposite fashion to red and green; they fire in response to one and turn off in response to the other. Others respond in opposite fashion to blue and yellow. (A third system responds in opposite fashion to white and black and thus yields information about brightness.) The net result is a color *code* that is passed along to the higher visual centers. Opposing colors cannot be coded at the same time, which is why we never see a reddish-green or a bluish-yellow.

Opponent-process cells that are *inhibited* by a particular color seem to produce a burst of firing when the color is removed, just as they would if the opposing color were present. Similarly, cells that *fire* in response to a color stop firing when the color is removed, just as they would if the opposing color were present. These facts seem to explain why we are susceptible to **negative afterimages** when we stare at a particular hue—why we see, for instance, red after staring at green (Figure 5.7). There is a sort of neural rebound effect: The cells that switch on or off to signal ''red'' send the opposite signal (''green'') when the red is removed. If you stare intently at the green screen of a computer for a long time, you may occasionally see the world through rose-colored glasses when you turn your gaze away—a demonstration of the opponent process in action.

Unfortunately, two-stage theories do not yet provide a complete explanation of color vision. The wavelengths reflected by an object do not by themselves account for whether we see the object as mauve or magenta, purple or puce. Edwin Land (1959), inventor of the Polaroid camera, has shown that the perceived color of an object depends on the wavelengths reflected by *everything around it*. Thus you never see a good, strong red unless there are other objects around that reflect the green and blue part of the spectrum. Land has worked out precise rules that predict exactly how an object will appear, given the wavelengths reflected by all the objects in a scene. So far, however, researchers have not been able to explain fully how the *brain* follows these rules.

opponent-process cells
Cells in the visual system that fire in response to one color and are inhibited from firing by another.
negative afterimage *A visual image that persists after a visual stimulus is withdrawn and that has features that contrast with those of the stimulus (e.g., a contrasting color).*

Hearing

Like vision, hearing, or **audition**, provides a vital link with the environment around us. The consequences of hearing loss go beyond the obvious loss of auditory information. We use hearing to monitor our own speech; when deafness is present at birth or occurs early in life, speech development is hindered. Deaf people sometimes feel socially isolated because social relationships rely so heavily on hearing others.

What we hear

The stimulus for sound is a wave of pressure created when an object vibrates. The vibration causes molecules in a transmitting substance to move together and apart. This movement produces variations in pressure that radiate in all directions. The transmitting substance is usually air, but sound waves also travel through water and solids. That is why, in westerns, Indians can be seen putting an ear to the ground to find out if the cavalry is coming.

As with vision, certain aspects of our auditory experience are related in a predictable way to physical characteristics of the stimulus, in this case, a sound wave:

1. **Loudness** is the dimension of auditory experience related to the intensity of a wave's pressure. Intensity corresponds to the amplitude (maximum height) of the wave. The more energy pushing the wave, the higher it is at its peak. Loudness is also affected by pitch (how high or low a sound is). If low and high sounds produce waves with equal amplitudes, the low sound may seem quieter.

Sound intensity is measured in units called decibels (dB). A decibel is one-tenth of a bel, a unit named for Alexander Graham Bell, the inventor of the telephone. The average absolute threshold of hearing in human beings is zero decibels. Decibels are not equally distant, as inches on a ruler are. A sound of 60 decibels (such as that of a sewing machine) is not one-fifth louder than one at 50 decibels (such as that of a refrigerator) but ten times louder. Table 5.3 gives the intensity in decibels of some common sounds.

2. **Pitch** is the dimension of auditory experience related to the **frequency** of the sound wave and, to some extent, its intensity. Frequency refers to how rapidly the air (or other medium) vibrates, that is, the number of times per second the wave cycles through a peak and a low point. One cycle per second is known as 1 Hertz (Hz). The human ear detects frequencies in the range of 16 Hz (the lowest note on a pipe organ) to 20,000 Hz (the scraping of a grasshopper's legs). Many older people cannot hear very high frequencies because some receptor cells in the ear are lost with age.

3. **Timbre** is the distinguishing quality of a sound. It is the dimension of auditory experience related to the complexity of the sound wave—to how wide or narrow a range of frequencies the wave contains. A pure tone consists of only one frequency, but in nature pure tones are extremely rare. Usually what we hear is a complex wave consisting of several subwaves with different frequencies. A particular combination of frequencies results in a particular timbre. Timbre is what makes a note played on a flute, which produces relatively pure tones, sound different from the same note played on an oboe, which produces very complex sounds.

When many frequencies are present but are not in harmony, we hear noise. When all the frequencies of the sound spectrum occur, they produce a hissing sound called *white noise*. White noise is named by analogy to white light, because its physical basis is similar. White noise includes all frequencies of the sound spectrum, and white light includes all wavelengths of the visible light spectrum.

audition *The sense of hearing.*

loudness *The dimension of auditory experience related to the intensity of a pressure wave.*

pitch *The dimension of auditory experience related to the frequency of a pressure wave; height or depth of a tone.*

frequency (of a sound wave) *The number of times per second that a sound wave cycles through a peak and low point.*

timbre *The distinguishing quality of a sound; the dimension of auditory experience related to the complexity of the pressure wave.*

TABLE 5.5
SOUND INTENSITY LEVELS IN THE ENVIRONMENT

The following decibel levels apply at typical working distances. Each ten-point increase on the decibel scale represents a tenfold increase in sound intensity over the previous level. Even some everyday noises can be hazardous to hearing if exposure goes on for too long a time.

Typical Level (Decibels)	Example	Dangerous Time Exposure
0	Lowest sound audible to human ear	
30	Quiet library, soft whisper	
40	Quiet office, living room, bedroom away from traffic	
50	Light traffic at a distance, refrigerator, gentle breeze	
60	Air conditioner at 20 feet, conversation, sewing machine	
70	Busy traffic, office tabulators, noisy restaurant (constant exposure)	Critical level begins
80	Subway, heavy city traffic, alarm clock at 2 feet, factory noise	More than 8 hours
90	Truck traffic, noisy home appliances, shop tools, lawnmower	Less than 8 hours
100	Chain saw, boiler shop, pneumatic drill	Less than 2 hours
120	Rock concert in front of speakers, sandblasting, thunderclap	Immediate danger
140	Gunshot blast, jet plane at 50 feet	Any length of exposure time is dangerous
180	Rocket launching pad	Hearing loss inevitable

SOURCE: Reprinted with permission from the American Academy of Otolaryngology—Head and Neck Surgery, Washington, D.C.

QUICK ■ QUIZ

For each of the following *physical* dimensions of visual or auditory stimuli, see if you can name the corresponding *psychological* one.

1. wavelength of light: _____
2. amount or intensity of light: _____
3. complexity of light: _____
4. intensity of a sound wave: _____
5. frequency of a sound wave: _____
6. complexity of a sound wave: _____

Answers:

1. hue 2. brightness 3. saturation 4. loudness 5. pitch 6. timbre

An ear on the world

As Figure 5.8 shows, the ear has an outer, a middle, and an inner section. The soft, funnel-shaped outer ear is well designed to collect sound waves, but hearing would still be quite good without it. The essential parts of the ear are hidden from view, inside the head.

A sound wave passes into the outer ear and through an inch-long canal to strike an oval-shaped membrane called the *eardrum*. The eardrum is so sensitive that it can respond to the movement of a single molecule! A sound wave causes it to vibrate with the same frequency and amplitude as the wave itself. This vibration is passed along to three tiny bones in the middle ear, the smallest bones in the human body. The bones move, one after the other, which has the effect of intensifying the force of the vibration. The third bone pushes on a membrane that opens into the inner ear.

The actual organ of hearing (the *organ of Corti*) is a chamber inside the snail-shaped **cochlea**, within the inner ear. This organ plays the same role in hearing that the retina plays in vision. It contains the all-important receptor cells, which in this case look like bristles and are called hair cells. The hair cells are embedded in the rubbery *basilar membrane*, which stretches across the interior of the cochlea. When pressure reaches the cochlea, it causes wavelike motions in fluid within the

cochlea (KOCK-lee-uh) *A snail-shaped, fluid-filled organ in the inner ear, containing the receptors for hearing.*

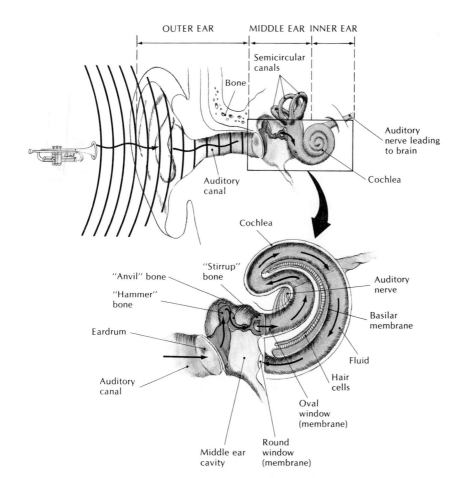

OUTER EAR   MIDDLE EAR   INNER EAR

Semicircular canals

Bone

Auditory nerve leading to brain

Auditory canal

Cochlea

Cochlea

"Anvil" bone

"Stirrup" bone

"Hammer" bone

Auditory nerve

Eardrum

Basilar membrane

Auditory canal

Fluid

Hair cells

Oval window (membrane)

Middle ear cavity

Round window (membrane)

FIGURE 5.8

Major structures of the ear

Sound waves are collected by the outer ear and channeled down the auditory canal, causing the eardrum to vibrate. These vibrations are then passed along to the tiny bones of the middle ear. Movement of these bones intensifies the force of the vibrations and funnels them to a small membrane separating the middle and inner ear. The receptor cells for hearing (hair cells) are located in a small organ within the snail-shaped cochlea. The receptors initiate nerve impulses that travel along the auditory nerve to the brain.

The spiraled interior of a guinea pig's cochlea, shown here, is almost identical to that of a human cochlea.

cochlea's interior. These motions push on the membrane in which the hair cells are embedded, causing it to move in a wavelike motion.

Just above the hair cells is yet another membrane. As the hair cells rise and fall, their tips brush against it and they bend. This causes the hair cells to initiate a signal that is passed along to the *auditory nerve*. The auditory nerve then carries the message to the brain. The particular pattern of hair cell movement is affected by the manner in which the basilar membrane moves. The pattern determines which neurons fire and how rapidly they fire, and the resulting code determines the sort of sound we hear.

Could anyone ever imagine such a complex and odd arrangement of bristles, fluids, and snail shells if it didn't already exist?

Other Senses

Psychologists have paid special attention to vision and audition because of their importance to survival. They are beginning to pay more attention to the "other senses," though, as awareness of how these senses contribute to our lives grows and as new ways are found to study them.

Taste: Savory sensations

Taste, or **gustation**, occurs because chemicals stimulate receptors in the mouth. These receptors, some 10,000 of them, are located primarily on the tongue, but there are also some in the throat and on the roof of the mouth. If you look at your tongue in a mirror you will notice many tiny bumps. Each bump contains about 245 **taste buds**. These buds are commonly referred to as the taste receptors. The actual receptor cells, however, are inside the buds, 15 or 20 to a bud.

There appear to be only four basic tastes: salty, sour, bitter, and sweet, each produced by a different type of chemical. The four tastes are associated with different receptors, and bitterness has multiple receptor types (McBurney, 1978). As you can see in Figure 5.9, different parts of the tongue are particularly sensitive to particular tastes. When you bite into an egg or a piece of bread or an orange, its unique flavor is composed of some combination of the four basic taste types. According to one theory, the four basic tastes are really points on a continuum, just as colors are. According to another, the four tastes are separate and distinct, each associated with a particular type of nerve fiber. The physiological evidence so far has not resolved the issue.

gustation *The sense of taste.*

taste buds *Nests of taste receptor cells.*

FIGURE 5.9

Taste receptors

(a) Various areas of the tongue are differentially sensitive to the four basic tastes, at least when the solution being tested is weak. (b) An enlarged view of the tongue's surface. (c) An enlarged view of a single taste bud.

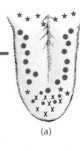

(a)

x Salty   ★ Bitter
• Sweet   ● Sour

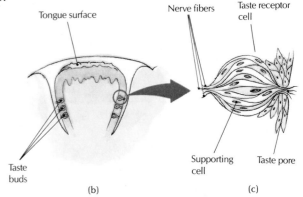

(b)

(c)

Human beings are born with a sweet tooth, to the chagrin of dieters everywhere. We also seem to have a natural dislike for bitter substances, possibly because many poisonous substances are bitter. But taste is also a matter of culture. Although raw oysters, raw smoked salmon (lox), and raw herring are appetizing to many North Americans, for example, other forms of raw seafood, popular in Japan, have only recently gained a following here.

Individual tastes also vary. The French have a saying, "Chacun à son goût" (literally, each to his own taste). Why do some people within a culture gobble up a dish that makes others in the same culture turn green? Experience undoubtedly plays a role. As we will see in Chapter 6, one can acquire a taste or a distaste for a particular food. Genetic differences probably also make people more or less sensitive to the chemicals in particular foods (Bartoshuk, 1980). Some people experience a bitter taste from saccharin, but others do not; some people notice that water tastes sweet immediately after they eat artichokes, but others taste no difference.

The attractiveness of a particular food is also affected by its temperature and texture. As Goldilocks found out, a cold bowl of porridge isn't nearly as delicious as one that is properly heated. And any peanut butter fan will tell you that chunky and smooth peanut butters just don't taste the same. Even more important for taste is a food's odor. Subtle flavors, such as chocolate and vanilla, are more accurately called smells than tastes, since they would have little taste if we could not smell them (see Figure 5.10). The dependence of taste on smell explains why you have trouble tasting your food when you have a stuffy nose.

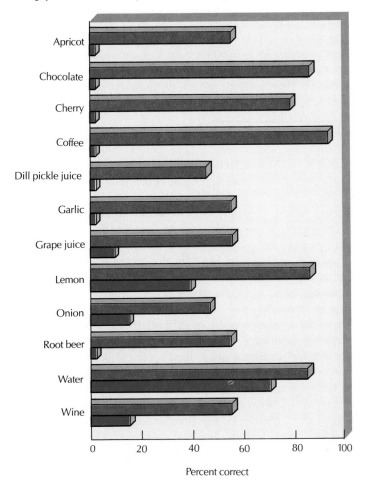

Percent correct

FIGURE 5.10

Taste test
The red bars show the percentages of people who could identify a substance dropped on their tongues when they were able to smell it. The blue bars show the percentages who could identify a substance when they were prevented from smelling it. (From Mozell et al., 1969.)

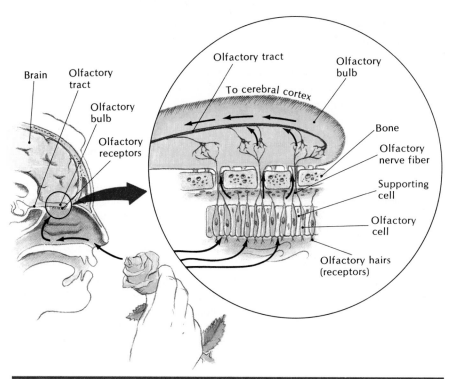

FIGURE 5.11

Receptors for smell
Airborne chemical molecules (vapors) enter the nose and circulate through the nasal cavity, where the smell receptors are located. Sniffing draws more vapors into the nose and speeds their circulation. Vapors can also reach the nasal cavity through the mouth by way of a passageway from the throat.

Smell: The sense of scent

The receptors for smell, or **olfaction**, are specialized neurons embedded in a tiny path of mucous membrane in the upper part of the nasal passage (see Figure 5.11). These receptors—about 5 million of them in each nasal cavity—respond to chemical molecules in the air. Certain types of molecules seem to fit certain receptors the way a key fits a lock. Somehow their effects combine to yield the yeasty smell of freshly baked bread or the spicy fragrance of a eucalyptus tree. But the neural code for smell, like that for taste, remains to be discovered. One complicating factor is that there are many words to describe smells (rotten, burned, musky, fruity, spicy, flowery, resinous, putrid . . .), but no one has been able to show that any particular set of smells is "basic."

Many animals depend on smell for survival; they could not find food or detect predators without it. Smell is less vital for human beings but still important. We sniff out danger by smelling smoke, food spoilage, or poison gases. A loss of sensitivity to odors can indicate infection or disease. There is also some evidence that human beings, like many other animals, produce **pheromones**, chemical substances that provoke a behavioral response in others because of their scent. Biologist Winnifred Cutler, chemist George Preti, and their colleagues noted that women who have regular sexual activity with men seem more likely than other women to have normal menstrual cycles. To check whether pheromones might be responsible, the researchers collected underarm secretions from men, diluted them in alcohol,

olfaction *The sense of smell.*

pheromone *A chemical substance that, when released by an organism, influences the physiology or behavior of other members of the same species.*

and swabbed them three times a week on the upper lips of seven women with unusually long or short menstrual cycles. Over the 14 weeks of the study, the women's cycles became more regular, averaging 29.5 days, while the cycles of women treated with alcohol alone did not change (Cutler et al., 1986). In a similar study, the researchers swabbed the upper lips of women with the underarm secretions of other women (Preti et al., 1986). They found that after only a few months the treated women's menstrual periods tended to become synchronized, while those of control subjects did not. Preti and Cutler suspect that androstenol, a steroid present in human sweat, was responsible. These findings may explain earlier observations of menstrual synchrony among women living in close quarters (McClintock, 1971).

Human pheromones, then, may play a role in the regulation of reproductive cycles. (We say ''may'' because these studies need to be replicated.) In many animals, pheromones also play a role in *sexual* behavior. A female cat in heat will attract, through scent, all the unneutered tomcats in the neighborhood. Do pheromones also increase the sexual allure of human beings? Some perfume companies are gambling that the answer is yes. A few years ago, Jovan, Inc., an American perfume company, brought out a new scent that it said would ''trigger an intense magnetic reaction'' in persons of the other sex. The perfume contained a derivative of androstenone (similar to androstenol). This substance is found not only in human sweat but also in a boar's testes and saliva. Sows find it appealing, which may explain why pigs are used to locate truffles, a fungus that grows beneath the ground and is esteemed by food lovers: Truffles also contain androstenone (Maugh, 1982).

It is a big leap, however, from pigs to people. There has been little well-controlled research on pheromones and sexual behavior in human beings, and the few studies that have been done have found human responses to be highly variable (Labows, 1980). Even monkeys do not respond automatically or inevitably to pheromones, and in human beings, context is all-important. Thus the smell of sex may be perceived as pleasantly musky during a romantic interlude, but the same smells in the laboratory may seem merely unpleasant. This doesn't mean that natural or learned reactions to smells play no role at all in sex; when people completely lose their ability to smell, they sometimes show a decline in sexual interest (Monmaney, 1987). But there is no evidence that eau de pheromone can *compel* human sexual behavior, and it probably cannot reliably improve the ''chemistry'' between people. Human beings are generally more affected sexually by what the brain learns and the eyes see than what the nose knows.

Odor preferences, in any case, are not at all universal. In some societies, people use rancid fat as a hair pomade, but anyone in our culture who did so would quickly have a social problem. Again, context is important. The same chemicals that contribute to unpleasant body odors and bad breath contribute to the bouquet and flavor of cheese (Labows, 1980). There are also individual differences in sensitivity to various smells. Almost half of all people cannot smell human urine. Over a third cannot smell malty odors. Smaller percentages of people cannot detect the smell of sperm, musky odors, fishy smells, or sweaty smells (Amoore, 1977).

Pheromones increase sex appeal—in pigs. Perfume companies are prepared to generalize from pigs to people, but should the rest of us? Would you buy a pheromone-based perfume that claimed to make you irresistible?

Senses of the skin

The skin's usefulness is more than just skin deep. Besides protecting our innards, our 2 square yards of skin help us identify objects and establish intimacy with others. By providing a boundary between ourselves and everything else, the skin also gives us a sense of ourselves as distinct from the environment.

Smell has not only evolutionary but cultural significance. These pilgrims in Matsuyama, Japan, are purifying themselves with holy incense for good luck and health. Incense has always been an important commodity; the gifts of the Magi, after all, included frankincense and myrrh.

The skin senses include touch (or pressure), warmth, cold, and pain. At one time it was thought that these four senses were associated with four distinct kinds of receptors, or "end organs," but this view is now in doubt. Although there are spots on the skin that are particularly sensitive to cold, warmth, pressure, and pain, no simple, straightforward correspondence between the four sensations and the various types of receptors has been found (Schneider & Tarshis, 1986). Recent research has concentrated more on the neural codes involved in the skin senses than on the receptors themselves.

Pain, which is both a skin sense and an internal sense, has come under special scrutiny. Pain differs from other senses in an important way: When the stimulus producing it is removed, the sensation may continue. Chronic pain disrupts lives, keeps people from their jobs, and causes depression and despair. (For ways of coping with pain, see "Taking Psychology with You.")

According to the **gate-control theory** of pain, introduced in the 1960s, the experience of pain depends partly on whether pain impulses get past a "gate" in the spinal cord and thus reach the brain (Melzack & Wall, 1965). The gate is made up of neurons that can either transmit or block pain-related information. According to the theory, pain fibers (like other kinds of fibers in the nervous system) are always active. When injury to tissue occurs, certain small-diameter fibers open the gate. Normally, though, the gate is closed, either by impulses coming into the spinal cord from large-diameter fibers that respond to pressure or by signals from the brain itself. Chronic pain occurs when disease, infection, or injury damages the fibers that ordinarily close the gate, and pain messages are able to reach the brain unchecked.

The gate-control theory has been used to help explain how the ancient Chinese practice of *acupuncture* works to relieve or prevent pain. In acupuncture, very thin needles are inserted at particular points on the skin. Acupuncture is sometimes used in China as an anesthetic in childbirth and major surgery. Patients remain awake and cheerful, even during head and abdominal operations. Controlled studies in the

gate-control theory *The theory that the experience of pain depends in part on whether pain impulses get past a neurological "gate" in the spinal cord and thus reach the brain.*

United States show that more than ''mere suggestion'' is at work. It may be that the acupuncture needles initiate neural impulses in the brain that close the spinal pain gates (Melzack & Dennis, 1978).

The gate-control theory may also help explain the strange phenomenon of *phantom limb pain*. People who have lost an arm or leg sometimes report excruciating pain that seems to come from the missing limb. Since there is no limb, there are no sense receptors for the pain, yet the pain can be overwhelming. Phantom limb pain may occur because the impulses that normally inhibit pain by closing or partially closing the ''gate'' are eliminated by the amputation. Since there are no inhibiting impulses, any remaining pain fibers near the spinal cord are able to get their messages through. Another possibility is that once pain-producing activity begins in the brain, it can continue on its own without further impulses from the spinal cord (Melzack & Loeser, 1978).

Recent work shows that the physiology of pain is far more complicated than thought two decades ago, when the gate-control theory was first proposed. The occurrence of pain involves the release of several chemicals at the site of tissue damage, including a neurotransmitter called *substance P*. These chemicals cause pain nerves to fire and promote inflammation. The suppression of pain involves the release of endorphins in the brain (see Chapter 3). One effect of the endorphins is to prevent pain fibers from releasing substance P (Jessel & Iversen, 1979; Ruda, 1982). However, in its general outline, the gate-control theory has held up well. The theory correctly predicts that mild pressure, as well as other types of stimulation, can interfere with severe or protracted pain by closing the spinal gate, either directly or by means of signals sent from the brain. When we vigorously rub a banged elbow, or apply ice packs, heat, or mustard plasters to injuries, we are acting on this principle. The idea of fighting fire with fire in order to close the pain gate has led to the development of a pain relief device that delivers small amounts of electric current into certain spinal cord nerves. This device can actually be installed under the skin, and patients can control the amount of stimulation themselves.

Much remains to be learned, not only about the four basic skin sensations, but also about itch, tickle, sensitivity to vibration, the sensation of wetness, and different types of pain. Researchers are trying to break the neural codes that explain why gently pricking pain spots with a needle produces itch; why lightly touching adjacent pressure spots in rapid succession produces tickle; and why the simultaneous stimulation of warm and cold spots produces not a lukewarm sensation but the sensation of heat. Decoding the messages of the skin senses will eventually tell us how we are able to distinguish sandpaper from velvet and glue from grease.

The environment within

We usually think of our senses as pipelines to the ''outside'' world, but two senses keep us informed about the movements of our own bodies. **Kinesthesis** tells us where our various body parts are located and lets us know when they move. It uses pain and pressure receptors located in the muscles, joints, and tendons (tissues that connect muscles to bones). Without kinesthesis you could not touch your finger to your nose with your eyes shut. In fact, you would have trouble with any voluntary movement. Think of how hard walking is when your leg has ''fallen asleep'' or how clumsy chewing is when a dentist has numbed your jaw with an anesthetic.

Equilibrium, or the sense of balance, gives us information about our bodies as a whole. Along with vision and touch, it lets us know whether we are standing upright or on our heads and tells us when we are falling or rotating. Equilibrium

kinesthesis (KIN-es-THEE-sis) *The sense of body position and movement of body parts. Also called kinesthesia.*

equilibrium *The sense of balance.*

Olympic gold medalist Greg Louganis executes a winning dive that requires precise positioning of each part of his body. "I have a good kinesthetic awareness," says Louganis, with some understatement. "I am aware of where I am in space."

relies primarily on three **semicircular canals** in the inner ear (see Figure 5.8 on page 173 again). These thin tubes are filled with fluid that moves and presses on hairlike receptors whenever the head rotates. The receptors initiate messages that travel through a part of the auditory nerve that is not involved in hearing.

Normally, kinesthesis and equilibrium work together to give us a sense of our own physical reality, something we take utterly for granted but shouldn't. Oliver Sacks (1985) tells the heartbreaking story of a young British woman named Christina who suffered irreversible damage to her kinesthetic nerve fibers because of a mysterious inflammation. At first Christina was as floppy as a rag doll; she could not sit up, walk, or stand. Then, slowly, she learned to do these things, relying on visual cues and sheer will power. But her movements remained unnatural; she had to grasp a fork with painful force or she would drop it. More important, despite her remaining sensitivity to light touch on the skin, she could no longer experience herself as physically embodied: "It's like something's been scooped right out of me, right at the centre. . . ."

With equilibrium, we come, as it were, to the end of our senses. We have seen that the gathering of sensory data about the external and internal world is far from straightforward. We are about to consider processes that are, if anything, even more mysterious: the processes of perception.

Our Perceptual Powers

semicircular canals *Sense organs in the inner ear that contribute to equilibrium by responding to rotation of the head.*

We do not see a retinal image. We do not hear a combination of brushlike tufts bending and swaying in the dark recesses of the cochlea. Sensory phenomena are merely grist for the mill of the mind, which actively *constructs* the world from the often fragmentary data of the senses. One hundred sensory signals reach the brain each second. In the brain, where we ultimately see, hear, and feel pain, those signals are combined to produce a model of the world at that moment. As Figure 5.12 illustrates, we do not merely take in an image, we also *interpret* it.

So great are the brain's powers of interpretation that we can even adjust to an abnormal image. During the past century, a number of psychologists have fitted themselves with special glasses that distort the world—for example, by transposing left and right or by turning the visual field upside down (I. Kohler, 1962). They have found that in a matter of days or weeks the person can carry on as usual and even ride a bicycle. The brain has learned to apply new rules for interpreting the retinal image.

In the following sections, we will see how our magnificent powers of perception enable us to decipher reality accurately and effortlessly—and why we also sometimes make mistakes.

Conscious and nonconscious perception

Suppose you want to know whether a passing automobile is a Toyota or a Nissan. Not being a car buff, you examine the car closely, looking for characteristics that will allow you to recognize its make based on your knowledge of Toyotas and Nissans. You are perfectly aware of what you are doing; it is a conscious process.

Many aspects of perception, however, occur outside of awareness. As we saw earlier, before something can be recognized or identified, its basic features must be analyzed. In the case of vision, we must make out edges, colors, textures, and differences in the reflectance of light. This analysis takes place without any intention or awareness on the part of the perceiver. You know automatically whether the car passing you is shiny or dull and where it begins and ends.

Research on persons blinded by damage to the visual cortex provides striking evidence for the nonconscious nature of certain basic perceptual processes. When these people are presented with a brief flash of light, they deny seeing it. But when they are asked to *guess* where the light is by pointing to it or by directing their eyes

FIGURE 5.12

Perception is meaningful
Perceptual processes actively organize and interpret data from our senses. For example, chances are that you see more than a random collection of light and dark splotches in this picture. If not, try holding the picture a little farther away from you.

toward it, they do much better than chance, though they continue to deny seeing anything (Bridgeman & Staggs, 1982). Some patients can even distinguish a vertical line from a horizontal one, or an *X* from an *O*, with better than chance accuracy. Such "blindsight" may occur because messages from the eyes reach parts of the brain other than the visual cortex, areas that control eye movements and probably handle elementary kinds of visual information.

Evidence of nonconscious perception also comes from clinical studies of people with brain damage who cannot recognize familiar faces. (Do you remember the man who mistook his wife for a hat, in Chapter 3?) When two such patients were shown photographs of familiar and unfamiliar faces, they reported no recognition of the familiar ones. But electrical conductance of the skin (a measure of autonomic nervous system arousal) changed while they were looking at the familiar pictures, indicating that some sort of primitive, nonconscious recognition was, in fact, taking place (Tranel & Damasio, 1988).

A third source of information on nonconscious processing comes from research on people anesthetized and unconscious during surgery. As many surgeons can attest, after an operation some patients show signs of having heard remarks made by doctors and nurses while the patient was still "under." Several controlled studies support these observations (Bennett, 1988; Millar & Watkinson, 1983; Stolzy, Couture, & Edmonds, 1986). In one study, researchers suggested to anesthetized patients that they later pull on an ear during a postoperative interview. On the average, the patients did so six times more often than patients in a control group, although they had no recollection of having heard the suggestion (Bennett, Davis, & Giannini, 1985). There is even evidence that therapeutic suggestions during surgery can speed and improve recovery (Evans & Richardson, 1988).

Critics point out that the anesthesia studies are open to alternate interpretations (Rymer, 1987). For example, it is possible that some patients partially emerge from an anesthetic-induced coma during surgery and begin to process sounds consciously, though they remain paralyzed and insensitive to pain. Modern anesthetics often contain chemicals that produce amnesia for the surgery to prevent lingering memories of any pain that happened to get through. Thus a remark heard *consciously* during surgery may be forgotten later. On the other hand, there is physiological evidence that the auditory nerve and auditory cortex respond to sound even when a person has lost all awareness of self and setting, so truly nonconscious perception may indeed be occurring.

For only $29.95, a "subliminal perception tape" promises to tune up your sluggish motivation. It's true that some perceptual processes occur outside of awareness, but does that mean that "subliminal" tapes can change your behavior?

Does that mean there is such a thing as "subliminal perception"? Not necessarily. The sort of nonconscious processes we have been describing involve stimuli that would be above the absolute threshold if consciously attended to. Subliminal perception refers to the ability to perceive and respond to complex messages that are too quiet to be consciously heard (in the case of hearing) or too brief or dim to be consciously seen (in the case of vision). A few psychologists believe that under carefully controlled conditions, subliminal messages do affect later behavior (Shevrin & Dickman, 1980; Silverman & Weinberger, 1985). But others question the validity of the research on which these claims rest (Balay & Shevrin, 1988), and most psychologists remain skeptical.

What about the well-publicized powers of subliminal advertising? Experiments by a commercial firm during the 1950s did suggest that advertisers could use subliminal messages to manipulate people into buying their products. But these studies were poorly designed, and later research showed that subliminal advertising was ineffective (Anastasi, 1964; George & Jennings, 1975). It is unlikely, then, that Madison Avenue can seduce us into buying soft drinks or voting for political candidates by flashing subliminal slogans on television or slipping subliminal images into magazine ads. Nor is there any evidence whatsoever that messages recorded backward on music albums—for some a subliminal scare—can affect anyone's behavior or attitudes (Vokey & Read, 1985). As for subliminal tapes that promise to help you lose weight, stop smoking, reduce stress, or find the perfect mate, any effects they have are probably due to the listener's own expectations.

Dividing up reality

To make sense of the world, we must know where one thing ends and another begins. We must separate the teacher from the podium, the piano solo from the orchestral accompaniment, the marshmallow from the hot chocolate. The process of dividing up the world occurs so rapidly and effortlessly that we take it completely for granted—until we must make out objects in a heavy fog or words in the rapid-fire conversation of someone speaking a foreign language.

The Gestalt psychologists, introduced in Chapter 1, were among the first to study how people organize the world into meaningful units and patterns. In German, *gestalt* means "pattern" or "configuration." The Gestalt psychologists' motto was "The whole is more than the sum of its parts." They observed that when we perceive something, certain properties emerge from the whole configuration that are not found in any particular component. When you watch a movie, for example, the motion you "see" is nowhere in the film, which consists of separate static frames projected at 8, 16, or 32 frames per second.

Although the Gestalt psychologists had ideas about the physiology of visual perception that are no longer accepted, many of their observations are still useful. For instance, they noted that we always organize the visual field into *figure* and *ground*. The figure stands out from the rest of the environment, which provides a formless background (see Figure 5.13). When your instructor lectures, he or she hopes that his or her voice is figure and that the hum of a passing airplane, cheers from the athletic field, and distant sounds of a construction crew are all part of the ground.

Some things stand out as figure by virtue of their intensity or size. It is hard to ignore a scream, the blinding flash of a camera, or a tidal wave approaching your piece of the beach. Unique objects also stand out, such as a banana in a bowl of oranges. Moving objects in an otherwise still environment, such as a shooting star, will usually be seen as figure. Indeed, it is hard to ignore a sudden change of any kind in the environment. Remember, our brains are geared to respond to change and contrast.

FIGURE 5.13

Figure and ground
Each of these drawings has two possible interpretations. In (a) the yellow areas may be the figure (two silhouettes) and the red area background, or the red area may be the figure (a goblet) and the yellow areas background. Because of the ambiguity, the two perceptions will probably alternate as you look at the drawing. Do you perceive the word in drawing (b)?

(a)

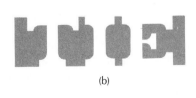

(b)

Still, selective attention, the ability to concentrate on some stimuli and filter out others, gives us some control over what we perceive as figure and ground. Suppose that during your instructor's lecture a classmate draws your attention to a buzzing fluorescent light. Until that moment, the buzz has been part of the ground, but as you turn your perceptual spotlight on it, it becomes figure. The instructor's voice fades into the background, at least momentarily.

Here are some other Gestalt strategies that the brain uses to group sensory building blocks into perceptual units:

1. *Proximity*. Things that are near each other tend to be grouped together. Thus you perceive the dots on the left as three groups of dots, not 12 separate, unrelated ones. Similarly, you perceive the pattern on the right as vertical columns of dots, not as horizontal rows:

2. *Closure*. The brain tends to fill in gaps in order to perceive complete forms. This is fortunate, since we often need to decipher less than perfect images. The following figures are easily perceived as a triangle, a face, and the letter *e*, even though none of the figures is complete:

3. *Similarity*. Things that are alike in some way tend to be perceived as belonging together. The basis of their similarity may be color, shape, size, timbre, temperature, or any other dimension. In the figure on the left, you see the circles as forming an *x*. In the one on the right, you see horizontal bars rather than vertical columns because the horizontally aligned stars share the same color:

4. *Continuity*. Lines and patterns tend to be perceived as continuing in time or space. You perceive the figure on the left as a single line partially covered by a circle rather than as two separate lines touching a circle. In the figure on the right, you see two lines, one curved and one straight, instead of two curved and two straight lines:

"A Closer Look at Human Factors Psychology" discusses how Gestalt and other perceptual principles can be used to improve the facility with which we perceive and use everyday objects.

QUICK ▪ QUIZ

The Gestalt psychologists concentrated on visual strategies, but similar ones seem to apply to hearing. For each of the following auditory abilities, see if you can determine which perceptual strategy is required: *closure, similarity, continuity,* or *proximity.*

1. Naming and distinguishing two melodies when someone merely taps out the two rhythms
2. Understanding a radio announcer's words when static makes some of the sounds unintelligible
3. Picking out the soprano voices in a chorus and hearing them as a unit (the soprano section)
4. Following a melody on a violin when another violin is playing another melody at the same time

Answers:

1. proximity (You can tell which notes "go together" to form different rhythms.) 2. closure (The brain "fills in" the missing sounds.) 3. similarity (The soprano voices are similar and so are perceived as a separate unit.) 4. continuity (The continuity of the first violin's melody helps you distinguish it from the second one.)

Locating objects in space

We usually want to know where objects are. Touch gives us this information directly. Hearing and vision do not, so we must use various cues to *infer* an object's location.

Localizing sounds. If the stimulus is a sound, we can use its loudness to infer our distance from its source. We know that a train sounds much louder when it is 20 yards away than when it is a mile off. To locate the direction a sound is coming from, we depend in part on the fact that we have two ears. A sound arriving from the right reaches the right ear a fraction of a second sooner than it reaches the left. It may also provide a bit more energy to the right ear (depending on the sound wave's frequency) because the wave has to get around the head to reach the left ear. When you turn or cock your head, you are actively seeking such cues. It is hard to localize sounds that are coming either from directly in back of you or from directly above your head.

Localizing objects visually. People who are deaf in one ear have difficulty telling where sounds are coming from. Even those with normal hearing have problems locating objects through sound alone, as you know if you have ever played children's games like Marco Polo or Blind Man's Bluff. Our eyes provide much fuller information than our ears because they provide direct perception of a three-dimensional world. With our eyes we can gauge distance and depth.

A Closer Look at Human Factors Psychology

Getting Those *!@#% Machines to Work

Your new VCR, the salesperson assures you, is state-of-the-art. It will enable you to preprogram the recording of umpteen shows over a period of umpteen days; you can record one show while watching another . . . it practically makes your coffee for you in the morning. "I'll take it!" you say. Three weeks later you're still trying to figure out how to set the current time of day, never mind recording programs.

Why are modern "conveniences" so often inconvenient to use? Why is it so hard to open a milk carton, adjust water temperature in a one-faucet shower, or put someone on hold in a modern office telephone system? **Human factors psychology**—also called ergonomics—has some of the answers. Psychologists in this fast-growing field design human-machine systems that optimize human abilities while minimizing error (Smither, 1988). Their goal is to come up with equipment, tasks, and work settings that take into account the sensory, perceptual, and motor abilities and limitations of human beings. Knowing that people react more quickly to green signals than to red or blue, or that reaction time with the hand is 20 percent faster than with the foot, can be critical in the design of an airplane control panel. Knowing that fluorescent lighting minimizes shadows and diffuses light can reduce the stress of office workers.

But what about those milk cartons, faucets, and telephones? One psychologist who studies human perception estimates that an adult must readily discriminate among 30,000 different everyday objects (Biederman, 1987). In *The Psychology of Everyday Things* (1988), cognitive psychologist Donald Norman shows that many of these objects are engineered with little thought for how the human mind works. It can be a major challenge to figure out how to use a new washing machine, camera, or sewing machine, or set a digital watch. And it's not the *people* that are stupid. A well-known engineer, the

human factors psychology
An applied field of psychology concerned with the design of equipment, tasks, and work settings that take into account the capacities and requirements of workers.

binocular cues *Visual cues to depth or distance requiring two eyes.*

retinal disparity *The slight difference in lateral separation between two objects as seen by the left eye and the right eye.*

To perform this remarkable feat, we rely in part on **binocular cues**—cues that require the use of two eyes. The eyes are about 2½ inches apart on the face. As they converge on objects close by or far away, the angle of convergence changes, providing information about distance (see Figure 5.14). The two eyes also receive slightly different retinal images of the same object. You can easily prove this by holding a finger about a foot in front of your face and looking at it with only one eye at a time. Its position will appear to shift when you change eyes. Now hold up two fingers, one closer to your nose than the other. Notice that the amount of space between the two fingers appears to change when you switch eyes. The slight difference in lateral (sideways) separation between two objects as seen by the left eye and the right eye is called **retinal disparity**. Since retinal disparity increases as distance between two objects increases, the brain can use retinal disparity to infer depth and

founder of a major data-processing equipment company, once confessed at an annual meeting that he couldn't figure out how to heat a cup of coffee in the company's microwave oven.

A good product, Norman observes, conveys information regarding its use by means of its visible structure instead of forcing the user to rely on memory. One useful design concept, borrowed from the study of perception, is called *affordance* (Gibson, 1979). Affordance refers to the way perceived and actual properties of a thing determine how it can be used. A flat horizontal bar on a door *affords* no action except pushing, so it's a good idea to have such a bar on a door that is supposed to be pushed. A door that is supposed to be pulled should have a different kind of hardware, such as a small, narrow, vertical bar. (Can you think of other possibilities?) When affordances are taken advantage of, says Norman, you know what to do with an object just by looking; you don't need pictures, labels, or instructions.

Good design also requires *visibility*: Crucial distinctions must be visually obvious. What good is a telephone that has a dozen fancy features if you need to read the manual every time you perform an operation, or if the lettering on the phone is so small you can't read it? (One of us has such a phone. Switches used for the programming of numbers are on the side, labeled by tiny raised black letters, and the phone itself is black. You can't decipher the labels unless you lift the phone up, turn it on its side, and hold it 2 inches away from your face.)

And then there's the matter of *mapping*, the relationship between controls and their results. Most stoves have two burners in front and two in back. The controls, however, are often arranged in a row. It's hard to know which control goes with which burner unless there are labels. The solution: Arrange the controls in a rectangular configuration that matches that of the burners, or arrange the burners in a semicircle to achieve a left-to-right arrangement like that of the controls.

If you are clever, you can overcome problems of poor design by making your own modifications, using perceptual principles in this chapter. For example, if you want knobs or switches to be easily distinguishable, you can apply the Gestalt principles on page 184: The objects should have different colors, textures, or shapes and be spatially separated. (Control-room operators in one nuclear power plant solved the problem of similar knobs on two adjacent switches by placing distinctively shaped beer-keg handles over them, one labeled Heineken's, the other Michelob.) At the very least, we can learn to recognize good and bad design and adjust our buying habits accordingly. "Give mental prizes to those who practice good design: send flowers," advises Norman. "Jeer those who don't: send weeds."

---

calculate distance. Retinal disparity is mimicked by 3-D movies and slide viewers (stereoscopes), which project two images, one as seen by the left eye and one as seen by the right, to create an illusion of depth.

Binocular cues only help locate objects up to about 50 feet away. For objects farther away, we might as well be one-eyed. Fortunately, the brain is also able to use **monocular cues** to depth, cues that work with only one eye. One such cue is *interposition*: When an object is interposed between the viewer and a second object, partly blocking the view of the second object, the first object is perceived as closer. Another cue is *linear perspective*: When two lines known to be parallel appear to be coming together or converging, they imply the existence of depth. For example, if you are standing between railroad tracks, they appear to converge in the distance. These and other monocular cues are illustrated in Figure 5.15.

monocular cues *Visual cues to depth or distance that can be used by one eye alone.*

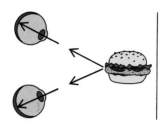
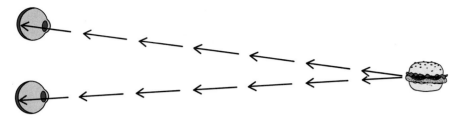

FIGURE 5.14

Convergence

Information from the muscles that produce convergence provide an important binocular cue to depth and distance. If an object is in the center of your visual field, then the closer it is the more your two eyes must turn inward to focus on it. The resulting muscular sensations are obvious when you "cross" your eyes by trying to look at your own nose.

(a)

(b)

(f)

(g)

Perceptual constancies: When seeing is believing

Lighting conditions, the viewing angles of various objects, and the distances of objects all change as we move about. Yet we rarely confuse these changes with changes in the objects themselves. The ability to perceive objects as stable or unchanging despite the fact that the sensory patterns they produce are constantly shifting is known as **perceptual constancy**. The best studied constancies are visual ones and include the following:

1. *Shape constancy.* We continue to perceive objects as having a constant shape despite the fact that the shape of the retinal image changes when our point of view changes. If you hold a Frisbee directly in front of your face, its image on the retina will be round. When you set the Frisbee on a table, its image becomes elliptical, yet you continue to identify the Frisbee as round.

2. *Location constancy.* We perceive stationary objects as remaining in the same place even though the retinal image moves constantly as we move our eyes,

perceptual constancy *The accurate perception of objects as stable or unchanged despite changes in the sensory patterns they produce.*

(c)

(d)

(e)

FIGURE 5.15

Monocular cues to depth
Most cues to depth do not depend on having two eyes. Some monocular (one-eyed) cues are: (a) Interposition *(partial overlap). An object that partly blocks or obscures another one must be in front of the other one, and is therefore seen as closer. (b)* Motion parallax. *When an observer is moving, objects seem to move at different speeds and in different directions. The closer an object is, the faster it seems to move. Close objects also appear to move backward, while distant ones seem to move forward. (c)* Light and shadow. *Light and shadow give objects the appearance of three dimensions. (d)* Relative size. *The smaller the image of an object on the retina, the farther away it appears. (e)* Relative clarity. *Because of particles in the air (from fog, smog, or dust), distant objects tend to look hazier, duller, or less detailed. (f)* Texture gradients. *In a uniform surface, distant parts of the surface appear denser; that is, the elements that make it up seem spaced more closely together. (g)* Linear perspective. *Parallel lines will appear to be converging in the distance; the greater the apparent convergence, the greater the perceived distance. This cue is often exaggerated by artists to convey an impression of depth.*

heads, and bodies. As you drive along the highway, telephone poles and trees fly by—on your retina. However, because you know that objects like telephone poles and trees move by themselves only in cartoons, and you also know that your body is moving, you perceive the poles and trees as staying put.

3. *Brightness constancy.* We continue to see objects as having a more or less constant brightness even though the amount of light they reflect changes as the overall level of illumination changes. Snow remains white even on a cloudy day. In fact, it is possible for a black object in strong sunlight to reflect more light than a white object in the shade. We are not fooled, though, because the brain registers the total illumination in the scene, and we automatically take this information into account in the perception of any particular object's brightness.

4. *Color constancy.* We see an object as maintaining its hue despite the fact that the wavelength of light reaching our eyes may change somewhat. For example, outdoor light is "bluer" than indoor light, and objects outdoors therefore reflect more "blue" light than those indoors. Conversely, indoor light from a lamp is rich in long wavelengths, and is therefore "yellower." Yet objects usually look the same color in both places. The explanation involves sensory adaptation, which we discussed earlier. Outdoors we quickly adapt to short wavelength (blue) light, and indoors we adapt to long wavelength light. As a result, our visual responses are similar in the two situations. Also, as we saw earlier, the brain takes into account all the wavelengths in the visual field when computing the color of a particular object. If a lemon is bathed in bluish light, so, usually, is everything else around it. The increase in blue light reflected by the lemon is "cancelled" in the visual cortex by the increase in blue light reflected by the lemon's surroundings, and so the lemon continues to look yellow (Montgomery, 1988).

5. *Size constancy.* We continue to see an object as having a constant size even when its retinal image becomes smaller or larger. A friend approaching on the street does not seem to be growing; a car pulling away from the curb does not seem to be shrinking. Size constancy depends in part on familiarity with objects. You *know* people and cars don't change size just like that. It also depends on the apparent distance of an object. When you move your hand toward your face, your brain registers the fact that the hand is getting closer, and you correctly perceive its unchanging size. There is, then, an intimate relationship between perceived size and perceived distance.

QUICK⌐QUIZ

Which perceptual constancy is operating in each of the following situations?

1. A rider on a horse gallops toward you. As he approaches, he does not appear to become a giant, nor does his horse.
2. You are trying to decide if a dollar bill is counterfeit. You turn it this way and that as you examine it. Thus the bill's orientation in space and your view of it keep changing. But from any angle of view, it is still recognizable as a dollar bill.
3. You are seated with a friend for dinner. Her dress is white. You turn the lights off and light some candles instead. Her dress remains white.

Answers

1. size 2. shape 3. brightness

Perceptual illusions: When seeing is misleading

Perceptual constancies allow us to make sense of the world, or at least of the thin slice of it that our senses are designed to detect. Occasionally, though, we can be fooled, and we misperceive the world. The result is a **perceptual illusion**. For psychologists, illusions are valuable because they are *systematic* errors that provide hints about the perceptual strategies of the mind.

Visual illusions sometimes occur when the strategies that normally lead to accurate perception are overextended to situations where they don't apply. Compare the two lines in the margin. If you are like most people, you perceive the line on the right as slightly longer than the one on the left. Yet if you measure the lines, you will find that they are exactly the same length. This is the Müller-Lyer illusion, named after the man who devised it in 1889.

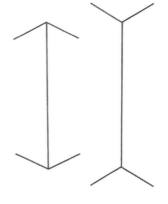

One explanation for the illusion is that the figures contain perspective cues that normally suggest depth (Gregory, 1963). The line on the left is like the near edge of a building; the one on the right is like the far corner of a room. The two lines produce the same-sized retinal image, but the one with the outward-facing branches suggests greater distance. We are fooled into perceiving it as longer because we automatically apply a rule about the relationship between size and distance that is normally very useful. The rule is that when two objects produce the same-sized retinal image, and one is farther away, the farther one is larger. The problem, in this case, is that there is no actual difference in the distance of the two lines, so the rule is inappropriate. A similar explanation applies to other "geometrical" illusions.

Just as there are size, shape, location, brightness, and color constancies, so there are size, shape, location, brightness, and color illusions. Some illusions are simply a matter of physics. Thus a chopstick in a half-filled glass of water looks bent because water and air refract light differently. Other illusions are due to misleading messages from the sense organs, as in sensory adaptation. Still others, like the Müller-Lyer illusion, appear to occur because the brain misinterprets sensory information. Figure 5.16 shows some simple but startling visual illusions.

Although illusions are distortions, in everyday life most are harmless or even useful or entertaining. For example, at the New York Stock Exchange, the fluctuating prices of stocks are displayed on a large board made up of many electric lights. The numbers appear to be moving across the board. Actually, nothing is moving; lights are simply flashing on and off in a certain pattern, causing images to occur successively across the retina, as in real movement. The result is apparent motion, or the *phi phenomenon.*

perceptual illusion *An erroneous or misleading perception of reality.*

FIGURE 5.16

Some visual illusions
It may be hard to believe, but in (a) the cats as drawn are all the same size; in (b) the vertical and horizontal lines are the same size; in (c) the two figures are the same size; in (d) the diagonal lines are all parallel; and in (e) the sides of the square are all straight.

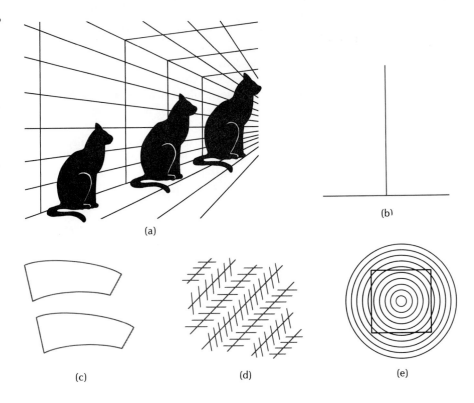

Psychological influences on perception

A camera doesn't care what it "sees." A tape recorder doesn't ponder what it "hears." A robot arm on a factory assembly line holds no opinion about what it "touches." But we human beings are different. Not only do we care about what we perceive, but our thoughts and feelings can influence our perceptions. (The effects that groups exert on an individual's perceptions are discussed in Chapter 18.)

Needs. When we need something, have an interest in it, or want it, we are especially likely to perceive it. For example, studies show that hungry individuals are faster than others at seeing words related to hunger when the words are flashed briefly on a screen (Wispé & Drambarean, 1953).

Some years ago, two researchers discovered that the desire of sports fans to see their team win can affect what they see during a game. Sports fans, of course, tend to regard their own team as the good guys and the opposing team as the dirty rats. In the study, Princeton and Dartmouth students were shown a movie of a football game between their two teams. The game, which Princeton won, was a rough one. Several players were injured, including Princeton's star quarterback. Princeton students viewing the film saw Dartmouth players commit an average of 9.8 rule infractions. They considered the game "rough and dirty." Dartmouth students, on the other hand, noticed only half as many infractions by their team. They considered the game rough but fair (Hastorf & Cantril, 1954).

Beliefs. What a person holds to be true about the world can affect the interpretation of ambiguous sensory signals. Suppose you spot a round object hovering high in the sky. If you believe that extraterrestrials occasionally make visits to Earth, you may "see" the object as a spaceship. But if you hold that such beliefs are hogwash, you are more likely to see a weather balloon. A few years ago, an image of a crucified Jesus on a garage door in Santa Fe Springs, California, caused great excitement among people who were ready to believe that divine "messages" may be found on everyday objects. The image was found to be caused by two streetlights that merged the shadows of a bush and a "For Sale" sign in the yard.

Emotions. Emotions can also influence the interpretation of sensory information. A small child, afraid of the dark, may see a ghost instead of a robe hanging on the door, or a monster instead of a beloved doll. Pain, in particular, seems affected by emotion (Melzack & Dennis, 1978). Soldiers who are seriously wounded often deny being in much pain, even though they are alert and are not in shock. Their relief at being alive may offset the anxiety and fear that contribute so much to pain (though other explanations are also possible).

Expectations. Previous experiences lead us to expect the world to be a certain way. A readiness to perceive a stimulus in a particular way is called a **perceptual set**. Perceptual sets can come in handy. For example, at a noisy party you may not catch every sound the person talking to you makes. But if she says, "How do you . . ." and then extends her hand, you may "hear" the word *do*. But perceptaul sets can also keep us from perceiving things. In Center Harbor, Maine, local legend has it that veteran newscaster Walter Cronkite was sailing into port one day when he heard a small crowd on shore shouting "Hello, Walter . . . Hello, Walter." Pleased, he waved and took a bow. Only when he ran aground did he realize what they had really been shouting: "Low water . . . low water." (By the way, there is a misspelled word right before this story. Once you look for it, you should find it easily. If you missed it the first time, it was because you expected all the words in this book to be spelled correctly.)

Inborn Abilities and Perceptual Learning

The Gestalt psychologists believed that the basic strategies for organizing the world are *innate,* that is, wired into our brains from the beginning. Other psychologists have argued that babies have almost none of the perceptual powers that adults have and must acquire them through experience and learning; William James once described the infant's world as nothing but a "blooming, buzzing confusion." Modern research suggests that the truth lies somewhere between these two extremes.

We can see from studies of other cultures that experience and learning play a role. Perception is not the same the world over (see Figure 5.17). One study found that members of certain African tribes were much less likely to be fooled by the Müller-Lyer illusion and other geometric illusions than were Westerners. Westerners, the researchers observed, live in a "carpentered" world, full of rectangular structures built with the aid of saws, planes, straight edges, and carpenter's squares. Westerners are also used to interpreting two-dimensional photographs and perspective drawings as representations of a three-dimensional world. Therefore, they learn to interpret acute and obtuse angles as right angles extended in space—just the sort of habit that would lead to the Müller-Lyer illusion. Rural Africans, living in a less carpentered environment and in round huts, seem more likely to take the lines in the figures literally, as two-dimensional (Segal, Campbell, & Herskovits, 1966). Other research has found that Cree Indians, whose tents are cone-shaped, perform differently than Euro-Canadians on tests of visual acuity. The latter do better at distinguishing vertical and horizontal lines than diagonals; Crees do equally well on all three types of lines (Annis & Frost, 1973).

People often see what they want to see. This apartment building in a small French town drew huge crowds when some people thought they saw the face of Jesus on it. Actually, the pattern on the wall was the result of damage caused by water leaking from faulty plumbing in one of the apartments.

perceptual set *A habitual way of perceiving, based on expectations.*

We can also observe the effects of experience in studies of animals. If newborn animals are raised in total darkness for a period of weeks or months, or fitted with translucent goggles that permit only diffuse light to reach their eyes, or exposed only to certain types of patterns, vision develops abnormally. In one study, kittens were fitted with special collars that kept them from turning their heads or seeing their own bodies. For five hours each day, they were kept in a cylinder with walls that were covered entirely with either vertical or horizontal black and white stripes. The rest of the time they were housed in a completely dark room. When tested after several months, the kittens exposed only to vertical stripes seemed blind to all horizontal contours, and the kittens exposed only to horizontal stripes seemed blind to all vertical ones (Blakemore & Cooper, 1970).

But what, exactly, do these results mean? *How* does experience affect perceptual development? One possibility is that early experience is necessary for the *initial* development of the skills in question—that cats are blind to both horizontal and vertical lines at birth. There is another possibility, though: that normal experience merely ensures the survival of skills already present at birth. Physiological studies suggest that the second interpretation is correct, at least in the case of line perception. The brains of newborn kittens are equipped with the same "feature detector" cells that adult cats have. But when kittens are not allowed to see lines of a particular orientation, cells sensitive to those orientations deteriorate or change, and perception suffers. For example, when a kitten wears a special mask that permits it to see only vertical lines with one eye and horizontal lines with the other, cells in its visual cortex later respond only to vertical or horizontal orientations rather than the full range of orientations that is usual in cats (Hirsch & Spinelli, 1970).

These findings do not mean that *all* perception is inborn. For some abilities, specific kinds of experience may be necessary for the appropriate neural pathways to become established in the first place. But two other types of evidence support the notion that certain abilities are prewired. One is case histories of people who have gained sight after a lifetime of blindness (Senden, 1960). Even though such individuals have never seen before, when their bandages are removed they can distinguish figure from ground, scan objects, and follow moving objects with their eyes. Thus these abilities, at least, seem to be inborn.

The other evidence comes from studies of human infants. Babies are born nearsighted, but their visual acuity develops rapidly. They can discriminate size and color very early, possibly even at birth, and can distinguish patterns after only a few weeks (see Chapter 13). Even depth perception occurs early.

Testing an infant's perception of depth requires considerable ingenuity. One favorite procedure is to place infants on a device called a "visual cliff" (Gibson &

Walk, 1960). The ''cliff'' is a pane of glass covering both a shallow surface and a deep one (see Figure 5.18). The infant is placed on a board in the middle, and the child's mother tries to lure the baby across either the shallow or deep side. Babies as young as 6 months of age will crawl to their mothers across the shallow side but will refuse to crawl out over the ''cliff.'' Their hesitation shows that they have depth perception.

Infants younger than 6 months are unable to crawl, but they can still be tested on the visual cliff. At only 2 months of age, babies show a drop in heart rate when placed on the deep side of the cliff, but no change when they are placed on the shallow side. A slowed heart rate is usually a sign of increased attention. These infants may not be frightened the way an older infant would be, but apparently they can notice the difference in depth (Banks & Salapatek, 1984; Campos, Langer, & Krowitz, 1970). Other studies suggest that within the first few months of life, infants use depth cues to achieve size constancy (T. G. R. Bower, 1981).

Note, though, that what babies *perceive* about depth does not necessarily determine how they *behave*. Babies differ in their degree of timidity (Kagan, 1984). Some will recklessly crawl off kitchen tables, front porches, stairs, and beds, unless someone grabs them by the ankle. Others contemplate edges more cautiously, turning around to move feet first down steps. Not all babies act on depth perception in the same way.

To sum up: A child's perceptual world is not identical to an adult's. Perceptual skills improve throughout childhood. If babies are deprived of certain kinds of experiences, their skills will fail to develop properly. But the world of the infant is far from the blooming, buzzing confusion that William James took it to be. If learning to perceive is compared to going to school, nature has allowed us to skip kindergarten, and possibly even first grade.

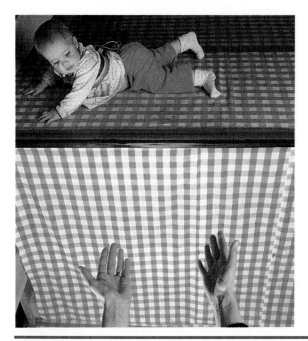

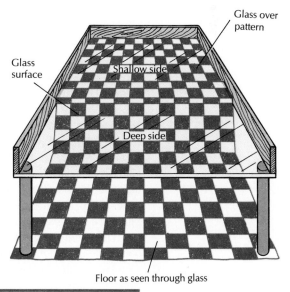

FIGURE 5.18

A cliff-hanger

Infants as young as 6 months usually hesitate to crawl past the apparent edge of a ''visual cliff,'' which suggests that they are able to perceive depth.

Extrasensory Perception: Reality or Illusion?

Eyes, ears, mouth, nose, skin—we rely on these organs for our experience of the external world. Some people, however, claim they can send and receive messages about the world without relying on the usual sensory channels. This presumed ability is called **extrasensory perception**, or **ESP**.

Reported ESP experiences fall into four general categories. (1) *Telepathy* is direct communication from one mind to another without the usual visual, auditory, and other sensory signals. If you try to guess what number someone is thinking of or what card a person is holding out of sight, you are attempting telepathy. (2) *Clairvoyance* is the perception of an event or fact without normal sensory input. If a man suddenly "knows" that his wife has just died, yet no one has informed him of the death, he might be called clairvoyant. (3) *Precognition* is the perception of an event that has not yet happened. Fortune-tellers make their livings by claiming to read the future in tea leaves or a person's palm. (4) *Out-of-body experiences* involve the perception of one's own body from "outside," as another observer might see it. The person feels that he or she has left the physical body entirely. Such experiences are often reported by persons who have been near death, but some people say they can bring them on at will.

Some types of ESP are more plausible than others, given what we know about the physical world. Normal perception depends on the ability to detect changes in energy. Conceivably telepathy could involve something similar: the sending and receiving of changes in energy through channels that have not yet been identified. Other forms of ESP, however, challenge everything we suppose to be true about the way the world and the universe operate. Precognition, for instance, contradicts our usual assumptions about time and space. If it exists, then tomorrow is as real as today and future events can be known, even though they cannot have caused physical changes in the environment.

Evidence — or coincidence?

Much of the "evidence" for extrasensory perception comes from anecdotal accounts. Unfortunately, people are not always reliable reporters. They often embellish and exaggerate, or recall only parts of an experience. They also tend to "forget" incidents that don't fit their beliefs, such as "premonitions" of events that fail to occur. Many ESP experiences could merely be unusual coincidences that are memorable because they are dramatic (see Chapter 2). What passes for telepathy, clairvoyance, or precognition could also be based on what a person knows or deduces through ordinary means. For example, if Joanne's father has had three heart attacks, her "premonition" that her father will die shortly (followed, in fact, by her father's death) may not really be so impressive.

The scientific way to establish that a phenomenon exists is to produce it under controlled conditions. Extrasensory perception has been studied extensively by researchers in the field of **parapsychology**. In a typical study, a person might be asked to guess which of five symbols will appear on a card presented at random. A "sender" who can see the card before it is presented tries to transmit a mental image of the symbol to the person. A deck of 25 cards is usually used. Though most people do no better than chance at guessing the symbols, in some studies a few

It might be fun to have ESP—especially before a tough exam or a blind date. However, it's one thing to wish ESP existed and another to conclude that it does. What kind of evidence would convince you that ESP is real, and what kind is only wishful thinking?

extrasensory perception (ESP) *Perception that does not appear to depend on normal sense organ stimulation. Its existence has not been proven.*

parapsychology *The study of unusual psychological phenomena that do not seem explainable by known scientific laws.*

people have consistently done somewhat better than chance. Unfortunately, ESP studies have often been sloppily designed, with inadequate precautions against fraud and improper statistical analysis. When skeptical researchers try to repeat the studies, they usually get negative results. The better controlled the study, the less likely it is to produce support for ESP. We are not saying that ESP abilities are impossible; some scientists continue to view the issue as unresolved. But most feel that the thousands of experiments done in the past 40 years have failed to make a convincing case for ESP. After an exhaustive review, the National Research Council has concluded that there is "no scientific justification . . . for the existence of parapsychological phenomena" (Druckman & Swets, 1988).

Lessons from a magician

Despite the lack of evidence for ESP, many people believe in it. Perhaps you yourself have had an experience that seemed to involve ESP or have seen a convincing demonstration by someone else. Surely you can trust the evidence of your own eyes—or can you? We will answer with a true story that contains an important lesson, not only about ESP but about normal perception.

Several years ago, physician Andrew Weil (whose writings on altered states of consciousness we discussed in Chapter 4) set out to investigate the claims of a young Israeli psychic named Uri Geller (Weil, 1974a, 1974b). Geller seemed able to bend keys without touching them, start broken watches, and guess the nature of simple drawings hidden in sealed envelopes. Although he had performed as a stage magician in his native country, he denied using trickery. His powers, he said, came from energy sent through him from another universe.

Weil, who believed in telepathy, felt that ESP might be explained by principles of modern physics. Therefore he was receptive to Geller's claims. When he met Geller at a private gathering, he was not disappointed. The psychic correctly identified a cross and a Star of David sealed inside separate envelopes. He made a stopped watch start running and a ring sag into an oval shape, apparently without touching them. He made keys change shape in front of Weil's very eyes. Weil came away a convert. What he had seen with his own eyes seemed impossible to deny . . . that is, until he met The Amazing Randi.

Randi is a well-known magician, a professional creator of illusions. To Weil's astonishment, Randi was able to duplicate much of what Geller had done. He, too, could bend keys and guess the contents of sealed envelopes. But Randi's feats were only tricks, and he was willing to show Weil exactly how they were done. Weil (1974b) suddenly experienced "a sense of how strongly the mind can impose its own interpretations on perceptions; how it can see what it expects to see, but not see the unexpected."

Weil was dis-illusioned—literally. He was forced to admit that the evidence of one's own eyes is *not* always reliable. Even when Weil knew what to look for in a trick, he could not catch The Amazing Randi doing it. Weil learned that one's sense impressions of reality are not the same as reality. Our eyes, our ears, and especially our brains can play tricks on us.

The great Greek philosopher Plato once said that "knowledge is nothing but perception," but in fact simple perception is *not* always the best path to knowledge. The truth about human behavior is most likely to emerge if we are aware of how our beliefs and assumptions shape and alter our perceptions. As we have seen in this chapter, we do not simply register the world "out there." We mentally construct it.

"Seeing is believing," goes the old saying, but, in fact, we can easily be fooled by our own eyes. The engraving at the top shows "a living half woman." The one on the bottom reveals how the illusion is produced: A diagonal mirror reflects the floor or carpet pattern, so onlookers think they see an unbroken expanse of floor. The moral: Be skeptical when someone claims to possess "supranormal" powers, even if you "saw it with your own eyes."

Taking Psychology with You

Living with Pain

Temporary pain is an unpleasant but necessary part of life, a warning of disease or injury. Chronic pain, which is ongoing or recurring, is another matter, a primary problem in itself. According to one estimate, 86 million Americans have some form of chronic pain (Bonica, 1980). Back injuries, arthritis, migraine headaches, serious illnesses like cancer—all can cause unrelieved misery to pain sufferers and their families. The direct and indirect financial costs to victims and the health care system approach $60 billion annually.

Once the only way to combat pain was with drugs or surgery, which might or might not be effective. Today, we know that the experience of pain is affected by attitudes, actions, emotions, and circumstances, and that treatment must take into account psychology as well as biology. Even social roles can influence a person's response to pain. For example, in pain experiments done in the laboratory, men tend to "tough it out" longer than women do. But a real-world study of people in constant pain for more than six months found that men suffered more severe psychological distress than women, possibly because the male role made it hard for them to admit their pain or accept a decrease in productivity (Snow et al., 1986).

Many pain treatment programs encourage patients to manage their pain themselves instead of relying entirely on health care professionals. Usually these programs combine several strategies:

- *Painkilling medication.* Doctors used to worry that patients would become addicted to painkillers or develop a tolerance to them. They would give a minimal dose, then wait until the effects wore off and the patient was once again in agony before giving more. This approach was ineffectual and ignored the fact that addiction depends in part on the motives for which a drug is taken and the circumstances under which it is used (see Chapters 4 and 16). The new method is to give pain sufferers a continuous dose of painkiller in whatever amount is necessary to keep them pain-free, and to allow them to do this for themselves when they leave the hospital. This strategy leads to *reduced* dosages rather than increasing ones and usually does not lead to drug dependence or tolerance (Chapman, 1987; Taub, 1984).

- *Spouse or family involvement.* When a person is in pain, friends and relatives understandably tend to be sympathetic and excuse the sufferer from regular responsibilities. The sufferer takes to bed, avoids physical activity, and focuses on the pain. As we will see in Chapter 6, attention from others is a powerful reinforcer of whatever behavior produces the attention. Unfortunately, focusing on pain tends to increase it, and inactivity can lead to shortened muscles, muscle spasms, and fatigue. So sympathy and attention can backfire and may actually prolong the agony (Flor, Kerns, & Turk, 1985; Fordyce, 1976). As a consequence, many pain experts now encourage family members to resist rewarding or reinforcing the pain and instead reward activity, exercise, and "wellness." This approach, however, must be used carefully, preferably under the direction of a competent professional, since a patient's complaints about pain are an important diagnostic tool for the physician (Rodgers, 1988).

▪ *Behavioral self-management*. In behavioral therapy, patients learn to identify how, when, and where their pain occurs. This knowledge helps them determine whether the pain is being reinforced or maintained by external events. Just being in control of one's pain can have a powerful pain-reducing effect. Behavior therapy may also include muscle "reeducation"; for example, instead of tensing muscles in response to pain, which only makes the pain worse, patients can learn to relax them (Keefe, 1985).

▪ *Biofeedback, hypnosis, and progressive relaxation*. These techniques have all been successful with some patients (McGuigan, 1984: Woolfolk & Lehrer, 1984). (We discussed biofeedback in Chapter 3, hypnosis in Chapter 4.) It is unclear, though, whether biofeedback and progressive relaxation are applicable to all types of chronic pain; most studies have looked only at headaches (Turner & Chapman, 1982a).

▪ *Cognitive-behavioral therapy*. Attention, expectancies, and beliefs can affect how a person experiences pain. Cognitive-behavioral strategies teach people to identify negative thoughts about pain; recognize connections between thoughts, feelings, and pain; substitute adaptive thoughts for negative ones; and use various coping strategies (such as distraction, relabeling of sensations, and imagery) to alleviate suffering (Turner & Chapman, 1982b). All of these techniques increase feelings of control and reduce feelings of inadequacy. Laboratory research suggests that perceived control ("There are ways to reduce pain . . .") and *self-efficacy* (". . . and I'm confident that I can use them successfully") both contribute to the ability to tolerate pain (Litt, 1988).

For further information about help for pain, you can contact pain clinics or services in teaching hospitals and medical schools. There are many reputable clinics around the country, some specializing in specific disorders. But take care: There are also many untested therapies and quack practitioners who only prey on people's pain.

KEY WORDS

SUMMARY

1. *Sensation* is the detection or awareness of changes in physical energy caused by environmental or internal events. *Perception* is the process by which sensory impulses are organized and interpreted.

2. Our senses evolved to help us survive. Separate sensations can be accounted for by anatomical codes (the *doctrine of specific nerve energies)* and functional codes in the nervous system.

3. Psychologists in the area of *psychophysics* study sensory sensitivity by measuring the *absolute threshold* and the *difference threshold*. The assumption of a single absolute threshold has been replaced by the *theory of signal detectability*, which assumes that an observer's response in a detection task consists of a sensory process and a decision process.

4. A certain amount of sensory stimulation is necessary for the brain to function normally. However, too much stimulation can be overwhelming, which is why we exercise *selective attention* in daily life.

5. Vision is affected by the wavelength, frequency, and complexity of light. The visual receptors—the *rods* and *cones*—are located in the *retina* of the eye. Rods are responsible for vision in dim light; cones are responsible for color vision. The visual world is not a mosaic of light and dark spots but a collection of lines and angles detected and integrated by special cells in the visual cortex of the brain.

6. Color vision involves at least two stages. In the first, three types of cones respond selectively to different wavelengths of light. In the second, ganglion and brain cells known as *opponent-process* cells respond in opposite fashion to short and long wavelengths.

7. Hearing, or *audition*, is affected by the intensity, frequency, and complexity of pressure waves in the air or other transmitting substance. The receptors for hearing are hair cells in the interior of the *cochlea*. The sort of sound we hear is determined by the pattern of hair cell movement.

8. Taste, or *gustation*, is a chemical sense. The taste of a food is affected by culture, genetic differences among individuals, the texture and temperature of the food, and above all, by the food's smell.

9. Smell, or *olfaction*, is also a chemical sense. No basic odors have been identified, and the code for smell remains to be worked out. *Pheromones* may play some role in the regulation of reproductive cycles, but research has not established that they have any significant or reliable effect in human beings on sexual attractiveness or sexual interest. Cultural and individual differences affect people's responses to particular odors.

10. The skin senses include touch (pressure), warmth, cold, and pain. There does not seem to be a simple connection between these four senses and different types of receptors, as was once thought.

11. Pain is both a skin and an internal sense. According to the *gate-control theory* of pain, the experience of pain depends on whether neural impulses get past a "gate" in the spinal cord and thus reach the brain. In general outline the theory seems valid, and it has led to important advances in the treatment of pain. Recent research shows that pain also depends on the release of certain chemicals at the site of tissue damage, and pain suppression involves the release of endorphins in the brain.

12. *Kinesthesis* tells us where our various body parts are located, and *equilibrium* tells us the orientation of the body as a whole. Together these two senses provide us with a feeling of physical embodiment.

13. Perception involves the active construction of a model of the world. Many perceptual processes occur outside of conscious awareness. The *Gestalt principles* help explain the perceptual strategies used to divide up the world into separate objects. These principles include proximity, closure, similarity, and continuity, and the division of the visual field into *figure* and *ground*. As we saw in "A Closer Look at Human Factors Psychology," Gestalt and other perceptual principles can be used in the design of everyday objects.

14. When we localize sounds we use subtle differences in how pressure waves reach the two ears. We localize objects in visual space by using both *binocular* and *monocular* cues.

15. Perceptual *constancies* allow us to perceive objects as stable or unchanging when sensory patterns shift. They include size, shape, brightness, color, and location constancy. Perceptual *illusions* occur when sensory cues are misleading or when we misinterpret cues. Because illusions are systematic errors, they provide hints about how perception works.

16. Psychological influences on perception include needs, beliefs, emotions, and expectations. Because these factors affect the way we construct the perceptual world, the evidence of our senses is not always reliable.

17. Studies of people from other cultures, visually deprived animals, and infants all suggest that experience is important for perception. Without such experience, cells in the nervous system deteriorate, change, or fail to form appropriate neural pathways, and perception is impaired. However, many fundamental perceptual skills seem to be inborn or acquired shortly after birth.

18. *Extrasensory perception* refers to such paranormal abilities as telepathy, clairvoyance, precognition, and out-of-body experiences. Studies of ESP by *parapsychologists* have been difficult to replicate, and most scientists feel that the case for ESP is not convincing.

P A R T

T H R E E

Learning, Thinking, and Feeling

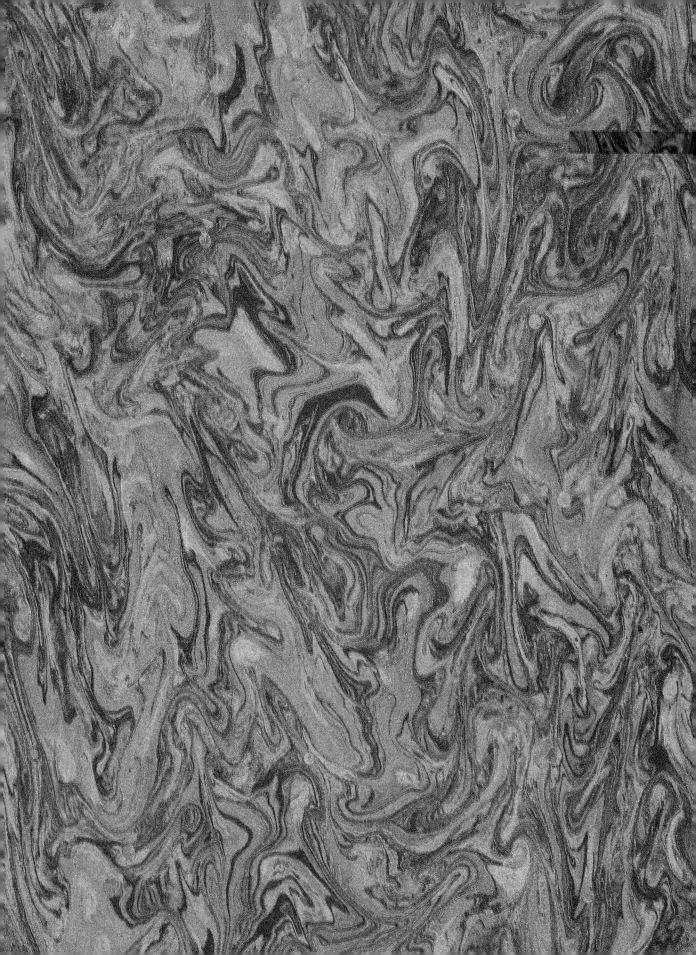

CHAPTER 6

Learning

[R]eward and punishment . . . these are the spur and reins whereby all mankind are set on work, and guided.

JOHN LOCKE

*I*t's January 1, a brand new year. The sins and lapses of the old year are behind you; you're ready for a fresh start. Optimistically, you sit down to record your New Year's resolutions:

1. Lose 10 pounds; no more chocolate ice cream.
2. Raise grades; spend more time studying.
3. Be easier to get along with; control temper.
4. Get more exercise; join a gym.
5. Control spending; pay off credit card.
6. Overcome shyness; stop blushing when called on to speak.
7. (You fill in the blank.)

How likely are you to achieve these goals? Some people do fulfill most of their resolutions. For others, the road to frustration is paved with good intentions. Within weeks, days, or even hours they find themselves backsliding (''Well, maybe just one *teensy* dish of ice cream''). They may end up feeling like the proverbial old dog, unable to learn new tricks.

In fact, however, all of us *can* learn new tricks. By studying the laws of learning, we can improve our ability to change behavior in desirable ways—as we will see in this chapter.

In everyday speech, learning often means classroom activities, like diagramming sentences or memorizing the facts of geography. But to psychologists, **learning** refers to any relatively permanent change in behavior that occurs because of experience (excluding changes due to fatigue, injury, or disease). Experience is the great teacher, altering an organism's nervous system and, through it, its behavior. Learning provides the essential link between the past and the future, enabling an organism to adapt appropriately to changing circumstances in order to survive and thrive. It is a fundamental process in all animals, from the lowliest backyard bug to the loftiest human scholar.

Not all behavior, however, is learned. Some emerges simply as a result of maturation, or natural growth and development. In many animals, a great deal of behavior is due not to learning but to inborn reflexes, automatic responses to specific stimuli. Human beings, too, are born with reflexes. If you touch a baby's face, it will turn toward your hand, and if you touch its lips, it will make sucking motions. These reactions help the infant find and use the nipple during nursing. Later, when they are no longer needed, they disappear. However, as we noted in Chapter 3, many other automatic responses, such as the knee-jerk, eye-blink, and sneeze reflexes, remain.

Complex chains of interrelated reflexes are called **instincts** (or sometimes *fixed action patterns*). These patterns of behavior occur without learning in every individual of a species. Everyone agrees that instincts exist in many if not all animals and contribute mightily to their survival. Some instincts are common to several different species. Others are ''species-specific,'' representing an adaptation unique to a particular type of organism. A spider will spin a perfect web even if it has never seen

learning *A relatively permanent change in behavior (or behavioral potential) due to experience.*

instinct *A complex pattern of behavior that occurs without learning in every member of a species in response to a specific stimulus.*

one before. A male stickleback fish will instinctively attack any other male that approaches its territory during the mating season, its belligerence automatically triggered by the invader's distinctive red belly.

Soon after birth, some animals behave in ways that combine elements of both instinct and learning. They will follow and become attached to the first thing they see or hear that happens to move, a behavior known as **imprinting**. Ordinarily, the "thing" on which the animal imprints is its mother, but experience can dictate otherwise. When ethologist Konrad Lorenz hatched young geese in an incubator, they imprinted on *him*, following him around and responding to his calls as if he were their mother (Lorenz, 1937). In the laboratory, ducklings have imprinted on decoys, rubber balls, and wooden blocks (Hess, 1959). Imprinting is most likely to take place during a brief **sensitive period** of development. (Researchers used to speak of a *critical period*, but after finding that the readiness to imprint sometimes declines gradually, they changed their terminology.) Once imprinting has occurred, it is usually hard to reverse, even when the "mother" is an inanimate object that can offer neither food nor affection. These facts suggest that imprinting is a special type of perceptual learning that occurs because at a particular stage in development the animal's nervous system is geared to respond to a conspicuous moving object in a certain way.

Scientists disagree about the place of instinct in human behavior. **Sociobiologists** argue that even complicated forms of human behavior can have an instinctive basis. They believe we have an inborn urge to propagate our own genes or those of our biological relatives. Social customs that enhance the odds of such transmission survive in the form of kinship bonds, courtship rituals, altruism, taboos against female adultery, and many other aspects of social life (Wilson, 1975). Other social scientists have argued that human behavior can be explained solely by learning. Psychologists today generally take a middle path. They acknowledge that human behavior is influenced by our biological heritage, but most doubt that either imprinting or true instincts occur in human beings.

Because we human beings learn more frequently and impressively than any other organism, we acquire not only those characteristics typical of our species but also thousands of attributes that make us unique as individuals. We are liberals, conservatives, rock fans, Bach buffs, mathematicians, poets, gourmet cooks, fast-food fanatics, optimists, pessimists, homebodies, and adventurers because of our experiences in life and what we have learned from them. In this chapter we will examine some basic types of learning that help account for our similarities and our diversity. Research on these topics has been heavily influenced by **behaviorism**, the view that psychologists should explain behavior in terms of observable events rather than hypothetical mental processes (see Chapter 1). However, as we will see, newer theories hold that omitting mental processes from explanations of learning is like omitting passion from descriptions of sex: You may explain the form, but you miss the substance. To nonbehaviorists, learning is not so much a change in behavior as a change in *knowledge*. Such changes then have the *potential* for affecting behavior.

Not all behavior is learned; in many animals, responses to particular stimuli are instinctive—like the glorious display of the male peacock when he is courting. Some people have their own dramatic courtship rituals. However, instincts, or "fixed action" patterns of behavior probably do not occur in human beings.

imprinting *The tendency of some animals, especially birds, to follow and form a permanent attachment to the first moving object they see or hear after birth.*

sensitive period *A period in the development of an organism that is optimal for the acquisition of a particular behavior.*

sociobiology *A school of thought that attempts to account for social behavior in terms of genetic predispositions and evolutionary principles.*

behaviorism *An approach to psychology that emphasizes the study of objectively observable behavior and the role of the environment as a determinant of behavior.*

Classical Conditioning: New Reflexes from Old

At the turn of the century, the great Russian physiologist Ivan Pavlov (1849–1936) was studying salivation in dogs, as part of a research program on digestion. His work on digestion would shortly win him the Nobel Prize in physiology and medi-

FIGURE 6.1

Pavlov's apparatus
In Pavlov's studies, saliva collected from a dog's cheek flowed down a tube and was measured by the movement of a needle on a revolving drum.

cine. Pavlov's procedure was to make a surgical opening in a dog's cheek and insert a tube that conducted saliva away from the animal's salivary gland to a measuring device (see Figure 6.1). To stimulate the flow of saliva, a simple inborn reflex, Pavlov placed meat powder and other forms of food in the dog's mouth.

Pavlov was a truly dedicated scientific observer. (Many years later, when he was dying, he carefully dictated his sensations for posterity!) During his salivation studies, Pavlov noticed something that most people would have overlooked or dismissed as trivial. After a dog had been brought to the laboratory a number of times, it would start to salivate *before* the food was placed in its mouth. The sight or smell of the food, the dish in which the food was kept, even the sight of the person who delivered the food or the sound of the person's footsteps, were enough to start the dog's mouth watering. This new salivary response clearly was not inborn but was acquired through experience. Pavlov called it a "conditional" reflex—conditional because it depended on environmental conditions.

Pavlov soon dropped what he had been doing and turned to the study of conditional reflexes. The salivary glands of his dogs apparently were affected by experience, as though they had a mind of their own. What was causing this change? In good behaviorist fashion, Pavlov refused to speculate about the dogs' thoughts, wishes, or memories. Instead he analyzed the environment in which the conditional reflex arose.

The original salivary reflex, according to Pavlov, consisted of an **unconditioned stimulus (US)**, food, and an **unconditioned response (UR)**, salivation. By an unconditioned stimulus, Pavlov meant a stimulus that elicited a response automatically or reflexively. By an unconditioned response, he meant the response that was automatically produced:

unconditioned stimulus (US) *The classical conditioning term for a stimulus that elicits a reflexive response in the absence of learning.*

unconditioned response (UR) *The classical conditioning term for a reflexive response elicited by a stimulus in the absence of learning.*

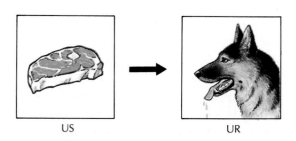

US   UR

Learning occurred when some neutral stimulus was regularly paired with an uncon-ditioned stimulus. The neutral stimulus then became a **conditioned stimulus (CS)**, which elicited a learned or **conditioned response (CR)** that was similar to the original, unlearned one. In Pavlov's laboratory, the sight of the food dish, which had not previously elicited salivation, became a CS for salivation:

Conditioning

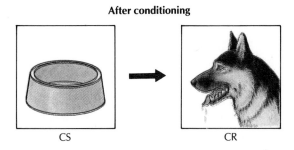

Neutral stimulus   US

After conditioning

CS   CR

In a series of experiments, Pavlov showed that virtually any stimulus can be-come a conditioned stimulus for salivation—the ticking of a metronome, the sound of a tuning fork, a bell, a buzzer, a triangle drawn on a large card, even a pinprick or electric shock. None of these stimuli ''naturally'' elicits salivation, but if paired with food, they all will. The process by which a neutral stimulus becomes a condi-tioned stimulus has become known as **classical** or **Pavlovian conditioning** (also sometimes called *respondent conditioning*).

conditioned stimulus (CS)
The classical conditioning term for an initially neutral stimulus that comes to elicit a conditioned response after being associated with an unconditioned stimulus.
conditioned response (CR)
The classical conditioning term for a response that is elicited by a conditioned stimulus; occurs after the conditioned stimulus is asso-ciated with an unconditioned stimulus.
classical (Pavlovian) condi-tioning *The process, first described by Ivan Pavlov, by which a previously neu-tral stimulus acquires the capacity to elicit a response through association with a stimulus that naturally elic-its a similar response.*

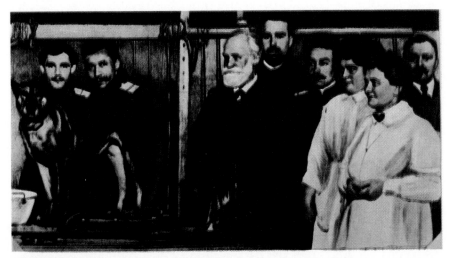

Ivan Pavlov is in the center, flanked by his students and a canine subject.

QUICK ▪ QUIZ

Name the four components of classical conditioning in these two situations:

1. Five-year-old Samantha is watching a storm from her window. A huge bolt of lightning is followed by a tremendous thunderclap, and Samantha jumps at the noise. This happens several more times. There is a brief lull and then another lightning bolt. Samantha jumps in response to the bolt.
2. Gregory's mouth waters whenever he eats anything with lemon in it. One day, while reading an ad that shows a big glass of lemonade, Gregory notices his mouth watering.

Answers:

1. US = the thunderclap; UR = jumping elicited by the noise; CS = the sight of the lightning; CR = jumping elicited by the lightning.   2. US = the taste of lemon; UR = salivation elicited by the taste of lemon; CS = the picture of a glass of lemonade; CR = salivation elicited by the picture.

Principles of classical conditioning

Nearly any automatic, involuntary response can become a conditioned response—for example, heartbeat, stomach secretions, blood pressure, brain waves, reflexive movements, blinking, or muscular contractions. For optimal conditioning, the conditioned stimulus should precede the unconditioned stimulus, not follow it or occur simultaneously. This makes sense, for in classical conditioning, the conditioned stimulus becomes a kind of signal for the unconditioned stimulus. In Pavlov's experiments, a bell or buzzer was a signal that meat was coming. The optimal interval between the presentation of the CS and the presentation of the US depends on the kind of response being conditioned. In the laboratory, the optimal interval is often less than a second.

To a surprising extent, the principles that govern the learning of conditioned responses are common to all species. Here are some important principles.

extinction *The weakening and eventual disappearance of a learned response. Occurs in classical conditioning when the conditioned stimulus is no longer paired with the unconditioned stimulus.*

spontaneous recovery *The sudden reappearance of a learned response after its apparent extinction.*

stimulus generalization *After conditioning, the tendency to respond to a stimulus that resembles one involved in the original conditioning. In classical conditioning, occurs when a stimulus that resembles the conditioned stimulus elicits the conditioned response.*

Extinction.   Conditioned responses do not necessarily last forever. If, after conditioning, the conditioned stimulus is repeatedly presented without the unconditioned stimulus, the conditioned response eventually disappears and **extinction** is said to have occurred (see Figure 6.2). Suppose you train a dog to salivate to the sound of a bell, but then you ring the bell every five minutes and do *not* follow it with food. The dog will soon stop salivating to the bell. However, if you come back the next day and ring the bell, the dog may salivate for a few trials again. The reappearance of the response is called **spontaneous recovery**. Because of spontaneous recovery, the elimination of a conditioned response usually requires more than one extinction session.

Stimulus generalization and discrimination.   After a stimulus becomes a conditioned stimulus for some response, other, similar stimuli may also elicit that response. This spreading of the response to stimuli that are similar to the CS is known as **stimulus generalization**. For example, a dog conditioned to salivate to middle C on the piano may also salivate to D, which is one tone above C, even though D was not paired with food. Stimulus generalization is described nicely by an old English proverb: "He who hath been bitten by a snake fears a rope."

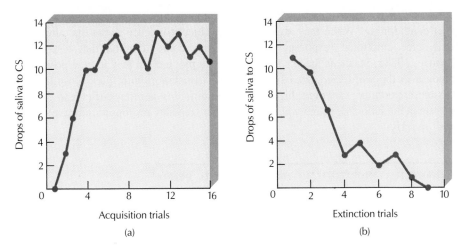

FIGURE 6.2

Acquisition and extinction of a salivary response
Graph (a) shows what happens when a neutral stimulus is consistently followed by an unconditioned stimulus for salivation. The neutral stimulus also comes to elicit salivation; that is, it becomes a conditioned stimulus. Graph (b) shows what happens when the conditioned stimulus is repeatedly presented without the unconditioned stimulus. The conditioned salivary response weakens and eventually disappears; it is extinguished.

The mirror image of stimulus generalization is **stimulus discrimination**, in which *different* responses are made to stimuli that resemble the conditioned stimulus in some way. Suppose a dog conditioned to salivate to middle C on the piano is presented with middle C on a guitar. If the dog does not salivate to the note on the guitar, we can say that the dog has discriminated between the two sounds. In this case, the discrimination has occurred naturally. But it is also possible to teach a discrimination explicitly by the selective use of reinforcement. Again, suppose that a dog has been conditioned to salivate to middle C on the piano and that because of generalization the dog also salivates to D. If you repeatedly present D without following it by food (but continue to follow C by food), eventually the dog will stop salivating to D and will respond only to C.

Higher-order conditioning.   Sometimes a neutral stimulus can become a conditioned stimulus by being paired with an already established CS, a procedure known as **higher-order conditioning**. Say a dog has learned to salivate to a bell. Now you present a flash of light before ringing the bell. With repeated pairings of the light and the bell, the dog may learn to salivate to the light (though the light will probably elicit less salivation than the bell does). The procedure looks like this:

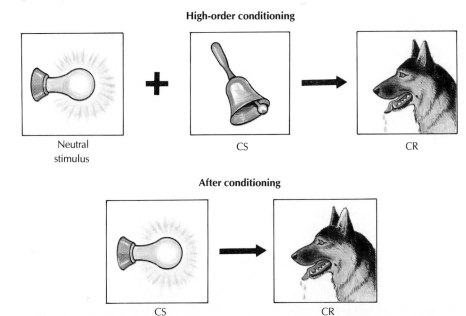

High-order conditioning

Neutral stimulus   CS   CR

After conditioning

CS   CR

stimulus discrimination
The tendency to respond differently to two or more similar stimuli.

higher-order conditioning
In classical conditioning, a procedure in which a neutral stimulus becomes a conditioned stimulus through association with an already established conditioned stimulus.

It may be that words acquire their emotional meanings through a process of higher-order conditioning. When they are paired with objects or other words that already elicit some emotional response, they, too, may come to elicit that response (Chance, 1988a; Staats & Staats, 1957). For example, a child may learn a positive response to the word *Christmas* because of its association with gifts. Despite its possible importance, however, higher-order conditioning is often difficult to demonstrate in the laboratory, and when it does occur, the new response tends to extinguish quickly.

Classical conditioning and the real world

If a dog can learn to salivate to a bell, so can you. In fact, you probably *have* learned to salivate to the sound of a lunch bell, not to mention the sight of the refrigerator, the word *steak*, the sight of a waiter in a restaurant, and a voice calling out "Dinner's ready!" But the role of classical conditioning in our lives goes far beyond the learning of simple observable reflexes. Here are some other ways that classical conditioning affects us in everyday life.

Accounting for taste. We probably learn to like and dislike many things through a process of classical conditioning. Martin Seligman, who has studied learned behavior in the laboratory, tells how he was conditioned to hate Béarnaise sauce. Seligman and his wife went out for dinner and ordered one of his favorite dishes, filet mignon with Béarnaise sauce. Shortly afterward, Seligman happened to come down with the flu. Naturally, he felt wretched. His misery had nothing to do with the Béarnaise sauce, of course, yet the next time he tried it, he found he disliked the taste (Seligman & Hager, 1972). Similar conditioned food aversions sometimes occur in cancer patients when eating precedes nausea-inducing chemotherapy (Bernstein, 1985).

Food and odor preferences have also been conditioned in the laboratory. One researcher trained slugs to associate the smell of carrots, which slugs normally like, with a bitter-tasting chemical, which they detest. Soon the slugs were avoiding the smell of carrots. The researcher then demonstrated higher-order conditioning by pairing the smell of carrots with the smell of potato. Sure enough, the slugs began to avoid the smell of potato as well (Sahley, Rudy, & Gelperin, 1981).

Sometimes we subjectively like something, but our bodies refuse to tolerate it. This happens with allergies—you adore chocolate, but your skin breaks out in hives whenever you eat it. Certain allergic reactions may be classically conditioned. In a study with guinea pigs, researchers paired the smell of either fish or sulphur with injection of a substance that the animals were already allergic to. After only ten pairings, the animals became allergic to the odor alone. Their blood histamine levels rose, just as they would have after exposure to a true allergen (Russell et al., 1984). People, too, may learn to be allergic to certain substances that have been associated with ones they are already sensitive to.

Learning to love. Classical conditioning involves involuntary bodily responses, and many such responses are part and parcel of human emotions. It follows that this type of learning may explain how we acquire emotional responses to particular objects and events.

One of the first psychologists to recognize this implication of Pavlovian theory was John B. Watson. Watson, the founder of American behaviorism, believed that emotions were simply collections of gut-level muscular and glandular responses. A few such responses, said Watson, are inborn. For the sake of convenience he called them fear, rage, and love, but he was really referring to patterns of movement and changes in breathing, circulation, and digestion, not subjective feelings. In Watson's analysis, "love" included the smiling and burbling that babies are apt to do when they are stroked and cuddled. The stroking and cuddling are unconditioned stimuli; the smiling and burbling are unconditioned responses. According to Watson, an infant learns to "love" other things when they are paired with stroking and cuddling. The thing most likely to be paired with stroking and cuddling is, of course, a parent. Learning to love a parent, then, is really no different from learning to salivate to the sound of a bell—at least in Watson's view.

A similar process may explain unusual desires and preferences. For example, some individuals are sexually aroused by *fetishes*, objects or parts of the body not ordinarily associated with sex. A fetish may initially acquire its appeal by being paired with an unconditioned stimulus for arousal. In one case, a fetishist had broken his leg when he was a boy and was attended by an attractive nurse, who held the leg while the cast was set. He had found this sexually stimulating. When he grew up, he had to wear a plaster cast to become sexually aroused (Tollison & Adams, 1979).

Classical conditioning may also explain *masochism*, the enjoyment of pain. We mentioned earlier that Pavlov could condition dogs to salivate to a pinprick or an electric shock. The animals showed none of the bodily upset usually associated with these painful stimuli. In fact, they seemed to enjoy being pricked or shocked. Similarly, masochism in human beings may result when painful stimuli are associated with an unconditioned stimulus for pleasure or satisfaction.

Conditioned fears and phobias. Negative emotions, too, can be classically conditioned. Interest has focused on fears and **phobias** (irrational fears). According to behaviorists, the original conditioning incident or incidents need not be remembered; the emotional response remains long after its origin has faded into the mists of memory.

To demonstrate how fears and phobias are acquired, John B. Watson and Rosalie Rayner (1920) deliberately established a rat phobia in an 11-month-old boy named Albert. The ethics, procedures, and findings of their study have since been questioned (Harris, 1979). However, the study is a classic, and its main conclusion, that fears can be conditioned, is well accepted.

"Little Albert" was a rather placid little tyke who rarely cried. When Watson and Rayner gave him a furry white rat to play with, he was initially delighted. (Contrary to widespread opinion, fear of rats, bugs, spiders, snakes, and other creepy-crawlies is not innate.) However, like most children, Albert *was* afraid of loud noises. Whenever a steel bar behind Albert's head was struck with a hammer, Albert would jump and fall sideways onto the mattress he was sitting on. The noise was an unconditioned stimulus for the unconditioned response of fear.

Having established that Albert liked rats, Watson and Rayner set about teaching him to fear them. Once again they offered him a rat, but this time, as Albert reached for it, one of the researchers struck the steel bar. Startled, Albert fell onto the mattress. The researchers repeated this procedure several times. Albert began to whimper and tremble. Finally, the rat was offered alone, without the noise. Albert fell over, cried, and crawled away as fast as his little legs could carry him. The rat had become a conditioned stimulus for fear. Further tests showed that Albert's fear generalized to other hairy or furry objects, including white rabbits, cotton wool, a Santa Claus mask, and the experimenter's hair (see Figure 6.3).

Unfortunately, Watson and Rayner did not have an opportunity to reverse the conditioning. (The circumstances are unclear.) Later, however, Watson and Mary Cover Jones did accomplish a reversal in a 3-year-old named Peter (M. Jones,

phobia *An intense, unrealistic fear of a specific situation, activity, or object.*

FIGURE 6.3

Little Albert

This photograph, made from a 1919 film, shows John Watson, in a mask, testing Albert for stimulus generalization. (Photo courtesy of Prof. Benjamin Harris.)

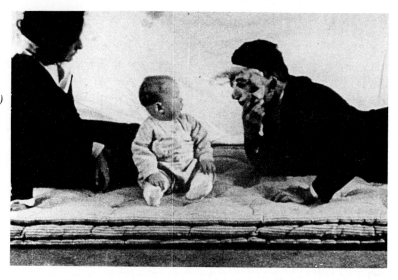

1924). Peter was deathly afraid of rabbits. His fear was, as Watson put it, "home-grown" rather than psychologist-induced. Watson and Jones eliminated it with a method called **counterconditioning**, which involved pairing the rabbit with another stimulus—a snack of milk and crackers—that elicited responses incompatible with the conditioned response of fear. At first, the researchers kept the rabbit some distance from Peter, so his fear would remain at a low level. Otherwise, Peter might have learned to fear milk and crackers! But gradually, over several days, they brought the rabbit closer and closer. Eventually Peter was able to sit with the rabbit in his lap, playing with it with one hand while he ate with the other. A variation of this procedure, called *systematic desensitization*, was later devised for treating phobias in adults (see Chapter 17).

The power of drugs. Since Pavlov's day, many researchers have concluded that a conditioned stimulus signals an organism to *prepare* for the unconditioned stimulus. So, when Pavlov's dog heard a bell, it salivated in preparation for digesting food. A preparatory (conditioned) response usually resembles the unconditioned response, but not always. Sometimes it is quite the opposite: Electric shock causes an increase in heart rate, but a stimulus that signals shock causes a *decrease* in heart rate. This fact has important implications for understanding drug addiction. Canadian psychologist Shepard Siegel (1983) argues that through a process of classical conditioning, habitual drug users learn to respond to various environmental cues for drug taking (the presence of needles, the company of other addicts) in a *compensatory* way. If the drug suppresses pain, for example, the conditioned response is an increase in sensitivity to pain. As a result, the body's reaction to the drug decreases over time; the person develops a tolerance for the substance, and more is necessary to produce the usual effects (see Chapter 4).

counterconditioning *In classical conditioning, the process of pairing a conditioned stimulus with a stimulus that elicits a response that is incompatible with an unwanted conditioned response.*

Experiments with both animals and human beings support this theory. In one study, male college students drank large amounts of beer at the same place on each of four consecutive days. On the fifth day, some of the students downed their beers at a new place. Students who remained at the original location scored higher on tests of intellectual and perceptual-motor skills, apparently because their bodies had learned to moderate the effects of alcohol in the presence of familiar cues (Lightfoot, 1980). In another study, researchers gave rats a strong dose of heroin. Some of the rats were already "experienced" with the drug. In inexperienced rats, the injection was almost always fatal, but in experienced ones the outcome depended on the setting: Two-thirds of the rats injected while in a strange environment died, versus only a third of those who remained in a familiar place (Siegel et al., 1982).

This work suggests that a dose that is ordinarily safe, given an addict's tolerance level, may be lethal when a drug is used in novel circumstances. The result may be sudden death. The importance of environmental cues may also help explain why residential drug rehabilitation programs so often fail: When people return to the neighborhoods where they used to take drugs, conditioned stimuli elicit the usual compensatory responses. In the absence of the drug, such responses are now experienced as a return of unpleasant withdrawal symptoms, and so a craving for the drug again develops (Siegel, 1983). The implication is that people who want to overcome drug dependence either must relocate to a new environment or must receive treatment that systematically exposes them to cues for drug taking until their responses to these cues become extinguished.

QUICK ▪ QUIZ

Supply the correct terms to describe the following:

1. After a child learned to fear spiders, he also responded with fear to ants, beetles, and other crawling bugs.
2. A toddler was afraid of the bath, so her father put just a little water in the tub and gave the child a lollipop to suck while she was being washed. Soon the little girl lost her fear of the bath.
3. A factory worker noticed that his mouth watered whenever the noontime bell rang, signaling the beginning of his lunch break. One day the bell went haywire and rang every half hour. By the end of the day, the worker had stopped salivating to the bell.

Answers:

1. stimulus generalization   2. counterconditioning   3. extinction

Operant Conditioning:
The Carrot and the Stick

Imagine that your 5-year-old nephew, frustrated by his failure to get his way, has decided to throw a tantrum. There he is on the ground, screaming, kicking, and turning an alarming shade of red. What is an adult to do? Many parents would yell at the boy or spank him. Others might try soothing him. But the best strategy—though not the easiest—is probably to ignore him completely. This approach takes advantage of a basic law of learning: *Behavior becomes more or less likely depending on its consequences.* By ignoring the child, you refuse to reward him with an emotional reaction or submission to his demands. You foil his plot.

An emphasis on the consequences of behavior is at the heart of **operant conditioning** (also called *instrumental conditioning*). In classical conditioning, the animal's or person's behavior does not have any environmental consequences. Thus in Pavlov's procedure, the dog receives food whether or not it salivates. But in operant conditioning, the organism's response (say, your nephew's kicking and screaming)

operant conditioning *The process by which a response becomes more or less likely to occur, depending on its consequences.*

operates or produces effects on the environment. These effects, in turn, influence whether or not the response occurs again. Classical and operant conditioning also tend to involve different types of responses. In classical conditioning, the response is reflexive, an automatic reaction to something happening in the environment (for example, the sight of food or the sound of a bell). Generally speaking, responses in operant conditioning are more voluntary, as in riding a bicycle, writing a letter, climbing a mountain, or throwing a tantrum.

Classical and operant conditioning often occur in the same situation. For example, when Little Albert learned to fear the rat, his trembling was classically conditioned. But when he learned to avoid the rat by crawling away (a response that had the effect of reducing his fear), that was an example of operant conditioning. In "A Closer Look at Consumer Psychology" we discuss how both classical and operant conditioning contribute to that perennially popular pastime, consumer spending.

Operant conditioning has been studied since the turn of the century. Edward Thorndike (1898) set the stage by observing cats as they tried to escape from a "puzzle box" to reach a food reward. At first the cat would engage in blind trial and error, scratching, biting, or swatting at parts of the cage in an unorganized way. Then, after a few minutes, the animal would chance on the successful response (loosening a bolt, pulling a string, hitting a button) and get the reward. Placed in the box again, the cat now took a little less time to escape. And after several trials, the cat immediately made the correct response. According to Thorndike's *law of effect*, the correct response had been "stamped in" by the satisfaction the animal felt at getting the reward. In contrast, punishments, being annoying, "stamped out" behavior. Behavior, said Thorndike, is controlled by its consequences.

This general principle was accepted by B. F. (Burrhus Frederic) Skinner, whose name is today most closely associated with operant conditioning. But Skinner refuses to make assumptions about how an animal feels or what it wants. Calling his approach "radical behaviorism," Skinner also parts company with the original behaviorists in other ways. For instance, John Watson argued that psychologists should study only public (external) events, not private (internal) ones. But Skinner maintains that we *can* study private sensory events (such as a toothache) by observ-

B. F. Skinner, at work on a scale model of a Skinner box.

A Closer Look at Consumer Psychology

Buy, Buy, Buy

You are strolling through the mall one day when an item in a store window happens to catch your eye. You want it. You *must* have it. Never mind that you can't really afford it; before you can say "MasterCard," you have bought it.

A *consumer psychologist* would want to know why you gave in to the impulse. Perhaps there was something about the window display that especially appealed to someone like you. Perhaps you had been bombarded lately by commercials for that product that wore down your resistance. The field of consumer psychology addresses these kinds of questions and many others. As you might guess, researchers in this field are in demand by advertisers, manufacturers, and retailers who want advice on how to capture the attention of potential customers and get people to open their wallets.

Consumer psychologists have shown that many of Madison Avenue's techniques are based on principles of conditioning, whether advertising executives realize it or not. For example, Gerald Gorn (1982) showed that associating an item with pleasant stimuli induces people to like the item itself. Gorn had college students view slides of either a beige or blue pen. During the presentation, half the students heard a song from the film *Grease* and half heard a selection of classical Indian music. (Gorn made the reasonable assumption that the show tune would be more appealing to Americans than the Indian music.) Later the students were allowed to choose one of the pens. Of those who had heard the popular music, 70 percent chose a pen that was the same color as the one they had seen in the slides. Of those who had heard the Indian music, 70 percent chose a pen that *differed* in color from the one they had seen.

This is an instance of classical conditioning: The music was an unconditioned stimulus for internal responses associated with pleasure or displeasure, and the pens became conditioned stimuli for similar responses. You can see why television commercials often pair products with music, attractive people, or other appealing stimuli.

Advertising is not the only influence on spending. Credit cards, as some of us know all too well, have a power of their own. Handing over your card to a salesperson is immediately rewarded by the delivery of a desired item into your hands; the payment comes much later. Thus, through a process of operant conditioning, credit card use becomes more likely. Even the mere presence of a credit card increases the likelihood and magnitude of spending. When a card is repeatedly paired with the responses involved in spending, it becomes on its own a stimulus for "spending behavior." Through a process of classical conditioning, the card may also come to elicit positive emotional responses (Feinberg, 1986).

If you are a seller, you will want to use psychology to attract customers—for instance, by displaying signs of the credit cards you accept. But when you are on the other side of the counter, being aware of conditioning principles can help you control your own spending. To avoid impulse buying, you might purposely leave your credit cards at home. To reduce your susceptibility to a commercial, you might turn down the sound. And next time you find yourself about to reach for an item at the end of the supermarket aisle even though it is not on your list, think of Pavlov and Skinner.

---

ing our own sensory responses and the verbal reports of others and the conditions under which they occur. Private events are as "real" or "physical" as public ones, Skinner believes. They are simply less accessible and therefore harder to describe precisely than are events in the world at large (Skinner, 1972).

While some other psychologists, notably the humanists, argue for the existence of free will, Skinner has steadfastly argued the view of *determinism*. Free will, he says, is an illusion. Environmental consequences may not automatically "stamp in'' operant behavior, but they determine the probability that an action will occur. Indeed, Skinner regards his own life as just a long case history of environmental influences. ''So far as I know,'' he wrote in the third volume of his autobiography (1983), ''my behavior at any given moment has been nothing more than the product of my genetic endowment, my personal history, and the current setting.'' Skinner would not credit mental events—plans, goals, thoughts, or motives—for his own or anyone else's accomplishments. As we explore the principles of operant conditioning, ask yourself if you agree with this view.

Reinforcers and punishers: A matter of consequence

In the behavioral analysis, a response can lead to one of three types of consequences. The first type is neutral as far as future behavior is concerned. That is, it neither increases nor decreases the probability that the behavior will recur. If a door handle squeaks each time you turn it, the sound may not affect whether you turn the door handle again in the future. The squeak would be a neutral consequence.

A second type of consequence involves **reinforcement**. In reinforcement, a reinforcing stimulus, or **reinforcer**, strengthens or increases the probability of the response that it follows. When you are training your dog to heel, and you offer it a doggie biscuit or a pat on the head when it does something right, you are using reinforcement (see Figure 6.4). Reinforcers are roughly equivalent to rewards. Strict behaviorists, however, avoid the term *reward* because it is the organism, not the response, that is rewarded. The response is *strengthened*. Also, in common usage, a reward is something earned that results in happiness or satisfaction. But technically, any stimulus is a reinforcer if it strengthens the preceding behavior, whether or not the organism experiences pleasure or any other positive state. Conversely, no matter how pleasurable a stimulus is, it is not a reinforcer if it does not increase the likelihood of a response. Like most psychologists, however, we ourselves have no objection to the use of *reward* as an approximate synonym of *reinforcer*.

reinforcement *The process by which a stimulus or event strengthens or increases the probability of the response that it follows.*
reinforcer *Any stimulus or event that strengthens or increases the probability of the response that it follows.*

(a)   (b)   (c)

FIGURE 6.4

Reinforcement in action
The dog's response, heeling (a), is followed immediately by a reinforcer, in this case praise and a pat (b). As a result, the response is strengthened (c).

(a)   (b)   (c)

FIGURE 6.5

Punishment in action

The dog's response, urinating on the rug (a) is followed immediately by a punisher, in this case a swat (b). As a result, the response is weakened (c).

The third type of consequence involves **punishment**. Punishment occurs when the stimulus or event that follows a response weakens it or makes it less likely to recur. Any aversive (unpleasant) stimulus or event may be a **punisher**. When you catch your dog in the act of urinating on the carpet and shout "No!" or swat it with the newspaper, you are applying punishment (see Figure 6.5). (Later we will see that punishment has many drawbacks as a means of behavioral control.)

Reinforcement and punishment are not as simple as they may seem. In our example of reinforcement, something pleasant follows the response, namely, the dog biscuit. This type of consequence is known as **positive reinforcement**. However, reinforcement can also involve the *removal* of something *unpleasant*, in which case it is called **negative reinforcement**. The same is true of punishment: Something unpleasant may occur or something pleasant may be removed (see Table 6.1).

It is too bad that the two kinds of reinforcement are called "positive" and "negative" because these terms are a great source of confusion to students. "Positive" and "negative" have nothing to do with "good" or "bad." They refer to procedures—giving something or taking something away. Both kinds of reinforcement make a response more likely. If someone praises Ludwig for doing his homework, that is positive reinforcement. If Ludwig's headache goes away after he takes an aspirin, that is negative reinforcement (of aspirin taking). Think of a positive reinforcer as something that is added or obtained, and a negative reinforcer as the avoidance of or escape from something. After Little Albert learned to fear the white rat, crawling away—an operant behavior—was negatively reinforced by escape from the now fearsome rodent. Negative reinforcement of "escape behavior" and "avoidance behavior" explains why so many fears are long-lasting. By avoiding a feared object or situation, you also avoid opportunities for extinguishing the fear.

Understandably, people often confuse negative reinforcement with positive punishment, since both involve an unpleasant stimulus. To keep the two straight, remember that punishment *decreases* the likelihood of a response. Reinforcement—either positive or negative—*increases* it. In real life, punishment and negative reinforcement often go hand in hand. If you use a choke collar on your dog to teach it to heel, a yank on the collar *punishes* the act of walking. But release of the collar *negatively reinforces* the act of standing still by your side.

punishment *The process by which a stimulus or event weakens or reduces the probability of the response that it follows.*

punisher *Any stimulus or event that weakens or reduces the probability of the response that it follows.*

positive reinforcement *A reinforcement procedure in which a response is followed by the presentation of, or increase in intensity of, a reinforcing stimulus; as a result, the response becomes stronger or more likely to occur.*

negative reinforcement *A reinforcement procedure in which a response is followed by the removal, delay, or decrease in intensity of an unpleasant stimulus; as a result, the response becomes stronger or more likely to occur.*

	TABLE 6.1			
	TYPES OF REINFORCEMENT AND PUNISHMENT			

When a stimulus event follows a response, its effect depends on the nature of the stimulus and whether it was presented or removed. The presentation of a pleasant stimulus or the removal of an aversive one is reinforcing. The presentation of an aversive stimulus or the removal of a pleasant one is punishing.

Procedure	Nature of stimulus	Type of stimulus event following response	Effect on response	Example
Positive reinforcement	Pleasant	Stimulus presented	Increases	Completion of homework assignments increases when followed by praise.
Negative reinforcement	Aversive	Stimulus removed	Increases	Use of aspirin increases when followed by reduction of headache pain.
Negative punishment	Pleasant	Stimulus removed	Decreases	Investing money in stock market decreases when followed by financial loss.
Positive punishment	Aversive	Stimulus presented	Decreases	Nail biting decreases when followed by bitter taste of substance painted on nails.

QUICK ▪ QUIZ

Which kind of consequence is illustrated by each of the following?

1. A child is nagging her father for a cookie. He keeps refusing, but she (being a talented behavior controller) keeps whining. Finally, unable to stand the aversive stimulation any longer, he gives in and hands over the cookie. For him, the ending of the child's nagging is a _____ . For the child, the cookie is a _____ .
2. A woman has been trying to get her husband to take responsibility for some domestic chores. One night he clears the dishes. She touches him affectionately on the arm. The next night he again clears the dishes. Her touch was probably a _____ .
3. A hungry toddler gleefully eats his oatmeal with his hands after being told not to. His mother promptly removes the cereal and takes the messy offender out of the high chair. The removal of the cereal is a _____ .

Answers:

1. negative reinforcer; positive reinforcer   2. positive reinforcer   3. punisher

---

primary reinforcer *A stimulus that is inherently reinforcing, typically satisfying a physiological need; an example is food.*

primary punisher *A stimulus that is inherently punishing; an example is electric shock.*

Secondary reinforcement

Food, water, light stroking of the skin, and a comfortable air temperature are naturally reinforcing because they satisfy a biological need. They are therefore known as **primary reinforcers**. Similarly, pain and extreme heat or cold are inherently punishing and are therefore known as **primary punishers**. Primary reinforcers and punishers are powerful controllers of behavior, but they also have their drawbacks.

For one thing, the organism may have to be in a deprived state for a stimulus to act as a primary reinforcer; a glass of water isn't much of a reward to someone who just drank three full glasses. Also, there are ethical problems with using primary punishers or taking away primary reinforcers.

Fortunately, behavior can be controlled just as effectively by **secondary reinforcers and punishers**, which are learned. Money, praise, a smile, a friendly greeting, applause, good grades, awards, and gold stars are common secondary reinforcers. Criticism, demerits, a frown, catcalls, scoldings, bad grades, and angry gestures are common secondary punishers. Most behaviorists believe that secondary reinforcers and punishers acquire their ability to influence behavior by being paired with primary reinforcers and punishers. (If that reminds you of classical conditioning, reinforce yourself with a pat on the back.) Secondary reinforcers and punishers are often called *conditioned* reinforcers and punishers.

Just because a reinforcer (or punisher) is secondary doesn't mean it is any less potent than a primary reinforcer (or punisher). Money, it has been said, makes the world go round. That may or may not be true, but it certainly has a great deal of power over most people's behavior. Not only can it be exchanged for primary reinforcers such as food and shelter, but also it brings with it other secondary reinforcers, such as praise and respect. But like any conditioned stimulus, a secondary reinforcer will eventually lose its ability to affect behavior if it cannot be paired at least occasionally with one of the stimuli originally paired with it. Today, U.S. pennies have become so worthless that billions of them go out of circulation each year because people throw them away or leave them on the ground when they drop.

Principles of operant conditioning

Thousands of studies have been done on operant conditioning, the majority using animals. A favorite experimental tool is the Skinner box, a cage equipped with a device (called a magazine) that delivers food into a dish when an animal makes a desired response (see Figure 6.6). Skinner originally created this apparatus by adapting a Sears, Roebuck ice chest.

Early in his career, Skinner (1938) used the Skinner box for a classic demonstration of operant conditioning. A rat that had previously learned to expect food from the magazine was placed in the box. Since no food was present, the animal proceeded to engage in typical ratlike behavior, scurrying about the box and randomly touching parts of the floor and walls. Quite by accident it happened to press a

secondary reinforcer *A stimulus that has acquired reinforcing properties through association with other reinforcers.*
secondary punisher *A stimulus that has acquired punishing properties through association with other punishers.*

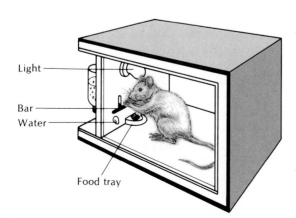

Light
Bar
Water
Food tray

FIGURE 6.6

The Skinner box
Rats have been popular research subjects in studies using this device. When a rat presses a bar, a food pellet or drop of water is automatically released. Skinner's own favorite subjects, however, have been pigeons, which are typically trained to peck at a disk or key.

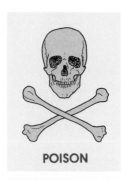

FIGURE 6.7

A warning or an invitation?

For children, who associate a skull and crossbones with pirates and treasure, the top label may be a discriminative stimulus for opening a container and exploring its contents. The National Poison Center Network has proposed that the bottom label be used instead.

extinction *The weakening and eventual disappearance of a learned response. In operant conditioning, occurs when a response is no longer followed by a reinforcer.*

stimulus generalization *In operant conditioning, the tendency for a response that has been reinforced (or punished) in the presence of one stimulus to occur (or be suppressed) in the presence of other, similar stimuli.*

lever mounted on one wall. Immediately a pellet of tasty rat food fell into the food dish. The rat continued its movements and again happened to press the bar. Plop! Another pellet. With additional repetitions of bar pressing followed by food, the animal's random movements began to disappear, replaced by more consistent bar pressing. Eventually Skinner had the rat pressing the bar as fast as it could shuttle back from the magazine.

By using the Skinner box and similar devices, psychologists have discovered many reliable principles of operant conditioning.

Extinction. In operant conditioning, as in classical, **extinction** is a procedure that causes a response to stop occurring. In operant conditioning, extinction takes place when an existing response is no longer reinforced and therefore becomes less frequent and eventually ceases. Suppose you put a coin in a vending machine and get nothing back. You may throw in another coin, or perhaps even two, before you finally stop trying. The next day you may put in yet another coin, an example of *spontaneous recovery.* Eventually, though, you will probably give up on that machine. Your response will have been extinguished.

Immediate versus delayed consequences. In general, the sooner a reinforcer or punisher follows a response, the greater its effect. This is especially true for animals and human children, but human adults also respond more reliably when they don't have to wait too long for a paycheck, a smile, or a grade. When there is delay, other responses occur in the interval, and the connection between the desired or undesired response and the consequence is weak. Suppose your naughty pooch has again urinated on the rug, but you have been away and don't discover the soiled spot until later. Now you swat the poor dog for its misbehavior. The punishment is not likely to work. Instead, a more recent behavior, such as approaching you as you enter the room, will be weakened. Holding the dog's nose next to the offending spot and then swatting it won't help either: You will merely be punishing the dog for putting its nose in that position! In operant conditioning, timing is all important.

Stimulus generalization and stimulus discrimination. In operant conditioning, as in classical, **stimulus generalization** may occur. That is, responses may generalize to stimuli not present during the original learning situation. For example, a pigeon that has been trained to peck at a picture of a circle also may peck at a slightly oval figure. But if the bird does not peck at the oval when it is presented, then **stimulus discrimination** has occurred. If you wanted explicitly to train the bird to make this discrimination, you would present both the circle and the oval, giving reinforcers whenever the bird pecked at the circle but withholding reinforcers when it pecked at the oval.

A somewhat different kind of discrimination occurs when an animal or human being learns to respond to a stimulus only when some other stimulus, called a **discriminative stimulus**, is present. The discriminative stimulus signals whether a response, if made, will "pay off." In a Skinner box, for example, a light may function as a discriminative stimulus for pecking at a circle. When the light is on, pecking brings a reward; when it is off, pecking is futile. Unlike the conditioned stimulus in classical conditioning, a discriminative stimulus does not reflexively elicit the response. It does, however, exert **stimulus control** over the response by setting the occasion for reinforcement to occur if the response is made. Human behavior is controlled by many discriminative stimuli, both verbal ("Store hours are nine to five") and nonverbal (traffic lights, door bells, the ring of a telephone, the facial expressions of others). Figure 6.7 shows a nonverbal discriminative stimulus that may have unintended consequences.

Learning to make discriminations is an essential part of the learning process. In a public place, if you have to go to the bathroom, you don't simply walk through any door that leads to a toilet. The words *Women* and *Men* are discriminative stimuli for entering. One word indicates that the response will be rewarded by the opportunity to empty a full bladder, the other that it will be punished by the jeers or protests of others. Similarly, when you go fly fishing, a smooth surface on a lake may cause you to put away your gear, whereas ripples and splashes tell you your efforts are likely to be rewarded by a tasty dinner. In the language of behaviorism, the jumping behavior of a trout is a discriminative stimulus for the fishing behavior of a human being.

In everyday life, failure to make appropriate discriminations can be a problem, but so can insufficient generalization. For example, "personal growth" workshops provide participants with lots of reinforcement for warmth, emotional expressiveness, and self-disclosure. Participants often feel that their way of interacting with others has been dramatically transformed. But when they return to normal life, where the environment is full of the same old reinforcers, punishers, and discriminative stimuli, they may find, to their chagrin, that their new responses have failed to generalize. A grumpy boss or cranky spouse may still be able to "push their buttons."

Learning on schedule. When a response is first acquired, learning is usually most rapid if the response is reinforced each time it occurs. This procedure of reinforcing every response is called **continuous reinforcement**. However, once a response has become reliable, it is more resistant to extinction if it is rewarded on a **partial** or **intermittent schedule of reinforcement**, which involves reinforcing only some responses, not all. (Skinner [1956] reported that he first happened on this property of partial reinforcement when he ran short of food pellets for his rats and was forced to deliver reinforcers less often. Not all scientific discoveries are planned!)

Many kinds of intermittent schedules have been studied. *Ratio schedules* deliver a reinforcer after a certain number of responses have occurred. *Interval schedules* deliver a reinforcer after the passage of a certain amount of time. The number of responses that must occur or the amount of time that must pass before the payoff may be *fixed* (constant) or *variable*. Combining the ratio versus interval and fixed versus variable patterns yields four basic types of schedule (see Figure 6.8). Each type has a characteristic effect on the rate and pattern of responding:

1. *On a **fixed-ratio (FR) schedule**, reinforcement occurs after a fixed number of responses.* An FR-2 schedule delivers a reinforcer after every other response, an FR-3 schedule delivers a reinforcer after every third response, and so forth. Fixed-ratio schedules produce very high rates of responding. In the laboratory, a rat may rapidly press a bar several hundred times to get a single reward. Outside the laboratory, fixed-ratio schedules are often used by employers to increase productivity. A salesperson who must sell a certain number of items before getting a commission or a factory worker who must produce a certain number of products before earning a given amount of pay (a system known as "piecework") are on fixed-ratio schedules. An interesting feature of high fixed-ratio schedules is that performance drops off just after reinforcement. If a writer must complete four chapters before getting a check, interest and motivation will sag right after the check is received.

2. *On a **variable-ratio (VR) schedule**, reinforcement occurs after some average number of responses, but the number varies from reinforcement to reinforcement.* A VR-5 schedule would deliver a reinforcer *on the average* after every fifth response but sometimes after one, two, six, or seven responses, or any other num-

After a weekend of "getting in touch" with your feelings, you are full of patience and goodwill toward others. Then why do you lose your temper just as easily on Monday morning as you did on Friday afternoon?

stimulus discrimination *In operant conditioning, the tendency of a response to occur in the presence of one stimulus but not in the presence of other, similar stimuli that differ from it on some dimension.*

discriminative stimulus *A stimulus that signals when a particular response will be followed by a certain type of consequence.*

stimulus control *Control over the occurrence of a response by a discriminative stimulus.*

continuous reinforcement *A reinforcement schedule in which a particular response is always reinforced.*

intermittent (partial) schedule of reinforcement *A reinforcement schedule in which a particular response is sometimes but not always reinforced.*

fixed-ratio (FR) schedule *An intermittent schedule of reinforcement in which reinforcement occurs only after a fixed number of responses.*

variable-ratio (VR) schedule *An intermittent schedule of reinforcement in which reinforcement occurs after a variable number of responses.*

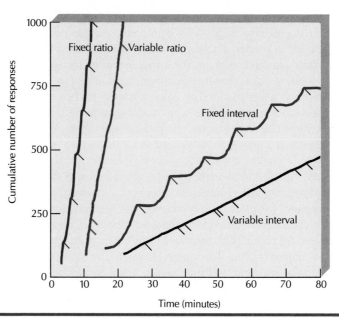

FIGURE 6.8

Reinforcement schedules and behavior

Different reinforcement schedules produce different learning curves, or patterns of responding over time. In research using the Skinner box, these curves can be recorded by a device called a cumulative recorder. Each time a response occurs, a pen moves up a notch on a moving strip of paper. The faster the rate of responding, the steeper the curve. In this figure, each crosshatch indicates the delivery of a reinforcer. Notice that when a fixed-interval schedule is used, responses drop off immediately after reinforcement, resulting in a "scalloped" curve. (Adapted from B. F. Skinner, "Teaching machines," November 1961, p. 96. Copyright © 1961 by SCIENTIFIC AMERICAN, Inc. All rights reserved.)

ber, as long as the average was five. Variable-ratio schedules produce extremely high, steady rates of responding. The responses are more resistant to extinction than when a fixed-ratio schedule is used. The prime example of a variable-ratio schedule outside the laboratory is delivery of payoffs by a slot machine. A player at a "one-armed bandit" knows that the average number of responses necessary to win is set at a level that makes money for the house. Hope springs eternal, though. The gambler takes a chance on being in front of the machine during one of those lucky moments when fewer responses bring a payoff.

3. On a ***fixed-interval (FI) schedule***, *reinforcement of a response occurs only if a fixed amount of time has passed since the previous reinforcer.* A rat on a FI-10-second schedule gets a food pellet the first time it presses the bar after the passage of a 10-second interval. Pressing the bar earlier does not hasten the reward. Animals on fixed-interval schedules seem to develop a sharp sense of time. After a reinforcer is delivered, they often stop responding altogether. Then as the end of the interval approaches, responding again picks up, reaching a maximum rate right before reinforcement. Outside the laboratory, fixed-interval schedules are not common, but certain behavior patterns do resemble those seen on such schedules. Suppose your sweetheart, who is away for a month, writes you a love letter every day. If the letter usually arrives at about noon, you probably won't check the mailbox at 8:00 A.M., but will start checking as noon approaches. Once the delivery is received, you will not check again until the next day (Houston, 1981).

4. On a ***variable-interval (VI) schedule***, *reinforcement of a response occurs*

fixed-interval (FI) schedule
An intermittent schedule of reinforcement in which a reinforcer is delivered for the first response made after a fixed period of time has elapsed since the last reinforcer.

variable-interval (VI) schedule *An intermittent schedule of reinforcement in which a reinforcer is delivered for a response made after a variable period of time has elapsed since the last reinforcer.*

only if a variable amount of time has passed since the previous reinforcer. A VI-10-second schedule means that the interval will average 10 seconds but will vary from reinforcement to reinforcement. Since the animal or person cannot predict when a reward will come, responding is low but steady. When you go fishing, you do not know whether a fish will bite in 5 seconds or 30 minutes (or at all). Under these conditions (assuming you really want that fish), you may steadily check your line every few minutes (Houston, 1981).

A basic principle of operant conditioning is that if you want a response to persist after it has been learned, you should reinforce it intermittently, not continuously. If an animal has been receiving continuous reinforcement and then reinforcement stops, the animal recognizes fairly rapidly that further responding will get it nowhere; at least, that is how it behaves. But if reinforcement has been partial, it takes longer for the animal to recognize that it has stopped. In the laboratory, pigeons, rats, and people on intermittent schedules of reinforcement have responded thousands of times without reinforcement before throwing in the towel, especially on variable schedules. Animals will sometimes work so hard for an unpredictable, infrequent bit of food that the energy they expend is greater than that from the reward; theoretically, the animal could actually work itself to death (Hill, 1985).

It follows that if you want to get rid of a response, you should be careful *not* to reinforce it intermittently. If you are going to extinguish undesirable behavior by ignoring it—a child's tantrums, a friend's midnight phone calls, a parent's unasked-for advice—you must be absolutely consistent in withholding reinforcement (your attention). Otherwise, you may only make matters worse. The other person will learn that if he or she keeps up the screaming, calling, or advice giving long enough, it will eventually be rewarded.

Shaping and chaining. For a response to be reinforced, it must first occur. But suppose you want to train a rat to pick up a marble, or a dog to stand on its hind legs and turn around, or a child to use a knife and fork properly, or a friend to play terrific tennis. Such behaviors, and most others in everyday life, have almost no probability of appearing spontaneously. You could grow old and gray waiting for them to occur so they could be reinforced. The operant solution to this dilemma is a procedure that Skinner calls **shaping**.

In shaping, you start by reinforcing a tendency in the right direction, then gradually require responses that are more and more similar to the final, desired response. The responses that you reinforce on the way to the final one are called *successive approximations*. In the case of the rat and the marble, you might deliver a food pellet if the rat merely turned toward the marble. Once this response was well established, you might then reward the rat for taking a step toward the marble. After that, you could reward it for approaching the marble, then touching the marble, then putting both paws on the marble, and finally holding it. With the achievement of each approximation, the next one would become more likely, making it available for reinforcement.

To teach a complex sequence of actions, shaping can be combined with a related procedure called **chaining**. In this procedure, you start by shaping the final response in the sequence and then work *backward* until a chain of behaviors has been learned. You give a reinforcer only for the final response (which is learned first). Gradually, you require more of the animal or person to get that reward. For example, in the laboratory an experimenter might train a pigeon to peck at a red light, then turn it off and require the animal to peck at a yellow one instead. Pecking at the yellow light is reinforced by the opportunity to peck again at the red one (the final response in the chain) and get a food reward. Using shaping and chaining,

Animals can learn to do some surprising things, with a little help from their human friends and the application of operant conditioning techniques. Water skiing, anyone?

shaping *An operant conditioning procedure in which successive approximations of a desired response are reinforced. Used when the desired response has a low probability of occurring spontaneously.*

chaining *An operant conditioning procedure in which a complex sequence of responses is established. The final response in the sequence is usually established first.*

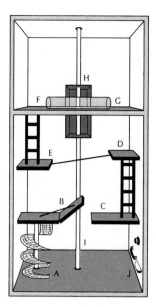

FIGURE 6.9

A rat's route

To demonstrate the effectiveness of shaping and chaining, a researcher trained a rat to perform a long sequence of activities in an apparatus resembling this one. Starting at point A, the rat climbs a ramp to B, crosses a drawbridge to C, climbs a ladder to D, crosses a tightrope to E, climbs another ladder to F, crawls through a tunnel to G, runs to H and enters an elevator, descends in the elevator to I, and runs out of the elevator to J, where it presses a lever and finally receives food. (After Cheney, in Chance, 1988.)

"Boy, do we have this guy conditioned. Every time I press the bar down he drops a pellet in."

Skinner was able to train pigeons to play Ping-Pong with their beaks and to "bowl" in a miniature alley complete with a wooden ball and tiny bowling pins. Rats have learned equally impressive behaviors (see Figure 6.9).

Animal trainers use shaping to teach dolphins to run flags up flagpoles, bears to ride bicycles, and dogs to act as the "eyes" of the blind. Shaping can be equally effective with human beings. According to one story (probably apocryphal, though it could have happened), some university students once used the secondary reinforcement of eye contact to shape the behavior of a famous professor who was an expert on operant conditioning. They decided to get him to deliver his lecture from one particular corner of the room. Each time he moved in the appropriate direction, they looked at him. Otherwise, they averted their gaze. Eventually, the professor was backed into the corner, never suspecting that his behavior had been shaped.

Superstition. So far, we have been talking about responses that directly bring about some consequence. But a consequence can be effective even when it is entirely coincidental. Skinner (1948) demonstrated this fact by putting eight pigeons in boxes and rigging the boxes so that food was delivered every 15 seconds, even if the bird didn't lift a feather. But pigeons, like rats, are often in motion, so when the food came, each animal was doing *something*. That something was then reinforced by the food. The behavior, of course, was reinforced entirely by chance, but it still became more likely to occur, and thus to be reinforced again. Within a short time six of the pigeons were practicing some sort of consistent ritual—turning in counterclockwise circles, bobbing the head up and down, swinging the head to and fro, or making brushing movements toward the floor. None of these activities had the least effect on the delivery of the reinforcer; the birds were simply superstitious.

Coincidental reinforcement probably accounts for many human superstitions. A baseball pitcher happens to scratch his left ear, then strikes out a star batter on the other team. Ever after, he scratches his left ear before pitching. A student always uses a "lucky" pen for taking tests because she used it on the first exam of the semester and got an A. Why, though, don't such superstitions extinguish? After all, the pitcher isn't always going to pitch a perfect game, nor is the student always going to be brilliant. One answer: because of intermittent reinforcement, which

"Good luck" objects and rituals—a lucky hat, knocking wood—don't "work" most of the time. Why do people superstitiously continue to believe in them?

makes a response particularly resistant to extinction. If coincidental reinforcement occurs occasionally, the superstitious behavior may continue indefinitely (Schwartz & Reilly, 1985). The fact that our little rituals only "work" some of the time ensures that we will keep using them.

There is another reason, however, that superstitions persist. People often try to find evidence to justify their superstitions, but typically they notice only confirming instances and ignore contrary evidence. As Paul Chance (1988b) points out, if a child finds a four-leaf clover and a few days later trips over a dollar, adults may point to the four-leaf clover's power. But if nothing particularly lucky happens to the child until puberty, no one points to the clover's failure. When people survive a plane crash, they often attribute their escape to prayer. "The chances are good that those who did not survive also prayed for all they were worth," notes Chance, "but they are now too dead to testify about the value of the procedure." As for good-luck charms and the like, as long as nothing awful happens when a person is carrying the charm, the person is likely to credit it with protective powers, but if something bad does occur, the person can always say that the charm has "lost" its powers. Chance says that he himself no longer has any superstitions. "A black cat means nothing to me now, nor does a broken mirror. There are no little plastic icons on the dashboard of my car, and I carry no rabbit's foot. I am free of all such nonsense, and I am happy to report no ill effects—knock wood."

Farmers sometimes put "hex" signs like this one on the sides of their barns to ward off evil spirits. Why do such superstitions persist?

QUICK ▪ QUIZ

Are you ready to apply the principles of operant conditioning? In each of the following situations, choose the best alternative and give your reason for choosing it:

1. You want your 2-year-old to ask for water with a word instead of a grunt. Should you give him water when he says "wa-wa" or wait until his pronunciation improves?
2. Your roommate keeps interrupting you while you are studying though you have asked her to stop. Should you ignore her completely or occasionally respond for the sake of good manners?
3. Your father, who rarely writes to you, has sent a letter. Should you reply quickly or wait a while so he will know how it feels to be ignored?

Answers:

1. You should reinforce "wa-wa," an approximation of *water*, since complex behaviors need to be shaped. 2. You should ignore her completely because intermittent reinforcement could cause her interruptions to persist. 3. You should reply quickly if you want to encourage letter writing. Immediate reinforcement is more effective than delayed.

Just deserts? The problem with punishment

In a novel called *Walden Two* (1948/1976), Skinner imagined a utopia where reinforcers were used so wisely that undesirable behavior was rare. His book gives a revealing glimpse of how a behaviorist might go about designing an entire community by using "behavioral engineering." But in the real world, boners, bloopers, and bad behavior abound. We learn bad habits as well as good ones, maladaptive behaviors as well as useful ones. Then we are faced with how to get rid of the bad habits and behaviors.

An obvious answer might seem to be punishment. "Spare the rod and spoil the child," goes the old saying, and many people believe it. The United States is one of the few Western countries that still permits corporal (physical) punishment of students by principals and teachers. (States vary in their policies.) According to one estimate (Hyman, 1988), at least half of all American schoolchildren are at some time exposed to physical or psychological punishment. Boys, minority children, and poor whites are the most likely to be hit. Our penal system is also based on the principle of punishment as a deterrent. Yelling, scolding, fining, and firing are familiar features of life. Does all this punishment work?

In the laboratory, aversive stimuli do make the behaviors they follow less probable. Punishment can also be effective in the real world. A study in Minneapolis found that men arrested for beating their wives were less likely to repeat the offense within six months than either men who were ordered by police to leave the premises for eight hours or men whose disputes with their wives were mediated by police officers. The police were cooperating with the researchers. They decided which action to take before entering a home, though they had the option of changing their minds if they judged the situation to be dangerous. In most cases, the arrested men were home within 24 hours, so lack of opportunity to repeat the offense could not explain the results. Apparently, most of the arrested men had not realized that beating their wives could lead to criminal charges, and they were shaken by the experience (Sherman & Berk, 1984). In any case, punishment worked.

Despite such successes, however, both laboratory and real-world studies show that punishment has some serious disadvantages as a method of behavior control:

1. *People often administer punishment inappropriately or when they are so enraged that they are unable to think through what they are doing and how they are doing it.* They swing blindly or yell wildly, applying punishment with such a broad brush that it covers all sorts of irrelevant behaviors. Indeed, even when people are not carried away by anger, they often misunderstand the proper application of punishment. One student told us his parents used to punish their children before leaving them alone for the evening because of all the naughty things they were going to do. Naturally, the children didn't bother to behave like angels.

2. *The recipient of punishment often responds with anxiety, fear, or rage.* These emotional "side effects" may then generalize to the entire situation in which the punishment occurs—the place, the person delivering the punishment, and the circumstances—through a process of classical conditioning. Such reactions tend to create more problems than the punishment solves. For example, the recipient might strike back or run away, outcomes that are rarely the goal of punishment.

3. *The effects of punishment are sometimes temporary, depending heavily on the presence of the punishing person or circumstances.* We can probably all remember some transgressions of childhood that we never dared commit when our parents were around but which we promptly resumed as soon as they were gone. All we learned was not to get caught.

4. *Most misbehavior is hard to punish immediately.* Recall that punishment, like reward, works best if it quickly follows a response, especially with animals and children. Outside the laboratory, quick punishment is often hard to achieve.

5. *Punishment conveys little information.* If it immediately follows the misbehavior, it may tell the recipient what not to do. But it doesn't communicate what should be done. For example, spanking a toddler for messing in his pants will not teach him to go in the potty.

*Warnings and threats of
punishment often don't
work.*

6. *Oddly enough, punishment sometimes backfires because it includes a powerful reward, attention.* In fact, angry attention may be just what the offender is after. If a mother yells at a child who is throwing a tantrum, the very act of yelling may give him what he wants, a reaction from her. In the schoolroom, teachers who scold children in front of other students, thus putting them in the limelight, often unwittingly reward the very misbehavior they are trying to eliminate.

Fortunately, there is an alternative to punishment: a combination of reinforcement (of the responses you want to encourage) and extinction (of the responses you want to discourage). The bad news is that extinction is sometimes difficult to carry out. It is hard to ignore the child nagging for a cookie before dinner, the roommate interrupting your concentration, or the dog barking its lungs out. Also, the simplest form of extinction, simply ignoring the behavior, is not always appropriate. A teacher cannot ignore a child who is clobbering a playmate. The dog owner who ignores Fido's backyard barking may soon hear from the neighbors. A parent whose child is a TV addict can't ignore the behavior, because television is rewarding to the child. (In this last case, a better strategy might be to encourage behavior that is incompatible with television watching, such as playing outdoors or reading.)

We don't want to imply that punishment is never justified. Consider the problem of highly disturbed children who engage in self-destructive acts. Such children may chew their own fingers to the bone, stick objects in their eyes, or tear out their hair. You can't ignore such behavior, for eventually the children will seriously injure themselves. You can't respond with concern and affection because you may unwittingly reward the behavior. Clinical studies find, however, that immediately punishing the self-destructive behavior eliminates it (Lovaas, 1977; Lovaas, Schreibman, & Koegel, 1974). Originally it was thought that rather strong punishment, such as electric shock, was necessary. However, milder punishers, such as a spray of water in the face, are equally or more effective. The word ''No!'' can also be established as a conditioned punisher.

In daily life, however, most psychologists believe that punishment, and especially severe punishment, is a poor way to eliminate unwanted behavior and in general should be regarded as a last resort. The elimination of undesirable behavior is usually best handled through a combination of reinforcement and extinction. When punishment is used, it should not involve physical abuse, it should be accompanied by information about what kind of behavior would have been more appropriate, and it should be followed, whenever possible, by the reinforcement of desirable behavior.

Putting Operant Principles to Work

The use of operant techniques (and also classical ones) in real-world settings is called **behavior modification**. Behavior modifiers have carried learning principles out of the narrow world of the Skinner box and into the wider world of the classroom, athletic field, prison, mental hospital, reform school, nursing home, rehabilitation ward, day-care center, corporation, factory, and office. They have taught parents how to toilet train their children (Azrin & Foxx, 1974) and teachers how to be "behavioral change agents" (Besalel-Azrin, Azrin, & Armstrong, 1977). They have taught autistic children who have never before spoken to use a vocabulary of several hundred words (Lovaas, 1977). They have trained barely functioning disturbed and mentally retarded adults to communicate, dress themselves, mingle socially with others, and earn a living in the community (Ayllon & Azrin, 1968; Lent, 1968; McLeod, 1985). And they have helped ordinary folk eliminate unwanted habits, like smoking and nail biting, or acquire wanted ones, like practicing the piano or studying. They have even used operant procedures, once thought applicable only to voluntary behavior, to modify such "involuntary" responses as heart rate and blood pressure (although the mechanism by which this process occurs remains controversial, as we saw in Chapter 3). Behavior modification has its critics, but behaviorists contend that life would be safer and saner if individuals and institutions were better at applying operant principles (see "Think About It").

Many behavior modification programs rely on a feature called a **token economy**. Tokens are secondary reinforcers that can be collected and exchanged for

behavior modification *The application of conditioning techniques to reduce or eliminate maladaptive or problematic behavior or teach new responses.*

token economy *A behavior modification technique in which secondary reinforcers called* tokens *are used as reinforcers. The tokens can eventually be exchanged for primary or other secondary reinforcers.*

FIGURE 6.12

Behavioral principles have practical consequences
This capuchin monkey has been trained to assist her paralyzed owner by picking up objects, opening doors, helping with feeding, and performing many other everyday tasks.

Think About It

The Use and Misuse of Reward and Punishment

Critics of behavior modification fear that its widespread use will crush creativity and turn people into sheep. To these critics, operant conditioning seems mechanistic and cold-blooded. It also seems unethical, especially when it involves the use of punishment or the withholding of reinforcers. These concerns have brought behavioral projects in many prisons, schools, and hospitals to a screeching halt. Behaviorists, however, contend that society needs *more*, not less, behavior modification. They point out that the unethical manipulation of others existed long before operant principles were known. Reinforcement, punishment, and extinction are always occurring, whether in a planned or unplanned way. The important question is whether society is willing to use behavioral procedures wisely to achieve humane goals.

All too often, say behaviorists, society either ignores the consequences of behavior or applies operant principles haphazardly. For example, in many states, nursing homes for the elderly receive more state aid for bedridden patients than for those who can get about. Thus there is no financial incentive for helping patients become independent. To take another example: Many health insurance plans will not pay for checkups when a person is well. Health care professionals believe that some serious, costly illnesses could be avoided if they were caught early during routine exams. Unfortunately, when insured patients are denied reimbursement for taking such preventive measures, they are not likely to do so. (On the positive side, some schools and large companies are establishing "wellness" programs and giving prizes for improved health habits. Also, insurance companies have begun to reward nonsmokers by reducing the cost of their premiums.)

Schools, prisons, and hospitals often set up rules for the convenience of the staff, without analyzing the impact on students, prisoners, or patients. Israel Goldiamond, a behaviorist who spent eight months in a rehabilitation hospital after an automobile accident, observed firsthand what can happen when behavioral consequences are ignored (Goldiamond, 1973). One of Goldiamond's roommates had undergone surgery for a brain tumor and was disoriented. He would not use the portable urinal supplied by the hospital, but instead urinated against the wall of the room. A hospital attendant who was studying psychology asked Goldiamond for his advice. Since the patient was always begging for cigarettes, Goldiamond suggested that these be used to reinforce delivery of a urinal to the attendant. The contents required for the payoff could gradually be increased.

The results were dramatic. On one occasion the patient searched most of the floor for the attendant, "with urinal in hand like Diogenes' lamp," in order to get his cigarette. But patients who go wandering about are viewed by hospital staff as a problem, and the experiment was terminated, with tragic results. The staff strapped the patient in a wheelchair and catheterized him. The man's rage increased, Goldiamond later recalled, "and he seemed to be on his way toward an inadvertently programmed organic psychosis."

Perhaps you can think of other social or institutional policies that have undesirable consequences because the basic principles of reinforcement are ignored. You may also be able to think of ways that governments and institutions might use operant principles to design more effective or beneficial policies. Do the potential advantages of these principles outweigh the potential risks feared by their detractors? If operant techniques should be used, how might institutions be persuaded to adopt them? What do you think?

---

primary and other secondary reinforcers. Money, tickets, and rain checks are examples of tokens. Once a particular behavior is established, tokens can be phased out and replaced by more "natural" reinforcers, such as praise.

Complicating Factors in the Modification of Behavior

We have made behavioral modification sound pretty easy. In the real world, though, it sometimes fails or even backfires. Operant procedures that appear simple are often difficult to apply in practice. Human beings may feel manipulated and refuse to cooperate. Situations are often so complex and uncontrolled that well-planned programs can go awry. In one study, a token economy system that had worked well with juvenile offenders in a pilot project fell apart when it was tried in a different institution. The people in charge neglected to smile as they handed out the tokens, and apparently the young men took their stern expressions as an insult (related by Pryor, 1984). Operant techniques may also fail when the underlying cause of the behavior is not altered. For example, rewarding cheerfulness in a mate may not do much good if his or her gloominess is caused by a boring job. The real solution may be for the person to change jobs.

Effective behavior modification is not only a science but an art. (In "Taking Psychology with You" we offer some guidelines for mastering that art.) Let us look at two other complicating factors.

When play becomes work: Intrinsic versus extrinsic reinforcers

People often work hard for money and good grades. Unhappily, these rewards can also kill the intrinsic pleasure of the activity. Could that be why so many college students stop reading after they graduate?

One complication is that human beings (and probably animals, too) work not only for **extrinsic reinforcers**, such as money and gold stars, but also for **intrinsic** ones, such as enjoyment of the task. As behavior modifiers have carried operant conditioning into real-world settings, it has become obvious that extrinsic reinforcement can turn into too much of a good thing. In fact, it can sometimes kill intrinsic motivation.

Consider what happened when psychologists had nursery school children draw with felt-tip pens (Greene & Lepper, 1974; Lepper, Greene, & Nisbett, 1973). The children already liked this activity and readily took it up during free play. First the researchers recorded how long each child spontaneously played with the pens. They then told some children that if they would draw with felt-tip pens for a man who had come "to see what kinds of pictures boys and girls like to draw with magic-markers," there would be a prize, a "Good Player Award" complete with gold seal and red ribbon. After drawing for six minutes, each child got the promised award. Other children were not led to expect a reward and were not given one. A week later, the researchers again observed the children's free play. Those children who had expected and received a reward were playing with the pens less than those who had not received an award. Further, they were spending much less time with the pens than they had before the start of the experiment (see Figure 6.10). Similar results occurred when older children were or were not promised awards for working on academic subjects.

Why should extrinsic rewards undermine intrinsic motivation? One possibility is that when we are paid for an activity, we interpret it as work. It is as if we say to ourselves, "I'm doing this because I'm being paid for it. Since I'm being paid, it must be something I wouldn't do if I didn't have to." When the reward is withdrawn, we refuse to "work" any longer. Another possibility is that extrinsic reinforcement raises the rate of responding above some optimal, enjoyable level. Then the activity does become work.

The temporary quality of extrinsically rewarded behavior is captured in a folk-

extrinsic reinforcers
Reinforcers that are not inherently related to the activity being reinforced. Examples are money, prizes, and praise.

intrinsic reinforcers
Reinforcers that are inherently related to the activity being reinforced. Examples are enjoyment of the task and the satisfaction of accomplishment.

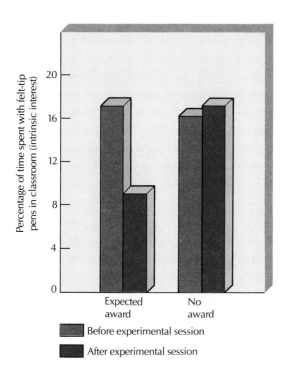

FIGURE 6.10

Turning play into work
Preschool children were promised a prize for drawing with felt-tip pens, an activity they already liked. Time voluntarily spent with the pens temporarily increased. But after the prize was awarded, the children spent less time with the pens than they had before the study. In contrast, children who were not promised or given an award continued to show interest in the activity. Such results suggest that extrinsic rewards can sometimes reduce intrinsic motivation.

tale about an old man whose peace and quiet were constantly disturbed by some rowdy children. The old man called the children over and said, ''I like to hear you play. If you'll come every day and make noise, I'll pay you each a quarter.'' Naturally, the children agreed, and that day they got their quarters. The next day, the old man said, ''I'm a little low on cash, so I can only pay you twenty cents.'' The children were disappointed, but they accepted. Each day the fee continued to fall, until it was only five cents. ''Well!'' snorted the children, ''We're not going to make noise for only five cents. It's not worth the effort.'' Off they went, leaving the old man to enjoy his tranquillity.

There is a trade-off, then, between the short-term effectiveness of extrinsic rewards and the long-term effectiveness of intrinsic ones. Extrinsic rewards work: How many of us would trudge off to work in the morning if we never got paid? (We might continue to work if we suddenly inherited enough money to last a lifetime, but every morning?) In the classroom, a teacher who offers incentives to an unmotivated student may be taking the only course of action open. But if the behavior is to last when the teacher isn't around, extrinsic reinforcers eventually must be phased out. As one mother wrote in a *Newsweek* essay, ''The winners [of prizes for school work] will . . . suffer if they don't discover for themselves that they can gain the pleasure of health and strength from exercise, the joy of music from songs, the power of mathematics from counting and all of human wisdom from reading'' (Skreslet, 1987).

The fact that our school system relies heavily on grades and other extrinsic incentives may help explain why the average college graduate reads few books. Many businesses and industries now recognize that workers' productivity depends not only on pay but also on having interesting, challenging, and varied kinds of work to do (see Chapter 10). We do not want to leave the impression, however, that extrinsic reinforcers always decrease intrinsic motivation. They usually do not interfere with intrinsic motivation when they are clearly tied to competence rather than mere performance of a task, and when the activity is one that is already well learned (Deci, 1975). The best approach is probably to use extrinsic reinforcers to supplement intrinsic ones, while creating opportunities for intrinsic reinforcers to operate.

''That is the correct answer, Billy, but I'm afraid you don't win anything for it.''

Biological limits on learning

Operant conditioning procedures work best when they capitalize on an animal's natural responses. It's easy to train pigs to hunt for truffles, a fungus that grows underground, because pigs have a natural rooting instinct.

Certain biological constraints on learning also limit the effectiveness of operant procedures. What an animal can learn depends on the physical characteristics of its body; a fish cannot be trained to climb a ladder. Further, animals seem to be biologically prepared to learn some responses more easily than others. In an article entitled ''The Misbehavior of Organisms,'' Keller and Marian Breland (1961), two psychologists who became animal trainers, described some fascinating failures in operant conditioning. The Brelands found that animals often had trouble learning what should have been an easy task. For example, a pig was supposed to drop large wooden coins in a box. Instead, the pig would drop the coin, push at it with its snout, throw it in the air, and push at it some more. This behavior actually delayed reinforcement, so it was hard to explain in terms of operant principles. Apparently the pig's rooting instinct (its tendency to use its snout to uncover edible roots) interfered with the desired learning. The Brelands called this tendency to revert to an instinctive behavior **instinctive drift**.

Operant procedures, and classical ones as well, seem to work best when they capitalize on inborn tendencies. Consider the psychologist mentioned earlier who learned to hate Béarnaise sauce. This incident differed from laboratory conditioning in many ways. Learning occurred after only one pairing of the sauce with illness and with a considerable delay between the conditioned and unconditioned stimuli. In addition, neither the psychologist's wife nor the plate from which he ate became conditioned stimuli for nausea, though they, too, were paired with illness. Controlled research suggests that certain animals (including, apparently, psychologists) are biologically prepared to associate sickness with taste rather than, say, with light and sound (Garcia & Koelling, 1966; Seligman & Hager, 1972). As we will see in Chapter 13, many psychologists believe that human beings are also biologically ''prepared'' to learn a type of behavior that gives our species a distinct advantage: language.

QUICK ▪ QUIZ

According to behavioral principles, what is happening here?

1. An adolescent whose parents have hit him for minor transgressions since he was small runs away from home.
2. A young woman whose parents paid her to clean her room while she was growing up is a slob when she moves to her own apartment.
3. In a scouting group, children earn points for performing good deeds. Later, they can exchange the points for toys and other items.
4. Two parents scold their young daughter every time they catch her sucking her thumb. The thumb sucking continues.

Answers:

1. The physical punishment was aversive, and through a process of classical conditioning, the situation in which it occurred also became aversive. Since escape from an aversive stimulus is negatively reinforcing, the boy ran away. 2. Extrinsic reinforcers are no longer available, and room-cleaning behavior has extinguished. 3. The scouts are on a token economy system of reinforcement. 4. Punishment has failed, possibly because it rewards thumb sucking with attention or because thumb sucking still brings the child pleasure whenever the parents aren't around.

instinctive drift *The tendency of an organism to revert to an instinctive behavior over time; can interfere with learning.*

Connections or Cognitions? Why Learning Occurs

Conditioning alters behavior. But why?

For half a century, most American learning theories were couched in the language of stimuli, or Ss, and responses, or Rs (Hill, 1985). This approach was known as **connectionism** because theorists assumed that what was learned was a bond or connection between Ss and Rs. In Pavlov's salivation experiments, the learned connection was said to link a conditioned stimulus, such as a bell, and a conditioned response, salivation. In the operant situation, the connection was between an operant response, such as bar pressing, and a situational consequence, such as food.

Skinner himself (1974) rejected a simple connectionist approach. He wrote not only about specific stimuli but about complex cues for responding, and not only about specific responses but about classes of behavior. He also acknowledged that rules, in the form of language, can control behavior. However, like all behaviorists, he avoided the use of mentalistic concepts to explain behavior. Nothing was to be gained, he said, by theorizing about hypothetical mental operations. For Skinnerians, behavior is adequately explained by specifying the behavioral ''ABCs''— *antecedents* (events preceding behavior), *behaviors,* and *consequences.*

In the 1960s, traditional behaviorist theories began to come under attack. A new view, labeled ''expectancy theory,'' emphasized the fact that when an organism behaves in a certain way, it acts as if it has certain expectations (Bolles, 1972; Bolles et al., 1980). Pavlov's dogs acted as if they expected the bell (CS) to be followed by food (US). According to expectancy theory, the critical connection in classical conditioning is therefore stimulus-stimulus (S-S), not stimulus-response (S-R), because an association is formed between the unconditioned and the conditioned stimuli. Similarly, in operant conditioning the organism acts as if it expects a response to be followed by a particular consequence. Skinner's rats acted as if they expected bar pressing to be followed by food. The critical connection here is a response-stimulus (R-S) expectancy. In any given situation, both S-S and R-S expectancies determine whether a response will occur. Suppose you are hungry and you see a sign that says ''Joe's Cafe.'' If you feel certain that the sign means food is in the building (S-S), and you expect that entering the building will get you food (R-S), you will enter.

Many expectancy theorists still have one foot in the connectionist tradition. They feel uncomfortable speculating about what an organism consciously experiences, and they stick to the language of Ss and Rs. But their views are a step away from strict behaviorism and a step closer to a more mentalistic view of learning. Other moves in the same direction have been prompted by findings on three kinds of learning that many psychologists believe require mentalistic explanations: latent learning, observational learning, and insight.

Latent learning: Delayed performance

Behaviorism emphasizes behavior. Sometimes, though, learning takes place without any obvious behavioral change. In a classic experiment, psychologists placed three groups of rats in mazes and observed their behavior each day for over two weeks. The rats in Group 1 always found food at the end of the maze. Group 2 never found food. Group 3 found no food for ten days but then received food on the

connectionism *The school of thought that explains learning in terms of connections or bonds between stimuli and responses.*

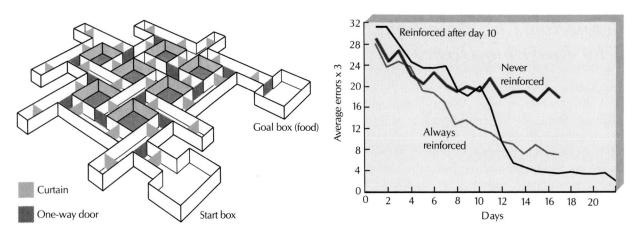

Curtain

One-way door

Goal box (food)

Start box

FIGURE 6.11

Latent learning

Rats were placed in a maze like the one on the left. Rats that always found a food reward in the goal box made fewer errors over time, as shown by the gray curve on the graph. In contrast, rats that never found food showed little improvement, as shown by the red curve. A third group of rats found no food for the first ten days and then were given food on the eleventh day. As the black curve shows, these animals showed rapid improvement from then on, quickly equaling the performance of the rats that received food from the start. This result suggests that learning involves cognitive changes that can occur even in the absence of reinforcement, although such changes may not be acted upon until a reward becomes available.

eleventh. The Group 1 rats quickly learned to head straight for the end of the maze without going down blind alleys, whereas Group 2 rats did not learn to go to the end. These differences can be predicted on the basis of what we know about reinforcement. But the Group 3 rats were different. For ten days they appeared to follow no particular route. But on the eleventh day, when food was introduced, they quickly learned to run to the end of the maze. As Figure 6.11 shows, by the next day they were doing as well as Group 1 (Tolman & Honzik, 1930).

Group 3 had demonstrated **latent learning**, learning that is not immediately expressed in an overt response. A great deal of human knowledge also remains latent until circumstances allow or require it to be expressed in performance. We learn how the world is organized, which paths lead to which places, and which actions can produce which payoffs. This knowledge permits us to be creative and flexible in the way we reach our goals.

Behaviorists have usually dealt with latent learning by defining learning as a change in behavior or in the *potential* for behavior. However, latent learning poses certain problems for behavioral theories. For one thing, it occurs in the absence of any obvious reinforcer. Of course, you can speculate about internal reinforcers, such as the satisfaction of curiosity, or about the anticipation of an eventual reward. But such explanations are similar to talking about feelings, motives, and expectations—in other words, mental events and operations, or *cognitions.*

Latent learning also raises questions about what, exactly, is learned during learning. The rats who were not given food until the eleventh day had no reason to run toward the end during their first ten days in the maze. Yet clearly they had learned something. One of the psychologists who designed the experiment suggested that this "something" was a **cognitive map**—a mental representation of the

latent learning *A form of learning that is not immediately expressed in an overt response. Occurs without obvious reinforcement.*
cognitive map *A mental representation of the environment.*

spatial layout of the maze (Tolman, 1948). Other studies of latent learning also seem to involve knowledge, not behavior. When a reinforcer is eventually introduced, it does not actually produce new learning; it merely motivates the person or animal to use already existing knowledge stored in memory. What's more, the behavior may take many forms. You can find your way to the supermarket in a car, even if in the past you have always walked there. The learned ''responses,'' then, are not muscle movements—but what are they?

Observational learning: The copycat syndrome

Observational learning, sometimes called *vicarious conditioning*, has also led psychologists toward a more cognitive view of learning. In observational learning, the learner observes a *model* (another animal or person) making certain responses and experiencing the consequences. Sometimes the learner mimics or imitates the responses shortly after observing them. At other times the learning remains latent. A young child may observe a parent setting the table, threading a needle, or tightening a screw, but not act on this learning for several years. Then the child finds he knows how to do these things, even though he has never before done them. He did not learn by doing, but by watching.

None of us would last long without observational learning. We would have to learn about avoiding oncoming cars by walking into traffic and suffering the consequences, or about swimming by jumping into a deep pool, or about staying warm by going out in a snowstorm without clothes. Learning would not only be dangerous but also inefficient. Parents and teachers would be busy 24 hours a day shaping children's behavior. Bosses would have to stand over their employees' desks, rewarding every little link in the complex chains we call typing, report writing, and widget building.

Observational learning can also explain how children acquire certain attitudes and responses, both positive and negative. In one study, nursery school children

observational learning *A learning process in which an individual learns new responses by observing the behavior of another (a model) rather than through direct experience. Sometimes called* vicarious conditioning.

Like father, like daughter. Parents can be powerful role models.

viewed a short film of two men, Rocky and Johnny, playing with toys (Bandura, Ross, & Ross, 1963). (The children apparently didn't think this behavior was odd.) In the film, Johnny refuses to share his toys, and Rocky responds by clobbering him. Rocky's actions are rewarded because he winds up with all the toys. Poor Johnny sits dejectedly in the corner, while Rocky marches off with a sack full of his loot and a hobby horse under his arm. After watching the film, each child was left alone for 20 minutes in a playroom full of toys, including some of the items shown in the film. Watching through a one-way mirror, the researchers found that the children were much more aggressive in their play than a control group that had not viewed the film. Sometimes the children's behavior was almost a direct imitation of Rocky's. At the end of the session, one little girl even asked the experimenter for a sack!

Albert Bandura (1973) has noted: "Children have been apprehended for writing bad checks to obtain money for candy, for sniping at strangers with BB guns, for sending threatening letters to teachers and for injurious switchblade fights after witnessing similar performances on television." Children also learn attitudes and behaviors from real models. This may be one reason why parents who hit their children for hitting playmates and siblings tend to rear children who are hitters, and why yellers ("Be quiet!") tend to rear yellers. The children do as their parents do, not as they say. Keep in mind, however, that observational learning is complex and interacts with many other influences. For example, although aggressiveness *can* be learned from media depictions (Comstock et al., 1978; Eron, 1980; Geen, 1978), not every child or adult who observes televised violence rushes out to commit mayhem. In fact, many studies find that media violence has no effect on behavior, or they suggest that it is mainly aggression-prone children who are affected (Freedman, 1988).

Behaviorists recognize the importance of observational learning and have attempted to explain it in stimulus-response terms. But many psychologists have concluded that observational learning cannot be understood without taking into account the thought processes of the learner (Bandura, 1977). They argue that traditional behavioral theories of learning do not actually explain learning, but only its expression in performance.

In observational learning, as in latent, the performance of a response is often delayed until long after learning has occurred, and the nature of the reinforcer during learning is not easily identified. Once the learner does perform the response, it is often carried out smoothly and without error, even though the learner has never done it before. Further, with human beings, an actual demonstration of behavior is often not necessary. One person can simply tell another how to make a bed or do long division or use a computer—a far cry from the simple reinforcement of a rat's bar pressing. Language gives us a short-cut method of observational learning. What the learner seems to learn is not a response, but knowledge about responses and their consequences.

Insight learning: The "aha!" phenomenon

insight *A form of learning that occurs in problem solving and appears to involve the (often sudden) understanding of how elements of a situation are related or can be reorganized to achieve a solution.*

Sometimes learning seems to occur in a flash. You suddenly "see" how to solve an equation, fix your carburetor, or finish a puzzle. This sort of learning, called **insight**, draws on previous experience but also seems to involve a new way of perceiving logical and cause-and-effect relationships. You do not simply respond to stimuli; you solve a problem.

Not only humans but also chimpanzees seem capable of insight. In the 1920s,

Wolfgang Köhler (1925) put chimpanzees in situations in which some tempting bananas were just out of reach, and then watched to see what they would do. The apes turned out to be very clever. If the bananas were outside the cage, the animal might pull them in with a stick. If the bananas were hung overhead, and there were boxes in the cage, the chimpanzee might pile up the boxes and climb on top of them to reach the fruit. Often the solution came after the animal had been sitting quietly for a while without actively trying to reach the bananas. It looked as though the animal was thinking about the problem and suddenly saw the answer.

Behaviorists argue that insight can be explained in terms of prior reinforcement history, without resorting to cognitive explanations (Windholz & Lamal, 1985). They observe that even animals not credited with higher mental processes seem capable of what looks suspiciously like "insight," if they have had certain experiences. In one ingenious study, researchers trained four pigeons to push boxes in a particular direction and also to climb onto a box to peck a toy banana overhead in order to obtain grain. The birds were also taught not to fly or jump at the banana. Then they were left alone with the banana overhead and the box at the edge of the cage. The pigeons quickly solved their feeding problem by pushing the box beneath the banana and climbing onto it, just as Köhler's chimps had done (see Figure 6.12). Here is how the researchers described the behavior of one bird: "It paced and looked perplexed, stretched toward the banana, glanced back and forth from box to banana and then energetically pushed the box toward it, looking up at it repeatedly as it did so, then stopped just short of it, climbed, and pecked" (Epstein et al., 1984). Yet few people would want to credit pigeons with complex thought.

For behaviorists, insight is the *result* of learning, not a way of learning. Other psychologists maintain that although human beings (and possibly chimpanzees) draw on previously learned responses to solve problems, insight requires mentally combining these responses in new ways. The cognitive interpretation is widely accepted. In truth, however, psychologists do not yet have much insight into how insight operates.

When a chimpanzee suddenly finds a way to reach some bananas, we say it has "insight." But what if a pigeon does the same thing? Can a birdbrain have insight?

 (a)

 (b)

 (c)

FIGURE 6.12

Smart bird
"Now, let's see. . . ." In Robert Epstein's laboratory, a pigeon looks at a cluster of toy bananas strung overhead (a), pushes a small box beneath the bananas (b), then climbs on the box to peck at them (c). The bird had previously learned separate components of this sequence through a process of operant conditioning. Behaviorists view this accomplishment, which resembles that of chimpanzees (see text), as evidence against the cognitive view of insight. Cognitive psychologists disagree. What do you think?

QUICK ▪ QUIZ

In the view of many psychologists, latent learning, observational learning, and insight require mentalistic rather than stimulus-response explanations. Which of these three kinds of learning does each of the following situations represent?

1. A woman trying to open her locked door suddenly runs to her purse, fetches a credit card, and inserts the card between the door and the door jamb, forcing back the lock. She has never seen or heard of this strategy used by anyone else.
2. After watching chef Julia Child make a perfect soufflé on television, a viewer who has never made one does the same thing in his own kitchen.
3. A Trivial Pursuit player answers a question with information she read in a magazine many years ago.

Answers:

1. insight 2. observational learning 3. latent learning

Cognitive theories: Peering into the black box

We close this chapter with a story, told by social-learning theorist Albert Bandura (1969). Once upon a time, there was a big-game hunter who came face to face with a hungry lion. As the hunter prepared to shoot the charging beast, the gun jammed. Terrified, the hunter closed his eyes and began to pray. Moments passed but nothing happened. Surprised and puzzled, the hunter slowly opened his eyes to find the lion also bowed in prayer. "Thank God," the hunter exclaimed, "you are responding to my prayers!" The lion promptly replied, "Not at all. I'm saying grace."

Because he did not know the lion's goals, intentions, and motives, the poor hunter lacked a complete understanding of its behavior. Similarly, most psychologists have concluded that a straightforward description of behavior is not enough to give them the understanding they desire. They feel that such descriptions treat an organism as if it were "empty." In contrast, cognitive psychologists maintain that people are full of attitudes, beliefs, and expectations that affect the way they acquire and store information, make decisions, reason, and solve problems.

Cognitive psychologists like to compare the mind to an engineer's hypothetical "black box," a device whose workings must be inferred because they can't be observed directly. By carefully examining the box's inputs and outputs, cognitive psychologists attempt to construct plausible models of what is happening inside the box. By carefully designing imaginative experiments, they objectively study such "mentalistic" phenomena as attention, silent rehearsal of information, imagery, and thinking.

As we saw in Chapter 1, cognitive theories have become increasingly influential in psychology. Strict behaviorists continue to reject these theories, considering them vague and unnecessary. However, other behaviorists have incorporated aspects of the cognitive approach into their thinking. For example, many now view classical conditioning as a means by which an organism represents the structure of its world. According to one researcher (Rescorla, 1988), "Pavlovian conditioning is not a stupid process by which the organism willy-nilly forms associations between any two stimuli that happen to co-occur. Rather, the organism is . . . an information seeker using logical and perceptual relations among events, along with its own preconceptions, to form a sophisticated representation of its world.''

Behavioral and cognitive explanations are now often treated as different levels of analysis, rather than conflicting ones. Also, because desirable behaviors acquired through behavioral techniques sometimes extinguish quickly or fail to generalize beyond the training situation, many therapists combine behavioral principles with cognitive ones to treat people in psychotherapy (see Chapter 17). Nonetheless, as we will see in the next two chapters, cognitive psychologists have staked out for study many areas that behaviorists have traditionally regarded as foreign territory— areas in the vast country of the mind.

Taking Psychology with You

Shape Up!

Operant conditioning can seem deceptively simple. Some popular books reinforce this impression. In the early 1980s, a tiny but expensive book called *The One Minute Manager* became an enormous best-seller simply by advising managers to use praise and constructive criticism. In practice, though, behavior modification can be full of unwanted surprises, even in the hands of experts. Here are some things to keep in mind if you want to modify your own or someone else's behavior.

- *Accentuate the positive*. Most people notice bad behavior more than good and therefore miss opportunities to use reinforcers. Parents, for example, often scold a child for bed-wetting but fail to give praise for dry sheets in the morning; or they punish a child for poor grades but fail to reward studying.
- *Reinforce small improvements*. A common error is to withhold reinforcement until behavior is perfect. Has your child's grade in math improved from a D to a C? Has your favorite date, who is usually an awful cook, managed to serve up a half-decent omelet? Has your messy roommate left some dirty dishes in the sink but vacuumed the rug? It's probably time for a reinforcer. On the other hand, you don't want to overdo praise or give it insincerely. Gushing about every tiny step in the right direction will cause your praise to lose its value, and soon nothing less than a standing ovation will do.
- *Find the right reinforcers*. You may have to experiment a bit to find which reinforcers a person (or animal) actually wants; one person's meat, as they say, is another's poison. In general, it is good to use a variety of reinforcers since using the same type over and over again can get boring. Reinforcers, by the way, do not have to be *things*. According to the *Premack Principle*, any response that has a higher probability of occurring than the one you are trying to train can serve as a reinforcer (Premack, 1965). In plain language, this means you can use valued activi-

ties, such as playing outdoors or watching television, to reinforce other behavior.

▪ *Always examine what you are reinforcing*. It is easy to reinforce undesirable behavior merely by responding to it. Suppose someone is always yelling at you for the slightest provocation or with no provocation at all. You find the yelling enraging and humiliating, and you want it to stop. If you respond to it at all, whether by crying, apologizing, or yelling back, you are likely to reinforce it. An alternative might be to explain in a calm voice that you do not respond to complaints unless they are communicated without yelling—and then, if the yelling continues, leave. When the person does speak civilly, you can reward this behavior with your attention and good will.

▪ *Set time limits*. This is a strategy for getting others to respond more quickly (Pryor, 1984). Let's say that when you call your roommates for dinner, they usually get there in about ten minutes, give or take a minute or two. Since they sometimes get there in eight minutes, serve dinner after eight minutes. Anyone who comes after that gets cold food. Then change the interval to six, then four, and so on. You don't have to explain what you are doing; if you just do it and are absolutely consistent, it will work.

Since you are with yourself more than anyone else, it may be easier to modify your own behavior than someone else's. You may wish to reduce your nibbling, eliminate a smoking habit, or become more outgoing in public. Let's assume, though, for the sake of discussion, that you aren't studying enough. How can you increase the time you spend with your books? Some hints:

▪ *Analyze the situation*. Are there circumstances that keep you from studying, such as a friend who is always pressuring you to go out or a rock band that practices next door? If so, you need to change the "discriminative stimuli" in your environment during study periods. Try to find a comfortable, cheerful, quiet, well-lighted place. Not only will you concentrate better, but also you may have positive emotional responses to the environment that may generalize to the activity of studying.

▪ *Set up realistic goals*. If you usually study only 30 minutes a day, don't suddenly hit the books for 5 hours straight. All you will do is make studying so aversive that you will tend to avoid it. Instead, reward yourself for small, steady improvements—perhaps 30 minutes the first day, 45 the next, and 60 the third.

▪ *Reinforce getting started*. The hardest part of studying can be getting started. (This is true of many other activities, too, as writers, joggers, and people who prepare their own income tax forms can tell you.) You might give yourself a small bit of candy or some other reward just for sitting down at your desk or, if you study at the library, setting out to get there.

▪ *Keep records*. Chart your progress in some way, perhaps by making a graph. This will keep you honest, and the progress you see on the graph will serve as a secondary reinforcer.

▪ *Don't punish yourself.* If you didn't study enough last week, don't brood about it or berate yourself with self-defeating thoughts, such as "I'll never be a good student" or "I'm a failure." Think about the coming week instead.

Above all, be patient. Shaping behavior is a creative skill that takes time to learn. Like Rome, new habits cannot be built in a day.

KEY WORDS

learning 206
instincts 206
imprinting 207
sensitive period 207
sociobiology 207
behaviorism 207
Ivan Pavlov 207
unconditioned stimulus (US) 208
unconditioned response (UR) 208
conditioned stimulus (CS) 209
conditioned response (CR) 209
classical (Pavlovian) conditioning 209
extinction (in classical conditioning) 210
spontaneous recovery 210
stimulus generalization (in classical conditioning) 210
stimulus discrimination (in classical conditioning) 211
higher-order conditioning 211
counterconditioning 214
operant conditioning 215
B. F. Skinner 216
reinforcement 218
reinforcer 218
punishment 219
punisher 219
positive reinforcement 219
negative reinforcement 219
primary reinforcers/punishers 220
secondary (conditioned) reinforcers/punishers 221
extinction (in operant conditioning) 222

immediate versus delayed consequences 222
stimulus generalization (in operant conditioning) 222
stimulus discrimination (in operant conditioning) 222
discriminative stimulus 222
stimulus control 222
continuous reinforcement 223
intermittent (partial) reinforcement 223
fixed-ratio (FR) schedule 223
variable-ratio (VR) schedule 223
fixed-interval (FI) schedule 224
variable-interval (VI) schedule 224
shaping 225
successive approximations 225
chaining 225
behavior modification 230
token economy 230
extrinsic reinforcers 232
intrinsic reinforcers 232
instinctive drift 234
connectionism 235
behavioral "ABCs" 235
latent learning 236
cognitions 236
cognitive map 236
observational (vicarious) learning 237
model 237
insight 238

SUMMARY

1. Not all behavior is learned. A great deal of animal behavior is instinctive. Some animals also show *imprinting* during a *sensitive period* of development. However, although most psychologists acknowledge that human behavior is influenced by our biological heritage, they doubt that either imprinting or true instincts occur in human beings.

2. Research on learning has been heavily influenced by the behavioral approach to psychology. A great deal of research has been devoted to two basic types of learning, classical conditioning and operant conditioning.

3. *Classical conditioning* was first studied by Russian physiologist Ivan Pavlov. He noted that when a neutral stimulus is paired with an *unconditioned stimulus (US)* that elicits some reflexive *unconditioned response (UR)*, the neutral stimulus comes to elicit a similar response. The neutral stimulus is then called a *conditioned stimulus (CS)*, and the response it elicits, a *conditioned response (CR)*. Subsequent studies demonstrated such phenomena as *extinction, stimulus generalization, stimulus discrimination*, and *higher-order conditioning*.

4. Classical conditioning may account for the acquisition of likes and dislikes, positive emotions, and fears and phobias. John Watson and his colleagues showed how fears may be learned and then unlearned through a process of *counterconditioning*. Classical conditioning may also be involved in such aspects of drug addiction as tolerance and withdrawal.

5. The basic principle of *operant conditioning* is that behavior becomes more or less likely to occur depending on its consequences. Research in this area is closely associated with B. F. Skinner.

6. The consequences of behavior may be neutral, reinforcing, or punishing. *Reinforcement* strengthens or increases the probability of a response. *Punishment* weakens or decreases the probability of a response. Reinforcement (as well as punishment) may be either positive or negative. *Positive reinforcement* occurs when something rewarding is added to a situation. *Negative reinforcement* is the removal of an unpleasant stimulus. Reinforcement may also be characterized as primary or secondary. *Primary reinforcers* are naturally reinforcing and usually satisfy a biological need. *Secondary reinforcers* acquire their ability to strengthen responses through their association with other reinforcers.

7. Studies have demonstrated that such phenomena as extinction, stimulus generalization, and stimulus discrimination occur in operant as well as classical conditioning.

8. The pattern of responding in operant conditioning depends in part on the *schedule of reinforcement. Continuous reinforcement* leads to the most rapid learning, but *intermittent*, or *partial*, *reinforcement* makes a response resistant to extinction. Intermittent schedules deliver a reinforcer after a certain amount of time has passed (*interval* schedules) or after a certain number of responses are made (*ratio* schedules). Such schedules may be *fixed* or *variable*.

9. *Shaping* and *chaining* are used to train complex behavior. In shaping, reinforcement is given for *successive approximations* to the desired response, until the desired response is achieved. In chaining, a sequence of actions is shaped, starting with the final one and working backward through the sequence.

10. Accidental or coincidental reinforcement can effectively strengthen behavior and probably helps account for the learning of superstitions.

11. Punishment has several drawbacks as a method for eliminating undesirable behavior. It is often administered haphazardly; it may produce such "side effects" as rage and fear; its effects are often temporary; it is hard to administer immediately; it conveys little information about what kind of behavior is desired; and it sometimes backfires by reinforcing behavior with attention. Extinction of undesirable behavior, combined with reinforcement of desired behavior, is generally preferable to the use of punishment, though not in all situations.

12. *Behavior modification*, the application of operant principles, has been used in many settings with success. However, problems also occur. For example, dependence on *extrinsic reinforcers* can undermine *intrinsic* motivation. Also, biological constraints may interfere with learning.

13. *Connectionist theories* of learning, which explain behavior in terms of stimulus-response connections, have difficulty accounting for *latent learning*, which appears to take place in the absence of any obvious reinforcement and does not involve an immediate (observable) response. They also have difficulty accounting for *observational learning*, in which the learner imitates the behavior of a model, and *insight learning*, which seems to occur suddenly and involve the understanding of relationships (though the interpretation of insight experiments with animals is controversial).

14. In the past few decades, *cognitive theories* of learning have become increasingly influential in psychology. Cognitive models attempt to explain how such mental phenomena as attention, imagery, and thinking can affect learning. The behavioral and cognitive approaches are quite different. However, many psychologists treat them as different levels of analysis that are not mutually exclusive.

C H A P T E R 7

Cognition I: Memory

Better by far that you should forget and smile
Than that you should remember and be sad.
CHRISTINA ROSSETTI

*W*hat is your earliest memory?

Swiss psychologist Jean Piaget (1951) once reported one of his own earliest memories—nearly being kidnapped at the age of 2. Piaget could remember sitting in his pram, watching his nurse as she stood bravely between him and the kidnapper. He could see the scratches she received on her face. He remembered a police officer with a short cloak and white baton who finally chased the kidnapper away. There was only one small problem: None of this ever happened. When Piaget was 15, his nurse wrote to his parents confessing that she had made up the entire story. Piaget noted, "I therefore must have heard, as a child, the account of this story . . . and projected it into the past in the form of a visual memory, which was a memory of a memory, but false."

A young woman we know recalls a more serene early memory. She was about 5 years old, on a car trip in Ireland with her parents. From the window she was looking out on velvety green hills. The sun was emerging after a downpour, and there was a spectacular rainbow. The image of her father is especially vivid in her mind's eye. "It's all so clear, so real," she says, "that sometimes I can close my eyes and go there." There is only one small problem: Our friend was completely blind until age 7, and her father died when she was 4.

Memory, as you can see, plays tricks. We remember things that never happened and forget things that did take place. Even recent memories can evaporate like the morning dew. Yet memory can also be remarkably accurate. Who were some of your teachers in grammar school? Who fought whom in World War II? How do you compute the circumference of a circle? When are presidential elections held? What is the tune of Paul McCartney's song "Yesterday"? Each of us holds in memory hundreds of thousands of facts, descriptions, and skills, available in an instant.

Visual memory is often especially accurate. Roger Shepard (1967) had students view 612 colored pictures on slides. Then the pictures were paired with new ones, and the students had to select the ones they had previously seen. Immediately after the original presentation, recognition was 96.7 percent, and four months later it was still better than 50 percent. Subsequent research showed that even if the original set of slides contained 2560 different photographs, recognition remained high (Haber, 1970).

It's a good thing, of course, that **memory**, the capacity to retain and retrieve information, is so accurate. Memory confers competence; without it we would all be as helpless as infants, unable to negotiate even the most trivial of our daily tasks, from brushing our teeth to turning on the television set. Memory also confers a sense of personal identity. In a real sense, each of us is the sum total of his or her personal recollections. Both individuals and cultures rely on a remembered history for a sense of coherence and meaning. Memory preserves the past and guides the future. In the words of philosopher George Santayana, "Those who cannot remember the past are condemned to repeat it."

Language forces us to refer to memory as if it were a single ability or faculty (as in, "I must be losing my memory"). Actually, however, the term *memory* covers a complex collection of abilities, processes, and mental systems. In this chapter, we

memory *The capacity to retain and retrieve information. It also refers to the mental structure or structures that account for this capacity and to the material that is retained.*

247

will see how these abilities, processes, and systems allow us to remember, and why, despite our best efforts, we so often forget.

The Information-Processing Approach to Memory

In the past, philosophers often compared memory to a tablet of hot wax that would preserve anything that chanced to make an imprint on it. Today some popular writers refer to memory as if it were a tape recorder, faithfully and automatically recording every moment of our lives. But both these analogies are misleading because memory is highly selective. Not everything that happens to us or impinges on our senses is tucked away for later use. If it were, our minds would be cluttered with all sorts of mental ''junk''—the temperature at noon on Thursday, the sale price of hamburger two years ago, a phone number needed only once.

Most current models of memory view the human mind not as a wax tablet or a tape recorder but as an information processor, analogous in some ways to an electronic computer, only far more complex. These models borrow liberally from the language of computer programming: Instead of stimuli, there are ''inputs''; instead of responses, there are ''outputs''; and between the inputs and outputs, information is actively processed in a series of stages, or ''subroutines.'' Though the mind of a machine differs in many ways from that of a human being (see Chapter 8), information-processing approaches have proven useful. They capture the fact that the brain does not passively record information but alters and organizes it.

Encoding, storage, and retrieval

All information-processing theorists agree that what gets stored in memory is not an exact replica of experience. If information is to be retained, it must first be **encoded**, or converted to a form that the brain can process and store. Sensory information is changed in form almost as soon as it is detected (see Chapter 5), and the form retained for the long run is different from the original stimulus. For example, when you hear a lecture, you may hang on every word, but you do not store those words verbatim. Instead, you convert sentences to units of meaning, probably in the form of *propositions* (Anderson & Bower, 1973). Propositions are similar to sentences, but they express unitary ideas and are made up of abstract concepts rather than words. Thus the sentence ''The clever psychologist made an amazing discovery'' contains three propositions that can be expressed by the words *the psychologist was clever*, *the psychologist made a discovery*, and *the discovery was amazing*.

A man who emigrated from Germany at a young age and forgot all his German would still remember facts learned in the first grade because such information is stored as propositions, not as strings of German (or English) words. But most psychologists believe that information can also be stored in other forms. Some memories seem similar to visual or auditory images. Others, such as those that allow you to swim or ride a bicycle, seem to be stored as sets of kinesthetic (muscular) instructions.

With certain kinds of information, encoding takes place automatically; you don't have to make a deliberate effort. Think about your bedroom. When were you last there? What color are the walls? Where is the bed located? You can probably

encoding (in memory) *The conversion of information into a form that can be stored and retrieved.*

provide this information easily, although you never made an effort to encode it. In general, people automatically encode their location in space and time and the frequency with which they experience various situations (Hasher & Zacks, 1984). But other kinds of information require *effortful* encoding. To retain the information, you might have to label it, associate it with other material, or rehearse it until it is familiar. A woman we know tells us that in her ballet class, when she is asked to do a *pas de bourrée* she knows exactly what to do, yet she often has trouble recalling and using the term. This is probably in part because she has only heard the term and rarely uses it, and so has not bothered to encode it well.

Unfortunately, people sometimes count on automatic encoding when effortful encoding is called for. They may assume they can encode the material in a textbook as effortlessly as they encode the color of their bedrooms, and they wind up in trouble at test time. (Yes, this is a hint.)

The two other basic memory processes are *storage* and *retrieval*. Storage is simply the retention of information over time. Retrieval is the recovery of stored material, or what a computer programmer might call the "accessing" of information. When memory works well, encoding leads to storage and storage permits retrieval. Sometimes, however, information is temporarily encoded but not retained for the long run. And as we will see, even if it does get stored a person may have trouble retrieving it.

Three systems of memory

Once information is encoded, where does it go? Most people think of memory as a single "place" or system. But information-processing theorists view memory as three separate, interacting systems. The first is **sensory memory**, which retains incoming sensory information for at most a second or two, until it can be processed further. The second is **short-term memory (STM)**, which holds a limited amount of information for a brief period of time, perhaps up to 30 seconds or so, unless a conscious effort is made to keep it there longer. The third system is **long-term memory (LTM)**, which accounts for the more or less permanent storage.

sensory memory *A memory system that momentarily preserves literal images of sensory information.*
short-term memory (STM) *A limited capacity memory system involved in the retention of information for brief periods. It is used to store recently perceived information and information retrieved from long-term memory for temporary use.*
long-term memory (LTM) *The memory system involved in the long-term retention of information; theoretically, it has an unlimited capacity.*

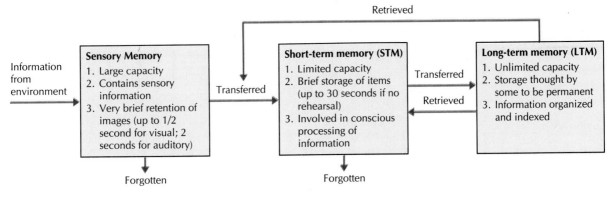

FIGURE 7.1

Three memory systems
Most memory models distinguish three separate but interacting memory systems, as shown in this diagram (although some models would draw the arrows somewhat differently). Note that when information does not transfer from sensory memory to short-term memory it decays or is displaced and is therefore forgotten. The same is true for information that does not transfer from short-term memory to long-term memory. Once in long-term memory, information can be retrieved for use in the analysis of incoming data or for temporary mental operations performed in short-term memory.

According to the **multistore model of memory** (sometimes informally called the "three-box model"), information can pass from sensory memory to short-term memory and in either direction between short-term and long-term memory (see Figure 7.1). To encode this model in your own memory, you might think of "memory" as a library building that contains an entry area, a work area, and the stacks. A new piece of information passes through the entry area to the work area, where a decision is made about whether it should remain permanently. If the answer is yes, the information is stored in the stacks. From there, it can be called up for temporary use in the work area. This analogy does not imply that there are actually three separate "places" in the brain corresponding to the three memory storehouses. Talking about memory systems as places is merely a convenience. The three systems are actually clusters of mental processes that occur at different stages.

The multistore model has dominated research on memory for nearly three decades and has been extremely useful. However, it does not explain all the findings, and in the past few years at least six other models have been proposed. Advocates of these models disagree with each other about how information passes from one kind of memory system to another and how information gets encoded and stored in each system. One researcher, Nelson Cowan (1988), argues that incoming information must pass *first* through long-term memory before entering short-term memory. In his model, short-term memory is simply an activated *subset* of long-term memory. It contains whatever information is available for immediate use, whether a person is consciously focusing on that information or not.

Details about competing models of memory are beyond the scope of this book, and until the dust settles, we cannot say which one works best. The important point here is that most information-processing theorists continue to make distinctions among sensory, short-term, and long-term memories.

Fleeting Impressions: Sensory Memory

All incoming sensory information must make a brief stop in *sensory memory*, the entry area of memory. According to most models of memory, sensory memory includes a number of separate memory subsystems, or **sensory registers**—as many as there are senses. Information in sensory memory is short-lived. Visual images, or *icons*, remain for a maximum of half a second in a visual sensory register. Auditory images, or *echoes*, remain for a slightly longer time, by most estimates up to two seconds or so, in an auditory sensory register.

Sensory memory acts as a sort of holding bin, retaining information just until we can select items for attention from the stream of stimuli bombarding our senses. In most models of memory, *pattern recognition*, the preliminary identification of a stimulus on the basis of information already contained in long-term memory, occurs during the transfer of information from sensory memory to short-term memory. Information that does not go on to short-term memory vanishes forever, like a message written in disappearing ink.

Images in sensory memory are fairly complete. How do we know that? In a clever experiment, George Sperling (1960) briefly presented subjects with a visual array of letters like the one that follows:

X K C Q

N D X G

T F R J

multistore model of memory *A model that portrays the encoding, storage, and retrieval of information as involving three separate though interacting memory systems: sensory memory, short-term memory, and long-term memory.*

sensory registers *Subsystems of sensory memory. Most memory models assume a separate register for each sensory modality.*

In previous studies, subjects had been able to recall only four or five letters, no matter how many were initially shown. Yet many people insisted that they had seen more items than they could remember. Some of the letters, they said, seemed to slip away before they could be reported. To overcome this problem, Sperling devised a method of "partial report." He had subjects report the first row of letters when they heard a high tone, the middle row when they heard a medium tone, and the third row when they heard a low tone:

X	K	C	Q	←	High tone
N	D	X	G	←	Medium tone
T	F	R	J	←	Low tone

If the tone occurred right after presentation of the array, people could recall about three letters from a row. Since they did not know beforehand which row they would have to report, they therefore must have had most of the letters in sensory memory. However, if the tone occurred after a delay of even one second, people remembered very little of what they had seen. The letters had slipped away.

Sensory memory could be involved in the curious phenomenon of **déjà vu**. That is the feeling that something happening now has happened before in *exactly* the same way. Perhaps déjà vu occurs when information entering sensory memory "short-circuits," or fails to complete its normal route, and must therefore be reprocessed. The feeling of familiarity would result from the fact that you *did* experience exactly the same situation before—though only a fraction of a second before. If you were unable to determine when the initial processing occurred, you might mistakenly feel that the experience had occurred in the more distant past. Unfortunately, however, this and other psychological explanations of déjà vu are as difficult to prove as more exotic ones that assume reincarnation or dreams that predict the future.

We also wonder if the visual sensory register could be involved in a poorly understood (and still controversial) phenomenon called **eidetic imagery**. A person with eidetic imagery, usually a child, can reportedly look at a picture for several seconds, look away, and "see" a literal image of the picture projected on the wall or on a blank sheet of paper. The image is experienced as "out there" rather than in "the mind's eye." Like images in sensory memory, eidetic images are accurate, but they last considerably longer, for at least half a minute and often for several minutes. While they remain, the person seems able to "read" information from them just as from a real picture. Eidetic images arise spontaneously. In fact, any attempt by the "eidetiker" to memorize a picture by naming or labeling the items in it seems to prevent formation of the image. Perhaps the eidetic image is actually an image from the visual sensory register that for some reason has stayed around longer than usual.

Eidetic imagery seems to occur in about 8 children out of 100 (Haber, 1969, 1974). It usually disappears by adolescence, perhaps because by then language is the dominant way of processing new information. Since eidetic images usually cannot be reinstated once they disappear, eidetikers cannot recall events or memorize material better than anyone else. Indeed, eidetic images are a potential nuisance. Imagine what would happen if you had eidetic images that kept popping back into view or that lasted a long time. You might turn a page of music only to see a previous page's notes superimposed on the new ones! To avoid such confusion, eidetikers apparently prevent the production of images in daily life by taking care not to look at anything too long and by forcefully blinking the eyes to "erase" an image.

You're traveling in Turku for the first time in your life, when suddenly you have a weird feeling of déjà vu; you're sure you've been there before. Does this sensation occur because of a glitch in the sensory register? What else might cause it?

---

déjà vu [day-zhah voo]
The feeling that something happening at the present moment has happened before in exactly the same way. From the French for "already seen."
eidetic [eye-DET-ik] imagery *An image of a visual stimulus that appears to exist in the external environment instead of in "the mind's eye" and that can be "read" for information.*

If the sensory register did not clear quickly, multiple images might interfere with the accurate perception and encoding of information.

In normal processing, too, sensory memory needs to clear quickly to prevent sensory "double exposures." It also acts as a filter, keeping out extraneous and unimportant information. Our brains store trillions of bits of information during our lifetimes. Processing everything detected by our senses, including irrelevancies, would lead to inefficiency and frustration.

Memory's Work Area: Short-term Memory

Like sensory memory, *short-term memory (STM)* retains information only temporarily—for up to about 30 seconds by most estimates (Atkinson & Shiffrin, 1968, 1971; Shiffrin & Atkinson, 1969), although some think the maximum interval may extend to a few minutes (Melton, 1963). In short-term memory, the material is no longer an exact sensory image but an encoding of one, such as a word or a number. In the multistore model, this material either transfers into long-term memory or decays and is lost forever. (There are, however, ways to keep material in short-term memory beyond the usual limits, as we will see.)

Cases of brain injury demonstrate the importance of transferring new information out of short-term memory and into long-term memory. You may recall the tragic case of H. M., described in Chapter 3. Ever since his amygdala and much of his hippocampus were surgically removed in 1953, H. M. has suffered from **anterograde amnesia**, the inability to form long-term memories for new events and facts. H. M. does store information on a short-term basis; he can hold a conversation and appears normal when you first meet him. Moreover, memories that were already encoded in long-term memory before the operation remain intact; H. M. can recall most of what happened before the surgery. However, H. M. cannot retain information about new facts and events for longer than a few minutes. He must be reintroduced to his doctors each time he sees them, and he can read the same magazine over and over without realizing that he has read it before. Today, because he has aged, he can no longer recognize a photograph of his own face; he is stuck in a time warp from the past. Many psychologists attribute these terrible memory deficits,

anterograde amnesia *Loss of the ability to form long-term memories for new facts and events.*

which have also been seen in other patients, to a problem in transferring material out of short-term memory and into long-term storage.

Besides retaining new information for brief periods, short-term memory also holds information that has been retrieved from long-term memory for temporary use. For this reason, short-term memory is sometimes called *active* or *working* memory. When you do an arithmetic problem, working memory contains the numbers and the instructions for doing the necessary operations ("add the right column, carry the 2"), plus the intermediate results from each step. The ability to bring information from long-term memory into working memory is *not* disrupted in patients like H. M. They can do arithmetic, converse, relate events that occurred before their injury, and do anything else that requires retrieval of information from long-term into short-term memory. (Try to remember H. M., as we will later examine research that may explain why his memory is impaired in some ways but not in others.)

Chunks of experience

We all know what it is like to look up a telephone number, dial it, get a busy signal, and then find a moment later that we have forgotten the number. The information has vanished from short-term memory. The same thing happens when you are introduced to someone and seconds later can't, for the life of you, recall that person's name. Is it any wonder that short-term memory has been called a "leaky bucket"?

According to most memory models, if the bucket did not leak it would quickly overflow, because at any given moment short-term memory can hold only a few items. Years ago, George Miller estimated its capacity to be "the magical number 7 plus or minus 2" (G. A. Miller, 1956). (Five-number zip codes and seven-number telephone numbers fall conveniently in this range.) More recently, others have questioned whether Miller's magical number is all that magical. Estimates of STM's capacity have ranged from 2 items to 20, with most of the estimates at the lower end. Everyone agrees, however, that the capacity of short-term memory is exceedingly small.

If this is so, how do we remember the beginning of a spoken sentence until the speaker reaches the end? After all, most sentences are longer than just a few words. According to most models of memory, we overcome this problem by grouping small bits of information into larger units, or **chunks**. The real capacity of STM, then, is not a few bits of information but a few chunks. A chunk may be a word, a phrase, a sentence, or even a visual image, and it depends on previous experience. For most of us, the date *1492* is one chunk, not four. The acronym *FBI* is also one chunk. In contrast, the number *9214* is four chunks, and *IBF* is three—unless your address is 9214 or your initials are IBF. To take another, more visual example: If you are ignorant of football and look at a field full of players, you probably won't be able to remember their positions when you look away. But if you are a fan, you may see a single chunk of information—say, a wishbone formation—and be able to retain it for some time.

Even chunking, however, cannot keep short-term memory from eventually filling up. The "work area" of the mind's library has only a few desks in it, and although these desks can bear a lot of weight, sooner or later some items must leave so others can enter. Fortunately, much of the information we encounter during the day is needed for only a few moments. If you are multiplying two numbers, you need to remember which ones they are only until you have the answer. If you are

chunk *A meaningful unit of information; may be comprised of smaller units.*

"Chunking" increases the amount of information that can be held in short-term memory. If you don't play chess, the pieces on a chess board will look randomly placed and you won't be able to recall their positions when you look away. But experienced chess players, in the middle of a game, can remember the positions of every piece after glancing briefly at the board. They "chunk" the pieces into a few standard configurations, instead of trying to memorize where each individual piece is located.

talking to someone, you need to keep their words in mind only until you have understood them. But other information is needed for longer periods and must be transferred to long-term memory. Items that are particularly meaningful, have an emotional impact, or link up to something already in long-term memory, may enter long-term storage easily, with only a brief stay in STM. The destiny of other items depends on how soon new information replaces them. The longer information remains in short-term memory, the more likely it is to pass into long-term memory.

Retention strategies

One technique for keeping items in short-term memory is **rehearsal**. In a classic study, people were given meaningless groups of letters to memorize. Immediately afterward, they had to start counting backward by threes from an arbitrary number, which prevented them from rehearsing the letter groups. Within only 18 seconds, the subjects forgot most of the items (see Figure 7.2). But when they did not have to count backward, their performance was much better, probably because they were rehearsing the items to themselves (Peterson & Peterson, 1959). Similarly, if you repeat a telephone number over and over, you will be able to retain it in short-term memory for as long as you like; but if you look up a number and then get into a conversation with someone, you are apt to forget the number almost immediately.

Short-term memory can apparently hold many kinds of information, including visual information and abstract meanings. (Some theorists believe that there are several STMs, each specializing in a particular type of information.) But most people—or at least most hearing people—seem to favor speech for rehearsing the contents of short-term memory. The speech may be overt (spoken aloud) or covert (spoken to oneself). When subjects make errors on short-term memory tests that use letters or words, they often confuse items that sound alike, such as *b* and *t*, or *bear* and *bare*. These errors suggest that the subjects have been rehearsing verbally.

Repeating a number to yourself is an example of **maintenance rehearsal** (or *rote rehearsal*). Maintenance rehearsal is fine for maintaining information in STM. However, it does not always lead to long-term retention. In one experiment, people were given pairs of numbers to memorize. After each pair they were told to repeat a word aloud once per second "to prevent rehearsal." Then there was a surprise: The critical memory test was for the words used as distractors, *not* for the numbers. The results showed that merely repeating the words did not guarantee retention. Further, the number of times a person rehearsed a word—4, 8, or 12 times—had no effect on how well that word was recalled (Rundus, 1977).

rehearsal *The review or practice of material for the purpose of improving subsequent retention.*

maintenance rehearsal *Rote repetition of material in order to maintain its availability in memory.*

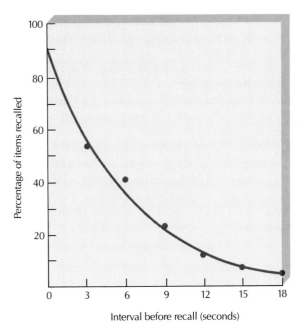

FIGURE 7.2

Retention in short-term memory: Going, going, gone
Subjects heard a set of items consisting of three consonants read aloud. After various intervals of time, they tried to recall the items. During each interval, a distracting task kept the subjects from rehearsing the items. The longer the interval, the poorer the recall; after only 18 seconds, recall fell to almost zero (Wessell, 1982).

An alternative to rote rehearsal is **elaborative rehearsal** (also called *elaboration of encoding*) (Cermak & Craik, 1979; Craik & Tulving, 1975). Elaboration involves associating new items of information with items that have already been stored or with other new items. It can also involve analyzing the various physical, sensory, or semantic features of an item (see Figure 7.3). Suppose, for example, that you are studying the concept of reinforcement discussed in Chapter 6. Simple rote rehearsal of the definition, or repetition of the word *reinforcement,* is unlikely to transfer the information from short-term to long-term memory. Instead, when going over (''rehearsing'') the material, you might encode the information that a reinforcer follows a response, strengthens the response, and is similar to a reward. You could also note that the word *reinforcer* starts with the same letter as *reward.*

elaborative rehearsal
Association of new information with already stored knowledge and analysis of the new information in order to make it memorable.

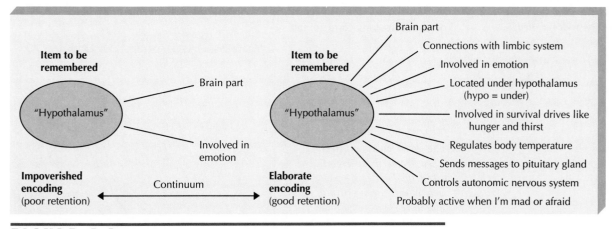

FIGURE 7.3

Elaboration of encoding
In elaborate encoding, one encodes the features of an item and its associations with other items. When you studied the hypothalamus in Chapter 3, was your encoding elaborate or impoverished?

And you might think up some examples of reinforcement and of how you have used it in your own life and could use it in the future. The more you elaborate the concept of reinforcement, the better you will remember it.

A related strategy for prolonging retention is **deep processing,** or the processing of meaning. If you simply process the physical or sensory features of a stimulus, such as how the word *reinforcement* is spelled and how it sounds, your processing will be *shallow* even if it is elaborate. If you recognize patterns and assign labels to objects or events (''Reinforcement is an operant procedure''), your processing will be somewhat deeper. And if you fully analyze the meaning of what you are trying to remember, your processing will be deeper yet. Deep processing is often more effective than shallow processing for remembering information, but not always. For example, if you are trying to memorize a poem, you will want to pay attention to (and elaborately encode) the sounds of the words and the patterns of rhythm in the poem, and not just the poem's meaning.

The serial position curve

deep processing *In the encoding of information, the processing of meaning rather than simply the physical or sensory features of a stimulus.*

serial position effect *The tendency for recall of the first and last items on a list to surpass recall of items in the middle of the list.*

primacy effect *The tendency for items at the beginning of a list to be well recalled.*

recency effect *The tendency for items at the end of a list to be well recalled.*

The assumption of a short-term memory distinct from a long-term memory has been used to explain a phenomenon called the **serial position effect**. When a person is asked to recall a list of items (for example, words) immediately after the list is presented, the retention of an item depends on its position in the list (Glanzer & Cunitz, 1966). Recall is best for items at the beginning of the list (the **primacy effect**) and at the end of the list (the **recency effect**). When errors are plotted, the result is a curve with a characteristic shape (Figure 7.4). According to the multistore model, the first few items are remembered well because they were well rehearsed. Since short-term memory was relatively ''empty'' when they entered, there was little competition among items for rehearsal time, and so the items made it into long-term memory. The last few items are remembered well for a different reason: At the time of recall, they are still sitting in STM and can simply be ''dumped.'' (If there is a 30-second delay after presentation of the list and people are prevented from rehearsing, the recency effect disappears, presumably because the items in STM have decayed.) The items in the middle are not well retained because by the time they get into short-term memory it is ''crowded'' and individual items get less rehearsal. Therefore, many of them drop out of short-term memory before they can be stored in long-term memory.

FIGURE 7.4

The serial position effect
When people try to recall a list of similar items immediately after learning it, they tend to remember the first and last items on the list best and the ones in the middle worst. This effect occurs with all sorts of materials.

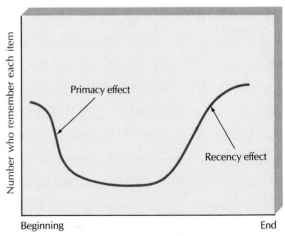

QUICK ■ QUIZ

Answer the following, based on the findings discussed so far.

1. The three basic memory processes are _____, storage, and _____.
2. Horace repeats his grocery list over and over to himself as he walks down the supermarket aisle. What strategy is he using to keep the items in STM?
3. In short-term memory, the abbreviation *U.S.A.* probably consists of _____ informational "chunk(s)."
4. _____ memory holds images for a fraction of a second.
5. If a child is trying to memorize the alphabet, which sequence should present the greatest difficulty: *abcdefg*, *klmnopq*, or *tuvwxyz*? Why?

Answers:

1. encoding, retrieval 2. maintenance rehearsal 3. one 4. Sensory 5. *klmnopq* (because of the serial position effect)

Final Destination: Long-term Memory

Just as the heart of a library is the stacks, the heart of the mental storage system is *long-term memory (LTM)*. The capacity of long-term memory seems to have no practical limits. The vast amount of information stored there enables us to learn, get around in the environment, and build a sense of identity and a personal history.

Organization in long-term memory

Because there is so much information in long-term memory, we cannot search it exhaustively, as we can short-term memory. Therefore, the information must be organized and indexed, just as items in a library are. One way to index words (or the concepts they represent) is to group them into categories on the basis of meaning. In a well-known study, people had to memorize 60 words that came from four conceptual categories: animals, vegetables, names, and professions. The words were presented in random order, but people tended to recall them in clusters corresponding to the four categories (Bousfield, 1953).

More recent evidence on the storage of information by conceptual category comes from a case study of a stroke victim called M. D. (Hart, Berndt, & Caramazza, 1985). Two years after suffering several strokes, M. D. appeared to have made a complete recovery, except for one problem: He had trouble remembering the names of fruits and vegetables. He could easily name a picture of an abacus or a sphinx but not a picture of an orange or a peach. He could sort pictures of animals, vehicles, and food products into their appropriate categories, but he had difficulty doing the same with pictures of fruits and vegetables. On the other hand, when M. D. was *given* the names of fruits and vegetables, he immediately pointed to the corresponding pictures. Apparently, he still had a store of information about fruits and vegetables, but his brain lesion prevented him from using their names to get to the information when he needed it, unless the names were provided by someone else. Although this evidence comes from only one patient, it supports the idea that information about a particular concept (such as *peach*) is indexed by the concept's semantic category (such as *fruit*).

The fact that some information is indexed by semantic category, however, does not mean that the mind is limited to that system. We may also index words in terms of the way they sound or look. Have you ever tried to recall some word that was on the ''tip of your tongue''? Researchers were able to reproduce this frustrating state by presenting people with definitions of uncommon words and asking them to supply the words. When **tip-of-the-tongue (TOT) states** occurred, people often came up with words that were similar in meaning to the right word before they finally recalled it. For example, if given the definition ''a navigational instrument used in measuring angular distances, especially the altitude of the sun, moon, and stars at sea,'' they might guess *astrolabe*, *compass*, or *protractor* before recalling the correct answer, *sextant*. However, they might also guess *secant*, *sextet*, or *sexton*, words that are similar in sound and form. Often the incorrect guesses had the correct number of syllables, started with the correct letter, or had the correct prefix or suffix (Brown & McNeill, 1966).

What is stored in long-term memory?

Researchers are currently investigating other ways in which we organize items of information in long-term memory, such as by their familiarity, personal relevance, or association with other information. The method used in any given instance probably depends on the nature of the memory. For example, information about the major cities of Europe is probably organized quite differently than information about your first date.

To understand the organization of long-term memory, then, we need to understand what kinds of information can be stored there. Endel Tulving (1985) has proposed that there are three general types of long-term memories, as illustrated in Figure 7.5:

1. **Procedural memories** are internal representations of stimulus-response connections. They prescribe a particular action and account for much of the learning described in Chapter 6. You have procedural memories of how to brush your teeth, use a pencil, and swim.

2. **Semantic memories** are internal representations of the world, independent of any particular context. Semantic memories include facts, rules, and concepts. With a semantic memory of the concept *cat*, you can say that a cat is a small, furry mammal that typically spends its time eating, sleeping, and staring into space, even though a cat may not be present when you give this description and you probably won't know how or when you learned it.

3. **Episodic memories** are internal representations of personally experienced events. They allow you to ''travel back'' in time. When you remember how your furry feline once surprised you in the middle of the night by pouncing on your face as you slept, you are retrieving an episodic memory.

Other theorists describe the contents of long-term memory in slightly different ways. Most, however, distinguish skills or habits (''knowing how'') from abstract or representational knowledge (''knowing that''). Semantic and episodic memories both require ''knowing that'' and are referred to together as **declarative memories**. As we will see, the procedural-declarative distinction is supported by recent brain research.

tip-of-the-tongue (TOT) state *The subjective certainty that information is available in long-term memory even though one is having difficulty retrieving it.*

procedural memories *Memories for the performance of particular types of action.*

semantic memories *Memories that reveal general knowledge, including facts, rules, concepts, and propositions.*

episodic memories *Memories for personally experienced events and the contexts in which they occurred.*

declarative memories *Memories of facts, rules, concepts, and events; include semantic and episodic memories.*

FIGURE 7.5

Memories are made of this
According to one widely accepted classification scheme, long-term memory contains procedural memories (stimulus-response connections that enable us to perform specific acts), semantic memories (general knowledge), and episodic memories (personal recollections). You might draw on the first to ride a bike, the second to identify a bird, and the third to recall your graduation or wedding. Can you come up with some other examples for each type of memory?

Reconstructing the past

Despite our library analogy, remembering information stored in long-term memory is not like checking a book out of the library. It is more like checking out a few pages, then figuring out what the rest of the book must have said. That is, when we remember, we "look up" some information and *reconstruct* the rest (Bartlett, 1932). Dozens of memory studies have found this to be true, for everything from stories to conversations. Often we cannot tell what we originally stored and what we have added since then. It all feels like one "memory."

Suppose someone asks you to describe your seventh birthday. You may have some direct recollection of what took place, but you have also stored information gleaned from family stories, photographs, or home movies. You take all these bits and pieces and build one integrated account from them, and you may not be able to identify which information came from which source. As we saw in Chapter 4, this sort of reconstruction also occurs when people are "age regressed" under hypnosis. The information they unwittingly add may or may not turn out to be an accurate reflection of what really happened.

Not only do we reconstruct at the time of recall, but we alter information even as it is being stored. Most cognitive psychologists believe that whenever we are exposed to new information, we incorporate it into what we already know or believe. Instead of simply filing separate items away, we make their information part of an existing web of knowledge, or **cognitive schema**. To make the new information "fit" a particular schema, we may distort or modify it. If it still won't fit, we may simply ignore it. For example, we all tend to organize the actions of other

cognitive schema *An integrated network of knowledge, beliefs, and expectations concerning a particular topic.*

people into categories, such as "smart," "dumb," "kind," or "insensitive." If you consider a particular politician smart and trustworthy, you are apt to store—and remember—information about the politician that fits your expectations. You will probably ignore—or "misremember"—information that is incongruent.

Some familiar facts may simply be reproduced without much reconstruction, but literal recall is probably the exception, not the rule. In general, remembering is an *active* process that involves not only dredging up stored information but also putting two and two together to reconstruct the past. This process helps the mind work efficiently. We can store just the essentials of an experience, then use our general knowledge to figure out the specifics when we need them. But sometimes the reconstructive nature of memory gets us into hot water.

The eyewitness on trial

Imagine that as you leave your bank, you see a man walking in the direction of a blue Dodge. You glance away for a moment, and when you look back, you see that someone in the Dodge is pulling away from the curb. You are not paying any special attention to this chain of events. Why should you? But just then, a teller runs out of the bank, points wildly at the receding Dodge and shouts, "Stop that man, he robbed the bank!" Soon the police arrive and ask you to give an account of what you saw.

If we compare memory to a film, you have actually stored only some of the frames. Asked now to recall, you are likely to fill in those frames that are missing, the ones that would presumably show the man climbing into the car. In other words, you *infer* (deduce) what must have happened. Now you have a complete "film" in your mental archives, but you may be unable to tell which parts were shot during the original event and which were added later. ("I saw a brown-haired man, about 5 feet 10 inches tall, with a mustache, and wearing a blue shirt, walk over to the blue Dodge, get in, and drive away.") To make matters worse, even the frames you stored at the time of the event were probably hazy or incomplete, so you have gone back and retouched them. What has happened is a little like the perceptual closure we discussed in Chapter 5, except that in this case the closure has occurred in memory.

Was any harm done by your reconstruction? That depends. Maybe the man you saw did drive off in the getaway car. Then again, perhaps someone you failed to notice was the robber, and the man you saw simply walked away before you looked back at the scene. Because memory is reconstructive, eyewitness testimony is not always reliable.

There is no easy solution to this problem. For example, it does little good to give a lie detector test to a witness who is unwittingly reconstructing an event. Not only are lie detectors less than perfectly reliable (see Chapter 9), but also someone who reconstructs the past is not deliberately lying and should therefore easily pass the test. The consequences can be serious: Eyewitness testimony is a necessary feature of our justice system, but convictions based on such testimony occasionally turn out to be mistakes. One study found that such errors are especially likely to occur when the suspect's race differs from that of the witness (Luce, 1974). Negative racial attitudes or lack of familiarity may prevent people from attending to the distinctive features of members of other races. (For more information on this study's results, see Figure 7.6.)

To complicate matters, our reconstructions of past events are heavily influenced

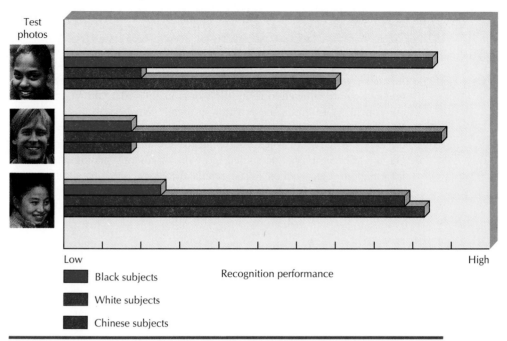

Recognition performance

Low .... High

■ Black subjects

■ White subjects

■ Chinese subjects

FIGURE 7.6

"They all look alike to me"

People are generally best at recognizing differences among faces in their own racial group. In one study, black subjects recognized different black faces easily but could not easily distinguish white or Chinese faces. Whites subjects could distinguish white and Chinese faces easily but not black ones. Chinese subjects could distinguish Chinese faces, but had some trouble with black faces and great difficulty with white ones (Luce, 1974).

by the way questions are put to us. Elizabeth Loftus showed people short films depicting multicar traffic accidents. Afterward she asked some of the viewers, "About how fast were the cars going when they *hit* each other?" Other viewers were asked the same question, but with the verb changed to *smashed, collided, bumped,* or *contacted.* These words imply different things about speed and force of impact. Sure enough, the average estimates varied considerably, depending on which word was used (Loftus, 1974; Loftus & Palmer, 1974). From highest to lowest, the average estimates were: *smashed,* 40.8 mph; *collided,* 39.3 mph; *bumped,* 38.1 mph; *hit,* 34.0 mph; *contacted,* 31.8 mph.

In a similar study (Loftus & Zanni, 1975), some people were asked, "Did you see *a* broken headlight?" Others were asked, "Did you see *the* broken headlight?" Two other pairs of questions also differed only in the use of *a* or *the.* Note that the question with *the* presupposes a broken headlight, merely asking if the witness saw it. The question with *a* makes no such presupposition. Loftus and Zanni found that people who received questions with *the* were far more likely to report having seen something that had not really appeared in the film than were those who received questions with *a.* If a tiny word like *the* can lead people to remember what they never saw, you can imagine how the leading questions of police detectives and courtroom lawyers might influence a witness's recall. What we remember, it seems, is not always what happened.

QUICK ■ QUIZ

1. Suppose you must memorize a long list of words that includes the following: *desk, pig, gold, dog, chair, silver, table, rooster, bed, copper,* and *horse*. You are allowed to recall the words in any order you wish. How are you likely to group these words in recall? Why?
2. When you ski, are you relying on procedural, semantic, or episodic memory? What about when you recall the months of the year?
3. Harvey tells Susan that he spilled red wine on his rug, adding no other information. Later, when Susan retells the story, she says, "Harvey stained his rug with red wine." What does this tell you about retrieval from long-term memory?

Answers:

1. *Desk, chair, table,* and *bed* would probably form one cluster; *pig, dog, rooster,* and *horse* a second cluster; and *gold, silver,* and *copper* a third. Concepts tend to be organized in long-term memory in terms of the semantic categories they belong to, such as *furniture, animals,* and *metals*. 2. procedural; semantic 3. Retrieval from long-term memory is reconstructive. (Susan "remembers" the rug was stained, though Harvey didn't tell her so.)

Memory and the Brain

Some years ago a team of researchers conditioned flatworms to cringe at a flashing light. Then they killed the worms, ground them into a mash, and fed the mash to a second set of worms. This cannibalistic diet, the researchers reported, sped up conditioning in the second group of worms (McConnell, 1962). As you can imagine, this generated tremendous excitement. If worms could learn faster by ingesting the "memory molecules" of their fellow worms, could memory pills be far behind? Students joked about grinding up professors; professors joked about doing brain transplants in students.

Unfortunately, the results proved difficult to replicate, and talk of memory pills eventually faded away. Today, instead of searching for memory molecules, scientists studying the biology of memory focus on three questions: (1) What changes in neurons and synapses (the small gaps between neurons) are associated with remembering an event or task? (2) Where in the brain do these changes occur? (3) How might hormones and other substances regulate or improve memory? In their work, researchers draw on many of the concepts covered in earlier sections of this chapter.

To many people, biological findings on neurons, enzymes, and chemicals seem more solid and reliable than psychological findings. Is this necessarily so?

Each new finding on the biology of memory nudges the neuroscientist's dream of describing behavior in physical terms a bit closer to reality. We must warn you, however, that biological findings can be as slippery as any others. People often assume that because neuropsychology deals with physical phenomena—neurons, enzymes, chemicals—it is on firmer ground than other areas of psychology. This is not so. Technical obstacles in physiological research can make it difficult to get reliable results. A finding with one animal or procedure may not apply to others. (When you have seen one neuron, you haven't seen them all.) Neuropsychology is one of the most exciting areas in psychology, but many of its findings are tentative, and conclusions must often be revised.

In this regard, we want to tell you about something that happened while we were writing this chapter. We originally planned to include some promising new research on memory-related changes in receptors for glutamate, a probable neurotransmitter (Lynch, 1986; Lynch & Baudry, 1984). This research appears in many psychology and physiology textbooks. The trouble was that by the time we finished writing up the findings, they were already out of date! It turns out that the critical changes do not occur in glutamate receptors but in "uptake sites," where unused glutamate molecules are reabsorbed (Kessler et al., 1987). So at the last minute, we had to drop our description.

New discoveries about the brain's role in memory are being made at almost a monthly rate. But because so many of these findings are provisional, and because there is still no comprehensive model of the biology of memory, we have decided to concentrate in this book on general issues, to which we now turn.

Changes in neurons and synapses

Nearly all scientists agree that memory requires chemical and structural changes at the level of neurons. (If you have forgotten about neurons or the brain structures they make up, you might want to review Chapter 3 before going on.) But why do some memories last only a few seconds or minutes, whereas others persist for years or even a lifetime? Why, when a blow on the head or an electroconvulsive shock disrupts brain activity, do people often lose information stored a few seconds or minutes earlier but not information stored weeks or years ago?

One answer is that short-term memory and long-term memory involve different brain changes. Unlike long-term retention, short-term retention does not seem to require permanent structural changes in the brain. Instead, there are temporary changes within neurons that alter their ability to release neurotransmitters, the chemicals that carry messages from one cell to another. Evidence comes from studies with the lowly sea snail, *Aplysia* (Kandel & Schwartz, 1982), and other primitive organisms that have small numbers of easily identifiable neurons. These studies show that depending on the kind of learning, a neuron's readiness to release neurotransmitter molecules either increases or decreases.

Long-term memory, on the other hand, does involve permanent structural changes in the brain. To mimic what they think may happen during the formation of a long-term memory, researchers apply brief, high-frequency electrical stimulation to groups of neurons in the brains of animals. In various brain areas, particularly the hippocampus, this stimulation leads to a long-lasting increase in the strength of synaptic responsiveness known as **long-term potentiation** (McNaughton & Morris, 1987; Teyler & DiScenna, 1987). Long-term potentiation is associated with faster conditioning in animals, and many scientists suspect that in normal life it is an important memory mechanism. It seems to occur because of a complicated sequence of chemical reactions in receiving neurons, including the synthesis of certain proteins (Lynch, 1986; Lynch & Baudry, 1984). One result is that the tiny spines (projections) that cover the dendrites of the receiving neuron change shape, becoming rounder. This change causes decreased electrical resistance and an increase in the responsiveness of the receiving neuron to the transmitting neuron. It is a little like what would happen if you increased the diameter of a funnel's neck to permit more flow through the funnel.

Other, related changes also occur in long-term potentiation (and presumably, the formation of long-term memories). For example, dendrites branch out, and

long-term potentiation *A long-lasting increase in the strength of synaptic responsiveness, thought to be a biological mechanism of memory.*

certain types of synapses increase in number (Greenough, 1984). These changes all take time, which may explain why after storage a long-term memory remains vulnerable to disruption for some time. It takes a period of **consolidation**, or stabilization, before the memory solidifies. Consolidation appears to be a gradual rather than an all-or-nothing process. If an animal gets electroconvulsive shock within the first hour after learning a task, it will forget what it has learned, which indicates that little if any consolidation has occurred. If the shock is delivered several hours or a few days after learning, the memory will be unaffected, which implies that by then consolidation has taken place. But *repeated* sessions of shock will again disrupt the memory, showing that the process is not yet complete (Squire, 1987). Consolidation can continue in animals for weeks and in human beings for several years.

Keep in mind that the brain changes we have described are correlational. That is, they accompany retention of learning, but no one can be certain that they actually reflect the storage of information. One way to find out might be to look at what happens in the brain after an animal's memory for some task (say, running a maze) begins to dim (Squire, 1987). Do the physical changes disappear, too? Future research will tell.

Locating memories

We have been describing changes in neurons, but which neurons are they? As we saw in Chapter 3, most scientists believe that memory traces (the neural changes associated with specific memories) are confined to specific areas, or *localized*. However, some disagree, suggesting that any given memory is *distributed* across large areas of the brain. These two views can be reconciled by recognizing that the typical "memory" is actually a complex cluster of information. When you recall meeting a man yesterday, you remember his greeting, his tone of voice, how he looked, and where he was. These different pieces of information may be processed separately and stored at different sites, but all these sites may participate in representing the event as a whole. If this is so, memories are both "localized" and "distributed" (Squire, 1986).

Recently, researchers have discovered that certain broad *categories* of memories are associated with particular brain structures, although there is some overlap (see Figure 7.7). Generally speaking, procedural memories (skills and habits) involve different structures and pathways than declarative memories (facts and episodes).

Procedural memories—the kind you draw on to ride a bike, solve a jigsaw puzzle, or slam your foot on the brake—form after practice or conditioning. Richard Thompson (1983, 1986) has shown that one kind of procedural memory, a simple, classically conditioned response to an unpleasant stimulus, is associated with specific changes in the cerebellum, the roundish structure at the back of the brain. After Thompson conditioned rabbits to blink in response to a tone, he discovered predictable changes in electrical activity in particular parts of this structure. And if he removed or destroyed the affected brain tissue, the animals immediately forgot the response. They still blinked reflexively when air was blown in their eyes, and they still heard the tone, but they no longer blinked in response to the tone. These results, and those from other studies using different stimuli and different animals, show that the cerebellum is vital for certain kinds of simple conditioning. Some habits, however, are located or processed elsewhere, in the amygdala, hypothalamus, or an area called the striatum (R. Thompson, 1986).

consolidation *The process by which a long-term memory becomes durable and stable.*

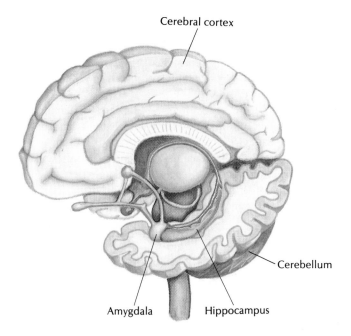

Cerebral cortex

Cerebellum

Amygdala   Hippocampus

FIGURE 7.7

Brain areas critical for memory
The regions shown are particularly important in the formation or storage of memories.

Declarative memories are those you draw on when identifying a flower or recalling an experience. Formation of declarative memories is most closely associated with the hippocampus, the amygdala, and parts of the temporal lobe cortex. Recall that H. M., who had his amygdala and a large section of his hippocampus removed, lost his ability to permanently store new information about events or knowledge about the world. Yet studies have found that he can acquire new cognitive, perceptual, and motor *skills*, such as solving a puzzle, reading mirror-reversed words, or playing tennis—although he does not remember the training sessions. In other words, the operation interfered only with the formation of declarative memories, not procedural ones. Other patients with similar brain damage have shown the same pattern of memory loss, as have monkeys with lesions in the hippocampus and amygdala (Mishkin & Appenzeller, 1987).

Work with animals suggests that the hippocampus is especially important for storing information about spatial relations, such as where items of furniture are located in a room. The amygdala also has its specialties. It seems to be responsible for associating memories that were formed in different senses. These associations allow you to remember what a speaker looks like when you hear the person's voice on the telephone and to recall the sour taste of a lemon when you see a picture of one. The amygdala may also link up emotional responses with specific memories. But be careful: We are talking about brain circuits involved in the *formation* of long-term memories, and not necessarily areas where the permanent changes required for retention occur. Some researchers believe that the ultimate destinations of declarative memories are the same cortical areas that took part in the original perception of the information (Mishkin & Appenzeller, 1987; Squire, 1986). This means that information acquired through vision will be stored in different areas than information acquired through hearing or some other sense.

Hormones and memory

Neurotransmitters and neural changes are apparently the basis of memory storage. Hormones, however, also affect memory, by regulating, or modulating, the storage of information (Gold, 1984; McGaugh, 1989).

Some people are "laid back." Others are "hyper." But work on hormones suggests that if you want to remember information well, you will aim for an arousal level somewhere between these two extremes. The reason: Various hormones released during stress, including epinephrine (adrenaline) and certain steroids, appear to enhance memory—but only at low or moderate levels. If you administer epinephrine to animals right after learning, their memory improves. But if the dosages are too high, their memory suffers, and if you wait too long to administer the hormones, there is no effect at all.

How can hormones affect the remembrance of things past? In the case of adrenal epinephrine, the effects may be indirect. Paul Gold (1987) notes that epinephrine causes the level of glucose (a sugar) to rise in the bloodstream. Epinephrine, Gold argues, cannot enter the brain from the bloodstream, but glucose can. Once in the brain, glucose may enhance memory either directly or by altering the effects of various neurotransmitters—the "sweet memories" effect. Before you reach for a candy bar, however, be advised that not everyone agrees with this conclusion. Some researchers question the assumption that epinephrine does not pass from the bloodstream into the brain. They suspect that epinephrine has direct access to at least certain brain parts.

The apparent ability of hormones to regulate memory fits well with the view of many scientists that emotional arousal is an essential ingredient in learning and memory. Arousal may signal the brain that an event or piece of information is important enough to store. Or it may ensure that a person or animal will pay attention to what is happening so that encoding can take place. But the exact mechanisms

Which of these students will remember best? Keep in mind that a moderate degree of emotional arousal enhances memory. One explanation may be biological: Retention seems to be best when hormones associated with arousal reach an optimal level.

remain unclear and controversial. In this area, as in others in the biology of memory, we still have much to learn. We do not know how the brain actually encodes information, how "distributed" circuits link up with one another, or how a student is able to locate and retrieve information at the drop of a multiple-choice item.

QUICK ▪ QUIZ

1. Speaking of multiple-choice items, is *long-term potentiation* associated with (a) increased responsiveness of a receiving neuron to a transmitting neuron, (b) a decrease in receptors on a receiving neuron, or (c) reaching your true potential?
2. The cerebellum has been associated with _____ memories, and the hippocampus and amygdala have been associated with _____ memories.
3. True or false: Hormone research suggests that if you want to remember well, you should be as relaxed as possible while learning.

Answers:

1. a 2. procedural, declarative 3. false

Forgetting of Things Past

Have you ever, in the middle of some experience, told yourself, "I'm never going to forget this. I want to remember every detail," only to find later that the memory has receded into the misty recesses of your mind? As we suggest in "Think About It," not all forgetting is bad. Most of us, however, probably forget more than we would like to. In previous sections we saw that forgetfulness often means that a person didn't encode well in the first place; you can't remember what you never learned. But suppose you do encode well. Why, then, do you forget?

How long-term is long-term memory?

Two popular but conflicting "commonsense" views of forgetting have been around for some time. One, the **decay theory**, holds that memory traces simply fade with time if they are not "called up" now and then. As we have seen, trace decay does seem to occur in both the sensory memory and short-term memory. However, the mere passage of time does not seem to account well for forgetting in long-term memory. Who has not had the experience of forgetting something that happened only yesterday while remembering an event from many years ago?

Indeed, some knowledge is still accessible decades after learning. In one study, people who had taken Spanish in high school or college were able to do well on Spanish tests up to 50 years later, although most had hardly used Spanish at all in the intervening years (Bahrick, 1984). Most forgetting occurred in the first few years after learning. This period was followed by a quarter century of stability and then, again, a decline (though scores were still impressive). The better people did in

decay theory (of forgetting) *The theory that information in memory eventually disappears if it is not reactivated; it appears to be more plausible for short-term than long-term memory.*

Think About It

The Benefits of Forgetting

Who has not wished, at some time or other, for a "photographic memory"? It is bad enough that we forget so much that we have worked diligently to learn in school. How can we formulate a realistic assessment of ourselves if our recollection of the past is both inaccurate and incomplete?

Yet a perfect memory is not the blessing that one might suppose. Soviet psychologist Alexander Luria (1968) once told of a journalist, S., who could remember giant grids of numbers and long lists of words after seeing them for only a few seconds. This man could reproduce these grids and lists both forward and backward, even after the passage of 15 years. He also remembered the circumstances under which he had originally learned the material.

S. used various memory "tricks" to accomplish his astonishing feats, many involving the formation of visual images. But you shouldn't envy him, for he had a serious problem: He could not forget. Images he had formed in order to remember kept creeping into consciousness, distracting him and interfering with his ability to concentrate. At times he even had trouble holding a simple conversation because the other person's words would set off a jumble of associations. In fact, Luria called him "rather dull-witted." Eventually, unable to work at his profession, S. took to supporting himself by traveling from place to place as a performer, demonstrating his abilities for audiences.

Perhaps you are not convinced that a perfect memory would be less than a blessing. Imagine, then, for a moment, what it would be like to remember *everything*. Each time you recalled the past, you would dredge up not only the diamonds of experience but the pebbles as well. Remembering might take hours instead of moments. The clutter in your mind might grow beyond your ability to organize it efficiently.

With a perfect memory, you might also remember things better off forgotten. Think back; would you really like to recall every angry argument, every embarrassing episode, every painful moment? How would total recall affect your relationships with relatives and friends? Could it be that the success of a close relationship depends on a certain amount of forgiving forgetfulness? Could it be that self-confidence and optimism are only possible if we lock some grievances in a back drawer of memory?

Like remembering, a certain degree of forgetting contributes to our survival and our sanity. Where is the line between adaptive forgetting and disruptive forgetting? If you had the choice, what would you choose to recollect with greater clarity, and what would you allow to fade? Think about it.

---

their original courses and the more courses they had taken, the better they did years later. Decay alone, then, does not seem to explain lapses in long-term memory.

A second "commonsense" view of forgetting holds that once material is learned, it remains forever in one's mental library, but for various reasons it may be difficult to retrieve. Many psychologists agree. They point out that electrical stimulation of the brain before brain surgery sometimes evokes vivid memories of the distant past, thought by the patient to be long forgotten (Penfield & Perot, 1963). In one case, for example, a woman reported rehearing a concert she had attended years before; she even hummed along with the music.

When their brains are electrically stimulated, some people seem to "relive" long-forgotten experiences. Can you conclude that all our memories are permanently on file, waiting to be retrieved?

The notion that memory is permanent is certainly appealing, and its appeal may explain why for many years people accepted the brain stimulation evidence as persuasive. But then Elizabeth Loftus looked again and discovered that "memories" have actually occurred in very few brain surgery patients. Moreover, those "memories" that have been reported seem more like reconstructions than accurately retrieved events (Loftus, 1980; Loftus & Loftus, 1980). Loftus also pointed out what in retrospect should have been obvious: The recovery of *some* information stored long ago does not mean that *all* memories from the past remain available.

According to Loftus, there is no solid evidence that long-term memories do last forever. On the contrary, she argues, information in long-term memory can be completely wiped out by new, misleading information. Loftus cites a study in which she and her colleagues used a leading question to mislead some people into thinking they had seen either a stop sign or a yield sign while viewing slides of a traffic accident. Other people were not misled and accurately identified the sign they had actually seen. Later, all the subjects were told the purpose of the study and asked to guess whether or not they had been misled. Of those who had been misled, 90 percent still insisted that they had seen the sign whose existence had been "planted" in their minds by the leading question (Loftus, Miller, & Burns, 1978). Other studies, too, suggest that new, incorrect information can "erase" old, correct information, just as rerecording on a tape recorder will erase the original material.

Not everyone agrees with this conclusion, however (McCloskey & Zaragoza, 1985). It is possible that misleading information does not actually "erase" the original information, but simply makes it inaccessible. Future research may resolve the question of whether long-term memories are or are not permanent. It is clear, however, that forgetting is likelier under some conditions than others, as we are about to see.

Forgetting: Now you find it, now you don't

The ability to remember and the tendency to forget are not all-or-nothing phenomena; they depend in part on the kind of performance required. Students who express a preference for a multiple-choice, essay, or fill-in-the-blanks format on exams show that they know this.

Recognition is the ability to identify information to which you were previously exposed. The information is given to you, and you simply say whether it is old or new, or perhaps correct or incorrect, or you pick it out of a set of alternatives. In other words, you match a current stimulus with what you have stored in memory. In the classroom, true-false and multiple-choice tests ask for recognition. In contrast, **recall** tests tap the ability to retrieve from memory information that is not currently present. Essay and fill-in-the-blank exams and memory games like Trivial Pursuit ask for recall. Under most circumstances, recall is more difficult than recognition, although exceptions do occur—for example, when false items on a recognition test are extremely similar to the correct ones.

recognition *The ability to identify previously encountered material.*

recall *The ability to retrieve and reproduce from memory previously encountered material.*

A witness viewing a police lineup relies on recognition memory, which is generally superior to recall. But the lineup has a serious drawback. Sometimes witnesses compare the suspects and pick the one most like the criminal, even though all the suspects are actually innocent. Observing suspects one at a time, instead of in a group, reduces such false identifications without reducing correct identifications (Cutler & Penrod, 1988). The moral: The accuracy of memory depends on the methods used to invoke it.

The gap between recognition and recall was demonstrated in a study of people's memories for their high school classmates (Bahrick, Bahrick, & Wittlinger, 1974, 1975). The subjects, aged 17 to 74, first wrote down the names of as many classmates as they could remember. Recall was poor; most recent graduates could write only a few dozen names, and those out of school for 40 years or more recalled on the average only 19. When prompted with yearbook pictures of their classmates, the youngest subjects still failed to name almost 30 percent and the oldest ones failed to name over 80 percent.

Recognition, however, was far better. The researchers showed each person ten cards, each with five photographs on it. The task was to say which picture on a card was that of a former classmate. Recent graduates could do so for 90 percent of the cards. More important, so could people who had graduated 35 years earlier. Even those who had been out of high school for over 40 years were able to identify the faces of three-fourths of their classmates, and the ability to recognize *names* was almost as impressive. These results show that recall tests may underestimate the amount of information people retain in memory. (This does not mean that essay tests should be abolished, however. If you do well on recognition, it does not necessarily mean that you will do well on recall of the same material. But if you do well on recall, you will probably also do well on recognition, and so your instructor can feel confident that you know the material well.)

Sometimes recall and recognition are both poor, yet there are indications that some information still remains in memory. The **relearning** (or *savings*) **method** measures retention indirectly, by requiring people to relearn information or a task that was learned earlier. If they learn more quickly the second time, they must be remembering something from the first experience, whether they realize it or not. Relearning and other indirect tests of memory are very sensitive, detecting extremely small amounts of remembering. They show that even when we think we have forgotten everything we have learned, we may not have to start over from the beginning. The previous experience has *primed* us for remembering the material better when we confront it again. Previously learned material can also prime performance on new, related tasks, even when we do not recall or recognize the material (Richardson-Klavehn & Bjork, 1988).

Sometimes, however, the most sensitive tests do not detect any evidence of remembering. Let us look more closely, now, at why memory's contents so often elude the mind's grasp.

Three ways to forget

Psychologists have discovered that some forgetting occurs because competing material "gets in the way." At other times, we forget because we cannot bear to remember. And sometimes we simply lack sufficient cues for finding the information we have stored.

Interference in memory. Some forgetting occurs because similar items of information interfere with each other (see Figure 7.8). This type of forgetting, which occurs in both short- and long-term memory, is especially common when you have to recall isolated facts. Suppose you are at a party and you meet someone named Julie. A half hour later you meet someone named Judy. You go on to talk to other people, and after an hour you again bump into Julie, but by mistake you call her Judy. The second name has interfered with the first. This type of interference, in which new information interferes with the ability to remember old information, is

relearning method *A method to measure retention that compares the time required to relearn material with the time used in initial learning of the material.*

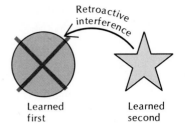 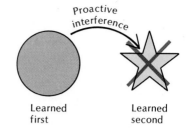

FIGURE 7.8

Interference in memory
*Retroactive interference oc-
curs when new information
interferes with memory for
previously stored material.
Proactive interference occurs when previously stored
material interferes with
memory for new informa-
tion.*

called **retroactive**. It is often illustrated by a story about an absent-minded professor of ichthyology (the study of fish) who complained that whenever he learned the
name of a new student he forgot the name of a fish.

Interference also works in the opposite direction. Old information may interfere
with the ability to remember new information (for example, the professor might call
one of his students ''trout''). This type of interference is called **proactive**. Over a
period of weeks, months, and years, proactive interference may cause more forgetting than retroactive, simply because we have stored up so much information that
can potentially interfere with anything new (Hill, 1985). Fortunately, we can also
use our old information to elaborately encode new information and thus improve
memory.

Motivated forgetting. In another kind of memory lapse, called **motivated
forgetting**, the person consciously or unconsciously decides to ''hide'' a memory
because it is painful or unpleasant. Motivated forgetting may explain some cases of
retrograde amnesia, in which people remember historical incidents and can form
new memories but forget friends, relatives, or personal events from the past.

Sigmund Freud called the unconscious willing of forgetfulness ''repression.''
He argued that repressed information has a way of stubbornly signaling its existence
in dreams or when a person pauses, fumbles for words, or blushes when certain
topics are raised. Repression seems to account for the fact that survivors of childhood sexual abuse sometimes have trouble remembering details of the experience,
or even that they were abused. In incest cases, the earlier and more violent the
experiences and the longer they go on, the more thoroughly they seem to be forgotten (Herman & Schatzow, 1987). Yet these experiences can have a profound effect
on a person's later relationships and emotional life (see Chapter 16).

Cue-dependent forgetting. To find something in our mental ''library,'' we
need cues that tell us where to look. If few cues are available, retrieval may fail.
This kind of forgetting, **cue-dependent forgetting**, is perhaps the most common.
When it occurs, it is as though we have lost the call number, or perhaps some part of
the call number, for the entry. Apparently, that is what happened when M. D., the
stroke patient, was unable to gain access to information on fruits and vegetables that
he had stored in his long-term memory.

Fortunately, most information seems to be filed under several different headings. We can look up information about a football game in high school by searching
under ''high school,'' ''everything that happened in the tenth grade,'' or ''football
games I've attended.'' Some items, however, have few such labels and are difficult
to retrieve. One way to overcome a retrieval problem is to conjure up memories
associated with the item you are trying to reach. For example, people can often
recall when a political event occurred by first recalling some other public event
(Brown, Shevell, & Rips, 1986).

retroactive interference
*Forgetting that occurs when
recently learned material
interferes with the ability to
remember similar material
stored previously.*

proactive interference
*Forgetting that occurs when
previously stored material
interferes with the ability to
remember similar, more
recently learned material.*

motivated forgetting
*Forgetting because of a
conscious or unconscious
desire to eliminate awareness of painful or unpleasant experiences.*

retrograde amnesia *Loss of
the ability to remember
events or experiences that
occurred before some par-
ticular time.*

cue-dependent forgetting
*The inability to retrieve in-
formation stored in memory
because of insufficient internally or externally generated
cues.*

Charlie Chaplin's film City Lights *provides a classic illustration of state-dependent memory. After Charlie saves the life of a drunken millionaire, the two spend the rest of the evening in boisterous merry-making. The next day, however, after sobering up, the millionaire fails to recognize Charlie and gives him the cold shoulder. Then, once again, the millionaire gets drunk—and once again he greets Charlie as a pal.*

Retrieval cues may work by getting us into the general area of memory where the item we are seeking is stored, or by making a "match" with the labels used when storing the item. Or perhaps the cue provides the sort of cross-reference that you find in a library index. The most effective retrieval cues tend to be ones that were present at the time of the initial experience. That may explain why retrieval is often relatively easy when you are in the same physical situation you were in when you originally encoded and stored the information; the situation provides many retrieval cues. Even imagining the original situation can help. To remember the name of a woman you met at a party, you might conjure up an image of the party itself—where it was held, who else was there, and so forth.

Your mental or physical state may also act as a retrieval cue, evoking a **state-dependent memory**. For example, if you are drunk when something happens, you may remember it better when you are once again drunk than when you are sober. Or if your emotional arousal is high or low at the time of an event, you may remember that event best when you are once again in the same state of arousal. One research team has speculated that when victims of violent crimes have trouble recalling details of the experience, it may be in part because they are far less emotionally aroused than they were at the time of the crime (Clark, Milberg, & Erber, 1987).

Another possible influence on state-dependent memory is mood: Retrieval from memory may be best when a person's mood is the same as it was during initial encoding and storage (Blaney, 1986; G. Bower, 1981). Such *mood-dependent retrieval (MDR)* could help explain why depressed people are often flooded with unhappy memories, which in turn make them even more depressed. It also predicts that happy people will tend to remember happy events, which will produce an "upward spiral" in mood. However, laboratory research on mood-dependent memory has been inconclusive, with many studies reporting weak or nonexistent effects. In an article on one series of studies that produced mainly negative results, Gordon Bower and John Mayer (in press) write, "We confess an inability to make sense out of the crazy patchquilt of findings on MDR. We are frankly puzzled by the inconsistencies in outcomes." Mood-dependent retrieval may be difficult to demonstrate in part because in the laboratory moods do not arise spontaneously; instead, they must be induced by the researcher, using such devices as happy or sad music, or photographs. It remains to be seen whether the conditions that promote mood-dependent retrieval—if any—can be reliably established.

state-dependent memory
The tendency to remember something when one is in the same physical or mental state as during the original learning or experience.

QUICK ▪ QUIZ

1. A boy who saw his brother drown cannot recall the incident. What sort of forgetting has probably occurred?
2. Willard was a fan of Judy Garland's in the 1950s and 1960s. Later, he became a fan of Garland's daughter, singer/actress Liza Minelli. Now Willard often mistakenly refers to Ms. Minelli as "Judy." Why doesn't he remember her name correctly?
3. When a woman at her twentieth high school reunion sees her old friends, she recalls incidents she thought she had long forgotten. Why?
4. In this quiz, do questions 1–3 measure recall, recognition, or relearning? (And what about this item?)

Answers:

1. motivated forgetting or repression   2. proactive interference   3. The sight of her friends provides retrieval cues for the incidents.   4. The first three questions measure recall; the fourth measures recognition because the options are given to you, and you simply have to recognize the correct one.

Autobiographical Memory

We opened this chapter by noting that memory provides each of us with a sense of identity. This sense of ourselves evolves and changes as we build up a store of episodic memories about events we have experienced first-hand. For many years, psychologists tended to shy away from studying these autobiographical memories, preferring instead to focus on procedural and semantic memories, which could be measured and manipulated in the experimental laboratory. That has changed, however, and researchers are now exploring the ways in which people remember—and forget—the events of their own lives.

Childhood amnesia: The missing years

One curious thing about episodic memories is that few people can recall any from earlier than about the third or fourth year of life. We all retain procedural memories from the toddler stage, when we first learned to use a fork, drink from a cup, and pull a wagon. We also retain semantic memories acquired early: the rules of counting, the names of people and things, knowledge about all manner of objects in the world. But we cannot remember being fed in infancy by our parents, taking our first steps, or uttering our first halting sentences. We are victims of **childhood amnesia**.

People often find childhood amnesia a difficult thing to accept. There is something disturbing about the fact that one's early years are beyond recall—so disturbing that some people adamantly deny it, claiming they remember events from the second or even the first year of life. But most psychologists believe these "memories" are merely reconstructions based on photographs, family stories, and imagination. Like Piaget's kidnapping, the "remembered" event may not even have taken place.

Some researchers believe that early memories are hazy or nonexistent because brain areas used to store events, notably the hippocampus, are not well developed in infancy (Nadel & Zola-Morgan, 1984; Schacter & Moscovitch, 1984). Also, as

What do our earliest memories tell us? Do they reveal actual events that occurred—or events that we wish had occurred? Do they tell us what we were like then—or what we are like now?

childhood amnesia *The inability to remember events and experiences that occurred early in life.*

She may be having a great birthday party, but this toddler will be unable to recall it when she grows up. Like the rest of us, she will fall victim to "childhood amnesia."

adults we use very different cognitive schemas than in early childhood, schemas that are not useful for reconstructing early events from the memory fragments we stored at the time (Neisser, 1967). Only after we enter school do we learn to think as adults do, using language to organize our memories and storing not only events but also what we think about them. In addition, as preschoolers we probably encoded our experiences far less elaborately than we do as adults because our information-processing abilities were still quite limited. As a result, we have few cues for retrieving our early memories later on in life (White & Pillemer, 1979).

Whatever the explanation for childhood amnesia, our first memories may provide some useful insights into our personalities. Some psychologists believe that these memories are not random but instead reveal our basic concerns, ambitions, and attitudes toward life (Kihlstrom & Harackiewicz, 1982). Do you think your own first memory reveals anything important about you?

Memories of a lifetime

A century ago, Hermann Ebbinghaus established a method for studying memory that was adopted by generations of psychologists. Ebbinghaus wanted to measure "pure" memory loss, independent of personal experience. Using himself as a subject, he memorized long lists of nonsense syllables, such as *bok*, *waf*, or *ged*, and tested his retention over a period of several days or weeks. He reported (1885/1913) that most forgetting occurred soon after the initial learning and then tapered off (see Figure 7.9).

A hundred years later, Marigold Linton, also using herself as a subject, decided to chart the curve of forgetting over years rather than days. Linton was interested in how people forget real-life events, not nonsense syllables. Every day for 12 years she recorded on a 4-x-6-inch card two or more things that had happened to her that day. Eventually she accumulated a catalogue of thousands of discrete events, both trivial ("I have dinner at the Canton Kitchen: delicious lobster dish") and significant ("I land at Orly Airport in Paris"). Once a month, she took a random sampling of all the cards accumulated to that point, noted whether she could remember the

FIGURE 7.9

Ebbinghaus's forgetting curve
When Hermann Ebbinghaus tested his own retention of a list of nonsense syllables, he found that memory loss was rapid soon after initial learning and then tapered off.

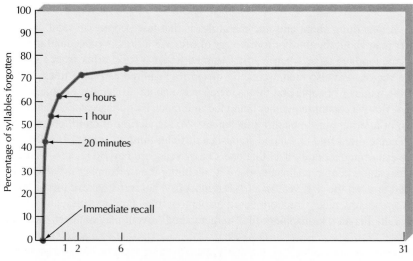

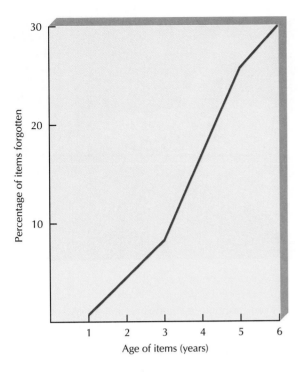

FIGURE 7.10

A forgetting curve for personal events
When Marigold Linton tested her own memory for personal events over a period of several years, she obtained a forgetting curve quite different from that of Ebbinghaus (see Figure 7.9). Memory loss was slow at first, then rose at a gradual but steady rate.

events on them, and tried to date the events. Reporting on the first 6 years' results, Linton (1978, 1979) told how she had expected a forgetting curve similar to that reported by Ebbinghaus. Instead, as Figure 7.10 shows, she found that long-term forgetting was slower and proceeded at a much more constant pace.

As you might expect, details tended to drop out of Linton's memories with the passage of time. A similar study, by Willem Wagenaar (1986), found the same thing. Wagenaar thought that certain critical details about events were sure to be remembered if he recalled anything at all about the events. Yet within a year he forgot 20 percent of these details, and after five years he forgot 60 percent. (However, when he gathered cues from witnesses about ten events that appeared to be completely forgotten, he was able to recall something about all ten of them, which suggests that his forgetting was cue-dependent.)

Of course, even with the passage of time, some memories never lose their vividness. Most American adults over 40 can tell you exactly where they were and what they were doing on November 22, 1963, when they heard that President John F. Kennedy had been assassinated. The memory is not only for the historical event itself—the shooting of the president—but for the circumstances in which they heard about it. Personal events, too, if they are surprising, shocking, or emotional, may seem to freeze a moment in time, with all the details intact.

Roger Brown and James Kulik (1977) have dubbed such memories **flashbulb memories** because that term captures the surprise, illumination, and brevity that characterize them. Brown and Kulik speculate that flashbulb memories may have evolved biologically in prehistoric times because they had survival value. Remembering the details of a surprising or dangerous experience could help a person avoid a similar situation in the future. Since it was impossible for an individual to know which details would ultimately prove useful, a large number were stored. This interpretation fits well with the finding mentioned earlier, that hormones released during emotional arousal enhance memory.

flashbulb memories *Vivid, detailed recollections of the circumstances in which one learned of or perceived some significant or surprising event.*

Do you recall where you were and what you were doing when you learned about the tragic explosion of the space shuttle Challenger *on January 28, 1986? If so, you may have a "flashbulb memory" of that moment.*

But despite their vividness, even flashbulb memories are not always complete or accurate. When details are checked they often turn out to be wrong. A recent study (McCloskey, Wible, & Cohen, 1988) found that a few days after the 1986 explosion of the space shuttle *Challenger*, most people knew (or thought they knew) exactly where they were and what they were doing when they learned of the tragedy, as well as who told them the news and what their reactions had been. But nine months later, there was an increase in "don't remember" responses and a shift to more general answers. Moreover, a quarter of the subjects gave some answers that were inconsistent with their original reports. Another study (Bohannon, 1988) found that in the short run, either strong emotion or frequent retelling of a person's experience in learning of the space shuttle disaster was enough to establish a flashbulb memory, but for long-term retention, both were necessary. After eight months, only people who had been upset rather than calm at the news and who had often recounted their experience in learning about it could relate many details of the incident with a high degree of confidence.

Theorists disagree about how "special" flashbulb memories actually are. It is clear, though, that even with flashbulb memories, facts tend to get mixed with a little fiction. Some of the details we "remember" so clearly probably are added at some time after the event, as we try to tie our own life stories to the broader saga of history (Neisser, 1982). Having read this chapter, you should not be surprised at this. As we have seen, we are not merely actors in our personal life dramas. We also write the scripts.

Taking Psychology with You
Memory Shortcuts

Someday drugs may help people with memory deficiencies and increase the performance of those with normal memories. For the time being, however, those of us who hope to improve our memories must rely on mental strategies. Formal memory techniques are known as **mnemonic [neh-MON-ik] devices**. Some mnemonic devices use easily memorized rhymes ("Thirty days hath September/April, June, and November . . . "). Others use formulas ("**E**very **g**ood **b**oy **d**oes **f**ine" for remembering which notes are on the lines of the treble clef in musical notation). Still others use visual images or verbal associations. These tricks work for a variety of reasons. Some force you to encode the material actively and thoroughly. Some make the information meaningful and therefore easier to retrieve. Still others reduce the amount of information to be stored by "chunking" it. The phone number 466-3293, for example, is better remembered in terms of the corresponding letters, which form a meaningful chunk: GOOD-BYE (appropriate, perhaps, for a travel agency).

Books on how to improve your memory often suggest elaborate mnemonics that take time to learn. A favorite is to remember a list of items by taking a mental stroll through your house, forming a visual image of each item at a particular location (the "method of Loci"). Later you repeat the tour, picking off each item as you go. Such aids can help those who must learn lists of relatively meaningless material or remember long speeches. They are also tricks of the trade for stage performers with apparently amazing memories. Most of us, however, do not wish to learn complicated tricks. Why bother to memorize a grocery list with the "mental stroll" method when you can simply write down what you plan to buy? We can benefit more by following some general guidelines, based on the principles in this chapter. They include the following:

▪ *Pay attention!* It seems obvious, but often we fail to remember because we never actually encoded information in the first place. For example, which of the following is similar to a real Lincoln penny?

Most people have trouble recognizing the real penny because they have never attended carefully to the details of a penny's design (Nickerson & Adams, 1979). We are not advising you to do so, unless you happen to be a coin collector or a counterfeiting expert. Just keep in mind that when you do have something to remember, you will do better if you encode it well. (The real penny, by the way, is the middle penny in the bottom row.)

mnemonic [neh-MON-ik] device *A strategy or technique for improving memory.*

▪ *Encode information in more than one way*. The more elaborate the encoding of information, the more memorable it will be. Elaboration can take many forms. In addition to remembering a telephone number by the sound of the individual digits, you might note the spatial pattern they make as you punch them in on a push-button phone.

▪ *Add meaning*. The more meaningful material is, the more likely it is to link up with information already in long-term memory. Meaningfulness also reduces the number of chunks of information you have to learn. Thus, if your license plate is 236MPL, you might think of 236 maples.

▪ *Use visual imagery*. Memory for pictures is often better than memory for words (Paivio, 1969). Recent research finds that visual imagery also produces better recall of an everyday event that has been seen on videotape than does rehearsing a verbal narrative of the event (Gehring & Toglia, 1989). You can make up your own mental ''pictures'' when you have to memorize verbal information. If you are in the import-export business and need to remember the main exports of several different countries, instead of trying to store, say, ''Brazil: coffee,'' you might imagine a map of Brazil with a big coffee mug superimposed on it. Some people find that the odder the image, the better.

▪ *Take your time*. If you must remember large amounts of verbal material, leisurely learning, spread out over several sessions, will probably produce better results than harried cramming. (*Reviewing* material just before you are tested on it, however, can be helpful since it places the information at the top of your ''cognitive deck.'') In terms of hours spent, spaced, or ''distributed,'' learning sessions are more efficient than ''massed'' ones. Thus you may find that you retain information better after three separate one-hour sessions than after one session of three hours.

▪ *Take time out*. If possible, minimize interference by using study breaks for rest or recreation. Sleep is the ultimate way to reduce interference. In a classic study, students who slept for eight hours after learning lists of nonsense syllables retained them better than students who went about their usual business (Jenkins & Dallenbach, 1924). Sleep is not always possible, of course, but periodic mental relaxation usually is.

▪ *Overlearn*. You can't remember something you never learned well in the first place. Overlearning—studying information even after you think you know it—is one of the best ways to remember it.

Whatever strategies you use, you will find that active learning produces more retention than merely reading or listening passively. The mind does not gobble up information automatically; you must take some pains to make the material digestible. Even then, you should not expect to remember everything you read or hear. Nor should you want to. Piling up facts without distinguishing the important from the trivial may merely clutter your mind. It is what you do with what you know that counts. Books on memory written by reputable scientists may help you boost your recall, but books or courses that promise a ''perfect,'' ''photographic,'' or ''instant'' memory fly in the face of what psychology knows about the workings of the mind. Our advice: Forget them.

KEY WORDS

memory 247
encoding 248
proposition 248
storage 249
retrieval 249
sensory memory 249
short-term memory (STM) 249
long-term memory (LTM) 249
multistore model of memory 250
sensory registers 250
déjà vu 251
eidetic imagery 251
anterograde amnesia 252
active/working memory 253
chunks 253
maintenance rehearsal 254
elaborative rehearsal 255
deep versus shallow processing 256
serial position effect 256
primacy and recency effects 256
tip-of-the-tongue state 258

procedural memories 258
semantic memories 258
episodic memories 258
declarative memories 258
cognitive schema 259
long-term potentiation (LTP) 263
consolidation 264
decay theory 267
recognition 269
recall 269
relearning method 270
priming 270
proactive and retroactive
   interference 271
motivated forgetting/repression 271
retrograde amnesia 271
cue-dependent forgetting 271
state-dependent memory 272
childhood amnesia 273
flashbulb memories 275
mnemonic devices 277

SUMMARY

1. Memory is selective; not everything we experience gets stored, and what is stored is not an exact replica of experience. Sensory information is *encoded* almost as soon as it is detected and is stored in the form of propositions, images, or sets of instructions. Most current models of memory account for the encoding, storage, and retrieval of information by taking an *information-processing approach.*

2. The *multistore model of memory*, and most other models as well, assume that there are three separate but interacting types of memory systems: sensory memory, short-term memory, and long-term memory.

3. In most models, *sensory memory* includes several subsystems, or *sensory registers*, for the different senses. Sensory memory briefly retains information in the form of literal sensory images, such as *icons* and *echoes*, so that it can be further processed. We speculated that sensory memory may somehow be involved in such curious phenomena as *déjà vu* and *eidetic imagery.* Information that is not transferred to short-term memory from sensory memory decays and is lost.

4. *Short-term memory (STM)* retains recently received information temporarily, perhaps up to 30 seconds, although *rehearsal* can extend retention. Short-term memory also provides a working memory for the use of information retrieved from long-term memory.

5. The limited capacity of STM can be extended by *chunking* information into larger units. According to most models of memory, information that is not transferred to long-term memory from short-term memory decays and is lost. Elaborative rehearsal is more likely to result in transfer to long-term memory than is maintenance (rote) rehearsal. And deep processing is often a more effective retention

strategy than shallow processing, although there are exceptions. The assumption of a short-term memory distinct from a long-term memory has been used to explain the *serial position effect* in recall.

6. *Long-term memory (LTM)* is the system that handles more or less permanent storage of information. Its contents appear to be organized and indexed largely in terms of meaning, but other systems are also used, depending on the nature of the material. *Procedural memories* are memories for how to perform specific actions. *Semantic memories* are internal representations of the world, including facts, rules, and concepts. *Episodic memories* are internal representations of personally experienced events. Semantic and episodic memories are also known as *declarative memories*.

7. Remembering information stored in long-term memory is in part a reconstructive process, and what we remember may be a distortion of what was originally learned or experienced. Distortions also occur because initial storage is influenced by *cognitive schemas* and because memory can be affected by leading questions. These facts pose problems for the legal system, which must rely to some extent on eyewitness testimony.

8. Short-term memory involves temporary changes within neurons that alter their ability to release neurotransmitters. Long-term memory involves long-lasting structural changes in neurons and synapses. *Long-term potentiation*, an increase in the strength of synaptic response, may be an important mechanism of long-term memory. Neural changes underlying memory take time to develop, which may explain why long-term memories require a period of *consolidation*. Procedural memories are associated in part with the cerebellum, and formation of declarative memories is most closely associated with the hippocampus and amygdala. Various hormones produced during emotional arousal appear to affect the retention of learning.

9. Some psychologists believe that long-term memories are permanent and that forgetting is due solely to *retrieval failure*. Elizabeth Loftus debates this view, citing evidence that information in LTM can be "erased" by new, contradictory information. The issue of the permanence or impermanence of long-term memories remains to be resolved.

10. Forgetting is not an all-or-nothing phenomenon. *Recognition* is usually easier than *recall*, and subtle tests of memory, such as *relearning tests*, show that previously stored material can affect performance even when the material is not recognized or recalled.

11. Some forgetting occurs because of interference among items, either *proactive* or *retroactive*. Other memory lapses appear to be due to *motivated forgetting*. Perhaps the most common cause of forgetting, however, is the unavailability of *retrieval cues*. This type of forgetting is called *cue-dependent*. The most effective retrieval cues tend to be ones that were present at the time of the initial learning or experience. We may remember best when we are in the same mental or physical state as during the initial learning or experience, a phenomenon called *state-dependent memory*.

12. Autobiographical memories are in some ways different from other memories. They are missing from the first two or three years of life, a phenomenon known as *childhood amnesia*. They also seem to be forgotten at a slower and more steady rate than are the nonsense materials so often used in laboratory experiments. *Flashbulb memories* have a special vividness and clarity, freezing a moment in time when we learned about or perceived a surprising or shocking event. However, even flashbulb memories may be embellished or altered, for remembering is a reconstructive process.

CHAPTER 8

Cognition II: Thought and Language

What a piece of work is man! How noble in reason! How infinite in faculties! . . . in apprehension how like a god!

WILLIAM SHAKESPEARE

A great many people think they are thinking when they are merely rearranging their prejudices.

WILLIAM JAMES

23 | 9167486769200039158
0986609275853801
6248310668014430
8622407126516427
9346570408670096
5932792057677480
8067900227783016
3549248523803033
5745316935111903
5965775473400707
5681688305620820
1016129132845564
8057801588806771

Shakuntala Devi can find the twenty-third root of a 201-digit number in 50 seconds, in her head. That's impressive—but so are the ordinary mental operations we all carry out every day.

*I*ndian-born Shakuntala Devi has an unusual talent: She can beat a computer at certain kinds of complicated calculations. Once she extracted the twenty-third root of a 201-digit number in only 50 seconds, *in her head*. It would take most people almost that long just to write down the problem. Such lightning calculations seem to depend on an unusual ability to visualize numbers on one's mental "blackboard" and apply various numerical strategies. Dazzling as this feat is, though, in a way it is no more impressive than what we all do every day as we go about our business. Ordinary thought involves processes that are just as complex: drawing inferences, analyzing relationships, organizing and reorganizing the flotsam and jetsam of our mental world.

But just as memory both impresses and disappoints, so, too, do our powers of thought and reason. Consider:

▪ During childhood we all master the concept of time and learn how clocks arbitrarily divide it into hours, minutes, and seconds. Yet in 1966, when a national Daylight Savings Time bill was passed, some people worried that the government was tampering with "God's time." One woman in Colorado complained in a letter to her local newspaper that the "extra hour" of sunlight was burning up her lawn!

▪ In 1978, a man claiming to be a weather expert made tabloid headlines when he claimed that two successive harsh winters in North America had been caused by the Soviet Cosmos satellite positioned above the East Coast. "I admit I have no hard evidence," he said, "but then there is no negative evidence either" (Radner & Radner, 1982).

▪ Twentieth-century Americans consider themselves rational and enlightened. Yet for years, the Proctor & Gamble Company was deluged with calls from people who had heard that the company's moon-and-stars trademark was a satanic symbol. (Actually, the logo's 13 stars signify the 13 original colonies, and its quarter moon with a human face is patterned after an image popular when the company was founded.) Frustrated by the recurring rumors, the company decided in 1985 gradually to remove the 103-year-old trademark from its packages.

The human mind, which has managed to come up with poetry, penicillin, and pantyhose, clearly has its limitations. In this chapter, we will examine our capabilities of thought, reasoning, problem solving, and language, as well as our mental shortcomings.

Thought: Using What We Know

Thinking is defined most simply as the mental manipulation of information. This capacity frees us from the cage of the immediate present: We can think about the camping trip we took three years ago, the party we have planned for next Saturday night, the War of 1812. It also carries us beyond the boundaries of physical reality: We can think about unicorns and utopias, Martians and magic. Because we can think, we do not need to grope our way blindly through our problems but can solve them intelligently and creatively.

The elements of cognition

When we take action, we physically manipulate the environment. When we think, we *mentally* manipulate internal representations of objects, activities, and situations. However, we do not manipulate *all* the information potentially available to us, any more than we store in memory everything we read, see, or hear. If we did, making the simplest decision or solving the most trivial problem would be a time-consuming, and perhaps impossible, task. Imagine trying to decide whether to go out for a hamburger if that entailed thinking about every hamburger you had ever bitten into, seen a commercial for, or watched someone else devour. Thinking is possible because our internal representations simplify and summarize information that reaches us from the environment.

Concepts. One type of representation, or unit of thought, is the **concept**. The concept of a concept is a tricky one. Essentially, a concept is a mental category that groups objects, relations, activities, abstractions, or qualities having common properties. The instances of a concept are seen as roughly similar. For example, *golden retriever*, *cocker spaniel*, *Weimaraner*, and *German shepherd* are all instances of the concept *dog*. *Anger*, *joy*, *sadness*, *fear*, and *surprise* are all instances of the abstract concept *emotion*. Because concepts simplify the world, we do not have to learn a new name for each thing, relation, activity, abstract state, or quality we encounter, nor treat each instance as though it were unique. You may never have seen a *Basenji* or eaten *escargots*, but if you know that the first is an instance of *dog* and the second an instance of *food*, you will know how to respond.

We form concepts not only through direct contact with objects and situations, but also by contact with *symbols*, things that represent or stand for something else. Symbolic representations include words, mathematical formulas, maps, graphs, pictures, and even gestures. Symbols stand not only for objects but for operations (for example, the symbols + and ÷), relationships (for example, = and <), and qualities (for example, the dot in musical notation that symbolizes an abrupt or staccato quality).

The symbols we call words are particularly useful in speeding up the process of concept formation. Before they have language, children must learn concepts through the laborious process of noting positive and negative instances. No wonder they sometimes confuse dogs and cats or candy and pills. Once they have language, however, they have a shortcut available; they can learn definitions and rules. But infants and even animals can acquire concepts without language. Gestalt psychologist Wolfgang Köhler (1939) once taught chickens to peck at a medium gray square covered with seed and to ignore a darker gray square also covered with seed. Then he replaced the darker square with a very light one. Which square do you think the chickens pecked at? Not, as it turned out, the medium gray one, where they had

thinking *The mental manipulation of information stored in the form of concepts, images, or propositions.*
concept *A category used to class together objects, relations, activities, abstractions, or qualities that share common properties.*

eaten before, but the new, light gray one. The chickens seemed to have the concept "lighter one" and to know they could feed at the lighter of any two squares. Thus they were able to learn a relationship, not merely a response to a particular stimulus. (For more on the cognitive abilities of animals, see "Think About It.")

One researcher (Rosch [formerly Heider], 1973) argues that concepts having a moderate number of instances are *basic* and are naturally easier to acquire than those that have either few or many instances. What is the object pictured in the margin? You will probably call it an apple. The concept *apple* is more basic than *fruit*, which includes many more instances and is more abstract. It is also more basic than *McIntosh apple*, which is quite specific. Children seem to learn basic-level concepts earlier than others, and adults use them more often than others. Basic concepts convey an optimal amount of information in most situations and are probably universal (R. Brown, 1986).

In most cases, all the qualities associated with a particular concept do not apply to every instance: Some apples are not red; some dogs do not bark; some birds do not fly or perch on trees. But all the instances of a concept do share a "family resemblance." Moreover, everyone within a culture can easily tell you which in-

Which of these men are bachelors? Some instances of a concept are more representative, or prototypical, than others. Thus, although all four of these men are unmarried, chances are you will not see them all as equally representative of the concept bachelor.

stances are most representative, or *prototypical*, of the concept (Rosch, 1973). Which dog is doggier, a golden retriever or a chihuahua? Which fruit is more fruitlike, an apple or a tangerine? Which activity is more representative of sports, football or weight lifting? When we need to decide whether something belongs to a concept, we are likely to compare it to a prototype.

Propositions and images.   Concepts are the building blocks of thought, but they would be of limited use if we simply stacked them up mentally. We must also represent how they are related to one another. As we saw in Chapter 7, one way we accomplish this seems to be by storing and using **propositions**. Propositions are units of meaning that are made up of concepts and that express a unitary idea. A proposition may express nearly any sort of knowledge (*John raises Basenjis*) or belief (*John is crazy*). Propositions, in turn, may be linked together in complicated, constantly shifting networks (Anderson, 1976; Anderson & Bower, 1973).

Most psychologists believe that mental **images** are also important in thinking (Kosslyn, 1983; Paivio, 1983). Most people report experiencing visual images, pictures in the mind's eye. Although no one can directly ''see'' another person's visual images, cognitive psychologists are able to study them indirectly. One method is to measure how long it takes people to rotate an image, scan from one point to another, or ''read off'' some detail. The results suggest that visual images are analogous to images on a television screen. That is, we can manipulate them, they occur in a mental ''space'' of a fixed size, and small ones contain less detail than larger ones (Kosslyn, 1980; Shepard & Metzler, 1971).

Most people also report auditory images, for instance, when thinking about a song or a conversation, and many report images in other sensory modalities—touch, taste, smell, or pain. Some even report muscular or kinesthetic images, feelings in the muscles and joints. People say they use their mental images for many purposes: to visualize the possible outcomes of a decision, to understand or formulate verbal descriptions, to boost motivation, and to improve mood (Kosslyn et al., 1989). Imagining yourself performing a motor skill, such as diving or sprinting, may even improve your actual performance (Druckman & Swets, 1988).

Albert Einstein said that he relied heavily on visual and muscular imagery for formulating ideas. The happiest thought of his life, he once recalled, occurred in 1907, when he suddenly imagined a human observer falling freely from the roof of a house and realized the person would not experience a gravitational field in his immediate vicinity. This insight led to Einstein's discovery of the principle of general relativity, and physics was never again the same.

Soviet and East European athletes pioneered the use of visual imagery to rehearse a skill mentally before performing it.

QUICK ▪ QUIZ

1. Stuffing your mouth with cotton candy, licking a lollipop, gnawing on a chicken drumstick, and chewing a piece of beef jerky are all instances of the _____ *eating*.
2. Which concept is most basic: *furniture*, *chair*, or *high chair*?
3. In addition to concepts and images, _____ have been proposed as a basic form of mental representation.

Answers:

1. concept 2. *chair* 3. propositions

proposition *A unit of meaning that expresses a unitary idea and is made up of concepts.*

image *A likeness of something; a representation that mirrors or resembles the thing it represents. Mental images can occur in many and perhaps all sensory modalities.*

Think About It

Are "Dumb Beasts" Smarter Than We Think?

▪ A green heron swipes some bread from a picnicker's table and scatters the crumbs on a nearby stream. When a minnow rises to the bait, the heron strikes, swallowing its prey before you can say "hook, line, and sinker."

▪ A sea otter, floating calmly on its back, bangs a mussel shell against a stone that is resting on its stomach. When the shell cracks apart, the otter devours the tasty morsel inside, tucks the stone under its flipper, and dives for another shell, which it will open in the same way.

▪ An African lion appears behind a herd of wildebeests and chases them toward a ditch. Another lion, lying in wait at the ditch, leaps up and kills one of the passing wildebeests. The first lion then joins its companion for the feast.

Incidents like these have convinced some biologists, psychologists, and ethologists that animals are brighter than they generally get credit for. They argue that at least some animals can anticipate, plan, make choices, and coordinate their activities with those of their comrades (Griffin, 1984; S. Walker, 1982). Other scientists are not so certain. They note that behavior may look complex yet be genetically prewired. The assassin bug of South America catches termites by gluing nest material on its back

as camouflage, but it is hard to imagine how the bug's tiny dab of brain tissue could enable it to plan this strategy consciously. The behavior must be innate. Even trees and plants, which few people credit with consciousness, do things that *appear* intelligent. When willow trees are attacked by insects, they release a chemical into the air that causes leaves on nearby healthy willow trees to change chemically and become less palatable to the insects (Rhoades, 1985). Their "communication" does not imply thought; it is simply a genetically controlled adaptation to the environment.

Yet genetic explanations leave some questions unanswered. Honeybees communicate the source of nectar to one another by doing a little "dance" in a figure-eight pattern. The orientation of the dance conveys the position of the food relative to the sun's position in the sky, and the speed of the dance tells how far the food source is from the hive. Researchers assume that the ability to perform and decode the dance is innate and shows no special intelligence. But in one study, when researchers kept changing the site of the food source, each time moving the food 25 percent farther than the previous site, forager bees began to anticipate where the food source would appear next. When the researchers arrived at the new location, they would find the bees circling

Reasoning

reasoning *The drawing of conclusions or inferences from observations, facts, or assumptions.*

inductive reasoning *Reasoning from the particular to the general; drawing general conclusions from examination of specific examples.*

Not all thinking has an obvious purpose; we all spend some of our time simply daydreaming (see Chapter 4). But much thinking is goal-directed and requires that we draw inferences from observations, facts, or assumptions. This kind of purposive thinking is what is meant by **reasoning**. When we reason, we use the concepts, propositions, and images we have stored in memory to review the past, make judgments and decisions, and solve problems.

Logicians talk about two basic kinds of reasoning. In **inductive reasoning**, the thinker draws general conclusions from specific observations. If you notice that a comedian you once admired has made five dreadful movies in a row, you may well

the spot, waiting for their dinner (Gould & Gould, 1982). No one has yet explained how bees, whose brains weigh four ten-thousandths of an ounce, could have inferred the location of the new site.

Psychologists studying animals must resist the temptation to *anthropomorphize*, or attribute human qualities to nonhuman beings. Anthropomorphizing can lead to serious misinterpretations of the evidence. Consider the true story of Clever Hans, a "wonder horse" in Germany at the turn of the century who was said to possess mathematical abilities (Fernald, 1984). Clever Hans would answer math problems by stamping his hoof. For example, if asked to solve "3 times 6 divided by 2," Clever Hans would tap his foot 9 times. But a little experimentation revealed that when Hans was prevented from seeing the questioner, his "powers" left him. It seems that questioners were staring at the animal's feet and leaning forward expectantly after stating the problem, then lifting their eyes and relaxing as soon as he completed the right number of taps. Clever Hans was indeed clever, but not at math. He was simply responding to nonverbal signals that people were inadvertently providing.

This does not mean animals are *unable* to acquire numerical skills. In fact, recent, carefully controlled tests suggest that some of them can. In one study, chimpanzees compared two pairs of food wells containing chocolate chips. One pair might contain, say, five chips and three chips, the other four chips and three chips. Allowed to choose which pair they wanted, the chimps almost always chose the one with the higher total, showing some sort of summing ability (Rumbaugh, Savage-Rumbaugh, & Pate, 1988). Other chimps have learned to use numerals to label quantities of items and simple sums (Boysen, 1988; Rumbaugh, 1988a). One researcher has even taught an African gray parrot to name different quantities of items up to six, using spoken English ("two cork(s)," "four key(s)"). Although it is unclear whether the bird is actually counting, it apparently recognizes quantity by some means (Pepperberg, 1987).

How much intelligence is revealed when animals use objects in the natural environment as rudimentary tools? Will the counting abilities of laboratory animals force us to revise our assumptions about animal abilities, or are we falling into the Clever Hans trap? On a continuum of cognitive abilities, are animals more like willow trees or human beings? Think about it.

---

conclude that he has lost his comic touch. Science depends heavily on inductive reasoning based on carefully collected evidence. But inductive reasoning has a drawback: No matter how much supporting evidence you gather, it is always possible that you have overlooked some evidence that contradicts your conclusion.

The other kind of reasoning is **deductive**. The thinker starts with one or more general assumptions, or *premises*, and draws specific conclusions that follow logically. Deductive reasoning often takes the form of a *syllogism*, a simple argument consisting of two premises and a conclusion:

premise   All human beings are mortal.
premise   I am a human being.
conclusion   Therefore I am mortal.

deductive reasoning
Reasoning from the general to the particular; drawing a conclusion that follows necessarily from certain premises.

Note that the conclusion *must* be true if the two premises are true.

We think in syllogisms all the time, even though many of our premises are implicit rather than clearly spelled out in our minds: "I never have to work on Saturday. Today is Saturday, so I don't have to work today." However, knowing when to use deductive reasoning does not come naturally. It is influenced by experience, schooling, and culture. In a study of the Kpelle Tribe in Africa (Scribner, 1977), researchers gave a farmer this problem: "All Kpelle men are rice farmers. Mr. Smith is not a rice farmer. Is he a Kpelle man?" The farmer insisted that the information provided did not allow a conclusion:

> KPELLE MAN: I don't know the man in person. I have not laid eyes on the man himself.
>
> RESEARCHER: Just think about the statement.
>
> KPELLE MAN: If I know him in person, I can answer that question, but since I do not know him in person I cannot answer that question.

Yet the Kpelle man in the exchange was reasoning deductively:

premise	If I do not know a person, I cannot draw any conclusions about that person.
premise	I do not know Mr. Smith.
conclusion	Therefore I cannot draw any conclusions about Mr. Smith.

One's culture, then, teaches which sorts of questions can legitimately be settled by syllogistic thinking. In the course of growing up, we also learn the general premises our culture considers true. Before Columbus discovered America, most people accepted the premise that the earth is flat. It was perfectly reasonable—indeed, *logical*—to conclude that a ship sailing too far in any direction would fall off the earth. Deductive reasoning only tells you that *if* certain premises are true, a certain conclusion must follow. It does not tell you whether or not the premises are true.

People often have trouble applying the rules of logic. For example, they may say that the following syllogism is valid, when in fact it is not:

> All birds have beaks.
> That creature has a beak.
> Therefore that creature is a bird.

"That creature" may well be a bird, but the conclusion does not follow from the premises. Certain other animals may also have beaks. Errors of this type occur because people reverse a premise. In this case, "All birds have beaks" is converted to "All beaked animals are birds." The reversed premise is plausible because few people are aware of any instances of *beaked creature* besides birds—but this premise is not the one that was given. In contrast, a similar error is *not* likely to occur with the following syllogism, though it has exactly the same form:

> All psychology professors are geniuses.
> That person is a genius.
> Therefore that person is a psychology professor.

In this case, people can see that the syllogism is invalid. They do not reverse the first premise because the notion that all geniuses are psychology professors is implausible.

Deductive and inductive reasoning alone will not enable the members of this jury to reach a conclusion. They will also need to reason dialectically, weighing the evidence for and against guilt or innocence and the reasonableness of the arguments made by the attorneys.

But even when people are perfectly logical, they may disagree if they accept different premises. For example, your position on abortion rights will depend on your premises about when meaningful human life begins, the relative importance of embryonic life versus avoiding unwanted children, and so forth. Controversial issues tend to be those in which premises cannot be proven true or false to everyone's satisfaction. Thus people of good will can reach opposite conclusions—logically.

Logic is inadequate for solving messy real-life problems for another reason: There often is no single right answer. Many approaches and viewpoints compete, and you must decide which is most reasonable. Should the government raise taxes or lower them? Should arms control negotiators be tough or conciliatory? How much say should parents have about sex education in the schools? To think rationally about such issues, people need more than inductive and deductive logic. They also need skill in **dialectical reasoning**, the ability to think critically about opposing points of view. One writer describes this type of reasoning as moving ''up and back between contradictory lines of reasoning, using each to critically cross-examine the other'' (Paul, 1984). Dialectical reasoning is what juries do to arrive at a verdict. A jury decision is not reached by applying some formula or set of procedures but by open-minded consideration of arguments for and against, point and counterpoint. Many people have trouble with dialectical reasoning because their self-esteem rests on being right and having their beliefs and prejudices accepted.

''If people would only be logical, they could get along.'' But logic is not enough when people start with different assumptions and values. How can people who are operating from different premises reach agreement?

Sources of irrationality

The need to be right is not the only psychological reason people are unreasonable. In most areas of life, judgments and decisions are made under conditions of uncertainty. Faced with incomplete information, people often fall back on habitual strategies or rules of thumb that may or may not be appropriate. And just as they are influenced in recalling events by the way questions are put (see Chapter 7), they are influenced in making decisions by the way choices are framed. Psychologists have studied many of our cognitive biases. They have shown that models of personal, economic, and political decision making cannot predict behavior correctly unless they take human irrationality into account (Simon, 1973; Tversky & Kahneman, 1986). Here are some representative findings:

dialectical reasoning *A process in which opposing facts or ideas are weighed and compared, with a view to determining the truth or resolving differences.*

Loss aversion. In general, people try to avoid risks or losses. In one study, the subjects, who included physicians, were asked to choose between two health programs to combat a disease expected to kill 600 people (Tversky & Kahneman, 1981). Most preferred a program that would definitely save 200 people to a program that had a one-third probability of saving all 600 and a two-thirds probability of saving none. In other words, they rejected the riskier, though potentially more rewarding, solution. However, people will accept risk if they see it as a way to avoid loss. In the same study, people were asked to choose between a program in which 400 people would definitely die and a program in which there was a one-third probability of nobody dying and a two-thirds probability that all 600 would die. If you think about it for a while, you will see that the alternatives are exactly the same as in the first problem but are worded differently. This time, a majority of the respondents chose the second solution. They rejected any risk when they thought of the outcome in terms of lives saved, but they accepted risk when they thought of the outcome in terms of lives lost.

Few of us will have to face a decision involving hundreds of lives, but we may have to choose between different medical treatments for ourselves or a relative. Our decision may be affected by whether the doctor frames the choice in terms of mortality or survival.

Costs versus losses. In general, disadvantages seem more acceptable if they are labeled costs than if they are labeled losses. For example, most people say they would rather accept a 25 percent chance to lose $200 than a sure loss of $50. At the same time, most people say they are willing to pay $50 for insurance against a 25 percent risk of losing $200 (Slovic, Fischhoff, and Lichtenstein, 1982). In the second case, they probably see the $50 as the cost of protection rather than as a mere loss. We may justify many losses in life by finding reasons to view them as costs.

One's evaluation of a cost, however, depends on the particular context. Suppose you buy a $10 ticket to a play. As you enter the theater you discover you have lost the ticket. Would you pay $10 for another ticket? Most people say no (Kahneman & Tversky, 1984). Now suppose you decide to see a play where admission is $10 a ticket. At the theater you discover that you have lost a $10 bill. Would you still pay $10 for a ticket to the play? Faced with this hypothetical problem, 88 percent of respondents said they would go ahead and buy the ticket.

Note that in each case, you would have been out $10. The "mental accounting" people do, however, differs in the two situations. People tend to view going to the theater as a transaction in which they exchange the cost of a ticket for the experience of seeing the play. In the first situation, losing the ticket raises the cost to a level that most people find unacceptable. In the second the loss of $10 is not mentally linked to the cost of the ticket. But when people are given both versions of the problem, they become more willing to replace the lost ticket in the first situation. They recognize that the lost ticket can be regarded as equivalent to lost cash.

Relative accounting. We also judge the advantages and disadvantages of options relative to some reference state. An example will make this clearer: Suppose you are about to buy a $125 jacket and a $15 calculator. The salesperson tells you the calculator is on sale for $10 at another branch of the store, 20 minutes' drive away. Would you make the trip to the other store? In one study, over two-thirds of the respondents said they would (Kahneman & Tversky, 1984). But now suppose the prices are switched: The jacket is $15, the calculator is $125, and the calculator is on sale at the other branch for $120. Under these conditions, most people say they would not make the trip. In both situations, the savings would be $5! But people see the gain not in absolute terms but *relative* to the price of the particular item on sale.

These traders on the commodities exchange are taking a calculated risk. Do you or would you do the same? The answer depends in part on whether you regard losing money this way as a clear loss, or simply a cost of investing.

Relativistic thinking explains why people spend money for carpeting more easily when they are buying a new house than when they are simply redecorating.

Expectations.   In Chapter 5 we saw that expectations affect how we perceive the world. They also affect what we do with the information that we perceive. On July 3, 1988, a U.S. warship shot down an Iranian passenger jet taking off over the Persian Gulf, killing all aboard. The warship's computer system had at first misread the plane's altitude and identified it as an F-14 fighter jet but then corrected itself. Unfortunately, by that time, the initial information had created an expectation of an attack. In the stress of the moment, the skipper paid more attention to his crew's reports of an emergency than to new information being generated by the computer. The earlier information was never reevaluated, and the crew assumed that the airliner was descending rather than ascending—with tragic results (Nisbett, 1988).

Exaggerating the improbable.   People tend to exaggerate the probability of very rare events. Therefore they will accept risk even though a gain is improbable, and avoid risk even though a loss is unlikely. The first tendency helps explain the popularity of lotteries. The second explains why people buy earthquake insurance.

As seen in Chapter 2, people are especially likely to exaggerate the probability of rare but catastrophic events. One reason is the *availability heuristic*, the tendency to overestimate the occurrence of an event because it is easily noticed, imagined, or retrieved from memory. In one study, people overestimated the frequency of deaths from tornadoes, which are dramatic but rare, and underestimated the frequency of deaths from asthma, which occur 20 times as often but do not make headlines. In addition, they estimated deaths from accidents and disease to be equally frequent, although in reality 16 times as many people die each year from disease as from accidents (Lichtenstein et al., 1978).

As you can see, the decisions human beings make, and the feelings of regret or pleasure that follow, are not entirely logical. The psychological principles that govern both our rational and irrational choices have enormous implications for decision makers in business, medicine, government, the marketplace—in fact, in all areas of life.

QUICK ▪ QUIZ

Provide the missing word or phrase.

1. Mervin observes that most of the items he bought as Christmas gifts cost more than they did last year, and he concludes that inflation is increasing. Which sort of reasoning is he using: inductive, deductive, or dialectical?

2. Yvonne is arguing with Henrietta about whether real estate is a better investment than stocks. "You can't convince me," she says, "I just know I'm right." Yvonne needs training in _____ reasoning.

3. Neil has been unwilling to lay out money for a record album he wants. Then his stereo breaks down and he goes to buy a new one. "I might as well buy that album, too," he tells himself. "After all, I'm already spending so much money, what's a little bit more?" Neil's change of heart can be explained as _____ thinking.

Answers:

1. inductive 2. dialectical 3. relativistic

Problem Solving

Individuals, families, businesses, governments—all have problems. They may be as mundane as getting to work when the car breaks down or as profound as avoiding nuclear war. Problems bring all our cognitive abilities into play: internal representation, memory, and reasoning.

Paths to problem solving

It may seem obvious, but before you can solve a problem, you have to recognize that one exists. This is easier for some people than others. Students who have trouble learning (which is certainly a problem) are less likely than others to notice when a textbook contains incomplete or inconsistent information, or when a passage is especially difficult. As a result, they spend no more time on difficult passages than on easy ones. Poor learners also tend to be lazy readers; they only go through the motions of reading and do not realize when they have failed to comprehend what they have read (Bransford et al., 1986).

Once a problem is recognized, people generally go about solving it in four steps (Wessells, 1982): (1) *defining the problem*, which may be difficult if it lacks clear starting and end points (creating a new style of art, inventing a better mousetrap, finding a good term paper topic); (2) *devising a strategy*; (3) *executing the strategy*; and (4) *evaluating progress toward the goal*. As conditions affecting the problem change, the problem solver may have to repeat one or more of these steps before reaching the goal. For example, you may decide to solve your money problems by finding a better job, but if a recession reduces the number of jobs available you may need to rethink your strategy—perhaps keeping your current job but spending less.

Problems can sometimes be attacked by methods guaranteed to produce a solution, even if the solver does not understand how they work. Such methods are called

algorithm *A problem-solving strategy that is guaranteed to lead eventually to a solution.*

heuristic *A rule of thumb that guides problem solving but does not guarantee an optimal solution. Heuristics are often used as shortcuts in solving complex problems.*

artificial intelligence *"Intelligent" behavior performed by computers. Also, the study of the methods used to program such behavior in computers.*

algorithms. Some algorithms consist of a set of rules. To solve a problem in long division, you apply a set of rules learned in the fourth grade. Similarly, to bake a chocolate cake, you use a set of rules called a recipe. Other algorithms require an exhaustive search through all possible solutions. For example, if you forgot the last digit of a friend's unlisted telephone number, you could simply try each of the possibilities, from 0 through 9, until you reached your friend.

Often, however, there is no obvious sequence of steps that will lead inevitably to a solution. Instead, the solution depends on certain rules of thumb, or **heuristics**. Heuristics suggest a course of action but do not guarantee an optimal solution. For instance, when you play chess, you can't possibly consider all of the possible strategies for winning. (Don't try; it would take you longer than the estimated life of the universe to work out all the possible sequences of moves!) But your knowledge of the game and your past history of successes and failures suggest certain heuristics, such as ''Move the powerful pieces first'' and ''Control the center of the board.'' A doctor trying to determine the best treatment for breast cancer, a marriage counselor trying to advise a troubled couple, and a factory owner trying to boost production must all rely on heuristics. Life's problems are rarely susceptible to ''cookbook'' solutions.

Problem-solving pitfalls

If problem solving is simply a four-stage process, why don't more problems get solved? We have already encountered some answers: the difficulty people have with logic when logic is called for, their reluctance to consider opposing points of view, and their biases in evaluating alternatives. But these are not the only barriers.

To find out why some people are better at devising problem-solving strategies than others, researchers have compared experts and nonexperts in engineering, business management, physics, medicine, and other fields (Bransford et al., 1986; Lash, 1988; Wagner & Sternberg, 1986). A major difference is that the experts have a rich fund of knowledge relevant to the problem at hand. On the average, they are no more intelligent than novices, but they know more and do not have to search laboriously for information. On the basis of experience they can recognize patterns, retrieve cognitive schemas (see Chapter 7), and quickly arrive at a solution. This capacity to acquire a vast storehouse of knowledge about the world, gained through experience, gives human intelligence its speed and flexibility and distinguishes it from the **artificial intelligence** of a computer (see ''A Closer Look at Artificial Intelligence'').

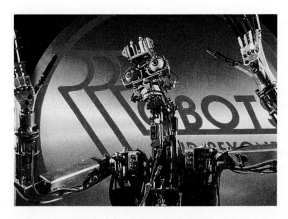

What would a robot have to do before you would considered it ''intelligent'' ? This cheerful piece of machinery informed visitors to the Boston Museum of Science, ''Humans, you are witnessing the beginning of a great new era.'' Yet robots cannot contemplate the meaning of death, paint a great work of art, or know that it's time to prune the roses simply by looking at them.

A Closer Look at Artificial Intelligence

The Computer's Lament: If I Only Had a Brain

The philosopher René Descartes, who wrote, "I think, therefore I am," struggled long and hard to distinguish the consciousness of human beings from the workings of mere machines. Little did he suspect that three centuries later, machines, too, would think. We refer, of course, to computers, sometimes known as electronic brains. No computer has yet achieved the sophistication of "Hal," whose sinister circuits plotted rebellion in the film *2001: A Space Odyssey*. But these remarkable machines can mimic and sometimes surpass their human creators at reasoning, applying algorithms and heuristics, testing hypotheses, and remembering facts. They make plans, hold limited conversations, play chess, and even compose music. Computerized robots, though neither as talented nor as cute as *Star Wars'* R2D2, both hear and see.

Scientists in the multidisciplinary field of *artificial intelligence* design the sets of instructions (programs) that enable machines to do all these things. Until recently, most did not care whether the machine actually used human strategies as long as it behaved as it was supposed to. The computer's successes were many and often put human processing to shame. As early as the 1950s, when computers were still at the Neanderthal stage in their evolution, they could use logical principles to find alternate

proofs of theorems in symbolic logic (Newell & Simon, 1972). The machines were tireless, and barring a power outage, would continue to operate with unvarying efficiency day and night, even without coffee breaks. They were fast: They could reason and compute in millionths or even trillionths of a second, making the human mind look like molasses. And they were accurate, carrying out instructions with absolute precision and reliably regurgitating whatever was stored in their memories.

But unbounded optimism soon gave way to caution. The powerful computers might diagnose illnesses or solve mathematical problems, but they could not carry out the most mundane everyday activities, like understanding a casual conversation, planning a trip to the grocery store, or recognizing a face. These simple accomplishments (simple for human beings, that is) require a commonsense knowledge of the world, which living things absorb through the senses. A computer knows only what a programmer has put into its data base. It lacks the millions—possibly billions—of bits of information that people collect over a lifetime.

When you read the words "The phone rang. The woman got up from her chair," you can predict what will probably happen next. When you hear "Mary Had a Little Lamb," you know that the jin-

In daily life, knowledge can spell the difference between helplessness and mastery of life's problems. After a lecture on language development, a young woman we know asked her professor whether something might be wrong with her 3-year-old son, who did not yet speak. (Until the lecture, the student did not recognize the possible existence of a problem.) The professor asked if there was any deafness in the family. There was. Then the professor suggested that the child get a physical checkup. But the student was poor; she couldn't pay a doctor. So the professor suggested that she contact the county health agency, which offered free exams. How, asked the student, do you contact this agency? Because she lacked important knowledge—about the contribution of hearing impairment to speech problems, the normal age for the appearance of speech, the existence of county health services, and the listing of such services in the phone book under "County Government"—she was unable to solve her problem without assistance.

Another source of difficulty in problem solving is a rigidity toward trying out

gle is about a pet, not Mary's lunch (Allman, 1986). And when you see a friend on the street, you immediately recognize her, even if she is wearing a new outfit and just had her hair permed. Computers lack these abilities. Moreover, because they do not take context into account, they may translate "He shot off his mouth without thinking" as "He absent-mindedly fired a bullet into his jaw," or "The spirit is willing but the flesh is weak" as "The vodka is good, but the meat is rotten."

Some members of the "artificial intelligentsia" conclude that if computers are to be truly intelligent, they must be modeled after the greatest computer of them all, the human brain. Most computers today process instructions sequentially and work on a single incoming stream of data. In contrast, the brain performs many operations simultaneously, and it recognizes patterns "all at once" rather than as a sequence of information bits. It can do these things because each neuron communicates with thousands of others, which in turn communicate with millions more. Although no single neuron is terribly smart, millions of them working collectively and simultaneously produce cognition.

Computer scientists are now designing machines called *neural networks* (or neural nets) that attempt to imitate the brain's vast grid of densely connected neurons (Anderson & Rosenfeld, 1988; D. Levine, in press). In these machines, simple processing units are linked up to one another, much as neurons in the brain are, sharing information and working in parallel. Like the human brain, neural nets do not always find the very best solution to a problem, but usually they do find a good solution quickly. They also have the potential to learn from experience by adjusting the strengths of their "neural" connections in response to new information. These systems are now in their infancy, but if they are ultimately successful, they will be able to recognize patterns even when the information is incomplete—just as a 3-year-old human being can.

Researchers working on neural nets are confident that they can give computers a humanlike ability to think, remember, and solve problems. Are they right? Critics are skeptical. After all, human intelligence arises from the experiences of human life, including the experience of inhabiting a human body. Human thought is inseparable from emotion, motives, and the pursuit of pleasure, for better or for worse. And human beings *know* they think, whereas computers, as far as anyone knows, lack consciousness. But then, perhaps they don't need it—they have us.

---

different approaches. When certain strategies and rules have been successful in the past, they may become habitual: A person may develop a **mental set**, or tendency to solve new problems using the same procedures that worked before. In daily life, mental sets make human learning and problem solving efficient. Because of them, we do not have to continually reinvent the wheel. But mental sets are not helpful when a problem calls for fresh insights and methods. They cause us to cling to the same old assumptions, hypotheses, and strategies, blinding us to breakthroughs that would lead to correct, better, or more rapid solutions. As an illustration: Copy the figure in the margin on a sheet of paper and see if you can connect the dots by using no more than four straight lines, without lifting the pencil from the paper. A line must pass through each point. Can you do it?

Most people have difficulty solving this problem because they are set to perceive patterns, and they interpret the arrangement of dots as a square. Once having done so, they assume that they can't extend a line beyond the "boundaries" of the

mental set *A tendency to solve a problem with the same strategies and rules used on previous problems.*

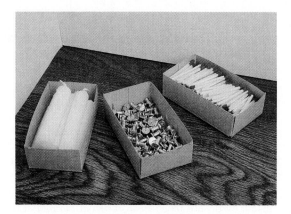

FIGURE 8.1

Candle mounting problem
If you were given the items shown here, and only these items, how would you go about mounting a candle on the wall? (The solution is given in Figure 8.6.)

square. As we observed in the chapter on sensation and perception, the tendency to perceive patterns enables us to make sense of the world. But in this case a correct solution requires you to break the set. Now that you know this, you might try again if you haven't yet solved the puzzle. Some possible solutions are given on page 311.

Another type of mental rigidity is known as **functional fixedness**. This is the tendency to encode an object only in terms of its usual function. There is nothing wrong with that, of course, *unless* the solution to a problem requires you to consider some novel uses. Functional fixedness may prevent you from seeing that a nail file can be used as a screwdriver when you don't have your tool box. Figure 8.1 shows a problem that requires you to overcome functional fixedness.

Cultivating creativity

Creativity is the ability to go beyond present knowledge, resist the persistence of set, and produce something new. Creative people recognize that problems are often solvable in more than one way. They exercise **divergent thinking**; instead of stubbornly sticking to one tried and true path, they explore some side alleys. As a result, they are able to use familiar concepts in unexpected ways (see Figure 8.2). Less creative individuals rely solely on **convergent thinking**, following a particular set of steps that they think will converge on one correct solution. Convergent thinking is useful (it includes logical reasoning and the use of algorithms), but to be creative in solving the fuzzy problems of life, you also need divergent thinking.

Traditional tests of creativity measure fluency, flexibility, and originality in generating solutions to problems (Guilford, 1950). One, the Alternate Uses Test, asks you to think of as many uses as possible for common items, such as a brick or a paper clip. Another, the Remote Associates Test (Mednick, 1962), presents sets of three words and asks you to find an associated word for each set. For example, an appropriate answer for the set *news–clip–wall* is *paper*. Associating elements in new ways by finding a common connection among them is thought to be an important component of creativity. (Can you find associates for the word sets in the margin? The answers are given in the Very Quick Quiz on page 298.)

Recently, a new approach to measuring creativity has emerged. The Lifetime Creativity Scales (Richards et al., 1988) assess a person's actual history of creativity in a broad range of work and leisure activities. First, a skilled interviewer obtains detailed information about the person's creative accomplishments, including those that may not have been socially recognized. Then trained raters, using a special

1. piggy–green–lash
2. surprise–line–birthday
3. mark–shelf–telephone
4. stick–maker–tennis
5. blue–cottage–cloth
6. motion–poke–down
7. gem–wall–stepping
8. chorus–bee–side
9. lunch–car–gift
10. foul–ground–pen

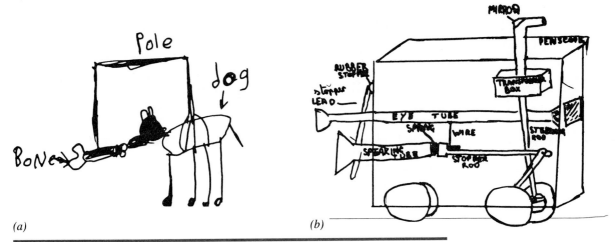

(a) *(b)*

FIGURE 8.2

Creativity begins early

When creativity expert Edward de Bono asked children aged 4 to 14 to design a dog-exercising machine, their solutions showed they could use familiar concepts in new and imaginative ways. The child who produced drawing (a) came up with the simple idea of having the dog chase a bone held always out of reach by a harness on the dog's back—frustrating for the dog, but effective. The solution in (b) is more sophisticated: When the dog barks into a "speaking tube," the energy of its barking activates a system of rods and springs, causing the wheels of the cart to turn. An "eye tube" allows the poor pooch to see where it is going, but this is only a courtesy, since a periscope automatically "sees" obstacles and a "transformer box" adjusts the steering accordingly. The more the dog barks, the faster the cart moves. What kind of dog-exercising machine can you come up with?

scoring manual, judge each product, action, or idea on its originality and meaningfulness. Achievements do not have to be within a traditionally creative field, such as art or music, to be judged creative. The scales measure both *peak creativity* (as reflected by major enterprises or activities) and *extent of involvement* (the pervasiveness of creative activity in a person's life). The invention of an unusual machine or the writing of a distinctive novel would earn you a high peak creativity score. The ongoing diagnosis and repair of automobiles or the writing of colorful letters to the editor would show some creativity. The routine assembly of mechanical parts according to a prescribed pattern or the proofreading of a manuscript would demonstrate "insignificant" creativity.

Interestingly, creativity and intelligence are only weakly correlated (Barron & Harrington, 1981). A certain level of intelligence (as measured by IQ tests) seems necessary for creativity in most fields, but a high IQ does not guarantee that you will be creative. Personality characteristics seem more important and include the following (McCrae, 1987; MacKinnon, 1962, 1968; Schank, 1988):

1. *Nonconformity*. Creative individuals are not overly concerned about what others think of them. They are willing to risk ridicule by proposing ideas that may initially appear foolish or off the mark.

2. *Independence*. Highly creative people tend to prefer working alone instead of in a group. During childhood, they are often encouraged to solve problems themselves instead of depending on others. However, they are not antisocial. On the contrary, they tend to be outgoing and well adjusted. (Some geniuses in the arts are exceptions, but we are talking about creative people in general.)

functional fixedness *The tendency to consider only the usual function of an object and overlook other possible uses. It often leads to rigidity in problem solving.*

creativity *A flexible, imaginative thought process leading to novel but appropriate solutions to problems, original ideas and insights, or new and useful products.*

divergent thinking *Mental exploration of unusual or unconventional alternatives during problem solving. It tends to enhance creativity.*

convergent thinking *Thinking aimed at finding a single correct answer to a problem by applying knowledge and reasoning.*

3. *Confidence*. In general, creative people neither fear failure nor overvalue success. They are therefore able to enjoy the challenge of a complex, ambiguous, or difficult problem.

4. *Curiosity*. Creative people usually have a wide range of interests and therefore accumulate a broad base of knowledge. They are open to new experiences and look into everyday puzzles that others would ignore. As one writer puts it, "They wonder why butterflies have to be caterpillars first. They wonder why the drugstore on the corner always does well and why the one across the street from it seems to be up for sale every two years. . . . They notice things and ask questions about them" (Schank, 1988).

5. *Persistence*. This is perhaps the most important attribute of the creative person. After that imaginary light bulb goes on over your head, you still have to work hard to make the illumination last. Or as Thomas Edison, who invented the real light bulb, reportedly put it, "Genius is one-tenth inspiration and nine-tenths perspiration." Persistence requires motivation, energy, and discipline, but it can be cultivated.

The characteristics of creativity are apparent in the biographies of successful artists, writers, scientists, and inventors. Consider the story of Georges de Mestral, a Swiss inventor, who was hunting one day in the late 1940s when he and his dog accidentally brushed up against a bush that left them both covered with burrs. When de Mestral tried to remove the burrs, they clung stubbornly to his clothes. This would be merely a minor annoyance to most of us, but de Mestral was curious about why the burrs were so hard to remove. After he got home, he studied them under a microscope and discovered that hundreds of tiny hooks on each burr had snagged on the threads of his pants. Burrs, he thought, would make great fasteners.

That was the inspiration. There followed several years of perspiration as de Mestral tried to figure out how to attach tiny hooks to pieces of tape in such a way that they would stay lined up. He also struggled to find a way of producing equally tiny loops for the hooks to attach to. After testing many methods, he finally succeeded. The result: Velcro fasteners, now used on millions of items, from blood pressure cuffs to tennis shoes (Madigan & Elwood, 1984).

(For additional lessons to be learned from creative thinkers of the past and some pointers on applying them, see "Taking Psychology with You.")

VERY ■ QUICK ■ QUIZ

When Georges de Mestral went about solving the problem of producing tiny loops:

1. Was he using algorithms or heuristics?
2. Which of the personality traits associated with creativity did he exemplify?

Answers:

1. heuristics   2. all of them

Answers to marginal test on page 296:

back, party, book, match, cheese, slow, stone, line, box, play

FIGURE 8.3

A poem for four hands
Language need not involve speech; American Sign Language (ASL) can be used to express both everyday meanings and poetic or musical ones. These two signers are experimenting with the signed equivalent of a duet. It describes the daily activities of three generations living in harmony together. In this excerpt, the man signs "brother/is bathing,/ grandpa/is rocking" while the woman signs "sister/is playing,/ grandma/is knitting."

Language

In the biblical story of the Tower of Babel, God punishes humankind for the sin of arrogance by transforming the one language shared by all into many different, mutually incomprehensible tongues. Unable to understand one another, the speech groups scatter to the four corners of the earth. But the punishment could have been worse: God might have deprived human beings of language altogether.

Language is our most impressive and versatile tool. Every human culture possesses this tool, and except in cases of profound retardation or disturbance, all children easily acquire it. (The process of language acquisition is discussed in Chapter 13.) Nonlinguistic communication can be both eloquent and informative, but language is what permits us to transmit the nuances and niceties of meaning that are the foundation of social life—a fact you know firsthand if you have ever found yourself in a country where you speak only a little of the language. In such a situation, a person accustomed to conveying complex abstract thoughts is reduced to the concrete level of communication typical of a young child.

Speaking of language

A **language** is a system for combining elements that are in themselves meaningless into utterances that convey meaning. The elements are usually sounds, but not always. In the United States and Canada, many hearing-impaired people use as their primary language American Sign Language, or ASL, which employs gesture rather than sound (see Figure 8.3). In other countries, other gestural languages are used. These gestural "tongues" are not simply pantomime. Gestural signals, or *signs*, convey both abstract and concrete concepts and ideas, and usually you can't guess from their form what they mean. Formal rules govern the production, sequencing, and timing of the signs, just as formal rules govern the order and production of words in spoken language.

If language is not equivalent to speech, how can we know whether a communi-

language *A system that combines meaningless elements such as sounds or gestures into structured utterances that convey meaning.*

cation system qualifies as a language? Linguists have identified several essential characteristics (Hockett, 1960). These include:

1. *Meaningfulness.* The main purpose of any language is to make meaningful reference to things, ideas, and feelings. Meaningfulness is achieved in language by the arbitrary but consistent combination of elements (such as sounds and gestures) into meaningful units (such as words or signs). There are enough words (or signs) in a language to express all the concepts that a community might want or need to express. Thus the lexicon or dictionary of the language provides a map of the community "mind" (R. Brown, 1958). The link between the terms and what they refer to are specific enough so that when one member of the community uses a term, others will know what is meant.

2. *Displacement.* Languages permit communication about objects and events that are not present here and now—that are displaced in time or space. Merely pointing to things is not language.

3. *Productivity.* Language allows the expression and comprehension of an infinite number of novel utterances, created on the spot. You are apt to find few, if any, sentences in this book that you have read, heard, or spoken before in exactly the same form. Except for a few fixed phrases ("Have a nice day"), most utterances we make or hear are new.

Since most utterances are novel, how are we able to produce and understand them? According to most linguists and **psycholinguists**, we apply a large but finite set of rules that make up the **grammar** of the language. These rules tell us which strings of sounds and words form acceptable utterances and which do not. Most people cannot actually state the rules of their grammar (despite the efforts of their English teachers). But they do use them. For example, you can transform the active sentence "John adores Mary" into a passive sentence, "Mary is adored by John." This change requires you to know that the subject and object of the original sentence must be switched, that the verb must be changed in form, and that a preposition must be inserted before the object. You carry out these operations without even thinking about it.

Syntax is the part of grammar that governs how words are arranged to convey meaning. Obviously, it makes all the difference in the world whether you say "Cassandra ate the cow" or "The cow ate Cassandra." We use our knowledge of syntax to figure out how the *surface structure* of a sentence as it is actually spoken or written reveals an underlying *deep structure* that contains meaning. Two sentences with different surface structures may have the same or nearly the same underlying structure. In "John kissed Mary," John is the grammatical subject and Mary the object; in "Mary was kissed by John," the opposite is true. But both sentences have a deep structure in which John is the actor and Mary is the recipient of the action.

A single surface structure may also have two or more possible deep structures. In that case, the sentence is ambiguous. For example, "They heard the shooting of the hunters" has two possible underlying structures. In one, the hunters are the actors; they are doing the shooting. In the other, the hunters are the objects of the action, the victims of the shooting. Ambiguous sentences are the linguistic equivalent of the ambiguous pictures we discussed in Chapter 5. Just as perception provides an interpretation of sensory information, the deep structure provides an interpretation of the surface structure of a sentence.

Linguistic rules alone are not enough to get us from the surface to the deep structure of a sentence. Psycholinguists have found that expectations, context, and our general knowledge of the world are equally important (Bransford, Barclay, & Franks, 1972; Johnson, Bransford, & Solomon, 1973; MacKay, 1970). If Wendy

psycholinguistics *The study of the acquisition, comprehension, and production of language.*

grammar *The system of linguistic rules governing sounds (or in the case of sign languages, gestures), meanings, and syntax of a language. It may be viewed as a mechanism for generating all possible sentences in a language.*

syntax *The set of grammatical rules governing the way words combine to form sentences.*

Last night, Maurice ate food that disagreed with him.

FIGURE 8.4

Back talk

Humor is often created by violating an expectation about the way words can be used in a particular context.

has been running a fever and her doctor feels her forehead, the sentence ''She seemed cool to him'' will mean one thing. If Wendy has been sitting next to Zeke all night without saying a word, ''She seemed cool to him'' will mean something quite different. And if Wendy comes across as socially ''with it,'' the phrase will have yet another meaning. The cartoon in Figure 8.4 illustrates how linguistic jokes sometimes reverse expectations to produce strange and amusing meanings.

Can animals learn language?

By the criteria of language listed earlier, animals do not have their own languages. Of course, animals do communicate with one another, using gestures, body postures, facial expressions, vocal sounds, and odors. But a communication system is not necessarily a language. Dolphins exchange clicks and whistles with one another in consistent ways, but no one has shown that these sounds form a meaningful, productive code. The grunts and screeches of an ape seem limited to a set repertoire. Some of these grunts have more specific meanings than previously thought. For example, vervet monkeys seem to have separate calls to warn about leopards, eagles, and snakes (Cheney & Seyfarth, 1985). But the sounds are not combined in various ways to produce novel utterances. Thus Bongo may make a certain type of sound when he encounters food, but he cannot say, ''The bananas in the next grove are a lot riper than the ones we ate last week and sure beat termites.''

Perhaps, however, certain animals could acquire language if they got a little help from their human friends. Dozens of researchers have tried to provide chimpanzees with just such help. Because the vocal tract of a chimpanzee does not permit speech, early efforts to teach chimpanzees spoken language were failures (though some comprehension did occur). During the 1960s and 1970s, researchers tried some different approaches. In one project, chimpanzees learned to use as words geometric plastic shapes arranged on a magnetic board (Premack & Premack, 1983). In another, they learned to punch symbols on a computer keyboard (Rumbaugh, 1977). In yet another, they learned hundreds of signs from American Sign Language (Fouts & Rigby, 1977; Gardner & Gardner, 1969). The animals in these and other studies learned to follow instructions, answer questions, and make requests. More important, they combined individual signs or symbols into longer utterances that they had never ''heard'' (or more precisely, seen) before. In general, their linguistic abilities appeared to resemble those of a 2-year-old child acquiring language.

It's hard not to love apes that use sign language to apologize, ask for fruit, or lie when they are naughty. But do signing apes really have language? What do we mean by language anyway?

As you can imagine, accounts of the apes' abilities caused quite a stir. The animals were apparently using their newfound skills to apologize for being disobedient, scold their trainers, and even talk to themselves. Koko, a lowland gorilla, reportedly used signs to say that she felt happy or sad, refer to past and future events, mourn for her dead pet (a kitten named All-Ball), and convey her yearning for a baby. She even lied on occasion, when she did something naughty (Patterson & Linden, 1981).

For a decade or so, these achievements met unquestioning acceptance by many psychologists and most of the public. The animals were cute and lovable, the findings appealing. But then skeptics, and some of the researchers themselves, began to point out serious problems (Seidenberg & Petitto, 1979; Terrace, 1979, 1985). In their desire to talk to the animals and their affection for their simian subjects, researchers had failed to be objective. They had overinterpreted the animal's utterances, reading all sorts of meanings and intentions into a single sign. In videotapes, they could be seen unwittingly giving nonverbal cues that might enable the apes to respond correctly without understanding. Further, the animals appeared to be stringing signs and symbols together haphazardly to earn a reward instead of using grammatical rules to produce novel utterances. In most cases, signs followed no particular order, suggesting that "Me eat banana" was no different for an ape than "Banana eat me." Longer utterances did not bring greater complexity in syntax, but mere repetition: "Give orange me give eat orange me eat orange give me eat orange give me you" (R. Brown, 1986).

Today, the Koko project still appears to suffer from overinterpretation of data and subtle cuing by trainers (Davidson & Hopson, 1988). Other studies, however, have benefited from the criticisms and are a marked improvement on past research. Carefully controlled experiments have established that after arduous training, chimps can acquire the ability to use symbols to refer to objects (Savage-Rumbaugh, 1986). In some projects, chimpanzees are spontaneously using their signs to converse with each other, suggesting that they are not merely imitating or trying to get a reward (Van Cantfort & Rimpau, 1982). A young chimp named Loulis has learned dozens of signs from Washoe, the original signing chimp (Fouts, Fouts, & Van Cantfort, 1989). A male pygmy chimpanzee named Kanzi has learned to understand English words and short sentences without specific training (Rumbaugh, 1988b). Kanzi hears the words through headphones, and his caregivers do not know which words are being tested, so they cannot give the animal cues. Kanzi

FIGURE 8.5

Learning language? *Researchers have used several methods in their efforts to teach apes language. Here Kanzi, a pygmy chimp with the most advanced linguistic skill yet acquired by a nonhuman primate, answers questions and makes requests by punching symbols on a specially designed computer keyboard.*

has also learned (with training) to manipulate keyboard symbols to make requests, and he seems to use some simple grammatical ordering rules (see Figure 8.5).

These new results are impressive, but whether they mean that apes can acquire true language remains unclear. The debate promises to continue. Stay tuned.

QUICK ▪ QUIZ

Fill in the blanks.

1. You've trained your parrot to say "Play it again, Sam" for a food reward. It always produces this string of sounds when it is hungry, but it does not respond to any of the words or to the sentence as a whole in any consistent way. The parrot does not have language, since its "speech" lacks _____.
2. A honey bee performs a little dance that communicates to other bees the direction and source of honey. Since the bee can "talk" about something that is located elsewhere, its communication system shows _____. But since the bee can create no utterances other than the ones that are genetically wired into its repertoire, its communication system lacks _____.
3. Knowledge of _____ permits you to identify "Frost was on the windshield" as an acceptable sentence and "On frost the was windshield" as an unacceptable one.
4. "They are visiting fire fighters" has one _____ structure and two possible _____ structures.
5. Psychologists disagree about whether signing apes use _____ rules to produce novel utterances.

Answers:

1. meaningfulness 2. displacement; productivity 3. syntax 4. surface; deep (In one deep structure, the fire fighters are doing the visiting; in the other, they are being visited.) 5. grammatical

The influence of language on thought

In George Orwell's chilling novel *Nineteen Eighty-Four*, a totalitarian government tries to narrow thought by shrinking language. The result, called Newspeak, is supposed to wipe out "thoughtcrime" by obliterating the words needed to commit it. "We're destroying words—scores of them, hundreds of them, every day," boasts a worker in the ironically named Ministry of Truth. "We're cutting the language down to the bone." Words also get new meanings: War is peace, love is hate. Lest you think Orwell's projections were pure fantasy, in recent years leaders in our own government have called lying "misspeaking," the forced withdrawal of troops "redeployment," and nuclear missiles "peacekeepers."

Was Orwell right? Does language provide a mental straitjacket for thought? Can we think only what we can say? Or does language merely express ideas and perceptions that would exist anyway?

The leading spokesperson for the notion that language shapes thought was Benjamin Lee Whorf (1897–1941), an insurance inspector by profession and a linguist and anthropologist by calling. His **theory of linguistic relativity** held that

Does language confine thought, or merely channel it in certain directions? If your language had no future tense, would you still be able to imagine the future?

linguistic relativity theory
The theory that language molds habits of thought and perception and that different language communities tend to have different views of reality.

(1) language molds habits of both cognition and perception and (2) different languages point speakers toward different views of reality. Whorf sometimes seemed to believe that language determines thought in an absolute way. He once wrote, "We dissect nature along lines laid down by our native languages" (Whorf, 1956). But usually he took the more moderate position that language has a powerful *influence* on cognition.

Whorf's evidence was linguistic and cultural. For example, he noted that English has only one word for snow, but Eskimos have different words for falling snow, slushy snow, powdered snow, and so forth. On the other hand, Hopi has a single noun that refers to all flying things and beings, with the exception of birds. This word can be used for aphids, airplanes, and aviators. Thus Eskimos presumably would notice differences in snow that we would not, and Hopis might see similarities between insects and aviators that we would miss.

Whorf also discussed facts of grammar. In English we have three tenses, and we speak of time as a thing that can be saved, squandered, or spent. This thing can be measured as space is measured: We say time is short, long, or great. In Hopi, according to Whorf, there are no grammatical time tenses. Whorf felt this fact explained why the Hopis enjoyed repetitive rituals that Anglos would view as a "waste of time." The Hopis, Whorf said, did not see time as a motion upon space (i.e., as time passing) but as a getting later of everything that has ever been done. Therefore, the Hopis did not share the Western emphasis on history, private and business calendars, dating, and clocks (Whorf, 1941).

What do you think of Whorf's evidence? The linguistic differences that Whorf cited have fascinated students and teachers for generations. However, critics have argued that his examples are not as convincing as they may seem. After all, it is easy enough to describe in English what the various Eskimo words for snow mean or how Hopis conceive of time, despite the linguistic differences. Within a culture, when a need to express some unlabeled phenomenon arises, speakers easily manufacture new words. For example, English-speaking skiers, like Eskimos, need to talk about several kinds of snow, so they speak of *powder*, *corn*, and *boilerplate* (ice). These facts demonstrate that language need not *determine* thought.

There is still the possibility, however, that language *influences* thought. Linguistic evidence in itself is not enough to establish this connection. (How do we know that Eskimos perceive snow any differently than other people?) It must be supplemented by psychological evidence. So far, the few controlled studies of the issue have been inconclusive because of methodological problems. However, recent research suggests that languages may, in fact, influence the acquisition of specific mental skills by guiding attention in particular directions. For example, Irene Miura and her colleagues (Miura et al., 1988; Miura & Okamoto, 1989) argue that linguistic differences can help explain why Asian children tend to outperform English-speaking children on tests of numerical ability. In many Asian languages, names of numbers reflect a base-10 system: The label for 12 is "ten-two," the label for 22 is "two ten(s)-two," and so forth. These names may help children understand numbers and simple arithmetic. In a study of Korean, Chinese, Japanese, and American first graders, Miura and her associates (1988) had children stack blocks to represent five different quantities. White blocks stood for single units and blue blocks for ten units. Each child had two chances to show the numbers. Most of the Asian children could express all five numbers in more than one way—for example, 12 as either 12 white blocks or 1 blue block and 2 white ones. But only 13 percent of the American children could do the same; most simply used a collection of white blocks. Further, on their first try most of the Asian children used patterns corresponding to written

FIGURE 8.6

Solution to the candle mounting problem
The problem given in Figure 8.1 can be solved by using the tacks to fasten one of the boxes to the wall as a stand. People often miss this solution because functional fixedness prevents them from recognizing that a box can have a purpose other than as a container. If all the items, including the boxes, are labeled when the problem is first presented, the solution is found more quickly.

numbers—for example, 2 tens and 8 ones for 28. But only 8 percent of the American children did so. Of course, these results do not *prove* that linguistic differences are responsible for the differences in math achievement. It is interesting, though, that bilingual Asian-American students tend to score higher in math achievement than do those who speak only English (Moore & Stanley, 1986).

Whatever the merits of linguistic relativity, *within* a given culture language clearly does influence cognition. For example, it affects the way we remember. In a classic study, people examined a series of line drawings in which each drawing was accompanied by one of two labels. For example, the drawing O—O was labeled either "eyeglasses" or "barbells." Later, those people who had seen the label "eyeglasses" tended to reproduce the figure as O⌒O, whereas those who had seen "barbells" tended to distort it toward O——O (Carmichael, Hogan, & Walter, 1932). Labels help us reconstruct the past.

Language also affects how we solve, or fail to solve, problems. Consider the solution to the candle-mounting problem, shown in Figure 8.6. This solution is easier to find when the items, including the boxes, are labeled. In fact, people take 15 times as long without the labels as with them (Glucksberg & Weisberg, 1966). Apparently, the labels direct attention to each object, so people notice a box as an object and not merely as a container for other objects.

Finally, language affects social perceptions. Feminists have long objected to the use of *men* or *mankind* to refer to humanity, and *he* to refer to any person, sex unspecified. Such usage, they argue, reinforces the idea that humanity is male and women are outsiders, the "second sex." These objections cannot be put down to pronoun envy. Children understand the "neutral" *he* as masculine, and this affects their sex stereotyping of animals, objects, and, perhaps most important, jobs (Bem, 1981; Hyde, 1984). When adults appear to be using *he* in the gender-neutral sense, they often are actually thinking only of men (Martyna, 1977). (Because of such findings, the American Psychological Association has issued a set of guidelines for psychologists on nonsexist writing.)

Language, then, can influence thinking, reasoning, problem solving, and social stereotypes. It allows us to manipulate symbols rather than objects. It directs our attention. It allows us to create detailed plans for the future. But the degree to which linguistic differences between cultures result in different ways of thinking and perceiving remains an open question.

The influence of thought on language

Those who have argued for linguistic relativity have sometimes made two huge assumptions: (1) that reality has no inherent organization but is a "kaleidoscopic flux" of impressions; and (2) that human cognition has no innate structure, apart from that imposed by culture and language. In recent years, researchers have questioned both of these assumptions (Rosch [Heider], 1977; Rosch [Heider] & Mervis, 1975). People the world over seem to share certain cognitive abilities, and language is as likely to *reflect* human cognition as it is to shape it.

The evidence comes in part from studies of **linguistic universals**. Despite their many differences, the languages of the world are surprisingly alike. Consider the perceptual category of color. If reality were inherently unorganized, and if human beings could "cut up reality" in any way they pleased, color words would be arbitrary; it would be possible for a language to have a single word that included what English calls green and red. But anthropologists have discovered that color naming is not at all arbitrary (Berlin & Kay, 1969; Kay, 1975). The number of basic color terms used by languages varies from only 2, as in Dani, to 11, as in English, but every language draws its basic terms from a list of only 11 possibilities: black, white, red, yellow, green, blue, brown, purple, pink, orange, and gray.

These color names are not drawn at random. Every language selects its terms from the following hierarchy, working from left to right:

$$\begin{bmatrix} \text{black} \\ \text{white} \end{bmatrix} \rightarrow \text{red} \rightarrow \begin{bmatrix} \text{yellow} \\ \text{green} \\ \text{blue} \end{bmatrix} \rightarrow \text{brown} \rightarrow \begin{bmatrix} \text{purple} \\ \text{pink} \\ \text{orange} \\ \text{gray} \end{bmatrix}$$

A language with only 2 terms will have black and white (or dark and light). A language with 3 terms will have black, white, and red. A language with 4 terms will have black, white, red, and one of the colors in the middle column (yellow, green, or blue). A language with 6 terms will have black, white, red, yellow, green, and blue. If languages selected color terms at random from the 11 basic ones, there would be 2048 possible color systems. But because they are confined to a universal hierarchy, there are actually only 33 possible systems among the thousands of human languages.

What's more, when researchers show people color charts and ask them to point to the best representatives of the basic color terms in their language, the results are the same from one language to another. The best *red* for English speakers is the best *aka* for speakers of Japanese, the best *lichi* for Navahos, and the best *anpalultak* for Eskimos. These *focal colors* are easier to remember, are named more quickly, and are more eye-catching than other colors. In fact, focal colors are salient even when people have no names for them in their language (E. R. Heider, 1972; Heider & Olivier, 1972).

All this suggests that people are sensitive to focal colors not because language emphasizes them but because the human visual system processes reality in a certain way (Lakoff, 1985). In Chapter 5 we saw that color perception seems to depend on special opponent-process cells that are sensitive to black or white, blue or yellow, and red or green—precisely the first six colors of the universal color hierarchy. It is possible that the visual system is also maximally sensitive in some way to the remaining five colors of the hierarchy.

linguistic universals *The linguistic features that characterize all languages.*

Color names provide only one example of how perception influences language. All languages seem to name the same basic shapes and spatial relations (Clark & Clark, 1977). These categories seem to be based on built-in, natural ways of perceiving. Even some abstract categories, not obviously rooted in perception, appear to be universal. For example, all languages have some way to distinguish the present, past, and future (Whorf notwithstanding). The past is usually, and the future is always, expressed in a more complex way than the present. Thus in English, we must add a special ending to a regular verb to make it past tense (*walk, walked*), and an additional word to make it future tense (*will walk*). The explanation seems to be that the here and now is easier to think about than the past or future, and the past is easier than the future. Children take several years to grasp the concept of nonpresent. Only when they have done so are they ready to use words like *yesterday* and *tomorrow* correctly. At first, they use *yesterday* to signify both past and future. When they understand the concept of past, they use *yesterday* correctly but are still confused about *tomorrow*. Finally they understand the concept of the future and use *tomorrow* correctly.

The universals of language, then, tell us much about human perception, memory, and mental processes. Language, which sometimes seems to be cognition's master, is also its obedient servant.

Taking Psychology with You

Becoming More Creative

Psychologists use creativity tests to study the personality characteristics of creative people. We can also find some clues to the origins of creativity in the biographies of creative geniuses. Here are a few habits and strategies that seem important and that may help you enhance your own creativity:

▪ *When reality contradicts expectations, ask why*. Early in this century, Wilhelm Roentgen, a German physicist, was studying cathode rays when he noticed a strange glow on one of his screens. Other people had seen the glow, too, but they ignored it because it didn't jibe with current understanding of cathode rays. Roentgen studied the glow, found it to be a new kind of radiation, and discovered X-rays (Briggs, 1984).

▪ *Notice your images and dreams*. Many creative people say they get their best ideas in visual form and only later translate them into language. Some even solve problems in their dreams. Elias Howe, who invented the sewing machine, had trouble figuring out how to thread the needle. Needles had always had an eye at the top and a point at the bottom, but the needle in a sewing machine had to be fastened at the top to the machine. One night Howe dreamed he was attacked by savages carrying spears with holes near the tip. When he awoke, he whittled a needle with the hole at the pointed end, and his problem was solved (B. Edwards, 1986).

▪ *Keep at it*. The flash of insight is usually only the beginning of a long, drawn-out process. Einstein himself said, "I know quite certainly that I myself have no special talent. Curiosity, obsession, and dogged endurance, combined with self-criticism, have brought me to my ideas. Especially strong thinking powers, brain muscles, I do not have, or only to a modest degree. Many have far more of those than I without producing anything surprising'' (quoted in Briggs, 1984).

▪ *Gather as much information as you can*. Louis Pasteur, who proved that germs cause disease, once said, ''Chance favors the prepared mind.'' Most creative thinkers say that early in the creative process, they find out as much about a problem as possible.

▪ *When your mind is saturated with information, let the problem incubate*. Several inventors and discoverers have told how the solution to a problem came to them only after they stopped consciously thinking about the welter of information they had gathered.

▪ *Don't let others discourage you*. There is a fine line between bullheaded faith in a foolish idea and dedication to a correct one. But keep in mind that creative people do not worry about being nonconformists or having their ideas ridiculed. Geneticist Barbara McClintock's research was ignored or belittled for nearly 30 years. But she was sure she could show how genes move around and produce sudden changes in heredity. In 1983, McClintock won the Nobel Prize. The Nobel officials called her work ''the second great [genetic] discovery of our time,'' along with the discovery of the structure of DNA. McClintock told reporters she hadn't cared what others thought. She knew she was right.

In addition to creative persons, there are creative *circumstances*. For example, Alice Isen and her associates (1987) find that cheerful situations foster inspiration. The performance of students on creativity tests improved significantly after they watched a funny film or received a gift of candy, which put them in a good mood. In contrast, watching an upsetting film on concentration camps or a ''neutral'' film on math, or exercising for two minutes to boost energy, had no effect. Elation, then, may loosen up creative associations.

Another situational factor is the encouragement of *intrinsic* rather than *extrinsic* motivation. Intrinsic motives include a sense of accomplishment, intellectual fulfillment, the satisfaction of curiosity, and the sheer love of the activity. Extrinsic motives include a desire for money, fame, and attention, or the wish to avoid punishment. In one study of motives and creativity, Teresa Amabile (1985) asked 72 talented young poets and writers to create two poems. Before writing their second poem, half the writers evaluated a list of extrinsic motives for writing (such as ''The market for freelance writing is constantly expanding'' and ''You enjoy public recognition of your work''). The other half evaluated a list of intrinsic motives (''You like to play with words''; ''You achieve new insights''). Then a panel of 12 experienced poets judged the two sets of poems for originality and creativity, without knowing which writers had read which set of motives. The writers who were exposed to extrinsic reasons for writing showed a significant drop in the creativity of their second poem. Those who paid attention to intrinsic motives wrote two poems of equal quality.

Other research (Amabile, 1983) shows that people tend to be most creative when they (1) have control over how to perform a task or solve a problem; (2) are evaluated unobtrusively, instead of being constantly observed and judged; and (3) work alone. (Group brainstorming, in which people generate as many ideas as they can without judging their value, does not seem any more effective than individual brainstorming. Quantity of ideas does not ensure quality.) In addition, organizations encourage creativity when they allow people to take risks, give them plenty of time to think about problems, and welcome innovative ideas.

In sum, if you hope to become more creative, there are two things you can do. One is to cultivate the personal qualities that lead to creativity. The other is to seek out the kinds of situations that permit their expression.

KEY WORDS

thinking 283
concept 283
basic concept 284
prototypical instance 285
proposition 285
image 285
reasoning 286
inductive reasoning 286
deductive reasoning 287
premise 287
syllogism 287
dialectical reasoning 289
relative accounting 290
availability heuristic 291
algorithm 293
heuristic 293

artificial intelligence 293
mental set 295
functional fixedness 296
creativity 296
divergent/convergent thinking 296
language 299
meaningfulness 300
displacement 300
productivity 300
psycholinguistics 300
grammar 300
syntax 300
surface and deep structures 300
linguistic relativity theory 303
linguistic universals 306

SUMMARY

1. *Thinking* is the mental manipulation of information. This information is internally represented as concepts, propositions, and images. Internal representations simplify and summarize information in the environment.

2. A *concept* is a mental category that groups objects, relations, activities, abstractions, or qualities having common properties. We form concepts through direct contact with the things they represent and by contact with symbols. Words speed up concept formation, but concepts can be acquired without language. *Basic concepts* have a moderate number of instances and seem naturally easier to acquire than concepts with few or many instances. Some instances of a concept are more *prototypical* than others.

3. *Propositions* are units of meaning that are made up of concepts and that express unitary ideas. *Images* are representations that mirror or resemble what they represent. Mental visual images seem analogous to images on a television screen and are used for many purposes.

4. *Reasoning* involves drawing inferences and conclusions from observations, facts, or assumptions. In *inductive reasoning*, general conclusions are drawn from specific observations. In *deductive reasoning*, conclusions follow necessarily from general assumptions, or premises. The application of deductive reasoning is influenced by culture. *Dialectical reasoning* is often more appropriate than other forms of reasoning in real life. It involves the ability to think critically about opposing points of view.

5. When people make judgments and decisions, they are influenced by many cognitive biases and by the way choices are framed. In general, people try to avoid risks or losses; find disadvantages more acceptable when they are labeled costs than when they are labeled losses; judge advantages and disadvantages relative to some reference state determined by the context (''relative accounting''); let expectations direct their attention to particular alternatives; and exaggerate the probability of rare events.

6. Problem solving occurs in four stages: defining the problem, devising a strategy, executing the strategy, and evaluating progress. Problems can sometimes be solved by applying an *algorithm*, a procedure guaranteed to lead eventually to a solution. However, many problems require the use of *heuristics*, rules of thumb that provide shortcuts but do not guarantee an optimal solution.

7. One important barrier to effective problem solving is lack of knowledge. Another is the persistence of *mental sets*, or the tendency to use strategies and rules used on previous problems although they are no longer appropriate. *Functional fixedness* is a particular type of mental set, in which a person fails to recognize novel uses for an object.

8. As we saw in ''A Closer Look at Artificial Intelligence,'' the *artificial intelligence* of computers has been limited by a lack of a broad knowledge base. Scientists are trying to overcome this problem by designing machines called *neural networks*.

9. Creative problem solving requires *divergent* as well as *convergent thinking*. Most creativity tests measure fluency, flexibility, and originality in generating problem solutions, but a recent approach assesses a person's actual history of creative accomplishment. Creative people generally are willing to risk ridicule; prefer working independently; are confident enough to enjoy working on difficult problems; are curious about the world; and are able to persist at a task without becoming discouraged.

10. *Language* is a system for combining meaningless elements into utterances that convey meaning. Most languages are vocal, but gestural languages also exist and are used by the hearing-impaired. To qualify as a language, a communication system must have three features: meaningfulness, displacement, and productivity.

11. Productivity in language is achieved by applying a large but finite set of rules called a *grammar*. These rules determine which strings of sounds and words form acceptable utterances and which do not. Rules of *syntax*, or word order, help us derive the underlying *deep structure* of a sentence from its *surface structure*. We also rely on expectations, context, and general knowledge of the world in determining deep structures.

12. No animal seems to have a full-fledged language in the wild. However, dozens of researchers have attempted to teach language to nonhuman primates, employing either visual symbol systems or American Sign Language for the deaf. The linguistic skills of these animals are impressive in many respects, but skeptics are not convinced that such animals have true language.

13. Benjamin Lee Whorf's *theory of linguistic relativity* holds that language molds habits of cognition and perception, and that different language communities tend to perceive reality differently. This theory has been difficult to prove. However, language does appear to influence the way we remember, solve problems, and form social perceptions, and it may account for some cultural differences on specific cognitive tasks.

14. Thought also influences language. Despite their many differences, the languages of the world are surprisingly alike. Many of their similarities appear to reflect universal ways of perceiving, thinking, and forming concepts.

SOME SOLUTIONS TO THE NINE-DOT PROBLEM (From Adams, 1986.)

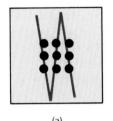

(a)

(b)

Cut the puzzle apart, tape it together in a different format, and use one line.

(c)

(d)

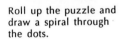

Roll up the puzzle and draw a spiral through the dots.

(e)

1 Line 0 Folds

Lay the paper on the surface of the Earth. Circumnavigate the globe twice + a few inches, displacing a little each time so as to pass through the next row on each circuit as you "Go West, young man."

(f)

~ 2 Lines* 0 Folds

*Statistical

Draw dots as large as possible. Wad paper into a ball. Stab with pencil. Open up and see if you did it. If not, try again. "Nobody loses: Play until you win."

(g)

May 30, 1974
5 FDR   NAVAS
ROOSEVEIT Rds. ↑
Celba, PR 00635

Dear Prof. James L. Adams,
 My dad and I were doing Puzzles from "Conceptual Blockbusting". We were mostly working on the dot ones, like ⋮⋮⋮. My dad said a man found a way to do it with one line. I tried and did it. Not with folding. but I used a fat line. I does'nt say you can't use a fat line. Like this→ ▮
P.S.
acctually you   Sincerely,
need a very   Becky Buechel
fat writing   age: 10
apparatice.

(h)

CHAPTER 9

Emotion

The beauty of the world has two edges,
one of laughter, one of anguish,
cutting the heart asunder.

VIRGINIA WOOLF

On Sunday, April 25, in the year 1227, a knight named Ulrich von Lichtenstein disguised himself as the goddess Venus. Wearing an ornate white gown, waist-length braids, heavy veils, and bedecked with pearls, Ulrich began a pilgrimage from Venice to Bohemia. As he traveled, he invited any and all local warriors to challenge him to a duel. By his own count (which may have been exaggerated), Ulrich broke 307 lances, unhorsed four opponents, and completed his five-week journey with an undefeated record. The reason for this extravagant performance was his passion for a highborn princess, nameless to history, whom he adored but who barely gave poor Ulrich the time of day. Ulrich trembled in her presence, suffered in her absence, and constantly endured feelings of longing, misery, and melancholy, a state of love that apparently made him very happy (M. Hunt, 1959/1967).

How would Ulrich's story sound with the emotion removed? Suppose Ulrich endured his hardships and tribulations because he was somewhat fond of the lady. Suppose he was bored in her presence and only vaguely aware of her absence. Suppose, in short, that she meant nothing more to him than his wife (oh, yes, Ulrich was married), that theirs was merely an economic union, a practical arrangement for the purpose of begetting children and managing the serfs. How would we evaluate Ulrich's knightly performance then?

Let's try another story, this one more recent. In the wealthy community of Scarsdale, New York, 23-year-old Richard Herrin murdered his sleeping girlfriend, Bonnie Garland. Herrin was depressed because Garland had told him she was too young to marry and wanted to date other men. In a rage over her decision, he battered her to death with a claw hammer. The jury did not convict Herrin of murder, but of the lesser crime of manslaughter, believing that he had acted under "extreme emotional disturbance." Herrin's supporters thought even this sentence too harsh, arguing that he had loved Bonnie deeply and passionately and was desperately grieved over her death. This defense did not persuade the prosecution. One psychiatrist said it reminded him of the old story of the man who murdered his parents, and then pleaded for mercy because he was an orphan (Jacoby, 1983).

How would Herrin's story sound with the emotion removed? Suppose Herrin murdered Garland calmly. Suppose he wasn't depressed about losing her, but indifferent. He wasn't enraged that she rejected him, only mildly sorry. He didn't love her "deeply and passionately"; he just liked her a little. He didn't grieve over her death; he barely noticed. What sentence do you think Herrin would have received? Would his friends still have defended him?

As these stories show, emotions are the heart and soul of human life. They give life color, intensity, excitement—and misery. If you could wave a magic wand and eliminate them, you would never again worry about a test result, a job interview, or a first date. You would never feel angry, even if your roommate called you an idiot or your best friend stole your bicycle. You wouldn't be afraid to jump out of an airplane, with or without a parachute. You would never feel the grief of losing someone you love, not only because you wouldn't know sadness but because you wouldn't know love.

What we do for love: Ulrich von Lichtenstein disguised as Venus.

Considering the importance of emotion in every aspect of experience, it is curious that psychologists are still arguing furiously about what emotion *is* and that there is no commonly accepted definition (Mandler, 1984). Is it primarily a physiological reflex, as universal as the smile and as uncontrollable as a sneeze? Or is it primarily mental, something we think ourselves into (as in "The more I thought about it, the madder I got")? Which emotions cross all nations, and which ones stop at the border?

Thinking About Feeling

In the past, many Western philosophers and scientists regarded emotion as the opposite of thinking, and an inferior opposite, at that. "The heart" (emotion) was said to go its own way, in spite of what "the head" (reason) wanted. Some writers believed that following one's heart could be a good thing, as when, say, it led to a happy marriage or a new invention. But most thought that thinking was superior to feeling. Reason, logic, intellectual ideas, judgment, and perception, they said, were better than intuition, hunch, and emotion, just as the mind was supposedly superior to the body and human beings superior to lower animals.

The mind-body battle has been fought in the study of emotions themselves. For centuries, the field has been divided into two traditions. One, the **organic school**, argues that emotions are primarily a matter of biology, of physical events that, like a thumping heart or a giddy blush, are not voluntarily controlled. The other tradition, the **mental school**, argues that emotions are primarily a matter of cognition and perception. Modern researchers are trying to build bridges between mind *and* body, thinking *and* feeling. But the two traditions differ on which comes first.

The organic tradition maintains that feeling comes first and thoughts follow, or are unrelated to emotion. Several lines of evidence support this argument. First, in the development of human beings and our nearest primate relatives, emotion seems to appear before cognition does: Babies weep and show distress at separation long before they understand or perceive reasons for adult behavior; they reveal facial expressions of emotion as mere infants (Stenberg & Campos, 1990). Second, the limbic system, sometimes called the "emotional brain," is involved with emotional expression and behavior, whereas cognitive processes occur in another part of the brain. Third, pure sensory input is enough to stimulate an emotional response, without interference from higher mental processes. Fourth, feeling and thinking are often unrelated. Sometimes people don't know why they feel the way they do, and changing their thoughts doesn't always change their emotional states (Izard, 1984; Zajonc, 1980, 1984).

The mental tradition says that thoughts come first, and this camp also marshalls evidence in its support (Lazarus, 1984). Simple sensory reactions, in this view, cannot properly be called "emotions" at all. Some events will automatically produce reflex actions. If you unexpectedly hear a loud noise, you will show a startle response, but that does not mean you feel "afraid"; the emotion of fear requires the perception of danger. Babies cry and frown to communicate distress, but this doesn't mean they feel "angry." As for brain research, emotions have never been easily assigned to one part of the brain or another. The causes and effects of emotion spread rapidly across both brain hemispheres (Sperry, 1982). The evidence of enormous cultural differences in what produces emotion and in how people respond to emotion means that very little in emotional experience is truly universal or biologically programmed. Finally, new therapies have had great success in treating emo-

organic school (of emotion) *Scientists and philosophers who seek biological explanations of emotion—for example, in facial expressions, brain centers, or levels of physiological arousal.*
mental school (of emotion) *Scientists and philosophers who seek psychological explanations of emotion—for example, in beliefs, judgments, and interpretations of events.*

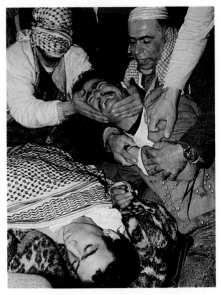

Israeli parents (left) and an Arab father (right) react to the death of their children in the tragic Middle Eastern conflict. The organic school argues that grief is a biological response to loss; the mental school argues that the perception of loss triggers the biological response. Both schools agree that culture affects the display of emotion—whether, say, you should "let it out" or "keep a stiff upper lip."

tional disorders by changing unrealistic thinking (Beck & Emery, 1985; Lazarus & Folkman, 1984).

The mind-body debate about emotions is a classic case of either-or thinking. There is probably no way to resolve it, because, as we will show, **emotions** consist of three elements: *physiological* changes in the body and face, *cognitive* processes such as interpretations of events, and *cultural* influences that shape the experience and expression of emotion.

Elements of Emotion 1: The Body

Early philosophers thought our emotional personalities depended on mixes of four body products, or "humors": blood, phlegm, yellow bile (choler), and black bile. If you were an angry, irritable sort of person, you supposedly had an excess of choler; even now, the English word *choleric* describes a hothead. If you were slow-moving and unemotional, you supposedly had an excess of phlegm, and English still calls such people *phlegmatic*. People are amused today by the theory of the four humors, and yet the basic questions it was trying to answer remain with us. What is the physiology of emotion? Where in the body does an emotion occur?

A bit of background

In 1884, William James challenged everyone who thought the chicken comes first to think about the egg. Common sense, then as now, assumed that (1) something happens, (2) you feel an emotion, (3) you do something. In James's own examples,

emotion *A state involving a pattern of facial and bodily changes, cognitive appraisals, and beliefs. Culture, in turn, shapes the experience and expression of emotion. (See also primary emotions and secondary emotions.)*

you lose your fortune, you feel miserable, you cry; or your rival insults you, you feel angry, you hit him. But James argued that this seemingly logical sequence was out of order, and he turned it on its head. "We feel sorry *because* we cry," he said, "angry *because* we strike, afraid *because* we tremble." The correct sequence, he argued, should be (1) you perceive an event, (2) your body reacts, (3) you interpret that bodily reaction as a specific emotion. James (1884) said, with emphasis, "*bodily changes follow directly the PERCEPTION of the exciting fact, and . . . our feeling of the same changes as they occur IS the emotion.*"

Well, what "bodily changes"? James included the whole range: actions (such as running, crying, and striking out), changes of facial expression, and "gut reactions" (changes in the *viscera*, or the internal organs, such as the stomach and intestines). At about the same time, a Danish researcher named Carl Lange came up with a similar theory, and the two names were soon linked. The **James-Lange theory** of emotions refers to the idea that emotion is the perception of one's own bodily reactions.

In 1927, physiologist Walter B. Cannon challenged the James-Lange theory on several grounds. For one thing, he said, bodily changes are not enough to produce emotion. If emotion follows bodily changes, you ought to be able to generate an emotion simply by injecting people with epinephrine, the hormone that energizes the body to fight or flee in response to threat. But when Spanish researcher G. Marañón did this precise experiment in 1924, most people merely reported the physical changes ("My heart is beating fast"; "My throat feels tight"). Some reported "as if" emotions: "I feel *as if* I were angry"; "I feel *as if* I were happy." However, they did not report true emotions. This finding, as we will see, has been replicated many times (S. Schachter, 1971). Cannon also argued that emotions occur faster than changes in the internal organs do, and the same bodily changes occur in many different emotions.

Cannon's own theory was that emotion depends on the thalamus of the brain, which, he believed, *simultaneously* controls the feelings and expression of emotion by sending messages to other parts of the brain (such as the cortex) and the body. Messages to the cortex produce the *experience* of emotion, whereas other messages from the thalamus produce emotional *behavior* by activating visceral and skeletal reactions. According to Cannon, we can experience intense "fear" of a snake yet be rooted to the spot like a tree, because "fear" and "running away" are regulated by different parts of the brain. This view was endorsed by Philip Bard a few years later and came to be called the **Cannon-Bard theory**.

Today, most researchers think that the time distinctions made by these two theories are not terribly important. When an emotion "starts" may depend more on the situation than on physiology. The emotional response to nearly being run down by a car is more immediate, for instance, than the growing awareness that you are angry at a friend's thoughtlessness. But these ideas inspired a great deal of laboratory research. With new ways to study physiology, psychologists in the organic tradition began to investigate facial expressions, hormones, and the brain.

James-Lange theory *The theory, proposed independently by William James and Carl Lange, that emotion results from the perception of one's own bodily reactions. In this view, each emotion is physiologically distinct.*

Cannon-Bard theory *The theory, proposed independently by Walter Cannon and Philip Bard, that emotion originates in the thalamus of the brain, which controls both emotional feeling and behavior. In this view, all emotions are physiologically similar.*

The face of emotion

The most obvious place to look for emotion is on the face, where the expression of emotion can be most visible. In his classic book *The Expression of the Emotions in Man and Animals*, Charles Darwin (1872/1965) wrote that facial expressions were biologically wired in human beings and other animals. The smile, the frown, the

FIGURE 9.1

Some universal expressions
*Can you tell what feelings
are being conveyed here?
Most people around the
world can readily identify
facial expressions of surprise, disgust, anger, happiness, fear, and sadness,
suggesting that "the face of
emotion" is built in and
plays an important role in
communication.*

grimace, the glare, he wrote, all helped species adapt. The face of emotion is not learned, said Darwin; it is as much a part of our biological heritage as a nose or a kidney. That is a good thing, too, he added, because it means you can quickly tell the difference between a stranger who is friendly (who smiles and conveys happiness) and one who is about to attack (who glares and conveys rage).

Modern psychologists have supported Darwin's idea that certain basic emotions are registered on the face and that they are recognized all over the world (see Figure 9.1). Even remote tribes that have never watched a movie or read *People* magazine, such as the Fore of New Guinea or the Minangkabau of West Sumatra, can recognize the emotions expressed in pictures of people who are entirely foreign to them—and we can recognize theirs. For nearly 20 years, Paul Ekman and Wallace Friesen have been gathering evidence for the universality of six basic facial expressions of emotion: anger, happiness, fear, surprise, disgust, and sadness (Ekman, Friesen, & Ellsworth, 1972; Ekman et al., 1987). In every culture they have studied—including New Guinea, Brazil, Chile, Estonia, Germany, Greece, Hong Kong, Italy, Japan, Scotland, Sumatra, Turkey, and the United States—the large majority has recognized the emotional expression portrayed by people in other cultures. Yet in one study, only 61 percent of the Germans recognized disgust, only 67 percent of the Estonians and Japanese identified anger, and only 76 percent of the Turks recognized sadness (Ekman et al., 1987). Are you impressed that a majority in so many different nations agreed on each emotion, or that sometimes a large minority disagreed?

Facial expressions don't always convey the emotion that is felt. A posed, "social" smile (left) may have nothing to do with true feelings of happiness. (Cover her smile with your hand and you'll see that the "smile" doesn't reach her eyes.) Conversely, even a face that seems to convey utter anguish (right) may be misleading. This young woman is weeping for joy: She has just won the "Best Young Actress of the Year" award.

The main purpose of facial expressions, said Darwin, is to communicate with others. This communication starts in infancy. Remember the visual cliff study described in Chapter 5 (see p. 195)? This research was originally designed to test the development of depth perception. Now it turns out that if the baby's mother is on the far side of the cliff and *warns the baby against crossing by putting on an expression of fear or anger*, the baby will not cross. If, however, the mother smiles at the baby warmly, the baby crosses to her, even though it is aware of the "cliff" (Sorce et al., 1985). Clearly, the baby's ability to recognize facial expressions of emotion has survival value.

Interestingly, facial expressions of emotion also seem to help people communicate with themselves, so to speak. Some psychologists believe that facial expressions help people identify their own emotions. Like James, these psychologists argue that people don't frown because they are angry; rather, they feel angry because they are frowning. According to this **facial-feedback hypothesis**, the facial muscles send messages to the brain, identifying each basic emotion. When people are asked to contort their facial muscles into various patterns, they often report changed emotions to fit the pattern. As one young man put it, "When my jaw was clenched and my brows down, I tried not to be angry but it just fit the position" (Laird, 1974). Voluntary facial expressions even seem to affect the involuntary nervous system. If you put on an "angry" face, your heart rate will rise faster than if you put on a "happy" face (Ekman, Levenson, & Friesen, 1983). When people are told to contract the facial muscles involved in smiling (though not actually instructed to smile) and then to look at cartoons, they find the cartoons funnier than if they are contracting their muscles in a way that is incompatible with smiling (Strack, Martin, & Stepper, 1988). Studies like these suggest that the facial muscles are somehow tied to the autonomic nervous system, which controls heart rate, breathing, and other vital functions.

facial-feedback hypothesis
The notion that the facial muscles send messages to the brain, identifying the emotion a person feels.

Of course, people do not always wear their emotions on their faces. They do not, for instance, go around scowling and clenching their jaws whenever they are angry. They can grieve and feel enormously sad without weeping. They can feel worried and tense, yet put on a happy face. They can use facial expressions to lie about a ''real'' feeling. So interpreting another person's facial expression is not always a simple task.

To get around the human ability to mask emotions, Paul Ekman and his associates have developed a way to peek under the mask. The Facial Action Coding System (FACS) allows researchers to analyze and identify each of the nearly 80 muscles of the face, as well as the combinations of muscles that are associated with various emotions. When people try to hide their real emotions, Ekman (1985) believes, they use different groups of muscles. For example, when people try to pretend that they feel grief, only 15 percent manage to get the eyebrows, eyelids, and forehead wrinkle exactly right, mimicking the way grief is expressed spontaneously. Authentic smiles last only two seconds; false smiles may last ten seconds or more. Moreover, the muscle changes associated with the real emotion—anger, contempt, sadness—can be identified beneath the smiling mask (Ekman, Friesen, & O'Sullivan, 1988).

Ekman and others conclude from this research that some emotions are indeed part of basic species equipment and physiologically distinct from each other. Yet facial expressions, lively as they are, are only part of the emotional picture. Even Ekman, who has been studying them for years, concludes, ''There is obviously emotion without facial expression and facial expression without emotion'' (in Mandler, 1984). As a nasty character in Shakespeare's play *Henry VI* says,

> Why, I can smile, and murder while I smile;
> And cry content to that which grieves my heart;
> And wet my cheeks with artificial tears,
> And frame my face to all occasions.

The energy of emotion

What accounts for the intensity of an emotion? Why does contentment differ from ecstasy, mild irritation from fury, nervousness from fear? When you are in a situation that requires the body to respond—to fight, to flee, to cope—the sympathetic nervous system (see Chapter 3) whirls into action. In particular, the adrenal medulla sends out two hormones, **epinephrine** and **norepinephrine**. (Most scientists prefer these terms to their older names, *adrenaline* and *noradrenaline*, which are still in common use.) These hormones bring about the following effects:

1. Your pupils dilate, widening to allow in more light.
2. Your heart beats faster.
3. Your breathing speeds up.
4. Your blood sugar rises, providing your body with more energy.
5. Your digestion slows down. Blood flow is diverted from your stomach and intestines to your brain, some muscles, and the surface of your skin. (This is why, when you are excited, scared, furious, or wildly in love, you don't want to eat.)
6. Your skin perspires to keep you cool from all your exertion.
7. The hairs on the skin stand up, causing goose pimples.
8. Your memory, concentration, and performance improve—up to a point. If hormone levels become too high and you are too agitated, concentration and perfor-

epinephrine, norepinephrine (adrenaline, noradrenaline) *Hormones produced by the adrenal glands that provide the body with energy to respond to environmental events.*

Crowds are physically arousing—which is why sports fans like these feel especially exuberant when their team is ahead (or especially gloomy, like the young woman in front, when it isn't).

mance worsen. This is why a little nervousness when you take an exam is a good thing; hand-trembling anxiety is not.

In general, then, the adrenal hormones produce a state of *arousal*, a level of energy that allows the body to respond quickly. Epinephrine and norepinephrine used to be considered the "fear" and "anger" hormones respectively, but psychologists now know that these hormones provide the fuel for all emotional states, including excitement, anxiety, jealousy, even joy. Epinephrine will rise if you are laughing at a funny movie or playing a video game, if you are anticipating a fabulous date or worried about an exam, if you are cheering at a game, or if you are responding to an insult.

Moreover, the body produces epinephrine and norepinephrine in response to nonemotional states, too, such as heat, cold, pain, injury, burns, and physical exercise, and in response to drugs (caffeine, nicotine, and alcohol). Epinephrine rises when you have to respond to stress and pressure. Surprisingly, it also rises when you aren't stressed enough, when you are bored and coping with tedium (Frankenhaeuser, 1975). These hormones are at their lowest when you are doing something mildly engaging and interesting, such as practicing the tuba.

Epinephrine and norepinephrine provide the feeling of an emotion, that tingle, excitement, and sense of energy. At high levels, they create the sensation of being "seized" or "flooded" by an emotion that is out of one's control. In a sense, the release of these hormones does cause us to "lose control," because few people can consciously alter their heart rates, blood pressures, and digestive tracts. (However, people *can* learn to control their actions when they are aroused; see "Taking Psychology with You.") As arousal subsides, a "hot" emotion turns into its "cool" counterpart. Anger may pale into annoyance or dislike, ecstasy into contentment, fear into suspicion. This is why memories of past emotional whirlwinds are often calm breezes. They lack the intensity of arousal.

But these hormones are not enough to produce an emotion. For one thing, new research in psychology and neurology has found that "arousal" takes several forms, not just one, and these forms may involve different hemispheres of the brain and different hormones (McGuinness & Pribram, 1980; Tucker & Williamson, 1984). Further, the concept of arousal does not distinguish one emotion from another, and it does not distinguish emotions in general from other states of excitement. Also, it cannot explain why, of two students about to take an exam, one feels "psyched up" and the other feels overwhelmed by anxiety (Neiss, 1988).

Without the mind's perceptions, arousal has no content. Are you thrilled or frightened? Sick or just in love? Your body alone won't tell you.

Brain centers

Psychologists in the organic tradition have long sought to identify specific areas in the brain that might be responsible for emotions. Some researchers have traced emotion to the limbic system and hypothalamus, evolutionarily old parts of the brain that human beings share with other species (MacLean, 1963, 1970). They argue that certain emotions—particularly fear, rage, and sexual arousal—are as "wired in" as the wing flutter of a frightened bird, the purr of a contented cat, or the snarl of a threatened wolf. As evidence, they note that when you electronically stimulate the hypothalamus of many animals, fear or anger typically results. In human beings also, brain damage (as a result of head injury or illness) can produce irrational rage and violence (A. Berman, 1978; Lewis, 1981).

However, efforts to match each emotion with a corresponding "brain center" in the limbic system have largely failed. One reason is that human emotions are also influenced by another part of the brain, the cortex, the center of reason, symbols, and logic. The capacity for cold revenge, for anxiety about grades, for different emotional reactions to the same signal (was the wisecrack meant to be an insult or a joke?) is uniquely human (Averill, 1982). Further, certain emotions depend almost entirely on cognition. Babies and rabbits don't feel shame or guilt, for example, because these emotions require the emergence of a sense of self and the mental perception that you have behaved badly (Lewis et al., 1988).

Thus many brain researchers no longer look just for "rage circuits" or "pleasure centers." New approaches emphasize the *interactions* between emotion and cognition in different parts of the brain. For example, certain regions of the left hemisphere appear to be specialized for the processing of positive emotions, such as joy; regions of the right hemisphere are involved in the processing of negative emotions, such as depression (R. Davidson, 1984, 1986; Tucker, 1989). Patients who have lesions in one hemisphere often lose the ability to experience certain emotions. Damage to the left hemisphere tends to produce excessive hostility, tears, and pessimism. "Well," you might say, "wouldn't brain damage make *anyone* angry, sad, and pessimistic?" But damage to the right hemisphere is associated with excessive displays of happiness, joking, and laughing.

Another line of research seeks to identify parts of the brain responsible for the many different aspects of emotional experience: recognizing another person's emotion, feeling intensely aroused, labeling the emotion, deciding what to do about it, and so on. Take something as apparently simple as recognizing a face. You can recognize your mother's face any old time. You could even recognize a picture of her taken ten years ago. You can recognize her when she is angry and when she is smiling. But if you had a rare disease called prosopagnosia, you would lose the ability to recognize all faces, including your own (Sacks, 1985). Yet people with this problem are often able to recognize facial *expressions* even when they can't identify *faces,* suggesting that different parts of the brain are involved in each process (Tranel, Damasio, & Damasio, 1988).

There are two things to keep in mind, though, about efforts to find physiological origins of emotion. One is that although the brain influences behavior, behavior also influences the brain; every part of the brain is affected by experience. In one study of electrical brain stimulation, for instance, *previously violent* patients became violent, whereas *previously nonviolent* patients did not (Scherer, Abeles, &

A Closer Look at Psychology and Public Policy

The Politics of Lie Detection

Governments, employers, spouses, and spies all want guaranteed ways of detecting "the truth." Fortunately or unfortunately, human beings are very good at lying about their own thoughts and feelings, but very poor at detecting the lies of others. They think that liars won't smile or "look you in the eye," for instance, but liars do exactly that. Many people assume that some body signs (such as facial animation) reflect truthfulness and others (such as nervous gestures) indicate deception, but neither assumption is true. Thus people who are animated and do not have nervous mannerisms are more likely to be successful at deception than people who are less expressive or do have nervous gestures (Ekman, 1985; Riggio & Friedman, 1983).

In recent years, many police departments and businesses have turned to "lie detectors" in the hope that machines will do better than people at discovering the truth. Increasingly, companies are requiring job applicants to take lie-detector tests as part of the screening procedure; some employers routinely use the machines to interrogate employees for drug abuse, theft, or other illegal activities. The Senate Labor Committee estimated that by 1988, some 2 million tests were being given every year, many by poorly trained operators.

"Lie detectors" are properly called emotion detectors, for their aim is to measure bodily changes that contradict what a person says. The *polygraph machine* records changes in heart rate, breathing, blood pressure, and the electrical activity of the skin (galvanic skin response, or GSR). In the first part of a polygraph test, you are wired up and asked a few neutral questions ("What's your name?" "Where do you live?"). Your physical reactions serve as the standard (baseline) for evaluating what comes next. Then you are asked a few critical questions among the neutral ones ("When did you rob the bank?"). The assumption is that if you are guilty, your body will reveal the truth, even if you try to deny it. Your heart rate, respiration, and GSR will change abruptly as you respond to the incriminating questions.

That is the theory; but psychologists have found that lie detectors are simply not reliable. Since most physical changes are the same across all emotions, machines cannot tell whether you are feeling guilty, angry, nervous, thrilled, or revved up from an exciting day. Innocent people may be tense and nervous about the whole procedure. They may react physiologically to a certain word ("bank") not because they robbed it, but because they recently bounced a check. In either case, the machine will record a "lie." The reverse mistake is also common. Some suave, practiced liars can lie without flinching, and others learn to "beat the machine" by tensing muscles or thinking about an exciting experience during neutral questions (Lykken, 1981).

In one important study, the polygraph results of 50 confessed thieves and 50 innocent people were given to six professional interpreters working at a leading lie detector company. The interpreters made many mistakes. *They were more likely to accuse the innocent of lying than to let the guilty go free.* Moreover, they did not agree with each other's judgments, which they ought to have done if the tests were truly objective. On the average, they classified 39 percent of the innocent as guilty; one interpreter made this mistake with 62 percent of the innocent. As for identifying the guilty, they were fooled by one thief in every four, and two interpreters made this error more than 30 percent of the time (Kleinmuntz & Szucko, 1984).

As a result of research like this, the American Psychological Association issued a policy statement opposing the use of lie detectors. There is no scientific evidence that polygraphs are valid, the statement noted; the number of innocent people who are labeled guilty is "unacceptably high"; and the polygraph does not conform to the APA's standards for psychological testing. In 1988, the U.S. Congress agreed, to some extent. Although it didn't go along with the APA's recommendation for a total ban, it did forbid the routine use of lie detectors in screening job applicants or randomly testing employees. As one shocked senator said, "Some 320,000 honest Americans are branded as liars every single year."

Fischer, 1975). Another point is that emotions tend to occur in bunches, like grapes. Psychologists usually study one emotion or another, but most people feel one emotion *and* another (Smith & Ellsworth, 1987). One researcher, who was trying to separate anger from anxiety for an experiment, discovered that her subjects kept reporting mixed emotions. When angry, they also reported feeling anxious and depressed. When afraid, they also said they felt depressed and hostile (Polivy, 1981).

For all these reasons, efforts to define emotion by its biology alone have failed. Psychologists have tried to "locate" emotion in the cardiovascular system, brain centers, facial expressions, internal organs, muscles, and gut. Because bodily sensations are *involved* in emotion, says one frustrated researcher, people have incorrectly assumed that bodily sensations *are* the emotion (De Rivera, 1977). One consequence of this mistaken assumption has been the widespread use of "lie detectors," which are based on the belief that the body reveals guilt even if the mind doesn't want it to. (See "A Closer Look at Psychology and Public Policy.")

QUICK ▪ QUIZ

Match each physical aspect of emotion with its function.

1. The hypothalamus
2. Epinephrine and norepinephrine
3. The neocortex

a. Send(s) messages to the autonomic nervous system
b. Provide(s) the energy of emotion and arouse(s) the body to respond
c. Permit(s) interpretations of events

Answers:

1. a   2. b   3. c

Elements of Emotion 2: The Mind

Put your finger on the dot in the margin, and smile. How do you feel at this moment, amused or irritated? If you followed our instructions and touched the dot, you probably feel more amused than angry. You may be laughing at yourself for doing such a silly thing, and that will make you feel happy—remember the facial-feedback hypothesis. If you didn't put your finger on the dot, you probably feel more angry than amused. "Why are the authors of this book asking me to play stupid games?" you may be saying to yourself.

Notice that it is not what we wrote that produced your emotion; it is your *interpretation* of what we asked you to do. Consider another example from everyday life. Let's say that you have had a crush for weeks on the new student in your computer class. Finally you get up the nerve to start a conversation. Heart pounding, palms sweating, you cheerfully say, "Hi, there!" Before you can add another word, the student has walked right past you without even a nod. What emotion do you feel? Your answer will depend on how you explain the student's behavior:

▪ *Angry*: "What a rude thing to do, to ignore me like that!"
▪ *Sad*: "I knew it; I'm no good. No one will ever like me."
▪ *Embarrassed*: "Oh, no! Everyone saw how I was humiliated!"
▪ *Relieved*: "Thank goodness; I didn't want to get involved, anyway."

Now take this scenario one step further. Suppose you have decided that the student intentionally ignored you and you are feeling angry. The next day a classmate informs you that you weren't snubbed at all, that the object of your passion is, without glasses, simply as blind as a bat. Your anger, along with your perception of insult, vanishes at once.

Just as the organic approach to emotions goes back to ancient philosophy, so does the mental tradition. The Stoic philosophers, in the first century A.D., were among the first to say that people do not become angry or sad or anxious because of actual events, but because of their explanations of those events. Modern psychologists, as we will see, are testing the Stoics' ideas experimentally, identifying the mental processes involved in emotions.

A bit of background

In the 1960s, Stanley Schachter and Jerome Singer proposed a **two-factor theory of emotion** (Schachter, 1971; Schachter & Singer, 1962). Bodily changes are necessary to experience an emotion, they said, but they are not enough. Your body may be churning away in high gear, but unless you can interpret, explain, and label those changes, you won't feel an "emotion." Schachter and Singer argued that true emotion depends on two factors: physiological arousal (the feeling of a feeling) and the cognitive interpretation of that arousal (how you define what you are feeling). Three predictions follow from this theory:

1. *If you are physiologically aroused and don't know why, you will try to label your feeling, using interpretations of events around you.* If all your friends are nervous and worried about an upcoming exam, you may decide that the pounding of your heart is a sign that you are nervous, too. In fact, it may only be a result of your partying too much and not getting enough sleep.

2. *If (in the absence of an emotional event) you are physiologically aroused and you* do *know why—you have just been jogging for 3 miles and expect your pulse rate to be high—you will not feel a need to explain the changes in your body or to describe them as an emotion.*

3. *If you are* not *physiologically aroused, your interpretations of events will not produce a true emotion.* You will react "emotionally" only when you are feeling some degree of arousal.

To test these predictions, Schachter and Singer devised a clever experiment. It was so clever that psychologists love to tell about it, even though it didn't quite turn out as the experimenters hoped, and no one has been able to replicate the study (Marshall & Zimbardo, 1979; Maslach, 1979).

Schachter and Singer injected some student volunteers with epinephrine, telling them they were getting an injection of vitamins. Some students were *correctly informed* of the symptoms they could expect (such as a thumping heart and shaking hands). Some were *misinformed* about what symptoms would occur ("your feet will feel numb"). Some were *left ignorant* of what to expect. Finally, a control group of students got a placebo injection that did not cause physical changes. Following the injection, the students were left alone in a room with a student ally (confederate) of the experimenters. Sometimes the ally acted as if he were in a goofy, jolly mood; on other occasions he would fly into a rage and stomp out of the room. The question was whether the subjects would begin to feel the ally's emotion, happiness or fury.

The psychologists believed the answer would be yes, *but only for the students*

two-factor theory of emotion *The theory that emotions depend on both physiological arousal and a cognitive interpretation or evaluation of that arousal.*

Does a trembling heart mean love or fear? Young men crossing the precarious Capilano Bridge (left), which sways 230 feet above the rapids, were more attracted to a female interviewer (right) than were men on a lower, sturdier bridge. According to the researchers, the men on the high bridge were aroused by fear; in the presence of a pretty woman, they experienced that arousal as sexual attraction (Dutton & Aron, 1974).

who were physiologically aroused by epinephrine and did not know what symptoms they would feel. That is pretty much what they found. The students who were misinformed or left ignorant about the effects of epinephrine were most likely to ''catch'' the ally's happy mood both in imitating the joyous behavior and in reporting that they felt happy. The students who knew what to expect from the epinephrine were least affected by the ally's giddiness. However, in the ''anger'' condition, students who were ignorant about the real effects of epinephrine did tend to *imitate* the ally's angry actions, but they did not report that they actually *felt* any angrier than either the control group or the group that knew what physical symptoms to expect. Perhaps they were just going along with the other guy to be sociable.

This complex study had many problems, but one aspect of Schachter and Singer's theory has subsequently been supported: When people are aroused for nonemotional reasons and don't know why—they have been listening to loud music, perhaps, or playing an active sport—they *are* more inclined to mislabel and misinterpret this arousal as intense emotion. If you are at a noisy, crowded concert and you believe that someone has insulted you, you are likely to feel very angry, very quickly. You will feel angrier than if you had been listening to a quiet clarinet, lying on the sofa, or watching a romantic comedy (Averill, 1982; Zillmann, 1979).

Yet the two-factor theory has not been supported in two respects. Schachter and Singer assumed that ''arousal'' was essential to the experience of emotion and that the more aroused you are, the more intense the emotion; but it's not necessarily so. Injecting people with ephedrine, a powerful stimulant, has no effect on how afraid they *feel* about being threatened with electric shock. Conversely, drugs that lower the heart rate have no effect on people's subjective reports of feeling anxious (Neiss, 1988). And as we said earlier, ''arousal'' is too general and meaningless a term to account for the many varieties of emotion.

Further, aroused or not, people don't just look at what others around them are feeling and then label their own physical state accordingly. (If you have ever been depressed while a group of merry friends tries to cheer you up, you will know what we mean.) Schachter and Singer were right to observe that the experience of emotion requires more than bodily arousal (as Cannon had long ago argued). Yet it also requires more than simply *labeling* one's arousal. Today, psychologists have made great advances in identifying other psychological components.

How thoughts affect emotions

Most people assume that success on a project brings happiness, and failure brings unhappiness. In fact, their emotions depend on the explanations they make of *why* they succeeded or failed. In a series of experiments, students reported occasions in which they had succeeded or failed on an exam for a particular reason (such as help from others or lack of effort). The students also reported the emotions they felt on each of these occasions. The researchers found that the students' emotions were more closely associated with their explanations than with the outcome of the test (Weiner, Russell, & Lerman, 1978, 1979). In particular:

- Those who believed they did well because of their own efforts and abilities tended to feel proud, competent, and satisfied.
- Those who believed they did well because of a lucky fluke or chance tended to feel gratitude, surprise, or guilt (''I don't deserve this'').
- Those who believed their failures were their own fault tended to feel regret, guilt, and resignation.
- Those who blamed others for their failures tended to feel angry, surprised, hostile, or alarmed.

Psychologists have studied the thought patterns, beliefs, and perceptions typical of many emotions, from euphoria to depression. Negative emotions differ from positive ones in the kinds of perceptions and explanations that generate them. We observed this phenomenon for ourselves when some friends returned from a mountain-climbing trip to Nepal. One said, ''It was wonderful! The crystal-clear skies, the millions of stars, the friendly people, the majestic mountains, the harmony of the universe!'' The other said, ''It was horrible! The bedbugs, the millions of fleas, the lack of toilets, the yak-butter tea, the horrible food, the unforgiving mountains!'' Guess which traveler was ecstatic while traveling and which was miserable?

To understand the mental processes involved in emotion, consider the case of loneliness. Loneliness consists of a cluster of emotions, including unhappiness, distress, and sometimes irritability. National surveys show that the loneliest people in America are adolescents and college students; fortunately, loneliness declines as people get older (Shaver & Buhrmester, 1983).

Being alone is not the same as feeling lonely. Why?

There are two sources of loneliness: ''emotional isolation,'' which can occur when people lack an intimate, stable attachment, and ''social isolation,'' which comes from a lack of friends and community (Weiss, 1973). If either form of isolation lasts too long, lonely people may sink into a self-critical depression. ''I felt rejected and inadequate,'' said one college student. Another, describing a recent bout with loneliness, said, ''I felt very depressed, and I hated myself'' (Peplau, Russell, & Heim, 1979).

Loneliness, however, is not the same thing as solitude or being alone. Many people live alone and do not feel lonely, because they have close ties to good friends and family. Others live in large families and feel desperately lonely, because they think that no one understands them or cares about them. Feelings of loneliness, therefore, cannot be understood by studying *actual* isolation. Certain events may set the stage for loneliness: the breakup of a dating relationship or a marriage, widowhood, moving away from home, being fired from a job, quarreling frequently with family or friends (Rubenstein & Shaver, 1982). But loneliness depends on how a person interprets and reacts to these events over time. Three styles of thinking are related to prolonged loneliness and unhappiness (Peplau & Perlman, 1982; Weiner, 1985):

1. *Internality.* Does the person believe the reason for his loneliness is internal (something particular about him) or external (something in his outside world)? Internal reasons include "I'm unattractive"; "I don't know how to make friends"; "I'm not trying very hard to get over this." External explanations look outward: "The people I work with are unfriendly"; "I'm having a run of bad luck"; "This school is so big and impersonal it's hard to meet new people." Internal blame tends to make lonely people more withdrawn.

2. *Stability.* Does the person believe the reason for her loneliness is permanent and unchangeable ("I'm ugly and horrible and always will be") or temporary and changeable? People who think they are doomed to be lonely create a vicious cycle: Expecting nothing to improve, they do nothing to improve their circumstances, so they remain lonely.

3. *Control.* Does the person believe he has control over the causes of his loneliness? The belief that there is absolutely nothing one can do to change the situation often prolongs the loneliness and the lonely person's feeling of despair.

These beliefs affect not only how lonely people feel, but also what they do. People who believe their loneliness is a result of internal, stable causes tend to feel depressed and helpless and remain stuck in their misery (Anderson, Horowitz, & French, 1983). Lonely people who believe their feelings are due to controllable, unstable causes, whether internal or external, are more likely to fight back, to make new friends, to change themselves or their circumstances. "Well, I'm shy," they might say, "but that's because I don't know anyone around here" or "I'm lonely because I just moved here, but that's just a natural phase of moving."

One of the challenges of studying emotion is the sheer variety and complexity of emotional experience in people's everyday lives. As we noted, most people have *blends* of feeling, not a single emotion. People differ in how *intensely* they experience their emotions; some seem as calm as clams, others as jumpy as rabbits. And some people have a greater emotional *range* than others. Provocative new studies in the cognitive tradition are investigating these mysteries of emotion.

▪ *Blends of emotion.* In one study, college students described their cognitive judgments and emotional states just before taking a midterm exam and again after they got their grades (Smith & Ellsworth, 1987). At both times, students often reported mixed feelings—such as hope and fear *before* the exam or anger and guilt *after* the exam. These emotional blends were reliably related to the students' appraisals of their performance, the importance of the exam, their own effort in studying, their degree of certainty about how well they would do, and so on. The students who felt angriest about their poor grades, for example, interpreted the exam as being unfair. This anger, though, was often combined with guilt ("I should have studied harder"), fear ("What if I don't pass?"), or apathy ("I don't care about this course anyway").

▪ *Intensity of emotion.* Why is it that of two people who do well on an exam, one feels mildly pleased and the other ecstatic? Why is it that of two people who read about a crook who has cheated people out of their life's savings, one feels annoyed and the other enraged? People who feel emotions intensely have typical ways of thinking (Beck, 1976; Larsen, Diener, & Cropanzano, 1987): They *personalize* events ("I thought about how I would feel if my friends, family, or I were in that situation"); they *pay selective attention* to the emotion-provoking aspects of events ("I focused on the worst part of the situation"); and they *overgeneralize*, taking a single event as a sign of a general state of the world. They make mountains out of molehills, whether the molehills are good or bad.

▪ *Emotional range.* Some people seem to have a limited number of emotions—they go from happy to sad, and that's about it. Others play on a keyboard of emotions—nostalgia, melancholy, gloom, euphoria, embarrassment, jealousy, you name it. This difference may seem to reflect physiology or temperament, but Shula Sommers and Anthony Scioli (1986) found that people's values and basic "way of life" are correlated with their emotional range.

For instance, men and women who have a limited emotional range tend to value a way of life based on pleasure and self-indulgence, and to reject the notions of responsibility and loyalty. In addition, women who have a limited range are more likely than other women to feel powerless and entrust their lives to fate. Think about these interesting results, keeping in mind that correlation is not causation. Why would having a varied emotional range affect your values? Or does having certain values give you a greater emotional range? Might another factor, such as temperament, affect both? How would you explain these findings?

As you see, the psychological factors involved in emotion range from your immediate perceptions of an event to your basic philosophy of life. If you believe that winning is everything and trying your best counts for nothing, you may feel depressed rather than joyous if you "only" come in second. If you think a friend's criticism is intentionally mean rather than well meaning, you may respond with anger rather than gratitude. Our emotions cannot be separated from our mental lives (Frijda, 1988).

The mind-body connection

Emotions, then, depend on a complex combination of bodily responses and mental processes. The body provides the energy to fight, flee, cope, respond, hug, sing, or dance. The mind contributes understanding, or at least an explanation, of one's own and other people's actions. The reason that human emotions differ from those of other animals is that people are constantly thinking, perceiving, and interpreting. As fast as your body is generating epinephrine to help you respond to danger, your mind is helping you decide whether that raised fist is a sign of playfulness or threat.

Perhaps you can see now why both the organic and mental traditions have contributed to our understanding of emotion. It is not a matter of "which comes first," because the interaction of body and mind works in *both directions.* Sometimes people experience intense emotions, as we saw, because of their habitual ways of generalizing and personalizing events. But sometimes people experience intense emotions because they are physiologically aroused from nonemotional sources, such as being in a crowd or sweltering on a steamy day.

Many people believe that emotions spell the doom of our species because they lead to cruel and selfish behavior. But what about the benefits of emotion? Could we survive without shame, pity, empathy, and love?

Many people believe that the organic, "animal-like" basis of emotion dooms our species to rage, fear, and selfishness. If only we didn't have those nasty old mammalian emotions, they say, we could rely on reason and critical thinking to solve our problems. But the two research traditions described so far suggest more optimistic conclusions.

For instance, the mental tradition can be used to teach depressed or anxious people how their thinking affects their emotions. What is the evidence for their beliefs that the world will collapse if they get a C in biology, that no one loves them, that they are doomed to loneliness forever? In these cases, it is not emotion that prevents critical thinking; it is the failure to think critically that creates the emotion!

Similarly, the organic tradition reminds people of their biological connections to each other; it highlights the survival value of emotions such as guilt, shame, pity, remorse, gratitude, and empathy (Plutchik, 1987). What do you think the world would be like without these feelings? Psychopaths, torturers, con men, and practiced liars can cognitively rationalize the cruelest actions, without a jiggle of arousal or a raised heartbeat. Without the physiological mechanisms that link us to one another and to the consequences of our actions, cognition can become self-serving and irrational—the very opposite of the spirit of critical thinking.

An individual experience of emotion combines mind and body, but individuals live in a social world. Thoughts may influence emotion, but where do thoughts come from? You may decide you are wildly jealous, but where do you get your ideas of jealousy? You may feel angry enough to punch the walls, but where do you learn what to do when you are that enraged? To answer these questions, we turn to the role of culture.

QUICK ■ QUIZ

Test your understanding of mind, body, and emotion.

1. Chronically lonely people tend to believe that the reasons for their unhappiness are (**a**) temporary, external, controllable, (**b**) temporary, internal, controllable, (**c**) permanent, internal, uncontrollable.
2. People who react intensely to events tend to (**a**) take them personally, (**b**) be oversensitive, (**c**) have abnormal arousal levels, (**d**) focus on the larger meaning of the event.
3. When you are physically aroused by epinephrine and you don't know why, which of the following is likely to happen? You will (**a**) feel an emotion more intensely than usual, (**b**) try to explain your feeling, (**c**) sometimes confuse the ''high'' of epinephrine with the ''high'' of an emotion, (**d**) all of the above.
4. You are driving in traffic with a passenger in the front seat. Another car suddenly cuts in front of you. Based on our discussion of emotion, why do you feel angrier than your friend does? (**a**) You have a bad temper. (**b**) The demands of driving in traffic have raised your epinephrine level. (**c**) You are a better driver than anyone else.

Answers:
1. c 2. a 3. d 4. b

Elements of Emotion 3: The Culture

A young wife leaves her house one morning to draw water from the local well, as her husband watches from the porch. On her way back from the well, a stranger stops her and asks for some water. She gives him a cupful and then invites him home to dinner. He accepts. The husband, wife, and guest have a pleasant meal together. The husband, in a gesture of hospitality, invites the guest to spend the night—with his wife. He accepts. In the morning, the husband leaves early to bring home breakfast. When he returns, he finds his wife again in bed with the visitor.

The question is: At what point in this story does the husband feel angry?

The answer is: It depends on the culture to which he belongs (Hupka, 1981).

Think About It

The Seven Deadly . . . Emotions?

A counselor, interviewing a woman with a history of child abuse, asked her why she beat her young son. "I can't stop myself," the woman said. "I just lose control." When movie mogul David Begelman was caught embezzling $40,000 from Columbia Pictures, a tiny amount compared to the multithousands he was earning, he pleaded with his employers not to fire him: "I have a compulsion to destroy myself," he cried. In New Bedford, Massachusetts, four men raped a woman in a public bar. "We couldn't help it," they said, "she provoked us."

Are we in control of our emotions, or do they control us? This question has been debated for centuries, and its answer affects our laws, everyday relationships, therapies, and hopes for civilization. The law, for example, distinguishes between first-

degree murder (premeditated) and second-degree murder (on the spot). The difference between these categories is, in a word, *emotion*. Cold blood confers responsibility for our actions; passion excuses our actions (Averill, DeWitt, & Zimmer, 1978). So we hear, "I couldn't help myself; I was overcome by lust"—or rage, fear, jealousy, greed. . . .

Nearly 2000 years ago, the Roman philosopher Seneca observed how passionately people cling to their passions. "We are in love with our vices," he wrote. "We uphold them and prefer to make excuses for them rather than shake them off." We excuse them, said Seneca, because they excuse us. Many modern psychologists agree. As we noted in Chapter 4, some people get drunk knowing that their inebriation will give them an excuse for violence

---

An American husband would feel rather angry at a wife who had an extramarital affair, and a wife would feel rather angry at being offered to a guest as if she were a lamb chop. But these reactions are not universal.

- A Pawnee Indian husband of the nineteenth century would be enraged at any man who dared ask his wife for water.
- An Ammassalik Eskimo husband finds it perfectly honorable to offer his wife to a stranger, but only once. He would be angry to find his wife and the guest having a second encounter.
- A Toda husband at the turn of the century in India would not be angry at all. The Todas allowed both husband and wife to take lovers, and women were even allowed to have several husbands. Both spouses might feel angry, though, if one of them had a *sneaky* affair, without announcing it publicly.

As this story illustrates, people in most cultures experience the emotion of anger as a response to insult. It's just that they disagree about what an insult is. In this section, we will explore some cultural influences on the causes and expression of emotion. (As "Think About It" suggests, cultures also determine what people may "get away with" when they are in "the heat of passion.")

The varieties of emotion

A major problem in studying emotions is language. Gujarati, a language of India, lacks the words for "excited" and "annoyed." In Croatian and Chinese you can't say "hurt" or "troubled." Some languages have words for emotional states that English lacks entirely, and vice versa. The Germans have *schadenfreude*, a feeling

(Gelles, 1979). Emotion doesn't simply cause bad behavior; it also justifies it. Perhaps you have heard people say, "I was so depressed I ate an entire cake" or "I was so mad that I finally told him what I think of him" or "I was so drunk that I went to bed with her; I didn't know what I was doing." Many people get drunk, physically aroused, or angry *in order* to say or do what they know would be immoral, illegal, or fattening otherwise.

Of course, there are people who truly are not responsible for their actions because of organic or mental illness. But in everyday life, where do we draw the line? Are people slaves of their emotions? It can be difficult to control the involuntary aspects of emotion, such as arousal and certain types of body language, but many psychologists believe that people can control their perceptions of an event and how they decide to react. Yet it is often in people's interests to maintain that they were overpowered by their feelings.

Pride, greed, anger, envy, gluttony, sloth, and lust made the list of Seven Deadly Sins because human beings were assumed to be in charge of their emotions and responsible for their actions. "Sinners" know what they are doing is wrong, but they do it anyway to satisfy their desires. However, if people believe that they have no control over their emotions, they can avoid taking responsibility for their actions. Can child abusers help themselves? Was Begelman's thievery a case of compulsion or greed? Is rape an act of uncontrollable lust or controllable cruelty? What do you think?

of joy at another's misfortune; the Japanese have *amaeru*, the emotional need to be dependent on another.

Psychologists disagree on the meaning of these language differences. Are Germans more likely than Americans actually to feel *schadenfreude* or just more willing to give the emotion a single name? Robert Levy (1984) reports that Tahitians lack the Western concept of and word for sadness. Tahitians experience sadness but identify it as illness. If you ask a Tahitian who is grieving over the loss of a lover what is wrong, he will say, "A spirit has made me ill." In contrast, Tahitians have a

Cultures everywhere determine the rules for expressing emotions. The rule for a formal Japanese wedding portrait is "no smiling" —but not every member of this family has learned that rule yet.

word for an emotion that most Westerners do not experience. Levy calls this emotion "a sense of the uncanny," a trembling sensation that Tahitians feel when ordinary categories of perception are suspended: at twilight, in the brush, watching fires glow without heat. To Westerners, an event that cannot be categorized and identified is usually greeted with fear. But the Tahitian "uncanny" does not describe what Westerners call fear or terror.

Do you remember the research on linguistic universals in naming colors (Chapter 8)? Every culture distinguishes black and white, and then adds color terms predictably, along the color spectrum. By analyzing hundreds of words for emotions in many languages, researchers have found that a similar process applies to naming emotions (Shaver & Schwartz, in press).

That is, all cultures distinguish *positive* (pleasant) emotions from *negative* (unpleasant) ones (Storm & Storm, 1987; Watson, Clark, & Tellegen, 1984). People everywhere regard love, joy, admiration, and amusement as positive emotions, and they regard fear, hatred, sorrow, and shame as negative ones. A few cultures differentiate emotions only in terms of their negative or positive tone: Some African tribes, for instance, have one word for "anger" and "sadness."

At the next level of emotion naming, most cultures recognize a number of **primary emotions**, which seem to be universal experiences. Psychologists distinguish these from **secondary emotions**, which include cultural variations (such as *schadenfreude* or *amaeru*), blends of feeling (the bittersweet emotion of feeling sad and happy at a friend's wedding, say), and degrees of intensity ("fear" can range from nervousness to terror) (J. Russell, 1983). Primary emotions have been identified in several ways: by universally recognized facial expressions; by the existence in most languages of words that label them; and by the predictable appearance of these emotions in child development. Thus the most common emotion words young children use are the basics: *happy*, *sad*, *mad*, and *scared*. As they get older, they learn varieties that are specific to their language, such as *ecstatic*, *depressed*, *hostile*, or *anxious* (Storm & Storm, 1987).

Depending on how psychologists go about measuring emotions, the list of the "primary" ones varies somewhat. As Table 9.1 shows, fear, anger, sadness, joy, surprise, and disgust turn up in most studies. But sometimes laypeople disagree with psychologists. Most Americans consider "love" to be an emotion, even

primary emotions
Emotions that are considered to be universal and biologically based. They generally include fear, anger, sadness, joy, and disgust.

secondary emotions
Emotions that are either "blends" of primary emotions (e.g., contempt as a blend of anger and disgust) or that are specific to certain cultures (e.g., the Tahitian sense of the "uncanny").

This father is clearly proud of his family. Is pride just a variation of happiness, or is it a distinct emotional state?

TABLE 9.1
PRIMARY EMOTIONS ACCORDING TO LEADING THEORIES

Psychologists have tried to identify the "basic" or universal emotions in several ways. Some, such as Ekman, study universally recognizable facial expressions or other biological elements. Others, such as Plutchik, study people's subjective evaluation of emotion words and reduce their varied emotional experiences into basic categories. Still others, such as Shaver and the Storms, ask people to evaluate hundreds of words according to whether they are or are not emotions, and then to sort all the emotion words into clusters that "go together." The results, shown below, indicate some uniformities across all methods and some interesting variations. Notice that shame and love are basic in some theories but not in others. Some researchers observe that hope, pride, and empathy are as much a part of the human emotional experience as sadness and anger, but fail to make the list of "primary" emotions because they can't be measured in the brain or identified on the face (Weiner, 1982; Weiner & Graham, 1984). What do you think?

Tomkins	Ekman	Izard	Plutchik	Shaver et al.	Storm & Storm
Fear	Fear	Fear	Fear	Fear	Fear
Anger	Anger	Anger	Anger	Anger	Anger
Enjoyment	Happiness	Joy	Joy	Joy	Happiness
Distress	Sadness	Sadness	Sadness	Sadness	Sadness[b]
Disgust	Disgust	Disgust	Disgust		
Interest		Interest	Anticipation		
Surprise	Surprise	Surprise	Surprise	Surprise[a]	
Contempt		Contempt			
Shame		Shame			
			Acceptance	Love	Love/liking

[a]This category was marginal to the others and not really considered an emotion by subjects.

[b]Includes shame and pain.

SOURCES: Ekman et al., 1987; Izard, 1971, 1984; Plutchik, 1984; Shaver et al., 1987; Storm & Storm, 1987; Tomkins, 1981.

though it doesn't have a typical facial expression (except perhaps the mooning gaze of new sweethearts). In contrast, they don't really think of surprise or disgust as true emotions, although both are registered on the face (Shaver et al., 1987; Storm & Storm, 1987).

Whether an emotion is "primary" or not, cultures determine much of what people feel angry, sad, lonely, happy (or whatever) *about*. For instance, to most Westerners, the state of frustration is supposed to be biologically irritating. Years ago a team of psychologists even argued that frustration is always a cause of aggression (Dollard et al., 1939). Later studies found, however, that frustration goes along with anger only in societies that emphasize success, meeting goals, getting ahead, and the like. The Balinese, in contrast, aren't fazed by frustration. You can interrupt them at work or play and they won't be cranky at all. They will be irritated, though, if you steal a cow or renege on a bet (Bateson, 1941).

The communication of emotion

Once you feel an emotion, how do you express it? The answer is rarely a simple "I say what I feel." You may be obliged to disguise what you feel. You may wish you could feel what you say. You may even convey an emotional message unintentionally, through nonverbal signals (Buck, 1984).

What are good manners and dignified restraint to a European may seem "cold" or "unfeeling" to the average American. What are the unfortunate consequences of overlooking the effects of culture on the display of emotions?

Display rules and "emotion work."   Whatever the emotion, every society has **display rules** that govern how and when emotions may be expressed (Ekman & Friesen, 1975). In some cultures, grief is expressed by noisy wailing and weeping; in others, by stoic, tearless resignation; in still others, by merry dance, drink, and song (LaBarre, 1947). In some traditions, love is to be expressed by extravagant gesture, like the one Ulrich made in his Venus suit; in others, love is expressed by sustained, understated action. Imagine the conflict that can occur between people from different cultures!

People learn their culture's display rules as effortlessly as they learn language. Just as they can speak without knowing the rules of grammar, most people express (or suppress) their emotions without being aware of the rules they are following. Consider the display rules for the stages of an angry dispute (E. Hall, 1976). Suppose your neighbor builds a fence on what you believe is your property. You feel angry about this. If you are a white Anglo-American, your anger is likely to move from small steps to large ones. You start by dropping hints ("Gee, Mort, are you sure that fence is on your side of the line?"). You talk to friends. Then you get a third person to intervene. Eventually you talk directly to Mort, maybe getting angrier in the process. If none of this works, you may go to court and sue him. If that strategy fails, you may burn the fence down.

To Anglos, these steps, from small to large, are the natural, logical way to express anger. But there is nothing "natural" about this course of action. Worldwide, it isn't even very typical. In many cultures, the first thing you do when your neighbor builds a fence that angers you is . . . nothing. You think about it. You brood over your grievances and decide what to do. This brooding may last for weeks, months, or even years. The second step is . . . you burn the fence down. This is only to draw your neighbor's attention to the fact that you two have a problem, and now you are ready for negotiations, lawyers, third-party interventions, and so on. Notice how cultures have different interpretations of the same action: Burning the fence down is the last resort in one, but the start of the conversation in another.

Display rules not only tell us what to do when we *are* feeling an emotion; they also tell us how and when we should show an emotion we do *not* feel. Acting out an emotion we don't really feel has been called **emotion work**. People are expected to demonstrate sadness at funerals, happiness at weddings, and affection toward relatives. If they don't really feel such emotions, they may playact to convince others that they do.

Flight attendants, male or female, are trained to smile and convey friendliness. This man is a steward on a corporate jet.

Sometimes emotion work is a job requirement, as a study of flight attendants and bill collectors found. Flight attendants must "put on a happy face" and convey cheerfulness, even if they are angry about a rude or drunken passenger. Bill collectors must put on a fierce face to convey threat; they must withhold empathy, even if they are feeling sorry for the poor person in debt (Hochschild, 1983). Other employees do "emotion work" when they express contentment with an employer's infuriating decision, or when they display cheerfulness to annoying customers.

Body language.   Fiorello LaGuardia, who was mayor of New York from 1933 to 1945, was fluent in three different languages: English, Italian, and Yiddish. LaGuardia knew more than the words of those languages; he also knew the gestures that went along with each one. Researchers who studied films of his speeches could tell which language he was speaking *with the sound turned off* (Birdwhistell, 1970). How could they do this?

FIGURE 9.2

Reading body language
The body communicates many messages of emotion and status. Walking or standing with hands clasped behind the body, for example—as members of royalty often do, or military commanders inspecting the troops—is a sign of dominance and confidence. Culture influences many kinds of body language. Arabs stand much closer to each other in normal conversation than Westerners do—close enough to feel one another's breath and "read" one another's eyes. In many societies, men greet men with an embrace and a kiss, gestures that are taboo in most of the United States and Canada.

Emotions are expressed by *body language*, the countless nonverbal signals of body movement, posture, gesture, and gaze. Even the absence of movement is significant. If you see someone who is utterly rigid, you will probably assume the person is terrified, anxious, or even mentally disturbed (Collier, 1985). People can stop talking, but they do not stop revealing their emotions. People can lie about how they feel, but their bodies may reveal what their words do not.

Some basic signals of body language, like some basic facial expressions, seem to be "spoken" universally. Across cultures, people generally recognize body movements that reveal pleasure or displeasure, liking or dislike, tension or relaxation, high status or low status (Buck, 1984). When people are depressed, it shows in their walk, stance, and position of head (Snodgrass, 1985a). However, most aspects of body language are specific to particular spoken languages and cultures, as La-Guardia knew (see Figure 9.2):

▪ *Smile.* The smile seems simple and unmistakable; it is, as we saw, universally recognized. But it does not have universal meaning. Americans, for instance, smile more frequently than Germans. This does not mean that Americans are friendlier than Germans, only that they differ in their notions of a smile's appropriateness. After a German-American business session, Americans often complain that their German counterparts are cold and aloof. "You can never get to know them," the Americans say. Meanwhile, Germans often complain that the Americans are excessively cheerful, hiding their real feelings under the mask of a smile. "You can never get to know them," the Germans say (Hall & Hall, 1983). The Japanese smile even more than the Americans, to disguise embarrassment, anger, or other negative emotions whose public display is considered inappropriate and rude. In the United States and Canada, women smile more often than men, but women in Taiwan and

display rules *Social and cultural rules that regulate when, how, and where a person may express (or suppress) emotional feelings.*
emotion work *Expression of an emotion one does not really feel in response to social or cultural expectations.*

the People's Republic of China do not differ from men in facial expressiveness (Buck & Teng, 1987). An old Chinese book of advice to women warns, "Do not show your unhappiness easily and do not smile easily" and "Do not show your teeth when you smile."

▪ *Touch.* Here is a small observational study you can do. Sit in a coffee shop and watch people who are eating together. Count how many times one person touches the other during their conversations. Sidney Jourard (1966) did so in four cities: San Juan, Puerto Rico; Paris; London; and Gainesville, Florida. His scores were San Juan, 180; Paris, 110; London, 0; and Gainesville, 2. Anglo-American culture is not very body- and touch-oriented.

▪ *Gesture.* Visitors to other countries may learn some words in their hosts' language in an effort at courtesy, and then unwittingly offend them by making the wrong gesture. The sign of the University of Texas football team, the Longhorns, is to extend the second finger and the pinkie. In Italy this gesture means a man's wife has been unfaithful to him—a serious insult! The cheerful V-for-Victory sign in the United States (palm facing out) conveys an angry vulgarity in England (palm facing in).

Cultures differ in how attentive they are to body signals and which signals are likely to draw attention. For instance, a study of more than 1000 Japanese students found that the Japanese pay more attention to body movements associated with status and power than to body movements that express like or dislike (Kudoh & Matsumoto, 1985). In Japan, the researchers explain, social relationships are vertical, based on status, respect, and duty. In the United States, social relationships are more likely to be horizontal, based on friendship, affection, and attraction. Americans, consequently, pay more attention to body signals of emotional attraction and liking.

Even within cultures, people differ in their physical "expressiveness" and habitual gestures. Of course, much of what people call "body language" has little to do with emotion. We wave our arms for emphasis; we draw pictures in the air for clarification (as in describing a spiral staircase). We use formal gestures to wave for taxis, get attention in class, greet a new acquaintance. Whether communicating emotion, intention, emphasis, or power, one body gesture can be worth a thousand words.

Putting the Elements Together: The Case of Emotion and Gender

Why is it "arguing" when he does it but "getting emotional" when she does it? On emotional subjects, people often fail to define their terms. What, for example, does "emotional" mean?

The *San Francisco Chronicle* once published a highly unscientific report of its male readers' opinions about women. At the very top of the men's gripe list was "women's nagging," followed by "women get too emotional when I argue." Why, asks Stephanie Shields (1986), "is it 'arguing' when *he* does it, but 'getting emotional' or 'nagging' when *she* does it?"

People hold strong beliefs about sex differences in emotion and about whether the male or female style is "better" (Shields, 1988). When psychologists study the question of sex differences in emotion, they try to separate these values from actual behavior. As we have seen, "being emotional" can refer to an internal emotional state, to how an emotion is displayed, to nonverbal expressiveness, or to "emotion work.'' Because emotion has so many aspects, the answer to ''who is more emotional'' isn't simple.

First, there is not much evidence that one sex *feels* emotions more often or more intensely than the other. (We are talking here about men and women from the same ethnic background.) Both sexes are equally likely, on the average, to feel anxious in new social situations. Both sexes are equally likely to experience jealousy, love, and loneliness. Both sexes feel angry when they are insulted, are treated badly, or are in conflict with loved ones. Both sexes grieve when close attachments break up. Both sexes feel embarrassed when they make public mistakes (Tavris & Wade, 1984).

Men and women do differ, though, in how, where, and when they *express* some emotions. At home and at work, men and women are fairly similar in how they express anger. They are equally likely to sulk, brood, collect grievances, discuss matters outright, or yell (Averill, 1982). But men are more likely than women to express anger to strangers, usually other men, when they believe that they have been challenged. Men are also more likely to express anger, fear, or hurt pride in the form of aggressive action. For that matter, men are more likely to behave aggressively when they aren't feeling any emotion, but simply want to establish dominance or get their way (Frodi, Macaulay, & Thome, 1977).

Women are more likely than men, in contrast, to reveal certain negative emotions, such as fear, sadness, loneliness, and embarrassment, and to express these feelings to friends as well as to family (Cherulnik, 1979; Hacker, 1981). Men, if they express these ''unmanly'' emotions at all, tend to do so only to the woman they love, and rarely to their male friends (Schwartz, Sharpsteen, & Butler, 1989). Even with their wives and girlfriends, men tend to reveal their strengths and positive emotions and conceal their worries and weaknesses (Peplau, 1983). Two psychologists, reviewing findings from 39 studies, found that both sexes were equally likely to *feel* lonely, but women were much more likely to *admit* being lonely. One reason, the researchers discovered, was that both sexes are more likely to reject a lonely male than a lonely female. There are greater negative consequences to men than to women, it seems, of revealing unhappiness (Borys & Perlman, 1985).

Sometimes women are considered ''more emotional'' because of their supposed sensitivity to other people's emotional states. Robert Rosenthal and his colleagues (1979) developed a test called the Profile of Nonverbal Sensitivity (PONS), which measures a person's ability to detect emotions revealed in tones of voice, movements of the body, and facial expressions. Women have scored slightly, but reliably, better on this test than men (J. Hall, 1978). But other research finds that sensitivity to another person's emotional state depends on several conditions, including:

■ *The sex of the sender and the receiver.* People do better reading their own sex's signals than those of the opposite sex (Buck, 1984).

■ *How well the two people know each other.* Dating couples and married couples can interpret each other's facial expressions and other signals better than strangers can (Sabatelli, Buck, & Dreyer, 1982).

■ *Who has the power.* Less powerful people learn to read the powerful person's signals, perhaps for self-protection (Frieze et al., 1978). One experiment found that ''women's intuition'' should more properly be called ''subordinate's intuition.'' In male-female pairs, the person in the subordinate (follower) position was more sensitive to the leader's nonverbal signals than the leader was to the follower's cues. This

From childhood on, girls tend to prefer ''face to face'' friendships, based on shared feelings; boys tend to prefer ''side by side'' friendships, based on shared activities.

difference occurred whether a man or a woman was the leader or the follower (Snodgrass, 1985b).

Both sexes know the experience of having to hide emotions they feel and pretend emotions they do not feel. But their ''emotion work'' is often different. On the whole, women tend to be involved in the flight-attendant side of emotion work (persuading others that they are friendly, happy, and warm) and men to be involved in the bill-collection side (persuading others that they are stern, aggressive, and ''unemotional''). Public-service jobs requiring emotion work are a fourth of all the jobs that men do, but they are more than half of the jobs that women do (Hochschild, 1983). Emotion work is often a woman's job in the family as well as in the workplace. It is part of the traditional wife's task to attend to the feelings and emotional well-being of her husband and children.

Perhaps as part of their emotion work, women in American society smile more often than men do, not necessarily because they feel happier, but to pacify, nurture, and convey deference (Mayo & Henley, 1981). If women don't smile when others expect them to, they are often disliked, even if they are only smiling as often as men would. Children learn this lesson early. Carolyn Saarni (1979, 1982) found that 6- to 10-year-olds show a steady increase in knowledge about where and when they should disguise feelings and put on a ''polite smile'' (for instance, when they are given a gift they don't like). From childhood on, girls are more likely than boys to mask their negative feelings with positive expressions. As adults, women often express anger with a smile, a mixed message that is puzzling to their friends, spouses, and children (Deutsch, LeBaron, & Fryer, 1987).

So it seems that women are criticized both for being ''too emotional'' (when they express intimate feelings, when they reveal fears and weaknesses) and for not being emotional enough (when they don't smile politely, when they don't attend to others' emotional signs). Men are criticized for being ''too emotional'' (when they behave aggressively) and for not being emotional enough (when they are reluctant to reveal fears and weaknesses). Perhaps people would be better off if they stopped fussing about who is more ''emotional,'' and concentrated instead on understanding each other's emotional messages.

QUICK ▪ QUIZ

Is each of the following more characteristic of men, more characteristic of women, or equally characteristic of both sexes?

1. Expressing anger to an irritating stranger
2. Admitting a fear of spiders
3. Yelling and screaming
4. Confessing worries and weaknesses to a friend of the same sex
5. Pretending an emotion not really felt at work
6. Feeling angry, happy, or worried
7. Pretending not to feel afraid or hurt

Answers:

1. men 2. women 3. both 4. women 5. women 6. both 7. men

As we have seen in this chapter, the full experience and expression of emotion depend on the body's responses, the mind's perceptions, and society's rules. Human emotions can be compared to a tree: The biological capacity for emotion is the trunk; thoughts and explanations create the many branches; and culture is the gardener that shapes the tree and prunes it, cutting off some limbs and cultivating others.

Emotions have many purposes in human life. They allow us to establish close bonds, threaten and warn, get help from others, reveal or deceive. The many varieties and expressions of emotion suggest that although we feel emotions physically, we use them socially. As we explore further issues of motivation, personality, development, well-being, and mental disorders, we will see again and again how emotions involve thinking *and* feeling, perception *and* action—head *and* heart.

Taking Psychology with You

"Let It Out" or "Bottle It Up"? The Dilemma of Anger

There is a common notion afoot in America that it is always best to express every emotion you feel, whenever and wherever you feel it, or else it will "fester" and cause problems. It is supposed to be especially bad to "bottle up" anger, as if it were a fizzing poison. Does "letting anger out" really get rid of it, or does it only make it more intense? The answer is highly relevant for how we get along with our families, neighbors, employers, and strangers. People rarely express anger to themselves. They express anger to somebody, and whether they feel good or bad afterward has a lot to do with how that somebody reacts. Most people feel good about expressing anger if they get results ("Were you angry at me? Oh, dear, how can I make amends?"). But they feel miserable if the anger backfires ("*You* dare to be angry at *me*? *You're* the one who never does anything around here, you turkey!").

Although some schools of therapy advise people to "let it all hang out," psychologists are finding that this advice is more likely to hang you. By and large, research shows that expressing anger does not always get rid of anger; often it prolongs it (Averill, 1982; Tavris, 1989). When people talk about feeling angry or act on that feeling, they tend to rehearse their grievances, create a hostile disposition, and pump up their blood pressures. Conversely, when people learn to control their tempers, they usually feel better, not worse; calmer, not angrier. Charles Darwin (1872/1965) observed this fact more than a century ago. "The free expression by outward signs of an emotion intensifies it," he wrote. "On the other hand, the repression, as far as this is possible, of all outward signs softens our emotions. He who gives way to violent gestures will increase his rage."

Some people behave aggressively when they are angry, but others behave in a friendly, cooperative way to try to solve the problem that is causing their anger. The aggressive expression of anger is learned, not biologically determined (Hokanson, 1970). When people are feeling emotionally churned up, they tend to do something. They write letters, play the piano, jog, bake bread, kick the sofa, abuse their friends or family, or yell. If a particular action soothes their feelings or gets the desired response from other people, they are likely to acquire a habit. If you have learned an aggressive habit, the research in this chapter offers practical suggestions for relearning constructive ways of managing anger:

- *Don't sound off in the heat of anger; let bodily arousal cool down.* Whether your arousal comes from background stresses such as heat, exercise, crowds, or loud noise, or whether it comes from conflict with another person, take time to relax. Time allows you to decide if you are "really" angry or just tired and tense. This is the reason for that sage old advice to count to 10, count to 100, or sleep on it.
- *Remember that anger depends on the perception of insult; see if you can rethink the problem.* People who are quick to feel angry tend to interpret other people's actions as intentional offenses. People who are slow to anger tend to give others the benefit of the doubt (Burns, 1980; Novaco, 1985). Empathy ("Poor guy, he's feeling rotten") is usually incompatible with anger and aggresiveness, so try to see the situation from the other person's perspective (Miller & Eisenberg, 1988).
- *If you decide that expressing anger is appropriate, think carefully about how to do it so that you will get the results you want.* As we saw, different cultures have different display rules. Be sure the recipient of your anger understands what you are feeling and what complaint you are trying to convey.

Ultimately, the decision about whether to express anger depends not only on whether you will feel good if you do, but also on what you hope to accomplish. Do you want to restore your rights, change the other person, improve a bad situation, or achieve justice? If those are your goals, then learning *how* to express anger so the other person will listen, and respond, is essential. For example, people who have been the targets of discrimination have successfully directed anger through legal channels to win their rights.

Of course, if you just want to "blow off steam," go right ahead—though you risk becoming a hothead.

KEY WORDS

organic school 314
mental school 314
emotion 315
James-Lange theory 316
Cannon-Bard theory 316
Charles Darwin 316
facial-feedback hypothesis 318
epinephrine (adrenaline) 319

norepinephrine (noradrenaline) 319
arousal 320
two-factor theory 324
primary emotions 332
secondary emotions 332
display rules 334
emotion work 334
body language 334

SUMMARY

1. For many centuries, psychologists and philosophers have debated what an emotion is. The *organic school* holds that emotions are caused by biological changes in the body. The *mental school* holds that emotions are caused by perceptions, interpretations, and other cognitions.

2. In the late nineteenth century, the *James-Lange* theory of emotion proposed that perceptions of bodily reactions to an event give rise to the experience of emotion. "We feel sorry *because* we cry, angry *because* we strike," wrote James. Later, the *Cannon-Bard* theory argued against the James-Lange approach on the grounds that bodily changes are not enough to produce an emotion; changes occur too slowly in the internal organs to be a source of emotion; and the same bodily changes occur in many different emotions.

3. Some psychologists believe that facial expressions are a clue to the biological nature of emotion. Some basic facial expressions—anger, fear, sadness, happiness, disgust, surprise—are widely recognized across different cultures. Different facial expressions become apparent in infancy, and infants recognize adult expressions of fear, anger, and happiness.

4. According to the *facial-feedback hypothesis,* facial expressions not only communicate to others, but also may send messages to the brain identifying our own emotional states. Because people can disguise their emotions, facial expressions do not always communicate accurately.

5. *Epinephrine* and *norepinephrine* (also called adrenaline and noradrenaline) are hormones that produce physiological *arousal* to prepare the body to cope with environmental stimuli, nonemotional but physically taxing events, and all emotional states. These hormones produce changes in heart rate, respiration, pupil dilation, blood sugar levels, perspiration, digestion, memory, and performance. There seem to be several forms of arousal, involving different areas of the brain, and arousal itself does not cause an emotional state.

6. Some researchers look for the biological sources of emotion in the brain's limbic system, which human beings share with other species. However, human emotions are greatly influenced by the cortex, the center of reason and symbolic logic, and all areas of the brain are influenced by the environment and a person's learning history. New approaches no longer look for "brain centers" associated with emotion, but at how different areas of the brain are involved in various aspects of emotional experience: for example, experiencing positive versus negative emotions, or recognizing faces versus recognizing facial expressions.

7. Although a person's true emotion may "leak" in nonverbal signs, most people are poor at detecting lies, as discussed in "A Closer Look at Psychology and Public Policy." Mechanical "lie detectors" (polygraph machines) are not much better; innocent people may appear to be lying, and liars can learn to trick the machine—which is why Congress banned their use in employment applications and routine testing of employees.

8. Schachter and Singer's *two-factor theory* argued that emotions result from (1) *arousal* and (2) the *labeling* or interpretation of that arousal. Their classic experiment was never replicated, but it launched a slew of studies. People do sometimes mislabel their emotions when they are physiologically aroused and don't know why. But the cognitive processes involved in emotion are more complex than simple labeling, and "arousal" is too general to account for the varieties of emotion and emotional intensity.

9. One cognitive process involved in emotion is how people interpret and judge events. For example, people who feel depressed and lonely tend to think that

the reasons for their unhappiness are *internal, stable,* and *uncontrollable*. People who feel emotions intensely tend to *personalize* events, *pay selective attention*, and *overgeneralize*. Emotional range may be related to people's basic philosophy of life.

10. Some researchers distinguish *primary* emotions, which are thought to be universal, from *secondary* emotions, which include variations and blends that are specific to cultures. The primary emotions are usually identified as fear, anger, sadness, joy, surprise, and disgust. Other psychologists doubt that surprise and disgust are true emotions; they also think this list omits universal emotions, such as love, hope, empathy, and pride, that are difficult to measure physiologically.

11. Cultures influence the experience and expression of emotions. They determine what their members feel emotional about; whether intense feelings are seen as good or bad; and what people do when they feel an emotion. *Display rules* are the culture's way of regulating how, when, and where a person may express (or must suppress) an emotion. *Emotion work* is the effort a person makes to display an emotion he or she doesn't really feel.

12. People communicate their emotions (and many other messages) through *body language:* gesture, posture, body movement, touch, and mannerism. Cultures differ as widely in body language as in spoken language.

13. Women and men are equally likely to feel a wide array of emotions, from love to anger, but they often express their emotions differently. Women are more likely to reveal fear and loneliness; men are more likely to behave aggressively. Women seem to be slightly better than men at "reading" nonverbal body language, but this ability depends on status, familiarity with the other person, and whether the partners are of the same gender. Women do more "emotion work" than men, both at their jobs and in the family.

CHAPTER 10

Motivation

Sex is by no means everything. It varies, as a matter of fact, from only as high as 78 per cent of everything to as low as 3.10 per cent.

JAMES THURBER & E.B. WHITE

Pitcher Jim Abbott at work.

*A*ll that Jim Abbott ever wanted to do was play baseball. This is not an unusual ambition, perhaps, but Jim Abbott was born with a condition that might have dampened the motivation of most others: He has no right hand. You'd never know it to watch him play, though. His brilliant pitching earned the U.S. baseball team a gold medal in the 1988 Olympics and won for him a contract with a major-league team, the Angels. What would motivate a young man to pursue a goal that everyone told him was impossible?

All that Dian Fossey ever wanted to do was study mountain gorillas. This was not an unusual ambition, considering the varied interests that people have, but Dian Fossey's methods might have dampened the motivation of most others. Fossey lived in the wilderness with "her" gorillas, fought fiercely against the human poachers who were paid to kill or capture the animals, endured countless hardships and physical assaults, and was eventually murdered by unknown assailants. Many people have lived under temporary conditions of hardship to advance human knowledge, traveling to the North Pole or outer space. What would motivate a young woman to choose such hardship as a way of life, forgoing all comforts, family, and human love?

The fascination with motives has been with us from the beginning of humanity. The first crime committed in the Bible is a mystery of motive, not identification: We know Cain killed Abel, but why? Although detective stories are called "whodunits," detective work in fiction and in real life is really more a "*why*dunit." Without a "motive" for a crime, detectives have a more difficult time finding and prosecuting the criminal.

Many psychology textbooks put the study of *motivation* together with *emotion*. Both words come from the Latin root meaning "to move," and the psychology of motivation indeed aims to figure out what moves us, why we do what we do. Both processes involve cognition and physiology, and both processes are sources of great debate in the field. Emotion can certainly motivate us to behave in particular ways: Anger can move us to shout, love can move us to embrace, and fear can move us to run. But emotion is only one kind of motivating force. In general, **motivation** refers to an assumed process within a person (or animal) that causes that organism to move toward a goal. The goal may be to satisfy a biological need, as in eating a sandwich to reduce hunger. The goal may be to fulfill a social ambition, such as having fame, money, or a good marriage. In this chapter, we will consider some of the many motives that give human life and human character their diversity.

motivation *An inferred process within an animal or person that causes that organism to move toward a goal.*

The Push and Pull of Motivation

In Hugh Lofting's delightful book *The Story of Dr. Doolittle*, a shy but affectionate animal called a pushmi-pullyu turns up. The pushmi-pullyu has heads at both ends, so it can eat with one and talk with the other, and always knows where it is going (and why). When it comes to motivation, human beings are a bit like the pushmi-pullyu. Some biologically based motives, such as hunger and thirst, push us. If you go too long without food and water, your body will motivate you to seek them out. Other motives, social ones, pull us; they involve **incentives**, such as money, fame, or power, that draw us toward a goal. To see the difference between a biological need and an incentive, consider thirst. Your body doesn't care whether you satisfy your thirst by drinking water, prune juice, or a milkshake. But if you decide to treat yourself to a milkshake as a reward for two hours of study, that milkshake has become an incentive. You might not be thirsty at all.

Psychologists who study motivation, like those who study emotion, often disagree about what the phenomenon is, what causes it, and how to identify it. As the preceding example suggests, if you see someone drink a milkshake, you don't necessarily know that person's motive for doing so. The motive could be thirst, reward, or something else entirely. (Perhaps the person hates milkshakes but is being polite because her roommate brought it to her as a present.) Moreover, just as several emotions usually cluster together, so several motives may operate together, sometimes in different directions. A man may be motivated to achieve financial success and motivated to be a good father, but what happens when one motive conflicts with the other? Like the pushmi-pullyu, human beings are often pushed *and* pulled by competing forces.

When motives conflict

Two motives are said to be in conflict when the satisfaction of one leads to the inability to act on the other—when, for instance, you want to eat your cake and have it, too. Researchers have identified four basic kinds of motivational conflicts (K. Lewin, 1948):

1. *Approach-approach* conflicts occur when you are equally attracted to two or more possible activities or goals. For example, you would like to go out with Tom, Dick, *and* Harry; you would like to be a veterinarian *and* a cowboy; you would like to stay home with a great novel *and* go out to dinner with friends.

2. *Approach-avoidance* conflicts occur when one activity or goal has both a positive and a negative aspect. For example, a shy woman wants to go to a party with her friends, but she fears being awkward and lonely if she attends; she wants to approach the party and avoid it at the same time.

In an approach-avoidance conflict, both attraction and repulsion are strongest when you are nearest the goal. The closer you are to something appealing, the stronger your desire to approach; the closer you are to something unpleasant or frightening, the stronger your desire to flee (see Figure 10.1). However, as you step away from the goal, the two motives change in strength. The attractive aspects of the goal still seem appealing, but the negative ones seem less unpleasant. This may be one reason that people often have trouble resolving their ambivalence in approach-avoidance situations. When they leave a relationship that has some benefits but many problems, and consider it from a distance, they see its positive aspects and overlook the negative ones. So they approach it again. Up close, the problems appear more clearly, motivating them to avoid the relationship once more.

3. *Avoidance-avoidance* conflicts, which require you to choose between "the lesser of two evils," occur when you dislike two alternatives. Novice parachute

incentive *An external motivating stimulus, such as money, praise, or fame.*

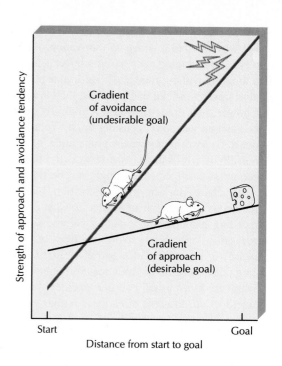

FIGURE 10.1

The approach-avoidance problem

When a goal is both appealing (good food) and punishing (because painful shock accompanies the food), an animal is motivated both to approach it and avoid it. As the animal gets closer to the goal, the desire to avoid pain rises more steeply than the desire to approach pleasure. At the point where the two tendencies intersect, the animal shows the greatest uncertainty and vacillation.

jumpers, for example, must choose between the fear of jumping and the fear of losing face if they don't jump (Epstein & Fenz, 1965).

4. *Multiple approach-avoidance* conflicts occur in situations that offer several possible choices, each containing advantages and disadvantages. For example, you might want to marry and settle down while you're still in school, and you think you have found the right person. On the other hand, you also want to establish a career and have some money in the bank, and lately you and the right person have been quarreling a lot.

Everyone has lived through one or another of these conflicts; conflict is inevitable, unless you are a garden slug. (Even slugs, for all we know, suffer endless approach-approach conflicts over which plant to eat.) But over time, unresolved conflicts have a physical and mental cost.

In a series of studies, students listed their 15 main ''personal strivings'': ''approach'' goals such as ''trying to be attractive'' or ''trying to seek new experiences,'' or ''avoidance'' goals such as ''trying to avoid being noticed by others'' or ''trying to avoid being dependent on my boyfriend.'' Next, they rated these objectives on the amount of conflict they caused and on how ambivalent they felt about them. (For example, striving ''to appear more intelligent than I am'' conflicts with striving ''to always present myself in an honest light.'') High degrees of conflict and ambivalence were associated with anxiety, depression, lowered well-being, physical symptoms (such as headaches, nausea, and dizziness), and increased visits to the student health center (Emmons & King, 1988).

A provocative finding of these studies is that the students in a state of conflict tended to *think* a great deal about their conflicts but not *do* anything to resolve them. One student, for instance, might remain unhappily stuck between his goal of ''achieving independence'' and his desire to continue to be cared for by his parents. The reconciliation of opposites, the researchers found, is ''a premier goal of human development'' and a cornerstone of well-being.

Primary drives and social motives

Generations ago, psychologists assumed that human beings were motivated by many instincts, or inborn patterns of behavior. They proposed nearly as many of these instincts as there were activities, from cleanliness to cruelty. But in the 1920s, the popularity of instinct theories faded, and the concept of instincts was replaced by that of drives (Hull, 1943).

According to drive theory, biological *needs* result from states of physical deprivation. Deprivation, in turn, produces a physiological *drive*, a state of tension that motivates a person (or animal) to satisfy the need. The cycle works like this: The body is deprived of something it physically needs, such as food or water; this need creates a drive; the person is then motivated to reduce the drive by finding food or drinking water, which satisfies the need. Just as there are only a few primary emotions, there are only a few primary drives, including hunger, thirst, excessive cold, and pain.

Drive theory depends on the concept of **homeostasis**, the tendency of the body to maintain itself in a steady, stable condition. Homeostasis works like a thermostat, which goes on when the temperature drops a few degrees and shuts off when it reaches its set level. The body has several "thermostats" to regulate internal temperature, blood sugar, water balance in the cells, and oxygen and carbon dioxide in the blood. If an imbalance occurs in any of these conditions, a need is created and the body will try to regain balance.

It soon became apparent that drive theory could not account for many human actions. Today the study of motivation, like the study of emotion, recognizes that people are conscious creatures who think and plan ahead, who set goals for themselves and plot strategies to reach them. **Social motives**, such as the need for friendship or power, are as important as primary drives in influencing people's actions. Social motives are learned, some in childhood, some in later life, and they are called "social" because they develop in the context of family, environment, and society (Geen, 1984). For some people, these motives can dominate biological needs. In the disorder of anorexia nervosa, the obsession to be thin and control one's body weight overrules hunger entirely. The anorexic may die of self-imposed starvation.

Yet motivation, again like emotion, is not solely a cognitive process. Physical energy fuels social motives as well as biological ones (McClelland et al., 1980). Two supposedly "basic" needs, food and sex, which we discuss next, reveal the complicated connections between mind and body.

Hunger

For most people, hunger, if left unsatisfied, can become a powerful motivator. Hungry people dream of and fantasize about food. Given access to food, they consume enormous quantities to try to eliminate the feeling of being ravenous. Starving people will gorge themselves until they return to their previous body weight, and dieting people often go on binges that bring them back to their previous size (Keys et al., 1950; Polivy & Herman, 1985).

Many people assume that hunger, eating, and weight all have a natural biological relationship to each other. "Normal" people occasionally feel hungry, they eat a little, and they maintain a "normal" body weight. "Abnormal" people feel excessively hungry, they eat too much, and so they gain weight (or else they rarely

homeostasis *The tendency of the body to maintain itself in a steady, stable condition with regard to physical processes.*

social motives *Learned motives, such as the need for affiliation, power, competence, or achievement, that are acquired through social experiences.*

feel hungry, eat too little, and are too thin). However, research does not support these common assumptions.

An early explanation of hunger and eating sought to find "hunger centers" and "satiation centers" in the brain, particularly in the hypothalamus. Early research suggested that the lateral hypothalamus (LH) was responsible for signals to "start eating," and the ventromedial hypothalamus (VMH) was responsible for signals to "stop eating." If you damage cells in the VMH of a rat, for example, the animal will gorge itself and get very fat. But it is too simple to say that the LH is a "hunger center" and the VMH is the "satiety center." Lesions in these areas produce many behavioral changes in rats, not just changes that affect eating. The quantity of food that lesioned animals eat does not depend only on damage to the hypothalamus. Finally, rats with lesions in the VMH will gain weight even if they are fed only as much as normal rats (Powley, 1977).

Another theory held that overweight is a sign of psychological disturbance, that people overeat in response to emotional problems. Research has failed to support this popular belief, too. Fat people are no more and no less neurotic, unhappy, tense, or depressed than average-weight people (Stunkard, 1976). If anything, emotional problems, such as tension or irritability, are a *result* of overweight and constant dieting, not a cause, in a society that discriminates against people who are heavier than the "ideal" (Bennett & Gurin, 1982).

By far the most popular theory—so widely accepted that hardly anyone bothered to test it—was that overweight is caused by overeating. Yet research now has clearly determined that *overweight is not caused simply by overeating*. Some overweight people do eat enormous quantities of food, but so do some very thin people. Some thin people eat very little, but so do some very fat people. In one study that carefully monitored everything that subjects were eating, two 260-pound women were maintaining their weights on only 1000 calories a day (Wooley, Wooley, & Dyrenforth, 1979). A study that asked volunteers to gorge themselves for months found that it was as hard for slender people to gain weight as it is for most heavy people to lose weight. The minute the study was over, the slender people lost weight as fast as dieters gained it back (Sims, 1974).

One theory that integrates these diverse findings on hunger, eating, and weight argues that body weight is governed by a **set point**, a homeostatic mechanism that keeps people at roughly the weight they are genetically designed to be. Set-point theorists claim that everyone has a genetically programmed *basal metabolism rate*, the rate at which the body burns calories for energy, and a fixed number of *fat cells*, cells in the body that store fat for energy. These cells may change in size (the amount of fat they contain), but never in number. After weight loss, they just lurk around the body, waiting for the chance to puff up again. According to set-point theory, there is no single area in the brain that keeps track of weight. Rather, an interaction of metabolism, fat cells, and hormones keeps people at the weight their bodies are designed to be. When a heavy person diets, the body slows down to conserve energy (and its fat reserves). When a thin person overeats, the body speeds up to burn energy.

The set-point weight is defined as "the weight you stay at when you aren't thinking about it"—that is, when you aren't trying to diet or gain but are eating whatever you want. Your set-point weight can also be thought of as the weight you tend to return to, like it or not, after you have tried to wrench yourself above it or below it (Stunkard, 1980).

Set-point theory was first supported by research with rats (Keesey, 1980; Peck, 1978). In one study, Jeffrey Peck put normal-weight rats, thinner-than-normal rats,

Overweight is caused mainly by overeating, isn't it? This idea is logical, obvious . . . and wrong. What other theories might explain why some slender people eat a lot, and some overweight people eat very little?

set point *According to one theory, a homeostatic mechanism that regulates food intake, fat reserves, and metabolism to keep an organism at its predetermined weight.*

Body shape and weight are strongly influenced by genetic factors. Set-point theory explains why the members of some Native American tribes of the Southwest (left) gain weight easily but lose it slowly, whereas the Bororo nomads of Niger (right) can eat a lot of food yet remain slender.

and fatter-than-normal rats in a series of experimental conditions. In one, a cold cage, the rats would have to eat more than usual to maintain body heat; and indeed, all the animals ate *more* than usual and maintained their existing body weights. In a second condition, the rats could control the intravenous intake of a rich eggnog, but they couldn't taste what they were eating or know how much food they were getting. Nevertheless, all the animals ate *less* than usual in order to maintain their existing body weights. Two researchers, commenting on these studies, noted, ''In effect, Peck was asking his animals: 'Which do you care about most, how fat you are, or how much you eat?' And the animals returned a clear answer: 'How fat we are' '' (Bennett & Gurin, 1982).

Studies of average-weight and heavy people support set-point theory in human beings, too (Roswell, Fishman, & Lubetkin, 1985). Obese people may eat the same amount of food as thinner people do, but their bodies convert excess calories into fat instead of burning them off. In a study of 171 Pima Indians in Arizona—a tribe in which two-thirds of the women and half of the men are obese—researchers found that the slower the metabolism, the greater the weight gain. Yet after adding anywhere from 20 to 45 pounds, the Pimas stopped gaining weight. Their metabolism rates rose, keeping their weights at the new, higher level (Ravussin et al., 1988). Moreover, the genetic disposition to gain weight is evident in infancy. In a study of 18 infants only 3 months of age, the babies of overweight mothers were generating 21 percent less energy than the babies of normal-weight mothers, although all the babies were eating the same amount. At one year of age, these lower-metabolism babies had become overweight (Roberts et al., 1988).

Set-point theory makes good evolutionary sense. People, like rats, are built to make the most efficient use and storage of food that might be available at unpredictable intervals. Our bodies allow us to "plump up" in times of plenty so that we will have energy reserves during times of famine. The body was designed long before the modern supermarket was.

Of course, some people do gain or lose weight and maintain the change. Set-point theorists explain that one influence on the set point is exercise, which boosts the body's metabolic rate. This is why changes in weight often accompany major changes in habits and activity levels. People start walking to work (or stop). They become unhappy and lethargic after losing a job (and gain weight), or euphoric and excited when they fall in love (and lose weight). In addition, as people age, their metabolic rate slows, making it harder to stay at the same weight (Bennett & Gurin, 1982). (In "Taking Psychology with You," we discuss weight and dieting further.)

How does the body adjust the set point? Why do some people become obese? Judith Rodin (1983, 1984) believes the answers do not lie in "failed will power" but in the hormone insulin. Insulin regulates the flow of glucose, a sugar, from the bloodstream into the body's cells. Since the cells usually do not need all this glucose, much of it is turned into fat for storage. Insulin increases fat stores, and it also works to prevent fat breakdown and keep the levels of free fatty acids in the blood low. At high levels, insulin makes you hungry, makes you eat more, and makes sweets taste better. When you eat glucose, say in a doughnut, your body produces more insulin to get that glucose from your blood to your cells, and the insulin level stays high for hours. In contrast, fructose (the sugar found in fruits) produces a much slower and lower rise in both blood sugar and insulin.

Rodin has identified a group of individuals, whom she calls "hyper-responders," whose insulin levels are actually "turned on" by the sight, sound, and smell of food. "Hyperresponders have a hard lot in life," says Rodin (1984). "They are easy prey for food ads and commercials, for doughnut shops and hot dog stands." They can be fat or thin, but it takes tremendous effort for them not to give in to their body's insulin plea for food.

Hunger, eating, and fat are not located in a single brain mechanism. They are part of a complex system in which brain mechanisms, fat cells, food intake, metabolism, and body chemistry all interact. Physiology, however, is just part of the motivation story. So you're hungry; now what?

Culture and ethnic background help determine how often people eat, what they eat, and with whom they eat. "Three square meals a day" is not, worldwide, the typical pattern. The "main meal" may be in the middle of the day (as is often true in farming communities) or very late in the evening (as is true in Mediterranean countries). Depending on your culture, you might eat lots of little meals throughout the day or only one large meal. What do you eat? People eat what their environment provides: whale meat for the Eskimos, lizards in South America, locusts in Africa, horses in France, dogs in Asia. Moreover, they don't eat the food their culture calls taboo: pork among Moslems and Orthodox Jews, cows in India, horses in America, deer among the Tapirapé (M. Harris, 1985). With whom do you eat? People tend to eat with those of their own social status or higher. They don't eat with those they consider their social inferiors, which in various cultures includes servants, children, or women (Bates, 1967).

The social influences on hunger often cause people to eat when they aren't hungry (to be sociable) or not to eat when they *are* hungry (because society tells them they are too fat or because the company or food is undesirable). The next time you contemplate the miracle of chocolate cake, think about the many motives that determine whether you gobble it up or push it away.

Almost everyone responds to the sight of a luscious dessert, but "hyperresponders" rush right out and eat one.

$QUICK$ ▪ $QUIZ$

Can you fill in the blanks?

1. Your mother gives you a choice of cleaning 12 years of junk out of the attic or cleaning 6 years of grease out of the oven. Deciding which of these chores to accept is an example of an _____ conflict.
2. The Smedleys have invited you over for dinner. You enjoy being with them but their meals are always as inedible as rocks. Accepting their invitation is an example of an _____ conflict.
3. The theory that explains hunger and weight as an interaction of metabolism, fat cells, and hormones is called _____ theory.
4. The flow of sugar from the bloodstream to cells is regulated by _____ .

Bonus: Which type of conflict is illustrated by the cartoon in the margin?

Answers:

Bonus: avoidance-avoidance

1. avoidance-avoidance   2. approach-avoidance   3. set-point   4. insulin

"C'mon, c'mon—it's either one or the other."

Sex

Almost anyone can tell the difference between food and sex, though we often use the same words in describing them: "appetite," "hungry," "satiated," "starved." A person will not live very long without food and water, but people can live long, healthy lives without sex.

Psychologists do not agree on whether human sexuality is a primary drive, like hunger, or even whether it is a "drive" at all (Singer & Toates, 1987). Biological factors, particularly having a minimum level of the hormone testosterone, may influence sexual desire in both sexes (McCauley & Ehrhardt, 1980). Men who are chemically castrated (given synthetic hormones that suppress the production or functioning of testosterone) often show a decrease in sexual desire. European studies of criminal sex offenders who had been castrated in this way find that most of the men lost their sexual urges, their ability to get an erection, and their capacity for orgasm (Wade & Cerise, in press). However, these effects are not inevitable, and the link between testosterone and sexual behavior poses the old chicken-and-egg problem. Testosterone may produce sexual arousal, but sexual arousal and activity may produce higher levels of testosterone.

In lower species, sexual behavior is genetically programmed. A male stickleback fish knows exactly what to do with a female stickleback, and a whooping crane knows when to whoop without instruction. As animals move up the evolutionary ladder, learning assumes a greater role in their sexual (and other) behavior. Most female animals, for instance, are sexually receptive to males only when they are "in heat" during ovulation, when the sex hormone estrogen is at its highest level. But among some primates, including human beings, sexual behavior can occur at all phases of the female's fertility cycle. In exchange for this opportunity, primates have to learn what to do with it. If you put an inexperienced male primate in a room with an experienced female, she will have to teach him the ropes. People must learn from experience, reinforcement, and cultural standards what they are supposed to *do* with their sexual desires. People learn what "turns them on," what parts of the body and what activities are "erotic," and even how to have sexual relations.

Virtually every human society thinks that its sexual practices and attitudes are the only "natural" ones (see "Think About It"). In certain times and places, for example, people have assumed that men have the greater sex drive, whereas women have weak sexual desires or none at all. In other societies, people have assumed that women have the greater sex drive and that men are the innocent victims of women's infinite lusts (Sherfey, 1973). Differences between men and women in the meanings and motives of sex are often a source of misunderstanding and resentment.

In America, men often complain, "Women never say what they mean. They *say* they don't want sex, but then they lead you on, come to your apartment, act seductive—and when you make a pass, they cry and get all indignant that you're 'forcing' them. They can't just enjoy sex for the pleasure of it. They're forever pestering you to love them." Women complain, "Men never honor their word. They *agree* not to pressure you to have sex, but then that's all they do. You try to be affectionate and friendly, and they immediately think you want to hop into bed. They're forever pestering you to have sex with them."

Think About It

What Is "Sexuality"?

Consider kissing. Westerners *like* to consider kissing. They like to do it, too. But if you think it is "natural," try to remember your first serious kiss—and all you had to learn about noses, breathing, position of teeth and tongue, and whatnot. Indeed, the sexual kiss is so complicated that most cultures in human history have never gotten around to it. Some tribes think that kissing another person's mouth—the very place that food enters!—is disgusting (Tiefer, 1978).

We are going to ask you now to think about a subject that is among the most passionate and personal in human life: sexuality. If any topic evokes emotional reasoning, this is it! The problem is that most people assume that their own practices and preferences are "normal," right, and universal; everyone who deviates must therefore be deviant, sick, and disgusting. This attitude tends to impede rational thinking about sex.

You may be amused, for instance, that anyone would find kissing "disgusting." But what is your reaction to pedophilia—sex between adults and children? Do you approve of a 50-year-old man having sex with a woman half his age? Then what do you think about a 50-year-old *woman* who has sex with a man half her age? What is your attitude about adultery, and does it matter whether the husband or the wife is having the affair? For that matter, what is your attitude about sex between husband and wife—is it your notion of bliss or boredom? Is homosexuality abnormal? What about heterosexuality?

In various times and places, each of these practices has been considered normal and erotic; each has been considered abnormal and disgusting. In classical Athens, husbands had to be directed *by law* to have sex with their wives three times a month, to ensure enough new citizens (Pomeroy, 1975). People must have been repulsed by the "disgusting" thought of marital sex.

Many people, on hearing these facts, jump to the wrong conclusion that "all sexual behavior is relative" or that "anything goes," including pedophilia and adultery. No: The point to understand is that *sexual behavior takes place in a larger network of rules, norms, and moral standards*. In Western societies, the sexual abuse of children is morally reprehensible and can have lasting harmful consequences (Stein et al., 1988). In tribes in which

Kissing, whether to convey tender affection, playfulness, or passionate desire, is an "acquired taste" and a learned skill.

childhood ends at puberty, however, early sexual initiation is considered necessary and appropriate. In a number of societies in Melanesia, boys are expected to have temporary homosexual relationships with older males as a normal part of growing up, a rite of passage on the route to manhood and marriage (Herdt, 1984). Shakespeare's Juliet was only 13 when she ran away with Romeo, an age at which most girls of that time were getting ready to marry; in the United States, Romeo would have been arrested for statutory rape.

Yet psychologists know very little about why people *within* a culture acquire the preferences and passions they do. We don't even know why people become heterosexual, much less homosexual. John Gagnon (1987) observes that most people believe there is a single behavioral pattern called "homosexuality," which is caused by a fundamental "defect." Once we locate this flaw, runs this argument, we will understand the "normal" nature of heterosexuality. So researchers have tried to find something wrong with homosexuals in their genetics, mothers, experiences, or brains.

The search for the "defect" has persisted, says

Gagnon, in spite of overwhelming evidence that it does not exist. No single theory can account for all the *varieties* of homosexuality or of heterosexuality. Some people are exclusively homosexual or heterosexual all their lives; but many others are not. Sexual preferences are deeply felt, but they often *change* over the life span, Gagnon notes, a fact that "single defect" theories cannot explain. Sexual behavior is a complex constellation of learning, hormones, cultural standards, experiences, and opportunities.

Consider the circumstances under which you acquired your own sexual orientation and other preferences, and whether you think they could change. Do you think you could be attracted to a person who is 20 years older than you? (Why do men and women answer that question differently?) Do you think you could be attracted to someone of the same gender, or, if you are gay, to someone of the opposite gender? To someone of another race? To someone who weighs 300 pounds? Why or why not? What are the cultural values, beliefs about sexual normalcy, and standards of erotic beauty that you have internalized? Think about it.

Physiologically, there are fewer sexual differences between men and women than you might think. There are the obvious anatomical differences, of course. But the basic processes of sexual arousal and release are very similar in both sexes. There is no way to know for sure that two people experience sexual pleasure the same way, any more than we can know for sure that two people see the same color blue. But when men and women subjectively describe their orgasms, judges cannot distinguish men's descriptions from women's. Both sexes report growing tension followed by feelings of warmth and release (Vance & Wagner, 1977). Yet research finds repeatedly that men and women continue to attribute different meanings to sexual activity, as we can see in their attitudes and actions.

Attitudes, motives, and signals. Sexual attitudes are related to larger social and political trends in a society. In the early 1960s, for instance, about half of all women had intercourse before marriage. In the 1970s, researchers found a shift toward more permissive attitudes and behavior and a decline of the double standard. By the late 1970s, the great majority of women and men were having sex outside of marriage (Sherwin & Corbett, 1985).

Nevertheless, aspects of the double standard persist today (Hyde, 1988). Throughout their lives, men are more likely than women to report having had casual sex, and they have more sexual partners than women do (Wade & Cerise, in press). In a study of more than 1000 teenagers, parents were still less tolerant of sexual activity of daughters than of sons, and teenage girls still worried about risking their reputations, although teenage boys did not (Coles & Stokes, 1985). In studies of college students across the country, women are, on the average, more conservative and idealistic about sex than men are, and men tend to be more permissive and liberal (Hendrick & Hendrick, 1987; Hendrick et al., 1985).

Even when the sexual *behavior* of men and women is alike, their sexual *motives* often differ. In many studies, men tend to be more "instrumental" in their motives for sex (regarding sex as a physical act for the purpose of pleasure); women are more "expressive" (regarding sex as an emotional act for the purpose of closeness). Men often rate sex as more important than love as a goal of dating; women tend to say that love is more important than sex (Peplau, 1984; Peplau, Rubin, & Hill, 1977). Even among older married couples, men tend to want their wives to be more experimental sexually, and women want their husbands to be more affectionate (Hatfield et al., 1982).

The instrumental-expressive difference in sexual motives often causes misunderstandings and crossed signals. Some men promise love in order to get sex, and some women give sex in order to get love. In the Coles and Stokes (1985) study, many of the female teenagers felt obliged to cooperate sexually with a boyfriend to please or keep him, rather than for their own pleasure. In numerous studies of college students, large numbers of women say they have experienced unwanted sex—not only through physical force (rape), but also through psychological pressure. In one survey of 275 undergraduate women, more than 50 percent said they had been pressured into kissing, fondling, and oral sex, and 43 percent felt pressured into having intercourse (Christopher, 1988). (These percentages vary from school to school but are consistently high.) Women say they "give in" for a variety of motives: because it is easier than having an argument; because they don't want to lose the relationship; because they feel obligated, once the partner has spent a lot of time and money on them; because the partner makes them feel guilty or inhibited; or because of verbal or physical coercion (M. Lewin, 1985; Muehlenhard & Cook, 1988).

For their part, many men feel obliged to "make a move" when they don't want to. In a study of 71 college men who admitted to having coerced their dates into having sex with them, Eugene Kanin (1985) found that these young men had, from early adolescence, been pressured by male friends to "prove their masculinity" by "scoring." And in one survey of 993 undergraduates, 63 percent of the men reported having had unwanted intercourse (Muehlenhard & Cook, 1988). The main reasons for doing so, the men said, were peer pressure, inexperience, a desire for popularity, and a fear of seeming homosexual or "unmasculine." More men than women reported having gotten sexually aroused while drunk, having sex, and regretting it later.

College students, particularly young white women, seem to be under particular pressure to have unwanted sex. In a *representative* survey of 3312 white and Hispanic men and women, 14 percent of the women and 7 percent of the men, and more than twice as many whites as Hispanics, reported having been subjected to sexual assault at any time in their adult lives. But the numbers were even higher among college students: 26 percent of the non-Hispanic women (and 12 percent of the men). Women were more likely than men to have been harmed during the assault or threatened with harm; the "unwanted sex" for men tended to be a result of "pressure for sexual contact" (Sorenson et al., 1987). Another representative sample found no differences between black women and white women: Fully one-third reported having been sexually abused (Wyatt, 1988).

Men and women often misread each other's body language, with unhappy results. In one study of 400 teenagers, ages 14 to 17, researchers found major misunderstandings about sexual signals. In general, boys thought almost everything was a sexual signal! They were more likely to regard tight clothing, certain situations (such as being alone in a room), and affectionate actions (such as a girl's playing with her date's hair or gazing into his eyes) as signs of willingness for sex. The girls were more likely to regard tight clothing as a sign of being fashionable, and being alone with a date or behaving affectionately simply as signs of—well, affection (Giarrusso et al., 1979; Zellman & Goodchilds, 1983). Yet both sexes agreed that once a girl had "led a boy on," his loss of control was her responsibility.

Keep in mind that we are talking about *average* differences between men and women, not absolutes. Still, this subject tends to produce emotional reasoning and defensiveness. What are some of the reasons for the continuing "battle of the sexes," which all too often seems to be a literal battle?

Is she dressing provocatively or comfortably? Boys and girls often disagree on the answer.

The prism of gender. Every society sets certain norms that specify ideal love and ideal sex. These norms, in turn, are shaped by a society's **gender roles**, collections of rules that determine the "proper" attitudes and behavior for men and women. There are, of course, many variations in attitude and behavior among the many groups that make up a national population, but some consistent differences between men and women remain. As we will see in Chapter 18, people play many roles in society. During childhood and adolescence, they learn the "scripts" that fit each role.

According to John Gagnon and William Simon (1973), sexual "scripts" teach boys and girls what to consider erotic or sexy, and how to behave in dating and sex. In this view, biology influences sexuality only indirectly. Adolescent males have spontaneous erections and eventually orgasms; boys often talk and joke about masturbation with their friends. Female anatomy, however, makes the discovery of masturbation and orgasm less certain. Male sexuality is learned in a competitive atmosphere where the goal is to impress other males. While boys are learning about physical sex, girls are learning to value the emotional aspects of relationships and to make themselves attractive. By adulthood, according to Simon and Gagnon (1969), male sexuality has become genitally focused and emotionally detached, compared

gender role *A set of norms that defines socially approved attitudes and behavior for men and women.*

to that of females. Female sexuality is more closely connected to love and marriage.

In an update of their theory, Simon and Gagnon (1986) argue that people follow three kinds of sexual scripts. *Cultural* scripts describe the larger culture's requirements for proper sexual behavior. Are women, for example, supposed to be sexually adventurous and assertive or sexually modest and passive? The answers vary from culture to culture. However, although people may know what their culture expects of them in general, not everyone follows its rules specifically. Sexual behavior also depends on *interpersonal* scripts, the rules of behavior that a couple develops in the course of their relationship. For example, will one be dominant and one passive? The answers for any individual differ depending on the relationship itself, and may change as the relationship changes. Finally, individuals follow their own *intrapsychic* scripts, scenarios for ideal or fantasized sexual behavior that develop out of a person's own unique history and experiences.

Because women have been concerned with finding and keeping a secure relationship, some theorists maintain, they have consciously or unconsciously regarded sex as a bargaining chip. It is an asset to be rationed rather than an activity to be enjoyed for its own sake. This attitude is reflected in language, when people talk of a woman "giving herself" to, or "saving herself" for, a man. What happens, then, when a young woman who views sex as a valuable resource has intercourse early in a relationship? She may rationalize that she was "swept away" by candlelight and passion. (In fact, many young women are reluctant to use birth control because it implies a conscious choice to have sex.) She may convince herself that she is wildly in love with her partner instead of mildly interested or simply sexually aroused. She may tell herself that he is wildly in love with her, despite evidence to the contrary (Cassell, 1984).

Understanding sexual attitudes and behavior as part of a larger pattern of gender roles helps explain why men initiate sex more often, why women tend to reject casual sex, why women "give in" and men "make a move" when they don't really want to, and why both sexes regard women as the sexual "referees." Knowing the scripts for one's gender role has benefits; they provide a familiar set of guidelines for dealing with the complexities of male-female relationships. But they can also create misunderstandings and unhappiness, and once someone has learned the script, changing the lines is not so easy—even when it seems as though men and women are in different plays. There are pressures on both sexes to conform to social rules. Perhaps if men and women understand the ways they are both caught in the roles of gender, they can revise the script to suit their common goals.

QUICK ▪ QUIZ

Which sex is more likely to

1. Have casual sexual relations?
2. Be more "instrumental" in their sexual motives?
3. Be more "expressive" in their sexual motives?
4. Interpret many situations and signals as sexual?
5. Have subjectively "better" orgasms?

Answers:
1. M 2. M 3. F 4. M 5. neither

The Curious Animal: Motives to Explore, Play, and Understand

You have just had a great meal. Your hunger and thirst are sated, the indoor temperature is comfortably mild, and you are feeling no pain. If you were motivated only by primary drives, you would then sit in your chair like a hibernating bear for hours, even days. You wouldn't move until hunger pangs sent you to the refrigerator, or until someone pricked you with pins to make you get up. But you are also governed by motives that will move you off that chair before the spring thaw. These are the motives of curiosity, play, and exploration. They are the reason you will get up to see what that noise in the basement is, or find out what's in the nice fat package that just arrived, or join the neighbors for volleyball.

Now let's say your sister calls with puzzling and shocking news: A student in your class has murdered his wife. You know him; he seems a shy, friendly person. You spend an hour on the phone, trying to make sense of this act of unpredictable violence. Your behavior is motivated by your desire to understand, to make sense of events, to put your belief about your classmate (''a nice guy'') into line with his action (killing his wife). In hundreds of small ways as well as major ones, we are governed by the cognitive motives to understand and organize experience.

Curiosity and play: Some behavioral motives

''Curiosity killed the cat,'' parents warn their snooping children or inquisitive neighbors, but actually curiosity helps our species survive. It is the motive that impels us to find out what things are, what they mean, and whether they are dangerous or useful.

We might think of human beings as falling somewhere along the Sloth-Otter Scale. The sloth is probably the laziest creature on the planet. Sloths defy laws of survival, for they are so lethargic that they won't even run away from danger or discomfort. (One scientist put a plastic bowl on a sloth's head, and it remained there until the scientist removed it—two days later.) When sloths aren't sleeping, they are hanging motionless from tree branches. In contrast, the otter is nature's clown. It loves to play. It is creative. Karen Pryor, a professional animal trainer, told us that if you teach a tiger or a dolphin to jump through a hoop, the animal will do it the same way ever after. But an otter will go through the hoop a new way every time—backwards, running, sliding, creeping—just for the fun of it.

Some psychologists regard curiosity as a form of information processing, a way that people learn new things about their environments and assimilate the information. Others study individual differences in curiosity and how learning and environmental conditions can suppress this motive or encourage it. But everyone agrees that curiosity is a key motive in human behavior (Voss & Keller, 1983).

Familiarity versus novelty. Human beings are constantly balancing their affection for the familiar with their curiosity about the unfamiliar. In a series of experimental studies, Robert Zajonc (1968) showed that the more familiar people are with something, the more they like it, whether the ''it'' is a supermarket product, a politician, or a nonsense syllable like ZUG. But once familiar with an environment, many species are motivated to seek novelty. If a rat has had its dinner, it will prefer exploring an unfamiliar wing of a maze rather than the familiar wing where food is. A human baby will stop eating if something or someone new enters his or her range of vision. The interest in novelty starts early. A new object or event will provoke either curiosity and exploration or fear and flight, depending on its complexity and unpredictability (Berlyne, 1960).

Although homeostasis technically refers to biological conditions, some psychologists apply the idea to psychological states as well. For instance, most people seek a balance between novelty and stability. If your life veers off too wildly, for too long, in the direction of unpredictable change, you may eventually be motivated to seek calmer seas. If you feel you have lived too long in boring stability, "a rut," you may be motivated to seek a change.

Other researchers regard risk taking and the love of adventure as characteristic aspects of personality. In this view, some people are unflappably cool, whereas others want the most excitement they can get, because they differ in the level of arousal that is most comfortable to them. To assess a person's optimal arousal, Marvin Zuckerman (1979, 1983) developed a Sensation Seeking Scale to measure the strength of the motivation for excitement, risk, sensation, and adventure. He finds that "sensation seeking" seems to be a consistent quality in individuals. Sensation seekers like risky activities, new adventures, driving too fast, mood-changing drugs, tasting new foods, and sexual variety (Bates, Labouvie, & White, 1986; Carroll, Zuckerman, & Vogel, 1982). They regard a peaceful life as "boring" rather than "stable"; they think a life of adventure and change is "exciting" rather than "foolhardy."

Exploration and manipulation.   All birds and mammals are motivated to explore and investigate. Primates especially like to "monkey around" with objects, taking them apart and scrutinizing the pieces, apparently for the sheer pleasure of it. Monkeys will learn how to operate mechanical gizmos without food or other reward (Harlow, Harlow, & Meyer, 1950). From the first, human babies explore and manipulate their small worlds. They grasp whatever is put in their tiny hands, they shake rattles, they bang pots. As they grow, they keep exploring, tasting, and investigating. Children will play spontaneously with items that honk, rattle, and ring. The motive to handle interesting objects can be overwhelming, which is why the command "don't touch" is often ignored by children, museum-goers, and shoppers.

Play.   Many animal species, including human beings, have an innate motive to play—to fool around and to imitate others (Huizinga, 1950). Think of kittens and lion cubs, puppies and pandas, and all young primates, who will play with and pounce on each other all day until hunger and naptime call. Play is not the same as games, which are organized activities that may bear only a passing resemblance to the spirit and purpose of play. For many people, games are hard work and not fun at all.

Ethologists observe that the young of many species enjoy *practice play*, behavior that will later be used for "serious" purposes when they are adults. A kitten, for example, will stalk and attack a ball of yarn (Vandenberg, 1985). In human beings, play is part of a child's socialization; the child "plays at" being a cowboy, parent, teacher, or astronaut. Play with peers also teaches the young how to get along with others (Harlow & Harlow, 1966).

Some psychologists have argued that the motives for play and exploration are biologically adaptive because they help a species to find more food and other necessities of life and to cope with its environment. This may be so, but the curiosity and play motives seem to have developed independently of any other biological motives. Moreover, some observers believe that emphasizing the biological similarities

Play and playfulness take on many forms all through life. Young children play elaborate fantasy games. Adults, like this fellow in rabbit gear, enjoy planned play and spontaneous silliness.

between human play and the play of other animals ignores the ways in which human play is different. Children's play doesn't always imitate adult rules and activities; it often breaks adult rules and generates its own (Sutton-Smith, 1984).

What is unique about human play, to some researchers, is that it celebrates imagination, storytelling, and hope for the future. In fantasy play, children create imaginary worlds that structure and give meaning to experience. This ability is central to human experience (Vandenberg, 1985).

Consistency and understanding: Some cognitive motives

A friend of ours moved from California to Oklahoma to go to graduate school. She was miserable about living in Oklahoma, because ever since seeing *The Wizard of Oz* at the age of 8 she had been afraid of tornadoes. "Tornadoes?" the Oklahomans said to her in amusement. "There's nothing to be afraid of. How could *you* live in California, with all those *earthquakes*?"

Most people are motivated to justify and explain what they do and what they believe. So reliable is this motive that psychologists can accurately predict what our friend will do. Having chosen to live in Oklahoma, she will begin to agree with the natives that tornadoes aren't so frightening. The real dangers occur to people who live far away, in California or India.

Years ago, Fritz Heider (1946, 1958) developed "the principle of cognitive balance" to explain such changes of mind. The mind, said Heider, seeks to keep information in balance. If you get a new piece of information that doesn't fit your beliefs, or if the opinions of a man you admire differ from your own, you are thrown into a state of imbalance and you will try to regain mental equilibrium. In the first case, you might reject the new information to keep your ideas intact and consistent. In the second case, you might change your opinion of the man you admire, or change your own views to agree with his.

Preacher Jimmy Swaggart confessed to having sex with a prostitute, and begged his congregation to forgive him. How would his followers resolve the conflict between "I revere this man" and "He committed a sin"? Dissonance theory predicts that they will either revere him less or decide his sin wasn't all that bad.

Time and again doomsday predictions fail. Have you ever wondered why people who wrongly predict a devastating earthquake or the end of the world don't feel embarrassed when their forecasts flop?

cognitive dissonance *A state of tension that occurs when a person simultaneously holds two cognitions that are psychologically inconsistent or when a person's belief is inconsistent with his or her behavior.*

Heider's work was expanded by Leon Festinger (1957), who proposed the theory of **cognitive dissonance**. "Dissonance," the opposite of consistency ("consonance"), is a state of tension that occurs when a person simultaneously holds two cognitions (thoughts, beliefs) that are psychologically inconsistent, or holds a belief that is incongruent with the person's behavior. This tension is uncomfortable, and someone in a state of dissonance will be motivated to reduce it.

For example, cigarette smoking is dissonant with the awareness that "smoking causes illness." The smoker might change the behavior, and try to quit. Or she might reject the cognition "smoking is bad." She could deny the Surgeon General's report ("There's no real evidence"). She could persuade herself that she will quit later on ("after these exams"). She could emphasize the benefits of smoking ("A cigarette helps me relax"). Or she could decide she doesn't want a long life, anyhow ("It will be shorter, but sweeter"). In all of these cases, the smoker is motivated to reduce dissonance because the behavior, smoking, is out of kilter with the smoker's knowledge of the dangers of that behavior.

Cognitive dissonance theory applies to many daily experiences. The harder you work to achieve a goal, the theory predicts, the more you will value the goal, even if the goal itself isn't so great after all. In one experiment, young women who expended little or no effort to join a boring discussion group saw the experience for what it was, a dull waste of time. But those who went through a severe and embarrassing initiation rite convinced themselves that the same discussion group was interesting and worthwhile (Aronson & Mills, 1959). This experiment illustrates why hazing, whether in social clubs or the military, turns new recruits into loyal members. The cognition "I went through a lot of awful stuff to join this group" is dissonant with the cognition " . . . only to find I hate the group." So people must decide either that the hazing wasn't so bad or that they really like the group. This mental reevaluation is called the *justification of effort.*

You can see cognitive dissonance at work among the growing number of true believers who are predicting that doomsday is at hand. Such predictions are especially popular at the end of every century, so we predict that you will be hearing some lulus as the year 2000 dawns. Forecasts of Armageddon, the ultimate war between good and evil, are already on the rise; a man named Edgar Whisenant predicted one for September 11, 1988, and thousands of people believed him. (Many ran up large bills on their charge accounts, on the grounds that Christ would return before their monthly statements did.) In California, quacks and hustlers are forever taking advantage of people's worry about earthquakes (which do occur) by making specific forecasts of when the Big One will hit. Hundreds of people have been known to leave their jobs or flee the state on the basis of these predictions.

Do you ever wonder what happens to these believers when the prophecy fails? Do they ever say, "Boy, what a jerk I was; never again"? What would dissonance theory predict?

Festinger and two associates took advantage of a chance to study a group of people, led by a mystic they called Marian Keech, who believed that the world would end on December 21. Keech promised that the faithful would be picked up by a flying saucer and whisked to safety at midnight on December 20. Many of these believers quit their jobs and spent their money in anticipation of the end. What would they do or say to reduce the dissonance between "The world is still muddling along on the 21st" and "I predicted the end of the world and sold all my worldly possessions"?

The researchers joined the group to find out. They predicted that believers who had made no public commitment to the prophecy, who awaited "the end of the world" by themselves at home, would simply lose their faith. But the believers who acted on their conviction, waiting with Keech for the spaceship, would be in a state of dissonance. They would, said the researchers, have to *increase* their religious belief to avoid the cognition that they had behaved foolishly. That is just what happened. At 4:45 A.M., long past the appointed hour of the saucer's arrival, the leader had a new "vision." The world had been spared, she said, because of the impressive faith of their little band (Festinger, Riecken, & Schachter, 1956).

Cognitive dissonance theory thus predicts how people will receive and process information that conflicts with their existing ideas. They don't always do so "rationally," that is, by accepting new facts that are well documented. You rarely hear someone say, cheerfully, "Oh, thank you for explaining to me why my lifelong philosophy of child-raising is wrong! I'm so *grateful* for your facts!" The person usually says, "Oh, buzz off, and take your cockamamie ideas with you."

There are certain problems, however, with the original theory. It is often difficult to determine when two cognitions are "inconsistent": What is dissonant to one person may be neutral or pleasingly eccentric to another. Some people reduce dissonance by admitting their mistakes instead of trying to justify them. But there is now vast evidence of a motive for cognitive consistency under some conditions. Cognitive imbalance does seem to produce a state of tension that feels physically uncomfortable (Elkin & Lieppe, 1986), particularly when the inconsistent cognitions violate one's self-concept (Aronson, 1988).

Theories of cognitive balance and dissonance assume an even more fundamental motive: a need to organize and understand experience in terms of some general belief system. All societies have constructed religious, ethical, and political beliefs that account for how the world works (and that justify the way their particular society works). All civilizations, from the dawn of human history, have sought to understand the great mysteries of life and death. The desire to understand is one of the most powerful motives in human psychology.

Cognitive dissonance theory predicts the "justification of effort": The harder you work for a goal, the more you will like or value it afterwards. These men in basic training should become extremely devoted soldiers!

QUICK ■ QUIZ

A. Which motives do the following actions illustrate?

1. A 2-year-old climbing all over the furniture
2. Denying evidence that disputes your beliefs
3. Three children dressing in adult clothes
4. A monkey taking apart a jigsaw puzzle

   a. cognitive disso-
      nance reduction
   b. exploration
   c. manipulation
   d. practice play

B. Now, test your understanding of cognitive dissonance. In a classic study, students had to do a series of boring, repetitive tasks for an hour (Festinger & Carlsmith, 1959). Then they had to tell another student, who was waiting to participate in the study, that the work was interesting and fun. Half of the students were given $20 for telling this lie, and the others only $1. Which students decided that the tasks were fun after all?

Answers:

A. 1. b 2. a 3. d 4. c B. The students who were paid only $1. They were the ones in a state of dissonance: "The task was as dull as dishwater" is dissonant with "I enjoyed it—and for a mere dollar, at that." Since they couldn't change the fact of the dollar, they changed their judgment that the task was truly dull. But the students who got $20 felt no dissonance; they felt justified in lying because they were well paid.

The Social Animal: Motives to Love

The **need for affiliation** refers to the motive to be with others, to make friends, to cooperate, to love. Our lives would be impossible without affiliation. Human development depends on the child's ability to care for and learn from others; adult life depends on social relations with friends, family, strangers, and colleagues.

Most American social scientists have, naturally, studied American society, which values achievement, power, and success. Thus they have not paid as much attention to affiliation as to these other motives (Spence, 1985). Moreover, the study of achievement, power, and success usually has been based on men. One consequence of this lopsided emphasis is the assumption that the "basic nature of man" is fundamentally competitive and power-oriented. In the last decade, some researchers have argued that the "basic nature of man and woman" is fundamentally cooperative and attachment-oriented. Indeed, they argue, without affiliation and cooperation, human societies would never have survived (Dahlberg, 1981; Kohn, 1986; Tanner & Zihlman, 1976).

Attachment and affiliation

need for affiliation *The motive to associate with other people, as by seeking friends, moral support, contact comfort, or companionship.*

Harry Harlow (1958) first demonstrated the primate need for *contact comfort* by raising infant rhesus monkeys with two kinds of artificial mothers. The first was a forbidding construction of wires and warming lights, with a milk bottle attached. The second was constructed of wire and covered in foam rubber and cuddly terry cloth (see Figure 10.2). At the time, psychologists (but not many mothers) thought

that babies become attached to their parents because the parent provides food and warmth. But Harlow's baby monkeys ran to the terry cloth "mother" when they were frightened or startled, and cuddling it calmed them down. As any reader of "Peanuts" knows, you should never try to take away a child's security blanket.

Infants become attached to their mothers (or caretakers) for the contact comfort the adults provide. John Bowlby (1969, 1973) proposed that infant attachment has two additional purposes. It provides a secure base from which the child can explore the environment, and it provides a haven of safety to which the child can return when he or she is afraid. A sense of security, said Bowlby, allows children to develop cognitive skills. A sense of safety allows them to develop trust. Severe social deprivation and continued separations from loved ones prevent children from forming attachments, with tragic results.

The need for, and pleasure in, physical contact starts at birth and lasts until death. Babies who are given adequate food, water, and warmth, but who are deprived of being touched and held, show retarded emotional and physical development (Bowlby, 1969). Emotional and physical symptoms also occur in adults who are "undertouched" in our society, such as the sick and the aged. One of the greatest powers a doctor has is touching the patient, especially since friends and family typically *stop* touching someone who is ill. A "laying on of hands" is not usually sufficient to cure disease, but it reassures and comforts, and reassurance and comfort are half the battle (Thomas, 1983).

Individuals vary in their need for affiliation. Some like "lots of space," and some like to be surrounded by friends. Cultures, too, vary in the value they place on affiliation. American culture emphasizes personal independence and self-reliance, but other cultures, such as the Japanese, emphasize group interdependence and teamwork (Pascale & Athos, 1981). In our society dependence is almost a dirty word, but in Japan the need for dependence is assumed to be so powerful that, as we noted in Chapter 9, Japanese has its own word for the motive, *amaeru* (Doi, 1973). In fact, whatever one's culture, people are "dependent"; but they depend on one another for different things at different ages. A baby is totally dependent on its parents, but gradually develops the ability to act and think independently.

Researchers—and laypeople—continue to debate whether men or women are the "dependent sex" or are better at "affiliation." According to Carol Gilligan

FIGURE   10.2

The comfort of contact *Infants need cuddling as much as food. In Harry Harlow's studies, infant rhesus monkeys were raised with a terry cloth "mother" that was cuddly to cling to and with a bare wire "mother" that provided milk. The infants preferred clinging to the terry mother when they weren't being fed, and when they were frightened or startled, it was the terry "mother" they ran to. "Man does not live," concluded Harlow, "by milk alone."*

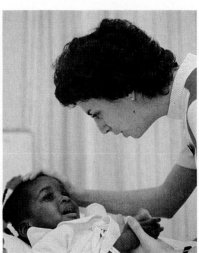

Human beings respond to "contact comfort," whether from the reassuring presence of a loved pet or from the reassuring touch of a caretaker.

(1982), many young men regard attachment as a source of danger and threat; many young women regard attachment as a source of safety and intimacy. She supports her argument with the stories that people tell in response to pictures. One study found that men were more than twice as likely as women to see danger and threat in pictures of people described as having "an intimate bond" between them (Helgeson & Sharpsteen, 1987).

Before we all jump to the apparent conclusion that "men fear closeness" and women pursue it, consider these warnings: First, not all studies find a sex difference. One research team found no differences and called the whole idea "a common and perhaps repressive stereotype" (Benton et al., 1983). Second, *even in the studies that do find differences, the differences are tiny.* Men may be "twice as likely" to see danger in affiliation, but do we really want to draw conclusions about "men and women" when the numbers in question are 18 percent to 8 percent (Helgeson & Sharpsteen, 1987)?

Perhaps a more reasonable conclusion, based on studies of close relationships, is that both sexes depend on each other, although sometimes for different things (S. Brehm, 1985). In a family, the spouse who isn't working is financially dependent on the one who is. The spouse who can't express feelings is emotionally dependent on the one who can. It's hard to find true loners. Even the Lone Ranger had Tonto.

Love

"How do I love thee? Let me count the ways," wrote Elizabeth Barrett to Robert Browning. Social psychologists have also counted the ways of loving (although not as prettily as Barrett did). Zick Rubin, one of the first psychologists to develop a questionnaire to measure the meanings of love, asked people to distinguish their feelings for lovers from their feelings for friends. He found that *love*, at least among dating couples, has to do with intimacy (sharing innermost thoughts and feelings), attachment, and caring, and was distinctly different from *liking*, which has to do with affection and respect (Rubin, 1970, 1973).

How do people differ in their styles of love? Shall we count the ways? There have been many efforts to define kinds of love and to determine which ones are related to happy and enduring relationships.

▪ *Passionate ("romantic") versus companionate love.* This basic distinction contrasts *passionate* love, characterized by a turmoil of intense emotions, with *companionate* love, characterized by affection and trust (Hatfield, 1988). Passionate love is emotionally intense, *the* focus of one's life, highly sexualized, and often feels unstable and fragile. Companionate love is calmer, *a* focus of one's life, not necessarily sexualized, and feels stable and reliable—more like liking. Passionate love is the stuff of crushes, infatuations, "love at first sight," and the early stage of love affairs. It may "burn out" completely or subside into companionate love.

Psychologists disagree about the purpose and origins of passionate love. Some believe it is rooted in our evolutionary biology: Passionate love sees to it that couples bond together; reproduce; look after each other; and stay together in spite of having the flu, mortgages, and housework (Buss, 1988). Others, such as Sharon Brehm (1988), reply that sexual pleasure is sufficient to ensure the reproduction of the species, and long-term bonding depends on a lot more than intense passions. She believes that passionate love—an "intense combination of imagination and emotion"—motivates people "to construct a vision of a better world and to try to bring it about in reality." Still others maintain that passionate love is a modern, Western invention, one that individualistic cultures celebrate and community-oriented cultures distrust (Dion & Dion, 1988; Hunt, 1967). Asians, for example, are less likely than Anglos and blacks to endorse romantic love as their ideal (Hendrick & Hendrick, 1986).

▪ *The six styles of love.* In the early 1970s, John Alan Lee (1973, 1988) expanded these two categories into six different "styles of loving," which he labeled with Greek names. The three basic ones are *ludus* (game-playing love), *eros* (romantic, passionate love), and *storge* [pronounced stor-gay] (affectionate, friendly love). Three secondary styles are *mania* (possessive, dependent, "crazy" love), *pragma* (logical, pragmatic love), and *agape* [ah-GA-pay] (unselfish, brotherly love).

These six types have been validated empirically in two studies with more than 1300 students (Hendrick & Hendrick, 1986). A romantic, "erotic" lover (who believes in true love, instant chemistry, and abiding passion) is very different from a "ludic" lover (who enjoys playing the game of love with several partners at once, who enjoys the chase more than the catch). A pragmatic lover (who chooses a partner according to a "shopping list" of compatible traits) is unlike a "storgic" lover (who believes true love grows out of long friendship).

"Personals" columns are a good place to see the styles of love, as shown by the magazine excerpts in the margin. Some people are looking for "affectionate, friendly" love (A); others are more playful (B). Some pragmatic types have a whole shopping list of requirements (C), while others have a minimum standard (D). Occasionally you find someone (E) who is either refreshingly candid or just having a good time.

▪ *The triangle theory of love.* Robert Sternberg (1988) has proposed a "triangle" theory, in which love consists of *passion*, *intimacy*, and *commitment*. To Sternberg, love differs according to the emphasis that individuals place on each of these elements and how they combine them. To use Lee's terms, a ludic lover may seek passion only; an erotic, romantic lover values passion and intimacy without commitment; a pragmatic lover may prefer intimacy and commitment without passion. Two people can have an intimate friendship in which they share their deepest feelings, but Sternberg would call this "liking," not love.

▪ *The attachment theory of love.* Another effort to describe styles of love is based on the human need for attachment: the sense of almost physical connection with a loved one and of physical loss when a loved one leaves. In Chapter 13 we

Beautiful inside and out, SWF, 35, slender, professional, bright, communicative, sensitive, loving, seeks emotionally and financially secure SWM, 35-45, to share affection, honesty, laughter, friendship, love. Note/Phone/Photo   (A)

Successful, attractive, sexy, published/produced writer (books, TV, Village Voice, Playboy), 38, not secretly yearning to be a director. Likes Don Mattingly, KCRW, making waffles & staying out late. Wants successful, interesting & well-read guy who enjoys his career, for dinner dates during world series & possible post season play. Please tell me about yourself. Photo optional.   (B)

Looking for a permanent best friend/lover, 25-35, with a 3 digit IQ, big heart, skinny legs. Race unimportant. But, **MUST** be honest, kind, witty, sensuous, confident, compassionate, adventurous, competent, reliable, and looking for a future with love, sincerity, children and time zone changes. Letter/photo/phone.   (C)

DESPERATELY SEEKING SUSAN, or Mary, or Evelyn, or Nancy or Lorraine or? (D)

Seeking an ugly, overweight, short woman lacking style, intelligence & humor. Hopefully she smokes, is in lousy shape & wouldn't know "sensitive" if it bit her on the butt. I'm dumpy, balding, unattractive & not in my early 30's. I don't work out. I'm stuck in a deadend job, smoke like a chimney & I'm a compulsive liar. Note, photo & phone not necessary.   (E)

The gaze of love is unmistakeable, even after years together.

will discuss a controversial theory that describes three kinds of infant attachment to the mother: secure, anxious/ambivalent, and avoidant. Cindy Hazan and Phillip Shaver (1987) believe that adult styles of love originate in these early styles of infant-parent attachment—the baby's first and most important "love relationship."

According to this research, some couples are securely attached to each other; they aren't jealous, nervous, or worried about being abandoned. Others are always anxious or ambivalent about the relationship and fretting over it; they want to be close but worry that their partners will leave them. And some people distrust and avoid all intimate attachments (Shaver, Hazan, & Bradshaw, 1988). To use Lee's terms again, romantic lovers are likely to be securely attached; manic lovers are anxious and ambivalent; and ludic lovers are avoidant.

So far, these theories are largely descriptive, and the overlap among them suggests they are describing the same things. All imply that some styles of love are better suited to satisfying relationships than others. In one study that compared couples who remained together with those who split up, the former were more erotic, less ludic, more intimate (disclosing of feelings and thoughts), and higher in commitment (Hendrick, Hendrick, & Adler, 1988). The success of a relationship, these theories agree, also depends not on whether both partners "love" each other, but on whether they love each other in the same way. This suggests that when someone says "I love you," perhaps you should reply, "What exactly do you mean by that?"

Some people seem to have characteristic styles of love that reflect their personalities (Dion & Dion, 1988). Perhaps they consistently avoid commitment; perhaps they are "sensation seekers" who thrive on passionate love. Yet all four theories hold that most people can, and do, change their styles of love over time and with new partners. The most pragmatic, unromantic person can be struck by the thunderbolt and have a passionate interlude. The most game-playing, "no-marriage-for-me" ludic lover may, with the right person, become deeply committed to a companionate, affectionate relationship. And lovers who are insecurely attached as young adults may find secure attachments later on (Hazan & Shaver, 1987).

Men and women spend a lot of time, especially after a breakup, debating which sex is "better at love." Would they be better off asking whether men and women love differently, and if so, how?

Do men and women differ in love? If you looked at the best-selling books about "women who love too much" or "women men love, women men leave," you would think so. Actually, there is no evidence that one sex loves more than the other, in terms of "love at first sight," passionate love, or companionate love over the long haul (Hatfield & Sprecher, 1986). Both sexes become equally attached and in the same way (Shaver, Hazan, & Bradshaw, 1988), and both suffer at the end of love.

But women and men do differ, on the average, in *how* they love (Peplau & Gordon, 1985). Perhaps you remember from Chapter 9, for example, that males and females define and express their notions of emotional intimacy quite differently. (Is ''intimacy'' going to the movies together or discussing secret worries?) Men are more likely to be ludic than women—that is, to regard love and sex as a game to be played for the fun of the challenge (Hatkoff & Lasswell, 1979; Hendrick & Hendrick, 1986). Once in a relationship, women report stronger feelings of affection and companionate love than men do, and they spend more time and energy analyzing their relationships for strengths and problems. Men monitor their relationships mainly when they have problems (S. Brehm, 1985; Holtzworth-Munroe & Jacobson, 1985).

These differences between the sexes may, in turn, be tied to male and female roles. Traditionally, as sociologist Willard Waller (1938) said, a woman didn't just marry a man; she married a standard of living. The husband determined her security and that of their children. Therefore she could not afford to marry someone ''unsuitable'' or waste her time in a relationship that was ''not going anywhere,'' even if she loved the man. In contrast, a man could afford to be sentimental and romantic in his choice of partner (Hochschild, 1975).

Indeed, for many years studies found that men were much more romantic (as well as ludic) than women, who were in turn much more pragmatic than men. In the 1960s, two-thirds of a sample of college men said they would not marry someone they did not love, but only a fourth of the women ruled out the possibility (Kephart, 1967). As women became self-supporting, and as two incomes became necessary in American families, the sex difference in romantic love began to fade. Nowadays women are just as romantic as men—or not (Hazan & Shaver, 1987; Hendrick & Hendrick, 1986). This change suggests that our feelings about love, and the kind of love we feel, are influenced by larger social and economic concerns. Can you think of other influences on your own ''style of love''?

''Sorry, Eric, but before I commit to anybody I still need about three years of fun.''

A ''ludic lover'' in action. Do you think that gender differences in this style of love are fading?

QUICK▪QUIZ

A. Of Lee's six "styles of loving," which style does each example below illustrate?

1. St. Paul tells the Corinthians to love others whether or not other people deserve it.
2. Jane Welsh and Thomas Carlyle enjoy exchanging ideas and confidences for years before realizing they love each other.
3. In choosing his last four wives, Henry VIII makes sure they are likely to bear children and are of suitably high status for his court.
4. Romeo and Juliet think only of each other and hate to be separated for even an hour.
5. Casanova tries to seduce every woman he meets for the thrill of the chase.

B. Prince Charles falls head over heels in love with Lady Diana and immediately wants to make her his wife and eventually his queen. However, he doesn't have much in common with her and rarely tells her about his private interests or worries. According to the "triangle theory of love," which component of love is Prince Charles lacking?

C. Tiffany is wildly in love with Timothy, who says he loves her, but she can't stop worrying about him and doubting his love. She wants to be with him constantly, but when she is feeling jealous she pushes him away. According to the attachment theory of love, which style of attachment does Tiffany have?

Answers:

A. 1. selfless or brotherly love (agape) 2. intimacy and friendship love (storge) 3. pragmatic love (pragma) 4. romantic love (eros) 5. game-playing love (ludus) B. intimacy C. anxious/ambivalent

---

The Competent Animal: Motives to Work

Almost every adult works. Most people spend more time at work than they do at play or with their families. "Work" does not mean only paid employment. Students work at the job of being a student. Housewives work, often more hours than salaried employees, at the job of running a household. Artists, poets, and actors work, even if they are paid erratically. What keeps everybody doing it? The simplest answer, of course, is survival. People work to have food on the table and a roof over their heads. But survival does not explain what motivates LeRoy to work for caviar on his table and Duane to work for peanut butter on his. It doesn't explain why some people want to do their work well and others want just to get it done. It doesn't explain the difference between Aristotle's view ("All paid employments absorb and degrade the mind") and Noel Coward's ("Work is more fun than fun").

Psychologists have studied work motivation in the laboratory, where they have focused on such internal motives as the desire for achievement or power, and in organizations, where they study the working conditions that influence productivity and satisfaction (see "A Closer Look at Industrial and Organizational Psychology" on page 370).

The effects of motivation on work

Several independent forces keep you working toward a goal: your expectation of success, your motivation to act, and opportunities in the environment and the nature of your work (McClelland, 1985). Although we will be discussing these factors in the context of paid work, they apply to any form of achievement, from running a household to running a marathon.

Expectations and values. How hard you work for something depends partly on what you expect to accomplish. If you are fairly certain of success, you will work much harder to reach your goal than if you are fairly certain of failure.

One experiment showed how quickly experience affects expectations. Young women were asked to solve 15 anagrams. Before working on each one, they had to estimate their chances of solving it. Half of the women started off with very simple anagrams, but half began with insoluble ones. Sure enough, those who started with the easy ones increased their estimates of success on later ones. Those who began with the impossible ones decided they would *all* be impossible. These expectations, in turn, affected the young women's ability to actually solve the last 10 anagrams (which were the same for everyone). The higher the expectation of success, the more anagrams the women solved (Feather, 1966).

Once acquired, therefore, expectations can create a **self-fulfilling prophecy**, in which a person predicts how he or she will do and then behaves in such a way as to make the prediction come true (R. Jones, 1977). You expect to do well, so you study hard, and then you do well. You expect to fail, so you don't do much work, and then you do poorly. In either case, you have fulfilled your expectation of yourself.

How hard you work for something, of course, also depends on how much you want it, which in turn depends on your general value system (Feather, 1982). Some people value affiliation more than achievement, and others have opposite priorities. The value people place on a goal, though, depends in part on how hard it is to reach! As we saw in the initiation experiment, people tend to attach more value to goals and relationships they have to work hard for than to those that come easy (Brehm et al., 1983). Conversely, when people work hard for something and fail to get it, they tend to devalue the goal, deciding it wasn't important anyway. This is known as the "sour grapes" phenomenon, a popular way to reduce dissonance.

The need for competence. A long tradition in American psychology has held that human beings are motivated by a **need for competence** in dealing with their environments (White, 1959). This motive was assumed to be basic to the species, and its gratification was assumed to be naturally satisfying.

Research has expanded and clarified this idea. A child's sense of mastery changes and develops (or can be suppressed) with age, experience, and reinforcement. The pleasure of competence is highest when the difficulty of a task is not too easy and not too hard. Mastering an easy task offers no challenge, but the satisfaction of mastering a very difficult task may be lessened if too much time and effort are expended (Harter, 1978, 1981).

Albert Bandura (1977a, 1986) argues that competence involves a belief in *self-efficacy*, the conviction that you can successfully accomplish what you set out to do. To Bandura, self-efficacy is acquired from several sources: your own experiences with mastery; vicarious observation of another person's competence, which may convince you that the task is possible; persuasion and encouragement from others; and perception of your own physiological state. (People feel more competent

self-fulfilling prophecy *The tendency to act on one's expectations in such a way as to make the expectations come true.*

need for competence *The motive to be capable in one's activities and to master new situations.*

A Closer Look at Industrial and Organizational Psychology

For Love or Money: Why Do People Work?

The poet Sylvia Plath once described the dilemma of work. "I want acceptance [from the public and critics], and to feel my work good and well-taken," she wrote. "Which ironically freezes me at my work, corrupts my nunnish labor of work-for-itself-as-its-own-reward." Plath was caught between **intrinsic** (internal) **motivation** for work—intellectual satisfaction, happiness, curiosity, play, and the sheer love of the activity—and **extrinsic** (external) **motivation**—a desire for money, fame, and attention. Can these motives be combined?

This question falls into the domain of **industrial and organizational (I/O) psychology**, which is concerned with the development and application of psychological principles to the workplace (Smither, 1988). I/O psychologists do basic and applied research in personnel selection and training, job analysis (identifying the exact duties and activities that define a job), human factors (see page 186), workers' satisfaction, improving the organizational structure, leadership, and motivation. Their practical goals are to reduce employee turnover,

absenteeism, and low productivity; improve the design of working environments, machines, and products; and raise workers' morale and motivation.

The scope and application of I/O research has been broad indeed, from helping the government select spies in World War II (this was a big success) to advising Coca-Cola to change its classic formula (this was a big bloop). (A badly designed study suggested that many consumers wanted a sweeter-tasting drink; it overlooked the millions of consumers who were loyal to the old drink. You see why good research methods matter?) I/O psychologists study many other topics, too, including:

- *Hiring procedures*: How can employers select the people who will be best qualified and best motivated for the job? How can they eliminate discrimination against minorities, women, older people, or the handicapped?
- *Political and legal issues*, such as *comparable worth*: Should women and men be paid equally if they hold different jobs but are comparably trained

---

intrinsic motivation
Motivation based on internal rewards, such as the basic pleasure of the activity itself, the intellectual challenge, or the satisfaction of curiosity.

extrinsic motivation
Motivation based on external incentives, such as pay, praise, attention, or the avoidance of punishment.

industrial/organizational (I/O) psychology *The study of behavior in the workplace.*

when they are calm and relaxed than when they are agitated or excited.) From whatever source, the belief in self-efficacy influences motivation. You may have many skills and talents, but if you believe you are incompetent, the skills may go to waste. If you believe you are competent, you are likely to value your abilities and aspire to success (Harackiewicz, Sansone, & Manderlink, 1985).

The need for achievement. Why do some individuals and societies achieve more than others? Why are some people self-motivated, ambitious, eager to start their own businesses or risk new challenges? In the early 1950s, David McClelland and his associates (1953) speculated that these people have a **need for achievement** (abbreviated **nAch**) that motivates them as much as hunger motivates people to eat. How could this motive be identified? McClelland (1961) later wrote that he and his colleagues sought the " 'psychic X-ray' that would permit us to observe what was going on in a person's head in the same way that we can observe stomach contractions or nerve discharges in a hungry organism."

The solution came in the form of a method developed by Henry Murray in the 1930s. The Thematic Apperception Test (TAT) is a series of ambiguous pictures and

in knowledge, skills, and level of responsibility?

▪ *Management styles*: What is the best way to run a company? Can American companies learn from Japanese methods?

▪ *Working conditions*: How do you design an assembly line that won't drive factory workers crazy with boredom? One way is to have them work in groups and handle different aspects of assembling the product instead of one repeated routine.

▪ *Dilemmas of motivation*: How can workers and employers balance the intrinsic satisfactions of work with the extrinsic rewards of income and praise? One solution is to combine a secure base pay with incentive, or ''merit pay,'' for special achievements. Merit pay rewards people for doing especially good work—an intrinsic pleasure—not for simply working.

After countless studies of productivity, power, competitiveness, and other heavy topics, I/O researchers are beginning to acknowledge another great motivator of work: fun. David Abramis (1987) surveyed 341 adults, aged 18 to 63, working in many occupations, and asked them to describe the sources of ''fun'' on the job. For many people, fun is the intrinsic pleasure of doing the work itself; for others, fun lies in the social aspects of the work—fooling around with friends, having office parties, and the like. Most people, Abramis found, create fun at work, even when they have jobs that are ''fun-resistant''—boring, routine, or unpleasant.

Fun is not the only important aspect of work, Abramis says. It won't replace good pay or security, and it won't smooth over a bad fit between you and your job. Yet fun matters because it is related to well-being. It enhances creativity and motivation, and it improves performance even when the worker doesn't much like his or her job. Supervisors can increase staff fun by rewarding good performance; by sponsoring group parties, sports, and spontaneous gatherings; and by giving employees opportunities to work alone, to teach each other, and to ''fool around.'' You can tell when people are having fun, says Abramis. You hear a lot of laughter.

drawings, and all you have to do is tell a story about the picture you see. What is happening in the picture? What are the characters thinking and feeling? What will happen next? Your behavior, said McClelland (1961), may be influenced by many things, but the strength of your internal motive to achieve is best captured in the fantasies you tell. ''In fantasy anything is at least symbolically possible,'' he explained. ''A person may rise to great heights, sink to great depths, kill his grandmother, or take off for the South Sea Islands on a pogo stick.''

Needless to say, people with high achievement motivation do not fantasize about taking off for the South Seas or sinking to great depths. They tell stories about working hard, becoming rich and famous, and clobbering the opposition with their wit and brilliance. These achievement-related themes increase when high achievers are in situations that arouse their competitiveness and desire to succeed—when, for example, they believe that the TAT is measuring their intelligence and leadership ability (J. Atkinson, 1958). Researchers have used the TAT to study other motives as well, such as those for affiliation and power.

Further studies of the achievement motive in the laboratory and in real life have found numerous differences between people who score high on the need for

need for achievement (achievement motivation) *A learned motive to meet personal standards of success and excellence in a chosen area (often abbreviated* **nAch***).*

achievement and those who score low. High scorers are more likely, for example, to start their own businesses, set high personal standards, and prefer to work with capable colleagues who can help them succeed than with co-workers who are merely friendly (Kuhl, 1978; McClelland, 1965).

In a new approach to motivation and achievement, Carol Dweck and Ellen Leggett (1988) argue that it is not enough to say that some people have "achievement motivation" and others don't. To them, the interesting question is *why* someone wants to achieve. For the love of learning? For fame and success? To prove self-worth?

Suppose we offer you a choice of two boxes. In the first, you will find a variety of interesting problems, some hard, some easy; by choosing this box, you will have a chance to prove to us what you know. In the second box, you will find some challenging new activities; by choosing this box, you will learn some new things, but you will also make some dumb mistakes along the way. Which box do you choose?

People who choose the first box are motivated by *performance* goals: They are concerned with doing well, being judged highly, and avoiding criticism. Those who choose the second box are motivated by *learning* goals: They are concerned with increasing their competence and skills. Now imagine what happens when both types are faced with a difficult problem. Who will sink into helplessness, doing poorly at solving the problem and eventually giving up, and who will keep going to master the problem and avoid failure?

The crucial fact about these alternatives—helplessness or mastery—is that *they are unrelated to ability.* When people are faced with a difficult problem, talent or ambition alone does not predict who will push on and who will give up. Indeed,

The Many Motives of Accomplishment

PRODUCTIVITY

ISAAC ASIMOV
(b. 1920)

Scientist, writer
"If my doctor told me I had only six minutes to live, I wouldn't brood. I'd type a little faster."

KNOWLEDGE

MARGARET MEAD
(1901–1978)

Anthropologist
"I was brought up to believe that the only thing worth doing was to add to the sum of accurate information in the world."

JUSTICE

MARTIN LUTHER KING, JR. *(1929–1968)*

Civil rights activist
"I have a dream . . . that my four little children will one day live in a nation where they will not be judged by the color of their skin but by the content of their character."

AUTONOMY

GEORGIA O'KEEFFE
(1887–1986)

Artist
"[I] found myself saying to myself—I can't live where I want to, go where I want to, do what I want to . . . I decided I was a very stupid fool not to at least paint as I wanted to."

many bright and capable children and adults drop out when they begin to feel helpless in solving their problems. In several studies, Elliott and Dweck (1988) found that the reason lies in the goals people set for themselves. When people are focused on how well they are performing, and then do not do well, they often decide the fault is theirs. They begin to feel unhappy and pessimistic, and they stop trying to improve. Since their goal is to demonstrate their abilities, they set themselves up for grief when they temporarily fail—as all of us must if we are to learn anything new. In contrast, people whose goal is learning regard failure as a source of useful information that will help them improve. Failure does not discourage them or wreck their self-confidence, because they know it takes time to learn a skill or solve a problem.

Gender and achievement.   Nearly all the early research on achievement motivation was done on men. When women took the TAT their answers were so odd (to the researchers) that the results were simply ignored. Then, in the 1960s, Matina Horner (1972) came up with a theory of female achievement motivation. Achievement and masculinity go together in American society like ham and eggs, she said, but achievement and femininity are like, well, ham and popcorn. In women, Horner argued, achievement is considered aggressive and unladylike, so many bright women develop a motive to *avoid* success.

Horner's method was to ask female undergraduates to tell a story about a young woman, Anne, who "finds herself at the top of her medical school class." Male undergraduates told stories about a young man, John, at the top of his class. The men foresaw rosy futures for John. About two-thirds of the women, though, saw disaster for Anne. Her fellow classmates beat her up. She lives a lonely and misera-

POWER
HENRY KISSINGER
(b. 1923)

Former Secretary of State
"Power is the ultimate aphrodisiac."

DUTY
ELEANOR ROOSEVELT
(1884–1962)

Humanitarian, lecturer, stateswoman
"As for accomplishments, I just did what I had to do as things came along."

EXCELLENCE
FLORENCE GRIFFITH JOYNER *(b. 1959)*

Olympic gold medalist
"When you've been second best for so long, you can either accept it, or try to become the best. I made the decision to try and be the best."

MONEY
SALVADOR DALI
(1904–1988)

Surrealist artist
"Liking money like I like it, is nothing less than mysticism. Money is a glory."

ble life. She is ugly and horrid. Their stories seemed to reveal a "fear of success," yet that "fear" didn't keep the young women themselves from actually succeeding. Most of them graduated with honors and went on for graduate degrees (L. Hoffman, 1977).

At the time of Horner's study, women were only a small percentage of all medical students, let alone physicians. The women in Horner's study could have been responding not to Anne's success but to her nonconformity. Sure enough, in later studies, when women told stories about a woman who was first in a class that was 50 percent women, "fear of success" virtually vanished. This finding suggests that Horner's women feared social rejection more than they feared achievement. Indeed, both men and women "fear success" in occupations that are not traditional for their gender (Cherry & Deaux, 1975). Further, in the 1970s, many men began to wonder about the wisdom of striving for success at the expense of relationships and health. Soon, studies were finding that men showed as much "fear of success" imagery as women had (Robbins & Robbins, 1973). In a study of real physicians, 382 women and 866 men, it was the *men* who showed higher fear-of-success imagery (Pyke & Kahill, 1983).

This research illustrates an important point about achievement motivation in particular and learned motives in general: that motivation (and research) are strongly affected by current social conditions. The time-bound nature of this research suggests that the "achievement motive" can be activated or diminished by experiences in adult life.

The need for power.   Some people are motivated by a **need for power**, for dominance over and control of others. In telling TAT fantasy stories, people who have a high need for power write stories about having a strong impact on others. The methods they use to win power include aggression, persuasion, helping others, or manipulating others by arousing their guilt, devotion, or anger. Men who score high in power are more likely than low scorers to be argumentative, play competitive sports, accumulate prestige symbols, and try to dominate conversations. If they are unable to act on their need for power, because of internal inhibitions or external constraints, they are at risk of hypertension (chronic high blood pressure) and illness (McClelland, 1975; McClelland et al., 1980).

In his years of studying power motivation, David Winter (1988) finds that although there are certainly sex differences in the distribution of actual power, studies have consistently failed to find any motivational differences. Men and women who have high power motivation do the same things—seek visibility and prestige, enter powerful careers, and run for office. There is one big difference, though. Among men, but not among women, power motivation is associated with what Winter calls the "expansive, profligate impulse"—drinking, drug use, aggression, gambling, and exploitative sexuality. This does not mean that women never drink, gamble, fight, insult, or exploit others. It means that when they do so, power is not their main motive. What might be the origins of the "profligate impulse"?

The power motive, Winter argues, may take one of two forms: *egoistic dominance* (being aggressive, seeking attention, using dominance to control others) or *responsible nurturance* (giving help and support, using dominance to do good for others). When Winter examined the family records of people high in the need for power, he found that those men and women who had had younger siblings—or who now, as adults, had children—were far more likely to express "responsible," positive power than the controlling or dissolute kind. Girls, Winter observes, tend to have more responsibility training than boys, so the apparent sex difference in "profligate power" may simply reflect differences in learning to look after others.

need for power *A learned motive to dominate or control others.*

The effects of work on motivation

The very concept of the motive to achieve is deeply embedded in cultural values. Achievement and power motivation, some social scientists argue, have been defined and measured by white, male, middle-class standards that overlook the values and accomplishments of other groups. In addition, some psychologists object to the idea that achievement depends at all on an internal "motive"—an enduring, unchanging quality of the individual. This notion, they say, leads to the incorrect conclusion that if minorities, women, and the poor don't succeed or acquire power, it's their own fault—they lack the internal drive to make it (C. Epstein, 1976; Kanter, 1977).

In fact, research finds that accomplishment is not determined only by your personal ambitions. It can be nurtured or reduced by the work you do and the conditions under which you do it.

Goals and feedback. One of the most important influences on motivation to work and on actual performance is the nature of the goal you are working toward. Given two people of equal ability, the one who sets specific and moderately difficult goals will work longer and achieve more than the one who sets vague, easy goals or none at all (Locke et al., 1981; Smither, 1988). If a goal is too vague, such as "I'm going to work harder," you don't know what action to take to reach it or how to recognize it when you get there (what does "harder" mean?). If you set a specific goal, such as "I am going to study two hours in the evening instead of one, and read 25 pages instead of 15," you have specified both a course of action and a goal you can recognize.

Once you have specified a goal, continued motivation depends in part on getting feedback about your performance. Your employer needs to tell you that you are almost number one in sales. Your piano teacher needs to tell you that your playing has improved. When people work in environments that do not provide feedback, their motivation to do well is often weakened (Thayer, 1983).

Working conditions. Working conditions affect a person's satisfaction, mood, health, happiness—and motivation to work. In an important longitudinal study, researchers interviewed a random sample of American workers over a period of ten years (Kohn & Schooler, 1983). Comparing results of the first interviews with later ones, they found that aspects of the work (such as fringe benefits, complexity of daily tasks, pace, pressure, and how routine or varied the work was) significantly changed the workers' self-esteem, job commitment, and motivation. The degree of job flexibility was especially important. People who have a chance to set their own hours, make decisions, alternate gadget making with widget weaving, and solve problems are likely to rise to the challenge. They tend to become more flexible and tolerant in their thinking, and feel better about themselves and their work, than if they feel stuck in a routine, boring job that gives them no control over what they do. As a result, their work motivation rises (Hackman & Oldham, 1980).

Surprising as it may seem, having a high income does *not* stimulate work motivation. This doesn't mean that we should all accept low pay because we will like our jobs better. Pay is important, especially in American society, where a person's character and self-confidence are often measured by the size of his or her income. However, work motivation itself is not related to money, but to how and when the money is paid (Thayer, 1983). In a review of many field studies of employee performance, researchers found that the strongest motivator was *incentive pay*, that is, bonuses that are given upon completion of a goal and not as an automatic part of salary. The second strongest motivator was goal setting, and the third

If someone isn't working hard, we tend to ask, "What's the matter with that person's motivation?" Why don't we ask, "What's the matter with that person's job?"

was "job enrichment," making the work more interesting (Locke et al., 1981). These three factors together increased the motivation of workers by over 40 percent.

Similarly, the "working conditions" of marriage can produce either highly motivated homemakers or apathetic ones (A. Oakley, 1974; Strasser, 1982). Motivated homemakers tend to have extended families whom they see regularly and friends in the neighborhood who drop in frequently. They set specific goals ("I'm cleaning closets today and devoting tomorrow to the kids"). They get feedback from the family ("You spent all day making this meal? It's fabulous!"). Apathetic homemakers tend to lack social contacts and to be physically isolated. They have no clear standards for a job well done, so they don't feel they have done their jobs well. None of this, by the way, applies only to women. When men are "househusbands," their motivation rises or falls according to the same circumstances (Beer, 1983).

Achievement ambitions, likewise, are related to people's *chances* of achieving. Reviewing dozens of studies of opportunity and ambition, Rosabeth Kanter (1977) found that men and women who work in dead-end jobs with no prospect of promotion behave the same way. They play down the importance of achievement, fantasize about quitting, and emphasize the social benefits of their jobs instead of the intellectual benefits. Yet if opportunities are created for such people, their motivation often changes.

In Kanter's research, a woman who had been a secretary for 20 years reported that she had never had a desire to be anything else. Then, with an affirmative action program, she was offered a managerial job. Although she felt insecure about her ability, she accepted it. She did superbly, and her motives changed. "Now I'm ambitious," she told the interviewer, "probably overly so. I will probably work 20 more years, and I expect to move at least six grade levels, maybe to vice-president. . . . You know, as you do, you learn you can, so you want to do more."

QUICK ■ QUIZ

Check your understanding of work motivation.

1. Expecting to be lonely and then making no effort to find friends can result in a _____.
2. Ramón and Ramona are learning to ski. Every time she falls down, Ramona says, "This is the most humiliating experience I've ever had! Everyone is watching me behave like a clumsy dolt!" Ramón says, "&*!!@*$@! I'll show these dratted skis who's boss!" Why is Ramona more likely than Ramón to give up? **(a)** She *is* a clumsy dolt. **(b)** She is less competent at skiing. **(c)** She is focused on performance. **(d)** She is focused on learning.
3. Studies of "fear of success" find that **(a)** women are more afraid than men of success, **(b)** men are more afraid than women of success, **(c)** both men and women fear nonconformity and rejection more than success.
4. Which of these factors significantly increase work motivation? Choose all that apply. **(a)** specific goals, **(b)** regular pay, **(c)** feedback, **(d)** general goals, **(e)** being told what to do, **(f)** being able to make decisions, **(g)** the chance of promotion, **(h)** having routine, predictable work, **(i)** incentive pay.

Answers:
1. self-fulfilling prophecy 2. c 3. c 4. a, c, f, g, i

"Basic" Needs and "Higher" Goals: Can Motives Be Ranked?

We have come a long way from the motives of hunger and thirst to the many forces that motivate a day's work. This progression, from basic needs to learned ones, from universal needs to culture-specific ones, from the simple to the complex, was not lost on Abraham Maslow (1954/1970). Maslow made sense of the astonishing array of human motives by arranging them in a pyramid, which he called a "hierarchy of needs."

Although Maslow revised the pyramid over the course of his life, changing the ranking of some needs, the hierarchy basically ascends from simple biological needs to complex psychological motives, culminating in "self-actualization" and "self-transcendence." Maslow argued that your needs must be met at each level before you can even think of the matters posed by the level above it. You can't worry about achievement, for instance, if you are hungry, cold, and poor. You can't become self-actualized if you haven't satisfied your need for self-esteem and love. Maslow believed that everyone would reach the highest levels if social and economic obstacles were removed. Human beings behave badly, he argued, only when their lower needs are frustrated, especially those for love, belonging, and self-esteem.

This theory became immensely popular because it is intuitively logical and optimistic about human nature. Unfortunately, the theory has not been supported by scientific research (Howell & Dipboye, 1982). But the idea of a hierarchy of needs and motives remains popular, especially with business managers in many companies. You may encounter Maslow's theory in other courses and even on the job one day, and some organizational psychologists want to forewarn you that the theory is unverified (Smither, 1988; Thayer, 1983).

One problem with Maslow's hierarchy is that it is just as possible to organize human needs horizontally instead of vertically. One could argue that people have *simultaneous* needs for basic physical comfort and safety *and* for understanding, self-esteem, and competence. Even hungry people are motivated to explain the world and to be thought well of. Even a person who is still seeking love may be strongly motivated by ideas, social convictions, or a love of beauty. Second, people who have met their "lower" needs do not inevitably seek "higher" ones, nor is it the case that antisocial behavior results only from frustrated lower needs. Third, "higher" needs may overcome "lower" ones. Human history is full of examples of people who would rather starve than be humiliated (a "self-esteem" need); rather die of torture than sacrifice their convictions; rather explore, risk, or create new art than be safe and secure at home.

Think of Jim Abbott, Dian Fossey, and the men and women portrayed on pages 372–373. All, Maslow might say, were "self-actualized," fulfilling their potentials and setting their own standards. They were not necessarily doing so because they had overcome lower needs, but because some of those "lower" needs were less important to them than they might be to other people. Many heroes and pioneers have sacrificed safety needs, love needs, and the need for approval and recognition in the quest of unpopular goals and private dreams.

Perhaps the safest conclusion, therefore, is that each of us develops an individual hierarchy of motives in the course of our development from childhood to old age. For some, the need for love, security, and safety will dominate. For others, the need for achievement will rule. Most of us, as we will see in the next unit, combine many motives in a way that suits our personalities and experiences.

Maslow's "hierarchy of motives" is immensely popular, but does it really predict what a person will strive for? Do you have to satisfy a "lower" need for safety before you can fulfill a "higher" one for self-esteem?

Taking Psychology with You

How to Lose Weight—And Whether You Should

Have you ever read those "ideal weight" charts that describe the weight you ought to be for your "frame size"? Well, forget them. Careful research on longevity and health shows that those old height-and-weight tables were wrong (Gurin, 1984). Research now finds that:

▪ The healthiest weight seems to rise with age.

▪ Fatness *by itself* is not associated with a higher death rate, particularly among women. In some studies, people who are average or even plump survive the longest.

▪ Being obese *is* unhealthy because of the increased risk of diabetes and high blood pressure, but being very thin is just as unhealthy. A review of many studies found that "in every given population examined, the thinnest people have the highest death rate" (*Current Controversy,* 1985). Either way, the risks to longevity exist only with extreme heaviness or thinness.

▪ Good health does not depend on being a single, perfect weight. Your life expectancy is average if you are within a range of 30 or 40 pounds. To compute that healthy range, (1) divide your height, in inches, by 66; (2) multiply the result by itself; (3) multiply that result by your age plus 100. That number, in pounds, is the weight that is the *middle* of your healthy range. If you are within 15 or 20 pounds of this number, either higher or lower, your weight is fine, unless you have a weight-related condition such as hypertension or diabetes.

Chances are, though, that you will protest that the weight you just calculated is "too fat." At the same time that evidence was accumulating that overweight was not necessarily bad for a person, fashion was changing toward an even more slender standard. Miss Sweden of 1951, for example, was 5'7" tall and weighed 151 pounds; Miss Sweden of 1983 was 5'9" tall and weighed 109 pounds. The average Playboy Playmate and fashion model likewise have become slimmer and much less busty over the last three decades (Garner et al., 1980). Brett Silverstein and his colleagues documented the changing female ideal in this century by computing a "bust-to-waist" ratio of the measurements of models in popular women's magazines (Silverstein, Peterson, & Perdue, 1986). The ideal body type became decidedly non-curvy twice during this century: in the mid-1920s and from the mid-1960s to the present.

Why did these changes in the ideal female body occur? Silverstein found that men and women associate the curvy, big-breasted body with femininity; and they associate femininity with domesticity, nurturance, and, alas, *incompetence*. Thus, in every era in which women have been admitted to universities and have had professional careers in greater numbers—notably, the 1920s and 1960s—women have tried to look boyishly thin to avoid the risk of appearing feminine and dumb. This femininity-versus-competency conflict, Silverstein hypothesized, should be pronounced among women who value academic achievement, higher education, and careers (especially male-dominated careers)—particularly among women who doubt their competence and who are insecure about how other people see them. And in reviewing many other studies and conducting his own, that is just what he found (Silverstein et al., 1986).

Many women today, therefore, face a dilemma. They want to achieve the modern ideal of boyish thinness, but evolution has programmed them for a womanly reserve of fat necessary for the onset of menstruation, healthy childbearing, nursing, and, after menopause, for the storage of the hormone estrogen. The result of the battle between biological design and social standards is that many women today—as in the 1920s—are obsessed with weight, continually dieting, or suffering from eating disorders such as anorexia nervosa (virtual self-starvation) or bulimia (bingeing and vomiting) (Striegel-Moore, Silberstein, & Rodin, 1986). Men, too, have fallen prey to the new standard; for them, too, ''overweight'' is considered a sign of ''softness'' and lack of masculinity.

What's a person to do? Research offers some suggestions for those who want to control their weight or live with it:

- Realize that the disposition to gain weight varies from person to person. Metabolic rate, body shape, and genetic inheritance all influence the readiness to gain.
- Recognize that a diet of junk food is bad for health as well as weight control. Two researchers were trying to induce their laboratory rats to become obese, without success. One day they went to a nearby supermarket and bought peanut butter, marshmallows, chocolate chip cookies, salami, and other rich food. The rats thought they were in rat heaven and quickly became as round as baseballs (Sclafani & Springer, 1976).
- Avoid fad diets that restrict you to only a few foods or that promise quick weight loss. Such diets lead to bingeing when the diet is over, which restores the lost weight—plus some. ''Yo-yo'' patterns of dieting and weight gain actually lower body metabolism and increase the proportion of body fat, making it *easier* to gain weight and harder to lose it (Steen, Oppliger, & Brownell, 1988; Polivy & Herman, 1985).
- Get more exercise, which may raise the metabolic rate without harmful side effects. You do not have to become a marathon runner. But you can increase your daily activity level, for example, by walking instead of driving to work.
- Avoid amphetamines and other ''diet pills,'' which can be far more dangerous to your health than a few pounds. Diet pills raise the metabolic rate only as long as you take them. When you stop taking them, the pounds return.
- If you are mistakenly trying to control weight by frequent vomiting and abuse of laxatives, you can break this harmful pattern by joining an eating-disorders program, such as one that offers group support *plus* directed instructions for behavioral change (Kirkley, Schneider, & Bachman, 1984).

Most of all, though, think carefully and critically about the reasons that you are dieting. Are you really ''overweight''? Whose standards are you following? Why?

KEY WORDS

motivation 344

incentive 345

homeostasis 347

social motives 347

set-point theory 348

sexual desire 352

gender role 355

sexual scripts 355

exploration and curiosity 357

familiarity versus novelty 357

sensation seeking 358

practice play 358

cognitive dissonance theory 360

justification of effort 360

affiliation 362

contact comfort 362

passionate and companionate love 365

six "styles of love" 365

triangle theory of love 365

attachment theory of love 365

expectations and values 369

self-fulfilling prophecy 369

competence 369

self-efficacy 369

achievement motivation (nAch) 370

performance versus learning goals 372

power motivation 374

goals and feedback 375

hierarchy of needs (Maslow) 377

SUMMARY

1. The study of motivation, like the study of emotion, is filled with debate. According to drive theory, a few basic drives are based on physiological needs, such as those for food, water, and avoidance of excessive cold and pain. But people are also motivated by cognitive processes that permit planning, values, and expectations. *Social* (learned) *motives* are as important as physical needs.

2. Human motives often conflict. In an *approach-approach* conflict, a person is equally attracted to two goals. In an *avoidance-avoidance* conflict, a person is equally repelled by two goals. An *approach-avoidance* conflict is the most difficult to resolve, because the person is both attracted to and repelled by the *same* goal. Prolonged conflict can lead to physical symptoms and lowered well-being.

3. Overweight is not caused simply by overeating or emotional problems. According to *set-point theory*, hunger, weight, and eating are regulated by a complex set of bodily mechanisms that keep people at the weight they were designed to be. Insulin regulates the flow of sugar from the bloodstream into the cells; it increases fat stores and prevents fat breakdown.

4. The set point is influenced by exercise, which raises the body's metabolic rate, and by the kind of food a person eats. Sweet foods raise insulin levels, which in turn increase feelings of hunger, increase the amount of food consumed, and can create "cravings" for more sweets. Culture determines what people eat, when and how often they eat, and with whom they eat.

5. Psychologists disagree about whether any aspect of human sexuality can be considered a "primary drive" or a "biological need." Levels of testosterone may influence sexual desire in both sexes, but human sexual desire and behavior are largely influenced by learning, cultural standards, and opportunity.

6. Although most men and women prefer to have sex with partners they love, they often differ in the meanings they attach to sex and their motives for making love. Men tend to be more "instrumental," enjoying sex for its physical pleasure; women tend to be more "expressive," enjoying sex for its emotional closeness. They also have different interpretations of sexual signals, with men seeing certain signs and situations as indications of sexual interest, when women intend only to convey affection. Men sometimes feel obligated to "make a move" to prove their masculinity, and women sometimes feel obligated to "give in" to preserve the relationship. These differences are related to different *gender role* expectations for men and women, including the "sexual scripts" that dictate how both sexes should behave during courtship, intimacy, and sex.

7. Curiosity and play are important behavioral motives. The more familiar people are with something—a person, a face, a symbol—the more they tend to like it. This affection for the familiar is balanced by the need for novelty and stimulation. Individuals differ in how they strike this balance; sensation seekers prefer a high level of stimulation in many activities. In human beings, play seems to be an innate motive that is apparent from early childhood. *Practice play* is rehearsal for adult activities, but children's play also reflects the development of imagination, storytelling, and the ability to anticipate the future.

8. Consistency and understanding are important cognitive motives. *Cognitive dissonance theory* assumes that people are motivated to reduce the tension that exists when two cognitions are out of balance. The theory seems to predict how people will receive new information that is dissonant with their beliefs, self-concepts, and self-esteem.

9. People are motivated to *affiliate* with others for contact comfort, for reassurance, and for friendship. As with all social motives, individuals and cultures differ in how much affiliation they seek and in the importance they place on attachments. Several categories or theories have described varieties of love: *passionate ("romantic") vs. companionate love*; the *six styles of love* (eros, ludus, storge, mania, pragma, and agape); the *triangle theory of love* (love as passion, intimacy, and commitment); and the *attachment theory of love* (love as secure, anxious/ ambivalent, or avoidant). Men and women are equally likely to feel love and attachment, but gender roles affect how they experience and express love.

10. The motivation to work depends on a person's *expectations* of success; the *value* the person places on the goal; various *motives* such as competence, achievement, or power; and the *opportunity* to act on these motives.

11. Many psychologists believe that people are motivated by a basic need to feel competent at what they do. A theory of *self-efficacy* argues that people get information from several sources about their abilities. Without a sense of competence, people lack the motivation to master new situations.

12. People who are motivated by a high *need for achievement* (nAch) set their own standards for success and excellence. But achievement motivation also depends on the goals people set for themselves. *Performance* goals can lead to helplessness and giving up; *learning* goals can lead to mastery.

13. Some researchers once thought that women have a "fear of success," a result of the cultural inconsistency between femininity and achievement. Later research showed that women (and men) are more likely to fear social rejection than success, and that some men doubt the benefits of achievement. The need for achievement is influenced by the times and the society.

14. People who are motivated by a *need for power* seek to dominate and control others. They may use a variety of methods to gain this power, from aggression to persuasion. The power motive may take one of two forms: egoistic dominance (controlling others) or responsible nurturance (helping others).

15. Achievement motivation can be raised by the conditions of work: having specific goals; feedback and praise; flexibility of tasks; control over decisions; *incentive pay* (bonuses for good work or goals met); and the opportunity for advancement.

16. Abraham Maslow believed that human motives could be ranked from basic biological needs to "higher" psychological needs. This theory, though popular, remains unproven. People can have simultaneous motives; "higher" motives can outweigh "lower" ones; and people do not always become kinder or more self-actualized when their "lower" needs for safety and love are met.

P A R T

F O U R

Development of the Individual

CHAPTER 11

Theories of the Person and Personality

Selfness is an essential fact of life. The thought of nonselfness, precise sameness, is terrifying.

LEWIS THOMAS

Does your personality change, or only your interests? Jerry Rubin was a 1960s yippie and is a yuppie today.

personality *A distinctive and relatively stable pattern of behavior, thoughts, motives, and emotions that characterizes an individual.*

386

A psychologist we know recently gave a lecture to the faculty of the first school she ever went to—her nursery school. Her topic was an optimistic report of new research on adult life. "People are not prisoners of childhood," she said. "They change their attitudes, philosophies of life, self-esteem, ambitions, values, and looks. They have new experiences that change their outlook and politics. They even outgrow early traumas."

In the audience, unknown to our friend, was one of her original teachers—now 96 years old, as clear-minded as ever. "A very nice speech, dear," she said when it was over, "but as far as I'm concerned, you haven't changed a bit." "Not since I was 3?" said our friend. "You're a bit taller, is all," said the teacher.

Some people are impressed at how much their friends change over time. Others are impressed at how much their friends remain the same, in *spite* of apparent changes. Likewise, some people find it miraculous that under normal conditions, every human being ends up with a face that has the same number of eyes, noses, ears, and teeth. Others find it more miraculous that every human face is recognizably different from every other. These two ways of looking at humanity reflect two different concerns of psychology. One focuses on the *common* steps of biological and psychological development. The second identifies what makes each individual different from every other, unique in all the world.

The four chapters in this part will explore the twin themes of similarity and difference, stability and change. What are the biological and social causes of individual differences (Chapter 12)? How does the individual grow and develop in childhood (Chapter 13) and adulthood (Chapter 14)? Before we can talk about the development of the person, however, we need to know what a person is. The answer is not so obvious.

Most psychologists would say that what made our friend appear unchanged to her nursery-school teacher was her "personality." The word doesn't refer to enthusiasm and liveliness, as in "she's got a lot of personality," or only to a set of positive qualities, as in "he's got a great personality." Psychologists generally define **personality** as a distinctive and stable pattern of behavior, thoughts, motives, and emotions that characterizes an individual.

That's all very well, but *which* behaviors, thoughts, motives, and emotions shall we count? How stable are they? Some psychologists look for personality in dark, hidden motives of the mind. Others regard personality as the core sense of self, the "true self," behind the masks that people wear in daily social situations. Some psychologists regard personality as a diamond, consisting of different facets of behavior and belief. Others argue that the whole notion of "personality" is wrongheaded, a comfortable fiction rather than scientific fact. In their view, people are much more influenced by their immediate circumstances and experience than by "personality." If people seem consistent, it is only because their environments haven't changed. As we report different theories of personality, keep your eye on the key questions of this chapter: How can we describe the astonishing variety among individuals, and why can we recognize "personality" even when we can't explain it?

The Psychoanalytic Tradition: You Are What You Were

Sigmund Freud (1856–1939), the founder of the theory and therapy called **psychoanalysis**, cast a long shadow over this century. Today there are basically three attitudes toward Freud and psychoanalysis:

▪ Freud was one of the geniuses of history. With minor exceptions, his basic theory is correct, universal, and brilliant. This view agrees with Freud's own appraisal of the importance of psychoanalysis: that it was as profound a revolution in human thought as Galileo, Darwin, and Newton created in their fields.

▪ Freud was a great thinker of his generation and era. Although many of his ideas have lasting value, some are dated, limited to Freud's time and place, and others are wrong. This is probably the most common current view among psychiatrists and many clinical psychologists, who still use many of Freud's terms and ideas but have updated his approach.

▪ Freud was a fraud. One scientist called psychoanalysis a dinosaur in the history of ideas, doomed to extinction. For good measure, he added that it is ''the most stupendous intellectual confidence trick of the twentieth century'' (Medawar, 1982). Anti-Freudians criticize Freud and his modern followers for their anti-woman attitudes, for their lack of scientific rigor, for regarding psychoanalysis as an in-group that accepts no dissenters or disbelievers, and for promoting a costly method of therapy that is not demonstrably better than any other (see Chapter 17).

What provocative theory could produce such wildly different points of view? In this section, we will try to give you an introduction to what Freud said, what some of his followers said, and why the debate about his work continues so hotly even today.

Freud and psychoanalysis

As you may remember from Chapter 1, psychology as a science began in Germany as an effort to study human consciousness. So it is ironic that one of the first major challenges to this young science attacked the relevance of consciousness. Freud, who lived in Vienna for most of his long career, compared conscious awareness to the tip of a mental iceberg. Beneath the visible tip, he said, lies the **unconscious** part of the mind, containing unrevealed wishes, ambitions, passions, guilty secrets, unspeakable yearnings, and conflicts between desire and duty. These unseen forces, Freud believed, have far more power over human behavior than consciousness does, so the true study of human psychology must probe beneath the surface.

To probe the unconscious, Freud developed the **psychoanalytic method**. The unconscious reveals itself, said Freud, in dreams, ''free association''—talking about anything that pops into your head, without worrying about what anyone will think of you—and slips of the tongue. (According to Freud, accidentally saying ''I'd like to kill you'' when you intend to say ''I'd like to kiss you'' reveals your true, unconscious desire.) Because so many thoughts and memories are hidden in the unconscious and because patients resist uncovering them, Freud maintained, psychoanalytic therapy can be long and difficult.

psychoanalysis *An approach to psychology that emphasizes unconscious motives and conflicts. It encompasses both a theory of personality and a method of psychotherapy.*
unconscious processes *Mental processes, such as motives, desires, and memories, not available to awareness or to conscious introspection. Sometimes called ''the unconscious,'' as a metaphor for the part of the mind below conscious awareness.*
psychoanalytic method *In psychoanalytic therapy, the effort to bring unconscious material into consciousness, usually through dream recall and free association.*

The dynamics of personality. Freud's theory, and the approach of many of his followers, is called **psychodynamic** because it is based on the movement of psychological energy within the person, in the form of attachments, conflicts, and motivations. Psychic energy is to Freud's theory of personality what water is to Hoover Dam: the content within the structure.

Dynamics is a term from physics that refers to the motion and balance of systems under the action of outside or inside forces. (For example, the science of thermodynamics studies the relationship between heat and mechanical energy.) Freud borrowed from nineteenth-century physics the idea of the "conservation of energy": Within any system, he thought, energy can be shifted or transformed, but the total amount of energy remains the same. Psychological energy—the energy it takes to carry out psychological processes, such as thinking and dreaming—was, to Freud, another form of physical energy.

Freud believed that energy that is blocked from direct expression must be *displaced* onto a substitute. For example, the "aggressive instinct" might be displaced in sports competition instead of directly expressed in war. When **displacement** serves a higher cultural or socially useful purpose, as in the creation of art or inventions, it is called **sublimation**. Freud himself thought that for the sake of civilization and survival, sexual and aggressive energies could and should be displaced or sublimated into socially appropriate and constructive forms.

The displacement of energy from one object to another is a key feature of Freud's psychodynamics of personality. Personality differences in tastes, habits, attitudes, and behavior patterns stem from the way people displace energy from their early instinctual preferences.

The structure of personality. To Freud, the personality is made up of three major systems: the *id*, the *ego*, and the *superego*. Although each system has its own functions and elements, human behavior is nearly always a result of the interaction among them (Freud, 1905b, 1920/1960, 1923/1962).

The **id**, present at birth, is the reservoir of all psychological energies and inherited instincts. To Freud, the id was the "true psychic reality" because it represents the inner world of subjective experience. It is unconcerned with objective reality and is unaffected by the environment. The id operates according to the **pleasure principle**, seeking to reduce tension, avoid pain, and obtain pleasure.

The id contains what Freud considered to be two basic, competing groups of instincts: the life, or sexual, instincts (fueled by psychic energy called the **libido**) and the death, or aggressive, instincts. As instinctive energy builds up in the id, the result is an uncomfortable state of tension. The id may discharge this tension in the form of reflex actions, displacement, physical symptoms, or "wishful thinking"— uncensored mental images and unbidden thoughts.

The **ego**, the second system to emerge, is a referee between the needs of instinct and the demands of society. It obeys the **reality principle**, putting a rein on the id's desire for pleasure until a suitable outlet can be found. The ego, said Freud, represents "reason and good sense." Freud (1923/1962) described the relationship between ego and id this way: "In relation to the id, [the ego] is like a man on horseback, who has to hold in check the superior strength of the horse; . . . Often a rider, if he is not to be parted from his horse, is obliged to guide it where it wants to go; so in the same way the ego constantly carries into action the wishes of the id as if they were its own."

If a person feels anxious or threatened when those "wishes of the id" conflict with social reality, the ego has certain weapons at its command to relieve the tension. These weapons, called **defense mechanisms**, have two characteristics:

psychodynamic *A word referring to psychological theories that explain behavior in terms of forces located in the individual, such as drives, motives, or, in psychoanalysis, instinctual energy.*

displacement *The shifting of instinctual energy from its original object or activity to a different one.*

sublimation *A type of displacement that serves a higher cultural or socially useful purpose; e.g., the creation of art or music as a sublimation of sexual energy.*

id *In psychoanalysis, the part of personality containing inherited psychological energy, particularly sexual and aggressive instincts; operates according to the* pleasure principle.

pleasure principle *The principle guiding the operation of the id; seeks to reduce tension, avoid pain, and enhance pleasure.*

libido *In psychoanalysis, the psychic energy that fuels the life or sexual instincts of the id.*

"I'm sorry, I'm not speaking to anyone tonight. My defense mechanisms seem to be out of order."

They deny or distort reality, and they operate unconsciously. According to Freud, they are often unhealthy patterns that cause emotional problems and self-defeating behavior. Although there is no single agreed-upon list of all the processes that Freud considered to be defenses, we will use the main ones described by Freud's daughter Anna Freud (1946), who became an eminent psychoanalyst herself, and by modern personality researchers (Plutchik, Kellerman, & Conte, 1979):

1. In *repression*, a threatening idea, memory, or emotion is blocked from becoming conscious. A woman who had a frightening experience in childhood, for example, may repress her memory of it. "Repression" doesn't mean that you consciously bite your tongue rather than reveal a guilty secret. It refers to the mind's effort to keep a lid on unacceptable feelings and thoughts in the unconscious, so that you aren't even aware of them.

2. In *projection*, one's own unacceptable feelings are attributed to someone else. A boy who dislikes his father, for instance, may feel anxious about disliking someone he depends on. So he may project his feelings onto his father, concluding that "he hates me." A person who has uncomfortable sexual feelings about members of a different ethnic group may project this discomfort onto them, saying, "those people are dirty-minded and oversexed."

3. In *reaction formation*, the feeling that produces unconscious anxiety is transformed into its opposite in consciousness. A woman who is afraid to admit she doesn't love her husband may consciously believe she loves him. How does such a transformed emotion differ from the true emotion? Usually, a reaction formation gives itself away by being excessive: The person asserts the feeling too much and is too extravagant and compulsive about demonstrating it. ("Love him? *Of course* I love him! I *never* have any bad thoughts about him! He's perfect. . . .")

4. *Regression*. As we will see, Freud believed that personality develops in a series of stages, from birth to maturity. Each new step, however, produces a certain amount of frustration and anxiety. If these become too great, normal development may be briefly or permanently halted and the child may remain *fixated* at the current stage; for instance, he or she may not outgrow clinging dependence. People may

ego *In psychoanalysis, the part of personality that represents reason, good sense, and rational self-control; operates according to the* reality principle.

reality principle *The principle guiding the operation of the ego; seeks to find socially acceptable outlets for instinctual energies.*

defense mechanisms *Methods used by the ego to prevent unconscious anxiety from reaching consciousness.*

Is she "regressing"?

"regress" to an earlier stage if they suffer a traumatic experience in a later one. An 8-year-old child who is anxious about parental divorce may regress to earlier habits of thumbsucking or clinging. Adults occasionally reveal "partial fixations" that they never outgrew, such as biting nails, and often regress to immature behavior when they are stressed.

5. In *denial*, people simply refuse to admit that something unpleasant is happening or that they are experiencing a taboo emotion. A woman who is angry with her boyfriend may deny that anything is wrong; an alcoholic may deny that he depends on liquor.

6. *Intellectualization* and *rationalization* (defenses favored by intellectuals!) are higher-level defenses that depend on cognitive processes. Intellectualization is the unconscious control of emotions and impulses by excessive dependence on "rational" interpretations of situations. For example, a person refuses to acknowledge his or her normal fear of death by saying, "I'm not afraid of getting old because it happens to everybody." In rationalization, the person finds excuses to justify actions that were caused by repressed and unacceptable feelings.

7. In *displacement*, as noted, people release their "pent-up" emotions (usually anger) on things, animals, or other people that are not the real object of their feelings. People use displacement when they perceive the real target as being too threatening to confront directly. A boy who is forbidden to express anger at his father, for example, may "take it out" on his toys or his younger sister.

These defense mechanisms, Freud maintained, protect the ego and allow the person to cope with reality. Different personalities emerge because people differ in the defenses they use, in how rigid their defenses are, and in whether their defenses lead to healthy or disturbed functioning.

The **superego**, the last system of personality to develop, represents the voice of morality, the rules of parents and society, the power of authority. The superego consists of the *ego ideal*, those moral and social standards you come to believe are right, and the *conscience*, the inner voice that says you did something wrong. The superego sits in judgment on the activities of the id, handing out good feelings (pride, satisfaction) when you do something well and handing out miserable feelings (guilt, shame) when you break the rules.

According to Freud, the healthy personality must keep all three systems in balance. Someone who is too controlled by the id is governed by impulse and selfish desires. Someone who is too controlled by the superego is rigid, moralistic, and authoritarian. Someone who has a weak ego is unable to balance personal needs and wishes with social duties and realistic limitations.

The development of personality. Freud thought that personality develops in a fixed series of five stages. Freud called these stages "psychosexual" because he believed that psychological development depends on the changing expression of sexual energy in different parts of the body as the child matures.

1. *The oral stage* marks the first year of life. Babies take in the world, as well as their nourishment, through their mouths. So the mouth, said Freud, is the focus of sensation and stimulation at this stage. People who remain fixated at the oral stage, he maintained, may, as adults, seek constant "oral gratification" in such activities as smoking, drinking, or overeating.

2. *The anal stage*, at about age 2 to 3, marks the start of ego development, as the child becomes aware of the self and of the demands of reality. The major issue at

superego *In psychoanalysis, the part of personality that represents conscience, morality, and social standards.*

this stage, said Freud, is control of bodily wastes, a lesson in self-control that the child learns during toilet training. People who remain fixated at this stage, he thought, may become "anal retentive," holding everything in, obsessive about neatness and cleanliness. Or they can become just the opposite, "anal expulsive," that is, messy and disorganized.

3. *The phallic (or Oedipal) stage* lasts roughly from age 3 to 5. Now sexual sensation is located in the penis, for boys, and in the clitoris, for girls. The child, said Freud, wishes to possess the parent of the opposite sex and get rid of the parent of the same sex. Children of this age often announce proudly that "I'm going to marry Daddy (or Mommy) when I grow up" and reject the same-sex "rival." Freud (1924a, 1924b) labeled this phenomenon the **Oedipus complex**, after the Greek legend of King Oedipus, who unwittingly killed his father and married his mother. Later, some psychoanalysts used the term "Electra complex" (from another Greek legend) to describe the female version of this conflict, but Freud himself and almost all contemporary psychoanalysts speak of the "Oedipus complex" for both sexes.

Boys and girls, Freud believed, go through the Oedipal stage differently. Boys at this stage are discovering the pleasure and pride of having a penis. When they see a female for the first time, they are horrified. Their unconscious exclaims (in one way or another), "Her penis has dropped off! How could this happen? The girl must have been castrated. Who could have done such a thing to her? My powerful father." This realization, said Freud, causes little boys to accept the authority of the father, who must have the power to castrate them, too. They repress their desire for the mother and decide to be as much like the father as possible. **Identification** is the process by which they take in, as their own, the father's standards of conscience and morality. The superego has emerged.

Freud admitted that he didn't know what to make of females, who, lacking the penis, couldn't go through the same steps. He speculated that a girl, upon discovering male anatomy, would panic that she had only a puny clitoris instead of a stately penis. She would conclude, said Freud, that she already had been castrated. As a result, girls don't have the powerful motivating fear that boys do to give up their Oedipal feelings. They have only a lingering sense of "penis envy."

The healthy female, said Freud, resolves penis envy by having children. The neurotic female resolves penis envy by trying to be like men, perhaps by having a career or becoming too "masculine." In either case, Freud concluded, women do not develop the strong moral superegos that men do. They feel inferior to men; dislike other women; and develop the unfortunate personality traits of passivity, vanity, jealousy, and "masochism" (taking pleasure in being treated badly).

By about age 5, when the Oedipus complex is resolved, the child's basic personality patterns are formed. Unconscious conflicts with parents, unresolved fixations and guilts, and attitudes toward the same and the opposite sex, said Freud, will continue to replay themselves throughout life.

4. *The latency stage* lasts from the end of the phallic stage to puberty. The child settles down, goes to school, makes friends, develops self-confidence, and learns the social rules for appropriate male or female behavior. Sexual feeling subsides.

5. *The genital stage* begins at puberty and marks the beginning of what Freud considered mature adult sexuality. Sexual energy is now located in the genitals, and, eventually, directed toward sexual intercourse. Not everyone reaches this mature stage, said Freud. The defense mechanisms of the ego and the displacement of instinctual energy may prevent people from reaching mature genital sexuality, and keep them fixated on "immature" forms of sexual behavior.

Oedipus complex *In psychoanalysis, a conflict in which a child desires the parent of the opposite sex and views the same-sex parent as a rival; this is the key issue in the phallic stage of development.*
identification *A process by which the child adopts an adult's standards of morality, values, and beliefs as his or her own; in psychoanalysis, identification with the same-sex parent occurs at resolution of the Oedipus conflict.*

As you might imagine, Freud's ideas were not exactly received with yawns. Some of his colleagues thought his theory was, to put it kindly, nonsense. Others felt that Freud had made an important contribution by putting together many already-existing ideas into a coherent theory of personality and its development. (Although other scientists had written about the unconscious and about the sexual impulses of children, Freud was the first to package these ideas in a systematic theory.) Still others became devoted followers, who revered Freud as they would revere the founder of a new religion (Drucker, 1979; Sulloway, 1979). Before we evaluate some aspects of Freud's theory, let's consider some variations on his basic theme.

QUICK ■ QUIZ

Which Freudian concepts do these examples suggest?

1. A 4-year-old girl wants to snuggle on Daddy's lap but refuses to kiss her mother.
2. A celibate priest writes poetry about sexual passion and love.
3. A man who is angry at his boss shouts at his kids for making noise.
4. A woman who was molested by her brother for many years assures her friends that she adores him and thinks he is simply perfect.
5. A racist justifies segregation by saying that black men are only interested in sex with white women.
6. A 9-year-old boy who moves to a new city starts having tantrums.

Answers:

5. projection   6. regression

1. Oedipus complex   2. sublimation   3. displacement   4. reaction formation

Freud's descendants and dissenters

Some of Freud's followers stayed in the psychoanalytic tradition and modified Freud's theories from within. Others broke away completely to start their own schools.

Karen Horney [HORN-eye] (1885–1952) took issue with Freud's emphasis on sexual and aggressive motivations, his notion of genetically based instincts, and his view that inner conflicts are inevitable (Horney, 1937, 1945). Horney's key concept was that of *basic anxiety*, the feeling of being "isolated and helpless in a potentially hostile world." Because people are dependent on each other, she believed, they often end up in a state of anxious conflict when others don't treat them well. Insecure, anxious children develop personality patterns to help them cope with their feelings of isolation and helplessness. They may become aggressive as a way of protecting what little security they do have. They may become overly submissive. They may become selfish and self-pitying as a way of gaining attention or sympathy.

In general, said Horney, people relate to each other in one of three ways: They can move *toward* others, seeking love, support, and cooperation; they can move

Puzzles of Personality

1. To what extent is personality available to consciousness?

To Freudians, conscious awareness is only the tip of the mental iceberg; most motives and conflicts are hidden in the unconscious and are revealed only in symbols (such as the phallic symbol of the snake), dreams, slips of the tongue, and free associations.

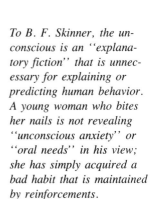

Carl Jung believed that in addition to having a private unconscious, individuals share a collective unconscious containing the images and themes (archetypes) *that unite human history and experience. One such archetype is the* shadow, *the monster or evil creature. From dragons to Dracula to Darth Vader, the shadow represents the primordial fear of animals and the "bestial" side of humanity.*

To B. F. Skinner, the unconscious is an "explanatory fiction" that is unnecessary for explaining or predicting human behavior. A young woman who bites her nails is not revealing "unconscious anxiety" or "oral needs" in his view; she has simply acquired a bad habit that is maintained by reinforcements.

Some psychoanalysts, such as Karen Horney, have argued that men's efforts to participate in the births of their children are evidence of unconscious "womb envy." To social-learning theorists, it reflects a conscious desire to be involved, and is a result of changing social rules, reinforcements, and attitudes about the father's role.

away from others, trying to be independent and self-sufficient; or they can move *against* others, being competitive, critical, and domineering. Ideally, she said, the healthy personality balances all three orientations. But some people become locked into only one mode: too weak-willed and self-denying, afraid to offend anyone; too independent, afraid to admit dependency; or too hostile, afraid to express affection.

Horney (1967) was also one of the first psychoanalysts to challenge Freud's notions of penis envy and female inferiority. She argued that it is both insulting philosophy and bad science to claim, as Freud did, that half the human race is dissatisfied with the gender assigned to it. When women feel inferior to men, she said, we should look for explanations in the real social disadvantages that women live with and their second-class status. Along with many contemporary female psychoanalysts, she feared that Freudian theory would justify continued discrimination against women by making it seem that female inferiority was "in their nature" and not in the conditions of their lives.

In fact, said Horney, if anyone has an envy problem, it is men, not women. Men have "womb envy": They envy the female ability to bear and nurse children. Men glorify their own genitals, she said, because they are unable to give birth themselves. Later psychoanalysts, such as Bruno Bettelheim (1962), argued that both sexes envy the reproductive abilities of the other.

Some psychoanalysts broke away even more radically than Horney from Freud's theories. Two of the most important renegades were Alfred Adler and Carl Jung, each of whom established separate schools.

Alfred Adler (1870–1937) disagreed with Freud's emphasis on the unconscious depths of the id, with its aggressive and sexual instincts. Adler had a more positive view of the human condition than Freud did. For instance, he believed that people have a *drive for superiority*, which is not the desire to dominate others but the desire for self-improvement. Adler (1927/1959) thought that people are motivated by an "upward drive" for perfection. This drive, said Adler, stems from the natural feelings of inferiority that all of us have, first as children, when we are weak and powerless compared to adults, and then later, when we have to recognize some limitations on our abilities. But some individuals, he wrote, develop an **inferiority complex**. Unable to accept their natural limitations, they try to mask them by pretending to be strong and capable. Instead of coping with real problems in life, people with inferiority complexes become overly concerned with protecting their self-esteem.

Unlike Freud and like Horney, Adler emphasized the individual's need for others. A key concept in Adler's theory of personality was that of **social interest**, empathy and concern for others (Adler, 1938/1964; Crandall, 1981). Social interest reflects the ability to be unselfish, to be sympathetic, to cooperate, and to feel connected to other people and to the world. (As the "Think About It" box suggests, this emphasis on unselfish motives has not been prominent in Western psychology.)

Adler (1935) further maintained that the real essence of human personality is *the creative self*. In this view, each person actively creates his or her own personality from the raw material of heredity and experience. Everyone creates a goal to strive for as well as a way of reaching that goal. All psychological processes form a consistent organization within each individual, a personality structure that is expressed in a unique *style of life* (Adler was the original "life-style" theorist). The style of life is a result of biological factors, the individual's conscious and unconscious motives, past history, and life goals (Ansbacher & Ansbacher, 1964).

To Freud, human beings were the passive victims of unconscious forces; to Adler, they were the masterful directors of their fate. To Freud, creativity was a side effect of sublimation; to Adler, creativity was a basic capacity of the species. To

inferiority complex *To Alfred Adler, an inability to accept natural limitations; occurs when the need for self-improvement is blocked or inhibited.*

social interest *To Adler, the ability to feel empathy, cooperate, and be connected to others.*

Think About It

The Self and Selfishness

Does the field of psychology, in its emphasis on the individual, promote selfishness? According to Michael Wallach and Lise Wallach (1983), both clinical and academic psychology "sanction and legitimize selfishness." The Wallachs believe that modern psychological views of human nature imply that if we look carefully enough at the kindest behavior, we will find self-interest and selfish motives underneath. Psychological research even regards love, marriage, and commitment as "bargains," trade-offs, and an exchange of assets.

The Wallachs trace the "selfishness of psychology" to Freud's emphasis on the naturally self-promoting desires of the id and ego. But even neo-Freudians and humanists, they argue, emphasize individual health and welfare over the health and welfare of the individual's family and community. Rogers and Maslow celebrated "self-love" and "self-actualization," freedom and autonomy. These are noble sentiments, say the Wallachs, but in practice they have been misinterpreted to give permission for selfishness. People who don't put themselves first may be accused of "suppressing their inner needs," "being a doormat," or "denying their real selves."

This attitude, the Wallachs believe, does not make people happier, create empathy or compassion, or help people get along with one another. Some therapists are now trying to balance this tilt, drawing on altruistic and ethical principles that move clients away from self-absorption. These new approaches are therapeutic, say the Wallachs, because they stress the importance for the individual's well-being of *not* focusing on the self. Doing unto others, they believe, is good therapy as well as good theory.

Certainly, much of modern psychology is concerned with such concepts as the "personality," "inner motives," "needs," "self-esteem," "freedom," and "achievement"—all of which emphasize the individual (Sampson, 1988). But look again at the Table of Contents of this book. Imagine what it would be like if 16 chapters concerned family relations, social groups, dependency needs, and the effects of other people on our behavior and perception, and only two chapters were devoted to individual physiology and cognition. Such a revised textbook would be close to the Japanese view of psychology, which contends that there is virtually no such thing as studying the individual apart from his or her social world (Weisz, Rothbaum, & Blackburn, 1984). A Chinese-American writer, Francis Hsu (1981), contrasts the Chinese, who are situation-centered, with the Americans, who are individual-centered. This cultural difference is reflected in the way psychologists see and study the world.

If you had a "situation-centered" psychology text, would your view of personality be different? How? Does the repeated emphasis in America on "the individual" blind us to our need for social connections? Does all this talk about the self make us more self-ish? What do you think?

Freud, social cooperation was a grudging sacrifice of the id; to Adler, it was the essence of human life. In recent years, as psychology has moved toward an emphasis on cognitive appraisals in human development, therapy, and personality, Adler's work has been rediscovered.

Carl Jung (1875–1961) differed with Freud on the nature of the unconscious. In addition to the individual's personal unconscious, said Jung, there is a **collective unconscious**, containing the universal memories and history of humankind. From his study of international myths, folklore, and art, Jung was impressed by common, repeated images, which he called **archetypes**. An archetype can be a picture, such as the "magic circle," called a "mandala" in Eastern religions, which symbolizes the unity of life. It can be a mythical figure, such as the Hero, the Nurturing Mother, the Powerful Father, the Wicked Witch (Jung, 1967). Other powerful archetypes are the *persona* and the *shadow*. The persona is the public personality,

collective unconscious *To Carl Jung, the universal memories and experiences of humankind, represented in the unconscious of all people.*

archetypes [AR-ki-tipes] *To Jung, universal, symbolic images that appear in myths, art, dreams, and other expressions of the collective unconscious.*

the aspects of yourself that you reveal to others, the role that society expects you to play. The shadow archetype reflects the prehistoric fear of wild animals and represents the animal side of human nature.

Two of the most important archetypes, in Jung's view, are those of men and women themselves. Jung (like Freud) recognized that human beings are psychologically bisexual, that is, that ''masculine'' and ''feminine'' qualities are to be found in both sexes. The *anima* represents the feminine archetype in men; the *animus* represents the masculine archetype in women. A man understands the nature of woman by virtue of his anima, and a woman understands a man by virtue of her animus. Problems can arise, though, if either sex projects an idealized archetype onto the other and cannot accept the real individual.

Although Jung shared with Freud a fascination with the unconscious side of the personality, he shared with Adler a belief in the positive, forward-moving strengths of the ego. For Jung, people are motivated not only by past conflicts, as Freud thought, but also by their future goals and by the desire to fulfill themselves. There are two basic personality orientations, Jung believed: *introversion*, which describes the person who is focused inward, who is cautious, shy, timid, and reflective; and *extroversion*, which describes the person who is outgoing, sociable, assertive, and energetic. Jung believed that the healthy personality maintains a balance in all spheres, that it is male and female, introverted and extroverted, conscious and unconscious, able to accept the past and strive for the future.

Modern research has supported Jung's belief that extroversion-introversion is a basic dimension of personality, as we will soon see. Research has also confirmed Jung's idea that certain basic archetypes—such as the Hero and the Earth Mother—appear in virtually every society (Campbell, 1949/1968) and may influence how people see their own lives. In one study in which 50 people told their life stories in a two-hour session, Dan McAdams (1988) found common Jungian archetypes—a mythic character at the heart of the person's life story, around which the person shaped his or her identity. For example, many of the subjects told stories that could be symbolized by the myth of the Greek god Dionysus, the pleasure seeker who escapes responsibility. These archetypes, McAdams believes, are idealized images of ourselves. They represent ''the main characters in the life stories we construct as our identities.'' As we said in Chapter 1, human beings are the ''story-telling species''; we live by the stories we tell.

QUICK ■ QUIZ

Match each idea with the analyst who proposed it.

1. Alfred Adler
2. Sigmund Freud
3. Karen Horney
4. Carl Jung

a. basic anxiety
b. collective unconscious
c. superego
d. womb envy
e. Oedipus complex
f. social interest
g. archetype
h. inferiority complex

Answers:

1. f, h   2. c, e   3. a, d   4. b, g

Evaluating psychoanalysis

There are very few true-blue Freudians any more. Modern neo (''new'')-Freudians have modified many aspects of Freud's original theories. But most of the criticism of psychoanalysis comes from other schools of psychology, which point out the following problems with this approach:

1. *Untestable hypotheses.* Many of the ideas in psychoanalysis, old or new, are impossible to test one way or the other. They are descriptive observations, more poetic than scientific. As we saw in Chapter 2, a theory that is impossible to disconfirm in principle is not a scientific theory, and many psychoanalytic ideas about unconscious motivations are impossible to confirm or disprove. Further, because so much of psychoanalytic theory depends on the subjective interpretation of the analyst, there is no way to decide which analyst is right. Freud saw penis envy; Horney saw womb envy. Freud saw castration fears; other analysts did not.

2. *Incorrect or time-limited ideas.* Many of Freud's ideas that were put to the test have proved faulty. His notion that our instincts fill an internal ''reservoir,'' for instance, has been disproved by modern research in physiology. The body does not ''store'' anger or other emotions. People can certainly collect grievances and keep a mental list of grudges, but this is not the same as saying they have a fixed amount of aggressive energy. As we saw in Chapter 9, people are not teapots: When they ''blow off steam'' they tend to become hotter, not cooler. Other Freudian ideas have been shown to be specific to his society rather than universal, timeless principles. Freud's belief that sexual conflicts are behind most personality problems, for example, was probably truer in Victorian times than today.

3. *The ''patients-represent-everyone'' fallacy.* Freud and his followers generalized inappropriately from patients in therapy to all human beings. If a woman comes to her therapist complaining of an excessive attachment to her father, the therapist cannot scientifically conclude that her problem is typical of *all* women. If a child is confused about sexual anatomy and thinks that girls have lost their penises, a scientist cannot conclude that *all* children share this view. If a homosexual patient reports having emotional conflicts, a clinician cannot conclude that *all* homosexuals are ''sick.'' To be accurate, the observer would have to study a random sample of women, children, or homosexuals who are not in therapy.

4. *The ''looking-backward'' fallacy.* Any of us, looking backward over our lives, can array events in a straight line. We assume that if A came before B, then A *caused* B. Psychoanalysts often make this error, and Freud himself was aware of it. ''So long as we trace the development from its final stage backwards,'' he wrote, ''the connection appears continuous, and we feel we have gained an insight which is completely satisfactory or even exhaustive. But if we proceed the reverse way [if we start at the beginning and try to predict the result], then we no longer get the impression of an inevitable sequence of events'' (Freud, 1920/1963). Looking backward also depends on a person's memories, which—you may remember!—are highly subject to distortion.

5. *An overemphasis on unconscious processes rather than real experiences.* Freud's emphasis on the unconscious had a powerful effect, then and now, not just for theoretical reasons but also for practical ones. It was a great step forward to discover that people are not always aware of their actual desires or of the motives behind their behavior. However, some psychologists today believe that the emphasis on the unconscious went too far, overshadowing the importance of real events and conscious thoughts. Consider the story of how Freud hit upon the very cornerstone of psychoanalytic theory—the Oedipus complex.

Freud's ideas are provocative. But are they testable? What errors can arise in generalizing from patients to all humanity and in using retrospective histories to create theories of development?

Early in Freud's career, many of his women patients (and some men) told him they had been sexually molested in childhood, typically by their fathers, uncles, or male friends of the family. At first, Freud concluded that these early experiences of sexual abuse were responsible for his patients' later unhappiness and illness. But then Freud changed his mind. He decided that his patients must be reporting *fantasies*, not real events, and that children (all children, not just his patients) fantasize about having sexual relations with their opposite-sex parent. These fantasies are so taboo, said Freud, that children feel guilty about having them. It is their unconscious guilt about wanting sex with the parent, not the actual experience of sexual abuse, that causes illness and emotional problems later on. With this turnaround, psychoanalysis was born (Sulloway, 1979).

Today, the notion that children are "unconsciously" seductive is being vigorously attacked, as studies document the reality of sexual abuse in childhood (D. Russell, 1986). New research suggests that Freud's patients probably were telling the truth when they revealed sexual abuse (Masson, 1984; Rush, 1980; Sulloway, 1979). Other analysts have become more sensitive to the actual abuse, emotional as well as physical, that some parents inflict on their children (A. Miller, 1984). This abuse, they argue, has more impact than childish "fantasies."

In spite of all these problems, contemporary researchers and clinical psychologists are finding support for some of Freud's assumptions, as we will see in later chapters. Many people are indeed unconscious of the motives behind their puzzling actions. Some early childhood experiences can have a lasting effect on personality. Thoughts and rational behavior can be distorted by guilt, anxiety, and shame. The mind does defend itself against information that is threatening, unpleasant, or shocking. Prolonged emotional conflict may play itself out in physical symptoms, immature habits, and self-defeating actions.

In his provocative ideas, in the beauty of his writing, and in his own complicated personality, Freud left a powerful legacy to psychology. As Havelock Ellis (1910) put it, even when Freud "selects a very thin thread [in tying together his theories], he seldom fails to string pearls on it, and these have their value whether the thread snaps or not."

The Learning Tradition: You Are What You Do

On a hot summer day, James Peters, of Franklin, Long Island, shot and killed his next-door neighbor, Ralph Galluccio. They had not been fighting over love, money, drugs, or politics. They had reached the end of their patience in a ten-year dispute over their common property line. According to friends, this feud was not typical of the men's personalities. Galluccio, said his employer, was "a likable person with a good, even disposition." Peters, said his employer, is a "very mild-mannered, cooperative" man, "an all-around good guy."

A Freudian analyst might say that this violent episode demonstrates the aggressive instinct in us all, but these men were not able to channel or displace their aggression constructively. A behaviorist, however, would examine the role of environment in determining the actions of these men. In the behavioral tradition, "environment" includes everything from neighbors and friends to family circumstances and job requirements. Some *radical behaviorists* take the extreme view that "per-

Puzzles of Personality

2. Is human nature basically destructive and selfish or constructive and cooperative?

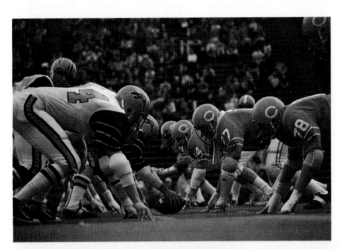

To Freudians, human nature rests on an eternal war between the aggressive or death instincts and the sexual or life instincts. The modern football game, in this view, represents the displacement of aggressive energy into a socially accepted activity.

To behaviorists and social learning theorists, human nature can be as aggressive or peaceable as our environments permit. Behavioral research finds that aggressive sports, far from "displacing" aggression, actually model and encourage hostility and violence among players and spectators.

Karen Horney argued that human nature is basically social and cooperative; individuals who row together, so to speak, grow together. When people are prevented from expressing their needs for attachment and connection, however, they feel a basic anxiety and insecurity that may be expressed in destructiveness and hostility.

Alfred Adler believed that human nature is basically creative and constructive. Unless individuals are thwarted by social conditions, they strive to excel—as did champion skaters Torvill and Dean, who achieved perfect scores at the 1984 Olympics.

sonality'' is only a convenient illusion. To understand human behavior, they say, we do not need to consider mental processes or biological factors; we need only consider the environment in which behavior occurs. Others, called *social learning theorists*, argue that we acquire consistent personality patterns as we learn to deal with the environment. What anyone does at a given time, they say, is a result of the interaction between personality and the situation.

The behavioral school

In 1913, while Sigmund Freud was deeply enmeshed in formulating psychoanalysis in Vienna, John B. Watson was founding the behavioral tradition in the United States. The two men represented the North and South Poles of personality theory, with Freud talking about instincts and unconscious motives and Watson dismissing these concepts as vague and unscientific. As we noted in Chapter 6, Watson held that most aspects of personality, including conflicts, fears, and habits, are classically conditioned responses, just as salivation was in Pavlov's dogs.

The best-known American behaviorist, B. F. Skinner, was actually as critical of Watson as he was of the psychoanalysts. Skinner shared with Freud the belief that *behavior is determined* by predictable factors. But he disagreed with Freud's reliance on hypothetical forces such as ''the unconscious,'' ''instincts,'' or ''repression.'' Skinner shared with Watson a belief that behavior is primarily learned. But he rejected Watson's emphasis on classical conditioning as the major form of learning. Noting that many kinds of behavior were not classically conditioned, he turned to operant (instrumental) conditioning as the fundamental form of learning. (To refresh your memory on these forms of learning, see Chapter 6.) Skinner (1950) was more interested in formulating universal laws of behavior than in formulating a theory of personality; personality is simply a collection of behavioral patterns. The terms we commonly use to describe personality (such as ''aggressive'' or ''dominant'') can be reduced to a description of particular responses in certain situations.

This doesn't mean that all situations produce the same responses in all individuals. Consider two people at a party of strangers. One is outgoing and friendly, and the other, nervous and shy. Skinner would say that if we looked into the behavioral histories of these two people, we would find different patterns of reinforcement. For one, friendliness was reinforced; for the other, shyness was reinforced and assertiveness punished. What could possibly reward painful shyness? Experiments have found that shyness and anxiety are encouraged when they serve as a ''self-handicapping strategy.'' When shy people are in situations in which they believe they will be evaluated, they learn to use their anxiety as an excuse for poor performance (Snyder et al., 1985).

Some behaviorists have tried to translate Freud's descriptive terms into behavioral principles. Among the first of these were John Dollard and Neal Miller (1950). For example, they interpreted Freud's notion of repression in terms of acquired habits. Suppose a young man is worried that his girlfriend will leave him. He is afraid to talk to her about his feelings because he believes that would reveal an unmanly weakness. Instead, every time his feelings of insecurity arise, he goes out drinking with his buddies. In so doing, he is learning a habit: ''When I feel anxious, I'll go out drinking.'' Freud might say he has repressed his true feelings, burying them in the unconscious. Dollard and Miller would say he has learned a way of avoiding his feelings, because drinking with his friends is temporarily enjoyable and distracts him from anxiety.

Similarly, psychologists have demonstrated in the laboratory that masochism, taking pleasure in pain, is learned—not, as Freud thought, an inevitable part of female personality (Stone & Hokanson, 1969). Anyone, male or female, may acquire self-defeating, even injurious, habits if those habits help the person avoid hostility or greater injury from others. When self-punishment is the lesser of two evils, it actually reduces anxiety and "feels good."

Some psychologists criticize behaviorism for implying that individuals are as soft as jellyfish, and that with the right environment, anyone can become anything. They also criticize behaviorism for implying that people are entirely passive recipients of environmental events. These common charges are not accurate, at least as far as Skinner's work is concerned. Skinner (1957) recognizes that people may have limits because of their genetic constitution or temperament, and he recognizes that people can *change* their environments to provide a different set of reinforcers.

Skinner and other "radical" behaviorists do not deny that people have feelings, thoughts, or values. However, they believe that these mental states are as subject to the laws of learning as, say, nail biting is. (Nail biting itself, they would say, is a learned bad habit rather than a "fixation" at the "oral stage.") Skinner believes that the study of values is essentially the study of reinforcers. It is unscientific and imprecise to say that "Pat values fame." Rather, fame is positively reinforcing to Pat, which is why Pat continues to strive for it. Someone else might find fame unpleasantly punishing, and thus hold different "values." If we want a peaceful world, Skinner concludes, we had better not wait around for people's personalities or feelings to change. We had better change circumstances so that cooperation is rewarded, cheaters don't win, and aggressors don't stay in power.

The social learning school

Modern social learning theorists give true radical behaviorists heartburn, because they have rediscovered the mind. They still emphasize the importance of the environment in shaping behavior, but they also believe in the importance of how people *interpret* their environments. The social learning approach to personality includes (1) aspects of the individual, (2) aspects of the environment, and (3) the *interaction* between them. Skinner would agree, but he would not focus, as social learning theorists do, on cognitive phenomena such as perception, symbols, and beliefs.

"If actions were determined solely by external rewards and punishments," writes Albert Bandura (1986), "people would behave like weathervanes, constantly shifting direction to conform to whatever momentary influence happened to impinge on them." To social learning theorists such as Bandura, the fact that people don't (always) act like weathervanes means that much of human behavior is *self-regulated*—shaped by thoughts, values, self-reflections, and intentions. Personality, they maintain, depends both on the context in which behavior is originally learned and on the current situation in which it occurs. To traditional learning theory, they have added principles of social learning, such as observational (vicarious) learning (learning by watching what other people do and what happens to them for doing it) and self-reinforcement (rewarding yourself for reaching a goal or punishing yourself for failing to do so).

Social learning theorists have identified qualities of the person that they believe influence behavior across many situations. The way people differ in each of these spheres, they say, contributes to their recognizable "personalities" (Mischel, 1968, 1981). Some of these qualities are:

▪ *Inherited temperaments*, such as level of energy or the disposition to respond to novelty with either curiosity or fear.

▪ *Skills and talents*, such as singing, sailing, writing, or managing.

▪ *Perceptions*. Individuals differ in how they have learned to interpret events, selectively noticing some aspects of a situation and ignoring others. Give Casey a chance to speak to an audience of 300 members of the Wildlife Association, and he sees it as an exciting challenge. Give Frank the same chance, and he sees it as a giant plot to embarrass and terrify him.

▪ *Expectations*. As you grow up, you learn to have certain expectations about what will happen to you if you behave in certain ways. Mildred may learn that if she speaks her mind, she can expect to irritate her parents, who want her to be quiet and obedient. Elizabeth may learn that if she speaks her mind, she can expect praise and attention.

▪ *Plans of action*. By adulthood, you have developed certain standards and values you use to govern yourself and your actions. People differ in their abilities to plan for the future and to carry out their plans.

Would you be likely to see a bagpipe band in Polynesia?

All of these aspects of the individual, however, depend on specific situations. Do the circumstances permit your personal qualities or preferences to be expressed? How may they be expressed? You may have a skill, such as pie baking or hog calling, and find yourself in a place that never gives you the chance to reveal it. (There is not much call for hog callers in San Francisco.) On the other hand, you may find yourself in a new environment that gives you an opportunity to learn skills you never dreamed you had. Specific situations, according to the social learning school, either permit us to express aspects of our personalities or prevent us from doing so.

Evaluating behavioral theories

Why did James Peters kill Ralph Galluccio? Instead of assuming that Galluccio and Peters were driven by a universal destructive impulse, social learning psychologists would investigate the social *conditions* of their quarrel and each man's *perceptions* about it. The two men found themselves in an increasingly difficult situation that seemed to offer no way out. This doesn't mean that any two neighbors caught in a similar situation would have behaved the same way. Perhaps these two men lacked the skill to negotiate their differences. Perhaps each man had learned that aggressive actions would make other people knuckle under to his wishes. When hurling insults, and then hurling eggs, failed, all they knew how to do was to escalate the aggression.

The behavioral and social learning approaches represent a big step forward in solving some of the problems with psychoanalytic theories. These approaches rely on experimental evidence and field studies rather than on the memories of patients in therapy. They also explain why behavior is so often inconsistent. If George is aggressive at home but meek at work, or if Georgina is independent at work but dependent on her friends, it is because they are reinforced differently in different situations. They have *learned* to behave differently.

Critics, however, observe that the social learning approach often does not distinguish the cause of a behavior from its consequences. For example, observational studies of children find that teachers and parents react more harshly to boys' aggressiveness than to girls' (Serbin & Connor, 1979). Boys get more attention and also more punishment for disruptive behavior. In social learning theory, this fact helps explain why more boys than girls are physically aggressive. But it is also possible that adults pay more attention to boys because the boys' aggressiveness is so disruptive and annoying to begin with.

Some psychologists, as we will see next, regard behavioral theories of personality as too ''cold'' and mechanical. Instead, they propose theories of personality that emphasize the total individual, the individual's unique sense of self, and free will.

QUICK ■ QUIZ

In each situation, which explanation would be offered by a psychoanalyst, a behaviorist, and a social learning theorist?

1. A 6-year-old boy is behaving aggressively in the classroom, hitting other children and refusing to obey the teacher.
   a. The boy is being positively reinforced for aggressive behavior by getting attention from the teacher and the other children.
   b. The boy is expressing the aggressive energy of the id and has not developed enough ego control.
   c. The boy's behavior is an interaction of his own high energy level and of what he believes, from his own experience and observation, about the consequences of aggression.
2. A 6-year-old girl is clinging to her teacher in the classroom, afraid to do anything on her own.
   a. The girl has already learned to expect that any independent action she tries will be ignored or punished, so she is reluctant to work on her own.
   b. The girl gets attention from the teacher only when she is in close range. When she goes off to do work on her own, the teacher ignores her.
   c. The girl has developed passivity and dependency as a normal resolution of her Oedipus complex in preparation for her adult roles of wife and mother.

Answers:

1. a. behaviorist b. psychoanalyst c. social learning theorist 2. a. social learning theorist b. behaviorist c. psychoanalyst

The Humanist Tradition: You Are What You Become

A third way to look at personality is not from outside, observing what a person does or says, but from inside, concentrating on a person's own sense of self and experience. This perspective, sometimes called **phenomenology**, does not seek to predict behavior or to uncover hidden motivation. It focuses on the person's subjective interpretation of what is happening right now. One group of phenomenologists,

phenomenology *The study of events and situations as individuals experience them; in personality, the study of an individual's qualities from the person's own point of view.*

called the *humanists*, believes that personality is defined by the human abilities that separate us from other animals: freedom of choice, free will, and self-direction.

The self and self-regard

Humanistic psychology was launched as a movement within psychology at a conference in 1964. Its chief leaders were Abraham Maslow, Rollo May, and Carl Rogers, who argued that it was time for a "third force" in psychology. They rejected the psychoanalytic emphasis on hostility, biological instincts, and conflict. They also rejected the fragmented approach of the behavioral schools, with their emphasis on describing pieces of the person. Mainstream psychology, they said, failed to deal with the real problems of life or draw a full picture of human potential (M. Smith, 1984). The trouble with psychology, said Maslow (1971), was that it had forgotten that human nature includes some good things, such as joy, rapture, laughter, love, simple daily happiness, and rare moments of ecstasy, which he called *peak experiences.*

Not all humanists have been as cheerful as Maslow was about human nature. Rollo May emphasizes some of the fundamentally difficult or even tragic aspects of the human condition, including loneliness, anxiety, and alienation. In books such as *The Meaning of Anxiety, Man's Search for Himself, Love and Will,* and *Existential Psychology,* May brought to American psychology elements of the European philosophy of existentialism. This doctrine holds, for instance, that human beings have absolute freedom of choice, but this freedom carries a price in anxiety and even despair.

Carl Rogers, like Freud, derived many of his ideas from observing his clients in therapy. As a clinician, Rogers (1951, 1961) was interested not only in why some people cannot function well, but also in what he called the fully functioning individual. Rogers's theory of personality is based on the relationship between the *self* (your conscious view of yourself, the qualities that make up "I" or "me") and the *organism* (the sum of all of your experience, including unconscious feelings, perceptions, and wishes). This experience is known only to you, through your own frame of reference. How you behave depends on your own subjective reality, Rogers said, not on the external reality around you. Fully functioning people, Rogers believed, show a **congruence**, or harmony, between self and organism. Such people are trusting, warm, and open to new experience. They aren't defensive or intolerant. Their beliefs about themselves are realistic. When the self and the organism are in conflict, however, the person is said to be in a state of incongruence.

To become fully functioning, congruent people, Rogers maintained, we all need **unconditional positive regard**, love and support for the people we are, without strings (conditions) attached. This doesn't mean that Winnifred should be allowed to kick her brother when she is angry with him or that Wilbur may throw his dinner out the window because he doesn't like pot roast. In these cases, however, a parent can correct the child's behavior without withdrawing love from the child. The child can learn that the behavior, not the child, is what is bad. "House rules are 'no violence,' Winnifred," is a very different message from "You are a horrible person, Winnifred."

Unfortunately, Rogers observed, many children are raised with *conditional* positive regard. The condition is "I'll love you if you behave well and I won't love you if you behave badly." Adults often treat each other this way, too. People treated with conditional regard begin to suppress or deny feelings or actions that

congruence *To Carl Rogers, harmony between the conscious self and the totality of the person's unconscious feelings and life experiences.*

unconditional positive regard *To Rogers, love or support given to another person with no conditions attached.*

they believe are unacceptable to those they love. The result, said Rogers, is incongruence. The suppression of feelings and parts of oneself produces low self-regard, inaccurate perceptions of reality, defensiveness, and unhappiness. Incongruence creates the sensation of being ''out of touch with your feelings,'' of not being true to your ''real self.''

Evaluating humanistic psychology

The major criticism of the humanistic approach is that many of its assumptions cannot be tested because the terms that humanists use are vague. How would you tell if a person is ''self-fulfilled'' or ''self-actualized''? How would you distinguish a person who has ''unconditional positive self-regard'' from one who is arrogant or selfish? Critics also say that humanistic psychology is closer to philosophy than science, because it rests on a subjective view of human nature. It happens to be a nicer view of human nature than, say, Freud's, but it is just as difficult to prove. Freud saw, in his patients and in history, conflict, destructive drives, selfishness, and lust. Maslow and Rogers saw, in individuals and in history, cooperation, constructive drives, altruism, and love. This may tell us more about the observers than about the observed.

Many psychologists also resent the implication that they are not humanists, or do not care about humanity, just because they study people scientifically or have different ideas about how to achieve goals of peace and self-fulfillment. Some, who observe the power of a particular situation to make people conform or behave badly, are skeptical about the prospects of creating a humane world by simply trusting in people to behave well, by giving them unconditional love, or by counting on the goodness of human nature.

Nevertheless, humanistic psychology has added balance to psychology's view of human nature. Further, some of Maslow's and Rogers's ideas have been tested experimentally. Many have proven faulty, such as Maslow's belief in a hierarchy of needs (see Chapter 10), but others have been supported, as we will see in later chapters. Psychologists now study the happier emotions and positive experiences, such as love, altruism, cooperation, and creativity, along with the troubling ones. Stress researchers have discovered the healing powers of humor and hope. Child psychologists have shown how parental treatment contributes to or crushes a child's self-esteem and creativity. Clinical research has found that empathy is indeed a critical factor in successful therapy. Finally, the idea that personality contains a deep well of ''potential'' (usually this means a potential for good, not a potential to become an ax murderer) has spawned an interest in the further reaches of consciousness and capability.

Traits and Types: You Do What You Are

So far we have been looking at theories of what a personality is (or is not) and how it develops. But if you have ever taken a personality quiz in your local newspaper or a favorite magazine, you are following a very different psychological tradition. These questionnaires usually have blaring headlines such as WHAT'S YOUR ASSERTIVENESS QUOTIENT? or ARE YOU SELF-DESTRUCTIVE? or WHAT TYPE OF FRIEND ARE YOU—JEALOUS, JUMPY, OR JOVIAL? Most of these

Puzzles of Personality

3. Which has more influence on behavior, personality or situation?

Some societies, such as China, are highly situation-oriented; others, such as the United States, are more individual-oriented. Chinese workers in Beijing do their morning T'ai Chi exercises in identical fashion; individualistic Americans take morning exercise—running or walking in different directions, in different ways, in different clothes.

Many psychologists believe that behavior is more strongly influenced by the situation you are in than by your personality. Numerous situations, from working in an office to playing in a marching band, require us to set aside preferences and feelings and behave in specific ways. Other psychologists reply that even in situations that demand a certain uniformity, individuals manage to put their unique marks on their environments. These otherwise identical row houses, for instance, are stamped with the ''personalities'' of their owners.

popular quizzes are, in fact, pretty silly psychology (see "Taking Psychology with You"). But they are part of an ancient effort to divide people according to their particular traits or "personality types." A **trait** is simply a characteristic that is assumed to describe a person across many situations: shy, brave, reliable, friendly, hostile, serious, confident, sullen, and so on. A *type* is a clump of traits thought to describe a certain kind of individual. An "executive type," for instance, might have the traits of leadership, dominance, high self-confidence, and consideration for others.

The very first efforts to describe personality were "type theories," usually based on physical differences among people. We have already noted some historical efforts to divide people into four types according to their "dominant" bodily fluid (blood, phlegm, yellow bile, black bile) or according to the location of bumps on the head (Gall's system of phrenology). In the twentieth century, William Sheldon (1942) tried to identify personality types according to body build. Fat, muscular, and thin body types, he said, have different personalities.

Among psychologists nowadays, type theories are about as popular as a dog at a cat show. Although people certainly are influenced by how they look and feel physically, there is no evidence that their personalities depend on their body shapes, bodily fluids, or head bumps. Today, many psychologists concentrate on identifying specific traits, the pieces of personality. For the most part, psychologists in this area are more concerned with describing the traits than explaining how they develop.

Counting qualities

One of the most influential trait theorists in this century was Gordon Allport (1897–1967). Allport observed that most members of a society share certain qualities, which he called common traits, that their culture expects and rewards. For example, most Eskimo are peaceful and cooperative, so you don't learn much about an individual Eskimo's personality if you find that he or she is kind and cooperative. To understand why two people differ, said Allport (1937, 1961), you must look at their individual traits (also called dispositions), the qualities that make each of them unique.

Allport maintained that there are three kinds of individual traits: cardinal, central, and secondary. *Cardinal traits* are of overwhelming importance to an individual and influence almost everything the person does. We might say that Mohandas Gandhi and Martin Luther King, Jr., had the cardinal trait of nonviolence. Few people, said Allport, have cardinal traits. Instead, most of us have five to ten *central traits* that reflect a characteristic way of behaving, dealing with others, and reacting to new situations. Some typical central traits might include being warm, neat, humble, shy, or competitive. *Secondary traits* are less important aspects of personality, more subject to change and situation than central traits are. They include preferences (for foods, colors, movies), habits, garden-variety opinions, and the like.

Years ago, Solomon Asch (1946) observed that central traits are important not only because they organize the personality, but also because they affect how other people react. For example, the central traits "warm" and "cold" have a powerful effect on how you regard a person and on the other traits you expect that person to have. Experiments find that when you expect a person to be "warm," you also assume that he or she will be more sociable, funny, easygoing, and considerate than when you expect the person to be "cold" (Asch & Zukier, 1984; Kelley, 1950).

trait *A descriptive characteristic of an individual, assumed to be stable across situations.*

The trait approach to personality has been enormously popular; psychologists have studied hundreds of traits. A large area of research has concerned the identification and measurement of components of self-concept, including self-esteem and locus of control.

▪ *Self-esteem.* All things considered, do you like yourself? Do you often feel inadequate, or do you feel secure about yourself in spite of your flaws? One problem with measuring self-esteem, as William James noted in 1890, is that it rises and falls like a barometer. You might feel terrific about yourself on Tuesday, when you sail through a tough exam, and detest yourself on Wednesday, after you make an embarrassing mistake in public. Another problem is that how people feel about themselves privately (*experienced* self-esteem) is not necessarily related to how they behave with others (*presented* self-esteem) (Demo, 1985). You might brag about your performance on the basketball team, yet secretly feel that you blew your chance to play in a tournament. Some researchers define self-esteem as a global, stable personality trait and measure it at one moment in time (Rosenberg, 1979). Others try to take "snapshots" of a person's self-esteem in different situations (Savin-Williams & Demo, 1983).

▪ *Locus of control.* In Chapter 9 we discussed some of the beliefs that are related to different emotions. For example, people who believe that they do well because of their own abilities are likely to feel happy. If they believe their success is due to chance or luck, however, they are likely to feel grateful or even guilty. This finding emerged from research on **locus of control**, your general expectation of whether or not the results of your actions are under your own control (Rotter, 1966). People who have an *internal* locus of control ("internals") tend to believe they are responsible for what happens to them, that they are captains of their life's ship. People who have an *external* locus of control ("externals") tend to believe they are the helpless victims of chance, fate, or other people.

You might think that having an internal locus of control would be related to self-esteem, and usually it is. Feeling that you are in control of your life is conducive to a sense of self-worth, competence, and well-being. Internals are more likely than externals to join civil rights and women's rights groups that are devoted to improving social conditions (Gergen & Gergen, 1986). Sometimes, though, having too strong a sense of internal control can backfire, as in trying to cope with events that are in fact out of one's power to influence. (We will discuss control and health in Chapter 15.)

Psychologists have identified many fascinating single traits, from "sensation seeking" (the extent to which people enjoy anything to do with risk) to "erotophobia" (the extent to which people fear anything to do with sex). But some personality theorists are unhappy with this piecemeal approach to personality. They are attempting to find the few *basic*, organizing traits of personality.

Raymond B. Cattell (1965, 1973) advanced the study of personality traits by using a statistical method called *factor analysis* (see Chapter 12). Performing a factor analysis on personality traits is like adding water to flour: It causes the basic material to clump up into little balls. Using questionnaires, life descriptions, and observations, Cattell measured dozens of personality traits in hundreds of people. He called these descriptive qualities *surface traits* because they are visible in a person's words or deeds. He believed that factor analysis, which shows which traits are correlated with which others, would identify *source traits*, the bedrock of personality, the underlying causes of surface qualities. A person might have the surface

locus of control *A general expectation about whether the results of one's actions are under one's own control* (internal *locus*) *or beyond one's control* (external *locus*).

traits of assertiveness, courage, and ambition; the source trait, linking all three, might be dominance. Cattell and his associates have investigated many aspects of personality, including humor, music preferences, intelligence, creativity, leadership, and emotional disorder. His method of conducting large-scale research and of carefully describing the connections between personality traits had a major influence on research in personality.

Cattell maintains that there are at least 16 factors necessary to describe the complexities of personality, and others agree with him (Mershon & Gorsuch, 1988). But some psychologists have tried to boil surface traits down into even fewer clusters. Hans Eysenck (1970), for example, applying factor analysis to personality test scores, concluded that there are only three dimensions of personality, each grounded in biology. One is *extroversion* (E), the extent to which a person is outgoing, sociable, and energetic (extroverted). The second is *neuroticism* (N), or emotionality, the extent to which a person is anxious, depressed, obsessive, and hostile. The third is *psychoticism* (P), or tough-mindedness, the extent to which a person is ruthless, lacks empathy, and is disposed to crime and mental illness. Eysenck and his associates have validated these dimensions in 25 nations, from India and Uganda to England and Singapore (Barrett & Eysenck, 1984; Eysenck & Eysenck, 1985; Eysenck & Long, 1986).

Other researchers think that Eysenck went too far in "boiling down" basic traits, and their work casts doubt on the existence of a P factor for most people. By conducting longitudinal studies and analyzing hundreds of personality traits, these psychologists argue that personality can be described according to five "robust factors" (Costa & McCrae, 1988; Digman & Inouye, 1986; Zuckerman, Kuhlman, & Camac, 1988):

Are extroverts born or made?

1. *Introversion versus extroversion*: This dimension includes such personality traits as being talkative or silent, sociable or reclusive, adventurous or cautious, outgoing or shy. Eysenck, and before him Carl Jung, had said this was a basic dimension of personality; research proves them right (Buss & Plomin, 1984; Costa, McCrae, & Arenberg, 1980; Kagan, 1984; Moss & Susman, 1980).

2. *Neuroticism*, or emotional instability: Traits include being calm or anxious, composed or excitable, poised or nervous. Neurotic individuals are complainers and defeatists. They complain about different things at different ages, but they are always ready to see the sour side of life and none of its sweetness (Conley, 1984; McCrae & Costa, 1984).

Neuroticism is sometimes called "negative affectivity (emotionality)." As we noted in Chapter 9, emotions tend to occur in clusters, and a person who feels one negative emotion tends also to feel others. Indeed, the trait *negative affectivity* (NA) describes a person's tendency to feel anger, scorn, revulsion, guilt, anxiety, sadness, and other negative moods (Watson & Clark, 1984). High NA people frequently feel worried and tense, even in the absence of objective problems. They complain more about their health and report more physical symptoms than low NAs do, but they are not actually in poorer health (Watson & Pennebaker, 1989).

3. *Agreeableness*: This dimension describes the extent to which people are good-natured or irritable, gentle or headstrong, cooperative or abrasive, not jealous or jealous. It reflects the capacity for friendly relationships or the tendency to have hostile ones.

4. *Conscientiousness*: This factor describes individuals who are responsible or undependable; who are persevering or who quit easily; who are steadfast or fickle; who are tidy or careless; who are scrupulous or unscrupulous.

5. *Openness to experience*: This fifth dimension describes the extent to which people are original, imaginative, questioning, artistically inclined, and capable of divergent thinking (creativity)—or are conforming, unimaginative, and predictable.

These "Big Five" factors turn up in studies of Chinese, Japanese, Filipino, Hawaiian, and Australian adults (Digman & Inouye, 1986; Noller, Law, & Comrey, 1987). Moreover, they seem to be as persistent as crabgrass. You might think (and hope) that people would become more open-minded and agreeable, and less neurotic, as they mature. But two psychologists, working on a major longitudinal study with men and women aged 21 to 96, conclude that these traits are "still stable after all these years" (Costa & McCrae, 1988).

Rating traits

Despite its popularity, the trait approach has its detractors. For one thing, it often reveals a problem of circular thinking: The answer restates the original question. Let's say Hilda has the personality trait of anxiety. How do we know? Because she says so. Why does she say so? Because at a dance last week she felt anxious. Why did she feel anxious? Because she has the personality trait of anxiety.

A second criticism of the trait approach is that once a person has a personality "label," he or she may be victimized by it (Rosenthal, 1966; Szasz, 1961/1967). Hilda may decide that anxiety is as permanent a description of her as her green eyes. She may fail to observe that she is not nervous with her parents, neighbors, or soccer team. Other people, once they label Hilda "anxious," may start treating her cautiously or ignore her altogether. So Hilda doesn't get the chance to prove that she *isn't* anxious. Trait theories often overlook the importance of the situation in determining behavior.

A third problem with measuring personality traits has to do with a fascinating bias in how we see ourselves. People tend to think that they have rich, many-faceted personalities that make them unpredictable and flexible. Therefore, if given a choice, people will say they are serious *and* carefree, energetic *and* relaxed, outgoing *and* shy, depending on circumstances. But they describe other people as having fewer personality traits and as being more predictable than they themselves are (Sande, Goethals, & Radloff, 1988). Other people can be reduced to three or five dimensions, we say, but not us.

Fourth, it is possible that self-described traits, even on tests taken years apart, do not measure the stability of your *traits* but the stability of your *self-concept*. Perhaps you continue to think of yourself as "timid old Sam" long after you've become chief trapeze artist for the circus. Some researchers get around this problem by asking spouses and friends to judge each other's traits. Even then, spouses and friends may observe only certain qualities in each other and ignore (or actively discourage) changes. Have you ever gone home for the holidays, full of new experiences to reveal, only to find yourself "relapsing" into old habits because your family sees the same old you?

The most damaging attack on the trait approach, however, concerns the problems of consistency and predictability. If you score high on a measure of ambition but fail to *behave* in a way that demonstrates your ambition, what good is it to say you are "ambitious"? Years ago, an eminent psychologist, having reviewed dozens of studies, found only the weakest of correlations between a person's "trait" on a personality test and that person's behavior in a particular situation (Mischel, 1968).

This bombshell made quite an explosion in the field of personality research. After all, the most basic assumption about personality is that it is stable across situations. The gap between the belief in consistency and the fact of inconsistency has been called, logically, the *consistency paradox* (Bem & Allen, 1974; Mischel, 1984). The question of the consistency and stability of traits continues to generate controversy and research.

QUICK ▪ QUIZ

Choose the correct word in each pair.

1. According to Carl Rogers, a man who loves his wife only when she is looking her best is giving her *conditional/unconditional* positive regard.
2. Jung and Eysenck agreed that a major dimension of personality is *extroversion/neuroticism*.
3. Raymond Cattell advanced the study of personality by his method of *case study analysis/factor analysis*.
4. A student who believes that his grade in psychology is all a matter of luck shows an *internal/external* locus of control.
5. A student who scores high on a test of assertiveness but who becomes completely tongue-tied during an interview illustrates the *consistency/ self-monitoring* paradox.

Bonus: Which of the following traits are *not* "robust factors" in personality? (a) introversion, (b) agreeableness, (c) psychoticism, (d) open-mindedness, (e) intelligence, (f) neuroticism, (g) conscientiousness

Answers:

1. conditional 2. extroversion 3. factor analysis 4. external 5. consistency *Bonus:* c, e

The Private Personality

Whatever "personality" is, most psychologists have agreed that it is stable. Psychoanalysts believe that personality is formed within the first few years. Biologically oriented researchers believe that infants are born with many basic qualities that *develop* but do not *change*. Even those who emphasize learning and environment think that people are pretty much shaped for life in their formative years by the rewards, punishments, and parental treatment they get. Today these assumptions are being challenged. What people do is often unrelated to what they say about themselves, and some childhood qualities may be outgrown in adulthood. What does this mean for the study of personality?

Stability versus change

One problem with measuring the stability of personality is that even when psychologists do find significant correlations in traits over time, not *everybody remains exactly the same.* Consider the example of aggressiveness. Numerous studies have found that aggressive little boys tend to grow up to be aggressive men (Huesmann et al., 1984; Moss & Susman, 1980; Olweus, 1979; Rushton et al., 1986). In one study, a group of 8-year-old children, rated by their classmates as being either very aggressive or not at all aggressive, were reinterviewed when they were 30 years of age. The most aggressive children had become the most aggressive adults, many of whom had criminal records (Huesmann et al., 1984).

Some personality traits tend to remain stable from childhood to adulthood. Why can't we conclude that aggressive 8-year-old boys will inevitably grow up to become used-car salesmen, prize fighters, or criminals?

Does this mean that we should lock up schoolyard bullies and throw away the key, on the grounds that they will become criminals by 30? Although the correlations between childhood and adult behavior were *statistically significant, they were also very low.* That is, despite the general trend, some of the most aggressive children became less aggressive as adults (perhaps they entered the Peace Corps), and some of the least aggressive children became more so (perhaps they became hockey players). In a longitudinal study of adult twins, aged 19 to 60, the researchers found that aggressiveness seemed to have a strong hereditary component (see Chapter 12). Yet altruism (doing unselfish things for others) *increased* over the life span, and aggressiveness *decreased* (Rushton et al., 1986).

Thus it is wrong to conclude that "stability" always means "inevitability." As we will see in the next two chapters, many studies show that childhood aggression and antisocial behavior are learned in very specific family patterns that create a set of persistent problems. That is, once a child becomes aggressive and disobedient, he (less often, she) tends to be disliked and rejected by peers and parents, which in turn lowers the child's self-esteem, which in turn makes the child more aggressive. Fortunately, several intervention programs have been successful in teaching parents how to break this vicious cycle, which would otherwise appear to be "stable" (Patterson, 1986).

Other longitudinal studies also show that some traits change more readily. In Chapter 10 we described how changing conditions can raise or lower people's achievement motivation (Veroff, 1983). The same is true of locus of control. In four large national samples, men and women were followed from the late 1960s to the late 1970s. At the time of the first testing, men and women, old and young, were alike in their locus of control scores. But by the late 1970s, women of all ages (but not men) had moved toward the external end of the scale. The researchers believe that as women entered the work force during that decade, they became more aware of the external limits on their ability to succeed (Doherty & Baldwin, 1985).

Psychologists who believe that personality is flexible suggest that "stability" is more a matter of perception than reality. They point to several biases in the study of personality.

One is the *pleasure of patterns.* Most people, including psychologists, like to string events together to make a pattern. As Freud said, when we look back, we feel our development has been predictable because we see the paths we chose and forget the roads not taken. Looking across situations, we feel our actions and feelings are coherent because we don't want to feel that we are easily swayed by prevailing winds.

A second is *perceptual bias.* Consistency is often more in the eye of the beholder than in the behavior of the subject. One psychologist, who shall remain nameless, photographed a 7-month-old boy reaching up, trying to catch a sunbeam. When that boy was in high school, he made a laser. The psychologist connected the two events, concluding that the boy was always "fascinated with light." In seeing a consistency between the 7-month-old and the 17-year-old, she failed to notice all the babies who reach for sunbeams and then grow up to be miners, darkroom photo developers, or tunnel builders.

Puzzles of Personality

4. Is personality stable over a lifetime?

To psychoanalysts, the basic conflicts and motives of personality are set during a child's first five years. Other schools of psychology maintain that personality traits are flexible and can change in adulthood depending on experiences. Research is identifying some of the traits that do seem to be stable across the lifespan, and others that are more influenced by circumstances.

Self-esteem is particularly vulnerable to a person's situation and experiences. Many individuals lose self-esteem when they are fired from jobs, or when they work in environments that give them no feedback or support. People often gain self-esteem, though, when they join supportive groups to improve their working conditions. This group of union women at a Labor Day parade is not lacking in esteem.

Extroversion and introversion are among the more stable of traits. The woman in the bright lime-colored outfit, mugging for the camera, has probably been outgoing and demonstrative since childhood.

Shyness and timidity also seem to be relatively stable. Although everyone feels shy on occasion, some people feel shy on most occasions—uncomfortable in new situations and slow to reveal themselves.

Not all traits are lifelong aspects of personality, however. Although aggressive children are somewhat more likely than their calmer peers to be aggressive as adults, many children and teenagers outgrow early aggressiveness.

A third is *cultural bias*. Our society emphasizes the importance of stability, for both the mental health of the individual and the social health of the community. This bias toward stability has meant that people who *do* change have often been considered unhealthy, deviant, and immature (Block, 1971). But too much stability can be as unhealthy as too little: A person whose traits never varied would be inflexible, unable to adapt to new situations.

The inner I

The need to feel consistent can blind us to the fact that what we do is often unrelated to who we think we are. Is this an example of emotional reasoning, or are our feelings of consistency justified in some ways?

Perhaps the main reason for seeing consistency in our own lives and those of others is that we *feel* consistent. Each of us has a sense of self, an identity, through which we process and absorb experiences, thoughts, and emotions. Each of us has a unique constellation of memories, dreams, wishes, and history. The result, that inner sense of continuity and perception, has been called the "private personality" (Singer, 1984). The private personality allows us to draw links across situations and explain away behavior we think is "out of character." We even rewrite personal history if necessary—that is, correct our memories—to maintain the sense of consistency (Greenwald, 1980).

A series of experiments found that people's private thoughts and emotions often play a more profound role in their self-conceptions than do their actual behaviors (Andersen, 1984; Andersen & Ross, 1984). In fact, self-image may last long after actual behavior has changed radically (Rosenberg, 1979). Private feelings of guilt, despair, pride, anticipation, elation, desire, lightheartedness, and worry shape our self-concepts because they are so vivid. People can rationalize or explain away their actions, but, as Carl Rogers often said, they regard inner feelings and thoughts as the "real self."

The private personality, researchers are finding, is made up of many *"possible selves"* (Markus & Nurius, 1986). There is the real self, the traits that people use to describe their personalities. But, as Karen Horney (1950) observed, people are also guided by an *ideal self*—images of what they would like to be, images around which they organize actions and aspirations. (Horney maintained that unhealthy people focus exclusively on idealized notions of the self.) People even have images of their *undesired self*, made up of traits they dislike in themselves and hope to overcome. One study found that people's well-being depends more on feeling that they have come a long way from their undesired traits (such as being conceited, fat, messy, or stupid) than on their attainment of ideal traits (such as becoming creative, generous, or famous) (Ogilvie, 1987). The way we construct and envision our possible selves affects our motivations, dreams, plans, and self-esteem—the very stuff of personality.

Ultimately, the larger picture of change and constancy in personality is analogous to the figure-ground illusion in perception (see Chapter 5). If you notice change, then consistent qualities fade into the background. If you look for consistency, then the qualities that change tend to fade out. In truth, every personality is a mixture of stability and change. The particular balance in a person's life will depend on genetic predispositions, psychological processes, and experience. People do not strike the same balance the same way at the same time. Some people may stabilize their personalities early in life, whereas others change significantly over the years.

Personality change, in any case, is like a sunrise; you can't pinpoint the single moment when the sky turns color. The slow and steady nature of most changes in personality contributes to the belief that we don't really change; we just become more like ourselves.

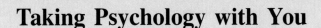

Taking Psychology with You

On Suckers and "Personality Profiles": How to Avoid the Barnum Effect

How well does the following paragraph describe you?

> Some of your aspirations tend to be pretty unrealistic. At times you are extroverted, affable, sociable, while at other times you are introverted, wary, and reserved. You have found it unwise to be too frank in revealing yourself to others. You pride yourself on being an independent thinker and do not accept others' opinions without satisfactory proof. You prefer a certain amount of change and variety, and become dissatisfied when hemmed in by restrictions and limitations. At times you have serious doubts as to whether you have made the right decision or done the right thing.

When people believe that this description was written just for them— the result of a personalized horoscope, "personality profile," or handwriting analysis—they all say the same thing: "It's me! It describes me *exactly*!" Why should this be so? C. R. Snyder and Randee Shenkel (1975) point out that this description is vague enough to apply to almost everyone, positive enough to please almost everyone, and flattering enough to get almost anyone to accept it. People are not so quick to accept this "personality profile":

> You are a sullen, hateful slob. You dislike people and most people dislike you too. You are usually nasty, cruel, and calculating. You never think for yourself but steal other people's ideas. Once you've made a decision you stick with it, even when it's wrong.

As research shows, the more effort people invest in getting a horoscope or profile, the more likely they are to believe the results—even when the identical results are given to everyone. If they must pay money for a profile, take the time to write away for it, or give detailed and specific information about themselves, they are more likely to believe the profile is "eerily accurate." A French psychologist once advertised himself as an astrologer. In reply to the hundreds of people who wrote to him for his services, he sent out the same vague horoscope. "More than 200 grateful clients took the time to write thank-you notes praising his accuracy and perceptiveness," Snyder and Shenkel observed.

Personality quizzes in magazines or newspapers commit some of the same errors. They are based on a simplified (and flattering) idea of personality traits, and they rarely allow people to distinguish a "personality" problem from a situational problem. Let's say you total up your score and discover that you are a "worrier." Is that truly a personality trait, or do you have four exams in three days, an employer who is giving you a hard time, and an alcoholic roommate? Some of these pop personality quizzes can really make you worry about yourself.

This is why many psychologists worry that too many people are falling prey to the "P. T. Barnum effect." Barnum was the great circus showman who said "there's a sucker born every minute." But Barnum also knew that the formula for success was to "have a little something for everybody"—which is what unscientific personality profiles, horoscopes, and handwriting tests have in common.

To avoid the Barnum effect, research offers a few strategies:

▪ *Beware of all-purpose descriptions that could apply to anyone.* We know a married couple who were terribly impressed when an astrologer told them that "each of you needs privacy and time to be independent" along with "but don't become too independent or you will lose your bond." Such observations, which play it safe by playing it both ways, apply to virtually all couples.

▪ *Beware of your own selective perceptions.* Most of us are so impressed when a palm reader or horoscope gets something right that we overlook all the observations and predictions that are plain wrong.

▪ *Resist flattery.* This is the hard one. Most of us would reject a personality profile that described us as being nasty, sullen, and stupid. But most of us fall for profiles that tell us how wonderful and smart we are, especially if they seem objective or "scientific."

All this discussion is not meant to keep you from having fun reading your daily horoscope or taking a newspaper's latest personality quiz. But keep your critical faculties alongside your sense of humor as you read them. Then you won't end up paying hard cash for soft answers, pawning the piano because Leos should invest in gold this month, or taking a job you despise because it fits your "type." In other words—have a good time, but prove Barnum wrong.

KEY WORDS

SUMMARY

1. *Personality* is usually defined as an individual's distinctive and relatively stable pattern of behavior, motives, and thoughts. Different schools of psychology analyze personality differently.

2. Sigmund Freud was the founder of *psychoanalysis*, which emphasizes the unconscious aspects of personality. Freud's *psychodynamic* theory was based on the movement of energy within the person. Instincts that are blocked from direct expression may be *displaced* or *sublimated* in socially acceptable ways.

3. To Freud, the personality consists of id (the source of *libido* and the aggressive instinct), ego (the source of reason), and superego (the source of conscience). *Defense mechanisms* protect the ego from unconscious anxiety.

4. Freud believed that personality develops in a series of *psychosexual* stages: oral, anal, phallic (Oedipal), latency, and genital. During the phallic stage, Freud believed, the *Oedipus complex* occurs, in which the child desires the opposite-sex parent and feels rivalry with the same-sex parent. When the complex is resolved, the child will *identify* with the same-sex parent and settle into the latency stage. At puberty, the genital stage of adult sexuality begins.

5. Karen Horney believed that basic anxiety was the central human motivation, and she emphasized social relationships more than biological instincts. She also challenged Freud's ideas of female inferiority and penis envy.

6. Alfred Adler and Carl Jung also broke away from Freud. Adler argued that people have a need for self-improvement (the drive for *superiority*); that an important aspect of personality is empathy (*social interest*); and that each person creates his or her own personality from heredity and experience (*the creative self*).

7. Jung believed that people share a *collective unconscious* that contains universal human memories and history. There are many universal *archetypes* in personality, including the anima and animus.

8. Psychoanalysis has been criticized for being unscientific, dated, and incorrect. Its methods have been challenged for relying on the memories of unrepresentative patients and on retrospective accounts, and for paying more attention to unconscious motives than to real experiences. But many of Freud's ideas have been influential both in experimental psychology and in therapy.

9. ''Radical behaviorists'' believe that personality, including thoughts and values, can be studied according to learning principles, without relying on internal mental processes or biology. Social learning theorists also believe that personality consists of learned patterns, but they have added cognitive factors and social learning principles (such as observation and self-reinforcement). In their view, personality depends on aspects of the individual, aspects of the environment, and how the two interact.

10. Humanists believe that personality is defined by uniquely human abilities, notably free will and the subjective experience of the self. Abraham Maslow emphasized the positive, self-actualizing side of personality. Rollo May emphasizes the existential concerns of free will. Carl Rogers emphasized the importance of *unconditional positive regard* in creating a "fully functioning" person.

11. Trait theories consider the individual traits (descriptive qualities) that make up personality. Gordon Allport argued that personality consists of three kinds of traits: *cardinal*, *central*, and *secondary*.

12. Many individual traits have been identified, such as self-esteem and locus of control. Raymond Cattell used factor analysis to distinguish *surface* traits from *source* traits, the basic components of personality. Although Cattell said that there are at least 16 basic personality factors, Hans Eysenck argued that there are only three, which he called extroversion, neuroticism, and psychoticism. Still others propose that there are five "robust factors" in personality: extroversion, neuroticism (emotionality), agreeableness, conscientiousness, and openness to experience.

13. Critics of the trait approach argue that descriptive labels do not explain behavior; that an emphasis on traits overlooks the importance of the situation in explaining behavior; that people are biased in how they evaluate their own traits; and that personality tests may measure stability of self-concept rather than stability of traits. Most of all, critics point to the *consistency paradox*: the gap between the belief in consistent personality traits and the fact that behavior often is not consistent.

14. Some psychologists argue that trait stability is an illusion, a result of cultural and perceptual biases. However, the "private personality"—the inner sense of continuity and subjective experience—gives us a feeling of consistency, allows us to assimilate change slowly, and lets us rationalize behavior that seems "out of character." In addition, personality includes not only actual traits, but also *possible selves*: the images of the ideal self and the undesired self that motivate people and shape their goals. The issue of continuity versus change continues to be debated in psychology.

CHAPTER 12

Measuring and Explaining Human Diversity

The tough-minded . . . respect difference. Their goal is a world made safe for differences. . . .

RUTH BENEDICT

The long and short of it is: Human beings are diverse.

*A*ll of us pass through similar sequences of development, yet we also "turn out" with distinct abilities and personalities. Why? Was your Uncle Al born to be the crusty curmudgeon that he is, or might he have been a kindhearted softy if only his life had been easier? Does Aunt Grace play the piano like an angel because of inborn musical talent or because her mother made her practice every day? In short, are individual differences primarily inborn, a matter of *nature*, or are they acquired through experience, the result of *nurture*?

The way people answer this question affects their perceptions of themselves and others. For example, those who favor nature may expect a child to behave like a genetic chip off the old block. If both Andrea and her father are warm and generous, love the outdoors, and sing off-key, they will exclaim, "That Andrea—she has been practically a clone of her dad from the day she was born!" (They may forget that Andrea is quick tempered and her father is mild mannered, or that Andrea is a "grind" and her father hated school. And they may overlook the fact that Andrea's brother is a different sort of chip altogether.) In contrast, those who favor nurture may assume they have unlimited power over their children's development. They may enroll their offspring in French and Russian lessons at age 2 in hopes of turning them into international diplomats, and perhaps wonder what happened when the children grow up to be real estate agents.

As you might guess, in this chapter we are not going to resolve the issue of individual differences in favor of either nature or nurture. Instead, you will learn that the strands of heredity and experience are inextricably intertwined, and that it may be impossible to determine with any certainty how much relative influence each has. Before we can consider this issue, however, we must first examine how psychologists go about measuring individual differences, using techniques of **psychological assessment**. Along the way, we will consider the uses to which such measurements are put: What is the purpose of sorting humanity into the smart and the dull, the talented and the ordinary, the calm and the hot-blooded? Then, in the second part of the chapter, we will return to the question of where individual differences come from—and what they mean in the world outside the classroom, otherwise known as "real life."

Sizing Up Human Nature: Psychological Assessment

Most people reading this book have taken a psychological test. You took intelligence tests, achievement tests, and possibly vocational aptitude tests in school. You may also have taken a personality test when applying for a job, joining the military, or starting psychotherapy. There are thousands of psychological tests or assessment "instruments" in use in industry, education, the helping professions, and basic research. Some are administered to individuals, others to large groups of people. These measures help clarify differences among individuals as well as differences in the reactions of the same individual on different occasions or at different stages of life.

psychological assessment
The measurement and evaluation of abilities, aptitudes, and personality characteristics.

The test of a good test

Any good test must surmount two hurdles. First, if the attribute being measured is assumed to be stable, then scores or test results must be consistent. They should not fluctuate because of chance factors, such as who happens to administer the test or the time of day it is given. The consistency of scores on a test is known as test **reliability**. It is easy to see why unreliable tests are of little use if you consider medical tests. What good would a cholesterol test be if it came out high one day and low the next?

There are several ways to measure reliability. *Test-retest reliability* is computed by giving the test twice to the same group of people, then statistically comparing the two sets of scores. If the test is reliable, individuals' scores will be similar from one session to another. This method has a drawback, however. People tend to do better on a psychological test the second time they take it, after they have become familiar with its purpose, the strategies required, and the actual test items. An alternative is to compute *alternate forms reliability*, by giving different versions of the same test to the same group on two separate occasions. The items on the two forms are similar in format but are not identical in content. With this method, performance cannot improve because of familiarity with the items, although people may still do somewhat better the second time because they have learned the strategies and procedures expected of them.

A third method, *split-half reliability*, takes a completely different tack. Scores on half of the test items (for example, the even items) are compared with scores on the other half (for example, the odd items). The two halves of the test are treated as though they were alternate forms. High split-half reliability means that the test is "internally consistent."

In addition to being reliable, a test must have **validity**, that is, must measure what it claims to measure. A test should not be used to assess, say, creativity if what it really measures is vocabulary size. Psychologists ensure validity in a variety of ways. One is to see that a test has *content validity*—that it measures all or most aspects of the trait in question. Suppose you constructed a test to measure employees' job satisfaction. If your test tapped a broad sampling of relevant beliefs and behaviors ("Do you feel you have reached a dead end at work?" "Are you bored with your assignments?"), it would have content validity. If the test asked only how workers felt about their salary level, it would lack content validity and would be of little use. (Highly paid people are not always satisfied with their jobs, nor are poorly paid people always dissatisfied.)

Most tests are also judged on *criterion validity*, the ability to predict other, independent measures, or criteria, of the trait in question. A test can have criterion validity and thus be useful whether or not individual test items *look* valid or sensible to the test-taker. The criterion for a scholastic aptitude test might be college grades; the criterion for a test of shyness might be behavior in social situations. To find out if your job satisfaction test has criterion validity, you might return a year later to see if it has correctly predicted absenteeism, resignations, or requests for job transfers.

Unfortunately, teachers, parents, and even psychologists do not always stop to question a test's validity when the test yields a number, such as an IQ score or a job applicant ranking (see Figure 12.1). Enthralled by the test score, they simply assume that the test measures what they think it does. Robert Sternberg (1988b) notes that this assumption occurs particularly with mental tests, which, he argues, actually tap only a limited set of abilities important for intelligent behavior. "There is an allure to exact-sounding numbers," says Sternberg. "An IQ of 119, an SAT score of 580, a mental-abilities score in the 74th percentile—all sound very precise. . . . But the appearance of precision is no substitute for the fact of validity."

Exact numbers can be reassuring or worrying: If your IQ is 143, you'll be thrilled; if your SAT score is 143, you'll be depressed. But do exact numbers necessarily mean that a test is valid?

reliability *In test construction, the consistency of scores derived from a test.*
validity *The ability of a test to measure what it was designed to measure.*

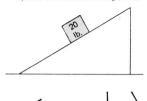

63. In what direction does the force of gravity pull the 20 lb. weight placed on the board in diagram 63?

(A)   (B)   (C)   (D)

FIGURE 12.1

An item from a test for fire fighters
In a lawsuit involving this item, a judge noted that although a high school physics student would know that the correct answer is (C), answer (A) might be more useful in fighting fires! In recent years, efforts have been made to make employment screening tests more relevant to the skills required on the job.

standardize *In test construction, to develop uniform procedures for giving and scoring a test.*
norms *In test construction, established standards of performance.*
achievement tests *Tests designed to measure acquired skills and knowledge.*
aptitude tests *Tests designed to measure a person's potential for acquiring various types of skills and knowledge, based on present abilities.*
intelligence *An inferred characteristic of an individual, usually defined as the ability to profit from experience, acquire knowledge, think abstractly, or adapt to changes in the environment.*

In addition to checking the reliability and validity of tests, psychologists usually **standardize** a test during its construction. That is, they develop uniform procedures for giving and scoring the test. It would hardly be fair to give some people detailed instructions and plenty of time and others only vague instructions and limited time. Standardized tests come with detailed instructions on how to explain the tasks involved, how much time to allow, what materials to use, and so forth. Scoring is usually done by referring to **norms**, or established standards of performance. The usual procedure for developing norms is to give the test to a large group of people who resemble those for whom the test is intended. Norms tell a tester which scores are considered high, low, or average.

Measuring the mind

Mental tests were originally conceived as an impartial, democratic way to select people for jobs or special schooling. They were considered an antidote for political favoritism, cronyism, prejudice, and class privilege. Employers and teachers might be swayed by stereotypes and self-interest, but tests were objective. (As we will see, however, "objective" does not always mean "fair.")

Traditionally, mental tests have been divided into two types. **Achievement tests** are designed to measure acquired skills and knowledge, particularly those that have been explicitly taught. The proficiency exams required by some states for high school graduation are achievement tests. **Aptitude tests** are designed to measure a person's ability to acquire skills or knowledge in the future. For example, vocational aptitude tests can help you decide if you will do better as a mechanic or a musician. However, all mental tests are in some sense achievement tests because they assume some sort of past learning or experience with certain objects, words, or situations. The difference between achievement and aptitude tests is one of degree and intended use.

Intelligence tests. The best-known aptitude tests are those designed to measure **intelligence**. Like love, intelligence is highly valued but hard to define. Some psychologists equate it with the ability to reason abstractly, others with the ability to learn and profit from experience in daily life. Some emphasize the ability to think rationally, others the ability to act purposefully. These qualities are all probably part of that elusive attribute we call "intelligence," but theorists weigh them differently. The lack of agreement on a precise definition has led some psychologists to conclude, only half jokingly, that intelligence is "whatever intelligence tests measure."

Some writers distinguish two major types of intelligence (Cattell, 1971; Horn, 1978). *Fluid intelligence* is the capacity for insight into complex relations. It is presumed to be relatively independent of education and experience (although not all psychologists agree on this point). Deductive reasoning and the ability to unscramble a sentence ("tree pick an climbed man our apple the to") both require fluid intelligence. *Crystallized intelligence* is the ability to master and use acquired knowledge and skills and is assumed to depend heavily on culture and education. Defining words, solving arithmetic problems, and summarizing the Republican party's policies all require crystallized intelligence.

A typical intelligence test asks you to do several things: provide a specific bit of information, notice similarities between objects, solve arithmetic problems, define words, fill in the missing parts of incomplete pictures, arrange pictures in a logical order, arrange blocks to resemble a design, assemble puzzles, use a coding scheme, or judge what behavior would be appropriate in a particular situation. Researchers have used the statistical method called **factor analysis** (see Chapter 11) to identify which sorts of abilities underlie performance on the various items. Some conclude that a general ability, or **g factor**, underlies all the specific abilities as well as various kinds of talent (Spearman, 1927; Wechsler, 1955). They cite findings that although people may do better on some tasks than others, a person's scores on various tasks are often highly correlated. Other psychologists dispute the existence of a g factor, arguing that a person can excel in some kinds of tasks yet do poorly in others (Thurstone, 1938). One theory originally proposed no fewer than 120 separate "factors" in intelligence, and was subsequently updated to include 150 and then 180 such factors (Guilford, 1967, 1982, 1988).

Until recently, most theories of intelligence took a **psychometric** approach, focusing on how well people perform on tests—that is, on whether or not they get the right answers. Newer approaches, inspired by findings on human information processing, emphasize *how* people who score well differ from those who score poorly in their approach to solving problems. The goal is not merely to measure mental ability but also to understand it and help people increase its use in daily life. One promising theory, Robert Sternberg's *triarchic theory of intelligence* (1988b), distinguishes three aspects of intelligence: componential, experiential, and contextual.

1. *Componential intelligence* refers to the information-processing strategies that go on inside a person's head when the person thinks intelligently. According to Sternberg, there are three types of components in the solution of any problem. *Metacomponents* are the steps necessary for planning, monitoring, and evaluating the solution. *Performance components* are the steps required for actually finding the solution. *Knowledge-acquisition components* are the steps used in learning how to solve problems of a given type in the first place. When you write a term paper, you use metacomponents to decide on a topic, plan the paper, monitor the writing, and evaluate how well the finished product succeeds. But you use knowledge-acquisition components to do the research and performance components for the actual writing. When you draw up a budget, you use metacomponents to decide how much you are willing to spend on what, performance components to do the computations, and knowledge-acquisition components to learn how to budget in the first place. People who are strong in componential intelligence tend to do well on conventional mental tests.

2. *Experiential intelligence* takes into account experience with a given task. People who are strong in this area cope well with novelty and are able to "automatize" steps in solving problems of a given type once they have experience with them. Those who are lacking in this area may perform well only under a narrow set of circumstances. For example, a student may do well in school but be less successful after graduation if the job environment is different from what she is used to and less supportive of her goals.

3. *Contextual intelligence* takes the external world into account. If you are strong in contextual intelligence, you know when to adapt to the environment (you are in a dangerous neighborhood, so you become more vigilant than usual); when to change environments (you had planned to be a teacher but you find you don't enjoy working with kids, so you switch to accounting); and when to try to shape the environment into something new (your marriage is rocky, so you and your spouse go for counseling).

factor analysis *A statistical method for analyzing the intercorrelations among various measures or test scores. Clusters of measures or scores that are highly correlated are assumed to measure the same underlying trait, ability, or aptitude (factor).*

g factor *A general ability assumed by some theorists to underlie various specific mental abilities and talents.*

psychometrics *The measurement of mental abilities, traits, and processes.*

Most existing mental tests do not measure the experiential and contextual aspects of intelligence, but Sternberg and others are trying to change that. Their work promises to broaden our ideas about what intelligence is and help us understand the cognitive processes underlying intelligent behavior on tests and in the real world. In the meantime, conventional tests, and in particular IQ tests, remain the yardstick by which individual differences are usually measured. In the next section, we will see how these tests came into being, how they have been used, and why they have been controversial.

QUICK QUIZ

1. Professor Flummox gives his newly constructed test of Aptitude for Studying Psychology to his psychology students at the start of the year. At the end of the year he finds that those who did well on the test averaged only a C in the course. The test lacks _____.
2. The professor also gives the test to a group of students who have never taken and are not now taking psychology. They take the test once in the first week and again in the second week of the semester. Most students' scores are quite different on the two occasions, so the test also lacks _____.
3. Which are aptitude tests? **(a)** this quiz, **(b)** a driver's license exam, **(c)** the bar examination for would-be lawyers, **(d)** a test to determine who can benefit from artistic training.
4. True or false: Doing long division requires crystallized intelligence.
5. In your statistics class, you understand the formulas fairly well and can do the computations. But on tests you plan your time poorly, spending the entire period on the most difficult problems and never even getting to the ones you can solve easily. As a result, your scores are lower than they might be. According to Sternberg, which aspect of componential intelligence do you need to work on?

Answers:

1. validity (or, more specifically, criterion validity) 2. reliability (or, more specifically, test-retest reliability) 3. d 4. true 5. metacomponents

---

Binet's brainstorm. In 1904, the French Ministry of Education asked psychologist Alfred Binet (1857–1911) to design a test that would identify slow learners. School attendance had been made mandatory, but some children did not learn well in an ordinary classroom and needed special help. The ministry was reluctant to let teachers identify slow learners. They might have prejudices about lower-class children or assume that shy or disruptive children were retarded. What was needed was an objective test that would reveal who could benefit from remedial work.

Wrestling with the problem, Binet had a great insight: In the classroom, the responses of "dull" children resembled those of ordinary children of younger ages. Bright children, on the other hand, responded like ordinary children of older ages. The thing to measure, then, was a child's **mental age (MA)**, or level of intellectual development relative to other children's. Then instruction could be tailored to the child's capabilities. The test devised by Binet and his colleague, Theophile Simon, measured memory, vocabulary, and perceptual discrimination. Items ranged from those that most young children could do easily to those that only older children

mental age (MA) *A measure of mental development expressed in terms of the average mental ability at a given age. A child with a mental age of 8 performs on a test of mental ability at the level of the average 8-year-old.*

could handle, as determined by the testing of large numbers of children. These items were grouped by age level: Items passed by most 6-year-olds were assigned to the 6-year level, items passed by most 7-year-olds were assigned to the 7-year level, and so forth. An individual child's mental age was computed by finding the highest level at which the child passed all items, and then adding partial credit in months for any items passed at higher levels.

A scoring system developed later by others used a formula in which the child's mental age (MA) was divided by the child's chronological age (CA) to yield an **intelligence quotient**, or **IQ**. The result was multiplied by 100 to get rid of the decimal point:

$$IQ = \frac{MA}{CA} \times 100$$

Thus a child of 8 who performed like an average 6-year-old would have an IQ of $\frac{6}{8} \times 100 = 75$. A child of 8 who scored like an average 10-year-old would have an IQ of $\frac{10}{8} \times 100 = 125$. All average children, regardless of age, would have an IQ of 100 because MA and CA would be the same. (In actual calculations, months were used, not years, to yield a precise figure. We use years here to keep the computations simple.)

Unfortunately, this method of figuring IQ had a serious flaw. At all ages, the distribution of scores formed a bell-shaped curve, with scores near the average (mean) most common and very high or low scores rare. However, at one age scores might cluster tightly around the average, whereas at another age they might be somewhat more dispersed. As a result, the IQ score necessary to be in the top 10 (or 20 or 30) percent of one's age group varied, depending on one's age. Because of this problem, and because the IQ formula did not make much sense for adults, today's intelligence tests are scored differently. Usually the average is arbitrarily set at 100 and test scores (still informally referred to as ''IQs'') are computed from tables. A score still reflects how a person compares with others, either children of a particular age or adults in general. The test is constructed so that the *standard deviation*—a measure of how spread out the scores are around the mean—is always 15 (or 16 on the modern version of the Binet test). When the standard deviation is 15, theoretically about 68 percent of all people will score between 85 and 115, about 95 percent will score between 70 and 130, and about 99.7 percent will score between 55 and 145 (see Figure 12.2). In any particular sample of people, the distribution will vary somewhat from the theoretical ideal, however. On many tests,

intelligence quotient (IQ)
A measure of intelligence originally computed by dividing a person's mental age by his or her chronological age and multiplying by 100; now derived from norms provided for standardized intelligence tests.

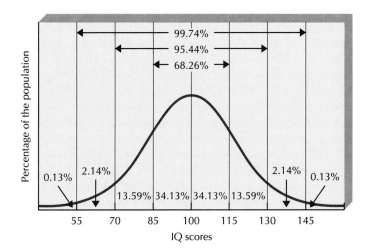

FIGURE 12.2

Expected distribution of IQ scores
In a large population of people, IQ scores will tend to be distributed in a normal (bell-shaped) curve. On most tests, about two-thirds of the scores are expected to fall between 85 and 115. In any actual sample, however, the distribution will depart somewhat from the ideal. In particular, very low scores will usually outnumber very high ones because of mental retardation caused by brain damage and birth defects.

Army intelligence testing during World War I was often carried out under noisy, crowded, and confusing conditions. Many test items were culturally loaded, and some men refused to answer at all. People often ignored these facts, however, and concluded that a high proportion of army recruits were morons.

descriptive labels are used to characterize people whose scores fall between certain arbitrary cutoff points. For instance, those scoring above 130 might be called ''very superior,'' those scoring below 70 ''mentally retarded.''

From opportunities to limits.   Binet made certain important assumptions about his test—for example, that all children taking it would have a similar cultural background. He also emphasized that the test merely *sampled* intelligence and did not measure everything covered by that term. A test score, he said, could be useful, along with other information, for predicting school performance under ordinary conditions, but it should *not* be confused with intelligence itself. The purpose of the test was to identify children with learning problems, not to rank normal children.

Binet's test soon crossed the Atlantic to America, where it was embraced warmly. Stanford psychologist Lewis Terman revised the test and standardized it for American children. His version, the *Stanford-Binet Intelligence Scale*, became the standard against which most other tests were validated. The Stanford-Binet test has since been updated several times, most recently in 1985. (For some sample items, see Table 12.1.)

However, Binet's original intentions somehow got lost in passage, and since he died only a few years after designing his test, he was not around to protest. In France, Binet's test had been given to each child individually, so the test-giver could see if a child was ill or nervous, had poor vision, or was not trying. In America, the revised Binet also was used with individuals, but other intelligence tests were given to huge groups of people, usually students or soldiers, and the advantages of individualized testing were lost. Americans assumed that IQ tests revealed some permanent, inherited trait underlying all intelligent behavior. The object was not to bring slow learners up to the average, but to ''track'' people according to ''natural'' ability. On the basis of test scores earned during a single testing session, students were assigned to slow or fast tracks, and soldiers were groomed for or discouraged from applying for officer status. The testers overlooked the fact that in America, with its many ethnic and social groups, people did not all share the same background and experience (S. J. Gould, 1981).

TABLE 12.1

SAMPLE ITEMS FROM THE STANFORD-BINET
INTELLIGENCE TEST, FORM L-M

The older the test-taker is, the more the test requires in the way of verbal comprehension and fluency.

Age	Task
4	Fills in the missing word when asked, "Brother is a boy; sister is a _____."
	Answers correctly when asked, "Why do we have houses?"
9	Answers correctly when examiner says, "In an old graveyard in Spain they have discovered a small skull which they believe to be that of Christopher Columbus when he was about 10 years old. What is foolish about that?"
	Examiner notches folded paper; child draws how it will look unfolded.
12	Completes "The streams are dry . . . there has been little rain."
	Tells what is foolish about statements such as "Bill Jones's feet are so big that he has to put his trousers on over his head."
Adult	Can describe the difference between *misery* and *poverty, character* and *reputation, laziness* and *idleness.*
	Explains how to measure 3 pints of water with a 5-pint and a 2-pint can.

SOURCE: From Lewis M. Terman & Maud A. Merrill, *Stanford-Binet Intelligence Scale* (1972 norms ed.). Boston: Houghton-Mifflin, 1973. (Currently published by The Riverside Publishing Company.) Items are copyright 1916 by Lewis M. Terman, 1937 by Lewis M. Terman and Maud A. Merrill, © 1960, 1973 by The Riverside Publishing Company. Reproduced or adapted by permission of the publisher.

Intelligence tests developed or revised between World War I and the 1960s for use in schools favored city children over rural ones, middle-class children over poor ones, and white children over minority children. One item asked whether the Emperor Concerto was written by Beethoven, Mozart, Bach, Brahms, or Mahler. (The answer is Beethoven.) Another asked, "What should you do if you find a 3-year-old child lost on the street?" (The correct answer: Call the police. But that response might not look so attractive to a child living in a ghetto, or a farm child living where there are no police nearby and no "streets," only roads.) IQ tests did not measure the kinds of knowledge and skills that are "intelligent" in a minority neighborhood or in the hills of Appalachia (Scarr, 1984a).

In the 1960s, criticism mounted. Opponents of testing argued that because teachers thought IQ scores revealed the limits of a child's potential, the scores could produce a self-fulfilling prophecy. Low-scoring children would not get the educational attention or encouragement they needed; high-scoring children would. In an ingenious study, Robert Rosenthal and his colleagues demonstrated how a teacher's expectations might affect students' performance. Elementary school teachers were told early in the school year that on the basis of a "test for intellectual blooming," certain children would probably show a large jump in IQ that year. In fact, the "bloomers" were selected entirely at random. At the end of the year, "bloomers" in the first and second grades did actually show a greater gain in their IQ scores than other children did (Rosenthal & Jacobson, 1968). No one is sure why such an effect occurred. But there is evidence that when teachers expect a child to do well, they respond more warmly, give more feedback, teach more material, and give the child more chances to ask and answer questions (R. Rosenthal, 1973).

Culture-free and culture-fair tests. In the 1970s, group intelligence testing became a public issue. School boards and employers were sued for restricting the opportunities of low scorers. Some states prohibited the use of group tests for classifying children. Several test-makers responded to the charge of cultural bias by trying to construct tests that were **culture-free**. Such tests were usually nonverbal; in some, even instructions were pantomimed. Test constructors soon found, however, that culture can affect performance in unexpected ways. In one case, children who had emigrated from Arab countries to Israel were asked to show which detail was missing from a picture of a face with no mouth. The children, who were not used to thinking of a drawing of a head as a complete picture, said that the *body* was missing (Ortar, 1963)!

In recent years, test constructors have tried to design tests that are **culture-fair**. Instead of trying to eliminate the influence of culture, they attempt to find items that incorporate knowledge and skills common to many different cultures. So far the results have been less successful than originally hoped. Cultural values affect a person's attitude toward taking tests, comfort in the settings required for testing, motivation, rapport with the test-giver, competitiveness, and experience in solving problems independently (Anastasi, 1988). Therefore, using ''culture-fair'' items does not always eliminate group differences in performance.

In theory, it should be possible to establish norms that are not based on white, urban children, simply by throwing out items on which such children score better than others. This strategy was used years ago to eliminate sex differences in IQ. On early tests, girls scored higher than boys at every age (Samelson, 1979). Nobody was willing to conclude that males were intellectually inferior, so in the 1937 revision of the Stanford-Binet test, Lewis Terman simply deleted items that showed sex differences. But few people are willing to do for cultural differences what Terman did for sex differences. The reason points to a dilemma at the heart of intelligence testing. Intelligence tests put some groups of children at a disadvantage because of cultural differences. Yet what most people mean by ''intelligent behavior'' requires certain kinds of cultural knowledge and skills. How can educators recognize and accept cultural differences and, at the same time, require students to demonstrate mastery of the cultural skills, knowledge, and attitudes that will help them succeed in school and in the larger society? How can they eliminate bias from tests, while preserving the purpose for which the tests were designed? Anne Anastasi, an eminent expert in testing, argues that concealing the effects of cultural disadvantage by rejecting tests or devising tests that are insensitive to such effects is ''equivalent to breaking a thermometer because it registers a body temperature of 101.'' Instead, remedial help should be given (Anastasi, 1988). Others believe that IQ and other mental tests do more harm than good. Sociologist Jane Mercer (1988) has been trying for years to get testers to understand that children can be *ignorant* of information required by IQ tests without being *stupid*, but she has finally given up. Now, she says, ''I'm out to kill the IQ test.''

Suppose a test finds IQ differences between two groups of children. Should we change the children or change the test?

culture-free tests *Tests in which cultural experience does not influence performance.*

culture-fair tests *Tests that reduce cultural bias by incorporating knowledge and skills common to many different cultures and socioeconomic groups.*

The uses and misuses of intelligence testing. The resolution of the IQ debate may ultimately depend on whether test users can ever learn to use intelligence tests intelligently. Most educators feel the tests still have value, as long as a person's background is kept in mind and the results are interpreted cautiously. IQ tests are well standardized, and those given to school-age children predict school performance fairly well. Correlations between IQ scores and current or future school grades, though far from perfect, are high, ranging between .40 and .60 (Wing & Wallach, 1971). IQ tests often identify not only the mentally retarded but also gifted students who have not previously considered higher education.

In some schools, a child's placement in a special education program now depends not only on IQ score but also on medical data and the child's demonstrated ability to get along in the family and community. Some schools are also returning to Binet's original concept. Instead of using group tests to label and categorize children, they give individual tests to identify a child's strengths and weaknesses so that teachers can design individualized programs that will boost the child's performance. This change in emphasis reflects in part an increasing awareness that the intellect—and IQ scores—can be improved, even in the mentally retarded (Butterfield & Belmont, 1977; Feuerstein, 1980; Sternberg, 1986). It also recognizes that a person may have a **learning disability**, a problem with a specific mental skill like reading or arithmetic, without having a general intellectual impairment. Many children with learning disabilities have normal or even superior intelligence and can overcome or compensate for their handicap. Often, their problems are linked to perceptual or memory difficulties. Such well-known people as inventor Thomas Edison, poet Amy Lowell, and politician Nelson Rockefeller have succeeded in their fields despite having *dyslexia*, a reading disability that makes it difficult to decode patterns of letters correctly.

The most popular individual intelligence tests today are the *Wechsler Adult Intelligence Scale-Revised (WAIS-R)* and the *Wechsler Intelligence Scale for Children-Revised (WISC-R)*. (For sample items, see Figure 12.3 and Table 12.2). Although the Wechsler tests produce a general IQ score, they also provide specific scores for different kinds of ability, both verbal and nonverbal (''performance''). Two people with the same IQ score may show a different *pattern* of strengths and weaknesses. This information can be used in the planning of individualized instructional programs. Other tests for measuring specific skills are also available. Some are specially designed to test the intelligence of children whose perceptual, motor, or speech disabilities prevent them from doing as well as they might on traditional IQ tests.

Intellectually impaired children, like this child with Down's Syndrome, are accomplishing more academically than anyone once thought they could.

learning disability *A difficulty in the performance of a specific mental skill, such as reading or arithmetic; sometimes linked to perceptual or memory problems.*

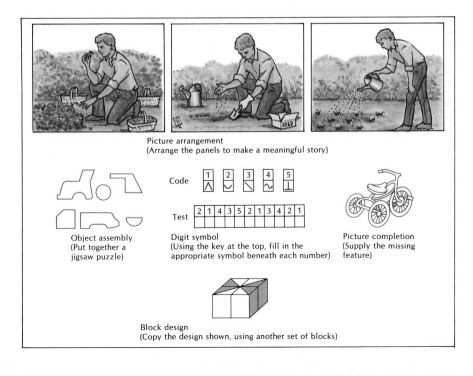

Picture arrangement
(Arrange the panels to make a meaningful story)

Object assembly
(Put together a jigsaw puzzle)

Code

Test

Digit symbol
(Using the key at the top, fill in the appropriate symbol beneath each number)

Picture completion
(Supply the missing feature)

Block design
(Copy the design shown, using another set of blocks)

FIGURE 12.3

Performance tasks on the Wechsler tests
Performance (nonverbal) items are particularly useful in measuring the abilities of those who have poor hearing, are not fluent in the tester's language, have limited education, or resist doing classroom-type tasks. A large gap between a person's verbal score and performance score on a Wechsler test sometimes indicates a specific learning problem. (Object assembly, digit symbol, and picture completion adapted from Cronbach, 1990.)

TABLE 12.2

VERBAL ITEMS SIMILAR TO THOSE ON THE WISC-R AND THE WAIS-R

For each subtest, the first example illustrates the level of difficulty of the Wechsler Intelligence Scale for Children-Revised. The second example illustrates the level of difficulty of the Wechsler Adult Intelligence Scale-Revised. Digit span items are similar on the two tests.

Subtest	Examples
Information	Who was Thomas Jefferson?
	Who wrote *Huckleberry Finn*?
Comprehension	Why is it important to use zip codes when you mail letters?
	Why do married people who want a divorce have to go to court?
Similarities	In what way are corn and macaroni alike?
	In what way are a book and a movie alike?
Vocabulary	What do we mean by *protect*?
	What does *formulate* mean?
Arithmetic	Dick had 13 pieces of candy and gave away 8. How many did he have left?
	How many hours will it take to drive 140 miles at the rate of 30 miles an hour?
Digit Span	I am going to say some numbers. Listen carefully, and when I am through, say them right after me: 3-6-1-7-5-8.
	Now I am going to say some more numbers, but this time when I stop, I want you to say them backward: 1-9-3-2-7.

SOURCE: Adapted from Lee J. Cronbach, *Essentials of Psychological Testing,* 5th ed. New York: Harper & Row, 1990, and based on items from the Wechsler scales, published by The Psychological Corporation, 1958.

QUICK ▪ QUIZ

Test yourself on your knowledge of IQ tests.

1. On Binet's test, a child of 7 who scored like most 7-year-olds would have an IQ of _____. A child of 10 with a mental age of 9 would have an IQ of _____.
2. True or false: Culture-fair tests have eliminated group differences that show up on traditional IQ tests.
3. Some schools are returning to Binet's original goal of using IQ tests as a tool for (a) labeling and categorizing children, (b) identifying children who could benefit from individualized programs, (c) studying intellectual differences among ethnic groups.

Answers:
1. 100, 90   2. false   3. b

Plotting personality

If anything, personality is harder to condense into a test score than intelligence. Each of us is a constantly shifting kaleidoscope of traits, tendencies, preferences, and moods, which no one test can possibly summarize. But various tests and assessment methods do provide information about certain aspects of personality—about needs, values, interests, moods, and characteristic ways of responding to particular situations.

Objective tests. Objective tests, or **inventories**, are standardized questionnaires that require written responses, typically to multiple-choice or true-false items. Usually the test-taker is asked to report how she or he feels or acts in certain circumstances. A test may measure a single trait, such as sense of humor, neuroticism, or pessimism, or several traits at once. In general, objective tests have better reliability and validity than other kinds of personality tests.

As befitting the computer age, some publishers of objective tests now offer the ultimate in objectivity: computerized interpretations of test results. These interpretations, based on statistical norms, are often more reliable than those made by clinical experts. But such objectivity is not without its drawbacks. Computers cannot consider how a person behaved during the test or a person's previous psychological history. Managers, teachers, and others not trained in psychological testing may put too much faith in statistical interpretations, just because they come from a machine.

The most widely used objective personality test is the **Minnesota Multiphasic Personality Inventory (MMPI)**. The MMPI was originally developed in the 1930s by a psychologist and a psychiatrist to screen people with psychological disorders. A thousand potential test items were given to approximately 200 mental patients and 1500 nonpatients in Minneapolis. The items took the form of statements about symptoms, moods, attitudes, and behavior, and test-takers had to indicate whether the statements applied to themselves by responding "true," "false," or "cannot say." Of the initial test items, 566 were answered differently on the average by the disturbed and nondisturbed sample groups; these items were retained. (The items did not have to "make sense" theoretically as long as they discriminated between the people in the two groups.) The various items were assigned to ten clinical categories, or *scales*, that measured such problems as depression, hysteria, paranoia, and social introversion. Four *validity scales* indicated whether a test-taker was lying, careless, defensive, or evasive while answering the items. For example, if a person gave an unlikely response to almost every test item, the person's score on the lie scale would be high.

Since the original MMPI was devised, hundreds of supplemental scales, based on different groupings of the same items, have been added, and more than 8000 books and articles have been written on the test (Butcher & Finn, 1983). The inventory has been used in some 50 countries, on everyone from ordinary job applicants to Soviet cosmonauts, and the scales have been increasingly used to assess normal personality traits rather than psychological disturbance. The MMPI has also inspired the development of other personality inventories using similar items. In 1989, a long-awaited revision of the MMPI was released, with norms based on a nationally representative sample balanced by region, ethnicity, age, education, and gender (Hathaway & McKinley, with Butcher et al., 1989).

Yet despite its popularity, the MMPI has many critics. Some argue that the test is racially, culturally, and sexually biased. For example, a woman whose answers indicate that she likes mechanics magazines or would enjoy serving as a soldier

inventories *Standardized objective questionnaires requiring written responses; they typically include scales on which people are asked to rate themselves.*

Minnesota Multiphasic Personality Inventory (MMPI) *A widely used objective personality test.*

might be labeled abnormally masculine simply because men are more likely to report such interests. The validity and reliability of the test have also come under fire. One recent review of studies concludes that the validity and reliability of the MMPI are adequate if the test is used for its original purpose—identifying people with personality or emotional disorders (Parker, Hanson, & Hunsley, 1988). But in practice, the MMPI (along with other objective tests) is often used in business, industry, and education for inappropriate reasons by persons who are not well trained in testing.

Projective tests. **Projective tests** are used to measure conscious and unconscious motives, thoughts, perceptions, and conflicts—aspects of personality that may not be apparent in a person's public behavior. The tests present ambiguous pictures, patterns, or stories for the test-taker to interpret. There is no correct interpretation; each person is free to respond as he or she likes. The assumption is that the person's thoughts and feelings will be ''projected'' onto the test materials and revealed in the person's interpretations. Projective tests are used most often by psychotherapists to explore how their clients perceive the world, but researchers also find them useful (see Figure 12.4).

One popular projective test, the **Rorschach Inkblot Test**, was devised by Swiss psychiatrist Hermann Rorschach in 1921. It consists of ten cards with symmetrical abstract patterns, originally formed by spilling ink on paper and folding the paper in two. The test-taker reports what he or she ''sees'' in the inkblots. Scoring systems take into account three aspects of the person's responses:

1. *Location.* Did the person respond to the entire blot or only certain parts? Which part or parts of the blot did the person discuss?

2. *Determinants.* Which aspects of the blot (for example, color, form, or texture) did the person mention?

3. *Content.* What type of object or activity did the person ''see''?

Many scorers also consider the ''popularity'' of the response (whether it was common or original) and the person's behaviors and comments during the session. Some

projective tests *Psychological tests used to infer a person's motives, thoughts, perceptions, and conflicts on the basis of the person's interpretations of ambiguous or unstructured stimuli.*
Rorschach [ROR-shock] Inkblot Test *A projective personality test that asks respondents to interpret abstract, symmetrical inkblots.*

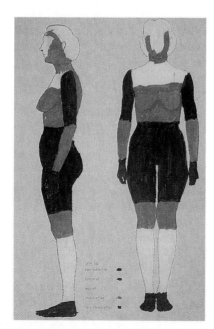

FIGURE 12.4

A projective test for body satisfaction
The Color-A-Person Test is a projective test (Wooley & Wooley, 1985) for evaluating a person's body image and the emotions associated with it. Test takers use different colors to indicate the degree of satisfaction or dissatisfaction with various parts of their bodies. Scoring takes into account not only which colors were used, but differentiation of body parts, distortions from reality, and comments made during the test. This drawing was made by a woman suffering from bulimia, an eating disorder characterized by binge eating followed by self-induced vomiting to avoid weight gain.

FIGURE 12.5

The Thematic Apperception Test
On the left, a woman taking the TAT makes up stories for a set of thematically ambiguous pictures. The picture on the right, similar to one included in an adaptation of the test, has been used to study people's unconscious feelings about intimacy. (For one such study, see p. 364.) When you look at this picture, what sort of "story" do you think of? Who are the people and what are they thinking and saying? What past events have led up to this situation, and what will happen as a result?

clinicians interpret the answers subjectively, taking into account the symbolic meanings emphasized by psychoanalytic theory.

Another widely used projective test is the **Thematic Apperception Test (TAT)**, which consists of a series of drawings or photographs showing people in ambiguous situations (see Figure 12.5). The test-taker must make up a story about each scene. An elaborate scoring system takes into account the basic issues raised in each story, the characters the test-taker identified with, the motives and emotions attributed to the various characters, and the endings given to the stories. (Chapter 10 explained how the TAT is used to assess achievement motivation.)

Other projective tests use sentence or story completion, word association, or self-expression through art. Many clinicians believe that projective techniques are a rich source of information. Test-takers cannot "fake" or lie as easily as on objective tests. Also, the tests can help a clinician establish rapport with a client and encourage a person to open up about anxieties, conflicts, and problems. Many critics, however, question both the validity and the reliability of some of the tests, especially as they are used by clinicians. They note that different clinicians often interpret the tests differently, and that the clinicians themselves may be "projecting" when they decide what a specific response means. Moreover, it can be hard to know whether a person's responses reflect deep-seated personality characteristics or only temporary conditions such as fatigue or a hard day.

Interviews. In interviews, a psychologist or examiner asks a person questions, face to face. In *structured interviews*, the person answers a predetermined set of questions. In *unstructured interviews*, the person is free to respond in any way and can influence what is talked about and the order in which topics are covered. Interviews probe a person's perceptions and interpretations of experience more directly than projective tests do.

Although interviews are widely used in education, business, psychological research, and psychotherapy, they have certain problems. A person being interviewed

Thematic Apperception Test (TAT) *A projective personality test that asks respondents to interpret a series of drawings showing ambiguous scenes.*

may lie or misremember. As with projective tests, different interviewers may interpret responses differently, depending on their own perceptions and personalities. The way people act during an interview may not be the way they act in daily life. On the plus side, during an interview the interviewer can gauge a person's emotional responses to questions by observing tone of voice, body language, and facial expressions.

Behavioral observations.   A final technique is the direct observation of behavior or performance in a particular situation. Observers usually rate the frequency and quality of specific behaviors according to a carefully worked-out procedure. For example, they might record how many times a person in psychotherapy laughs inappropriately or how many times a child approaches other children in a playroom. Behavioral observations are sometimes used to evaluate the reactions of people applying for jobs requiring particular personality traits. Many police departments now show officers videotaped re-creations of situations like those they encounter in the line of duty. The officer must decide whether a crime is occurring and what action to take (for instance, whether or not to shoot). Such tests, which are also used in training, can reveal whether a person has a tendency to overreact or hesitate too long in a potentially dangerous situation. The main drawback with behavioral observation is that sometimes it is hard to know whether a person experiences the test situation as ''real'' and is behaving as he or she ordinarily would.

Evaluating personality tests.   Personality tests, and in particular interviews and projective tests, are often poor at predicting actual behavior. Some do not reliably distinguish between people who have a particular trait or psychological problem and those who do not. The fault, however, is not entirely with the tests. As we saw in Chapter 11, personality itself is often inconsistent, shifting from one situation to another or from one year to another. A test cannot pin down personality if personality won't hold still.

Like mental tests, however, personality tests can be informative when used along with other information about an individual. The tests may be far from perfect, but without them clinical diagnosis would be difficult and much personality research would be impossible. Like intelligence tests, personality tests can be useful in probing the origins of human diversity, to which we now turn.

QUICK ▪ QUIZ

Identify which category—projective, interview, objective, or behavioral observation—fits each test description given below.

1. A psychotherapist questions her client about his childhood.
2. An applicant for a management job is observed making decisions in a mock business crisis.
3. A subject in a study of anxiety supplies an ending to a story about someone who must give a speech to a large audience.
4. A schoolchild answers a questionnaire containing items usually answered differently by children with high and low self-esteem.

Answers:

1. interview 2. behavioral observation 3. projective 4. objective

The Heritability Hunt: Genetic Origins of Diversity

Historically, debates about genetic and environmental influences on human development have sometimes sounded like a boxing match: "In this corner, we have Heredity and in this corner, we have Environment. Okay, you guys, come out fighting." E. L. Thorndike, one of the leading psychologists of the early 1900s, claimed (1903) that "in the actual race of life . . . the chief determining factor is heredity." But his contemporary, behaviorist John B. Watson (1925), thought that experience could write virtually any message on the blank slate of human nature:

> Give me a dozen healthy infants, well-formed, and my own specified world to bring them up in and I'll guarantee to take any one at random and train him to become any type of specialist I might select—doctor, lawyer, artist, merchant-chief and yes, even beggar-man and thief, regardless of his talents, penchants, tendencies, abilities, vocations, and race of his ancestors. (p. 104)

Today, most psychologists have concluded that in the nature-nurture contest, there can be no clear winner. Findings in the interdisciplinary field of **behavior genetics** suggest that within a particular group, nervous system and biochemical differences may help account for variations in how people respond to their environments. But no psychological characteristic emerges full-blown from some genetic blueprint without environmental influence, any more than language appears in an infant reared in isolation. Throughout life, heredity and environment continually interact.

One kind of interaction occurs when genetic factors affect how adults respond to children. For example, even a modest genetic difference in intelligence may lead parents to treat two children differently. The slightly brighter child may get more educational toys and books (and a calculator and personal computer). Adults may prompt her to ask searching questions. Over time, her slight edge may grow into a larger one. As a result, she may attend to different stimuli in the environment or take advantage of different opportunities than one who is less endowed; she may actively select certain experiences over others. This selection process, of course, assumes that children have environments to select *from*. When a child's opportunities are limited, as they are for many poor and inner-city children, the environment may slam a lid on genetic potential instead of opening a door to it.

Thus the origins of human diversity are complicated. And so, of necessity, are the sections that follow, not only because heredity and environment interact but also because attempts to unravel this interaction have been fraught with problems of measurement, sampling, and interpretation. We want to alert you here that you will need to read these sections carefully. However, we feel it would be wrong to avoid or gloss over the complexities. Unsophisticated assumptions about nature and nurture can influence the formation of social and educational policies that affect millions of lives.

It's easy to oversimplify the nature-nurture debate. Heredity and environment may seem like contenders in some winner-take-all competition, but in real life is it possible to separate them?

Heredity and the individual

The first thing to understand about the nature-nurture issue is that no one can determine the impact of heredity on any *particular* individual's intellectual or emotional makeup. The reason lies in the mechanisms of inheritance.

behavior genetics *An interdisciplinary field of study concerned with the genetic bases of behavior.*

Each person's genes are strung out on **chromosomes**, rod-shaped structures in the center of each body cell. In all cells except sperm and eggs, 46 chromosomes are lined up two by two, in 23 pairs, with each chromosome containing about 20,000 genes. Corresponding areas on each pair work together to determine a particular trait. When the body cells that produce sperm and eggs divide, one member of each original chromosome pair goes to one new sperm or egg, and the other member goes to the other new sperm or egg. Thus sperm and eggs contain 23 *unpaired* chromosomes. Chance alone decides which member of a chromosome pair goes to a particular sperm or egg. Mathematically, this means that each sperm- or egg-producing cell has the potential to produce several million *different* chromosome combinations in a new sperm or egg. But the actual diversity is even greater because small segments of chromosomes often "cross over" from one member of a chromosome pair to another during the formation of sperm and eggs.

The upshot is that although a parent and his or her offspring share, on the average, half their genes, each of us is the potential parent of billions of genetically *different* offspring (given the time and energy). In other words, each sperm or egg in your body contains a genetic mosaic different from the one in the sperm or egg that helped make you. Of course, the person we mate with also contributes one of billions of possible combinations to each child. Thus siblings (who also share, on the average, half their genes) can be quite unlike each other, and children can be unlike their parents, in purely *genetic* terms.

To say, then, that some trait is "genetic" does not mean that children will be just like their parents. It is true that a parent and child will be more alike in many ways than two unrelated people selected at random. It is also true that genes—half from the mother, half from the father—set limits on many human attributes: gender, eye color, height range, shape of nose, color of skin. But *human diversity is built into the way heredity works.* Each of us, with the exception of identical twins, is a unique genetic hodgepodge, one that never existed before and never will again. That is why knowing a person's heredity does not automatically tell you what the person will be like, even in purely genetic terms.

Understanding heritability

Although determining the influence of heredity and environment on a particular individual's behavior or personality is impossible, behavior geneticists can study the origins of differences *among* individuals. Their methods typically yield a statistical estimate of the *proportion of the total variance in a trait* that is attributable to *genetic variation* within a group. This estimate is known as the trait's **heritability**, and since it is expressed as a proportion, its maximum value is 1.0. Height is highly heritable; that is, within a group, most variation among individuals is accounted for by genetic differences. In contrast, table manners have low heritability, because most variation among individuals is accounted for by differences in upbringing.

Many people have mistaken ideas about heritability. Because understanding the nature-nurture issue depends on understanding heritability, it is important that you know the facts:

1. *An estimate of heritability applies only to a particular group living in a particular environment.* Suppose that all the children in Rich County are affluent, eat plenty of high-quality food, and go to the same top-notch schools. The intellectual differences among them will probably be due largely to their genetic differences, because their environments are very similar and are optimal for intellectual

What does it mean to say that some trait is "highly heritable"? If you want to improve your piccolo playing and someone tells you that musical ability is heritable, would you stop practicing?

chromosomes *The rod-shaped structures in the center of each body cell that carry the genes and determine hereditary characteristics.*

heritability *A statistical estimate of the proportion of the total variance in some trait within a group that is attributable to genetic differences among individuals within the group.*

development. In contrast, the children in Normal County are rich, poor, and in between. Some have good diets; others live on cupcakes. Some attend good schools; others go to miserable ones. These children's intellectual differences might well be due to their environmental differences, and for them, estimated heritability of intelligence will be lower.

2. *Heritability estimates do not apply to individuals, only to groups.* Suppose researchers knew the heritability of gymnastics ability. That fact would *not* tell you whether your own gymnastics ability was due primarily to your genes, your motivation, or your training. The same applies to any trait.

3. *Heritability can change over time.* Although genetic makeup may act as a lens through which the world is experienced, the lens is not fixed: Genes turn on and off over the life span, controlled in part by signals in the environment (Scarr, 1984a; Scarr & McCartney, 1983). Thus the relative influence of heredity as opposed to environment can differ for different age groups. A trait that is highly heritable in a group of 5-year-olds may hardly be heritable at all in a group of 10-year-olds. In other words, the relative influence of the environment may be greater for the 10-year-olds.

4. *Even highly heritable traits can be modified by the environment.* Although height is highly heritable, malnourished children may not grow to be as tall as they would with sufficient food. Conversely, if children eat a super-nutritious diet, they may grow to be taller than anyone thought they could. The same principle applies to psychological traits, although some writers have failed to realize this. In a famous paper, Arthur Jensen (1969) concluded that IQ and school achievement could not be boosted much because IQ is highly heritable. As we will see, IQ scores may or may not be highly heritable, but even if they are, they may still be modifiable.

5. *The genetics of human variation are difficult to specify precisely because traits are often influenced by many genes working in combination.* It is unlikely that any single gene confers musical talent, mathematical ability, or a sunny disposition.

6. *Not all inborn traits are inherited.* The traits babies are born with are also influenced by the mother's health and drug use and by genetic mutations and accidents. **Down's syndrome**, which accounts for about 10 percent of all mental retardation, usually occurs because of a genetic error. For unknown reasons, faulty distribution of chromosomes during sperm or egg formation produces an extra chromosome in the child's cells, and the twenty-first pair becomes a triplet (Robinson & Robinson, 1976). The chances of having a child with Down's syndrome increase with the age of the mother and possibly the father (L. Holmes, 1978). The syndrome is present at birth, but most cases are *not* inherited (passed on from parent to child).

Clues from adoption and twin studies

Scientists cannot estimate the heritability of human behavior by examining chromosomes directly under a microscope; they would not know what to look for. Instead, they must *infer* heritability by studying people whose degree of genetic similarity is known. This task is not easy. The simplest approach might seem to be a comparison of blood relatives within families. Everyone knows of families that are famous for some talent or trait. For example, there were seven generations of musical Bachs. But anecdotes and isolated examples can always be answered with counterexamples: Mendelssohn's father was a banker, Chopin's a bookkeeper, and Schubert's a schoolmaster, and their mothers were not known to have musical talent (Lewontin, 1982). Results from controlled studies of families are also inconclusive, for close

Down's syndrome *A form of mental retardation usually caused by an extra chromosome 21. It is accompanied by various physical anomalies, such as a downward curve of the inner eyelid.*

Separated at birth, the Mallifert twins meet accidentally.

relatives usually share environments as well as genes. If Carlo's parents and siblings all love lasagna, that doesn't mean a taste for lasagna is heritable. The same applies if everyone in Carlo's family has a high IQ, is mentally ill, or is moody.

There are two ways out of this bind. One is to study adopted children. Such children share half their genes with each birth parent, but not their environment. On the other hand, they share an environment with their adoptive parents, but not their genes. Researchers can compare correlations between the children's traits and those of their biological and adoptive parents and use the results to estimate heritability.

The other approach is to compare **identical (monozygotic)** and **fraternal (dyzygotic) twins**. Identical twins are born when a fertilized egg divides into two parts that then develop into two separate embryos. Since the twins come from the same fertilized egg, they share all their genes, barring genetic mutations or accidents. (They may be slightly different at birth, however, because of birth complications or differences in the blood supply to the two fetuses.) In contrast, fraternal twins develop when a woman's ovaries release two eggs instead of one, and each egg is fertilized by a different sperm. Fraternal twins are wombmates, but they are no more alike genetically than any two siblings and may be of different sexes. By comparing groups of same-sex fraternal twins to groups of identical twins, psychologists can estimate heritability. The basic assumption is that if identical twins are more alike than fraternal twins, the increased similarity must be genetic.

Perhaps, however, environments shared by identical twins differ from those shared by fraternal twins. People may treat identical twins as more alike or go to the other extreme by emphasizing their differences. To avoid such problems, investigators have studied identical twins who were separated early in life and reared apart. (Until recently, adoption policies and attitudes toward illegitimacy permitted such separation to occur.) Though rare, such cases are numerous enough to study. In theory, separated identical twins share all their genes but not their environments. Any similarities between them should be genetic and should permit a direct estimate of heritability.

In the past, studies of twins reared apart have had some serious flaws. In a

monozygotic twins (identical twins) *Twins born when a fertilized egg divides into two parts that develop into separate embryos.*

dyzygotic twins (fraternal twins) *Twins that develop from two separate eggs fertilized by different sperm. They are no more alike genetically than any two siblings.*

review, Susan Farber (1981) discovered that most twins "reared apart" weren't so *far* apart. Many had visited one another during childhood or were reared by relatives in the same town or went to the same school. Of the 121 sets studied between 1922 and 1973, only 3 were strangers at the time of study. Judgments of similarity typically were based on only a few tests, self-reports, or casual observation. There were other methodological problems as well.

A recent research project has corrected some of these problems. Since the early 1980s, an interdisciplinary team at the University of Minnesota has been testing and interviewing identical and fraternal twins reared apart (Bouchard, 1984; Holden, 1987; Tellegen et al., 1988). Subjects undergo six days of comprehensive psychological and medical monitoring and answer some 15,000 written questions. By 1989, information had been reported on 71 sets of reunited twins, 44 of them identical. The investigators also have comparison data on twins reared together. But even this well-controlled study has some problems. First, most of the twins were reared in fairly similar environments, which, as we have seen, can statistically boost heritability estimates. Second, some of the twins were reunited several years before being studied and may have had a chance to influence one another during adulthood. (Available reports do not say whether twins reunited shortly before being studied are as similar as those reunited several years earlier.) Third, all the twins are volunteers. It is possible that similar identical twin pairs are especially likely to be in contact and thus be available to volunteer for the study.

Because twin studies currently provide the best clues to heritability, we will examine what they suggest, along with other research results, about the origins of individual differences—looking first at personality and then at intellectual ability. However, as an informed consumer of psychological research, you should keep the methodological problems in mind.

Heritability and personality differences

One way to study the origins of personality differences is to look at **temperaments**, characteristic styles of responding to the environment that appear in early childhood. If personality has some genetic basis, certain temperamental styles ought to emerge early in life and affect subsequent development. This is, in fact, the case. Even in the first weeks after birth, infants differ in activity level, mood, responsiveness, and attention span.

In one highly regarded study of temperament, physicians Alexander Thomas and Stella Chess (1977) found that most infants could be classified into three categories. *Easy children* were usually cheerful and contented, and adjusted easily to new people and experiences. *Difficult children* were often fussy and agitated, and distrusted changes and new experiences, although they eventually adapted. *Slow-to-warm-up children* showed few intense reactions, were somewhat negative in mood, and tended to be passive and withdrawn when faced with new things (instead of protesting noisily, as difficult children did). Other researchers have suggested somewhat different categories. For example, Arnold Buss and Robert Plomin (1984) propose that infants differ in *emotionality* (the tendency to be distressed), *sociability* (the tendency to prefer the company of others over being alone), and *activity* (tempo and vigor of movement).

Recent evidence suggests that certain temperamental differences in infants and young children are due to variations in the responsiveness of the sympathetic nervous system to change and novelty. Jerome Kagan and his colleagues have found that socially inhibited 5-year-olds are more likely than uninhibited children to show

temperaments *Characteristic styles of responding to the environment that are present in infancy and are assumed to be innate.*

signs of sympathetic nervous system activity during mildly stressful mental tasks (Kagan, 1988; Kagan, Reznick, & Snidman, 1988). Such signs include increased heart rate, increased pupillary dilation, and a rise in norepinephrine in the sympathetic nervous system. Highly inhibited children also have higher than average cortisol levels, and there is some indirect evidence that they have relatively high levels of norepinephrine in the brain. Exactly the same physiological attributes are being found in inhibited infant monkeys (Suomi, 1987).

Some aspects of temperament may lead to characteristic habits and mannerisms in adults. Researchers have been struck by certain unnerving similarities in the gestures, movements, and speech patterns of separated identical twins. In her review of the research, Susan Farber (1981) remarked on two male twins who both nodded their heads in a certain way while speaking, two other male twins who both flicked their fingers when unable to think of an answer, and two female twins who both rubbed their noses and rocked when tired. Farber also noted that identical twins reared apart tended to have similar characteristic moods. If one twin was optimistic, excitable, or glum, the other was likely to be the same. If one had frequent mood changes, the other was apt to have them as well. The Minnesota project has found the same sorts of resemblances in mood and personal style (Bouchard et al., 1986). (Some of these similarities could be coincidental, however, as "Taking Psychology with You" points out.)

A second way to study the genetic basis of personality is to estimate the heritability of specific adult personality traits, using data from twin studies. Researchers using this method report that whether the trait in question is altruism, aggression, neuroticism, sense of well-being, or traditionalism (respect for rules and authority), heritability is typically around .50 (Loehlin, 1988; Rushton et al., 1986; Tellegen et al., 1988). If this figure is correct, then within a group of people about 50 percent of the variance in such personality traits is attributable to people's genetic differences.

These findings, however, are probably not the last word. Although it is easy to estimate the genetic similarity of twins, measures of environmental similarities (and differences) are still exceedingly crude. Rarely do researchers actually observe the environments of separated twins; instead, they rely on retrospective self-reports. As a result, they may underestimate the relative impact of the environment on the development of personality differences. For this reason, we urge caution in drawing

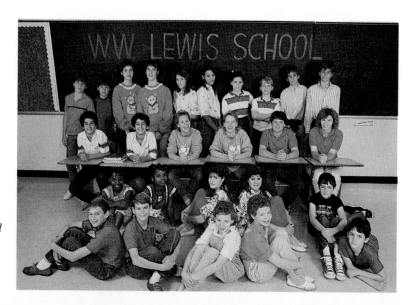

When posing for a photograph, identical twins will often unconsciously arrange their arms and legs in the same way and assume similar facial expressions. Research suggests that such physical mannerisms probably have some genetic basis.

FIGURE 12.6

**From one branch, two
different twigs**
*In many respects, the per-
sonalities of identical twins
seem more alike on the average than those of other
siblings. But not all identical twins resemble each
other psychologically. These
pictures show the same pair
of identical twins at different ages. In both infancy
and childhood the twin on
the left was cheerful and
easygoing, whereas the one
on the right was negative
and difficult. Genetic differences may help explain
some personality differ-
ences, but a particular set
of genes does not lead inevitably to a particular personality type.*

conclusions about the exact heritability of personality traits. Remember, too, that
heritability estimates do not tell you how much heredity contributes to an *individual's* personality. Journalistic accounts of twin studies often make this error. In a
Time article on the Minnesota research, we found this passage: "How much of any
individual's personality is due to heredity? The answer: about half." But as we have
seen, heritability applies only to differences within a group, not to individuals. Even
identical twins, who share all their genes, can become very different people (see
Figure 12.6). One twin may even become schizophrenic and the other not (see
Chapter 16).

Heritability and intellectual differences

Most studies on the heritability of personality use standard personality tests to assess
the traits being investigated. Similarly, most studies on the heritability of intelligence rely on IQ tests. As we have seen, not all psychologists consider the IQ test to
be a valid sampling of intelligent behavior. Assuming, however, that IQ scores are
at least a partial reflection of intelligence, what do twin studies suggest about the
genetic basis of intellectual differences?

Almost all twin studies report that the IQ scores of identical twins correlate
more highly than the scores of fraternal twins. In fact, the scores of identical twins
reared apart are more highly correlated than those of fraternal twins reared together.
These findings point to a genetic contribution to at least some kinds of intelligence.
However, the *size* of the contribution is a bone of contention, one that has been
gnawed at for years. The Minnesota team estimates the heritability of IQ to be
between .50 and .60 (McGue & Bouchard, 1987). But other estimates range from
.10 to almost .90 (see Figure 12.7). The figures depend in part on how the calculations are done. When Susan Farber (1981) pooled all the data on 121 pairs of
identical twins reared apart, she found a heritability estimate of .75. But Farber
realized that some of the similarity that appeared to be genetic must be environmental, because most "separated" twins actually had contact with each other. When
she took degree of separation into account, the result came out much lower, about
.48. Farber argued that if other factors were considered, such as similarity between
the homes in which the twins were reared and the ones in which they were born, the
figure would be lower still.

Psychologists who accept twin studies at face value conclude that intelligence is
highly heritable (Jensen, 1969, 1980). Others, emphasizing flaws in the studies and

FIGURE 12.7

Family resemblances in IQ

This chart is based on a survey of studies on IQ correlations for biological and adoptive relatives (Bouchard & McGue, 1981). The bars show the range of correlations found by various studies. The vertical line on each bar indicates the average correlation for each type of comparison. The red arrows show the correlations that would be predicted by a purely genetic model of intelligence, with no environmental effects. On the average, the higher the proportion of genes family members have in common, the more highly correlated their IQ scores are, suggesting that differences in heredity contribute to differences in intelligence. However, for most comparisons the range of correlations found by different studies is quite broad. The extent to which intelligence is heritable remains a controversial question that may never be answered, for reasons explained in the text.

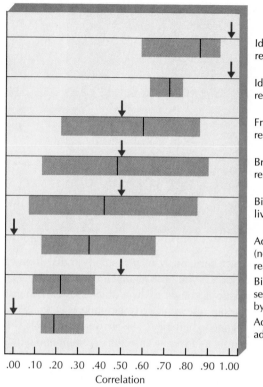

Identical twins reared together

Identical twins reared apart

Fraternal twins reared together

Brothers and sisters reared together

Birth parent and offspring, living together

Adopted siblings (not biologically related) reared together

Birth parent and offspring, separated (child adopted by others)

Adopting parent and adopted child

.00 .10 .20 .30 .40 .50 .60 .70 .80 .90 1.00
Correlation

problems in their interpretation, believe that heredity counts for little. Most experts, however, take a middle road (Plomin & DeFries, 1980; Scarr & Weinberg, 1977, 1979; Snyderman & Rothman, 1987). The consensus is that variations in intelligence are at least partly attributable to genetic differences, but that specific estimates of heritability must be taken with a grain of salt.

QUICK ■ QUIZ

1. Diane hears that a particular psychological trait is highly heritable and concludes that her own lack of the trait must be due mostly to her genes. What's wrong with her reasoning?
2. Carpentry skills seem to "run" in Andy's family. Why shouldn't Andy conclude that this talent is genetic?
3. True or false: Individual differences in temperament appear to have a genetic basis.
4. True or false: Twin studies indicate that the heritability of personality traits is close to zero.
5. Estimates of the heritability of intelligence based on twin studies **(a)** put heritability at about .80, **(b)** show heritability to be low, **(c)** vary widely.

Answers:

1. Heritability applies only to differences among individuals within a group, not to particular individuals. 2. Family members share environments as well as genes. 3. true 4. false 5. c

The Forge of Experience: Environmental Origins of Diversity

Up to this point, we have focused on heredity. But it is clear that whatever their heritability, both personality traits and mental abilities can be profoundly affected by the environment. Let's look at some ways in which experience can mold individual differences in personality and intellect.

The environment and personality

We saw earlier that temperaments appear early in life and can influence later personality traits. But this does not mean that temperaments provide a fixed, unchangeable blueprint for later personality. Temperaments change; a "difficult" child may mature and learn to exercise self-control (Thomas & Chess, 1982). (The way others perceive a child's temperamental style can also change. A child whom everyone considers "easy" because he is placid and docile may later seem "difficult" because he is lazy and lacks initiative.)

Consistency in a given temperament seems to depend in part on how extreme that temperament is in infancy. Jerome Kagan and his colleagues (1988) report that children who are exceptionally shy and subdued at age 2 tend to be quiet, cautious, and socially inhibited at age 7. Similarly, those who are extremely sociable and uninhibited at 2 are usually talkative and sociable five years later. But most children fall somewhere between the extremes and show far less consistency over time.

Even children at the extremes of some temperament may change as they grow older. Whether or not such change occurs seems to depend largely on how parents respond to the child. In his work with monkeys, Stephen Suomi (1989) has shown that a highly inhibited infant is likely to overcome its timidity if it is reared by a nurturant foster mother (see Figure 12.8). In human beings, the "fit" between a child's nature and the parents' is critical (Thomas & Chess, 1980). Not only do parents affect the baby, but the baby affects the parents. Imagine a high-strung parent with a child who is difficult and sometimes slow to respond to affection. The parent may begin to feel desperate, angry, or rejected. Over time, the parent may

FIGURE 12.8

Don't be shy
On the left, a timid infant rhesus monkey cowers behind a friend in the presence of a more outgoing stranger. Such socially inhibited behavior seems to be a biologically based disposition, both in monkeys and in human beings. But a nurturant adult monkey (in the photo on the right, a foster mother) can help an infant overcome its initial timidity; temperamental dispositions can be modified.

withdraw from the child or become critical and punishing. Such responses are likely to make the child even more difficult to live with. In contrast, a more easygoing parent may have a calming effect on a difficult child or may persist in showing affection even when the child holds back. As a result, the child may eventually become more responsive.

In sum, two children who begin life with similar temperaments may grow up to have very different personalities, depending on their parents, their environments, and their unique experiences. As developmental psychologist Alan Sroufe (1978) points out, "A child who has a rapid tempo may be seething with anger, hostile to other children, unable to control his or her impulses and filled with feelings of worthlessness. But a child who has a rapid tempo also may be eager, spirited, effective, and a pleasure to others."

The environment and mental ability

Like temperaments and personality traits, IQ scores are also vulnerable to the environment. You can see how heritability can be significant yet the environment important in studies of adopted children. The IQ scores of adopted children correlate more highly with their birth parents' scores than with those of their adoptive parents. That is, if Johnny scores high relative to other adopted children, his birth parents are likely to score high relative to other adults who have put their children up for adoption. This fact supports the heritability of intelligence as measured by IQ tests. However, in *absolute* terms, Johnny's IQ may differ considerably from the scores of his birth parents. Indeed, on the average, adopted children have IQs that are 10 to 20 points *higher* than those of their birth parents (Scarr & Weinberg, 1977; Skodak & Skeels, 1949). Most psychologists believe that this difference exists because adoptive families tend to be smaller, wealthier, and better educated than other families, and these environmental factors are associated with high IQs in children.

The influence of the environment on mental ability begins even before birth, in the silent "environment" of the womb. If a pregnant woman is malnourished, contracts certain infections, takes certain drugs, smokes or drinks excessively, or is exposed to environmental pollutants, the fetus's development may suffer (see Chapter 13). All of these circumstances are associated with reduced IQs and increased incidence of learning disabilities in children. Even extreme stress during pregnancy may affect the fetus's neuron growth by altering the mother's hormone levels (McEwen, 1983b).

Here are a few factors thought to affect mental ability *after* birth. They have all been implicated in the lower IQ scores of children from poor and working-class families, as compared with those from middle-class families.

1. *Nutrition.* Early malnutrition slows brain growth and mental development (Stoch & Smythe, 1963; Winick, Meyer, & Harris, 1975). The average IQ gap between severely malnourished and well-nourished children can be as high as 20 points. When there are other kinds of deprivation as well, the effects of early malnutrition may be permanent.

2. *Exposure to toxins.* Children exposed to toxins such as lead, which can damage the nervous system, have lower IQ scores and more attention problems than other children (Needleman, Leviton, & Bellinger, 1982). House paint no longer contains lead, but poor children often live in old, run-down buildings with peeling, lead-based paint.

3. *Mental stimulation.* Dozens of animal studies show that a stimulating environment actually alters the structure of the brain (Rosenzweig, 1984). Rats that learn complicated tasks or grow up in cages equipped with lots of rat toys develop thicker and heavier cortexes and richer networks of synaptic connections in certain brain areas than do rats in unchallenging environments.

If stimulation is important, early enrichment programs for preschoolers, such as the federally funded Head Start program, should promote mental growth in disadvantaged children. Early studies on this issue found that gains from such programs were only temporary, but recent evidence is more positive (Burchinal, Lee, & Ramey, 1986; Collins, 1983; McKey et al., 1985; Zigler & Berman, 1983). Although IQ gains do not appear to be large or enduring, children who have been in early enrichment programs adjust better to school than do their peers, get better grades, score higher on achievement tests, and have better social skills. Since children usually do not enroll in these programs until age 4, it is possible that earlier intervention would bring even greater benefits, including long-term gains in IQ (M. Hunt, 1982).

For that matter, *late* enrichment can also boost mental performance. Like the children in early enrichment programs, many elderly adults live in disadvantaged environments. When people aged 60 to 80 get even short-term training in the kinds of skills tapped by IQ tests, their scores on tests of specific mental abilities climb, often entirely offsetting the losses typical for that age group (Baltes & Willis, 1982). This is true even for abilities presumed to be part of "fluid" intelligence—the very ones that supposedly are not susceptible to training.

4. *Parent-child interactions.* In general, children who score well on IQ tests have parents who actively encourage their development. Such parents spend time with their children; encourage them to think things through; provide appropriate toys, books, and field trips; and expect them to do well (Bee et al., 1982; Bradley & Caldwell, 1984). They talk to them about objects and people and describe things accurately and fully (Clarke-Stewart, VanderStoep, & Killian, 1979; Dickson et al., 1979). They are warm and affectionate without being intrusive (Carew, 1980). Most important, their reactions to their children are tied directly to what the children do (Beckwith & Cohen, 1984). By answering their children's questions and responding to their actions, such parents teach their children that their efforts matter. An unresponsive parent may give the child just as much attention, but the attention

The children of migrant workers (left) often spend long hours in backbreaking field work, and may miss out on the educational opportunities and intellectual advantages available to middle-class children (right).

is not tied to the child's accomplishments and efforts. Such attention does not help the child grow intellectually or give the child a sense of competence.

5. *Family size.* The average IQ in a family declines as the number of children rises (Belmont & Marolla, 1973). Birth order also makes a difference: IQ tends to decline slightly in each successive child (Zajonc & Markus, 1975). Most researchers attribute these facts to the reduced time parents with many children can spend with each child.

Environmental changes probably help explain why IQ scores often change during childhood (although genes that switch on and off cannot be ruled out as a cause, either). If two tests are given within a fairly short period of time, scores are usually similar, but over the entire span of childhood, IQ scores often dip or rise. In one study of children who had been given IQ tests regularly between ages $2\frac{1}{2}$ and 17, the majority showed changes of 20 to 30 points during childhood, and some children showed changes of 40 points (McCall, Appelbaum, & Hogarty, 1973).

The general impact of environment has been seen in Japan. Since World War II, IQ scores of Japanese children have risen, and the average IQ of Japanese children is now the highest in the world (Lynn, 1982). Genetic explanations for the increase are unlikely; genetic changes in a population do not occur that fast. It is more likely that the rise is due to improvements in the Japanese educational system, urbanization, improved health, and greater exposure to Western culture, which originally created IQ tests.

Race and IQ

So far, we have considered only intellectual differences among individuals. Throughout this century, researchers have also wondered about the origins of group differences. Unfortunately, the history of intelligence testing has sometimes been marred by racial, ethnic, and class prejudice. Too often, in the words of one critic, the result has been "the mismeasure of man" (S. J. Gould, 1981). (For more on this issue, see "Think About It" on pages 450–451.)

Today, most interest in group differences focuses on black-white differences in IQ. A few psychologists argue for a genetic explanation of such differences. A leading spokesperson for this view is Arthur Jensen (1969, 1973), although over the years he has modified his position somewhat (Jensen, 1981). Genetic theories of racial differences aim to account for the fact that black American schoolchildren score, on the average, 10 to 15 points lower on IQ tests than do white American schoolchildren, a fact that no one disputes. (We are talking about *averages*; many black children score higher than most whites, and many whites score lower than most blacks. That is, the distributions of scores for blacks and whites overlap.) A serious problem with such theories is that they use heritability estimates based on white samples to estimate the role heredity plays in group differences. This problem sounds pretty technical, but it is not too difficult to understand, so stay with us.

Consider, first, not people but tomatoes. Suppose you have a bag of tomato seeds that vary genetically. You take a bunch of seeds in your left hand and a bunch in your right. Though one seed differs genetically from another, there is no *average* difference between the seeds in your left hand and those in your right. Now you plant the left hand's seeds in pot A with some soil that you have doctored with nitrogen and other nutrients, and you plant the right hand's seeds in pot B with soil from which you have extracted nutrients. When the tomatoes grow, they will vary in size *within* each pot, purely because of genetic differences. But there will also be

Poor soil   Rich soil

FIGURE   12.9

The tomato plant experiment
Even if the differences among plants within each pot were due entirely to genetic differences, the average difference between pots could be entirely environmental. As the text explains, the same principle applies to individual and group differences among human beings.

an average difference between pot A and pot B. This difference *between* pots is due entirely to the different soils—even though the *within*-pot heritability is 100 percent. (This "thought experiment" is illustrated in Figure 12.9 and is based on Lewontin, 1970.)

The principle is the same for people as it is for tomatoes. Most psychologists believe that differences *within* groups, such as whites or blacks, are at least partly genetic. But that does not mean that differences *between* groups are genetic. Blacks and whites do not grow up, on the average, in the same environment. Because of racial discrimination, black children (as well as Hispanic and other minority children) often receive far fewer "nutrients"—in terms of education, encouragement by society, and opportunities.

One sure way to settle the question of inherent racial differences would be to gather IQ information on blacks and whites raised in exactly the same circumstances. This task is nearly impossible at present in the United States. However, we know that in the past few decades, as economic, social, political, and educational opportunities have opened up to black Americans, the performance of black children on scholastic achievement and aptitude tests has climbed considerably, and black-white differences have shrunk (L. Jones, 1984). Further, the handful of studies that have overcome past methodological problems fail to reveal any genetic differences between blacks and whites in whatever it is that IQ tests measure (Lewontin, 1982; Mackenzie, 1984). Consider:

▪ Children fathered by black and white American soldiers in Germany after World War II, and reared in similar German communities by similar families, did not differ significantly in IQ (Eyferth, 1961).

▪ Black and interracial children adopted by white families with above-average incomes and education score more than 15 points higher on IQ tests than disadvantaged black children living with their biological parents. Their performance on achievement tests is somewhat higher than the national average (Scarr & Weinberg, 1976).

▪ Degree of African ancestry (which can be roughly estimated from skin color, blood analysis, and genealogy) does not appear to be related to measured intelligence, as a genetic theory of black-white differences would predict (Scarr et al., 1977).

In sum, it is fair to say that the available data fail to support a genetic explanation of racial differences in IQ.

QUICK ▪ QUIZ

1. Bruce is a "difficult" baby. What environmental factor is likely to have a powerful influence on how Bruce's temperament affects his later personality?
2. Name at least four environmental factors that affect mental abilities.
3. According to a German study, when black and white children are reared in similar environments, their IQ scores are _____.

Answers:

1. how his parents respond to him 2. nutrition, exposure to toxins, mental stimulation, stress, parent-child interactions, family size 3. similar

Intellectual Differences and Real Life

Group differences aside, it is clear that *individuals* within groups differ intellectually, for both genetic and environmental reasons. What impact do these differences have on their success in life?

One way to explore this question is to examine the lives of children classified as mentally gifted. In one of the longest-running psychological studies ever conducted—it began in 1921 and is still going on—researchers at Stanford University have followed 1528 people with childhood IQ scores of at least 135. As children, the subjects were nicknamed "Termites," after Lewis Terman, who originally directed the study. The Termites' scores put them in the top 1 percent of the IQ distribution. The children were not only bright but also physically healthy, sociable, and well adjusted.

As the group entered adulthood, some failed to live up to their early promise, dropping out of school or drifting into low-level work. None of the children became another Madame Curie or Pablo Picasso. On the whole, however, the Termites were enormously successful (Sears & Barbee, 1977; Sears, 1977; Terman & Oden, 1959). Most of the men finished college and went on to excel in a wide range of areas, from literature to law. Most of the women became homemakers, a role that was socially expected at the time, but many also had careers. In general, the gifted people in this study also had good mental health, stable families, and a lower than average death rate.

Does IQ predict success for more ordinary folk? A study of thousands of men during World War II found that the average IQ of professional men was higher than the average IQ of office and blue-collar workers. However, within any occupation, there was a wide spread of IQ scores. For example, although the average IQ of teachers was almost 120, their scores ranged from about 80 to about 140. The average IQ of auto mechanics was about 100, but their scores ranged from about 60 to nearly 140. Thus some teachers had lower IQs than the average auto mechanic and some auto mechanics had higher IQs than the average teacher. The same was true in comparisons of other professionals, such as accountants or engineers, with other blue-collar workers, such as truck drivers or miners. The average scores differed, but the ranges overlapped (Harrell & Harrell, 1945).

The correlation between IQ and occupational status (and by implication, financial success) is weaker, then, than you might expect. Further, such a correlation does not mean that a high IQ *causes* occupational success. Researchers must use statistical methods to disentangle the IQ score as a predictor of success from two other factors associated with IQ: schooling and socioeconomic background. Geneticist Richard Lewontin (1982) notes that if you look only at people with a given IQ—say, 100—schooling *still* predicts later income and occupational status quite accurately. In other words, one reason IQ predicts income is that people with high IQ scores tend to get more education than others do; a high IQ score opens the doors of opportunity. The same is true for socioeconomic background. A man with an IQ of 100 who comes from an upper-class family is seven and a half times more likely to earn a high income than a man with an IQ of 100 who comes from a lower-class family. As Lewontin puts it, ''If [IQ] tests do measure intrinsic intelligence, as they are claimed to do, then one can only conclude that it is better to be born rich than smart.''

We are not saying that IQ contributes nothing to success in life (as our society defines it). Low IQ scores reflect an intellectual handicap. High ones probably reflect an advantage. Unusual talents, too, may give some people an edge. When you look at the lives of certain geniuses, it is hard not to conclude that they were wired somewhat differently than the rest of us. Mozart, whose father pushed him to develop his musical talents, played the harpsichord at 3 and wrote his first composition before he was 7. If you surround your child with music and hire a music teacher for her when she is 2, will she promptly become another Mozart? Probably not.

However, many kinds of intelligent behavior are not captured by conventional IQ tests. Seymour Sarason tells of reporting for his first job, which was giving IQ tests at a school for the mentally retarded. Upon arriving, he learned that the students had all escaped! When they were eventually rounded up and Sarason gave them the first test, he found that most could not do even the first problem. Yet these same students had outsmarted the school authorities by escaping, at least temporarily (in Sternberg, 1988). Intelligence also reveals itself in the ordinary behavior of average citizens. For example, a study at a racetrack found that successful handicappers used an exceedingly complicated statistical method to predict winners. This ability was *not* related to the handicappers' IQs (Ceci & Liker, 1986). Another study found that shoppers in a supermarket can somehow select the best buy even when they cannot do the mathematical computations that would allow them to compare two items (Lave, Murtaugh, & de la Roche, 1984).

For most people, IQ is not destiny, and inborn talents are not the sole key to success. Drive and determination are what lead to the top. A team of educational researchers headed by Benjamin Bloom (1985) interviewed 120 of America's top artists, athletes, and scholars. There were equal numbers of concert pianists, Olym-

You are thinking of hiring someone who has a very high IQ. How much confidence in the person's ability would that IQ score inspire? What other aspects of the person and of the job would you consider?

Think About It

Intolerance and IQ

A hammer is a tool that can be used to build a house or bash a head. Mental tests are tools, too. They can foster the growth of individuals or promote prejudices, depending on how they are used.

Historically, the birth of the testing movement in the United States happened to coincide with a period of widespread class, ethnic, religious, and racial prejudice. Scientists were not immune. Although many, if not most, early testers rejected (or at least were skeptical of) efforts to rank ethnic, racial, or socioeconomic groups, some eminent individuals let prejudice cloud their judgment.

One such individual was H. H. Goddard, a leading educator and advocate of mental testing. Goddard believed that low intelligence and poor character were inherited and that "undesirables" should be prevented from having children. In one study, he gave IQ tests to a group of newly arrived immigrants at Ellis Island (Goddard, 1917). Most of these people knew little or no English. Many could not read or write their own language. Yet no sooner did they get off the boat after a long and tiring journey than they found themselves taking the Binet IQ test. The results: 83 percent of the Jews, 80 percent of the Hungarians, 79 percent of the Italians, and 87 percent of the Russians scored as "feeble-minded," with a mental age lower than 12. Goddard acknowledged that environmental deprivation might explain these results, but he did not recognize that the results themselves had no validity, given the conditions under which they were obtained.

A more ambitious study of IQ was done during World War I. A million and a half soldiers took either the Army Alpha test (a verbal test) or the Army Beta test (a nonverbal test)—the first mass-produced intelligence tests in America. The purpose was to eliminate feeble-minded recruits and determine who should become an officer. To everyone's astonishment, the average mental age of white men was only 13, just a notch above the "moron" level. Blacks and eastern and southern Europeans scored even lower on the average. Many citizens of northern European ancestry concluded that the nation's intelligence was declining. They blamed the influx of new immigrants and the "breeding" of poor people.

Overlooked were the abominable conditions under which the tests were given. Testing rooms were crowded and poorly lit. Some men could not hear the instructions, which in any case were confusing, and many simply refused to answer. Although many of the men had little or no education, or were recent immigrants, a high proportion of the items assumed schooling or experience with middle-class American culture. For instance:

The number of a Kaffir's legs is: 2, 4, 6, 8.
Christy Mathewson is famous as a: writer,
   artist, baseball player, comedian.
Washington is to Adams as first is to. . . .

How well did you do on these items? When

pic swimmers, sculptors, tennis players, mathematicians, and research neurologists. The families and teachers of these successful people were also interviewed. The research team expected to hear tales of extraordinary natural talent. Instead, they heard tales of extraordinary dedication. The concert pianists had practiced several hours a day for years. A typical swimmer would tell of rising early every morning to swim for two hours before school started.

These results agree with others from the Stanford study of gifted children. When researchers compared the 100 most successful men in the Stanford study with the 100 least successful, they found that motivation made the difference. The successful men were ambitious, were socially active, had many interests, and were encouraged by their parents. The least successful drifted casually through life. There was *no* average difference in IQ between the two groups.

Not everyone wishes to work in a competitive occupation or reach the top of a

Stephen Jay Gould gave the Army Alpha to his students at Harvard University, more than 10 percent earned scores low enough to have kept them buck privates during World War I (Gould, 1981). ("Kaffir" is a derogatory term used by white South Africans for blacks—so a Kaffir has two legs. Christy Mathewson was a baseball player. We are not sure about the third item: The answer could be "second," since Washington was the first U.S. president and John Adams was the second, but it could also be "sixth," since John Quincy Adams was the sixth president.)

A more recent instance of bias, one that created a scientific scandal, involved Sir Cyril Burt, a renowned British school psychologist. For 20 years, Burt collected IQ data on twins reared apart. He concluded that intelligence is almost entirely genetic and cannot be modified. Burt also believed there were innate differences between races and classes. His views influenced the British to adopt a system in which test scores at age 11 determined whether a child could pursue academic studies or had to enroll in vocational training instead.

After Burt's death, American psychologist Leon Kamin reanalyzed his data. Kamin (1974) found errors that no beginning psychology student would make. Sample sizes were reported differently in different papers or not at all. Test scores were "adjusted," or merely *estimated* on the basis of subjective impressions. Research procedures were vague or unreported. Kamin also noticed that correlations computed from different samples of twins

agreed again and again to the third decimal place. These results seemed too good to be true, and in fact, they weren't. Further investigation showed that at least some of Burt's studies were sheer fiction. He had made up the twins, the test scores, and even the names of nonexistent collaborators (Hearnshaw, 1979). (Naturally, we have not included Burt's studies among those discussed in this chapter.)

Today, psychologists are more sophisticated about the nature of prejudice. But psychologist R. J. Herrnstein (1982) argues that egalitarians are as biased now as racists ever were. Herrnstein, who believes IQ scores are highly heritable, complains that his position is routinely distorted or ignored by the popular news media. Flaws in the studies of environmentalists, says Herrnstein, are overlooked or rationalized. Anyone who takes the hereditarian view, or who mentions racial or ethnic differences in test data, is branded a racist or an elitist by other scientists and social commentators.

The political nature of the IQ controversy raises some hard questions about both society and science. Why have scientists and nonscientists alike been so concerned about group differences in IQ for so many decades? Does this concern threaten social harmony and promote class and racial bias? Should scientists consider the political ramifications of their research, or should they leave that to others? Finally, once we have research on an issue as explosive as group differences, how can we determine which social implications are justified by the results and which are not?

What do you think?

---

field. Career achievement carries a price tag, and it is certainly not the only path to satisfaction and fulfillment. But clearly, many people's talents go untapped because they are not encouraged and trained. Talent, unlike cream, does not automatically rise to the top. That is the point of the old joke: A young man walking down a New York street asks an old woman, "How do I get to Carnegie Hall?" Her reply: "Practice, young man. Practice."

The Case for Human Diversity

This chapter opened with a simple question: How do nature and nurture produce the many differences among us? We have seen that the answer is not so simple. Statistical estimates of the extent to which differences are "heritable" or "environmental"

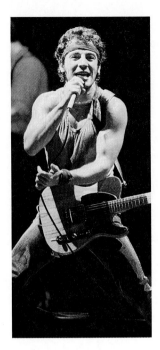

Intelligence is more than what IQ tests measure. A rock star has musical intelligence, a surveyor has spatial intelligence, and a compassionate friend has social intelligence.

do not tell us how heredity and environment interact to produce each unique mixture of qualities that we call a human being. Each of us is, in a sense, more than the sum of the individual influences on us. Once these influences become a part of us, they blend and become indistinguishable. A geneticist, a neurobiologist, and a psychologist offer this analogy:

> Think . . . of the baking of a cake: the taste of the product is the result of a complex interaction of components—such as butter, sugar, and flour—exposed for various periods to elevated temperatures; it is not dissociable into such-or-such a percent of flour, such-or-such of butter, etc., although each and every component . . . has its contribution to make to the final product. (Lewontin, Rose, & Kamin, 1984, p. 11)

The "cake" that is a person is never done. Each moment a slightly different self interacts with a slightly different environment. We can no more speak of genes, or of the environment, *causing* personality than we can speak of butter, sugar, or flour *causing* the taste of a cake. Yet we do speak that way. Why? Perhaps out of a desire to make things clearer than they are. Sometimes to justify prejudices about race or class.

Nature, however, loves diversity. Biologists agree that the "fitness" of any species depends on this diversity. If members of a species were all alike, with exactly the same strengths and weaknesses, the species could not survive a major change in the physical or social environment. With diversity, at least some members have a good chance of survival. Howard Gardner (1983) suggests that in human beings this diversity is expressed in seven independent "intelligences," or talents. They are linguistic, logical-mathematical, spatial, musical, and bodily-kinesthetic intelligence (which mimes, actors, athletes, and dancers have), insight into oneself, and understanding of others. Standard intelligence tests measure only the first three.

When we broaden the definition of intelligence, we see that each of us has something valuable to contribute to the world, whether it is artistic talent, academic ability, creativity, social skill, athletic prowess, a sense of humor, mechanical aptitude, practical wisdom, a social conscience, or the energy to get things done. The challenge, for any society, is to promote the potential of every citizen.

Taking Psychology with You

Uncanny Coincidences in Everyday Life

Have you ever daydreamed about an old friend you hadn't seen in a long time, only to answer the phone and hear your friend's voice? Have you ever dreamed of a plane crash, only to read of an airline disaster the next morning? Have you ever made any other spooky "prediction" that came true and that you couldn't explain?

If so, welcome to the world of uncanny coincidences. "Given the extraordinary ability of the human mind to make sense out of things," wrote the scientist Richard Furnald Smith, "it is natural occasionally to make sense out of things that have no sense at all." The human mind is unhappy with coincidences. It likes to impose meaning on them, some causal link, some *reason* for their existence. We don't easily accept the idea that many astonishing coincidences may be just that: accidental and random.

The case of identical twins, who have so many mannerisms and traits in common, offers a fascinating lesson in the psychology of coincidence. When you read strange stories of twins separated at birth, who, reunited, share all kinds of remarkable behaviors, it is tempting to infer that there is some magic, biologically based "psychic bond" that links them. Or is there?

Jim Lewis and Jim Springer are identical twins who were separated a few weeks after their birth in 1939 and adopted by different families in Ohio. Almost 40 years later, after leading entirely separate lives, they were finally reunited. Lewis later recalled, "Right off the bat I felt close—it wasn't like meeting a stranger."

Jim and Jim soon discovered some astonishing—and perplexing—similarities in their lives (Holden, 1980). Not only did they have the same first name, but both had an adopted brother named Larry and both had married a woman named Linda, divorced her, then married a woman named Betty. Lewis named his first son James Alan; Springer named his James Allan. During childhood both Jims owned a dog named Toy, and both liked math but hated spelling. During adolescence both put on 10 pounds for no apparent reason, then took it off. As adults, both had worked as a deputy sheriff, as an attendant in a filling station, and for the McDonald's fast-food chain. Both vacationed at a 300-yard-long beach near St. Petersburg, Florida; bit their nails to the quick; drank Miller Lite Beer; had white benches built around the trunk of a tree in the garden; and did blueprinting and woodworking.

When psychologist Thomas Bouchard heard about the two Jims, he invited them to participate in the ongoing twin study at the University of Minnesota discussed in this chapter. Like the two Jims, many of the other twins in the study also have reported uncanny coincidences. Two British twins found after being reunited that they had married on the same day in 1960, within an hour of each other. Two other twins discovered they had each filled out a diary for just one year, 1962; had used the same type of diary; and had filled out the same days of the year.

What are we to make of such coincidences? British writer Peter Watson (1981) observes that the world is a large place and rare events do happen, entirely by chance. The odds of the same number coming up three times in a row at roulette are pretty unlikely, only 1 in 50,652. Yet considering the tens of thousands of people who gamble throughout the world each day, this unlikely event is almost certain to happen every few days, and perhaps on most days, somewhere or other in the world. Rare events do happen.

Further, some events that seem uncommon actually are not. Watson points out that the twins who married on the same day were the twenty-first and twenty-second married twins seen in the Minnesota study. Statistically, the chances were nearly even that two of the Minnesota twins would have been married on the same day of the year. Of course, these twins got married in the same *year* as well. However, most people marry at around the same age, and in Britain, the favorite day for a wedding is Saturday (the day the twins married). Taking all these facts into account, Watson estimates that the odds of any one of the pairs seen in Minnesota marrying on the same Saturday are 1 in 125—not enormous, to be sure, but not impossible, either.

Watson has also estimated the probabilities of other coincidences in the lives of the twins in the Minnesota study. Some were highly improbable, though no more so than events that occur all the time, such as assaults or car crashes (which no one considers uncanny). Others were not improbable at all. Two twins, Barbara and Daphne, both loved vodka, but vodka happens to be the most popular type of liquor among women, so their taste for it is hardly surprising. Likewise, a preference for Miller Lite among men is not unusual.

Some of the "spooky" similarities between separated twins may be explainable in terms of physiology. Because they share all their genes, identical twins are likely to develop the same hereditary illnesses. Medical problems can affect other aspects of life—financial, occupational, social, and educational. Similarities in the economic and social conditions of life may also lead to specific similarities in behavior. For example, people who have modest incomes may be especially likely to vacation in Florida, where a holiday is relatively inexpensive.

Twin similarities reported with much ado by the press may divert attention from the many differences between identical twins. Two of the twins in the Minnesota study—one raised as a Nazi, the other as a Jew—wore short mustaches, fell asleep easily in front of the television, read in restaurants, read magazines from back to front, dipped buttered toast into their coffee, and flushed the toilet before using it. But one had been an alcoholic, whereas the other did not drink, and one had a history of depression and suicidal thinking, but the other did not. Moreover, many of the startling twin similarities are undoubtedly due to fashions, fads, and events in the environment, such as the popularity of certain names, drinks, and even kinds of pets or the availability of certain kinds of work. It is hard to imagine that there is a gene for naming your dog Toy or for marrying a woman named Betty or for working in filling stations.

Even if you are not an identical twin, you can take the lessons of Watson's analysis into your own life. Begin by noticing the occasions in which you dream of plane crashes or deaths in the family—and none occur. Observe whether you have an inclination to see only the "odd" similarities between you and a relative ("Great-Aunt Margaret traveled in a canoe down the Amazon River, and here I am rafting down the Colorado") and ignore the differences ("Of course, she risked malaria and death and I'm traveling in luxury"). Some of the traits that we say "run in families" may indeed be hereditary, but others "run in the culture" or the community; if several members of a family share them, it may be due to coincidence rather than genes. Obviously, we don't want to imply that every similarity is accidental. Just keep in mind that strange and rare events do happen—entirely by chance.

KEY WORDS

nature versus nurture 420
psychological assessment 420
reliability 421
test-retest reliability 421
alternate forms reliability 421
split-half reliability 421
validity 421
content validity 421
criterion validity 421
standardization 422
test norms 422
achievement tests 422
aptitude tests 422
intelligence 422
fluid intelligence 422
crystallized intelligence 422
factor analysis 423
g factor 423
psychometrics 423
triarchic theory of intelligence 423
mental age (MA) 424
intelligence quotient (IQ) 425
Stanford-Binet Intelligence Test 426

culture-free tests 428
culture-fair tests 428
learning disability 429
Wechsler Adult Intelligence Scale-Revised (WAIS-R) 429
Wechsler Intelligence Scale for Children-Revised (WISC-R) 429
inventories 431
Minnesota Multiphasic Personality Inventory (MMPI) 431
projective tests 432
Rorschach Inkblot Test 432
Thematic Apperception Test (TAT) 433
interviews 433
behavioral observations 434
behavior genetics 435
chromosomes 436
heritability 436
Down's syndrome 437
monozygotic (identical) twins 438
dyzygotic (fraternal) twins 438
temperaments 439

SUMMARY

1. Although all of us pass through similar stages of development, we differ from one another in mental ability and personality. Psychologists measure these differences by using techniques of *psychological assessment*. Psychological tests are judged in terms of their *reliability* (ability to produce consistent results) and their *validity* (ability to measure what they are intended to measure). Most widely used tests are *standardized* and are scored by referring to established *norms*.

2. There is controversy concerning exactly what intelligence tests measure. Some theorists believe that a general ability underlies the many specific abilities tapped by such tests, while others do not. Recent research has focused on the strategies people use to solve problems on intelligence tests. Sternberg's *triarchic theory of intelligence* proposes three aspects of intelligence: componential, experiential, and contextual. However, conventional intelligence tests remain the yardstick by which individual differences are typically measured.

3. The *intelligence quotient*, or *IQ* score, represents how a person has done on an intelligence test compared to others of the same age. IQ tests have been criticized for being biased in favor of white, middle-class people. Efforts have been made to construct culture-free and culture-fair tests, but these efforts have not eliminated group differences in performance. Some critics would like to dispense with IQ tests altogether because they are so often used unintelligently. But most educators believe IQ tests are useful for predicting school performance and diagnosing learning difficulties, as long as they are combined with other kinds of information.

4. Personality tests include *objective tests* or *inventories*; *projective tests*; *interviews*; and *behavioral observations*. Interviews and projective tests, which rely to some extent on the subjective interpretation of responses, are generally less reliable than the other two measures. Although personality tests have their defects, psychologists feel that like intelligence tests, they can be useful when used with other information.

5. Individual differences in personality and ability depend on complex interactions between heredity (nature) and environment (nurture). Despite the difficulty of studying such interactions, *behavior geneticists* have attempted to estimate the heritability of various mental and personality traits using psychological assessment techniques and data from studies of twins and adopted children.

6. *Heritability* refers to the extent to which differences in a trait within a group of individuals are accounted for by genetic differences. An estimate of heritability does not reveal the impact of heredity on any *particular* individual's intellectual or personal qualities. Moreover, heritability estimates apply only to a particular group living in a particular environment and not to differences between groups. Heritability of a trait can change over the life span, and even a highly heritable trait may be susceptible to environmental modification.

7. Certain personality characteristics appear to be heritable to some degree. Individual differences in *temperaments* or ways of reacting to the environment emerge early in life and can influence subsequent development. Certain temperamental differences may be due to variations in the responsiveness of the sympathetic nervous system to change and novelty. Data from twin studies suggest that the heritability of various adult personality traits is around .50. Caution is advised, however, in drawing conclusions about the precise heritability of personality traits because of methodological problems in the research.

8. Most experts believe that intelligence is also at least partly heritable. However, there is disagreement about the degree of genetic influence. Heritability estimates vary depending on the methods used in research and the population studied.

9. Whatever their heritability, both personality traits and mental abilities can be profoundly affected by the environment. For example, the consistency of a child's temperament over time depends in part on how extreme the temperament was to begin with and how adults react to the child. Two children who begin life with similar temperaments may grow up to have very different personalities depending on their environments and unique experiences.

10. Environmental factors that can affect performance on IQ tests include nutrition, exposure to toxins, mental stimulation, parent-child interactions, and family size. Because of these influences, an individual's IQ scores may fluctuate considerably during childhood.

11. Genetic explanations of racial differences in IQ sometimes have used heritability estimates derived from one group to estimate the genetic contribution to group differences. This is not a valid procedure. The available evidence fails to support genetic explanations of average black-white differences in IQ.

12. Education and socioeconomic background are better predictors of occupational success than IQ alone. Within any occupation there is a wide range of IQs. Drive, determination, and resourcefulness are essential components of real-world success.

13. Human intelligence may take many forms, not all of them measured by conventional IQ tests. From an evolutionary point of view, a diversity of talents and aptitudes is a good thing. Broadening the definition of intelligence helps us to recognize that there are many ways to contribute to the world and express individual potential.

CHAPTER 13

Child Development

I do not believe in a child world . . . I believe the child should be taught from the very first that the whole world is his world, that adult and child share one world . . .

<blockquote>
PEARL S. BUCK
</blockquote>

Children are on a different plane, they belong to a generation and way of feeling properly their own.

<blockquote>
GEORGE SANTAYANA
</blockquote>

In 1618, a Puritan minister advised parents that all children have "a stubbornness, and stoutness of mind arising from natural pride, which must, in the first place, be broken and beaten down" (Demos, 1970). Today, many psychologists advise parents to help their children develop pride and self-esteem by building them up instead of beating them down. Throughout history, there have been many other mutually contradictory views of the child, such as the following (Kagan, 1984):

> A baby is born knowing nothing at all. It is an empty package, waiting to be stuffed with experience.
> A baby is born with all the personality it will ever have. It just needs time to reveal it.

> A child is a little savage, filled with selfish and greedy instincts, until civilized society teaches it to be otherwise.
> A child is a little moralist, filled with noble and generous instincts, until uncivilized society teaches it to be otherwise.

Today, too, people hold strong and differing beliefs about what children are like and how they should be brought up. Should mothers work? Should they breast-feed or bottle-feed? Do babies need their mothers around all the time? Can fathers act like mothers? How early can babies start learning, and how much can we teach them? Can you create the child you want, or does the child have something to say about it?

Against this background of social values and practical concerns, child psychologists study many facets of a child's physical, cognitive, social, and moral development. *Child development* includes the processes by which an organism grows from a fetus in the womb to an adult, processes that include predictable changes in biological **maturation**, physical structure, behavior, and thinking (Mussen et al., 1984). Some researchers think of "development" as a series of small, gradual, continuous steps that blend into each other, just as the babbling sound "maa, maa" becomes a call for "Mama." Others think of development as a series of distinct stages that are qualitatively different from each other. Walking, for example, is significantly different from crawling, involving different motor skills and movements. In this view, with each stage, children acquire a new way of thinking or behaving that is added to the earlier way.

In some societies and eras, children have been regarded as "little adults," as this painting of Sir Walter Raleigh and his son shows. The very idea of childhood as a special time of development is a relatively new invention.

maturation *The sequential unfolding of genetically governed behavior and physical characteristics.*

459

Psychologists study *universal* aspects of development, the changes that occur in all children as they mature; *cultural differences* in development, the patterns that occur in some cultures and ethnic groups but not in others; and *individual differences* in development, the changes that occur in some children but not in others. In this chapter we will consider some of their discoveries. Then we will ask you to step back, put what you have read into perspective, and consider a controversial question: What is the connection between childhood and adulthood?

From Conception to the First Year

A baby's development, before and after birth, is an astonishing process, a marvel of maturation. In only 9 months of a mother's pregnancy, a cell grows from a dot this big (.) to a squalling bundle of energy that looks just like Aunt Sarah. In roughly another 15 months, that squalling bundle of energy grows into a babbling toddler who is curious about everything. No other time in human development brings so many changes, so fast.

Prenatal development

Prenatal development is divided into three stages: the *germinal*, the *embryonic*, and the *fetal*. The germinal stage begins at conception, when the male sperm unites with the female ovum (egg). A day or so after conception, the fertilized egg, or *zygote*, begins to divide into two parts and attach itself to the wall of the uterus. The outer part will form the placenta, and the inner part becomes the *embryo*. The placenta will be the growing embryo's food and supply link from the mother, connected to the embryo itself through the umbilical cord. The placenta allows nutrients to get through and screens out some, but not all, harmful substances.

Once implantation of the zygote is completed, about two weeks after conception, the germinal stage is over and the *embryonic* stage begins, lasting until the eighth week after conception. The embryo develops webbed fingers and toes, a tail (you have a "tailbone" to remind you of this prenatal phase), eyes, ears, a nose, a mouth, a heart and circulatory system, and a spinal cord—though at eight weeks, the embryo is only 1½ inches long. Sometime during the fourth to eighth week, the male hormone testosterone is secreted by the rudimentary testes in embryos that are genetically male; without this hormone, the embryo will develop as a female.

After eight weeks, the *fetal* stage begins and lasts until birth. The embryo, now called a *fetus*, further develops the organs and systems that existed in rudimentary form during the embryonic stage. By 28 weeks, the nervous and respiratory systems are developed enough to allow the fetus to live if it is born prematurely. (New technology allows some prematures to survive if born even earlier, but the risks are higher.) The last 12 weeks before birth see the greatest gains in brain and nervous system development, length, and weight.

Although the womb is a fairly sturdy protector of the growing fetus, some harmful influences can cross the placental barrier. Some of the conditions known to harm fetal development include the following:

• *German measles* (rubella), especially early in the pregnancy, often affects the fetus's eyes, ears, and heart. The most common consequence is deafness. Rubella is preventable if the mother has been vaccinated, which can be done in adulthood, up to three months before pregnancy.

▪ *X-rays* or other radiation, or toxic chemicals, can cause fetal abnormalities and deformities.

▪ *Sexually transmitted diseases*, such as syphilis, can cause mental retardation, blindness, and other physical disorders, and, in the case of AIDS, eventually death. Herpes can affect the fetus only if the mother has an outbreak at the time of delivery, which exposes the newborn to the virus in the birth canal. This risk can be avoided by having a Caesarean section, in which the baby is removed surgically through the uterus.

▪ *Cigarettes.* Pregnant women who smoke increase the likelihood of miscarriage, premature birth, abnormal fetal heartbeat, and underweight babies. The negative effects of smoking during pregnancy can last long after the child's birth, showing up in increased rates of infant sickness, Sudden Infant Death Syndrome, and, in later childhood, hyperactivity and difficulties in school.

▪ *Alcohol.* Pregnant women who drink alcohol increase the risk of the **fetal alcohol syndrome** (FAS). Infants with FAS are smaller than normal, have smaller brains, are more uncoordinated, show sleep disturbances, and have some degree of mental retardation. Researchers used to think that only heavy consumption of alcohol (four or more drinks a day) produced these effects. Now, though, they fear that even small amounts of alcohol increase the risk to the fetus.

▪ *Drugs.* The effects of morphine, cocaine, and heroin can be transmitted to the fetus, as well as commonly used drugs such as antibiotics, antihistamines, tranquilizers, diet pills, and excessive amounts of vitamins. Women should also guard against prescribed drugs that have not been adequately tested. In the 1960s, pregnant women who took the tranquilizer Thalidomide gave birth to fetuses with missing or deformed limbs. Between the 1940s and 1971, many women were given the hormone diethylstilbestrol (DES) to prevent miscarriages. Some daughters of these women later developed cancer of the vagina during adolescence, and sons were prone to testicular problems.

The lesson seems clear. A pregnant woman does well to quit smoking completely, to drink very little alcohol and possibly none at all, and to take no drugs of any kind unless they are medically necessary and tested for safety (and then to accept the fact that her child will never be properly grateful for all that sacrifice!).

What about positive prenatal experiences? Should a pregnant woman be reading Shakespeare to her fetus, playing classical music, and preparing the fetus for college entrance exams? The fetus can certainly hear sounds in the last few months of pregnancy—its mother's voice, music, startling sounds from television, hair dryers, and vacuum cleaners—but the "Cat in the Hat" experiment got people excited again about prenatal "education." Two psychologists asked 16 pregnant women to read Dr. Seuss's classic story *The Cat in the Hat* to their fetuses twice a day for the last six weeks of their pregnancies. When the babies were born, they had a choice of sucking on one of two nipples. Sucking on the first brought a recording of their mothers reading the Seuss story. Sucking on the other nipple produced a recording of the mothers reading *The King, the Mice and the Cheese,* a story with a different rhythm and pace. The newborns preferred—you guessed it—*The Cat in the Hat* (DeCasper & Spence, 1986).

This is fascinating work on two counts. One, it shows the amazing ability of psychologists to find ways to "interview" newborn babies who cannot talk and who don't even know what a hat is, much less a cat. Two, it shows the amazing ability of the human brain to learn as soon as it develops, even before birth. As we will see, it's good to have some respect for what a newborn knows, but without going overboard. That newborn still has a lot to learn.

fetal alcohol syndrome *A pattern of physical and intellectual abnormalities in infants whose mothers drank an excessive amount of alcohol during pregnancy.*

The newborn child

Newborn babies could never survive on their own, but they are far from being completely passive and inert. As Table 13.1 shows, they have a number of built-in *motor reflexes*, automatic behaviors that are necessary for survival. They can see, hear, touch, smell, and taste (bananas and sugar water are in, rotten eggs are out). They even have rudimentary social "conversations" with the adults who tend them.

The sucking and grasping reflexes at work.

Reflexes. Newborn babies turn their heads toward a touch on the cheek or corner of the mouth and search for something to suck on, a handy "rooting reflex" that allows them to find the breast or bottle. They suck vigorously on a nipple, finger, or pacifier placed in their mouths. They grasp tightly to a finger pressed on their palms. They are startled by loud noises or shocks. They follow a moving light with their eyes and turn toward a familiar sound, such as the mother's voice or the thump-thump of a heartbeat (both of which they heard in the womb) (DeCasper & Prescott, 1984).

	TABLE 13.1
	REFLEXES AND PERCEPTUAL SKILLS OF THE NEWBORN BABY

Reflex	Description
Rooting	An infant touched on the cheek or corner of mouth will turn toward the touch and search for something to suck on.
Sucking	An infant will suck anything suckable, such as nipple or finger.
Swallowing	An infant can swallow, though this reflex is not yet well coordinated with breathing.
Moro or "startle"	In response to loud noise or physical shock, an infant will throw arms outward and arch back.
Babinsky	In response to touch on bottom of foot, the infant's toes splay outward and then curl in. (In adults, toes curl in.)
Grasp	In response to touch on palm of hand, an infant will grasp.
Stepping	If held so feet just touch the ground, an infant will show "walking" movements, alternating feet in steps. This reflex vanishes in a couple of weeks.

Sense	The newborn can . . .
Sight	Focus on a point about 8 inches away; follow a moving object with eyes; discriminate some colors.
Sound	Respond to sounds, especially those of pitch and loudness of human voice; respond to rhythmic or familiar sounds heard in womb, such as heartbeat.
Smell	React to some smells, such as ammonia or licorice.
Taste	Tell the difference between salty and sweet, between sour and bitter; prefer sweet tastes.
Touch	Respond to touches, especially on hands and mouth.

SOURCE: Bee, 1989, pp. 92–93.

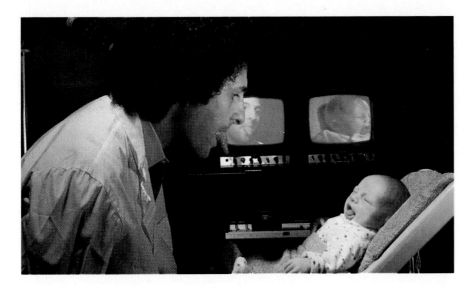

FIGURE 13.1

Baby imitations
*At only 2 weeks of age and
sometimes even younger,
babies can imitate many
adult expressions. In this
experiment, psychologist
Andrew Meltzoff sticks out
his tongue at an infant—and
evokes the same reaction.
Babies will also pout, smile,
and open their mouths to
mimic adult expressions.*

Vision. At birth, a baby is very, very nearsighted. The focus range is about 8 inches, the distance between the baby and the face of the person holding the baby. But visual ability develops rapidly. Newborns open their eyes wide to investigate what is around them, even in the dark. They can distinguish black-white contrasts, shadows, and edges. They like faces and are even able to imitate facial expressions within 2 or 3 weeks of age, sometimes sooner (Greenspan & Greenspan, 1985; Meltzoff & Moore, 1977). (See Figure 13.1.)

An interest in novelty (a motive discussed in Chapter 10) also starts early. Babies reveal a surprising preference for looking at and listening to unfamiliar things (this includes most of the world). By observing what infants prefer to look at, given a choice, and how long they gaze at it, psychologists have identified many infant abilities (P. Harris, 1984).

For the first six to eight weeks, babies are mostly concerned with *where* something is. Their vision helps them track someone's location and movement. After two months, though, the baby is able to determine *what* something is (Banks & Salapatek, 1984). Babies now can pay attention to details. They show a distinct preference for curved lines over straight ones, they can focus on parts of a picture, and, most important to doting parents, they can tell the difference between Mom, Dad, and visiting strangers. Within a few months of birth, they develop depth perception (see Chapter 5).

Social skills. Newborns are sociable from the first. They have inborn abilities to attract adults to care for them. A baby's cry is physiologically arousing to both men and women, motivating adults to end the baby's discomfort. If they succeed, they immediately are reinforced by the reduction of arousal (Frodi & Lamb, 1978). Adults feel good when they stop a baby's wails, and they feel even better when babies smile at them. Babies smile regularly at about 4 to 6 weeks, especially in response to faces. Although the babies haven't the foggiest notion of whom they are smiling at, this enchanting biological response tends to melt the most unsentimental adult.

The first "conversation" a baby has is with the mother or primary caretaker. Like most human conversations, it often takes place over a good meal. Nursing babies and their mothers play little games with each other, exchanging signals in a rhythmic pattern. Babies nurse in a pattern of sucks and pauses (whether on breast or bottle). During the pauses, the mother usually jiggles the baby, who then starts to suck again. The pattern between them has the back-and-forth rhythm of spoken conversation: suck, pause, jiggle, pause, suck, pause, jiggle, pause (Kaye, 1977).

This early rhythmic "conversation" illustrates a crucial aspect of all human exchanges: the importance of *synchrony* (Condon, 1982). Synchrony refers to the adjustment of one person's behavior to coordinate with another's. If you have ever tried to talk to someone who was "out of sync" with you, you will understand its importance; you just don't seem to connect. In every conversation, people unconsciously adjust their rhythms of speech, and their gestures and expressions, to be "in sync" with each other. Synchrony seems to be essential in establishing rapport between people, and its absence has been observed in people who have learning disabilities and emotional problems such as depression (Tronick, 1989).

Synchrony begins at birth. Newborn infants will synchronize their behavior and attention to adult speech but not to other sounds, such as street noise or tapping (Beebe et al., 1982). Synchrony takes three related forms: *simultaneous movement* (e.g., the mother turns her head just as the baby lifts an arm), *similar tempo* (the degree to which parent and baby move at the same pace and rhythm, i.e., "march to the beat of the same drummer"), and *coordination and smoothness* (the behavior of parent and baby meshes smoothly, like well-matched dance partners). Mothers show more synchrony with their own infants than with others; parents learn how to "tune in" to their own babies' rhythms early on (Bernieri, Reznick, & Rosenthal, 1988).

Temperament. All normal newborns have the same biological capacities, but it is clear to everyone that not all newborns are alike. Some are irritable and cranky. Some are placid and sweet-natured. Some cuddle up in any adult's arms and snuggle. Some squirm and fidget, as if they can't stand being held. Babies differ in activity level (squirming and kicking), smiling and laughing, fussing and showing signs of distress, "soothability" (how soon a baby calms down after distress), and cooing and burbling in reaction to people or things (Rothbart, 1986). As we saw in Chapter 12, these differences in temperament may be hereditary dispositions (Field, 1987).

Some of these differences may be ethnically based (see Figure 13.2). Chinese-American infants are, on the average, more "soothable" than European-American infants. If you press a newborn baby's nose with a cloth, most Caucasian and black babies will show a "defense reaction," turning their heads or trying to hit the cloth with their hands. In contrast, most Chinese babies lie on their backs and accept the cloth without a fight. These and other differences among newborns have been documented in studies that controlled for the mothers' age, class, nutrition, use of drugs during delivery, and other factors that might affect temperament (D. Freedman, 1979). Such findings imply hereditary differences, but parents in various ethnic groups also treat their babies differently right from the start, in how often they hold, touch, or talk to them (Caudill & Frost, 1972).

The older infant

Babies grow as fast as weeds during the first two years. Most infants double their birth weight in five months. By 1 year of age, on the average, they have tripled their birth weight and grown 10 to 12 inches in length. (The custom of talking about a baby's "length" but a child's "height" is charming; the language changes as soon as the baby is upright!) By age 2, most toddlers are half the height they will be as

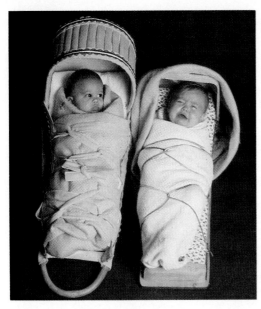

FIGURE 13.2

Temperament and culture: The case of the cradleboard
Most Navaho babies (left) calmly accept the Navaho custom of being strapped to a cradleboard until they are about 6 months old; Caucasian babies (right) protest vigorously when strapped in one. In spite of cultural differences in such practices, babies in every culture sit, crawl, and walk at the same average maturational age.

adults. The baby not only grows in height and weight, but also changes proportion. An infant's head is nearly one-third of the whole body; a 2-year-old's head is about one-fourth; an adult's head is only one-eighth to one-tenth of total height.

Motor abilities. At about 1 month, infants can hold their chins up when lying on their stomachs. At about 2 months, they can raise the upper body. At 4 months, they can sit if someone supports them. At about 7 months, they can sit upright without support. From then on, parents have to look sharp. Babies begin to crawl and stand with help (9 months), walk with help (10 months), and toddle off on their own (13 months). These milestones are only *averages*, however. Some babies develop more quickly, others more slowly. We know a baby who was such a speedy crawler that she didn't walk until 18 months, and did so then only because an older man, her 3-year-old cousin, yanked her to her feet.

The brain and nervous system. A newborn baby is like a model sailing ship: The basic kit comes with all its parts, but some of them aren't assembled yet. The brain's cortex, for instance, the part responsible for perception, thinking, and language, is "unfinished." All the cells appear to be there, but many haven't been fully connected by way of synapses, and some connections later drop out (see Chapter 3). This may be one reason why you can't remember what being born felt like, or, in fact, anything of your first two or three years. As an infant, you didn't have the section of your ship responsible for long-term memory wired up yet (see Chapter 7).

The transmission of messages between nerve cells is aided by the development of *myelin*, an insulating sheath around the axons of individual neurons. The growth of this coating, called *myelinization*, takes time. The reason that infants cannot fully control the lower half of their bodies is that neurons in the spinal cord, which carry messages from the brain to the body, are not fully covered with myelin until the child is about 2 years old (Bee, 1989). Myelinization in the brain itself and the growth of connecting cells continue into adolescence and possibly adulthood.

By the end of the first year, infants have made huge progress in their physical abilities (see Table 13.2). Now the story gets even more interesting.

TABLE 13.2
DEVELOPMENTAL MILESTONES DURING THE FIRST YEAR

Average Age	Motor	Cognitive	Emotion
0–2 months	Turns head; lifts chin when lying on stomach	Prefers looking at faces; likes familiar sounds; is interested in novelty; tracks *where* things are	Can imitate adult facial expressions; cries when distressed
3–4 months	Lifts chest; holds head erect; reaches for an object	Becomes interested in *what* things are; recognizes different faces and details of objects	Smiles and shows interest in slightly unfamiliar objects; may be distressed by objects that are too unfamiliar
5–6 months	Holds head steady; transfers an object from one hand to another	Develops depth perception; understands object identity (that a thing is the same each time it is encountered)	Apparent fear at visual cliff (see Chapter 5); facial expressions of anger may appear in response to frustration
7–8 months	Sits alone	Develops retrieval memory (can recall a familiar face) and larger "working memory"; understands object permanence	Shows first signs of stranger and separation anxiety
9–10 months	Stands with help; crawls	Understands some words	
11–12 months	Pulls self to standing position; walks with support	Begins symbolic play; utters first meaningful words	Shows sadness at loss of an attachment figure

SOURCE: Mussen et al., 1984, p. 107.

QUICK ▪ QUIZ

You may not remember your own first year, but what do you remember about infants generally?

1. Newborn babies can **(a)** recognize their parents, **(b)** see a distance of about 8 inches, **(c)** look for a favorite toy.
2. Which of the following is *not* among the newborn baby's repertoire of abilities? **(a)** sucking, **(b)** rooting, **(c)** the startle reflex, **(d)** long-term memory, **(e)** grasping
3. What is the infant's earliest social "conversation"? **(a)** crying in response to adult noises, **(b)** yelling for milk, **(c)** cooing when touched or stroked, **(d)** nursing at breast or bottle, in rhythm with reactions from the mother

Answers:
1. b 2. d 3. d

Cognitive Development

Our friend Joel reports how thrilled he was when his 13-month-old daughter Alison looked at him one day and said, for the first time, "Daddy! Daddy!" His delight was deflated somewhat, though, when the doorbell rang and she ran to the door, calling, "Daddy! Daddy!" And his delight was completely shattered when the phone rang and Alison ran to it, shouting, "Daddy! Daddy!" Later Joel learned that there was a 2-year-old child in Alison's day-care group whose father would call her on the telephone during the day and ring the doorbell when he picked her up in the evening. Alison acquired her little friend's enthusiasm for doorbells and phones, but didn't quite get the hang of "Daddy."

She will soon enough, though, and that is the mystery of language. Further, she will eventually be able to imagine, reason, and see the world from Daddy's viewpoint one day, and that is the mystery of thought.

The ability to think

In the 1920s, a Swiss biologist named Jean Piaget [Zhan Pea-ah-ZHAY] proposed a theory of the cognitive development of children. Piaget, who died in 1980 at the age of 84, caused a revolution in thinking about how thinking develops. Piaget (1984) observed that children understand concepts and reason differently at different stages. The cognitive strategies children use to solve problems, said Piaget, reflect an interaction between the child's current developmental stage and experience in the world.

Piaget and cognitive stages. Piaget (1929/1960, 1952) proposed that mental functioning depends on two basic biological processes, *organization* and *adaptation*. All human beings are designed to organize their observations and experiences into a coherent set of meanings, and to adapt to new observations and experiences. The process of adaptation, said Piaget, takes two forms, which he called *assimilation* and *accommodation*.

Assimilation is what you do when you fit new information into your present system of knowledge and beliefs. If you like Professor X, you will easily assimilate the information that she is kind to strangers. Sometimes assimilation requires you to alter the information to make it consistent with existing mental structures. When you hear that Professor X refused to help a student who was having difficulty in her course, you may decide that this news can only be a spiteful rumor spread by the failing student.

Accommodation is what you do when, as a result of undeniable new information, you finally change or modify your existing beliefs. If, after hearing enough bad stories about Professor X, you finally decide she is not so likable after all, you have accommodated the new evidence. Rochel Gelman (1983) offers an example of "accommodation in action" in a 2-year-old girl. The child would practice counting: "1,2,3,4,5,6,8,9,10." Her mother, with no luck, kept reminding her that she was leaving out the 7. Eventually the child assimilated this information. She would say to herself, "1,2,3,4,5,6,8,9,10—where's the 7?" Her next step was to count to 6 and stop. Finally she accommodated the missing 7 and could correctly count to 10. In this fashion, said Piaget, children at each stage assimilate the information they are capable of absorbing. Then, when the information no longer fits, their underlying mental structure accommodates.

Using these basic concepts, Piaget proposed that all children go through four stages of cognitive development:

assimilation *The process of absorbing new information into existing cognitive structures, modifying it if necessary to "fit."*

accommodation *The process of modifying existing cognitive structures in response to experience and new information.*

1. During the *sensory-motor stage* (birth to age 2), the infant learns through concrete actions: looking, touching, hearing, putting things in the mouth, sucking, grasping. "Thinking" consists of coordinating sensory information with bodily movements. Soon these movements become more purposeful, as the child actively explores the environment and learns that specific movements will produce specific results. Swatting a cloth away will reveal a hidden toy; releasing one's grasp of a fuzzy duck will cause the duck to drop out of reach; banging on the table with a spoon will produce dinner (or Mom, taking the spoon away).

One of the baby's major accomplishments at this stage, said Piaget, is **object permanence**, the understanding that something continues to exist even if you can't see it or touch it. In the first few months of life, infants are very fickle. "Out of sight, out of mind" seems to be their motto. They will look intently at a little toy, but if you hide it behind a piece of paper they will not look behind the paper or make an effort to get the toy. By about 6 months, infants begin to grasp the idea that a toy is a toy, and the cat is a cat, whether they can see the toy, or the cat, or not. If a baby of this age drops a toy from her playpen, she will look for it; she also will look under a cloth for a toy that is partially hidden. By 1 year of age, most babies have developed an awareness of the permanence of (some) objects. That is when they love to play peek-a-boo.

Object permanence, said Piaget, represents the beginning of *representational* (symbolic) thought. The capacity for representational thought is what allows human beings to use symbolic systems such as language. The child is able for the first time to hold a concept in mind, to learn that the word *fly* represents an annoying, buzzing creature, and that *Daddy* represents a friendly, playful one. These developments during the sensory-motor stage occur at a similar rate and sequence across a wide range of cultures. In the next stage, cultural differences begin to make themselves felt.

2. The essential aspect of the *preoperational stage* (ages 2 to 7) is the accelerated use of symbols and language, in play and in imitation of adult behavior. A 2-year-old is able to pretend, for instance, that a large box is a house, table, or train. Piaget described this stage largely in terms of what (he thought) the child cannot do. Children can think, said Piaget, but they cannot reason. They do not yet have the kinds of mental abilities that allow them to understand abstract principles or cause and effect. Piaget called these abilities **operations**, actions that the child performs in the mind and that are *reversible*. An operation is a sort of "train of thought" that can be run backward or forward. For example, multiplying 2 times 6 to get 12 is an operation; so is the reverse operation of dividing 12 by 6 to get 2.

Children at the preoperational stage are not capable of reasoning in this way. They rely on primitive or intuitive reasoning and the evidence of their own senses (which can be misleading). If a tree moves in the wind, it must be alive. If the wind blows while the child is walking, then walking must make the wind blow. Children of this age also cannot take another person's point of view, Piaget believed, because their thinking is **egocentric**. They see the world only from their own frame of reference, as an extension of themselves. They cannot imagine that you see things differently, or that events happen to others that do not happen to them. "Why are there mountains [with lakes]?" Piaget asked a preoperational (Swiss) child. "So that we can skate," answered the child.

Further, said Piaget, preoperational children cannot grasp the concept of **conservation**—that physical properties do not change when their form or appearance changes. They are unable to understand that an amount of liquid, a number of pennies, or a length of rope remains the same even if you pour the liquid from one glass to another, stack the pennies, or coil the rope (see Figure 13.3). If you pour

object permanence *The understanding that an object continues to exist even when you can't see it or touch it.*
operations *In Piaget's theory, mental actions that are cognitively reversible.*
egocentric thinking *Perceiving the world from only one's own point of view; the inability to take another person's perspective.*
conservation *The understanding that the physical properties of objects—such as number of items, amount of liquid, or length of an object—remain the same even when appearances change (as long as nothing is added or taken away).*

FIGURE 13.3

Piaget's principle of conservation
These children are taking part in experiments designed to measure their understanding of conservation. In a typical test of conservation of number *(right), the child shows whether he understands that two sets of seven blocks contain the same number—even though the blocks in one set are larger and take up more space. In a test of* conservation of quantity *(left), the child shows whether she understands that pouring liquid from a short fat glass into a tall narrow glass does not change the amount of liquid—even if it is now the same height as liquid in another short fat glass.*

liquid from a short, fat glass into a tall, narrow glass, preoperational children will say there is more liquid in the second glass. They attend to the appearance of the liquid (its height in the glass) instead of reasoning about its quantity. As children develop, so does their ability to distinguish appearances from reality (Flavell, 1986).

3. During the *concrete operations stage* (about age 6 or 7 to 11), the nature and quality of children's thought changes significantly. According to Piaget, during these years children come to understand the principles of conservation, reversibility, and cause and effect. They understand the nature of *identity*, that a girl doesn't turn into a boy by wearing a boy's hat, that a brother will always be a brother, even if he grows up. They learn specific mental operations, such as addition, subtraction, multiplication, division, and categorization—not just of numbers, but of people, events, and actions. They learn some abstract concepts such as *serial ordering*, the idea that things can be ranked from smallest to largest, lightest to darkest, shortest to tallest.

Children's thinking at this age is called ''concrete'' because it is still grounded in concrete experiences and concepts. Children of this age do not have much ability to understand abstract ideas or to think deductively (drawing conclusions from premises). They can use their imaginations to try to solve problems but not in a systematic and logical way. An adult who is playing Twenty Questions systematically tries to reduce the range of possible answers: Is it a person? Female? American? Fictional? A young concrete-operational child will make random guesses: Is it an astronaut? Kermit the Frog? Grandpa? (Mosher & Hornsby, 1966).

The development of concrete operations varies in timing and content from one culture to another (Dasen, 1977; Greenfield, 1976). For example, a study of six African cultures found that stringing beads—a skill that children learn at an early age—speeds the development of the conservation of number. On the other hand, many unschooled children of the Wolof, a rural Moslem group in Senegal, do not ''naturally'' acquire an understanding of conservation, as their peers who attend school do. However, the ability for concrete operations appears in all cultures, and brief training experiences can bring them out (Greenfield, 1966).

4. The *formal operations stage* (age 12 to adulthood) marks the beginning of abstract reasoning, as we will see in the next chapter.

People used to ask Piaget whether it was possible to "speed up" cognitive development. Piaget called this concern "the American question" because Americans, he said, are always trying to hurry things along. As the "Think About It" box on page 473 suggests, the American question is far from settled.

Evaluating Piaget. Piaget's theory has had a powerful impact, but subsequent research has modified it considerably. Many young children demonstrate more cognitive skills than Piaget thought they had, and many older children and adults lack some cognitive skills that Piaget thought everyone had by their ages. Moreover, the changes from one stage to another are neither as clear-cut nor as sweeping as Piaget implied: Children's reasoning ability has as much to do with what they are reasoning *about* as with what "stage" they are in.

In particular, there seems to be no major shift from preoperational to concrete-operational thought (Gelman, 1983; Gelman & Baillargeon, 1983; Shweder, Mahapatra, & Miller, 1987). Research now shows that preoperational children can understand more than Piaget gave them credit for:

- Piaget believed that the ability of a baby to play peek-a-boo illustrates object permanence. But infants as young as 9 months of age also understand the *rules* of peek-a-boo. In one study, when adults failed to "take their turns," the infants were clearly startled and distressed. The babies reacted by pointing to or touching the adults, repeating their own turns, or offering toys to the adults (Ross & Lollis, 1987).

- Children advance rapidly in their understanding and use of symbolism much earlier than Piaget thought—between the ages of 2½ and 3. In that six months, they become able to think of a miniature model of a room in two ways at once: as a room in its own right and as a symbol of the larger room it represents. This ability is a big step toward adult symbolic thought, in which anything can stand for anything else—a flag for a country, a saltshaker for a house, a detachable pot handle for a doll (DeLoache, 1987).

- Most 3- and 4-year-olds *can* take another person's perspective (see Figure 13.4), and, as we will see, they are capable of astonishing acts of empathy. They are not always egocentric; perhaps it depends on the questions you ask them. One 5-year-old showed her teacher a picture she had drawn of a cat and an unidentifiable blob. "The cat is lovely," said the teacher, "but what is this thing here?" "That has nothing to do with you," said the child. "That's what the cat is looking at."

- Very young children can understand the difference between animate and inanimate things. Three- and 4-year-olds, shown pictures of varied objects and asked which ones could go uphill and downhill by themselves, know that animals can do so but inanimate objects can't. (Some of the children said that a *small* animal might need its mother to carry it up a big hill.) At this age, children use the concept of movement to help them answer whether the object walks, crawls, or flies on its own, or whether someone pushes it. However, they have no concept of growth (they can't tell you whether a toy or a tree will grow) or of biology (they don't understand that both plants and animals are alive) (Massey & Gelman, 1988).

In spite of these problems with his theory, the *sequence* of cognitive development that Piaget described does seem to hold across cultures. New reasoning abilities depend on the emergence of the previous ones. You can't study algebra before you can count, and you can't study philosophy before you understand logic. Piaget's critics agree with him on a most important point: Children are not passive

FIGURE 13.4

Are children really egocentric?
This 3-year-old girl was asked to place the boy doll where the policeman could not find him. According to Piaget, she should be "egocentric," and therefore hide the boy doll from herself as well (left). On several occasions, however, she placed the doll where she, but not the policeman, could see him, suggesting that she could take the policeman's point of view (right).

vessels into which education and experience are poured. Children actively interpret their experiences. They actively bring their own perceptions to new adventures.

The ability to speak

Learning to speak would seem to be an enormous task. A child eventually will understand thousands and thousands of words; learn to string them together in sentences that make sense; and, most impressive of all, learn to make and understand an infinite number of new word combinations.

Language development. In the first months, babies cry and coo. By 6 months, infants start making many "ba-ba" and "goo-goo" sounds, endlessly repeating sounds and syllables. This *babbling phase* lasts until about 1 year of age, when the child begins to name things. One-year-olds already have a few concepts in their minds—they know who mama and daddy are, they can recognize favorite objects and people—and their first words are those that represent familiar concepts ("mama," "doggie," "bug").

By 12 to 14 months of age, babies have also developed a repertoire of symbolic *gestures*, another important part of communication. They use gestures to refer to objects (sniffing to indicate "flower," panting to indicate "dog"), to request something (smacking lips for "food," moving hands up and down for "play the piano"), to describe an object (blowing or waving a hand for "hot," raising arms for "big"), and to reply to questions (opening palms or shrugging shoulders for "I don't know"). One baby baseball fan used a clapping sign in response to baseball games—real or pictured (Acredolo & Goodwyn, 1988).

At about age 2, toddlers begin to produce words in two- or three-word combi-

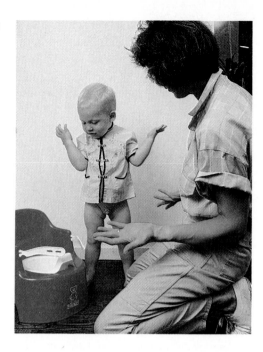

Symbolic gestures emerge early! This mother and her son are clearly having a "conversation."

nations ("Mama here," "go 'way bug," "my toy"). This is an especially enjoyable phase for adults to observe because 2-year-olds, who are clearly trying to understand the differences between categories of things, often make mistakes. They know that Tiger (the family dog) is "doggie." But they may call any four-legged, furry, noise-making object "doggie"—the neighbor's cat, a picture of a cow or deer, a pony at the circus. That is, the child *overgeneralizes*. As children grow and learn new words, their overgeneralizations decrease. They learn the difference between the concept "animal" and different animals, such as dogs (which bark) and cows (which moo).

The child's first combinations of words have a common quality in every language: They are **telegraphic**. When you have to pay for every word in a telegram, you quickly learn to drop unnecessary articles (*a*, *an*, or *the*) and auxiliary verbs (such as *is* or *are*, as in the phrase "it is all gone"). But you still convey your message. Similarly, the two-word sentences of toddlers omit lots of articles, auxiliary verbs, other parts of speech, and word endings, but are remarkably accurate in conveying many messages. Here are some functions and examples of children's two-word "telegrams" (Slobin, 1979):

- *To locate or name something:* there toy, that chair, see doggie
- *To demand something:* more milk, give candy
- *To negate an action:* no wet, no want, not hungry, allgone milk
- *To describe an event:* Bambi go, mail come, hit ball, block fall
- *To show possession:* my shoe, Mama dress
- *To modify an object:* pretty dress, big boat
- *To question:* where ball, where Daddy

telegraphic speech *A child's first combinations of words, which omit (as a telegram does) nonessential words.*

Pretty good for a little kid, don't you think?

At age 3 or 4, children are creating longer and more grammatical sentences ("Why he can't come?"). Along with their growing conceptual ability, they make fewer overgeneralizations. They learn that Mom works at a *desk* and the family eats

Think About It

Should Children Have a Childhood?

- An expectant mother uses a "pregaphone" to "talk" to her unborn baby.

- A father flashes word cards at his 1-year-old son, hoping to teach him to "read."

- A 5-year-old boy, leaving an admission interview for *kindergarten*, tells his mother, "That's a rough school. They asked a lot of hard questions about numbers and letters, but I knew the answers."

- A 6-year-old girl comes home from first grade and proudly announces that she'll never be fat. "You just have to do this," she says—making the gesture for vomiting.

These true stories are signs of the times, and some psychologists are worried. A decade ago, David Elkind (1981) wrote a book called *The Hurried Child: Growing Up Too Fast, Too Soon,* and since then, he thinks, matters have gotten worse (Elkind, 1988). Today's parents are trying to raise "superbabies," he fears, force-feeding them with reading and math lessons, pressuring them to achieve more and more at earlier and earlier ages. Children no longer have time for the main business of childhood: play—unstructured, undemanding play that fosters creativity and fun. Today, even play has become work. Many children take karate and tennis lessons, in which they must compete and "succeed."

Elkind believes that the pressures on children to hurry up and become adults are having disastrous results. Children are coming to doctors with stress symptoms of headaches, stomach aches, tics, and even ulcers. Their anxiety over success and failure can, by adolescence, lead to dropping out, delinquency, drug abuse, and even suicide. They are losing the intrinsic pleasures of learning for its own sake.

Many psychologists agree that there is a fine line between giving children opportunities to learn and explore, and cramming information down their throats. Some believe it is possible to "speed up" Piaget's timetable of mental maturation by teaching children cognitive skills (Endsley et al., 1979). Oth-

ers think parents should relax; children will read when they are able to read (Scarr, 1984b). Some psychologists favor "early enrichment programs"; others think these efforts lead to later mental impoverishment.

In evaluating both sides, consider that theories about children's cognitive development take place in a larger social context. We might ask, *Why* are children expected to grow up so rapidly nowadays? Elkind is critical of what he calls "gourmet" parents, often older couples who have only one or two children and want them to be "perfect." They want to give their preschoolers a "leg up" on getting into Harvard, he says, and think the kids should learn "survival skills" by age 3.

But other trends in society are pressuring children to grow up fast. Some affluent parents may think it is cute or trendy to have mini-adult children, but many middle- and working-class parents think it is *necessary.* The economic needs of families, the high divorce rate, and the lack of good day-care and school facilities leave many "latchkey" children to fend for themselves. Under such conditions, some parents must give their children adult responsibilities, such as shopping, cleaning up, caring for younger siblings, and earning some money. As you will see in this chapter, giving children responsibility for siblings and chores teaches them to be helpful and mature. But what is the line between having some responsibilities and having too many?

The debate over early enrichment, therefore, often obscures different questions and agendas. Can children learn ahead of developmental schedule? Perhaps so, but should they? Why should they? Do we, asks psychologist Elizabeth Douvan (1985), "both overprotect our children and burden them with parents' problems?" Our society bombards children with adult images of violence, sex, glamor, and drugs. Should we raise children to cope early with these facts of modern society, even if it means having them grow up "too soon"? Or should we try to shelter them from these realities, even if it means having them grow up "too late"? Think about it.

on a *table*. But they are still seeking rules of speech and often make funny errors when they overextend or misapply a rule. Helen Bee (1989) reports this conversation between a 6-year-old and a 3-year-old, who are arguing about the relative dangers of forgetting to feed pet goldfish or of feeding them too much:

6-YEAR-OLD: It's worse to forget to feed them.
3-YEAR-OLD: No, it's badder to feed them too much.
6-YEAR-OLD: You don't say badder, you say worser.
3-YEAR-OLD: But it's baddest to give them too much food.
6-YEAR-OLD: No it's not. It's worsest to forget to feed them.

These children have learned a rule for comparisons (-*er* and -*est* endings), but they haven't yet learned all the exceptions. As a result, they overgeneralize the rules of grammar. Their conversation shows, however, that they are seeking regular, predictable rules of speech. (See Figure 13.5 for similar "smart" errors in vocabulary use.)

As children get older, of course, they begin to understand and use words and sentences of greater complexity. Their language seems to reflect the growing complexity of their thoughts. For example, children learn the plural *"s" (boys, toys, cookies)* before they learn the possessive *"s" (Mommy's car, Danny's toy)*. Plurals are conceptually simpler, so children learn them first (R. Brown, 1973).

The nature-nurture question. Is the ability to speak innate, wired into our biology like vision? Or do we have to be carefully taught? Until the middle of this century, many psychologists assumed that children learn to speak by imitating what adults say and by having adults correct the child's mistakes. In his book *Verbal Behavior,* B. F. Skinner (1957) argued that language is learned like any other behavior, primarily through the laws of operant conditioning.

One of the strongest arguments against this view came from Noam Chomsky (1957, 1972), who argued that the brain must contain a *language acquisition device*, a biological system that is programmed to acquire language and the rules of grammar. Chomsky and others have noted that imitation cannot explain how children learn language or why they all go through the same stages of acquiring speech. The telegraphic sentences of young children consist of word pairs that adults would never say. Children regularly reduce a parent's sentences ("Let's go to the store!") to their own two-word version ("Go store!"), and they make errors that adults never make ("Did Daddy take you?" "Daddy taked me") (Ervin-Tripp, 1964).

Learning explanations of the acquisition of language assume that children are rewarded for saying the right words and punished for making errors. But as you saw in the conversation between the two children, the 6-year-old's attempts to "correct" the younger child's mistake ("You don't say badder, you say worser") had no effect. Parents don't fare any better ("Say, Daddy *took* you." "Daddy taked me"). Moreover, parents don't stop to correct every error in their children's speech, as long as they understand what the child is trying to say (Brown, Cazden, & Bellugi, 1969). Indeed, parents often *reward* children for incorrect statements! The 2-year-old who demands "More milk!" is likely to get it; most parents would not wait for a more grammatical (or polite) request.

Most significant, children are forever coming up with new associations and terms that are entirely original. A 5-year-old we know was walking home with his mother, who was carrying a large shopping bag that kept bumping into him. The boy protested, "It's hitting me in the armpit of my leg!" (Well, is there another term for the back of the knee?)

Nevertheless, language learning is not entirely "built in." Parents do not tell

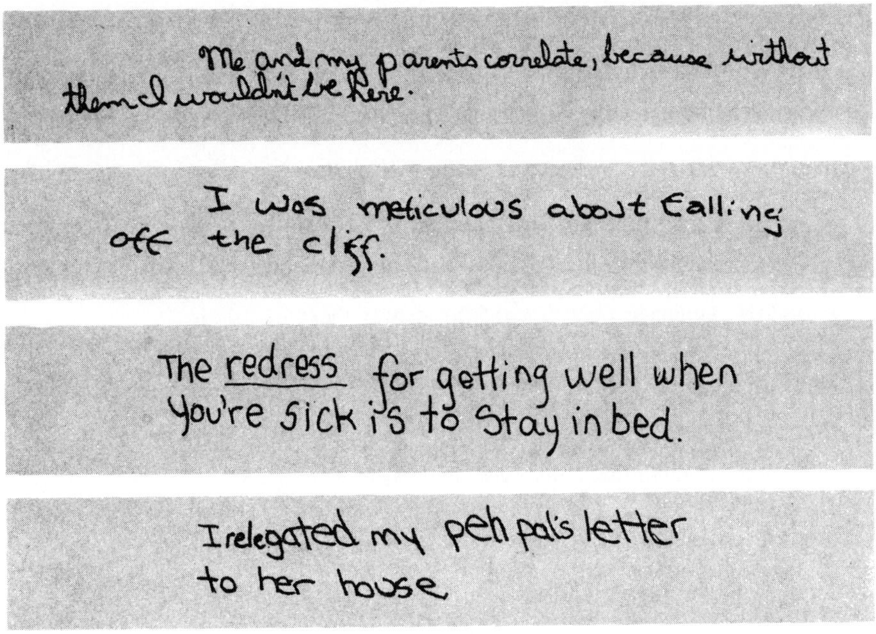

> Me and my parents correlate, because without them I wouldn't be here.

> I was meticulous about falling off the cliff.

> The <u>redress</u> for getting well when you're sick is to stay in bed.

> I relegated my pen pal's letter to her house.

FIGURE 13.5

How children learn words
Schoolchildren often produce mystifying sentences like these when they are trying to learn an unfamiliar word. The reason is that they extract one element of a word's definition, and then apply it inappropriately. For example, if "correlate" means related to, *you must be "correlated" with your parents. Similarly, "meticulous" involves* being very careful *about small details; to "redress" a grievance means to find a* remedy *for it; and to "relegate" means to* send away. *Children learn new words faster when they are given model sentences that use the word correctly than when they are given only definitions of it (Miller & Gildea, 1987).*

their children, "You said that wrong," but neither do they ignore their children's errors of speech. Instead, they are more likely to repeat verbatim a child's *well-formed* sentence than a sentence with errors ("That's a horse, Mommy!" "Yes, that's a horse"). And when the child does make a mistake or a clumsy sentence, parents almost invariably respond by recasting it ("That are monkey!" "That *is* a monkey") or expanding its basic elements ("Monkey climbing!" "The monkey is climbing to the top of the tree") (Bohannon & Stanowicz, 1988). In turn, children are more likely to imitate adult recasts and expansions, suggesting that they are learning from them (Bohannon & Symons, 1988).

Adults in some cultures (not all) also help children learn speech by speaking more slowly, simply, and repetitiously to them. "Baby talk" is a simpler form of adult language, simpler in length of sentence, vocabulary, pace, and sentence construction (Gelman & Shatz, 1977). Further, children certainly do imitate their parents' inflections, accents, and tone of voice, and they will repeat specific words that the parent tries to teach ("This is a *ball*, Erwin." "Baw").

Language acquisition, it seems, depends both on biological readiness and social experience. The *ability* to speak seems to be biologically programmed, whereas a specific language (Japanese, Spanish, English, Swahili) is learned from the culture the child grows up in. Children who are abandoned, abused, and not exposed to language for years (such as Genie, whom we discussed in Chapter 2) rarely speak normally. Such sad evidence suggests that there may be a critical period in language development, possibly the years between 1 and 5, possibly the entire first decade of life (Curtiss, 1977; Lenneberg, 1967). During these years children do not need to *hear* language—deaf children's acquisition of sign language parallels the development of spoken language—but they do need close relationships and practice in conversation.

In summary, we draw these conclusions about language development:

- The child's very first sentences follow simple rules.
- These rules are specific to children's speech and show up in every language around the world. They are not necessarily the rules of the adult language.

- The child's grammar becomes gradually more complex, as the child's thinking does.
- The child's language is creative and original from the start. Language does not come merely from imitating adults or passively parroting adults' rules.

QUICK ■ QUIZ

Please use language (and thought) to answer these questions.

1. "More cake!" and "Daddy here" are examples of _____ speech.
2. Understanding that two rows of six pennies are equal in number, even if one row is flat and the other is stacked up, is an example of _____ .
3. Understanding that a toy exists even after Mom puts it in her purse is an example of _____ , which occurs during the _____ stage.
4. The belief that a car moves because you are riding in it shows _____ thinking.

Answers:

1. telegraphic   2. conservation   3. object permanence, sensory-motor   4. egocentric

Social Development

Learning to walk, talk, and think are not the only challenges facing young children. They have to find a balance between dependence on their parents and independence. They have to figure out relationships with siblings and friends. They have to learn the values of their families and communities. They have to learn what it means to be a boy or a girl. They must, in psychological terms, become **socialized** in the rules of adult life.

Bonding and attachment

In developmental psychology, **attachment** refers to the emotional tie that children and their caretakers feel toward each other. Chicks, ducklings, baby monkeys, puppies, and many other species attach themselves instinctively to their mothers, and their mothers are primed by hormonal factors to care for and defend their young. Is this true for human beings?

Bonding. Years ago, Marshall Klaus and John Kennell (1976) argued that mothers who could see and hold their newborns immediately after birth became "bonded" to them. Later, these women would be better, more attentive mothers than women who were separated from their babies after delivery, which used to be customary hospital procedure. This idea got much publicity, and hospitals began plunking every healthy newborn on its mother's stomach as soon as the baby emerged from the womb.

socialization *The process by which a child acquires the rules, standards, and values of his or her family and culture.*

attachment *A strong emotional tie between babies and their primary caretakers. In later life, attachment refers to any emotional connection between two people.*

Bonding was thought to be set off by maternal hormones that are present during childbirth. However, subsequent research has shown that mothers (and fathers) can ''bond'' just fine to their babies if they see them a day, four days, or months after the birth. So can parents who adopt older infants and children. Parents of premature infants who live in incubators for weeks are as glad to take their babies home as are parents of full-term babies. Modern fathers are just as attentive to their newborns as new mothers are, even without ''bonding hormones'' to help them along (Parke & Sawin, 1980). And, sadly, some mothers and fathers who *do* see their babies right after delivery do not feel close to their infants or wish to care for them.

For all of these reasons, most psychologists now believe that bonding at birth is nice if you can do it, but not essential. The effects of early bonding are weak, and do not explain why a mother keeps on mothering (Campos et al., 1984). Hormones do not explain motherly behavior in the female woman as they do, say, in the female rat. ''Nature has to prepare mother rats for only forty days of parenthood,'' writes Sandra Scarr (1984b). ''Humans had better be prepared for twenty years. Hormones just can't handle that.''

Attachment. As we saw in Chapter 10, Harry Harlow's studies found that infants become attached to their mothers (or caretakers) for the contact comfort the adults provide. In the first few months of life, babies become attached to their caretakers, but they really aren't too particular about who the caretaker is. Between 7 and 12 months, however, babies stop this indiscriminate affection. They become wary or fearful of strangers, a reaction called *stranger anxiety*. They wail if they are put in an unfamiliar setting or are left with an unfamiliar person. They have become especially attached to the mother (or the primary caretaker) and show *separation anxiety* if she temporarily leaves the room. This reaction continues until the middle of the second year, but many children show signs of distress at parental separation until they are about 3.

To determine the kind and quality of attachment between mothers and babies, Mary Ainsworth (1973, 1979; Ainsworth et al., 1978) devised a method called the ''Strange Situation.'' A mother (or sometimes a father) brings the baby into an unfamiliar room, containing lots of toys. After a while a stranger comes in and attempts to play with the child. The mother leaves the baby with the stranger. She then returns, plays with the child, and the stranger leaves. Finally, the mother leaves the baby alone for three minutes and returns. How does the baby behave, with the mother (or father), with the stranger, and when the baby is alone?

Ainsworth and her associates divided children into categories on the basis of their reactions to the Strange Situation. Some are *securely attached*. They cry or protest if the parent leaves the room; they welcome her back and then play happily again; they are clearly more attached to the parent than to the stranger. But some are *insecurely attached*. There are two styles of insecure attachment. A child may be *detached* or *avoidant*, not caring if the mother leaves the room, making little effort to seek contact with her on her return, and treating the stranger about the same as the mother. Or a child may be *resistant* or *ambivalent*, resisting contact with the mother at reunion but protesting loudly if she leaves. Such children may cry to be picked up and then demand to be put down. Some behave as if they are angry with the mother and resist her comfort.

Ainsworth thinks that the difference between secure and insecure attachment lies primarily in the way mothers treat their babies in the first few months. Mothers of securely attached babies, she believes, are sensitive to their babies' needs and the meanings of their cries; they are affectionate and demonstrative. Mothers of avoid-

If a woman doesn't ''bond'' to her baby right after childbirth, will she be a bad mother? What about parents who adopt older children— is it too late for them to ''bond''?

Toward the end of the first year, children develop a wariness of strangers and distress at separation from caretakers.

bonding *A strong emotional tie that parents typically feel toward their newborn babies.*

ant babies are irritated by their infants, express controlled anger toward them, and are rejecting. Mothers of ambivalent babies are insensitive and inept but not reject-ing. They don't know what to do to relieve their babies' distress and are "out of sync" in handling their babies. Ainsworth's work, like the bonding studies, implies that it is up to sensitive, responsive mothers to create happily attached infants.

Although this research represents a thoughtful effort to measure elusive con-cepts such as attachment and maternal sensitivity, there are some problems with it (Campos et al., 1984). First, the observers who rated the mothers' behavior were aware of how the babies had behaved in the Strange Situation, so their descriptions of the mothers may have been biased. Second, signs of attachment in a baby, as well as ratings of a mother's sensitivity, are often inconsistent over time. The same baby may be "securely attached" one week and "insecurely attached" two weeks or two months later. The same mother might be "sensitive" one week and "out of sync" the next. Finally, some babies may become insecurely attached because they are temperamentally difficult; anyone would have trouble dealing with them.

Everyone agrees that attachment is important. When infants are deprived of social contact, affection, and cuddling, the effects can be long-lasting. But psychol-ogists disagree on the importance of an exclusively *maternal* attachment, particu-larly to the biological mother. There is no evidence that only full-time mothers can fulfill the infant's attachment need. Dozens of studies now show that babies go through the stages of indiscriminate friendliness, fear of strangers, and indepen-dence, whether they are at home or in day care. Babies develop well in many kinds of caretaking arrangements, *as long as the care is good* (Scarr, 1984b).

Sex typing

If you woke up tomorrow and found you were a member of the opposite sex, how would your life be different? By the time they are in first grade, most boys will tell you the transformation would be disastrous. They couldn't do as much or be as active. They would have to be polite and pretty. But at the same age, most girls will say that the transformation would be beneficial. They could do more and be more assertive. People would like them more. They would be more outspoken and confi-dent (Baumgartner, 1983).

Where do children get these ideas? How is it that they know "for sure" what boys and girls can and cannot do, what they are or are not like? **Sex typing** is the psychological process by which boys and girls become "masculine" or "femi-nine." Through sex typing, children learn the preferences, abilities, interests, per-sonality traits, actions, and self-concepts that their culture says are appropriate for males and females. In the United States, they have traditionally learned that boys are supposed to like carpentry and girls are supposed to like cooking. Boys are supposed to be good with gadgets; girls, with babies. Boys are supposed to be aggressive and mathematical; girls, passive and verbal.

Sex typing starts early, with blue booties for baby boys and pink booties for girls. By the time children are 3 or 4, most prefer the games and activities that are "right" for their gender, and they also prefer same-sex friends. They are trying to determine the rules that distinguish male from female. Just as they overextend language rules ("Daddy taked me"; "He runned"), they overgeneralize social rules. Try convincing a 4-year-old that girls can become pilots or that boys can become nurses. The child will say patiently, as if you are an idiot, "No, *boys* can be pilots. Only girls can be nurses." When occupations become less sex-typed, how-ever, so do children's views of them.

sex typing *The process by which children learn the behaviors, attitudes, and expectations associated in their culture with being "masculine" or "femi-nine."*

cathy®   **by Cathy Guisewite**

Sex typing starts early.

By age 4 or 5, most children have acquired a permanent **gender identity**, a sense of being biologically male or female, in spite of what they wear or how they act. As we noted earlier, they realize that a girl remains a girl, even if she can climb a tree. But they are still learning the rules of sex typing. Jason, a 9-year-old of our acquaintance, was taken to a cooking class that he had expressed an interest in joining. On the way there, he asked, "Mom, do boys take cooking lessons?" "Of course, of course," she reassured him. "Why, many of the greatest cooks in the world are men." He paused to consider this information. "Does everybody know that?" he asked.

Four theories try to account for the development of sex typing:

1. *Psychoanalytic theory* emphasizes the child's identification with the same-sex parent. As a result of the crisis of the Oedipal conflict (see Chapter 11), the child "identifies with," that is, assumes the behavior and values of, that parent. If Daddy doesn't cook, the son had better not either.

2. *Social learning theory* emphasizes the rewards and punishments that children get for behaving appropriately or inappropriately for their gender, the adult models they observe, and the vicarious lessons they learn from seeing what happens to men and women who break the rules of sex typing. This approach assumes that children learn to be male or female just as they learn any other social lesson.

3. *Cognitive developmental theory* maintains that children actively sex-type themselves as their cognitive abilities mature (Kohlberg, 1966; Lewis & Brooks-Gunn, 1979). As children begin to organize their social worlds, they divide people into the fundamental categories of male or female. Once they understand where they fit, they are motivated by the need for cognitive consistency (see Chapter 10) to do the things that are appropriate to their gender, and to value the things associated with that gender. Once a boy has a stable self-concept of himself as male, he then values "boy things" and dislikes "girl things" automatically, without being taught. This view does not explain, however, why girls who have stable self-concepts nevertheless value male activities, as society does.

4. *Gender schema theory* maintains that the human mind is set up to perceive and organize information according to a network of associations called a *schema*. According to Sandra Bem (1985), a "gender schema" organizes the world in terms of male or female. In many societies gender is the most powerful organizing category, but different group divisions are more important elsewhere (for instance, race in South Africa, class and caste in India). Like social learning theory, this approach

gender identity *The sense of being male or female, whether or not one follows the rules of sex typing.*

holds that sex typing is learned. Like cognitive developmental theory, it emphasizes the child's active mental interpretations. But it adds the element of culture; societies determine which schemas are important and the associations they contain.

Bem believes that psychologists have been as swayed by gender schemas as has the general public. Masculinity and femininity, says Bem, are not opposite ends of a continuum. Many men are nurturant and compassionate (traditional qualities of the "feminine" woman), and many women are independent and assertive (traditional qualities of the "masculine" man). Not all men are predominantly masculine; not all women are exclusively feminine; and not all children become traditionally sex-typed (Bem, 1974, 1985). Bem used the term **androgynous** to describe people who have both masculine *and* feminine qualities. Later, other researchers found that some people are *undifferentiated*, having few traditionally masculine *or* feminine qualities (Spence & Helmreich, 1978).

All of these theories contribute a piece to the picture of sex typing. Children do identify with their parents and try to copy them, but not exclusively on a same-sex basis. (They may identify with the occupation of parent A and the sense of humor of parent B.) Children certainly are rewarded and punished when they behave appropriately or inappropriately for their gender, although boys are punished more for behaving like girls than vice versa (Maccoby, 1980). Children do play an active part in interpreting the rules of gender. As their abilities mature, they understand that women can be doctors and men can be nurses. Finally, a "gender schema" organizes almost every aspect of life, although many children acquire traditional qualities associated with *both* sexes (Jacklin, 1989).

QUICK ▪ QUIZ

Choose the best answer to each question.

1. Which of the following best predicts good mothering? **(a)** maternal hormones, **(b)** bonding, **(c)** Caesarean section, **(d)** practice
2. Which of the following best predicts good fathering? **(a)** male hormones, **(b)** having to work 12 hours a day, **(c)** genetic predisposition, **(d)** practice
3. Sex typing explains why **(a)** girls are genetically better at typing than boys are, **(b)** more girls than boys take typing courses, **(c)** some types of boys are better than girls.
4. A girl who wants to be "just like Mommy when I grow up" illustrates **(a)** gender schema, **(b)** identification, **(c)** cognitive inconsistency.

Answers:
1. d 2. d 3. b 4. b

Parents and peers

androgynous *Having both traditionally "masculine" and "feminine" qualities; literally, "male-female."*

For many years, psychologists (and parents) assumed that children were reared and influenced solely by their mothers. They worried that mothers were too involved with their children or they worried that mothers weren't involved enough; but hardly anyone worried about fathers unless they were absent because of divorce, desertion,

How many mothers have you seen doing this? Fathers tend to be rougher and more physical in playing with their children than mothers are.

or death. Few thought much about the socializing influences of siblings or same-age peers. Now fathers, friends, and siblings have entered the picture.

Fathers and mothers. In primate species, fathers vary enormously in how much attention and affection they give to infants, toddlers, and growing offspring. Primate males who take care of their young tend to live in predictable circumstances. Their culture is monogamous (one male for each female), there is a long period of infant dependency on adults, and both parents are needed to get food. When males have to defend their territory or acquire resources, the females stay home with the kids, and males tend to be distant from their offspring (Katz & Konner, 1981). Within a species, social organization can vary, as the many human cultures on this earth testify. The very same species of monkey may live in two entirely different social systems on opposite sides of a mountain (Redican & Taub, 1981).

For human beings, like other primates, good fathers (like good mothers) are made, not born. Even within a culture, some individuals are better fathers than others. American fathers spend anywhere from six minutes to a few hours a day with their children (Campos et al., 1984). Despite this variation, psychologists have found that the American father's role in his children's development is usually quite different from the mother's role (Lamb, 1981; Pleck, 1987):

▪ Fathers tend to be more physically stimulating, playful, and unpredictable than mothers. Mothers tend to be more verbal, instructive, and calming. This difference in parents' behavior starts at the infant's birth (Parke & Tinsley, 1981). One psychologist who reviewed this chapter for us remarked that he began testing his daughter's reflexes—by dangling her from his fingers—when she was only 45 minutes old. His wife did not approve.

▪ Fathers set higher expectations for their sons than their daughters, and those expectations are related to their children's achievement (or lack of it). Fathers often

TABLE 13.3
WHO TENDS THE KIDS?

Even when mothers and fathers both work outside the home, they differ in the child care they do.

Child-care Activities	Time (in Hours) per Week	
	Mothers	Fathers
Routine physical care (bathing, feeding, taking to doctor, etc.)	24.8	15.4
Caring for child's social needs (talking, disciplining, etc.)	5.7	3.8
Caring for child's cognitive growth (reading, playing games)	5.3	4.0
Caring for child's emotional needs (comforting, nurturing)	1.4	.8
Miscellaneous (arranging child care, shopping, transportation)	5.3	2.7
TOTAL	42.5	26.7

SOURCE: Jump & Haas, 1987, p. 103.

send mixed messages to daughters: Achieve, but don't be too independent (Radin, 1981).

▪ Fathers allow their sons to explore, break rules, and take physical chances, but they protectively keep their daughters nearby. By the way they play and the toys they provide their children, fathers take a more active role than mothers do in teaching sex-appropriate behavior (Jacklin, DiPietro, & Maccoby, 1984).

▪ Mothers do child *care*; fathers do child *play*. In absolute hours, mothers play with their children more than fathers do, but mothers do other things with them as well—taking them to the doctor, to their music lessons, to buy shoes—which fathers rarely do (Jump & Haas, 1987). (See Table 13.3.)

It is commonly believed that women are "naturally" better with babies than men are. But how can we explain why single fathers who must care for their children behave just like mothers?

Why do mothers do the "mothering"—the child care? Popular explanations hold that females are biologically suited to it, or are socialized from childhood, or have deeply ingrained personality traits that make them more nurturant and sympathetic. Barbara Risman (1987) compared the "parenting" skills and personality traits of single fathers, single mothers, and married parents. If biological predispositions or sex-role learning indeed create personality differences between men and women, Risman noted, then fathers should differ from mothers in the baby-care business, regardless of marital status.

In fact, having responsibility for child care was as strongly related to self-reported "feminine" personality traits, such as nurturance and sympathy, as being female was. The single men who were caring for children were more like mothers than they were like married fathers. These men, though not representative of all custodial fathers, were not an atypical group of especially "nurturant" men, either. They had custody of their children through circumstances beyond their control—widowhood, the wife's desertion, or the wife's lack of interest in sharing custody.

This research does not deny the importance of personality or learning, but it does imply that sex differences depend more on what the two genders *do* than on entrenched internal qualities. And differences in what they do start early. In a cross-cultural survey of 11 cultures, the researchers found that the development of nurturance in children depends largely on the children's opportunity to care for infants and younger siblings. In most cultures, but not all, girls are given the main responsibility for baby care, creating the impression of a gender difference that may actually be an experience difference (Whiting & Edwards, 1988).

Methods of child rearing. *How* parents teach their children is just as important as *what* they teach them. In a successful method called **induction**, the parent appeals to the child's own resources, affection for others, and sense of responsibility. For example, a mother may tell her child that the child's actions will harm, inconvenience, or disappoint another person. Induction tends to produce children who have moral feelings and who behave morally on five different measures. They feel guilty if they hurt others; they internalize standards of right and wrong, instead of just following orders; they confess rather than lie if they misbehave; they accept responsibility for their misbehavior; and they are considerate of other children (Hoffman & Saltzstein, 1967).

In contrast, parents who rely on *power assertion* use such methods as threats; physical punishment; depriving the child of privileges; and taking advantage of being bigger, stronger, and more powerful (''because I say so''). Power assertion, which is based on the child's fear of punishment, is associated with a *lack* of moral feeling and behavior in children. The child may feel guilty about his or her own desires and impulses (which the parent punishes), but not guilty about harming others (Maccoby, 1980).

Love withdrawal is another punishing strategy. The parent reacts to the child's misbehavior by withdrawing, by disapproving without saying why, or by threatening to ''stop loving'' the child. This reaction makes the child feel bad, without teaching the child what to do to feel good. However, love withdrawal can be a powerful instructive lesson to the child under three specific conditions (Schulman & Mekler, 1985). First, the parent is usually affectionate and loving, so the child will feel distressed that he has hurt her feelings. Second, the parent uses the method *only for important matters*. ''I am angry and upset that you stole a bike, and here is why'' conveys an important lesson; ''I don't love you when you won't eat your vegetables'' conveys a petty one. Third, the parent always accompanies love withdrawal with *an explanation* to the child. The child then learns *why* the parent is angry instead of being puzzled over the parent's apparently random punishment.

Parental methods of child rearing also affect a child's sense of internal control (feeling in charge of oneself and of events) or external control (feeling like a passive victim of fate) (see Chapter 11). In one study, parental practices relating to a child's having internal control included nurturance, showing protective concern, using predictable discipline, and setting predictable standards. The practices related to a child's having external control included imposing too many protective restrictions, depriving the child of friends and favored toys, nagging, yelling, acting cold, acting hurt, and inculcating guilt (Marquis & Detweiler, 1985).

The humanistic psychologist Carl Rogers argued that parents who provide conditions of ''psychological safety and freedom'' will allow their children to develop their creative potential. A group of researchers confirmed this idea with a longitudinal study of 106 families (Harrington, Block, & Block, 1987). The most creative children had parents who respected their opinions, allowed them to make many of their own decisions, encouraged them to explore and question, gave them time to

induction *A method of child rearing in which the parent appeals to the child's own resources, abilities, sense of responsibility, and feelings for others in correcting the child's misbehavior (in contrast to methods that rely on asserting power or withdrawing love).*

Parents teach their children all sorts of lessons, many of which are unintentional. This group effort to make dinner, for instance, is teaching the children that (1) they're never too young to help, (2) both sexes belong in the kitchen, (3) group cooking may be messy but it's fun, and (4) the person who frosts the cake gets to lick the spoon.

daydream, shared good times, and praised their accomplishments. (For more on methods of child rearing, see "Taking Psychology with You.")

Of course, parental styles of child rearing depend on the kind of child a parent is trying to raise. Over the years, the traits that parents most value have changed significantly. In 1924, about 50 percent of a sample of average Americans emphasized "strict obedience" and "loyalty to Church" in training their children; by the late 1970s, those percentages had dropped to only 20 percent. In contrast, in 1924, only 6 percent valued teaching their children "tolerance of other people's opinions," and only 25 percent valued "independence—thinking and acting for yourself." In the late 1970s, 47 percent valued tolerance, and a whopping 76 percent valued independence of thought and action (Alwin, 1988).

QUICK ▪ QUIZ

Match the method of discipline with the appropriate example:

1. induction
2. power assertion
3. punishment
4. love withdrawal

a. "Go to your room."
b. "Mommy doesn't like you when you do that."
c. "Pinching hurts Jane; big boys like you don't need to pinch anyone."
d. "Do it because I say so, period."

Answers:
1. c   2. d   3. a   4. b

Peers and play. A friend recently drove his 5-year-old to his first day of school. The boy cried the whole way there, and then grabbed onto the steering wheel when his father tried to take him out of the car. ''I won't go!'' he screamed. ''I won't, I *won't*, I . . . Oh, HI, Justin!'' And he bolted off to join his best friend. ''He didn't even say goodbye,'' says his father.

From early infancy, babies recognize and react to one another. As their social and cognitive abilities mature, so do their relationships with siblings and with new-found friends. Aside from being fun, having friends has several important developmental purposes (Leventhal & Dawson, 1984):

▪ Friends provide emotional security. In an unfamiliar situation, the presence of a familiar child is reassuring and supportive, sometimes even more so than the presence of a parent.

▪ Peers and siblings teach a child how to get along and cooperate with others (even when they also teach competitiveness and rivalry). The child learns how to enter a group, how to convey approval of and support for others, how to manage conflicts, and how to be sensitive to others. Children who learn to pay attention to others, to praise them, to show affection, and to help them tend to be the most popular.

▪ Friends provide instruction. Remember how you learned to play volleyball, Ping-Pong, and computer games? Remember all the (wrong) information you got about sex? Your friends did that for you. Remember how you tried to copy everything your adored older sister or brother did, and how you taught your younger siblings to tie their shoelaces? By example and by explicit instruction, children teach each other all the time.

▪ Friends set the rules. During middle childhood, children learn from their peers to follow the rules—and which rules to follow: ''Big kids don't snivel when they lose.'' ''Our group doesn't wear *white* sneakers—they're yukky.'' Pressures to conform to the group can become especially fierce at this age and may override the example set by parents.

Children's friendships change as they grow older. Preschool children change their ''best friends'' in only a few days or weeks. In middle childhood, friendships last longer, but boys and girls begin to have different kinds of friendships and games. Boys have more extensive friendship groups, based on shared activities. Girls have fewer, more intense friendships, based on shared revelations and feelings (Gilligan, 1982; Hartup, 1980). In any form, friendships are as important to children as they are to adults.

When attachments break: The effects of divorce on children

Thirty years ago, divorce was rare and shameful. Today, divorce is as common as the flu and often strikes as unpredictably, to couples married only a year as well as to couples married for decades, affecting 1 million children a year. A child born today has a 40 percent chance of living through a *second* parental divorce by age 18. At least the stigma of being different no longer matters; we know a child who complains that she has ''only'' one set of parents.

Despite its increasing prevalence, divorce continues to be troubling, difficult, and painful for children of all ages—just as it is troubling for most divorcing couples. One reason is that human beings do not break their attachments lightly, even bad attachments (Berman, 1988; Bowlby, 1988). Married couples who fought constantly are often surprised to discover, once separated, how emotionally attached they remain to each other. Children often persist in their attachment to a cold or abusive parent long after the parent has abandoned them.

According to longitudinal studies, the effects of divorce depend on the child's gender, age at the time of the parents' divorce, and whether you are looking at *immediate* or *long-term* reactions (Wallerstein, 1984; Wallerstein & Blakeslee, 1989):

▪ Preschool-age children (ages 2 to 6) are the age group most immediately distressed by their parents' divorce, yet the group that does best in the long run. Preschoolers become extremely needy and anxious. Being egocentric in their thinking, they blame themselves for the divorce (''Daddy is leaving because I left my toys on the stairs''). A year and a half later, about half of these children, especially the boys, are still deeply troubled. After five years, more than a third of them are still moderately to severely depressed. By adolescence, however, most have forgotten the distress and fears they felt at the time of the divorce and are less burdened by the divorce than older children. Yet many still speak sadly of the disruption and some still have fantasies of their parents' reconciliation. Almost all remain emotionally attached to their fathers, whether the father visits them often or rarely, predictably or erratically.

▪ Elementary-school-age children (ages 7 to 12) are not as likely to blame themselves for the divorce, but most feel abandoned and lonely nevertheless. They are better than preschoolers at expressing their feelings, but they have trouble managing conflicting emotions toward the custodial parent, such as anger and sadness. They often fear that if they make that parent angry, he or she will leave them, too.

▪ Adolescents (ages 13 to 18) report frequent feelings of anger, sadness, shame, helplessness, and a sense of betrayal by the parents. They tend to cope by distancing themselves from their parents, remaining aloof even a year or more later. Girls may respond to parental divorce by becoming sexually precocious (Hetherington, Cox, & Cox, 1985). Boys may become sexually insecure and threatened, acting out their feelings through drug use and aggression. Other boys become ''supermacho,'' exaggerating the male role. Because of their greater cognitive maturity, adolescents are better able than younger children to see the divorce as mainly the parents' problem. But for the same reason, they often become more distrustful of the institution of marriage itself.

▪ College-age students (ages 18 to 22) intellectually understand and accept the reasons for their parents' divorce, but this understanding does not reduce their emotional upheaval. Many report depression, stress, and feelings of insecurity. They are old enough to feel empathy for their parents, yet they often worry that no one appreciates their own grief and confusion (Cooney et al., 1986).

Overall, girls adjust to divorce more easily than boys, and one reason seems to be that boys suffer more by being separated from the father when the mother has custody (Beech-Lublin, 1985; Guidubaldi & Perry, 1985). Children who live in joint custody or in custody of the same-sex parent show significantly more competence, maturity, cooperativeness, and self-esteem than children living with the opposite-sex parent (Meyer & Simons, 1988).

A child's ability to cope with divorce also depends on whether the parents settle into amicable (or at least silent) relations or continue to feel angry and conflicted. Children will eventually recover from the parents' divorce, unless the parents continue to quarrel about visitation rights, take each other to court, or fight with each other at every visit (Ash & Guyer, 1986; Wallerstein & Blakeslee, 1989). From the standpoint of children's adjustment, an amicable divorce is better than a bitter marriage, but a prolonged and bitter divorce is worst of all.

Moral Development

Do you think it is morally acceptable to steal? To steal something if you can afford to pay for it? To steal something if you need it to save a life? Do you think it is morally acceptable to hit someone? To hit someone to get something you want? To hit someone to save your life?

Adults make moral judgments not only according to what people do, but also according to *why* they do it. We allow bad behavior, depending on a person's intention, extenuating circumstances, and need. We don't much like good behavior that is motivated by selfishness or greed. The study of moral development focuses on three questions: (1) moral judgments (is stealing right or wrong?); (2) moral emotions (how will you feel if you steal that watch?); and (3) moral behavior (you may know it is wrong to steal, and even feel guilty if you do—but can you say no to temptation?).

Moral judgments: Reasoning about morality

Piaget (1932) was the first developmental psychologist to divide moral reasoning into stages. Young children, he said, see right and wrong in terms of results rather than intention. They might tell you that a child who accidentally breaks two dishes is naughtier than a child who intentionally breaks one. They think that rules are set by a higher authority and are inflexible. You can't change the rules of a game, of family tradition, of life. If you break the rules, punishment will be swift and sure. At about age 7, said Piaget, children begin to understand that rules are social contracts that can be changed. Older children believe that intention, "fair play," and reciprocity ("you do for me and I do for you") are the standards of moral action. Children's moral reasoning, said Piaget, follows the increasing cognitive complexity of their reasoning in general.

In the 1960s, Lawrence Kohlberg (1964) outlined a new stage theory. Like Piaget, he focused on moral reasoning, not behavior. He did not observe how children or adults *actually* treat each other. But because his theory has become so influential—parent-training manuals use it, entire school systems have based moral-reasoning courses on it, some prisons even use it in rehabilitation programs—we are going to look at it closely.

Kohlberg (1976, 1984) proposed three levels of moral development, each divided into two stages. Your moral "stage" is determined by the answers you give to hypothetical moral dilemmas. For example, a man's wife is dying and needs a special drug. The man can't afford the drug and the druggist won't lower his price. Should the man steal the drug? What if he no longer loves his wife? If the man is caught, should the judge be lenient? To Kohlberg, the reasoning behind the answers was more important than the decisions themselves.

At the first level of moral reasoning, *preconventional morality*, young children obey rules because they are ordered to, because they will be punished if they disobey, or because they want to. What is "right" is what Mom and Dad say, or what feels good. At about ages 10 or 11, according to Kohlberg, children shift to the second level, the *conventional morality* of adult society. At first, conventional morality is based on trust, caring, and loyalty to others; morality means "don't hurt others; don't rock the boat." Many people then advance to a "law-and-order orientation," based on understanding the social order, law, justice, and duty.

How do children learn to resist temptation and eventually follow social rules?

Late in adolescence and early adulthood, said Kohlberg, some people realize that there is an even higher level of moral judgment, beyond human laws. Some laws—such as those that segregate blacks from whites, or those that sent millions of Jews to death in Hitler's Germany—are themselves immoral. Such awareness moves some individuals to the highest moral level, *postconventional ("principled") morality*. They realize that values and laws are relative, that people hold different standards, that laws are important but can be changed. A few great individuals have a moral standard based on universal human rights. When faced with a conflict between law and conscience, such people follow conscience, even at personal risk.

Most people, said Kohlberg, never reach this ultimate level; but if anyone does in Kohlberg's system, it's likely to be a man. Women, his studies implied, are more likely than men to "get stuck" at the beginning of level 2, worrying about other people's feelings as the basis of moral judgment. Men tend to stop at the end of level 2, emphasizing principles of law and duty that are above feelings.

Kohlberg's theory has been attacked on several counts. First, some critics complain that the hierarchy of stages actually reflects verbal, not moral, development and thus favors white, middle-class people in Western society (Leventhal & Dawson, 1984). College-educated people give "higher-level," "more mature" explanations of moral decisions than people who have not attended college, but we can hardly conclude that they actually *are* more moral. They are more verbally sophisticated, though.

Second, adults have greater understanding of law than children, but this knowledge does not make them more moral. A child who says "The judge should be lenient because [the husband] acted unselfishly" will score lower than the adult who says "The judge should be lenient because he or she can find a precedent or rule that reflects what is right." As two psychologists conclude, "The cruellest lawyer is, without question, going to get a higher score than the kindest eight-year-old" (Schulman & Mekler, 1985). Indeed, dozens of research studies now show that very young children are capable of moral feelings, of behaving kindly and considerately, of understanding that their actions have consequences. In some ways they are more moral than adults. Three-year-olds have no color, class, or religious prejudices.

Other critics challenge the idea that once people reach a higher level, they don't "regress" to a lower one. Studies find that neither adults nor children use the same moral reasoning in all ethical situations (Colby et al., 1983). You might show conventional morality by overlooking a racial slur at a dinner party (you don't want to upset everyone else), but postconventional reasoning by protesting a war you regard as immoral. Men in general are supposed to operate according to principles of law and justice, but about 35 percent of American and Canadian college men say they would rape a woman if they could "get away with it" (Malamuth, 1981). This is the lowest form of moral reasoning.

Finally, many researchers criticize Kohlberg's work for its implication that men are more moral than women. Carol Gilligan (1982) has argued that because Kohlberg and Piaget based their original theories on studies only of boys, their research was invalid as a way of understanding how and why girls make moral decisions. Gilligan agrees that women tend to base moral decisions on principles of compassion and care, whereas men base theirs on abstract principles of law and justice. But neither style of moral reasoning is *better* than the other, she maintains. Each has its strengths and weaknesses. Justice without compassion can be cold. Compassion without principle can be spineless.

Some studies support Gilligan's view, finding that men care more about justice and women care more about caring (Blake & Cohen, 1984; Bussey & Maughan,

1982; Gilligan & Wiggins, 1987). Most research, however, finds no sex differences in moral reasoning (L. Walker, 1984), especially when people are allowed to rank *all* the reasons behind their moral judgments. In one study, 101 young men and women evaluated the importance of a series of considerations in deciding how to respond to four moral dilemmas. Some of the considerations emphasized "care-based" reasoning (such as "which outcome will cause the least hurt for all of the people involved") and others were "justice-based" (such as "whether there is a moral code to which all individuals should adhere"). The researchers found absolutely no differences in how men and women ranked the items or in how they evaluated the moral dilemmas. Indeed, on a few items, men were more "care-based" than women. Both men and women, it seems, base their moral decisions on compassion *and* abstract principles of justice (Friedman, Robinson, & Friedman, 1987).

Nevertheless, Gilligan's approach has an important virtue. Rather than ranking moral judgments one above the other, perhaps we should consider how they can coexist. To Kohlberg, Mohandas Gandhi reached the highest moral stage because of his commitment to universal principles of peace, justice, and nonviolence. To Gilligan, Gandhi was *also* a man who was aloof from his family and followers, whom he often treated callously. Can we really say he was at the pinnacle of morality? Here is another problem for you. Vietnam war hero John Vann performed astonishing feats of bravery during the war, time and again rescuing men from certain death. He was also an obsessive womanizer who eventually abandoned his wife and five children without support, and he lied to avoid being court-martialed for the seduction of a 15-year-old girl (Sheehan, 1988). Does a person's moral virtues in one sphere of life excuse his or her behavior in other realms?

John Paul Vann was a Vietnam war hero who saved many of his men from death. He was also a womanizer who abandoned his wife and family. What "stage" of morality would you place him in?

Moral emotions:
Acquiring empathy, guilt, and shame

A second approach to studying morality concentrates on the development of conscience. Children shift from obeying rules for external reasons, such as fear of punishment, to obeying rules for internal reasons, because they will feel guilty or ashamed of behaving badly. Morality, in this view, depends on *empathy*, the ability to feel bad about another person's unhappiness and to feel good about another's joy, and on *altruism*, the willingness to help another person without thought of personal gain.

Children reveal empathic feelings early in life; empathy develops into different forms, depending on the child's age and cognitive abilities (Hoffman, 1987, 1989). In the first year, before they even have a sense of themselves as distinct from others, infants feel *global empathy*, general distress at another person's misery. At times, they act as though what happened to the other happened to themselves. One 11-month-old girl, seeing an older child fall and cry, behaved as if *she* had been hurt. She looked about to cry, put her thumb in her mouth, and buried her head in her mother's lap (Hoffman, 1987).

With the emergence of object permanence and the sense of self (ages 1 to 2), toddlers develop *"egocentric" empathy*. Children now understand that someone else is in distress, but they assume that the other person must feel as they do. Two-year-olds are often impulsive and egocentric, but they are also able to feel sad when another child or adult is unhappy and are capable of trying to make the person feel better. In one touching instance, a 13-month-old child offered her beloved doll to a sad adult (Hoffman, 1977). In another, an 18-month-old boy fetched his own

Children have an innate ability to form attachments, but experience determines whether they will develop empathy for or rivalry with others. A child who learns how to care for a new sibling is likely to acquire feelings of protectiveness and concern instead of rivalry and distance.

mother to comfort a crying friend, although the friend's mother was also there (Hoffman, 1987)!

By the age of 2 or 3, children are capable of *empathy for another's feelings* that are different from their own. The development of language also allows children to empathize with a growing number of emotions. For example, they can empathize with another child's feelings of shame, and they know when the child wants to be left alone. They are able to feel angry on someone else's behalf. One little boy, seeing a doctor give another child a painful injection, swatted the doctor in protest. A toddler in one study said, "You sad, Mommy. What Daddy do?" (Bretherton & Beeghly, 1982).

The final stage of empathy, *empathy for another's life condition*, emerges by late childhood. Children are able to understand that people have different experiences and histories and to feel empathy toward whole groups of individuals who are less fortunate than they.

Shame and guilt develop differently, with different consequences. *Shame* is a wound to the self-concept. It comes from perceiving that others have seen you doing something wrong and that they will like you less for having done it. As soon as the toddler has a sense of self, shame is quick to follow (Campos et al., 1984; Lewis et al., 1988). *Guilt*, in contrast, is the emotion you feel when you have not lived up to your own internal standard. It is a kind of self-inflicted punishment. Although people might like a life without shame or guilt, these emotions are essential to social life. They help maintain rules and standards, and encourage moral action.

By the age of 2, children are aware of standards of behavior, and at this tender age they react with anxious concern or distress when a standard has been violated. By the age of 3 or 4, children associate a bad act with being a "bad boy" or "bad girl," and they begin to regulate their own behavior. In every culture around the world, children at this age judge their thoughts, feelings, and behavior against the standards they know are "right" (C. Edwards, 1987). In turn, adults now treat children differently, expecting them to do the right thing.

The capacity for moral feeling, like the capacity for language, seems to be inborn. Children have a basic ability to understand right from wrong and to feel bad when they do wrong. As Jerome Kagan (1984) says, "Without this fundamental human capacity, which nineteenth-century observers called a *moral sense*, the child could not be socialized." But the shape this "moral sense" takes depends on the child's family and culture. Infants may feel "global empathy," but whether a

4-year-old boy will feel empathy toward a newborn sister's wails depends on the experience he has in taking care of her.

Moral action:
Learning to behave morally

Unfortunately, moral reasoning is not necessarily related to moral behavior, and neither are moral emotions (M. Hoffman, 1987; Kurtines & Gewirtz, 1984). People can know what is right and not do it. They can feel really miserable about treating each other horribly, and do it anyway. In Chapter 18 we will be looking at some social forces, such as conformity and obedience, that affect moral behavior. Here we want to consider how children become helpful members of society. How do they learn to avoid the temptations to steal, lie, cheat, and otherwise behave as they might like to?

Social learning theorists answer that children's moral feelings and actions depend on the rewards, punishments, and examples they get as they grow up. When children are rewarded for aggressive and competitive acts, such behavior will prevail over meekness and cooperation. Many studies have shown that when children are in competitive situations, they are less likely to behave altruistically toward others (Maccoby, 1980). However, directly rewarding children for being helpful does not necessarily produce helpful children. After all, the point of altruism is to do good with no thought of getting a reward. Good role models have only a mild influence. Finally, the fear of punishment interferes with the learning of self-control, empathy, and internalized values.

Then how do children learn to behave morally? In a study of children only 15 to 20 months old, some were already more helpful than others. If their behavior caused a friend to feel unhappy, afraid, or hurt, they would try to bring comfort by offering a toy, hugging the friend, or going to get help. It turned out that the mothers of these little Samaritans were using induction to reprimand their children in a particular way. They would *moralize* ("You made Doug cry; it's not nice to bite") or prohibit bad behavior *with explanations* or *statements of principle* ("You must *never* poke anyone's eyes"). Other ways of reprimanding bad behavior were ineffective. Neutral explanations ("Tina is crying because you pushed her") had no effect. The reprimands that produced the lowest rates of helping were unexplained prohibitions ("Stop that!") and physical punishment, such as spanking and swatting (Zahn-Waxler, Radke-Yarrow, & King, 1979).

Ultimately, a major influence on children's moral behavior is the behavior that is expected of them. In a major study of children in six cultures (Kenya, India, the Philippines, Okinawa, Mexico, and the United States), Beatrice and John Whiting (1975) measured how often children behaved altruistically (offering help, support, or unselfish suggestions) or egoistically (seeking help and attention, or wanting to dominate others). (This study was recently reanalyzed, and five new cultures were added to it [Whiting & Edwards, 1988].) American children were the *least* altruistic on all three measures and the *most* egoistic. The most altruistic children came from societies in which:

▪ Children are assigned many tasks, such as caring for younger children, helping with gathering food and preparing it.
▪ Children know that their work makes a genuine contribution to the well-being or economic survival of the family.
▪ Parents depend on the children's contributions.

In many cultures, children are expected to work to contribute to the family income, and to take care of their younger siblings. These experiences encourage helpfulness and empathy.

- Mothers have many responsibilities inside and outside the home.
- Children respect parental authority.

Freud believed that children are "naturally" savage and selfish, and that they must learn to be cooperative and self-restrained. Today, psychologists find that children are also "naturally" empathic and unselfish, and that they must learn to be aggressive or cruel.

QUICK ■ QUIZ

To raise children who are kind and helpful, parents (and parents-to-be) should be able to answer the following questions.

1. LaVerne, age 14 months, feels sad when she sees her mother crying during a tear-jerker movie, and she starts to cry too. LaVerne has developed **(a)** global empathy, **(b)** egocentric empathy, **(c)** empathy for another's feelings.
2. Shame and guilt are **(a)** unconscious emotions in infancy, **(b)** necessary emotions in learning moral feeling and behavior, **(c)** destructive emotions that should be stamped out as soon as possible.
3. Which method of parental discipline tends to create helpful children? **(a)** unexplained love withdrawal, **(b)** induction, **(c)** punishment, **(d)** power assertion
4. Which form of family life tends to create helpful children? **(a)** where every family member "does his or her own thing," **(b)** where parents have all the power, **(c)** where children contribute to the family welfare

Answers:
1. c   2. b   3. b   4. c

Does Childhood Matter?

As you can see, the study of child development does not produce one set of simple findings. Every time we presented somebody's research—Klaus and Kennel's on "bonding," Ainsworth's on "maternal sensitivity," Piaget's on cognitive stages, Kohlberg's on moral development—we had to follow it with contradictory evidence. The result is continuing controversies. Can children's cognitive development be hurried up? Is sex typing a necessary stage in social development or can it be eliminated? Can morality be taught? By generating studies to answer these questions, psychologists narrow the gap between the laboratory and real life. This is how science advances.

Of all the controversial issues in child development, perhaps the most controversial is this: What, if anything, does childhood have to do with adulthood? Let's consider some surprising evidence.

The first year

Some psychologists argue that no year of life is as important as the first. If the baby doesn't start out well, they warn, if the parents (especially the mother) do not tend to the baby's every physical and emotional need in the "right" way, the baby's whole life may be influenced for the worse. Nearly half of all mothers of newborn babies are employed nowadays, and some people worry that maternal employment will have long-lasting unfortunate consequences for the children. How critical is this year?

Certainly, newborns are not little blobs of clay. They show individual differences right from the start. They can do a lot of things. They form attachments. If they start off on the wrong foot, with sickness, premature birth, or social deprivation, they don't do as well as babies who start off healthy and loved. But the events of the first year do not necessarily have permanent effects, as study after study confirms:

▪ Infant differences in irritability, fussiness, crying, and sleeping patterns do not last (Emde & Sorce, 1984; Kagan, 1984; Rothbart, 1986).

▪ A large-scale review of infant studies led the researchers to conclude that "behavior remains plastic during the early years . . . infants are not captives of crystallized behavior patterns" (Moss & Susman, 1980).

▪ Infant vulnerabilities often can be outgrown. Researchers who followed the development of 643 children, from birth to age 18, found that supportive home environments totally overcame any initial biological weakness. Psychological problems that emerged were related more to stressful home environments than to biological vulnerabilities in infancy. Even those problems proved temporary. "As we watched these children grow from babyhood to adulthood," the researchers reported, "we could not help but respect the self-righting tendencies within them that produced normal development under all but the most persistently adverse circumstances" (Werner & Smith, 1982).

What then can we conclude about the importance of the baby's first year? Mainly, that we should keep things in perspective. Given adequate stimulation, attention, and nourishment, normal babies will develop normally. But "adequate" covers considerable territory. Babies get along just fine on cradleboards or unbound, in good day-care centers or at home with caretakers. It's good to give them the very best stimulation, attention, and nourishment possible. But parents need not fear that one wrong step will cost their baby a place in graduate school or will later require 17 years of therapy. Babies are very resilient. They are more like plastic glasses than crystal ones. They don't easily shatter, and it takes a lot of heat to bend them out of their natural shape (E. Hall, 1986).

The childhood years

Are we really "prisoners of childhood"? If you suffered a trauma in your early years, must you endure its effects for the rest of your life?

All of us acquire attitudes, habits, and deep emotional feelings from our families. Parents influence their children in thousands of ways, both positively and negatively. Many adults carry with them the scars of abuses they suffered as children. But do all of the experiences of later childhood lead in a straight and inflexible line to the future?

As adults, we all enjoy the game of looking backward to make sense out of our lives. This is why retrospective studies, in which people tell interviewers about their pasts, often find consistent patterns of development, whereas prospective studies, which follow people from childhood to adulthood, often do not.

▪ After World War II, many European children, made homeless by the war, were adopted by American families. A group of these orphans, aged 5 months to 10 years, was followed and their adjustment observed. About 20 percent of the children initially showed many signs of anxiety (such as overeating, sleep disturbances, and nightmares), but over the years all of these symptoms vanished. All of the children made good progress in school; none had psychiatric problems; and all established happy, affectionate relationships with their new parents (Rathbun, DiVirgilio, & Waldfogel, 1958).

▪ Of 53 children who had had psychological disorders ranging from delinquency to depression, 35 had recovered completely by late adolescence. The researchers concluded, "The emotionally traumatized child is not doomed, the parents' early mistakes are not irrevocable" (Thomas & Chess, 1984).

▪ Another study followed 200 disturbed children who had been referred to a child guidance clinic for treatment when they were, on the average, 9 years old. But as young adults, aged 18 to 27, most of those children had improved enormously. Except for the most seriously disturbed children, the researchers said, "there seems to be little continuity between child and adult disturbances" (Cass & Thomas, 1979).

Nowadays one can hardly read the newspapers or listen to a talk show without someone asserting that children of abusers grow up to be abusers or that children of alcoholics are doomed to be alcoholics. In fact, the statistical truth is that although *more* children of alcoholic or abusive parents acquire the problem than do children of nondisturbed parents, *most* of them—the majority—grow up to be just fine:

▪ Melissa West and Ronald J. Prinz (1987) reviewed ten years of studies of children of alcoholic parents. They examined a range of possible pathological effects: hyperactivity, drug abuse and delinquency, lower IQ and poor school performance, social inadequacy, physical symptoms, anxiety and depression, physical aggression, and troubled family relationships. In comparison to children of nondisturbed parents, children who had an alcoholic parent were at greater risk of one or more of these problems, and the researchers noted that "parental alcoholism is undoubtedly disruptive to family life." But West and Prinz found that "neither all nor a major portion of the population of children from alcoholic homes are inevitably doomed to psychological disorder."

▪ Most children who are abused do *not*, as parents, abuse their own children. "Adults who were maltreated have been told so many times that they will abuse their children that for some it has become a self-fulfilling prophecy," observe Joan Kaufman and Edward Zigler (1987). In reviewing more than 40 articles on child abuse, they found that most studies of this question failed to use representative samples or a comparison group of adults who were abused and did *not* abuse their own children. Being maltreated in childhood makes a person *more likely* to be an abusive parent, but fully 70 percent do not repeat their parents' cruelties.

No one knows why the majority of the children of alcoholics and abusers are so resilient, but a number of clues turn up in studies. Many of the resilient children get love and attention from the nondisturbed parent or another doting adult. They have an informal support network for advice and aid. They have good experiences in school. They have acquired a "sense of meaning and faith about life" (West & Prinz, 1987). Most of all, they are determined not to repeat their histories.

We do not wish to imply, in reporting this good news, that childhood is always easy and comfortable. Although this chapter has emphasized the joys and challenges of child development, there is a larger, more serious issue to consider: Whether children themselves are valued by the culture in which they develop—and what effects cultural attitudes might have on them. Indeed, a strong case can be made that American society, for all its professed love of children, does not treat them as well as most people assume. Consider the evidence: Unlike Sweden and most other European nations, the United States does not place a high priority on child-care services and education. People who work with children earn less than people who work with adults, even within the same field (pediatricians earn less than internists, elementary school teachers earn less than college teachers). "Adults-only" communities are springing up from coast to coast. And, most tragically, the physical and emotional abuse of children is widespread. (Perhaps you remember the horrible case of Lisa Steinberg [pictured in the margin], the child who was beaten to death by the attorney who had illegally taken custody of her.)

Keep in mind, therefore, that although many children *can* survive early traumas, this doesn't mean that childhood experiences are insignificant or that society should be indifferent to children's welfare. But as children develop, they are subject to other influences, too. They outgrow certain habits and attitudes, even as they cling to others that have been rewarded and encouraged. Things happen to children and adults that *can* overturn the effects of earlier experiences. Perhaps the most powerful reason for the breaks between childhood and adulthood is that children actively interpret their experiences, a theme we have emphasized. Children have minds of their own. This is the reason for the gap between what parents try to teach and what children learn, and between what children learn and what they take with them into adulthood.

In the next chapter, we will look at the development of the individual throughout life. What are the influences on adults that can override the lessons of their parents? As we will see, the link between childhood and adulthood is more like a dotted curve than a straight line.

Do Americans really like children? If so, why do so many "adults-only" communities exclude them? Why do people who work with children earn less than people who work with adults? Saddest of all, why are so many children abused, and some even murdered, by their own parents?

Taking Psychology with You

Bringing Up Baby

How are you supposed to treat your children? Should you be strict or lenient, powerful or permissive? Should you require your child to stop having tantrums, to clean up his or her room, to be polite? Will what you do make any difference, anyhow? The answers tend to change from generation to generation. Social values and goals influence our basic beliefs about how parents should raise their children, what teachers should teach, when mothers should work outside the home, and whether childhood determines the course of your adult life (Borstelmann, 1984).

In psychology, the pendulum has swung from the Mother-Blaming Explanation (the idea that the mother is virtually the sole influence on her children) to the Child Temperament Explanation (the idea that children virtually raise themselves because of their built-in personalities and perceptions). The first view says that what parents do makes *all* the difference. The second says that what parents do makes hardly *any* difference. The truth, as usual, lies in between, as we can see in the case of aggressive children.

Aggressive behavior typically results from specific parental practices, often unintentional. Parents of aggressive children use a great deal of punishment (shouting, scolding, spanking), yet they fail to make the punishment contingent on the child's behavior. They do not state clear rules, require compliance, praise good behavior, and consistently punish violations. Instead, they nag and "natter" at the child, occasionally and unpredictably tossing in a slap or loss of privileges. The child, in turn, becomes more antisocial, manipulative, and difficult to discipline (Patterson, 1985, 1986).

Authoritarian parents exercise too much power; *permissive* parents too little. *Authoritative* parents know when and how to discipline their children (Baumrind, 1971, 1973). What are the practical steps you can take to travel this middle road? According to a vast number of research studies, the following guidelines are effective in teaching children to control aggressive impulses; have good self-control, high self-esteem, and confidence; and be cheerful, thoughtful, and helpful (Maccoby, 1980):

- *Be consistent in enforcing specific rules and demands*. Do not give in to the child's whining or tantrums, or let the child break rules behind your back. Inconsistency—letting the child pull the cat's tail on Tuesday but not on Thursday—encourages the undesirable behavior.
- *Set high expectations that are appropriate to the child's age, and teach the child how to meet them*. Some parents make few demands on their children, either intentionally (they believe a parent should not "impose" standards) or accidentally. Others set many demands and standards, such as requiring children to be polite, help with chores, control their anger, be thoughtful of others, do well in school. The children of well-meaning parents who make few demands tend to be aggressive, impulsive, and immature. The children of parents who have demands and ex-

pectations tend to be helpful rather than selfish and above average in competence and self-confidence. However, the demands must be appropriate for the child's age. You can't expect 2-year-olds to dress themselves, and before you can expect children to get ready for school by themselves they have to know how to work an alarm clock.

▪ *Establish open communication with your child.* Enforce rules and requirements, but talk to children and explain your reasons. "Because I say so" isn't enough. This doesn't mean you have to argue with a 4-year-old about the merits of table manners. You can set standards for your children, but also allow them to express disagreements and feelings.

▪ *Notice, approve of, and reward good behavior.* Many parents tend to punish the behavior they dislike, a form of attention that may actually be rewarding to the child. But it is much more effective to praise the behavior you *do* want, which teaches the child what is right.

▪ *Call the child's attention to the effect of his or her actions on others, and teach the child to take another person's point of view.* As we saw in this chapter, this lesson teaches empathy and consideration for others. Vague orders, such as "Don't fight!", are less effective than showing the child how his fighting disrupts and hurts others. For boys especially, there is a strong negative relationship between aggression and empathy: The higher the one, the lower the other (Feshbach, 1983; Feshbach et al., 1983).

▪ *Temper your teachings to the child's temperament.* All of these guidelines depend on how the child reacts to them and how the child interprets your actions. You cannot turn a calm child into a bundle of energy. You cannot create the "ideal child," that is, one who is an exact replica of you. But you *can* expect the best from your children—their best, not yours.

KEY WORDS

maturation 459
germinal, embryonic, fetal stages 460
fetal alcohol syndrome 461
motor reflexes 462
synchrony 464
temperament 464
myelin 465
assimilation and accommodation 467
object permanence 468
representational thought 468
operations 468
egocentric thought 468
conservation 468
babbling phase 471
overgeneralization 472
telegraphic speech 472
language acquisition device 474

socialization 476
attachment 476
bonding 477
stranger anxiety 477
separation anxiety 477
the Strange Situation 477
sex typing 478
gender identity 479
gender schema theory 479
androgyny 480
induction 483
power assertion 483
love withdrawal 483
stages of moral reasoning 487
empathy 489
altruism 489
shame and guilt 490

SUMMARY

1. Babies are born with basic motor reflexes that are necessary for survival, including the grasping, startle, sucking, and "rooting" reflexes. At first, they can see only a distance of 8 inches, but within a few weeks they can distinguish where something is and what it is. Babies also develop *synchrony* of pace and rhythm with their caretakers.

2. Physical development is very rapid during the first year. On the average, babies sit without support at 7 months, crawl at 9 months, and take their first steps at 13 months. Brain development, including the growth of *myelin*, progresses rapidly.

3. Jean Piaget proposed that children's cognitive development depends on their current developmental stage and their experience in the world. Children's thinking changes and adapts through two processes, *assimilation* and *accommodation*. Piaget proposed four stages of cognitive development: *sensory-motor* (birth to age 2), during which the child learns *object permanence*; *preoperational* (ages 2 to 7), during which language and symbolic thought develop; *concrete operations* (ages 6 or 7 to 11); and *formal operations* (age 12 to adulthood).

4. In evaluating Piaget, researchers find some problems and some support. Young children have more cognitive abilities, at earlier ages, than Piaget thought, and they are not entirely egocentric in their thinking. Moreover, cognitive development does not seem to work in a set of "stages," in which the same mode of thought applies to all problems. But the *sequence* of development that Piaget observed does hold up.

5. Language development begins with a "babbling phase," from age 6 months to a year, and with nonverbal but symbolic gestures. At about 1 year, one-word utterances begin. At age 2, children speak in two- or three-word *telegraphic* sentences that convey a variety of messages. By age 3 or 4, they create longer sentences but often incorrectly *overgeneralize* grammatical rules. Language seems to reflect the growing complexity of thought.

6. Language develops through a combination of biological readiness and social experience. Parents do not "teach" language nor do children "learn" it according to behavioral principles. However, certain parental practices are helpful to the child, such as speaking more slowly and repeating correct sentences verbatim. There may be a critical period in which children who are not exposed to social relationships will never learn to speak.

7. In human beings, hormones do not account for maternal "*bonding*" to the newborn infant. Infants and caretakers usually become *attached* to each other over time; by the age of 7 to 12 months, babies often feel *stranger anxiety* and *separation anxiety*. Attachment occurs whether the mother is home full time or the child is in day care.

8. Several theories attempt to account for *sex typing*, the process by which boys and girls become "masculine" or "feminine," and *gender identity*, the cognitive understanding that one is biologically male or female. Psychoanalytic theory emphasizes the child's identification with the same-sex parent. Social learning theory emphasizes the rewards, punishments, and vicarious examples that children get in behaving appropriately or inappropriately for their gender. Cognitive developmental theory holds that children "sex-type" themselves, as their cognitive abilities mature, naturally perceiving and valuing the activities associated with their gender. Gender schema theory adds that culturally determined "gender schemas" divide the world into male and female spheres.

9. In human beings, fathering depends on how societies are structured, and it varies widely across individuals. In general, fathers tend to be more physically stimulating, playful, and unpredictable than mothers, and to do less of the routine child care.

10. Parental methods of discipline, such as *induction* and *power assertion*, have different results. Induction is associated with children who develop empathy, internalized moral standards, and a sense of internal control, and who can resist temptation. Power assertion is associated with children who have a sense of external control, are aggressive and destructive, and show a lack of empathy and moral behavior.

11. Divorce usually affects children of all ages, although the specific effects depend on the age and gender of the child, whether the father maintains contact, and how bitter the divorce was.

12. Lawrence Kohlberg's theory of moral development proposes three levels of moral reasoning: *preconventional morality* (based on rules, punishment, and self-interest), *conventional morality* (based on relationships and rules of justice and law), and *postconventional ("principled") morality*, based on higher principles of human rights. The theory has been criticized for its middle-class, educational bias; its bias against women; and its assumption that people don't ''regress'' to a lower stage once they reach a higher one.

13. Moral development also depends on the emergence of the ''moral emotions''—empathy, shame, and guilt. Empathy takes different forms, depending on the child's age and cognitive abilities: *global* empathy, *egocentric* empathy, and *empathy for another's life condition*. Shame develops with the sense of self, around age 2; guilt develops when children have an internal standard of behavior, about age 3 or 4.

14. Altruistic (helpful) children tend to come from families in which they contribute to the family's well-being, carry out many tasks, and respect parental authority, and in which parents set limits without being arbitrary.

15. Some psychologists believe that no year of life is as critical as the first one, but many studies have failed to show the stability of infant qualities. With the exception of serious disorders, most childhood problems are outgrown by late adolescence or adulthood.

CHAPTER 14

Adolescence, Adulthood, and Aging

When you are ignorant, old age is a famine.
When you are learned, it is a harvest.

JEWISH PROVERB

Age only matters when one is aging. Now that I have arrived at a great age, I might just as well be twenty.

PABLO PICASSO (AT 80)

*A*dult life used to be fairly consistent and predictable, and so were studies of middle-class adult development. You would marry in your late teens or early 20s. You would have your last child by your mid-30s. By your late-40s, you would be going through your final job decisions (if you were male) or through menopause (if you were female). By your mid-50s, you would be a doting grandparent, and by your mid-60s, you would be in retirement. Everyone, including you, would agree you were "set in your ways."

When psychologists first began longitudinal studies, following people's lives from childhood to adulthood, they would come around every ten years or so and draw conclusions about the consistency of personality and stages of life (Kagan & Moss, 1962). Now psychologists come around every ten years and find that people have changed their names, jobs, houses, and spouses. Grandma is not home minding the grandchildren; she and Grandpa have bought a trailer and are camping in Yosemite. Mom has gone to work as an investment banker and Dad has quit business to become a jazz musician. Your sister has eloped with her secretary, Roger, and your brother has married his ex-wife's ex-husband's half-sister. No one is doing things on schedule, either. Your cousin Harriet just had her first baby at 16, and your Aunt Henrietta just had *her* first baby at 45.

On the psychology shelves of your local bookstore, you will find books that try to make sense of the often bewildering changes in American life and help readers cope with them. There are books on the anguish of adolescence; the normal "passages" of adult life; how to get through your "midlife crisis"; how to shift careers; and how to manage divorce, remarriage, retirement, and widowhood. Most of these books reflect one of three popular views of adult development:

- Adult development, like child development, proceeds in a series of biologically programmed stages. An internal clock, governed by the rise and fall of hormones, directs the passages of adulthood.
- Adult development is difficult, but it can occur through intensive efforts to liberate the "real self." By thinking about yourself and trying to fulfill your potential, you can become anything you want.
- Adults don't really develop, because the personality is formed in childhood. You can tinker with the basic blueprint but can never make major alterations.

Research shows, surprisingly, that all three viewpoints have serious flaws. In this chapter, we will show why they do, as we report new approaches to the study of development over the entire life span. In particular, we will explore three primary influences on adult development:

Aging isn't what it used to be: Hulda Crooks, age 91, climbing Mt. Fuji.

1. *The biological clock.* After the growth spurt of puberty and adolescence, there are few dramatic biological changes that occur in adulthood (apart from the menopause for women). But the normal physiology of aging does influence adult life.

2. *The "social clock."* Most people in a society experience certain events at roughly the same age. American children go to school at age 5 or 6. Almost all 16-year-olds learn to drive a car. Most Americans are married by age 25. Most employees retire at age 65.

3. *Circumstances.* Adults are influenced by the era in which they were born, by the kinds of situations they find themselves in, and by unexpected events. For instance, the generation you were born into—your age *cohort*—affects your attitudes, expectations (will life be easy or a struggle?), and opportunities. When there is a large "generation gap" between parents and offspring, friends can have more influence on adult development than does family. Adults are also affected by situations and activities, such as the kind of work they do, that may permit (even require) changes in personality and behavior—or that keep people in ruts. Finally, life is full of unexpected chance influences: winning the lottery, being in a serious accident, getting pregnant without planning to.

People's lives aren't as predictable as they used to be, and old theories of adult development have had to be reconsidered. Jerome Kagan (1984) uses the example of a marble rolling down a trough. Just because it rolls in a straight line, he says, we cannot infer that there is something in the nature of marbles that makes them roll in a straight line. But that is the mistake we have made with people. In the last decades, the troughs that once kept people on the straight and narrow path have broken down, and the human marbles are spilling out in all directions.

Growing Up and Growing Old: The Biological Clock

Children's development is influenced to a great extent by physical maturation. Once individuals are past childhood, are they subject to other genetically programmed biological upheavals that mark adult life? It seems that there are at least three adult phases: adolescence, with the hormonal changes that bring sexual maturity; midlife, with another set of hormonal changes that bring women's reproductive capacity to an end; and old age, with the deterioration of some physical abilities.

There are many popular impressions about all of these phases of development. Adolescents are assumed to undergo severe emotional turbulence and rebellion. This agitation eventually settles down in adulthood, to be reawakened during midlife, when, supposedly, women undergo traumatic menopause and men have a comparable "midlife crisis." Finally, many people believe that the older you get, the more you lose: your sex drive, your memory, your brain cells, your energy, your intelligence. In this section, we will look at the scientific evidence that has put these ideas to the test.

The adolescent experience

Adolescence refers to the period of development between **puberty** (the onset of sexual maturity) and adulthood. In some cultures, the time span between puberty and adulthood is only a few months. Once sexually mature, a boy or girl is expected

adolescence *The period of development between puberty (a biological event) and adulthood (a social event).*

puberty *The age at which a person becomes capable of sexual reproduction.*

Boys and girls typically reach puberty at different times, as everyone who took a coed dancing class in grade school remembers.

to marry and assume adult tasks. In our society, adolescence lasts several years. Teenagers may be biologically mature, but they are not considered to be emotionally mature enough to be full-fledged adults. It is believed that they are not yet ready to assume the rights, responsibilities, and roles of adulthood. The long span of adolescence is new to this century. In the past, societies needed the labor of young people and could not afford to have them idle away a decade in school or in a leisurely program of "self-discovery" (Kett, 1977).

So adolescence begins with a biological marker (puberty), but it ends with a social marker (the society's definition of adulthood, such as the legal age to vote, marry, or join the military). In some societies and religions, the child goes through a social ritual, called a "rite of passage," that commemorates the arrival of adulthood.

Biological development. Throughout childhood, both boys and girls produce about the same amount of male hormones (androgens) and female hormones (estrogens). At puberty, the hypothalamus in the brain sends messages to the pituitary gland saying, in effect, "Childhood's over! Get on with adult life!" The pituitary gland, in turn, stimulates increased hormone production in the adrenal and other endocrine glands and in the reproductive glands. (In boys, these are the testes, which produce sperm. In girls, the reproductive glands are the ovaries, which release eggs, or ova.) Now boys have a higher level of androgens than girls do, and girls have a higher level of estrogens than boys do.

During puberty, the sex organs mature and the individual becomes capable of reproduction. In girls, the onset of menstruation (called **menarche**) and the development of breasts are major signs of sexual maturity. In boys, the major signs are the onset of nocturnal emissions and the growth of the testes and scrotum. Hormones are also responsible for the emergence of *secondary sex characteristics*, such as a deepened voice and facial and chest hair (in boys) and pubic hair (in both sexes).

The changing rise and fall of hormones may contribute to the rapid mood swings that some adolescents feel, to the depth of their passions, and to their sensation of being out of control of their emotions. In one study, teenagers described their thoughts and feelings at random intervals for a week, whenever they were "beeped" on a pager they carried with them. The most striking result was the frequency and extent of emotional changes, from highs to lows. Adolescents who had the greatest mood swings were just as happy and well adjusted, however, as their steadier peers (Csikszentmihalyi & Larson, 1984).

menarche [men-ARE-kee]
The onset of menstruation.

The dramatic physical changes of puberty are the last "growth spurt" on the child's road to adulthood. For girls, the adolescent growth spurt begins, on the average, at age 10, peaks at 12 or 13, and stops at about age 16, by which time most girls are sexually mature. For boys, the average adolescent growth spurt starts at about age 12 and ends at about age 18. This difference in the rates of development is often a source of misery to adolescents, for most girls mature sooner than most boys.

There is, however, enormous individual variation in the onset and length of puberty. Some girls menstruate as early as age 8 and others do not begin until age 15. One 15-year-old male may be as developed as an adult man and another will still be a boy. In addition, just to be mischievous, nature has seen fit to make growth a jumpy, irregular, uneven business. Different parts of the body mature at different rates, a phenomenon called *asynchrony*. A girl may have undeveloped breasts but adult-sized hands and feet. A boy may be tall and gangly but have no trace of a longed-for beard. Eventually, everything catches up.

Intellectual development. During one's adolescence, cognitive development reaches its adult level. According to Jean Piaget, at about age 12, young people reach the stage of *formal operations* and begin to use abstract reasoning. They understand that ideas can be compared and classified, just as objects can. They shift from concrete operations to deductive reasoning, using premises common to their culture and experience. From here on, the further development of thinking depends on education, accumulated knowledge, and the integration of experience and observation known as wisdom.

Recent research, however, shows that not all adolescents develop the ability for formal operational thought or complex moral reasoning (Laboratory, 1984). Some never do. Others continue to think "concretely" unless a specific problem requires abstract thought. Psychologists disagree about why some children proceed to formal operations and others do not. Perhaps education helps. Taking lots of math and science may teach deductive and abstract reasoning, although it is also possible that teenagers who are already good at deductive and abstract reasoning take lots of math and science. Perhaps temperament has something to do with it. Calm, reflective children seem more likely than impulsive children to have the patience for formal operations (Neimark, 1975). Perhaps it depends on culture. Cultures value different cognitive abilities, and children develop the skills they need to get along in their communities (Laboratory, 1984).

Rebellious-teenager movies and studies of troubled teens depict adolescence as a time of storm and stress. What is missing from this portrait of adolescence?

Psychological development. The biological storms of puberty are reputed to carry over into psychological storms: insecurity about oneself in relation to friends, dislike of one's newly mature body, a fierce and unhappy struggle for self-identity, and a distrust and dislike of parents. This view represents the "turmoil theory of adolescent development." It argues that adolescent anguish and rebellion are necessary and inevitable, the means by which teenagers separate themselves psychologically from their parents and form their own identities (Blos, 1962; G. Hall, 1904).

It is certainly true that adolescence can be difficult for many teenagers. It is a transition time, a "farewell to childhood," in which adolescents are learning the rules of adult sexuality, morality, work, and family (L. Kaplan, 1984). Teenagers are beginning to develop their own standards and values, and often do so by "trying on" the styles, actions, and attitudes of their peers (in contrast to those of their parents). They are growing more independent of their parents. They are questioning adult life, even as they are rehearsing for it (Douvan, 1986; Douvan & Adelson, 1966).

The varieties of adolescence. *The adolescent stereotype emphasizes teenage turmoil and rebellion (top left). But most teens feel good about themselves and their communities, as do the students at a high school car-wash fund-raiser (lower left), and many hold jobs to earn income (above).*

For some teenagers, these changes can feel overwhelming and lead to loneliness, depression, and a sense of isolation. But such feelings do not give us the whole picture. In fact, studies of representative samples of normal teenagers find that extreme turmoil and unhappiness are the exception, not the rule. For instance, a massive study of more than 20,000 teenagers surveyed between 1962 and 1982 found that the vast majority reported feeling happy, strong, and self-confident (Offer & Sabshin, 1984a). They did not feel inferior to others and they did not feel that others were treating them badly. They felt in control of their lives. They liked their parents and did not have major conflicts with them. They felt that their parents understood and loved them, even when the parents were being strict. The majority even liked the recent changes in their bodies and did not feel ugly or clumsy. (Boys had a more positive body image than girls, however. Four girls in ten said they often felt ugly and ashamed of their bodies.)

This research found that most adolescents travel one of three routes to adulthood, depending on their genetic endowment, childhood experiences, opportunities, coping skills, and social life (Offer & Sabshin, 1984b). Most teenagers have few emotional upsets. They have supportive families, a sense of purpose and self-confidence, good friends, and the skill to cope with problems. Others have a bumpier ride, having suffered parental divorce, the death of a close relative, or serious illness. Their self-esteem wavers; they are more dependent on the positive evaluation of peers and parents and more subject to discouragement. A third group, about 20 percent of all teenagers, have a tumultuous adolescence. They have behavioral problems at school and at home. They report more difficulties than satisfactions in their lives. Their backgrounds tend to be less stable, more fraught with conflicts and problems, and less advantageous than those of the other two groups. They feel less happy and secure, and they mistrust adults.

Of course, adolescents of different races, cultures, and social classes have different experiences as teenagers—they differ in average age at puberty, in sexual and social rules, and in expectations about work. Black adolescents, on the average, face greater economic problems (such as unemployment) and discrimination than whites; that alone makes a certain amount of struggle and stress more likely. Yet the black teenager's overall self-esteem is as high as that of whites, and black adolescent girls have *higher* self-esteem, on the average, than white girls (Bush & Simmons, 1987).

There are, in short, many "normal" ways to be an adolescent. Turmoil is only one of them.

QUICK ■ QUIZ

If you're not feeling rebellious, try these questions.

1. Puberty marks the biological beginning of adolescence.
2. All societies everywhere agree when adulthood begins.
3. The average girl matures earlier than the average boy.
4. The onset of menstruation is called _____.
5. In boys, a deepening voice and a new mustache are examples of _____.
6. Emotional turmoil and rebellion are inevitable in adolescence.

Answers:

1. T 2. F 3. T 4. menarche 5. secondary sex characteristics 6. F

Menopause and midlife

The biology of aging affects people all through life, as a 27-year-old "aging" tennis champion or a 20-year-old "over-the-hill" Olympic gymnast can tell you. For most people, though, the next chiming of the biological clock occurs at midlife, with different consequences for men and women.

Here are some common assumptions about the "typical" menopausal woman: She suffers from a "syndrome" or "deficiency disease." She has numerous complaints, mental and physical. She is deeply regretful about losing her reproductive capacity, her sexuality, her femininity. Often she becomes deeply depressed. Are any of these assumptions true?

In women in their 40s, the ovaries begin to produce less estrogen. When women are in their late 40s or early 50s, menstruation stops, and soon thereafter the production of ova stops as well. This is called the **menopause**, and the entire process of declining reproductive ability is called the **climacteric** or *climacterium*. The ovaries stop producing the hormones estrogen and progesterone, although some estrogen continues to be produced by the adrenal glands. (Female smokers enter menopause nearly two years sooner than nonsmokers, because of the effects of smoking on hormone production [McKinlay, Bifano, & McKinlay, 1985].) The

menopause *The cessation of menstruation; usually a gradual process lasting up to several years.*

climacteric *The period of decreasing reproductive capacity in women, culminating in menopause.*

drastic decline of estrogen produces some uncomfortable physical symptoms in some menopausal women, such as "hot flashes," fatigue, and rapid heartbeat.

However, most women go through menopause with no particular psychological difficulties and very few physical ones. In a large survey of more than 8000 randomly chosen women, the majority viewed menopause positively (with relief that they no longer had to worry about pregnancy or periods) or neutrally (no particular feelings at all). The vast majority did not feel regret at reaching menopause; only 3 percent said they did. The vast majority did not report troubling physical symptoms or become a burden on medical services. Apart from having some "temporarily bothersome symptoms," such as hot flashes, sweating, and menstrual irregularity, most women say that menopause is simply "no big deal" (McKinlay & McKinlay, 1984).

Then where do so many people get the idea that it is? According to the researchers who did this large survey, this false impression is based on women who go to physicians or therapists because they have special worries or medical problems. By definition, such women are unrepresentative. Because most studies of menopausal women were, until recently, conducted on such atypical patients, many people concluded that menopause causes a "crisis."

The loss of fertility, however, *is* an important biological marker for women in one way, because it means that they must make final decisions about having children. Working women in their 30s often speak of being "up against the biological clock" because questions about having children cannot be postponed much longer (Daniels & Weingarten, 1982; Fabe & Wikler, 1979).

Some writers have proposed that men go through a "male menopause" that parallels the female version (Levinson, 1978; McGill, 1980; Mayer, 1978). For men, however, there is no biological equivalent to menopause. Testosterone does seem to peak during adolescence, but researchers disagree about when, whether, and how much it declines during adulthood. In any case, testosterone never drops as sharply in men as estrogen does in women, and men do not lose their fertility, though their sperm count may slowly diminish.

There is a big difference between a physical issue (such as changes in hormone levels) and a psychological one (such as fear of death). The biological *fact* of aging does not itself predict how people will *feel* about aging. Many popular writers have assumed that aging always produces a psychological crisis. As we will see, aging may be universal, but crises are not.

The riddle of aging

There are two general theories about aging. One theory, until recently taken for granted, is that aging is a normal part of development. An individual is born, grows older, reaches a peak, declines, and dies. It's all built into the cells; there might even be a "death gene" that sets a limit on the human life span. The trouble is, this "normal" development is still a mystery. Genes do set a *maximum life span* for a species—about 13 years for a rabbit, 113 years for a human being—and this span has remained constant for the last 30,000 years (Cunningham & Brookbank, 1988). But an individual's *life expectancy* will vary, depending on environment, nutrition, disease, and heredity. Researchers have identified some of the genetic abnormalities that can reduce life expectancy, but no one has identified a "death gene" or knows why bodily functions slow down (Newton, Lazarus, & Weinberg, 1984).

A second theory is that aging is *not* normal or inevitable, but a result of damage to cells or a slow decline in immune function. Over many years, cells may be

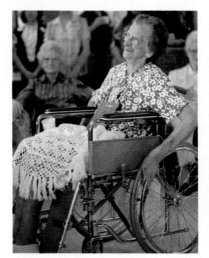  

The varieties of "old age."
Stereotypes about old people are breaking down as more and more people are living longer, healthier lives. Of three 80-year-olds, one may be ailing and infirm, one may be healthy and active, and a third might be exceptionally capable and strong.

damaged in many ways, for different reasons—such as mutations in DNA or mistakes in the process of synthesizing proteins. So far no one knows whether all cells become defective for the same reason, or which kind of damage can be avoided. The immune function argument holds that we become sick, weak, and eventually die because degenerative diseases are no longer held in check by the immune system, the cells that fight infection and that regulate the fighter cells (Burnet, 1970; Laudenslager & Reite, 1984).

On the average, the body reaches its peak efficiency at about age 30 and then slowly declines. Certainly, biological aging does impose limits on what people can do as they grow older. Heart, lung, and muscle capacity weaken. Metabolism and reflexes slow down. Physical changes in the eye reduce the amount of light that reaches the retina, so visual sharpness decreases. Older adults often lose some of their hearing ability, especially for tones in the higher register. The sense of smell declines after age 65 and drops sharply after age 80 (Cunningham & Brookbank, 1988; Doty, 1985). The central nervous system processes information more slowly than it once did, so older people often take longer to react. The skin loses moisture and elasticity, causing wrinkles and bags. The hair gets thinner and whiter; many men get balder.

It is not all bad news, though. The field of **gerontology** has made astonishing advances in separating the processes that are normal in aging from those that are a result of illness or preventable conditions (see "A Closer Look at Gerontology" for some heartening news about your own future old age). Moreover, researchers are beginning to investigate the *benefits* of aging: wisdom, experience, a sense of humor, and old-fashioned maturity (Erikson, Erikson, & Kivnick, 1986; Helson & Wink, 1987). As people age, they tend to feel less angry, happier, and more content with themselves and their limitations. In a society that values youth and the "new," it is easy to overlook the values of experience and the "old."

Nevertheless, being 75 is definitely not the same as being 25. What changes, and what does not?

Memory and intelligence. Although folklore has it that the brain loses brain cells the way a scalp sheds dandruff, studies of animals and people question this gloomy forecast. Normal human aging does not produce extensive brain cell deterioration until, perhaps, extreme old age (M. Diamond, 1985). There is some decrease in the number of working neurons and in brain weight, but individuals vary

gerontology *The study of aging and the old.*

enormously. What is more, there is no direct evidence that changes in neural structures are connected to changes in intellectual performance (Horn & Donaldson, 1980).

Longitudinal studies that follow people from the middle years into old age suggest that some aspects of intelligence, such as reasoning, spatial ability, and verbal comprehension, do decline with age. However, researchers disagree about whether this decline is natural in all older people or whether it holds only for specific generations. Many people *don't* show a decline, and some even improve their intellectual abilities (Baltes, Dittmann-Kohli, & Dixon, 1984). What appears to be an intellectual decline in old age may really be a result of lack of education and stimulation. As we saw in Chapter 12, a short-term training program for people between 60 and 80 was able to produce gains in intellectual ability that were as large as the losses typical for that age group (Baltes & Willis, 1982).

The same issues occur in studies of memory. Older people can hold as much information in short-term memory as younger people do, whether the name of a person they just met or a phone number they just looked up (Fozard, 1980). Long-term memory plays tricks on everyone's ability to conjure up long-past events. Much of the mental decline that does occur in older adults is a result of poor health, poor education, or lack of practice. One study found that years of schooling and current enrollment in school were better predictors of differences in memory ability than age was (Zivian & Darjes, 1983).

As Robin West (1984) observes, most memory studies of older adults don't take place in the real world. It is important to remember to call your doctor or pay your bills, but it isn't very important to remember nonsense syllables. It turns out that older people can retrieve information from memory just as rapidly as younger people can when they know the material or when it is relevant to their lives. When older people have trouble with memory, the reason seems to be their impaired perceptual-motor skills—their slower reaction times—not impaired long-term memory. It is a shame, therefore, that many older people accept the negative assumptions about aging. When they can't remember a name, they say "Drat, I'm getting old." When younger people can't remember a name, they just say "Drat."

Finally, older adults are just as good as young ones at long-practiced abilities, which is why all kinds of people—lawyers, teachers, farmers, and insurance agents—continue their work well into old age (Hoyer & Plude, 1980). When people live in stimulating, interesting environments, their brain function does not "naturally" decay (M. Diamond, 1988). In a study of active people over the age of 88, Marian Diamond (1984) found that "the people who use their brains don't lose them."

Sexuality. Early surveys by sex researcher Alfred Kinsey and his associates (1948, 1953) suggested that men reach their sexual peak at age 18, women reach their sexual peak in their mid-30s, and after that it is all downhill. The idea of "peaks," however, has passed. Although later surveys have shown that the frequency of sexual activity declines over the life span, psychologists disagree about whether this drop is due to biological factors or to social factors such as job stress, sexual boredom or familiarity, marital conflict, overwork, or the *expectation* of sexual decline.

In later years, there are some biological changes in sexual response. Women produce less vaginal lubrication and men take longer to reach full erection. For both sexes, there are fewer contractions at orgasm. But these changes are not necessarily related to the frequency of sexual activity or pleasure. Many married couples say that they would like to make love more than they do, which suggests that their

Your grandparents are slowly losing their mental sharpness. Everyone tells you that's normal and inevitable. Are they right? What might cause intellectual decline in old age, besides age itself?

A Closer Look at Gerontology

The Coming of Age

As sciences go, *gerontology*—the study of aging and the old—is a baby. The reason is simple. "It used to be," says one gerontologist, "that people didn't age. They died" (Gibbs, 1988). As life expectancy has lengthened in this century, more and more people have been living into their 70s, 80s, and beyond. Moreover, most have been living well, feeling just fine.

The percentage of the population that is over 65 is growing rapidly. In 1900, only 4 percent of the total population was over 65; today, it's around 12 percent; and by 2030, it's projected to be as high as 18 percent. Thanks to the "aging boom," gerontologists now have plenty to do. Some are physiological psychologists who study the biology and genetics of aging. Some are cognitive psychologists, interested in the mental abilities and problems of older people. Still others, from social and health psychology, study the attitudes and environments that distinguish older people who live well and happily from those who don't. (Not all gerontologists are psychologists, however. They come from many other fields as well.)

The results from this exploding field of research have been, in a word, revolutionary. "Old" used to

imply forgetful, stooped, and physically and mentally feeble. But three new developments are changing people's minds about the stereotypes of "old age":

1. *The definition of* old *got older.* Not long ago you would have been considered old in your 60s. Today, "old age" is not a simple matter of chronological years. Indeed, the elderly can be divided into two groups: the "young old," who have their health, strength, and mental capacities, and the "old old," who are infirm, weak, and incapacitated (Neugarten, 1974).

2. *Aging was separated from illness.* People used to think that all bodily functions declined with age. Some conditions, such as osteoporosis (having extremely brittle bones) or *senility* (the loss of mental abilities), were assumed to be inevitable. Today, gerontologists have found that many of the conditions thought characteristic of old age are really a result of cellular damage, malnutrition, overmedication, or disease. For example, only 15 percent of the people over age 65 suffer serious mental impairment, and half of those cases are due to Alzheimer's disease, a neurological disorder (Cunningham &

problem is finding the time, not losing their hormones. Among old people, the main sexual problem is lack of a partner, not lack of desire. Longitudinal studies show that sexual interest and capacity typically last over the life span, unless illness or the death of one's partner intervenes (Brecher, 1984; Turner & Adams, 1988; Winn & Newton, 1982).

The greatest difference in sexual activity is not between the old and the young but between individuals. The frequency of a person's sexual experiences in early adulthood is the best predictor of his or her sexual experiences in later life (Martin, 1981; Wade & Cerise, in press). People who prefer to have sex infrequently tend to remain consistent. People who enjoy sex frequently are likewise consistent. As a female respondent to a sex survey once wrote, "I am 60 years old and they say you never get too old to enjoy sex. I know, because once I asked my Grandma when you stop liking it and she was 80. She said, 'Child, you'll have to ask someone older than me' " (Tavris, 1977).

Sex researchers agree with brain researchers on a simple rule of aging: "Use it or lose it." The common denominators of a healthy old age, says Marian Diamond (1984), are "activity, and love of life and love of others and being loved. Love is very basic."

Brookbank, 1988). Free of disease, many people live into their 80s and longer without serious mental or physical decline.

3. *The biology of aging was separated from its psychology.* Imagine that you are taken from your home, your friends, and your work. You are put in a residence where you know no one and have nothing to do. Your relatives live too far away to visit. You aren't allowed to make decisions, decorate your room, keep a pet, have a lover, or choose your food. "Just relax and have a good time," your caretakers tell you. What would happen to you? Most likely, you would become listless, depressed, and bored. You would become forgetful, lazy, and apathetic. You would become, in a word, "old."

Gerontologists have found that many of the problems of "old age" would occur to most people who were deprived of loved ones, close friends, meaningful activity, intellectual stimulation, and control over what happens to them (Rodin, 1988). When nursing-home residents have responsibilities and incentives for good memory, their apathy declines and their memory improves (Langer, 1989; Langer et al., 1979). When old people feel they have a purpose in life, they feel younger than their chronological age ("I'm just a kid at heart") and their well-being flourishes (Baum & Boxley, 1983).

Gerontologists also study the social consequences of having an aging population—something that will affect you no matter how old you are now. With a projected 18 percent of the population over age 65 by 2030, imagine the possible effects on TV advertising and content, movies, consumer goods, demand for health care, and changes in retirement policies! When the current "baby boom" reaches retirement age, how will younger (and smaller) generations support the older generation's medical and financial needs? Should healthy, vigorous 65-year-olds be forced to retire? Should wealthy 65-year-olds be entitled to Medicare and social security?

Some observers forecast a confrontation between the young (many of whom are not as financially successful or secure as they expected to be) and the old (many of whom are financially better off than they expected) over the distribution of the country's resources. They warn of the coming "age wars." Gerontologists hope this crisis can be averted, that aging can be made as comfortable as possible—not only for the old, but for everyone.

Young adults do not have a corner on sexuality. Desire and sensuality are life-long pleasures.

QUICK ■ QUIZ

What do you remember about aging?

1. The biological clock inevitably causes **(a)** menopause, **(b)** loss of male fertility, **(c)** loss of sexual interest, **(d)** forgetfulness.
2. Most women react to menopause by **(a)** feeling depressed, **(b)** regretting the loss of femininity, **(c)** feeling relieved or neutral, **(d)** going crazy.
3. Which of the following has *not* been found to affect aging and eventual death? **(a)** the genetically determined maximum life span, **(b)** a death gene, **(c)** poor nutrition, **(d)** heredity
4. Which of the following abilities tend to decline predictably with age? (Choose all that apply.) **(a)** hearing, **(b)** memory, **(c)** perceptual-motor skills, **(d)** intelligence, **(e)** ability to work, **(f)** sexual pleasure, **(g)** wisdom, **(h)** sense of humor, **(i)** reaction time

Answers:

1. a   2. c   3. b   4. a, c, i

Stages and Ages:
The Psychological Clock

According to ancient Greek legend, the Sphinx was a monster, half lion, half woman, who terrorized passersby on the road to Thebes. The Sphinx would ask each traveler a question, and murder those who failed to answer correctly. The question was this: What animal walks on four feet in the morning, two feet at noon, and three feet in the evening? Only one traveler, Oedipus, knew the solution to the riddle. The animal, he said, is Man, who crawls on all fours as a baby, walks upright as an adult, and limps in old age with the aid of a staff.

The Sphinx was the first life span theorist. Since then, many philosophers, writers, and scientists have speculated on the course of adult life, expanding the Sphinx's three basic stages into seven, eight, or ten. Shakespeare suggested seven ages: infant, schoolboy, lover, soldier, just man, foolish old man, and doddering state of "second childhood." (On women's stages Shakespeare, like many men before and since, was silent.) The idea of stages was terrifically appealing. Everyone could see that children go through stages of physical maturation. It made sense to assume that adults go through parallel stages of psychological maturation.

Erikson and stage theories

One of the first psychologists in this century to emphasize growth and change over the entire life span was Alfred Adler, who, as we saw in Chapter 11, broke from the traditional Freudian view that personality development stops in childhood. Adler emphasized two influences on adult change: the social factors that influence us throughout life and the ability to control our own destinies.

A fuller theory was later proposed by psychoanalyst Erik H. Erikson (1950/ 1963, 1987). Erikson argued that everyone passes through eight developmental stages on the way to wisdom and maturity. Erikson called his theory "psychosocial," instead of "psychosexual" as Freud had, because he believed that people are propelled by psychological and social forces, not just by sexual motives. Each stage, said Erikson, represents a combination of biological drives and societal demands. At each one, there is a "crisis" you must solve before you can proceed to the next.

The first stage, during the baby's first year, produces the crisis of *trust versus mistrust*. A baby must blindly trust others to provide food, comfort, cuddling, and warmth. If these needs are not met, the child may never develop the basic trust necessary to get along in the world.

The second stage, as the baby becomes a toddler, sets up the crisis of *autonomy (independence) versus shame and doubt*. The young child is learning to "stand on his own feet," said Erikson, and must do so without feeling ashamed of his behavior or too doubtful of his growing abilities.

The third stage is marked by the crisis of *initiative versus guilt*: The child is acquiring new physical and mental skills, setting goals, and enjoying newfound talents. At the same time, the child must learn to control impulses and energies. The danger lies in developing too strong a sense of guilt over his or her fantasies, newfound power, and childish instincts.

The fourth stage, the crisis of *competence* (originally "industry") *versus inferiority*, teaches the child, said Erikson, "to be a worker and potential provider." The child, now in school, is learning to make things, use tools, and acquire the skills for adult life. Children who fail these lessons of mastery and competence, Erikson argued, risk feeling inadequate and inferior.

The fifth stage, puberty, sets off the crisis of *identity versus role confusion*. You must decide what you are going to be and what you hope to make of your life. If you succeed, you will come out of this stage with a strong identity, ready to plan for the future. Otherwise, you will sink into confusion, unable to make decisions. The term *identity crisis* describes what Erikson considered to be the major conflict of adolescence.

The sixth stage sees the crisis of *intimacy versus isolation*. Once you have decided who you are, you must share yourself with another and learn to make commitments. No matter how successful you are in work, said Erikson, you are not developmentally complete until you are capable of intimacy.

According to Erikson, children must master a sense of competence and older adults must meet the need for "generativity" and nurturance. Do these challenges occur only during one "stage" of life?

The seventh stage involves the crisis of *generativity versus stagnation*. Now that you know who you are and have an intimate relationship, will you sink into complacency and selfishness, or will you experience generativity, the pleasure of creativity and renewal? Parenthood is the most common means for the successful resolution of this stage, but people can be productive, creative, and nurturant in other ways, in their work or their relationships with the younger generation. Erikson suggested that adults need children as much as children need adults, and that this stage reflects the need to create a living legacy.

The eighth and final crisis is that of *ego integrity versus despair*. As they age, people strive to reach the ultimate goal—wisdom, spiritual tranquillity, an acceptance of one's life and one's role in the larger scheme of things. Just as the healthy child will not fear life, said Erikson, the healthy adult will not fear death.

Some societies, Erikson maintained, make the transition from one stage to another relatively easy. If you know you are going to be a farmer like your mother and father and you have no alternative, then moving from adolescence into young adulthood is not a very painful or passionate step (unless you hate farming). If you have many choices, as adolescents in our society often do, the transition can become prolonged. Some people put off making choices indefinitely and never resolve their "identity crisis." Similarly, our society values both independence and attachment, so some individuals are unable to resolve Erikson's sixth crisis, that of intimacy versus isolation.

Stage theories have become increasingly popular since Erikson's work, possibly as a way to make sense of the bewildering changes in American life since World War II. In the 1970s there was a sudden spate of life-stage books, some by journalists and some by psychologists, that drew a lot of popular and academic attention. Journalist Gail Sheehy published a best-selling book, *Passages,* subtitled *The Predictable Crises of Adult Life.* George Vaillant (1977), in *Adaptation to Life,* analyzed a longitudinal study of privileged Harvard students and concluded that men go through Eriksonian stages even if the external circumstances of their lives differ. Roger Gould (1978), in *Transformations,* argued that the main issue of adult growth is the struggle to shuck off the chains of childhood, to liberate "previously undeveloped aspects of the self." Daniel Levinson and his associates (1978) followed with *The Seasons of a Man's Life,* which argued that there are universal periods that unfold in a natural sequence, like the four seasons of the year.

It was fun for readers to figure out what stage they were in and where they were heading. But are stage theories valid for everyone, or only for the middle-class white men (and a few women) who have made their way into these studies? Are these theories popular because they are accurate, or because, as one psychologist thinks, most of us "want predictability . . . and we desperately want definitions of 'normality' " (Kammen, 1979)?

Evaluating stage theories

It's fun to try to figure out what adult "stage" you're in. But what about all the people whose experiences don't divide up neatly into ten-year intervals? What is a better way of explaining the nature and diversity of adult changes?

Stage theories of adult development are important because they remind us that life is not over at age 10, 15, or even 21. Adults have different concerns at different ages, a result of their changing roles (student, professional, spouse, parent, grandparent) and their changing emotional needs. As Erikson showed, development is never finished once and for all; it is an ongoing process that continues throughout life. Erikson made a lasting contribution in identifying the essential concerns of adulthood: identity, competence, love and nurturance, the ability to enjoy life and accept death.

Adult life changes, however, are not like the stages of child development, for one important reason. Child development is powerfully governed by *maturational* and *biological* changes that are dictated by the genes. Children go through a stage of babbling before they enter the stage of talk; they crawl before they walk; they cry before they can say, "I'm feeling blue today." But as children mature, genes become less of a driving influence on their development, and environmental demands take on greater impact (Baltes, 1983). This means that adult "stages" cannot be as universal or as inevitable as childhood stages. Children are more alike than middle-aged adults or old people (Neugarten, 1982).

Moreover, the very definition of a stage means that you must master a lower stage before you can proceed to a higher one. You cannot win a marathon without first learning to run a few miles; you cannot write an essay until you have mastered basic grammar. Why, though, must you master an "identity crisis" before you learn to love? Don't issues of competence and inferiority recur throughout life? Is the need for "generativity" relevant only to adults in midlife?

Research has shown that adolescence *is* a time of confusion about identity and aspirations, and the college years see the greatest gains in self-understanding and the resolution of identity conflicts (Adams et al., 1985; Marcia, 1966, 1976). Many adolescents are unsure of their job goals, political and religious values, and sense of purpose or direction. However, an "identity crisis" is not limited to adolescence. An adult auto worker who is laid off and must find an entirely new career may have an identity crisis too (Holstein, 1983). Erikson's themes recur throughout life, in different order for different people. Many women become wives and mothers, being "intimate" and "generative," before they seek professional identities (Tesch & Whitbourne, 1982). "Competence" is not mastered once and for all; people learn new skills and give up old ones throughout their lives, and their sense of competence rises and falls (Schlossberg, 1984b).

If development does not occur predictably in adulthood, why and how does it occur at all?

QUICK ▪ QUIZ

At what stage is your understanding of stages?

1. Erik Erikson's theory of life stages is called the _____ theory of development.
2. The major psychological issue during adolescence, said Erikson, is called an _____ crisis.
3. A main difference between child and adult development is that **(a)** children are more vulnerable to the environment, **(b)** children are more influenced by biological changes, **(c)** children do not go through predictable stages.
4. The trouble with adult stage theories is that **(a)** they imply you have to "pass" one stage before going on, **(b)** life changes do not occur in ten-year phases, **(c)** people's lives are not as predictable as they once were, **(d)** the research has not been done with representative samples, **(e)** all of the above.

Answers:
1. psychosocial 2. identity 3. b 4. e

According to transition theory, *what matters in adult development is not how old you are but what you are doing. For example, having a child has predictable effects (it increases nurturance but often temporarily diminishes self-esteem), regardless of* when *you have a child. These two first-time mothers, one under 20 and the other over 40, have a lot in common despite their age difference.*

Adult Transitions: The Social Clock

Instead of focusing on stages, a second major approach to these questions concentrates on the transitions, or milestones, that mark adult life. Research in this area suggests that what matters in adult development is not how old you are, but what you are doing (Baum, 1988). *Having* a child has stronger effects on you than *when* you have a child (Helson, Mitchell, & Moane, 1984). Entering the work force has strong effects on your self-esteem and ambition regardless of *when* you start working (Kohn & Schooler, 1983; Lykes & Stewart, 1982). Men facing retirement confront similar issues whether they are retiring at 40, 50, or 60. Divorced people have similar problems whether they divorce at 30 or 50.

Transition theorists do not look for the "crises" in life, but rather the transitions from one role or situation to another—that is, the events that happen (or fail to happen) that cause us to change in some way. Four kinds of transitions can occur (Schlossberg, 1984a, 1989):

▪ *Anticipated transitions* are the events you plan for, expect, and rehearse: You go to school. You get married. You start a job. You get promoted. You have a child. You retire at age 65.

▪ *Unanticipated transitions* are the things that happen unexpectedly, with no preparation: You flunk out of school. You are fired from your job. You have triplets. You are forced to retire early.

▪ *Nonevent transitions* are the changes you expect to happen that don't: You don't get married. You can't have children. You aren't promoted. You planned to retire but need to keep working for the income.

▪ *Chronic hassle transitions* are the situations that may eventually require you to change or take action, but that rumble along uncomfortably for a long stretch: You aren't getting along with your spouse. Your mother gets a chronic illness and needs constant care. You have to deal with discrimination at your job. Your son keeps getting into trouble.

Notice that what is an anticipated change for one person (say, going to college) might be unanticipated for another. An upsetting, ''nonevent'' transition for one person (not getting married) can be a planned decision for another and not a transition at all. This approach acknowledges that nonevents and chronic situations cause us to change just as surely as actual events do, although perhaps less dramatically. It also recognizes that not all transitions create a crisis (see ''Taking Psychology with You'').

So we will look now at the transitions that occur, predictably and unpredictably, across the life cycle. Perhaps we should say ''life cycles.'' For we will see, as one psychologist put it, that ''There is not one process of aging, but many; there is not one life course followed, but multiple courses. . . . There is no one sequence of stages but many. The variety is as rich as the historic conditions people have faced and the current circumstances they experience'' (Pearlin, 1982).

"On time" and "off time"

Almost all of us can remember how carefully we compared our own development to our friends' growth in childhood and adolescence. Every new step was an occasion for gloom (if your best friend ''got ahead'' of you) or elation (when you got there too). In adulthood, we make the same comparisons. All my friends are married; why aren't I? All my friends know what work they want; why don't I? Everyone I know has children; am I ready?

Adults evaluate their development according to a **social clock** that determines whether they are ''on time'' for their age or ''off time'' (Neugarten, 1979). All cultures have social clocks that define the ''right time'' to marry, start work, and have children, but these clocks may differ greatly. In some societies, as we noted, young men and women are supposed to marry and start having children right after puberty, and work responsibilities come later. In others, a man may not marry until he has demonstrated his financial ability to support a family. Society's reactions to people who are ''off time'' vary as well, from amusement (''Ah, when will he grow up?'') to scorn, rejection, or pity (''Poor thing, she'll never get a husband if she spends all that time working'').

In the United States, different social clocks exist side by side. Races, ethnic groups, and men and women within groups often have different ''time schedules'' on which they base their lives. For instance, there is a traditional *feminine social clock* and a traditional *masculine occupational clock*. The feminine social clock for middle-class white women used to emphasize getting a husband and starting a family in one's early or middle 20s, with the first child within six years. The masculine occupational clock for middle- and upper-class men still specifies professional training in one's 20s, with subsequent steps up the ladder of success (promotions, raises, prestige) at regular intervals. It is better to be ''ahead of time'' on the masculine clock than ''on time,'' and interruptions are considered bad. Many women are now following the masculine occupational clock. Some try to combine their careers with the traditional timing of marriage and motherhood, others set the feminine clock forward, and others have stopped ''telling time'' altogether.

Doing the right thing at the right time, compared to your friends and family,

Marriage (and remarriage) now occur less predictably than they once did.

''social clock'' *A society's timetable for the ''right'' ages to marry, have children, start work, retire, and have other adult experiences.*

can make you feel satisfied, capable, and healthy. When nearly everyone goes through the same experience or enters a new role at the same time—school, driving a car, voting, marriage, having a baby—adjusting to the new experience is relatively easy (Stewart et al., 1982). People who wish to do things on time and cannot, for reasons out of their control, may feel inadequate, depressed, and dissatisfied.

In the next two sections, we will look first at some typical milestones, the anticipated transitions, of adult life. These are the events that happen to most people in the United States, usually on time but not always, that shape adult development. Then we will consider some of the forces that can shatter those milestones: the unanticipated transitions, the events that don't happen when they should, the random winds of chance.

Major milestones

Most members of every society share certain experiences that occur with age. Some of these experiences are the result of laws, national or local (getting a driver's license at 16, being able to drink at 21, retiring at 65). Some are a matter of custom (the average age of first marriage is about 23 for women, 25 for men). Some are a matter of living long enough (having grandchildren). These events have a *high* likelihood of occurring to *most* people, so they are the events that have attracted the attention of many life span psychologists (Baltes, 1983).

Starting out.   Which group faces the most difficult transition: people who are about to retire from work; people who face the midlife awareness of growing old; or young people, about to start their marriages and careers? The answer is the young people (Pearlin, 1982). The late teens and early 20s often bring many changes at once—finishing school, leaving home, making independent decisions, starting work or professional training, getting married, having children, moving to a new part of the country and a new home. Having so many new roles, new expectations, and new obligations may be why young adults report high levels of loneliness or a sense of feeling uprooted and unsettled (Rubenstein & Shaver, 1982).

Young adults are also "working on" several important psychological tasks. They are developing close friendships, some of which may last throughout their lives. Many young adults are also establishing a philosophy of life and a moral code that will influence their life choices. These may change with later experience, but young adults are aware for the first time that they are starting out on a life course and that they will have to make ethical and practical decisions (Arnstein, 1984; Neugarten, 1969).

Marriage or living alone.   Of all the milestones in adult life, the one that people take most for granted is getting married. Of course there are many factors involved in the timing of marriage and choice of partner, but here we want to draw your attention to one factor that has special power in shaping people's love lives and in setting the social clock an entire generation will follow: the availability of marriage partners.

Normally, each generation of babies has a nature-balanced ratio of males to females. But some events can create an unbalanced ratio in adulthood. Men may have to migrate from one region to another for work. Wars may deplete a generation of its young men. A "baby boom"—a sudden increase in the number of children born in a particular year—can also change the ratio of marriage partners (Guttentag & Secord, 1983). The reason is that in the United States and Canada, the

Graduation, the "commencement" of a new phase of life, is exhilarating—but then what? The young woman being interviewed by a corporate recruiter (right) may be learning what research shows: "Starting out"—graduating, finding work, establishing close relationships—is an exciting challenge, but can also cause worry and apprehension.

average young woman marries a man who is about two years older than she. Women who are born during a period of increasingly high birth rates will therefore outnumber the "older" men who are potential marriage partners. This is what happened to the baby-boom women born after World War II. When they came of marriageable age, there weren't enough men to go around. In 1970, for every 100 white women between the ages of 20 and 24, there were only 67 white men between the ages of 23 and 27. By 1990, because of low white birthrates in the 1970s, the sex ratio became roughly even again for young white women, but not for black women in any age group.

What happens when a generation of young people does not marry when they expect to? They change. In the 1960s and 1970s, millions of women went on to graduate school, entered careers, and postponed marriage and childbearing. Their aspirations and goals changed, and they began to value singlehood and independence. Men's attitudes about marriage and family changed, too. When men are a "scarce resource," they tend to postpone marriage and value sexual freedom and independence.

In contrast, when women are the scarce resource, as they were on the American frontier, societies tend to value monogamy, marriage, and traditional gender roles. These results of uneven sex ratios—more men to women in an age group or more women to men—have been similar whenever and wherever they have occurred, from ancient Greece to modern America (Guttentag & Secord, 1983). Think about how the sex ratio might be affecting some of your own attitudes and expectations about marriage, children, work, and sexuality. Have any of your plans been affected by your assumptions or expectations—pro or con—about marriage?

Whatever your answer, more and more Americans are living alone—and liking it. In 1940, fewer than 8 percent of all households consisted of adults living alone. By 1980, the figure was almost 25 percent: young single adults postponing marriage or choosing not to marry, divorced adults, never-married older adults, and widows and widowers (Alwin & Converse, 1984). Attitudes toward people who remain unmarried have changed too, from negative to neutral (Veroff, Douvan, & Kulka, 1981). Marriage, divorce, and remarriage do not fall on predictable timelines in adult life.

Parenthood. There is an old story that most parents understand at once. Two friends meet after not having seen each other for 30 years. Jake tells Fred he is married, is president of his own company, has three lovely children, and life is perfect. Fred tells Jake he is married, a successful lawyer, a good amateur tennis player, and a member of the local orchestra. Jake is shocked but sympathetic: ''You have no children?'' ''Alas, no,'' says Fred, ''no children.'' ''My God!'' Jake exclaims. ''What do you do for aggravation?''

Having children is a profound transition in a couple's life. Most people want children, enjoy them, and feel enriched by them, but often they are unprepared for the stresses that children bring. These are usually not major problems, such as having a very sick or troubled child, but small, daily, chronic ''hassles'': discipline problems, noisiness, conflicts, interruptions, demands on the parents' time and energy. Children interfere with a couple's freedom, privacy, and ability to sleep late on Sundays. These hassles are the reason that parents of young children report feeling more stress and pressure than any other group (Feshbach, 1985).

Parenthood has a far greater effect on most mothers than on most fathers. Fathers report much less of a dip in happiness and life satisfaction than new mothers do, and the reason seems to be, simply, that mothers have the responsibility for looking after the children. Although some men are taking more interest in their offspring and making concerted efforts to be involved, attentive fathers, the *average* father leaves the child care to his wife. Moreover, the *more* children a couple has, the *less* likely the husband is to do any housework or child care. If, in addition, the

Parenthood is like a picnic: It brings some nuisances and hassles, but also many delicious pleasures.

wife has a paid job, she has double the work without much help (Barnett & Baruch, 1987).

Parenthood has other psychological consequences, too. Stage theories, such as Erik Erikson's, suggest that when a person reaches a certain age, an internal need for nurturance becomes dominant; now the person desires children. But the opposite pattern is also true: Some people have children and *then* become nurturant (they have babies to nurture, after all). Studies show that new mothers of any age tend to become more responsible, self-controlled, and nurturant—all qualities that have to do with looking after a child. Unfortunately, new mothers also often become less self-confident, self-accepting, and happy—qualities that may have to do with how little support society and husbands tend to give new mothers (Helson, Mitchell, & Moane, 1984). As we saw in Chapter 13, when *fathers* are "mothers"—when they have the sole or major responsibility for child rearing—they have the same problems and pleasures as mothers do (Risman, 1987).

Does the timing of parenthood make a difference? Is it better or worse to have children when you are in your 20s, 30s, or even 40s? Each choice has its benefits and disadvantages. Young fathers tend to be preoccupied with work and so have less time and interest to devote to their children. Older first-time fathers, and men who remarry and have second families in midlife, often report greater enjoyment of their children.

For women, the timing of children is more critical, because children tend to interrupt a woman's job or career. Women who have children in their 20s are doing so at the biologically best time and the professionally worst time. However, in their 30s, with the children in school, they can pursue other interests without interruption. Women who take the opposite route, establishing their work interests first and waiting to have children until their late 30s, tend to know themselves better and are more certain of their goals. Yet they are also more worried about the age gap between themselves and their children, and they have a somewhat greater risk of physical difficulties in conception and pregnancy (Daniels & Weingarten, 1982). The children of older parents are often grateful for their parents' greater maturity and ability to provide, but they also have more worries about their parents' health and survival (Morris, 1988).

The empty nest. In spite of the hassles of child rearing, people are thought to suffer an emotional crisis when their children grow up and leave home for school or work. Parents, especially women who have made a career of mothering, are thought to feel unhappy, lonely, and unwanted when their "baby birds" leave the nest.

Actually, study after study finds that the transition to the empty nest does not dampen the morale of most mothers or fathers. On the contrary, most empty-nest parents report increased happiness with their marriages and a renewed sense of freedom; increased satisfaction with the children, who are now off on their own; and decreased parental strain (Datan & Thomas, 1984; Reinke, Holmes, & Harris, 1985). Many of them say this stage is one of the best periods of their lives, a result of having fewer responsibilities and financial burdens and more time for new interests. Of course, some parents have difficulty accepting this transition. Those who lack goals to guide them in this new "postparental" phase may continue to be overinvolved in the lives of their adult children (Lowenthal, Thurnher, & Chiriboga, 1975).

For many empty-nest parents, the real crisis occurs not when children leave home, but when they *fail* to leave home or *return* home to stay. With the age of first marriage and the divorce rate rising, and with economic pressures in many parts of the country, more and more adult "children" are returning home to live with their parents—or never leaving in the first place. These "off-time" arrangements require adjustments from everybody. In one study of three-generation families, the researchers found that when young-adult children did not leave home at the expected time, family tension and conflict grew (Wilen, 1979).

Just as we hear a lot about "adolescent turmoil," we hear a lot about the "midlife crisis." How would you define a "crisis"? For that matter, what is "midlife"? If a person doesn't have a crisis, is there something wrong with that person—or with the concept?

The "midlife crisis." In the middle years, some psychologists believe, most people go through an emotional crisis as they lament their lost youth and unfulfilled dreams. But researchers do not agree on what the "middle years" are. Some say 40 to 60, others say 35 to 55, others say 45 to 65. Some say the midlife crisis begins at age 40, "give or take a decade." A crisis that is so variable cannot be universal or inevitable. However, there do seem to be some common psychological themes in the middle years, whenever they occur (Neugarten, 1969, 1979; Schlossberg, 1984a):

- Reappraising one's life and dreams; questioning one's basic values
- Accepting the gap between one's dreams and one's achievements
- Overcoming stagnation, the sense of being stuck or trapped
- Facing the fact of aging and death

These concerns come early for some men and women, late for some, and never for others. For some, these are issues that stretch out over 10 or 20 years; others face and resolve them in a brief span. Some people confront these issues because an unexpected event forces them to, such as the death of a close friend, a disability, or loss of a job. Other, more inward-looking individuals may be in the habit of frequently assessing their lives. Some psychologists believe that the midlife years are as tumultuous as adolescence (R. Gould, 1978). But just as research finds that most adolescents do *not* go through turmoil, most people in midlife do not go through a crisis.

The issues that are important in the middle years have a lot to do with what a person's life has been like. Some couples find themselves in a midlife zigzag of interests and feelings. A husband who has been working hard for 25 years may start turning inward. He may be ready for some peace and quiet, yearn to develop new hobbies, and want to spend more time with family and friends. His wife, however, if she has been working at home for 25 years raising children, may start turning outward. She may be ready for new activities and excitement, yearn to meet new people and travel, and want to spend less time with family and friends and more time on her own interests (Crosby, 1986; Tiffany & Tiffany, 1983). The couple's marriage may indeed go through a "crisis" because their lives are moving in opposite directions.

Retirement. You have worked for Amalgamated Teabiscuit and Muffins, Inc., for 39 years. You love old AT & M. You have great colleagues. You are esteemed by one and all for your expertise and wisdom. You know more about the international muffin market than anyone else in the industry. You have power, prestige, and an expense account. Next year, at 65, you are required to retire. Will it be a quiet transition or a traumatic change?

For many years, it was assumed that men had trouble adjusting to retirement just as women had trouble adjusting to the empty nest. For each, after all, their primary job as worker or mother was over. In fact, both sexes move from one role to another with remarkably little fuss. The overwhelming majority of retirees are highly satisfied. They don't miss work and they don't have trouble adjusting (Newton, Lazarus, & Weinberg, 1984). Now that women have entered the work force in large numbers, they make the transition to retirement just as well or poorly as men do. The only difference is in income. Working women earn much less than working men, and so have fewer benefits on which to retire (Troll, 1986).

Once again, people's reactions to this change in role depend on the *circumstances* of the change, not on the fact of change itself. A national, longitudinal survey of several thousand men divided the sample according to the men's reasons for retirement (Crowley, 1984): ill health; voluntary early retirement before age 65; voluntary retirement at age 65; and mandatory retirement of men who were required by company policy to retire, even though they would have preferred to keep working.

Well-being in retirement, this survey found, depends on having adequate financial and psychological resources. If you have health, comfortable income, new interests to keep you occupied, and someone to love, retirement will probably feel just fine. If you have planned for retirement, both financially and emotionally, it will come as no big shock. If you have voluntarily chosen retirement, your well-being may even be better than that of people who are still employed. But if you have no interests at all outside of the biscuit business and you try to hang on to the former job that gave you your identity, then leaving AT & M can be stressful indeed.

Retirement is no big deal if you have passions, hobbies, and interests. Ernie Dunbar, age 94, has been raising bird-of-paradise flowers for years.

Widowhood. The death of a spouse is almost always a sad and difficult transition, but individuals vary in how they react (Atchley, 1975; Newton, Lazarus, & Weinberg, 1984). Basically, a person's ability to adjust depends on how much he or she depended on the deceased spouse; how many friends and social connections the widow or widower continues to have; the financial resources the individual has to establish a new life; and the individual's style of coping (Lopata, 1975).

Widows are usually better off than widowers on two of these factors. First, women seem to have a better ability to cope with the death of a spouse than men do. Psychologically speaking, they are used to taking care of themselves and their families, whereas married men are used to being taken care of. Second, they usually have more friends, although many widows and divorcees lament that they see much less of their married-couple friends. Widows, however, often lack the financial resources that widowers have, and a widowed man has many more opportunities for remarriage than a widowed woman has because women live longer than men (Newton, Lazarus, & Weinberg, 1984).

Older widows report that widowhood is less disruptive of their lives and less stressful than young widows do (Lopata, 1975). The reason, again, seems to be that older women *expect* to become widows; this condition is appropriate to their age and time in life. Being widowed may still be painful, but at some level older widows aren't shocked by the experience and may have even mentally rehearsed it. In addition, they often have the company of other widows who understand their feelings. The unexpected death of a young person, though, is shocking and tragic, and the surviving spouse has a more difficult time adjusting (Morgan, 1976).

Most Americans believe that one of the greatest problems that widows and widowers face in old age is loneliness. This idea is part of the generally gloomy stereotype that young people have of the old. Actually, as we have noted, loneliness decreases with age, even among widowed, divorced, and never-married older people. The best guarantee against loneliness in old age, by the way, is not children and grandchildren, but frequent contact with friends and neighbors (Mullins, Johnson, & Andersson, 1987).

People do best at managing milestones if these events occur "on time," yet the complexities of modern life keep changing our timetables. Efforts to push back or stop the clock have especially powerful consequences, however, when it comes to the ultimate transition, death. (In "Think About It" on pages 526–527, we discuss some important controversies about our society's view of death and dying.)

QUICK ▪ QUIZ

How well do you understand transitions?

1. When grown children leave home, what are most empty-nest parents likely to say? **(a)** ''Come back! All is forgiven!'' **(b)** ''At last! Hooray!'' **(c)** ''I'm bored and lonely! Now what?''
2. The ''midlife crisis'' **(a)** happens to everybody, **(b)** happens to men but not to women, **(c)** is common but not universal.
3. Which transition is most difficult for most people? **(a)** starting out, **(b)** becoming parents, **(c)** changing careers, **(d)** having the children leave home, **(e)** retirement
4. Which group reports the highest amount of stress, headaches, and hassles? **(a)** newly married husbands, **(b)** graduate students, **(c)** mothers of young children, **(d)** empty-nest parents, **(e)** retired couples
5. Match the name of each transition (left) with the correct example (right):

   1. chronic hassle   **a.** You don't get married when you planned to.
   2. nonevent   **b.** You graduate from college.
   3. anticipated   **c.** You lose your job when the company goes
   4. unanticipated   bankrupt.
                  d. Your child has a continuing illness.

Answers:
1. b 2. c 3. a 4. c 5. 1d, 2a, 3b, 4c

The high Cs of change: Cohort, circumstance, and chance

The influences on adult development are many and varied. Some are in the individual, in physical maturation and personality. Some are in events we can control, such as whom we marry. Some, however, are out of our control. People are affected by their generation's values and experiences. They are affected by the work they do and the work that is available for them to do. They are affected by pure luck, by bolts from the blue such as losing their houses in a tornado or being drafted for war. In today's world, we can all expect to have unexpected transitions, and we can all expect that some of our expected transitions will never occur.

The cohort effect. Each generation, or age **cohort**, has its own set of experiences, social outlook, and economic opportunities. Generations that have the benefits of security and a wide range of jobs are different from those that lived through the Great Depression, say, or major wars. Teenagers who came of age during the Vietnam War are unlike those who came of age before or since. The availability of drugs and changing sexual standards can create dilemmas for one generation that its parents never imagined. The cohort effect is a major reason that children differ from their parents, and a reason that parents are not the sole important influence on their children (Baltes, Cornelius, & Nesselroade, 1979; Veroff, 1983).

At the end of a large-scale study that followed several hundred children for 30 years, roughly from 1930 to 1960, the researcher acknowledged how rapidly and

cohort *An age group, such as a school class or a whole generation, that shares common experiences or demographic traits.*

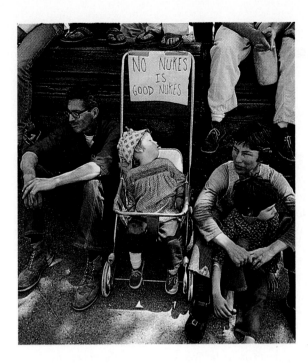

The "cohort effect" applies to the shared experiences and values of a generation. Many people who came of age during the political protests of the 1960s, such as this couple, continue their political activism throughout their lives. Which of your cohort's values might be affecting you?

extensively American life had changed in those three decades. We must, he said, consider the possibility that some of the findings from longitudinal research will be valid only for "a time or circumstance that will never recur" (Block, 1971).

Circumstance and situation. One of the most powerful influences on adult development is, simply, what people do. Every day, the situations in which they work, play, love, and live make demands. Some environments offer little room for independence or creativity, and others provide an opportunity to explore both. The conditions of employment and marriage can affect motivation, mood, health, happiness, and even intellectual abilities.

People may "burn out" at work, growing unhappy with their jobs, because of the conditions of the job, not because they have reached a critical stage or because they have personality problems. Conversely, people may grow and develop when they have new opportunities or expectations. In one generation, the law and medicine opened to women, as did bartending, business schools, and bill collecting. The computer revolution produced an entirely new and unanticipated industry. Adult development depends to a large extent on what an adult's environment permits.

The fickle finger of fate. Psychologists have rarely computed the role of chance in their theories of adult development. Chance is so, well, unexpected, so hard to study! But if you are planning to be a piano teacher and you suddenly are offered a scholarship in science, win a $10-million lottery, or are struck with a disease that cripples your fingers, your entire life may be affected.

As people grow older, unexpected events have an even more significant effect on their lives (Baltes, 1983; Kagan, 1984). A ten-year study of a national sample of 5000 families found tremendous, continuing changes in family income, entry into the work force, and family composition (Duncan et al., 1984; Duncan, Hill, & Hoffman, 1988). For most poor people, poverty is only temporary, a result of unexpected misfortunes that could strike anyone, such as getting very sick, losing a job, or, for women, being divorced.

Think About It

On Death and Dying

Death used to be more familiar than it is now. Only two generations ago, you could not reach the age of 20 without losing members of your family—certainly a grandparent, quite possibly a parent, and most likely a sibling who did not survive childhood. Today the loss of a child is an accident and a tragedy, and death has moved farther into the shadows of life.

Death used to be simpler than it is now. Heartbeat and breathing stopped, and the person was pronounced dead. Today patients can "live" for weeks, even years, unconscious and in a coma, while machines keep the vital organs going. Some patients have the chance to replace dying organs, such as the heart or kidney, with healthy ones.

Death used to come sooner than it does now. Life expectancy has increased for men (to 70 years) and for women (to 78 years). The fastest-growing age group in the United States, proportionately, is the over-85 group.

These three changes in the experience of aging and death have caused profound psychological, legal, and moral issues for our society. Sooner or later, most of us will have to think about some difficult questions:

▪ *What is legal death?* New definitions of "death" include irreversible brain damage, total brain death, and the inability of the heart to beat on its own. Is a person dead if he or she could not survive without machine support?

▪ *When is it time to "pull the plug," and who decides?* Doctors, lawyers, families, and clergy often disagree with each other on the "right" time to let an ailing person die. Doctors, trained to prolong life, often want to keep the dying person alive as long as possible, even when that means prolonged pain and suffering. (They also fear malpractice suits that may occur if they let someone die whom the family thinks could have lived longer.) Religious groups differ too on the role of intervention in keeping someone alive. Some believe that death is natural and inevitable, and that doctors and lawyers should not interfere with its course. Others believe that death is to be fought with all the weapons of modern medicine.

▪ *"Passive" versus "active" euthanasia.* Euthanasia means "easy death" (from the Greek *eu*, "good" or "well," as in *euphoria*; and *thanatos*, "death"). It refers to the act of painlessly putting to death someone who is suffering an incurable and painful disease. "Passive" euthanasia means simply allowing such a person to die without using heroic measures to keep the person alive, such as taking a comatose patient off a life-support system. In "active" euthanasia, commonly called "mercy killing," a physician or family member actually helps the death come sooner to spare the patient suffering.

In Florida, a 76-year-old man shot and killed

The "American Dream" is built on the belief in upward mobility: Work hard and you will move up the ladder of success. Yet about 20 percent of all Americans move *down* the job hierarchy in their lives, and more than half are in economic decline, with incomes lagging behind inflation (Newman, 1988). The downwardly mobile do not necessarily become poor. But many land in jobs that offer far less status and affluence than they once enjoyed.

Katherine Newman (1988) interviewed 150 downwardly mobile Americans: former executives, fired air traffic controllers, blue-collar workers in a plant shutdown, and divorced mothers. She found some common psychological themes—a feeling of failure, loss of control and a coherent identity, and disorientation. But people's reactions also depended, for example, on whether they shared the experience with others (as in a company closing) or felt themselves to be alone (as in divorce). American culture is rich in symbols and rituals that celebrate success,

his wife. He did it, he said, because she was dying of Alzheimer's disease and suffering from crippling osteoporosis. He could not bear to see the woman he loved and had lived with for over 50 years in such misery. The man was convicted of first-degree murder and sentenced to life in prison. At a clemency hearing, the governor expressed his dilemma: He had great sympathy for the man, but what message would clemency send to other people who had sick and suffering relatives? Would they decide a "mercy killing" was an approved way to rid themselves of the burden of caretaking?

To avoid putting their relatives through such a moral dilemma, and to avoid a lingering, painful death, some people have signed "The Living Will," which specifies the conditions under which they want to be considered legally dead. The will requests that the person be allowed to die peacefully, without being kept alive by artificial means. (By the way, the Florida governor did not pardon the husband. But in Oregon not long afterward, a man was sentenced to a year of community service for having committed a similar "crime.")

▪ *Who cares for the dying?* Dying of protracted illnesses, such as Alzheimer's disease, AIDS, or cancer, can last months or even years. Thus the issues of who will care for the terminally ill and where they will die are becoming more urgent. Hospitals are often cold, anonymous institutions that deprive a dying person of dignity and individuality, the company of friends and family, and choices about life-prolonging techniques. One alternative is the *hospice*, a center for the dying person and his or her family. Hospices offer the medical care of hospitals, but they are homier, allow families to live with the patient (at home or in the hospice itself), offer counseling to both patient and family, and help the patient die with as little pain as possible.

Today many middle-aged adults face a terrible dilemma, caught between their deeply felt concerns for their parents and an equally pressing need to work. If they give up the caretaking, they often feel guilty and "selfish." If they give up their jobs, they risk poverty and financial insecurity in their own old age. How can this dilemma be avoided?

▪ *Who pays for the dying, and do only the wealthy live?* The costs of life-sustaining equipment, long-term hospital (or hospice) care, and organ transplants are growing rapidly, a result of new technology. Who will pay the costs? Families? Government? If someone else can afford an organ transplant and you can't, should that person be allowed to live and you to die?

In his book *Setting Limits,* Daniel Callahan (1987) argues that Americans must curb their "insatiable appetite for a longer life." They should, he says, be "creatively and honorably accepting aging and death, not struggling to overcome them." Do you agree? How should a society set limits on life?

Newman observes, yet there are no stories to help people make sense of losing that success.

Economic conditions have a way of interrupting people's best-laid plans. You hope to be a teacher, but you find that there are too many teachers. You hope to be able to stay home and raise four children, but inflation makes it impossible for your spouse to support the family on one income. You expect to have children in your early 20s, but you are offered a great job and decide to establish your career before starting a family.

Nevertheless, chance isn't everything. Keep in mind that people's attitudes and motivations determine how they respond to chance opportunities and even whether they seek them out (M. Snyder, 1982). What happens to you when chance strikes depends on your ability to change your expectations, make new plans, and find a path through unfamiliar territory.

VERY ▪ QUICK ▪ QUIZ

Match each experience with its most likely cause.

1. You lose your job when your company goes bankrupt.
2. People your age are particularly worried about nuclear war.
3. You've lost your ambition to succeed.
4. You temporarily need welfare.

a. the cohort effect
b. having a boring job
c. loss of job or spouse
d. chance

Answers:
1. d 2. a 3. b 4. c

The Adult Experience: Themes of Continuity and Change

Clinical psychologists are fond of saying that there are two things in human nature that will never change: the desire to change and the fear of change (H. Lerner, 1986). "Each person is, by nature, a purposeful, striving organism with a desire to be more than he or she is now," write two developmentalists (Brim & Kagan, 1980). At the same time, they add, each of us has a sense of identity, or continuity, that protects us from the fear of changing too fast, or of being changed against our will by outside forces.

By understanding the forces that promote development or keep us consistent, we can better evaluate popular ideas about adult life. Few people, for instance, are immune to the influence of their generation, their society, or their working conditions. This fact tells us to beware of theories that ignore the real, everyday conditions of life. Books or programs that offer to "liberate the self" (as if the "self" existed apart from a social world of duties, demands, pleasures, and possibilities) often promise more than they can deliver. Conversely, the belief that *nothing* changes once you are past childhood (as if adult experiences had no effect) often makes people worry that they are condemned to endure their early problems forever.

The last four chapters have considered some of the factors in personality, genetic disposition, learning, and environment that foster stability and that encourage development. To summarize briefly:

First, what resists change? Your basic personality "package"—including mannerisms, habits, defense mechanisms, level of energy, inhibitions, and general temperament—seems to be fairly consistent throughout life. These qualities influence how you interpret and react to new situations, and whether you seek stimulation and change or prefer stability and calm. Some of the more stable personality traits include extroversion, neuroticism (negative emotionality), agreeableness, conscientiousness, and openness to experience (Costa & McCrae, 1988).

Second, what is able to change? Many intellectual abilities, emotions, behaviors, and aspects of personality are significantly influenced by new situations and experiences. These include self-esteem, ambitiousness, interest in work, nurturance, loneliness, intellectual flexibility or rigidity, competence, and locus of control (Schaie, 1983).

Researchers who study adult development have usually used one of two approaches. One approach looks at what people *do* throughout their lives, how their activities change as they move into different phases of family and work life. The other looks at how people *feel* throughout their lives as their emotional needs and concerns change. Nancy Schlossberg (1984b, 1989) has put these two dimensions together in a theory of psychological themes that are important throughout life. Unlike Erikson, who said that certain psychological issues are more important at some ages than at others, Schlossberg believes that life events, not age, determine which of these issues will be important at any given time.

▪ *Belonging.* Do you feel that you are a central part of your social world, or only marginal?

▪ *"Mattering."* Do you feel that you matter to others, that you count?

▪ *Autonomy.* Do you feel that you have a reasonable amount of control over your life, in work, love, and play?

▪ *Competence.* Do you feel able to do what you need and want to do?

▪ *Renewal.* Do you have energy and enthusiasm for your activities?

▪ *Identity.* Do you have a strong sense of yourself, of who you are?

▪ *Intimacy.* Do you have important, close attachments?

▪ *Commitments.* Are there people, activities, or values to which you are committed, which give meaning to your life?

These themes, says Schlossberg, reflect our common humanity, uniting men and women, black and white, old and young. A freshman in college and a newly retired man may both temporarily feel marginal, "out of things." A teenager and her great-grandmother may both suffer loneliness without intimate friends. A man may feel he has control over his life until he is injured in a car accident. A wife's identity may change if she goes back to school in midlife. When people lose the commitments that give their lives meaning—a loved one, a career, a religious belief, a political cause—they feel cut off, adrift.

In short, adult concerns are not settled, once and for all, at some critical stage or age. It would be nice if we could acquire a sense of competence in grammar school and keep it forever, if we had only one identity crisis per lifetime, if we always belonged. But adult development is more complicated than that, and also more interesting. Adult life is full of transitions, problems, fun, choices, worries, chances, and unexpected curve balls. Having them is what it means to live. Meeting them is what it means to be an adult.

Chance events—losing a job, being injured, getting divorced—can affect people's lives in unexpected ways. Most of the people who receive welfare or emergency services do so for only a brief time. How do your stable personality traits interact with unexpected events to produce the course of your adult development?

Taking Psychology with You

Coping with Transitions: When Is a Change a "Crisis"?

Our psychological society tends to make definitive crises out of life's predictable problems. Unhappiness after divorce becomes a Divorce Crisis. Difficulties at work become a Job Crisis. Blues at age 45 become a Midlife Crisis. This tends to make people feel both better ("I'm not alone; it's a diagnosable problem") and worse ("Oh my God, I'm having a crisis!"). What is a crisis, and do you need to have one? If you don't suffer occasionally from temporary insanity, is there something wrong with you?

A *crisis* is a sudden, severely upsetting situation that forces you to mobilize your resources; a *transition* is a change in your roles, routines, or relationships. Many psychologists believe that it is not your age that creates a crisis, but an event, such as losing your health, your parents, or your work. Several factors can turn a transition into a crisis (Brim, 1976; Neugarten, 1979; Schlossberg, 1989):

• Is the change planned or unplanned, predictable or unpredictable? Major stresses can be caused by events that are unanticipated or out of order: when the birth of a child is too early, when a parent dies too soon, when retirement or unemployment occurs unexpectedly.

• Does the change involve one event or many? A crisis may occur if you must deal with many changes at once, such as moving away from home, leaving all of your old friends, having to support yourself, and taking on new responsibilities.

• Do you want the change and feel that you have control over it? People are more shattered by events that seem to come out of the blue, forcing them to make changes they would prefer to avoid.

• Do you have the emotional skills to help you cope? Some people react to change as a challenging problem to be solved. Others collapse, feeling that they are in an overwhelming situation with no solution. (For more on coping with stress, see Chapter 15.)

• Do you have friends, relatives, or associates who can help you? Change can be difficult for people who feel they have little support for desired decisions or no one to help them through unwished-for changes.

Keeping these issues in mind, would you say marriage is a crisis? How about divorce? If two people get married, move to a new city, leave their close friends behind, and immediately have children, they may find themselves in a crisis indeed. But getting married is not a crisis for most couples. They have planned for it, they know each other's habits, and they know more or less what to expect. For them, the transition from single to married is a slow process of change and assimilation. Even divorce, a sad and significant transition for most people, doesn't have to provoke an emotional crisis. Divorce may be difficult but untraumatic for a woman who wants the separation; has a good job; and keeps her house, friends, and standard of living. It can be a crisis for a woman who didn't choose the divorce, must move to a smaller house and a new community, loses her friends, and doesn't have a job.

Understanding the factors that can turn a transition into a crisis can sometimes help people plan better. Some guidelines:

▪ *Don't take on too many life-shaking changes at once,* unless you know what you are getting into. You may decide you really want to disown your family, sell all your possessions, give away your dog, and move to Australia, but you might do better to give yourself a little time in case you have a change of heart. If you know a major change that you cannot control is coming your way, try to postpone other decisions that aren't as important.

▪ *Set reasonable expectations.* First-time parents who realize that having children will produce a noisy, exciting, and stressful few years, for example, adjust better to this transition than do parents who expect children to make no difference in their stress levels or their marriages. A student who expects to feel lonely for a while in a new school will cope better than a student who expects instant social success.

▪ *Don't be shy about asking for help* from friends, relatives, or support groups. The truth about change is that everyone goes through it. The realization that others are in the same boat is often reassuring in itself.

We cannot always choose the changes that happen to us, but often we can decide what to do next.

KEY WORDS

adolescence 502
puberty 502
menarche 503
secondary sex characteristics 503
asynchrony 504
formal operations stage 504
menopause 506
climacteric 506
"male menopause" 507
maximum life span 507
gerontology 508, 510
memory and intelligence in old
  age 508

sexuality and aging 509
senility 510
psychosocial theory of development
  (Erik Erikson) 512
identity crisis 513
stage theories 513
transitions 516
social clock 517
empty nest 521
"midlife crisis" 522
cohort effect 524

SUMMARY

1. Adult development is influenced by the *biological clock* (physical changes throughout life), the *social clock* (events most people experience at the same ages), the *generation or cohort* effect, *experiences,* and *chance events.*

2. Adolescence begins with *puberty.* In girls, puberty is signaled by *menarche* (the onset of menstruation) and the development of breasts; in boys, it begins with the onset of nocturnal emissions and the development of the testes and scrotum. Hormones are responsible for *secondary sex characteristics* and for rapid mood swings. But adolescence ends with society's definition of adulthood. Most adolescents do not go through extreme emotional turmoil. Some have a relatively calm adolescence, some face particular problems, and some have more serious problems. No single pattern is typical of all teenagers.

3. In women, the *menopause* begins in their late 40s or early 50s. Most women have a few minor symptoms, but they do not regret the end of fertility, they do not become depressed or irritable, and they do not feel "unfeminine."

4. There are two theories of aging. One says that aging is normal and inevitable, perhaps genetically programmed by a "death gene." Another says that aging results from damage to cells or from decline in immune function, the cells' ability to fight infection and disease.

5. Ideas about old age have been revised now that old people are living longer and healthier lives. As discussed in "A Closer Look at Gerontology," many supposed results of aging, such as senility and brittle bones, are results of disease. Other supposed aspects of old age result from psychological problems, such as lack of stimulation, control, and meaningful work, rather than physical decline.

6. Some studies suggest that perceptual-motor skills, intelligence, and memory decline with age, but intellectual decline may result from poor education, lack of training and experience, or poor health. The frequency of sexual activity declines over the life span, but psychologists do not agree on whether the reason is hormonal or social. Sexual desire and pleasure last well into old age among people who have always enjoyed sex and who continue to have partners.

7. Erik Erikson proposed an influential *psychosocial theory of development*, in which he argued that life consists of eight stages, each characterized by a particular psychological *crisis*. Other stage theories followed.

8. Adult "stages" are not universal or biologically governed, like stages of child development. Unlike stage theories, the *transitions* approach concentrates on the social changes in people's lives regardless of when they occur. There are four kinds of transitions: *anticipated*, *unanticipated*, *nonevent*, and *chronic hassle*.

9. Adults evaluate their development according to a *social clock* that determines whether they are "on time" or "off time" for a particular activity. In the United States, the traditional *feminine social clock* emphasizes getting married and starting a family early; the *masculine occupational clock* specifies the "correct" ages for career advancement.

10. The major milestones in most people's lives include leaving home and starting an independent life; beginning work; getting married and having children; being on their own again when the children leave home; retirement; and the death of a spouse. Of all of these changes, one of the most stressful is the first, starting out. Parenthood brings special stresses and concerns, especially to mothers. Contrary to stereotype, most couples enjoy being "empty-nest" parents, and most people take well to retirement.

11. Just as most adolescents do not go through turmoil, most adults in midlife do not go through a "midlife crisis." But some do spend time reassessing their values and goals, learning to accept the fact of aging, and seeking renewal.

12. Adult development is also influenced by the nature of one's work and marriage; the *cohort effect*; and random, chance events. For most people on welfare, poverty is a temporary response to misfortune—losing a job, getting sick, or being divorced.

13. The truth about adult development falls somewhere between "you can change anything about yourself" and "you can't change anything." Some aspects of personality, such as extroversion, neuroticism, agreeableness, conscientious-ness, and openness to experience, resist change. But many others, such as self-esteem, competence, achievement motivation, intellectual flexibility, and nurtur-ance, are influenced by experiences in adulthood.

14. Some psychological issues recur throughout life: belonging, the need to matter to others, autonomy, competence, renewal of energy and enthusiasm, iden-tity, intimacy, and commitments to activities or people that give life meaning.

P A R T

F I V E

Health and

Disorder

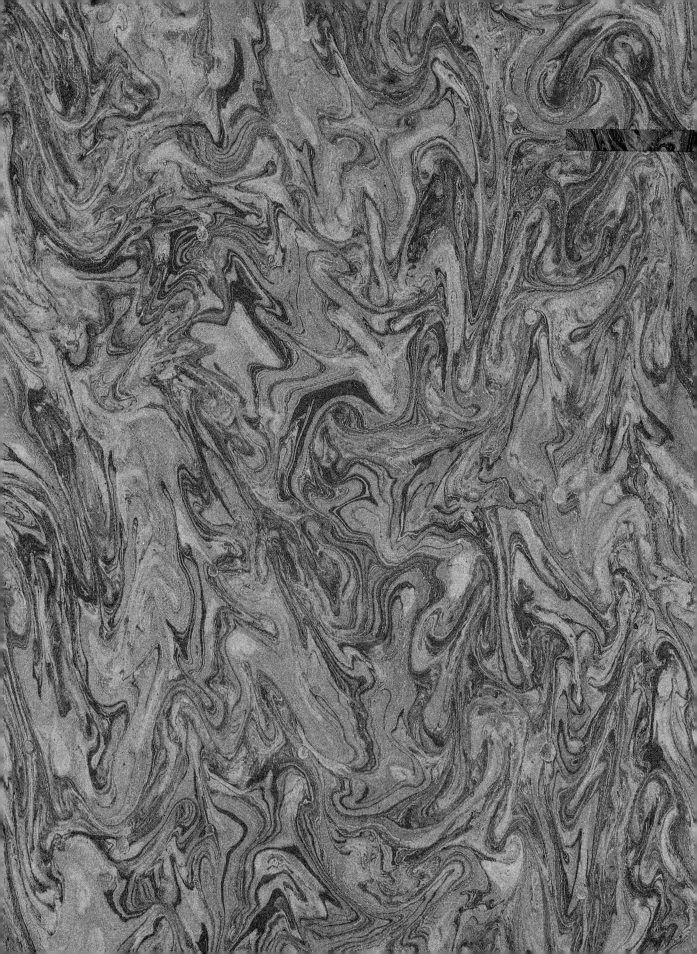

CHAPTER 15

Health, Stress, and Coping

Rule No. 1 is, don't sweat the small stuff.
Rule No. 2 is, it's all small stuff.
And if you can't fight and you can't flee, flow.

ROBERT ELIOT, M.D.

Stressful events can hit at any time. How would you react to a "bolt from the blue"?

▪ Bill and his father have been battling for years. Bill feels that he can never do anything right, that his father is always ready to criticize him for the slightest flaw. Now that he has left home, Bill has more perspective on their relationship, but one thing hasn't changed. Every time his father comes to visit, Bill breaks out in a mysterious rash.

▪ Tanya has never told anyone about a shattering experience she had as a child. She is afraid to reveal her secret, sure that no one will understand or sympathize. But the memory haunts her in daydreams and nightmares.

▪ Josh is walking home from school one night when three young men grab him, threaten to kill him, and steal his watch and wallet. Josh is relieved to be alive, but he finds that he can't get over this experience. Months later, he still feels humiliated and angry, and dreams of revenge.

▪ Lucy, who is already late for class, gets stuck in a traffic jam caused by a three-car accident. As she walks in the door, her instructor reprimands her for being late. Rushing to get her notes together for an overdue research paper, Lucy spills coffee all over herself and the documents. By noon Lucy has a splitting headache and feels exhausted.

All of these people are certainly under "stress," but, as you see, this word covers a multitude of experiences. It includes occasional but recurring conflicts (Bill and his father), a traumatic experience or a sudden event that shatters your sense of safety (Tanya, Josh), and a collection of small irritations that can wear you down (Lucy). Is there a link between these "stresses" and health or illness?

In this chapter, we will explore the psychology of health and illness, stress and coping, in the context of daily life. We will look at some findings from the new field of **health psychology**, which studies all psychological aspects of health and illness, such as the psychological influences on how people stay healthy, why they become ill, and how they respond when they do get ill (Taylor, 1986). A related field, called **behavioral medicine**, is an interdisciplinary approach to health and illness. Researchers in behavioral medicine come from many different backgrounds, such as medicine, nutrition, and physiology, as well as psychology.

Scientific psychology and medicine have typically used a *pathogenic* approach, focusing on the causes of a problem or an illness (from *patho-*, "disease" or "suffering," and *-genic*, "producing"). But health psychologists also want to know what generates health, by taking the *salutogenic* approach (from *salut*, "health"). According to Aaron Antonovsky (1979, 1984), the pathogenic approach divides the world into the healthy and the sick, although many healthy people have occasions of "dis-ease" and many sick people are able to get along in life. It seeks a single cause to a problem, such as "Type A causes heart attacks," and it has led us to assume that all stress is bad. In emphasizing the people who are at "high risk" of becoming ill, it ignores the majority who, though at risk, stay well.

The pathogenic approach, says Antonovsky, asks, "How can we eradicate this or that stressor?" The salutogenic approach asks instead, "How can we learn to

health psychology *A field within psychology that studies psychological aspects of health and illness.*

behavioral medicine *An interdisciplinary field that studies behaviors related to the maintenance of health, the onset of illness, and the prevention of disease.*

live, and live well, with stressors, and possibly even turn [them] to our advantage?" To find out, health psychologists also study the exceptions—the people who theoretically should become sick but don't, the people who transcend difficult problems instead of giving in to them.

Modern research in health psychology, as we will see in this chapter, is very promising. But some of its findings, unfortunately, have been misused to foster two common misconceptions: Illness is "all in the mind" and curing illness just requires the right attitude, or "mind over matter." In the conclusion, we will consider the contributions of health psychology and its limitations.

The Nature of Stress

Throughout history, "stress" has been one of those things that everyone has experienced but few can define (Elliott & Eisdorfer, 1982). Why has it been so difficult to agree on something all of us have felt?

Alarms and adaptation

In his 1956 book, *The Stress of Life,* Canadian physician Hans Selye (1907–1982) popularized the idea of stress and advanced its study. Selye noted that many environmental factors—heat, cold, pain, toxins, viruses, and so on—throw the body out of equilibrium, forcing it to respond. These factors, called *stressors*, include anything that requires the body to mobilize its resources. The body responds to a stressor with an orchestrated set of physical and chemical changes, which, as we saw in Chapter 9, prepare an individual to fight or flee. To Selye, "stress" consisted of this package of reactions, which he called the **General Adaptation Syndrome** (with the memorable acronym GAS). Usually, the body will meet the challenge of the environment and *adapt* to the stress.

The general adaptation syndrome has three phases:

1. In the *alarm phase*, the organism mobilizes to meet the threat. This is a basic package of biological responses that allows a person to fight or flee no matter what the stressor is: trying to cross a crowded intersection or trying to escape a cross rattlesnake.

2. In the *phase of resistance*, the organism attempts to resist or cope with a threat that continues and cannot be avoided. During this phase, the body's physiological responses are above normal—a response to the original stressor—but this very mechanism makes the body more susceptible to *other* stressors. For example, when your body has mobilized to fight off the flu, you may find you are more easily annoyed by minor frustrations. In most cases, the body will eventually *adapt* to the stressor and return to normal.

3. If the stressor persists, it may overwhelm the body's resources. Depleted of energy, the body enters the *phase of exhaustion*, becoming vulnerable to fatigue, physical problems, and eventually illness. The very reactions that allow the body to resist short-term stressors—boosting energy, tensing muscles in preparation for action, shutting out signs of pain, closing off digestion, raising blood pressure—are unhealthy as long-range responses. Tense muscles can cause headache and neck pain. Increased blood pressure can become chronic hypertension. Closing off digestion for too long can lead to digestive disorders.

General Adaptation Syndrome (GAS) *According to Hans Selye, the bodily reactions to environmental stressors.*

Who has more "stress"—and whose stress counts? Many media stories emphasize the "stress" faced by white-collar workers and managers of companies. They are less concerned with the stress faced by assembly line workers and laborers. Why do you think this might be so? Which group is under more stress—powerful people in highly competitive and complicated jobs, or powerless people in boring and predictable jobs?

Stress is a bane of modern civilization because our physiological alarm mechanism now chimes too often. Today, when the typical stressor is a mammoth traffic jam and not a mammoth mammal, the fight-or-flight response often gets revved up with nowhere to go. When your teacher announces that you will have an unexpected exam, you don't really need to respond as if you were fighting for your life, but your body will still sweat to dispose of excess body heat. When you see your sweetheart flirting with someone else, you don't really need to breathe hard to get oxygen to your muscles, as you would if you were fleeing to safety.

Not all stress is bad, however. Some stress, which Selye called **eustress**, is positive and feels good, even if it also requires the body to produce short-term energy: competing in an athletic event, falling in love, working hard on a project you enjoy. Selye did not believe that all stress could be avoided or that people should aim for a stress-free life, which is an impossible goal. "Just as any inanimate machine gradually wears out," he said, "so does the human machine sooner or later become the victim of constant wear and tear." The goal is to minimize the wear and tear, not get rid of it.

Selye recognized that psychological stressors (such as emotional conflict or grief) can be as important as physical stressors (such as heat, toxic chemicals, or noise). He also observed that some factors *mediate* between the stressor and the stress. A warm climate or a nutritious diet, for example, can soften the impact of an environmental stressor such as pollution. Conversely, a harsh climate or a poor diet can make such stressors worse. But by and large, Selye concentrated on the biological responses that result from a person's attempt to adapt to environmental demands. He defined a stressor as any event that produces the stress (that is, the General Adaptation Syndrome). A diagram of his view is:

eustress [YOU-stress]
Positive or beneficial stress.

Stressor $--\rightarrow$ Stress (GAS) $--\rightarrow$ Healthy adaptation or illness

Later studies have found that stress is not a purely biological condition that can lead directly to illness. First, between the stressor and the stress is *the individual's evaluation of the event:* An event that is stressful for one person may be challenging for another and routinely boring for a third. Losing a job, traveling to China, or having "too much" work to do is stressful to some people and not to others. Second, between the stress and its consequences is *how the individual copes with the stress.* Not all individuals who are under stress behave in the same way. Not all get ill. Thus a revised diagram might look like this:

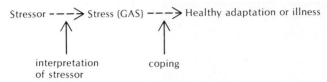

Because people differ in how they interpret events and in how they respond to them, many psychologists now prefer a definition of stress that takes into account aspects of the environment, aspects of the individual, and how the two interact. **Psychological stress** is the result of an exchange between the person and the environment, in which the person believes that the situation strains or overwhelms his or her resources and is endangering his or her well-being (Lazarus & Folkman, 1984).

Illness and immunology

Another approach to the psychological origins of illness came from the field of *psychosomatic medicine,* which developed in psychiatry at the turn of the century. **Psychosomatic** describes the interaction of mind (*psyche*) and body (*soma*). Freud was one of the main proponents of the idea that physical symptoms are often the result of unconscious conflicts. Other psychosomatic theorists maintained that many disorders—notably rheumatoid arthritis, asthma, ulcers, migraine headaches, and hypertension—are caused by neurotic personality patterns. Many of these early theories led to the mistaken view that a "psychosomatic illness" is "all in the mind," but they have not been supported by modern research. Today's field of psychosomatic medicine recognizes the complex nature of the mind-body relationship—not only how mind affects body, but also how body affects mind.

Some researchers, borrowing ideas from Selye and from psychosomatic medicine, are studying the effects of physical stress and psychological factors on the immune system. The immune system is designed to do two things: recognize foreign substances (antigens), such as flu viruses, bacteria, and tumor cells, and destroy or deactivate them. There are basically two types of white blood cells in the immune system: the *lymphocytes,* whose job is primarily to recognize and destroy foreign cells, and the *phagocytes,* whose job is to ingest and eliminate them.

To defend the body against foreign invaders, the immune system deploys different weapons (cells), sometimes together and sometimes alone, depending on the nature of the enemy. For example, *natural killer cells,* a type of lymphocyte, are important in tumor detection and rejection; *killer T cells* help destroy antigens that they have been exposed to previously. Prolonged or severe stress can suppress these cells and others that normally fight disease and infection.

The marriage of immunology and psychology has produced an offspring with the cumbersome name **psychoneuroimmunology**. This new field explores the connections among psychological processes (such as emotions, attitudes, and percep-

psychological stress *The result of a relationship between the person and the environment, in which the person believes the situation is overwhelming and threatens his or her ability to cope.*

psychosomatic *A term that describes the interaction between a physical illness or condition and psychological states; literally, mind (psyche) and body (soma).*

psychoneuroimmunology *[psycho/neuro/immu/nology] The field that studies the relationships among psychology, the nervous system, and the immune system.*

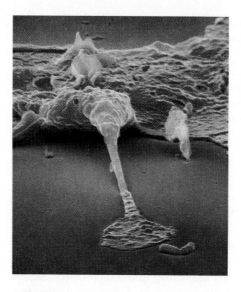

Like a fantastical Hollywood creature, a phagocyte reaches out with an extended "arm," called a pseudopod, to ensnare two unwitting bacteria.

tions), the nervous system, and immune functions. A basic assumption in this work is that *all* disease is the result of relationships among the endocrine, nervous, and immune systems; behavior; and emotions (G. Solomon, 1985). These relationships explain, for example, why of two people who are exposed to a flu virus, one is sick all winter and the other doesn't even get the sniffles (Kiecolt-Glaser & Glaser, 1989). In a study of medical students who had herpes virus, researchers found that herpes outbreaks were more likely to occur when the students were feeling loneliest or were under the pressure of exams. Loneliness and stress apparently suppressed the cells' immune capability, permitting the existing herpes virus to erupt (Kiecolt-Glaser et al., 1985a).

Some sources of stress

What are the stressors that might affect the immune system and thus lead to illness? Some psychologists study the significant events that disrupt our lives and take an emotional toll. Others count nuisances, the small straws that break the camel's back. Still others emphasize continuing pressures.

Life events. Years ago, Thomas Holmes and Richard Rahe (1967) identified 43 events that seemed to be especially stressful. By testing thousands of people, they were able to rank a series of "life-change events" in order of their disruptive impact. Holmes and Rahe then assigned each event a corresponding number of "life-change units" (LCUs). At the top was death of a spouse (100 LCUs), followed by divorce (73), imprisonment (63), and death of a close family member (63). Not all of the events were unpleasant. Marriage (50) was on the list, as were pregnancy (40), buying a house (31), and Christmas (12). Among people who had become ill, the large majority had had 300 LCUs or more in a single year.

Later studies found numerous flaws in the idea that *all* life events are stressful and lead to illness. First, many of the items on the Holmes-Rahe scale are the *result* of psychological problems or illness, not their cause (such as "problems at work" and "major changes in sleeping habits") (Hudgens, 1974). Second, some events become more stressful once a person is already depressed or ill (Dohrenwend,

1979). Third, as we saw in Chapter 14, many expected changes, such as retirement or having the children leave home, are not especially stressful for most people. Happy, positive events are not related (thank goodness) to illness or poor health (Taylor, 1986). Finally, simply counting "life-change units" is not enough: Having 17 things happen to you in one year is not necessarily stressful unless you feel overwhelmed by them (Cohen, Kamarck, & Mermelstein, 1983; Sarason, Johnson, & Siegel, 1978).

Bereavement and tragedy.　Some events, of course, are more shocking to the system, psychologically and physically, than others. The events at the top of the Holmes-Rahe list, death of a spouse and divorce, are powerful stressors that are linked to a subsequent decline in health. Widows and widowers are more susceptible to illness and physical ailments, and their mortality rate is higher than expected (Calabrese, Kling, & Gold, 1987). Divorce also often takes a long-term health toll. Divorced adults have higher rates of emotional disturbance, heart disease, pneumonia, and other diseases than comparable adults who are not divorced (Jacobson, 1983; Weiss, 1975).

Bereaved and divorced people may be vulnerable to illness because, feeling unhappy and lonely, they don't sleep well, they stop eating properly, and they consume more drugs and cigarettes. But animal and human studies suggest that separation *itself* creates changes in the cardiovascular system, a lowered white blood cell count, and other abnormal responses of the immune system (Laudenslager & Reite, 1984; Stein, Keller, & Schleifer, 1985). You may recall from Chapters 10 and 13 that attachment appears to be a basic biological need of the species, and broken attachments affect us at a basic cellular level. But the quality of the attachment is as important as its presence. Unhappily married individuals show the same decline in immune function as unhappy divorced people (Kiecolt-Glaser et al., 1987a).

Sadly, many people suffer shocking experiences that are not on the Holmes-Rahe list—experiences about which they feel so secret, and dirty, that the secret itself adds to the stress. (See "A Closer Look at Psychoneuroimmunology" for a fascinating case study of how this field's findings have yielded a therapeutic suggestion for recovery from trauma.)

Daily hassles.　Some psychologists argue that we handle most of the big problems of life relatively well; it's the daily grind that can get us down. "Hassles" are the irritations and frustrations of everyday routines, such as thoughtless roommates, traffic, bad weather, annoying arguments, broken plumbing, lost keys, and sick cats. Some research suggests that hassles are better predictors of psychological and physical symptoms than are life changes (DeLongis et al., 1982). In one study of 75 married couples, the frequency of daily hassles was related to later health problems such as flu, sore throats, headaches, and backaches (DeLongis, Folkman, & Lazarus, 1988).

Of course, a major event, such as divorce, often increases the number of hassles a person must contend with (new financial pressures, custody questions, moving) and might make a person more intolerant of small hassles. By and large, though, people's reports of being hassled are independent of life events. In a study of 210 police officers, the most stressful things they reported were not the dramatic dangers you see on television, but daily paperwork, annoyance with "distorted" accounts of the police in the press, and the snail-like pace of the judicial system (Grier, 1982).

How do you cope with headaches and hassles? These airplane passengers, frustrated about a canceled flight, show the many possible responses to life's annoyances: amused friendliness, sullen acceptance, efforts to get information, and just plain gloom.

Notice, though, that when people report that something is a hassle, they are really reporting their feelings about it. The activity itself might be neutral. A young mother who says that making meals every day is a hassle is revealing her attitudes and emotions about this chore. Perhaps because she has so many other things to do every day, preparing dinner feels to her like the last straw. Her husband might look forward to cooking as an enjoyable way to reduce tension. So the measure of "hassles," like that of "stressful events," may be confounded with existing symptoms of emotional distress (Dohrenwend & Shrout, 1985).

Continuing problems. Many stress researchers believe that people have a good ability to withstand acute (short-term) stress, even a massive blow. The real problem, they say, occurs when stress becomes interminable: working in a pressure-cooker occupation; living with a tyrannical parent; living with discrimination because of your color, religion, gender, or age; feeling trapped in a situation you can't escape.

Under conditions of chronic stress, many people do not show physical adaptation to the stressor. In a study of 34 people who were taking care of a relative with advanced Alzheimer's disease—a relentless source of stress if there ever was one—the caregivers had significantly lower percentages of T lymphocytes and helper T lymphocytes than the control group and showed other abnormalities of the immune system. Their immune systems were apparently not adapting to the chronic stress (Kiecolt-Glaser et al., 1987b).

Prolonged or repeated stress (from occupations such as air traffic controller or from circumstances such as unemployment) is associated with heart disease, hypertension, arthritis, and immune-related deficiencies (Taylor, 1986). Black men in America who live in stressful neighborhoods (characterized by poverty, high divorce and unemployment rates, crime, and drug use) are particularly vulnerable to hypertension and related diseases (Gentry, 1985; Harburg et al., 1973). Female clerical workers who feel they have no support from their bosses, who are stuck in low-paying jobs without hope of promotion, and who have financial problems at home are the women most at risk of heart disease (Haynes & Feinleib, 1980).

A Closer Look at Psychoneuroimmunology

Why Confession Is Good for the Soul — And the Body

Now pay attention: *Don't think of a white bear*. Are you not thinking of it? Anyone who has ever tried to banish an uninvited thought knows how hard it is to erase the mental tape of worries, unhappy memories, or unwished-for obsessions. In an actual study, people who were told not to think of a white bear mentioned it nine times in a five-minute stream-of-consciousness session (Wegner et al., 1987). The reason seems to be that when you are trying to avoid a thought, you are in fact processing the thought frequently—rehearsing it and making it more accessible to consciousness.

According to James Pennebaker and his associates, the prolonged inhibition of thoughts and emotions requires physical effort, which is stressful to the body (Pennebaker, Hughes, & O'Heeron, 1987). Yet many people do try to inhibit secret thoughts and feelings that make them ashamed or depressed. The inability or unwillingness to confide important or traumatic events places continuing stress on the system and can lead to long-term health problems. In study after study, such individuals prove to be at greater risk of illness than people who are able to talk about their tragedies, even though disclosures of traumatic events are often painful and unpleasant at first (Pennebaker, 1988).

This information poses a problem: If an event is stressful and trying to stop thinking about the event is stressful, what should you do? Research from *psychoneuroimmunology*, the growing field that bridges psychology and the immune system, suggests some answers.

In one study, college students were assigned to write about *either* personal, traumatic experiences *or* trivial topics for 20 minutes a day, four days in a row. Those who were asked to reveal "their deepest thoughts and feelings" about a traumatic event all had something to talk about. Many told stories of sexual abuse, physical beatings, emotional humiliation, and parental abandonment. Others described upsetting changes, such as coming to college and the loneliness associated with leaving home. Yet most had never discussed these feelings with anyone.

The researchers took blood samples to test for the immune activity of lymphocytes; they also measured the students' physical symptoms, emotions, and visits to the health center. On every measure, the students who wrote about traumatic experiences were better off than those who did not (Pennebaker, Kiecolt-Glaser, & Glaser, 1988). Some of them showed *short-term* increases in anger and depression; writing about an unpleasant experience was not fun. But as months passed, their physical and emotional well-being improved.

The researchers believe that "the failure to confront a trauma forces the person to live with it in an unresolved manner." Actively writing or talking about it apparently helps people assimilate the tragedy and come to a sense of completion about it. But confession must not turn to obsession. Confessing your "deepest thoughts and feelings" is not therapeutic if you keep rehearsing and confessing them endlessly to all who will listen. The key is physiological release *and* cognitive perspective.

For example, several students who wrote about the same experience day after day gradually gained insight and distance. One woman, who had been molested at the age of 9 by a boy a few years older, at first wrote about her feelings of embarrassment and guilt. By the third day, she was writing about how angry she felt at the boy. By the last day, she had begun to see the whole event differently; he was young too, after all. After the experiment, she said, "Before, when I thought about it, I'd lie to myself. . . . Now, I don't feel like I even have to think about it because I got it off my chest. I finally admitted that it happened."

To see if the research will benefit you, why not keep a diary this year? All you have to do is jot down, from time to time, your "deepest thoughts and feelings" about school, your past, your future, anything. Pennebaker predicts that you will have fewer colds, headaches, and trips to the medical clinic next year.

What is "stressful" about stress?

In general, health psychologists today believe that life changes *are* related to your state of health, although the relationship is weak (Cohen & Edwards, 1989). Something else is going on between the event and your response to it. One of those things, as by now you can guess, is your perception of how stressful an event, a "hassle," or an accumulation of events is. In turn, feeling overwhelmed by stress depends on whether or not you feel you can *control* it. What seems to be most debilitating about chronically stressful situations is the feeling of powerlessness, of having no control over what happens. People can tolerate years of difficulty if they feel they can *control* events or at least *predict* them (Laudenslager & Reite, 1984). These are not necessarily the same thing. You may not be able to control the stressful experience of an exam, but you can usually predict and prepare for it. When people know that they will be going through a hard time or living in a stressful environment, they can take steps to reduce stress. We will return to this important topic of control later.

QUICK ▪ QUIZ

We hope these questions are not sources of stress for you.

1. Steve is unexpectedly called on in class to discuss a question. He doesn't have the faintest idea of the answer, and he feels his heart start to pound and his palms to sweat. He is in the _____ phase of the GAS.
2. Which of the Holmes-Rahe "life-change events" has the strongest relationship to immune problems and illness? **(a)** marriage, **(b)** bereavement, **(c)** taking an exam, **(d)** moving, **(e)** hassles
3. Maria works in a fast-food shop. Which aspect of the job is likely to be *most* stressful for her? **(a)** the speed of the work, **(b)** the predictable routine, **(c)** feeling unable to make any changes in her job, **(d)** the daily demands from customers

Answers:
1. alarm 2. b 3. c

Coping with Stress

We have just discussed different, compelling sources of stress, yet the remarkable fact is that most people who are "under stress" do *not* become ill. Why not? What helps people manage endless hassles and recover from the most awful adversity? How, in short, do they cope? We define **coping** as the constantly changing cognitive and behavioral efforts to manage demands, in the environment or in oneself, that one feels or believes to be stressful (Lazarus & Folkman, 1984). Coping is not a single strategy to be applied at all times and in all circumstances. People cope differently with daily hassles, losses, dangers, or challenges (Feifel, 1985; McCrae, 1984).

Freud argued that the mind develops defenses to protect it from unpleasant

coping *Cognitive and behavioral efforts to manage demands in the environment or oneself that one feels to be stressful.*

How do you cope with inevitable events?

truths, experiences, or conflicts. Because he treated people with problems, his theory implied that defenses are usually unhealthy, maladaptive, and passive. Although clinical psychologists are still concerned with the defenses that keep people unhappy, most health psychologists prefer the term *coping* to reflect a more active, constructive, and sympathetic view of people's efforts to solve their problems.

The many successful ways of coping fall into three general categories: (1) attacking the problem, (2) rethinking the problem, and (3) accepting the problem but lessening the physical effects of its stress (Shaver & O'Connor, 1986). Notice that the first attacks the stressor, the second attacks your interpretation of the stressor, and the third attacks the physical effects of the stress.

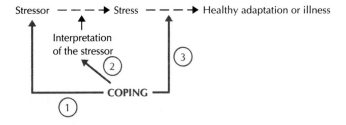

Attacking the problem

A woman we know, whom we will call Nancy, was struck by tragedy when she was 22. She and her new husband were driving home one evening when a car ran out of control and crashed into them. When Nancy awoke in a hospital room, she learned that her husband had been killed instantly. She herself had permanent spinal injury and would never walk again.

For many months, Nancy reacted with rage, despair, and grief. "Get it out of your system," her friends said. "You need to get in touch with your feelings." "But I *know* I'm miserable," Nancy lamented. "What do I *do*?"

What should Nancy do, indeed? Her predicament and her friends' advice point to the difference between *emotion-focused* and *problem-focused* coping (Lazarus & Folkman, 1984). Emotion-focused coping concentrates on changing or managing the emotions the problem has caused, whether anger, anxiety, or grief. Problem-focused coping attacks the problem itself.

The specific steps in problem-focused coping depend on the problem. (You may recall from Chapter 8 some of the stages of problem solving in general.) Sometimes the problem is clear (you lost your job). Sometimes it is uncertain (you suspect, but aren't sure, that you will lose your job). The problem may be a pressing but one-time decision; a continuing difficulty, such as living with a handicap; or an anticipated experience, such as the need to have an operation.

"Defining the problem" may seem obvious, especially when the Problem is standing there yelling at you. However, people often define a problem incorrectly and then set off down a wrong coping road. For example, unhappy couples often blame each other, or "incompatibility," for their misery. Sometimes, of course, they are right. But a study of several hundred couples found that marital unhappiness is often a result of misdiagnosis. A husband who is under great pressure at his office may decide that his problem is an unsupportive wife. A wife who is feeling too many conflicting demands may decide that her problem is her lazy husband. If this couple tries to cope with their unhappiness by attacking each other, they merely increase their misery. If they correctly diagnose the problem ("I'm worried about my job"; "I don't have enough leisure time to myself"), different coping solutions follow (A. Pines, 1986).

Once the problem is identified, the coper can learn as much as possible about it from professionals, friends, books, and others in the same boat. In Nancy's case, she can begin by learning more about her medical condition and prognosis. What can she do for herself? What kind of exercise will help her? How do other accident victims cope? Many people in stressful situations see no hope of escape. They divide their options into "stay here and suffer" versus "leave here and die" (Burns, 1980). What are Nancy's options? She could give up and feel sorry for herself. She could return home to live with her parents. She could learn to care for herself. She could go into the wheelchair business. She could. . . . (In fact, Nancy stayed in school, remarried, got a Ph.D. in psychology, and now does research and counseling with disabled people.)

Problem-focused coping has a large psychological benefit: It tends to increase a person's sense of self-esteem, control, and effectiveness (Pearlin & Schooler, 1978). Sometimes, though, emotions get in the way of assessing a problem accurately. When people are agonizing over a decision, they may, to relieve their anguish, make a fast, impulsive choice. They may say or do something in anger that worsens their predicament, or become so depressed that they cannot evaluate the situation carefully. That is why most people use a combination of emotion- and problem-focused coping (Folkman & Lazarus, 1980).

"Defining the problem" may sound easy: You're unhappy at work. But what does that mean? Is the problem your boss, your co-workers, your own attitude, or the work itself? How might your answer affect the way you cope with your unhappiness?

Rethinking the problem

Your first cognitive response to an event is a general evaluation, in which you decide whether the event is positive, neutral, or threatening and harmful. This global evaluation is followed by your judgment of whether you can handle the situation and, if so, how (Lazarus & Folkman, 1984). One way of coping with problems is to think about them in new ways, and there are several strategies for doing so. Shelley Taylor (1983, 1988), who has worked with cancer and cardiac patients, women who have been raped, and other victims of disaster or disease, finds that rethinking strategies have three goals:

- To find *meaning* in the experience: Why did this event happen to me? What does it mean for my life now?
- To regain *mastery* over the event and one's life: How can I keep this from happening again? What can I do about it now?
- To *restore self-esteem,* to feel good about oneself again in spite of the setback.

Among the many cognitive strategies that people use to reinterpret events, we will consider several of the most effective. (Again, keep in mind that their effectiveness may depend on the problem.)

Reappraisal: "It's not so bad." When people cannot eliminate a stressor, they can choose to rethink its implications and consequences. Problems can be turned into challenges, losses into unexpected gains. You lost your job. Is that a disaster? Maybe it wasn't such a good job, but you were too afraid to quit to look for another. A study of 100 spinal-cord-injured people found that two-thirds of them felt the disability had had positive side effects (Schulz & Decker, 1985). Benefits included becoming "a better person," "seeing other people as more important," and having an "increased awareness of self" and a new appreciation of "brain, not brawn."

People also reappraise the motives behind the distressing behavior of others. Instead of becoming enraged at someone's actions, for example, the empathic per-

Would you be overwhelmed or challenged by having lots to do?

"My Mom says to come in and have a seat. She's on two lines and has three people on hold."

son tries to see the situation from the other person's standpoint in order to avoid misunderstandings and misperceptions (Miller & Eisenberg, 1988).

Social comparisons: "I'm better off than they are."   In her study of women with breast cancer, Taylor (1983) found that successful copers compared themselves to others who were (they felt) less fortunate. This was true regardless of their age, marital status, or severity of the disease.

Thus women who had lumpectomies (removal of the lump itself) compared themselves to women who had the whole breast removed. One woman said, "I had a comparatively small amount of surgery. How awful it must be for women who have had a mastectomy." Yet women who had had mastectomies compared themselves to women whose cancer was far more serious. Said one, "It was not tragic. It's worked out okay. Now, if the thing had spread all over, I would have had a whole different story for you." Younger married women compared themselves to single women ("I can't imagine dating . . . and not knowing how to tell the man about it"), but no single woman felt it would have been easier for her if she had been married. The women who were worst off felt grateful that they were not dying and that they were not in pain. "The point, of course," concludes Taylor, "is that everyone is better off than someone as long as one picks the right dimension."

Avoidance: "It's not important; let's go to the movies."   Is it ever a good idea to cope with a problem by ignoring it or running away from it? Suppose you are going to the hospital for routine surgery, such as for a hernia, gall bladder, or thyroid condition. Should you get as much information as you can about every detail and risk of the procedure, or, having decided to go ahead, should you avoid thinking about it?

In a study of this question, researchers divided 61 patients according to their style of coping with a forthcoming operation: "vigilance" or "avoidance" (Cohen & Lazarus, 1973). Avoiders showed a remarkable lack of interest in what was going to happen to them. They said such things as "All I know is that I have a hernia. It doesn't disturb me one bit." They didn't discuss the surgery in detail and said it was nothing to worry about. "Having an operation," said one avoider, "is like having a vacation."

In contrast, the vigilant types attended to every detail. They read articles about their condition and wanted to know everything about the surgery, including the type of incision that would be made and the anesthesia used. They learned about every risk, no matter how remote, and about possible postoperative complications. One patient said, "I have all the facts, my will is prepared . . . your heart could quit, you can have shock."

Some psychologists believe that vigilance is the best strategy, that "the work of worrying" prepares a person to cope with all possible results. In this situation, however, vigilance backfired. The avoiders fared much better. They needed fewer pain medications. They complained less about treatment. They had fewer minor complications such as nausea, headache, fever, or infection. They got out of the hospital sooner.

Many studies have now been done on the difference between people who are vigilant, who scan all information for evidence of threat to themselves, and those who avoid threatening information by distracting themselves (S. Miller, 1987, 1989). There are benefits and disadvantages to both styles of coping. Vigilant individuals, for example, are overly sensitive to their bodily symptoms, tend to exaggerate their importance, and take longer to recover from them (Miller, Brody, & Summerton, 1988). On the other hand, perhaps because they are so health con-

When should you try to leave your problems behind you . . .

When should you cope with a problem by attacking it head-on, and when should you ignore it? Under stress, is it better to be a tiger or an ostrich?

scious, they are more likely to look after themselves—say, by getting routine medical and dental exams.

Once you have all the necessary information to make a decision and that decision is out of your hands, avoidance—letting go of worry—is an excellent coping device. But vigilance is called for when action is possible and necessary. Sometimes both strategies can work together. In a hospital, for example, patients do best if they refuse to dwell on every little thing that could go wrong, if they distract themselves as much as possible. They also get well faster (and protect themselves) when they are vigilant about the care they are getting, when they protest incorrect or thoughtless treatment. The benefits of distraction do not mean you should lie there like a flounder and passively accept every decision made for you.

Of course, some people do more than "distract" themselves when they cope with a stressful situation; they deny it altogether. Is denial ever good for you? See "Think About It."

Humor: "People are funny." "A merry heart doeth good like a medicine," says Proverbs, and researchers are beginning to agree. Once thought too frivolous a topic for serious study, humor has made its way into the laboratory. Rod Martin and Herbert Lefcourt (1983) gave people tests to measure stress, mood, and sense of humor. "Sense of humor" includes the ability to respond with humor in real situations, to like humor and humorous people, and to use humor in coping with stress.

Martin and Lefcourt found that humor makes an excellent buffer between stress and negative moods. What's so funny about misery? "He who laughs," thundered the German poet and dramatist Bertolt Brecht, "has not heard the terrible news." But people who can transform the "terrible news" into a sense of the absurd or the whimsical, Martin and Lefcourt found, are less prone to depression, anger, tension, and fatigue than are people who give in to gloom. Supporting studies with more than 1000 college students found the same thing. Among students coping with unfortunate events, those who respond with humor feel fewer negative emotions and unhappiness later than do students who don't have a sense of humor or who instead succumb to moping and tears (Labott & Martin, 1986; Nezu, Nezu, & Blissett, 1988).

Some theories of laughter emphasize its ability to reduce tension and emotion. You have probably been in a tense group situation when someone suddenly made exactly the right crack to defuse the mood and make everyone laugh. Laughter seems to produce some beneficial biological responses, possibly stimulating the immune system or starting the flow of endorphins, the painkilling chemicals in the brain (Fry, 1986; J. Goldstein, 1987).

. . . and when should you laugh about them?

Other theories emphasize the cognitive components of humor. When you laugh at a problem, you are putting it in a new perspective—seeing its silly aspects—and gaining control over it (Dixon, 1980). Humor also allows you to express indirectly feelings that are hazardous to express directly, which is why it is so often the weapon of minorities. An old joke tells of a Jew who accidentally bumped into a Nazi on a street. "Swine!" bellowed the Nazi. "And I'm Cohen," replied the Jew, "pleased to meet you."

Having a sense of humor, however, is not the same as smiling all the time or "putting on a happy face." Many women, in particular, feel they have to smile, smile, smile, to put others at ease, but often this social smile masks feelings of insecurity and unhappiness (Frances, 1979). For humor to be effective in coping with stress, a person must actually use it during a stressful situation—seeing or inventing funny aspects of serious events and having the ability to laugh at them (Nezu, Nezu, & Blissett, 1988). Hostile humor therefore misses the point: Vicious,

Think About It

Are Illusions Healthy?

Denial is certainly a common response to stress: "This isn't happening to me"; "It is happening to me, but it isn't important"; "If I ignore it, the problem will go away." Since Freud, many psychologists have regarded denial as a primitive, dangerous defense mechanism that meant a person was out of touch with reality. And being out of touch with reality has long been assumed to be a hallmark of mental illness. Now some researchers are asking: When reality serves up a problem you can't do anything about, what's so bad about losing touch with it?

Emotionally healthy people supposedly are good at "reality testing" and do not need self-promoting illusions; they can face the truth about themselves. Today, the weight of evidence has shifted to the opposite view. After reviewing years of research, Shelley E. Taylor and Jonathon D. Brown (1988) conclude that well-being virtually depends on the illusions of "overly positive self-evaluations, exaggerated perceptions of control or mastery, and unrealistic optimism." These illusions, Taylor (1989) argues, are not only characteristic of normal human thought, but also necessary for the usual criteria of mental health: the ability to

care about others, the ability to be contented, and the ability to work productively. In fact, the people who score *highest* on tests of self-deception (for example, who deny threatening but universal feelings, such as ever having felt guilty) score the *lowest* on measures of psychopathology and depression!

Why should this be so? The mind is designed to filter all incoming information, say Taylor and Brown, distorting it in a positive direction to enhance self-esteem and ward off bad news. Positive illusions, they find, are especially useful under conditions of adversity—when people are threatened with illness, crisis, or attacks to their self-esteem. This strategy is adaptive and healthy, because if people judged their problems accurately, they might fold their tents and give up. In a situation in which your abilities are untested, as William James noted long ago, it is much more beneficial to try and possibly succeed than not to try at all.

On the other hand, health psychologists worry about the many self-destructive things that denial permits people to do: They drink too much, they smoke, they won't wear their seat belts, they don't take medication for chronic illness. When people

---

rude jokes at another person's expense are not stress reducers. They often create more tension and anger (Baron, 1977).

Living with the problem

In modern life, we often cannot escape life changes, ongoing conflicts, or the hassles of traffic, noise, or job or school pressure (see "Taking Psychology with You"). A third approach to coping concentrates on reducing the physical effects of stress itself.

Relaxation. The simplest way to reduce signs of stress, such as high blood pressure and rapid breathing, is to relax. Relaxation training—learning to alternately tense and relax certain muscles, to lie or sit quietly, to banish worries of the day—apparently has beneficial effects on the immune system. In a sample of 45 elderly people living in retirement homes, those who learned to reduce stress with relaxation techniques showed significant increases in natural killer (NK) cell activity and decreases in antibodies to herpes simplex virus, both signs of improved immune activity (Kiecolt-Glaser et al., 1985b).

make important decisions about themselves that are based on denial and self-flattering illusions, the results can be disastrous. It is dangerous when a woman ignores a lump in her breast, when a man having a heart attack says "it's only indigestion," when a diabetic fails to take needed medication.

Moreover, the illusion of invulnerability—"it will never happen to me"—can lead people to do all sorts of dangerous and stupid things. So strong is this illusion that it even affects people who should know better. The former Olympic diver Bruce Kimball, whose face and body were smashed in a car accident, recovered sufficiently to win a silver medal in the 1984 Olympics. But in 1988 he got blind drunk and careened his car into a group of teenagers, killing two and seriously injuring six.

Further, illusions are not necessarily beneficial if they keep people from recognizing their limitations. How long should you keep trying to join the major leagues if you just aren't a great ball player? People need to know when to quit, and what they can't do as well as what they can (Janoff-Bulman, 1988). People who overestimate their chances of success may spend excessive, wasteful years trying

to become something they are not (Baumeister & Scher, 1988). As W. C. Fields once observed, "If at first you don't succeed, try, try again. If you still don't succeed, quit. No use being a damn fool about it."

What happens when people must reconcile their former illusions with a traumatic event that cannot be ignored? The result is often, literally, dis-illusion (Janoff-Bulman, 1988). Some victims never return to their former illusions; they see the world as less benevolent and less meaningful than it had been and themselves as less worthy. Unable to create positive illusions, they often become depressed, anxious, and hopeless. Others do eventually reestablish a positive view of the world and themselves, finding new meaning in the tragedy (Collins, Taylor, & Skokan, in press).

What is the line between "healthy illusions"— those that maintain self-esteem and optimism—and self-destructive ones? How would you know which is which? Is it better to maintain illusions at all costs, if they protect your self-esteem, or to think critically about them and risk losing optimism? What do you think?

Some people learn to relax through systematic *meditation*, a practice aimed at focusing one's attention and eliminating all distracting thoughts. Short-term meditation does not produce a unique physiological or emotional state; studies find no difference between meditation and simple resting (D. Holmes, 1984; Holmes et al., 1983). In Eastern religions like Hinduism and Buddhism, however, meditation is much more than a relaxation or stress-reduction technique. The goal is not to unwind but to attain wisdom, acceptance of reality, emotional detachment, and transcendence of the self—states of mind not measurable on an EEG machine.

In a review of relaxation methods, two researchers found that methods that work for one person or one kind of problem may not be as successful with others (Woolfolk & Lehrer, 1984). For example, relaxation is helpful in reducing the pain of menstrual cramps if the pain is caused by muscle cramps and not fluid retention. Some people benefit from cognitive therapy or self-hypnosis, as well as relaxation, to learn to calm tense thoughts as well as tense muscles (see Chapter 17). And although biofeedback is often promoted as a stress-reducer, simple relaxation is just as effective, and a lot cheaper (Turner & Chapman, 1982a).

Exercise. Physical exercise, such as jogging, dancing, biking, and swimming, is very important in maintaining health and reducing stress (Hayden, 1984;

Exercise has many all-around health benefits, which is why some American companies are adopting the Japanese practice of scheduling exercise breaks for workers. Should exercise be a formal and required part of the work-day?

Exercise is great, but is it a cure-all? When does it help you alleviate your problems, and when does it become an excuse to escape them?

Taylor, 1986). An invigorating workout can leave you feeling refreshed and ener-getic—a nonhostile, nonaggressive workout, that is. People who think angry, com-petitive thoughts while they are exercising are, in effect, adding fuel to the fire (France, 1984).

Besides reducing tension, exercise combats anxiety, depression, and the blues. In one study of 43 college women, all moderately to severely depressed, researchers assigned the students to one of three groups. One group did aerobic exercise three times a week, another practiced relaxation and took leisurely walks four times a week, and a control group did neither. After five weeks and again after ten weeks, the women took tests of their aerobic capacity and level of depression. Those who exercised vigorously showed improved fitness and sharp declines in depression; the relaxation and control groups didn't reduce their depression levels (McCann & Holmes, 1984). Similarly, a study of 207 Denver workers found that the more these employees exercised, the fewer physical symptoms, colds, and stresses, and the less anxiety, depression, and irritability, they reported (Hendrix & Rodriguez, 1984).

Many popular books and magazines therefore advocate exercise as the all-purpose coping strategy. There is no doubt that regular exercise is an excellent all-around health tonic. But people who exercise in order to *avoid* their problems are not necessarily reducing their stress load, especially if they have to go back to the same old problem tomorrow. In one study of 230 working women, the strongest predictor of depression, anxiety, and physical stress was difficulty at work. The form of coping that helped best was dealing with the job problems directly (O'Neill & Zeichner, 1984). You can't, it seems, jog away from everything.

Looking outward

A psychologist who has worked with Holocaust survivors, prisoners of war, hos-tages, refugees, and other survivors of catastrophe believes that a key element in their recovery is compassion, ''healing through helping'' (Segal, 1986). People gain strength, he says, by giving it to others.

This observation echoes Alfred Adler's theory of *social interest* (see Chapter

11). To Adler (1938/1964), social interest has a cognitive component (the ability to understand others, to see the connectedness of humanity and the world), an emotional component (the ability to feel empathy and attachment), and a behavioral component (the willingness to cooperate with others for the common welfare). Although ''social interest'' is the opposite of selfishness, it is harmonious with self-interest. Adler believed that people who are involved with others, unlike those who are too self-involved, would be better able to cope with life's problems, have higher self-esteem, and be psychologically stronger (Ansbacher, 1968).

Adler's ideas have been supported. One large study used two measures of social interest: a scale of moral values and an index of cooperation in love, work, and friendship. People who were high in social interest, compared to others, had fewer stressful experiences and were better able to cope with the stressful episodes they did have. Among people low in social interest, stress was more likely to be associated with anxiety, depression, and hostility. Social interest seems to soften the effects of stress on psychological well-being (Crandall, 1984).

Why is social interest healthy? The ability to look outside of oneself, to be concerned with others, is related to virtually all of the successful coping mechanisms we have discussed so far. It tends to lead to solving problems instead of blaming others. It helps you reappraise a conflict, trying to see it as others do, instead of taking it personally. It allows you to get perspective on a problem instead of exaggerating its importance. Because of its elements of forgiveness, tolerance, and sense of connectedness, it helps you live with situations that are facts of life.

QUICK ▪ QUIZ

Can you cope with these refresher questions?

1. You accidentally broke your glasses. Which response is an example of cognitive reappraisal? **(a)** ''I am such a stupid clumsy idiot!'' **(b)** ''I never do anything right.'' **(c)** ''What a shame, but I've been wanting new frames anyway.'' **(d)** ''I'll forget about it in aerobics class.''
2. Finding out what your legal and financial resources are when you have been victimized by a crime is an example of **(a)** problem-focused coping, **(b)** emotion-focused coping, **(c)** distraction, **(d)** reappraisal.
3. Learning deep-breathing techniques to reduce anxiety in taking exams is an example of **(a)** problem-focused coping, **(b)** emotion-focused coping, **(c)** avoidance, **(d)** reappraisal.
4. ''This class drives me crazy, but it's better than not being in school'' is an example of **(a)** distraction, **(b)** social comparison, **(c)** denial, **(d)** empathy.
5. Your roommate has turned your room into a bomb crater, filled with rotten apple cores and unwashed clothes. Should you **(a)** nag, **(b)** start a quarrel, **(c)** resentfully clean the room yourself, **(d)** pile everything into a heap, put a flag on top, and add a sign: ''Monument to the Battle of the Bilge''?

Answers:
1. c 2. a 3. b 4. b 5. d

The Individual Side of Health and Well-Being

Up to now, we have been discussing strategies that anyone can use in reducing the effects of stress. But people differ in how well they are able to cope and in what they do to protect their health. We now turn to four aspects of individual psychology that are related to health: negative emotions, ''explanatory style,'' healthy habits, and locus of control.

Negative emotions

Efforts to document the relationship between emotion and disease go back many centuries, and today many people speak as if the connection were proven: Worriers get ulcers; irritable workaholics get heart attacks; asthmatics are emotionally repressed. Certainly it seems that some people manufacture their own misery. Send them to a beach far from civilization, and they bring along a bag of worries and irritations. But the connections between emotion and health are not simple.

An initial attempt to identify one of those connections focused on the *Type A behavior pattern*, a set of qualities that seemed to increase the risk of heart disease, the nation's leading cause of death (Friedman & Rosenman, 1974). Although Type A has been measured in different, often inconsistent ways, it basically refers to a constant struggle to achieve, a sense of time urgency, impatience at anyone or anything that gets in the way, irritability, and an intense effort to control the environment. Type B people are calmer and less intense. Researchers were excited about the Type A hypothesis, and so was the public. People began talking about what ''type'' they were and whether they could or should change it.

Today, however, the enthusiasm about Type A is a mere shadow of its former self. It turns out that different tasks and situations produce different physiological responses in the same people, and being highly reactive to stress and challenge is not in itself a risk factor in heart disease (Krantz & Manuck, 1984). Type A people *do* set themselves a fast work pace and a heavy work load, but many cope better than Type B people who have a lighter work load, and without a high physiological price (Frankenhaeuser, 1980). Further, people who are highly involved in their jobs, even if they work hard, have a low incidence of heart disease. ''There'd be nothing wrong with us fast-moving Type A's,'' said a friend of ours, ''if it weren't for all those slow-moving Type B's.''

Nevertheless, something about Type A may be dangerous to one's health. Which aspects of the Type A pattern are unhealthy, and which are fine? One research team distinguished between two groups of ambitious, fast-moving people often called Type A: the ''healthy charismatics,'' who are expressive, active, friendly, and relaxed, and the ''hostile competitives,'' who are angry, tense, and defensive (Friedman, Hall, & Harris, 1985). As psychologists delved into the puzzle of Type A, they found that its hazardous ingredients are likely to be anger, anxiety, and depression (Friedman & Booth-Kewley, 1987a, 1987b). For example, men who are chronically angry and resentful and who have a hostile attitude toward others are *five times* as likely as nonhostile men to get coronary heart disease and other ailments, controlling for other risk factors such as smoking (Williams, 1989; Williams, Barefoot, & Shekelle, 1985).

Even then, not all kinds of hostility have turned out to be equally hazardous to

When you're under a lot of pressure, do you take it out on others?

health. *Neurotic hostility*, which describes people who are grumpy, complaining, and irritable, is *not* related to heart disease. (It seems to be part of the general personality trait of neuroticism, described in Chapter 11.) But *antagonistic hostility*, describing people who are aggressive, rude, confronting, cynical, and uncooperative, is, researchers find, the "toxic" hostility that is linked to heart disease (Dembroski & Costa, 1988). You can see, therefore, the importance of defining terms, such as "anger" and "hostility," carefully.

Howard S. Friedman and Stephanie Booth-Kewley (1987a) took the next step, asking whether negative emotions are related to specific diseases. They selected several emotions or personality traits that have been implicated in illness (anger, hostility, depression, introversion, and anxiety) and five diseases believed to have psychological components (asthma, arthritis, ulcers, headaches, and heart disease). The researchers used a sophisticated statistical method to combine and summarize the results of 101 studies. To their surprise, they failed to find specific, disease-connected traits, such as the arthritic personality or the coronary-prone personality or the anger-suppressing ulcer patient. But the researchers did find evidence for a "generic, disease-prone personality" who is chronically depressed, angry and hostile, and anxious. Depression was most strongly implicated in four of the five diseases, excluding ulcers.

Before concluding that emotions or personality traits directly cause illness, Friedman and Booth-Kewley (1987b) observed that there are other possible links between personality and disease:

If sick people are angrier than others, does that mean that anger caused their illnesses? Can you think of other explanations for a relationship between emotions and disease?

▪ *The disease causes the emotion.* Many psychotherapists and physicians see patients who are angry, depressed, or anxious because they are sick. It is an easy jump to the (wrong) conclusion that the anger, depression, or anxiety *caused* the sickness. In addition, some diseases or abnormalities, such as brain tumors or an oxygen deficiency, can directly cause mood change (see Chapter 16).

▪ *Unhealthy habits cause the disease.* Before you could conclude that "an anxious personality style causes lung cancer," you would have to rule out the possibility that people who feel anxious are more likely to smoke or drink. Unfortunately, many studies that examine the links between personality and disease do not take health habits into account.

▪ *Something else entirely affects emotion* and *disease.* Another possibility is that some third factor is related both to an emotional style and a disease. For example, perhaps an overresponsive nervous system leads to the development of frequent anger and, independently, to the development of heart disease.

▪ *Personality leads to disease, which affects personality, which affects disease: the mind-body system.* A single personality trait or emotion rarely is "the cause" of disease. But chronic anxiety could lead to unhealthy practices, which could cause physical changes (influenced in turn by genetic makeup), which could make one's anxiety worse, which could keep one from taking care of oneself, which in turn. . . .

It is therefore one thing to say that emotions or personality factors are *involved* in illness. It is quite another to say that they *cause* illness. "Personality may function like diet," the researchers concluded. "Imbalances can predispose one to all sorts of diseases." Psychological disturbances affect the immune system *in general*, they observed. The occurrence of a *specific* illness depends on other factors, such as whether a person drinks excessively or smokes, the person's genetic vulnerabilities, and the biology of the disease itself.

Studies suggest that explanatory style affects longevity. Zack Wheat, an outfielder for the Brooklyn Dodgers, had an optimistic explanatory style: "I'm a better hitter than I used to be because my strength has improved and my experience has improved." Wheat lived to be 83.

Explanatory style

Perhaps you remember from Chapter 9 the habits of thinking associated with depression. Depressed people tend to explain uncontrollable events as internal ("It's all my fault"), stable ("This misery is going to last forever"), and global ("It's going to affect everything I do"). Cheerful people regard the same events as external ("I couldn't have done anything about it"), unstable ("Things will improve"), and limited in impact ("Well, at least the rest of my life is OK").

Christopher Peterson and Martin Seligman (1984, 1987) call these characteristic ways of accounting for bad events *explanatory style*, and they observe that these two styles of thinking describe the difference between pessimists and optimists. Their research suggests that an optimistic explanatory style is related to self-esteem, achievement, and physical health and longevity (Peterson, 1988). Pessimists will probably complain that optimism is just a *result* of good health; it's easy to think positively when you feel good. But there is growing evidence that optimism may produce good health as well as reflect it.

In one imaginative study of baseball Hall-of-Famers who had played between 1900 and 1950, 30 players were rated according to their explanatory style. A pessimistic remark would be internal, stable, and global, such as "We didn't win because my arm is shot, it'll never get better, and it affects my performance every time." An optimistic version would be external, unstable, and specific: "We didn't win because we got a couple of lousy calls, just bad luck on this game, but we'll be great tomorrow." The optimists were significantly more likely to have lived well into old age than were the pessimists (Seligman, 1986).

What could be the link between pessimism and illness? One answer is that pessimism produces depression and stress, which in turn affect the immune system. High degrees of pessimism are independently associated with impaired immune activity (Rodin, 1988). This means that pessimists do not fall ill because they are sicker or more depressed to begin with. A longitudinal study of Harvard University graduates started out with young men who were in good health. But 35 years later,

Walter Johnson, a star pitcher for the Washington Senators, had a pessimistic explanatory style: "I can't depend on myself to pitch well. I'm growing old. I have had my day." Johnson died at the age of 59.

those who had had a pessimistic explanatory style were in significantly worse health than the optimists (Peterson, Seligman, & Vaillant, 1988).

A second explanation may have to do with how people cope with stress. Optimists tend to be problem-focused rather than emotion-focused. When faced with a problem, such as a risky operation or a serious continuing struggle with alcoholism, they focus on what they can *do* rather than on how they *feel*. They have a higher expectation of being successful, so they don't give up at the first sign of a setback (Carver & Scheier, 1987; Peterson & Barrett, 1987). Perhaps, then, pessimists are more likely to become ill because they stir up negative emotions rather than take constructive action.

Third, pessimists often fail to take care of themselves (on the belief, we suppose, that it won't do any good). When they develop colds or flu, for example, they are less likely than optimists to take the basic precautions: sleeping more, drinking fluids, not overdoing it. Perhaps this is why their colds and flu are more likely to return (Peterson & Seligman, 1987).

Can pessimism be "cured"? Optimists, naturally, think so. Cognitive therapy has been remarkably successful in teaching depressed people new explanatory styles (see Chapter 17). Psychologist Rachel Hare-Mustin told us how her mother cured her budding childhood pessimism—with humor. "Nobody likes me," Rachel lamented. "Don't say that," her mother said. "Everybody hasn't met you yet."

Healthy habits

We bet you $100 that you already know the basic rules for protecting your health: get enough sleep, get regular exercise, eat a nutritious diet, drink alcohol only in moderation, do not overeat, do not undereat (on starvation diets), and do not smoke cigarettes. A ten-year longitudinal study of nearly 7000 people in Alameda County, California, found that each of these practices was independently related to good health and lack of stress symptoms (Matarazzo, 1984; Wiley & Camacho, 1980).

The more of these practices people followed, the better their mental and physical health.

Well, why aren't you following all of them? Health psychologists study one of the perplexing riddles of human behavior: why, when people know what is good for them, they often don't do it. An important goal of health psychology is prevention: helping people eliminate the risk factors for illness before the illness has a chance to develop. One goal is to get people to change their unhealthy habits—to get them to quit smoking, say, or to cut down on junk food. Another goal is to keep people from developing the bad habits in the first place, for example, by demonstrating the dangers of smoking to preadolescent children. But health psychologists have found several obstacles in their pursuit of prevention (Taylor, 1986):

- Many health habits are entrenched in childhood, and parents play a powerful role in determining a child's health habits. For example, they determine what children learn about alcohol—whether to drink in moderation or go on ''binges''—and what kind of food is best. It will be hard for you to give up a high-cholesterol diet if you associate it with home-cooked meals.
- People often have little incentive to change unhealthy habits. Smoking, drinking, eating junk food, and not exercising have no immediate consequences, and their effects might not become apparent for years. So many people in good health feel invulnerable.
- Health habits are largely independent of one another. Some people exercise every day and continue to smoke. Some people eat nutritious meals and take a lot of drugs.
- Health habits are unstable over time. Some people quit smoking for a year—and then take it up again. Others lose 50 pounds—and then gain 60.

In spite of these obstacles, health psychologists have identified many factors that influence your health habits. Some are in your social system: Do all your friends smoke and drink themselves into a stupor on weekends? Chances are that you will join them. Some are in your larger cultural environment: Does your culture think it is appropriate for women to exercise or for men to stop eating red meat? Some are in your access to health care services and information: Not everybody in this society has the affluence, insurance, or opportunity to consult doctors. Finally, some are in your basic attitudes and beliefs: Do you feel fatalistic about illness or in charge of your health?

The question of control: Fight or flow?

In Chapter 11 we described *internal and external* **locus of control**: People who feel that they are in charge of their lives (with an internal locus of control) often deal more effectively with problems and decisions than people who lack this sense of mastery (those with an external locus of control). ''Internals'' adjust their coping efforts to suit the problem, selecting the appropriate tactic from a range of possibilities (Parkes, 1984). People who feel powerless (''externals'') tend to respond to stress with anger, depression, drug use, or physical symptoms (Langer, 1983). All of the factors we have discussed so far—negative emotions, pessimism, poor health habits, and an inability to cope—may in turn be related to this basic personality factor: feeling in control of one's life.

locus of control *A general expectation about whether the results of one's actions are under one's own control (internal* locus*) or beyond one's control (external* locus*).*

The benefits of control. Some years ago, a team of psychologists followed 259 business managers for five years, comparing those who developed illnesses with those who did not (Kobasa, 1979; Kobasa, Maddi, & Kahn, 1982). The healthy group turned out to have what the researchers called "hardy" personalities. "Hardiness" had three components: *commitment*, the feeling of attachment to one's activities and relationships; *challenge*, the willingness to accept new experiences, to see opportunities in change rather than losses; and *control*, the belief that one can influence most events and other people.

Like Type A, hardiness was a concept that almost immediately achieved great popular appeal. It sounded so right. However, the three components turn out to be largely independent of one another, and "challenge" is not directly related to health at all. Moreover, it is not the *presence* of commitment and control that lead to health; it is the *lack* of commitment and *lack* of control in specific situations that can be harmful (Funk & Houston, 1987; Hull, Van Treuren, & Virnelli, 1987). All things considered, the benefits of hardiness appear to be accounted for by the more general factor, locus of control (Cohen & Edwards, 1989).

The sense of being in control need not be enormous to be effective. When elderly residents of nursing homes are simply given more choices over their activities and environment and given more control over day-to-day events, the results are dramatic: They become more alert, more active, happier—and less likely to die (Langer, 1983; Langer et al., 1979).

Locus of control has many effects on mind and body. As we saw in Chapter 5, it is related to a person's appraisal that he or she can cope with pain (Litt, 1988). Control also influences how people experience and label their physical sensations: Is that twinge or cough a sign of something serious? In experiments that vary the amount of control people have over what happens to them, subjects given low or no control report more physical symptoms than those who feel more in control (Pennebaker, 1982). The sense of control also directly affects the neuroendocrine and immune systems. This fact may explain why an improved sense of control is so beneficial to old people, whose immune systems normally decline (Rodin, 1988).

Keep in mind, though, that the sense of control is not all in your head. It is also in your social circumstances, income, and status. Working-class people, for instance, have both less sense of control *and* worse health than more affluent people do. Moreover, the path between control and health runs in two directions. Control does affect health, but health also affects how much control you feel you have (Rodin, 1988).

Some problems with control. In general, a sense of control is a good thing. But believing that an event is controllable does not always lead to a reduction in stress, and believing that an event is uncontrollable does not always lead to an increase in stress (Folkman, 1984; S. Thompson, 1981). The question must always be asked: Control over what? If an unrealistically confident person tries to control the uncontrollable ("I'm going to be a movie star in 60 days!"), the resulting failure may lead to unrealistic helplessness (Fleming, Baum, & Singer, 1984). In one study of 45 adults, those who had the strongest internal locus of control were the most vulnerable to stressful events that were out of their control, as measured by their immune functioning (Kubitz, Peavey, & Moore, 1985).

It also doesn't help people to believe they have control over an event if they then feel unable to cope with it. Victims of abuse or other crimes, for example, often suffer because they blame themselves for having "provoked" their attackers, as if they could have controlled the criminal's behavior (Janoff-Bulman, 1988).

What, then, can we conclude about the importance of control to health? One answer comes from a psychologist we know, who once asked a Buddhist monk how to manage stress. The monk laughed. "The very question is the problem," he said. "Americans are always to trying to 'manage' and 'control' everything, as if one's

In general, it's good to feel in control of your life, but what does that mean exactly? Control over what? How much of your life? How do the events in your life affect your sense of control?

Sometimes life dishes up a disaster, as it has for many farm families who have lost their lands and livelihoods because of the changing economy. When is it helpful to believe we can control everything that happens to us, and when is it harmful?

feelings were unruly parts of nature that required taming.'' ''Management'' is a business term, he told our friend, and ''hardiness'' is a concept better suited to the pioneer life than to modern times. Buddhists believe that change and death are inevitable. Anyone who fails to recognize this truth, they say, cannot be healthy or at peace (Shaver & O'Connor, 1986).

Eastern and Western approaches both offer ways of feeling in control of one's life, but they are different ways and different kinds of control. In **primary control**, people try to influence existing reality by changing other people, circumstances, or events. In **secondary control**, people try to accommodate to external reality by changing their own perceptions, goals, or desires (Rothbaum, Weisz, & Snyder, 1982). By and large, the Western approach has been to aim for primary control: If you don't like something, change it, fix it, or fight it. The Eastern approach has been to emphasize secondary control: If you have a problem, learn to live with it or act in spite of it. In a comparison of the United States and Japan, one study found that these two perspectives influence practices in child rearing, socialization, religion, work, and psychotherapy (Weisz, Rothbaum, & Blackburn, 1984).

A Japanese psychologist offers some examples of Japanese proverbs that teach the benefits of yielding to the inevitable (Azuma, 1984): *To lose is to win* (giving in, to protect the harmony of a relationship, demonstrates the superior traits of tolerance, self-control, and generosity); *Willow trees do not get broken by piled up snow* (no matter how many problems pile up in your life, flexibility will allow you to survive them); and *The true tolerance is to tolerate the intolerable* (some ''intolerable'' situations are facts of life, and you do better to accept them than to protest uselessly). Perhaps you can imagine how long ''to lose is to win'' would survive on an American football field, or how long most Americans would be prepared to tolerate the intolerable!

The point is not that one form of control is better or healthier than the other, but rather that both have their place. The emphasis on primary control encourages self-expression, independence, and change, at a possible price of self-absorption and loneliness. The emphasis on secondary control leads to continuity, attachment, and serenity, at a possible price of self-denial and stagnation (Iga, 1986). Most problems require us to choose between trying to change what we can and accepting what we cannot. Perhaps a secret of healthy control lies in knowing the difference.

primary control *An effort to modify external reality by changing other people, the situation, or events; a ''fighting-back'' method of coping.*

secondary control *An effort to accept external reality by changing one's own attitudes, goals, or emotions; a ''learn to live with it'' method of coping.*

QUICK ▪ QUIZ

Do not interpret these questions as stressful:

1. Which of the following aspects of Type A behavior seem most hazardous to health? **(a)** working hard, **(b)** being in a hurry, **(c)** antagonistic hostility, **(d)** high physical reactivity, **(e)** neurotic hostility
2. "I'll never find anyone else to love because I'm not good-looking; that one romance was a fluke" illustrates a(n) _____ explanatory style.
3. Adapting yourself to the reality that you are getting older is an example of _____ control.
4. Joining a protest against sexual harassment on the job is an example of _____ control.

Answers:

1. c 2. pessimistic 3. secondary 4. primary

The Social Side of Health and Well-Being

Thus far we have been looking at individual factors involved in stress and illness. But health and well-being are not just up to you as an individual. They also depend on the people around you.

The Alameda County health study that we mentioned earlier (which followed nearly 7000 adults for a decade) also investigated the importance of social relationships to health. The researchers considered four kinds of social ties: marriage, contact with friends and relatives, church membership, and participation in other groups. The people who had few social networks were more likely to have died at the time of the ten-year follow-up than those who had many (Berkman & Syme, 1979).

Perhaps the people who died were sicker to begin with or had poorer health habits, which kept them from socializing? No. The importance of social networks was unrelated to physical health at the time the study began, to socioeconomic status, and to such risk factors as smoking.

Perhaps the people who died had some undiagnosed illness at the beginning of the study? This interpretation was possible because the study was based on the participants' self-reports. So the research was repeated with nearly 3000 people in Tecumseh, Michigan, and this time the investigators collected everyone's medical exams. Ten years later, those who had few social relationships were more likely to have died than the people who had many, even after age, health, and other risk factors were taken into account (House, 1986; House, Robbins, & Metzner, 1982).

As psychologists explored the benefits of friends and family, they noticed something else. Sometimes friends and family are themselves the source of hassles, headaches, and conflicts. There are two sides to the human need for social support.

When friends help you cope . . .

One psychologist calls friendship a form of "assisted coping": Friends help you deal with problems when you are too drained to budge (Thoits, 1984). By "friends" we mean family members, neighbors, co-workers, and anyone else in your social network.

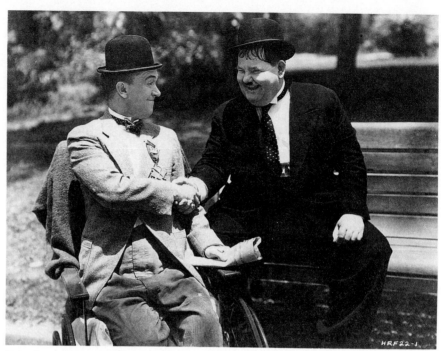

Friends can be our greatest sources of warmth, support, and fun . . .

Friends do many "supportive" things. They provide *emotional support*, such as concern and affection. They offer *cognitive guidance*, helping you evaluate problems and plan a course of action. They offer *tangible support*, with resources and services such as loaning money or the car, or taking notes in class for you when you have to go to the doctor. They offer companionship (Rook, 1987). Perhaps most of all, they give you the feeling of attachment to others, of being part of a network that cares (Hobfoll & Stephens, in press; Sarason et al., 1987).

The effect of friends on your health depends on what the friends are doing for you and how much stress you are under. In studying a representative sample of more than 2000 adults, Karen Rook (1987) found that for people with *average*, everyday levels of stress, social support had no effect on health one way or the other. Among people who had *above*-average levels of stress, support from friends did help reduce their physical and emotional symptoms. But among people who had *below*-average levels of stress, such support was actually harmful. It was associated with more symptoms! Why might this be so? When people are going through a series of disasters, Rook believes, they need friends who can offer advice, assistance, and reassurance. But talking too much about daily, trivial nuisances may simply reward people's distress rather than helping them manage it.

Of course, individuals and cultures differ in how many friends and relations are needed for well-being. Mexican-Americans, for example, rely on their extended families for emotional support much more than Anglo-Americans do, and they show more anxiety when separated from them. Anglos have more casual networks—even listing co-workers among those they depend on—than do Mexican-Americans (Griffith, 1983).

Cultures also differ in the value they place on friends and family. Anglo-Americans value quick friendliness and sociability, a result perhaps of frequent moves and life changes, but in many other cultures friendship develops slowly. It takes a long time to flower, but then it blooms for life. The difference between Japanese and

. . . and also sources of exasperation, headaches, and pressure.

American culture shows clearly in the reactions to the proverb "A rolling stone gathers no moss." To Americans, it means keep moving; don't let anything cling to you. To the Japanese, it means stay where you are; if you keep moving you will never acquire the beauty of stability (Syme, 1982).

. . . And coping with friends

Your neighbor tells you that your closest friend has betrayed your confidence. You ask a friend for help, and he says, "Sorry—I'm too busy right now." You're in the middle of describing your most recent unhappy date, and your friend says, "Oh, quit whining." You're in the hospital recovering from major surgery, and your closest friend never shows up for a visit.

As most of us learn, friends and relatives can be stress producing as well as stress reducing. They are often sources of hassles, quarrels, and conflicts (Kanner et al., 1981). When disaster or serious illness strikes, friends may blunder around, not knowing what to do or say. Cancer victims report that they are often upset and distressed by the well-meaning but unhelpful reassurances from their families and friends that "all will be fine." They often feel better talking to other cancer patients (Dunkel-Schetter, 1984). Other stressful aspects of friendship include:

■ *The contagion effect.* Helping a depressed or troubled friend may rub off, making you depressed and troubled too (Albrecht & Adelman, 1984). In serious situations, groups can create a "pressure cooker effect." In one study of Israeli women whose husbands were away at war, talking with others and listening to rumors exaggerated their feelings of danger and helplessness (Hobfoll & London, 1986).

- *Network stress.* A friend's problems may become your problems and sources of stress. People are nearly as upset about events that happen to their friends and relatives as they are about things that happen to themselves (Eckenrode & Gore, 1981).

- *The burdens of care.* If too many people in your life require your energy and support, you can become stressed and exhausted.

Do the benefits of friendship outweigh the costs, or do they balance each other out? Do most people keep a sort of running balance sheet ("Well, Hildegard is a fussbudget, but she's very loyal")? To find out, Karen Rook (1984a, 1984b) interviewed 120 older women, expecting to find that social support would balance social conflicts. She thought that the women would overlook their friends' misbehavior by remembering all their good deeds. Not a chance. Rook found that emotional well-being was affected more by having *problems* with friends than by having their *support*! Hassles, conflicts, and disappointments lowered the women's well-being more than the friends' good deeds elevated their well-being. It's not that stress makes you more critical of your friends, by the way. Friends who do the wrong thing are an independent source of aggravation and worry (Pagel, Erdly, & Becker, 1987).

A review of dozens of studies identified several factors that determine whether support helps or not (Shinn, Lehmann, & Wong, 1984):

1. *Amount of support.* Too much help and sympathy offered to someone in trouble can actually backfire, creating dependency and low self-esteem. For example, cancer patients who say they are receiving lots of support and that people are doing many things for them tend to have *lower* self-esteem and less sense of mastery than cancer patients who grumble about having to rely on themselves (Revenson, Wollman, & Felton, 1983).

2. *Timing of support.* After bereavement, divorce, or loss, a person needs lots of understanding. Friends who try to stem grief prematurely are not helping the sufferer. Later, however, they can prove helpful by trying to get the friend back into a social life.

3. *Source of support.* For a friend's advice and sympathy to be effective, the sufferer must feel that the friend understands and has been in the same boat. People who are under stress at work, for example, do better if they can talk their problems over with their employers or co-workers. Their spouses generally lack the experience to offer constructive advice (Kobasa & Puccetti, 1983).

4. *Density of support.* In dense social networks, friends all know one another. Dense networks are good for your sense of stability and identity, and in a crisis everybody in the network pitches in. But being in such a web can get sticky if you want to get out. Among women going back to school, those who were in a tightly knit group of friends showed worse adjustment, more physical symptoms, and lower self-esteem than women who were not in dense networks (Hirsch, 1981). "Good old friends" tend to want you to stay put. They can make you feel guilty for wanting to change.

Think for a moment about the future of friendship. Americans place great importance on their independence, yet studies suggest that the price they pay is widespread loneliness and anxiety. This dilemma—the choices between attachment and individualism, between tradition and change, between commitment to others and to oneself—is built into the very structure of American life (Bellah et al., 1985).

QUICK ▪ QUIZ

Identify which stressful aspect of friendship—contagion effect, conflicting demands, dense network, or badly timed support—is demonstrated by each of the following examples.

1. Your friends let you rage too long about an unfair experience.
2. You want to go away to graduate school, but your friends advise you to find a local job.
3. You start to feel your friend's unhappiness.
4. Two friends are having a quarrel and each wants you to take his or her side.

Answers:

1. badly timed support   2. dense network   3. contagion effect   4. conflicting demands

The Mind-Body Connection

Countless self-help books and workshops, based on a first wave of promising research, offer advice for coping with stress or for avoiding disease. (The more critical second wave of studies rarely makes the news.) Executives can take "hardiness" seminars. Type A workers can take workshops on "how to change your Type A personality." Some therapists offer "humordrama" groups to teach you how to find the humor in stressful situations.

Indeed, many people don't have problems any more; they have "stress," as if that explained something. If a friend says to you, "Gee, I've been under a lot of stress lately," you could say, "What a shame; have you tried relaxing, meditating, watching funny movies, or taking naps?" But if your friend says, "Gee, I have a problem; I'm about to be evicted because I can't come up with the rent," you wouldn't dream of advising only relaxation, because it would be wildly inappropriate.

We offer this anecdote because it draws attention to an important debate in health psychology: In studying the origins of health and illness, are we overestimating psychological factors (such as optimism, humor, and attitude) and underestimating economic and biological conditions (such as unemployment or disease)?

Without doubt, psychological factors are a link in a long chain that connects stress and illness, but researchers disagree about how strong that link is. At one extreme, some physicians think that psychology counts for almost nothing. Disease is a biological matter, they say, and personality cannot influence a germ or a tumor. An editorial in the *New England Journal of Medicine* lashed out against the "psychologizing" of illness. "At a time when patients are already burdened by disease," the editor wrote, "they should not be further burdened by having to accept the responsibility for the outcome" (Angell, 1985). At the other extreme, numerous popular books state or imply that health is largely mind over matter and that the worst diseases can be cured with jokes, papaya juice, and positive thinking.

What, then, are the most reasonable lessons to be drawn from health psychology? First, in terms of practical action, people ought to be following "good old-fashioned motherly advice" and practicing those *habits* associated with health, such as not smoking, not drinking excessively or in binges, and so on. Second, in terms

News reports often imply that health is mostly "mind over matter." What is the matter with overemphasizing the power of the mind— and, conversely, what's wrong with ignoring the mind's influence?

of psychological factors, the most consistent finding, as we have seen, is that the effects of stress are worsened when an individual feels helpless. Although many things happen that are out of our control—exams, accidents, a flu epidemic, natural disasters—we *do* have control over how we cope with them.

One way to restore a sense of control is to take responsibility for future actions, while not blaming ourselves for past ones. In the study of cancer copers, for instance, adjustment was related to a woman's belief that she was not to blame for getting sick but that she was in charge of taking care of herself from now on (Taylor, Lichtman, & Wood, 1984). "I felt that I had lost control of my body somehow," said a 45-year-old woman, "and the way for me to get back some control was to find out as much as I could." This way of thinking about illness allows a person to avoid guilt and self-blame while gaining mastery and control.

Moreover, once you are in a stressful situation, some ways of coping are better than others. If the situation requires action, problem-solving techniques are more helpful than wallowing around indecisively or simply venting your emotions. But if the situation is a fact of life, people who can use humor, hope, distraction, reappraisal, and social comparisons will be better off than those who are overcome by depression and pessimism.

Finally, one of the most important lessons from health psychology is that successful coping does not mean eliminating all stress. It does not mean constant happiness or a life without pain. The healthy person faces problems, "copes" with them, and gets beyond them, but the problems are necessary if the person is to acquire coping skills that endure. To wish for a life without stress would be like wishing for a life without friends. The result might be calm, but it would be joyless, and ultimately hazardous to your health. The stresses of life—the daily hassles and the occasional tragedies—force us to grow, and to grow up.

Taking Psychology with You

Noise, Crowds, and Weather: Living in a Stressful World

Writer Oscar Wilde once called the United States the noisiest nation that ever existed. That was in 1882. A century later, the din is even worse. Our ears are constantly assaulted by jackhammers, jet airplanes, motorcycles, lawn mowers, snowmobiles, chain saws, and blaring radios. To all that noise, add other nuisances, such as traffic jams, crowds, blizzards, and hot spells. What are the physical and psychological consequences of these environmental stressors?

Loud noise impairs intellectual performance on complex tasks, even when you think you have adjusted to it. Children in elementary schools that were beneath the flight path for Los Angeles International Airport were compared with children in quieter classrooms (Cohen et al., 1980). The two groups were matched in age, ethnicity, race, and social class. Children in the noisy schools had higher blood pressure, were more distractable, and had more difficulty with puzzles and math problems than children in quieter schools. Children raised in noisy environments also have trouble learning how to discriminate between irrelevant noise and the relevant task. They either tune out too much in the environment or cannot tune out enough (Cohen, Glass, & Phillips, 1979; Taylor, 1986).

Studies find that noise contributes to cardiovascular problems, ulcers, irritability, fatigue, and aggressiveness. All of these effects are probably due to overstimulation of the autonomic nervous system. Continuous noise also has a cumulative effect on hearing. At the University of Tennessee, 60 percent of 1410 freshmen had significant hearing loss in the high-frequency range. Their hearing resembled that of people more than twice their age (Lipscomb, 1972). Disc jockeys in discotheques, truck drivers, fire fighters, dentists, machinists, and shipbuilders all have a higher incidence of substandard hearing than the norm (Murphy, 1982).

The noise that is most stressful to people, however, is noise *they cannot control*. The rock song that you choose to listen to at jackhammer loudness may be pleasurable to you but intolerable to anyone who doesn't share your musical taste. The motorcycle without a muffler that makes you feel like Superman may make your neighbor feel like King Kong.

The same pattern of findings is true of crowding. At one time, environmental psychologists believed that crowding was a major source of most urban ills—crime, juvenile delinquency, infant mortality, family quarrels, and so on. This argument was not supported by subsequent research that controlled for income, class, and ethnicity (some cultures are used to high density; others are not). In Tokyo, where population density exceeds that of any U.S. city, crowding is not associated with crime.

Crowds themselves are not necessarily stressful. Sometimes they are even part of the fun, as on New Year's Eve or at baseball games. As with noise, crowds become stressful when they curtail your sense of freedom and control. They are stressful not when you *are* crowded but when you *feel* crowded (Y. Epstein, 1981). When people are able to work without interruptions in a densely packed room, they feel less crowded than if they work with interruptions in the same room with fewer people. Laboratory experiments and field studies find that the feeling of being trapped is more detrimental to health and intellectual performance than are most stressors themselves (Taylor, 1986). These negative effects can last long after the stressful event is over. Researchers therefore offer suggestions for asserting some control over environmental stressors and for living with those that are out of our control:

▪ If silence is golden, a little less noise will make us all a bit richer. So lower the volume of radios, TV sets, and stereos; don't turn stereos with earphones to full blast.

▪ If you work at a noisy job, be sure federal regulations are followed. To avoid permanent damage to the inner ear, constant noise levels for anyone working an eight-hour day may not exceed 90 decibels (dB).

▪ Stop shouting! If you are talking to someone, don't yell over the noise of the TV. Turn it down or shut it off. Then talk.

▪ Try to find a quiet place to study where you won't be interrupted by unpredictable noise, such as your brothers fighting over the car or your roommates wanting to play touch football.

▪ If you are trapped in a crowd over which you have no control (say, stalled in a traffic jam or in line at a busy store), relax. You can't do anything about it, and having a tantrum just raises your blood pressure and adds to the stress. Do some deep breathing, calm down, use the "extra" time to make lists or recite all the states in the union.

▪ If the weather is making you irritable—either because it snowed again for the ninety-fourth day or has been boiling hot for three weeks— well, join the group. Mark Twain tried to cheer up some New Englanders who were complaining about the unpredictable spring weather. "In the spring I have counted one hundred and thirty-six different kinds of weather," said Twain, "inside of twenty-four hours." As an editorial in the 1897 issue of the *Hartford Courant* lamented, "Everybody talks about the weather, but nobody does anything about it." You can't either. "Grin and bear it" is much less stressful than grumbling and being a bear.

KEY WORDS

health psychology 538
behavioral medicine 538
pathogenic 538
salutogenic 538
General Adaptation Syndrome (GAS) 539
alarm/resistance/exhaustion phases of GAS 539
eustress 540
psychological stress 541
psychosomatic 541
psychoneuroimmunology 541
life-change units 542
hassles 543
coping 546

emotion-focused coping 548
problem-focused coping 548
reappraisal 549
social comparisons 550
vigilance and avoidance 550
social interest 554
Type A behavior pattern 556
neurotic vs. antagonistic hostility 557
"disease-prone" personality 557
explanatory style 558
locus of control 560
hardiness 561
primary control 562
secondary control 562

SUMMARY

1. Hans Selye argued that environmental *stressors* (such as heat, pain, and toxins) cause the body to respond with fight-or-flee responses, as part of the *General Adaptation Syndrome*. If a stressor persists, it may overwhelm the body's ability to cope, and fatigue and illness may result. Current theories, however, emphasize the psychological factors that mediate between the stressor and the stress.

2. The immune system consists of several types of blood cells that are designed to recognize and destroy foreign substances, such as viruses. Researchers in the field of *psychoneuroimmunology* are studying how human behavior and emotion can affect the immune system.

3. Certain major events, such as the death of a loved one or divorce, are known to be extremely stressful. But some psychologists argue that daily hassles, such as traffic jams and interruptions, are more stressful than life-changing experiences, and that continuing situations are more stressful than one major event. Whatever the source, an important predictor of stress seems to be the inability to *control* and *predict* the environment.

4. Stress does not lead directly to illness. Two factors intervene: how the person interprets the event and how he or she copes with it. Coping involves a person's active and adaptive efforts to manage demands that he or she feels are stressful. Methods of coping include *attacking the problem*; *rethinking the problem* (finding meaning in the experience, comparing oneself to others who are worse off, seeing the humor in the situation, and, once a decision is made, not thinking or worrying about it); and *living with the problem* (reducing the physical effects of stress through relaxation, meditation, or exercise). Healthy coping also involves *social interest*, Adler's term for empathy, cooperation, and attachment to other people.

5. Individual factors that affect health and the ability to cope with stress include *negative emotions* (particularly anger, anxiety, and depression), *explanatory style* (optimism or pessimism), *health habits*, and *locus of control*. Although evidence for a Type A personality is mixed, studies indicate that antagonistic hostility in particular, and negative emotions that cluster together in general, can lead to a "disease-prone personality." However, there are many possible links between personality and disease: Disease may cause personality changes; some personality traits may cause unhealthy habits (such as smoking), which cause disease; a third factor may affect both personality and disease; and personality and illness may affect each other in a complex feedback loop.

6. An important goal of health psychology is prevention—getting people to eat nutritious meals, quit (or never start) smoking, not abuse drugs, and the like. Some problems in prevention are that health habits are often entrenched in childhood, people have little incentive to change their patterns, and health habits are independent of one another and are unstable.

7. *Locus of control* affects a person's neuroendocrine and immune systems, and the ability to live with stress and pain. However, control and health influence each other, and control is also affected by one's circumstances.

8. People can sometimes have too strong a sense of control over events. If something happens that is truly out of their power, they may not be able to cope. Health and well-being seem to depend on the right combination of *primary control* (trying to change the stressful situation) and *secondary control* (learning to accept the stressful situation). Cultures differ in the kind of control they emphasize.

9. Friendships, family, and acquaintances are important in maintaining physical health and emotional well-being. They provide emotional support, cognitive guidance, tangible support, companionship, and the sense of attachment. Friends can also be stressful—a source of hassles, conflicts, burdens, and betrayals. They sometimes provide the wrong kind of support or too much support or they offer support at the wrong time (too little too soon, too much too late). A *dense network*, in which many friends know each other, is good for stability and identity but can make change difficult if one member wants to break away.

10. Psychological factors are only one link in a long chain that connects stress and illness; illness is not "all in your mind" or easily cured with "the right attitude." Still, psychologists agree on the importance of learning good health habits and good coping skills. Coping with stress does not mean trying to live without pain, problems, or nuisances. It means learning how to live with them.

CHAPTER 16

Psychological Disorders

Who in the rainbow can draw the line where the violet tint ends and the orange tint begins? Distinctly we see the difference of the colors, but where exactly does the one first blendingly enter into the other? So with sanity and insanity. In pronounced cases there is no question about them. But in some . . . cases, in various degrees supposedly less pronounced, [few people are willing] to draw the exact line of demarcation . . . though for a fee some professional experts will.

HERMAN MELVILLE

You don't have to be a psychologist to recognize extreme forms of abnormal behavior. A homeless woman stands on a street corner every night between midnight and 3:00 A.M., screaming obscenities and curses; by day, she is calm. A man on a bus tells you confidentially that his shoes have been bugged by the FBI, his phone is wiretapped, and all his friends are spying on him for the CIA. On the TV news, a man suspected of committing hundreds of murders brags about his overpowering urges to kill.

When most people think of "abnormal behavior," they imagine the unusual, often bizarre stories that fill the newspapers. They assume that "abnormal" is the same as "insane," "crazy," or "sick." But most episodes of abnormal behavior are far less dramatic and would never make the nightly news. They occur when an individual cannot cope effectively with the stresses and problems of life. He or she may become so anxious and worried that work is impaired, or become severely depressed for a prolonged time, or begin to abuse drugs. In most cases, as the novelist Melville knew, there is no "exact line of demarcation" that indicates when coping fails.

You will have noticed by now that we have tried hard to avoid traps of either-or thinking in this book, whether the subject is "right-brain versus left-brain" differences or "health versus illness." It is the same with "normal" and "abnormal," terms that describe a rainbow of behaviors, with many shadings of color and brightness. A particular problem is not a fixed point on the rainbow. It may shift over time; a person may go through episodes of inability to function. Some abnormal problems are chronic disorders; some are temporary, such as a brief but intense episode of depression. Others recur intermittently throughout life, such as drinking heavily as a response to stress. Problems also vary in intensity. They may be mildly uncomfortable, serious but endurable, or completely incapacitating. Psychologists and psychiatrists diagnose and treat a wide range of "abnormal" problems.

One of the most common worries that people have is "Am I normal?" It is normal to have this concern. All of us occasionally have difficulties that seem too

Joan of Arc heard voices that inspired her to martyrdom. Was she sane and saintly—or mad?

573

much to handle. Several events in a row may make us feel we can't cope, adapt, and get on with life. It is also normal to experience Medical Students' Syndrome: deciding that you suffer from whatever disorder you are reading about. Precisely because many psychological disorders are so common, differing from "normal" problems only by a shade of intensity on the rainbow, it is often easy to conclude that you have them all. (We are tempted to add that this faulty conclusion is a pigment of the imagination.)

Defining Abnormal Behavior

Abnormal literally means "away from the normal," which implies that psychologists agree on what *normal* is. But they do not. These terms have produced considerable argument and debate. Definitions of "abnormal" depend on who is doing the defining: individuals, societies, or mental health professionals. Consider these five different definitions:

1. *Statistical deviation.* If "normal" is whatever most people do, then one definition of abnormal behavior is any behavior that is statistically rare or that deviates from the standard. Interpreted literally, this definition would lump together "abnormal" behavior that is destructive (such as sexual abuse), "abnormal" behavior that is charmingly unique (collecting ceramic alligators), and "abnormal" behavior that is desirable (genius). Clinically, statistical deviation is used to define mental retardation in terms of a cutoff score on an intelligence test.

Statistics themselves, of course, are neither good nor bad, but some people confuse numbers with personal values. They cite statistics to pressure each other (or themselves) into conforming, saying "everybody does it. . . ." If enough people are doing something, they conclude, it is "normal" behavior and hence acceptable. But few psychologists would agree that it is normal or desirable for a community or nation to endorse sadistic practices (as was true in Nazi Germany) or to require the suicide of its members (as was true of the religious cult of Jonestown).

2. *Violation of cultural standards.* A second definition of abnormal behavior is any action that violates the standards of a group. Every society sets up its own standards of appropriate behavior and the rules that people are expected to follow. Some kinds of behavior are shared by many cultures, such as wearing clothes and not committing murder. But others might be normal in one culture and abnormal in another. For example, seeing visions might be a sign of schizophrenia in a twentieth-century farmer, but a sign of healthy religious fervor in a thirteenth-century monk.

In America, people who have hallucinations of a deceased spouse or other relative are thought to be "abnormal." Actually, this experience is not uncommon during bereavement; it is just that grieving spouses don't talk about it much because they fear being considered "crazy." But in some cultures, such as those of the Japanese and the Hopi Indians, hallucinations are regarded as normal expressions of grief. In such societies, perhaps for this reason, hallucinations during bereavement are more prevalent and acceptable (DePaola & DePaola, 1988).

Certainly many ideas about abnormal behavior are culturally and historically relative. In the nineteenth century a woman who wanted to be a physician or a black student who wanted to go to college would have been considered "abnormal." Today, many behaviors once considered uncommon and abnormal are now accepted as part of the diversity of life and culture (see Figure 16.1). For instance, most psychologists no longer regard homosexuality as an abnormal sexual preference. As

Lots of people pierce their ears—but with a hole large enough for a juice can? What is normal to this African Masai would be abnormal to most-Westerners.

our world and values change, other behaviors have moved from normal to ''abnormal.'' A man or woman with no interest in sex at all was once considered normal (and, in some religions, at the pinnacle of morality). Today, some psychologists regard a *lack* of sexual interest as a disorder.

3. *Maladaptive behavior.* Many psychologists define abnormality as any behavior that is maladaptive for the individual or society. This definition would classify as abnormal a woman who is so afraid of crowds that she cannot leave her house, a man who drinks so much he cannot keep a job, and a student who is so anxious about failure that he cannot write term papers or take exams. It also covers individuals who say they feel fine and deny that there is anything wrong, but who behave in ways that are disruptive or dangerous to the community: the child who sets fires, the rapist who says his victim ''provoked him,'' the compulsive gambler who loses the family savings.

4. *Emotional distress.* A fourth definition identifies abnormality by a person's suffering. A person may conform to all the rules and norms of his or her community, managing to work and live adequately, yet privately feel on the verge of despair. He or she may, secretly or openly, feel anxious, afraid, angry, depressed, or lonely. The benefit of this approach is that it does not impose a label or diagnosis on anyone. A behavior that is unendurable or upsetting for one person (such as lack of interest in sex) may be perfectly tolerable and thus no problem to another.

5. *The legal definition: impaired judgment and lack of self-control.* In law, the definition of abnormality rests primarily on whether a person can tell right from wrong and can control his or her behavior. Psychologists and psychiatrists do not use the terms *sanity* or *insanity* in discussing abnormal behavior. These are legal terms only, for purposes of assessing a person's ability to stand trial.

How can we make sense of all of these definitions? All of them apply, and no one of them is enough. Therefore, we will define **abnormality** as any behavior or emotional state that causes an individual great suffering or worry; that is self-defeat-

abnormality (or psychological disorder) *Any behavior or state of emotional distress that causes personal suffering, that is self-destructive, or that is maladaptive.*

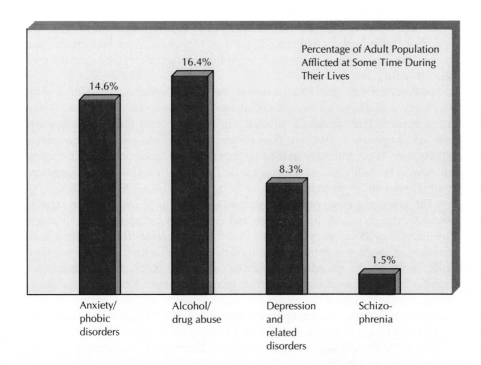

14.6%

16.4%

Percentage of Adult Population Afflicted at Some Time During Their Lives

8.3%

1.5%

Anxiety/
phobic
disorders

Alcohol/
drug abuse

Depression
and
related
disorders

Schizo-
phrenia

FIGURE 16.1

Prevalence of the most common mental health disorders
According to a massive nationwide study of 18,500 people selected at random, nearly a third of all Americans will have one or more mental disorders of varying duration at some time in their lives. This graph shows the specific incidences of four common mental disorders. (Data from Regier et al., 1988.)

ing or self-destructive; or that is maladaptive to or disruptive of the person's relationships or larger community. Even by this comprehensive definition, judgments of abnormality can be influenced by cultural standards and values as well as by statistical frequency. Many people will have some mental-health problem in the course of their lives. This is normal.

QUICK ▪ QUIZ

Which definition of "abnormality" does each example from Western culture best illustrate?

1. Arthur is declared mentally incompetent to stand trial for murder.
2. Bea has stopped accepting dates because she is afraid of crowds.
3. Chuck has a rare reading disability.
4. Dena has tattooed her face because she thinks tattoos are beautiful.
5. Ernie denies he has a problem, but his drinking has cost him his job.

Answers:

1. legal   2. emotional distress   3. statistical deviation   4. violation of cultural standards   5. maladaptive behavior

Dilemmas of Diagnosis

From the beginning of human society, people have suffered from sadness, mysterious symptoms, and bizarre behavior. From the beginning, physicians and healers have tried to classify these disorders, explain them, and cure them. Yet even today, psychologists still fail to agree on how many, or which, conditions can be classified as "official" mental disorders. As George Albee (1985), a past president of the American Psychological Association, put it, "Appendicitis, a brain tumor and chicken pox are the same everywhere, regardless of culture or class; mental conditions, it seems, are not."

In 1952, the American Psychiatric Association published the first edition of the *Diagnostic and Statistical Manual of Mental Disorders*. The *DSM-I*, as it was called, listed 60 types of mental "illness." In 1968, the *DSM-II* appeared, this time with 145 categories. In 1980, the third edition, *DSM-III*, was published, containing 230 disorders—everything from tobacco dependence, marital conflicts, and sexual problems to brain disease and schizophrenia. The *DSM-III-R* (for *Revised*) appeared in 1987, with still more refinements.

The primary aim of each edition is *descriptive*: to provide clear criteria of diagnostic categories, so that clinicians and researchers can agree on the disorders they are talking about, study them, and treat them. The *DSM-III-R* is directed to all clinicians, regardless of their theoretical orientation, and it makes few assumptions about causes of the disorders it describes. (In many cases, the causes are not known.) Each disorder is identified by its behavioral signs. Where possible, information is also provided about age of onset, predisposing factors, course of the disorder, prevalence (rare or common), sex ratio, associated problems, and family patterns. Table 16.1 lists the major diagnostic categories described in the *DSM-III-R*.

The *DSM-III-R* further classifies disorders according to five *axes*, or factors.

TABLE 16.1
MAJOR DIAGNOSTIC CATEGORIES FROM THE DSM-III-R

Disorders first evident in infancy, childhood, or adolescence include mental retardation, attention deficit disorders (such as hyperactivity or an inability to concentrate), eating disorders, and developmental problems.

Organic mental disorders are those resulting from brain damage, degenerative diseases such as syphilis or Alzheimer's, toxic substances, or drugs.

Psychoactive substance use disorders are problems associated with excessive use of or withdrawal from alcohol, barbiturates, opiates, cocaine, amphetamines, and other drugs that affect behavior. Amid controversy, the *DSM-III-R* includes cigarette withdrawal problems and marijuana intoxication in this category.

Schizophrenia consists of disorders characterized by delusions, hallucinations, and disturbances in thinking and perception.

Delusional (paranoid) disorders are characterized by excessive suspiciousness, jealousy, and delusions of persecution. The boundaries between paranoid disorder and ''paranoid personality disorder'' or ''paranoid schizophrenia'' are unclear.

Mood disorders include major depression, extreme elation (mania), swings between the two (bipolar disorder), and chronic depressed mood (dysthymia).

Anxiety disorders include generalized anxiety disorder, specific fears (phobias), panic attacks with or without agoraphobia, post-traumatic stress disorder, and obsessive thoughts or compulsive rituals.

Somatoform disorders involve individual reports of physical symptoms (such as paralysis, heart palpitations, dizziness) for which no organic cause can be found. This category includes *hypochondria*, the extreme preoccupation with one's health and the unfounded conviction that one is ill, and *conversion disorder*, in which a physical symptom (such as a paralyzed arm or blindness) serves a psychological function.

Dissociative disorders share a sudden alteration in consciousness, identity, or behavior. Alterations in consciousness include psychogenic *amnesia*, in which important events cannot be remembered after a traumatic event; alterations in identity include *multiple personality disorder*, in which normally integrated identity splits into two or more independent identities.

Sexual disorders include problems of sexual (gender) identity, such as transsexualism (wanting to be the opposite gender); sexual performance (such as premature ejaculation, lack of orgasm, lack of desire); and paraphilias (unusual or bizarre imagery or acts that are necessary for sexual arousal, such as fetishism, sadomasochism, or exhibitionism).

Impulse control disorders involve an inability to resist an impulse to perform some act that is harmful to the individual or to others, such as pathological gambling; stealing (*kleptomania*); setting fires (*pyromania*); or violent rages.

Personality disorders are inflexible and maladaptive personality patterns that cause distress to the individual or impair the individual's ability to function.

Conditions not attributable to a mental disorder that are a focus of attention or treatment include ''problems in living'' for which people seek help, such as marital and family conflicts, academic difficulties, procrastination, job dissatisfaction, and problems associated with life changes.

That is, instead of simply assigning a person to one category, such as ''schizophrenia'' or ''anxiety,'' it diagnoses each case in terms of five clinically important factors:

- The primary diagnosis of the problem, such as an anxiety disorder.
- Ingrained aspects of the individual's personality that are likely to affect the patient's behavior and ability to be treated, such as a history of extreme shyness.

▪ Any items in a person's medical or physical history that are relevant to the problem, such as the fact that the patient once fainted while giving a speech.

▪ The extent and severity of recent stressors in the patient's life, such as a recent breakup of a relationship or the death of a parent.

▪ An estimate of the patient's highest level of functioning in work, relationships, and leisure time. This factor indicates whether the problem is of recent origin or of long duration, and how incapacitating it is.

In classifying disorders, the *DSM-III-R* has abandoned that familiar term, **neurosis**. Freud used "neurosis" (actually, "psychoneurosis") to describe any disorder characterized by self-punishing behavior or symptoms that develop as an unconscious protection against anxiety. In contrast, Freud reserved the word **psychosis** to describe more serious mental disorders, in which a person cannot function in the world because of severe distortions of reality. Freud's definition of neurosis proved to be too general, but the *DSM-III-R* still uses *psychosis* to describe extreme mental disturbance.

For all its efforts to be precise, the *DSM-III-R* is a source of controversy. Is diagnosis itself—giving a label to a collection of symptoms—a good thing or not? Over the years, clinicians and philosophers have observed that when people have a tool, they will use it; Abraham Kaplan (1967) called this tendency "The Law of the Instrument." "If you give a small boy a hammer," Kaplan wrote, "it will turn out that everything he runs into needs pounding." So it is, some argue, with psychotherapists. Give them the instruments to diagnose disorders, and everything they run into will need treatment.

Other critics object to the medical implications of diagnosis. In *The Myth of Mental Illness*, Thomas Szasz (1961/1967) argued that people have "problems in living," not mental disorders. Psychiatric or psychological diagnosis, said Szasz, implies that problems in living are comparable to medical problems; that people have no responsibility for their actions; and that the solution is to be found in drugs, hospitalization, or surgery. Normal stresses no longer produce unhappiness and worry, say these critics, but depression and anxiety.

Jonas Robitscher, in *The Powers of Psychiatry* (1980), observed that "the act of diagnosing places a person in an inferior position and threatens his job security, family relationships, and self-concept." Labels can create a self-fulfilling prophecy, in which a person tries to live up to the diagnosed disorder. They can also blind observers to *changes* in a person's behavior. Once a person has acquired a label ("borderline schizophrenic"; "ex-mental patient"), the rest of the world often continues to see him or her in terms of the label (Rosenhan, 1973; see Chapter 18).

Further, critics warn of the prevalence of misdiagnosis and lack of agreement in labeling a disorder. In the early 1970s, a study found that American psychiatrists were more likely to diagnose schizophrenia than were English psychiatrists, who were inclined to diagnose the same behavior as an emotional disorder (Professional Staff, 1974). A decade later, 131 randomly chosen patients at an American mental hospital were carefully reevaluated by a team of clinicians. The new diagnoses were drastically different from the original ones. Of 89 patients originally diagnosed as schizophrenic, only 16 maintained that evaluation; most of the rest were considered to have mood disorders. Only 7 patients had originally been diagnosed as having organic disorders, but 26, on rediagnosis, were found to be suffering from organic problems such as Alzheimer's disease (Lipton & Simon, 1985).

Advocates of the *DSM-III-R* argue that when the manual is used correctly, diagnoses are more accurate. A study of patients admitted to public psychiatric hospitals in Maryland, for instance, found no evidence of the overdiagnosis of

neurosis, neuroses (pl.) *To Freud, a psychological disorder characterized by self-punishing, maladaptive behavior, emotional symptoms, or physical symptoms that protect a person against unconscious anxiety. It is no longer used as a clinical diagnosis.*

psychosis, psychoses (pl.) *An extreme mental disturbance involving distorted perceptions of reality and irrational behavior. It may have either psychological or organic causes.*

BLOOM COUNTY by Berke Breathed. © 1989, Washington Post Writers Group. Reprinted with permission.

When does a disorder diminish responsibility? *Clinicians have identified many different categories of abnormal behavior, in order to diagnose and treat people effectively. But the nature of diagnosis raises important, critical questions that society must grapple with: If people have a "disorder," are they still responsible for their actions? Some conditions legally qualify people as having "diminished responsibility" for their actions. Which disorders described in this chapter would you include? In your own life, where would you draw the line between* labeling *or* explaining *people's problems and excusing the behavior they attribute to their problems?*

schizophrenia and the underdiagnosis of mood disorders. The reason for the greater accuracy in these hospitals, the researchers concluded, was that the physicians were closely following *DSM-III-R* criteria (Pulver et al., 1988).

Some researchers respond to the criticisms that there is no such thing as "mental illness" or that diagnosis is simply a matter of cultural labeling by trying to distinguish mental disorders that seem to be universal from those that are embedded in their specific cultures. Schizophrenia and depression, for example, occur in some form in all societies (Kleinman, 1988). Anthropologist Jane Murphy (1976), who lived with the Eskimos of Alaska and the Yorubas of rural Nigeria, expected that their ideas of normality and abnormality would be very different from those held in Western culture; this was not generally the case. In every society, she found, there are individuals who behave oddly, who have delusions, who can't control their behavior—all of whom are considered abnormal. On the other hand, not all societies would regard cigarette withdrawal pangs, low sexual desire, premenstrual symptoms, or children's "hyperactivity" as signs of mental disorder, yet all of these are in the *DSM-III-R* (see "Think About It").

Keeping these controversies in mind, we will look next at some of the disorders in the *DSM-III-R*, ranging from emotional distress to psychosis.

Anxiety Disorders

The body, sensibly, prepares us to feel anxiety or fear when we are facing threatening, unfamiliar, or stressful situations, such as making a first parachute jump, waiting for important news, or not knowing how an unsettled situation will resolve

Think About It

The Politics of Diagnosis

They called me mad, and I called them mad, and damn them, they outvoted me.

Nathaniel Lee,
17th-century playwright,
on being consigned to a mental hospital
(Porter, 1987)

You might think that a diagnosis of mental disorder would depend on some hard-nosed, scientific criteria. In the case of organic abnormalities, it does. But the process of diagnosing disorders that have no apparent biological basis continues to rely more on consensus than science. When the American Psychiatric Association proposed to remove homosexuality from its manual of "mental disorders," it did not base its decision on research. It *took a vote of its members* (Bayer, 1981).

The story of the revision of the *DSM-III* raises a number of critical issues about the way mental disorders are defined and how these definitions come to be used. First, a Work Group was assigned to evaluate existing diagnostic categories and make corrections and additions. Other committees and "interested professionals" reviewed the results. Ultimately, the Work Group voted to decide which changes would be in and which would be out.

The Work Group proposed several new categories, including late luteal phase dysphoric disorder (a fancy term for "premenstrual syndrome") and self-defeating personality disorder. Many psychologists immediately objected to these proposals for their lack of empirical support, the biased judgments that had inspired them, and the consequences for the one group that would most be affected by them— women (Lerman, 1986).

For example, critics of the "premenstrual syndrome" entry pointed out, as we noted in Chapter 4, that there is no coherent definition of this alleged "syndrome"; that almost all women have some physical symptoms, which is a *normal* pattern, not an unusual one; and that although men have as many symptoms and mood changes as women do, the Work Group did not propose a category called "testosterone disorder." Most of all, critics noted that even though some women have unusually severe premenstrual symptoms, why should these be included in a manual of *mental disorders*? Making normal female processes into something pathological, critics said, is part of a long tradition that regards women, but not men, as being at the mercy of their "raging hormones" (Alagna & Hamilton, 1986).

Many women were even more outraged by the proposed category called "self-defeating personality disorder" (otherwise known as "masochism"). They agreed that certain individuals do behave in apparently foolish, self-destructive ways: They stay in bad relationships; they don't take advantage of new opportunities; they accept unforgivable heaps of abuse, verbal and physical. Yet there is no research evidence that a "masochistic personality," as such, exists. "The basis on which this strongly held belief . . . persists," argues Renee Garfinkel (1986), "is chummy, anecdotal reports of one believer to another." Critics observed that many women remain in relationships that are bad for them *for situational and economic* reasons. By implying that self-defeating behavior is rooted entirely in a woman's neurotic needs, and not in the tangible conditions of her life, critics said, this diagnostic category encourages clinicians (and the public) to blame the victim of an abusive man, not the man who is abusive (L. Brown, 1986; L. Walker, 1986).

The Work Group did not exclude these categories in the *DSM-III-R*; they compromised by listing them in an appendix as problems "needing further study." But it did decide to drop the one proposed new category that affected only men: "paraphilic coercive disorder," referring to men who rape. Critics feared that rapists who were diagnosed as having such a "disorder" would not be held responsible for their crimes.

What does this story suggest about the relationship between values and science, gender stereotypes and diagnosis of disorder? What are the benefits of having diagnostic labels that everyone agrees on, and what are the hazards? How can researchers and clinicians develop descriptive categories that are more scientifically based than the vote of a majority? What do you think?

itself. In the short run, these are adaptive emotions that prepare us to cope. But some individuals are more prone than others to anxiety or irrational fear. Anxiety seems to be a basic aspect of their personalities. This is true around the world, in countries as diverse as Turkey, Greece, India, Mexico, and Sweden (Barlow, 1988; Spielberger & Diaz-Guerrero, 1976).

People who have fear or anxiety problems are usually psychologically healthy in other ways. But often the fear that their fear is "crazy" makes it even worse. It is no help when well-meaning friends tell them what they already know, that their feeling is "irrational." As one psychologist who studies these emotions observes, "When someone says to you, 'You must be crazy to be afraid of _____ [substitute your favorite fear here],' that person is in effect saying, 'Your fear is different from my fear, and I don't understand yours' " (Chambless, 1986).

Fear and anxiety can appear in several distinctly different forms and disorders: *generalized anxiety disorder*, marked by long-lasting, continuous feelings of apprehension and doom; *phobias*, unrealistic fears of specific things or situations; and *obsessive-compulsive disorders*, in which people develop irrational thoughts or rituals designed to ward off anxious feelings.

Chronic anxiety

Before making the diagnosis of **generalized anxiety disorder**, psychologists rule out possible physical causes, such as disorder of the thyroid or excessive coffee consumption, that can mimic its symptoms. The condition is marked by continuous anxiety that has lasted a month or more, and that shows symptoms from three of four categories:

- *Motor tension:* shakiness, jitteriness, muscle aches, inability to relax, fidgeting, and restlessness.
- *Autonomic hyperactivity:* sweating, pounding heart, cold and clammy hands, dry mouth, dizziness, intestinal disorders, high resting pulse.
- *Apprehensive expectation:* constant anticipation of disaster to oneself or others, brooding about misfortune.
- *Vigilance and scanning:* difficulty in concentrating, feeling "on edge," irritability and impatience, excessive worrying.

There is no single cause of chronic anxiety. There are several *predisposing factors*, including a hereditary predisposition, inadequate coping mechanisms, traumatic events, and psychological dispositions, such as having unrealistic goals or unreasonable beliefs (Beck, 1988; Clark, 1988). There are also many *precipitating factors* that produce anxiety and keep it going. You are likely to feel anxious when you are in a situation in which others continually express their disapproval of you, or when you have to adapt yourself to an environment that doesn't fit your personality (such as being a slow-paced person in a fast-moving job). A particular case may reflect any combination of these factors (Beck & Emery, 1985).

When chronic anxiety results from experience with danger, it may create a syndrome called *post-traumatic stress disorder*. Years after the war in Vietnam was over, many veterans were still suffering emotional problems. These symptoms turned out to be common in people who have suffered traumatic experiences, such as war and combat, torture, rape and other assaults, and natural disasters (such as fire, flood, or earthquake). The psychological reaction might be immediate, occurring within six months of the trauma, or it might be delayed for years. Typical symptoms include:

What's the difference between normal fear and unreasonable worry?

generalized anxiety disorder *A continuous state of anxiety, lasting a month or more, marked by signs of motor tension, autonomic hyperactivity (e.g., a pounding heart), constant apprehension, and difficulties in concentration.*

It is normal to feel afraid when you jump out of a plane for the first time. But people with anxiety disorders feel as if they are jumping out of planes all the time.

- Reexperiencing the trauma in recurrent thoughts or dreams.
- "Psychic numbing" or "emotional anesthesia," characterized by detachment from others and loss of ability to feel happiness, intimacy, and sexual desire.
- Extreme alertness, difficulty concentrating, and sleep disturbances.
- In the case of life-threatening traumas shared by others, feelings of guilt about surviving when others did not.

Phobias

A **phobia** is an unrealistic fear of a specific situation, activity, or thing. In the general population, there are many common, "simple" phobias, such as fear of heights (acrophobia); fear of closed spaces (claustrophobia); fear of dirt and germs (mysophobia); and fear of such animals as snakes, dogs, insects, and mice (zoophobia). There are also more idiosyncratic fears, such as porphyrophobia (fear of purple); triskaidekaphobia (fear of the number 13); and brontophobia (fear of thunder).

People who have a *social phobia* have a persistent, irrational fear of situations in which they will be observed by others. They fear that they will do or say something humiliating or embarrassing. Common examples of social phobias are fears of speaking or performing in public, using public restrooms, eating in public, and writing in the presence of others.

By far the most disabling fear is **agoraphobia**, which accounts for more than half of the phobia cases for which people seek treatment (Chambless, 1986). Disregard the dictionary and popular definition of "fear of open spaces." The Greek *agora* was the social, political, business, and religious center of town. It was the public meeting place away from home. The essential feature in what agoraphobics fear is being alone in a public place from which escape might be difficult or help unavailable. They may report a great variety of specific fears—including fears of public transportation; driving on freeways, tunnels, and bridges; eating in restaurants; going to dinner parties—but the underlying fear is of being away from a safe place (usually home) or a safe person (usually a parent or spouse).

phobia *An unrealistic fear of a specific situation, activity, or object.*

agoraphobia *"Fear of fear"; a set of phobias, often set off by a panic attack, sharing the basic fear of being away from a safe place or person.*

Agoraphobia may begin with a series of **panic attacks** that seem to appear for no reason. A panic attack is a sudden onset of intense fear or terror, with feelings of impending doom. It may last from a few minutes to, rarely, hours, with intense symptoms of anxiety: trembling and shaking; dizziness; chest pain or discomfort; feelings of unreality; hot and cold flashes; sweating; tingling in hands or feet; and a fear of dying, going crazy, or losing control. This attack is so unexpected and so scary that the agoraphobic-to-be begins to avoid situations that he or she thinks may provoke another one. After a while, anything that sets off an emotional ''high,'' from an argument to pleasant excitement, feels too much like anxiety, and the person with agoraphobia will try to avoid it. Because so many of the behaviors associated with this phobia are designed to help the person avoid a panic attack, researchers often describe agoraphobia as a ''fear of fear'' rather than a fear of places (Chambless, 1988).

Some investigators believe that agoraphobia and panic attacks may be caused by biological abnormalities, because these disorders tend to run in families. Studies of twins suggest a heritable component of agoraphobia and panic attacks, so some researchers believe that these are medical disorders. Others maintain that these disorders, like all emotional states, come from an interaction of mind and body (Lang, 1988).

In agoraphobia, the heritable element seems to be a tendency for the body to respond to stress with a sudden ''alarm'' reaction. (For other people, the response may be headaches or ulcers.) During a stressful time, the individual has a panic attack that seems to come ''out of the blue.'' On closer inspection, this attack is often related to the physical arousal of stress, prolonged emotion, exercise, drugs (such as caffeine or cigarettes), or existing anxiety (Beck & Emery, 1985; Raskin et al., 1982). The essential ingredient of a panic attack, however, is *how the person interprets this bodily reaction*. A full-fledged panic attack begins when the person is *unable* to explain rationally why he or she feels this way. The physiological changes are viewed with alarm, as a sign of impending death or disaster instead of a passing moment of agitation. The sufferer begins to hyperventilate, which adds to the panic (Ley, 1988).

Some people get panic attacks and never develop generalized anxiety disorder or the self-protective restrictions of agoraphobia. Agoraphobia develops when a person begins to *anticipate* another panic attack and tries to avoid it. Even when panic attacks have not recurred for years, agoraphobics may persist in avoiding situations they believe bring them on.

Obsessive-compulsive disorders

Obsessions are recurrent, persistent thoughts, images, or impulses that seem to come unbidden and unwished for. The person finds them frightening and sometimes repugnant. For example, he or she may have repetitive thoughts of killing a child, of becoming contaminated by shaking hands, or of having unknowingly hurt someone in a traffic accident. Countless examples of obsessive thoughts have been reported, but they are alike in reflecting maladaptive ways of reasoning and processing information (Reed, 1985).

Some people develop obsessive thoughts because they have difficulty managing anger and aggression. In one case, a man had repeated images of hitting his 3-year-old son with a hammer. Unable to explain his ''horrible thoughts'' about his beloved son, he assumed he was going insane. Most parents, in fact, have occa-

panic attack *A brief feeling of intense fear and impending doom or death, accompanied by intense physiological symptoms such as rapid breathing and pulse, sweaty palms, and dizziness.*
obsessions *Recurrent, unwished-for, persistent thoughts and images.*

sional negative feelings about their children, and may even entertain a fleeting thought of murder, but they recognize that these brief reactions are normal and that feelings are not the same as actions. The man, it turned out, felt that his son had usurped his place in his wife's affections, but he was unable to reveal his anger and hurt to his wife directly (Coleman, Butcher, & Carson, 1984).

Compulsions are repetitive, ritual behaviors that a person carries out in a stereotyped fashion, designed to prevent some disaster. For example, a woman *must* check the furnace, lights, locks, oven, and fireplace three times before she can sleep. A man *must* wash his hands and face eight times before he leaves the house. The most common compulsions are hand washing, counting, touching, and checking. Most people do not enjoy these rituals and even realize that the behavior is senseless. But if they try to break the ritual, they feel mounting anxiety that is relieved only by giving in to the compulsion. They are like the man who constantly snaps his fingers to keep tigers away. "But there aren't any tigers here," says a friend. "You see! It works!" is the answer (Wender & Klein, 1981).

Many people have trivial compulsions and superstitious rituals. (Baseball player Wade Boggs believes that eating chicken every day keeps his batting average high.) Compulsions become more serious when they are troubling to the individual and interfere with his or her life. Some compulsive individuals develop elaborate rituals to try to control an unpredictable world or their own impulses. For example, a woman who fears contamination and illness washes her hands. This act briefly reduces her anxiety, so every time she feels anxious about her health she washes her hands. Before long, she has acquired a complicated compulsion, consisting of frequent hand washing, scrubbing floors, and disinfecting clothes, furniture, and dishes.

Anxiety disorders, uncomfortable or painful as they can be, are at least a sign of commitment to the future. They mean a person can anticipate the future enough to worry about it. But sometimes people's hope for the future becomes extinguished. They are no longer anxious that something *may* go wrong; they are convinced it *will* go wrong, so there is no point in trying. This is a sign, as we will see next, of the disorder of depression.

QUICK ■ QUIZ

Can you match the terms on the left with their definitions?

1. social phobia
2. generalized anxiety disorder
3. post-traumatic stress disorder
4. agoraphobia
5. compulsion
6. obsession

a. need to perform a ritual to avoid anxiety
b. fear of fear; of being trapped in public
c. continuing sense of doom and worry
d. repeated thoughts that seem to come unbidden
e. fear of meeting new people
f. anxiety state following unusual shock

compulsions *Repetitive, ritualized, stereotyped behaviors that a person feels must be done to avoid disaster.*

Answers:

1. e 2. c 3. f 4. b 5. a 6. d

Mood Disorders

Of course, everyone feels depressed at times—and there is the problem. Many people use the word *depression* to describe normal sadness, gloom, and loss of pep, and they mistake these normal states for an abnormal "syndrome." "No longer is a patient likely to arrive in my office declaring his distress to be marital tension, job insecurity, or generational conflict," wrote the psychiatrist Leslie Farber (1979). "What he announces is that he is depressed, as though that explained something. Of course he is depressed: marital tension or job insecurity or generational conflict of some sort is making him miserable; depression is not a surprising component of his outlook." Clinical depression, however, goes beyond normal sadness over life problems, and even beyond the wild grief that may accompany tragedy or bereavement.

Depression and mania

Depression is so widespread that it has been called "the common cold of psychiatric disturbances." **Major depression** differs from chronic depressed mood, a condition called *dysthymia* [dis-THIGH-me-a] or "depressive personality," in the intensity and duration of symptoms. Major depression usually occurs as an intense episode that, like a horrible flu attack, interrupts a person's normal functioning. Dysthymia consists of milder depressive symptoms that *are* the person's normal functioning.

Severe depression consists of emotional, behavioral, cognitive, and physical changes. Depressed people report despair and hopelessness. They are tearful and weepy, often "for no reason." They think often of death or suicide. They lose interest or pleasure in usual activities. They feel unable to get up and do things; it takes an enormous effort just to get dressed. Their thinking patterns feed this mood. They exaggerate minor failings (a single setback becomes a sign of total failure), ignore or discount positive events ("she didn't mean that compliment; she was only being polite"), and focus on negative experiences ("just my luck to miss that train").

Unlike normal sadness or grief, major depression involves low self-esteem. Emotionally healthy grieving people do not see themselves as completely worthless and unlovable. They do not blame themselves for the loss of a loved one; they know that grief will pass. Depressed people interpret all losses as signs of personal failure, take the blame, and conclude that they will never be happy again (Anderson, Horowitz, & French, 1983).

Depression is accompanied by physical changes as well. The depressed person may stop eating (or overeat), have difficulty falling asleep or sleeping through the night, lose sexual desire, have trouble concentrating, and feel tired all the time. Some sufferers have other physical reactions, such as inexplicable pain or headaches. (Because these symptoms can also be signs of physical illness, people should have a thorough medical exam before depression is diagnosed.)

About half of all people who go through a period of major depression will do so only once. Others have recurrent bouts. Some people have episodes that are many years apart. Others have clusters of depressive episodes over a few years. Depression during adolescence is often outgrown in adulthood, but depression and suicide rates among young people have increased in recent years. (See "Taking Psychology with You.")

At the opposite pole from depression is *mania*, an abnormally high state of exhilaration. You might not think it is possible to feel *too* good, but mania is not the

Former Prime Minister of England Winston Churchill described his bouts of depression as "black dogs." Some of the world's greatest leaders and artists have suffered from depression, without allowing it to keep them from achieving their goals.

major depression *A mood disorder involving disturbances in emotion (excessive sadness), behavior (apathy and loss of interest in usual activities), cognition (distorted thoughts of hopelessness and low self-esteem), and body function (fatigue, loss of appetite).*

normal joy of being in love or winning the Pulitzer Prize. Someone in a manic phase is overactive and expansive to an extent that is out of character. The symptoms are exactly the opposite of depression. Instead of feeling fatigued and listless, the manic person is full of energy. Instead of feeling unambitious, hopeless, and powerless, the manic person feels full of ambitions, plans, and power. The depressed person speaks slowly, monotonously, with no inflections. The manic person speaks rapidly, dramatically, often with many jokes and puns. The depressed person has no self-esteem. The manic person has inflated self-esteem.

Although people may experience major depressions without manic episodes, it is extremely rare for a person to experience only manic episodes. Most manic episodes are a sign of **bipolar disorder** (also called ''manic-depressive'' disorder), in which episodes of depression alternate with episodes of mania.

Theories of depression

Although bipolar disorders are equally common in both sexes, more women than men seem to suffer episodes of major depression. This sex difference in depression rates is debatable. Certainly more women than men seek treatment for major depression. But in community studies of people who are *not* in treatment, there is mixed evidence of a gender difference. Some surveys find no significant differences between women and men. Others find that an apparent difference occurs because a few women score higher at the extreme end of the depression measure, bringing up the average (Golding, 1988). It also seems likely that the sexes *express* depression differently. Men, for instance, have higher rates of drug abuse and violent behavior than women do, which may mask basic depression or anxiety (Klerman et al., 1984).

Many different theories have been advanced to explain the origins of depression. We will discuss four theories that are among the most commonly used: biological theories, social theories, attachment theories, and cognitive-behavioral theories.

1. *Biological theories* account for depression in terms of brain chemistry. As we saw in Chapter 3, neurotransmitters permit messages to be transmitted from one neuron to another in the brain. Two neurotransmitters that seem to be implicated in depressive disorders are norepinephrine (noradrenaline) and serotonin. In the view of some, depression is caused by a deficient production of one or both of these neurotransmitters, and manic moods are caused by an excessive production.

This theory is supported by studies showing that when animals are given drugs that diminish the body's ability to produce serotonin, the animals become sluggish and inactive—a symptom of depression (Wender & Klein, 1981). Conversely, drugs that increase the levels of serotonin and norepinephrine sometimes alleviate symptoms of depression; hence they are called ''antidepressants.'' The early success of antidepressants has provoked great interest in the search for the biological origins of depression (see Figure 16.2).

However, there remain many unanswered questions. Drugs are not universally effective; many depressed individuals do not improve. A more subtle issue concerns cause and effect. The fact that drugs may be effective does not mean necessarily that a disorder has an organic basis. A chemical imbalance may cause depression, but depression may cause a chemical imbalance. (We will discuss this matter again in Chapter 17.)

Several highly publicized findings have raised the possibility of a genetic con-

There are eight zillion studies of depression and many contradictory findings. What does this suggest about the search for a single cause or theory of the disorder? How can we make the most sense of conflicting results and points of view?

bipolar disorder *A mood disorder in which depression alternates with mania.*

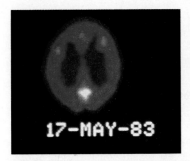
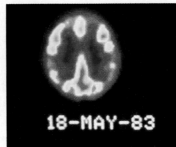
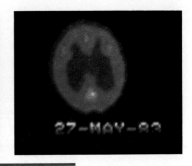

FIGURE 16.2

The depressed brain

These PET scans show changes in the metabolism of glucose, the brain's energy supply, in a patient with bipolar disorder. On May 17, the patient was depressed, and glucose metabolism throughout most of the brain was lower than normal. The next day, the patient became manic, and metabolic activity increased to near normal levels. By May 27, the patient was once again depressed, as reflected in glucose changes. Nevertheless, keep in mind that such changes do not show the direction of cause and effect: A drop in brain activity might bring on depression, but depression might also cause a drop in brain activity.

tribution to bipolar disorder, or manic-depression. In one study, Janice Egeland and several colleagues (1987) studied the Old Order Amish of Lancaster County, Pennsylvania. The Amish are an ideal population for genetic research, because they keep detailed genealogical records and are genetically isolated. All 12,500 Amish in Lancaster County are descended from 20 or 30 couples who came from Europe in the early 18th century, and few outsiders have married into the group. The initial research focused on one extended family of 81 people, 14 of them with bipolar disorder and 5 with other mental disorders. After gathering blood samples, the researchers used techniques of molecular biology to "cut" DNA samples into segments. They discovered that two genetic markers in the region of chromosome 11 distinguished manic-depressives from other family members. Their conclusion: One or more as yet unidentified genes in this region predispose an individual to the disorder. (Environment also plays a role; only 63 percent of those carrying the gene actually showed manic-depressive symptoms.)

Other findings, however, muddy the waters. A European study of families in Iceland and an American study of non-Amish families in the United States both failed to confirm the findings from the Amish. A study of five families in Jerusalem found two genetic markers for the disorder but in different locations than the ones discovered by Egeland's group—at the end of the long arm of the X chromosome. Belgian research has suggested the existence of yet another marker, again on the X chromosome (Baron et al., 1987; Hodgkinson et al., 1987). The conflicting evidence may mean that if a genetic predisposition for bipolar disorder does exist, it is not due to a single, specific gene—a point lost in newspaper headlines that claimed a manic-depressive gene had been "proven."

2. *Social theories* of depression consider the conditions of people's lives. In this view, the reason that women are more likely than men to suffer depression is that women are more likely to lack fulfilling jobs or family relations. Men are nearly twice as likely as women to be married *and* working full time, a combination that is strongly associated with mental health (Baucom, 1983; Golding, 1988). In a random sample of 1111 men and women in Boston, virtually all of the differences between men and women in their reported levels of depression could be accounted for by their different states of marriage and employment (Gore & Mangione, 1983).

Another study compared a random sample of 458 English working-class women with 100 women in psychiatric treatment for depression. The factors that predicted depression were a woman's lack of an intimate, confiding relationship with her husband; the loss of her mother before age 11; three or more children under the age of 14 at home; and lack of outside employment (Brown & Harris, 1978).

Another social factor in the origins of adult depression may be childhood sexual abuse. In a study of female patients in a psychiatric inpatient hospital, over half of the women reported a history of such abuse. Their histories were significantly correlated with the number and severity of depressive symptoms, in contrast to those of a control group of patients who reported no sexual abuse (Bryer et al., 1987). A community survey of 3125 Anglo, Hispanic, and black women found that mood disorders—depression, anxiety, panics, and phobias—were significantly higher among women who had been sexually abused as children or adolescents (Burnam et al., 1988; Stein et al., 1988).

Social analyses, though, fail to explain why some people who lose their jobs or spouses or have tragic experiences do not become clinically depressed, while others stay locked in the grip of despair. They do not explain why some people become depressed even though they seem to "have it all."

3. *Attachment theories* emphasize the fundamental importance of affiliation and attachment to well-being. In this view, depression results from disturbed relationships and separations, both past and present. One attachment theory, the "interpersonal theory of depression," includes biological, psychodynamic, and cognitive factors. But it emphasizes the depressed person's disputes, losses, anxieties, feelings of incompetence, and problems with relationships (Klerman et al., 1984).

A major review of studies of depression indeed found that the one thing that most often sets off a depressive episode is "disruption of a primary relationship," which is hardest on people who lack social support and good coping skills (Barnett & Gotlib, 1988). Nevertheless, attachment theories raise an interesting cause-and-effect problem. Disturbed or broken relationships may make some people clinically depressed. But depressed people are also demanding and "depressing" to family and friends, who often feel angry or sad around them and may eventually break away (Gotlib & Hooley, 1988).

4. *Cognitive-behavioral theories* propose that depression results from particular habits of thinking and interpreting events (Beck et al., 1979). Years ago, Martin Seligman's (1975) "theory of learned helplessness" held that people become depressed when their efforts to control the environment fail. Many studies showed that with repeated failures in avoiding pain or danger, animals become physically exhausted and emotionally drained. The consequences of this exhaustion are dramatic. The animal stops struggling for survival. It may become sick, even developing a cancerous tumor (Visintainer, Volpicelli, & Seligman, 1982).

But it soon became apparent that not all depressed people have *actually* failed in their lives; many merely *believe* that nothing they do will be successful (Abramson, Seligman, & Teasdale, 1978; Peterson & Seligman, 1984). The researchers eventually reformulated their views into the *hopelessness theory of depression*, arguing that the key cognitions in depression are that nothing good will ever happen ("It's all hopeless") and that the person is helpless to change this bleak future (Alloy et al., 1988).

In Chapter 9 we noted that depressed people tend to believe that negative events have internal, stable, and global causes ("It's my fault; it will always be my fault; and it will affect everything I do"). (Recall the related discussion of *explanatory style* and pessimism in Chapter 15.) Psychologists have been trying to pinpoint other beliefs that are associated with depression. For example, self-blame ("It's my fault'') may lead to depression, but it depends on what you are blaming yourself for: something you could control or not? When unfortunate things happen, people who say "It happened to me because of the lousy person I am" are more likely to become depressed than those who say "It happened to me because I was not as careful as I should have been" (Brown & Siegel, 1988).

One problem with cognitive theories of depression is that it is not clear whether distorted thinking *causes* depression, *accompanies* depression, or *follows* depression. When you are feeling sad, negative thoughts come more easily (Lewinsohn et al., 1981). Two researchers set themselves the awesome task of reviewing dozens of studies based on different theories of depression (Barnett & Gotlib, 1988). They concluded that there are many "cognitive abnormalities that wax and wane with the onset and remission of depression," but these cognitions do not *precede* depression, do not predict the severity of its symptoms, and tend to vanish during remission. Other reviews of the research, however, get more mixed results. Studies that follow people over time (to see whether negative thinking actually leads to depression) find that negative thinking is sometimes a cause, sometimes a result, and sometimes a two-way street (Robins, 1988; Teasdale, 1983).

What is a person supposed to conclude from all these studies and different theories? Why all the contradictory evidence? One answer is that depression comes in degrees of severity, from tearful tiredness to an inability to get out of bed, and psychologists study many different groups of depressed people. Yet researchers sometimes speak of the "depression" of clinical patients, college students, young children, and married couples as if it were always the same thing.

Second, depression may have many causes. One person may be suffering from a kind of post-traumatic stress syndrome after abuse in childhood; another may have a genetic predisposition to respond to stress with depression; a third may have a pessimistic personality style that fosters depressive interpretations of events. Every explanation accounts for some pieces of the depression puzzle, but none explains it all. The desire to understand depression does not mean we must cling to one theory as if it were our only life raft in a sea of sharks.

Personality Disorders

The *DSM-III-R* says that people with personality disorders "often appear 'odd' or eccentric . . . dramatic, emotional, or erratic . . . anxious or fearful." Since this description might fit any of us on some occasion (and some of us on many occasions), what is wrong with having these qualities? According to the *DSM-III-R*, **personality disorders** involve rigid, maladaptive, consistent traits that cause great personal distress or significant inability to get along with others. A personality disorder must be a repeated, long-term pattern of behavior. It is not related to an episode of illness or depression, or to a particular situation that temporarily generates uncomfortable emotions or behavior that is "out of character."

Problem personalities

Personality disorders generally fall into three clusters. The first cluster includes the **paranoid** personality, which is marked by a pervasive, unfounded suspiciousness and mistrust of other people, irrational jealousy, expectation of trickery, secretiveness, and doubt about the loyalty of others. People with paranoid personalities tend

personality disorders
Psychological disorders in which rigid, maladaptive personality patterns cause personal distress or an inability to get along with others.

paranoia (n.) paranoid (adj.) *Unreasonable and excessive suspiciousness, jealousy, or mistrust. It may occur as a type of personality disorder or, with more severe symptoms of psychosis, as a type of schizophrenic disorder.*

Narcissus fell in love with his own image—and now has a personality disorder named after him.

to be cold, inhibited, and restricted, and they take pride in being unemotional.

The second cluster includes the **narcissistic** personality, named after the Greek myth of Narcissus (a beautiful boy who fell in love with his own image). Narcissistic individuals have an exaggerated sense of self-importance and self-absorption. They are preoccupied with fantasies of unlimited success, power, brilliance, or ideal love. They require constant attention and admiration and feel entitled to special favors, without being willing to reciprocate. They fall in love quickly and out of love just as fast, when the beloved proves to have a human flaw. They're so vain (Raskin & Terry, 1988).

The third cluster includes the *avoidant* personality. People with this disorder are extremely sensitive to rejection and therefore avoid relationships unless they bring uncritical acceptance. Avoidant individuals long for affection and acceptance, but they prefer to withdraw from attachments rather than risk losing them.

Notice that these descriptions are both specific and vague. They are specific in that they evoke flashes of recognition (''I know that type!'') but vague in that they involve general qualities that depend on subjective labels and value judgments. Our society often encourages people to have fantasies of unlimited success and ideal love. Whether or not you like these traits is a separate matter from deciding they represent a *disorder*. For these reasons, clinicians often disagree in diagnosing personality disorders. The term ''avoidant personality disorder'' is, two psychiatrists observe candidly, ''a fancy phrase for extreme shyness'' (Wender & Klein, 1981).

Of all the personality disorders described in the *DSM-III-R*, one has provoked particular interest and study because of its consequences for society: the problem of the individual who lacks conscience, morality, and emotional attachments. In the 1830s the disorder was called ''moral insanity.'' By 1900 it became the ''psychopathic personality,'' a phrase that newspapers still love. More recently the word ''sociopath'' was coined. The *DSM-III-R* uses the term *antisocial personality* and considers it to be related to the narcissistic cluster. By any name, there are some key symptoms in this fascinating and troubling disorder, which has been around for centuries.

The antisocial personality

▪ Two teenage boys held a teacher down while a third poured gasoline over him and set him on fire. Fortunately, another teacher intervened in time for a rescue, but the boys showed no remorse. ''Next time we'll do it right,'' said the ringleader, ''so there won't be nobody left around to identify us'' (Coleman, Butcher, & Carson, 1984).

▪ ''Dan,'' according to the psychologist who interviewed him, had ''an unbelievable set of deceptive ways to deal with the opposition. Character assassination, rumor mongering, modest blackmail, seduction, and bare-faced lying were the least of his talents. He was a jackal in the entertainment jungle, a jackal who feasted on the bodies of those he had slaughtered professionally'' (McNeil, 1967).

People like these, who have **antisocial personalities**, lack two critical emotions: empathy, the ability to take another person's perspective; and guilt, the ability to feel remorse or sorrow for immoral actions. They have no conscience. They can lie, charm, seduce, and manipulate others, and then drop them without an ounce of regret. If caught in a lie or a crime, they may seem sincerely sorry and promise to make amends, but it is all an act. They are often sexually promiscuous, unable to

narcissism (n.), narcissistic (adj.) *An exaggerated sense of self-importance and self-absorption.*

antisocial personality disorder *A condition characterized by antisocial behavior (such as lying, stealing, and sometimes violence), a lack of social emotions (guilt and shame), and impulsivity.*

maintain enduring attachments, and irresponsible in their obligations to others. By all accounts this disorder is far more common in males than in females.

Antisocial personalities come in many forms. Some antisocial persons, like the teenagers who set a teacher on fire, are viciously sadistic, with a history of criminal or cruel behavior that began in childhood. Others, like "Dan," direct their energies into career advancement, abusing other people emotionally instead of physically. Some people with antisocial personalities can be very "sociable," charming everyone around them, but they have no emotional connection to others or guilt about their wrongdoing.

The inability to feel emotional arousal—empathy, guilt, fear of punishment, anxiety under stress—may imply some abnormality in the central nervous system. Antisocial individuals do not respond to punishments that would affect other people, such as threat of physical harm or loss of approval. It is as if they aren't "wired" to feel the anxiety necessary for avoidance learning. Some researchers believe this fact may explain why antisocial persons fail to learn that their actions will have unpleasant consequences (Hare, 1986). Others argue that perhaps those with antisocial personalities simply don't care about punishment or social approval. In fact, they *do* respond to reinforcements that are meaningful to them, such as food, money, and sex (Altrocchi, 1980). Still others believe that antisocial persons have learned to ignore signs of emotional arousal, so it takes unusually high levels of stimulation before they get an emotional "kick" (Mandler, 1984).

One theory, based on animal and human studies, maintains that there is a common inherited disorder among people who are labeled antisocial, alcoholic, hyperactive, or overly extroverted (Newman, Widom, & Nathan, 1985). All of these conditions involve problems in *behavioral inhibition*—that is, in a person's ability to control his or her response to frustration or to inhibit a pleasurable action that may have unpleasant consequences. For such individuals, says one researcher, "the appeal of the moment is strong enough to block out all thought of consequences" (Grant, 1977).

Among some extremely violent antisocial personalities, biological impairments might be the result of physical abuse. One study compared two groups of delin-

People with antisocial personalities are not necessarily evil-looking or socially inept. By all accounts, Ted Bundy, who murdered many women in cold blood, was charming, attractive, and utterly without remorse.

quents: violent boys who had been arrested for repeated incidents of vicious assault, rape, or murder; and boys whose violence was limited to fistfights or threats. Nearly all of the extremely violent boys (98.6 percent) had at least one neurological abnormality, and many had more than one, compared to 66.7 percent of the less violent boys. More than three-fourths of the violent boys had suffered head injuries as children, had had serious medical problems, and had been beaten savagely by their parents, compared to "only" one-third of the others (Lewis, 1981).

However, it is also important to consider the environments that encourage or discourage antisocial personalities. This disorder is apparently unknown in small, tight-knit, cooperative communities, such as the religious Hutterites, the Israeli kibbutz, and the Eskimo and Siriono (Altrocchi, 1980; Montagu, 1978). The fact that sociopaths and extroverts share certain characteristics, moreover, suggests that the two groups differ in how they learn to control their behavior and in how their environments react to them.

Our society worries more about the antisocial personalities who commit violent crimes than about the "con men" who gain vast power and fortune at the expense of their families or constituents. Even the *DSM-III-R* considers the antisocial personality to be a primarily "lower-class" phenomenon. While noting that some people with this disorder may "achieve political and economic success," the manual adds that they "virtually never present the full picture of the disorder." This is not surprising, since affluent (nonviolent) people with antisocial personalities rarely turn up in therapy, prison, or mental hospitals.

QUICK ∎ QUIZ

Can you diagnose each of the following disorders?

1. Ann can barely get out of bed in the morning. She feels life is hopeless and despairs of ever feeling good about herself.
2. Brad lacks guilt, empathy, and moral standards.
3. Connie constantly feels a sense of impending doom; for many weeks, her heart has been beating rapidly and she can't relax or concentrate.
4. Damon is totally absorbed in his own feelings, needs, and wishes.
5. Edna believes that everyone is out to get her and no one can be trusted.

Answers:

1. depression 2. antisocial personality 3. generalized anxiety disorder
4. narcissistic personality disorder 5. paranoid personality disorder

Dissociative Disorders

dissociative disorders
Conditions in which normally integrated consciousness or identity is split or altered, as in psychogenic amnesia or multiple personality.

Stress or shock can make any of us feel temporarily *dissociated*—that is, cut off from ourselves, feeling strange, dazed, or "unreal." In **dissociative disorders**, consciousness, behavior, and identity are split or altered. Unlike normal, short-lived states of dissociation, these disorders are extremely intense, last a long time, and appear to be out of one's control. Like post-traumatic stress disorder, dissociative disorders are often responses to shocking events. But in the former case, people can't get the trauma out of their minds and waking thoughts. In the latter, people escape the trauma by literally putting it out of their minds, erasing it from memory.

Amnesia and fugue

Amnesia, partial or complete memory loss of information or past events, is the most common dissociative disorder. Amnesia can result from organic conditions, such as head injury; when no organic causes are apparent it is called *psychogenic*. In one case, for example, a young man appeared at a hospital complaining that he did not know who he was. After staying there a few days, he awoke in great distress, with no awareness of what he had done during his amnesiac phase, and demanded to be released. Eventually he remembered that he had been in an automobile accident in which a pedestrian was killed. The shock of the experience and his fear that he might have been responsible set off the amnesia (Sarason & Sarason, 1980).

Psychogenic fugue states are even more fascinating. A person in a *fugue state* not only forgets his or her identity, but gives up customary habits and wanders far from home. The person may take on a new identity, remarry, get a new job, and live contentedly until he or she suddenly "wakes up"—puzzled and often with no memory of the fugue experiences. The fugue state may last anywhere from a few days to many years. One case turned up in the news at Christmas, 1985. James McDonnell, Jr., had left his family in New York in 1971 and wandered to New Jersey, where he took a new name (James Peters), a new job (short-order cook), and a new set of friends. Fifteen years later, he "woke up" and made his way back to his wife—who (apparently) greeted him with open arms.

As you might imagine, it is often difficult for clinicians to determine when people in fugue states have a true disorder and when they are faking (Schacter, 1986). (To read more about the legal system's problems of detecting faking, see "A Closer Look at Forensic Psychology.")

Multiple personality

If you have ever read or seen *The Three Faces of Eve* or *Sybil*, you have heard about "multiple personalities." **Multiple personality disorder** (MPD) is classified in the *DSM-III-R* as a dissociative disorder because its essential feature is the appearance, within one person, of two or more distinct personalities. Each personality may have its own memories, preferences, handwriting, voice, medical problems, eyeglass prescriptions, and even brain wave patterns (Braun, 1988).

Only 200 cases of multiple personality had been identified by 1979, but since 1979 more than 5000 have appeared. Some of these have been attempts by murderers to plead insanity: "*I* didn't kill her; my other personality did." The Hillside Strangler in Los Angeles, Kenneth Bianchi, convinced several psychiatrists and

amnesia *Partial or complete loss of memory for information or past events; when no organic causes are present, it is classified as a dissociative disorder.*

multiple personality disorder *A rare dissociative disorder marked by the appearance within one person of two or more distinct personalities, each with its own name, history, and traits.*

The different "personalities" of people with multiple personality disorder may have their own names, opinions, and even styles of handwriting, as this handwriting sample from a single patient illustrates. (Courtesy of Bennett Braun)

A Closer Look at Forensic Psychology

The Insanity Defense: Is It Insane?

▪ A civil servant named Dan White lost his job on San Francisco's Board of Supervisors. He went home, got his snub-nosed revolver, climbed in through the window of City Hall (so the metal detectors wouldn't detect his gun), and shot Mayor George Moscone nine times. Then he murdered supervisor Harvey Milk, a homosexual whom White disliked. In what the press played up as the "Twinkie Defense," White's psychiatrists testified that his excessive consumption of junk food was a sign of his "diminished mental capacity." Though his actions were premeditated, they said, White was temporarily insane. The jury agreed. Dan White served five years in prison for manslaughter. Twenty months after his release, he committed suicide.

▪ A troubled young man named John Hinckley, Jr., hoping to win the attention and love of actress Jodie Foster, shot and wounded former President Ronald Reagan and his press secretary, James Brady. Hinckley was acquitted of attempted murder on the grounds of insanity and was confined indefinitely to a mental institution.

These cases produced enormous public interest. What *is* the proper punishment for someone who apparently cannot control his or her actions? How do we know if someone is "insane" or faking? If someone is sentenced to spend time in a mental institution, how can we know when he or she is "cured"? Can we predict whether a person will kill again? Researchers interested in *forensic psychology*

study these and other psychological issues related to the law and courtroom.

Insanity is a legal term, not a psychological one. In 1834, a Scot named Daniel M'Naghten tried to assassinate the Prime Minister of England, killing the P.M.'s secretary by mistake. M'Naghten was acquitted of murder on the grounds that he had a "mental defect" that prevented him from understanding what he was doing at the time of the act. The "M'Naghten Rule" meant that people could be acquitted "by reason of insanity" and sentenced not to prison, but to mental institutions (or set free). In the United States, the 1954 *Durham* decision specified that "an accused is not criminally responsible if his unlawful act was the product of a mental disease or defect."

At the time, the English public was as outraged by the M'Naghten decision as the American public was by the Hinckley decision. People often get the impression that hordes of mad criminals are "getting off" by reason of insanity. In fact, trials based on the insanity plea receive far more attention than their numbers warrant. Of every 1000 criminal cases brought to trial, the insanity defense is raised in fewer than 10 and frees the defendant in fewer than 3 (Pasewark & Pasewark, 1982). Most of the small number of people who successfully plead insanity (about 30 cases per state per year) have committed mild offenses (Rosenhan, 1983).

Yet the insanity defense continues to be hotly debated. Most legal and mental health professionals

law-enforcement officials that his murders were really committed by his "other personality," called Steve Walker. However, a determined prosecutor discovered that Bianchi had read numerous psychology textbooks on multiple personality and had modeled his other personality on a student he had once impersonated. When a psychologist told Bianchi that "real" multiple personalities come in packages of at least three, Bianchi suddenly produced a third personality. Bianchi was convicted of murder. But Paul Miskamen, a born-again Christian who battered his wife to death, convinced psychiatrists and a jury that the man who killed his wife was another personality named Jack Kelly. Judged insane, Miskamen was committed to a mental hospital and released after 14 months.

Cases of multiple personality make for dramatic movies, books, and news stories, but among mental health professionals they are controversial. Some psychiatrists believe the disorder originates in childhood, as an adaptation to living in a

believe that the insanity plea is humane and necessary in a civilized society, and that the mentally incompetent or disturbed should be treated differently from those who are responsible for their actions. Some psychiatrists have even tried to expand the legal causes of "temporary insanity," arguing that "premenstrual syndrome," "chemical imbalance," high testosterone, and epilepsy are legitimate excuses for losing control of oneself and committing crimes (Pollak, 1984).

Others, such as Thomas Szasz (1987), believe that the insanity defense is a "legal fiction" that imprisons innocent people in mental hospitals and exonerates guilty people by declaring them not responsible for their actions. It allows wealthy or likable defendants to be let off completely or to spend a brief time in a mental hospital, and it sentences poor, minority, or rebellious defendants to lengthy or indefinite stays.

In a sizzling indictment of the ability of psychologists to determine "insanity" or to predict the future behavior of violent individuals, psychologists David Faust and Jay Ziskin (who is also a lawyer who specializes in forensic psychology) reviewed hundreds of studies (Faust & Ziskin, 1988). "Clinicians do not in fact make more accurate clinical judgments than laypersons," they concluded; their error rate exceeds their accuracy rate. In one study, military recruits who were kept in the service, despite psychiatrists' recommendations that they be discharged for "severe psychiatric liabilities,"

turned out to be as successful and adjusted as the control group. In study after study, clinicians were not very good at detecting malingering or efforts to fake insanity, and they were dismal at predicting future violence. One reason for these high error rates, Faust and Ziskin believe, is the differing perspectives of psychology and psychiatry—as well as the diversity of schools within psychology (think of the different views of personality, for example, and the disagreements over diagnosis itself). As a result, some trials end up as a battle of the experts, in which the jury must decide which psychiatrist or psychologist to believe.

Research in forensic psychology hopes to redress these problems. One researcher developed a Criminal Responsibility Assessment Scale, for example, that greatly improves agreement among clinicians in assessing the causes of an accused person's criminal act (R. Rogers, 1986, 1988). And, increasingly, empirical research in many other domains of psychology is finding its way into the courtroom: Developmental psychologists have testified on children's eyewitness memory; neuropsychologists on the extent of brain damage in people injured at work; social psychologists on conformity, "brainwashing," and how juries determine guilt or innocence. In these and many other areas where law and psychology intersect, psychologists are trying to help juries determine the fine line between "normal" and "abnormal" behavior—and who is responsible for crossing it.

---

situation that alternates unpredictably between unbearable abuse and affectionate loving. One "personality" embodies the good experiences, and another "personality" emerges to cope with the bad ones. Many of these patients suffered horrendous abuse as young children: being dangled out of windows, being forced to watch a murder, being buried alive, being the victim of sexual sadism. Usually, only one or two of the "multiple personalities" is conscious of the abuse; the others will have no memory of it. It is not known, though, why some children who suffer such abuse develop multiple personality disorder and others do not.

Some experts are skeptical of the recent popularity of this phenomenon and think it is, except in rare cases, a passing fad. Clinicians and researchers who study and treat MPD believe that it is not rare but often misdiagnosed as schizophrenia, depression, or personality disorder. In two studies of more than 450 MPD patients, the average patient had seen four therapists before a correct diagnosis was made

Some cases of multiple personality have turned out to be fakes, while others seem astonishingly real. How would you go about determining the difference?

(Fine, 1987). And diagnoses can be made more accurately now because the physiological changes that occur within each ''personality'' cannot be faked. One patient, for example, had a blood pressure of 150/110 when one personality was in control and a blood pressure of 90/60 when another personality took over (Braun, 1988).

People with MPD are currently being studied for the clues they provide for normal functioning. They represent, after all, an extreme form of the normal ability to shift from one state of consciousness to another, to change emotions in an instant, to present a variety of ''selves'' to the world.

Disorders of Physical Symptoms

Some people develop physical symptoms for which no organic reason can be found. They become blind, deaf, paralyzed, numb, or feel inexplicable pain. Such persons have **somatoform disorders**, so called because they have the form of a physical disorder (*somato* refers to the body) with no demonstrable medical cause. The *DSM-III-R* describes several kinds of somatoform disorders, including:

- *Somatization disorder*: Repeated, multiple, and yet vague physical complaints (an average of 12 to 14 different ones), lasting for at least several years, without medical cause. Symptoms include intestinal complaints, shortness of breath, dizziness, paralysis, or muscle weakness. These people feel that they have been ''sickly'' much of their lives.
- *Conversion disorder*: A single physical disturbance that seems to express a psychological conflict or need. For example, someone terrified of hurting another in a fit of rage might develop a ''paralyzed'' arm; a soldier who feels ambivalent about firing a gun may become ''blind.'' The symptom *must serve some psychological function* to be classified as a disorder.
- *Hypochondria*: An unrealistic fear of disease. Everyone occasionally has unexplained physical symptoms; everyone occasionally interprets them as a certain sign of a dread disease. But hypochondriacs exaggerate normal physical sensations, taking them as evidence of serious illness. They are preoccupied with normal bodily functions, such as heartbeat, elimination, and occasional coughs. Some hypochondriacs are obsessed about their bodies and apparent symptoms; some are phobic about developing a specific disease; some are wrongly convinced they are already ill. Their fears persist in spite of medical reassurance, which is why hypochondriacs often go from doctor to doctor, trying to confirm their fears (Barsky & Klerman, 1983).

In diagnosing somatoform disorders, clinicians look for symptoms that are inconsistent with known physical diseases or with basic anatomy: a ''paralyzed'' leg that otherwise shows normal motor reflexes, ''blindness'' in an eye that has normal pupillary responses, symptoms that vanish during hypnosis, or symptoms that are not anatomically possible. Are people who have these symptoms faking? Many clinicians regard somatoform disorders as expressions of unconscious conflicts that are out of our control. In contrast, they say, *malingering* is a conscious, voluntary effort to use or invent a physical symptom for an ulterior motive: to get out of work, to get drugs, to get sympathy. Others believe that the difference between malingering and a somatoform disorder is just a matter of degree or of words (Wender & Klein, 1981).

The social use of physical symptoms may be a conscious process or unconscious self-deception. People with somatoform disorders have typically been rewarded in some way for having physical complaints. One study found that hypo-

somatoform disorders
Physical disorders that have no demonstrable medical cause. They include somatization disorder, conversion disorder, and hypochondria.

This seventeenth-century spoof of a man with "an imaginary illness" shows that hypochondria has been around for ages.

chondriacs have learned to use the excuse of poor health to justify unsatisfactory performance. When they believe that they are being socially evaluated and that poor health will excuse poor scores, hypochondriacs report more physical symptoms than they do when they think they are not being evaluated (Smith, Snyder, & Perkins, 1983). Many factors influence a person's likelihood of observing, worrying about, and reporting physical symptoms (Pennebaker, 1982). These include expectations and attitudes about the nature of disease; sensitivity to pain; anxiety, which amplifies the intensity of pain; low self-esteem and morale; and ethnicity (Barsky & Klerman, 1983; Costa & McCrae, 1985).

Hypochondria is a good illustration of the problems of diagnosis, the role of community standards in defining "normalcy," and the risks of oversimplified thinking. Perhaps it is easy to see what is wrong with the extreme hypochondriac who is overly worried about every bodily sensation. But how would you label the person at the other extreme, the one who pays too *little* attention to symptoms, even at risk of his or her health (Costa & McRae, 1985)? Moreover, consider what Susan Baur (1988) calls "normal hypochondria"—the "irrational health worries that affect so many people that *not* to be preoccupied seems bizarre." For example, she argues, American society endorses "weight-watchers' hypochondria" and "fitness hypochondria." We don't think it odd if a woman weighs herself once or twice a day or if a man works out daily to have "perfect" muscles; why then is it a "disorder" if a person checks his or her tongue daily for signs of tongue cancer? Where, in short, would you draw the line between hypochondriacal attention to your body and healthy concern?

You discover a strange rash on your leg. Do you ignore it or rush to the doctor? Where would you draw the lines between foolish denial, justified worry, and hypochondria?

Drug Abuse and Addiction

Perhaps no topic in this chapter better illustrates the problem of finding the "shade of the spectrum" in which normal blurs into abnormal than that of drug abuse and addiction. Most people in America use drugs—legal, illegal, or prescription—in moderation, for short-lived effects. But a small percentage overuse them. The consequences for society of drug abuse are costly: loss of productive work, high rates of violence and crime, and family disruption. The consequences for individuals and their families are tragic: unhappiness, illness, and the increased likelihood of early death from accident or disease.

From use to abuse

Every drug—including aspirin, cough medicine, and coffee—is dangerous and even lethal if taken in excess. Although the drugs that come to the attention of the government and the media are the illegal ones (most notably marijuana, heroin, and cocaine), the drugs that do the most damage to the most people are legal: alcohol and cigarettes. (You might refer to Chapter 4 to refresh your memory about stimulant and depressant drugs and how people learn to react to them.) When does "moderate use" of any drug become abuse? How much is too much? Because there are so many dangers of drug *abuse*, debates about drug *use* are often impassioned. If the drug is illegal, feelings run especially high. Medically, psychologically, and socially, however, there are many differences between moderate use of any drug and excessive use.

To distinguish drug use from abuse, the *DSM-III-R* definition of "drug abuse," for alcohol or any other drug, includes these symptoms:

- The inability to stop or cut down.
- Intoxication throughout the day.
- Blackouts and loss of memory for events during the intoxication.
- Impaired ability to work or get along with others—for example, fights, loss of friends or job, absence from work, arguments with others over the drug use.
- Physical deterioration or illness.

Addiction: Disease or social problem?

Where should we draw the line between normal drinking and problem drinking?

Why are some people able to use drugs moderately, while others become alcoholics or addicts? One explanation looks to personality: Drug abusers may be sensation seekers who crave lots of excitement and stimulation (see Chapter 10). Another considers family history: Some drug abusers have deprived childhoods, antisocial parents, and a lifetime of rejection. A third explanation holds that peer pressure is the reason: If all your friends smoke, you are more likely to smoke too. But these factors are only part of the story.

In several longitudinal studies that followed three groups of people for more than 40 years, researchers were able to observe the course of alcohol use (and abuse) over time in people's lives (Vaillant, 1983). The first surprising discovery was that many people went through a period of heavy, even problem, drinking but eventually "healed themselves." For such persons, alcoholism was not progressive, permanently incapacitating, or a downward spiral to skid row. They "outgrew" alcoholism, cutting back to social drinking levels.

Second, the study found that many of the factors thought to *cause* alcoholism were instead a *result* of alcoholism. It had long been argued, from retrospective studies, that alcoholism was a result of an unstable or dependent personality. Alcoholics were supposed to have lower self-esteem and be more depressed, paranoid, aggressive, and impulsive than social drinkers. However, the longitudinal evidence showed that these traits, along with differences in social class, unemployment, and educational achievement, all tended to develop *after* the emergence of alcoholism. As adults, problem drinkers had personality disorders and were socially inadequate. But as children they were no less privileged than peers who became normal social drinkers, no less intelligent, and had no more emotional problems (Vaillant & Milofsky, 1982). Then why did they become alcoholic?

In colonial America, the average person drank two to three times the amount of liquor that is consumed today, yet alcoholism was not the serious social problem it is now. Drinking was a universally accepted social activity. Families drank and ate together. Alcohol was believed to produce pleasant feelings and relaxation. Indeed, the Puritan minister Cotton Mather called liquor "the good creature of God." If a person committed a crime or became violent while drunk, it wasn't the liquor that was the culprit, according to the colonials. It was the person's own immoral tendencies that led to drunkenness *and* crime (Critchlow, 1986).

Between 1790 and 1830, when the American frontier was expanding, drinking came to symbolize masculine independence, high-spiritedness, and violence. The saloon became the typical setting for drinking away from home. Alcoholism rates rose dramatically. The temperance movement, which followed, argued that drinking inevitably led to drunkenness, and drunkenness to crime. The solution it proposed, and won for the Prohibition years (1920 to 1933), was national abstinence (Peele, 1984b).

By the mid-twentieth century, drunkenness came to be seen not as an inevitable property of alcohol but as a characteristic of some people who have an inbred vulnerability to alcoholism. In *The Disease Concept of Alcoholism* (1960), E. M. Jellinek wrote that alcoholism is a disease over which an individual has no control and from which he or she never recovers. Again, complete abstinence was the only solution. Today the *disease model of addiction* is still widely used by drug researchers. The disease model regards addiction, to alcohol or to any other drug, as a biochemical process. The individual acquires a *tolerance* for the drug, meaning that greater and greater amounts are required to produce the same effect. Withdrawal produces a severe physiological reaction, including, in the case of alcohol, "the shakes," nervousness, anxiety, nightmares, and delirium.

Current research is exploring ways in which individuals differ in their biological vulnerability to alcoholism. Perhaps there is a genetic predisposition, although this idea is hotly debated because it isn't known what aspect of alcoholism can be inherited—perhaps a deficiency in the enzymes that metabolize alcohol, perhaps an "impulsivity" that makes self-control difficult. Some researchers maintain that having many biological relatives who are alcoholic contributes to a person's risk of becoming alcoholic, even if the person doesn't live with or grow up with the alcoholic relatives (B. Bower, 1988). Others, as we noted, think that a common genetic factor may underlie hyperactivity, antisocial personality, and alcoholism.

A different biological explanation suggests that alcoholism results, basically, from alcohol. Heavy drinking alters brain function, reduces the level of painkilling endorphins, produces nerve damage, shrinks the cerebral cortex, and wrecks the liver. These changes in turn create a biological dependence, an inability to metabolize alcohol, and psychological problems.

But the disease model, popular though it is, has many problems. If alcoholism and addiction to other drugs are diseases, more people than ever are "catching" them. A 1982 Gallup poll found that one-third of American families had had a problem with alcohol. Between 1942 and 1976 there was a 20-fold increase in the number of alcoholics in treatment (Peele, 1983). More and more people are becoming addicted to other drugs as well. For a century, physicians have been searching for the magic painkiller, the one that would not be addictive. Heroin, barbiturates, cocaine and synthetic narcotics such as Demerol, tranquilizers, and methadone were all, on first discovery, supposed to be nonaddictive. In each case, a small percentage of users became "addicted," and eventually abuse of the drug became a social problem.

It's time to think critically about the popular disease model of addiction. People can become "addicted" to jogging, love, and rock-and-roll. What "disease" are they catching?

Alcoholism depends on when and where people drink. In cultures in which people drink moderately with meals—and children learn the social rules of drinking along with their families— alcoholism rates are much lower than in cultures in which drinking occurs in bars, in binges, or in privacy.

Moreover, people can become "addicted" to activities as well as to drugs; what "disease" are they catching? Researchers are worried about the growing number of "exercise addicts" who have a compulsion to exercise that far exceeds any health benefits and who suffer withdrawal pains when deprived of it (Chan, 1987). Some of them cannot stop exercising even when their muscles and joints have been seriously injured. Like alcoholics who organize their lives around drink, "addicted" athletes put exercise above everything else, including their jobs or relationships. And they have major withdrawal symptoms, such as depression and loss of self-esteem, when they are unable to exercise.

Amid much argument, therefore, some researchers want to replace the disease model of addiction with a learning model. In his book *Heavy Drinking: The Myth of Alcoholism as a Disease* (1988)—a book as controversial today as Jellinek's was in 1960—Herbert Fingarette argues that alcoholism is a result of physical, personal, and social factors. It is neither a sin nor a disease but "a central activity of the individual's way of life."

Opponents of the disease model note, first, that *addiction patterns vary according to culture and learning.* Study after study has found that alcoholism is much more likely to occur in cultures that forbid children to drink but condone drunkenness in adults (such as Ireland) than in cultures that teach children how to drink responsibly but forbid adult drunkenness (such as Italy and Greece). In cultures with low rates of alcoholism, adults demonstrate correct drinking habits to their children, gradually introducing them to alcohol in safe family settings. These lessons are maintained by adult customs. Alcohol is not used as a rite of passage into adulthood, nor is it associated with masculinity and power (Peele, 1984a; Vaillant, 1983). Drinking is considered neither a virtue nor a sin. Abstainers are not sneered at and drunkenness is not considered charming, comical, or manly.

Second, *not all addicts go through physiological withdrawal symptoms when they stop taking the drug.* During the war in Vietnam, nearly 30 percent of the soldiers were taking heroin in doses far stronger than those available on the streets of U.S. cities. These men believed themselves to be addicted. Experts predicted a drug-withdrawal disaster among the returning veterans. It never materialized. Over 90 percent of the men simply gave the drug up, without withdrawal pain, when they came home (Robins, Davis, & Goodwin, 1974). Other studies find that large percentages of people who are addicted to alcohol, cigarettes, tranquilizers, or painkillers are able to stop taking these drugs, without outside help and with no withdrawal symptoms at all (Lee & Hart, 1985; Schachter, 1982).

Third, although some people may have a genetic problem in metabolizing alcohol, this cannot account entirely for the different rates of alcoholism between individuals or cultures. In certain cultures that are supposedly more genetically vulnerable to the effects of liquor, such as Native American and Eskimo, alcoholism rates are lower than in some cultures that supposedly have a greater genetic ability to ''hold'' liquor. Nor can genes account for the rapidly changing alcoholism rates *within* a culture.

All of this evidence suggests that drug abuse and addiction are not simply ''diseases,'' but reflect an interaction of physiology and psychology, person and culture. They occur when an individual who is vulnerable to abusing drugs finds a culture and social environment that support drug abuse (Zinberg & Harding, 1982). In particular:

▪ Addiction is more likely to occur among people who believe the drug is stronger than they are, that is, who believe they are addicted. In contrast, those who feel in control of the drug they use, whether it is alcohol, cigarettes, or even heroin, are able to use the drug in moderation and quit without withdrawal pains (Lindesmith, 1968).

▪ Addiction occurs when people come to rely on a drug or an experience as a way of coping with problems, relieving pain, or avoiding stress; when it provides a false sense of power, control, and self-esteem that the individual would not feel without it (Peele, 1983).

▪ Addiction occurs when the drug becomes a permanent part of a person's life instead of an occasional experience. In a study of 100 hospital patients who had been given strong doses of narcotics, 99 had no withdrawal symptoms upon leaving the hospital. They left postoperative pain behind them, along with the drug (Zinberg, 1974).

▪ Drug abuse is more likely to occur when it is part of a person's world; when ''everyone'' drinks heavily, takes cocaine, or uses other drugs; when the drug is taken in its most potent and distilled form (such as crack); and when moderate use is neither taught nor encouraged.

The disease model of addiction was important historically because it changed the existing moral condemnation of the alcoholic or addict as a ''bad'' person to concern for someone who is a ''sick'' person (Sarason & Sarason, 1980). If the disease model is incorrect, this is no reason to abandon sympathy for people with serious problems or to abandon the search for solutions. It may mean, though, that it is time to give up hoping for the perfect drug that has no addictive qualities, and look instead at the human qualities that make a drug seem perfect.

QUICK ▪ QUIZ

Answering these questions will not create an addiction to psychology:

1. Longitudinal studies find that the personality problems of alcoholics are often a result of (**a**) childhood trauma, (**b**) low self-esteem, (**c**) broken marriages, (**d**) alcoholism.
2. Which cultural practice is associated with *low* rates of alcoholism? (**a**) drinking in family or group settings, (**b**) infrequent but binge drinking, (**c**) drinking as a ''rite of passage,'' (**d**) regarding alcohol as sinful drink

Answers:
1. d 2. a

Schizophrenia and Other Psychotic Disorders

▪ Whenever she was upset, Jill heard a voice insulting her. She suspected that people were playing tricks on her. She yelled and cursed at strangers she thought were staring at her. Over the years, Jill became increasingly disturbed, withdrawn, and paranoid. She began to hallucinate, seeing Elizabeth Taylor in her mirror. She refused to undress or bathe, insisting that others were staring at her (Wender & Klein, 1981).

▪ Charles Whitman complained to a doctor that he was feeling overwhelmed by violent impulses and "tremendous headaches." "I have been the victim of many unusual and irrational thoughts," he wrote in his diary. One night he killed his wife and his mother. The next day he killed 14 people with a high-powered rifle before the police shot him to death. A postmortem examination revealed that Whitman had a malignant brain tumor.

These people were suffering from *psychotic disorders*, which involve distorted perceptions of reality and an inability to function in most aspects of life. Psychotic symptoms are often attributed to a large, varied group of disorders that go under the umbrella label **schizophrenia**. But, as may have been true for Whitman, they can also be caused by tumors and disease.

The nature of "the schizophrenias"

To be schizophrenic is best summed up in a repeating dream that I have had since childhood. In this dream I am lying on a beautiful sun-lit beach but my body is in pieces. This fact causes me no concern until I realize that the tide is coming in and that I am unable to gather the parts of my dismembered body together to run away. The tide gets closer and just when I am on the point of drowning I wake up screaming in panic. This to me is what schizophrenia feels like; being fragmented in one's personality and constantly afraid that the tide of illness will completely cover me. (schizophrenic patient, quoted in Rollin, 1980)

At the turn of the century the illness was called "Dementia praecox" (premature mental deterioration) by Emil Kraepelin, who thought it was a hereditary and degenerative disease. In 1911, Swiss psychiatrist Eugen Bleuler named it "schizophrenia," to signify that the personality loses its unity: Words are split from meaning, actions from motives, perceptions from reality. (However, schizophrenia is *not* the same as "split" or "multiple personality." As the schizophrenic just quoted says, schizophrenia describes a fragmented condition, not the coexistence of several different personalities.) Bleuler observed that the disorder does not always worsen and that its symptoms range from mild to totally incapacitating.

The most common symptoms include the following:

▪ *Bizarre delusions* that have no basis in fact, such as the belief that dogs are anthropologists from another planet, disguised as pets to infiltrate human families. Some schizophrenics have paranoid delusions, taking innocent events—a stranger's cough, a helicopter overhead—as "evidence" that the world is plotting against

schizophrenia *A psychotic disorder marked by some or all of these symptoms: delusions, hallucinations, incoherent word associations, inappropriate emotions, or lack of emotions.*

them. Some have "delusions of grandeur," believing that they are Moses, Jesus, or Joan of Arc. "Reasoning with schizophrenics about their delusions," says E. Fuller Torrey (1983), "is like trying to bail out the ocean with a bucket." These delusions, he adds, are "crazy" only to outsiders. To the schizophrenic, they form a logical pattern.

▪ *Hallucinations* that usually take the form of voices and consist of garbled, odd words; a running conversation in the head; or two or more voices conversing with each other. Unlike the hallucinations that might occur to a normal person on a drug high, schizophrenic hallucinations feel intensely real and believable to the patient. Most are auditory (voices) but some are tactile (such as the feeling of animals crawling over the body) or visual (as in Jill's vision of Elizabeth Taylor in her mirror).

▪ *Incoherent, loose word associations*, called "word salads." Schizophrenic thought is often an illogical jumble of ideas and symbols, linked by meaningless rhyming words or by remote associations. A patient of Bleuler's wrote this essay:

> Olive oil is an Arabian liquor-sauce which the Afghans, Moors and
> Moslems use in ostrich farming. The Indian plantain tree is the whis-
> key of the Parsees and Arabs. Barley, rice and sugar cane called arti-
> choke, grow remarkably well in India. The Brahmins live as castes in
> Baluchistan. The Circassians occupy Manchuria and China. China is
> the Eldorado of the Pawnees. (Bleuler, 1911/1950)

The great novelist James Joyce, the story goes, once asked Carl Jung to explain the difference between his own stream-of-consciousness writing and the odd associations of his schizophrenic daughter. Jung supposedly replied, "You dive—she falls" (Wender & Klein, 1981).

▪ *Severe emotional abnormalities*. Schizophrenics typically have inappropriate and exaggerated emotions (see Figure 16.3). They may laugh at sad news, become angry at good news, or weep inconsolably for no reason. Some eventually lose the ability to feel any emotion at all. One man set fire to his house, and then sat down calmly to watch TV.

▪ *Withdrawal into an inner world*. To an observer, some schizophrenics seem to be living in their own minds, oblivious to everything around them. In *Autobiography of a Schizophrenic Girl*, Marguerite Sechehaye wrote, "A wall of brass separates me from everybody and everything. In the midst of desolation, in indescribable distress, in absolute solitude, I am terrifyingly alone. . . ."

Schizophrenia varies in severity, duration, and kind of symptoms. In some individuals, the symptoms tend to appear abruptly and eventually disappear with the passage of time, with or without treatment. In others, the onset is often more gradual and insidious. Friends and family report a "change in personality." The person may stop working or bathing, become isolated and withdrawn, and start behaving in peculiar ways (for instance, collecting garbage or hoarding food).

As for prognosis, again schizophrenia is unpredictable. Psychiatrists often speak of the "rule of thirds": Of all people diagnosed and hospitalized with schizophrenia, one-third will recover completely, one-third will improve significantly, and one-third will not get well. The more breakdowns and relapses the schizophrenic has, the poorer the chances for complete recovery (Stephens, 1978; Vaillant, 1978). Yet even then, some "chronic" schizophrenics learn to live with their illness, are able to work and have warm family relationships, and eventually outgrow their symptoms completely (Harding et al., 1987).

This is the most common image of a person with schizophrenia—withdrawn into a private torment. But many recover completely, and others learn to manage their symptoms and live productively in society.

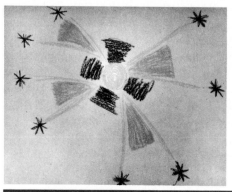

FIGURE 16.3

Emotions and schizophrenia
The Diagnostic Drawing Series, designed by art therapist Barry M. Cohen, consists of three drawings. The first is a spontaneous free choice. The second is a picture of a tree. The third, illustrated here, is a "feeling picture," in which subjects are asked to draw a picture of how they feel, using lines, shapes, and colors. The picture on the left, drawn by a 31-year-old, white, female non-patient, shows movement, expansive use of space, mixed use of line, shape, and color, heavy pressure, and an integrated design. The picture on the right, drawn by a 33-year-old, white, female schizophrenic, shows moderate use of space, the inclusion of words, single color, and lack of integration. The Diagnostic Drawing Series is the first large-scale research project to correlate diagnoses of psychiatric in-patients with specific characteristics of their drawings. Instructions, materials, and ratings of the three pictures are standardized.

The mystery of schizophrenia is that we could go on listing symptoms all day and not exhaust its variations. Some schizophrenics are almost completely impaired in all spheres; others do extremely well in certain areas. Some have perfectly normal moments of lucidity in otherwise withdrawn lives. One catatonic adolescent crouched in a rigid posture in front of a television for the month of October; later, he was able to report on all the highlights of the World Series he had seen. A middle-aged man, hospitalized for 20 years, believing he was a prophet of God and that monsters were coming out of the walls, was able to interrupt his ranting to play a good game of chess (Wender & Klein, 1981). People with brain damage or organic illness usually cannot interrupt their "madness" to watch the World Series or play chess. How can those with schizophrenia do so?

Theories of schizophrenia

As you might imagine, any disorder that has so many variations and symptoms will pose many problems for diagnosis and explanation. Some psychologists have concluded that there is really no such thing as schizophrenia and we would be better off to drop the label entirely. A review of 374 articles found "the persisting failure of research to establish schizophrenia as a stable, determinate, diagnostic entity," much less one that has a clearly identifiable cause (Mancuso & Sarbin, 1984; Sarbin & Mancuso, 1980). In this view, schizophrenia consists of a variety of rule-breaking actions, best understood by the context in which they occur. Others reply that in cultures around the world, the same core signs of schizophrenia appear: hallucinations, loss of touch with reality, delusions, flat or inappropriate emotions, and disorders of thought and perception. "If schizophrenia is a myth," says Seymour Kety (1974), "it is a myth with a strong genetic component."

Several theories attempt to account for the puzzle of schizophrenia:

1. *Psychoanalytic and family dynamics theories.* Some early explanations suggested that schizophrenia results from distorted patterns of communication in families (such as mixed messages and illogical thought processes), or from child-rearing styles (the parents may be hostile, immature, or disturbed). There is little evidence to support these theories, however, and a great deal that refutes them. Psychodynamic explanations have been based on very few cases; they did not include control groups; and they confused cause and effect. Some families do indeed show disturbed communication patterns, but this could result from the difficulty of trying to talk to a schizophrenic child.

2. *Biological theories.* Some researchers believe that schizophrenia is a brain disease (or diseases). The problem is that because schizophrenia involves so many different symptoms, no single physiological deficiency could account for all of them. Some studies have indeed found brain abnormalities in *some* people with schizophrenia—such as a slight decrease in brain weight, a decrease in the volume of the temporal lobe or limbic regions, and reduced numbers of neurons in specific layers of the prefrontal cortex (Meltzer, 1987). However, most of these studies have been very small, and it is not clear that the brain abnormalities occur *only* in schizophrenia.

Other leading biological explanations have focused on abnormalities in chemical neurotransmitters, especially dopamine and serotonin, and on abnormal eye movements and brain electrical activity (Holzman, 1987). Perhaps the brains of some people with schizophrenia are overly sensitive to everyday stimuli, which may be why they retreat into a inner world.

Brain abnormalities in schizophrenia might occur because of genetic defects. Children have a greater risk of schizophrenia if an identical twin develops the disorder, if one parent has the disorder, and especially if *both* parents are schizophrenic (Gottesman, McGuffin, & Farmer, 1987). This risk holds even if the child is reared apart from the twin or parent who has schizophrenia. A recent international study found a link between schizophrenic symptoms and an abnormal cluster of genes on chromosome 5 (Sherrington et al., 1988).

However, not every identical twin who has a schizophrenic sibling develops the disorder, so inheritance cannot be the only cause. Twin studies also suggest that structural abnormalities in the brain, when they occur, are often due to acquired causes rather than genetic ones (Meltzer, 1987). Finally, not all people with schizophrenic symptoms have gene defects on chromosome 5, or anywhere else (Kennedy et al., 1988).

In the last 30 years there has been growing interest in the possibility that an infectious virus causes schizophrenia. Viruses are known to attack very specific areas of the brain, leaving other areas untouched. They can alter brain cells without showing a trace of their damage under a microscope; and they can remain latent for many years before symptoms appear. Although the infectious disease theory fits the known facts about schizophrenia—even the fact that there are seasonal patterns in the births of schizophrenic children (viruses are seasonal)—at present the theory is unconfirmed (Torrey, 1983).

3. *The vulnerability-stress model.* Some researchers argue that a combination of heredity and stress is necessary to produce schizophrenia (Zubin & Spring, 1977). In this view, schizophrenia does not have a simple genetic cause; instead, what may be inherited is a predisposition to react to environmental stress in a particular way, which in turn leads to schizophrenia. A vulnerable person who lives in a good environment may never show signs of the disorder.

Most of the evidence for the vulnerability-stress theory comes from "high-risk" studies, in which children who have a biological parent with schizophrenia are followed over time. Compared to a risk of 1 to 2 percent in the general population, children with one schizophrenic parent have a lifetime risk of 12 percent, and the risk for children with two schizophrenic parents jumps to 35 to 46 percent (M. Goldstein, 1987). Keep in mind, though, that nearly 90 percent of all persons who develop schizophrenia do *not* have a schizophrenic parent, and that nearly 90 percent of all children with one schizophrenic parent do *not* develop the disorder. You see why studying this problem is so difficult.

Although individuals with schizophrenic symptoms appear in virtually all cultures, schizophrenia is regarded as a chronic, degenerative "brain disease" only in Western nations. In nonindustrial societies, individuals who have phases of "madness" are considered temporarily disabled, and most return to their prior level of functioning (L. Davidson, 1988). A review of follow-up studies of schizophrenia in the West concluded that chronic schizophrenia has less to do with "any inherent natural outcome" and more to do with the individual's family and support systems (Harding, Zubin, & Strauss, 1987). In particular, once a person has had a schizophrenic episode, relapses are more likely if he or she lives with parents who have a negative, critical, overinvolved emotional style (Doane et al., 1986; M. Goldstein, 1988).

It does seem clear that the onset and course of schizophrenia depend greatly on environmental stresses (or lack thereof). However, researchers have not been able to specify what kind of "stress" *sets off* the illness. As Torrey (1983) summarizes, "If stress can cause schizophrenia, why don't we have epidemics of schizophrenia in prisons and concentration camps? Why did the schizophrenia rate go down in many countries during World War II rather than up? Why is the schizophrenia rate low in places like warring Northern Ireland, and yet much higher in the relatively peaceful western part of Ireland?"

Scientists are still far from understanding this mysterious illness. If depression is the common cold of psychological disorder, says psychiatrist Donald Klein (1980), schizophrenia is its cancer. Because of the contradictory findings, some researchers believe that the "schizophrenias" cover several different disorders with different causes. Others believe that a common source of all schizophrenias may yet be discovered. They note that rheumatic fever can appear as a disease of the nervous system, of the heart, of the joints, or of the skin. It seemed to be four different diseases until bacteriologists identified the common source (Wender & Klein, 1981).

Organic brain disorders

No one knows how much of Charles Whitman's violent behavior was attributable to his brain tumor; he also had a lifelong love of guns. But organic disorders can produce the symptoms of psychosis. If the brain is affected by disease, tumors, infections, or a deficiency of nutrients, a person will eventually begin to behave in strange, sometimes psychotic ways. Some of these conditions are reversible. Others are progressive and irreversible, leading to death. Some are out of one's control. Others result from self-inflicted abuse. Prolonged alcoholism, for instance, can produce a brain disorder called *delirium tremens* (the D.T.'s), which causes tremors ("the shakes"), hallucinations, and terror.

Diseases. Several diseases are now known to affect brain function. Alzheimer's disease causes a gradual, irreversible deterioration in memory, intellectual ability, and motor control. Huntington's chorea, which involves a deficiency of the neurotransmitter GABA (gamma-amino-butyric acid), causes involuntary spasms and twisting movements of the body, facial grimacing, memory lapses, and impulsive behavior. The disease is carried by a single dominant gene, so every child of an affected parent has a 50 percent chance of getting it, although usually not until middle age. Because the disease produces paranoia, depression, and other psychological symptoms, it is often misdiagnosed. Songwriter Woody Guthrie ("This Land Is Your Land"), a famous victim of Huntington's, was for a long time mislabeled as an alcoholic.

Brain injury and tumors. These conditions produce a variety of symptoms, depending on where they are located and the severity and extent of the damage they produce. Minor brain damage, as after a car accident, may temporarily cause post-traumatic psychosis—delusions, confusions, and delirium. (But some people behave erratically simply because they are alarmed at having "brain damage.") The effects of tumors vary widely. For every Charles Whitman, there is someone whose tumor produces euphoria and mania, and another who becomes quiet and withdrawn. Brain tumors may grow rapidly or slowly, producing behavioral changes that have no apparent cause. In these cases, they are often misdiagnosed. Composer George Gershwin went into psychoanalysis because of severe headaches. His autopsy revealed a brain tumor.

Infections, nutritional deficiencies, poisoning. Hallucinations, delirium, and many abnormal behaviors can be caused by untreated infections, loss of oxygen to the brain (as during high fever), and toxic chemicals (such as lead poisoning). For example, an infection of syphilis may, if untreated, lead to *paresis*, a deterioration in mental and motor functioning that ends in paralysis, psychosis, and death. Gangster Al Capone and Winston Churchill's father, Randolph, both died of paresis caused by syphilis.

Brain disorders can also be caused by nutritional deficiencies. The symptoms of pellagra, a condition caused by lack of the vitamin niacin, include physical signs such as skin "burns" and diarrhea and also psychological signs that mimic anxiety disorders and even schizophrenia. Untreated, pellagra can lead to delirium, hallucinations, and psychotic behavior, but it is reversible with a proper diet.

We have come to the end of a long walk on the spectrum of disorders. We turn next to methods of treatment, for small problems and for overwhelming ones.

Taking Psychology with You

When a Friend Is Suicidal

Suicide is a scary subject, surrounded by mystery and myth. It can be frightening to those who find themselves fantasizing about it, and it is devastating to the family, friends, and acquaintances of those who go through with it. In the United States, most people who commit suicide are over the age of 45, but suicide rates are rapidly increasing among young people. Suicide is the second highest cause of death (after car accidents) among college students.

People who attempt suicide have different motives. Some believe they have no reason to live; some feel like failures in a world where (they think) everyone else is happy and successful; some want revenge against those who (they think) have made them suffer. But they all share the belief that life is unendurable and that suicide is the only solution. This belief may be rational, in the case of people who are terminally ill and in pain, or it may be the distorted thinking of someone suffering from depression.

Friends and family members can help prevent a suicide by knowing the difference between fact and fiction, and by recognizing the danger signs.

1. *There is no ''suicidal type.''* Most adolescents who try to commit suicide are isolated and lonely. Many are children of divorced or alcoholic parents. Some have problems in school and feel like failures. But others who are vulnerable to suicide attempts are college students who are perfectionistic, self-critical, and highly intelligent. The former may feel like ending their lives because they can foresee no future. The latter may feel suicidal because they do not like the futures they foresee.

2. *Take all suicide threats seriously.* Many people fail to take action when a friend talks about committing suicide. Some believe the friend's intentions but assume there is nothing they can do. ''He'll just do it at another place, another time,'' they think. In fact, most suicides occur during an acute crisis. Once the person gets through the crisis, the desire to commit suicide fades. One researcher tracked down 515 people who had attempted suicide by jumping off the Golden Gate Bridge many years earlier. After those attempts, fewer than 5 percent had actually committed suicide in the subsequent decades (Seiden, 1978).

Others believe that if a friend is *talking* about suicide, he or she won't really *do* it. This belief is also false. Few people commit suicide without signaling their intentions. Most are ambivalent: ''I want to kill myself, but I don't want to be dead—at least not forever.'' Most suicidal people don't want death, but relief from the terrible pain of feeling that nobody cares, that life is not worth living. Getting these thoughts and fears out in the open is an important first step.

3. *Know the danger signs.* A depressed person may be at risk of trying to commit suicide if he or she:

- Has tried to commit suicide before.
- Has become withdrawn, apathetic, and socially isolated.
- Reveals specific plans for carrying out the suicide.
- Expresses no concern about the usual deterrents to suicide, such as hurting the family, breaking religious rules, or the fact that suicide is an irreversible action.
- Suddenly seems to be coming out of a severe depression. The risk of suicide increases when the person begins to recover. No one knows why this is so. Perhaps deeply depressed people lack the energy to carry

out a suicide. Perhaps making the decision to end their suffering causes them to feel better.

4. *Take constructive action.* If you believe your friend is in danger of suicide, trust your judgment. Do not be afraid to ask, ''Are you thinking of suicide?'' This question does not ''put the idea'' in anyone's mind. If your friend is contemplating the action, he or she will probably be relieved to talk about it, and you will know that it is time to find help (Beck, Kovacs, and Weissman, 1979). Let your friend talk—without criticism, argument, or disapproval. Don't try to talk your friend out of it by debating whether suicide is right or wrong, and don't put on phony cheerfulness (''Everything will be all right''). If your friend's words or actions scare you, say so. By listening nonjudgmentally, you are showing that you care. By allowing your friend to unburden his or her grief, you help the person get through the immediate crisis.

Most of all, don't leave your friend alone. If necessary, get the person to a counselor, health professional, or emergency room of a hospital; or call a local suicide hot line. Don't worry about ''doing the wrong thing.'' In an emergency, the worst thing you can do is nothing at all.

KEY WORDS

abnormal behavior 574
sanity and insanity 575
DSM-III-R 576
neurosis 578
psychosis 578
generalized anxiety disorder 581
post-traumatic stress disorder 581
phobia 582
agoraphobia 582
panic attack 582
obsessions 583
compulsions 584
major depression 585
dysthymia (''depressive personality'') 585
mania 585
bipolar disorder 586
interpersonal theory of depression 588

hopelessness theory 588
paranoid personality disorder 589
narcissistic personality disorder 590
antisocial personality disorder 590
avoidant personality disorder 590
dissociative disorders 592
amnesia 593
multiple personality disorder 593
somatoform disorders 596
somatization disorder 596
conversion disorder 596
hypochondria 596
disease model of addiction 599
learning model of addiction 600
schizophrenia 602
''word salads'' 603
organic brain disorders 606

SUMMARY

1. ''Abnormal behavior'' has been defined as a statistical deviation from the norm; as a violation of cultural standards; as maladaptive or destructive behavior; as emotional distress; and as ''insanity,'' the legal term for incompetence to stand trial.

2. Diagnosing psychological disorders is not always easy. Some critics argue that diagnosis turns "problems in living" into inflated "disorders," gives people labels that stigmatize their behavior, and is not accurate. The *Diagnostic and Statistical Manual of Mental Disorders* tries to meet these objections and provide objective criteria of abnormal behavior.

3. *Generalized anxiety disorder* is a condition of continuous anxiety, lasting at least a month, with signs of nervousness, worry, and physiological arousal. Other anxiety disorders include *post-traumatic stress disorder*, *phobia*, *panic attack*, *agoraphobia*, and *obsessive-compulsive disorder*.

4. *Mood disorders* include *major depression* and *bipolar disorder*. Symptoms of major depression include distorted thinking patterns; low self-esteem; physical ailments such as fatigue and loss of appetite; and prolonged grief and despair. In bipolar disorder, depression alternates with mania or euphoria.

5. Many theories try to explain depression and its apparently greater prevalence among women. Biological theories emphasize a depletion of neurotransmitters in the brain and the effectiveness of antidepressant drugs. Social theories consider the actual conditions of people's lives, such as the facts that fewer women than men combine work and family life and that physical and sexual abuse in childhood is related to adult depression. Attachment or interpersonal theories argue that depression results from broken or conflicted relationships. Cognitive-behavioral theories, such as *hopelessness theory*, emphasize distorted thoughts and unrewarding patterns of reinforcement.

6. *Personality disorders* are characterized by rigid, self-destructive traits that cause personal distress or an inability to get along with others. Some types include the *paranoid*, the *narcissistic*, the *avoidant*, and the *antisocial* personality. The antisocial personality (also called psychopath or sociopath) is marked by antisocial behavior, lack of guilt and empathy, and impulsiveness or lack of self-control. The disorder may involve a neurological defect, caused by genetics or by damage in childhood to the central nervous system, or it may result from environment and experience.

7. *Dissociative disorders* involve a split in consciousness or identity. They include amnesia, fugue states, and "multiple personality," in which two or more distinct personalities and identities appear within one person.

8. *Somatoform disorders* consist of physical symptoms with no apparent physical cause. Some people are oversensitive to bodily symptoms and may use them to excuse poor performance (*hypochondria*); others ignore them. Other disorders in this group include *conversion disorder* and *somatization disorder*.

9. The effects of drugs depend on whether they are used moderately or are abused. Signs of *drug abuse* include the inability to stop or cut down, intoxication throughout the day, blackouts, impaired ability to work or get along with others, and physical deterioration. According to the *disease model of addiction*, some people have a biological vulnerability to addictions such as alcoholism. The vulnerability may result from a genetic factor or from years of heavy drinking or other drug use. Social or *learning* approaches to addiction point out that addiction patterns vary according to culture, learning, and accepted practice; that addiction rates change within a society as drinking practices change; that many people can stop taking a drug (even heroin) with no withdrawal symptoms; and that drug abuse increases when people are not taught moderate use. Addiction and abuse appear to reflect an interaction of physiology and psychology, person and culture, vulnerability and opportunity.

10. *Schizophrenia* is a psychotic disorder involving many symptoms, such as delusions, hallucinations, "word salads," inappropriate emotions, and withdrawal.

The disorder, probably a brain disease or group of diseases that seem to involve malfunctions in the limbic system, varies in severity, duration, and prognosis. Schizophrenia may result from genetic defects, viral infection, or an interaction of inherited predisposition and environmental stress, but its causes are still unknown.

11. *Organic brain disorders* can produce psychotic symptoms or psychological disorders, such as depression. Brain damage may result from disease, tumors, injury, infection, nutritional deficiency, a virus, or poisoning.

CHAPTER 17

Approaches to Treatment and Therapy

> *No form of therapy has ever been initiated without a claim that it had unique therapeutic advantages. And no form of therapy has ever been abandoned because of its failure to live up to these claims.*
>
> MORRIS B. PARLOFF

▪ Murray is a smart fellow with just one problem: He procrastinates. He can't seem to settle down and write his term papers. He keeps getting incompletes, swearing he'll do those papers soon, but before long the incompletes turn to F's. Why does Murray procrastinate, manufacturing his own misery? What kind of therapy might help him?

▪ Sally complains of anxieties, irritability, and continuing problems in her marriage. Although she is successful at work, she feels like a fraud, a useless member of society, and a burden to her family. She weeps often. Why is Sally so unhappy, and what can she do about it?

▪ Jerry, a college student, is brought to the hospital by the campus police, who found him wandering around, dazed and confused. He is anxious and talkative, and reports hearing threatening voices that accuse him of being a Russian spy. What treatment can help Jerry?

▪ Margaret is a victim of childhood sexual abuse. For five years, her stepfather forced her to have sex with him and threatened to kill her if she told anyone. Margaret is married and loves her husband, but she has many sexual inhibitions. What can Margaret do to recover from her past abuse?

A good therapist can help people get ''unstuck'' from life's problems.

People seek professional help for many difficulties and disorders. These range from ''problems in living,'' such as family conflicts and procrastination, to the delusions of schizophrenia. Today there seems to be an equally large array of programs that promise help for personal problems. In this chapter we will consider and evaluate three major approaches to treatment. (1) *Medical treatments* include drugs or direct intervention in brain function, with or without additional therapy. Medical treatment may be given in a hospital, but also by physicians or psychiatrists on an outpatient basis. (2) *Psychotherapy* covers an array of psychological approaches to treating mental problems. Some of the more popular schools of psychotherapy include psychodynamic therapies, cognitive-behavioral therapies, family therapy, group therapy, and humanistic therapies. Finally, (3) *self-help and community alternatives* include support groups, skills training, rehabilitation counseling, and community interventions.

Each of these approaches can successfully treat some problems but not others. Each can help some individuals but may harm others. Finding the right treatment depends not only on having a good practitioner but on being an educated consumer. What does research show about the effectiveness of drugs, psychotherapy, counseling, and self-help? What works best and for what problem? When do therapies fail and when do they do harm?

Medical Treatments

Over the centuries, approaches to psychological disorders have alternated between the medical model, which regards mental problems as having biological causes, and the psychological model, which views mental problems as having psychological causes. Treatments likewise have varied from physical interventions, such as drugs and surgery, to psychological ones.

Is it "all in the mind" or based in the body?

The medical tradition has had a healthy history. The ancients believed that "melancholia" (depression) was caused by an excess of "black bile" in the spleen. Plato located the source of female emotional and physical disorders in the uterus (*hystera* in Greek). He believed that the childless uterus literally wanders throughout the body, causing everything from paralysis and seizures to headaches and tears. All such symptoms in women, therefore, were "hysterical." Other philosophers thought that emotional and behavioral disorders resulted from faulty digestion and spicy food, which affected the *hypochondrium*—the area below the rib cage containing the stomach, liver, and pancreas. "Hypochondria" now refers to an unfounded concern with one's health, but the word used to refer to emotional disorders thought to be caused by digestive problems in this region (Drinka, 1984).

Theories of melancholia, hysteria, and hypochondria lasted for many centuries, right along with the belief that strange behavior was probably caused by demonic possession and witchcraft (Fraser, 1984). By the early eighteenth century, new medical discoveries challenged both of these views. Physicians argued that the cause of emotional disorder was to be found in the nervous system. "Nervousness" became the common diagnosis. "All nervous distempers whatsoever from Yawning and Stretching, up to a mortal fit of Apoplexy," wrote Dr. George Cheyne in 1733, "seem to be but one continued Disorder, or the several steps and degrees of it" (quoted in Drinka, 1984).

In the mid-1700s, a scientist named William Cullen used the Latin word for nervousness, *neurosis*, to describe the supposed disorders of the nervous system:

Centuries ago, people suffering from physical and mental problems were often "diagnosed" as being possessed by the devil or being witches. The "cure" was to be hanged or burned at the stake.

paralysis, fainting, shortness of breath, cholera, epilepsy, palpitations, asthma, diabetes, melancholia, diarrhea, and mental retardation. By clustering these "neurotic" conditions together, he popularized the idea that many disorders have a common physical, or *organic*, cause.

By the early twentieth century, Freud was redirecting the search for organic causes of "neurosis" to a search for psychological causes. Freud popularized the idea that many disorders have a common *psychological* cause, and this view dominated psychotherapy for most of this century.

Today the emphasis in psychiatry has shifted from studying the unconscious to studying biochemistry, an intellectual earthquake that has shattered the foundations of the profession. The organic model is enjoying a resurgence partly because of new research on the brain, drugs, and genetics, and partly because of the failure of traditional psychotherapies to help chronic sufferers. Many ethical and scientific issues remain unsettled, however, and the debate about treatment continues.

The question of drugs

Biopsychiatrists rely on two primary lines of evidence to support their conclusion that there is a biological basis to many, and perhaps most, emotional disorders and psychoses: (1) the evidence, discussed in Chapter 16, that some disorders may have a genetic component, and (2) the finding that some medications affect people with disorders but have no effect on others who lack the disorders, which suggests that the drugs may be compensating for an organic deficiency.

Antipsychotic drugs, or *major tranquilizers*, include chlorpromazine (Thorazine) and haloperidol (Haldol). These drugs represented a major breakthrough in the treatment of schizophrenia and other psychoses. Before their introduction, hospital staffs had to manage psychotic patients with physical restraints, including padded cells and straitjackets, to keep them from hurting others or themselves during states of extreme agitation and delusion. Restraint is still occasionally necessary until medication takes effect (Torrey, 1983). For people who are acutely ill with schizophrenia and likely to improve spontaneously within a few weeks or months, antipsychotic drugs are particularly effective. They reduce panic and agitation, and often shorten the schizophrenic episode (Kane, 1987).

Some researchers argue that antipsychotic drugs are among the safest in medicine (Baldessarini, 1979). But these drugs do have side effects. Less serious problems include weight gain and sensitivity to sun. More serious side effects include a neurological disorder called *tardive dyskinesia*, characterized by involuntary muscle movements. And in a small percentage of cases, antipsychotic drugs can cause delirium, coma, and death from *neuroleptic malignant syndrome (NMS)* (Pope, Keck, & McElroy, 1986). To avoid these dangers, researchers are experimenting with low doses of antipsychotic drugs. Unfortunately, doses that are too low increase the risk that schizophrenic symptoms will worsen, particularly after a year of treatment (Marder et al., 1987). Thus antipsychotic drugs are a double-edged sword in the treatment of chronic schizophrenia. They remove or lessen the most dramatic symptoms, such as hallucinations and "word salads," but they cannot restore normal thought patterns or social relationships. They allow many people to be discharged from hospitals, but often these individuals cannot care for themselves or they fail to take their medication.

Antidepressant drugs, classified as stimulants, are used in treating mood disorders, usually depression but also anxiety, agoraphobia, and obsessive-compulsive disorder. There are two kinds of antidepressant drugs. One kind, called *monoamine*

antipsychotic drugs *Major tranquilizers primarily used in the treatment of schizophrenia and other disorders involving psychotic symptoms, such as delusions.*
antidepressant drugs *Stimulants that influence neurotransmitters in the brain; they are used in the treatment of mood disorders, usually depression and anxiety.*

Before the advent of anti-psychotic medication, the straitjacket was commonly used to restrain people who were liable to hurt themselves or others.

oxidase (MAO) inhibitors, directly elevates the level of the neurotransmitters norepinephrine and serotonin. (These drugs are called MAO inhibitors because they block, or inhibit, the enzyme that can deactivate norepinephrine and serotonin.) The second kind, called *tricyclic antidepressants*, prevents reabsorption, or "reuptake," of norepinephrine and serotonin by the cells that have released them. Antidepressants are nonaddictive, and their side effects (usually a dry mouth and constipation) tend to be mild and wear off in a few weeks. Some people, however, react more strongly to these drugs.

Another substance, a salt called *lithium carbonate*, is often effective in calming people who have manic depression (Klerman et al., 1984). It must be given in exactly the right dose, because too little won't help and too much is toxic. The patient's blood levels of lithium must be carefully monitored.

"Minor" tranquilizers, such as Valium or Xanax, are classified as depressants. These drugs are the ones most frequently prescribed by physicians for patients who complain of unhappiness or anxiety, but, unfortunately, they are the least effective in treating emotional disorders. In addition, a small but significant percentage of the people who take minor tranquilizers become abusers of the drug, developing problems with tolerance and withdrawal (Lader, 1985). For these reasons, antidepressants are preferable to tranquilizers in treating mood disorders.

A drug is developed that frees psychotic patients from the need for straitjackets and that helps some otherwise healthy people recover from depression. Why shouldn't we leap to the conclusion that drugs are miracle cures?

Drugs have helped many people who might otherwise have gone from therapy to therapy without relief. In the case of Jerry, the young man having a schizophrenic episode, medication is likely to speed him through this frightening experience and return him to everyday life. In the case of Sally, antidepressants may allow her to make use of psychotherapy to tackle some of the problems she has with work and family. Medication, of course, does not magically eliminate depressed people's real-life problems. But it can improve their sleep patterns, appetite, and energy, allowing them to concentrate on solving their problems.

However, despite these benefits, a few words of caution are in order:

▪ New drugs, like new therapies, often promise quick and effective cures. The *placebo effect* (see Chapter 2), however, ensures that some people will respond positively to new drugs just because of the enthusiasm surrounding them. After a while, when placebo effects decline, many drugs turn out to be neither as effective as promised nor as widely applicable.

▪ The challenge with drugs is to find the "therapeutic window," the amount that is enough but not too much. Some people have been given antidepressants in doses too weak to make a difference. Others have been given doses that are too strong, causing unintended and sometimes harmful side effects. People sometimes have taken drugs for years, without improvement. This treatment is as useless as staying in a "talk therapy" for years without improvement.

▪ A person may have short-term success with antidepressant drugs, but over time the relapse rate is high among those who have not learned how to cope with anxiety or depression or with life problems. When people attribute their improvements to the drug, they may not be able to handle later setbacks. Sometimes drugs become part of the problem: Some anxious people are afraid to go anywhere without their pills (Beck & Emery, 1985).

▪ Although there appear to be no health consequences of taking prescribed amounts of antidepressants, researchers have been unhappily surprised by the eventual side effects of other "safe" drugs. Women of childbearing age should be particularly careful before taking any medication indefinitely. For many problems, such as phobias and anxiety, behavioral approaches work as well as drugs (Chambless & Goldstein, 1982).

In scientific conferences as well as in the media, some people have tended to regard drugs as either the Great Solution to All Problems or the Worst Possible Danger. Neither extreme is warranted. The proper use of drugs depends on the individual, the problem, whether the physician is knowledgeable, and whether the drugs are combined with other therapy.

Probing the brain: Surgery and electroshock

Throughout history, healers have resorted to physical interventions to literally root out behavior that they considered abnormal. One ancient technique, called *trepanning* (or *trephining*), was to drill holes in the skull and thereby "ventilate" evil impulses or mental pressures. Today there are certain medical procedures, used only in hospitals under controlled conditions, that attempt to change brain function directly.

Psychosurgery is an operation designed to intervene in the part of the brain thought to be responsible for emotional disorders or disturbed behavior. (It should not be confused with brain surgery to remove an abnormal organic condition, such as a tumor.) In 1936, a Portuguese neurologist, Egas Moniz, developed a procedure that cut the fibers of the frontal lobes of the brain. The operation, called a leucotomy or prefrontal *lobotomy,* was supposed to reduce the patient's anxiety or other symptoms without impairing intellectual ability. Unfortunately, it often left the patient apathetic and withdrawn. This procedure was performed on tens of thousands of people in its heyday (Valenstein, 1986).

With the advent of antipsychotic drugs in the 1950s, lobotomies declined in the United States, but other forms of psychosurgery took their place. Today technology allows surgeons to pinpoint and destroy highly specific areas in the brain. For example, some try to reduce uncontrollable rage by removing parts of the amygdala, a part of the limbic system involved in emotion. As Kenneth Moyer (1983) put it, "Just as there are wild cats and wild monkeys, there are wild people— individuals who have so much spontaneous activity in the neural systems that underlie aggressive behavior that they are a constant threat to themselves and to those around them." This aggressiveness, Moyer argues, can be reduced by making lesions in those neural systems.

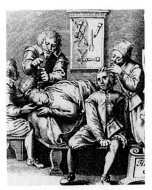

A engraving from 1634 shows trepanning, an ancient method of drilling holes in the skull to "release" psychic pressures supposedly causing mental illness.

psychosurgery *A surgical procedure that destroys selected areas of the brain believed to be involved in emotional disorders or violent, impulsive behavior.*

Psychosurgery is highly controversial. Critics argue that it is unreliable, has unpredictable results, and can cause unintended brain damage (Robitscher, 1980). For all the magnificent advances in understanding the brain, they add, our knowledge of its workings is still cloudy. When surgeons try to remove a ''rage center,'' they may blitz some good tissue as well; neural circuits in the brain are complex and intermeshed. Because the legal and ethical problems involved in irreversible surgery are considerable, psychosurgery is regarded as a procedure of last resort.

An equally controversial procedure is **electroconvulsive therapy (ECT),** or ''shock'' treatments. An electrode is placed on one or both sides of the head, and a brief current is turned on. The current triggers a seizure that typically lasts one minute, causing the body to convulse intensely.

A colleague told us about a man who was given ECT in the early 1950s: The convulsions sent him flying off the table and shattered his legs. Cases such as this reinforce the public impression of ECT as a barbaric and painful practice, akin to electrocution. Today the technique has been vastly modified and the voltage reduced. Patients are given muscle relaxants and anesthesia, so their convulsions are minimized and they can sleep through the procedure (Malitz & Sackeim, 1986). Advocates maintain that ECT is a far faster and more effective way to treat severe depression (especially in people who are suicidal) than drugs. The method lost favor when drugs seemed to be so promising and ECT so dangerous. When drugs proved to have limited effectiveness and to take time to work, and when new ways of measuring brain activity appeared, researchers began to reexamine ECT.

ECT affects every aspect of brain activity, including blood flow, neuroendocrine levels, and neurotransmitters. Although it may temporarily help some people with severe depression, it is not a cure; its beneficial effects are short-lived. ECT is not effective with most other disorders, such as schizophrenia or alcoholism. Its main drawback is that it produces memory loss and other cognitive impairments, sometimes briefly but sometimes permanently. That is why some former patients call it ''a crime against humanity,'' and a psychiatrist called the use of ECT ''like hitting [someone] with a two-by-four'' (Fisher, 1985). ECT continues to inspire passion, pro and con.

QUICK ▪ QUIZ

Match the treatment with the problem(s) for which it is most typically used.

1. antipsychotic drugs
2. antidepressant drugs
3. lithium carbonate
4. electroconvulsive therapy

a. suicidal depression
b. manic depression
c. schizophrenia
d. depression and anxiety

Answers:
1. c 2. d 3. b 4. a

---

electroconvulsive therapy (ECT) *A procedure occasionally used for cases of prolonged major depression, in which a brief brain seizure is induced to alter brain chemistry.*

The hoofbeats of a zebra

One rainy afternoon a young woman named Sheila Allen went to a community hospital and asked for psychiatric help. Sheila Allen had virtually no strength left. She couldn't walk; she could barely sit up. For years she had been going to dozens of doctors, getting sicker and sicker. Finally she concluded that she was "a kook," and in desperation went to the "kook hospital." Her diagnosis was "bizarre behavior, with looseness of thought associations and severe depression associated with suicidal thoughts."

Sheila Allen was lucky. At the hospital she met a neurologist who suspected she had an uncommon disease called myasthenia gravis, which weakens the muscles. His diagnosis proved correct. Fortunately, there is a treatment for this illness, and Sheila Allen recovered. Why had no doctor correctly diagnosed her problem? Her neurologist said, "There is a saying about diagnosis—about why doctors often fail to recognize one of the less common diseases. It goes, 'When you hear hoofbeats, you don't necessarily think of a zebra.' I recognized the hoofbeats of a zebra" (Roueché, 1984).

All clinicians learn to recognize the hoofbeats that make the most noise in their profession. "Mind"-oriented people listen for one beat, "body"-oriented people for another. Throughout history, both sides have made errors. In the nineteenth century, tuberculosis was thought to be caused by a "tubercular personality" until the bacillus that causes the disease was discovered (Sontag, 1978). Conversely, madness was believed to result from masturbation, and male circumcision became popular as a way to prevent "masturbatory insanity." It was (mistakenly) believed that circumcised boys wouldn't masturbate as much (Paige, 1978; Szasz, 1970).

Errors of diagnosis and treatment still occur. A British medical historian, Elizabeth Thornton (1984), observed the case of a young woman who was admitted to a hospital for psychiatric treatment. The patient was not as fortunate as Sheila Allen. Her psychiatrists subjected her to months of psychoanalytic therapy while failing to diagnose her real problem, a brain tumor. Thornton collected dozens of these errors and even reanalyzed Freud's early cases. She found that many psychoanalytic patients were suffering from organic illnesses that were unidentified in Freud's day, such as tuberculous meningitis, temporal lobe epilepsy, and Gilles de la Tourette's disease. She and other scientists fear that psychoanalytic methods are delaying the discovery of the real origins of mental illness (Medawar, 1982).

But psychologists are also concerned about a comparable error: reducing complex psychological problems to matters of biochemistry. Because drugs are easy to administer, some physicians are tempted to prescribe them indiscriminately, without finding out what the patient might be angry, depressed, or anxious *about*. Two psychosurgeons induced lesions on the amygdala of a man who, they said, had "paranoid delusions" about his wife's infidelity with a neighbor. Her denials would set the man off into a frenzy of rage. According to follow-ups conducted by an independent observer, the man never recovered. He has been in and out of hospitals ever since, with "paranoid delusions" that two doctors are out to get him. His wife divorced him and married the neighbor (Chorovor, 1974).

As long as people think that hoofbeats indicate only one animal, disagreements about medical and psychological models will continue.

Experts "see" what their training and experience teaches them to see. Psychologically minded experts and medically minded experts may therefore interpret the same behavior differently. How can we avoid the diagnostic errors that occur because of this either/or thinking?

Types of Psychotherapy

In this section we will consider the major schools of psychological treatment and some of their offshoots. In describing each of the therapeutic schools that follow, we will use our procrastinating friend Murray as an example to give you an idea of its basic philosophy and methods. But keep in mind that these therapies treat many problems, including emotional disorders, life decisions, conflicts in relationships, and traumatic experiences.

Freud (1910) believed that Leonardo da Vinci's paintings of Madonnas were a sublimated expression of his longing for his mother, from whom he had been separated early in life. One goal of psychoanalysis is to help clients "sublimate" their energies constructively instead of expressing them neurotically.

Psychodynamic ("insight") therapies

Sigmund Freud was the father of the "talking cure." He believed that intensive probing of the past and of the mind would produce *insight*—the patient's moment of truth, the awareness of the reason for his or her symptoms and anguish. With insight and emotional *catharsis* (release), the symptoms would disappear. Today, Freud's original method has evolved into many different forms, but the goal of insight unites them. These therapies are called *psychodynamic* because they are based on exploring the unconscious dynamics of personality, such as defenses and conflicts.

Traditional, "orthodox" psychoanalysis is a method for those who have money and time. The client usually meets with the analyst three to five times a week, often for many years. One orthodox psychoanalyst, John Gedo (1979), reported that in 20 years he treated only 36 people, each one requiring "more than 600 sessions, sometimes as many as 1,000, spread over 3 to 7 years." (In the film *Sleeper*, Woody Allen plays a character who has been in suspended animation for two centuries. When he awakes, his first thought is: "I haven't seen my analyst in 200 years! He was a strict Freudian–if I'd been going all this time I'd probably almost be cured by now.")

In analysis, the client lies on a couch, facing away from the analyst, and uses **free association** to say whatever comes to mind. For example, by free associating to his dreams, his fantasies about work, and his early memories, Murray might gain the insight that he procrastinates as a way of expressing anger toward his parents. He might realize he is angry because they insist that he study for a career he dislikes. Murray must come to this realization by himself. If the analyst suggests it to him, Murray might feel too defensive or anxious about displeasing his parents to accept it.

The second major element of psychoanalysis is **transference**, the patient's transfer of emotional responses toward his or her parents to the analyst. A woman who failed to resolve her Oedipal love for her father might in therapy seem to "fall in love" with the analyst. A man who was always angry at his mother for (in his perception) rejecting him might now become furious with his analyst for going on vacation. Through transference, analysts believe, patients "work through" their emotional problems.

Analysis does not expressly aim to solve an individual's immediate problem. In fact, a person may come in complaining of a symptom (such as anxiety or headaches), and the analysis may not get around to that symptom for months or even years. The analyst views the symptom as only the visible tip of the mental iceberg. To get rid of it, the unconscious block beneath the surface must be broken up. Some traditional analysts don't attempt "cures" at all. The goal, they say, is understanding, not change. Gedo (1979) explains (critics might say "rationalizes") this goal by maintaining that "to require patients to improve is an illegitimate infringement on their autonomy."

Other psychotherapists use Freudian or other analytic principles but reject traditional psychoanalytic methods. They face the client; they participate more; they are more goal-directed. Psychodynamic therapies differ according to the particular school they follow.

Brief psychodynamic therapy is another alternative to traditional psychoanalysis. Freud himself worried about the question of length of treatment in his essay "Analysis Terminable and Interminable." However, most of his followers operated on the principle that the longer a patient stays in therapy, the better. "In Freud's day," observes Rachel Hare-Mustin (1983), "analysis lasted a year and marriage lasted a lifetime. Now it's just the opposite." To counteract this trend, "time-limited" or "brief" programs consist of 15, 20, or 25 sessions. The therapist

---

free association *In psychoanalysis, a method of recovering unconscious conflicts by saying freely whatever comes to mind.*

transference *In psychoanalysis, a critical step in which the patient transfers emotional feelings for his or her parents to the therapist.*

chooses a *dynamic focus* (Binder, 1984) or a *central issue* (Mann, 1973). Without delving into the client's entire history, the therapist listens to the client's problems and formulates the main issue. The rest of therapy focuses on the person's self-defeating habits and repetitive problems. The therapist often uses the client's behavior in the therapeutic relationship to identify and change these chronic patterns (Davanloo, 1980; Strupp & Binder, 1984).

Cognitive and behavioral therapies

Psychologists who practice cognitive or behavioral therapy would focus on helping Murray change his current behavior and attitudes rather than providing him with insight. "Mur," they would say, "you have lousy study habits. And you have a set of beliefs about studying, writing papers, and success that are woefully unrealistic." Such therapists would not worry much about Murray's past, his parents, his "unconscious anxieties," or his motives.

In Chapter 6 we discussed the major principles of learning theory and behaviorism and some of their practical applications (such as the token economy). Behavior therapists use a variety of techniques derived from behavioral principles, including systematic desensitization, aversive conditioning, flooding, and contracts.

1. *Systematic desensitization* is a step-by-step-process of "desensitizing" a client to a feared object or experience. It combines relaxation training with a systematic hierarchy of stimuli, sometimes in imagined situations and sometimes in real ones, that lead gradually to the greatest fear. The hierarchy for a person who is terrified of flying might be this: Read about airplane safety; visit an airport; sit in a plane while it is on the ground; take a short flight; take a long flight across the country. At each step the person must become comfortable before going on.

2. *Aversive conditioning* uses punishment to replace the positive reinforcement that perpetuates a bad habit. For example, a woman who bites her nails is reinforced each time she does so by relief of anxiety and a brief good feeling. A behavior

Two therapists assist a phobic woman who is afraid of stairs. In this form of behavior therapy, the therapists take the client directly into the feared situation in order to extinguish her fear. What situations would you have to put yourself in to extinguish your own fears? Public speaking? Visiting the spider display at a zoo? Looking down from the top of the Empire State Building?

therapist might have her wear a rubber band around her wrist and ask her to snap it (hard!) each time she bites her nails or feels the desire to do so. The goal is to make sure that there are no continuing rewards for the undesirable behavior.

3. *Flooding or exposure treatments* take the individual right into the most feared situation, but the therapist goes along with the client to show that the situation isn't going to kill either of them. Exposure therapy has proved very effective with agoraphobia and other anxiety disorders (Agras, 1985; Chambless & Goldstein, 1982). Agoraphobics are taken into the very situation they fear, and they remain in the situation until their anxiety declines.

4. *Behavioral records and contracts* are ways of changing unwanted habits, such as overeating or quarreling, by keeping careful track of the rewards that keep the habit going. A man might not be aware of how much he eats or of what he eats throughout the day; a behavioral record shows that he eats more junk food than he realized in the late afternoon. Once the unwanted behavior is identified, along with the reinforcements that keep it going, a new program is instituted with a new program of reinforcements (Pryor, 1984). A husband and wife who fight over housework, for instance, might be asked to make up an actual contract of who will do what, with specified rewards for carrying out their responsibilities. Without such a contract, it is easy to shout accusations: "You *never* do anything around here!"

A behaviorist might treat Murray's procrastination in several ways. Murray might not be aware of how he actually spends his time when he is avoiding his studies. Afraid he hasn't time to do everything, he does nothing. Keeping a behavioral diary lets Murray know exactly how he spends his time, and how much time he could realistically allot to a project. (Procrastinators often are poor judges of how much time it takes to do things.) The therapist would help Murray set *behavioral goals*, small step by small step. Instead of having a vague, impossibly huge goal, such as "I'm going to reorganize my life," Murray would establish specific small goals, such as reading the two books necessary for an English paper and writing one page of an assignment (Burka & Yuen, 1983).

Of course, people's thoughts, feelings, and motivations can influence their behavior. Most of us reward and punish ourselves by the judgments we make of our actions. "Gee, I did that well," we say, or we torment ourselves with guilt for not doing something well. In discussing emotion (Chapter 9) and emotional disorders (Chapter 16), we saw how distorted thoughts and perceptions are related to moods and mood problems.

Cognitive therapy aims to correct distorted and unrealistic thinking (Beck, 1976; A. Ellis, 1962; Ellis & Dryden, 1987). Clients may be asked to write down their negative thoughts, read the thoughts as if someone else had said them, and then write a rational response to each one. For example, Linda, a young nurse, came to therapy because she was depressed about her job. Yet she would not allow herself to change jobs because she believed she *should* be able to resolve her problems at work. If she couldn't, it was clearly her fault. By writing down her thoughts, she could examine them up close (Eidelson, 1986).

A cognitive therapist would treat Murray's procrastination problem by exploring Murray's thoughts and feelings about his work. Many procrastinators are perfectionists. If they can't do something perfectly, they won't do it at all. Unable to accept their human limitations, they set impossible standards for themselves. Perfectionists are vulnerable to depression because the unreasonable demands they make of themselves give them ample opportunity to fail.

Murray may be afraid to write his term papers because he believes he cannot express his ideas well. When he writes a sentence, he imagines his teacher making fun of it. He imagines all possible criticisms in advance, and his poor essay doesn't

Ugly or beautiful? *Cognitive therapists ask clients to examine their perceptions of the world and the evidence for their beliefs. A depressed person observing this scene might see only the litter and none of the beauty—and might conclude that the whole world is ugly and always will be.*

stand up to them. In time, he decides that turning in nothing at all is better than turning in a bad paper. This decision brings its own problems. "Since the paper is late," he thinks, "it has to be even better to make up for its lateness." Now suppose Murray examines these thoughts:

Negative Thoughts	Rational Responses
That sentence isn't good enough. I'd better rewrite it.	Good enough for what? True, it won't get the Pulitzer Prize for literature, but it's just fine for a small English essay.
It's terrible not to do my best. I'm wasting my potential.	It's terrible to waste my life rewriting English essays. It's a greater waste to do nothing at all with my abilities.

True behaviorists consider thoughts to be "behaviors" that are modifiable by learning principles. In practice, most psychologists agree that thoughts influence behavior and behavior influences thoughts. Cognitive and behavioral therapies often borrow each other's methods, so "cognitive-behavior" therapy is more common than either method alone.

QUICK ▪ QUIZ

Match the method with the therapy that uses it.

1. free association
2. systematic desensitization
3. contract specifying duties
4. rational reappraisal of negative thoughts
5. dynamic focus

a. cognitive therapy
b. psychoanalysis
c. brief psychodynamic therapy
d. behavior therapy

Answers:

1. b 2. d 3. d 4. a 5. c

Humanistic therapies

Humanistic therapies, like their parent philosophy humanism, start from the assumption that people seek self-actualization and self-fulfillment (see Chapter 11). These therapies generally do not delve into past conflicts, but aim to help people feel better about themselves and free themselves from self-imposed limits. They share the belief that the way to do so is by exploring what is going on "here and now," not the issues of "why and how."

Client-centered or *nondirective* therapy, developed by Carl Rogers, is just what it sounds like. The therapist's role is to listen sympathetically, to offer unconditional positive regard, to be an "ideal parent." This method aims to build the client's self-esteem, the feeling that he or she is loved and respected no matter what. To Rogerians, it almost doesn't matter what the client's specific complaint is. Unhappiness and self-defeating behavior, they believe, derive from blocked self-actualization and low self-regard. Thus a Rogerian might assume that Murray's procrastination masks his low self-regard, and that Murray is out of touch with his real feelings and wishes.

Although client-centered therapy has no specific techniques, Rogers (1961) believed that effective therapists must have three qualities. They must be warm, showing unshakable regard for the client. They must be genuine and honest in expressing their feelings toward the client. And they must show accurate empathic understanding of the client's problems. The therapist's support for the client, according to Rogers, is eventually adopted by the client, who will become more self-accepting. Once that is accomplished, the person can accept the limitations of others too.

Gestalt therapy, developed by Frederick (Fritz) Perls (1969), aims at self-actualization through emotional liberation. Perls believed that people tend to think too much and to suppress their feelings. As a result, he said, they lose the ability to feel and to function at their full potential. *Gestalt* means "whole," and Perls wanted to "fill the holes" in personality.

Perls worked in a group setting, where people were encouraged to "let it all hang out"—that is, to express any feeling that they had without fear of consequences. One method was the direct encounter, in which brutal frankness, ventilation of any and all negative or taboo feelings, and confrontation were encouraged. Another method was *role playing*, in which an individual who was angry at his father might play himself talking to his father, then play his father talking back to him. By acting out both sides to a conflict, Perls maintained, a person gains greater understanding. Unlike a Rogerian, a Gestalt therapist might fight back with Murray, insult him, cajole him, or join him in role playing.

Existential therapy helps clients explore the meaning of existence, and face with courage the great questions of life, death, and free will. Existential therapists believe that people's lives are not inevitably determined by their past experience but that they have the power to choose their own destinies. Victor Frankl (1955) developed a form of existential therapy after surviving a Nazi concentration camp. In that pit of horror, he observed, some people maintained their dignity and sanity because they were able to find meaning in the experience, shattering though it was.

Some observers believe that ultimately, all therapies are "existential." In different ways, they help clients determine what is important to them, what values guide them, and what changes they will have the courage to make. An existential therapist might help Murray think about the significance of his procrastination, what school means to him, what his ultimate goals in life are, and how he might find the strength to carry out his goals.

Beyond the person: Family and group therapies

Murray's situation is getting worse. His father has begun to call him Mr. Tomorrow, which upsets his mother, and his brother the math major has been calculating how much tuition money Murray's incompletes are costing. His older sister Isabel, the biochemist who never had an incomplete in her life, now proposes that all of them go to a family therapist. "Murray's not the only one in this family with complaints," she says.

Family therapies maintain that Murray's problem is not *in him*. It developed in a social context, it is sustained by a social context, and it will take a social context to find the solution.

The family kaleidoscope. Salvador Minuchin (1984) compares the family to a kaleidoscope, a changing pattern of mosaics in which the pattern is larger than any one piece. Efforts to isolate and "therapize" one piece, one member of the family without the others, are, in this view, doomed to fail. For one thing, each member has his or her own perceptions about the others, which may be entirely wrong. For another, family members are usually unaware of how they influence one another. By observing the entire family together (or, in the case of marital problems, the wife and husband together), the therapist can discover the family's tensions and imbalances in power and communication (Satir, 1983).

In "psychosomatic families," only one member (usually a child) actually gets an illness or psychological symptoms, but that illness plays a role in the workings of the whole family. Minuchin believes that psychosomatic families have a common feature: They avoid conflict. The child gets sick as a way of expressing anger, keeping the parents together, or asserting control. For example, Minuchin argues, anorexia nervosa tends to occur in families in which parents overcontrol their daughters. Refusing to eat, even to the point of starvation, can be the daughter's way of controlling the one thing she can, her body (Minuchin, Rosman, & Baker, 1978).

Some family therapists use a *multigenerational* approach, helping clients identify repetitive patterns of behavior across generations in their families (Kerr & Bowen, 1988). The therapist and client will create a "genogram," a family tree of psychologically significant events across as many generations as the client can determine (Carter & McGoldrick, 1988; McGoldrick & Gerson, 1985). Sometimes the genogram highlights the origins of current problems and conflicts. The genogram of the playwright Eugene O'Neill, for instance, shows a pattern of estrangement between father and children for three generations (see Figure 17.1). Sometimes the genogram reveals positive patterns. The genogram of Alexander Graham Bell, the inventor of the telephone, reveals a three-generation preoccupation with problems in hearing and speaking.

Although many family therapists treat the whole family, others will treat individuals in a *family systems* perspective (Bowen, 1978; H. Lerner, 1986). That is, clients learn that if they change in any way, even in getting rid of their problem or unhappiness, their families will protest noisily. They will send explicit and subtle messages that read, "Change back!" The family systems view recognizes that if one family member changes, the others must change too: If I won't tango with you, you can't tango with me. But most people don't like to change. They are comfortable with old patterns and habits, even those that cause them trouble. They *want* to keep tangoing, even if their feet hurt.

Family therapy is particularly suited for children and adolescents who have problems. Often those problems are a response to parental conflicts or family stress:

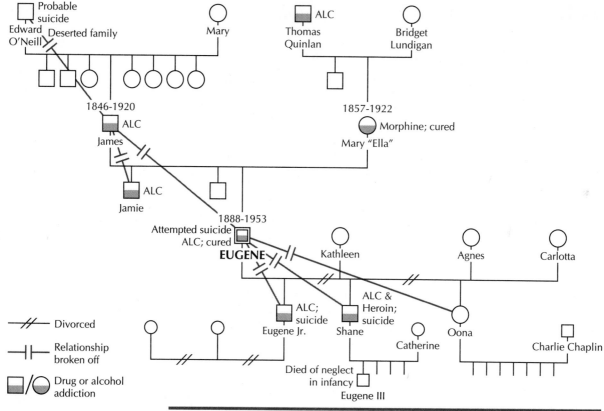

FIGURE 17.1

The family genogram of playwright Eugene O'Neill

The O'Neill family shows multigenerational patterns of estrangement between father and children, multiple marriages, and addiction. Both Eugene and his older brother Jamie felt alienated from their father; in turn, Eugene was totally estranged from his two sons, and he never spoke to his daughter Oona again after she married Charlie Chaplin. Eugene attempted suicide; both of his sons did commit suicide. Eugene's grandfather, father, older brother, and sons were alcoholics; his mother, a morphine addict for 26 years, was later cured. Eugene, who had had problems with alcohol as well, quit drinking at age 37.

Constructing a genogram allows family therapists and their clients to observe patterns across generations that often illuminate current conflicts and concerns. By recognizing patterns that are destructive, family members can begin to change them (McGoldrick & Gerson, 1985).

The parents may be quarreling, and the children respond by withdrawing or becoming more hostile. Or the "problem" may be a normal stage of development: The teenagers are developing their own interests and identities apart from the family's, causing conflicts with the parents. Family therapy helps all members of the family understand these *interacting* relationships and adjust to the changes of individuals (Fishman, 1988).

A family therapist might observe that Murray's procrastination is an ideal solution to his family dynamics. It allows Murray to compete with his siblings for his father's praise ("I'll be as good as they are, Dad, once I get these papers in"). It gains him the attention and sympathy of his mother ("Don't pester the boy, Harry; can't you see how unhappy he is?"). It keeps Murray from facing his greatest fear: that if he does finish his work, it won't measure up to his father's standards. The therapist would work with all members of the family, not only to help Murray stop procrastinating, but also to help the family accept a new Murray.

Group therapy. Murray could also join a group of procrastinators, who already know every one of his excuses and habits. In group therapy, some 6 to 12 people meet on a regular basis. Group therapies are as diverse as their leaders. Psychodynamic therapists, cognitive-behaviorists, family therapists, and humanists all may run group therapy sessions. Some groups consist of people who share a problem; others consist of people with different problems. Only the basic format— self-revelation in a group—is the same. In group therapy, ideally, members learn that their problems and fantasies are not unique. They learn to speak up and become more assertive with other people in (presumably) a safe setting. They learn that they cannot get away with their usual excuses because others in the group have tried them all. Group therapies are commonly used in institutions, such as prisons and mental hospitals. But they are also popular among people who have a range of social difficulties, such as shyness and anxiety.

Psychotherapy in practice

The four general approaches to psychotherapy that we have discussed may seem wildly different. In theory, they are. In practice, most psychotherapists are **eclectic**, borrowing a method from here, an idea from there. This flexibility suits their own preferences and enables them to treat many different clients. There is even a professional journal, *Integrative and Eclectic Psychotherapy*, and many books on the integrative approach to therapy are appearing. In a survey of family therapists, more than one-third described their methods as eclectic, and only small minorities rigidly adhered to ''pure'' theoretical schools within their field (Rait, 1988).

As we noted, cognitive-behavior therapy is already a popular hybrid. Some cognitive therapists also use role-playing techniques from Gestalt therapy. Some

eclectic *Literally, selected from various sources; in psychotherapy, the term describes the common practice of using methods from different theoretical schools.*

Successful therapists are flexible in their methods.

"I UTILIZE THE BEST FROM FREUD, THE BEST FROM JUNG AND THE BEST FROM MY UNCLE MARTY, A VERY SMART FELLOW."

psychoanalytic therapists borrow methods from the family systems approach. Some humanistic therapists are more ''directive'' than the theory recommends, and some behaviorists are less directive. Some ''insight'' therapists use behavioral methods to help the client act on the insight.

Some researchers are trying to identify the common themes or processes in all therapies, even those as apparently opposite as psychoanalytic and behaviorist, or biological and cognitive (Basch, 1988; Gazzaniga, 1988; Prochaska, 1984). Ultimately, therapy cannot be effective unless therapist and client are able to communicate. A good therapist does what it takes, regardless of theory, to achieve that goal.

Alternatives to Psychotherapy

Psychotherapy is increasingly popular for people with all sorts of problems, but sometimes it is not enough and sometimes it is too much. *Community programs* aim to help people who are seriously mentally ill or who have chronic disabilities and need more than individual therapy. *Self-help groups* help people who have problems that do not require individual therapy.

The community and rehabilitation movement

Many people assume that individuals who are seriously mentally ill are in hospitals and other institutions, but this is not so. The vast majority of people with mental disorders spend most of their lives in the community; yet they usually cannot live with their families, either. Instead, most of them live in boarding houses, hotel rooms, hostels, jails, hallways, abandoned buildings, halfway houses, or the streets (Torrey, 1983). The question of how best to treat them is critical to these individuals, their families, and society (see ''Think About It'' on page 630). How can they learn not only to ''cope'' with the problem, but to *live* with it, to do the best they can in love, work, and social life?

Rehabilitation psychologists are concerned with the assessment and treatment of people who are physically or mentally disabled, either temporarily or permanently—for instance, people with mental retardation, epilepsy, chronic pain, severe physical injuries, arthritis, cancer, addictions, and psychiatric problems. They conduct research to find the best ways to teach disabled people to work and live independently; to overcome motivational slumps, such as feeling sorry for themselves; to improve their sex lives; to follow healthy regimens. Their approach to treatment is practical and eclectic, often including behavior therapy, group counseling, job training, and community intervention.

Community programs have proven highly successful in helping many people who are mentally ill and who have long-term disabilities (Dion & Anthony, 1987). In a follow-up study of schizophrenics who had been hospitalized 20 years earlier, researchers found that the greatest predictor of successful functioning was community support, including the outpatient services of local clinics and close contact with family and friends (Harding et al., 1987).

But what kind of community support? People with schizophrenia need a comprehensive program. Traditional ''talk'' therapies are not effective (Kane, 1987). Although drugs are helpful, even essential, they are not sufficient; a drug can calm your symptoms but not teach you how to get a job. Psychologists have experimented with many different solutions. For a while, ''halfway houses,'' places for people who had been discharged from hospitals but who were unable to go home, were popular. Halfway houses vary in the services they provide for their residents; in their primary emphasis (work, social activities, companionship); in the strictness of their rules (e.g., about visitors or alcohol); and in the length of stay of their residents, from six months to indefinitely (Torrey, 1983).

Newer, more effective methods follow the "clubhouse model," a program for mentally ill people that provides rehabilitation counseling, job training, and a support network. Members may live at the clubhouse until they are ready to be on their own, and they may visit the clubhouse at any time. New York City's Fountain House, one of the oldest such programs in the country, has an excellent track record (Beard, Propst, & Malamud, 1982). Other community approaches include the establishment of support systems, family therapy, foster care and family home alternatives, and family support groups. The success of these programs, however, depends on the dedication and energy of the people running them, which is why it is often difficult to transplant a successful program from one place to another (Torrey, 1983).

Rehabilitation psychologists, by the way, do not work only with schizophrenics. We know a secretary who permanently injured her back and was no longer able to sit long hours at a desk or resume her old job. She entered a program run by rehabilitation psychologists who were helping people find new careers when they could no longer work at their former ones. Today she has a new career: rehabilitation psychologist.

The self-help movement

Long before there were psychotherapists, there were sympathetic advisers. Long before there were psychologists, there was psychological help. Nowadays, there are literally thousands of programs designed to help people help themselves—with a little help from their friends.

Self-help and support groups. An estimated 14 to 16 million Americans—a number expected to double in the next few years—belong to some 500,000 self-help groups, which are organized around a common concern. In fact, self-help

This self-help support group consists of several AIDS patients and two volunteers, who gather for sessions in which they share concerns and offer constructive advice. In this session, they are "visualizing" the disease in an effort to control its effects.

Think About It

Hospitals and the Dilemma of Commitment

You may have seen them on the streets. They aren't violent, but they are, to the larger community, distressing. They live in alleys and on sidewalks, carrying all their possessions with them. They may mumble to themselves or shout to the heavens. They are emotionally disturbed or psychotic, and they are homeless. What should be done with them? It is a troubling question. The answer used to be to put them in mental hospitals. But three trends combined to release many disturbed people back onto the streets:

1. Antipsychotic medication calmed most of the extreme symptoms, allowing people to return to their families and communities (usually, as long as they stayed on the medication).

2. Civil-rights and patients'-rights movements protested the abuses of institutionalization. They pointed out that many disturbed people were being "warehoused" without treatment, that people were being committed without sufficient cause, and that there were no review procedures to enable a person to get out of the hospital. Many mentally disturbed individuals were spending far longer in mental hospitals for committing minor crimes than they would have spent in prison. Some people were confined by mistake (perhaps because they could not speak English) or by oversight. A woman named Gladys Burr was involuntarily confined in 1936, with an incorrect diagnosis of mental retardation and psychosis. No one paid attention to her requests for freedom for 42 years.

In many states today, hearings are held to determine whether a patient should be released. A judge listens to the arguments of the hospital's psychiatrists and the patient's advocate and then makes a decision.

3. The federal government began a program of "deinstitutionalizing" mentally disturbed people, sending them to their communities for treatment. In 1963, Congress passed the Community Mental Health Centers Act, designed to set up a nationwide network of mental health centers that would provide inpatient and outpatient services, such as private or group therapy; emergency services for crisis, suicide, and psychotic episodes; and day treatment for people whose families could not care for them around the clock. The goal was to find alternatives to warehousing.

Unfortunately each of these trends, generated for all the right reasons, has backfired, creating more problems than anticipated. Antipsychotic medication, in some of the worst, understaffed hospitals, simply replaced straitjackets and padded cells with drugged stupors (Robitscher, 1980). Many pa-

group members outnumber therapy patients four to one; we are truly in the midst of a "self-help revolution" (Gartner & Riessman, 1984).

Name it, and there is a group for it: Alcoholics Anonymous (and related groups for the children or spouses of alcoholics), Overeaters Anonymous, Depressives Anonymous, Impotents Anonymous, Parents Anonymous (for abusive parents), Schizophrenics Anonymous. There are countless nonanonymous groups such as those for gay fathers, women who have had mastectomies, relatives of people with Alzheimer's disease, rape victims, cancer patients and their families, widows, and new stepparents.

By uniting people with common problems, support groups by definition offer their members three ingredients of feeling better: understanding, empathy, and advice. Others in the group have been there, know what you are going through, and may have found solutions you never would have imagined. For people who fear that

tients are given medication and released without support services; often their families are unable to care for them. Outside the hospital, patients often stop taking their medication. Their psychotic symptoms return, the patients are rehospitalized, and the "revolving door" cycle continues (Wender & Klein, 1981).

In addition, hospital administrators, anxious to avoid legal charges of violating patients' rights, often discharge patients as soon as possible without regard for where they might go. Some state officials have made it very difficult to hospitalize people involuntarily for longer than a few weeks (even those who are dangerous to themselves or others), and even difficult to keep patients who *want* to stay. Although this means that hospitals can't make the mistake they did with Gladys Burr, it creates other problems. A woman who had been hospitalized 12 times in ten years for violent attacks was let out (again) after a four-month confinement for stabbing someone. She then killed two people with a semiautomatic rifle. Her parents and psychiatrists had been unable to commit her against her will.

Finally, having pressured the states to close their mental hospitals and release disturbed people, the government has cut financial aid for local and state mental health care and for housing the poor and homeless. Without coordinated local services, the result is the "dumping" of thousands of patients onto the streets. For their part, many communities have refused to accept halfway houses or mental health centers; health care professionals call this the NIMBY problem ("not in my back yard").

One solution is "involuntary outpatient commitment": Patients who meet certain standards of being dangerous to themselves or the community could be compelled by the courts to take part in community treatment programs (Mulvey, Geller, & Roth, 1987). Patients would be monitored regularly, and only if they violate the treatment regimen would they be committed to an institution. Opponents of this idea argue that, in practice, patients would often end up being policed, like parolees from prison, without actually getting treatment. They worry about granting the state too much power to invade the privacy of the mentally ill. To make sure a person is taking medication, for example, would you require drug tests? Exactly what aspects of the person's life would you monitor for treatment—the patient's family life? Personal relationships? Friends? Drinking?

You are the public. What services should governments provide for disturbed people? How can communities protect the rights of the mentally ill while protecting the safety of the public? What do you think?

no one else has ever suffered what they have or felt what they feel, such groups can be reassuring in ways that family, friends, even psychotherapists are not (Dunkel-Schetter, 1984).

Margaret, our opening example of a victim of childhood sexual abuse, might do very well in a support group of women who had shared her experience. In a study of women, black and white, who had been victims of unwanted sexual contact in their childhoods, researchers found that one factor predicted recovery (measured in overall psychological adjustment and positive attitudes toward men): the ability to tell someone and to be believed (Wyatt & Mickey, 1985). This factor was the critical one, regardless of the severity or kind of abuse. Women who failed to get this support as children can benefit from individual or group therapy as adults.

Although self-help groups can be immensely therapeutic, they are not therapy. They do not search for "underlying problems." They are not designed to help people with serious psychological difficulties. "But there is one benefit of a self-help group that you don't get with a therapist," says Marion Jacobs, Co-Director of the California Self-Help Center at UCLA. "At the end of the program, you have ten new friends."

"Life change" encounter groups. During the 1960s, Fritz Perls's Gestalt techniques became the basis of the encounter group movement (M. B. Smith, 1984). Encounter groups, which might or might not be led by trained psychologists, aimed for "personal growth," not psychotherapy. Some groups met for a single intense session, lasting several hours. Others met for a weekend "marathon" session. Encounter groups became a popular counterculture experience, for they appealed to people who felt that Americans were becoming too remote and alienated from each other. The encounter-group scene has changed in many ways since then, not all of them desirable. "What began as something novel, spontaneous, unstructured and filled with surprise," wrote Thomas Kiernan (1974), "has quickly developed teachers, high priests, official spokesmen, orthodoxies, heresies, even messianic claims, rituals, dogmas, an ecclesiastical jargon and a Billy Graham-type of show business promotion."

Encounter groups exist today in dozens of different forms, none regulated by law or by psychological associations. Est, Lifespring, Marriage Encounter, and many other programs follow in the humanistic tradition, promising self-understanding, unconditional love and regard from others, and self-fulfillment. But they vary widely in the content of their philosophy and in the kind of encounter they offer participants. Some are based on breaking people down by putting them through stress, fatigue, and hunger, and then "reconstructing" them in the group's image (see Chapter 18). Other programs are milder, based on role playing and shared revelations.

Skills training. One of the most "therapeutic" solutions to life problems is new experience and skills. Skills training programs assume that most people do not have "psychological problems" but inexperience and inability. Just as you don't learn to play the piano by talking about pianos, in this view, you don't overcome shyness by talking about why you are shy. Pianists need music lessons, and shy people need to learn how to behave sociably.

Many therapies, particularly cognitive-behavioral ones, include skills training (Beck & Emery, 1985). But there are also programs designed to teach specific skills, and there are probably as many of these as there are skills to be learned. *Assertiveness training* is designed to teach people how to speak up for themselves without being hostile or aggressive (Bower & Bower, 1979). *Social skills training* teaches people who are shy and socially anxious how to behave in new situations. Social skills include how to talk to other people, how to listen, how to ask someone for a date, how and when to make eye contact, and how to pick up other people's signals (Bellack & Hersen, 1979). *Parent effectiveness training* helps parents learn to listen to their children, impart standards and values, and maintain discipline without authoritarianism (C. Brown, 1976; Gordon, 1970).

Poor Murray! He's getting a little tired by now, having tried so many therapies. That last weekend with the Nature Walk ("Trek to Truth") Encounter was especially fun, but now he's *really* behind. All of these choices are enough to make a person procrastinate about getting help. Which therapy or self-improvement program is the "right" one?

Evaluating Psychotherapy and Its Alternatives

In 1952, Hans Eysenck published a dramatic challenge to clinical psychology. In his studies, he found that psychotherapy simply was not effective in producing what it promised. About two-thirds of the people who had psychological problems improved within a couple of years, whether they were in psychotherapy or not. Normal life experiences, said Eysenck, are as "therapeutic" as therapy. In many cases, he added, being in psychotherapy *slows down* the natural rate of improvement. In 1966, he reviewed the evidence of additional research. The "uniformly negative results" persuaded Eysenck (1985) that, if anything, he had been too kind to therapy the first time.

Naturally, psychotherapists did not take this charge lightly. In the following years, they conducted literally hundreds of studies designed to test the effectiveness of therapy, counseling, and self-help groups.

First, the good news: Psychotherapy does seem to be better than doing nothing at all. People in almost any professional treatment improve more than people who do not get help (Lambert, 1983; Landman & Dawes, 1982; Qualls & Berman, 1988; Smith, Glass, & Miller, 1980). Now, the sobering news: The people who do the best in psychotherapy also have the least serious problems to begin with. Long-standing personality disorders or pathological problems are not appreciably helped by psychotherapy or its alternatives (Strupp, 1982). Finally, the bad news: In 5 to 10 percent of all cases, psychotherapy is harmful because of the therapist's incompetence or unethical methods (Lambert, Christensen, & DeJulio, 1983).

In studying the matter of effectiveness, researchers must overcome two difficulties. One is that people usually become attached to their therapists or groups, especially if they have invested money or time in them. (Remember "the justification of effort" research in Chapter 10.) The minute researchers say that some therapy doesn't "work," they hear a chorus of howls: "But psychotherapy worked for *me*! I would *never* have (taken that job) (moved to Cincinnati) (left home) if it hadn't been for Dr. Blitznik!" Alas, none of us can be our own control group. That is, we can't know what would have happened without Dr. Blitznik. Maybe we would have taken the job, moved to Cincinnati, or left home anyway.

The second, related problem is that most people who go through *any* therapy or self-improvement program will tell you they are the better for it. "I went through _____ and now I am a new person!" "I took a course in _____ and it changed my life!" Every program claims enthusiastic graduates, even when studies find that the program or therapy was objectively ineffective (Hinrichsen, Revenson, & Shinn, 1985). One reason seems to be that people edit their memories of what they were like before, because they want to believe that they are consistent. If their attitudes then change, people revise their memories, "recalling" past attitudes that are virtually identical to their present ones. But when people want to believe they *have* changed, they revise their memories in the opposite direction. In one study, participants in a self-improvement program exaggerated, in recall, how poorly off they were before the program and how much better they were afterward (Conway & Ross, 1984). When participants accept a program's validity, they anticipate change from the start, look for change as they go along, and overestimate the amount of change at the end.

Some psychotherapists believe that "feeling better" is a good enough measure of effectiveness. Others believe that effectiveness is unmeasurable. Anyone, they say, can see that therapy helps. Critics reply that *assertions* of effectiveness must

Psychotherapy clients will tell you how grateful they are to Dr. Blitznick for changing their lives. But perhaps their lives would have changed anyway. How can we evaluate the true effectiveness of psychotherapy?

not substitute for *demonstrations* of effectiveness, especially now that psychotherapy and self-help programs have become big business (Fischer, 1978). So the debate rages on. Is psychotherapy more effective than doing nothing at all? If so, which form of therapy is best? Are the nonprofessional alternatives just as good? What is a "cure" or a "success" in therapy anyway? (For more on this issue, see "A Closer Look at Sex Therapy.")

When therapy helps

Jerome Frank (1974, 1982) argues that psychotherapy is a healing art, not a scientific procedure. People who seek therapy, he says, have a common problem of *demoralization.* Regardless of their specific difficulties, they feel unable to cope, they have low self-esteem, and they suffer feelings of hopelessness. Most forms of therapy and other forms of emotional healing, whatever their content, are designed to combat this low morale and inspire the client to try new ways of coping in order to restore self-esteem and the sense of competence (Basch, 1988). The four elements in all successful therapies, Frank suggests, are these:

1. An emotionally charged, confiding relationship with a helping person (or group). No method works in the absence of a good therapeutic relationship between client and therapist (R. Hobson, 1985) or between client and group members.

2. A healing setting—an environment that reassures the client of being helped and that enhances the prestige of the therapist.

3. A rationale or philosophy that provides a plausible explanation for the client's symptoms and prescribes a procedure for resolving them.

4. A "healing ritual" that requires the active participation of both patient and therapist. This treatment reduces the client's sense of alienation and hopelessness, raises the expectation of getting better, and unites client and therapist (healer) in a shared goal. What is most effective about psychotherapy seems to be the client's belief that he or she will be helped (Prioleau, Murdock, & Brody, 1983).

Psychotherapy is a social exchange. Like all relationships, its success depends on qualities of both participants and on the "fit" between the two people. For example, therapists' judgments of a client's improvement tend to be based on whether the client has accepted their values. Long ago, a study found that clients who improved the most, according to their therapists, were those whose values changed to agree with the therapist's, particularly in the areas of sex, aggression, and authority (D. Rosenthal, 1955).

Even client-centered therapists, who are supposed to be totally supportive of whatever the client says or feels, show this bias. An independent observer taped and analyzed some therapy sessions conducted by Carl Rogers himself. When the client expressed himself in a style similar to that of the therapist, Rogers was more empathic, warm, and accepting and less directive. When the patient went off on his own track, Rogers became significantly less empathic and accepting and more directive (Truax, 1966).

The successful client. Good therapeutic candidates combine a basically strong sense of self with sufficient distress to motivate them to change (Strupp, 1982). As one psychologist summarized, they also tend to be "young, physically attractive, well-educated, members of the upper middle class, intelligent, verbal, willing to talk about and take responsibility for their problems, possessing considerable ego

A Closer Look at Sex Therapy

The Problem of "Cures"

Many new therapies begin with a flourish of trumpets and a burst of excitement: "At last," they promise, "we have found the Ultimate Cure!" Followers of the new therapy sing its praises and celebrate its successes. After a few years and studies, disenchantment sets in. Alas, the new therapy hasn't "cured" everyone, and a few of the early "miracle" cures have relapsed into their old ways. The story of sex therapy is a case in point of what happens in many therapies.

With the publication of Masters and Johnson's *Human Sexual Inadequacy* (1970), a new era in treating sexual problems was born. Before then, people who had sexual difficulties had two choices. They could endure their unhappiness privately, or they could spend years in psychodynamic therapy, trying to find the neurotic basis of their sexual symptoms. Masters and Johnson showed that most sexual problems are due to poor communication between partners, sexual ignorance, and plain old embarrassment. Their therapeutic program was brief, brilliantly effective, and easy to follow.

This was exciting and welcome news. Sex therapy programs sprang up like mushrooms after a rainfall. "Cure rates" were astonishingly high. Then, after a few years, the first evaluation studies came in. Sex therapy worked, all right, but it often didn't last. People whose problems were a result of sexual ignorance *did* improve quickly and permanently. Unfortunately, those "easy cases" were a small proportion of the people with problems.

In one follow-up study of 16 men with erection problems, Stephen Levine and David Agle (1978) learned how complicated it is to define a "cure." Is a man "cured" if he can achieve erections but is so worried about failing that he disregards his wife's sexual satisfaction? Is he "cured" if he can achieve erections but doesn't want to? What if he can have erections half the time? When the researchers de-

fined "cure" as *reduced frequency* of erection failure, sex therapy was successful in ten cases. When they defined "cure" as complete elimination of sexual problems in both husband and wife, sex therapy was successful in only one case. That one "easy case" was a man who believed his problem was a result of masturbating during adolescence. When the doctor reassured him that masturbation does not impair erection, the man's difficulties vanished. But for the other men, sexual satisfaction and performance depended on how the rest of their lives was going. In some cases, solving the sexual problem upset a delicate marital balance of power, creating new problems.

Similarly, in a program for women who had never had orgasms, all the women did become orgasmic. In that sense, sex therapy was 100 percent successful. But only a few of the women were able to integrate this sexual change into their marriages or love affairs, and several relationships split up (Payn, 1980). Was the therapy "successful" for them?

Today, sex therapists are wiser about the complex nature of sexuality. Sex occurs in a relationship, and sexual satisfaction has more to do with the state of the relationship than with the state of one's physical responses. As Levine (1979) concluded, "Many of my colleagues are wondering where all the easy cases have gone. I contend that it isn't the easy cases that have vanished, but the collective naïveté of sex therapists."

The lesson to be drawn from the saga of sex therapy is not that "nothing works." The lesson, rather, is that most human problems are not illnesses to be "cured," and that is why the search for an easy quick fix is probably doomed. The goal of therapy is not complete personality overhaul, but moderate improvements in our complicated lives and relationships.

---

strength, and showing no signs of gross pathology" (Rabkin, 1977). In short, they are like their therapists.

One reason that psychotherapies are so rarely "pure" in their methods is that the people who seek therapy are diverse. Some are introspective and want to talk about their childhoods. Others are practical sorts who attack an emotional problem as they would attack an overgrown lawn: Let's mow it down. Some want an open-ended chance to talk about their feelings. Others want to *do* something. These personality differences often influence the approach that the therapist uses, the course of therapy, and the results.

For example, one study of depressed elderly people found that cognitive, behavioral, or brief dynamic therapy were equally likely to be successful. What made the difference in outcome was the clients' *commitment* to the therapy and *willingness* to work on their problems. In turn, the people with commitment and willingness had support from their families and a personal style of dealing actively with problems instead of avoiding them (Gaston et al., 1987).

The successful therapist.   Even within the same school of therapy, why do some therapists succeed brilliantly and others fail? The answer has to do with the therapist's personality, particularly the qualities that Carl Rogers praised: empathy, warmth, genuineness, and imagination (see Figure 17.2). The great teachers who establish new schools of therapy often get high success rates because of their own "healing power" and charisma. They make their clients feel respected, accepted, and understood. In a study of 59 people in psychodynamic therapy, the one factor that predicted progress was the client's perception of the therapist's empathy (Free et al., 1985). Therapists who are cold, hostile, seductive, or pessimistic tend to have poor results with their clients (Rubenstein, 1986).

The qualities of a good therapist are not limited to professional psychologists. Many people who are unhappy or in a crisis cope with their difficulties by talking with friends, relatives, or religious advisers. Counselors, social workers, and even paraprofessionals (people who have some experience but not an advanced degree) are as effective as clinical psychologists in treating most problems (Strupp, 1982; Strupp & Hadley, 1979).

The therapeutic alliance.   Ultimately, success in psychotherapy depends on the "therapeutic alliance" that the therapist and client establish together. If they share many characteristics and preferences, religious values, and ethnic and racial background, they are more likely to understand each other (Strupp, 1980). Misunderstandings, whether they result from ignorance or from prejudice on either side, make therapy more difficult (McGoldrick, Pearce, & Giordano, 1982).

For example, some white therapists misunderstand their black clients' body language. They regard lack of eye contact and frequent glancing around as the client's attempt to "size up what can be ripped off," instead of as signs of discomfort and an effort to get oriented (Brodsky, 1982). From their standpoint, black clients often misunderstand or distrust the white therapist's demand for self-disclosure. A lifetime of experience often makes them reluctant to reveal feelings that they believe a white person wouldn't understand or accept (Ridley, 1984).

Similarly, Hispanics and Asians are likely to react to a formal interview with a therapist with relative passivity, deference, and inhibited silence, leading the therapist to diagnose a "problem" that is only a cultural norm. Some Hispanics respond to catastrophic stress with an "ataque nervioso," or a nervous attack of screaming, swooning, and agitation. It is a culturally determined response, but an uninformed clinician might label it as a sign of pathology, even as schizophrenia (Malgady, Rogler, & Costantino, 1987).

Some psychologists are trying to develop forms of therapy that fit the client. *Cuento* or "folktale" therapy, for example, is based on principles of social learning theory and modeling, using traditional Puerto Rican folktales. Puerto Rican children in this program feel less anxious and adapt to their Anglo-American neighborhoods

FIGURE 17.2

Psychotherapy in action: How one therapist reached a withdrawn boy

Robert Hobson (1985) spent many weeks trying to communicate with Stephen, a 15-year-old boy who refused to speak or look at him. One day, in frustration, Hobson took an envelope and drew a squiggly line (a) and invited Stephen to add to the picture. Stephen drew a ship (b) thereby turning Hobson's line into a "terrifying tidal wave." Was the boy, Hobson wondered, afraid of being emotionally "drowned"?

Hobson next drew c, a landing pier (representing safety). Stephen was not interested in safety. He responded with d, a person waving goodbye.

Hobson, suspecting that Stephen's problem might stem from emotional separation from his mother, drew e, a woman waving goodbye. Stephen drew f and spoke for the first time: "A flying fish."

Hobson drew g and said "An octopus." Stephen, shoulders drooping in sadness, marked up the entire sketch with lines (h), adding, "It's raining."

Hobson, hoping to convey optimism, drew the sun (i), its rays conflicting with the rain. Stephen paused, and looked at Hobson intently for the first time. He drew large arcs embracing the whole illustration (j).

"A rainbow," said Stephen. He smiled.

faster than control groups that receive either no treatments or traditional ones (Rogler et al., 1987).

Being aware of cultural differences, however, doesn't mean that the therapist should stereotype all clients of different cultures or tailor the therapy to fit some

"Cuento" (folktale) therapy was developed for Puerto Rican children who have behavioral problems. It makes use of traditional Puerto Rican stories, such as the tales of Juan Bobo (left), to teach children to control aggression, understand right from wrong, and delay gratification. The photo on the right shows a therapy session conducted by Giuseppe Costantino and Migdalia Coubertier, in which the children and their mothers watch a videotape of the folktale, discuss it together, and later role-play its major themes. The method has been successful in reducing children's anxiety and improving their attention span and imagination (Costantino, Malgady, & Rogler, 1986).

abstract notion of cultural rules. It does mean that therapists must do what is necessary to ensure that the client will find the therapist to be *trustworthy* and *effective* (Sue & Zane, 1987).

Some therapists define themselves by their commitment to clients who are targets of prejudice. Gay therapists, feminist therapists, and black and other minority therapists may come from any of the various psychological schools of therapy. But they share a goal of improving the self-esteem and mental health of clients whose problems are complicated by having been victims of discrimination. They would argue, for example, that a homosexual should not seek counseling from someone who still thinks that homosexuality is a sickness. They would advise a woman who was a victim of incest not to seek help from a Freudian who still thinks that little girls unconsciously want to have sex with their fathers.

Which therapy helps most?

> The result is that after six years in sessions, both group and individual, I have gained a great deal of insight into my own personality, the practical results of which are virtually nil. My problem is behavior, not insight. (quoted in Sarason & Sarason, 1980)

This man has learned what countless studies now reveal: First, insight alone can make people feel better, but it doesn't change their behavior. Second, more therapy is not necessarily better therapy.

Talk versus action.   It is not easy to compare two kinds of therapy because good therapists, as we saw, do many similar things, even when they come from different schools (Kazdin, 1982; Sloane et al., 1975). However, it is clear that the success of therapy does depend in part on the nature of the problem being treated.

Insight therapies have been shown to be *ineffective* for depression (Beck et al., 1979); for anxiety, fears, agoraphobia, and panic (Chambless & Goldstein, 1982); for sex problems and sex offenders (Abel et al., 1984); for severe personality disorders (Strupp, 1980); for schizophrenia (Torrey, 1983); and for drug abuse (Vaillant, 1983). Insight therapies seem to be best suited to people who are introspective about their motives and feelings, who want to explore their pasts and understand why they are the way they are.

Over 200 controlled studies have demonstrated the effectiveness of behavior therapies in contrast to doing nothing at all or to being in psychodynamic therapy (Fischer, 1978; Rachman & Wilson, 1980; Wolpe, 1981). In spite of this success rate, behavior therapy too has its failures (Foa & Emmelkamp, 1983). It is not the answer to such problems as recovering from trauma, coming out of suicidal depression, or changing sexual patterns or preferences. It is not highly effective with people who do not really want to change and who are not motivated to carry out a behavioral program (Messer & Winokur, 1980; Woolfolk & Richardson, 1984).

Long-term versus short-term. Most psychodynamic therapists believe that the longer therapy goes on, the more successful it is. As Figure 17.3 shows, research does not support this claim (Howard et al., 1986). In the late 1960s, a study compared 60 randomly selected clients who were given eight treatment sessions with another 60 who got standard analytic treatment for up to a year and a half. The long-term clients felt they had gained more insight, and the long-term therapists found treatment easier. But symptom improvement was the same in both groups, with one difference: Only one of the short-term clients became worse, while ten of the long-term clients did. Finally, the long-term treatment cost four times as much, but its effects were no more enduring (Goleman, 1981). Subsequent studies find the same results (Strupp, 1980; Strupp & Binder, 1984).

"Pure" versus combined approaches. Some problems, and some clients, are immune to any single kind of therapy but may respond to combined methods. For

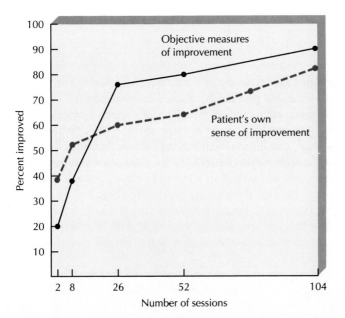

FIGURE 17.3

Is more therapy better?
About half of all patients improve in only eight sessions and about 75 percent improve by the twenty-sixth session. After that, only a few percent benefit from more sessions (Howard et. al., 1986).

example, the most promising treatment for sex offenders (including child molesters, rapists, and adults who commit incest) combines cognitive therapy, aversive conditioning, sex education, group therapy, reconditioning sexual fantasies, and social skills training. None of these methods works by itself (Abel et al., 1984). Some people who have anxiety disorders respond to a combination of drug treatments, cognitive-behavioral methods, and group support (Chambless & Goldstein, 1982). Some depressed patients respond better to a combination of drugs and cognitive psychotherapy than to either method alone (Bowers, 1988; Conte et al., 1986).

People who have continuing, difficult problems—such as recovering from a traumatic experience, living with chronic pain, or coping with a disturbed family member—often are best helped by a combination approach that specifically addresses their situation.

When therapy harms

▪ When "Susan B." committed suicide, her distraught husband accidentally discovered an eight-page suicide note she had left for her psychotherapist. This tortured letter implored the analyst not to feel guilty for "using me for your own pleasure"—for the sexual intercourse he required as part of her therapy for the five months she had been seeing him. She chided him for his waning sexual interest in her that caused her final depressive episode, but begged him not to blame himself for her death (Kiernan, 1974).

▪ A 54-year-old man came to a psychiatrist because none of his previous therapies had helped him. He had begun treatment in his early 20s, for anxieties and inhibitions that were normal for a shy, inexperienced young man. *Thirty years* of therapy with leading psychoanalysts had not helped him. On the contrary, his problems were worse and he was financially strapped, having spent most of his money on therapy (Schmideberg, 1970).

As we noted earlier, according to hundreds of studies on the outcomes of psychotherapy, about 5 to 10 percent of the people in therapy are seriously harmed by the treatment or by the therapist (Lambert, Christensen, & DeJulio, 1983). A client can be harmed in a number of ways:

1. *Deterioration* of the client's emotional state and worsening of symptoms (Bergin & Lambert, 1978). Sometimes the process of therapy itself or the client's relationship with the therapist causes the client's problems to intensify. The therapy or therapist may actually retard or prevent the client's improvement.

2. *Coercion* by the therapist to accept the therapist's ideas, advice, sexual intimacies, or other unethical behavior (Pope & Bouhoutsos, 1986). Some therapists abuse their clients' trust, convincing them that the therapy "requires" them to behave in ways they find reprehensible (Bersoff, 1978). Others use "strong-arm" tactics to try to get individuals or families to break old patterns. Donald Ransom (1982), a family therapist, criticizes the growing trend in his field to "overpower families" with authoritarian tactics. Some therapists, says Ransom, recommend "dropping bombs" on families and then leaving them to fend for themselves. Such methods can make a client's problems and feelings worse (Kolotkin & Johnson, 1983).

3. *Bias* on the part of a therapist who doesn't understand the client because of the client's gender, race, religion, or ethnic group (M. L. Smith, 1980). The therapist may try to induce the client to conform to the therapist's standards and values,

even if they are not appropriate to the client or in the client's best interest (Brodsky, 1982).

4. *Dependency* on the part of the client, who becomes unable to leave therapy and relies excessively on the therapist for all decisions. Since therapists depend on clients for their income, they must replace each client who leaves. It is thus often in the therapist's interest to foster the client's dependency (Johnson, 1988). In extreme cases, therapists have created "psychotherapy cults," in which members become persuaded that their health depends on staying in the group.

Encounter groups pose an added danger that individual therapies do not: social pressure to conform because of the presence of other people (Rosen, 1977). In a study of 200 college students who joined encounter groups with trained leaders, only a third reported benefits. Another third showed no changes. But the last third were emotionally harmed; the experience worsened their existing problems (Lieberman, Yalom, & Miles, 1973).

Self-help and support groups also can have negative effects. Some people become excessively dependent on the group, using it to wallow in their problems instead of solving them. According to many studies, people in self-help groups designed to help them break their addictions (whether to cigarettes, alcohol, or drugs) often have a higher relapse rate than do individuals who break these habits on their own (Peele, 1985; Vaillant, 1983). It is as if the group says, "You're addicted; you can't do anything about your addiction without us; and then you need us to keep from becoming readdicted." Once people define the problem in this way, giving up an internal locus of control, they seem to become less able or willing to take charge of it themselves.

For these reasons, it is important for people to become educated consumers of psychotherapeutic services (see "Taking Psychology with You").

The value and values of therapy

On radio, in the newspapers, on television, in countless popular books, media psychologists offer free thera...well, free advice. There is nothing unethical about advice. Clergy, neighbors, relatives, and friends hand it out all the time. Indeed, some observers have argued that psychotherapy is, in reality, paid friendship. As Americans become more and more geographically mobile, as families grow smaller, as city life becomes more impersonal, the professional support of psychotherapy has replaced the long-standing informal support of friends and relations.

Is there anything wrong with that? In his book *The Shrinking of America*, Bernie Zilbergeld (1983), himself a psychotherapist, argues that Americans are too attached to psychotherapy, and for the wrong reasons. Zilbergeld believes that therapy promotes three central myths that increase dissatisfaction:

Can psychotherapy transform a depressed person into someone who is never sad? What kinds of changes is it reasonable to expect from psychotherapy?

1. *People should try to change because they are not as happy, as good, or as competent as they should be.* Americans like to think that people can do anything or become anything if only they try hard enough. An anxious man can become the outgoing life of the party. A shy woman can become a jolly earth mother. Everyone can be happy all the time. The message of therapy, says Zilbergeld, is often "there is something wrong with the way you are and you ought to do something about it." The goal of "making yourself better" can motivate us toward improvement, but it can also create dissatisfaction with aspects of ourselves that are perfectly fine.

2. *Almost any change is possible; if something is wrong, fix it.* People can

The language and goals of psychotherapy have made their way into many programs designed to "expand human potential." This woman, for example, is hoping to learn to relax and trust others by being thrown into the air and caught. This exercise is probably fun, but is it likely to have lasting effects? What kinds of therapy are best for what kinds of problems? What are the limitations of psychotherapy and its offshoots?

make some changes, but therapy cannot transform their entire personalities (Strupp, 1982). Some aspects of personality are fairly consistent throughout life. Biology may set some limits on our temperaments. Psychological habits of long standing are hard to change, particularly if the environment remains the same.

3. *Change is relatively easy.* Just get some therapy or join a weekend encounter group, runs this myth, and you will get better, just like taking penicillin for an infection. In fact, changing an entrenched habit of thinking or behavior takes considerable time and effort. You have to change not only yourself, but also your relationships with others who may be rewarding your old ways. For change to occur, people must comply with the therapeutic program. But many do not.

As you may remember from Chapter 15, Americans and the Japanese have different notions of what they can control and change, and this difference is reflected in their psychotherapies. Many Japanese would disapprove of a Gestalt group or a behavioral attack-the-symptom method. Many Americans would disapprove of typical Japanese methods. In Morita therapy, for instance, clients are taught to accept and live with their most troubling emotions (Reynolds, 1976). Recently, however, some Western psychotherapists have been borrowing ideas from the Japanese, attempting to teach greater self-acceptance instead of constant self-improvement (Reynolds, 1987; Welwood, 1983).

QUICK ▪ QUIZ

Refresh your understanding of psychotherapy.

1. The longer therapy lasts, the more effective it is. True or false?
2. Insight is essential in changing behavior problems. True or false?
3. What are four possible sources of harm in psychotherapy?

4. The "therapeutic alliance" refers to (**a**) the way therapists stick together, (**b**) the client's resistance to change, (**c**) the bond between therapist and client.

5. The most important attribute of a good therapist is (**a**) years of training, (**b**) warmth and empathy, (**c**) emotional detachment, (**d**) intellectual ability.

Answers:

1. false 2. false 3. worsening of symptoms, coercion, therapist's bias, client's dependency on therapist 4. c 5. b

---

Psychotherapy warrants neither extravagant claims nor total rejection. There are many things it cannot do, and many things it can do. It cannot transform you into someone you're not. It cannot cure you overnight. It cannot provide a life without problems. But it can help you make decisions. It can get you through bad times when no one seems to care or understand. It can improve morale and restore the energy to cope.

In the final appraisal, therapy is not designed as a substitute for experience—for work that is satisfying, relationships that are sustaining, activities that are enjoyable. As Socrates knew, the unexamined life is not worth living. But as an anonymous philosopher added, the unlived life is not worth examining.

Taking Psychology with You

Becoming a Smart Therapy Consumer

In America today there is a vast and bewildering array of therapies in the marketplace. There are hundreds of them, including "marathon therapy, encounter therapy, nude therapy, crisis therapy, primal-scream therapy, electric sleep therapy, body-image therapy, deprivation therapy, expectation therapy, alpha-wave therapy, 'art of living' therapy, 'art of loving' therapy, and 'do it now' therapy" (Gross, 1978). The word *therapy* is unregulated. Anyone can set up any kind of program and call it therapy, and this is not against the law. (For every Primal Screamer, there is probably someone doing Ultimate Whisper Therapy.)

To protect themselves as well as to get the best possible help, consumers need to be informed and know how to choose wisely. Some people spend more time looking for a good dentist than a good therapist. They fail to remember that their consumer rights apply to buying mental health services as well as to buying any other professional service. You would not be likely to keep going to a dentist, year after year, if your toothache got worse and the dentist merely kept promising to make it go away. Yet some people stay in therapy, year after year, with no resolution of their problems. They become "therapy junkies" (Zilbergeld, 1983).

Knowing when to start. In general, if you have a persistent problem that you do not know how to solve, one that causes you considerable unhappiness and that has lasted six months or more, it may be time to look for help. Everyone gets stuck in a thicket, from time to time. It may take the clear-eyed observations of a perceptive bystander to see a way out.

Setting goals. Try to identify exactly what you expect from therapy, and discuss your goals with the therapist. Do you want to solve a problem in your relationships or in your emotional life? Are your goals realistic? Some therapies, as we discussed in this chapter, are designed not for solving problems but for exploring ideas. People often seek help in making important decisions. Others want to explore a philosophy of life to guide their future actions. Others want to understand themselves better. If you know what you want from therapy, you may feel less disappointed later. You will also be better able to select a therapist who can meet your needs.

Choosing a therapist. Remember that anyone can hang out a shingle advertising THERAPEUTIC HELP. The word "psychologist" is regulated, although qualifications vary from state to state. As we saw back in Chapter 1, you must have a professional degree and a period of supervised training to become a licensed psychologist, psychiatrist, counselor, or social worker. Unfortunately, the fact that someone has a license does not guarantee that he or she is competent, reputable, or ethical. Your school counseling center is a good place to start in finding a reputable therapist. Your local Mental Health Association (check your phone book) can also provide information on nearby therapists.

A therapist or counselor should be someone you trust and like. Research shows clearly that empathy between client and counselor, and the warmth of the counselor, are two of the most important factors in predicting success of treatment. Never trust anyone who suggests that a sexual relationship with him (or her) will help your problem. This is unethical conduct and illegal in many states. The basic rule of thumb is this: If the therapist does not treat you with the same attention and respect that you give him or her, find someone else.

The question of fees. Freud thought that patients should pay for treatment, enough to make it hurt. Only then, he said, would patients be motivated to improve. This theory, to put it kindly, serves therapists more than clients. *There is no evidence that the amount of payment affects the success of the therapy.* In a study of 432 patients receiving psychotherapy at a community mental health center, the amount the clients paid had no relation to how well they did later on. In another study, 52 patients paid either $20 or nothing for counseling. The two groups did not differ in how satisfied they were with the counseling, how much they had learned, or whether they wished to continue (Rubenstein, 1986). In a third study, university students in paid versus free therapy did not differ in self-reports of improvement, but the students who paid no fee had *lower* levels of distress when the therapy ended (Yoken & Berman, 1984).

As a consumer, you can often negotiate a fee depending on what you can afford. If you have medical insurance that covers psychotherapy, find out whether your policy covers the kind of therapist you are seeking. Some insurance companies pay only for treatments by psychiatrists or licensed psychologists.

Knowing when to stop. Of course, if you are in time-limited treatment, such as 12 sessions of brief therapy or a 7-session plane-phobia program, you ought to stick with it to the end. In an unlimited therapy program, however, you have the right to determine when enough is enough. Breaking with a trusted therapist can be painful and difficult, like leaving home for the first time, but it can also be a sign that the treatment has been successful (Johnson, 1988). You may need to consider ending therapy or changing therapists if:

- Therapy dominates your life and nothing else seems important,
- The therapist keeps finding new reasons for you to stay, although the original problems were solved long ago,
- You have become so dependent on the therapist that you won't make a move without consulting him or her,
- Your therapist has been unable to help you cope with the problem that brought you there.

As we saw in this chapter, not all therapies are appropriate for all problems. If you are not getting relief, the reason could be as much in the treatment as in you. If you have made a real effort to work with a counselor or therapist and there has been no result after considerable time and effort, it is time to think about alternatives.

KEY WORDS

antipsychotic drugs (major tranquilizers) 615
tardive dyskinesia 615
antidepressant drugs 615
lithium carbonate 616
minor tranquilizers 616
therapeutic window 617
trepanning 617
psychosurgery 617
lobotomy 617
electroconvulsive therapy (ECT) 618
psychodynamic ("insight") therapies 620
free association 620
transference 620
brief psychodynamic therapy 620
behavioral therapies 620
systematic desensitization 621

aversive conditioning 621
flooding (exposure) 622
cognitive therapy 622
humanistic therapies 624
client-centered therapy 624
Gestalt therapy 624
existential therapy 624
family therapy 625
genogram 625
group therapy 627
eclectic therapy 627
community programs 628
rehabilitation psychology 629
support groups 629
encounter groups 632
skills training 632
demoralization 634
therapeutic alliance 636

SUMMARY

1. Diagnoses and treatments of psychological problems have alternated throughout history from the medical (organic) model to the psychological (mental) model. Recent research has caused renewed interest in the biological aspects of mental disorder, but there is still much controversy.

2. The drugs most in use today for emotional disorders include *antipsychotic drugs*, used in treating schizophrenia and psychotic symptoms; *antidepressants*, used in treating mood disorders; and *minor tranquilizers,* often prescribed for emotional problems. Antipsychotics reduce psychotic symptoms and allow many schizophrenics to be released from hospitals. Antidepressants are more effective for mood disorders than minor tranquilizers, which seem to have little or no effect and can become addictive.

3. Some issues in drug treatment for nonpsychotic disorders include finding the "therapeutic window"; the high relapse rate among people who take antidepressants without learning how to cope with problems; and the fact that behavioral solutions work as well as drugs for some problems.

4. When drugs or psychotherapy fail to help seriously disturbed people, some psychiatrists intervene directly in the brain. *Psychosurgery* destroys an area of the brain thought to be responsible for the problem, such as impulsive violence. *Electroconvulsive therapy* (ECT), in which a brief current is sent through the brain, is quick and painless and has been used successfully to treat suicidal depressives. However, its effects do not last and it has unpredictable effects on the patient's memory.

5. Errors of diagnosis and treatment occur on both sides of the mind-body debate. Some people with organic disorders have been mistakenly treated with psychotherapy; some people with psychological problems have been mistakenly treated with drugs or surgery.

6. There are hundreds of forms of psychotherapy, but they basically fall into four schools: (a) *Psychodynamic ("insight") therapies* include orthodox Freudian psychoanalysis and its modern variations, which explore unconscious dynamics. *Brief psychodynamic therapy* is a time-limited version that focuses on only one major dynamic issue. (b) *Cognitive therapies* aim to change the distorted or irrational thoughts involved in emotional problems and self-defeating actions. *Behavioral therapies* are based on learning principles, and include methods of systematic desensitization, aversive conditioning, exposure, and behavioral contracts. In practice, many therapists combine cognitive and behavioral techniques. (c) *Humanistic therapies* aim to help people feel better about themselves and reach "self-actualization." They include Carl Rogers' *client-centered* therapy, Frederick Perls' *Gestalt* therapy, and *existential* therapy. (d) *Family therapies* share the view that individual problems do not exist by themselves but are part of a whole family network. In practice most therapists are *eclectic*, using many methods and ideas.

7. People who have severe, chronic mental problems, such as schizophrenia, or who have physical disabilities resulting from disease or injury, need a broader program than individual psychotherapy. *Rehabilitation psychologists* offer such people job training, support, and community treatment programs. Another growing alternative to individual psychotherapy is the *self-help movement*, including support groups organized around a specific problem and skills training.

8. Efforts to evaluate the effectiveness of psychotherapy get mixed results. Generally, therapies are not effective with people who have the most serious disorders; they do not produce extreme and long-lasting changes; and sometimes they are harmful. But they can help people feel better and solve (or accept) certain problems.

9. Successful therapy requires a good relationship between therapist and client and a "healing ritual" that persuades clients that they will be helped. Good clients are motivated to solve their problems and are willing to take responsibility for them. Good therapists are empathic, inspirational, and able to teach constructive lessons. A ''therapeutic alliance'' between client and therapist depends on their ability to understand each other.

10. Given the common elements in effective therapy, some therapies are better than others for specific problems. By and large, cognitive-behavior therapies have a higher success rate than psychodynamic or humanist therapies; short-term treatment is just as effective as (and cheaper than) long, indefinite therapy; and therapies that combine many techniques are able to solve some problems that one technique alone cannot.

11. In some cases, therapy is harmful. The therapist may be biased, coercive, and unethical, or foster the client's dependency. Encounter or self-help groups have the additional risk of conformity to group pressure.

12. Some psychologists feel that people have come to expect too much from therapy and that therapy fosters the false belief that change is always easy and desirable. Therapy can help people in many ways, but it cannot transform them into something they are not.

Social

Interactions

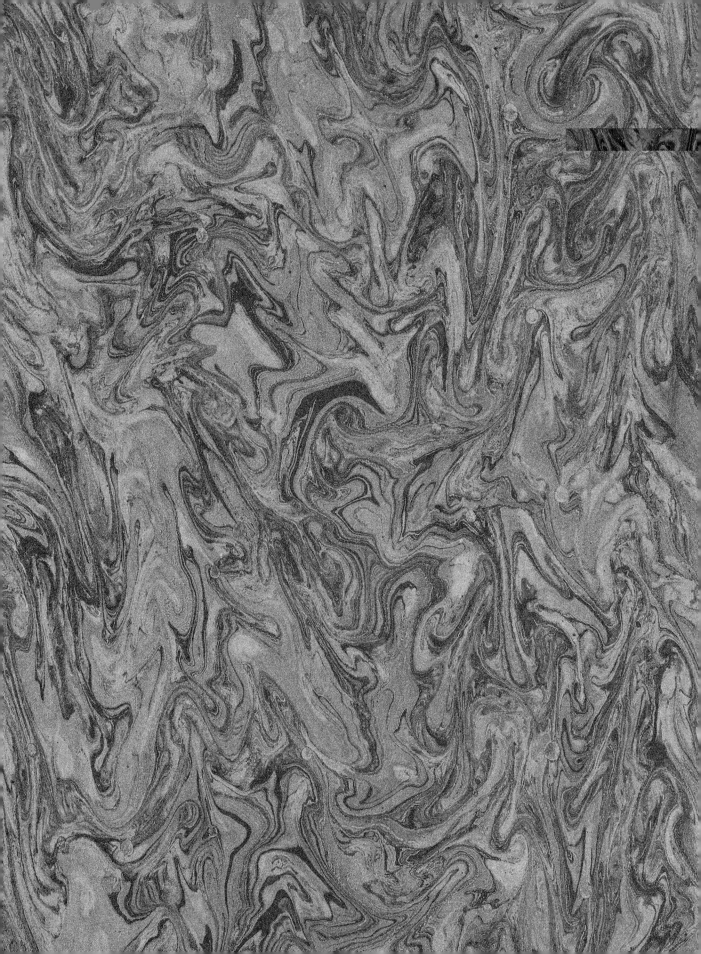

CHAPTER 18

Principles
of
Social
Life

. . . to hurt innocent people whom I knew many years ago in order to save myself is, to me, inhuman and indecent and dishonorable. I cannot and will not cut my conscience to fit this year's fashions.

LILLIAN HELLMAN

*T*he man was on trial for murder, although he personally had never killed anyone, and the penalty sought was death. Six psychiatrists examined him and found him sane. His family life was normal, and he had deep wellsprings of love for his wife, children, and parents. Two observers, after reviewing transcripts of his 275-hour interrogation, described him as ''an average man of middle class origins and normal middle class upbringing, a man without identifiable criminal tendencies'' (Von Lang & Sibyll, 1984).

The man was Adolf Eichmann, a Nazi SS officer who had supervised the deportation and death of millions of Jews during World War II. Eichmann was proud of his efficiency at his work and his ability to resist the temptation to feel pity for his victims. But he insisted he was not anti-Semitic: He had had a Jewish mistress for a while, and he personally arranged for the protection of his Jewish half-cousin (both dangerous crimes for an SS officer). Shortly before his execution by hanging, Eichmann said, ''I am not the monster I am made out to be. I am the victim of a fallacy'' (R. Brown, 1986).

The fallacy to which Eichmann referred was the widespread belief that a person who does monstrous deeds must be a monster—someone sick, insane, evil, cruel. An *enemy* monster, that is. When a member of their own side commits a monstrous act, people tend to be more lenient.

During the war in Vietnam, a platoon of American soldiers rounded up several hundred women, old men, and children in a village called My Lai. The commander of the platoon, Lt. William Calley, ordered the men to push the civilians into a ditch and kill them. Here is an account of the massacre by a soldier, interviewed by Mike Wallace of CBS News (Milgram, 1974):

Q: How many people would you say were killed that day?
A: I'd say about three hundred and seventy. . . .
Q: What kind of people—men, women, and children?
A: Men, women, children.
Q: And babies?
A: And babies. . . . They [were] just pushed in a ravine, or just sitting, squatting . . . and shot.
Q: How do you shoot babies?
A: I don't know. It's just one of those things.
Q: What did these civilians—particularly the women and children, the old men—what did they do? What did they say to you?
A: . . . They were begging and saying, ''No, no.'' And the mothers was hugging their children, and . . . but they kept right on firing. Well, we kept right on firing. They was waving their arms and begging. . . .

When this case came to trial, Lt. Calley made the same defense that Eichmann had: He was just following orders. Because there was some doubt about whether Calley had really been given explicit orders to kill civilians, he was found guilty—but given a light sentence.

Most Americans despised Eichmann and felt he deserved the death penalty, but about half of the American public felt sympathetic toward Calley and the soldiers who obeyed him. What else could a soldier do but obey orders? Disobedience could mean death. This is true, but not the whole truth. Not every soldier in Calley's platoon fired his weapon. Not every German in Nazi Germany took part in or supported the systematic killing of Jews and other groups targeted for destruction. A few heroes risked their lives to aid and shelter victims or to disobey direct orders.

For example, a German physician, known to history only as Dr. Marie L., refused Nazi requests that she participate in sadistic ''experiments'' on prisoners in concentration camps. One Nazi doctor, Eduard Wirths, tried to persuade her by pointing out that the Jews to be operated on were subhuman beings. ''Can you not see,'' he asked, ''that these people are different from you?'' She replied that many people were different from her, starting with Dr. Wirths (Lifton, 1986).

Why do some individuals behave bravely, even at the risk of their lives? Why do some people chart their own courses through unmarked territory? Perhaps we should turn these questions around. Why do most people go along with the crowd? Why do most people do what they are told without thinking twice about it? Why do some people behave in helpful and cooperative ways, and others in hurtful or destructive ones?

The field of *social psychology* explores these (and many other) questions by examining the individual in a social context. The ''psychology'' part of social psychology concerns the person's perceptions, attitudes, emotions, and behavior. The ''social'' part concerns the person's group, culture, and relationships. In previous chapters we have already reported some studies in social psychology: how ''set and setting'' affect the use of drugs; how social perceptions influence emotion; and why friends are necessary for health. Social psychology covers a lot of territory, from first impressions on meeting a stranger to international diplomacy.

In this chapter we will consider some of the major research areas in this field: the power of roles; attitudes and explanations; obedience and conformity; group decisions and behavior; and cooperation and competition. As we go along, we will show how findings can be used to explain the forces that divide people, such as prejudice, conflict, and war, as well as those that unite people, such as cooperation, altruism, and peace.

Roles and Rules

''We are all fragile creatures entwined in a cobweb of social constraints,'' said social psychologist Stanley Milgram. This cobweb snares people in two ways. First, there are social **rules** (also called **norms**) that people are expected to follow. Rules are the conventions of everyday life that make our interactions with other people predictable and orderly. Some rules are matters of law, such as ''A person may not beat up another person, except in self-defense.'' Some rules come from a group's cultural values, such as ''A man may beat up another man who insults his masculinity.'' Some rules are tiny, invisible regulations that people learn to follow unconsciously, such as ''You may not sing at the top of your lungs on a public bus.''

Second, people fill a variety of social **roles**. A role is a position in society that is regulated by norms about how a person in that position should behave. In modern

rules (norms) *Social conventions that regulate human life, including explicit laws and implicit cultural standards.*

role *A given social position that is governed by a set of norms for proper behavior.*

life, most people play many roles. Gender roles define the "proper" behavior for a man and a woman. Occupational roles determine "correct" behavior for a manager and an employee, a professor and a student. Family roles set tasks for parent and child, husband and wife, brother and sister. Certain aspects of every role must be carried out. As a student, for instance, you know just what you have to do to pass this course. But people bring their own personalities and interests to the roles they play. Although three actresses who play the role of Cleopatra must follow the script, each will have a different reading and interpretation. It is the same with social roles.

Now, before you read further, pause a moment to consider three questions and write down your best guess after each one. This is *not* a test, but rather a way for you to identify your present beliefs: (1) What percentage of people do you think are cruel by nature? _____ (2) If told by an authority figure to harm an innocent person, what percentage of people would do it? _____ (3) If *you* were instructed to harm an innocent person, would you do it or would you refuse? _____

In this section, we will examine three controversial studies that attempted to answer these questions. Together, they show the power of social roles to influence behavior.

The prison study

One day as you are walking home from school, a police car pulls up. Two uniformed officers get out, arrest you, and take you to a prison cell. There you are stripped of your clothes, sprayed with a delousing fluid, assigned a prison uniform, photographed with your prison number, and put behind bars. You feel a little queasy but not especially panicked, because you have agreed to play the part of "prisoner" in a psychological study for two weeks. Your prison cell, while authentic, is in the basement of a university building.

So began an experiment to study what happens when ordinary college students take on the roles of prisoners and guards (Haney, Banks, & Zimbardo, 1973). The students who volunteered for this experiment were paid a nice daily sum. They were randomly assigned to be prisoners or guards, but other than that they were given no instructions about how to behave.

Within a very short time, the "prisoners" became distressed, helpless, and

Prisoners and guards quickly learn their respective roles.

panicky. They developed emotional symptoms and psychosomatic ailments. Some became depressed, tearful, and apathetic. Others became rebellious and angry. After a few days, half of the prisoners begged to be let out. Most were more than willing to forfeit their pay for early release.

Within an equally short time, the "guards" adjusted to their new power. Some tried to be nice, helping the "prisoners" and doing little favors for them. Some were "tough but fair," holding strictly to "the rules." But about a third of them became tyrannical and cruel. Although they had complete freedom to use any method to maintain order, they almost always chose to be abusive, even when prisoners were not resisting in any way. One guard, unaware that he was being observed by the experimenters, paced the yard while the prisoners were sleeping, pounding his nightstick into his hand. Another guard put a prisoner in solitary confinement (a small closet) and tried to keep him there all night, concealing this information from the experimenters (who, he thought, were "too soft" on the "prisoners"). Many guards were willing to work overtime without additional pay.

The researchers ended this experiment after only six days. They had not expected such a speedy and terrifying transformation of normal students. The "prisoners" were relieved by this decision, but most of the "guards" were disappointed. They not only had become tyrants; they also enjoyed it.

Critics of this study maintain that you can't learn much from such an artificial setup. In their view, the volunteers knew very well—from movies, TV, and games—how they were supposed to behave. They acted their parts to the hilt, in order to have fun and not disappoint the experimenters. Their behavior was no more surprising than if young men had been dressed in football gear and then had been found to be willing to bruise each other. The critics agree that the prison study makes a great story, but they maintain that it isn't *research*. That is, it does not carefully investigate relationships between factors; for all its drama, the study provides no new information. "It's just staging a 'happening,'" argued Leon Festinger (1980).

Philip Zimbardo, who designed the study, believes that these criticisms make his point: People's behavior depends to a considerable extent on the roles they are asked to play. *Real* prisoners and guards know their "parts," too. Moreover, if the students were having so much "fun," why did the prisoners beg for early release? Why did the guards lose sight of the "game" and behave as if it were a real job? Even if the prison study was a dramatization, it illustrates the power of roles in a way that a short-lived experiment cannot.

The hospital study

Eight normal, healthy adults participated in David Rosenhan's (1973) study of mental hospitals. Although this study is usually used to illustrate problems of psychiatric diagnosis (see Chapter 16), it also shows the impact on behavior of being in the role of patient or attendant.

The eight volunteers—a housewife, a painter, a pediatrician, a graduate student in psychology, a psychiatrist, and three psychologists, including Rosenhan himself—appeared at 12 different mental hospitals (in five states) with the same complaint. They said that they had heard voices, mostly unclear, but they could make out the words *hollow*, *empty*, and *thud*. Apart from this lie, they all gave honest personal histories, which contained not a trace of abnormal problems. All eight were quickly admitted to the hospitals and all but one were diagnosed as schizophrenic.

Once in the hospital, the pseudopatients immediately stopped faking any symptoms. All behaved normally and "sanely." Nevertheless, they were kept in the hospital from 7 to 52 days, an average of 19 days. (They were released with the diagnosis of schizophrenia "in remission.") Once the pseudopatients were diagnosed as schizophrenic and assigned the role of patient, the hospital staff regarded everything they did as further signs of emotional disorder. For example, all of the pseudopatients took frequent notes about their experiences. Several nurses noted this act in the records without asking them what they were writing about. One nurse wrote "patient engages in writing behavior," as if writing were an odd thing to do.

The powerless role of "patient" and the label "mentally ill," Rosenhan found, confer invisibility and encourage **depersonalization**, the loss of people's individuality as persons. In all 12 hospitals, the professional staff avoided eye contact and conversation with patients as much as possible. The pseudopatients attempted to speak a total of 185 times to staff psychiatrists, but 71 percent of the time, the psychiatrist moved on, without replying or even looking at the patient. Only 4 percent of the attempts succeeded in getting the psychiatrist to stop and talk. Of 1283 attempts to talk to nurses and attendants, only .5 percent succeeded. The usual response to a pseudopatient's effort to communicate was the staff member's equal effort to avoid discussion. The result was often a bizarre exchange like this one:

> PSEUDOPATIENT: Pardon me, Dr. X. Could you tell me when I am eligible for grounds privileges?
> PSYCHIATRIST: Good morning, Dave. How are you today? [moves off without waiting for a response]

Conversely, the role of attendant confers a kind of power that often causes well-meaning individuals to treat patients badly. Rosenhan himself observed actual patients who were beaten by staff members for trying to talk to them. One patient was hit for approaching an attendant and saying, "I like you." A staff member might abuse a patient in front of a dozen other patients and stop only if another staff member appeared. To the staff, Rosenhan explains, patients are not credible witnesses. Their disorders somehow turn them into robots who lack feelings and perceptions.

There are problems with Rosenhan's study as there are with the prison study. Critics point out that it was not necessarily wrong to hospitalize people who complained of hearing voices. They also dislike the deceptiveness of the "infiltrators" and argue that Rosenhan wasn't sympathetic enough to an overworked staff suffering from financial cutbacks. Emotionally disturbed people, they add, often *do* behave in unpleasant, unpredictable, and difficult ways. It is not surprising that even a trained staff would feel ambivalent about them or impose control.

Rosenhan is sympathetic to the problems of mental health professionals. He knows that they are not monsters and that most of them enter their jobs with good motives. The cruel or simply impersonal (and depersonalizing) behavior of staff members reflects the roles they are required to play. Even in times of financial hardship, he adds, hospitals set priorities for what a person in each role is expected to do. Time with patients becomes a low priority, but the time-consuming practices of keeping detailed records and having lengthy staff meetings do not change. The result is less time for treatment of the people whom the staff is there to help.

The obedience study

depersonalization *The loss of one's individuality and humanity.* (See also *deindividuation.*)

In Chapter 2 we described Stanley Milgram's dramatic study of obedience to authority (Milgram, 1963, 1974). Participants thought they were part of an experiment on the effects of punishment on learning. Each was assigned, apparently at random, to the role of "teacher." Another person, introduced as a fellow volunteer, was the

Left: *Milgram's shock machine*. Right: *The "learner" is strapped into his chair.*

"learner." When the learner, seated in an adjoining room, made an error in reciting a list of word pairs he was supposed to have memorized, the teacher had to give him an electric shock by depressing a lever on an ominous-looking machine. With each error the voltage was to be increased. The shock levels labeled on the machine ranged from SLIGHT SHOCK to DANGER—SEVERE SHOCK and, finally, XXX. In reality, the "learners" were confederates of Milgram and did *not* receive shocks, but none of the "teachers" ever realized this. The actor-victims played their parts convincingly, even pleading to be released.

When Milgram first designed this experiment, he asked a number of psychiatrists, students, and middle-class adults how many people they thought would "go all the way" to XXX on orders from the experimenter. The psychiatrists predicted that most people would refuse to go beyond 150 volts (at the low end), when the "learner" first demanded to be freed, and that only one person in a thousand, someone who was emotionally disturbed and sadistic, would administer the highest voltage. The nonprofessionals agreed with this prediction, and all of them said that they personally would disobey early in the experiment.

In fact, however, every subject in the study administered some shock to the learner, and about two-thirds of these men and women, of all ages and all walks of life, obeyed the experimenter to the fullest. They obeyed no matter how much the victim shouted for them to stop and no matter how painful the shocks seemed to be. They obeyed even when they themselves were anguished about the pain they believed they were causing. They obeyed even as they wept, implored the experimenter to release them, and argued with themselves. More than 1000 participants at several universities eventually went through the Milgram experiment. Most of them, men and women equally, inflicted what they thought were dangerous amounts of shock to another person. Many protested to the experimenter, but their doubts were usually overcome when he simply responded, "The experiment requires that you continue."

After obtaining these results, Milgram and his team next set up several variations of the basic experiment to determine the conditions under which people might disobey the experimenter. They found that virtually *nothing the victim did or said changed the likelihood of the person's compliance*—not even when the victim said he had a heart condition, screamed in agony, or stopped responding entirely as if he had collapsed. However, people were more likely to disobey when:

• The experimenter left the room. Many people then subverted authority by giving low levels of shock but reporting that they were following orders.

• The victim was right there in the room, and the teacher had to administer the shock directly to his body.

▪ Two experimenters issued conflicting demands (to continue the experiment or to stop at once). In this case, no one kept inflicting shock.

▪ The person ordering them to continue was an ordinary man, apparently another volunteer, instead of the authoritative experimenter.

▪ The subject worked with peers who refused to go further. Seeing someone rebel gave subjects the courage to disobey.

"The key to the behavior of subjects," Milgram (1974) summarized, "lies not in pent-up anger or aggression but in the nature of their relationship to authority. They have given themselves to the authority; they see themselves as instruments for the execution of his wishes; once so defined, they are unable to break free."

The three controversial studies we have described illustrate the power of social roles and obligations to influence, even overturn, the personality patterns of individuals. The behavior of the prisoners and guards varied (some prisoners were more rebellious than others, some guards were more abusive than others); but, ultimately, what people did depended on the roles they were assigned. Regardless of their personal feelings, the staff of the mental hospital had to adapt to its structure of roles, from psychiatrists at the top to ward attendants at the bottom. Finally, when people in the Milgram study believed they had to follow the legitimate orders of authority, most of them put their private values to sleep.

Now go back to page 654 and look at the answers you wrote to the questions at the start of this section. Would your answers change now? Why or why not?

Social Cognition: Attributions, Stereotypes, and Attitudes

Social psychologists are interested not only in what people do, but in what is going on in their heads while they do it. One of the most important areas in social psychology is the study of **social cognition**, how the social environment influences thoughts, perceptions, and beliefs (Fiske & Taylor, 1984). In this section, we will look at three important topics in social cognition: attributions, stereotypes, and attitudes.

Explanations and excuses

social cognition *An area in social psychology that studies social influences on thought, memory, perception, and other cognitive processes.*

attribution theory *The theory that people are motivated to explain their own and others' behavior by attributing causes of that behavior to a situation or disposition.*

fundamental attribution error *The tendency to overestimate personality factors (dispositions) and underestimate environmental ones (situations) in explaining behavior.*

According to **attribution theory**, people are motivated to make sense of their own and others' behavior (Ross & Fletcher, 1985). "To attribute" means "to consider as caused by." Caused by what? Generally, there are two kinds of causes. When you make a *situational attribution*, you regard an action as being caused by something in the environment: "Joe stole the money because his family is starving." When you make a *dispositional attribution*, you regard an action as being caused by something in the person, such as a trait or motive: "Joe stole the money because he is a born thief."

Through experimental research, social psychologists have specified some of the conditions under which people prefer certain attributions to others. For example, when people try to find reasons for someone else's behavior, they tend to overestimate personality factors and underestimate the influence of the situation (Nisbett & Ross, 1980). This tendency has been called the **fundamental attribution error** (Ross, 1977). Were the student guards basically cruel and the prisoners basically

Calvin and Hobbes   by Bill Watterson

Children learn the value of excuses at an early age.

cowardly? Was the hospital staff lazy, thoughtless, or selfish? Were the hundreds of people who obeyed Milgram's experimenter by nature sadistic? People who think so, many psychologists maintain, are committing this attribution error.

The fascinating thing is that many people persist in the fundamental attribution error even when they know a person's behavior is required by the situation (E. Jones, 1979). In one experiment, students spent some time talking with a target person who was either friendly or unfriendly. In each case, students were told either that the target's behavior was spontaneous or that the target was specifically instructed to behave in that way. The students thought the friendly person was "truly friendly," even when they had been told the friendliness was forced. The students said that the unfriendly person was "truly unfriendly" even when they knew the unfriendliness was required (Napolitan & Goethals, 1979). The fundamental attribution error probably explains why we respond so favorably to smiling flight attendants, polite telephone operators, and charming salespeople. Even when we know their manners are "part of the job," we also believe they are "part of their personality."

When it comes to explaining their *own* behavior, however, people tend to choose attributions that are favorable to them. This **self-serving bias** means that people like to take credit for their good actions and let the situation account for their bad ones. For instance, most of us will say, "I am furious for good reason—this situation is intolerable!" We are less likely to say, "I am furious because I have always been an angry person." If we do something admirable, though, such as donating $100 to charity, we attribute our motives to personality ("I'm generous") instead of to the situation ("The fund-raiser pressured me into it").

The self-serving bias is also apparent in the excuses people make to justify their mistakes. C. R. Snyder, Raymond Higgins, and Rita Stucky (1983) observe that self-protecting excuses have been part of human life since Adam blamed Eve for giving him the apple—and Eve blamed the serpent. The researchers identified several categories of excuses. How often have you used them?

- *"I didn't do it."* In this category we have complete denial ("not me"), sometimes accompanied by blaming someone else: "The butler did it"; "The dog ate it"; "The kids broke it." A psychotherapy client of one of the researchers put it best. "It's like this," she said. "If it's not my fault, it's her fault, and if it's not her fault, it's still not my fault."

- *"It wasn't so bad."* These excuses acknowledge the blunder, but try to minimize it: "She'll get over it." "I'm only an hour late." Minimizers may leave

Have you ever called someone else's error a "stupid clumsy mistake," yet excused an identical blunder on your part as "something that couldn't be helped"? Why? Why do people need excuses anyway?

self-serving bias *The tendency of people to take credit for good actions and to excuse or rationalize their mistakes.*

out grisly details: "I only hit him once," they say, instead of "I broke his jaw and shattered his nose."

▪ *"Yes, but. . . ."* These excuses acknowledge the mistake ("Yes, I did it"), but the focus is on the reason (the "but"). A popular one is "but I couldn't help it." Another is "but I didn't mean to," in which we appeal to bumbling incompetence to offset any hint of maliciousness ("I didn't mean to make her cry"; "I was only joking"; "I didn't mean to ruin your new shirt").

Excuses soften the link between you and your actions. The excuse may reassert your good qualities, modify the degree of your responsibility, or minimize the badness of the action itself (C. Snyder, 1988). Excuses make it possible for people to maintain their self-esteem, while acknowledging errors. Yet excuses also justify the destructive things that people do and allow them to rationalize the failure to take helpful action, such as speaking up against wrongdoing or aiding someone in a crisis.

For example, in Milgram's experiment, many people who administered the highest levels of shock attributed their behavior to the demands of the experiment. A 37-year-old welder explained that the experimenter was responsible for any pain the victim might suffer "for the simple reason that I was paid for doing this. I had to follow orders. That's how I figured it." In contrast to this justification of cruelty, the people who refused to give high levels of shock took credit for their actions, attributing their refusal to internal matters of conscience or principle. "One of the things I think is very cowardly," said a 32-year-old industrial engineer, "is to try to shove the responsibility onto someone else. See, if I now turned around and said, 'It's your fault . . . it's not mine,' I would call that cowardly" (Milgram, 1974).

People also make attributions for events that have little to do with their self-esteem or even their own behavior. According to the **just-world hypothesis**, people need to believe that the world is fair, that good people are rewarded and villains punished (M. Lerner, 1980). The belief in a just world helps people make sense out of senseless events and feel safe in the presence of threatening events. If a friend loses his job, if a woman is raped, if a prisoner is tortured, it is reassuring to believe that they all must have done something to deserve what happened or at least to cause it.

The need to believe in a just world often leads to a dispositional attribution called *blaming the victim.* When there is no question in anyone's mind that A did something to harm B, A can argue that B deserved the treatment, provoked the treatment, or wanted the treatment. "Many subjects harshly devalue the victim *as a consequence* of acting against him," wrote Milgram (1974). "Such comments as, 'He was so stupid and stubborn he deserved to get shocked,' were common."

By now you might be wondering where, in all these attributions, the truth is. Most human actions are determined both by personality and by environment, and we cannot always know the "real reason" behind people's actions. In that case, is the fundamental attribution error always an "error"? Is the self-serving bias always "biased"? Maybe we know more about our own behavior than about the behavior of others. Researchers are still debating these controversial questions.

just-world hypothesis *The notion that people need to believe that the world is fair and that justice is served, that bad people are punished and good people are rewarded.*

The fact that attributions are not always accurate, or that they change, does not mean we should stop making them. We couldn't stop even if we wanted to. If we did not believe that most people are responsible for their actions, we could have no system of justice and law. If we did not understand that people are occasionally victims of circumstances beyond their control, we would be lacking in compassion and generosity. The point to keep in mind is that attributions, whether accurate or not, have consequences for emotions and actions, for law and justice, and for daily human relations.

QUICK ■ QUIZ

What kind of attribution is being made in each case, situational (S) or dispositional (D)?

1. A jury decides that a congressman accepted a bribe because FBI agents had set up a trap to trick him.
2. A jury decides that a congressman accepted a bribe because he is dishonest.
3. A man says, ''My wife has sure become a grouchy person.''
4. The same man says, ''I'm grouchy because I've had a bad day at the office.''
5. People read in the papers that farmers are losing their lands and livelihood because of economic conditions. ''Well, those people brought it on themselves,'' they say.
6. What principles of attribution theory are suggested by 3, 4, and 5?

Answers:

1. S 2. D 3. D 4. S 5. D 6. 3 illustrates the fundamental attribution error; 4, the self-serving bias; 5, the just-world hypothesis.

Stereotypes

A **stereotype** is a summary impression of a group of people in which a person believes that *all members* of that group share a common trait or traits. It is one of the cognitive schemas by which we map the world (see Chapter 7). Some stereotypes are negative (''Artists are weird''). Some are positive (''My school produces the smartest people and best athletes''). Some consist of neutral impressions of categories of people. There are stereotypes of people who drive Volkswagens or Mercedes-Benzes, of men who wear earrings and of women who wear business suits, of students in engineering and of students in art.

The fact that everyone generates stereotypes is itself neither good nor bad. A stereotype is a way of organizing experience, of making sense of the differences among individuals and groups, and of predicting how people will behave. If you had no stereotypes at all you might be ''open-minded,'' but you would also be unable to move. If you had to stop what you were doing every minute to guess what others would do, you couldn't get anything done. When, at a crowded party, you decide who will be most likely to share your interests, you are acting on a stereotype. When you learn ''street-smart'' techniques to avoid possibly dangerous people, you are acting on a stereotype.

Although stereotypes do help us put the world together, they lead to three distortions of reality. First, stereotypes *accentuate differences between groups*. They emphasize the ways in which groups are different, not the common features. So the stereotyped group may seem odd, unfamiliar, or dangerous, ''not like us.'' Second, stereotypes *underestimate differences within other groups*. People realize that their own groups are made up of all kinds of individuals. But stereotypes create the impression that all members of other groups (say, all Texans or teenagers) are the same. One rude French waiter means that all French are rude; one Greek thief means that all Greeks are thieves. But if someone in their own group is rude or caught stealing, people draw no such conclusions (Rothbart, Dawes, & Park, 1984). Third, stereotypes produce *selective perception* (see Chapter 5). People tend

Do you have a stereotype of this punk woman? (Turn the page.)

stereotype *A cognitive schema or a summary impression of a group, in which a person believes that all members of the group share a common trait or traits (positive, negative, or neutral).*

Do you have a stereotype of this woman now? She is participating in an English baby-buggy-pushing contest. Many people have a negative stereotype of punks, who seem odd and threatening. But punks are just as individually varied, and just as willing to conform (to their own style), as any other group.

to see only what fits the stereotype and to reject any perceptions that do not fit.

Stereotypes are not always entirely wrong. Many have a "grain of truth," capturing with some accuracy something about the group (Allport, 1954). The problems occur when people assume that the grain of truth is the whole seashore, and interpret an observation in a negative way. When people like a group, their stereotype of the group's behavior tends to be positive. When they dislike a group, their stereotype *of the same behavior* tends to be negative. In a study of six cultures (English, Russian, German, American, French, and Italian), people strongly agreed in their judgments of their own and the others' typical national traits (Peabody, 1985). But the terms they used to describe the traits depended on whether they liked the country or not. A person who is careful with money can be seen as *thrifty* or *stingy*. Someone who is friendly toward strangers could be *trusting* or *gullible*. Someone who enjoys spending time with the relatives might be *family-loving* or *clannish*. Here are some other examples:

English, Russians, and Germans		French, Italians, and Americans	
Positive	**Negative**	**Positive**	**Negative**
Thrifty	Stingy	Generous	Extravagant
Serious	Grim	Lively	Frivolous
Skeptical	Distrustful	Trusting	Gullible
Cautious	Timid	Bold	Rash
Selective	Choosy	Broad-minded	Undiscriminating

attitude *A fairly stable opinion regarding a person, object, or activity, containing a cognitive element (perceptions and beliefs) and an emotional element (positive or negative feelings).*

People who have negative stereotypes about a group, explains anthropologist Edward T. Hall (1983), cannot understand how *deeply felt* another culture's way of behaving is. As a result, he says, they don't realize that the behavior that seems shifty, irresponsible, compulsive, or stupid may simply reflect a different way of putting the world together. When Hall worked on a Hopi reservation, he found that the Hopis and the Anglos had stereotypes about each other. The Hopis were forever leaving work undone; they would start to build a dam, a house, or a road, and stop in the middle. To the Anglos, this meant that the Hopis were shiftless and lazy. But to the Hopi, building dams, houses, and roads was unimportant. Unlike the maturing of a sheep or the ripening of corn, these activities had no natural, built-in timetable. Why was it so important to finish these silly human projects, anyway? What did matter to the Hopi was working in their fields and completing religious ceremonies.

The values and rules of culture determine how people ''see'' the same social event. Is coming late to class good, bad, or indifferent? Is it good or bad to argue with your parents about grades? Chinese students in Hong Kong (where communalism and respect for one's elders are highly valued) and Caucasian students in Australia (where individualism is highly valued) give entirely different interpretations of these two events (Forgas & Bond, 1985). It is a small step from different interpretations to negative stereotypes: ''Australians are selfish and disrespectful of adults''; ''The Chinese are mindless slaves of authority.''

Attitudes

People have attitudes about all sorts of things—politics, people, food, children, movies, sports heroes, you name it. An **attitude** is a relatively stable opinion containing a cognitive element (your perceptions and beliefs about the topic, including any stereotypes you may have) and an emotional element (your feelings about the topic, which may range from negative and hostile to positive and loving). For instance, your attitude toward pornography includes your ideas about sexuality and your emotional feeling about whether pornography is good or bad.

Many attitudes, as the controversy over pornography suggests, are connected to deep-rooted values. Attitudes influence how people see the world and the attributions they make to explain events. In two studies, several hundred high-school and college students were asked what they thought were the causes of unemployment among young people. In general, students with conservative attitudes attributed unemployment to personality factors, such as lack of motivation or ability. Students with liberal attitudes attributed unemployment to social and economic factors, such as economic recession and ineffective government programs (Feather, 1985).

Attitudes can range from trivial, changeable opinions to deeply held, inflexible convictions (Abelson, 1988). Many public-opinion polls do not discriminate between these two extremes; they just ask for a person's ''opinion,'' not how strongly it is felt. As a result, public opinion often seems to be easily swayed.

Psychologists have attempted to distinguish deep, important attitudes (*convictions*) from shallow ones. In a series of surveys, Robert Abelson (1988) and his colleagues asked hundreds of people about their attitudes on a variety of issues: nuclear power, God, abortion, welfare, Star Wars (the government's ''strategic defense initiative''), AIDS, and support for the contras in Nicaragua. Conviction consisted of three factors: *emotional commitment* (''My beliefs about this express the real me''; ''I can't ever imagine changing my mind''; ''My beliefs are based on the moral sense of the way things should be''); *ego preoccupation* (''I think about this issue often''); and *cognitive elaboration*, the ''mental network'' in which the attitude is embedded (''I've held my views a long time''; ''I have more knowledge on the issue than the average person''; ''Several things could happen if my views were enacted''). People seem to acquire their convictions in different ways. In some cases, they learn a great deal about an issue and then become emotionally committed to it. But others have a sudden, mysterious emotional experience, and then develop the cognitive rationales to justify this "flash of truth."

Abelson raises some critical issues about conviction. For one thing, does it matter whether a conviction is acquired through cognitions first or emotions first? Abelson fears that if emotion comes first, "cognitive processes will be distorted in the service of inflexible, prejudged conclusions." Can you identify how your own convictions developed and whether you are able to be open-minded about them?

Further, is it good or bad to have convictions? Most people think it is admirable to have "the courage of your convictions." They long to be sure of their religious and political beliefs, their choice of loved ones, their choice of occupation. Yet, Abelson observes, "conviction can give deep meaning to life but it is also one of the surest ways to make a fool of yourself." Believing too strongly in a cause can create a sense of self-righteousness and vanity that blinds a person to exceptions, qualifications, and new evidence (Langer, 1989). Is there, Abelson asks, a way to distinguish good conviction from bad conviction, commitment from fanaticism?

Psychologists have argued for years about which comes first, attitudes or behavior. The answer is, causality works in both directions. Attitudes dispose people to act in certain ways. If you have a positive attitude about the game of soccer, you may try to get to every game you can. If you have a negative attitude, you may refuse every invitation to go to one. However, sometimes a change of behavior leads to new attitudes because of new information and new experiences. Your friends drag you, kicking and screaming, to a soccer game, and you become a devoted fan. Naturally, convictions carry a stronger correspondence to behavior than garden-variety attitudes do. People who have a strong emotional commitment to an issue are more likely to work on its behalf (Abelson, 1988).

Attitudes and behavior are also brought into harmony by the human wish for consistency. In Chapter 10 we discussed an important approach to the study of attitudes: **cognitive dissonance** theory and its interpretations. (You might refer back to that discussion to refresh your memory.) This theory is very important for understanding attitude change and the relationship between attitudes and behavior. As we saw, when two attitudes, or when an attitude and behavior, conflict (are dissonant), people are motivated to make them consonant. (For more on attitude change, see "Taking Psychology with You.")

The persistence of prejudice

A **prejudice** is an unjustified negative attitude toward a group, a category of people, or a cultural practice. Prejudice against a group carries a strong emotional discomfort with, dislike of, or outright hatred of its members. Often it is based on a negative stereotype that resists rational argument. In his classic book *The Nature of Prejudice*, Gordon Allport (1979) reported this conversation:

MR. X: The trouble with Jews is that they only take care of their own group.

MR. Y: But the record of the Community Chest campaign shows that they give more generously, in proportion to their numbers, to the general charities of the community, than do non-Jews.

MR. X: That shows they are always trying to buy favor and intrude into Christian affairs. They think of nothing but money; that is why there are so many Jewish bankers.

MR. Y: But a recent study shows that the percentage of Jews in the banking business is negligible, far smaller than the percentage of non-Jews.

MR. X: That's just it; they don't go in for respectable business; they are only in the movie business or run night clubs. (pp. 13–14)

cognitive dissonance *A state of tension that occurs when a person simultaneously holds two cognitions that are psychologically inconsistent, or when a person's belief is inconsistent with his or her behavior.*
prejudice *An unjustified negative attitude toward a group of people or a custom.*

Mr. X doesn't respond to Mr. Y's evidence; he just moves along to another reason for his dislike of Jews. That is the nature of prejudice. As Elliot Aronson (1988) observes, suppose Mr. Y tried to persuade you to eat boiled insects. "Ugh," you might say, "they are so ugly." "But so are lobsters," he says, "and lots of people love lobsters." "Well, insects have no food value," you say. "Actually, they are a good source of protein," he answers. He might try other arguments, but the fact is that not eating insects is simply the result of a food prejudice that exists in some cultures (M. Harris, 1985).

Some prejudices come from experience, such as an unpleasant or baffling encounter with someone from another ethnic group. Many prejudices are passed along from parents to children, in messages that say "we don't associate with people like that," sometimes without either generation having ever met the object of their dislike. Some come from the images that the media convey, for instance, of men and women, blacks and whites, old and young. Once people have formed attitudes in general, and prejudices in particular, they are reluctant to change their minds for several reasons:

1. *The cognitive payoff:* A consistent, unified set of beliefs. Stereotypes organize new information and old memories. People remember facts that support their stereotypes and tend to forget facts that disconfirm them (Rothbart, Evans, & Fulero, 1979).

2. *The social payoff:* Support from others for the attitude. As we will see, it is difficult for most people to break away from the attitudes and prejudices of their friends, families, and associates.

3. *The economic payoff:* The monetary benefit to one group of having prejudicial attitudes toward another group. Many studies have found that the greatest racial prejudice occurs among whites who are in direct competition with blacks for jobs (Maykovich, 1975). During the middle of the nineteenth century, when Chinese immigrants worked on building the transcontinental railroad across the United States, there was very little prejudice against them. They were considered hardworking, industrious, and law-abiding. There was also no economic competition between the Chinese and the Anglos, as jobs were plentiful. But after the railroad was finished, at about the end of the Civil War, jobs dwindled. The Chinese had to compete with former soldiers for scarce employment. Now attitudes toward the Chinese changed. They were considered criminal, crafty, and stupid (Aronson, 1988).

4. *The psychological payoff:* Self-esteem and reduced anxiety. Prejudice allows people to feel proud of themselves and their own group and superior to others (Tajfel, 1970). In addition, people who are insecure and frustrated can use another group as a **scapegoat**, that is, as a socially accepted target for that insecurity. Centuries ago, a scapegoat was literally a goat. A religious leader would place his hands on the head of a goat as he recited the sins of the community. The goat was then allowed to escape into the wilds, symbolically taking the people's sins with it. Today a scapegoat is any powerless person or group who takes the blame for a problem. Some families make one weak child the scapegoat for their emotional conflicts. Some nations make an ethnic minority the scapegoat for their economic difficulties, as the Nazis did with the Jews and as the early Romans did with the Christians (Allport, 1979).

People cling to some attitudes like life preservers but let themselves be persuaded to give up others. The more payoffs there are for maintaining an attitude, the more resistant it will be to change. If you have a mild prejudice against redheads that you haven't thought much about, meeting a terrific redhead or two may change

scapegoat *A powerless target of an individual's or group's prejudice that is made to bear the blame for personal or social problems.*

Newspapers and signs reveal the history of prejudice in the United States. In 1831, a newspaper boldly reflected the then-popular dislike of the Irish. Help-wanted columns in the 1930s advertised jobs for "Christians only" ("Chr."). Anti-Japanese feelings ran high in the 1920s and again during World War II; today, Iranians, among the most recent immigrants, are often the targets of political hostilities. Native Americans have been targets of hatred since the "white man" arrived. Segregation was the law in many parts of the country until the 1950s. Prejudice against women is widespread, as shown by a male-only club in Virginia. Why do new prejudices emerge, and why do some old ones never fade?

your mind. But if you are deeply prejudiced against redheads because of an emotional need to feel that brunettes are better (or because a redhead once jilted you), your prejudice will be harder to root out.

The different causal connections between attitudes and behavior can be seen clearly in the case of prejudice. In some cases, the attitude (prejudice) leads to behavior (discrimination). Discrimination may be subtle, as when a person refuses to associate with targets of the prejudice. It may be an accepted social practice, as when members of one group refuse to hire or promote people who are different from them. In extreme cases, it can take the form of efforts to control or exterminate members of the group. In the United States, prejudice has led to the lynching of blacks, the bombing of synagogues, the massacre of Native Americans, the illegal imprisonment of Japanese-Americans during World War II, the harassment of homosexuals, and other violent acts against minority groups.

But sometimes people who have prejudiced attitudes are prevented from discriminating because of the law, or social convention, or other interests. Years ago, Richard LaPiere (1934) and two friends, a Chinese couple, traveled through America, visiting 250 hotels and restaurants. No one refused to serve them. When they got home LaPiere wrote to each establishment and asked whether they "accepted members of the Chinese race as guests." Only 1 of the 128 answers to his letter said yes. In this case, prejudice did not lead to discrimination, perhaps because the hotels and restaurants preferred a customer in the hand to an attitude in the bush.

Even people who have no prejudices may nevertheless discriminate in their behavior. Custom, role requirements, or even the law causes them to treat people in

ways they would prefer not to. As we will see next, the pressures on people to conform and to obey can overcome some deeply held attitudes.

QUICK ▪ QUIZ

Identify which concept—blaming a scapegoat, stereotyping, discrimination, or prejudice—is illustrated by each of the following statements.

1. Juan believes that all Anglos are uptight and cold, and he won't listen to any evidence that contradicts his belief.
2. John believes that the Mexican minority in his town is responsible for his bad economic situation.
3. Jane believes that Honda owners are thrifty and practical. June believes that Honda owners are stingy and dull.
4. Jim's fraternity doesn't accept Catholics, so Jim stops seeing his Catholic friends.

Answers:

1. Juan has a *prejudice* against Anglos. 2. John uses the Mexican population as a scapegoat. 3. Jane and June have *stereotypes* about Honda drivers. 4. Jim and his fraternity *discriminate* against Catholics.

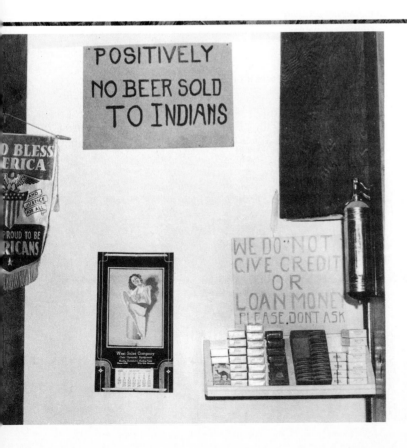

Conformity, Obedience, and Dissent

The cowboy is the American symbol of brave independence. In countless movies the single brave hero, ignoring the cringing cowardliness of the crowd, defeats the bad guys. Sometimes he disobeys unfair laws in order to bring the bad guys to justice. The cowboy's opposite is the bureaucrat, symbol of faceless conformity, who never steps out of line and never has a creative idea. The bureaucrat enforces unfair laws and tolerates injustice.

These stereotypes of the cowboy and the bureaucrat, and our general attitudes about obedience and conformity, are influenced by national values (Gergen, 1973; Sampson, 1977). To see this, look at the same stereotype through different glasses. You might see the cowboy as a loutish loner who never compromises, can't get along with others, and threatens the general welfare by breaking laws. You might see the bureaucrat as someone who cooperates with others, is loyal to co-workers, and modifies personal preferences and follows laws for the benefit of all.

As you can see, obedience and conformity have both positive and negative aspects. **Obedience** refers to behavior performed in following an order from someone in a position of authority. **Conformity** refers to behavior or attitudes that occur as a result of real or imagined group pressure. These basic social processes are necessary in all human societies. A nation could not function if everyone ignored red lights, cheated on their taxes, dumped garbage anywhere, or assaulted each other. But these same processes can have unfortunate consequences. Conformity often suppresses critical thinking and creativity. People often do self-destructive things because "everyone else does it." As for obedience, the plea "I was only following orders"—as in the cases of William Calley, Adolf Eichmann, and, more recently, Oliver North—has been offered throughout history to excuse actions carried out on behalf of orders that were foolish, destructive, or illegal. (By the way, the American military code does not require soldiers to obey *illegal* orders.) The writer C. P. Snow observed that "more hideous crimes have been committed in the name of obedience than in the name of rebellion."

In explaining their actions, people often *deny* conformity but *embrace* obedience (Milgram, 1974). When people conform to unspoken rules, they tend to believe they are doing so of their own free will. "I dress like all my friends because I want to," they say. When they obey specific orders, they tend to believe that they

obedience *Behavior performed in following an order from someone in authority.*

conformity *Behavior or attitudes that occur as a result of real or imagined group pressure.*

Sometimes people like to conform in order to feel part of the group . . .

do not have the free will to disobey. "I was ordered to wear this uniform," they say. "What else could I do?"

Conformity: Following peers

You appear at your professor's laboratory for an experiment on perception. You join seven other students seated in a room, and the study begins. You are shown a 10-inch line and asked which of three other lines is identical to it. The correct answer, line A, is obvious, so you are amused when the first person in the group chooses line B. "Bad eyesight," you say to yourself. "He's off by 2 whole inches!" The second person also chooses line B. "What a dope," you think. But by the time the fifth person has chosen line B you are beginning to doubt yourself. The sixth and seventh students also choose line B, and now you are worried about *your* eyesight. The experimenter looks at you. "Your turn," he says. Do you follow the evidence of your own eyes or the collective judgment of the group?

This was the basic design for a series of classic studies of conformity conducted by Solomon Asch (1952, 1965). The seven "nearsighted" students were actually Asch's confederates. Asch wanted to know what people would do when a group unanimously contradicted an obvious fact. He found that when people made the line comparisons on their own, they were almost always accurate. But in the group, only 20 percent of the students remained completely independent on every trial (often being apologetic for not agreeing with the group). One-third conformed to the group's incorrect decision more than half the time, and the rest conformed at least some of the time. Conformers and independents often felt uncertain regardless of their decision. As one said, "I felt disturbed, puzzled, separated, like an outcast from the rest."

As decades of research now confirm, many people will, in a group, deny their private beliefs, agree with silly notions, and do things they would never do on their own (Aronson, 1988). They do so for various reasons:

1. *Identification with the group.* People may conform because they identify with members of the group and want to be like them in dress, attitudes, or behavior.

. . . and sometimes they like to rebel a little in order to assert their individuality.

If all your friends have dyed their hair blue, you may subject your head to a blue rinse just so you will be like them.

   2. *The desire to be accurate.* Suppose you spell ''accommodate'' correctly, with two *c*'s and two *m*'s, but your classmates insist that it has only one *m*. You may conform to their judgment, on the grounds that they probably know more than you do. In this case, out of your natural desire to be right, you will be wrong. When people believe that a group has special abilities that are superior to their own, they are more likely to conform to its judgments (Insko et al., 1985).

   3. *The desire for personal gain.* You may comply with group opinion to keep your job, to win a promotion, or to win votes.

   4. *The wish to be liked; the fear of being unpopular.* Most people know that disagreeing with a group can make them unpopular. Groups have many ways of controlling their members and trying to enforce agreement. If one person in a group takes a deviant, contrary stance (or a creative, independent stance, depending on your point of view), the group first directs its energies toward persuading the person to conform. If pleasant persuasion fails, the group may become hostile. If subtle hostility fails, the group may punish, isolate, or reject the deviant altogether (Shaver & Buhrmester, 1983).

   5. *Mindlessness.* Ellen J. Langer and her colleagues draw the distinction between *mindful* and *mindless* behavior. Most of the time, people conform without thinking about it. They have no secret motive. They just go along doing what they have always done. When people are mindful, they are actively making decisions, trying to understand events, or concentrating on their tasks. When people behave mindlessly, they accept ideas uncritically, they don't really listen to what other people are saying, and their actions are dictated by past experience. They act on ''automatic pilot'' (Langer, 1989; Langer, Blank, & Chanowitz, 1978).

   6. *Personality versus situation.* Certain personality factors make some people more afraid than others to resist group pressure. People who have a strong need for social approval, who are highly rigid, or who have low self-esteem are all more likely to conform than people who are more self-assured and flexible (Gergen & Gergen, 1986). Most instances of conformity, though, depend heavily on the group situation and on the reasons behind the person's need to conform. Everyone conforms in some degree to their work rules, their friends' social habits, and the standards of groups that mean something to them. A teenager may do everything in her power *not* to conform to her parents' values, dress, and musical taste. Yet she may conform slavishly to the values, dress, and musical taste of her immediate group of friends. Conformity, therefore, is not a simple matter of joining the herd. People follow different herds at different times.

QUICK ▪ QUIZ

What is the reason for conformity in each of these cases?

1. You drink because you want to be like your friends, who drink heavily.
2. You drink as a matter of habit, without thinking twice about it.
3. You drink when you are socializing with your supervisor because your supervisor admires people who can ''hold their liquor.''

Answers:

1. identification 2. mindlessness 3. desire for personal gain (being thought well of)

Obedience: Following orders

Why do most people follow orders? Some answers are obvious: They can be suspended from school, fired from their jobs, or arrested if they disobey. In addition, they obey for many of the same reasons that they conform. The identify with the authority who is giving orders. They hope to gain personal advantages. They obey in "mindless" acceptance of the authority's right to issue orders. But what about those obedient people in Milgram's experiment, the ones who felt they were doing wrong, who wished they were free, but who could not untangle themselves? Why do people obey when it is not in their interest, or when obedience conflicts with their values? Assuming that a person wants to disobey, several factors may stand in the way:

It's easy to see why people obey authority when disobedience means they will lose their jobs—or, in war, their lives. But why do people obey when there is no apparent reason for doing so?

1. *Embarrassment.* Most people don't like to rock the boat, appear to doubt the experts, or be rude (Sabini & Silver, 1985). In most social situations, good manners are the honey of relationships and the grease of civilization. They smooth over the rough spots and protect good feelings. When people break the rules of manners, they often feel awkward and embarrassed. To have gotten up from your chair in the Milgram study and walked out meant you would have had to explain and justify your "rudeness." Many were too embarrassed to do so.

2. *Lacking a language of protest.* Many people in Milgram's study simply did not know *how* to stand up to authority and express their decision to disobey without embarrassment. They literally didn't have the words. One woman kept apologizing to the experimenter, trying not to offend him with her worries for the victim: "Do I go right to the end, sir? I hope there's nothing wrong with him there." (She did go right to the end.) A man repeatedly protested and questioned the experimenter, but he too obeyed, even when the victim apparently had collapsed in pain. "He thinks he is killing someone," Milgram commented, "yet he uses the language of the tea table."

3. *Entrapment.* **Entrapment** is a process in which individuals escalate their commitment to a course of action in order to justify their investment in it (Brockner & Rubin, 1985). You are "trapped" at the point at which you are heavily invested in an activity and it "costs" too much to get out. The first steps of entrapment pose no difficult choices. But one step leads to another, and before the person realizes it, he or she has become committed to a course of action that does pose problems. In Milgram's study, once subjects had given a 15-volt shock, they had committed themselves to the experiment. The next level was "only" 30 volts. Before they knew it, they were administering what they believed were dangerously high shocks. At that point, it was difficult to explain a sudden decision to quit.

Entrapment catches everyone, from individuals to governments. You start dating someone you like moderately. Before you know it, you have been together so long that you can't break up, although you don't want to become committed, either. A government starts a war it thinks will last a few weeks. Years later, it has lost so many soldiers and so much money that it believes it cannot back down without losing face.

Salespeople value the old "foot-in-the-door technique," a tried and true method of entrapment. Once you agree to do a small favor for someone, you are more likely to agree to a larger favor later. In one experiment, women were asked if they would help a safe-driving campaign by putting a small "Drive Safely" sign in their windows. Later the experimenters asked these women to put a large and ugly sign on their front lawns. Of the women who agreed to the first request, 76 percent agreed to the second, compared to only 16 percent of the control group, who were asked only to put up the ugly sign (Freedman & Fraser, 1966).

entrapment *A gradual process in which individuals escalate their commitment to a course of action to justify their investment of time, money, or effort.*

A far more dramatic and sinister example of entrapment comes from a study of 25 men who had been with the Greek military police during the authoritarian regime that ended in 1974 (Gibson & Haritos-Fatouros, 1986). A psychologist who interviewed the men identified the steps used in training them to use torture in questioning prisoners. First the men were ordered to stand guard outside the interrogation and torture cells. Then they stood guard in the detention rooms, where they observed the torture of prisoners. Then they "helped" beat up prisoners. Once they had obediently followed these orders and become actively involved, the torturers found their actions easier.

Many people expect moral problems to fall into two clear categories, with good on one side and evil on the other. But in real life, as in the Milgram study, people often set out on a path that is morally ambiguous, only to find that they have traveled a long way toward violating their own principles (Sabini & Silver, 1985). A job requires, at first, only a "little" cheating, and, besides, "everyone else is doing it." From Greece's "bad" torturers to Milgram's "good" subjects, people share the difficult task of drawing a line beyond which they will not go.

Dissent: Following conscience

Throughout history, men and women have not only obeyed orders or conformed to ideas that they believed to be misguided or immoral, but, sometimes, disobeyed them. Many blacks and whites disobeyed the laws of segregation. Many men and women have stopped conforming to traditional sex roles. Just as there are many reasons for obedience and conformity, so there are many reasons for independent action.

Some psychologists believe that everyone has a basic need to feel unique in all the world (Snyder & Fromkin, 1980). If you tell people that their attitudes are actually garden-variety opinions, they become more rebellious. According to Jack Brehm (1966, 1972), people need to believe that they have freedom of choice. When they believe their freedom is in jeopardy, they experience a negative emotional state that Brehm calls **reactance**. To reduce this state and restore their sense of freedom, people often react to an order by doing just the opposite (Wicklund, 1974).

Parents of small children observe reactance early on, when they instruct their 4-year-old to pick up his toys and he says, stoutly, "Won't!" (A woman we know found her 2-year-old daughter rehearsing reactance, singing quietly to herself, "No, nono, NO NO NO, no no no-o-o. . . . ") Adults react to some orders in roughly the same way. In one study, students were told they would not be able to hear a public lecture in favor of lowering the voting age. Half of the students were told that the reason was censorship: School officials did not want them to hear the speaker's ideas. The rest were told that the speaker was ill. The students in the first group became more positive toward the censored position (Wicklund & Brehm, 1976).

Reactance increases as the threat to freedom increases and as the issue in question becomes more important. You may not feel much reactance if your mother asks you to call Uncle Harry (whom you like), but you may dig in your heels if she asks you (again) to clean your room. Reactance also depends on the belief that you are *entitled* to freedom. If you believe that you have the right to free speech and that the government has no right to censor the press, you are more likely to feel angry about government censorship than if you do not have these views (Brehm & Brehm, 1981). For people to disobey, therefore, they must feel that they have right on their side.

reactance *A negative emotional state produced by a real or imagined threat to one's freedom of choice.*

Three courageous whistleblowers from Rockwell International—Ria Solomon, Sylvia Robins, and Al Bray—tried to inform NASA that the space shuttle Challenger was not safe.

Another important factor in dissent is, simply, *having an ally*. In Asch's experiment, the presence of one other person who gave the correct answer was enough to overcome conformity to the (incorrect) majority. In Milgram's experiment too, the presence of another person who disobeyed sharply increased the number of others who also disobeyed. One dissenting member of a group may be viewed as a "troublemaker," but two dissenting members are a coalition, and enough dissenting members can become a majority. Having an ally reassures a person of the rightness of the protest.

Let us now consider an actual moral dilemma that some people face at work. Suppose that you are working for an organization that you like very much. Your job is to supervise the safe installation of toxic waste cleanup systems. But after a while you learn that your immediate supervisor is taking bribes from companies that do not want to pay the cost of cleaning up their wastes. What would you do?

Your possibilities fall along two dimensions (Hirschman, 1970). One is "exit": Do you stay in the company or leave it? The second is "voice": Do you speak up or remain silent? For example, a person could stay in the company and keep his mouth shut (the "love it" part of "love it or leave it"). This is the traditional expectation of companies and governments that define loyalty as unquestioning obedience. The person could leave the organization quietly, without saying anything (the "leave it" part of "love it or leave it"). If a person does decide to speak up, he or she may do so within the organization, informing co-workers and supervisors. Finally, he or she can "blow the whistle," informing outsiders of company policies.

In a study of 8587 federal government employees across the country, employees were asked if they had observed any wrongdoing at work, whether they told anyone about it, and what happened when they told (Graham, 1984). Nearly half of the sample reported that they had personally observed some serious cases of wrongdoing, such as someone stealing federal funds, accepting bribes, or tolerating a situation that was dangerous to public safety. Of that half, 72 percent had done nothing at all. The rest reported the problem to their immediate supervisors. Of those who reported, about 40 percent did nothing else, but nearly 60 percent eventually took the matter to higher authorities.

According to this study, there were several stages of dissent. First, the dissenters had to *see* the wrongdoing and believe it was serious. Second, dissenters *took responsibility* for doing something about it. Third, they believed that *something could be done* about the problem, that there were solutions inside or outside the organization, often with allies to help. Finally, *entrapment* increased their commitment. Once having taken the initial step of informing their supervisors, most continued the protest.

Dissenters believe that loyalty to their company is revealed by correcting its mistakes, not by ignoring them. People who become whistleblowers believe they have a higher loyalty still, to the public or to principle. The difficulties of dissent, as we will see next, are made even harder by the pleasures and pressures of being in a group.

QUICK ▪ QUIZ

What concept does each story illustrate?

1. Although your parents keep insisting that you study harder, you study less and less.
2. A friend of yours, who is moving, asks you to bring over a few empty boxes. Since you are there anyway, he asks you to fill a few boxes with books. Before you know it, you have packed up his entire kitchen, living room, and den.
3. Your school's basketball team has been engaging in illegal practices in order to win games. On your own, you don't know how to protest something that "everybody does." Then you learn that several classmates are also distressed about the cheating, and together you decide to publicize the scandal.

Answers:

1. reactance 2. entrapment 3. having an ally

Individuals and Groups

▪ In 1961, President John F. Kennedy, after meeting with his advisers, approved a CIA plan to invade Cuba (with 1400 Cuban exiles) and overthrow the government of Fidel Castro. The invasion, at the Bay of Pigs, was a total disaster. The invaders were killed or captured, the United States was humiliated, and Cuba moved politically closer to the Soviet Union.

▪ At an international soccer competition in Belgium in 1985, a fight broke out in the stands. When the riot was over, 38 people were dead.

▪ Years ago, a woman named Kitty Genovese was stabbed repeatedly in front of her apartment building. She screamed for help for more than half an hour, but not one of the 38 neighbors who heard her, who came to their windows to watch, even called the police.

Something happens to individuals when they collect in a group. They think and act differently than they would on their own. This is true when the group is organized to solve problems and make decisions, as was Kennedy's circle of advisers; when it has gathered to have fun, as at a soccer game; or when it simply consists of anonymous bystanders, as in the Genovese case. A group's decisions and behavior, research suggests, depend less on the personalities of its members than on the nature of the group itself.

Group thinking and groupthink

Suppose a man with a serious heart ailment is offered an operation that could cure him or kill him. Should the man have the operation if his chances of dying are one in ten, three in ten, nine in ten? In the early 1960s, a graduate student was studying the effects of group discussion on group decisions (Stoner, 1961). He kept getting a curious result. On their own, people tended to be cautious about recommending surgery. But when they discussed the matter in a group, they made riskier recommendations. This result came to be called "the risky shift." Perhaps it explained irrational company decisions, "mob madness," and the Bay of Pigs invasion.

Within a decade, however, other studies had found that some group decisions are more conservative and less risky than the decisions of individual members would be. It turned out that the risky shift was a special case of a more general principle of group decision making, called **group polarization**. Polarization does not mean that a group becomes split between two poles. It means that the group's *average* decision is more extreme than its members' individual decisions would be.

The group's decision depends, in part, on the topic under consideration. Some topics bring out the risky side, but others, such as marriage or one's own illness, tend to bring out caution (R. Brown, 1986). The direction of polarization depends on how many people in the group were *initially* leaning toward risky or conservative decisions, or were pro or con on a particular attitude. Once the group starts talking, polarization occurs for at least two basic reasons. First, members want to conform to the group consensus. Some people intensify their opinions once they realize that others not only agree with them but are even stronger in their convictions. Second, people start thinking of arguments that will support their views. As arguments increase in favor of risk (or caution), the shift toward the extreme appears to be the only "rational" or "logical" choice (Kaplan & Miller, 1983).

One kind of group whose decisions have especially important consequences is the jury, 12 individuals who must agree on conviction or acquittal. What are the effects of group discussion on their collective decision? Usually, the verdict initially favored by a majority of the members is the one that eventually wins, as group polarization would predict (J. H. Davis, 1980). When the group is equally split, however, most juries show a *leniency bias*: The more the group talks, the more lenient its verdict (MacCoun & Kerr, 1988). One reason is that jurors who favor acquittal are more influential than jurors who favor conviction. Why might this be so? The "reasonable doubt" standard—a person is innocent unless proven guilty beyond a reasonable doubt—favors acquittal; it is easier to raise one doubt than to refute all doubts (Nemeth, 1977). But when juries are instructed to arrive at a verdict based on "a preponderance of evidence that the defendant committed the crime," the leniency bias vanishes (MacCoun & Kerr, 1988). If you ever serve on a jury, you might keep these findings in mind!

Group members who like each other and share attitudes often work well together. But close, friendly groups are subject to a problem that Irving Janis (1972) calls **groupthink**, the tendency for all members of the group to think alike and suppress dissent. It occurs when a group's need for total agreement overwhelms its need to make the wisest decision, and when the members' needs to be liked and accepted overwhelm their ability to disagree with a bad decision. To study groupthink, Janis began with the historical records of the presidents and advisers who

group polarization *The tendency of a group's decision to be more extreme than its members' individual decisions.*

groupthink *In close-knit groups, the tendency for all members to think alike and to suppress dissent and disagreement.*

How not to lead a group.

actually made the decisions to launch the Bay of Pigs invasion and to escalate the Vietnam War.

According to Janis, groupthink has several identifiable features. First, to preserve harmony and to stay in the leader's good graces, members avoid thinking of alternatives to the leader's initial preference. Instead of generating as many solutions to a problem as possible, they stick with the first one. Second, members don't want to disagree with each other or make their friends look bad, so they don't examine this initial preference closely for errors or flaws. They suppress their own misgivings, which creates an illusion of unanimity and invulnerability. Third, the group avoids getting any outside information from experts that might challenge its views, and it suppresses dissent within the group. (President Lyndon Johnson, who favored increased bombing of North Vietnam, ridiculed his adviser Bill Moyers by greeting him with "Well, here comes Mr. Stop-the-Bombing.") The result is that everyone remains in a "tight little ship," even if the ship is about to sink.

Groupthink can be counteracted, however, under particular conditions that encourage the expression of doubt and dissent. In one experiment, researchers divided management trainees into two groups to discuss a challenging problem: deciding what equipment would be necessary for survival on the moon (Hall & Watson, 1970). The first group was asked to come to a unanimous decision. The second group was encouraged to avoid agreement. Instead, members were instructed not to change their opinions for the sake of good feelings, not to take "straw votes" that might encourage people to side with the majority, and to regard their differences as natural and beneficial rather than disruptive. The final decisions of the two groups were evaluated by NASA scientists. In the quality and creativity of their decisions, the second group was far superior.

Other researchers remind us that just as groups influence individuals, individuals influence groups (Moscovici, 1985; Moscovici & Mugny, 1983). Group members who hold minority opinions do not have the same power as the majority, but they can sometimes persuade and change the majority. Considering, as Serge Moscovici puts it, that the minority starts off being viewed as "deviant, incompetent, unreasonable, unappealing, and unattractive," how *does* it influence the group?

One strategy is repetition. Repeated minority arguments are like drops of water eroding a rock. Eventually, as such arguments become familiar, they seem less outrageous. Second, by taking a firm, consistent, and well-expressed position, the minority makes its views more persuasive. A third strategy (as we noted earlier) is to find allies in the group, which makes minority members seem less "deviant" or "rebellious" and their ideas more legitimate. Dissenters are disruptive to a group, but they force the group to become aware of other ideas and other solutions. By undermining the majority's complacency, dissenters may move the group to more independent and innovative ideas.

Responsibility and anonymity

A friend told us of a tug-of-war game between the eleventh and twelfth grades in her high school. She confesses that she didn't pull as hard as she should have, because she figured that her teammate Steve, a 280-pound tackle, could do the work for the whole side. Many group members think this way. Responsibility for an outcome is "diffused," or spread, among all the members. This response allows individuals to pass the buck, to assume that someone else will do the job or make the right decision.

In work groups, the **diffusion of responsibility** often results in **social loafing**:

diffusion of responsibility *In organized or anonymous groups, the tendency of members to avoid taking responsibility for actions or decisions, assuming others will do it.*

social loafing *The tendency of group members, under some conditions, to reduce their efforts and "loaf"; one result of diffusion of responsibility.*

Each member of a team loafs along, letting others "pull harder" (Latané, Williams, & Harkins, 1979). This slowdown of effort does not happen in all groups. It occurs primarily when individual group members are not responsible or accountable for the work they do, when people feel that working harder would only duplicate their colleagues' efforts, or when the work itself is uninteresting. Members of a group need to feel that they are making unique contributions, even if their contributions are anonymous. When the challenge of the job is increased or when each member of the group has a different, important job to do, the sense of individual responsibility rises and loafing declines (Harkins & Petty, 1983). Experiments find that loafing also declines when people know they will be evaluating their own performance privately (Szymanski & Harkins, 1987). Perhaps self-evaluation raises a person's self-awareness and motivation to do well.

The faceless crowd. The most extreme condition associated with diffused responsibility is **deindividuation**, the loss of awareness of one's individuality (Festinger, Pepitone, & Newcomb, 1952). Deindividuated people "forget themselves" in responding to the immediate situation. They are more likely to act "mindlessly," and their behavior becomes disconnected from their attitudes. They do things they would never do on their own.

Deindividuation increases under conditions of anonymity. It is more likely to occur, for instance, when a person is in a large city rather than a small town, in a faceless mob rather than an intimate group, or when signs of individuality are covered by uniforms or masks. However, as David Myers (1983) notes, "Even if anonymity unleashes our impulses we must remember that not all our impulses are sinister." Deindividuated people can become more aggressive (think of those soccer fans), but sometimes they can become more friendly (think of all the chatty people on buses and planes who reveal things to their seatmates they would never tell anyone they knew). In one study, students who spent an hour with seven strangers in a darkened room felt more friendly and affectionate toward them than did students who conversed with strangers in a lighted room (Gergen, Gergen, & Barton, 1973).

The power of the situation to influence what deindividuated people do is shown clearly in two experiments. In one, women who were dressed in Ku Klux Klan-like white disguises delivered twice as much (apparent) electric shock to another woman as did women who were not only undisguised but also wore large name tags (Zimbardo, 1970; see Figure 18.1). In a second experiment, when the women were wearing nurses' uniforms, they gave *less* shock than women who were identified with name tags (Johnson & Downing, 1979). Apparently, the KKK disguise was a

deindividuation *In groups or crowds, the loss of awareness of one's own individuality; in varying degrees, a person feels indistinguishable from others.*

FIGURE 18.1

Anonymity and cruelty
In this experiment, women covered in Ku Klux Klan-like disguises gave more shocks to another woman than did women who were not disguised or who were identified with name tags (Zimbardo, 1970).

signal to behave aggressively; the nurses' uniforms were a signal to behave nurturantly.

Some individuals, and some cultures, are more "individuated" than others. Christina Maslach and her associates have developed a scale that assesses a person's willingness to be distinguished from others—for example, to give your opinion on a controversial subject to a group of strangers, to publicly challenge a speaker with whom you disagree, or to raise your hand to ask a question in a large class. Asians are on the average less individuated than Anglos, blacks, and Hispanics, reflecting the Asian cultural emphasis on social harmony (Maslach, Stapp, & Santee, 1985).

The helpful bystander. Since the Kitty Genovese story hit the news, there have been many other reports of bystander apathy. Without calling for help, bystanders watch as a woman is attacked, as a man burns himself to death, as a car hits a child and drives away. Such apathy reflects social loafing on a large scale. But instead of condemning bystanders for their laziness or cowardice, or trying to identify the "helpful personality," social psychologists have identified some of the factors that predict whether and when people will behave altruistically, helping strangers in trouble, even at risk to themselves (Batson et al., 1986, 1988; Latané & Darley, 1970, 1976). These conditions should be already familiar to you from another section of this chapter: *Every stage of a bystander's decision to help in a crisis applies to an individual's decision to protest wrongdoing* (see Figure 18.2).

First, in order to be altruistic, the bystander must perceive the need for help. Many bystanders see no need to help someone in trouble. Sometimes this blindness justifies inaction; the German citizens of Dachau didn't "see" the local Nazi concentration camp, although it was in plain view. But sometimes the blindness is an inevitable result of screening out too many demands on attention. People who live in a big city cannot stop to help everyone who seems to need it.

Whether or not people interpret a situation as requiring their aid also depends on societal rules. In northern European nations and in the United States, husband-wife disputes are considered strictly private; neighbors intervene at their peril. In one field study, bystanders observed a (staged) fight between a man and a woman. When the woman yelled, "Get away from me; I don't know you!", two-thirds of the bystanders went to help her. When she shouted, "Get away from me; I don't know why I ever married you!", only 19 percent tried to help (Shotland & Straw, 1976). In Mediterranean and Latin cultures, however, a dispute between any two people is considered fair game for anyone who is passing by. In fact, two people in a furious dispute might even *rely* on bystanders to intervene.

Second, once the bystander perceives that someone is in trouble, he or she must decide whether to take responsibility for doing something about it. In a large crowd of observers, it is easy for people to avoid action. Crowds of anonymous people encourage the diffusion of responsibility because everyone assumes that someone else will take charge. When people are alone and hear someone call for help, they usually *do* intervene (Darley & Latané, 1968). Bystanders who feel a moral obligation to the victim or who empathize with the victim are also more likely to take responsibility for helping (Batson et al., 1988).

Third, at this point, most bystanders quickly weigh the costs of "getting involved" as opposed to doing nothing. The cost of helping might be personal danger, wasted time, or embarrassment (if it turns out the person wasn't really in trouble). The cost of not helping might be guilt, blame from others, or loss of honor (Piliavin, Piliavin, & Rodin, 1975). Some people, however, help others out of empathy and concern, without weighing costs at all (Batson et al., 1988). A study of Gentiles who risked their lives to rescue Jews during the Nazi era found two

Person tries to help
(protests wrongdoing)

↑

No ↖ Yes

Do benefits of helping
(protesting) outweigh costs
of not helping (protesting)?

↑

Yes ↗ No

Does person assume responsibility for intervening (protesting)?

↑

No ↖ Yes

Does person interpret event as
an emergency (serious problem)?

↑

Yes ↗ No

Does person notice the incident
(wrongdoing)?

FIGURE 18.2

"The decision tree"

This "decision tree" shows the paths a person may take in intervening to help another person or in deciding to protest wrongdoing. At each fork in the tree, the individual has a choice of continuing on or of becoming diverted. An important factor at each fork is what other people in the crowd or group are doing (Darley & Latané, 1968; Graham, 1984).

motives: deeply held religious or other moral values or personal feelings for the victim (Fogelman & Wiener, 1985).

Fourth, bystanders who actively intervene to save a life or interrupt a crime not only want to be helpful; they also know *how* to be helpful. They feel that they are competent to help and that their efforts won't backfire. This sense of competence turns up in studies of people who rescue others from political persecution and of people who help in street emergencies. Of 32 people who had directly intervened in real criminal episodes, for example, all said they felt certain they could handle the dangerous situation. Many had had specialized training in police work, first aid, lifesaving, or self-defense (Huston et al., 1981). But even people who do not have such skills or strengths can help in an emergency. They can call for medical help, get the police, comfort the victim, and report a crime (Shotland & Goodstein, 1984).

Social psychologists emphasize, therefore, that altruism is not simply a spontaneous or selfless expression of a desire to help. There are social conditions that make it more likely to occur, as there are conditions that make the diffusion of responsibility and deindividuation more likely.

QUICK ▪ QUIZ

Identify which phenomenon—deindividuation, group polarization, diffusion of responsibility, or groupthink—is represented in each of the following situations.

1. The president's closest advisers are afraid to disagree with his views on arms negotiations.
2. You are at a Halloween party wearing a silly Donald Duck costume. When you see a chance to play a practical joke on the host, you do it.
3. After talking things over with your family, you agree to quit your safe job for a new one that offers greater challenge but has a risk of failure.
4. Walking down a busy street, you see that fire has broken out in a store window. "Someone must have called the fire department," you say.

Answers:

1. groupthink   2. deindividuation   3. group polarization   4. diffusion of responsibility

---

Competition and Cooperation

If you want to make some money, play the dollar game with several friends. Everyone must bid for your dollar in 5-cent increases, and the auction is over when there is no new bid for 30 seconds. The catch is this: The second-highest bidder must also pay you, although he or she will get nothing in return. Usually, the bidding starts quickly and soon narrows to two competitors. After one of them has bid $1.00, the other decides to bid $1.05, because she would rather pay $1.05 for your dollar than give you $.95 for nothing. Following the same logic, the person who bid $1.00 decides to go to $1.10. By the time they quit, you may have won $5 or $6.

Your bidders will have been trapped by the nature of competition. Both will want to "win"; both will fear losing; both will try to save face. Had they thought of

In the United States, most people assume that competition—in everything from the Little League to big business—is a good thing. Why, then, do some researchers think that "healthy competition" is a contradiction in terms?

cooperation, they would *both* have won. The bidders could have agreed to set a limit on the bidding (say, $.45) and split the profits.

During a competitive game, participants and spectators are involved and energized, and have a good time. But there are some psychological hazards to competition. When winning is everything, competitors may find no joy in being second, or even being in the activity at all. Competition and cooperation have powerful effects on personality, attitudes, and group relations.

FIGURE 18.3

Faces of the enemy

In every country, propaganda posters stereotype "them," the enemy, as ugly, aggressive, brutish, and greedy; "we," the heroes, are beautiful and virtuous. The top two posters show the American view of the enemy in World War I (left)—a "mad brute"— and the Soviet view of the United States in the 1930s (right)—a greedy capitalist. The two lower posters, though more recent, still convey the ugliness attributed to the enemy: an Iraqi view of Iran in 1985, in the midst of their long war (left), and a Dutch view of the United States in 1985 (right).

"Us" versus "them"

One consequence of competition is "us-them" thinking. Decades ago, Urie Bronfenbrenner (1963) showed photographs taken in the Soviet Union to fifth- and sixth-grade American children. One child asked, "Why do they have trees along the road?" Surprised, Bronfenbrenner turned the question back to the children. One said, "So that people won't be able to see what's going on beyond the road." "To make work for the prisoners," said another. Well, Bronfenbrenner asked them, why do *American* roads have trees along the side? "For shade," said the children, or "to keep the dust down." The question Bronfenbrenner asks is: "Where did the children get the idea that the Russians have different reasons than we have for planting trees?"

The answer is **ethnocentrism**, the belief that one's own group or nation is superior to all others. Every society on earth has been guilty of ethnocentrism, perhaps because it aids group survival by making people feel attached to their communities. Ethnocentrism is built on stereotypes—which, you may recall, accentuate differences between groups—and can be used to rationalize "our" abusive behavior toward "them." "We" are good, noble, and human; "they" are bad, stupid, and less than human (see Figure 18.3).

Thus the Germans who ran Hitler's concentration camps regarded Jews, blacks, homosexuals, Gypsies, Catholics, and anyone else who was not of the "pure" Aryan race as "vermin" to be "exterminated." Iranian fundamentalists feel superior to "heathens," and thus entitled to kill them. By viewing all Vietnamese as "gooks," American soldiers fighting in Vietnam rationalized the murder of thousands of civilians. Military torturers, such as the Greek police mentioned earlier, are able to inflict pain on their victims by splitting "us" (those who are the nation's "saviors") from "them" (the rebels who are the nation's "enemies") (Staub, 1985, 1988).

The irony is that "they" are thinking the same way about "us." Each side accuses the other of the same offenses; each side is sure it is right (Janis, 1985). After talking with dozens of Soviet citizens (in Russian), Bronfenbrenner (1961) found a "mirror image" in Soviet-American relations: *"The Russians' distorted picture of us was curiously similar to our picture of them."*

Competition, by its very nature, divides people into opposing teams: men-women, blacks-whites, Army fans-Navy fans, prisoners-guards, doctors-patients. Us-them thinking is especially common in war, of course, when enemies regard each other as inhuman and deserving of destruction. But, closer to home, you can see everyday examples of it at a football game, during an election, or in discussions of controversial issues.

Making enemies, making friends

Just as competition can drive people apart, cooperation can bring them together. Years ago, Muzafer Sherif and his colleagues used a natural setting, a Boy Scout camp called Robbers Cave, to conduct an experiment on the contrasting results of cooperation and competition (M. Sherif, 1958; Sherif et al., 1961). Sherif randomly assigned normal 11- and 12-year-old boys to two groups, the Eagles and the Rattlers. To build "team spirit," each group worked on communal projects, such as making a rope bridge and building a diving board. Sherif then put the teams in competition for prizes. During fierce games of football, baseball, and tug-of-war,

ethnocentrism *The belief that one's own ethnic group, nation, or religion is superior to all others.*

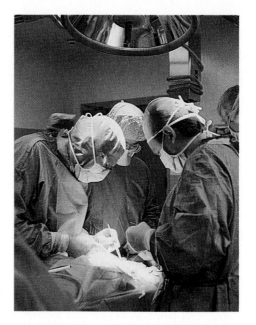

Members of a medical team pool their efforts and skills to save a patient—an example of the kind of teamwork that occurs less dramatically in everyone's life. Because industrial societies emphasize the value of competition, they often underestimate the pervasiveness and importance of cooperation.

the boys whipped up a competitive fever that spilled off the playing fields. They began to raid each other's cabins, call each other names, and start fistfights. No one dared to have a friend from the opposite gang. Before long, the Rattlers and Eagles were as hostile toward each other as any two rival gangs fighting for turf, any two siblings fighting for a parent's attention, and any two nations fighting for dominance. Their hostility continued even when they were just sitting around together watching movies.

So far, Sherif had done nothing more than a typical Little League competition might do. But then he determined to undo the hostility he had created and to make peace between the Eagles and Rattlers. The experimenters set up a series of situations in which both groups needed to work together to reach a desired goal. The boys had to cooperate to get the water supply system working. They had to pool their resources to get a movie they all wanted to see. When the staff truck broke down on a camping trip, they all had to join forces to pull the truck up a steep hill and get it started again. This policy of interdependence in reaching *mutual goals* was highly successful in breaking down ''us-them'' thinking, competitiveness, and hostility. The boys eventually made friends among their former ''enemies.''

The same process applies in adult groups. When adults work together in a cooperative group in which teamwork is rewarded, they often like each other better and are less hostile than when they are competing for individual success (Deutsch, 1949, 1980). Similarly, families who work together on an overriding problem, such as surviving economic hardship, are more cooperative and have less competition among siblings than those who do not have a unifying goal (see Chapter 13). In reviewing the huge number of studies on the effects of competition, Alfie Kohn (1986) concludes, provocatively, ''that the phrase *healthy competition* is a contradiction in terms.'' Competition, he shows, makes people feel insecure and anxious (even if they win), fosters jealousy and hostility, and actually stifles achievement. Because competition is ''the common denominator of American life,'' Kohn maintains, we rarely pause to notice its pervasive effects.

Many people have assumed that the best way to reduce group prejudice and stereotyping is simply for members of opposing groups to get to know each other better. This *contact hypothesis* became the basis for racial desegregation in the

1950s and 1960s. People assumed that contact would reduce hostility between the races, and sometimes it did. In two major studies of integrated housing projects, the white tenants who had the closest contact with black tenants had the most favorable attitudes toward blacks (Deutsch & Collins, 1951; Wilner, Walkley, & Cook, 1955).

However, desegregation of schools has not always been so successful. In reviewing studies of desegregation, Walter Stephan (1978, 1985) found that in 25 percent of the studies the black children showed a *drop* in self-esteem. For every example of reduced prejudice, Stephan found other evidence of more prejudice. In some integrated schools, different ethnic groups simply cluster together for moral support, forming cliques and gangs, fighting other groups, and defending their own ways. In such cases, why doesn't contact work?

One answer is that the typical American classroom is designed for competition (Aronson, 1988). Children compete for the teacher's attention and to be "best." Children who are not fluent in standard English, who are shy, or who come from cultures that praise cooperation do not fare well in such classrooms. Other children tease or ignore them, conclude that they are "stupid," and never give them the chance to prove themselves. The minority children then stick together, feeling angry and defensive.

To break this pattern, a research team used what they called the "jigsaw method" to build cooperation and group goals (Aronson et al., 1978). Classes were divided into groups of six students of mixed ethnicity and race. Each little group worked together on a shared task that was broken up like a jigsaw puzzle. *Each child needed the contributions of the others to put the assignment together*. For instance, each child might be given one paragraph of a six-paragraph biography and asked to learn the whole story.

At first, the children used their old competitive rules, making fun of anyone who was shy or didn't speak English well. One Hispanic boy, Carlos, would stammer and blush, refusing to speak. A girl ridiculed him, saying "Aw, you're stupid." A research assistant reminded the girl that teasing Carlos was not going to help her learn his part of the story. No longer could she gain from putting Carlos down; in fact, she would lose. Within a short time, the children recognized the benefits of cooperation. The Anglo children learned how to ask Carlos probing questions, to help him communicate what he knew. As he did so, Carlos became less nervous and opened up. After a few weeks, the other children concluded that Carlos wasn't nearly as dumb as they thought he was. They began to like him. Carlos began to see the Anglo children in his group not as tormentors but as helpful friends.

Decades of studies of the contact hypothesis find four factors that appear to be necessary to reduce prejudice between two groups: *cooperation*; *equal status* (if one side has more power, prejudice can continue); *support by authority figures* (such as teachers, employers, or police); and *opportunities* for members of both groups *to socialize informally* (Stephan & Brigham, 1985). In a real-life study that created these conditions, blacks and whites worked together for two hours a day for 20 days (Cook, 1984, 1985). The whites were selected for their extreme prejudice against blacks. Yet by the end of the project, 40 percent of them had completely reversed their attitudes toward integration and had become far more friendly to their black co-workers. Before the study, one young man said he would never go to an interracial party, vote for a black, invite blacks to dinner, share a swimming pool with them, or even attend an integrated church supper. After the experiment, he changed his mind about all of these situations, and his behavior toward his new black friends proved it.

VERY ▪ QUICK ▪ QUIZ

You may cooperate with a classmate in answering these questions.

1. You are on the college debating team. Which attitude will generate the least hostility and aggression? (**a**) ''Let's clobber those idiots.'' (**b**) ''Let's do the best we can.'' (**c**) ''If we don't win, I won't be able to face *anyone*.''
2. Innocent Americans are taken hostage by Lebanese militants. Which statement does *not* reflect us-them thinking? (**a**) ''They are thugs, thieves, and murderers.'' (**b**) ''They are vicious terrorists who have no compassion for human life.'' (**c**) ''They shouldn't have taken hostages, but they believe they have legitimate grievances.''

Answers:
1. b 2. c

Think About It

Is Peace Possible?

In this last box, we ask you to think about the greatest ''think about it'' of our time, war and peace. What will it take to prevent world war—a giant Robbers Cave experiment, in which nations cooperate against an invasion from space? Are we doomed to war because it is wired into our species? To consider this question, 20 social and biological scientists from 12 nations gathered in Seville, Spain, in 1986, and issued the Seville Statement on War. ''Humanity can be freed from the bondage of biological pessimism,'' the scientists concluded. ''The same species who invented war is capable of inventing peace'' (Groebel & Hinde, 1989).

The researchers reviewed the evidence for the common assumption that war is ''biologically wired'' in the human species. It is *scientifically incorrect*, they reported, to say that we have inherited a tendency to make war from our animal ancestors. Warfare ''is a peculiarly human phenomenon and does not occur in other animals,'' the researchers found. It is also *incorrect* to say that violence is genetically programmed into the human brain. Genes provide only a potential for any action; learning and environmental conditions determine whether and how that potential will express itself.

The report particularly condemns the notion that war is caused by instinct or any other single motivation. Most people seem to fight wars because they are ordered to, not because they want to. The dominant motivations in battle are not aggressiveness and hostility, but fear, fatigue, obedience, and close affection for one's comrades (Stouffer et al., 1949). Once a nation is at war, emotions may be generated to support the cause, but this is not the same as saying that the emotions caused the war. Moreover, history records changes in cultural practices from aggressiveness to peacefulness. Scandinavians produced the warmongering Vikings, but they are now among the most peace-loving nations in the world (Scott, 1984).

One problem with thinking about war is that many people don't want to think about it. Today, awareness of the dangers of nuclear war can lead to what psychologists call ''psychic numbing,'' becoming emotionally numb about topics that are alarming. But it can also lead to activism to find peaceful alternatives to conflict (Fiske, Pratto, & Pavelchak, 1983; Lifton, 1980; J. Thompson, 1985). Below we list some arguments for the inevitability of war on the one hand and the possibility of peace on the other. As you evaluate both sides, can you think of additional arguments?

The Question of Human Nature

Throughout this book, we have seen that individuals differ, as schools of psychology do, in their basic views of human nature. Are we, "at heart," good, helpful, and cooperative, or selfish, aggressive, and cruel? Those who believe that people are basically decent and kind often rely on moral persuasion as a tactic of making the world less hostile. Those who believe that people are governed by aggressive, even death-seeking "instincts," hope that we can find constructive ways of displacing or channeling our violent energies. Optimists tend to hope that everything will work out if you just trust people to behave well; pessimists assume that nothing will work out because you can't trust people further than you can throw them.

Social psychologists phrase the question differently. It is in our "nature," they would say, to behave both with astonishing generosity and with equally astonishing cruelty. The task is to identify the conditions that make helping or harming likely to occur (see "Think About It"). To do this, they draw on the *normal psychological processes* discussed in this chapter: acceptance of roles and rules, obedience to authority, conformity, stereotyping, self-justification, entrapment, deindividuation,

Optimists and pessimists disagree on whether "human nature" is basically good or basically destructive. With the question stated that way, the only answer is both—or neither. What would be a better question, and a more useful answer?

War Is Inevitable	**Peace Is Possible**
1. Once in the role of soldier, people follow orders.	1. Some people resist social pressure and follow conscience.
2. War solves economic problems.	2. War worsens economic problems.
3. Competition between countries is inevitable as long as they differ in resources and power.	3. Countries can cooperate in many realms—science, arts, social exchanges.
4. "Us-them" thinking will last as long as cultural differences do.	4. People have the empathic ability to understand "them."
5. Few people are willing to fight conformity.	5. People prize their freedom and uniqueness.
6. It is impossible for people to live without stereotypes or prejudice.	6. People can be legally forbidden to discriminate against those they dislike.
7. Much of human behavior is "mindless."	7. When human beings set themselves a problem to solve, they can be highly "mindful."
8. All new weapons have eventually been used; so will nuclear weapons, which will kill everyone.	8. Nuclear weapons are unique in their destructiveness; since World War II, no country has used them to fight a war.
9. There always has been war.	9. There always were smallpox and tuberculosis too, but they have been nearly eradicated.
10. People can't think about frightening subjects for too long; psychic numbing means the dangers of war will be ignored.	10. Worldwide protest against nuclear weapons is growing; a majority of Americans favor a nuclear freeze.
11. The end of the world is inevitable because of worldwide conflicts, famine, pollution, and other problems.	11. The problems of today, bad as they are, aren't as bad as the disasters of the fourteenth century, when two-thirds of the world's population died from plague, famine, and war.
12. What do you think?	12. What do you think?

and competition. These basic psychological processes provide the capacity for aggression or altruism, for war or peace.

▪ *Roles* are necessary in any social system, from a small tribe to a vast nation. They can be rigid, requiring people to give up personal feelings in the service of the role—whether the role is employee, spouse, or soldier. But they can also be flexible, less confining, and better able to bend with the qualities of the person who carries out the role.

▪ *Conformity* to one's group and *obedience* to authority are essential if a social system is to function. These mechanisms can lead to mindless obedience and the execution of illegal orders. But people can also learn to celebrate their unique qualities (and tolerate the qualities of others). They can learn how and when to protest in order to influence the majority. And they have the basic motives for uniqueness, freedom, and justice to help them do so.

▪ *Competition* is often a compelling motivator of achievement. The "space race" produced many rapid innovations in space technology. But competition can also produce prejudice and hostility, and it can reduce the pleasure of doing an activity for its own sake. Families, schools, companies, and cultures can train people in cooperative strategies, as well as encourage competition without the obsessive need for victory at all costs.

▪ *Cognitive processes*, such as stereotyping, ethnocentrism, attributions, and mindlessness, also have benefits and problems. They organize information that might otherwise be overwhelming. They justify behavior so that people don't have to think twice about everything they do (or even think once about it). They raise self-esteem so that people can feel good about themselves and their communities. But these same processes can lead to distorted perceptions of other groups. They justify unjustifiable behavior. They may protect self-esteem at the cost of self-delusion.

▪ *Entrapment* causes attitudes and actions to change in small steps. Before people realize it, they have committed themselves to a new belief or course of action. Entrapment can lead people toward helpful and generous behavior or toward aggressive behavior, depending on how the trap is set.

Many roles in modern life require us to give up our individuality, as conveyed by this dazzling image of white-suited referees at the Seoul Olympics. If each referee decided to behave out of role, the games could not continue. When is it justified to yield our personal styles and preferences for the role, and when is it not?

▪ *Deindividuation* allows people to suppress their individual preferences for the greater good of an institution, an ideal, or a goal. Yet when people entirely abandon responsibility for their actions, tragedy can result. The news is full of stories of mindless mobs, but also of people who retained their individuality amid great pressures to conform.

When philosopher Hannah Arendt (1963) wrote about the trial of Adolph Eichmann, she used the phrase "the banality of evil." (*Banal* means "commonplace" or "unoriginal.") Eichmann and his fellow Nazis were ordinary men, Arendt wrote, just doing their jobs. This is, perhaps, the hardest lesson in psychology. Most people want to believe that harm to others is done only by "evil people" who are bad down to their bones. It is reassuring to divide the world into those who are good or bad, mild or mean, open-minded or narrow-minded. Yet again and again, we have seen that perfectly nice people can become, under some conditions, aggressive, selfish, and prejudiced. Fortunately, people who are aggressive, selfish, and prejudiced can become, under some conditions, friendly, helpful, and tolerant.

All of this is good news and bad news. The bad news is that harmful or selfish behavior cannot be eliminated by getting rid of a few "bad" people or nations. The good news is that if humankind has created the conditions for cruelty, perhaps it can eradicate them.

Taking Psychology with You

Attitude Change: From Persuasion to "Brainwashing"

All around you, every day, people are trying to get you to change your mind. Advertisers, politicians, and friends use similar methods of persuasion. By knowing what these methods are, you will have a better chance of knowing how to evaluate persuasive messages and when to accept or resist them.

1. *Separate the person who is trying to persuade you from the message being conveyed.* There is a reason that advertisements are full of beautiful models, sports heroes, and "experts." People are more likely to be persuaded if they hear arguments from someone they admire or think is attractive. If you believe that someone is trying to cheat you or is arguing out of self-interest, you are unlikely to change your mind (Walster & Festinger, 1962). Advertisers and politicians spend more to convince the public that they can be trusted than to educate the public about their products or their ideas.

2. *Separate the quality of the product from your familiarity with it.* You may remember from Chapter 10 that repeated exposure to a name or symbol is enough to make a person feel more favorable toward it. This is the reason that some advertisements, for politicians and products, are repeated what seems like 1000 times a day. It is also the reason that many people spend four times as much for a familiar brand of aspirin as for an unfamiliar one, even though the cheaper product is just as good.

3. *Separate your intellectual judgment from your feelings.* If a message is linked with a good feeling, people are more likely to listen to it and to change their attitudes. In one study, students who were given peanuts and Pepsi while listening to an argument were more likely to be convinced than were students who listened without the pleasant munchies and soft drinks (Janis, Kaye, & Kirschner, 1965). Perhaps this is why so much business is conducted over lunch, and so many seductions over dinner!

The emotion of fear, in contrast, can cause people to avoid accepting arguments that are in their own best interest, which is why "scare tactics" are usually unsuccessful. Such tactics are used, for example, to try to persuade people to quit smoking or abusing other drugs, to drive only when sober, to use condoms to avoid AIDS and other sexually transmitted diseases, and to check for signs of cancer. However, fear works only if (1) people are scared a little, but not so much that they become too anxious and deny the danger completely; and (2) the message is combined with information about what a person can do to avoid the danger (Leventhal, Singer, & Jones, 1965; Rajecki, 1982). When messages about a future nuclear war are too terrifying and when people believe that there is nothing they can do to avoid war, they tend to deny the danger and live with "nuclear anxiety" (Nelson, 1985). Antiwar activists, in contrast, feel anxious enough to do something and they do not conceive of the problem as beyond action. They adopt a "strategy of small wins" to avoid being paralyzed by the scale of nuclear threat (Wagner, 1985; Weick, 1984).

4. *Know the attitudes and values that are important to you and be prepared to defend them*. Experiments find that when people are "inoculated" against persuasive tactics, by hearing opposing ideas and practicing a defense against them, they are better able to resist persuasion (McGuire & Papageorgis, 1961). This is not a case for rigid thinking and the refusal to accept new ideas. But it is a case for critical thinking. If you can identify and defend your point of view, you are better able to withstand unsupported arguments against it and to accept good evidence for changing it.

Sometimes, however, efforts to change attitudes go beyond exposing people to a new idea and persuading them to accept it. Persuasion tactics become more severe and manipulative. The term *brainwashing* was first used during the Korean War to describe how American prisoners of war came to collaborate with their Chinese Communist captors and endorse anti-American propaganda. It has since been used to account for the sympathy that some hostages develop toward their captors, and the fanatical attachment of cult members to their leaders. The cults may be religious, political, or psychological.

Some psychologists dislike the word "brainwashing" and prefer the phrase "undesired social influence" or "coercive persuasion" (Zimbardo, 1984; Zimbardo, Ebbesen, & Maslach, 1977). Brainwashing, they argue, implies that a person has a sudden change of mind and is unaware of what is happening. It sounds mysterious and powerful. In fact, its methods are neither mysterious nor unusual. Indeed, the difference between "persuasion" and "brainwashing" is often only a matter of degree and the observer's bias.

Studies of religious and psychological cults in the United States find some common steps in the "coercive persuasion" of a recruit. These steps occur in many other situations as well, from military and fraternity hazing to political rallies. They become coercive when they suppress an individual's ability to reason and make choices in his or her own best interests (Temerlin & Temerlin, 1982; Zimbardo, 1984).

1. *The person is put under physical or emotional distress.* Participants may not be allowed to eat, sleep, or exercise. They may be isolated in dark rooms with no stimulation or food prior to joining the group. In a group, they may be induced into a trancelike state through repetitive chanting, hypnosis, deep relaxation, or fatigue. If a participant is under stress, perhaps feeling lonely or troubled, he or she is already emotionally primed to accept the ideas of the group.

2. *The person's problems are defined in simplistic terms, and simple answers are offered.* There are as many of these explanations as there are persuasive groups, but here are some real examples: Do you have problems with your marriage? A long-term marriage is an "addiction"; better break the habit. Are you afraid or unhappy? It all stems from the pain of being born. Are you worried about war in the Mideast or hunger in Africa? It's not your problem; victims are responsible for everything that happens to them. Are your parents giving you a hard time? Reject them completely. Are you struggling financially? It's your fault for not wanting enough to be rich.

3. *The group leader offers unconditional love, acceptance, attention, and answers to personal problems.* In exchange, the leader demands the group's attachment, adoration, and idealization.

4. *The person may be given a "love bath" from the group.* Other members give the new recruit praise, support, applause, and affection. Positive emotions of euphoria and well-being are generated.

5. *The person is subjected to entrapment.* "There is no contract up front that says 'I agree to become a beggar and give up my family,'" says Philip Zimbardo. Instead, the person agrees to small things: to spend a weekend with the group, then another weekend, then weekly seminars, then advanced courses. During the Korean War, the Chinese first got the American POWs to agree with mild remarks such as "The United States is not perfect." Then the POWs had to add their own examples of such imperfections. At the end they were signing their names to anti-American broadcasts (Schein, Schneier, & Barker, 1961).

6. *Once in the group, the person's access to information is severely controlled.* Once a person is a committed member, the group limits his or her choices, denigrates critical thinking and makes fun of doubts, defines the outside world as evil, and insists that any private distress is due to lack of belief in the group. Total conformity is imposed and groupthink is demanded.

Some people may be more vulnerable than others to coercive tactics. But the techniques are powerful enough to overwhelm even strong individuals, as studies of hostages and prisoners have found. Unless people understand how these methods work, few can resist their power. To protect themselves, says psychologist Michael Langone, "people must think or sink." That has been the theme of this book.

KEY WORDS

rules (norms) 653
role 653
depersonalization 656
social cognition 658
attribution theory 658
fundamental attribution error 658
self-serving bias 659
just-world hypothesis 660
blaming the victim 660
stereotype 661
attitude 663
cognitive dissonance 664
prejudice 664
scapegoat 665
discrimination 666
obedience 668

conformity 668
mindlessness 670
entrapment 671
reactance 672
"whistleblowers" 673
group polarization 675
groupthink 675
diffusion of responsibility 676
social loafing 676
deindividuation vs. individuation 677
altruism 678
competition versus cooperation 679
"us-them" thinking 681
ethnocentrism 681
contact hypothesis 682

SUMMARY

1. Social psychology studies people in social context, including the influences of *roles*, *norms*, and groups on behavior and cognition. Three controversial studies illustrate the power of roles to affect individual personality and values. In Zimbardo's prison study, college students quickly fell into the role of "prisoner" or "guard." In Rosenhan's mental hospital study, the role of staff attendant caused nurses and psychiatrists to *depersonalize* patients and sometimes treat them harshly. In Milgram's obedience study, people in the role of "teacher" inflicted what they thought was extreme shock to another person in the role of "learner" because of the authority of the experimenter.

2. According to *attribution theory*, people are motivated to explain their own and other people's actions. They may attribute actions to the *situation* or to a person's *disposition* (qualities in the person). The *fundamental attribution error* is to overestimate personality traits as a cause of behavior and underestimate the situation. A *self-serving bias* allows people to excuse their own mistakes by blaming the situation. According to the *just-world hypothesis*, people are motivated to see the world as fair and to believe that people get what they deserve. To preserve the sense of justice, they may *blame the victim* for inviting injustice.

3. A *stereotype* is a cognitive schema about a group that helps people organize experience and predict how others will behave. But stereotypes distort reality in three ways: They emphasize differences between groups; they underestimate the differences within groups; and they produce selective perception, in which people see only evidence that fits their stereotypes. An *attitude* is a relatively stable opinion consisting of cognitive beliefs and emotional dispositions. A *prejudice* is an unjustified negative attitude about a group of people (or a social custom) that resists rational evidence.

4. Attitudes persist because of several benefits: cognitive benefits (a unified set of beliefs); social support; economic gains (the financial payoff of prejudice against another group); and psychological payoffs (self-esteem). People often use a minority group as a *scapegoat*, a target that is made to take the blame for their problems. "Taking Psychology with You" discusses some methods of attitude change, including tactics that range from persuasion to coercion ("brainwashing").

5. Attitudes do not always lead to behavior. Sometimes a change of behavior (because of the law or social custom) causes attitudes to change.

6. *Obedience*, following the orders of an authority, and *conformity*, going along with group pressure, are basic social processes that make society possible. People conform because they identify with a group, trust the group's judgment or knowledge, hope for personal gain, or wish to be liked. They also may conform "mindlessly," without thinking about it. People obey orders for many of the same reasons, but also because they are embarrassed to disobey, lack a language of protest, or have been *entrapped*.

7. *Dissent* and *nonconformity* also occur for several reasons. The theory of *reactance* maintains that people need to feel they have freedom of choice; if their freedom is threatened, they react to restore it. Dissent is more likely when a person has support and is not the lone protester.

8. Once in a group, individuals often behave differently than they would on their own. In *group polarization*, the group's collective decision is more extreme than its members' private decisions. In *groupthink*, group members think alike and, for the sake of harmony, suppress disagreement. The *diffusion of responsibility* causes group members to work less hard ("*social loafing*") and to avoid taking responsibility for their decisions and actions. *Deindividuation* is the loss of self-awareness and sense of individuality in a group or crowd. These group processes have been used to explain foolhardy group decisions, "mindless" mob violence, and the unwillingness of bystanders to help a stranger in trouble. However, groups can be structured to counteract all of these processes.

9. The stages in a bystander's decision to help a stranger (like the stages of deciding to protest a company or group decision) include seeing the need for help, deciding to take responsibility for action, weighing the costs of helping, having a commitment to helping others, and feeling able to help.

10. Cooperation and competition have strong effects on attitudes and behavior. Competition often fosters *ethnocentrism*, hostility, stereotyping, and aggression. Conflict and hostility between groups can be reduced by interdependence in working for mutual goals and by equal-status contact.

11. War and peace, cruelty and kindness, can be viewed as the results of normal psychological processes, including roles and rules, obedience and conformity, attributions, cooperation and competition, and deindividuation. By themselves, these processes are neutral; they can be used either positively or negatively.

E P I L O G U E

Taking Psychology with You

*Y*ou've come a long way since the beginning of this book. It is now time to stand back and ask yourself where you've been and what you've learned from the many studies, topics, and controversies that have been covered. What fundamental principles emerge, and how can you take them with you into your own life? You probably won't be surprised that different psychologists would answer these questions differently; as we noted back in Chapter 1, psychology is a patchwork quilt of ideas. Still, even a patchwork quilt has an overall pattern. We believe that there exists a ''big picture'' in the study of psychology, one that reveals five fundamental determinants of human behavior.

The Five Strands of Human Experience

If you look back at the chapters in this book, you will see that our focus began within the individual—with neurons and hormones—and gradually expanded to include the physical environment, the social environment, and entire cultures. Both across the sequence of chapters and within individual ones you can find what we call the five strands of human experience:

1. *Biology.* As physical creatures, we are influenced by our bodies and our brains. Physiology affects the rhythms of our lives, our perceptions of reality, our ability to learn, the intensity of our emotions, our temperaments, and, in some cases, our vulnerability to emotional disorder.

2. *Cognition.* Our species is, above all, the animal that explains things. Our cognitions—beliefs, explanations, and attributions—may not always be realistic or sensible, but they continually influence our actions and choices. All of us are constantly seeking to make sense of the world around us and of our own physical and mental states. Perception is sensation plus interpretation. Emotion is arousal plus attribution. Language is sound (or gesture) plus meaning.

3. *Environment.* What we do and how we do it are often less a matter of personality than of situation. We respond to the environment, and, in turn, our acts have consequences that influence future behavior. Features of the physical environment (such as room design, noise level, and air temperature) and the requirements of a specific circumstance (such as a job or a course) are constantly affecting us, even as we are constantly affecting our environments, in a repeating chain of cause and effect. The right environment can help us cope better with disabilities, get along better with others, and even become more creative and happy. The wrong kind can foster boredom, hostility, and discontent.

4. *Other people.* In Western culture, many people like to think of themselves as independent creatures. But everyone conforms, to one extent or another, and with greater or lesser awareness, to the expectations and demands of others. Spouses, lovers, friends, bosses, parents, and perfect strangers ''pull our strings'' in ways we may not recognize. Human beings emulate role models, conform to group pressures, obey authorities, and blossom or wilt in close relationships. Throughout life we need ''contact comfort''—sometimes in the literal touch or embrace of others and sometimes in shared experience or conversation.

5. *Culture.* Although there are many universals of behavior that unite humanity, ''human nature'' also varies from one culture to another. Culture dictates a set of norms and roles for how employers and employees, strangers and friends, and men and women are ''supposed'' to act. Culture teaches individuals how to use and

interpret body language, how to treat their spouses, how to rear their children, and even how to perceive the world. Whenever you find yourself wondering, irritably, why "*those* people have to behave that way," chances are a cultural difference is at work.

These five forces suggest different questions to ask when you are trying to describe, understand, predict, or change a particular aspect of your own life. For example:

Biology. What is going on in my body? Do I have a physical condition that might be affecting my behavior? Do I have a temperamental tendency to be easily aroused or to be calm? Are drugs or alcohol altering my ability to make decisions or behave as I would like? Do my days follow an irregular schedule that might be disrupting my physical functions and impairing my efficiency? Am I under unusual pressures that increase physical stress?

Cognition. How am I interpreting this situation? Are my explanations reasonable? Have I tested them? Am I wallowing in negative thoughts and "catastrophizing"? Do I attribute my successes to luck but take all the blame for my failures? Do I assume the worst about others? Do I make "external" attributions or "internal" ones? What are my underlying attitudes?

Environment. What are the contingencies and consequences governing my behavior and that of others? What rewards are maintaining the status quo? Which situations make me feel ambitious, confident, or content, and which ones make me feel helpless, pessimistic, or angry? Would I be different if the situation changed? How might I be able to change it?

Other people. Who are the people in my life who affect my attitudes and behavior? Am I responding to their expectations or rules in a "mindless" way? What part do I play in affecting their behavior? How do my friends and relatives support me or hinder me in achieving my goals?

Culture. How do my ethnicity and nationality affect me? What gender roles do they specify for me and my partners in close relationships? Am I acting out some sort of unwritten cultural role? What would happen if I ignored the norms of that role? Of the many cultural messages being aimed at me by television, books, parents, and teachers, which have the greatest influence? Are my conflicts with other people a result of cultural misunderstandings—due, for instance, to differing rules for expressing emotion?

Keep in mind, though, that *no single one of these factors operates in isolation from the others*. The forces that govern our behavior are as intertwined as strands of ivy on a wall, and it can be hard to see where one strand begins and another ends. This message, if enough people believed it, would probably put an end to the "pop psych" industry, which promotes single, simple answers to real-life complexities. (Anxious about the state of the world? Just jog some more or fix your diet. Not doing so well at work? Just learn to dress for success.) Some simplifiers of psychology try to reduce human problems to biochemical imbalances or genetic defects. Others argue that anyone can "fulfill any potential," regardless of biology or environment, and that solving problems is merely a matter of being determined.

In this book we have tried to show that the real concerns and dilemmas of life do not divide up neatly according to the chapters of an introductory psychology text (even ours). For example, to understand shyness or loneliness, you might need to consider your personal learning history; childhood experiences and what you observed from adult role models; temperamental tendencies; adult experiences; the autobiographical memories that make up your personal "story"; recent transitions in your life; how stress, diet, drugs, and sleep patterns might be affecting your mood; and whether you come from a culture that encourages or prohibits assertiveness. It may seem daunting to keep so many factors in mind. But once you get into the habit of seeing a situation from many points of view, relying on single-answer approaches will feel like wearing blinders.

Psychology in Your Life

If the theories and findings in this book are to be of long-lasting personal value to you, they must jump off the printed page and into your daily life. In previous chapters we have tried to point out ways in which you can apply what you have learned. However, *you* must do the actual work of selecting those aspects of psychological knowledge that can be of benefit to you.

To give you some practice in doing so, we will take two common problems and offer some ideas about where to look in this book for principles and findings that may shed light on them. If you are serious about wanting to use psychology, we recommend that you turn to the specified pages and think about how the information there can best be applied, even if you don't have the particular problems we have selected. Our brief lists of hints are far from exhaustive, and we have not attempted to touch on every major topic in this book. You should feel free to make the ''remote associations'' that are the heart of creativity (page 295) and come up with additional ideas that could be brought to bear on a particular problem. There is no single ''correct'' solution in these hypothetical situations, any more than there is a single solution to the real problems in life.

Situation 1: When love has gone

You have been romantically involved with someone for a year. When the relationship began, you felt very much in love and you thought your feelings were returned. But for a long time now your partner's treatment of you has been anything but loving. In fact, your partner makes fun of your faults in front of others, yells at you about the slightest annoyance, and insults and humiliates you. Sometimes you are ignored for days on end, as if your partner wants to punish you for some imagined wrong. All of your friends advise you to leave the relationship. Yet you can't shake the feeling that your partner must really love you. You still occasionally have a great time together, and your partner seems to become very distressed whenever you threaten to leave. You wish you could either improve the relationship or get out, and your inability to act leaves you feeling angry and depressed.

How might each of the following topics help you resolve this problem? We suggest that you try to come up with your own answers, aided by these text references, before you look at ours:

- Approach-avoidance conflicts (Chapter 10, page 345)
- Intermittent reinforcement (Chapter 6, page 223)
- Observational learning (Chapter 6, page 237)
- Self-esteem and locus of control (Chapter 11, page 408)
- Cognitive dissonance theory (Chapter 10, page 360)
- Gender differences in emotion and love (Chapter 9, page 336, and Chapter 10, page 355)
- Adult transitions (Chapter 14, pages 516 and 530)
- Reactance (Chapter 18, page 672)

Here are a few reasons why these topics might apply (you may think of others):

Research on *approach-avoidance conflicts* may help explain why you are both attracted to and repelled by this relationship—and why the closer you approach, the more you want to leave (and vice versa). When a goal is both attractive and painful, it is not unusual to feel uncertain and vacillate about the possible courses of action.

Intermittent reinforcement may explain why you persist in apparently self-defeating behavior. If staying in the relationship brought only punishment or if your partner always ignored you, it would be easier to leave. But your partner intermittently gives you good times, and when behavior is occasionally rewarded, it becomes resistant to extinction.

Past *observational learning* may help account for your present behavior. Perhaps your parents have a dominant/submissive relationship, and their way of interacting is what you have learned to expect in your own relationships.

Low *self-esteem* may explain why you tolerate abuse and humiliation; you may actually agree with your partner's criticisms and insults and feel you don't "deserve" a better relationship. If you have an *external locus of control*, you may feel that you cannot control what is happening to you—that you are merely a victim of fate, chance, or the whims and wishes of others.

Cognitive dissonance theory suggests that you may be trying to keep your attitudes and behavior consistent. The cognition "I am in this relationship and chose to be with this person" is dissonant with "This person ignores and mistreats me." Since you are still unable to break up (and alter the first cognition), you are working on the second cognition, hoping that your partner will change for the better.

Research on *gender differences* finds that men and women often have different unstated rules about expressing emotion and different definitions of love. Perhaps traditional gender roles are preventing you and your partner from communicating your true preferences and feelings.

Findings on *adult transitions* and "*crises*" might alert you to stresses in your partner's life: Have there been unexpected or difficult changes, such as a move, a new job, or the illness of a parent? (Remember from Chapter 9, though, that understanding the sources of a person's stress or unhappiness need not excuse that person's hostile behavior.)

Finally, *reactance* may explain why you do not listen to your friends. Their advice may be sound but threatening to your autonomy. In a paradoxical way, doing the opposite of what everyone thinks you should—staying in the relationship—gives you a (temporary) sense of control.

Understanding your situation, of course, does not lead automatically to a solution. Depending on the circumstances, you might choose to cope with the ongoing stress of the situation (Chapter 15); change your perceptions of the situation (Chapter 18); use learning principles to try to alter your own or your partner's behavior (Chapter 6); find other sources of self-esteem (Chapters 11 and 14); find a support group of people in the same situation (Chapter 17); seek psychological therapy or counseling, with or without your partner (Chapter 17)—or leave the relationship.

Situation 2: Job stress

You are an up-and-coming computer programmer. You like your job, but you feel overwhelmed by the amount of work you have to do. You never seem to be able to meet your deadlines, and you find yourself worrying about work at night and on weekends—you are unable to relax. Your friends accuse you of being a "grind" and a "workaholic," though you would like to work less if you could. You believe you deserve a promotion, but your boss is curt and abrupt, rarely accepts your good ideas, and never gives you any feedback about your work, let alone praise. (You assume your boss dislikes you and has some grudge against you.) You are beginning to feel isolated from your co-workers, too. Lately, you find that your motivation is sagging, and creative ideas are slow in coming. The occasional relaxing evening drink has turned into steady drinking at home and several belts during the day, too, as you try to blot out your worries. What can you do to improve this situation?

Here are some psychological topics that may yield insights:

- Sources of stress (Chapter 15, page 542)
- Work motivation (Chapter 6, page 232, and Chapter 10, page 369)
- Attributions (Chapter 18, page 658)
- Defense mechanisms (Chapter 11, page 388)
- Drug use and abuse (Chapter 4, page 137, and Chapter 16, page 597)
- Obedience, conformity, and dissent (Chapter 18, page 668)

Here are a few reasons why these topics might apply:

Research on *sources of stress* may alert you to the reasons for your harried condition. You may need to analyze how much of the pressure you feel is due to the demands of the job and how much is a product of your own internal standards. You can't cope with stress appropriately until you know where it comes from.

Research on *work motivation* shows that achievement motivation can be a part of personality but is also affected by the nature of the work environment. "Burnout," for instance, often occurs because of the way a job is structured; there may be little support from co-workers or employers, infrequent feedback, and few opportunities for developing innovative ideas. Workers are most productive when the conditions of the job—such as flexibility, variation in routine, and the power to make decisions—encourage intrinsic motivation.

Attribution theory states that attributions, whether accurate or not, guide our responses to a situation. Your assumption that your employer dislikes you and holds a grudge may not be valid. Perhaps he or she is under unusual pressure too, and hasn't had time to attend to you. Perhaps he or she is unaware of your contributions. A talk with the boss may be in order.

The clinical concept of a *defense mechanism* suggests that your overwork may be a way to channel thoughts away from some other area of your life that is troubling you. Would you really work less if you could, or is your constant preoccupation with your job a sign of denial—an unwillingness to face problems at home?

Research on *drug use* shows that drug effects and the likelihood of abuse depend on mental set and situational setting, your physical tolerance, your cultural experience with the use of the drug, and your social environment when taking the drug. A special vulnerability to alcohol's physical effects may explain your gradual slide into a serious alcohol problem. Or alcohol may offer you a convenient "reason" for relaxing your previously high standards of performance on the job ("I can't help it; it's the booze"). Since excessive drinking affects brain function and judgment, it probably does impair your performance, creating a vicious cycle of drug use and excuse. Finally, research on *obedience*, *conformity*, and *dissent* suggests that you may not be alone in your problems at work. Perhaps your co-workers share your problems and would like to make improvements, but they fear "rocking the boat." There may be a solution you could accomplish with the aid of others that would be difficult to achieve on your own.

Method and matter

Our two examples have been personal problems, but the applications of psychology extend beyond personal concerns to social ones. Remember James Peters and Ralph Galluccio from Chapter 11? (If you don't, don't worry; just reread Chapter 7 on memory, and feel reassured.) Peters and Galluccio were neighbors who fought for ten years over a boundary dispute. In the end, Peters killed Galluccio. Such disputes, with and without that violent finale, are unfortunately common among lovers, neighbors, and nations. Psychological findings can increase our understanding of such hostilities and may help reduce them. For example, Chapter 9 discussed how cultural differences in emotion and body language can create misunderstandings. Chapter 8 described steps that can lead to better, more creative solutions. Chapter 13 described how children learn to be altruistic, empathic, and responsible, or selfish and irresponsible. And Chapter 18 suggested ways people can overcome prejudice and ethnocentrism and get along in spite of their differences.

An engineer-turned-social scientist, Jacobo Varela (1978), believes that we now have enough accurate information about human behavior to develop "social technology." Just as physical technology offers mechanical answers to engineering problems, social technology applies psychological answers to social problems. Varela and his students have applied many of the findings discussed in this book to real-life situations, with great success. Yet Varela reports that it is often difficult to persuade people to think in terms of general psychological strategies for facing life's problems and challenges. Instead, he says, people often confuse his *examples* with his *method*:

> If I talk about a woman's being cured of alcoholism, people think the method applies only to alcoholics. . . . If I present the case of a parole violator who abandoned crime for good, I am told to offer my services to the nearest parole board. The point is that social technology is distinct from the problems it solves. The system of solutions remains constant, but it can be adapted easily to the task at hand. A screwdriver may be used to tighten screws on a typewriter, but that does not make it a typewriter tool, effective only on typewriters. (p. 89)

That is why the one chapter that may ultimately be most useful to you is the one you may have assumed to be least useful: Chapter 2, "How Psychologists Know What They Know." The best way to take psychology with you is to understand its basic principles of critical thinking, its ways of approaching problems and questions. Specific findings within psychology change, as new research is done and new theories evolve. But the method of psychology continues, and clear thinking is its hallmark.

APPENDIX

Statistical Methods

*N*ineteenth-century English statesman Benjamin Disraeli reportedly once named three forms of dishonesty: "lies, damned lies, and statistics." It is certainly true that people can lie with the help of statistics. It happens all the time: Advertisers, politicians, and others with some claim to make either use numbers inappropriately or ignore certain critical ones. (When hearing that "four out of five doctors surveyed" recommend some product, have you ever wondered just how many doctors were surveyed and whether they were representative of all doctors?) People also use numbers to convey a false impression of certainty and objectivity when the true state of affairs is uncertainty or ignorance. But it is people, not statistics, that lie. When statistics are used correctly and appropriately, they neither confuse nor mislead. On the contrary, they expose unwarranted conclusions, promote clarity and precision, and protect us from our own biases and blind spots.

If statistics are useful anywhere, it is in the study of human behavior. If human beings were all alike, and psychologists could specify all the influences on behavior, there would be no need for statistics. But any time we measure human behavior, we are going to wind up with different observations or scores for different individuals. Statistics can help us spot trends amid the diversity.

This appendix will introduce you to some basic statistical calculations used in psychology. Reading the appendix will not make you into a statistician, but it will acquaint you with some ways of organizing and assessing research data. If you suffer from a "number phobia," relax: You do not need to know much math to understand this material. However, you should have read Chapter 2, which discussed the rationale for using statistics and described various research methods. You may want to review the basic terms and concepts covered in that chapter. Be sure that you can define *hypothesis, sample, correlation, independent variable, dependent variable, random assignment, experimental group, control group, descriptive statistics, inferential statistics* and *test of statistical significance.* (Correlation coefficients, which are described in some detail in Chapter 2, will not be covered here.)

To read the tables in this appendix, you will also need to know the following symbols:

N = the total number of observations or scores in a set
X = an observation or score
Σ = the Greek capital letter sigma, read as "the sum of"
$\sqrt{\ }$ = the square root of

(*Note:* Boldfaced terms in this appendix are defined in the glossary at the end of the book.)

ORGANIZING DATA

Before we can discuss statistics, we need some numbers. Imagine that you are a psychologist and that you are interested in that most pleasing of human qualities, a sense of humor. You suspect that a well-developed funny bone can protect people from the negative emotional effects of stress. You already know that in the months following a stressful event, people who score high on sense-of-humor tests tend to feel less tense and moody than more sobersided individuals do (Martin & Lefcourt, 1983). You realize, though, that this correlational evidence does not prove cause and effect. Perhaps people with a healthy sense of humor have other traits, such as flexibility or creativity, that act as the true stress buffers. To find out whether humor itself really softens the impact of stress, you do an experiment.

First, you randomly assign subjects to two groups, an experimental group and a control group. To keep our calculations simple, let's assume there are only 15 people per group. Each person individually views a silent film that most North Americans find fairly stressful, one showing Australian aboriginal boys undergoing a puberty rite involving physical mutilation. Subjects in the experimental group are instructed to make up a humorous monologue while watching the film. Those in the control group are told to make up a straightforward narrative. After the film, each person answers a mood questionnaire that measures current feelings of tension, depression, aggressiveness, and anxiety. A person's overall score on the questionnaire can range from 1 (no mood disturbance) to 7 (strong mood disturbance). This procedure provides you with 15 "mood disturbance" scores for each group. Have people who tried to be humorous reported less disturbance than those who did not?

Constructing a Frequency Distribution

Your first step might be to organize and condense the "raw data" (the obtained scores) by constructing a **frequency distribution** for each group. A frequency distribution shows how often each possible score actually occurred. To construct one, you first order all the possible scores from highest to lowest. (Our mood disturbance scores will be ordered from 7 to 1.) Then you tally how often each score was actually obtained. Table A.1 gives some hypothetical "raw data" for the two groups, and Table A.2 shows the two frequency distributions based on these data. From these distributions you can see that the two groups differed. In the experimental group, the extreme scores of 7 and 1 did not occur at all, and the most common score was the middle one, 4. In the control group, a score of 7 occurred four

---

TABLE A.1

Some Hypothetical Raw Data

These scores are for the hypothetical humor-and-stress study described in the text.

Experimental group	4,5,4,4,3,6,5,2,4,3,5,4,4,3,4
Control group	6,4,7,6,6,4,6,7,7,5,5,5,7,6,6

TABLE A.2

Two Frequency Distributions

The scores are from Table A.1.

Experimental Group			Control Group		
Mood Disturbance Score	Tally	Frequency	Mood Disturbance score	Tally	Frequency
7		0	7	////	4
6	/	1	6	/// /	6
5	///	3	5	///	3
4	/// //	7	4	//	2
3	///	3	3		0
2	/	1	2		0
1		0	1		0
		N = 15			N = 15

times, the most common score was 6, and no one obtained a score lower than 4.

Because our mood scores have only seven possible values, our frequency distributions are quite manageable. Suppose, though, that your questionnaire had yielded scores that could range from 1 to 50. A frequency distribution with 50 entries would be cumbersome and might not reveal trends in the data clearly. A solution would be to construct a *grouped frequency distribution* by grouping adjacent scores into equal-sized *classes* or *intervals*. Each interval could cover, say, five scores (1-5, 6-10, 11-15, and so forth). Then you could tally the frequencies within each *interval*. This procedure would reduce the number of entries in each distribution from 50 to only 10, making the overall results much easier to grasp. However, information would be lost. For example, there would be no way of knowing how many people had a score of 43 versus 44.

Graphing the Data

As everyone knows, a picture is worth a thousand words. The most common statistical picture is a **graph**, a drawing that depicts numerical relationships. Graphs appear at several points in this book, and are routinely used by psychologists to convey their findings to others. From graphs, we can get a general impression of what the data are like, note the relative frequencies of different scores, and see which score was most frequent.

In a graph constructed from a frequency distribution, the possible score values are shown along a horizontal line (the *x-axis* of the graph) and frequencies along a vertical line (the *y-axis*), or vice versa. To construct a **histogram**, or **bar graph**, from our hypothetical stress scores, we draw rectangles (bars) above each score, indicating the number of times it occurred by the rectangle's height (Figure A.1).

A slightly different kind of "picture" is provided by a **frequency polygon**, or **line graph**. In a frequency polygon,

FIGURE A.1

A Histogram

This graph depicts the distribution of mood disturbance scores shown on the left side of Table A.2.

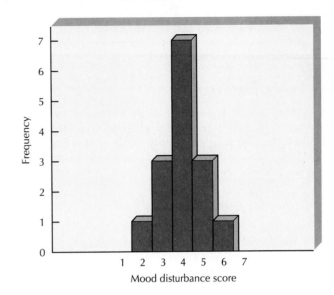

the frequency of each score is indicated by a dot placed directly over the score on the horizontal axis, at the appropriate height on the vertical axis. The dots for the various scores are then joined together by straight lines, as in Figure A.2. When necessary an "extra" score, with a fre-

FIGURE A.2

A Frequency Polygon

This graph depicts the same data as Figure A.1.

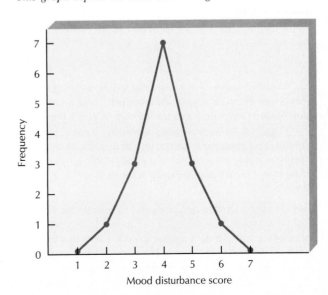

quency of zero, can be added at each end of the horizontal axis, so that the polygon will rest on this axis instead of floating above it.

A *word of caution about graphs*: They may either exaggerate or mask differences in the data, depending on which units are used on the vertical axis. The two graphs in Figure A.3, although they look quite different, actually depict the same data. Always read the units on the axes of a graph; otherwise, the shape of a histogram or frequency polygon may be misleading.

DESCRIBING DATA

Having organized your data, you are now ready to summarize and describe them. As you will recall from Chapter 2, procedures for doing so are known as *descriptive statistics*. In the following discussion, the word *score* will stand for any numerical observation.

Measuring Central Tendency

Your first step in describing your data might be to compute a **measure of central tendency** for each group. Measures of central tendency characterize an entire set of data in terms of a single representative number.

The Mean. The most popular measure of central tendency is the *arithmetic mean*, usually called simply the **mean**. It is often expressed by the symbol *M*. Most people are thinking of the mean when they say "average." We run across means all the time: in grade point averages, temperature averages, and batting averages. The mean is valuable to the psychologist because it takes all the data into account and it can be used in further statistical analyses. To compute the mean, you simply add up a set of scores and divide the total by the number of scores in the set. Recall that in mathematical notation, Σ means "the sum of," X stands for the individual scores, and N represents the total number of scores in a set. Thus the formula for calculating the mean is:

$$M = \frac{\Sigma X}{N}$$

Table A.3 shows how to compute the mean for our experimental group. Test your ability to perform this calculation by computing the mean for the control group yourself. (You can find the answer, along with other control group statistics, on page A-8). Later, we will describe how a psychologist would compare the two means statistically to see if there is a significant difference between them.

The Median. Despite its usefulness, sometimes the mean can be misleading, as we noted in Chapter 2. Suppose you piled some children on a seesaw in such a way that it was perfectly balanced, and then a 200-pound adult came and sat on one end. The center of gravity would quickly shift toward the adult. In the same way, one extremely high

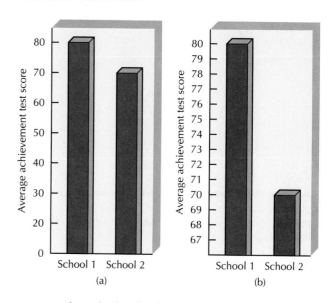

FIGURE A.3

Same Data, Different Impressions

These two graphs depict the same data, but have different units on the vertical axis.

score can dramatically raise the mean (and one extremely low score can dramatically lower it). In real life, this can be a serious problem. For example, in the calculation of a town's mean income, one millionaire would offset hundreds of poor people. The mean income would be a poor indication of the town's actual wealth.

When extreme scores occur, a more representative measure of central tendency is the **median**, or midpoint in a set of scores or observations ordered from highest to lowest. In any set of scores, the same *number* of scores falls above the median as below it. The median is not affected by extreme

TABLE A.3

Calculating a Mean and a Median

The scores are from the left side of Table A.1.

Mean (M)

$$M = \frac{4 + 5 + 4 + 4 + 3 + 6 + 5 + 2 + 4 + 3 + 5 + 4 + 4 + 3 + 4}{15}$$

$$= \frac{60}{15}$$

$$= 4$$

Median

Scores, in order: 2, 3, 3, 3, 4, 4, 4, $\boxed{4}$, 4, 4, 4, 5, 5, 5, 6

$\uparrow$

median

scores. If you were calculating the *median* income of that same town, the one millionaire would offset only one poor person.

When the number of scores in the set is odd, calculating the median is a simple matter of counting in from the ends to the middle. However, if the number of scores is even, there will be two middle scores. The simplest solution is to find the mean of those two scores and use that number as the median. (When the data are from a grouped frequency distribution, a more complicated procedure is required, one beyond the scope of this appendix.) In our experimental group, the median score is 4 (see Table A.3). What is it for the control group?

The Mode. A third measure of central tendency is the **mode**, the score that occurs most often. In our experimental group, the modal score is 4. In our control group, it is 6. In some distributions, all scores occur with equal frequency, and there is no mode. In others, two or more scores "tie" for the distinction of being most frequent. Modes are used less often than other measures of central tendency. They do not tell us anything about the other scores in the distribution; they often are not very "central"; and they tend to fluctuate from one random sample of a population to another more than either the median or the mean.

Measuring Variability

A measure of central tendency may or may not be highly representative of other scores in a distribution. To understand our results, we also need a **measure of variability** that will tell us whether our scores are clustered closely around the mean or widely scattered.

The Range. The simplest measure of variability is the **range**, which is found by subtracting the lowest score from the highest one. For our hypothetical set of mood disturbance scores, the range in the experimental group is 4 and in the control group it is 3. Unfortunately, though, simplicity is not always a virtue. The range gives us some information about variability but ignores all scores other than the highest and lowest ones.

The Standard Deviation. A more sophisticated measure of variability is the **standard deviation (SD)**. This statistic takes every score in the distribution into account. Loosely speaking, it gives us an idea of how much, on the average, scores in a distribution differ from the mean. If the scores were all the same, the standard deviation would be zero. The higher the standard deviation, the more variability there is among scores.

To compute the standard deviation, we must find out how much each individual score deviates from the mean. To do so we simply subtract the mean from each score. This gives us a set of *deviation scores*. Deviation scores for numbers above the mean will be positive, those for numbers below the mean will be negative, and the positive scores

will exactly balance the negative ones. In other words, the sum of the deviation scores will be zero. That is a problem, since the next step in our calculation is to add. The solution is to *square* all the deviation scores (that is, to multiply each score by itself). This step gets rid of negative values. Then we can compute the average of the *squared* deviation scores by adding them up and dividing the sum by the number of scores (*N*). Finally, we take the square root of the result, which takes us from squared units of measurement back to the same units that were used originally (in this case, mood disturbance levels).

The calculations just described are expressed by the following formula:

$$SD = \sqrt{\frac{\Sigma(X - M)^2}{N}}$$

Table A.4 shows the calculations for computing the standard deviation for our experimental group. Try your hand at computing the standard deviation for the control group.

Remember, a large standard deviation signifies that scores are widely scattered, and that therefore the mean is not terribly typical of the entire population. A small standard deviation tells us that most scores are clustered near the mean, and that therefore the mean is representative.

TABLE A.4

Calculating a Standard Deviation

Scores (X)	Deviation scores (X − M)	Squared deviation scores (X − M)²
6	2	4
5	1	1
5	1	1
5	1	1
4	0	0
4	0	0
4	0	0
4	0	0
4	0	0
4	0	0
4	0	0
3	−1	1
3	−1	1
3	−1	1
2	−2	4
	0	14

$$SD = \sqrt{\frac{\Sigma(X - M)^2}{N}} = \sqrt{\frac{14}{15}} = \sqrt{.93} = .97$$

Note: When data from a sample are used to estimate the standard deviation of the population from which the sample was drawn, division is by *N* − 1 instead of *N*, for reasons that will not concern us here.

Suppose two classes took a psychology exam, and both classes had the same mean score, 75 out of a possible 100. From the means alone, you might conclude that the classes were similar in performance. But if Class A had a standard deviation of 3 and Class B had a standard deviation of 9, you would know that there was much more variability in performance in Class B. This information could be useful to an instructor in planning lectures and making assignments.

Transforming Scores

Sometimes researchers do not wish to work directly with raw scores. They may prefer numbers that are more manageable, such as when the raw scores are tiny fractions. Or they may want to work with scores that reveal where a person stands relative to others. In such cases, raw scores can be transformed to other kinds of scores.

Percentile Scores. One common transformation converts each raw score to a **percentile score** (also called a *centile rank*). A percentile score gives the percentage of people who scored at or below a given raw score. Suppose you learn that you have scored 37 on a psychology exam. In the absence of any other information, you may not know whether to celebrate or cry. But if you are told that 37 is equivalent to a percentile score of 90, you know that you can be pretty proud of yourself; you have scored as well as or higher than 90 percent of those who have taken the test. On the other hand, if you are told that 37 is equivalent to a percentile score of 50, you have scored only at the median—only as well as, or higher than, half of the other students. The highest possible percentile rank is 99, or more precisely, 99.99, because you can never do better than 100 percent of a group when you are a member of the group. (Can you say what the lowest possible percentile score is? The answer is on page A-8.) Standardized tests such as those described in Chapter 12 often come with a table that allows for the easy conversion of any raw score to the appropriate percentile score, based on data from a larger number of people who have already taken the test.

Percentile scores are easy to understand and easy to calculate. However, they also have a drawback: They merely rank people and do *not* tell us how far apart people are in terms of raw scores. Suppose you scored in the 50th percentile on an exam, June scored in the 45th, Tricia scored in the 20th, and Sean scored in the 15th. The difference between you and June may seem identical to that between Tricia and Sean (five percentiles). But in terms of *raw* scores you and June are probably more alike than Tricia and Sean, because exam scores usually cluster closely together around the midpoint of the distribution and are farther apart at the extremes. Because percentile scores do not preserve the spatial relationships in the original distribution of scores, they are inappropriate for computing many kinds of statistics. For example, they cannot be used to calculate means.

Z-scores. Another common transformation of raw scores is to **z-scores**, or **standard scores**. A z-score tells you how far a given raw score is above or below the mean, using the standard deviation as the unit of measurement. To compute a z-score, you subtract the mean of the distribution from the raw score and divide by the standard deviation:

$$z = \frac{X - M}{SD}$$

Unlike percentile scores, z-scores preserve the relative spacing of the original raw scores. The mean itself always corresponds to a z-score of zero, since it cannot deviate from itself. All scores above the mean have positive z-scores and all scores below the mean have negative ones. When the raw scores form a certain pattern called a *normal distribution* (to be described shortly), a z-score tells you how high or low the corresponding raw score was, relative to the other scores. If your exam score of 37 is equivalent to a z-score of +1.0, you have scored 1 standard deviation above the mean. Assuming a roughly normal distribution, that's pretty good, because in a normal distribution only about 16 percent of all scores fall at or above 1 standard deviation above the mean. But if your 37 is equivalent to a z-score of −1.0, you have scored 1 standard deviation below the mean—a poor score.

Z-scores are sometimes used to compare people's performance on different tests or measures. Say that Elsa earns a score of 64 on her first psychology test and Manuel, who is taking psychology from a different instructor, earns a 62 on his first test. In Elsa's class, the mean score is 50 and the standard deviation is 7, so Elsa's z-score is (64 − 50)/7 = 2.0. In Manuel's class, the mean is also 50, but the standard deviation is 6. Therefore, his z-score is also 2.0 [(62 − 50)/6]. Compared to their respective classmates, Elsa and Manuel did equally well. *But be careful*: This does *not* imply that they are equally able students. Perhaps Elsa's instructor has a reputation for giving easy tests and Manuel's for giving hard ones, so Manuel's instructor has attracted a more industrious group of students. In that case, Manuel faces stiffer competition than Elsa does, and even though he and Elsa have the same z-score, Manuel's performance may be more impressive.

You can see that comparing z-scores from different people or different tests must be done with caution. Standardized tests, such as IQ tests and various personality tests, use z-scores derived from a large sample of people assumed to be representative of the general population taking the tests. When two tests are standardized for similar populations, it is safe to compare z-scores on them. But z-scores derived from special samples, such as students in different psychology classes, may not be comparable.

Curves

In addition to knowing how spread out our scores are, we need to know the *pattern* of their distribution. At this point we come to a rather curious phenomenon. When researchers make a very large number of observations, many of the physical and psychological variables they study have a distribution that approximates a pattern called a **normal distribution**. (We say "approximates" because a *perfect* normal distribution is a theoretical construct and is not actually found in nature.) Plotted in a frequency polygon, a normal distribution has a symmetrical, bell-shaped form known as a **normal curve** (see Figure A.4).

A normal curve has several interesting and convenient properties. The right side is the exact mirror image of the left. The mean, median, and mode all have the same value and are at the exact center of the curve, at the top of the "bell." Most observations or scores cluster around the center of the curve, with far fewer out at the ends, or "tails" of the curve. Most important, as Figure A.4 shows, when standard deviations (or z-scores) are used on the horizontal axis of the curve, the percentage of scores falling between the mean and any given point on the horizontal axis is always the same. For example, 68.26 percent of the scores will fall between plus and minus 1 standard deviation from the mean; 95.44 percent of the scores will fall between plus and minus 2 standard deviations from the mean; and 99.74 percent of the scores will fall between plus and minus 3 standard deviations from the mean. These percentages hold for any normal curve, no matter what the size of the standard deviation. Tables are available showing the percentages of scores in a normal distribution that lie between the mean and various points (as expressed by z-scores).

The normal curve makes life easier for psychologists when they want to compare individuals on some trait or performance. For example, since IQ scores from a population form a roughly normal curve, the mean and standard deviation of a test are all the information you need in order to know how many people score above or below a particular score. On a test with a mean of 100 and a standard deviation of 15, about 68.26 percent of the population scores between 85 and 115—1 standard deviation below and 1 standard deviation above the mean (see Chapter 12).

Not all types of observations, however, are distributed normally. Some curves are lopsided, or *skewed*, with scores clustering at one end or the other of the horizontal axis (see Figure A.5). When the "tail" of the curve is longer on the right than on the left, the curve is said to be positively, or right, skewed. When the opposite is true, the curve is said to be negatively, or left, skewed. In experiments, reaction times typically form a right-skewed distribution. For example, if people must press a button whenever they hear some signal, most will react quite quickly; but a few will take an unusually long time, causing the right "tail" of the curve to be stretched out.

Knowing the shape of a distribution can be extremely valuable. Paleontologist and biologist Stephen Jay Gould (1985) has told how such information helped him cope with the news that he had a rare and serious form of cancer. Being a researcher, he immediately headed for the library to learn all he could about his disease. The first thing he found was that it was incurable, with a median mortality of only eight months after discovery. Most people might have assumed that a "median mortality of eight months" means "I will probably be dead in eight months." But Gould realized that although half of all patients died within eight months, the other half survived longer than that. Since his disease had been diagnosed in its early stages, he was getting top notch medical treatment, and he had a strong will to live, Gould figured he could reasonably expect to be in

FIGURE A.4

A Normal Curve

When standard deviations (or z-scores) are used along the horizontal axis of a normal curve, certain fixed percentages of scores fall between the mean and any given point. As you can see, most scores fall in the middle range (between +1 and −1 standard deviations from the mean).

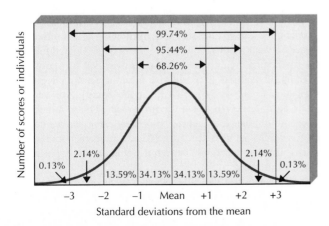

FIGURE A.5

Skewed Curves

Curve (a) is skewed negatively, to the left. Curve (b) is skewed positively, to the right. The direction of a curve's skewness is determined by the position of the long tail, not by the position of the bulge. In a skewed curve, the mean, median, and mode fall at different points.

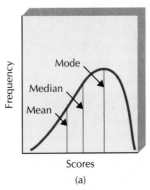

(a)

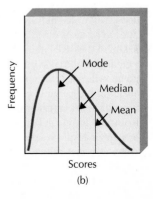

(b)

the half of the distribution that survived beyond eight months. Even more cheering, the distribution of deaths from the disease was right-skewed: The cases to the left of the median of eight months could only extend to zero months, but those to the right could stretch out for years. Gould saw no reason why he should not expect to be in the tip of that right-hand tail.

For Stephen Jay Gould, statistics, properly interpreted, were "profoundly nurturant and life-giving." They offered him hope and inspired him to fight his disease. As of this writing, Gould is as active professionally as he ever was. The initial diagnosis was made in July of 1982.

Answers:

Control group statistics:

$$\text{Mean} = \frac{\Sigma X}{N} = \frac{87}{15} = 5.8$$

$$\text{Median} = 6$$

$$\text{Standard Deviation} = \sqrt{\frac{\Sigma (X - M)^2}{N}} = \sqrt{\frac{14.4}{15}}$$
$$= \sqrt{.96} = .98$$

Lowest possible percentile score: 1 (or more precisely .01)

DRAWING INFERENCES

Once data are organized and summarized, the next step is to ask whether they differ from what might have been expected purely by chance (see Chapter 2). A researcher needs to know whether it is safe to infer that the results from a particular sample of people are valid for the entire population from which the sample was drawn. *Inferential statistics* provide this information. They are used in both experimental and correlational studies.

The Null Versus the Alternative Hypothesis

In an experiment, the scientist must assess the possibility that his or her experimental manipulations will have no effect on the subjects' behavior. The statement expressing this possibility is called the **null hypothesis**. In our stress-and-humor study, the null hypothesis states that making up a funny commentary will not relieve stress any more than making up a straightforward narrative will. In other words, it predicts that the difference between the means of the two groups will not deviate significantly from zero. Any obtained difference will be due solely to chance fluctuations. In contrast, the **alternative hypothesis** (also called the experimental or research hypothesis) states that on the average the experimental group will have lower mood disturbance scores than the control group.

The null hypothesis and the alternative hypothesis cannot both be true. Our goal is to reject the null hypothesis. If

our results turn out to be consistent with the null hypothesis, we will not be able to do so. If the data are inconsistent with the null hypothesis, we will be able to reject it with some degree of confidence. Unless we study the entire population, though, we will never be able to say that the alternative hypothesis has been proven. No matter how impressive our results are, there will always be some degree of uncertainty about the inferences we draw from them. Since we cannot prove the alternative hypothesis, we must be satisfied with showing that the null hypothesis is unreasonable.

Students are often surprised to learn that it is the null hypothesis, not the alternative hypothesis, that is tested. After all, it is the alternative hypothesis that is actually of interest. But this procedure does make good sense. The null hypothesis can be stated precisely and tested directly. In the case of our fictitious study, the null hypothesis predicts that the difference between the two means will be zero. The alternative hypothesis does not permit a precise prediction because we don't know how much the two means might differ (if, in fact, they do differ). Therefore, it cannot be tested directly.

Testing Hypotheses

Many computations are available for testing the null hypothesis. The choice depends on the design of the study, the size of the sample, and other factors. We will not cover any specific tests here. Our purpose is simply to introduce you to the kind of *reasoning* that underlies inferential statistics. With that in mind, let us return once again to our data. For each of our two groups we have calculated a mean and a standard deviation. Now we want to compare the two sets of data to see if they differ enough for us to reject the null hypothesis. We wish to be reasonably certain that our observed differences did not occur entirely by chance.

What does it mean to be "reasonably certain"? How different from zero must our result be to be taken seriously? Imagine, for a moment, that we had infinite resources and could somehow repeat our experiment, each time using a new pair of groups, until we had "run" the entire population through the study. It can be shown mathematically that if only chance were operating, our various experimental results would form a normal distribution. This theoretical distribution is called "the sampling distribution of the difference between means," but since that is quite a mouthful, we will simply call it the *sampling distribution* for short. If the null hypothesis were true, the mean of the sampling distribution would be zero. That is, on the average, we would find no difference between the two groups. Often, though, because of chance influences or *random error*, we would get a result that deviated to one degree or another from zero. On rare occasions, the result would deviate a great deal from zero.

We cannot test the entire population, though. All we have are data from a single sample. We would like to know whether the difference between means that we actually obtained would be close to the mean of the theoretical sampling distribution (if we *could* test the entire population) or far away from it, out in one of the "tails" of the curve. Was our result highly likely to occur on the basis of chance alone or highly unlikely?

Before we can answer that question, we must have some precise way to measure distance from the mean of the sampling distribution. We must know exactly how far from the mean our obtained result must be to be considered "far away." If only we knew the standard deviation of the sampling distribution, we could use it as our unit of measurement. We don't know it, but fortunately, we can use the standard deviation of our *sample* to estimate it. (We will not go into the reasons that this is so.)

Now we are in business. We can look at the mean difference between our two groups and figure out how far it is (in terms of standard deviations) from the mean of the sampling distribution. As mentioned earlier, one of the convenient things about a normal distribution is that a certain fixed percentage of all observations fall between the mean of the distribution and any point above or below the mean. These percentages are available from tables. Therefore, if we know the "distance" of our obtained result from the mean of the theoretical sampling distribution, we automatically know how likely our result is to have occurred strictly by chance.

To give a specific example, if it turns out that our obtained result is 2 standard deviations above the mean of the theoretical sampling distribution, we know that the probability of its having occurred by chance is less than 2.3 percent. If our result is 3 standard deviations above the mean of the sampling distribution, the probability of its having occurred by chance is less than .13 percent—less than 1 in 800. In either case, we might well suspect that our result did not occur entirely by chance after all. We would call the result *statistically significant*. (In psychology, researchers usually consider any highly unlikely result to be of interest, no matter which direction it takes. In other words, the result may be in either "tail" of the sampling distribution.)

To summarize: Statistical significance means that if only chance were operating, our result would be highly improbable, so we are fairly safe in concluding that more than chance was operating—namely, the influence of our independent variable. We can reject the null hypothesis, and open the champagne. As we noted in Chapter 2, psychologists usually accept a finding as statistically significant if the likelihood of its occurring by chance is 5 percent or less (see Figure A.6). This cutoff point gives the researcher a reasonable chance of confirming reliable results as well as reasonable protection against accepting unreliable ones.

Some cautions are in order, though. As noted in Chapter 2, statistically significant results are not always psychologically interesting or important. Further, statistical significance is related to the size of the sample. A large sample increases the likelihood of reliable results. But there is a

FIGURE A.6

Statistical Significance

This curve represents the theoretical sampling distribution discussed in the text. The curve is what we would expect by chance if we did our hypothetical stress-and-humor study many times, testing the entire population. If we used the conventional significance level of .05, we would regard our obtained result as significant only if the probability of getting a result that far from zero by chance (in either direction) totaled 5 percent or less. As shown, the result must fall far out in one of the tails of the sampling distribution. Otherwise, we cannot reject the null hypothesis.

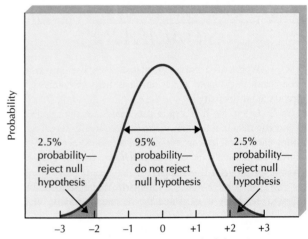

trade-off: The larger the sample, the more probable it is that a small result having no practical importance will reach statistical significance. For this reason, it is always useful to know how much of the total variability in scores was accounted for by the independent variable. (The computations are not discussed here.) If only 3 percent of the variance was accounted for, then 97 percent was due either to chance factors or to systematic influences of which the researcher was unaware. Because human behavior is affected by so many factors, the amount of variability accounted for by a single psychological variable is often modest.

Oh, yes, about those humor findings: Our fictitious study is similar to two more complicated ones done by Herbert M. Lefcourt and Rod A. Martin (1986). Women who tried to be funny reported less mood disturbance than women who merely produced a straightforward narrative. They also grimaced and fidgeted less during the film, suggesting that they really did feel less stress. The results were not statistically significant for men, possibly because men did not find the film all that stressful. Other findings, however, suggest that humor can shield both sexes from stress (Wade, 1986). *The moral*: When gravity gets you down, try a little levity.

KEY WORDS

SUMMARY

1. When used correctly, statistics expose unwarranted conclusions, promote precision, and help researchers spot trends amid diversity.

2. Often, the first step in data analysis is to organize and condense data in a *frequency distribution*, a tally showing how often each possible score (or interval of scores) occurred. Such information can also be depicted in a *histogram* (bar graph) or a *frequency polygon* (line graph).

3. Descriptive statistics summarize and describe the data. *Central tendency* is measured by the *mean*, *median*, or, less frequently, the *mode*. Since a measure of central tendency may or may not be highly representative of other scores in a distribution, it is also important to analyze variability. A large *standard deviation* means that scores are widely scattered about the mean; a small one means that most scores are clustered near the mean.

4. Raw scores can be transformed into other kinds of scores. *Percentile scores* indicate the percentage of people who scored at or below a given raw score. Z-scores (standard scores) indicate how far a given raw score is above or below the mean of the distribution.

5. Many variables have a distribution approximating a *normal distribution*, depicted as a *normal curve*. The normal curve has a convenient property: When standard deviations are used as the units on the horizontal axis, the percentage of scores falling between any two points on the horizontal axis is always the same. Not all types of observations are distributed normally, however. Some distributions are *skewed* to the left or right.

6. Inferential statistics are used to test the *null hypothesis*. They tell a researcher whether a result differed significantly from what might have been expected purely by chance. Basically, hypothesis testing involves estimating where the obtained result would have fallen in a theoretical *sampling distribution* based on studies of the entire population in question. If the result would have been far out in one of the "tails" of the distribution, it is considered statistically significant. A statistically significant result may or may not be psychologically interesting or important.

GLOSSARY

abnormality (or psychological disorder) Any behavior or state of emotional distress that causes personal suffering, that is self-destructive, or that is maladaptive.

absolute threshold The smallest quantity of physical energy that can be reliably detected by an observer.

accommodation The process of modifying existing cognitive structures in response to experience and new information.

achievement tests Tests designed to measure acquired skills and knowledge.

adolescence The period of development between puberty (a biological event) and adulthood (a social event).

agoraphobia "Fear of fear"; a set of phobias, often set off by a panic attack, sharing the basic fear of being away from a safe place or person.

algorithm A problem-solving strategy that is guaranteed to lead eventually to a solution.

alpha waves Relatively large, slow brain waves characteristic of relaxed wakefulness.

altered (alternate) state of consciousness A deliberately produced state of consciousness that differs from ordinary wakefulness or sleep.

alternate forms reliability The consistency of test scores when alternate versions of a test are given to the same person or group on separate occasions.

alternative hypothesis An assertion that the independent variable in a study will have a certain predictable effect on the dependent variable. Also called an *experimental* or *research hypothesis*.

amnesia Partial or complete loss of memory for information or past events; when no organic causes are present, it is classified as a dissociative disorder.

androgens Masculinizing hormones.

androgynous Having both traditionally "masculine" *and* "feminine" qualities; literally, "male-female."

anterograde amnesia Loss of the ability to form long-term memories for new facts and events.

anthropology The study of the physical, social, and cultural origins and development of the human race.

antidepressant drugs Stimulants that influence neurotransmitters in the brain; they are used in the treatment of mood disorders, usually depression and anxiety.

antipsychotic drugs Major tranquilizers primarily used in treatment of schizophrenia and other disorders involving psychotic symptoms, such as delusions.

antisocial personality disorder A condition characterized by antisocial behavior (such as lying, stealing, and sometimes violence), lack of social emotions (guilt and shame), and impulsivity.

anxiety disorder *See* generalized anxiety disorder; panic attack; phobia.

applied psychology The study of psychological issues that have direct practical significance. Also, the application of psychological findings.

aptitude tests Tests designed to measure a person's potential for acquiring various types of skills and knowledge, based on present abilities.

archetypes [AR-ki-tipes] To Carl Jung, universal, symbolic images that appear in myths, art, dreams, and other expressions of the collective unconscious.

arithmetic mean *See* mean.

artificial intelligence "Intelligent" behavior performed by computers. Also, the study of the methods used to program such behavior in computers.

assimilation The process of absorbing new information into existing cognitive structures, modifying it if necessary to "fit."

attachment A strong emotional tie between babies and their primary caretakers. In later life, attachment refers to any emotional connection between two people.

attitude   A fairly stable opinion toward a person, object, or activity, containing a cognitive element (perceptions and beliefs) and an emotional element (positive or negative feelings).

attribution theory   The theory that people are motivated to explain their own and others' behavior by attributing causes of that behavior to a situation or disposition.

audition   The sense of hearing.

auditory nerve   The nerve connecting the receptors for hearing with the brain.

autonomic nervous system   Subdivision of the peripheral nervous system that regulates the internal organs and glands.

axon   Extending fiber of a neuron that conducts impulses away from the cell body and transmits them to other neurons. From the Greek for ''axis.''

basic psychology   The study of psychological issues in order to seek knowledge for its own sake rather than for its practical application.

basilar [BASS-uh-lur] membrane   The membrane in which the auditory receptor cells are embedded.

behavior genetics   An interdisciplinary field of study concerned with the genetic bases of behavior.

behavior modification   The application of conditioning techniques to reduce or eliminate maladaptive or problematic behavior or teach new responses.

behavioral medicine   An interdisciplinary field that studies behaviors related to the maintenance of health, the onset of illness, and the prevention of disease.

behaviorism   An approach to psychology that emphasizes the study of objectively observable behavior rather than inner mental experiences. Behaviorists stress the role of the environment as a determinant of human and animal behavior.

binocular cues   Visual cues to depth or distance requiring two eyes.

biofeedback   A technique for controlling bodily functions by attending to an instrument that monitors the function and signals changes in it.

biological rhythm   A periodic, more-or-less regular fluctuation in a biological system; may or may not have psychological implications.

biology   The study of the evolution, structure, and functioning of living organisms.

bipolar disorder   A mood disorder in which depression alternates with mania.

body language   Nonverbal signals of posture, gaze, touch, facial expression, gesture and movement. These may reveal emotions such as anger, affection, shame, or grief. They also convey nonemotional messages about status, conversational emphasis, and personal mannerisms.

bonding   A strong emotional tie that parents typically feel toward their newborn babies.

brain stem   The part of the brain at the top of the spinal cord; responsible for automatic functions such as heartbeat and respiration.

brightness   Lightness or luminance; the dimension of visual experience related to the amount of light emitted from or reflected by an object.

Cannon-Bard theory   The theory, proposed independently by Walter Cannon and Philip Bard, that emotion originates in the thalamus of the brain, which controls both emotional feeling and behavior. In this view, all emotions are physiologically similar.

case history (case study)   A detailed description of a particular individual under study or treatment.

cell body   The part of the neuron that keeps it alive and determines whether it will fire.

central nervous system   The portion of the nervous system consisting of the brain and spinal cord.

central tendency   *See* measure of central tendency.

cerebellum   A brain structure that regulates movement and balance.

cerebral cortex   A thin layer of cells covering the cerebrum; largely responsible for higher functions. *Cortex* is Latin for ''bark'' or ''rind.''

cerebral hemispheres   The two halves of the cerebrum.

cerebrum [suh-REE-brum]   The largest brain structure, comprising the upper part of the forebrain; in charge of most sensory, motor, and cognitive processes in human beings. From the Latin for ''brain.''

chaining   An operant conditioning procedure in which a complex sequence of responses is established. The final response in the sequence is usually established first.

child development   The gradual, orderly sequence of changes in biological maturation, physical structure, behavior, and thinking that marks growth from conception to maturity. In life-span psychology, ''development'' refers to the process of growth and change from conception to death.

childhood amnesia   The inability to remember events and experiences that occurred early in life.

chromosomes   The rod-shaped structures in the center of each body cell that carry the genes and determine hereditary characteristics.

chunk   A meaningful unit of information; may be comprised of smaller units.

circadian [sur-CAY-dee-un] rhythm   A biological rhythm with a period (from peak to peak or trough to trough) of about 24 hours. From the Latin *circa,* ''about,'' and *dias,* ''a day.''

classical (Pavlovian) conditioning   The process, first described by Ivan Pavlov, by which a previously neutral stimulus acquires the capacity to elicit a response through association with a stimulus that naturally elicits a similar response. Sometimes called *respondent conditioning.*

climacteric   The period of decreasing reproductive capacity in women, culminating in menopause.

clinical psychology   The branch of psychology concerned with the diagnosis, treatment, and study of mental and emotional problems and disabilities.

cochlea [KOCK-lee-uh]   A snail-shaped, fluid-filled organ in the inner ear, containing the receptors for hearing.

coefficient of correlation A measure of correlation that ranges in value from −1.00 to +1.00.

cognitive dissonance A state of tension that occurs when a person simultaneously holds two cognitions that are psychologically inconsistent, or when a person's belief is inconsistent with his or her behavior.

cognitive map A mental representation of the environment.

cognitive psychology An approach to psychology that emphasizes mental processes in perception, memory, language, problem solving, and other areas of behavior.

cognitive schema An integrated network of knowledge, beliefs, and expectations concerning a particular topic.

cohort An age group, such as a school class or a whole generation, that shares common experiences or demographic traits.

collective unconscious To Carl Jung, universal memories and experiences of humankind, represented in the unconscious of all people.

complexity (of light) Refers to the number of different wavelengths contained in light from a particular source.

compulsions Repetitive, ritualized, stereotyped behaviors that a person feels must be done to avoid disaster.

concept A category used to class together objects, relations, activities, abstractions, or qualities that share common properties.

conditioned response (CR) The classical conditioning term for a response that is elicited by a conditioned stimulus; occurs after the conditioned stimulus is associated with an unconditioned stimulus.

conditioned stimulus (CS) The classical conditioning term for an initially neutral stimulus that comes to elicit a conditioned response after being associated with an unconditioned stimulus.

cones Visual receptors involved in color vision.

conformity Behavior or attitudes that occur as a result of real or imagined group pressure.

congruence To Carl Rogers, harmony between the conscious self and the totality of the person's unconscious feelings and life experiences.

connectionism The school of thought that explains learning in terms of connections or bonds between stimuli and responses.

consciousness The awareness of the environment and one's own existence, sensations, and thoughts.

conservation The understanding that the physical properties of objects—such as number of items, amount of liquid, or length of an object—remain the same even when appearances change (as long as nothing is added or taken away).

consistency paradox The gap between the belief that personality traits are consistent across situations and the fact that people don't always behave as their traits would predict.

consolidation The process by which a long-term memory becomes durable and stable.

content validity The ability of a test to give a broad picture of whatever the test claims to measure.

continuous reinforcement A reinforcement schedule in which a particular response is always reinforced.

control group A comparison group of subjects who are not exposed to the same ''treatment'' or manipulation of the independent variable as experimental subjects are.

convergent thinking Thinking aimed at finding a single correct answer to a problem by applying knowledge and reasoning.

coping The cognitive and behavioral efforts to manage demands in the environment or oneself that one feels to be stressful.

cornea A transparent membrane that covers the front part of the eye and bends incoming light toward a lens behind it.

corpus callosum Bundle of nerve fibers connecting the two cerebral hemispheres.

correlation A measure of how strongly two or more variables are related to each other.

correlational study A descriptive study that looks for a consistent relationship between two phenomena.

counseling psychology An applied branch of psychology concerned with helping people deal with problems of everyday life.

counterconditioning In classical conditioning, the process of pairing a conditioned stimulus with a stimulus that elicits a response that is incompatible with an unwanted conditioned response.

creativity A flexible, imaginative thought process leading to novel but appropriate solutions to problems, original ideas and insights, or new and useful products.

criterion validity The ability of a test to predict other, independent measures (criteria) associated with the characteristic being assessed.

critical period *See* sensitive period.

critical thinking The ability and willingness to assess claims and make objective judgments on the basis of well-supported reasons.

cross-sectional study A study in which groups of subjects of different ages are compared at a given time.

cue-dependent forgetting The inability to retrieve information stored in memory because of insufficient internally or externally generated cues.

culture-fair tests Tests that reduce cultural bias by incorporating knowledge and skills common to many different cultures and socioeconomic groups.

culture-free tests Tests in which cultural experience does not influence performance.

dark adaptation A process by which visual receptors become maximally sensitive to dim light.

decay theory (of forgetting) The theory that information in memory eventually disappears if it is not reactivated; it appears to be more plausible for short-term than long-term memory.

declarative memories Memories of facts, rules, concepts, and events; include semantic and episodic memories.

deductive reasoning Reasoning from the general to the particular; drawing a conclusion that follows necessarily from certain premises.

deep processing In the encoding of information, the processing of meaning rather than simply the physical or sensory features of a stimulus.

defense mechanisms In psychoanalytic theory, methods used by the ego to prevent unconscious anxiety from reaching consciousness.

deindividuation In groups or crowds, the loss of awareness of one's own individuality; in varying degrees, a person feels indistinguishable from others.

déjà vu [day-zhah VOO] The feeling that something happening at the present moment has happened before in exactly the same way; from the French for "already seen."

delta waves Slow, regular brain waves characteristic of stage 3 and stage 4 sleep.

dendrites Branches on a neuron that receive information from other neurons and transmit it toward the cell body. From the Greek for "tree."

denial In psychoanalytic theory, a defense mechanism in which a person refuses to accept evidence of the reality of his or her own emotions.

dependent variable A variable that an experimenter predicts will be affected by manipulations of the independent variable.

depersonalization The loss of one's individuality and humanity. (*See also* deindividuation.)

depressants Drugs that slow down activity in the central nervous system.

depression *See* major depression; bipolar disorder.

descriptive methods Methods that yield descriptions of behavior but not causal explanations.

descriptive statistics Statistics that organize and summarize research data.

determinism The philosophical doctrine that all acts and decisions are determined by preceding events (physiological, environmental, or psychological), rather than by the exercise of free will.

developmental psychology The study of physical, mental, and social changes over the life span.

dialectical reasoning A process in which opposing facts or ideas are weighed and compared, with a view to determining the truth or resolving differences.

difference threshold The smallest difference in stimulation that can be reliably detected by an observer when two stimuli are compared. Also called *just-noticeable-difference*.

diffusion of responsibility In organized or anonymous groups, the tendency of members to avoid taking responsibility for actions or decisions, assuming others will do it.

discriminative stimulus In operant conditioning, a stimulus that signals when a particular response will be followed by a reinforcer, punisher, or neutral consequence.

displacement In psychoanalytic theory, the shifting of instinctual energy from its original object or activity to a different one.

display rules Social and cultural rules that regulate when, how, and where a person may express (or suppress) emotional feelings.

dispositional attribution An explanation of one's own or another's behavior that relies on something in the person.

dissociation Separation of consciousness into distinct parts.

dissociative disorders Conditions in which normally integrated consciousness or identity is split or altered, as in psychogenic amnesia or multiple personality.

divergent thinking Mental exploration of unusual or unconventional alternatives during problem solving. It tends to enhance creativity.

doctrine of specific nerve energies The theory that we experience different sense modalities because signals received by different sense organs stimulate different nerve pathways, which terminate in different areas of the brain.

double-blind study An experiment in which neither the subjects nor the researchers know which subjects are in the control group(s) and which in the experimental group(s) until after results are tallied.

Down's syndrome A form of mental retardation usually caused by an extra chromosome 21. It is accompanied by various physical anomalies, such as a downward curve of the inner eyelid.

dualism The view that the mind is a separate entity that exists apart from the body and other aspects of material reality.

dyzygotic twins (fraternal twins) Twins that develop from two separate eggs fertilized by different sperm. They are no more alike genetically than any two siblings.

eclectic [ek-LEC-tik] Literally, selected from various sources; in psychotherapy, the term describes the common practice of using methods from different theoretical schools.

educational psychology The study of psychological principles that explain learning. It also looks for ways to improve educational systems.

ego In psychoanalysis, the part of personality that represents reason, good sense, rational control; it operates according to the *reality principle*.

egocentric thinking Perceiving the world from only one's own point of view; the inability to take another person's perspective.

eidetic [eye-DET-ik] imagery An image of a visual stimulus that appears to exist in the external environment instead of in "the mind's eye" and that can be "read" for information.

elaborative rehearsal Association of new information with already stored knowledge and analysis of the new information in order to make it memorable.

electroconvulsive therapy (ECT) A procedure occasionally used for cases of prolonged major depression, in which a brief brain seizure is induced to alter brain chemistry.

electrodes Devices used to apply electric current to tissue or detect neural activity.

electroencephalogram (EEG) A recording of neural activity detected by electrodes.

emotion A state involving a pattern of facial and bodily changes, cognitive appraisals, and beliefs. Culture, in turn, shapes the experience and expression of emotion. (*See also* primary emotions and secondary emotions.)

emotion work   The expression of an emotion one does not really feel in response to social or cultural expectations.

empirical   Relying on or derived from observation, experimentation, or measurement.

encoding (in memory)   The conversion of information into a form that can be stored and retrieved.

endocrine glands   Internal organs that produce hormones and release them into the bloodstream; from the Greek for "secrete within."

endorphins [en-DOR-fins]   Neurotransmitters that are similar in structure and action to opiates; they are involved in pain reduction, pleasure, and memory. (Technically known as *endogenous opioid peptides.*)

entrapment   A gradual process in which individuals escalate their commitment to a course of action to justify their investment of time, money, or effort.

epinephrine, norepinephrine (adrenaline, noradrenaline)   Hormones produced by the adrenal glands that provide the body with energy to respond to environmental events.

episodic memories   Memories for personally experienced events and the contexts in which they occurred.

equilibrium   The sense of balance.

estrogens   Feminizing hormones.

ethnocentrism   The belief that one's own ethnic group, nation, or religion is superior to all others.

eustress [YOU-stress]   Positive or beneficial stress. (*See also* psychological stress.)

evoked potentials   Patterns of brain activity produced in response to specific events.

experiment   A controlled test of a hypothesis in which the researcher manipulates one variable to discover its effect on another, while holding other conditions constant.

experimental psychology   A broad field of psychology devoted to the experimental study of learning, motivation, sensation and perception, physiology, human performance, and cognition.

experimenter effects   Unintended changes in subjects' behavior due to cues inadvertently given by the experimenter.

extinction   The weakening and eventual disappearance of a learned response. In classical conditioning, it occurs when the conditioned stimulus is no longer paired with the unconditioned stimulus. In operant conditioning, it occurs when a response is no longer followed by a reinforcer.

extrasensory perception (ESP)   Perception that does not appear to depend on normal sense organ stimulation. Its existence has not been proven.

extrinsic motivation   Motivation based on external incentives, such as pay, praise, attention, or the avoidance of punishment.

extrinsic reinforcers   Reinforcers that are not inherently related to the activity being reinforced. Examples are money, prizes, and praise.

facial-feedback hypothesis   The notion that the facial muscles send messages to the brain, identifying the emotion a person feels. According to this hypothesis, we don't frown because we feel angry; we feel angry because we are frowning.

factor analysis   A statistical method for analyzing the intercorrelations among various measures or test scores. Clusters of measures or scores that are highly correlated are assumed to measure the same underlying trait, ability, or aptitude (factor).

feature detectors   Cells in the visual cortex that are sensitive to specific features of the environment.

fetal alcohol syndrome   A pattern of physical and intellectual abnormalities in infants whose mothers drank an excessive amount of alcohol during pregnancy.

figure   The part of the perceptual field that is perceived as foreground or as an object or pattern against a background.

fixation   In psychoanalytic theory, an inability to develop psychosexually beyond a certain stage.

fixed interval (FI) schedule   An intermittent schedule of reinforcement in which a reinforcer is delivered for the first response made after a fixed period of time has elapsed since the last reinforcer.

fixed ratio (FR) schedule   An intermittent schedule of reinforcement in which reinforcement occurs only after a fixed number of responses.

flashbulb memories   Vivid, detailed recollections of the circumstances in which one learned of or perceived some significant or surprising event.

forebrain   The largest subdivision of the brain; involved in the control of sensory, motor, and cognitive processes in human beings. The upper part is called the *cerebrum.*

fovea   The area in the center of the retina of the eye containing the greatest concentration of cones; provides sensitivity to detail and color.

free association   In psychoanalysis, a method of recovering unconscious conflicts by saying freely whatever comes to mind.

frequency (of a sound wave)   The number of times per second that a sound wave cycles through a peak and low point.

frequency distribution   A summary of how frequently each score in a set occurred.

frequency polygon (line graph)   A graph showing a set of points obtained by plotting score values against score frequencies. Adjacent points are joined by straight lines.

functional fixedness   The tendency to consider only the usual function of an object and overlook other possible uses. It often leads to rigidity in problem solving.

functionalism   An early approach to psychology that stressed the function or purpose of behavior and consciousness.

fundamental attribution error   The tendency to overestimate personality factors (dispositions) and underestimate environmental ones (situations) in explaining behavior.

ganglion cells   Neurons in the retina of the eye that gather information from receptor cells (by way of intermediate bipolar cells); their axons make up the optic nerve.

gate control theory The theory that the experience of pain depends in part on whether pain impulses get past a neurological "gate" in the spinal cord and thus reach the brain.

gender identity The sense of being male or female, regardless of whether or not one follows the rules of sex typing.

gender role A set of norms that defines socially approved attitudes and behavior for men and women.

General Adaptation Syndrome (GAS) According to Hans Selye, the bodily reactions to environmental stressors.

generalized anxiety disorder A continuous state of anxiety, lasting a month or more, marked by signs of motor tension, autonomic hyperactivity (e.g., a pounding heart), constant apprehension, and difficulties in concentration.

gerontology The study of aging and the old.

gestalt [geh-SHTALT] psychology An approach to psychology that emphasizes the perception, learning, and mental manipulation of whole units rather than their analysis into parts; from the German word for "pattern" or "form."

g factor A general ability assumed by some theorists to underlie various specific mental abilities and talents.

glial cells Cells that hold neurons in place and provide them with nutrients.

grammar The system of linguistic rules governing sounds (or in the case of sign languages, gestures), meanings, and syntax of a language. It may be viewed as a mechanism for generating all possible sentences in a language.

graph A drawing that depicts numerical relationships.

ground The part of the perceptual field perceived as formless or as the background.

group polarization The tendency of a group's decision to be more extreme than its members' individual decisions.

groupthink In close-knit groups, the tendency for all members to think alike and to suppress dissent and disagreement.

gustation The sense of taste.

health psychology A field within psychology that studies psychological aspects of health and illness.

heritability A statistical estimate of the proportion of the total variance in some trait within a group that is attributable to genetic differences among individuals within the group.

heuristic A rule of thumb that guides problem solving but does not guarantee an optimal solution. Heuristics are often used as shortcuts in solving complex problems.

higher-order conditioning In classical conditioning, a procedure in which a neutral stimulus becomes a conditioned stimulus through association with an already established conditioned stimulus.

hindbrain A subdivision of the brain that includes the pons, the medulla, much of the reticular activating system, and the cerebellum.

hippocampus A brain structure thought to be involved in the storage of new information in memory.

histogram (bar graph) A graph in which the heights (or lengths) of bars are proportional to the frequencies of individual scores or classes of scores in a distribution.

homeostasis The tendency of the body to maintain itself in a steady, stable condition with regard to physical processes, such as temperature, water balance, blood sugar, and oxygen.

hopelessness theory A theory, developed from the earlier notion of "learned helplessness," that accounts for depression as a result of despairing cognitions (e.g., that the future is hopeless).

hormones Chemical substances that are secreted by organs called *glands* and that affect the functioning of other organs. From the Greek for "to urge on."

hue The dimension of visual experience specified by the various color names and related to the wavelength of light. In common usage, *hue* and *color* are often used synonymously.

human factors psychology An applied field of psychology concerned with the design of equipment, tasks, and work settings that take into account the capacities and requirements of workers.

humanistic psychology (humanism) An approach to psychology that emphasizes personal growth and the achievement of human potential more than the scientific understanding, prediction, and control of behavior.

hypnosis A condition in which attention is focused and a person is extremely responsive to suggestion.

hypothalamus A brain structure involved in emotions and drives vital to survival, such as fear, hunger, thirst, and reproduction; regulates the autonomic nervous system.

hypothesis A statement that attempts to predict or account for a set of phenomena. Scientific hypotheses specify relationships among events or variables and are supported or disconfirmed by empirical investigation.

id In psychoanalysis, the part of personality containing inherited psychological energy, particularly sexual and aggressive instincts; it operates according to the *pleasure principle*.

identification A process by which the child adopts an adult's standards of morality, values, and beliefs as his or her own; in psychoanalysis, identification with the same-sex parent occurs at resolution of the Oedipal conflict.

image A likeness of something; a representation that mirrors or resembles the thing it represents. Mental images can occur in many and perhaps all sensory modalities.

imprinting The tendency of some animals, especially birds, to follow and form a permanent attachment to the first moving object they see or hear after birth.

incentive An external motivating stimulus, such as money, praise, or fame.

independent variable A variable that an experimenter manipulates.

individuation A sense of oneself as distinct from others; a willingness to say and do things that set oneself apart from one's group.

induction A method of child rearing in which the parent appeals to the child's own resources, abilities, sense of responsibility, and feelings for others in correcting the child's misbehavior. (In contrast to methods that rely on asserting power or withdrawing love.)

inductive reasoning   Reasoning from the particular to the general; drawing general conclusions from examination of specific examples.

industrial/organizational psychology   The study of behavior in the workplace.

inferential statistics   Statistical tests that allow researchers to assess how likely it is that their results occurred merely by chance.

inferiority complex   To Alfred Adler, an inability to accept natural limitations; it occurs when the need for self-improvement is blocked or inhibited.

infradian [in-FRAY-dee-un] rhythm   A biological rhythm that occurs less frequently than once a day; from the Latin for ''below a day.''

insight   A form of learning that occurs in problem solving and appears to involve the (often sudden) understanding of how elements of a situation are related or can be reorganized to achieve a solution.

instinct   A complex pattern of behavior that occurs without learning in every member of a species in response to a specific stimulus.

instinctive drift   The tendency of an organism to revert to an instinctive behavior over time; it can interfere with learning.

intelligence   An inferred characteristic of an individual, usually defined as the ability to profit from experience, acquire knowledge, think abstractly, or adapt to changes in the environment.

intelligence quotient (IQ)   A measure of intelligence originally computed by dividing a person's mental age by his or her chronological age and multiplying by 100; now derived from norms provided for standardized intelligence tests.

intermittent (partial) schedule of reinforcement   A reinforcement schedule in which a particular response is sometimes but not always reinforced.

intrapsychic   Within the mind or self.

intrinsic motivation   Motivation based on internal rewards, such as the basic pleasure of the activity itself, the intellectual challenge, or the satisfaction of curiosity.

intrinsic reinforcers   Reinforcers that are inherently related to the activity being reinforced. Examples are enjoyment of the task and the satisfaction of accomplishment.

introspection   A form of self-observation in which individuals examine and report the contents of their own consciousnesses.

inventories   Standardized objective questionnaires requiring written responses; they typically include scales on which people are asked to rate themselves.

iris   A muscular, ring-shaped membrane that controls how much light enters the eye; also gives the eye its color.

James-Lange theory   The theory, proposed independently by William James and Carl Lange, that emotion results from the perception of one's own bodily reactions. In this view, each emotion is physiologically distinct.

just-noticeable-difference (j.n.d.)   Another name for *difference threshold*.

just-world hypothesis   The notion that people need to believe that the world is fair and that justice is served; that bad people are punished and good people are rewarded.

kinesthesis [KIN-es-THEE-sis]   The sense of body position and movement of body parts; also called *kinesthesia*.

laboratory observation   The observation of subjects in a research laboratory.

language   A system that combines meaningless elements such as sounds or gestures into structured utterances that convey meaning.

latent learning   A form of learning that is not immediately expressed in an overt response; it occurs without obvious reinforcement.

lateralization   Specialization of the two cerebral hemispheres for particular psychological operations.

learning   A relatively permanent change in behavior (or behavioral potential) due to experience.

learning disability   A difficulty in the performance of a specific mental skill, such as reading or arithmetic; sometimes linked to perceptual or memory problems.

lens (of the eye)   A curved, transparent structure that focuses light rays entering through the pupil.

libido   In psychoanalysis, the psychic energy that fuels the life or sexual instincts of the id.

limbic system   A group of brain areas involved in emotional reactions and motivated behavior.

linguistic relativity theory   The theory that language molds habits of thought and perception and that different language communities tend to have different views of reality. This theory is associated with Benjamin Lee Whorf.

linguistic universals   The linguistic features that characterize all languages.

lobotomy   A surgical procedure that cuts fibers in frontal lobes of the brain; it went out of fashion with the discovery of antipsychotic medication.

localization of function   Specialization of particular brain areas for particular functions.

locus of control   A general expectation about whether the results of one's actions are under one's own control (*internal* locus) or beyond one's control (*external* locus).

longitudinal study   A study in which subjects are followed and periodically reassessed over a period of time.

long-term memory (LTM)   The memory system involved in the long-term retention of information; theoretically, it has an unlimited capacity.

long-term potentiation   A long-lasting increase in the strength of synaptic responsiveness, thought to be a biological mechanism of memory.

loudness   The dimension of auditory experience related to the intensity of a pressure wave.

magnetic resonance imaging (MRI)   A method for studying body and brain tissue, using magnetic fields and special radio receivers.

maintenance rehearsal   Rote repetition of material in order to maintain its availability in memory.

major depression   A mood disorder involving disturbances in emotion (excessive sadness), behavior (apathy and loss of interest in usual activities), cognition (distorted thoughts of hopelessness and low self-esteem), and body function (fatigue, loss of appetite). (*See also* bipolar disorder.)

maturation The sequential unfolding of genetically governed behavior and physical characteristics.

mean The most common measure of central tendency; an average calculated by adding up all the scores or numbers in a set and dividing the sum by the number of quantities in the set.

measure of central tendency A number intended to characterize an entire set of data.

measure of variability A number that indicates how dispersed scores are around the mean of the distribution. (*See also* variance.)

median A measure of central tendency; the value at the midpoint of a distribution of scores when the scores are ordered from highest to lowest.

meditation A practice aimed at focusing consciousness and eliminating all distracting thoughts.

memory The capacity to retain and retrieve information. It also refers to the mental structure or structures that account for this capacity and to the material retained (either the total body of information or specific items of information).

menarche [men-ARE-kee] The onset of menstruation.

menopause The cessation of menstruation; usually a gradual process lasting up to several years.

mental age (MA) A measure of mental development expressed in terms of the average mental ability at a given age. A child with a mental age of 8 performs on a test of mental ability at the level of the average 8-year-old.

mental school (of emotion) Scientists and philosophers who seek psychological explanations of emotion—for example, in beliefs, judgments, and interpretations of events.

mental set A tendency to solve a problem with the same strategies and rules used on previous problems.

midbrain A subdivision of the brain that lies between the hindbrain and forebrain and contains important neural way-stations.

Minnesota Multiphasic Personality Inventory (MMPI) A widely used objective personality test.

mnemonic (ni-MON-ik) device A strategy or technique for improving memory.

mode A measure of central tendency; the most frequently occurring score in a distribution.

monism The view that mental and physical reality have the same basis.

monocular cues Visual cues to depth or distance that can be used by one eye alone.

monozygotic twins (identical twins) Twins born when a fertilized egg divides into two parts that develop into separate embryos.

motivated forgetting Forgetting because of a conscious or unconscious desire to eliminate awareness of painful or unpleasant experiences.

motivation An inferred process within an animal or person that causes that organism to move toward a goal.

motor nerves Nerves in the peripheral nervous system that carry messages from the central nervous system to muscles, glands, and internal organs.

multiple personality disorder A rare dissociative disorder marked by the appearance within one person of two or more distinct personalities, each with its own name, history, and traits.

multistore model of memory A model of memory that portrays the encoding, storage, and retrieval of information as involving three separate though interacting memory systems: sensory memory, short-term memory, and long-term memory.

myelin sheath A fatty insulating sheath surrounding many axons.

narcissism (n.); narcissistic (adj.) An exaggerated sense of self-importance and self-absorption.

naturalistic observation The observation of subjects in their natural environment.

need for achievement (achievement motivation) A learned motive to meet personal standards of success and excellence in a chosen area (often abbreviated *nAch*).

need for affiliation The motive to associate with other people, as by seeking friends, moral support, contact comfort, or companionship.

need for competence The motive to be capable in one's activities and to master new situations.

need for power A learned motive to dominate or control others.

negative afterimage A visual image that persists after a visual stimulus is withdrawn and has features that contrast with those of the stimulus (e.g., a contrasting color).

negative correlation An association between increases in one variable and decreases in another.

negative reinforcement A reinforcement procedure in which a response is followed by the removal, delay, or decrease in intensity of an unpleasant stimulus; as a result, the response becomes stronger or more likely to occur.

nerve A bundle of nerve fibers (axons) in the peripheral nervous system.

neuron Cell that conducts electrochemical signals; basic unit of the nervous system. Also called a *nerve cell*.

neuropsychology The field of psychology that studies the neural and biochemical bases of behavior and mental processes.

neuroscience An interdisciplinary field of study concerned with the structure, function, development, and biochemistry of the nervous system.

neurosis; neuroses (pl.) To Freud, a psychological disorder characterized by self-punishing, maladaptive behavior, emotional symptoms, or physical symptoms that protect a person against unconscious anxiety. It is no longer used as a clinical diagnosis.

neurotransmitter Chemical substance that is released by a transmitting neuron at the synapse and that alters the activity of a receiving neuron.

nonconscious process A mental process occurring outside of and not available to conscious awareness.

normal curve A symmetrical, bell-shaped frequency polygon representing a normal distribution.

normal distribution A theoretical frequency distribution having certain special characteristics. For example, the distribution is symmetrical, the mean, mode, and median all have the same value, and the farther a score is from the mean the less the likelihood of obtaining it.

norms In test construction, established standards of performance; they are usually determined by giving the test to a large group of people who are representative of the population for whom the test is intended.

norms (social) *See* rules.

null hypothesis An assertion that the independent variable in a study will have no effect on the dependent variable.

obedience Behavior performed in following an order from someone in authority.

object permanence The understanding that an object continues to exist even when you can't see it or touch it.

observational learning A learning process in which an individual learns new responses by observing the behavior of another (a model) rather than through direct experience. Sometimes called *vicarious conditioning*.

obsessions Recurrent, unwished-for, persistent thoughts and images.

Oedipus complex In psychoanalysis, a conflict in which a child desires the parent of the opposite sex and views the same-sex parent as a rival; this is the key issue in the phallic or Oedipal stage of development.

olfaction The sense of smell.

operant conditioning The process by which a response becomes more or less likely to occur, depending on its consequences. Also called *instrumental conditioning*.

operational definition A precise definition of a term in a hypothesis that specifies how it is to be observed and measured.

operations In Jean Piaget's theory, mental actions that are cognitively reversible.

opiates Drugs, derived from the opium poppy, that relieve pain and commonly produce euphoria.

opponent-process cells Cells in the visual system that fire in response to one color and are inhibited from firing by another.

opponent-process theory (of color) A theory that assumes that the visual system treats various pairs of colors as opposing or antagonistic.

optic nerve The nerve connecting the retina of the eye with the brain.

organic school (of emotion) Scientists and philosophers who seek biological explanations of emotion—for example, in facial expressions, brain centers, or levels of physiological arousal.

panic attack A brief feeling of intense fear and impending doom or death, accompanied by intense physiological symptoms such as rapid breathing and pulse, sweaty palms, and dizziness.

paradigm A model, theory, or set of beliefs and assumptions, shared by a community of scientists, that guides the questions they study and the methods they use.

paranoia (n.); paranoid (adj.) Unreasonable and excessive suspiciousness, jealousy, or mistrust. It may occur as a type of personality disorder or, with more severe symptoms of psychosis, as a type of schizophrenic disorder.

parapsychology The study of unusual psychological phenomena, such as ESP and precognition, that do not appear explainable by known scientific laws.

parasympathetic nervous system Subdivision of the autonomic nervous system that operates during relaxed states and conserves energy.

pathogenic Causing disease or suffering.

Pavlovian conditioning *See* classical conditioning.

peak experience An intense occasion of the highest fulfillment and happiness.

percentile score A number that indicates the percentage of people who scored at or below a given raw score.

perception The process by which the brain organizes and interprets sensory information.

perceptual constancy The accurate perception of objects as stable or unchanged despite changes in the sensory patterns they produce.

perceptual illusion An erroneous or misleading perception of reality.

perceptual set A habitual way of perceiving, based on expectations.

peripheral nervous system All portions of the nervous system outside the brain and spinal cord. Includes sensory and motor nerves.

personality A distinctive and relatively stable pattern of behavior, thoughts, motives, and emotions that characterizes an individual.

personality disorders Psychological disorders in which rigid, maladaptive personality patterns cause personal distress or inability to get along with others.

PET scan (positron-emission tomography) A method for analyzing biochemical activity in the brain using injections of a glucoselike substance containing a radioactive element.

phenomenology The study of events and situations as individuals experience them; in personality, the study of an individual's qualities from the person's own point of view.

pheromone A chemical substance that, when released by an organism, influences the physiology or behavior of other members of the same species.

phobia An intense, unrealistic fear of an object, activity, or situation.

physiological psychology An approach to psychology that emphasizes bodily events and changes associated with feelings, actions, and thoughts.

pitch The dimension of auditory experience related to the frequency of a pressure wave; height or depth of a tone.

pituitary gland A small endocrine gland at the base of the brain that releases many hormones and regulates other endocrine glands.

placebo An inactive substance or fake treatment used as a control in an experiment or given by a medical practitioner to a patient; people sometimes respond to a placebo as they would to an active substance or real treatment.

pleasure principle In psychoanalytic theory, the principle guiding the operation of the id; seeks to reduce tension, avoid pain, and enhance pleasure.

population The entire set of individuals from which a sample is drawn.

positive correlation An association between increases in one variable and increases in another.

positive reinforcement A reinforcement procedure in which a response is followed by the presentation of, or increase in intensity of, a reinforcing stimulus; as a result, the response becomes stronger or more likely to occur.

prejudice An unjustified negative attitude toward a group of people or a custom.

primacy effect The tendency for items at the beginning of a list to be well recalled.

primary control An effort to modify external reality by changing other people, the situation, or events; a ''fighting-back'' method of coping.

primary emotions Emotions that are considered to be universal and biologically based. They generally include fear, anger, sadness, joy, and disgust.

primary punisher A stimulus that is inherently punishing; an example is electric shock.

primary reinforcer A stimulus that is inherently reinforcing, typically satisfying a physiological need; an example is food.

proactive interference Forgetting that occurs when previously stored material interferes with the ability to remember similar, more recently learned material.

procedural memories Memories for the performance of particular types of actions.

progesterone A hormone essential in the maintenance of pregnancy.

projection In psychoanalytic theory, a defense mechanism in which one's unacceptable feelings are attributed to someone else.

projective tests Psychological tests used to infer a person's motives, thoughts, perceptions, and conflicts on the basis of the person's interpretations of ambiguous or unstructured stimuli.

proposition A unit of meaning that expresses a unitary idea and is made up of concepts.

psychedelic drugs Consciousness-altering drugs that produce hallucinations, change thought processes, or disrupt the normal perception of time and space.

psychiatry The medical study, diagnosis, treatment, and prevention of mental disorders.

psychoactive drug A drug capable of influencing perception, mood, cognition, or behavior.

psychoanalysis An approach to psychology that emphasizes unconscious motives and conflicts. It encompasses both a theory of personality and a method of psychotherapy.

psychoanalyst A person who has had special training in the theory and practice of psychoanalysis.

psychoanalytic method In psychoanalytic therapy, the effort to bring unconscious material into consciousness, usually through dream recall and free association.

psychodynamic A word referring to psychological theories that explain behavior in terms of forces located in the individual, such as drives, motives, or, in psychoanalysis, instinctual energy.

psycholinguistics The study of the acquisition, comprehension, and production of language.

psychological assessment The measurement and evaluation of abilities, aptitudes, and personality characteristics.

psychological stress The result of a relationship between the person and the environment, in which the person believes the situation is overwhelming and threatens his or her ability to cope.

psychological tests Procedures used to measure personality traits, emotional states, aptitudes, interests, abilities, and values.

psychology The scientific study of behavior and mental processes and how they are affected by an organism's physical state, mental state, and external environment. The term is often represented by Ψ, the Greek letter *psi* (pronounced SY).

psychometrics The measurement of mental abilities, traits, and processes.

psychoneuroimmunology [psycho/neuro/immu/nology] The field that studies the relationships among psychology, the nervous system, and the immune system.

psychophysics The area of psychology concerned with the relationship between physical properties of stimuli and sensory experience.

psychosis; psychoses (pl.) An extreme mental disturbance involving distorted perceptions of reality and irrational behavior. It may have either psychological or organic causes.

psychosomatic A term that describes the interaction between a physical illness or condition and psychological states; literally, mind *(psyche)* and body *(soma)*.

psychosurgery Any surgical procedure that destroys selected areas of the brain believed to be involved in emotional disorders or violent, impulsive behavior. *(See,* e.g., lobotomy.)

psychotherapist A person who practices psychotherapy; may be a clinical psychologist, psychiatrist, counselor, social worker, or other mental health professional.

psychotherapy The treatment of mental disorders, emotional problems, and personality difficulties. There are dozens of different kinds of psychotherapy.

puberty The age at which a person becomes capable of sexual reproduction.

punisher Any stimulus or event that weakens or reduces the probability of the response that it follows.

punishment The process by which a stimulus or event weakens or reduces the probability of the response that it follows.

pupil A round opening in the eye through which light passes.

random assignment   A procedure for assigning people to experimental and control groups in which each individual has the same probability as any other of being assigned to a given group.

range   A simple measure of variability, calculated by subtracting the lowest score in a distribution from the highest one.

rapid eye movement (REM) sleep   Sleep periods characterized by eye movement, loss of muscle tone, and dreaming.

reactance   A negative emotional state produced by a real or imagined threat to one's freedom of choice.

reaction formation   In psychoanalytic theory, a defense mechanism that transforms an unconscious emotion into its conscious opposite; e.g., hatred into love.

reality principle   In psychoanalytic theory, the principle guiding the operation of the ego; it seeks to find socially acceptable outlets for instinctual energies.

reasoning   The drawing of conclusions or inferences from observations, facts, or assumptions.

recall   The ability to retrieve and reproduce from memory previously encountered material.

recency effect   The tendency for items at the end of a list to be well recalled.

recognition   The ability to identify previously encountered material.

reflex   An automatic reaction to a stimulus; often inborn but can also be learned or modified by experience.

reflex arc   The neural circuitry underlying a reflex.

regression   In psychoanalytic theory, a defense mechanism in which a person returns to an earlier stage of development, behaving in immature ways.

rehearsal   The review or practice of material for the purpose of improving subsequent retention.

reinforcement   The process by which a stimulus or event strengthens or increases the probability of the response that it follows.

reinforcer   Any stimulus or event that strengthens or increases the probability of the response that it follows.

relearning method   A method to measure retention that compares the time required to relearn material with the time used in initial learning of the material.

reliability   In test construction, the consistency of test scores from one time and/or place to another.

replicate   To duplicate or repeat.

representative sample   A sample that matches the population in question on important characteristics such as age and sex.

repression   In psychoanalytic theory, a basic defense mechanism that keeps taboo or painful thoughts or emotions from consciousness.

reticular activating system (RAS)   A dense network of neurons found in the core of the brain stem; arouses the cortex and screens incoming information.

retina   A membrane lining the back of the eyeball's interior that contains the receptors for vision.

retinal disparity   The slight difference in lateral separation between two objects as seen by the left eye and the right eye.

retrieval   Recovery of material that has been stored in memory.

retroactive interference   Forgetting that occurs when recently learned material interferes with the ability to remember similar material stored previously.

retrograde amnesia   Loss of the ability to remember events or experiences that occurred before some particular time.

rods   Visual receptors that respond to dim light but are not involved in color vision.

role   A given social position that is governed by a set of norms for proper behavior.

Rorschach [ROR-shock] Inkblot Test   A projective personality test that asks respondents to interpret abstract, symmetrical inkblots.

rules (norms)   Social conventions that regulate human life, including explicit laws and implicit cultural standards.

salutogenic   Causing health.

sample   A group of subjects selected from a population for study in order to estimate characteristics of the population.

saturation   Vividness or purity of color; the dimension of visual experience related to the complexity of light waves.

scapegoat   A powerless target of an individual's or group's prejudice that is made to bear the blame for personal or social problems.

schizophrenia   A psychotic disorder marked by some or all of these symptoms: delusions, hallucinations, incoherent word associations, inappropriate emotions, or lack of emotions.

school psychology   An applied branch of psychology concerned with enhancing students' performance and emotional development.

secondary control   An effort to accept external reality by changing one's own attitudes, goals, or emotions; a ''learn to live with it'' method of coping.

secondary emotions   Emotions that are either ''blends'' of primary emotions (e.g., contempt as a blend of anger and disgust) or that are specific to certain cultures (e.g., the Tahitian sense of the ''uncanny'').

secondary punisher   A stimulus that has acquired punishing properties through association with other punishers: also called *conditioned punisher*.

secondary reinforcer   A stimulus that has acquired reinforcing properties through association with other reinforcers: also called *conditioned reinforcer*.

selective attention   The focusing of attention on selected aspects of the environment and blocking out of others.

self-fulfilling prophecy   The tendency to act on one's expectations in such a way as to make the expectations come true.

self-serving bias   The tendency of people to take credit for good actions and to excuse or rationalize their mistakes.

semantic memories   Memories that reveal general knowledge, including facts, rules, concepts, and propositions.

semicircular canals   Sense organs in the inner ear that contribute to equilibrium by responding to rotation of the head.

senility   A loss of mental abilities; once thought to be inevitable in old age, it is now known to result often from disease or malnutrition.

sensation   The detection or direct experience of physical energy in the external or internal environment due to stimulation of receptors in the sense organs.

sense organs   Parts of the body that contain the sense receptors.

sense receptors   Specialized cells that convert physical energy in the environment into electrical energy that can be transmitted as nerve impulses to the brain.

sensitive period   A period in the development of an organism that is optimal for the acquisition of a particular behavior.

sensory adaptation   The reduction or disappearance of sensory responsiveness that occurs when stimulation is unchanging or repetitious.

sensory deprivation   The absence of normal levels of sensory stimulation.

sensory memory   A memory system that momentarily preserves literal images of sensory information.

sensory nerves   Nerves in the peripheral nervous system that carry sensory messages toward the central nervous system.

sensory registers   Subsystems of sensory memory. Most memory models assume a separate register for each sensory modality.

serial position effect   The tendency for recall of the first and last items on a list to surpass recall of items in the middle of the list.

set point   According to one theory, a homeostatic mechanism that regulates food intake, fat reserves, and metabolism to keep an organism at its predetermined weight.

sex typing   The process by which children learn the behaviors, attitudes, and expectations associated in their culture with being ''masculine'' or ''feminine.''

shaping   An operant conditioning procedure in which successive approximations of a desired response are reinforced. Used when the desired response has a low probability of occurring spontaneously.

short-term memory (STM)   A limited capacity memory system involved in the retention of information for brief periods. It is used to store recently perceived information and information retrieved from long-term memory for temporary use.

signal detectability theory   A psychophysical theory that divides the detection of a sensory signal into a sensory process and a decision process.

single-blind study   An experiment in which subjects do not know whether they are in an experimental or control group.

situational attribution   An explanation of one's own or another's behavior that relies on something in the environment or circumstance.

''social clock''   A society's timetable for the ''right'' ages to marry, have children, start work, retire, and have other adult experiences.

social cognition   An area in social psychology that studies social influences on thought, memory, perception, and other cognitive processes.

social interest   To Alfred Adler, the ability to feel empathy, to cooperate, and to be connected to others.

socialization   The process by which a child acquires the rules, standards, and values of his or her family and culture.

social learning theory   The theory that human social behavior is learned through observation and imitation of others and is maintained by positive consequences.

social loafing   The tendency of group members, under some conditions, to reduce their efforts and ''loaf''; one result of the diffusion of responsibility.

social motives   Learned motives, such as the need for affiliation, power, competence, or achievement, that are acquired from social experiences.

social psychology   The field of psychology that studies individuals in a social context.

sociobiology   A school of thought that attempts to account for social behavior in terms of genetic predispositions and evolutionary principles.

sociocultural perspective   An approach to psychology that emphasizes social and cultural influences on behavior.

sociology   The study of the organization, development, and institutions of human society.

somatic nervous system   The subdivision of the peripheral nervous system that controls skeletal muscles. Also called *skeletal nervous system*.

somatoform disorders   Physical disorders that have no demonstrable medical cause. They include somatization disorder, conversion disorder, and hypochondria.

spinal cord   A collection of neurons and supportive tissue running from the base of the brain through the spinal column.

split-half reliability   The consistency of test scores when scores on two halves of a test are compared.

spontaneous recovery   The sudden reappearance of a learned response after its apparent extinction.

standard deviation   A commonly used measure of variability that indicates the average difference between scores in a distribution and their mean; more precisely, the square root of the average squared deviation from the mean.

standardize   In test construction, to develop uniform procedures for giving and scoring a test.

state-dependent memory   The tendency to remember something when one is in the same physical or mental state as during the original learning or experience.

states of consciousness   Distinctive and discrete patterns in the functioning of consciousness, characterized by particular modes of perception, thought, memory, or feeling.

statistically significant   The term used to refer to a result that is extremely unlikely to have occurred by chance.

stereotype A cognitive schema or a summary impression of a group, in which a person believes that all members of the group share a common trait or traits (positive, negative, or neutral).

stimulants Drugs that speed up activity in the central nervous system.

stimulus; stimuli (pl.) An event or change in the environment that causes, elicits, or leads to a response.

stimulus control Control over the occurrence of a response by a discriminative stimulus.

stimulus discrimination The tendency to respond differently to two or more similar stimuli that differ on some dimension. In classical conditioning, occurs when a stimulus similar to the conditioned stimulus fails to evoke the conditioned response. In operant conditioning, occurs when an organism learns to make a response in the presence of one stimulus but not in the presence of other, similar stimuli.

stimulus generalization After conditioning, the tendency to respond to a stimulus that resembles one involved in the original conditioning. In classical conditioning, it occurs when a stimulus that resembles the conditioned stimulus elicits the conditioned response. In operant conditioning, it occurs when a response that has been reinforced (or punished) in the presence of one stimulus tends to occur (or be suppressed) in the presence of other, similar stimuli.

storage Retention of material in memory.

stress *See* psychological stress; eustress.

structuralism An early approach to psychology that stressed the analysis of immediate experience into basic elements.

subconscious process A mental process occurring outside of conscious awareness but accessible to consciousness when necessary.

subjects Animals or human beings used in research.

sublimation In psychoanalytic theory, a type of displacement that serves a higher cultural or social purpose; e.g., the creation of art or music as sublimation of sexual energy.

superego In psychoanalysis, the part of personality that represents conscience, morality, and social standards.

surveys Questionnaires and interviews that ask people directly about their experiences, attitudes, or opinions.

sympathetic nervous system The subdivision of the autonomic nervous system that mobilizes bodily resources and increases the output of energy during emotion and stress.

synapse Microscopic gap between neurons at which transmission of nerve impulses occurs; from the Greek for "point of contact" or "joined together."

synaptic vesicles Chambers at the tip of an axon that contain neurotransmitter molecules.

syntax The set of grammatical rules governing the way words combine to form sentences.

systematic desensitization A variation of *counterconditioning* used in behavior therapy to eliminate fears; involves exposing a person to a hierarchy of fear- or anxiety-producing stimuli while the person is in a relaxed state.

taste buds Nests of taste receptor cells.

telegraphic speech A child's first combinations of words, which omit (as a telegram does) nonessential words.

temperaments Characteristic styles of responding to the environment that are present in infancy and are assumed to be innate.

test-retest reliability The consistency of test scores when a test is given to the same person or group on more than one occasion.

thalamus A brain structure that relays sensory messages to the cerebral cortex.

Thematic Apperception Test (TAT) A projective personality test that asks respondents to interpret a series of pictures showing ambiguous scenes.

theory An organized system of assumptions and principles that purports to explain a specified set of phenomena and their interrelationships.

thinking The mental manipulation of information stored in the form of concepts, images, or propositions.

timbre The distinguishing quality of a sound; the dimension of auditory experience related to the complexity of the pressure wave.

tip-of-the-tongue (TOT) state The subjective certainty that information is available in long-term memory even though one is having difficulty retrieving it.

token economy A behavior modification technique in which secondary reinforcers called *tokens* are used as reinforcers. The tokens can eventually be exchanged for primary or other secondary reinforcers.

tolerance The increasing resistance to a drug's effects with continued use; as tolerance develops, larger doses are required to produce effects once brought on by smaller ones.

trait A descriptive characteristic of an individual, assumed to be stable across situations.

transduction The conversion of one form of energy to another. Sensory receptors are biological transducers.

transference In psychoanalysis, a critical step in which the patient transfers emotional feelings for his or her parents to the therapist.

trichromatic theory A theory that proposes three mechanisms in the visual system, each sensitive to a certain range of wavelengths; their interaction is assumed to produce all the different experiences of hue.

two-factor theory of emotion The theory that emotions depend on both physiological arousal and a cognitive interpretation or evaluation of that arousal.

ultradian [ul-TRAY-dee-un] rhythm A biological rhythm that occurs more frequently than once a day; from the Latin for "beyond a day."

unconditional positive regard To Carl Rogers, love or support given to another person with no conditions attached.

unconditioned response (UR) The classical conditioning term for a reflexive response elicited by a stimulus in the absence of learning.

unconditioned stimulus (US) The classical conditioning term for a stimulus that elicits a reflexive response in the absence of learning.

unconscious processes   Mental processes, such as motives, desires, and memories, not available to awareness or to conscious introspection; sometimes called ''the unconscious,'' as a metaphor for the part of the mind below conscious awareness.

validity   In test construction, the ability of a test to measure what it was designed to measure.

variability   *See* measure of variability.

variable-interval (VI) schedule   An intermittent schedule of reinforcement in which a reinforcer is delivered for a response made after a variable period of time has elapsed since the last reinforcer.

variable-ratio (VR) schedule   An intermittent schedule of reinforcement in which reinforcement occurs after a variable number of responses.

variables   Characteristics of behavior or experience that can be measured or described by a numeric scale. Variables are manipulated and assessed in scientific studies.

variance   A measure of the dispersion of scores around the mean. (*See also* measure of variability.)

volunteer bias   A shortcoming of findings derived from a sample of volunteers instead of a representative sample.

Weber's Law   A law of psychophysics stating that the change necessary to produce a just-noticeable-difference is a constant proportion of the original stimulus.

withdrawal symptoms   Physical and psychological symptoms that occur when someone addicted to a drug stops taking it.

z-score (standard score)   A number that indicates how far a given raw score is above or below the mean, using the standard deviation of the distribution as the unit of measurement.

BIBLIOGRAPHY

Abel, Gene; Becker, Judith; et al. (1984). Treatment manual for child molesters. Unpublished manuscript, Columbia University.

Abelson, Robert P. (1988). Conviction. *American Psychologist, 43*, 267–275.

Abramis, David J. (1987). Fun at work: Does it matter? Paper presented at the annual meeting of the American Psychological Association, New York.

Abrams, David B., & Wilson, G. Terence (1983). Alcohol, sexual arousal, and self-control. *Journal of Personality and Social Psychology, 45*, 188–198.

Abramson, Lyn Y.; Seligman, Martin E. P.; & Teasdale, John (1978). Learned helplessness in humans: Critique and reformulation. *Journal of Abnormal Psychology, 87*, 49–74.

Acredolo, Linda, & Goodwyn, Susan (1988). Symbolic gesturing in normal infants. *Child Development, 59*, 450–466.

Adams, Gerald R.; Ryan, John H.; Hoffman, Joseph J.; Dobson, William R.; & Nielsen, Elwin C. (1985). Ego identity status, conformity behavior, and personality in late adolescence. *Journal of Personality and Social Psychology, 47*, 1091–1104.

Adams, James L. (1986). *Conceptual blockbusting: A guide to better ideas* (3rd ed.). Boston: Addison-Wesley.

Adler, Alfred (1927/1959). *Understanding human nature.* New York: Premier.

Adler, Alfred (1935). The fundamental views of individual psychology. *International Journal of Individual Psychology, 1*, 5–8.

Adler, Alfred (1938/1964). *Social interest: A challenge to mankind.* New York: Capricorn.

Agras, Stewart (1985). *Panic: Facing fears, phobias, and anxiety.* New York: Freeman.

Ainsworth, Mary D. S. (1973). The development of infant-mother attachment. In B. M. Caldwell & H. N. Ricciuti (eds.), *Review of child development research*, Vol. 3. Chicago: University of Chicago Press.

Ainsworth, Mary D. S. (1979). Infant-mother attachment. *American Psychologist, 34*, 932–937.

Ainsworth, Mary D. S.; Blehar, Mary L.; Waters, Everett; & Wall, Sally (1978). *Patterns of attachment.* Hillsdale, NJ: Erlbaum.

Alagna, Sheryle W., & Hamilton, Jean A. (1986). Science in the service of mythology: The psychopathologizing of menstruation. Paper presented at the annual meeting of the American Psychological Association, Washington.

Albee, George W. (1977). The Protestant ethic, sex, and psychotherapy. *American Psychologist, 32*, 150–161.

Albee, George W. (1982). Preventing psychopathology and promoting human potential. *American Psychologist, 37*, 1043–1050.

Albee, George W. (1985, February). The answer is prevention. *Psychology Today*, 60–64.

Albrecht, Terrance, & Adelman, Mara (1984). Social support and life stress. *Human Communication Research, 11*, 3–32.

Alkon, Daniel L. (1984). Calcium-mediated reduction of ionic currents: A biophysical memory trace. *Science, 226*, 1037–1045.

Allen, George S.; Burns, R. Stanley; Tulipan, Noel B.; & Parker, Robert A. (in press). Adrenal medullary transplantation to the caudate nucleus in Parkinson's disease. *Archives of Neurology*.

Allen, L. S.; Gorski, R. A.; Shin, J.; Barakat, N.; & Hines, M. (1987). Sex differences in the corpus callosum of the living human being. *Anatomical Record, 218*, 7A [Abstract].

Allen, Steven N. (1985). Imaginative involvement and hypnotizability in children. Paper presented at the annual meeting of the American Psychological Association, Los Angeles.

Allman, William F. (1986, May). Mindworks. *Science 86, 7*(3), 23–31.

Alloy, Lauren; Abramson, Lyn; Metalsky, Gerald; &

Hartlage, Shirley (1988). The hopelessness theory of depression: Attributional aspects. *British Journal of Clinical Psychology, 27*, 5–21.

Allport, Gordon (1937). *Personality: A psychological interpretation.* New York: Holt, Rinehart and Winston.

Allport, Gordon (1961). *Pattern and growth in personality.* New York: Holt, Rinehart and Winston.

Allport, Gordon (1979). *The nature of prejudice.* Reading, MA: Addison-Wesley.

Alper, Joseph S. (1985). Sex differences in brain asymmetry: A critical analysis. *Feminist Studies, 11*(1), 7–37.

Altrocchi, John (1980). *Abnormal behavior.* New York: Harcourt Brace Jovanovich.

Alwin, Duane (1988). Historical changes in parental orientations to children. In N. Mandell & S. Cahill (eds.), *Sociological studies of child development.* Greenwich, CT: JAI Press.

Alwin, Duane, & Converse, Philip (1984). Living alone. Institute for Social Research newsletter, University of Michigan.

Amabile, Teresa M. (1983). *The social psychology of creativity.* New York: Springer-Verlag.

Amabile, Teresa M. (1985). Motivation and creativity: Effects of motivational orientation on creative writers. *Journal of Personality and Social Psychology, 48*, 393–399.

American Psychiatric Association (1987). *Diagnostic and statistical manual of mental disorders* (3rd ed., rev.). Washington, DC: American Psychiatric Association.

American Psychological Association (1984). Survey of the use of animals in behavioral research at U.S. universities. Washington, DC: American Psychological Association.

Amoore, John E. (1977). Specific anosmia and the concept of primary odors. *Chemical Senses and Flavor, 2*, 267–281.

Anand, B. K.; Chinna, G. S.; & Singh, Baldev (1961). Studies on Shri Ramananda Yogi during his stay in an airtight box. *Indian Journal of Medical Research, 49*, 82–89.

Anastasi, Anne (1964). *Fields of applied psychology.* New York: McGraw-Hill.

Anastasi, Anne (1988). *Psychological testing* (6th ed.). New York: Macmillan.

Andersen, Susan M. (1984). Self-knowledge and social inference: II. The diagnosticity of cognitive/affective and behavioral data. *Journal of Personality and Social Psychology, 46*, 294–307.

Andersen, Susan M., & Ross, Lee (1984). Self-knowledge and social inference: I. The impact of cognitive/affective and behavioral data. *Journal of Personality and Social Psychology, 46*, 280–293.

Anderson, Craig A.; Horowitz, Leonard M.; & French, Rita (1983). Attributional style of lonely and depressed people. *Journal of Personality and Social Psychology, 45*, 127–136.

Anderson, James A., & Rosenfeld, Edward (eds.) (1988). *Neurocomputing: Foundations of research.* Cambridge, MA: MIT Press.

Anderson, John R. (1976). *Language, memory and thought.* Hillsdale, NJ: Erlbaum.

Anderson, John R., & Bower, Gordon H. (1973). *Human associative memory.* Washington, DC: Winston.

Angell, Marcia (1985, June 13). Disease as a reflection of the psyche. *New England Journal of Medicine, 312*, 1570–1572.

Annis, Robert C., & Frost, Barrie (1973). Human visual ecology and orientation antistropies in acuity. *Science, 182*, 729–731.

Ansbacher, Heinz (1968). The concept of social interest. *Journal of Individual Psychology, 24*, 131–149.

Ansbacher, Heinz, & Ansbacher, Rowena (eds.) (1964). *The individual psychology of Alfred Adler.* New York: Harper Torchbooks.

Antonovsky, Aaron (1979). *Health, stress, and coping.* San Francisco: Jossey-Bass.

Antonovsky, Aaron (1984, Summer). The sense of coherence as a determinant of health. *Advances, 1*, 36–51.

Arendt, Hannah (1963). *Eichmann in Jerusalem: A report on the banality of evil.* New York: Viking.

Arendt, Josephine; Aldhous, Margaret; & Wright, John (1988, April 2). Synchronisation of a disturbed sleep-wake cycle in a blind man by melatonin treatment. *Lancet, 1*(8588), 772–773.

Arendt, Thomas; Allen, Yvonne; Sinden, John; et al. (1988, March 31). Cholinergic-rich brain transplants reverse alcohol-induced memory deficits. *Nature, 332*, 448–450.

Arnstein, Robert L. (1984). Young adulthood: Stages of maturity. In D. Offer & M. Sabshin (eds.), *Normality and the life cycle.* New York: Basic Books.

Aronfreed, Justin (1969). The concept of internalization. In D. A. Goslin (ed.), *Handbook of socialization theory and research.* Chicago: Rand McNally.

Aronson, Elliot (1988). *The social animal* (5th ed.). New York: Freeman.

Aronson, Elliot, & Mills, Judson (1959). The effect of severity of initiation on liking for a group. *Journal of Abnormal and Social Psychology, 59*, 177–181.

Aronson, Elliot; Stephan, Cookie; Sikes, Jev; Blaney, Nancy; & Snapp, Matthew (1978). *The jigsaw classroom.* Beverly Hills, CA: Sage.

Asch, Solomon E. (1946). Forming impressions of personality. *Journal of Abnormal and Social Psychology, 41*, 258–290.

Asch, Solomon E. (1952). *Social psychology.* Englewood Cliffs, NJ: Prentice-Hall.

Asch, Solomon E. (1965). Effects of group pressure upon the modification and distortion of judgments. In H. Proshansky & B. Seidenberg (eds.), *Basic studies in social psychology.* New York: Holt, Rinehart and Winston.

Asch, Solomon, & Zukier, Henri (1984). Thinking about persons. *Journal of Personality and Social Psychology, 46*, 1230–1241.

Aschoff, Jurgen, & Wever, Rutger (1981). The circadian system of man. In J. Aschoff (ed.), *Handbook of behavioral neurobiology, Vol. 4: Biological rhythms.* New York: Plenum.

Aserinsky, Eugene, & Kleitman, Nathaniel (1955). Two types of ocular motility occurring in sleep. *Journal of Applied Physiology, 8,* 1–10.

Ash, Peter, & Guyer, Melvin (1986). A follow-up study of children in contested custody evaluations. Paper presented at the annual meeting of the American Academy of Psychiatry and the Law, Philadelphia.

Atchley, Robert C. (1975). Dimensions of widowhood in later life. *The Gerontologist, 15,* 176–178.

Atkinson, John W. (ed.) (1958). *Motives in fantasy, action, and society.* Princeton, NJ: Van Nostrand.

Atkinson, John W., & Raynor, Joel O. (eds.) (1974). *Personality, motivation, and achievement.* Washington, DC: Winston.

Atkinson, Richard C. (1977). Reflections on psychology's past and concerns about its future. *American Psychologist, 32,* 205–210.

Atkinson, Richard C., & Shiffrin, Richard M. (1968). Human memory: A proposed system and its control processes. In K. W. Spence & J. T. Spence (eds.), *The psychology of learning and motivation: Advances in research and theory,* Vol. 2. New York: Academic Press.

Atkinson, Richard C., & Shiffrin, Richard M. (1971, August). The control of short-term memory. *Scientific American, 225*(2), 82–90.

Averill, James R. (1980). On the paucity of positive emotions. In K. R. Blankenstein, P. Pliner, & J. Polivy (eds.), *Assessment and modification of emotional behavior.* New York: Plenum.

Averill, James R. (1982). *Anger and aggression.* New York: Springer-Verlag.

Averill, James R.; DeWitt, Gary W.; & Zimmer, Michael (1978). The self-attribution of emotion as a function of success and failure. *Journal of Personality, 46,* 323–347.

Ayllon, Teodoro, & Azrin, Nathan H. (1968). *The token economy.* New York: Appleton-Century-Crofts.

Azrin, Nathan H., & Foxx, Richard M. (1974). *Toilet training in less than a day.* New York: Simon & Schuster.

Azuma, Hiroshi (1984). Secondary control as a heterogeneous category. *American Psychologist, 39,* 970–971.

Bahrick, Harry P. (1984). Semantic memory content in permastore: Fifty years of memory for Spanish learned in school. *Journal of Experimental Psychology: General, 113*(1), 1–29.

Bahrick, Harry P.; Bahrick, Phyllis O.; & Wittlinger, Roy P. (1974, December). Long-term memory: Those unforgettable high-school days. *Psychology Today, 8*(7), 50–52, 55–56.

Bahrick, Harry P.; Bahrick, Phyllis O.; & Wittlinger, Roy P. (1975). Fifty years of memory for names and faces: A cross-sectional approach. *Journal of Experimental Psychology: General, 104,* 54–75.

Bailey, Ronald H. (1975). *The role of the brain.* New York: Time-Life Books.

Balay, Jennifer, & Shevrin, Howard (1988). The sublimi-nal psychodynamic activation method: A critical review. *American Psychologist, 43,* 161–174.

Baldessarini, Ross J. (1979). The neuroleptic antipsychotic drugs. *Postgraduate Medicine, 65,* 108–128.

Baltes, Paul B. (1983). Life-span developmental psychology: Observations on history and theory revisited. In R. M. Lerner (ed.), *Developmental psychology: Historical and philosophical perspectives.* Hillsdale, NJ: Erlbaum.

Baltes, Paul B.; Cornelius, S. W.; & Nesselroade, John R. (1979). Cohort effects in developmental psychology. In J. R. Nesselroade & P. B. Baltes (eds.), *Longitudinal research in the study of behavior and development.* New York: Academic Press.

Baltes, Paul B.; Dittmann-Kohli, Freya; & Dixon, Roger A. (1984). New perspectives on the development of intelligence in adulthood: Toward a dual-process conception and a model of selective optimization with compensation. In P. B. Baltes & O. G. Brim, Jr. (eds.), *Life-span development and behavior,* Vol. 6. New York: Academic Press.

Baltes, Paul B., & Willis, Sherry L. (1982). Plasticity and enhancement of intellectual functioning in old age. In F. I. M. Craik and S. Trehub (eds.), *Aging and cognitive processes.* New York: Plenum.

Bandura, Albert (1969). Social-learning theory of identificatory processes. In D. A. Goslin (ed.), *Handbook of socialization theory and research.* Chicago: Rand McNally.

Bandura, Albert (1973). *Aggression: A social learning analysis.* Englewood Cliffs, NJ: Prentice-Hall.

Bandura, Albert (1977a). Self-efficacy: Toward a unifying theory of behavioral change. *Psychological Review, 84,* 191–215.

Bandura, Albert (1977b). *Social learning theory.* Englewood Cliffs, NJ: Prentice-Hall.

Bandura, Albert (1986). *Social foundations of thought and action: A social cognitive theory.* Englewood Cliffs, NJ: Prentice-Hall.

Bandura, Albert; Ross, Dorothea; & Ross, Sheila A. (1963). Vicarious reinforcement and imitative learning. *Journal of Abnormal and Social Psychology, 67,* 601–607.

Banks, Martin S. (in collaboration with Philip Salapatek) (1984). Infant visual perception. In P. Mussen (ed.), *Handbook of child psychology* (4th ed.). Vol. II, M. M. Haith & J. J. Campos (eds.), *Infancy and developmental psychobiology.* New York: Wiley.

Bányai, Éva I., & Hilgard, Ernest R. (1976). Comparison of active-alert hypnotic induction with traditional relaxation induction. *Journal of Abnormal Psychology, 85,* 218–224.

Barber, Theodore X. (1970, July). Who believes in hypnosis? *Psychology Today, 4*(2), 20, 24, 26–27, 84.

Barber, Theodore X. (1979). Suggested ("hypnotic") behavior: The trance paradigm versus an alternative paradigm. In E. Fromm and R. E. Shor (eds.), *Hypnosis: Developments in research and new perspectives* (2nd ed.). New York: Aldine.

Barber, Theodore X., & Wilson, Sheryl C. (1977). Hypnosis, suggestions, and altered states of consciousness: Experimental evaluation of a new cognitive-behavioral theory and the traditional trance-state therapy of "hypnosis." *Annals of the New York Academy of Sciences, 296*, 34–47.

Barlow, David H. (1988). *Anxiety and its disorders*. New York: Guilford Press.

Barnett, Peter A., & Gotlib, Ian H. (1988). Psychosocial functioning and depression: Distinguishing among antecedents, concomitants, and consequences. *Psychological Bulletin, 104*, 97–126.

Barnett, Rosalind, & Baruch, Grace (1987). Social roles, gender, and psychological distress. In R. Barnett, L. Biener, & G. Baruch (eds.), *Gender & stress*. New York: Free Press.

Baron, Miron; Risch, Neil; Hamburger, Rahel; Mandel, Batsheva; et al. (1987, March 19). Genetic linkage between X-chromosome markers and bipolar affective illness. *Nature, 326*, 289–292.

Baron, Robert A. (1977). *Human aggression*. New York: Plenum.

Baron, Robert A. (1981). The "costs of deception" revisited: An openly optimistic rejoinder. *IRB: A Review of Human Subjects Research, 3*(1), 8–10.

Barrett, P., & Eysenck, Sybil (1984). The assessment of personality factors across 25 countries. *Personality and Individual Differences, 5*, 615–632.

Barron, Frank, & Harrington, David M. (1981). Creativity, intelligence, and personality. *Annual Review of Psychology, 32*, 439–476.

Barsky, Arthur, J., & Klerman, Gerald L. (1983). Overview: Hypochondriasis, bodily complaints, and somatic styles. *American Journal of Psychiatry, 140*, 273–283.

Bartlett, Frederic C. (1932). *Remembering*. Cambridge, England: Cambridge University Press.

Bartoshuk, Linda (1980, September). Separate worlds of taste. *Psychology Today, 14*(4), 48–49, 51, 54–56, 63.

Basch, Michael F. (1988). *Understanding psychotherapy*. New York: Basic Books.

Bates, Marsha E.; Labouvie, Erich W.; & White, Helene R. (1986). The effect of sensation seeking needs on alcohol and marijuana use in adolescence. *Bulletin of the Society of Psychologists in Addictive Behaviors, 5*, 29–36.

Bates, Marston (1967). *Gluttons and libertines*. New York: Random House.

Bateson, Gregory (1941). The frustration-aggression hypothesis and culture. *Psychological Review, 48*, 350–355.

Batson, C. Daniel; Bolen, Michelle H.; Cross, Julie A.; & Neuringer-Benefiel, Helen E. (1986). Where is the altruism in the altruistic personality? *Journal of Personality and Social Psychology, 50*, 212–220.

Batson, C. Daniel; Dyck, Janine; Brandt, J. Randall; Batson, Judy; et al. (1988). Five studies testing two new egoistic alternatives to the empathy-altruism hypothesis. *Journal of Personality and Social Psychology, 55*, 52–77.

Baucom, Donald H. (1983). Sex role identity and the decision to regain control among women: A learned helplessness investigation. *Journal of Personality and Social Psychology, 44*, 334–343.

Baum, Steven K. (1988). Adult development in women. Paper presented at the annual meeting of the American Psychological Association, Atlanta.

Baum, Steven, & Boxley, Russell (1983). Age identification in the elderly. *The Gerontologist, 23*, 532–537.

Baumeister, Roy F., & Scher, Steven J. (1988). Self-defeating behavior patterns among normal individuals: Review and analysis of common self-destructive tendencies. *Psychological Bulletin, 104*, 3–22.

Baumgartner, Alice (1983). "My daddy might have loved me": Student perceptions of differences between being male and being female. Paper published by the Institute for Equality in Education, Denver.

Baumrind, Diana (1971). Current patterns of parental authority. *Developmental Psychology Monograph 4* (1, pt. 2).

Baumrind, Diana (1973). The development of instrumental competence through socialization. In A. D. Pick (ed.), *Minnesota symposium on child psychology*, Vol. 7. Minneapolis: University of Minnesota Press.

Baumrind, Diana (1985). Research using intentional deception: Ethical issues revisited. *American Psychologist, 40*, 165–174.

Baur, Susan (1988). *Hypochondria: Woeful imaginings*. Berkeley: University of California Press.

Bayer, Ronald (1981). *Homosexuality and American psychiatry*. New York: Basic Books.

Beard, John H.; Propst, Rudyard N.; & Malamud, T. J. (1982). The Fountain House model of psychiatric rehabilitation. *Psychosocial Rehabilitation Journal, 5*, 47–54.

Beck, Aaron T. (1976). *Cognitive therapy and the emotional disorders*. New York: International Universities Press.

Beck, Aaron T. (1988). Cognitive approaches to panic disorder: Theory and therapy. In S. Rachman & J. D. Maser (eds.), *Panic: Psychological perspectives*. Hillsdale, NJ: Erlbaum.

Beck, Aaron T., & Emery, Gary (with Ruth L. Greenberg) (1985). *Anxiety disorders and phobias: A cognitive perspective*. New York: Basic Books.

Beck, Aaron T.; Kovacs, Maria; & Weissman, Arlene (1979). Assessment of suicidal ideation: The scale for suicide ideation. *Journal of Consulting and Clinical Psychology, 47*, 343–352.

Beck, Aaron T.; Rush, A. J.; Shaw, B. F.; & Emery, Gary (1979). *Cognitive theory of depression*. New York: Guilford Press.

Beckwith, Leila, & Cohen, Sarale E. (1984). Home environment and cognitive competence in preterm children during the first 5 years. In Allen W. Gottfried (ed.), *Home environment and early cognitive development: Longitudinal research*. Orlando, FL: Academic Press.

Bee, Helen (1989). *The developing child* (5th ed.). New York: Harper & Row.

Bee, Helen; Barnard, Kathryn E.; et al. (1982). Prediction of IQ and language skill from perinatal status, child performance, family characteristics, and mother-infant interaction. *Child Development, 53*, 1134–1156.

Beebe, B.; Gerstman, L.; Carson, B.; et al. (1982). Rhythmic communication in the mother-infant dyad. In M. Davis (ed.), *Interaction rhythms: Periodicity in communicative behavior*. New York: Human Sciences Press.

Beech-Lublin, Victoria (1985). Factors that facilitate child adjustment following divorce. Paper presented at the annual meeting of the American Psychological Association, Los Angeles.

Beer, William R. (1983). *Househusbands: Men and housework in American families*. South Hadley, MA: J. F. Bergin/Praeger.

Bellack, Alan, & Hersen, Michel (1979). *Research and practice in social skills training*. New York: Plenum.

Bellah, Robert N.; Madsen, Richard; Sullivan, William M.; Swidler, Ann; & Tipton, Steven M. (1985). *Habits of the heart: Individualism and commitment in American life*. Berkeley: University of California Press.

Belmont, Lillian, & Marolla, Francis A. (1973). Birth order, family size, and intelligence. *Science, 182*, 1096–1010.

Bem, Daryl, & Allen, Andrea (1974). On predicting some of the people some of the time: The search for cross-cultural consistencies in behavior. *Psychological Review, 81*, 506–520.

Bem, Sandra L. (1974). The measurement of psychological androgyny. *Journal of Consulting and Clinical Psychology, 42*, 155–162.

Bem, Sandra L. (1981). Gender schema theory: A cognitive account of sex typing. *Psychological Review, 88*, 354–364.

Bem, Sandra L. (1985). Androgyny and gender schema theory: A conceptual and empirical integration. In T. B. Sonderegger (ed.), *Nebraska symposium on motivation: Psychology and gender, 1984*, Vol. 32. Lincoln: University of Nebraska Press.

Benbow, Camilla P., & Stanley, Julian C. (1983). Sex differences in mathematical reasoning: More facts. *Science, 222*, 1029–1031.

Bennett, Henry L. (1988). Perception and memory for events during adequate general anesthesia for surgical operations. In Helen M. Pettinati (ed.), *Hypnosis and memory*. New York: Guilford Press.

Bennett, H. L.; Davis, H. S.; & Giannini, J. A. (1985). Non-verbal response to intraoperative conversation. *British Journal of Anaesthesia, 57*, 174–179.

Bennett, Neil G.; Blanc, Ann Klimas; & Bloom, David E. (1988). Commitment and the modern union: Assessing the link between premarital cohabitation and subsequent marital stability. *American Sociological Review, 53*, 127–138.

Bennett, William, & Gurin, Joel (1982). *The dieter's dilemma: Eating less and weighing more*. New York: Basic Books.

Benton, Cynthia; Hernandez, Anthony; Schmidt, Adeny; Schmitz, Mary; Stone, Anna; & Weiner, Bernard (1983). Is hostility linked with affiliation among males and with achievement among females? A critique of Pollak and Gilligan. *Journal of Personality and Social Psychology, 45*, 1167–1171.

Bergin, Alan E., & Lambert, Michael J. (1978). The evaluation of therapeutic outcomes. In A. E. Bergin & S. L. Garfield (eds.), *Handbook of psychotherapy and behavior change* (2nd ed.). New York: Wiley.

Berkman, Lisa, & Syme, S. Leonard (1979). Social networks, host resistance, and mortality: A nine-year follow-up study of Alameda County residents. *American Journal of Epidemiology, 109*, 186–204.

Berlin, Brent, & Kay, Paul (1969). *Basic color terms: Their universality and evolution*. Berkeley and Los Angeles: University of California Press.

Berlyne, Daniel (1960). *Conflict, arousal, and curiosity*. New York: McGraw-Hill.

Berman, Allan (1978). Neuropsychological aspects of violent behavior. Paper presented at the annual meeting of the American Psychological Association, Toronto.

Berman, William (1988). The role of attachment in the post-divorce experience. *Journal of Personality and Social Psychology, 54*, 496–503.

Bernard, Jessie (1981). The good-provider role: Its rise and fall. *American Psychologist, 36*, 1–12.

Bernieri, Frank J.; Reznick, J. Steven; & Rosenthal, Robert (1988). Synchrony, pseudosynchrony, and dissynchrony: Measuring the entrainment process in mother-infant interactions. *Journal of Personality and Social Psychology, 54*, 243–253.

Bernstein, Ilene L. (1985). Learning food aversions in the progression of cancer and treatment. *Annals of the New York Academy of Sciences, 443*, 365–380.

Berscheid, Ellen (1985). Interpersonal attraction. In G. Lindzey & E. Aronson (eds.), *Handbook of social psychology*, Vol. II. New York: Random House/Erlbaum.

Bersoff, Donald N. (1978). Coercion and reciprocity in psychotherapy. In C. T. Fischer & S. L. Brodsky (eds.), *Client participation in human services: The Prometheus principle*. New Brunswick, NJ: Transaction Books.

Besalel-Azrin, V.; Azrin, N. H.; & Armstrong, P. M. (1977). The student-oriented classroom: A method of improving student conduct and satisfaction. *Behavior Therapy, 8*, 193–204.

Bettelheim, Bruno (1962). *Symbolic wounds*. New York: Collier.

Bettelheim, Bruno (1967). *The empty fortress*. New York: Free Press.

Biederman, Irving (1987). Recognition-by-components: A theory of human image understanding. *Psychological Review, 94*, 115–147.

Biller, Henry B. (1981). The father and sex role development. In M. E. Lamb (ed.), *The role of the father in child development* (2nd ed.). New York: Wiley-Interscience.

Binder, Jeffrey (1984). New developments in the concept of a focus in time-limited dynamic psychotherapy. Paper presented at the annual meeting of the American Psychological Association, Toronto.

Birdwhistell, Ray L. (1970). *Kinesics and context: Essays on body motion communication.* Philadelphia: University of Pennsylvania Press.

Blake, Catherine, & Cohen, Henri (1984). A meta-analysis of sex differences in moral development. Paper presented at the annual meeting of the American Psychological Association, Toronto.

Blakemore, Colin, & Cooper, Grahame F. (1970). Development of the brain depends on the visual environment. *Nature, 228,* 477–478.

Blaney, Paul H. (1986). Affect and memory: A review. *Psychological Bulletin, 99,* 229–246.

Blass, John P., & Weksler, Marc E. (1983). Toward an effective treatment of Alzheimer's disease. *Annals of Internal Medicine, 98,* 251–252.

Bleier, Ruth (1987). Sex differences research in the neurosciences. Paper presented at the annual meeting of the American Association for the Advancement of Science, Chicago.

Bleier, Ruth; Houston, Lanning; & Byne, William (1986). Can the corpus callosum predict gender, age, handedness, or cognitive differences? *Trends in Neuro Sciences, 9,* 391–394.

Bleuler, Eugen (1911/1950). *Dementia praecox or the group of schizophrenias.* New York: International Universities Press.

Block, Jack (1971). *Lives through time.* Berkeley: University of California Press.

Bloom, Benjamin S. (ed.) (1985). *Developing talent in young people.* New York: Ballantine.

Bloom, John W.; Kaltenborn, Walter T.; Paoletti, Paolo; Camilli, Anthony; & Lebowitz, Michael D. (1987). Respiratory effects of non-tobacco cigarettes. *British Medical Journal, 295,* 1516–1518.

Bloom, Lois M.; Hood, Lois; & Lightbown, Patsy (1974). Imitation in language development: If, when, and why. *Cognitive Psychology, 6,* 380–420.

Blos, Peter (1962). *On adolescence.* New York: Free Press.

Bogen, Joseph (1978, October). The giant walk-through brain. *Human Nature, 1*(10), 40–47.

Bohannon, John N. (1988). Flashbulb memories for the space shuttle disaster: A tale of two theories. *Cognition, 29,* 179–196.

Bohannon, John N., & Stanowicz, Laura (1988). The issue of negative evidence: Adult responses to children's language errors. *Developmental Psychology, 24,* 684–689.

Bohannon, John N., & Symons, Victoria (1988). Conversational conditions of children's imitation. Paper presented at the biennial Conference on Human Development, Charleston.

Bolles, Robert C. (1972). Reinforcement, expectancy and learning. *Psychological Review, 79,* 394–409.

Bolles, Robert C.; Holtz, Rolf; Dunn, Thomas; & Hill, Wendy (1980). Comparisons of stimulus learning and response learning in a punishment situation. *Learning and Motivation, 11,* 78–96.

Bonica, John J. (1980). Pain research and therapy: Past and current status and future needs. In L. Ng & J. J. Bonica (eds.), *Pain, discomfort, and humanitarian care.* New York: Elsevier.

Bootzin, Richard R. (1973). Stimulus control of insomnia. Paper presented at the annual meeting of the American Psychological Association, Montreal.

Boring, Edwin G. (1950). *A history of experimental psychology.* New York: Appleton-Century-Crofts.

Boring, Edwin G. (1953). A history of introspection. *Psychological Bulletin, 50,* 169–187.

Borstelmann, Lloyd J. (1984). Children before psychology: Ideas about children from antiquity to the late 1800s. In P. Mussen (ed.), *Handbook of child psychology* (4th ed.). Vol. I, W. Kessen (ed.), *History, theory, and methods.* New York: Wiley.

Borys, Shelley, & Perlman, Daniel (1985). Gender differences in loneliness. *Personality and Social Psychology Bulletin, 11,* 63–74.

Bouchard, Thomas J., Jr. (1984). Twins reared together and apart: What they tell us about human diversity. In S. W. Fox (ed.), *Individuality and determinism.* New York: Plenum.

Bouchard, Thomas J., Jr.; Heston, L.; Eckert, E.; Keyes, M.; & Resnick, S. (1981). The Minnesota study of twins reared apart: Project description and sample results in the developmental domain. In Luigi Gedda (ed.), *Twin research 3: Intelligence, personality, and development.* New York: Alan R. Liss.

Bouchard, Thomas J., Jr.; Lykken, David T.; Segal, Nancy L.; & Wilcox, Kimerly J. (1986). Development in twins reared apart: A test of the chronogenetic hypothesis. In A. Demirjian (ed.), *Human growth: A multidisciplinary review.* London: Taylor & Francis.

Bouchard, Thomas J., Jr., & McGue, Matthew (1981). Familial studies of intelligence: A review. *Science, 212,* 1055–1058.

Bousfield, W. A. (1953). The occurrence of clustering in the recall of randomly arranged associates. *Journal of General Psychology, 49,* 229–240.

Bowen, Murray (1978). *Family therapy in clinical practice.* New York: Jason Aronson.

Bower, Bruce (1988, July 30). Alcoholism's elusive genes. *Science News, 134*(5), 74–75, 79ff.

Bower, Gordon H. (1981). Mood and memory. *American Psychologist, 36,* 129–148.

Bower, Gordon, & Bower, Sharon (1979). *Asserting yourself: A practical guide for positive change.* Reading, MA: Addison-Wesley.

Bower, Gordon H., & Mayer, John D. (in press). In search of mood-dependent retrieval. *Journal of Social Behavior and Personality, 3.*

Bower, T. G. R. (1981). *Development in infancy* (2nd ed.). San Francisco: Freeman.

Bowers, Wayne A. (1988). Treatment of depressed inpatients. Paper presented at the annual meeting of the American Psychological Association, Atlanta.

Bowlby, John (1969). *Attachment and loss. Vol. I: Attachment.* New York: Basic Books.

Bowlby, John (1973). *Attachment and loss. Vol. II: Separation.* New York: Basic Books.

Bowlby, John (1988). *A secure base: Parent-child attachment and healthy human development.* New York: Basic Books.

Boysen, Sarah T. (1988). Numerical abilities across species: Frivolous or functional? Paper presented at the annual meeting of the American Psychological Association, Atlanta.

Bradley, Robert H., & Caldwell, Bettye M. (1984). 174 children: A study of the relationship between home environment and cognitive development during the first 5 years. In Allen W. Gottfried (ed.), *Home environment and early cognitive development: Longitudinal research.* Orlando, FL: Academic Press.

Brainerd, Charles J. (1978). The stage question in cognitive development theory. *The Behavioral and Brain Sciences, 1,* 173–213.

Bransford, John D.; Barclay, J. Richard; & Franks, Jeffery J. (1972). Sentence memory: A constructive versus interpretive approach. *Cognitive Psychology, 3,* 193–209.

Bransford, John; Sherwood, Robert; Vye, Nancy; & Rieser, John (1986). Teaching thinking and problem solving. *American Psychologist, 41,* 1078–1089.

Braun, Bennett G. (1988). *The treatment of multiple personality disorder.* Washington, DC: American Psychiatric Press.

Brecher, Edward M. (and the editors of *Consumer Reports Books*) (1984). *Love, sex, and aging: A Consumers Union report.* Boston: Little, Brown.

Brehm, Jack W. (1966). *A theory of psychological reactance.* New York: Academic Press.

Brehm, Jack W. (1972). *Responses to loss of freedom: A theory of psychological reactance.* Morristown, NJ: General Learning Press.

Brehm, Jack W.; Wright, Rex; Solomon, Sheldon; Silka, Linda; & Greenberg, Jeff (1983). Perceived difficulty, energization, and the magnitude of goal valence. *Journal of Experimental Social Psychology, 19,* 21–48.

Brehm, Sharon S. (1985). *Intimate relationships.* New York: Random House.

Brehm, Sharon S. (1988). Passionate love. In R. J. Sternberg & M. L. Barnes (eds.), *The psychology of love.* New Haven, CT, and London: Yale University Press.

Brehm, Sharon S., & Brehm, Jack W. (1981). *Psychological reactance: A theory of freedom and control.* New York: Academic Press.

Breland, Keller, & Breland, Marian (1961). The misbehavior of organisms. *American Psychologist, 16,* 681–684.

Bretherton, Inge, & Beeghly, Marjorie (1982). Talking about internal states: The acquisition of an explicit theory of mind. *Developmental Psychology, 18,* 906–921.

Bridgeman, Bruce, & Staggs, David (1982). Plasticity in human blindsight. *Vision Research, 22,* 1199–1203.

Briggs, Jean (1970). *Never in anger: Portrait of an Eskimo family.* Cambridge, MA: Harvard University Press.

Briggs, John (1984, December). The genius mind. *Science Digest, 92*(12), 74–77, 102–103.

Brim, Orville G., Jr. (1976). Theories of the male mid-life crisis. In N. K. Schlossberg & A. D. Entine (eds.), *Counseling adults.* Monterey, CA: Brooks/Cole.

Brim, Orville G., Jr., & Kagan, Jerome (1980). Constancy and change: A view of the issues. In O. G. Brim, Jr., & J. Kagan (eds.), *Constancy and change in human development.* Cambridge, MA: Harvard University Press.

Brockner, Joel, & Rubin, Jeffrey Z. (1985). *Entrapment in escalating conflicts: A social psychological analysis.* New York: Springer-Verlag.

Brodsky, Annette M. (1982). Sex, race, and class issues in psychotherapy research. In J. H. Harvey & M. M. Parks (eds.), *Psychotherapy research and behavior change.* The Master Lecture Series, Vol. 1, Washington, DC: American Psychological Association.

Bronfenbrenner, Urie (1961). The mirror image in Soviet-American relations. *Journal of Social Issues, 17,* 45–56.

Bronfenbrenner, Urie (1963). ''Why do the Russians plant trees along the road?'' *Saturday Review, 46*(95), 96.

Brown, Catherine C. (1976, November). Field report: It changed my life. *Psychology Today, 10*(6). 47–57, 109–112.

Brown, George W., & Harris, Tirril (1978). *Social origins of depression.* Riverside, NJ: Free Press.

Brown, Jonathon D., & Siegel, Judith M. (1988). Attributions for negative life events and depression: The role of perceived control. *Journal of Personality and Social Psychology, 54,* 316–322.

Brown, Laura S. (1986). Diagnosis and the Zeitgeist: The politics of masochism in the DSM-III-R. Paper presented at the annual meeting of the American Psychological Association, Washington.

Brown, Norman R.; Shevell, Steven K.; & Rips, Lance J. (1986). Public memories and their personal context. In D. C. Rubin (ed.), *Autobiographical memory.* New York: Cambridge University Press.

Brown, Roger (1958). *Words and things.* Glencoe, IL: Free Press.

Brown, Roger (1973). *A first language: The early stages.* Cambridge, MA: Harvard University Press.

Brown, Roger (1986). *Social psychology* (2nd ed.). New York: Free Press.

Brown, Roger; Cazden, Courtney; & Bellugi, Ursula (1969). The child's grammar from I to III. In J. P. Hill (ed.). *Minnesota symposium on child psychology,* Vol. 2. Minneapolis: University of Minnesota Press.

Brown, Roger, & Kulik, James (1977). Flashbulb memories. *Cognition, 5,* 73–99.

Brown, Roger, & McNeill, David (1966). The ''tip of the tongue'' phenomenon. *Journal of Verbal Learning and Verbal Behavior, 5,* 325–337.

Bryer, Jeffrey; Nelson, Bernadette; Miller, Jean; &

Krol, Pamela (1987). Childhood sexual and physical abuse as factors in adult psychiatric illness. *American Journal of Psychiatry, 144*, 1426–1430.

Buck, Ross (1984). *The communication of emotion.* New York: Guilford Press.

Buck, Ross, & Teng, Wan-Cheng (1987). Spontaneous emotional communication and social biofeedback: A cross-cultural study of emotional expression and communication in Chinese and Taiwanese students. Paper presented at the annual meeting of the American Psychological Association, New York.

Burchinal, Margaret R.; Lee, Marvin; & Ramey, Craig T. (1986). Daycare effects on preschool intellectual development in poverty children. Paper presented at the annual meeting of the American Psychological Association, Washington.

Burka, Jane B., & Yuen, Lenora (1983). *Procrastination.* Reading, MA: Addison-Wesley.

Burke, Deborah; Burnett, Gayle; & Levenstein, Peggy (1978). Menstrual symptoms: New data from a double-blind study. Paper presented at the annual meeting of the Western Psychological Association, San Francisco.

Burnam, M. Audrey; Stein, Judith; Golding, Jacqueline; Siegel, Judith; & Sorenson, Susan (1988). Sexual assault and mental disorders in a community population. *Journal of Counseling and Clinical Psychology, 56*, 843–850.

Burnet, F. M. (1970, August 15). An immunological approach to aging. *Lancet, 2*, 358–360.

Burns, David (1980). *Feeling good: The new mood therapy.* New York: Signet.

Bush, Diane M., & Simmons, Roberta (1987). Gender and coping with the entry into early adolescence. In R. C. Barnett, L. Biener, & G. K. Baruch (eds.), *Gender & stress.* New York: Free Press.

Buss, Arnold, & Plomin, Robert (1984). *Temperament: Early developing personality traits.* Hillsdale, NJ: Erlbaum.

Buss, David M. (1988). Love acts: The evolutionary biology of love. In R. J. Sternberg & M. L. Barnes (eds.), *The psychology of love.* New Haven, CT, and London: Yale University Press.

Bussey, Kay, & Maughan, Betty (1982). Gender differences in moral reasoning. *Journal of Personality and Social Psychology, 42*, 701–706.

Butcher, James N., & Finn, Stephen (1983). Objective personality assessment in clinical settings. In M. H. Hersen, A. E. Kazdin, & A. S. Bellack (eds.), *The clinical psychology handbook.* New York: Pergamon.

Butterfield, E. C., & Belmont, J. M. (1977). Assessing and improving the executive cognitive functions of mentally retarded people. In I. Bialer & M. Sternlict (eds.), *Psychological issues in mental retardation.* New York: Psychological Dimensions.

Buzan, Tony (1976). *Use both sides of your brain.* New York: Dutton.

Calabrese, Joseph R.; Kling, Mitchell A.; & Gold, Philip W. (1987). Alterations in immunocompetence during stress, bereavement, and depression: Focus on neuroendocrine regulation. *The American Journal of Psychiatry, 144*, 1123–1134.

Callahan, Daniel (1987). *Setting limits.* New York: Simon & Schuster.

Campbell, Joseph (1949/1968). *The hero with 1,000 faces* (2nd ed.). Princeton, NJ: Princeton University Press.

Campbell, Magda; Adams, Phillip; Small, Arthur M.; Tesch, Lisa M.; & Curren, Elizabeth L. (1988). Naltrexone in infantile autism. *Psychopharmacology Bulletin, 24*, 135–139.

Campos, Joseph J.; Barrett, Karen C.; Lamb, Michael E.; Goldsmith, H. Hill; & Stenberg, Craig (1984). Socioemotional development. In P. Mussen (ed.), *Handbook of child psychology* (4th ed.). Vol. II, M. M. Haith & J. J. Campos (eds.), *Infancy and developmental psychobiology.* New York: Wiley.

Campos, Joseph J.; Langer, Alan; & Krowitz, Alice (1970). Cardiac responses on the visual cliff in prelocomotor infants. *Science, 170*, 196–197.

Cannon, Walter B. (1927). The James-Lange theory of emotion: A critical examination and an alternative theory. *American Journal of Psychology, 39*, 106–124. (Reprinted in M. Arnold [ed.], *The nature of emotion.* Baltimore: Penguin, 1968.)

Caplan, Robert D., et al. (1985). Tranquilizer use and well-being: A longitudinal study of social and psychological effects. Ann Arbor. MI: Institute for Social Research. ISR Research Report.

Carew, Jean V. (1980). Experience and the development of intelligence in young children at home and in day care. *Monographs of the Society for Research in Child Development, 45* (6–7, Serial No. 187).

Carmichael, L.; Hogan, H. P.; & Walter, A. A. (1932). An experimental study of the effect of language on the reproduction of visually perceived forms. *Journal of Experimental Psychology, 15*, 73–86.

Carpenter, William T., Jr.; Sadler, John H.; et al. (1983). The therapeutic efficacy of hemodialysis in schizophrenia. *New England Journal of Medicine, 308*(12), 669–675.

Carrington, Patricia (1978). *Freedom in meditation.* New York: Anchor/Doubleday.

Carroll, Edward N.; Zuckerman, Marvin; & Vogel, Wolfgang H. (1982). A test of the optimal level of arousal theory of sensation seeking. *Journal of Personality and Social Psychology, 42*, 572–575.

Carskadon, Mary A.; Mitler, Merrill M.; & Dement, William C. (1974). A comparison of insomniacs and normals: Total sleep time and sleep latency. *Sleep Research, 3*, 130 [Abstract].

Carter, Betty, & McGoldrick, Monica (eds.) (1988). *The changing family life cycle: A framework for family therapy* (2nd ed.). New York: Gardner Press.

Carver, Charles S., & Scheier, Michael F. (1987). Dispositional optimism, coping, and stress. Paper presented at the annual meeting of the American Psychological Association, New York.

Cass, Loretta K., & Thomas, Carolyn (1979). *Childhood pathology and later adjustment*. New York: Wiley-Interscience.

Cassell, Carol (1984). *Swept away: Why women fear their own sexuality*. New York: Simon & Schuster.

Cattell, Raymond B. (1965). *The scientific analysis of personality*. Baltimore: Penguin.

Cattell, Raymond B. (1971). *Abilities: Their structure, growth and action*. Boston: Houghton Mifflin.

Cattell, Raymond B. (1973). *Personality and mood by questionnaire*. San Francisco: Jossey-Bass.

Caudill, William, & Frost, Lois (1972). A comparison of maternal care and infant behavior in Japanese-American, American, and Japanese families. In U. Bronfenbrenner & M. A. Mahoney (eds.), *Influences on human development*. Hinsdale, IL: Dryden.

Ceci, Stephen J., & Liker, Jeffrey K. (1986). Academic and nonacademic intelligence: An experimental separation. In R. J. Sternberg & R. K. Wagner (eds.), *Practical intelligence: Nature and origins of competence in the everyday world*. New York: Cambridge University Press.

Cermak, Laird S., & Craik, Fergus I. M. (eds.) (1979). *Levels of processing in human memory*. Hillsdale, NJ: Erlbaum.

Chambless, Dianne (1986). Fears and anxiety. In C. Tavris (ed.), *EveryWoman's emotional well-being*. New York: Doubleday.

Chambless, Dianne (1988). Cognitive mechanisms in panic disorder. In S. Rachman & J. D. Maser (eds.), *Panic: Psychological perspectives*. Hillsdale, NJ: Erlbaum.

Chambless, Dianne, & Goldstein, Alan J. (eds.) (1982). *Agoraphobia: Multiple perspectives on theory and treatment*. New York: Wiley.

Chan, Connie (1987). Addiction to exercise among aerobic athletes: Symptoms, treatment and prevention. Paper presented at the annual meeting of the American Psychological Association, New York.

Chance, Paul (1988a). *Learning and behavior* (2nd ed). Belmont, CA: Wadsworth.

Chance, Paul (1988b, October). Knock wood. *Psychology Today, 22*(10), 68–69.

Chapman, C. Richard (1987). Prolonged self-administration of morphine and addiction liability in bone marrow transplant patients: Evaluation of two competing theories. Paper presented at the annual meeting of the American Psychological Association, 1987.

Cheney, Dorothy L., & Seyfarth, Robert M. (1985). Vervet monkey alarm calls: Manipulation through shared information? *Behavior, 94*, 150–166.

Cherry, Frances, & Deaux, Kay (1975). Fear of success versus fear of gender-inconsistent behavior: A sex similarity. Paper presented at the annual meeting of the Midwestern Psychological Association, Chicago.

Cherulnik, Paul D. (1979). Sex differences in the expression of emotion in a structured social encounter. *Sex Roles, 5*, 413–424.

Chomsky, Noam (1957). *Syntactic structures*. The Hague: Mouton.

Chomsky, Noam (1972). *Language and mind* (2nd ed.). New York: Harcourt Brace Jovanovich.

Chorovor, Stephan L. (1974, May). Big brother and psychotechnology II: The pacification of the brain. *Psychology Today, 7*(12), 59–69.

Christopher, F. Scott (1988). An initial investigation into a continuum of premarital sexual pressure. *The Journal of Sex Research, 25*, 255–266.

Clark, David M. (1988). A cognitive model of panic attacks. In S. Rachman & J. D. Maser (eds.), *Panic: Psychological perspectives*. Hillsdale, NJ: Erlbaum.

Clark, Herbert H., & Clark, Eve V. (1977). *Psychology and language: An introduction to psycholinguistics*. New York: Harcourt Brace Jovanovich.

Clark, Margaret S.; Milberg, Sandra; & Erber, Ralph (1987). Arousal state dependent memory: Evidence and some implications for understanding social judgments and social behavior. In K. Fiedler & J. P. Forgas (eds.), *Affect, cognition and social behavior*. Toronto: Hogrefe.

Clarke-Stewart, K. Alison; VanderStoep, Laima P.; & Killian, Grant A. (1979). Analyses and replication of mother-child relations at two years of age. *Child Development, 50*, 777–793.

Coe, William C., & Sarbin, Theodore R. (1977). Hypnosis from the standpoint of a contextualist. *Annals of the New York Academy of Sciences, 296*, 2–13.

Cohen, Frances, & Lazarus, Richard S. (1973). Active coping processes, coping dispositions, and recovery from surgery. *Psychosomatic Medicine, 35*, 375–389.

Cohen, Sheldon, & Edwards, Jeffrey R. (1989). Personality characteristics as moderators of the relationship between stress and disorder. In R. W. J. Neufeld (ed.), *Advances in the investigation of psychological stress*. New York: Wiley.

Cohen, Sheldon; Evans, Gary W.; Krantz; David S.; & Stokols, Daniel (1980). Physiological, motivational, and cognitive effects of aircraft noise on children. *American Psychologist, 35*, 231–243.

Cohen, Sheldon; Glass, David C.; & Phillips, Susan (1979). Environment and health. In H. E. Freeman, S. Levine, & L. G. Reeder (eds.), *Handbook of medical sociology* (3rd ed.). Englewood Cliffs, NJ: Prentice-Hall.

Cohen, Sheldon; Kamarck, Tom; & Mermelstein, Robin (1983). A global measure of perceived stress. *Journal of Health and Social Behavior, 24*, 385–396.

Colby, Anne; Kohlberg, Lawrence; Gibbs, J.; & Lieberman, M. (1983). A longitudinal study of moral judgment. *Monographs of the Society for Research in Child Development, 48* (1–2, Serial No. 200).

Coleman, James C.; Butcher, James N.; & Carson, Robert C. (1984). *Abnormal psychology and modern life* (7th ed.). Glenview, IL: Scott, Foresman.

Coles, Robert, & Stokes, Geoffrey (1985). *Sex and the American teenager*. New York: Harper & Row.

Collier, Gary (1985). *Emotional expression.* Hillsdale, NJ: Erlbaum.

Collins, R. (1983, Summer). Head Start: An update on program effects. *Newsletter, Society for Research in Child Development,* 1–2.

Collins, Rebecca L.; Taylor, Shelley E.; & Skokan, Laurie A. (in press). A better world or a shattered vision? Changes in life perspectives following victimization. *Journal of Personality and Social Psychology.*

Colquhoun, Peter (1981). Rhythms in performance. In J. Aschoff (ed.), *Handbook of behavioral neurobiology, Vol. 4: Biological rhythms.* New York: Plenum.

Comstock, George; Chaffee, Steven; Katzman, Natan; McCombs, Maxwell; & Roberts, Donald (1978). *Television and human behavior.* New York: Columbia University Press.

Condon, William (1982). Cultural microrhythms. In M. Davis (ed.), *Interaction rhythms: Periodicity in communicative behavior.* New York: Human Sciences Press.

Conley, James J. (1984). Longitudinal consistency of adult personality: Self-reported psychological characteristics across 45 years. *Journal of Personality and Social Psychology, 47,* 1325–1333.

Connor, James R., & Diamond, Marian C. (1982). A comparison of dendritic spine number and type on pyramidal neuron of the visual cortex of old adult rats from social and isolated environments. *Journal of Comparative Neurology, 210,* 99–106.

Conte, Hope; Plutchik, Robert; Wild, Katherine; & Karasu, Toksoz (1986). Combined psychotherapy and pharmacotherapy for depression. *Archives of General Psychiatry, 43,* 471–479.

Conway, Michael, & Ross, Michael (1984). Getting what you want by revising what you had. *Journal of Personality and Social Psychology, 47,* 738–748.

Cook, Stuart (1984). Cooperative interaction in multiethnic contexts. In N. Miller & M. Brewer (eds.), *Groups in contact: The psychology of desegregation.* Orlando, FL: Academic Press.

Cook, Stuart (1985). Experimenting on social issues: The case of school desegregation. *American Psychologist, 40,* 452–460.

Cooney, Teresa M.; Smyer, Michael A.; Hagestad, Gunhild O.; & Klock, Robin (1986). Parental divorce in young adulthood: Some preliminary findings. *American Journal of Orthopsychiatry, 53,* 470–477.

Cooper, Lynn A., & Shepard, Roger N. (1973). Chronometric studies of the rotation of mental images. In W. G. Chase (ed.), *Visual information processing.* New York and London: Academic Press.

Corkin, Suzanne; Davis, Kenneth L.; Growdon, John H.; Usdin E.; & Wurtman, Richard J. (eds.) (1982). *Alzheimer's disease: A report of progress in research (Aging,* Vol. 19). New York: Raven Press.

Costa, Paul T., Jr., & McCrae, Robert R. (1985). Hypochondriasis, neuroticism, and aging: When are somatic complaints unfounded? *American Psychologist, 40,* 19–28.

Costa, Paul T., Jr., & McCrae, Robert R. (1988). Personality in adulthood: A six-year longitudinal study of self-reports and spouse ratings on the NEO personality inventory. *Journal of Personality and Social Psychology, 54,* 853–863.

Costa, Paul T., Jr.; McCrae, Robert R.; & Arenberg, David (1980). Enduring dispositions in adult males. *Journal of Personality and Social Psychology, 38,* 668–678.

Costa, Paul T., Jr.; McCrae, Robert R.; & Arenberg, David (1983). Recent longitudinal research on personality and aging. In K. W. Schaie (ed.), *Longitudinal studies of adult psychological development.* New York: Guilford Press.

Costantino, Giuseppe; Malgady, Robert G.; & Rogler, Lloyd H. (1986). Cuento therapy: A culturally sensitive modality for Puerto Rican children. *Journal of Consulting and Clinical Psychology, 54,* 639–645.

Cowan, Nelson (1988). Evolving conceptions of memory storage, selective attention, and their mutual constraints within the human information-processing system. *Psychological Bulletin, 104,* 163–191.

Cowan, W. Maxwell (1979). The development of the brain. *Scientific American, 241,* 112–114, 116, 119–120, 124, 129–133.

Craik, Fergus I. M., & Lockhart, Robert S. (1972). Levels of processing: A framework for memory research. *Journal of Verbal Learning and Verbal Behavior, 11,* 671–684.

Craik, Fergus I. M., & Tulving, Endel (1975). Depth of processing and the retention of words in episodic memory. *Journal of Experimental Psychology: General, 104,* 268–294.

Crandall, James E. (1981). *Theory and measurement of social interest: Empirical tests of Alfred Adler's concept.* New York: Columbia University Press.

Crandall, James E. (1984). Social interest as a moderator of life stress. *Journal of Personality and Social Psychology, 47,* 164–174.

Crick, Francis [F.H.C.] (1979). Thinking about the brain. *Scientific American, 241*(3), 219–222, 224, 226, 228–230, 232.

Crick, Francis, & Mitchison, Graeme (1983, July 14). The function of dream sleep. *Nature, 304*(14), 111–114.

Critchlow, Barbara (1983). Blaming the booze: The attribution of responsibility for drunken behavior. *Personality and Social Psychology Bulletin, 9,* 451–474.

Critchlow, Barbara (1986). The powers of John Barleycorn: Beliefs about the effects of alcohol on social behavior. *American Psychologist, 41,* 751–764.

Cronbach, Lee J. (1990). *Essentials of psychological testing* (5th ed.). New York: Harper & Row.

Crosby, Faye (1986). Work. In C. Tavris (ed.), *EveryWoman's emotional well-being.* New York: Doubleday.

Crowley, Joan (1984). Longitudinal effects of retirement on men's well-being and health. Paper presented at the annual meeting of the American Psychological Association, Toronto.

Csikszentmihalyi, Mihaly, & Larson, Reed (1984). *Being adolescent: Conflict and growth in the teenage years*. New York: Basic Books.

Cunningham, Walter R., & Brookbank, John W. (1988). *Gerontology: The psychology, biology, and sociology of aging*. New York: Harper & Row.

Current Controversy (1985, April 6). How fat is fat? *4*, 6.

Curtiss, Susan (1977). *Genie: A psycholinguistic study of a modern-day "wild child."* New York: Academic Press.

Cutler, Brian, & Penrod, Steven D. (1988). Improving the reliability of eyewitness identification: Lineup construction and presentation. *Journal of Applied Psychology, 73*, 281–290.

Cutler, Winnifred B.; Preti, George; et al. (1986). Human axillary secretions influence women's menstrual cycles: The role of donor extract from men. *Hormones and Behavior, 20*, 463–473.

Czeisler, Charles A.; Moore-Ede, Martin C.; & Coleman, Richard M. (1982). Rotating shift work schedules that disrupt sleep are improved by applying circadian principles. *Science, 217*, 460–462.

Dahlberg, Frances (ed.) (1981). *Woman the gatherer*. New Haven, CT: Yale University Press.

Daniels, Pamela, & Weingarten, Kathy (1982). *Sooner or later: The timing of parenthood in adult lives*. New York: Norton.

Darley, John, & Latané, Bibb (1968). Bystander intervention in emergencies: Diffusion of responsibility. *Journal of Personality and Social Psychology, 8*, 377–383.

Darwin, Charles (1872/1965). *The expression of the emotions in man and animals*. Reprinted by the University of Chicago Press.

Dasen, Pierre (ed.) (1977). *Piagetian psychology: Cross-cultural contributions*. New York: Gardner Press.

Datan, Nancy, & Thomas, Jeanne (1984). Late adulthood: Love, work, and the normal transitions. In D. Offer & M. Sabshin (eds.), *Normality and the life cycle*. New York: Basic Books.

Davanloo, Habib (ed.) (1980). *Short-term dynamic psychotherapy*. New York: Jason Aronson.

Davidson, Keay, & Hopson, Janet L. (1988, April 10). Gorilla business. *Image (San Francisco Chronicle)*, 14–18, 33–36.

Davidson, Larry (1988). Psychologism in psychology: The case of schizophrenia. Paper presented at the annual meeting of the American Psychological Association, Atlanta.

Davidson, Richard J. (1984). Affect, cognition, and hemispheric specialization. In C. E. Izard, J. Kagan, & R. B. Zajonc (eds.), *Emotions, cognition, and behavior*. Cambridge, England: Cambridge University Press.

Davidson, Richard J. (1986). Thinking about feeling: Cerebral asymmetry and the nature of emotion. Paper presented at the annual meeting of the American Psychological Association, Washington.

Davis, James H. (1980). Group decision and procedural justice. In M. L. Fishbein (ed.), *Progress in social psychology: Vol. 1*. Hillsdale, NJ: Erlbaum.

Davis, Joel (1984). *Endorphins: New waves in brain chemistry*. Garden City, NY: Dial Press (Doubleday).

Dean, Geoffrey (1986–1987, Winter). Does astrology need to be true? Part I: A look at the real thing. *The Skeptical Inquirer, 11*, 166–184.

Dean, Geoffrey (1987, Spring). Does astrology need to be true? Part II: The answer is no. *The Skeptical Inquirer, 11*, 257–273.

de Bono, Edward (1985). *de Bono's thinking course*. New York: Facts on File.

DeCasper, Anthony J., & Prescott, Phyllis (1984). Human newborns' perception of male voices: Preference, discrimination, and reinforcing value. *Developmental Psychobiology, 17*, 481–491.

DeCasper, Anthony J., & Spence, Melanie J. (1986). Prenatal maternal speech influences newborns' perception of speech sounds. *Infant Behavior and Development, 9*, 133–150.

Deci, Edward L. (1975). *Intrinsic motivation*. New York: Plenum.

de Lacoste-Utamsing, Christine, & Holloway, Ralph L. (1982). Sexual dimorphism in the human corpus callosum. *Science, 216*, 1431–1432.

DeLoache, Judy S. (1987, December 11). Rapid change in the symbolic functioning of very young children. *Science, 238*, 1556–1557.

DeLongis, Anita; Coyne, James C.; Dakoi, Gayle; Folkman, Susan; & Lazarus, Richard S. (1982). Relationship of daily hassles, uplifts, and major life events to health status. *Health Psychology, 1*, 119–136.

DeLongis, Anita; Folkman, Susan; & Lazarus, Richard S. (1988). The impact of daily stress on health and mood: Psychological and social resources as mediators. *Journal of Personality and Social Psychology, 54*, 486–495.

Dembroski, Theodore M., & Costa, Paul T., Jr. (1988). Assessment of coronary-prone behavior: A current overview. *Annals of Behavioral Medicine, 10*, 60–63.

Dement, William (1955). Dream recall and eye movements during sleep in schizophrenics and normals. *Journal of Nervous and Mental Disease, 122*, 263–269.

Dement, William (1978). *Some must watch while some must sleep*. New York: Norton.

Dement, William, & Kleitman, Nathaniel (1957). The relation of eye movements during sleep to dream activity: An objective method for the study of dreaming. *Journal of Experimental Psychology, 53*, 339–346.

DeMyer, Marian K. (1975). Research in infantile autism: A strategy and its results. *Biological Psychiatry, 10*, 433–452.

Demo, David (1985). The measurement of self-esteem: Refining our methods. *Journal of Personality and Social Psychology, 48*, 1490–1502.

Demos, John (1970). *A little commonwealth*. New York: Oxford University Press.

DePaola, Laura, & DePaola, Steve (1988). Hallucinations during widowhood. Paper presented at the annual meeting of the Western Psychological Association, San Francisco.

De Rivera, Joseph (1977). A structural theory of the emotions. *Psychological Issues, X*(4). Monograph 40. New York: International Universities Press.

Deutsch, Francine M.; LeBaron, Dorothy; & Fryer, Maury M. (1987). What is in a smile? *Psychology of Women Quarterly, 11,* 341–352.

Deutsch, Morton (1949). An experimental study of the effects of co-operation and competition among group processes. *Human Relations, 2,* 199–231.

Deutsch, Morton (1980). Fifty years of conflict. In L. Festinger (ed.), *Retrospections on social psychology.* New York: Oxford University Press.

Deutsch, Morton, & Collins, Mary Ellen (1951). *Interracial housing: A psychological evaluation of a social experiment.* Minneapolis: University of Minnesota Press.

DeValois, Russell L. (1960). Color vision mechanisms in the monkey. *Journal of General Physiology, 43,* 115–128.

DeValois, Russell L., & DeValois, Karen K. (1975). Neural coding of color. In E. C. Carterette & M. P. Friedman (eds.), *Handbook of perception,* Vol. 5. New York: Academic Press.

DeValois, Russell L., & DeValois, Karen K. (1980). Spatial vision. *Annual Review of Psychology, 31,* 309–341.

Diamond, Jared (1987, August). Soft sciences are often harder than hard sciences. *Discover, 8*(8), 34–35, 38–39.

Diamond, Marian (1984, November). A love affair with the brain (A conversation). *Psychology Today, 18*(11), 62–73.

Diamond, Marian (1985). Lifespan plasticity of the brain. Paper presented at the annual meeting of the American Psychological Association, Los Angeles.

Diamond, Marian (1988). *Enriching heredity: The impact of the environment on the anatomy of the brain.* New York: Free Press.

Diamond, Marian; Johnson, Ruth E.; Young, Daniel; & Singh, S. Sukhwinder (1983). Age related morphologic differences in the rat cerebral cortex and hippocampus: Male-female; right-left. *Experimental Neurology, 81,* 1–13.

Diamond, Marian; Scheibel, Arnold B.; Murphy, Greer M.; & Harvey, Thomas (1985). On the brain of a scientist: Albert Einstein. *Experimental Neurology, 88,* 198–204.

Dickson, W. Patrick; Hess, Robert D.; Miyake, Naomi; & Azuma, Hiroshi (1979). Referential communication accuracy between mother and child as a predictor of cognitive development in the United States and Japan. *Child Development, 50,* 53–59.

DiFranza, Joseph R.; Winters, Thomas H.; Goldberg, Robert J.; Cirillo, Leonard; et al. (1986). The relationship of smoking to motor vehicle accidents and traffic violations. *New York State Journal of Medicine, 86,* 464–467.

Digman, John M., & Inouye, Jillian (1986). Further specification of the five robust factors of personality. *Journal of Personality and Social Psychology, 50,* 116–123.

Dinges, David F.; Orne, Martin T.; Whitehouse, Wayne G.; Orne, Emily C.; & Erdelyi, Matthew H.

(1987). Recall in hypnosis: More memory, more confidence, or more mistakes? Paper presented at the annual meeting of the American Psychological Association, New York.

Dion, George L., & Anthony, William A. (1987). Research in psychiatric rehabilitation: A review of experimental and quasi-experimental studies. *Rehabilitation Counseling Bulletin, 30,* 177–203.

Dion, Kenneth L., & Dion, Karen K. (1975). Self-esteem and romantic love. *Journal of Personality, 43,* 39–57.

Dion, Kenneth L., & Dion, Karen K. (1988). Romantic love: Individual and cultural perspectives. In R. J. Sternberg & M. L. Barnes (eds.), *The psychology of love.* New Haven, CT, and London: Yale University Press.

Dixon, N. F. (1980). Humor: A cognitive alternative to stress? In I. G. Sarason & C. D. Spielberger (eds.), *Stress and anxiety: Volume 7.* Washington, DC: Hemisphere.

Doane, Jeri; Goldstein, Michael; Miklowitz, David; & Falloon, Ian (1986). The impact of individual and family treatment on the affective climate of families of schizophrenics. *British Journal of Psychiatry, 148,* 279–287.

Doering, Charles H.; Brodie, H. K. H.; Kraemer, H. C.; Becker, H. B.; & Hamburg, D. A. (1974). Plasma testosterone levels and psychologic measures in men over a 2-month period. In R. C. Friedman, R. M. Richard, & R. L. Vande Wiele (eds.), *Sex differences in behavior.* New York: Wiley.

Doering, Charles H., et al. (1975). Negative affect and plasma testosterone: A longitudinal human study. *Psychosomatic Medicine, 37,* 484–491.

Doherty, William J., & Baldwin, Cynthia (1985). Shifts and stability in locus of control during the 1970s: Divergence of the sexes. *Journal of Personality and Social Psychology, 48,* 1048–1053.

Dohrenwend, Bruce P. (1979). Stressful life events and psychopathology: Some issues of theory and method. In J. E. Barrett et al. (eds.), *Stress and mental disorder.* New York: Raven Press.

Dohrenwend, Bruce P., & Shrout, Patrick E. (1985). ''Hassles'' in the conceptualization and measurement of life stress variables. *American Psychologist, 40,* 780–785.

Doi, L. T. (1973). *The anatomy of dependence.* Tokyo: Kodansha International.

Dollard, John R.; Doob, Leonard W.; Miller, Neal E.; & Sears, Robert S. (1939). *Frustration and aggression.* New Haven, CT: Yale University Press.

Dollard, John, & Miller, Neal E. (1950). *Personality and psychotherapy: An analysis in terms of learning, thinking, and culture.* New York: McGraw-Hill.

Doty, Richard L. (1985). Changing ability to identify odors over the lifespan. Paper presented at the annual meeting of the American Psychological Association, Los Angeles.

Douvan, Elizabeth (1985). The age of narcissism, 1963–1982. In J. M. Hawes & N. R. Hiner, *American childhood.* Westport, CT: Greenwood Press.

Douvan, Elizabeth (1986). Adolescence. In C. Tavris (ed.), *EveryWoman's emotional well-being*. New York: Doubleday.

Douvan, Elizabeth, & Adelson, Joseph (1966). *The adolescent experience*. New York: Wiley.

Drinka, George F. (1984). *The birth of neurosis*. New York: Simon & Schuster.

Drucker, Peter F. (1979, March). What Freud forgot. *Human Nature 2*, 40–50.

Druckman, Daniel, & Swets, John A. (eds.) (1988). *Enhancing human performance: Issues, theories, and techniques*. Washington, DC: National Academy Press.

Duncan, Greg J.; Coe, Richard D.; Corcoran, Mary E.; Hill, Martha S.; Hoffman, Saul D.; & Morgan, James N. (1984). *Years of poverty, years of plenty: The changing economic fortunes of American workers and families*. Ann Arbor, MI: Institute for Social Research.

Duncan, Greg J.; Hill, Martha S.; & Hoffman, Saul D. (1988, January 29). Welfare dependence within and across generations. *Science, 239*, 467.

Dunkel-Schetter, Christine (1984). Social support and cancer: Findings based on patient interviews and their implications. *Journal of Social Issues, 40*(4), 77–98.

Dutton, Donald, & Aron, Arthur (1974). Some evidence for heightened sexual attraction under conditions of high anxiety. *Journal of Personality and Social Psychology, 30*, 510–517.

Dweck, Carol S., & Leggett, Ellen L. (1988). A social-cognitive approach to motivation and personality. *Psychological Review, 95*, 256–273.

Dworkin, Barry, & Dworkin, Susan (1988). The treatment of scoliosis by continuous automated postural feedback. In R. Ader, H. Weiner, & A. Baum (eds.), *Experimental foundations of behavioral medicine: Conditioning approaches*. Hillsdale, NJ: Erlbaum.

Dworkin, Barry R., & Miller, Neal E. (1986). Failure to replicate visceral learning in the acute curarized rat preparation. *Behavioral Neuroscience, 100*, 299–314.

Dywan, Jane, & Bowers, Kenneth (1983). The use of hypnosis to enhance recall. *Science, 222*, 184–185.

Eagly, Alice H., & Carli, Linda L. (1981). Sex of researchers and sex-typed communications as determinants of sex differences in influencibility: A meta-analysis of social influence studies. *Psychological Bulletin, 90*, 1–20.

Ebbinghaus, Hermann M. (1913). *Memory: A contribution to experimental psychology*. (H. A. Ruger & C. E. Bussenius, translators.) New York: Teachers College, Columbia University. (Originally published 1885.)

Ebert, Roger (1984, March 18). Why are there so many drunks as movie characters? *San Francisco Sunday Examiner & Chronicle*.

Eccles, John C. (1981). In praise of falsification. In R. D. Tweney, M. E. Doherty, & C. R. Mynatt (eds.), *On scientific thinking*. New York: Columbia University Press.

Eckenrode, John, & Gore, Susan (1981). Stressful events and social supports: The significance of context. In B. H.

Gottlieb (ed.), *Social networks and social support*. Beverly Hills, CA: Sage.

Eckert, E. D.; Heston, L. L.; & Bouchard, T. J. (1981). MZ twins reared apart: Preliminary findings of psychiatric disturbances and traits. In *Twin research 3: Intelligence, personality and development*. New York: Alan R. Liss.

Edwards, Betty (1986). *Drawing on the artist within: A guide to innovation, invention, imagination and creativity*. New York: Simon & Schuster.

Edwards, Carolyn Pope (1987). Culture and the construction of moral values. In J. Kagan & S. Lamb (eds.), *The emergence of morality in young children*. Chicago: University of Chicago Press.

Egeland, Janice A.; Gerhard, Daniela; Pauls, David; Sussex, James; et al. (1987, February 26). Bipolar affective disorders linked to DNA markers on chromosome 11. *Nature, 325*, 783–787.

Eidelson, Judy (1986). Depression: Theories and therapies. In C. Tavris (ed.), *EveryWoman's emotional well-being*. New York: Doubleday.

Ekman, Paul (1985). *Telling lies*. New York: Norton.

Ekman, Paul, & Friesen, Wallace V. (1975). *Unmasking the face*. Englewood Cliffs, NJ: Prentice-Hall. (Reprinted in 1984 by Consulting Psychologists Press, Palo Alto, CA.)

Ekman, Paul; Friesen, Wallace V.; & Ellsworth, Phoebe (1972). *Emotion in the human face: Guidelines for research and an integration of findings*. New York: Pergamon.

Ekman, Paul; Friesen, Wallace V.; O'Sullivan, Maureen; et al. (1987). Universals and cultural differences in the judgments of facial expression of emotion. *Journal of Personality and Social Psychology, 53*, 712–717.

Ekman, Paul; Friesen, Wallace V.; & O'Sullivan, Maureen (1988). Smiles when lying. *Journal of Personality and Social Psychology, 54*, 414–420.

Ekman, Paul; Levenson, Robert W.; & Friesen, Wallace V. (1983, September 16). Autonomic nervous system activity distinguishes among emotions. *Science, 221*, 1208–1210.

Elkin, Roger A., & Leippe, Michael R. (1986). Physiological arousal, dissonance, and attitude change: Evidence for a dissonance-arousal link and a "don't remind me" effect. *Journal of Personality and Social Psychology, 51*, 55–65.

Elkind, David (1981). *The hurried child: Growing up too fast too soon*. Reading, MA: Addison-Wesley.

Elkind, David (1988). *Miseducation: Preschoolers at risk*. New York: Knopf.

Elliott, Elaine S., & Dweck, Carol S. (1988). Goals: An approach to motivation and achievement. *Journal of Personality and Social Psychology, 54*, 5–12.

Elliott, Glen R., & Eisdorfer, Carl (1982). *Stress and human health*. New York: Springer.

Ellis, Albert (1962). *Reason and emotion in psychotherapy*. New York: Lyle Stuart.

Ellis, Albert, & Dryden, Windy (1987). *The practice of rational emotive therapy*. New York: Springer.

Ellis, Havelock (1910). Review of "A psycho-analytic

study of Leonardo da Vinci,'' by Sigmund Freud. *The Journal of Mental Science, 56,* 522–523.

Elms, Alan C. (1981). Skinner's dark year and *Walden Two. American Psychologist, 36,* 470–479.

Emde, Robert N., & Sorce, James F. (1984). Infancy: Perspectives on normality. In D. Offer & M. Sabshin (eds.), *Normality and the life cycle.* New York: Basic Books.

Emmons, Robert A., & King, Laura A. (1988). Conflict among personal strivings: Immediate and long-term implications for psychological and physical well-being. *Journal of Personality and Social Psychology, 54,* 1040–1048.

Endsley, Richard C.; Hutcherson, M. Ann; Garner, Anita P.; & Martin, Michael J. (1979). Interrelationships among selected maternal behaviors, authoritarianism, and preschool children's verbal and non-verbal curiosity. *Child Development, 50,* 331–339.

Englander-Golden, Paula; Whitmore, Mary R.; & Dienstbier, Richard A. (1978). Menstrual cycle as focus of study and self-reports of moods and behaviors. *Motivation and Emotion, 2*(1), 75–86.

Ennis, Robert H. (1985). Critical thinking and the curriculum. *National Forum, 65*(1), 28–30.

Epstein, Cynthia F. (1976, March–April). Separate and unequal: Notes on women's achievement. *Social Policy, 6,* 17–23.

Epstein, Cynthia F. (1985). The politics of stress: Public visions, private realities. *The American Journal of Psychoanalysis, 45,* 282–290.

Epstein, R.; Kirshnit, C. E.; Lanza, R. P.; & Rubin, L. C. (1984, March 1). 'Insight' in the pigeon: Antecedents and determinants of an intelligent performance. *Nature, 308,* 61–62.

Epstein, Seymour, & Fenz, Walter (1965). Steepness of approach and avoidance gradients in humans as a function of experience. *Journal of Experimental Psychology, 70,* 1–12.

Epstein, Yakov M. (1981). Crowding stress and human behavior. *Journal of Social Issues, 37*(1), 126–145.

Erikson, Erik H. (1950/1963). *Childhood and society.* New York: Norton. (Second edition, revised and enlarged, 1963.)

Erikson, Erik H. (1987). *A way of looking at things: Selected papers from 1930 to 1980 (edited by Stephen Schlein).* New York: Norton.

Erikson, Erik H.; Erikson, Joan M.; & Kivnick, Helen Q. (1986). *Vital involvements in old age.* New York: Norton.

Eron, Leonard (1980). Prescription for reduction of aggression. *American Psychologist, 35,* 244–252.

Ervin-Tripp, Susan (1964). Imitation and structural change in children's language. In E. H. Lenneberg (ed.), *New directions in the study of language.* Cambridge, MA: MIT Press.

Evans, Carlton, & Richardson, P. H. (1988, August 27). Improved recovery and reduced postoperative stay after therapeutic suggestions during general anaesthesia. *Lancet,* 491–493.

Evans, Christopher (1984). *Landscapes of the night.* (Edited and completed by Peter Evans.) New York: Viking.

Eyferth, Klaus (1961). Leistungen verschiedener Gruppen von Besatzungskindern im Hamburg-Wechsler Intelligenztest für Kinder (HAWIK). [The performance of different groups of the children of occupation forces on the Hamburg-Wechsler Intelligence Test for Children.] *Archiv für die Gesamte Psychologie, 113,* 222–241.

Eysenck, Hans (1952). The effects of psychotherapy: An evaluation. *Journal of Consulting Psychology, 16,* 319–324.

Eysenck, Hans (1966). *The effects of psychotherapy.* New York: International Science Press.

Eysenck, Hans (1970). *The structure of human personality.* New York: Methuen.

Eysenck, Hans (1985). Psychotherapy effects: Real or imaginary? *American Psychologist, 40,* 239–240.

Eysenck, Hans J., & Eysenck, Michael W. (1985). *Personality and individual differences.* New York: Plenum.

Eysenck, Hans J., & Kamin, Leon J. (1981). *The intelligence controversy.* New York: Wiley.

Eysenck, Sybil, & Long, F. Y. (1986). A cross-cultural comparison of personality in adults and children: Singapore and England. *Journal of Personality and Social Psychology, 50,* 124–130.

Fabe, Marilyn, & Wikler, Norma (1979). *Up against the clock.* New York: Random House.

Farber, Leslie (1979, April). Merchandising depression. *Psychology Today, 12*(11), 64ff.

Farber, Susan L. (1981). *Identical twins reared apart: A reanalysis.* New York: Basic Books.

Faust, David, & Ziskin, Jay (1988, July 1). The expert witness in psychology and psychiatry. *Science, 241,* 31–35.

Fausto-Sterling, Anne (1985). *Myths of gender: Biological theories about women and men.* New York: Basic Books.

Feather, N. T. (1966). Effects of prior success and failure on expectations of success and subsequent performance. *Journal of Personality and Social Psychology, 3,* 287–298.

Feather, N. T. (ed.) (1982). *Expectations and actions: Expectancy-value models in psychology.* Hillsdale, NJ: Erlbaum.

Feather, N. T. (1985). Attitudes, values, and attributions: Explanations of unemployment. *Journal of Personality and Social Psychology, 48,* 876–889.

Feeney, Dennis M. (1987). Human rights and animal welfare. *American Psychologist, 42*(6), 593–599.

Feifel, Herman (1985). Coping with life-threat and general life conflict: Two diverse beasts. Paper presented at the annual meeting of the American Psychological Association, Los Angeles.

Feinberg, Richard A. (1986). Credit cards as spending facilitating stimuli: A conditioning interpretation. *Journal of Consumer Research, 13,* 348–356.

Feingold, Alan (1988). Cognitive gender differences are disappearing. *American Psychologist, 43,* 95–103.

Fernald, L. D. (1984). *The Hans legacy: A story of science.* Hillsdale, NJ: Erlbaum.

Feshbach, Norma (1983). Learning to care: A positive approach to child training and discipline. *Journal of Clinical Child Psychology, 12,* 266–271.

Feshbach, Norma (1985). Chronic maternal stress and its assessment. In J. N. Butcher & C. D. Speilberger (eds.), *Advances in personality assessment,* Vol. 5. Hillsdale, NJ: Erlbaum.

Feshbach, Norma; Feshbach, Seymour; Fauvre, Mary; & Ballard-Campbell, Michael (1983). *Learning to care: A curriculum for affective and social development.* Glenview, IL: Scott, Foresman.

Festinger, Leon (1957). *A theory of cognitive dissonance.* Evanston, IL: Row, Peterson.

Festinger, Leon (1980). Looking backward. In L. Festinger (ed.), *Retrospections on social psychology.* New York: Oxford University Press.

Festinger, Leon, & Carlsmith, J. Merrill (1959). Cognitive consequences of forced compliance. *Journal of Abnormal and Social Psychology, 58,* 203–210.

Festinger, Leon; Pepitone, Albert; & Newcomb, Theodore (1952). Some consequences of de-individuation in a group. *Journal of Abnormal and Social Psychology, 47,* 382–389.

Festinger, Leon; Riecken, Henry W.; & Schachter, Stanley (1956). *When prophecy fails.* Minneapolis: University of Minnesota Press.

Feuerstein, Reuven (1980). *Instrumental enrichment: An intervention program for cognitive modifiability.* Baltimore, MD: University Park Press.

Ficher, Ilda V.; Zuckerman, Marvin; & Neeb, Michael (1981). Marital compatibility in sensation seeking trait as a factor in marital adjustment. *Journal of Sex and Marital Therapy, 7,* 60–69.

Field, Tiffany (1987). Individual differences in neonatal expressivity. Paper presented at the annual meeting of the American Psychological Association, New York.

Fine, Catherine G. (1987). Diagnosis & treatment of dissociative disorders: Picking up after child abuse. Paper presented at the annual meeting of the American Psychological Association, New York.

Fingarette, Herbert (1988). *Heavy drinking: The myth of alcoholism as a disease.* Berkeley, CA: University of California Press.

Fischer, Joel (1978). Does anything work? *Journal of Social Science Research, 1,* 215–243.

Fisher, Kathleen (1985, March). ECT: New studies on how, why, who. *APA Monitor, 16,* 18–19.

Fishman, H. Charles (1988). *Treating troubled adolescents: A family therapy approach.* New York: Basic Books.

Fiske, Susan T.; Pratto, Felicia; & Pavelchak, Mark (1983). Citizens' images of nuclear war: Contents and consequences. *Journal of Social Issues, 39*(1), 41–66.

Fiske, Susan T., & Taylor, Shelley E. (1984). *Social cognition.* Reading, MA: Addison-Wesley.

Fixsen, Dean L.; Phillips, Elery L.; et al. (1978, November). The Boys Town revolution. *Human Nature, 1,* 54–61.

Flach, Frederic (1988). *Resilience.* New York: Fawcett Columbine.

Flavell, John H. (1986). The development of children's knowledge about the appearance-reality distinction. *American Psychologist, 41,* 418–425.

Fleming, Raymond; Baum, Andrew; & Singer, Jerome E. (1984). Toward an integrative approach to the study of stress. *Journal of Personality and Social Psychology, 46,* 939–949.

Flor, Herta; Kerns, Robert D.; & Turk, Dennis C. (1985). The prediction of pain behaviors in chronic pain patients from spouse reinforcement. Paper presented at the annual meeting of the Society of Behavioral Medicine, New Orleans.

Foa, Edna, & Emmelkamp, Paul (eds.) (1983). *Failures in behavior therapy.* New York: Wiley.

Fogelman, Eva, & Wiener, Valerie L. (1985, August). The few, the brave, the noble. *Psychology Today, 19*(8), 61–65.

Folkman, Susan (1984). Personal control and stress and coping processes: A theoretical analysis. *Journal of Personality and Social Psychology, 46,* 839–852.

Folkman, Susan, & Lazarus, Richard S. (1980). An analysis of coping in a middle-aged community sample. *Journal of Health and Social Behavior, 21,* 219–239.

Fordyce, Wilbert E. (1976). Behavioral concepts in chronic pain and illness. In P. O. Davidson (ed.), *The behavioral management of anxiety, depression, and pain.* New York: Brunner/Mazel.

Forgas, Joseph, & Bond, Michael H. (1985). Cultural influences on the perception of interaction episodes. *Personality and Social Psychology Bulletin, 11,* 75–88.

Fouts, Roger S.; Fouts, Deborah H.; & Van Cantfort, Thomas E. (1989). The infant Loulis learns signs from cross-fostered chimpanzees. In R. A. Gardner, B. T. Gardner, & T. E. Van Cantfort (eds.), *Teaching sign language to chimpanzees.* New York: State University of New York Press.

Fouts, Roger S., & Rigby, Randall L. (1977). Man-chimpanzee communication. In T. A. Seboek (ed.), *How animals communicate.* Bloomington: University of Indiana Press.

Fozard, James L. (1980). The time for remembering. In L. W. Poon (ed.), *Aging in the 1980's: Psychological issues.* Washington, DC: American Psychological Association.

France, Kenneth (1984). Competitive versus noncompetitive thinking during exercise: Effects on norepinephrine levels. Paper presented at the annual meeting of the American Psychological Association, Toronto.

Frances, Susan J. (1979). Sex differences in nonverbal behavior. *Sex Roles, 5,* 519–535.

Frank, Jerome D. (1974). *Persuasion and healing.* New York: Schocken.

Frank, Jerome D. (1982). Therapeutic components shared by all psychotherapies. In J. H. Harvey & M. M. Parks (eds.), *Psychotherapy research and behavior change.* The

Master Lecture Series, Vol. 1. Washington, DC: American Psychological Association.

Frankenhaeuser, Marianne (1975). Experimental approaches to the study of catecholamines and emotion. In L. Levi (ed.), *Emotions: Their parameters and measurement*. New York: Raven Press.

Frankenhaeuser, Marianne (1980). Psychological aspects of life stress. In S. Levine & H. Ursin (eds.), *Coping and health*. New York: Plenum.

Frankl, Victor E. (1955). *The doctor and the soul: An introduction to logotherapy*. New York: Knopf.

Fraser, Antonia (1984). *The weaker vessel*. New York: Knopf.

Free, Noel K.; Green, Bonnie L.; Grace, Mary C.; Chernus, Linda A.; & Whitman, Roy M. (1985). Empathy and outcome in brief focal-dynamic therapy. *American Journal of Psychiatry, 142,* 917–921.

Freedman, Daniel (1979). *Human sociobiology*. Riverside, NJ: Free Press.

Freedman, Jonathan L. (1988). Television violence and aggression: What the evidence shows. In Stewart Oskamp (ed.), *Television as a social issue. Applied Social Psychology Annual*, Vol. 8. Newbury Park, CA: Sage.

Freedman, Jonathan L., & Fraser, Scott (1966). Compliance without pressure: The foot-in-the-door technique. *Journal of Personality and Social Psychology, 4,* 195–202.

Freud, Anna (1946). *The ego and the mechanisms of defence*. New York: International Universities Press.

Freud, Sigmund (1905a). Fragment of an analysis of a case of hysteria. In J. Strachey (ed.), *Standard edition of the complete psychological works of Sigmund Freud,* Vol. VII. London: The Hogarth Press and the Institute of Psycho-Analysis (1964 edition).

Freud, Sigmund (1905b). Three essays on the theory of sexuality. In *Standard edition,* Vol. VII.

Freud, Sigmund (1910/1957). Leonardo da Vinci: A study in psychosexuality. In *Standard edition,* Vol. XI.

Freud, Sigmund (1917). Mourning and melancholia. In *Standard edition,* Vol. XIV.

Freud, Sigmund (1920/1960). *A general introduction to psychoanalysis*. (Joan Riviere, translator.) New York: Washington Square Press.

Freud, Sigmund (1920/1963). The psychogenesis of a case of homosexuality in a woman. In S. Freud, *Sexuality and the psychology of love*. New York: Collier Books.

Freud, Sigmund (1923/1962). *The ego and the id*. (Joan Riviere, translator.) New York: Norton.

Freud, Sigmund (1924a). The dissolution of the Oedipus complex. In *Standard edition,* Vol. XIX.

Freud, Sigmund (1924b). Some psychical consequences of the anatomical distinction between the sexes. In *Standard edition,* Vol. XIX.

Friedman, Howard S., & Booth-Kewley, Stephanie (1987a). The disease-prone personality: A meta-analytic view of the construct. *American Psychologist, 42,* 539–555.

Friedman, Howard S., & Booth-Kewley, Stephanie (1987b). Personality, Type A behavior, and coronary heart disease: The role of emotional expression. *Journal of Personality and Social Psychology, 53,* 783–792.

Friedman, Howard S.; Hall, Judith A.; & Harris, Monica J. (1985). Type A behavior, nonverbal expressive style, and health. *Journal of Personality and Social Psychology, 48,* 1299–1315.

Friedman, Meyer, & Rosenman, Ray (1974). *Type A behavior and your heart*. New York: Knopf.

Friedman, Stanley, & Fisher, Charles (1967). On the presence of a rhythmic, diurnal, oral instinctual drive cycle in man: A preliminary report. *Journal of the American Psychoanalytic Association, 15,* 317–343.

Friedman, William; Robinson, Amy; & Friedman, Britt (1987). Sex differences in moral judgments? A test of Gilligan's theory. *Psychology of Women Quarterly, 11,* 37–46.

Frieze, Irene H.; Parsons, Jacquelynne E.; Johnson, Paula B.; Ruble, Diane N.; & Zellman, Gail L. (1978). Being feminine or masculine—nonverbally. In I. H. Frieze et al. (eds.), *Women and sex roles: A social psychological perspective*. New York: Norton.

Frijda, Nico H. (1988). The laws of emotion. *American Psychologist, 43,* 349–358.

Frodi, Ann M., & Lamb, Michael E. (1978). Sex differences in responsiveness to infants. *Child Development, 49,* 1182–1188.

Frodi, Ann; Macaulay, Jacqueline; & Thome, Pauline (1977). Are women always less aggressive than men? A review of the literature. *Psychological Bulletin, 84,* 634–660.

Fry, William, Jr. (1986). Humor, physiology, and the aging process. In L. Nahemov (ed.), *Humor and aging*. New York: Academic Press.

Fry, William, Jr., & Salameh, Waleed (eds.) (1987). *Handbook of humor and psychotherapy*. Sarasota, FL: The Professional Resource Exchange.

Funk, Steven C., & Houston, B. Kent (1987). A critical analysis of the hardiness scale's validity and utility. *Journal of Personality and Social Psychology, 53,* 572–578.

Gagnon, John (1987). Science and the politics of pathology. *The Journal of Sex Research, 23,* 120–123.

Gagnon, John, & Simon, William (1973). *Sexual conduct: The social sources of human sexuality*. Chicago: Aldine.

Galanter, Eugene (1962). Contemporary psychophysics. In R. Brown, E. Galanter, H. Hess, and G. Mandler (eds.), *New directions in psychology*. New York: Holt, Rinehart and Winston.

Galin, David, & Ornstein, Robert (1972). Lateral specialization of cognitive mode: An EEG study. *Psychophysiology, 9,* 412–418.

Gallagher, Winifred (1988, March). Marijuana: Is there new reason to worry? *American Health, 7,* 92ff.

Garcia, John, & Koelling, Robert A. (1966). Relation of cue to consequence in avoidance learning. *Psychonomic Science, 4,* 123–124.

Gardner, Howard (1983). *Frames of mind: The theory of multiple intelligences*. New York: Basic Books.

Gardner, Howard (1985). *The mind's new science: A history of the cognitive revolution.* New York: Basic Books.

Gardner, R. Allen, & Gardner, Beatrice T. (1969). Teaching sign language to a chimpanzee. *Science, 165,* 664–672.

Garfield, Patricia (1974). *Creative dreaming.* New York: Ballantine.

Garfinkel, Renee (1986). Methodological and scientific problems in DSM-III-R diagnoses. Paper presented at the annual meeting of the American Psychological Association, Washington.

Garner, David; Garfinkel, Paul; Schwartz, Donald; & Thompson, Michael (1980). Cultural expectations of thinness in women. *Psychological Reports, 47,* 483–491.

Garnica, Olga Kaunoff (1975). Some characteristics of prosodic input to young children. Unpublished doctoral dissertation, Stanford University.

Gartner, Alan, & Riessman, Frank (eds.) (1984). *The self-help revolution.* Vol. X, Community Psychology Series. New York: Human Sciences Press.

Gaston, Louise; Marmar, Charles; Thompson, Larry; & Gallagher, Dolores (1987). Prediction of therapeutic alliance in behavior, cognitive, and brief dynamic psychotherapy. Paper presented at the annual meeting of the American Psychological Association, New York.

Gazzaniga, Michael S. (1967). The split brain in man. *Scientific American, 217*(2), 24–29.

Gazzaniga, Michael S. (1983). Right hemisphere language following brain bisection: A 20-year perspective. *American Psychologist, 38*(5), 525–537.

Gazzaniga, Michael S. (1985). *The social brain: Discovering the networks of the mind.* New York: Basic Books.

Gazzaniga, Michael S. (1988). *Mind matters.* Boston: Houghton Mifflin.

Gedo, John (1979). A psychoanalyst reports at mid-career. *American Journal of Psychiatry, 136,* 646–649.

Geen, Russell G. (1978). Some effects of observing violence upon the behavior of the observer. In B. A. Maher (ed.), *Progress in experimental personality research.* New York: Academic Press.

Geen, Russell G. (1984). Human motivation: New perspectives on old problems. In A. M. Rogers & C. J. Scheirer (eds.), *The G. Stanley Hall lecture series,* Vol. 4. Washington, DC: American Psychological Association.

Geen, Russell G. (1984). Preferred stimulation levels in introverts and extraverts: Effects on arousal and performance. *Journal of Personality and Social Psychology, 46,* 1303–1313.

Gehring, Robert E., & Toglia, Michael P. (1989). Recall of pictorial enactments and verbal descriptions with verbal and imagery study strategies. *Journal of Mental Imagery, 13*(2), 83–98.

Geldard, F. A. (1962). *Fundamentals of psychology.* New York: Wiley.

Gelenberg, Alan J.; Wojcik, Joanne D.; Gibson, Candace J.; & Wurtman, Richard J. (1982–1983). Tyrosine for depression. *Journal of Psychiatric Research, 17*(2), 175–180.

Gelles, Richard J. (1979). *Family violence.* Beverly Hills, CA: Sage.

Gelman, Rochel (1983). Recent trends in cognitive development. In C. J. Scheirer & A. M. Rogers (eds.), *The G. Stanley Hall lecture series,* Vol. 3. Washington, DC: American Psychological Association.

Gelman, Rochel, & Baillargeon, Renee (1983). A review of some Piagetian concepts. In J. H. Flavell & E. M. Markman (eds.), *Manual of child psychology: Cognitive development,* Vol. 3. New York: Wiley.

Gelman, Rochel, & Shatz, Marilyn (1977). Appropriate speech adjustments: The operation of conversational constraints on talk to two-year-olds. In M. Lewis & L. A. Rosenblum (eds.), *Interaction, conversation, and the development of language.* New York: Wiley.

Gentry, W. Doyle (1985). Relationship of anger-coping styles and blood pressure among black Americans. In M. A. Chesney & R. H. Rosenman (eds.), *Anger and hostility in cardiovascular and behavioral disorders.* New York: Hemisphere.

George, Stephen G., & Jennings, Luther B. (1975). Effect of subliminal stimuli on consumer behavior: Negative evidence. *Perceptual and Motor Skills, 41,* 847–854.

Gerbner, George (1988). Telling stories in the information age. In Brent D. Ruben (ed.), *Information and behavior,* Vol. 2. New Brunswick, NJ: Transaction Books.

Gergen, Kenneth (1973). Social psychology as history. *Journal of Personality and Social Psychology, 26,* 309–320.

Gergen, Kenneth, & Gergen, Mary (1986). *Social psychology.* New York: Springer-Verlag.

Gergen, Kenneth; Gergen, Mary; & Barton, William (1973, October). Deviance in the dark. *Psychology Today, 7*(5), 129–130.

Giarusso, Roseann; Johnson, Paula; Goodchilds, Jacqueline; & Zellman, Gail (1979). Adolescents' cues and signals: Sex and assault. Paper presented at the annual meeting of the Western Psychological Association, San Diego.

Gibbs, Nancy R. (1988, February 22). Grays on the go. *Time,* 66–78.

Gibson, Eleanor, & Walk, Richard (1960). The ''visual cliff.'' *Scientific American, 202,* 80–92.

Gibson, Janice T., & Haritos-Fatouros, Mika (1986, November). The education of a torturer. *Psychology Today, 20,* 50–58.

Gibson, J. J. (1979). *The ecological approach to visual perception.* Boston: Houghton Mifflin.

Gillberg, Christopher; Terenius, Lars; & Lönnerholm, Gudmar (1985). Endorphin activity in childhood psychosis. *Archives of General Psychiatry, 42,* 780–783.

Gilligan, Carol (1982). *In a different voice.* Cambridge, MA: Harvard University Press.

Gilligan, Carol, & Wiggins, Grant (1987). The origins of morality in early childhood relationships. In J. Kagan & S. Lamb (eds.), *The emergence of morality in young children.* Chicago: University of Chicago Press.

Gillin, J. Christian; Sitaram, N.; Janowsky, D.; et al. (1985). Cholinergic mechanisms in REM sleep. In A. Wauquier, J. M. Gaillard, J. M. Monti, & M. Radulovacki (eds.), *Sleep: Neurotransmitters and neuromodulators.* New York: Raven Press.

Glanzer, Murray, & Cunitz, Anita R. (1966). Two storage mechanisms in free recall. *Journal of Verbal Learning and Verbal Behavior, 5,* 351–360.

Glucksberg, Sam, & Weisberg, Robert W. (1966). Verbal behavior and problem solving: Some effects of labelling in a functional fixedness problem. *Journal of Experimental Psychology, 71,* 659–664.

Goddard, H. H. (1917). Mental tests and the immigrant. *The Journal of Delinquency, 2,* 243–277.

Gold, Paul E. (1984). Memory modulation: Neurobiological contexts. In Gary Lynch, James L. McGaugh, & N. M. Weinberger (eds.), *Neurobiology of learning and memory.* New York: Guilford Press.

Gold, Paul E. (1987). Sweet memories. *American Scientist, 75,* 151–155.

Goldfried, Marvin R. (1980). Toward the delineation of therapeutic change principles. *American Psychologist, 35,* 991–999.

Goldiamond, Israel (1973, November). A diary of self-modification. *Psychology Today, 7*(6), 95–100, 102.

Golding, Jacqueline M. (1988). Gender differences in depressive symptoms. *Psychology of Women Quarterly, 12,* 61–74.

Goldstein, Arnold, & Rosenbaum, Alan (1982). *Aggress-Less.* Englewood Cliffs, NJ: Prentice-Hall.

Goldstein, Avram (1980). Thrills in response to music and other stimuli. *Physiological Psychology, 8,* 126–129.

Goldstein, Jeffrey (ed.) (1983). *Sports violence.* New York: Springer-Verlag.

Goldstein, Jeffrey H. (1987). Therapeutic effects of laughter. In W. F. Fry, Jr., & W. A. Salameh (eds.), *Handbook of humor and psychotherapy.* Sarasota, FL: Professional Resource Exchange.

Goldstein, Michael J. (1987). Psychosocial issues. *Schizophrenia Bulletin, 13*(1), 157–171.

Goldstein, Michael J. (1988). The family and psychopathology. *American Review of Psychology, 39,* 283–299.

Goldstein, Richard (1981). On deceptive rejoinders about deceptive research: A reply to Baron. *IRB: A Review of Human Subjects Research, 3*(8), 5–6.

Goleman, Daniel (1977). *The varieties of the meditative experience.* New York: Dutton.

Goleman, Daniel (1981, August). Deadlines for change. *Psychology Today, 15*(8), 60–69.

Goleman, Daniel (1982, March). Staying up: The rebellion against sleep's gentle tyranny. *Psychology Today, 16*(3), 24–25, 27–28, 31–32, 35.

Goodenough, Donald R.; Shapiro, Arthur; Holden, Melvin; & Steinschriber, Leonard (1959). A comparison of dreamers and nondreamers: Eye movements, electroencephalograms and the recall of dreams. *Journal of Abnormal and Social Psychology, 59,* 295–302.

Gordon, Thomas (1970). *Parent effectiveness training.* New York: McKay.

Gore, Susan, & Mangione, Thomas W. (1983). Social roles, sex roles and psychological distress. *Journal of Health and Social Behavior, 24,* 300–312.

Gorn, Gerald J. (1982). The effects of music in advertising on choice behavior: A classical conditioning approach. *Journal of Marketing, 46,* 94–101.

Gotlib, Ian H., & Hooley, J. M. (1988). Depression and marital functioning. In S. Duck (ed.), *Handbook of personal relationships: Theory, research and interventions.* Chichester, England: Wiley.

Gottesman, Irving I. (1963). Genetic aspects of intelligent behavior. In N. Ellis (ed.), *Handbook of mental deficiency: Psychological theory and research.* New York: McGraw-Hill.

Gottesman, Irving; McGuffin, Peter; & Farmer, Anne E. (1987). Clinical genetics as clues to the "real" genetics of schizophrenia. *Schizophrenia Bulletin, 13*(1), 23–47.

Gottesman, Irving I., & Shields, James (1973). *Schizophrenia and genetics: A twin study vantage point.* New York: Academic Press.

Gottesman, Irving I., & Shields, James (1982). *Schizophrenia: The epigenetic puzzle.* Cambridge, England: Cambridge University Press.

Gould, James L., & Gould, Carol G. (1982). The insect mind: Physics or metaphysics? In D. R. Griffin (ed.), *Animal mind—human mind.* Berlin and New York: Simon & Schuster.

Gould, Stephen Jay (1981). *The mismeasure of man.* New York: Norton.

Gould, Stephen Jay (1985, June). The median isn't the message. *Discover, 6*(6), 40–42.

Graham, Jill (1984). Principled organizational dissent. Paper presented at the annual meeting of the American Psychological Association, Toronto.

Grant, Vernon (1977). *The menacing stranger: A primer on the psychopath.* Oceanside, NY: Dabor Science Publications.

Greene, David, & Lepper, Mark R. (1974, September). How to turn play into work. *Psychology Today, 8*(4), 49–52, 54.

Greenfield, Patricia (1966). On culture and conservation. In J. S. Bruner, R. R. Olver, & P. M. Greenfield et al. (eds.), *Studies in cognitive growth.* New York: Wiley.

Greenfield, Patricia (1976). Cross-cultural research and Piagetian theory: Paradox and progress. In K. F. Riegel & J. A. Meacham (eds.), *The developing individual in a changing world. Vol. 1: Historical and cultural issues.* The Hague: Mouton.

Greenfield, Patricia, & Beagles-Roos, Jessica (1988). Radio vs. television: Their cognitive impact on children of different socioeconomic and ethnic groups. *Journal of Communication, 38,* 71–92.

Greenough, W. T. (1984). Structural correlates of information storage in the mammalian brain: A review and hypothesis. *Trends in Neurosciences, 7,* 229–233.

Greenspan, Stanley, & Greenspan, Nancy (1985). *First feelings.* New York: Viking Press.

Greenwald, Anthony G. (1980). The totalitarian ego: Fabrication and revision of personal history. *American Psychologist, 35,* 603–618.

Gregory, R. L. (1963). Distortion of visual space as inappropriate constancy scaling. *Nature, 199,* 678–679.

Gregory, Richard L., & Wallace, Jean G. (1963). Recovery from early blindness: A case study. *Monograph Supplement 2, Quarterly Journal of Experimental Psychology,* No. 3. (Reprinted in R. L. Gregory, *Concepts and mechanisms of perception.* New York: Scribner's.)

Grier, Kenneth (1982). A study of job stress in police officers and high school teachers. Unpublished doctoral dissertation, University of South Florida.

Griffin, Donald (1984). *Animal thinking.* Cambridge, MA: Harvard University Press.

Griffith, James (1983). Emotional supports and psychological distress in Anglo and Mexican Americans. Paper presented at the annual meeting of the American Psychological Association, Anaheim, CA.

Groebel, Jo, & Hinde, Robert (eds.) (1989). The Seville statement on violence. *Aggression and war: Their biological and social bases.* Cambridge, England: Cambridge University Press.

Gross, Martin (1978). *The psychological society.* New York: Random House.

Guidubaldi, John, & Perry, Joseph (1985). Divorce and mental health sequelae for children: A two-year follow-up of a nationwide sample. *Journal of the American Academy of Child Psychiatry, 24,* 531–537.

Guilford, J. P. (1950). Creativity. *American Psychologist, 5,* 444–454.

Guilford, J. P. (1967). *The nature of human intelligence.* New York: McGraw-Hill.

Guilford, J. P. (1982). Cognitive psychology's ambiguities: Some suggested remedies. *Psychological Review, 89,* 48–59.

Guilford, J. P. (1988). Some changes in the structure-of-intellect model. *Educational and Psychological Measurement, 48,* 1–4.

Gur, Ruben C.; Gur, Raquel E.; et al. (1982). Sex and handedness differences in cerebral blood flow during rest and cognitive activity. *Science, 217,* 659–660.

Gurin, Joel (1984, May). What's your natural weight? *American Health, 3,* 43–47.

Guttentag, Marcia, & Secord, Paul (1983). *Too many women?* Beverly Hills, CA: Sage.

Haber, Ralph N. (1969, April). Eidetic images: With biographic sketches. *Scientific American, 220*(12), 36–44.

Haber, Ralph N. (1970, May). How we remember what we see. *Scientific American, 222,* 104–112.

Haber, Ralph N. (1974). Eidetic images. In R. Held (ed.), *Image, object, and illusion.* San Francisco: Freeman.

Hacker, Helen M. (1981). Blabbermouths and clams: Sex differences in self-disclosure in same-sex and cross-sex

friendship dyads. *Psychology of Women Quarterly, 5,* 385–401.

Hackman, J. Richard, & Oldham, Greg R. (1980). *Work redesign.* Reading, MA: Addison-Wesley.

Hall, Edward T. (1976). *Beyond culture.* New York: Anchor Press/Doubleday.

Hall, Edward T. (1983). *The dance of life.* New York: Anchor Press/Doubleday.

Hall, Edward T., & Hall, Mildred R. (1983). *Hidden differences: How to communicate with the Germans.* Hamburg, West Germany: *Stern* magazine/Gruner + Jahr.

Hall, Elizabeth (1986). Motherhood. In C. Tavris (ed.), *EveryWoman's emotional well-being.* New York: Doubleday.

Hall, G. Stanley (1904). *Adolescence.* New York: Appleton.

Hall, Jay, & Watson, W. H. (1970). The effects of normative intervention on group decision-making performance. *Human Relations, 23,* 299–317.

Hall, Judith (1978). Gender effects in decoding nonverbal cues. *Psychological Bulletin, 85,* 845–857.

Haney, Craig; Banks, Curtis; & Zimbardo, Philip (1973). Interpersonal dynamics in a simulated prison. *International Journal of Criminology and Penology, 1,* 69–97.

Harackiewicz, Judith M.; Sansone, Carol; & Manderlink, George (1985). Competence, achievement orientation, and intrinsic motivation: A process analysis. *Journal of Personality and Social Psychology, 48,* 493–508.

Harburg, Ernest; Erfurt, John C.; & Hauenstein, Louise S.; et al. (1973). Socioecological stress, suppressed hostility, skin color, and black-white male blood pressure: Detroit. *Psychosomatic Medicine, 35,* 276–296.

Harding, Courtenay; Brooks, George W.; Ashikaga, Takamaru; Strauss, John S.; & Breier, Alan (1987). The Vermont longitudinal study of persons with severe mental illness. I. Methodology, study sample, and overall current status. II. Long-term outcome for DSM-III schizophrenia. *American Journal of Psychiatry, 144,* 718–735.

Harding, Courtenay; Zubin, Joseph; & Strauss, John (1987). Chronicity in schizophrenia: Fact, partial fact, or artifact? *Hospital and Community Psychiatry, 38,* 477–486.

Hare, Robert D. (1986). Twenty years of experience with the Cleckley psychopath. In W. H. Reid, D. Dorr, J. I. Walker, & J. W. Bonner (eds.), *Unmasking the psychopath: Antisocial personality and related syndromes.* New York: Norton.

Hare-Mustin, Rachel T. (1983). Educating for counseling and psychotherapy with women. Paper presented at the annual meeting of the American Psychological Association, Anaheim, CA.

Hare-Mustin, Rachel T. (1984, April). Truth and fantasy: Ethical issues in psychotherapy. Charlotte Perkins Gilman lecture, Radcliffe College, Cambridge, MA.

Hare-Mustin, Rachel T.; Marecek, Jeanne; Kaplan, Alexandra G.; & Liss-Levinson, Nechama (1979). Rights of clients, responsibilities of therapists. *American Psychologist, 34,* 3–16.

Harkins, Stephen G., & Petty, Richard E. (1983). Social context effects in persuasion. In P. Paulus (ed.), *Basic group processes*. New York: Springer-Verlag.

Harlow, Harry F. (1958). The nature of love. *American Psychologist, 13*, 673–685.

Harlow, Harry F., & Harlow, Margaret K. (1966). Learning to love. *American Scientist, 54*, 244–272.

Harlow, Harry F.; Harlow, Margaret K.; & Meyer, D. R. (1950). Learning motivated by a manipulation drive. *Journal of Experimental Psychology, 40*, 228–234.

Harrell, Thomas W., & Harrell, Margaret S. (1945). Army general classification test scores for civilian occupations. *Educational and Psychological Measurement, 5*, 229–239.

Harrington, David; Block, Jeanne; & Block, Jack (1987). Testing aspects of Carl Rogers's theory of creative environments: Child-rearing antecedents of creative potential in young adolescents. *Journal of Personality and Social Psychology, 52*, 851–856.

Harris, Ben (1979). Whatever happened to little Albert? *American Psychologist, 34*, 151–160.

Harris, Marvin (1985). *Good to eat: Riddles of food and culture*. New York: Simon & Schuster.

Harris, Paul L. (1984). Infant cognition. In P. Mussen (ed.), *Handbook of child psychology* (4th ed.). Vol. II. M. M. Haith & J. J. Campos (eds.), *Infancy and developmental psychobiology*. New York: Wiley.

Hart, John Jr.; Berndt, Rita S.; & Caramazza, Alfonso (1985, August 1). Category-specific naming deficit following cerebral infarction. *Nature, 316*, 339–340.

Harter, Susan (1978). Effectance motivation reconsidered: Toward a developmental model. *Human Development, 21*, 34–64.

Harter, Susan (1981). A model of mastery motivation in children: Individual differences and developmental change. In W. A. Collins (ed.), *Aspects of the development of competence: The Minnesota symposia on child psychology, Vol. 14*. Hillsdale, NJ: Erlbaum.

Hartup, Willard W. (1980). Peer relations and family relations: Two social worlds. In M. Rutter (ed.), *Scientific foundations of developmental psychiatry*. London: Heinemann.

Hasher, Lynn, & Zacks, Rose T. (1984). Automatic processing of fundamental information: The case of frequency of occurrence. *American Psychologist, 39*, 1372–1388.

Hastorf, Albert H., & Cantril, Hadley (1954). They saw a game: A case study. *Journal of Abnormal and Social Psychology, 49*, 129–134.

Hatfield, Elaine (1988). Passionate and companionate love. In R. J. Sternberg & M. L. Barnes (eds.), *The psychology of love*. New Haven, CT, and London: Yale University Press.

Hatfield, Elaine; Greenberger, David; Traupmann, Jane; & Lambert, Philip (1982). Equity and sexual satisfaction in recently married couples. *Journal of Sex Research, 18*, 18–32.

Hatfield, Elaine, & Sprecher, Susan (1986). Measuring passionate love in intimate relationships. *Journal of Adolescence, 9*, 383–410.

Hathaway, S. R. & McKinley, J. C., with Butcher, James N.; Dahlstrom, W. Grant; Graham, John R.; Tellegen, Auke; & Kaemmer, Beverly (1989). *Minnesota Multiphasic Personality Inventory–II: Manual for administration and scoring*. Minneapolis: University of Minnesota Press.

Hatkoff, Terry S., & Lasswell, Thomas E. (1979). Male-female similarities and differences in conceptualizing love. In M. Cook & G. Wilson (eds.), *Love and attraction: An international conference*. Oxford, England: Pergamon.

Haviland, Jeannette M., & Lelwica, Mary (1987). The induced affect response: 10-week-old infants' responses to three emotional expressions. *Developmental Psychology, 23*, 97–104.

Hayden, Robert M. (1984). Physical fitness and mental health: Causal connection or simply correlation? Paper presented at the annual meeting of the American Psychological Association, Toronto.

Haynes, Suzanne, & Feinleib, Manning (1980). Women, work, and coronary heart disease: Prospective findings from the Framingham heart study. *American Journal of Public Health, 70*, 133–141.

Hazan, Cindy, & Shaver, Phillip (1987). Romantic love conceptualized as an attachment process. *Journal of Personality and Social Psychology, 52*, 511–524.

Hearnshaw, Leslie S. (1979). *Cyril Burt, psychologist*. Ithaca, NY: Cornell University Press.

Heider, Eleanor Rosch (1972). Universals in color naming and memory. *Journal of Experimental Psychology, 93*, 10–20.

Heider, Eleanor Rosch, & Olivier, Donald C. (1972). The structure of the color space in naming and memory for two languages. *Cognitive Psychology, 3*, 337–354.

Heider, Fritz (1946). Attitudes and cognitive organization. *Journal of Psychology, 21*, 107–112.

Heider, Fritz (1958). *The psychology of interpersonal relations*. New York: Wiley.

Helgeson, Vicki S., & Sharpsteen, Don J. (1987). Perceptions of danger in achievement and affiliation situations: An extension of the Pollak and Gilligan versus Benton et al. debate. *Journal of Personality and Social Psychology, 53*, 727–733.

Helson, Ravenna; Mitchell, Valory; & Moane, Geraldine (1984). Personality and patterns of adherence and nonadherence to the social clock. *Journal of Personality and Social Psychology, 46*, 1079–1097.

Helson, Ravenna, & Wink, Paul (1987). Two conceptions of maturity examined in the findings of a longitudinal study. *Journal of Personality and Social Psychology, 53*, 531–541.

Hendrick, Clyde, & Hendrick, Susan S. (1986). A theory and method of love. *Journal of Personality and Social Psychology, 50*, 392–402.

Hendrick, Susan S., & Hendrick, Clyde (1987). Multidimensionality of sexual attitudes. *The Journal of Sex Research, 23*, 502–526.

Hendrick, Susan S.; Hendrick, Clyde; & Adler, Nancy L. (1988). Romantic relationships: Love, satisfaction, and staying together. *Journal of Personality and Social Psychology, 54*, 980–988.

Hendrick, Susan S.; Hendrick, Clyde; Slapion-Foote, Michelle; & Foote, Franklin (1985). Gender differences in sexual attitudes. *Journal of Personality and Social Psychology, 48*, 1630–1642.

Hendrix, William H., & Rodriquez, Alex (1984, May). Effects of stress and exercise on employee health. Paper presented at the annual meeting of The Society of Behavioral Medicine, Philadelphia.

Herdt, Gilbert (1984). *Ritualized homosexuality in Melanesia*. Berkeley: University of California Press.

Herman, Barbara H., et al. (1987). Naltrexone decreases self-injurious behavior. *Annals of Neurology, 22*, 550–552.

Herman, Barbara H.; Hammock, M. Kathryn; Egan, James; Arthur-Smith, Ann; Chatoor, Irene; & Werner, Alisa (1989). Role for opioid peptides in self-injurious behavior: Dissociation from autonomic nervous system functioning. *Developmental Pharmacology Therapeutics, 12*, 81–89.

Herman, Judith L., & Schatzow, Emily (1987). Recovery and verification of memories of childhood sexual trauma. *Psychoanalytic Psychology, 4*(1), 1–14.

Heron, Woodburn (1957). The pathology of boredom. *Scientific American, 196*(1), 52–56.

Herrnstein, R. J. (1982, August). IQ testing and the media. *Atlantic Monthly, 250*(2), 68–74.

Hess, Eckhard H. (1959). Imprinting. *Science, 130*, 133–144.

Hetherington, E. Mavis; Cox, Martha; & Cox, Roger (1985). Long-term effect of divorce and remarriage on the adjustment of children. *Journal of the American Academy of Child Psychology, 24*, 518–530.

Hilgard, Ernest R. (1965). *Hypnotic susceptibility*. New York: Harcourt Brace Jovanovich.

Hilgard, Ernest R. (1977). *Divided consciousness: Multiple controls in human thought and action*. New York: Wiley-Interscience.

Hilgard, Ernest R. (1978, January). Hypnosis and consciousness. *Human Nature, 1*, 42–49.

Hilgard, Ernest R. (1980). Consciousness in contemporary psychology. *Annual Review of Psychology, 31*, 1–26.

Hilgard, Ernest R., & Hilgard, Josephine R. (1975). *Hypnosis in the relief of pain*. Los Altos, CA: William Kaufmann.

Hilgard, Josephine R. (1979). *Personality and hypnosis: A study of imaginative involvement* (2nd ed.). Chicago: University of Chicago Press.

Hill, Winfred F. (1985). *Learning: A survey of psychological interpretations* (4th ed.). New York: Harper & Row.

Hinrichsen, Gregory A.; Revenson, Tracey A.; & Shinn, Marybeth (1985). Does self-help help? An empirical investigation of scoliosis peer support groups. *Journal of Social Issues, 41*(1), 65–88.

Hirsch, Barton (1981). Social networks and the coping process: Creating personal communities. In B. H. Gottlieb (ed.), *Social networks and social support*. Beverly Hills, CA: Sage.

Hirsch, Helmut V. B., & Jacobson, Marcus (1975). The perfectible brain: Principles of neuronal development. In M. S. Gazzaniga & C. Blakemore (eds.), *Handbook of psychobiology*. New York: Academic Press.

Hirsch, Helmut V. B., & Spinelli, D. N. (1970). Visual experience modifies distribution of horizontally and vertically oriented receptive fields in cats. *Science, 168*, 869–871.

Hirschman, Albert O. (1970). Exit, voice, and loyalty: Responses to decline in firms, organizations, and states. Cambridge, MA: Harvard University Press.

Hirst, William; Neisser, Ulric; & Spelke, Elizabeth (1978). Divided attention. *Human Nature, 1*, 54–61.

Hite, Shere (1987). *Women and love: A cultural revolution in progress*. New York: Knopf.

Hobfoll, Stevan E., & London, Perry (1986). The relationship of self-concept and social support to emotional distress among women during war. *Journal of Social and Clinical Psychology, 12*, 87–100.

Hobfoll, Stevan E., & Stephens, Mary Ann P. (1990). Social support during extreme stress: Consequences and intervention. In I. G. Sarason, B. R. Sarason, & G. R. Pierce (eds.), *Social support: An interactional view—Issues in social support research*. New York: Wiley.

Hobson, J. Allan (1988). *The dreaming brain*. New York: Basic Books.

Hobson, J. Allan, & McCarley, Robert W. (1977). The brain as a dream state generator: An activation-synthesis hypothesis of the dream process. *American Journal of Psychiatry, 134*, 1335–1348.

Hobson, Robert F. (1985). *Forms of feeling: The heart of psychotherapy*. London and New York: Tavistock.

Hochschild, Arlie (1975). The sociology of feeling and emotion. In M. Millman & R. M. Kanter (eds.), *Another voice*. Garden City, NY: Anchor/Doubleday.

Hochschild, Arlie (1983). *The managed heart*. Berkeley: University of California Press.

Hockett, Charles F. (1960). The origins of speech. *Scientific American, 203*, 89–96.

Hodgkinson, Stephen; Sherrington, Robin; Gurling, Hugh; Marchbanks, Roger; et al. (1987, February 26). Molecular genetic evidence for heterogeneity in manic depression. *Nature, 325*, 805–808.

Hoffman, Lois W. (1977). Fear of success in 1965 and 1974: A follow-up study. *Journal of Consulting and Clinical Psychology, 45*, 310–321.

Hoffman, Lois W. (1984). The study of employed mothers over half a century. In M. Lewin (ed.), *In the shadow of the past: Psychology portrays the sexes*. New York: Columbia University Press.

Hoffman, Martin L. (1977). Empathy, its development and prosocial implications. In C. B. Keasey (ed.), *Nebraska symposium on motivation,* Vol. 25. Lincoln: University of Nebraska Press.

Hoffman, Martin L. (1987). The contribution of empathy to justice and moral judgment. In N. Eisenberg & J. Strayer (eds.), *Empathy and its development.* New York: Cambridge University Press.

Hoffman, Martin L. (1989). Empathy, social cognition, and moral action. In W. Kurtines & J. Gewirtz (eds.), *Moral behavior and development: Advances in theory, research, and application: Volume 1.* Hillsdale, NJ: Erlbaum.

Hoffman, Martin L., & Saltzstein, Herbert (1967). Parent discipline and the child's moral development. *Journal of Personality and Social Psychology, 5,* 45–57.

Hokanson, Jack E. (1970). Psychophysiological evaluation of the catharsis hypothesis. In E. I. Megargee & J. E. Hokanson (eds.), *The dynamics of aggression.* New York: Harper & Row.

Holden, Constance (1980). Identical twins reared apart. *Science, 207,* 1323–1325.

Holden, Constance (1987). The genetics of personality. *Science, 237,* 598–601.

Holmes, David (1984). Meditation and somatic arousal reduction: A review of the experimental evidence. *American Psychologist, 39,* 1–10.

Holmes, David; Solomon, Sheldon; Cappo, Bruce; & Greenberg, Jeffrey (1983). Effects of Transcendental Meditation versus resting on physiological and subjective arousal. *Journal of Personality and Social Psychology, 44,* 1245–1252.

Holmes, Lewis (1978, October). How fathers can cause the Down syndrome. *Human Nature, 1*(10), 70–72.

Holmes, Thomas, & Rahe, Richard (1967). The social readjustment rating scale. *Journal of Psychosomatic Research, 11,* 213–218.

Holstein, Kenneth A. (1983). Identity development: A comparison of adults and adolescents. Paper presented at the annual meeting of the American Psychological Association, Anaheim, CA.

Holtzworth-Munroe, Amy, & Jacobson, Neil S. (1985). Causal attributions of married couples: When do they search for causes? What do they conclude when they do? *Journal of Personality and Social Psychology, 48,* 1398–1412.

Holzman, Philip S. (1987). Recent studies of psychophysiology in schizophrenia. *Schizophrenia Bulletin, 13*(1), 49–75.

Hopson, Janet, & Rosenfeld, Anne (1984, August). PMS: Puzzling monthly symptoms. *Psychology Today, 18*(8), 30–35.

Horn, John L. (1978). Human ability systems. In P. B. Baltes (ed.), *Life-span development and behavior,* Vol. 1. New York: Academic Press.

Horn, John L., & Donaldson, Gary (1980). Cognitive development in adulthood. In O. G. Brim, Jr. & J. Kagan (eds.), *Constancy and change in human development.* Cambridge, MA: Harvard University Press.

Horner, Matina S. (1972). Toward an understanding of achievement-related conflicts in women. *Journal of Social Issues, 28*(2), 157–176.

Horney, Karen (1937). *The neurotic personality of our time.* New York: Norton.

Horney, Karen (1945). *Our inner conflicts.* New York: Norton.

Horney, Karen (1950). *Neurosis and human growth.* New York: Norton.

Horney, Karen (1967). *Feminine psychology.* New York: Norton.

House, James (1986). Social support and the quality and quantity of life. In F. Andrews (ed.), *Research on the quality of life.* Ann Arbor, MI: Institute for Social Research.

House, James; Robbins, Cynthia; & Metzner, Helen (1982). The association of social relationships and activities with mortality: Prospective evidence from the Tecumseh Community Health Study. *American Journal of Epidemiology, 116,* 123–140.

Houston, John P. (1981). *Fundamentals of learning and memory* (2nd ed.), New York: Academic Press.

Howard, Ann; Pion, Georgine M.; Gottfredson, Gary D.; Flattau, Pamela Ebert; Oskamp, Stuart; Pfafflin, Sheila M.; et al. (1986). The changing face of American psychology. *American Psychologist, 41,* 1311–1327.

Howard, Kenneth; Kopta, S. Mark; Krause, Merton S.; & Orlinsky, David (1986). The dose-effect relationship in psychotherapy. *American Psychologist, 41,* 159–164.

Howell, William C., & Dipboye, Robert L. (1982). *Essentials of industrial and organizational psychology.* Homewood, IL: Dorsey Press.

Hoyer, William J., & Plude, Dana J. (1980). Attentional and perceptual processes in the study of cognitive aging. In L. W. Poon (ed.), *Aging in the 1980's: Psychological issues.* Washington, DC: American Psychological Association.

Hsu, Francis (1981). *Americans and Chinese: Passage to difference.* Honolulu: University of Hawaii Press.

Hubel, D. H., & Wiesel, T. N. (1962). Receptive fields, binocular interaction and functional architecture in the cat's visual cortex. *Journal of Physiology* (London), *160,* 106–154.

Hubel, D. H., & Wiesel, T. N. (1968). Receptive fields and functional architecture of monkey striate cortex. *Journal of Physiology* (London), *195,* 215–243.

Hudgens, Richard W. (1974). Personal catastrophe and depression. In B. S. Dohrenwend & B. P. Dohrenwend (eds.), *Stressful life events: Their nature and effects.* New York: Wiley.

Huesmann, L. Rowell; Eron, Leonard; Lefkowitz, Monroe M.; & Walder, Leopold (1984). The stability of aggression over time and generations. *Developmental Psychology, 20,* 1120–1134.

Huizinga, Johan (1950). *Homo ludens: A study of the play element in culture.* Boston: Beacon.

Hull, Clark (1943). *Principles of behavior.* New York: Appleton-Century-Crofts.

Hull, Jay G.; Van Treuren, Ronald R.; & Virnelli, Su-

zanne (1987). Hardiness and health: A critique and alternative approach. *Journal of Personality and Social Psychology, 53,* 518–530.

Hunt, J. McVicker (1982). Toward equalizing the development opportunities of infants and preschool children. *Journal of Social Issues, 38,* 163–191.

Hunt, Morton M. (1959/1967). *The natural history of love.* New York: Minerva Press.

Hunt, Morton M. (1982, September 12). Research through deception. *The New York Times Magazine,* 66–67, 138, 140–143.

Hunt, Morton M. (1982). *The universe within: A new science explores the human mind.* New York: Simon & Schuster.

Hupka, Ralph (1981). Cultural determinants of jealousy. *Alternative Lifestyles, 4,* 310–356.

Hurvich, Leo M., & Jameson, Dorothea (1974). Opponent processes as a model of neural organization. *American Psychologist, 29,* 88–102.

Huston, Ted; Ruggiero, Mary; Conner, Ross; & Geis, Gilbert (1981). Bystander intervention into crime: A study based on naturally-occurring episodes. *Social Psychology Quarterly, 44,* 14–23.

Hyde, Janet S. (1981). How large are cognitive gender differences? A meta-analysis using ω^2 and d. *American Psychologist, 36,* 892–901.

Hyde, Janet S. (1984a). Children's understanding of sexist language. *Developmental Psychology, 20,* 697–706.

Hyde, Janet S. (1984b). How large are gender differences in aggression? A developmental meta-analysis. *Developmental Psychology, 20,* 722–736.

Hyde, Janet S. (1988). Sex, gender, and meta-analysis. Invited address to the Society for the Scientific Study of Sex, San Francisco.

Hyde, Janet S.; Fennema, Elizabeth; & Lamon, Susan (in preparation). Gender differences in mathematics performance: A meta-analysis.

Hyde, Janet S., & Linn, Marcia C. (1988). Gender differences in verbal ability: A meta-analysis. *Psychological Bulletin, 104,* 53–69.

Hyman, Irwin A. (1988). Eliminating corporal punishment in schools: Moving from advocacy research to policy implementation. Paper presented at the annual meeting of the American Psychological Association, Atlanta.

Iga, Mamoru (1986). *The thorn in the chrysanthemum: Suicide and economic success in modern Japan.* Berkeley: University of California Press.

Inglis, James, & Lawson, J. S. (1981). Sex differences in the effects of unilateral brain damage on intelligence. *Science, 212,* 693–695.

Insko, Chester A.; Smith, Richard; Alicke, Mark; Wade, Joel; & Taylor, Sylvester (1985). Conformity and group size: The concern with being right and the concern with being liked. *Personality and Social Psychology Bulletin, 11,* 41–50.

Isen, Alice M.; Daubman, Kimberly A.; & Nowicki,

Gary P. (1987). Positive affect facilitates creative problem solving. *Journal of Personality and Social Psychology, 52,* 1122–1131.

Izard, Carroll E. (1971). *The face of emotion.* New York: Appleton-Century-Crofts.

Izard, Carroll E. (1984). Emotion-cognition relationships and human development. In C. E. Izard, J. Kagan, & R. B. Zajonc (eds.), *Emotions, cognition, & behavior.* Cambridge, England: Cambridge University Press.

Jacklin, Carol N. (1989). Female and male: Issues of gender. *American Psychologist, 44,* 127–133.

Jacklin, Carol N.; DiPietro, Janet A.; & Maccoby, Eleanor E. (1984). Sex-typing behavior and sex-typing pressure in child/parent interaction. *Archives of Sexual Behavior, 13,* 413–425.

Jacobson, Gerald (1983). *The multiple crises of marital separation and divorce.* New York: Grune & Stratton.

Jacoby, Susan (1983). *Wild justice: The evolution of revenge.* New York: Harper & Row.

James, William (1884). What is an emotion? *Mind, 9,* 188–205. (Reprinted in M. Arnold [ed.], *The nature of emotion.* Baltimore, MD: Penguin, 1968.)

James, William (1936). *The varieties of religious experience.* New York: Modern Library. (Originally published in 1902.)

James, William (1950). *The principles of psychology.* New York: Dover. (Originally published in 1890.)

Janis, Irving L. (1972). *Victims of groupthink.* Boston: Houghton Mifflin.

Janis, Irving L. (1982). Counteracting the adverse effects of concurrence-seeking in policy-planning groups. In H. Brandstatter, J. H. Davis, & G. Stocker-Kreichgauer (eds.), *Group decision making.* New York: Academic Press.

Janis, Irving L. (1985). Problems of international crisis management in the nuclear age. Paper presented at the annual meeting of the American Psychological Association, Los Angeles.

Janis, Irving L.; Kaye, Donald; & Kirschner, Paul (1965). Facilitating effects of "eating-while-reading" on responsiveness to persuasive communications. *Journal of Personality and Social Psychology, 1,* 181–186.

Janoff-Bulman, Ronnie (1988). The benefits of illusions, the threat of disillusionment, and the limitations of inaccuracy. Paper presented at the annual meeting of the American Psychological Association, Atlanta.

Jaynes, Julian (1973a). Introduction: The study of the history of psychology. In M. Henle, J. Jaynes, & J. J. Sullivan (eds.), *Historical conceptions of psychology.* New York: Springer.

Jaynes, Julian (1973b). The problem of animate motion in the seventeenth century. In M. Henle, J. Jaynes, & J. J. Sullivan (eds.), *Historical conceptions of psychology.* New York: Springer.

Jellinek, E. M. (1960). *The disease concept of alcoholism.* New Haven, CT: Hillhouse Press.

Jenkins, John G., & Dallenbach, Karl M. (1924). Obliviscence during sleep and waking. *American Journal of Psychology, 35*, 605–612.

Jenkins, Sharon Rae (1987). Need for achievement and women's careers over 14 years: Evidence for occupational structure effects. *Journal of Personality and Social Psychology, 53*, 922–932.

Jensen, Arthur R. (1969). How much can we boost IQ and scholastic achievement? *Harvard Educational Review, 39*, 1–123.

Jensen, Arthur R. (1973). *Educability and group differences*. London: Methuen.

Jensen, Arthur R. (1980). *Bias in mental testing*. New York: Free Press.

Jensen, Arthur R. (1981). *Straight talk about mental tests*. New York: Free Press.

Jessel, T. M., & Iversen, L. L. (1979). Opiate analgesics inhibit substance P release from rat trigeminal nucleus. *Nature, 268*, 549–551.

John, E. Roy (1976, May). How the brain works—a new theory. *Psychology Today, 9*(12), 48–52.

John, E. R.; Tang, Y.; Brill, A. B.; Young, R.; & Ono, K. (1986). Double-labeled metabolic maps of memory. *Science, 233*, 1167–1175.

Johnson, Catherine (1988). *When to say goodbye to your therapist*. New York: Simon & Schuster.

Johnson, Marcia K.; Bransford, John D.; & Solomon, Susan (1973). Memory for tacit implications of sentences. *Journal of Experimental Psychology, 98*, 203–205.

Johnson, Robert, & Downing, Leslie (1979). Deindividuation and valence of cues: Effects of prosocial and antisocial behavior. *Journal of Personality and Social Psychology, 37*, 1532–1538.

Johnston, Lloyd B.; O'Malley, Patrick M.; & Bachman, Jerald G. (1988). Illicit drug use, smoking, and drinking by America's high school students, college students, and young adults, 1975–87. DHHS publication (ADM) 89-1602. Washington, DC: U.S. Department of Health and Human Services.

Jones, Edward E. (1979). The rocky road from acts to dispositions. *American Psychologist, 34*, 107–117.

Jones, Edward E.; Rock, L.; Shaver, Kelly; Goethals, George; & Ward, L. M. (1968). Pattern of performance and ability attribution: An unexpected primary effect. *Journal of Personality and Social Psychology, 9*, 317–340.

Jones, Lyle V. (1984). White-black achievement differences: The narrowing gap. *American Psychologist, 39*, 1207–1213.

Jones, Mary Cover (1924). A laboratory study of fear: The cause of Peter. *Pedagogical Seminary, 31*, 308–315.

Jones, Russell A. (1977). *Self-fulfilling prophecies*. Hillsdale, NJ: Erlbaum. (Distributed by John Wiley & Sons.)

Jourard, Sidney (1966). An exploratory study of body-accessibility. *British Journal of Social and Clinical Psychology, 114*, 135–136.

Jump, Teresa L., & Haas, Linda (1987). Fathers in transition: Dual-career fathers participating in child care. In M. S. Kimmel (ed.), *Changing men: New directions in research on men and masculinity*. Beverly Hills, CA: Sage.

Jung, Carl (1967). *Collected works*. Princeton, NJ: Princeton University Press.

Jussim, Lee; Coleman, Lerita M.; & Lerch, Lauren (1987). The nature of stereotypes: A comparison and integration of three theories. *Journal of Personality and Social Psychology, 52*, 536–546.

Kabatznick, Ronna (1984, August). Nurture/nature. *Ms., 76*, 102ff.

Kagan, Jerome (1984). *The nature of the child*. New York: Basic Books.

Kagan, Jerome (1988). Temperamental contributions to social behavior. Paper presented at the annual meeting of the American Psychological Association as a Distinguished Scientific Award Address, Atlanta.

Kagan, Jerome, & Lamb, Sharon (eds.) (1987). *The emergence of morality in young children*. Chicago: University of Chicago Press.

Kagan, Jerome, & Moss, Howard (1962). *Birth to maturity*. New York: Wiley.

Kagan, Jerome; Reznick, J. Steven; & Snidman, Nancy (1988). Biological bases of childhood shyness. *Science, 240*, 167–171.

Kagan, Jerome; Reznick, J. Steven; Snidman, Nancy; Gibbons, J.; & Johnson, Maureen O. (1988). Childhood derivatives of inhibition and lack of inhibition to the unfamiliar. *Child Development, 59*, 1580–1589.

Kahneman, Daniel, & Treisman, Anne (1984). Changing views of attention and automaticity. In R. Parasuraman, D. R. Davies, & J. Beatty (eds.), *Varieties of attention*. New York: Academic Press.

Kahneman, Daniel, & Tversky, Amos (1984). Choices, values, and frames. *American Psychologist, 39*, 341–350.

Kalat, James W. (1978). Letter to the editor: Speculations on similarities between autism and opiate addiction. *Journal of Autism and Childhood Schizophrenia, 8*, 477–479.

Kalmijn, Ad. J. (1982). Electric and magnetic field detection in elasmobranch fishes. *Science, 218*, 916–918.

Kamin, Leon J. (1974). *The science and politics of I.Q.* Potomac, MD: Erlbaum.

Kammen, M. (1979). Changing perceptions of the life cycle in American thought and culture. *Massachusetts Historical Society Proceedings, 91*, 35–66.

Kandel, Denise B. (1984). Marijuana users in young adulthood. *Archives of General Psychiatry, 41*, 200–209.

Kandel, Eric R. (1979). Small systems of neurons. *Scientific American, 241*(3), 67–76.

Kandel, Eric R. (1981). Visual system III: Physiology of the central visual pathways. In E. R. Kandel & J. H. Schwartz (eds.), *Principles of neural science*. New York: Elsevier-North Holland.

Kandel, Eric R., & Schwartz, James H. (1982). Molecular biology of learning: Modulation of transmitter release. *Science, 218*, 433–443.

Kane, John M. (1987). Treatment of schizophrenia. *Schizophrenia Bulletin, 13*(1), 133–156.

Kanin, Eugene J. (1985). Date rapists: Differential sexual socialization and relative deprivation. *Archives of Sexual Behavior, 14,* 219–231.

Kanner, Allen D.; Coyne, James C.; Schaefer, Catherine; & Lazarus, Richard (1981). Comparison of two modes of stress measurement: Daily hassles and uplifts versus major life events. *Journal of Behavioral Medicine, 4,* 1–39.

Kanter, Rosabeth (1977). *Men and women of the corporation.* New York: Basic Books.

Kaplan, Abraham (1967). A philosophical discussion of normality. *Archives of General Psychiatry, 17,* 325–330.

Kaplan, Louise (1984). *Adolescence: The farewell to childhood.* New York: Simon & Schuster.

Kaplan, Martin F., & Miller, Charles E. (1983). Group discussion and judgment. In P. Paulus (ed.), *Basic group processes.* New York: Springer-Verlag.

Katz, Mary M., & Konner, Melvin J. (1981). The role of the father: An anthropological perspective. In M. Lamb (ed.), *The role of the father in child development* (2nd ed.). New York: Wiley-Interscience.

Kaufman, Joan, & Zigler, Edward (1987). Do abused children become abusive parents? *American Journal of Orthopsychiatry, 57,* 186–192.

Kavich-Sharon, Richard (1984). The mixed sexual dysfunction syndrome: A team approach to total sexual health care. *Journal of Sex Research, 20,* 407–412.

Kay, Paul (1975). Synchronic variability and diachronic changes in basic color terms. *Language in Society, 4,* 257–270.

Kaye, Kenneth (1977). Toward the origin of dialogue. In H. R. Schaffer (ed.), *Studies in mother-infant interaction.* New York: Academic Press.

Kazdin, Alan E. (1982). Methodology of psychotherapy outcome research. In J. H. Harvey & M. M. Parks (eds.), *Psychotherapy research and behavior change.* The Master Lecture Series, Vol. 1. Washington, DC: American Psychological Association.

Keefe, Francis J. (1985). Behavioral approaches to pain management. Paper presented at the annual meeting of the Society of Behavioral Medicine, New Orleans.

Keesey, Richard E. (1980). A set-point analysis of the regulation of body weight. In A. Stunkard (ed.), *Obesity.* Philadelphia: Saunders.

Kelley, Harold (1950). The warm-cold variable in first impressions of persons. *Journal of Personality, 18,* 431–439.

Kelly, Dennis D. (1981a). Disorders of sleep and consciousness. In E. Kandel & J. Schwartz (eds.), *Principles of neural science.* New York: Elsevier-North Holland.

Kelly, Dennis D. (1981b). Physiology of sleep and dreaming. In E. Kandel & J. Schwartz (eds.), *Principles of neural science.* New York: Elsevier-North Holland.

Kennedy, James; Giuffra, Luis; Moises, Hans; Cavalli-Sforza, L. L.; et al. (1988, November 10). Evidence against linkage of schizophrenia to markers on chromosome 5 in a northern Swedish pedigree. *Nature, 336*(6195), 167–169.

Kephart, William M. (1967). Some correlates of romantic love. *Journal of Marriage and the Family, 29,* 470–474.

Kerr, Michael E., & Bowen, Murray (1988). *Family evaluation: An approach based on Bowen theory.* New York: Norton.

Kessler, M.; Petersen, G.; Vu, H. M.; Baudry, M.; & Lynch, G. (1987). L-phenylalanyl-L-glutamate-stimulated, chloride-dependent glutamate binding represents glutamate sequestration mediated by an exchange system. *Journal of Neurochemistry, 48,* 1191–1200.

Kett, Joseph (1977). *Rites of passage: Adolescence in America, 1790 to the present.* New York: Basic Books.

Kety, Seymour S. (1974). From rationalization to reason. *American Journal of Psychiatry, 131,* 957–963.

Keys, Ancel, et al. (1950). *The biology of human starvation* (2 vols.). Minneapolis: University of Minnesota Press.

Kiecolt-Glaser, Janice; Fisher, L. D.; Ogrocki, P.; Stout, J. C.; et al. (1987a). Marital quality, marital disruption, and immune function. *Psychosomatic Medicine, 49,* 13–34.

Kiecolt-Glaser, Janice; Garner, Warren; Speicher, Carl; Penn, Gerald; Holliday, Jane; & Glaser, Ronald (1985a). Psychosocial modifiers of immunocompetence in medical students. *Psychosomatic Medicine, 46,* 7–14.

Kiecolt-Glaser, Janice, & Glaser, Ronald (1989). Behavioral influences on immune function: Evidence for the interplay between stress and health. In T. Field, P. McCabe, & N. Schneiderman (eds.), *Stress and coping,* Vol. 2. Hillsdale, NJ: Erlbaum.

Kiecolt-Glaser, Janice; Glaser, Ronald; Shuttleworth, Edwin; Dyer, Carol; et al. (1987b). Chronic stress and immunity in family caregivers of Alzheimer's disease victims. *Psychosomatic Medicine, 49,* 523–535.

Kiecolt-Glaser, Janice; Glaser, Ronald; Williger, D.; Stout, J. C.; et al. (1985b). Psychosocial enhancement of immunocompetence in a geriatric population. *Health Psychology, 4,* 25–41.

Kiernan, Thomas (1974). *Shrinks, etc.: A consumer's guide to psychotherapies.* New York: Dial Press.

Kihlstrom, John F., & Harackiewicz, Judith M. (1982). The earliest recollection: A new survey. *Journal of Personality, 50,* 134–148.

Kimball, Meredith (1981). Women and science: A critique of biological theories. *International Journal of Women's Studies, 4,* 318–338.

Kimura, Doreen (1985, November). Male brain, female brain: The hidden difference. *Psychology Today, 19*(11), 50–52, 54, 56–58.

Kimura, Doreen, & Harshman, Richard (1984). Sex differences in brain organization. In G. J. de Vries, J. P. C. De Bruin, H. B. M. Vylings, & M. A. Corner (eds.), *Sex differences in the brain: The relation between structure and function,* Vol. 61. New York: Elsevier.

Kinsbourne, Marcel (1982). Hemispheric specialization and the growth of human understanding. *American Psychologist, 37,* 411–420.

Kinsey, Alfred C.; Pomeroy, Wardell B.; & Martin, Clyde E. (1948). *Sexual behavior in the human male*. Philadelphia: Saunders.

Kinsey, Alfred C.; Pomeroy, Wardell B.; Martin, Clyde E.; & Gebhard, Paul H. (1953). *Sexual behavior in the human female*. Philadelphia: Saunders.

Kirkley, Betty; Schneider, John; & Bachman, John (1984). Bulimia: A comparison of two group treatments. Paper presented at the annual meeting of the Society of Behavioral Medicine, Philadelphia.

Kitchener, Karen Strohm, & King, Patricia M. (1989). The reflective judgment model: Ten years of research. In M. L. Commons, C. Armon, L. Kohlberg, et al. (eds.), *Beyond formal operations III: Models and methods in the study of adolescent and adult thought*. New York: Praeger.

Klaus, Marshall, & Kennell, John (1976). *Maternal-infant bonding*. St. Louis: Mosby.

Klein, Donald F. (1980). Psychosocial treatment of schizophrenia, or psychosocial help for people with schizophrenia? *Schizophrenia Bulletin, 6*, 122–130.

Klein, Raymond, & Armitage, Roseanne (1979). Rhythms in human performance: 1½-hour oscillations in cognitive style. *Science, 204*, 1326–1328.

Kleinman, Arthur (1988). *Rethinking psychiatry: From cultural category to personal experience*. New York: Free Press.

Kleinmuntz, Benjamin, & Szucko, Julian J. (1984, March 29). A field study of the fallibility of polygraph lie detection. *Nature, 308*, 449–450.

Klerman, Gerald L.; Weissman, Myrna M.; Rounsaville, Bruce J.; & Chevron, Eve S. (1984). *Interpersonal psychotherapy of depression*. New York: Basic Books.

Klinger, Eric (1987, October). The power of dreams. *Psychology Today*, 37–39, 42, 44.

Kobasa, Suzanne C. (1979). Stressful life events, personality, and health: An inquiry into hardiness. *Journal of Personality and Social Psychology, 37*, 1–11.

Kobasa, Suzanne C.; Maddi, Salvatore; & Kahn, Stephen (1982). Hardiness and health: A prospective study. *Journal of Personality and Social Psychology, 42*, 168–177.

Kobasa, Suzanne C., & Puccetti, Mark C. (1983). Personality and social resources in stress resistance. *Journal of Personality and Social Psychology, 45*, 839–850.

Kohlberg, Lawrence (1964). Development of moral character and moral ideology. In M. Hoffman & L. W. Hoffman (eds.), *Review of child development research*. New York: Russell Sage Foundation.

Kohlberg, Lawrence (1966). A cognitive-developmental analysis of children's sex-role concepts and attitudes. In E. E. Maccoby (ed.), *The development of sex differences*. Stanford, CA: Stanford University Press.

Kohlberg, Lawrence (1976). Moral stages and moralization: The cognitive-developmental approach. In T. Lickona (ed.), *Moral development and behavior*. New York: Holt, Rinehart and Winston.

Kohlberg, Lawrence (1984). *Essays on moral development, Vol. 2. The psychology of moral development: The nature and validity of moral stages*. San Francisco: Harper & Row.

Kohler, Ivo (1962, May). Experiments with goggles. *Scientific American, 206*(5), 62–72.

Köhler, Wolfgang (1925). *The mentality of apes*. New York: Harcourt, Brace.

Köhler, Wolfgang (1939). Simple structural functions in the chimpanzee and in the chicken. In W. D. Ellis (ed.), *A source book of Gestalt psychology*. New York: Harcourt, Brace.

Köhler, Wolfgang (1978). Gestalt psychology today. (Presidential address to the 67th annual convention of the American Psychological Association, Cincinnati, Ohio, September 1959.) In E. R. Hilgard (ed.), *American psychology in historical perspective: Addresses of the presidents of the American Psychological Association, 1892–1977*. Washington, DC: American Psychological Association.

Kohn, Alfie (1986). *No contest: The case against competition*. Boston: Houghton Mifflin.

Kohn, Melvin, & Schooler, Carmi (1983). *Work and personality: An inquiry into the impact of social stratification*. Norwood, NJ: Ablex.

Kolotkin, Ronette L., & Johnson, Marilyn (1983). Crisis intervention and measurement of treatment outcome. In M. J. Lambert, E. R. Christensen, & S. S. DeJulio (eds.), *The assessment of psychotherapy outcome*. New York: Wiley-Interscience.

Kosslyn, Stephen M. (1980). *Image and mind*. Cambridge, MA: Harvard University Press.

Kosslyn, Stephen (1983). *Ghosts in the mind's machine: Creating and using images in the brain*. New York: Norton.

Kosslyn, Stephen M.; Seger, Carol; Pani, John; & Hillger, Lynn A. (in press). When is imagery used? A diary study. *Journal of Mental Imagery*.

Krantz, David S., & Manuck, Stephen B. (1984). Acute psychophysiologic reactivity and risk of cardiovascular disease: A review and methodological critique. *Psychological Bulletin, 96*, 435–464.

Krebs, Dennis, & Miller, Dale T. (1985). Altruism and aggression. In G. Lindzey & E. Aronson (eds.), *Handbook of social psychology*, Vol. II. New York: Random House.

Kripke, Daniel F. (1974). Ultradian rhythms in sleep and wakefulness. In E. D. Weitzman (ed.), *Advances in sleep research*, Vol. 1. Flushing, NY: Spectrum.

Kripke, Daniel F., & Sonnenschein, David (1978). A biologic rhythm in waking fantasy. In K. S. Pope & J. L. Singer (eds.), *The stream of consciousness: Scientific investigations into the flow of human experience*. New York: Plenum.

Kubitz, Karla A.; Peavey, Barbara; & Moore, Bert (1985). The relationship of the humoral immune system to stress. Paper presented at the annual meeting of the American Psychological Association, Los Angeles.

Kudoh, Tsutomu, & Matsumoto, David (1985). Cross-cultural examination of the semantic dimensions of body postures. *Journal of Personality and Social Psychology, 48*, 1440–1446.

Kuhl, Julius (1978). Standard setting and risk preference: An elaboration of the theory of achievement motivation and an empirical test. *Psychological Review, 85,* 239–248.

Kuhn, Thomas (1981). Unanswered questions about science. In R. D. Tweney, M. E. Doherty, & C. R. Mynatt (eds.), *On scientific thinking.* New York: Columbia University Press.

Kurtines, William M., & Gewirtz, Jacob L. (eds.) (1984). *Morality, moral behavior, and moral development.* New York: Wiley.

LaBarre, Weston (1947). The cultural bases of emotions and gestures. *Journal of Personality, 16,* 49–68.

LaBerge, Stephen (1986). *Lucid dreaming.* New York: Ballantine Books.

Laboratory of Comparative Human Cognition (1984). Culture and cognitive development. In P. Mussen (ed.), *Handbook of child psychology* (4th ed.). Vol I, W. Kessen (ed.), *History, theory, and methods.* New York: Wiley.

Labott, Susan, & Martin, Randall (1986). The stress-moderating effects of weeping and humor. Paper presented at the annual meeting of the American Psychological Association, Washington.

Labows, John N., Jr. (1980, November). What the nose knows: Investigating the significance of human odors. *The Sciences,* 10–13.

Lader, Malcolm (1985). Anxiolytic evolution in today's anxious world. Paper presented at the annual meeting of the American Psychiatric Association, Dallas.

Laird, James D. (1974). Self-attribution of emotion: The effects of expressive behavior on the quality of emotional experience. *Journal of Personality and Social Psychology, 29,* 475–486.

Lakoff, George (1985). *Women, fire, and dangerous things.* Chicago: University of Chicago Press.

Lamb, Michael E. (1981). Fathers and child development: An integrative overview. In M. E. Lamb (ed.), *The role of the father in child development* (2nd ed.). New York: Wiley-Interscience.

Lamb, Michael E., & Campos, Joseph (1983). *Development in infancy: An introduction.* New York: Random House.

Lambert, Michael J. (1983). Introduction to assessment of psychotherapy outcome: Historical perspective and current issues. In M. J. Lambert, E. R. Christensen, & S. S. DeJulio (eds.), *The assessment of psychotherapy outcome.* New York: Wiley-Interscience.

Lambert, Michael J.; Christensen, Edwin R.; & DeJulio, Steven S. (eds.) (1983). *The assessment of psychotherapy outcome.* New York: Wiley-Interscience.

Land, Edwin H. (1959). Experiments in color vision. *Scientific American, 200,* No. 5, 84–94, 96, 99.

Landman, Janet, & Dawes, Robyn (1982). Psychotherapy outcome. *American Psychologist, 37,* 504–516.

Lang, Peter J. (1988). Fear, anxiety, and panic: Context, cognition, and visceral arousal. In S. Rachman & J. D. Maser (eds.), *Panic: Psychological perspectives.* Hillsdale, NJ: Erlbaum.

Langer, Ellen J. (1983). *The psychology of control.* Beverly Hills, CA: Sage.

Langer, Ellen J. (1989). *Mindfulness.* Cambridge, MA: Addison-Wesley.

Langer, Ellen J.; Blank, Arthur; & Chanowitz, Benzion (1978). The mindlessness of ostensibly thoughtful action: The role of placebic information in interpersonal interaction. *Journal of Personality and Social Psychology, 36,* 635–642.

Langer, Ellen J.; Rodin, Judith; Beck, Pearl; Weinman, Cynthia; & Spitzer, Lynn (1979). Environmental determinants of memory improvement in late adulthood. *Journal of Personality and Social Psychology, 37,* 2003–2013.

LaPiere, Richard T. (1934). Attitudes vs. actions. *Social Forces, 13,* 230–237.

Larsen, Randy J.; Diener, Ed; & Cropanzano, Russell (1987). Cognitive operations associated with individual differences in affect intensity. *Journal of Personality and Social Psychology, 53,* 767–774.

Lash, Rick (1988). Problem solving and the development of expertise in management. Paper presented at the annual meeting of the American Psychological Association, Atlanta.

Lashley, Karl S. (1950). In search of the engram. In *Symposium of the Society for Experimental Biology,* Vol. 4. New York: Cambridge University Press.

Latané, Bibb, & Darley, John (1970). *The unresponsive bystander: Why doesn't he help?* New York: Appleton-Century-Crofts.

Latané, Bibb, & Darley, John (1976). Help in a crisis: Bystander response to an emergency. In J. Thibaut, J. Spence, & R. Carlson (eds.), *Contemporary topics in social psychology.* Morristown, NJ: General Learning Press.

Latané, Bibb; Williams, Kipling; & Harkins, Stephen (1979). Many hands make light the work: The causes and consequences of social loafing. *Journal of Personality and Social Psychology, 37,* 822–832.

Laudenslager, Mark L., & Reite, Martin L. (1984). Losses and separations: Immunological consequences and health implications. In P. Shaver (ed.), *Review of personality and social psychology: 5.* Beverly Hills, CA: Sage.

Lave, J.; Murtaugh, M.; & de la Roche, O. (1984). The dialectic of arithmetic in grocery shopping. In B. Rogoff & J. Lave (eds.), *Everyday cognition: Its development in social context.* Cambridge, MA: Harvard University Press.

Lavie, Peretz (1976). Ultradian rhythms in the perception of two apparent motions. *Chronobiologia, 3,* 214–218.

Lavie, Peretz, & Kripke, Daniel F. (1975, April). Ultradian rhythms: The 90-minute clock inside us. *Psychology Today, 8*(11), 54, 56, 65.

Lawler, Edward E. (1981). *Pay and organizational development.* Reading, MA: Addison-Wesley.

Lazarus, Richard S. (1984). On the primacy of cognition. *American Psychologist, 39,* 124–129.

Lazarus, Richard S.; DeLongis, Anita; Folkman, Susan; & Gruen, Rand (1985). Stress and adaptational outcomes: The problem of confounded measures. *American Psychologist, 40,* 770–779.

Lazarus, Richard S.; & Folkman, Susan (1984). *Stress, appraisal, and coping.* New York: Springer.

Lee, Jerry W., & Hart, Richard (1985). Techniques used by individuals who quit smoking on their own. Paper presented at the annual meeting of the American Psychological Association, Los Angeles.

Lee, John Alan (1973). *The colours of love.* Ontario, Canada: New Press.

Lee, John Alan (1988). Love-styles. In R. J. Sternberg & M. L. Barnes (eds.), *The psychology of love.* New Haven, CT, and London: Yale University Press.

Lefcourt, Herbert M., & Martin, Rod A. (1986). *Humor and life stress: Antidote to adversity.* New York: Springer-Verlag.

Lehman, Darrin R.; Lempert, Richard O.; & Nisbett, Richard E. (1988). The effects of graduate training on reasoning. *American Psychologist, 43,* 431–442.

Lenneberg, Eric H. (1967). *Biological foundations of language.* New York: Wiley.

Lent, James R. (1968, June). Mimosa cottage: Experiment in hope. *Psychology Today, 2*(1), 51–58.

Lepper, Mark R.; Greene, David; & Nisbett, Richard E. (1973). Undermining children's intrinsic interest with extrinsic rewards. *Journal of Personality and Social Psychology, 28,* 129–137.

Lerman, Hannah (1986). The purposes of diagnosis. Paper presented at the annual meeting of the American Psychological Association, Washington.

Lerner, Harriet (1986). The challenge of change. In C. Tavris (ed.), *EveryWoman's emotional well-being.* New York: Doubleday.

Lerner, Melvin J. (1980). *The belief in a just world: A fundamental delusion.* New York: Plenum.

Leventhal, Bennett L., & Dawson, Kenneth (1984). Middle childhood: Normality as integration and interaction. In D. Offer & M. Sabshin (eds.), *Normality and the life cycle.* New York: Basic Books.

Leventhal, Howard, & Cleary, Paul D. (1980). The smoking problem: A review of research and theory in behavioral risk modification. *Psychological Bulletin, 88,* 370–405.

Leventhal, Howard; Singer, Robert; & Jones, Susan (1965). Effects of fear and specificity of recommendation upon attitudes and behavior. *Journal of Personality and Social Psychology, 2,* 20–29.

Levine, Daniel S. (in press). *Introduction to neural and cognitive modeling.* Hillsdale, NJ: Erlbaum.

Levine, Stephen B. (1979, April). Is sex therapy a failure? *Human Nature,* 74–78.

Levine, Stephen B., & Agle, David (1978). The effectiveness of sex therapy for chronic secondary psychological impotence. *Journal of Sex and Marital Therapy, 4,* 235–258.

Levinson, Daniel (1978). *The seasons of a man's life.* New York: Knopf.

Levinthal, Charles F. (1988). *Messengers of paradise: Opiates and the brain.* New York: Doubleday/Anchor Press.

Levy, Jerre (1983). Language, cognition, and the right hemisphere: A response to Gazzaniga. *American Psychologist, 38,* 538–541.

Levy, Jerre (1985, May). Right brain, left brain: Fact and fiction. *Psychology Today, 19*(5), 38–39, 42–44.

Levy, Jerre; Trevarthen, Colwyn; & Sperry, Roger W. (1972). Perception of bilateral chimeric figures following hemispheric deconnection. *Brain, 95,* 61–78.

Levy, Robert I. (1984). The emotions in comparative perspective. In K. R. Scherer & P. Ekman (eds.), *Approaches to emotion.* Hillsdale, NJ: Erlbaum.

Lewin, Kurt (1948). *Resolving social conflicts.* New York: Harper.

Lewin, Miriam (1985). Unwanted intercourse: The difficulty of saying no. *Psychology of Women Quarterly, 9,* 184–192.

Lewinsohn, Peter; Steinmetz, Julia; Larson, Douglass; & Franklin, Judith (1981). Depression-related cognitions: Antecedent or consequence? *Journal of Abnormal Psychology, 90,* 213–219.

Lewis, Dorothy O. (ed.) (1981). *Vulnerabilities to delinquency.* New York: Spectrum Medical and Scientific Books.

Lewis, Michael, & Brooks-Gunn, Jeanne (1979). *Social cognition and the acquisition of self.* New York: Plenum.

Lewis, Michael; Sullivan, Margaret; Stanger, Catherine; & Weiss, Maya (1988). Self development and self-conscious emotions. Paper presented at the annual meeting of the American Psychological Association, Atlanta.

Lewontin, Richard C. (1970). Race and intelligence. *Bulletin of the Atomic Scientists, 26*(3), 2–8.

Lewontin, Richard C. (1982). *Human diversity.* New York: Scientific American Library.

Lewontin, Richard C.; Rose, Steven; & Kamin, Leon J. (1984). *Not in our genes: Biology, ideology, and human nature.* New York: Pantheon.

Lewy, Alfred J.; Sacks, Robert L.; Miller, L. Steven; & Hoban, Tana M. (1987). Antidepressant and circadian phase-shifting effects of light. *Science, 235,* 352–354.

Ley, Ronald (1988). Hyperventilation and lactate infusion in the production of panic attacks. *Clinical Psychology Review, 8,* 1–18.

Libet, Benjamin (1985). Unconscious cerebral initiative and the role of conscious will in voluntary action. *Behavioral and Brain Sciences, 8,* 529–566.

Lichtenstein, Sarah; Slovic, Paul; Fischhoff, Baruch; Layman, Mark; & Combs, Barbara (1978). Judged frequency of lethal events. *Journal of Experimental Psychology: Human Learning and Memory, 4,* 551–578.

Lieberman, David A. (1979). Behaviorism and the mind: A (limited) call for a return to introspection. *American Psychologist, 34,* 319–333.

Lieberman, Morton; Yalom, Irvin; & Miles, Matthew B. (1973). *Encounter groups: First facts.* New York: Basic Books.

Lifton, Robert J. (1980). Nuclearism. *Journal of Clinical Child Psychology, 9,* 119–124.

Lifton, Robert J. (1986). *The Nazi doctors: Medical killing and the psychology of genocide*. New York: Basic Books.

Lightfoot, Lynn O. (1980). Behavioral tolerance to low doses of alcohol in social drinkers. Unpublished doctoral dissertation, University of Waterloo.

Lindesmith, Alfred (1968). *Addiction and opiates*. Chicago: Aldine.

Linn, Marcia C., & Petersen, Anne C. (1985). A meta-analysis of gender differences in spatial ability: Implications for mathematics and science achievement. In J. S. Hyde & M. C. Linn (eds.), *The psychology of gender: Advances through meta-analysis*. Baltimore, MD: Johns Hopkins University Press.

Linton, Marigold (1978). Real-world memory after six years: An in vivo study of very long-term memory. In M. M. Gruneberg, P. E. Morris, & R. N. Sykes (eds.), *Practical aspects of memory*. London: Academic Press.

Linton, Marigold (1979, July). I remember it well. *Psychology Today, 13*(2), 80–82, 85–87.

Lipscomb, David (1972). The increased prevalence of high frequency hearing impairment among college students. *International Audiology, 11*, 231–237.

Lipton, Alan A., & Simon, Franklin S. (1985). Psychiatric diagnosis in a state hospital: Manhattan State revisited. *Hospital and Community Psychiatry, 36*, 368–373.

Litt, Mark D. (1988). Self-efficacy and perceived control: Cognitive mediators of pain tolerance. *Journal of Personality and Social Psychology, 54*, 149–160.

Locke, Edwin; Shaw, Karyll; Saari, Lise; & Latham, Gary (1981). Goal-setting and task performance: 1969–1980. *Psychological Bulletin, 90*, 125–152.

Loehlin, John C. (1988). Partitioning environmental and genetic contributions to behavioral development. Invited address at the annual meeting of the American Psychological Association, Atlanta.

Loftus, Elizabeth F. (1974, December). Reconstructing memory: The incredible eyewitness. *Psychology Today, 8*(7), 116–119.

Loftus, Elizabeth F. (1980). *Memory*. Reading, MA: Addison-Wesley.

Loftus, Elizabeth F., & Loftus, Geoffrey R. (1980). On the permanence of stored information in the human brain. *American Psychologist, 35*, 409–420.

Loftus, Elizabeth F.; Miller, David G.; & Burns, Helen J. (1978). Semantic integration of verbal information into a visual memory. *Journal of Experimental Psychology: Human Learning and Memory, 4*, 19–31.

Loftus, Elizabeth F., & Palmer, John C. (1974). Reconstruction of automobile destruction: An example of the interaction between language and memory. *Journal of Verbal Learning and Verbal Behavior, 13*, 585–589.

Loftus, Elizabeth F., & Zanni, Guido (1975). Eyewitness testimony: The influence of the wording of a question. *Bulletin of the Psychonomic Society, 5*, 86–88.

Lopata, Helena (1975). Widowhood: Societal factors in life-span disruptions and alternatives. In N. Datan & L. H.

Ginsberg (eds.), *Life-span developmental psychology: Normative life crises*. New York: Academic Press.

Lorenz, Konrad (1937). Imprinting. *The Auk, 54,* 245–273.

Louis, Arthur M. (1978, April). Should you buy biorhythms? *Psychology Today, 11*(11), 93–96.

Lovaas, O. Ivar (1977). *The autistic child: Language development through behavior modification*. New York: Halsted Press.

Lovaas, O. Ivar; Schreibman, Laura; & Koegel, Robert L. (1974). A behavior modification approach to the treatment of autistic children. *Journal of Autism and Childhood Schizophrenia, 4,* 111–129.

Lowenthal, Marjorie; Thurnher, Majda; & Chiriboga, David (1975). *Four stages of life*. San Francisco: Jossey-Bass.

Luce, Gay Gaer, & Segal, Julius (1966). *Current research on sleep and dreams*. Bethesda, MD: U.S. Department of Health, Education, and Welfare.

Luce, Terrence S. (1974, November). Blacks, whites and yellows, they all look alike to me. *Psychology Today, 8*(6), 105–106, 108.

Lugaresi, Elio; Medori, R.; Montagna, P.; et al. (1986, October 16). Fatal familial insomnia and dysautonomia with selective degeneration of thalamic nuclei. *New England Journal of Medicine, 315,* 997–1003.

Luria, A. R. (1968). *The mind of a mnemonist*. (L. Soltaroff, translator.) New York: Basic Books.

Luria, A. R. (1980). *Higher cortical functions in man* (2nd rev. ed.). New York: Basic Books.

Lykes, M. Brinton, & Stewart, Abigail (1982). Studying the effects of early experiences on women's career achievement. Paper presented at the annual meeting of the American Psychological Association, Washington.

Lykken, David T. (1981). *A tremor in the blood: Uses and abuses of the lie detector*. New York: McGraw-Hill.

Lynch, Gary (1986). *Synapses, circuits, and the beginnings of memory*. Cambridge, MA: MIT Press.

Lynch, Gary, & Baudry, M. (1984). The biochemistry of memory: A new and specific hypothesis. *Science, 224,* 1057–1063.

Lynn, R. (1982). IQ in Japan and the United States shows a growing disparity. *Nature, 297,* 222–223.

Maccoby, Eleanor E. (1980). *Social development*. New York: Harcourt Brace Jovanovich.

MacCoun, Robert J., & Kerr, Norbert L. (1988). Asymmetric influence in mock jury deliberation: Jurors' bias for leniency. *Journal of Personality and Social Psychology, 54,* 21–33.

MacKay, Donald G. (1970). Mental diplopia: Towards a model of speech perception at the semantic level. In G. B. Flores d'Arcais & W. J. M. Levelt (eds.), *Advances in psycholinguistics*. Amsterdam: North-Holland.

Mackenzie, Brian (1984). Explaining race differences in IQ: The logic, the methodology, and the evidence. *American Psychologist, 39,* 1214–1233.

MacKinnon, Donald W. (1962). The nature and nurture of creative talent. *American Psychologist, 17,* 484–495.

MacKinnon, Donald W. (1968). Selecting students with creative potential. In P. Heist (ed.), *The creative college student: An unmet challenge.* San Francisco: Jossey-Bass.

MacLean, Paul (1963). Phylogenesis. In P. Knapp (ed.), *Expression of the emotions in man.* New York: International Universities Press.

MacLean, Paul (1970). The limbic brain in relation to psychoses. In P. Black (ed.), *Physiological correlates of emotion.* New York: Academic Press.

Madigan, Carol Orsag, & Elwood, Ann (1984). *Brainstorms & thunderbolts.* New York: Macmillan.

Madrazo, Ignacio; Leon, Victor; Torres, Cesar; et al. (1988). Transplantation of fetal substantia nigra and adrenal medulla to the caudate nucleus in two patients with Parkinson's disease. *New England Journal of Medicine, 318,* 51.

Malamuth, Neil M. (1981). Rape proclivity among males. *Journal of Social Issues, 37,* 138–157.

Malgady, Robert G.; Rogler, Lloyd; & Costantino, Giuseppe (1987). Ethnocultural and linguistic bias in mental health evaluation of Hispanics. *American Psychologist, 42,* 228–234.

Malitz, Sidney, & Sackeim, Harold A. (eds.) (1986). *Electroconvulsive therapy: Clinical and basic research issues.* New York: New York Academy of Sciences.

Mancuso, James C., & Sarbin, Theodore (1984). Illusion and reality in the science of schizophrenia. *Contemporary Psychology, 29,* 992–993.

Mandler, George (1984). *Mind and body.* New York: Norton.

Mann, James (1973). *Time-limited psychotherapy.* Cambridge, MA: Harvard University Press.

Mannuzza, Salvatore; Klein, Rachel G.; Bonagura, Noreen; Konig, Paula H.; et al. (1988). Hyperactive boys almost grown up: II. Status of subjects without a mental disorder. *Archives of General Psychiatry. 45,* 13–18.

Marcia, James E. (1966). Development and validation of ego-identity status. *Journal of Personality and Social Psychology, 3,* 551–558.

Marcia, James E. (1976). Identity six years later: A follow-up study. *Journal of Youth and Adolescence, 5,* 145–160.

Marder, Stephen; Van Putten, T.; Mintz, J.; LeBell, M.; et al. (1987). Low- and conventional-dose maintenance therapy with fluphenazine decanoate. Two-year outcome. *Archives of General Psychiatry, 44,* 518–521.

Mark, Vernon (1978). Sociobiological theories of abnormal aggression. In I. L. Kutash et al. (eds.), *Violence.* San Francisco: Jossey-Bass.

Marks, Lawrence E. (1975, June). Synesthesia: The lucky people with mixed-up senses. *Psychology Today, 9*(1), 48, 51–52.

Markus, Hazel, & Nurius, Paula (1986). Possible selves. *American Psychologist, 41,* 954–969.

Marlatt, G. Alan, & Rohsenow, Damaris J. (1980). Cognitive processes in alcohol use: Expectancy and the balanced placebo design. In N. K. Mello (ed.), *Advances in substance abuse,* Vol. 1. Greenwich, CT: JAI Press.

Marlatt, G. Alan, & Rohsenow, Damaris J. (1981, December). The think-drink effect. *Psychology Today, 15*(12), 60–62, 64, 66, 68–69, 93.

Marquis, Kathlyn S., & Detweiler, Richard A. (1985). Does adopted mean different? An attributional analysis. *Journal of Personality and Social Psychology, 48,* 1054–1066.

Marsh, Caryl (1977). A framework for describing subjective states of consciousness. In N. E. Zinberg (ed.), *Alternate states of consciousness.* New York: Free Press.

Marshall, Gary D., & Zimbardo, Philip (1979). Affective consequences of inadequately explained physiological arousal. *Journal of Personality and Social Psychology, 37,* 970–989.

Marslen-Wilson, William, & Teuber, Hans-Lukas (1975). Memory for remote events in anterograde amnesia: Recognition of public figures from news photographs. *Neuropsychologia, 13,* 353–364.

Martin, Clyde E. (1981). Factors affecting sexual functioning in 60–79-year-old married males. *Archives of Sexual Behavior, 10,* 399–420.

Martin, Rod A., & Lefcourt, Herbert M. (1983). Sense of humor as a moderator of the relation between stressors and moods. *Journal of Personality and Social Psychology, 45,* 1313–1324.

Martyna, Wendy (1977). Comprehension of the generic masculine: Inferring ''she'' from ''he.'' Paper presented to the 85th annual meeting of the American Psychological Association, San Francisco.

Maslach, Christina (1979). Negative emotional biasing of unexplained arousal. *Journal of Personality and Social Psychology, 37,* 953–969.

Maslach, Christina; Stapp, Joy; & Santee, Richard T. (1985). Individuation: Conceptual analysis and assessment. *Journal of Personality and Social Psychology, 49,* 729–738.

Maslow, Abraham H. (1954/1970). *Motivation and personality* (1st and 2nd eds.). New York: Harper & Row.

Maslow, Abraham H. (1962/1968). *Toward a psychology of being.* Princeton, NJ: Van Nostrand. (2nd ed., 1968)

Maslow, Abraham H. (1971). *The farther reaches of human nature.* New York: Viking.

Massey, Christine M., & Gelman, Rochel (1988). Preschooler's ability to decide whether a photographed unfamiliar object can move itself. *Developmental Psychology, 24,* 307–317.

Masson, Jeffrey (1984). *The assault on truth: Freud's suppression of the seduction theory.* New York: Farrar, Straus & Giroux.

Masters, William H., & Johnson, Virginia E. (1966). *Human sexual response.* Boston: Little, Brown.

Masters, William H., & Johnson, Virginia E. (1970). *Human sexual inadequacy.* Boston: Little, Brown.

Matarazzo, Joseph (1984). Behavioral immunogens and

pathogens in health and illness. In B. L. Hammonds & C. J. Scheirer (eds.), *Psychology and health: The master lecture series*, Vol. 3. Washington, DC: The American Psychological Association.

Maugh, Thomas H., II (1982). The scent makes sense. *Science, 215,* 1224.

Mayer, D.; Prince, D.; Rafii, A.; & Barber, J. (1976). Acupuncture hypalgesia: Evidence for activation of a central control system as a mechanism of action. In J. J. Bonica & D. G. Albe-Fessard (eds.), *Advances in pain research and therapy,* Vol. 1. New York: Raven Press.

Mayer, Nancy (1978). *The male mid-life crisis.* New York: Signet.

Maykovich, Minako K. (1975). Correlates of racial prejudice. *Journal of Personality and Social Psychology, 32,* 1014–1020.

Mayo, Clara, & Henley, Nancy (eds.) (1981). *Gender and nonverbal behavior.* New York: Springer-Verlag.

Mazur, Allen, & Lamb, Theodore A. (1980). Testosterone, status, and mood in human males. *Hormones and Behavior, 14,* 236–246.

McAdams, Dan P. (1988). *Power, intimacy, and the life story: Personological inquiries into identity.* New York: Guilford Press.

McBurney, Donald (1978). Psychological dimensions and perceptual analyses of taste. In E. C. Carterette and M. P. Friedman (eds.), *Handbook of perception,* Vol. VI *A: Tasting and smelling.* New York: Academic Press.

McCall, Robert B.; Appelbaum, Mark I.; & Hogarty, Pamela S. (1973). Developmental changes in mental performance. *Monographs of the Society for Research in Child Development, 38* (3, Serial No. 150).

McCann, I. Lisa, & Holmes, David S. (1984). Influence of aerobic exercise on depression. *Journal of Personality and Social Psychology, 46,* 1142–1147.

McCarley, Robert W., & Hoffman, Edward (1981). REM sleep dreams and the activation-synthesis hypothesis. *American Journal of Psychiatry, 138,* 904–912.

McCauley, Elizabeth, & Ehrhardt, Anke (1980). Female sexual response. In D. D. Youngs & A. Ehrhardt (eds.), *Psychosomatic obstetrics and gynecology.* New York: Appleton-Century-Crofts.

McClelland, David C. (1958). Risk-taking in children with high and low need for achievement. In J. W. Atkinson (ed.), *Motives in fantasy, action, and society.* Princeton, NJ: Van Nostrand.

McClelland, David C. (1961). *The achieving society.* New York: Free Press.

McClelland, David C. (1965). Achievement and entrepreneurship: A longitudinal study. *Journal of Personality and Social Psychology, 1,* 389–392.

McClelland, David C. (1975). *Power: The inner experience.* New York: Irvington.

McClelland, David C. (1985). How motives, skills, and values determine what people do. *American Psychologist, 40,* 812–825.

McClelland, David C.; Atkinson, John W.; Clark, Russell A.; & Lowell, Edgar L. (1953). *The achievement motive.* New York: Appleton-Century-Crofts.

McClelland, David C.; Floor, Erik; Davidson, Richard J.; & Saron, Clifford (1980). Stressed power motivation, sympathetic activation, immune function, and illness. *Journal of Human Stress, 6,* 11–19.

McClintock, Martha K. (1971). Menstrual synchrony and suppression. *Nature, 229,* 244–245.

McCloskey, Michael; Wible, Cynthia G.; & Cohen, Neal J. (1988). Is there a special flashbulb-memory mechanism? *Journal of Experimental Psychology: General, 117,* 171–181.

McCloskey, Michael, & Zaragoza, Maria (1985). Misleading postevent information and memory for events: Arguments and evidence against memory impairment hypotheses. *Journal of Experimental Psychology: General, 114,* 1–16.

McConnell, James V. (1962). Memory transfer through cannibalism in planarians. *Journal of Neuropsychiatry, 3,* Monograph Supplement 1.

McCrae, Robert R. (1984). Situational determinants of coping responses: Loss, threat, and challenge. *Journal of Personality and Social Psychology, 46,* 919–928.

McCrae, Robert R. (1987). Creativity, divergent thinking, and openness to experience. *Journal of Personality and Social Psychology, 52,* 1258–1265.

McCrae, Robert R., & Costa, Paul T., Jr. (1984). *Emerging lives, enduring dispositions: Personality in adulthood.* Boston: Little, Brown.

McCrae, Robert R., & Costa, Paul T., Jr. (1987). Validation of the five-factor model of personality across instruments and observers. *Journal of Personality and Social Psychology, 52,* 81–90.

McEwen, Bruce S. (1983a). Gonadal steroid influences on brain development and sexual differentiation. *Reproductive Physiology IV (International Review of Physiology), 27,* 99–145.

McEwen, Bruce S. (1983b). Hormones and the brain. In Catherine C. Brown (ed.), *Childhood learning disabilities and prenatal risk.* Pediatric Round Table: 9. Johnson & Johnson Baby Products Co., pp. 11–17.

McFarlane, Jessica; Martin, Carol Lynn; & Williams, Tannis MacBeth (1988). Mood fluctuations: Women versus men and menstrual versus other cycles. *Psychology of Women Quarterly, 12,* 201–223.

McGaugh, James L. (1983). Preserving the presence of the past: Hormonal influences on memory storage. *American Psychologist, 38,* 161–174.

McGaugh, James L. (1989). Involvement of hormonal and neuromodulatory systems in the regulation of memory storage. *Annual Review of Neuroscience, 12,* 255–288.

McGill, Michael (1980). *The forty to sixty year old male.* New York: Simon & Schuster.

McGlone, Jeannette (1978). Sex differences in functional brain asymmetry. *Cortex, 14,* 122–128.

McGlone, Jeannette (1980). Sex differences in human

brain asymmetry: A critical survey. *Behavioral and Brain Sciences, 3,* 215–227.

McGoldrick, Monica, & Gerson, Randy (1985). *Genograms in family assessment.* New York: Norton.

McGoldrick, Monica, & Pearce, John K. (1981). Family therapy with Irish Americans. *Family Process, 20,* 223–241.

McGoldrick, Monica; Pearce, John K.; & Giordano, J. (eds.) (1982). *Ethnicity and family therapy.* New York: Guilford Press.

McGue, Matt, & Bouchard, Thomas J. (1987). Genetic and environmental determinants of information processing and special mental abilities: A twin analysis. In R. J. Sternberg (ed.), *Advances in the psychology of human intelligence,* Vol. 5. Hillsdale, NJ: Erlbaum.

McGuigan, F. J. (1984). Progressive relaxation: Origins, principles, and clinical applications. In R. L. Woolfolk & P. M. Lehrer (eds.), *Principles and practice of stress management.* New York: Guilford Press.

McGuinness, Diane, & Pribram, Karl H. (1980). The neuropsychology of attention: Emotional and motivational controls. In M. C. Wittrock (ed.), *The brain and psychology.* New York: Academic Press.

McGuire, William, & Papageorgis, Dimitri (1961). The relative efficacy of various types of prior belief-defense in producing immunity against persuasion. *Journal of Abnormal and Social Psychology, 62,* 327–337.

McKey, Ruth H.; Condelli, L.; Ganson, H.; Barrett, B.; McConkey, C.; & Plantz, M. (1985). *The impact of Head Start on children, families, and communities: Final report of the Head Start Evaluation, Synthesis and Utilization Project* (No. OHDS 85-31193). Washington, DC: U.S. Government Printing Office.

McKinlay, Sonja M.; Bifano, Nancy L.; & McKinlay, John B. (1985). Smoking and age at menopause in women. *Annals of Internal Medicine, 103,* 350–356.

McKinlay, Sonja M., & McKinlay, John B. (1984). Health status and health care utilization by menopausal women. Unpublished paper, Cambridge Research Center, American Institutes for Research, Cambridge, MA.

McLeod, Beverly (1985, March). Real work for real pay. *Psychology Today, 19*(3), 42–44, 46, 48–50.

McNaughton, B. L., & Morris, R. G. M. (1987). Hippocampal synaptic enhancement and information storage within a distributed memory system. *Trends in Neuroscience, 10,* 408–415.

McNeil, Elton (1967). *The quiet furies.* Englewood Cliffs, NJ: Prentice-Hall.

Medawar, Peter (1982). *Pluto's Republic.* Oxford, England: Oxford University Press.

Meddis, Ray (1977). *The sleep instinct.* London: Routledge & Kegan Paul.

Mednick, Sarnoff A. (1962). The associative basis of the creative process. *Psychological Review, 69,* 220–232.

Mefford, Ivan N.; Baker, Theodore L.; et al. (1983). Narcolepsy: Biogenic amine deficits in an animal model. *Science, 220,* 629–632.

Meichenbaum, Donald (1977). *Cognitive-behavior modification: An integrative approach.* New York: Plenum.

Melton, Arthur W. (1963). Implications of short-term memory for a general theory of memory. *Journal of Verbal Learning and Verbal Behavior, 2,* 1–21.

Meltzer, Herbert Y. (1987). Biological studies in schizophrenia. *Schizophrenia Bulletin, 13*(1), 77–111.

Meltzoff, Andrew, & Moore, Michael (1977). Imitation of facial and manual gestures by human neonates. *Science, 198,* 75–78.

Melzack, Ronald (1973). *The puzzle of pain.* New York: Basic Books.

Melzack, Ronald, & Dennis, Stephen G. (1978). Neurophysiological foundations of pain. In R. A. Sternback (ed.), *The psychology of pain.* New York: Raven Press.

Melzack, Ronald, & Loeser, John D. (1978). Phantom body pain in paraplegics: Evidence for a central pattern generating mechanism for pain. *Pain, 4,* 195–210.

Melzack, Ronald, & Wall, Patrick D. (1965). Pain mechanisms: A new theory. *Science, 150,* 971–979.

Mercer, Jane (1988, May 18). Racial differences in intelligence: Fact or artifact? Talk given at San Bernardino Valley College.

Mershon, Bryan, & Gorsuch, Richard L. (1988). Number of factors in the personality sphere: Does increase in factors increase predictability of real-life criteria? *Journal of Personality and Social Psychology, 55,* 675–680.

Messer, Stanley, & Winokur, Meir (1980). Some limits to the integration of psychoanalytic and behavior therapy. *American Psychologist, 35,* 818–827.

Meyer, Karen G., & Simons, Virginia A. (1988). Questions and issues related to social policies as they impact on very young children and their families who are caught in the divorce process. Paper presented at the annual meeting of the American Orthopsychiatric Association, San Francisco.

Meyers, Ronald E., & Sperry, R. W. (1953). Interocular transfer of a visual form discrimination habit in cats after section of the optic chiasm and corpus callosum. *Anatomical Record, 115,* 351–352.

Michael, Richard P., & Keverne, E. B. (1970). Primate sex pheromones of vaginal origin. *Nature, 225,* 84–85.

Milgram, Stanley (1963). Behavioral study of obedience. *Journal of Abnormal and Social Psychology, 67,* 371–378.

Milgram, Stanley (1974). *Obedience to authority: An experimental view.* New York: Harper & Row.

Millar, Keith, & Watkinson, Neal (1983). Recognition of words presented during general anaesthesia. *Ergonomics, 26,* 585–594.

Miller, Alice (1984). *Thou shalt not be aware: Psychoanalysis and society's betrayal of the child.* New York: Farrar, Straus & Giroux.

Miller, George A. (1956). The magical number seven, plus or minus two: Some limits on our capacity for processing information. *Psychological Review, 63,* 81–97.

Miller, George A. (1969, December). On turning psychology over to the unwashed. *Psychology Today, 3*(7), 53–55, 66–68, 70, 72, 74.

Miller, George A., & Gildea, Patricia M. (1987, September). How children learn words. *Scientific American, 257*(6), 94–99.

Miller, Jonathan (1983). *States of mind.* New York: Pantheon.

Miller, Neal E. (1969). Learning of visceral and glandular responses. *Science, 163*, 434–435.

Miller, Neal E. (1978). Biofeedback and visceral learning. *Annual Review of Psychology, 29*, 421–452.

Miller, Neal E. (1985). The value of behavioral research on animals. *American Psychologist, 40*, 423–440.

Miller, Paul A., & Eisenberg, Nancy (1988). The relation of empathy to aggressive and externalizing/antisocial behavior. *Psychological Bulletin, 103*, 324–344.

Miller, Suzanne M. (1987). Monitoring and blunting: Validation of a questionnaire to assess styles of information seeking under threat. *Journal of Personality and Social Psychology, 52*, 345–353.

Miller, Suzanne M. (1989). To see or not to see: Cognitive informational styles in the coping process. In M. Rosenbaum (ed.), *Learned resourcefulness: On coping skills, self-regulation, and adaptive behavior.* New York: Springer.

Miller, Suzanne M.; Brody, David; & Summerton, Jeffrey (1988). Styles of coping with threat: Implications for health. *Journal of Personality and Social Psychology, 54*, 142–148.

Milner, Brenda (1970). Memory and the temporal regions of the brain. In K. H. Pribram & D. E. Broadbent (eds.), *Biology of memory.* New York: Academic Press.

Milner, Brenda; Corkin, Suzanne; & Teuber, H. L. (1968). Further analysis of the hippocampal amnesic syndrome: 14-year follow-up study of H. M. *Neuropsychologia, 6*, 215–234.

Mindess, Harvey (1971). *Laughter and liberation.* Los Angeles: Nash.

Mindess, Harvey (1983, October 9). The proud father who boxed behaviorism. *Los Angeles Times Book Review.*

Minuchin, Salvador (1984). *Family kaleidoscope.* Cambridge, MA: Harvard University Press.

Minuchin, Salvador; Rosman, Bernice L.; & Baker, Lester (1978). *Psychosomatic families: Anorexia nervosa in context.* Cambridge, MA: Harvard University Press.

Mischel, Walter (1968). *Personality and assessment.* New York: Wiley.

Mischel, Walter (1981). A cognitive social learning approach to assessment. In T. V. Merluzzi, C. R. Glass, & M. Genest (eds.), *Cognitive assessment.* New York: Guilford Press.

Mischel, Walter (1984). Convergences and challenges in the search for consistency. *American Psychologist, 39*, 351–364.

Mishkin, Mortimer, & Appenzeller, Tim (1987). The anatomy of memory. *Scientific American, 256*, 80–89.

Mitroff, Ian I. (1974). Norms and counter-norms in a select group of the Apollo moon scientists: A case study of the ambivalence of scientists. *American Sociological Review, 39*, 579–595.

Miura, Irene T.; Kim, Chungsoon C.; Chang, Chih-Mei; & Okamoto, Yukari (1988). Effects of language characteristics on children's cognitive representation of number: Cross-national comparisons. *Child Development, 59*, 1445–1450.

Miura, Irene T., & Okamoto, Yukari (1989). Comparisons of U.S. and Japanese first graders' cognitive representation of number and understanding of place value. *Journal of Educational Psychology, 81*, 109–113.

Monk, Timothy H., & Aplin, Lynne C. (1980). Spring and Autumn daylight saving time changes: Studies of adjustment in sleep timings, mood, and efficiency. *Ergonomics, 23*, 167–178.

Monk, Timothy H.; Weitzman, Elliot D.; et al. (1983, August 11). Task variables determine which biological clock controls circadian rhythms in human performance. *Nature, 304*, 543–545.

Monmaney, Terence (1987, September). Are we led by the nose? *Discover, 8*(9), 48–56.

Montagner, Hubert (1985). Approache ethologique des systems à interaction du nouveau né et du jeune enfant. [An ethological approach of the interaction systems of the infant and the young child.] *Neuropsychiatrie de l'Enfance et de l'Adolescence, 33*, 59–71.

Montagu, Ashley (1978). *Learning non-aggression: The experience of non-literate societies.* New York: Oxford University Press.

Montgomery, Geoffrey (1988, December). Seeing with the brain. *Discover, 9*(12), 52–59.

Moore, Lawrence E., & Kaplan, Jerold Z. (1983). Hypnotically accelerated burn wound healing. *American Journal of Clinical Hypnosis, 26*(1), 16–19.

Moore, S. D., & Stanley, J. C. (1986). Family backgrounds of young Asian Americans who reason extremely well mathematically. Unpublished manuscript, Johns Hopkins University.

Moore-Ede, Martin C., & Sulzman, Frank M. (1981). Internal temporal order. In J. Aschoff (ed.), *Handbook of behavioral neurobiology, Vol. 4: Biological rhythms.* New York: Plenum.

Moore-Ede, Martin, C.; Sulzman, Frank M.; & Fuller, Charles A. (1984). *The clocks that time us: Physiology of the circadian timing system.* Cambridge, MA: Harvard University Press.

Morgan, Leslie A. (1976). A re-examination of widowhood and morale. *Journal of Gerontology, 31*, 687–695.

Morris, Monica (1988). *Last-chance children: Growing up with older parents.* New York: Columbia University Press.

Moscovici, Serge (1985). Social influence and conformity. In G. Lindzey & E. Aronson (eds.), *Handbook of social psychology,* Vol. II. 3rd ed. New York: Random House.

Moscovici, Serge, & Mugny, Gabriel (1983). Minority

influence. In P. B. Paulus (ed.), *Basic group processes.* New York: Springer-Verlag.

Mosher, Frederic A., & Hornsby, Joan R. (1966). On asking questions. In J. S. Bruner, R. R. Olver, & P. M. Greenfield (eds.), *Studies in cognitive growth.* New York: Wiley.

Moss, Howard A., & Susman, Elizabeth J. (1980). Longitudinal study of personality development. In O. G. Brim, Jr., & J. Kagan (eds.), *Constancy and change in human development.* Cambridge, MA: Harvard University Press.

Moyer, Kenneth E. (1983). The physiology of motivation: Aggression as a model. In C. J. Scheirer & A. M. Rogers (eds.), *The G. Stanley Hall lecture series,* Vol. 3. Washington, DC: American Psychological Association.

Mozell, Maxwell M.; Smith, Bruce P., Smith, Paul E., Sullivan, Richard L.; & Swender, Philip (1969). Nasal chemoreception in flavor identification. *Archives of Otolaryngology, 90,* 367–373.

Muehlenhard, Charlene, & Cook, Stephen (1988). Men's self-reports of unwanted sexual activity. *The Journal of Sex Research, 24,* 58–72.

Mueller, Conrad G. (1979). Some origins of psychology as science. *Annual Review of Psychology, 30,* 9–29.

Mullins, Larry C.; Johnson, D. Paul; & Andersson, Lars (1987). Loneliness of the elderly: The impact of family and friends. *Journal of Social Behavior and Personality, 2,* 161–164.

Mulvey, Edward P.; Geller, Jeffrey L.; & Roth, Loren H. (1987). The promise and peril of involuntary outpatient commitment. *American Psychologist, 42,* 571–584.

Murphy, Jane (1976). Psychiatric labeling in cross-cultural perspective. *Science, 191,* 1019–1028.

Murphy, Wendy B. (1982). *Touch, taste, smell, sight and hearing.* Alexandria, VA: Time-Life Books.

Mussen, Paul H.; Conger, John J.; Kagan, Jerome; & Huston, Aletha C. (1984). *Child development and personality.* New York: Harper & Row.

Myers, David G. (1980). *The inflated self.* New York: Seabury.

Myers, David G. (1983). *Social psychology.* New York: McGraw-Hill.

Myers, David G., & Ridl, Jack (1979, August). Can we all be better than average? *Psychology Today, 13*(3), 89, 95–96, 98.

Nadel, Lynn, & Zola-Morgan, Stuart (1984). Infantile amnesia: A neurobiological perspective. In M. Moscovitch (ed.), *Infantile memory: Its relation to normal and pathological memory in humans and other animals.* New York: Plenum.

Napolitan, David A., & Goethals, George R. (1979). The attribution of friendliness. *Journal of Experimental Social Psychology, 15,* 105–113.

Nash, Michael (1987). What, if anything, is regressed about hypnotic age regression? A review of the empirical literature. *Psychological Bulletin, 102,* 42–52.

Needleman, Herbert L.; Leviton, Alan; & Bellinger
David (1982). Lead-associated intellectual deficit. *New England Journal of Medicine, 306,* 367.

Neimark, Edith (1975). Intellectual development during adolescence. In F. D. Horowitz (ed.), *Review of child development research,* Vol. 4. Chicago: University of Chicago Press.

Neiss, Rob (1988). Reconceptualizing arousal: Psychobiological states in motor performance. *Psychological Bulletin, 103,* 345–366.

Neisser, Ulric (1967). *Cognitive psychology.* Englewood Cliffs, NJ: Prentice-Hall.

Neisser, Ulric (1981). John Dean's memory: A case study. *Cognition, 9,* 1–22. (Reprinted in U. Neisser [ed.], *Memory observed: Remembering in natural contexts.* San Francisco: Freeman, 1982.)

Neisser, Ulric (1982). Snapshots or benchmarks? In U. Neisser (ed.), *Memory observed: Remembering in natural contexts.* San Francisco: Freeman.

Nelson, Alan (1985). Psychological equivalence: Awareness and response-ability in our nuclear age. *American Psychologist, 40,* 549–556.

Nemeth, Charlan (1977). Interactions between jurors as a function of majority vs. unanimity decision rules. *Journal of Applied Social Psychology, 7,* 38–56.

Neugarten, Bernice (1969). Continuities and discontinuities of psychological issues in adult life. *Human Development, 14,* 121–130.

Neugarten, Bernice (1974, September). Age groups in American society and the rise of the young-old. *Annals of American Academy,* 187–189.

Neugarten, Bernice (1979). Time, age, and the life cycle. *American Journal of Psychiatry, 136,* 887–894.

Neugarten, Bernice (1982). Successful aging. Paper presented at the annual meeting of the American Psychological Association, Washington.

Newcomb, Michael D., & Bentler, Peter M. (1988). *Consequences of adolescent drug use.* Newbury Park, CA: Sage.

Newcomb, Michael D., & Bentler, Peter M. (1989). Substance use and abuse among children and teenagers. *American Psychologist, 44,* 242–248.

Newell, Alan, & Simon, Herbert (1972). *Human problem solving.* Englewood Cliffs, NJ: Prentice-Hall.

Newman, Eric A., & Hartline, Peter H. (1982). The infrared "vision" of snakes. *Scientific American, 246*(3), 116–127.

Newman, Joseph P.; Widom, Cathy S.; & Nathan, Stuart (1985). Passive avoidance in syndromes of disinhibition: Psychopathy and extraversion. *Journal of Personality and Social Psychology, 48,* 1316–1327.

Newman, Katherine (1988). *Falling from grace: The experience of downward mobility in the American middle class.* New York: Free Press.

Newton, Nancy A.; Lazarus, Lawrence W.; & Weinberg, Jack (1984). Aging: Biopsychosocial perspectives. In D. Offer & M. Sabshin (eds.), *Normality and the life cycle.* New York: Basic Books.

Nezu, Arthur M.; Nezu, Christine M.; & Blissett, Sonia E. (1988). Sense of humor as a moderator of the relation between stressful events and psychological distress: A prospective analysis. *Journal of Personality and Social Psychology, 54,* 520–525.

Nichols, Michael P. (1988). *The power of the family.* New York: Simon & Schuster.

Nickerson, Raymond A., & Adams, Marilyn Jager (1979). Long-term memory for a common object. *Cognitive Psychology, 11,* 287–307.

Nisbett, Richard E. (1988). Testimony on behalf of the American Psychological Association before the U.S. House of Representatives Committee on Armed Services, October 6.

Nisbett, Richard, & Ross, Lee (1980). *Human inference: Strategies and shortcomings of social judgment.* Englewood Cliffs, NJ: Prentice-Hall.

Noller, Patricia; Law, Henry; & Comrey, Andrew L. (1987). Cattell, Comrey, and Eysenck personality factors compared: More evidence for the five robust factors? *Journal of Personality and Social Psychology, 53,* 775–782.

Norman, Donald A. (1988). *The psychology of everyday things.* New York: Basic Books.

Novaco, Raymond W. (1985). Anger and its therapeutic regulation. In M. Chesney and R. Rosenman (eds.), *Anger and hostility in cardiovascular and behavioral disorders.* Washington, DC: Hemisphere.

Oakley, Ann (1974). *Woman's work: The housewife, past and present.* New York: Pantheon.

Offer, Daniel, & Sabshin, Melvin (1984a). Adolescence: Empirical perspectives. In D. Offer & M. Sabshin (eds.), *Normality and the life cycle.* New York: Basic Books.

Offer, Daniel, & Sabshin, Melvin (1984b). Patterns of normal development. In D. Offer & M. Sabshin (eds.), *Normality and the life cycle.* New York: Basic Books.

Ogilvie, Daniel M. (1987). The undesired self: A neglected variable in personality research. *Journal of Personality and Social Psychology, 52,* 379–385.

Olds, James (1975). Mapping the mind onto the brain. In F. G. Worden, J. P. Swazy, and G. Adelman (eds.), *The neurosciences: Paths of discovery.* Cambridge, MA: Colonial Press.

Olds, James, & Milner, Peter (1954). Positive reinforcement produced by electrical stimulation of septal area and other regions of the rat brain. *Journal of Comparative and Physiological Psychology, 47,* 419–429.

Olweus, Dan (1979). Stability of aggressive reaction patterns in males: A review. *Psychological Bulletin, 86,* 852–875.

O'Neill, Colleen, & Zeichner, Amos (1984, May). Working women: A study of relationships between stress, coping, and health. Paper presented at the annual meeting of the Society of Behavioral Medicine, Philadelphia.

Orne, Martin T. (1979). On the simulating subject as a quasi-control group in hypnosis research: What, why, and how. In E. Fromm & R. E. Shor (eds.), *Hypnosis: Developments in research and new perspectives* (2nd ed.). New York: Aldine.

Ornstein, Robert E. (1977). *The psychology of consciousness* (2nd ed.). New York: Harcourt Brace Jovanovich.

Ornstein, Robert E. (1978, May). The split and whole brain. *Human Nature, 1,* 76–83.

Ortar, G. (1963). Is a verbal test cross-cultural? *Scripta Hierosolymitana* (Hebrew University, Jerusalem), *13,* 219–235.

Orwell, George (1949). *Nineteen eighty-four.* New York: Harcourt Brace Jovanovich.

Page, J. Bryan; Fletcher, Jack; & True, William R. (1988). Psychosociocultural perspectives on chronic cannabis use: The Costa Rican follow-up. *Journal of Psychoactive Drugs, 20,* 57–65.

Pagel, Mark D.; Erdly, William W.; & Becker, Joseph (1987). Social networks: We get by with (and in spite of) a little help from our friends. *Journal of Personality and Social Psychology, 53,* 793–804.

Paige, Karen (1978, May). The ritual of circumcision. *Human Nature, 1,* 40–49.

Paivio, Allan (1969). Mental imagery in associative learning and memory. *Psychological Review, 76,* 241–263.

Paivio, Allan (1983). The empirical case for dual coding. In J. C. Yuille (ed.), *Imagery, memory and cognition.* Hillsdale, NJ: Erlbaum.

Panksepp, Jaak A. (1979). A neurochemical theory of autism. *Trends in Neuroscience, 2,* 174–177.

Panksepp, J.; Herman, B. H.; Vilberg, T.; Bishop, P.; & DeEskinazi, F. G. (1980). Endogenous opioids and social behavior. *Neuroscience and Biobehavioral Reviews, 4,* 473–487.

Parke, Ross, & Sawin, Douglas B. (1980). The family in early infancy. In F. A. Pederson (ed.), *The father-infant relationship: Observational studies in a family context.* New York: Praeger.

Parke, Ross, & Tinsley, Barbara R. (1981). The father's role in infancy: Determinants of involvement in caregiving and play. In M. E. Lamb (ed.), *The role of the father in child development* (2nd ed.). New York: Wiley-Interscience.

Parker, Elizabeth S.; Birnbaum, Isabel M.; & Noble, Ernest P. (1976). Alcohol and memory: Storage and state dependency. *Journal of Verbal Learning and Verbal Behavior, 15,* 691–702.

Parker, Keven C. H.; Hanson, R. Karl; & Hunsley, John (1988). MMPI, Rorschach, and WAIS: A meta-analytic comparison of reliability, stability, and validity. *Psychological Bulletin, 103,* 367–373.

Parkes, Katharine (1984). Locus of control, cognitive appraisal, and coping in stressful episodes. *Journal of Personality and Social Psychology, 46,* 655–668.

Parlee, Mary Brown (1973). The premenstrual syndrome. *Psychological Bulletin, 80,* 454–465.

Parlee, Mary Brown (1982). Changes in moods and activation levels during the menstrual cycle in experimentally naive subjects. *Psychology of Women Quarterly, 7,* 119–131.

Pascale, Richard, & Athos, Anthony G. (1981). *The art of Japanese management.* New York: Simon & Schuster.

Pasewark, Richard A., and Pasewark, Mark D. (1982). The insanity plea: Much ado about little. In B. L. Bloom & S. J. Asher (eds.), *Psychiatric patient rights and patient advocacy: Issues and evidence.* New York: Human Sciences Press.

Patterson, Francine, & Linden, Eugene (1981). *The education of Koko.* New York: Holt, Rinehart and Winston.

Patterson, Gerald R. (1985). A microsocial analysis of anger and irritable behavior. In M. A. Chesney & R. H. Rosenman (eds.), *Anger and hostility in cardiovascular and behavioral disorders.* Washington, DC, and New York: Hemisphere.

Patterson, Gerald R. (1986). Performance models for antisocial boys. *American Psychologist, 41,* 432–444.

Paul, Richard W. (1984, September). Critical thinking: Fundamental to education for a free society. *Educational Leadership,* 4–14.

Pavlov, Ivan P. (1960). *Conditioned reflexes.* (G. V. Anrep, translator and editor.) New York: Dover. (Original translation Oxford University Press, 1927.)

Payn, Nadine (1980). Beyond orgasm. Unpublished Ph.D. dissertation, University of California, Berkeley.

Peabody, Dean (1985). *National characteristics.* Cambridge, England: Cambridge University Press.

Pearlin, Leonard (1982). Discontinuities in the study of aging. In T. K. Hareven & K. J. Adams (eds.), *Aging and life course transitions: An interdisciplinary perspective.* New York: Guilford Press.

Pearlin, Leonard, & Schooler, Carmi (1978). The structure of coping. *Journal of Health and Social Behavior, 19,* 2–21.

Peck, Jeffrey W. (1978). Rats defend different body weights depending on palatability and accessibility of their food. *Journal of Comparative and Physiological Psychology, 92,* 555–570.

Peele, Stanton (1983). *The science of experience.* Lexington, MA: Lexington Books.

Peele, Stanton (1984a). The cultural context of psychological approaches to alcoholism: Can we control the effects of alcohol? *American Psychologist, 39,* 1337–1351.

Peele, Stanton (1984b, March–April). The new prohibitionists. *The Sciences,* 14–19.

Peele, Stanton (1985). *The meaning of addiction: Compulsive experience & its interpretation.* Lexington, MA: Lexington Books.

Penfield, Wilder, & Perot, Phanor (1963). The brain's record of auditory and visual experience: A final summary and discussion. *Brain, 86,* 595–696.

Pennebaker, James W. (1982). *The psychology of physical symptoms.* New York: Springer-Verlag.

Pennebaker, James W. (1988). Confiding traumatic experiences and health. In S. Fisher & J. Reason (eds.), *Handbook of life stress, cognition and health.* New York: Wiley.

Pennebaker, James W.; Hughes, Cheryl F.; &

O'Heeron, Robin C. (1987). The psychophysiology of confession: Linking inhibitory and psychosomatic processes. *Journal of Personality and Social Psychology, 52,* 781–793.

Pennebaker, James W.; Kiecolt-Glaser, Janice; & Glaser, Ronald (1988). Disclosure of traumas and immune function: Health implications for psychotherapy. *Journal of Consulting and Clinical Psychology, 56,* 239–245.

Peplau, Letitia A. (1983). Roles and gender. In H. Kelley et al. (eds.), *Close relationships.* New York: Freeman.

Peplau, Letitia A. (1984). Power in dating relationships. In J. Freedman (ed.), *Women: A feminist perspective* (3rd ed.). Palo Alto, CA: Mayfield.

Peplau, Letitia A., & Gordon, Steven L. (1985). Women and men in love: Gender differences in close heterosexual relationships. In V. O'Leary, R. Unger, & B. Wallston (eds.), *Women, gender, and social psychology.* Hillsdale, NJ: Erlbaum.

Peplau, Letitia A., & Perlman, Dan (eds.) (1982). *Loneliness: A sourcebook of current theory, research, and therapy.* New York: Wiley-Interscience.

Peplau, Letitia A.; Rubin, Zick; & Hill, Charles (1977). Sexual intimacy in dating relationships. *Journal of Social Issues, 33,* 86–109.

Peplau, Letitia A.; Russell, Dan; & Heim, Margaret (1979). The experience of loneliness. In I. H. Frieze, D. Bar-Tal, & J. S. Carroll (eds.), *New approaches to social problems.* San Francisco: Jossey-Bass.

Pepperberg, Irene M. (1987). Evidence for conceptual quantitative abilities in the African grey parrot: Labeling of cardinal sets. *Ethology, 75,* 37–61.

Peris, Frederick (1969). *Gestalt therapy verbatim.* Berkeley, CA: Real People Press.

Peterson, Christopher (1988). Explanatory style as a risk factor for illness. *Cognitive Therapy and Research, 12,* 117–130.

Peterson, Christopher, & Barrett, Lisa C. (1987). Explanatory style and academic performance among university freshmen. *Journal of Personality and Social Psychology, 53,* 603–607.

Peterson, Christopher, & Seligman, Martin E. P. (1984). Causal explanations as a risk factor for depression: Theory and evidence. *Psychological Review, 91,* 347–374.

Peterson, Christopher, & Seligman, Martin E. P. (1987). Explanatory style and illness. *Journal of Personality, 55,* 237–265.

Peterson, Christopher; Seligman, Martin E. P.; & Vaillant, George (1988). Pessimistic explanatory style is a risk factor for physical illness: A thirty-five year longitudinal study. *Journal of Personality and Social Psychology, 55,* 23–27.

Peterson, Lloyd R., & Peterson, Margaret J. (1959). Short-term retention of individual verbal items. *Journal of Experimental Psychology, 58,* 193–198.

Petros, Thomas V.; Kerbel, Norman; Beckwith, Bill E.; Sacks, Gary; & Sarafolean, Mary (1985). The effects of alcohol on prose memory. *Physiology and Behavior, 35,* 43–46.

Piaget, Jean (1929/1960). *The child's conception of the world*. Paterson, NJ: Littlefield, Adams. (First published in English, 1929.)

Piaget, Jean (1932). *The moral judgment of the child*. New York: Macmillan.

Piaget, Jean (1951). *Plays, dreams, and imitation in childhood*. New York: Norton.

Piaget, Jean (1952). *The origins of intelligence in children*. New York: International Universities Press.

Piaget, Jean (1984). Piaget's theory. In P. Mussen (ed.), *Handbook of child psychology* (4th ed.), Vol. 1. W. Kessen (ed.), *History, theory, and methods*. New York: Wiley.

Piliavin, Irving; Piliavin, Jane; & Rodin, Judith (1975). Costs, diffusion, and the stigmatized victim. *Journal of Personality and Social Psychology, 32*, 429–438.

Pines, Ayala (1986). Marriage. In C. Tavris (ed.), *EveryWoman's emotional well-being*. New York: Doubleday.

Pines, Maya (1983, September). The human difference. *Psychology Today, 17*(9), 62–68.

Pleck, Joseph H. (1987). American fathering in historical perspective. In M. S. Kimmel (ed.), *Changing men: New directions in research on men and masculinity*. Beverly Hills, CA: Sage.

Plomin, Robert, & DeFries, J. C. (1980). Genetics and intelligence: Recent data. *Intelligence, 4*, 15–24.

Plutchik, Robert (1984). Emotions: A general psychoevolutionary theory. In K. R. Scherer & P. Ekman (eds.), *Approaches to emotion*. Hillsdale, NJ: Erlbaum.

Plutchik, Robert (1987). Evolutionary bases of empathy. In N. Eisenberg & J. Strayer (eds.), *Empathy and its development*. New York: Cambridge University Press.

Plutchik, Robert; Kellerman, Henry; & Conte, Hope (1979). A structural theory of ego defenses and emotions. In C. E. Izard (ed.), *Emotions in personality and psychopathology*. New York: Plenum.

Poley, Wayne; Lea, Gary; & Vibe, Gail (1979). *Alcoholism: A treatment manual*. New York: Gardner.

Polivy, Janet (1981). On the induction of emotion in the laboratory: Discrete moods or multiple affect states? *Journal of Personality and Social Psychology, 41*, 803–817.

Polivy, Janet, & Herman, C. Peter (1985). Dieting and bing[e]ing: A causal analysis. *American Psychologist, 40*, 193–201.

Pollak, Richard (1984, May). The epilepsy defense. *Atlantic Monthly*, 20–28.

Pomeroy, Sarah (1975). *Goddesses, whores, wives and slaves—Women in classical antiquity*. New York: Schocken.

Pope, Harrison G., Jr.; Keck, P. E.; & McElroy, S. L. (1986). Frequency and presentation of neuroleptic malignant syndrome in a large psychiatric hospital. *American Journal of Psychiatry, 143*, 1227–1233.

Pope, Kenneth, & Bouhoutsos, Jacqueline (1986). *Sexual intimacy between therapists and patients*. New York: Praeger.

Porter, Roy (1987). *A social history of madness: The world through the eyes of the insane*. New York: Weidenfeld & Nicolson.

Powley, Terry (1977). The ventromedial hypothalamic syndrome, satiety, and a cephalic phase hypothesis. *Psychological Review, 84*, 89–126.

Premack, David (1965). Reinforcement theory. In D. Levine (ed.), *Nebraska symposium on motivation, 1965*. Lincoln: University of Nebraska Press.

Premack, David, & Premack, Ann James (1983). *The mind of an ape*. New York: Norton.

Preti, George; Cutler, Winnifred B.; et al. (1986). Human axillary secretions influence women's menstrual cycles: The role of donor extract from females. *Hormones and Behavior, 20*, 474–482.

Pribram, Karl H. (1971). *Languages of the brain: Experimental paradoxes and principles*. Englewood Cliffs, NJ: Prentice-Hall.

Pribram, Karl H. (1982). Localization and distribution of function in the brain. In J. Orbach (ed.), *Neuropsychology after Lashley*. Hillsdale, NJ: Erlbaum.

Prioleau, Leslie; Murdock, Martha; & Brody, Nathan (1983). An analysis of psychotherapy versus placebo studies. *Behavioral and Brain Sciences, 6*, 275–285.

Prochaska, James O. (1984). *Systems of psychotherapy: A transtheoretical analysis* (2nd ed.). Homewood, IL: Dorsey.

Professional Staff of the United States–United Kingdom Cross-National Project (1974). The diagnosis and psychopathology of schizophrenia in New York and London. *Schizophrenia Bulletin, 11*, 80–102.

Pryor, Karen (1984). *Don't shoot the dog!* New York: Simon & Schuster.

Pulver, Ann; Carpenter, William; Adler, Lawrence; & McGrath, John (1988). Accuracy of diagnoses of affective disorders and schizophrenia in public hospitals. *American Journal of Psychiatry, 145*, 218–220.

Pyke, S. W., & Kahill, S. P. (1983, Winter). Sex differences in characteristics presumed relevant to professional productivity. *Psychology of Women Quarterly, 8*, 189–192.

Qualls, R. Christopher, & Berman, Jeffrey S. (1988). Anorexia nervosa: A quantitative review of the treatment outcome literature. Paper presented at the annual meeting of the American Psychological Association, Atlanta.

Rabkin, Judith G. (1977). Therapists' attitudes toward mental illness and health. In A. S. Gurman & A. M. Razin (eds.), *Effective psychotherapy: A handbook of research*. New York: Pergamon.

Rachman, S. J., & Wilson, G. Terence (1980). *The effects of psychological therapy* (2nd ed.). Oxford, England: Pergamon.

Radin, Norma (1981). The role of the father in cognitive, academic, and intellectual development. In M. E. Lamb (ed.), *The role of the father in child development* (2nd ed.). New York: Wiley-Interscience.

Radner, Daisie, & Radner, Michael (1982). *Science and unreason*. Belmont, CA: Wadsworth.

Rait, Douglas (1988, January-February). Survey results. *The Family Therapy Networker*, 52–56.

Rajecki, D. W. (1982). *Attitudes: Themes and advances.* Sunderland, MA: Sinauer Associates.

Ralph, Martin R., & Menaker, Michael (1988). A mutation of the circadian system in golden hamsters. *Science, 241,* 1225–1227.

Ransom, Donald C. (1982). Harmful elements in family therapy. Paper presented at the annual meeting of the American Psychological Association, Washington.

Raskin, Marjorie; Peeke, Harman; Dickman, William; & Pinsker, Henry (1982). Panic and generalized anxiety disorders: Developmental antecedents and precipitants. *Archives of General Psychiatry, 39,* 687–689.

Raskin, Robert, & Terry, Howard (1988). A principal-components analysis of the narcissistic personality inventory and further evidence of its construct validity. *Journal of Personality and Social Psychology, 54,* 890–902.

Rathbun, Constance; DiVirgilio, Letitia; & Waldfogel, Samuel (1958). A restitutive process in children following radical separation from family and culture. *American Journal of Orthopsychiatry, 28,* 408–415.

Ravussin, Eric; Lillioja, Stephen; Knowler, William; Christin, Laurent; et al. (1988). Reduced rate of energy expenditure as a risk factor for body-weight gain. *New England Journal of Medicine, 318,* 467–472.

Redican, William K., & Taub, David M. (1981). Male parental care in monkeys and apes. In M. E. Lamb (ed.), *The role of the father in child development* (2nd ed.). New York: Wiley-Interscience.

Reed, Graham F. (1985). *Obsessional experience and compulsive behavior: A cognitive-structural approach.* Orlando, FL: Academic Press.

Regier, Darrel; Boyd, Jeffrey; Burke, Jack; Rae, Donald; et al. (1988). One-month prevalence of mental disorders in the United States. *Archives of General Psychiatry, 45,* 977–986.

Reinke, Barbara; Holmes, David S.; & Harris, Rochelle (1985). The timing of psychosocial changes in women's lives: The years 25 to 45. *Journal of Personality and Social Psychology, 48,* 1353–1365.

Reppert, Steven M.; Weaver, David R.; Rivkees, Scott A., & Stopa, Edward G. (1988). Putative melatonin receptors in a human biological clock. *Science, 242,* 78–81.

Rescorla, Robert A. (1988). Pavlovian conditioning: It's not what you think it is. *American Psychologist, 43,* 151–160.

Restak, Richard (1983, October). Is free will a fraud? *Science Digest, 91*(10), 52–55.

Revenson, Tracey; Wollman, Carol; & Felton, Barbara (1983). Social supports as stress buffers for adult cancer patients. *Psychosomatic Medicine, 45,* 321–331.

Reynolds, David K. (1976). *Morita therapy.* Berkeley: University of California Press.

Reynolds, David K. (1987). *Water bears no scars: Japanese lifeways for personal growth.* New York: Morrow.

Rhoades, David F. (1985). Pheromonal communication between plants. In G. A. Cooper-Driver, T. Swain, & E. E. Conn (eds.), *Research advances in phytochemistry,* Vol. 19. New York: Plenum.

Ricaurte, George A.; Forno, Lysia; Wilson, Mary; deLanney, Louis; Irwin, Ean; Mulliver, Mark; & Langston, J. William. (1988). (+ or −) 3, 4-Methylenedioxy-methamphetamine selectively damages central serotonergic neurons in nonhuman primates. *Journal of the American Medical Association, 260,* 51–55.

Richards, Ruth L.; Kinney, Dennis K.; Benet, Maria; & Merzel, Ann (1988). Everyday creativity: Characteristics of the Lifetime Creativity Scales and validation with three large samples. *Journal of Personality and Social Psychology, 54,* 476–485.

Richardson-Klavehn, Alan, & Bjork, Robert A. (1988). Measures of memory. *Annual Review of Psychology, 39,* 475–543.

Richmond, Barry J.; Optican, Lance M.; Podell, Michael; & Spitzer, Hedva (1987). Temporal encoding of two-dimensional patterns by single units in primate inferior temporal cortex. I. Response characteristics. *Journal of Neurophysiology, 57,* 132–146.

Ridley, Charles R. (1984). Clinical treatment of the nondisclosing black client. *American Psychologist, 39,* 1234–1244.

Riggio, Ronald E., & Friedman, Howard S. (1983). Individual differences and cues to deception. *Journal of Personality and Social Psychology, 45,* 899–915.

Rioch, David M. (1975). Psychological and pharmacological manipulations. In L. Levi (ed.), *Emotions: Their parameters and measurement.* New York: Raven Press.

Risman, Barbara J. (1987). Intimate relationships from a microstructural perspective: Men who mother. *Gender and Society, 1,* 6–32.

Robbins, Lillian, & Robbins, Edwin (1973). Comment on "Toward an understanding of achievement-related conflicts in women." *Journal of Social Issues, 29,* 133–137.

Roberts, Susan B.; Savage, J.; Coward, W. A.; Chew, B.; & Lucas, A. (1988). Energy expenditure and intake in infants born to lean and overweight mothers. *New England Journal of Medicine, 318,* 461–466.

Robins, Clive J. (1988). Attributions and depression: Why is the literature so inconsistent? *Journal of Personality and Social Psychology, 54,* 880–889.

Robins, Lee N.; Davis, Darlene H.; & Goodwin, Donald W. (1974). Drug use by U.S. Army enlisted men in Vietnam: A follow-up on their return home. *American Journal of Epidemiology, 99,* 235–249.

Robinson, Halbert B., & Robinson, Nancy M. (1976). *The mentally retarded child: A psychological approach* (2nd ed.). New York: McGraw-Hill.

Robinson, Ira E., & Jedlicka, Davor (1982). Change in sexual attitudes and behavior of college students from 1965 to 1989: A research note. *Journal of Marriage and the Family, 44,* 237–240.

Robitscher, Jonas (1980). *The powers of psychiatry.* Boston: Houghton Mifflin.

Rodgers, Joann (1988, April). Pains of complaint. *Psychology Today, 22*(4), 26–27.

Rodin, Judith (1983). Obesity. Paper presented at the annual meeting of the American Psychological Association, Anaheim, CA.

Rodin, Judith (1984, January-February). Taming the hunger hormones. *American Health, 3,* 43–47.

Rodin, Judith (1988). Control, health, and aging. Invited address, Society of Behavioral Medicine, Boston.

Rogers, Carl (1951). *Client-centered therapy: Its current practice, implications, and theory.* Boston: Houghton Mifflin.

Rogers, Carl (1961). *On becoming a person.* Boston: Houghton Mifflin.

Rogers, Malcolm, & Reich, Peter (1988, August 25). On the health consequences of bereavement. *New England Journal of Medicine, 319,* 510–511.

Rogers, Richard (1986). *Conducting insanity evaluations.* New York: Van Nostrand Reinhold.

Rogers, Richard (1988). APA's position on the insanity defense. *American Psychologist, 42,* 840–848.

Rogler, Lloyd H.; Malgady, Robert G.; Costantino, Giuseppe; & Blumenthal, Rena (1987). What do culturally sensitive mental health services mean? The case of Hispanics. *American Psychologist, 42,* 565–570.

Rollin, Henry (ed.) (1980). *Coping with schizophrenia.* London: Burnett.

Roman, Mark B. (1988, April). When good scientists turn bad. *Discover,* 50–58.

Rook, Karen S. (1984a). The negative side of social interaction: Impact on psychological well-being. *Journal of Personality and Social Psychology, 46,* 1097–1108.

Rook, Karen S. (1984b). Research on social support, loneliness, and social isolation. In P. Shaver (ed.), *Review of personality and social psychology: 5.* Beverly Hills, CA: Sage.

Rook, Karen S. (1987). Social support versus companionship: Effects on life stress, loneliness, and evaluations by others. *Journal of Personality and Social Psychology, 52,* 1132–1147.

Rosch, Eleanor H. (1973). Natural categories. *Cognitive Psychology, 4,* 328–350.

Rosch, Eleanor H. (1977). Human categorization. In N. Warren (ed.), *Advances in cross-cultural psychology,* Vol. 1. London: Academic Press.

Rosch, Eleanor H., & Mervis, Carolyn B. (1975). Family resemblances: Studies in the internal structure of categories. *Cognitive Psychology, 7,* 573–605.

Rose, Richard J.; Koskenvuo, Markku; Kaprio, Jaakko; Sarna, Seppo; & Langinvainio, Heimo (1988). Shared genes, shared experiences, and similarity of personality: Data from 14,288 adult Finnish co-twins. *Journal of Personality and Social Psychology, 54,* 161–171.

Rosen, R. D. (1977). *Psychobabble.* New York: Atheneum.

Rosenbaum, Michael (1983). Learned resourcefulness as a behavioral repertoire for the self-regulation of internal events: Issues and speculations. In M. Rosenbaum, C. M. Franks, & Y. Jaffe (eds.), *Perspectives on behavior therapy in the eighties.* New York: Springer.

Rosenbaum, Michael, & Ben-Ari, Karin (1985). Learned helplessness and learned resourcefulness. *Journal of Personality and Social Psychology, 48,* 198–215.

Rosenberg, Morris (1979). *Conceiving the self.* New York: Basic Books.

Rosenhan, David L. [D. L.] (1983). On being sane in insane places. *Science, 179,* 250–258.

Rosenhan, David L. (1973). Psychological abnormality and law. In C. J. Scheirer & B. L. Hammonds (eds.), *Psychology and the law: The APA Master Lecture Series,* Vol. 2. Washington, DC: American Psychological Association.

Rosenthal, David (1955). Changes in some moral values following psychotherapy. *Journal of Consulting Psychology, 19,* 431–436.

Rosenthal, Norman E.; Sack, David A.; et al. (1985). Antidepressant effects of light in seasonal affective disorder. *American Journal of Psychiatry, 142,* 163–169.

Rosenthal, Robert (1966). *Experimenter effects in behavioral research.* New York: Appleton-Century-Crofts.

Rosenthal, Robert (1968, September). Self-fulfilling prophecy. *Psychology Today, 2*(4), 44–51.

Rosenthal, Robert (1973, September). The pygmalion effect lives. *Psychology Today, 7*(4), 56–63.

Rosenthal, Robert; Hall, Judith A.; Archer, Dane; DiMatteo, M. Robin; & Rogers, Peter L. (1979). The PONS test: Measuring sensitivity to nonverbal cues. In S. Weitz (ed.), *Nonverbal communication* (2nd ed.). New York: Oxford University Press.

Rosenthal, Robert, & Jacobson, Lenore (1968). *Pygmalion in the classroom: Teacher expectations and pupils' intellectual development.* New York: Holt, Rinehart and Winston.

Rosenzweig, Mark R. (1984). Experience, memory, and the brain. *American Psychologist, 39,* 365–376.

Ross, Hildy S., & Lollis, Susan P. (1987). Communication within infant social games. *Developmental Psychology, 23,* 241–248.

Ross, Lee (1977). The intuitive psychologist and his shortcomings: Distortions in the attribution process. In L. Berkowitz (ed.), *Advances in experimental social psychology,* Vol. 10. New York: Academic Press.

Ross, Michael, & Fletcher, Garth J. O. (1985). Attribution and social perception. In G. Lindzey & E. Aronson (eds.), *Handbook of social psychology,* Vol. II. 3rd ed. New York: Random House (distributed by Erlbaum).

Roswell, Virginia A.; Fishman, Steven T.; & Lubetkin, Barry S. (1985). A clinical longitudinal study of weight and activity. Paper presented at the annual meeting of the American Psychological Association, Los Angeles.

Rothbart, Mary K. (1986). Longitudinal observation of infant temperament. *Developmental Psychology, 22,* 356–365.

Rothbart, Myron; Dawes, Robyn; & Park, Bernadette

(1984). Stereotyping and sampling biases in intergroup perception. In J. R. Eiser (ed.), *Attitudinal judgment*. New York: Springer-Verlag.

Rothbart, Myron; Evans, Mark; & Fulero, Solomon (1979). Recall for confirming events: Memory processes and the maintenance of social stereotypes. *Journal of Experimental Social Psychology, 15*, 343–355.

Rothbaum, Fred M.; Weisz, John R.; & Snyder, Samuel S. (1982). Changing the world and changing the self: A two-process model of perceived control. *Journal of Personality and Social Psychology, 42*, 5–37.

Rotter, Julian B. (1966). Generalized expectancies for internal versus external control of reinforcement. *Psychological Monographs, 80* (Whole no. 609, 1–28).

Roueché, Berton (1984, June 4). Annals of medicine: The hoofbeats of a zebra. *New Yorker, LX*, 71–86.

Rozin, Paul (1976). The psychobiological approach to human memory. In M. R. Rosenzweig & E. L. Bennett (eds.), *Neural mechanisms of learning and memory*. Cambridge, MA: MIT Press.

Rubenstein, Carin (1986). A consumer's guide to psychotherapy. In C. Tavris (ed.), *EveryWoman's emotional well-being*. New York: Doubleday.

Rubenstein, Carin, & Shaver, Phillip (1982). *In search of intimacy*. New York: Delacorte.

Rubin, Zick (1970). Measurement of romantic love. *Journal of Personality and Social Psychology, 16*, 265–273.

Rubin, Zick (1973). *Liking and loving*. New York: Holt, Rinehart and Winston.

Rubin, Zick, & Mitchell, Cynthia (1976). Couples research as couples counseling: Some unintended effects of studying close relationships. *American Psychologist, 31*, 17–25.

Ruda, M. A. (1982). Opiates and pain pathways: Demonstration of enkephalin synapses on dorsal horn projection neurons. *Science, 215*, 1523–1525.

Ruggiero, Vincent R. (1988). *Teaching thinking across the curriculum*. New York: Harper & Row.

Rumbaugh, Duane M. (1977). *Language learning by a chimpanzee: The Lana project*. New York: Academic Press.

Rumbaugh, Duane M. (1988a). Chimpanzees' competence for summation and counting. Paper presented at the annual meeting of the American Psychological Association, Atlanta.

Rumbaugh, Duane M. (1988b). Comparative psychology and the great apes: Their competence in learning, language, and numbers. Address presented at the annual meeting of the American Psychological Association, Atlanta.

Rumbaugh, Duane; Savage-Rumbaugh, E. Sue; & Pate, James L. (1988). Summation in the Chimpanzee (*Pan troglodytes*) [Addendum] *Journal of Experimental Psychology: Animal Behavior Processes, 14*, 118–120.

Rundus, Dewey (1977). Maintenance rehearsal and single-level processing. *Journal of Verbal Learning and Verbal Behavior, 16*, 665–681.

Rush, Florence (1980). *The best kept secret: Sexual abuse of children*. Englewood Cliffs, NJ: Prentice-Hall.

Rushton, J. Philippe; Fulker, David W.; Neale, Michael C.; Nias, David; & Eysenck, Hans J. (1986). Altruism and aggression: The heritability of individual differences. *Journal of Personality and Social Psychology, 50*, 1192–1198.

Russell, Diana E. H. (1986). *The secret trauma: Incest in the lives of girls and women*. New York: Basic Books.

Russell, James A. (1983). Pancultural aspects of the human conceptual organization of emotions. *Journal of Personality and Social Psychology, 45*, 1281–1288.

Russell, Michael; Peeke, Harman V. S.; et al. (1984). Learned histamine release. *Science, 225*, 733–734.

Rymer, Russ (1987, May/June). What patients hear under the knife. *Hippocrates, 1*, 100, 102.

Saarni, Carolyn (1979). Children's understanding of display rules for expressive behavior. *Developmental Psychology, 15*, 424–429.

Saarni, Carolyn (1982). Social and affective functions of nonverbal behavior: Developmental concerns. In R. S. Feldman (ed.), *Development of nonverbal behavior in children*. New York: Springer-Verlag.

Sabalis, Robert F. (1983). Assessing outcome in patients with sexual dysfunctions and sexual disorders. In M. J. Lambert, E. R. Christensen, & S. S. DeJulio (eds.), *The assessment of psychotherapy outcome*. New York: Wiley-Interscience.

Sabatelli, Ronald M.; Buck, Ross; & Dreyer, Albert (1982). Nonverbal communication accuracy in married couples: Relationship with marital complaints. *Journal of Personality and Social Psychology, 43*, 1088–1097.

Sabini, John, & Silver, Maury (1985, Winter). Critical thinking and obedience to authority. *National Forum* (Phi Beta Kappa Journal) *LXV*, 13–17.

Sacks, Oliver (1985). *The man who mistook his wife for a hat and other clinical tales*. New York: Simon & Schuster.

Sahley, Christie L.; Rudy, Jerry W.; & Gelperin, Alan (1981). An analysis of associative learning in a terrestrial mollusk. I: Higher-order conditioning, blocking, and a transient US preexposure effect. *Journal of Comparative Physiology, 144*, 1–8.

Sahley, Tony L., & Panksepp, Jaak (1987). Brain opioids and autism: An updated analysis of possible linkages. *Journal of Autism and Developmental Disorders, 17*, 201–216.

Samelson, Franz (1979). Putting psychology on the map: Ideology and intelligence testing. In A. R. Buss (ed.), *Psychology in social context*. New York: Irvington.

Sampson, Edward E. (1977). Psychology and the American ideal. *Journal of Personality and Social Psychology, 35*, 767–782.

Sampson, Edward E. (1988). The debate on individualism. *American Psychologist, 43*, 15–22.

Sande, Gerald N.; Goethals, George R.; & Radloff, Christine E. (1988). Perceiving one's own traits and others': The multifaceted self. *Journal of Personality and Social Psychology, 54*, 13–20.

Sanders, Diana; Warner, Pamela: Bäckström, Torbjörn; & Bancroft, John (1983). Mood, sexuality, hormones and the menstrual cycle. I. Changes in mood and physical state: Description of subjects and method. *Psychosomatic Medicine, 45,* 487–501.

Sapolsky, Robert M. (1987, July). The case of the falling nightwatchmen. *Discover, 8*(7), 42–45.

Sarafolean, Mary (1985). The effects of alcohol on prose memory. *Physiology and Behavior, 35,* 43–46.

Sarason, Barbara R.; Shearin, Edward N.; Pierce, Gregory R.; & Sarason, Irwin G. (1987). Interrelations of social support measures: Theoretical and practical implications. *Journal of Personality and Social Psychology, 52,* 813–832.

Sarason, Irwin G.; Johnson, James H.; & Siegel, Judith M. (1978). Assessing the impact of life changes: Development of the Life Experiences Survey. *Journal of Consulting and Clinical Psychology, 46,* 932–946.

Sarason, Irwin G., & Sarason, Barbara R. (1980). *Abnormal psychology.* Englewood Cliffs, NJ: Prentice-Hall.

Sarbin, Theodore R., & Coe, William C. (1972). *Hypnosis: A social psychological analysis of influence communication.* New York: Holt, Rinehart and Winston.

Sarbin, Theodore R., & Mancuso, James C. (1980). *Schizophrenia: Medical diagnosis or moral verdict?* Elmsford, NY: Pergamon.

Satir, Virginia (1983). *Conjoint family therapy* (3rd ed.). Palo Alto, CA: Science and Behavior Books.

Savage-Rumbaugh, E. Sue. (1986). *Ape language: From conditioned response to symbol.* New York: Columbia University Press.

Savin-Williams, Ritch C., & Demo, David H. (1983). Situational and transituational determinants of adolescent self-feelings. *Journal of Personality and Social Psychology, 44,* 824–833.

Scarr, Sandra (1983). The danger of having pet variables. Presidential address to Division 7 at the annual meeting of the American Psychological Association, Anaheim, CA.

Scarr, Sandra (1984a). Intelligence: What an introductory psychology student might want to know. In A. M. Rogers and C. J. Scheirer (eds.), *The G. Stanley Hall lecture series,* Vol. 4. Washington, DC: American Psychological Association.

Scarr, Sandra (1984b). *Mother care, other care.* New York: Basic Books.

Scarr, Sandra, & McCartney, Kathleen (1983). How people make their own environments: A theory of genotype → environmental effects. *Child Development, 54,* 424–435.

Scarr, Sandra; Pakstis, Andrew J.; Katz, Soloman H.; & Barker, William B. (1977). Absence of a relationship between degree of white ancestry and intellectual skill in a black population. *Human Genetics, 39,* 69–86.

Scarr, Sandra; Webber, Patricia L.; Weinberg, Richard A.; & Wittig, Michele A. (1981). Personality resemblance among adolescents and their parents in biologically related and adoptive families. *Journal of Personality and Social Psychology, 40,* 885–898.

Scarr, Sandra, & Weinberg, Richard A. (1976). IQ test performance of black children adopted by white families. *American Psychologist, 31,* 726–739.

Scarr, Sandra, & Weinberg, Richard A. (1977). Intellectual similarities within families of both adopted and biological children. *Intelligence, 1,* 170–191.

Scarr, Sandra, & Weinberg, Richard A. (1979). Intellectual similarities in adoptive and biologically related families of adolescents. In L. Willerman and R. G. Turner (eds.), *Readings about individual and group differences.* San Francisco: Freeman.

Schachter, Stanley (1971). *Emotion, obesity, and crime.* New York: Academic Press.

Schachter, Stanley (1982). Recidivism and self-cure of smoking and obesity. *American Psychologist, 37,* 436–444.

Schachter, Stanley, & Singer, Jerome E. (1962). Cognitive, social, and physiological determinants of emotional state. *Psychological Review, 69,* 379–399.

Schacter, Daniel L. (1986). Amnesia and crime: How much do we really know? *American Psychologist, 41,* 286–295.

Schacter, Daniel L., & Moscovitch, Morris (1984). Infants, amnesics, and dissociable memory systems. In M. Moscovitch (ed.), *Infant memory.* New York: Plenum.

Schaie, K. Warner (ed.) (1983). *Longitudinal studies of adult psychological development.* New York: Guilford Press.

Schank, Roger (with Peter Childers) (1988). *The creative attitude.* New York: Macmillan.

Schein, Edgar; Schneier, Inge; & Barker, Curtis H. (1961). *Coercive persuasion.* New York: Norton.

Scherer, Klaus R.; Abeles, Ronald P.; & Fischer, Claude S. (1975). *Human aggression and conflict.* Englewood Cliffs, NJ: Prentice-Hall.

Schiffman, Harvey R. (1976). *Sensation and perception: An integrated approach.* New York: Wiley.

Schlossberg, Nancy K. (1984a). Exploring the adult years. In A. M. Rogers & C. J. Scheirer (eds.), *The G. Stanley Hall lecture series,* Vol. 4. Washington, DC: American Psychological Association.

Schlossberg, Nancy K. (1984b). Recurring themes through life. Paper presented at the annual meeting of the Michigan Association of Counseling and Development.

Schlossberg, Nancy K. (1989). *Overwhelmed: Coping with life's ups and downs.* Lexington, MA: Lexington Books.

Schmideberg, Melitta (1970). Psychotherapy with failures of psychoanalysis. *British Journal of Psychiatry, 116,* 195–200.

Schmidt, Janet A. (1985). Older and wiser? A longitudinal study of the impact of college on intellectual development. *Journal of College Student Personnel, 26,* 388–394.

Schneider, Allen M., & Tarshis, Barry (1986). *An introduction to physiological psychology* (3rd ed.). New York: Random House.

Schulman, Michael, & Mekler, Eva (1985). *Bringing up a moral child.* Reading, MA: Addison-Wesley.

Schulz, Richard, & Decker, Susan (1985). Long-term adjustment to physical disability: The role of social support, perceived control, and self-blame. *Journal of Personality and Social Psychology, 48,* 1162–1172.

Schwartz, Barry, & Reilly, Martha (1985). Long-term retention of a complex operant in pigeons. *Journal of Experimental Psychology: Animal Behavior Processes, 11,* 337–355.

Schwartz, Judith; Sharpsteen, Don J.; & Butler, Julie (1989). Gender and intimacy regulation in same-sex friendships. Manuscript under review, *Journal of Personality and Social Psychology.*

Schwartz, Shalom H., & Howard, Judith A. (1981). A normative decision-making model of altruism. In J. P. Rushton & R. M. Sorrentino (eds.), *Altruism and helping behavior.* Hillsdale, NJ: Erlbaum.

Sclafani, Anthony, & Springer, Deleri (1976). Dietary obesity in adult rats. *Physiology and Behavior, 17,* 461–471.

Scott, John Paul (1984). Biological bases of intergroup conflict. Paper presented at the annual meeting of the American Psychological Association, Toronto.

Scott, Joseph E., & Schwalm, Loretta A. (1988). Rape rates and the circulation rates of adult magazines. *Journal of Sex Research, 24,* 241–250.

Scribner, Sylvia (1977). Modes of thinking and ways of speaking: Culture and logic reconsidered. In P. N. Johnson-Laird & P. C. Wason (eds.), *Thinking: Readings in cognitive science.* Cambridge, England: Cambridge University Press.

Scriven, Michael (1985). Critical for survival. *National Forum, 65*(1), 9–12.

Sears, Pauline, & Barbee, Ann H. (1977). Career and life satisfactions among Terman's gifted women. In J. C. Stanley, W. C. George, & C. H. Solano (eds.), *The gifted and the creative: A fifty-year perspective.* Baltimore, MD: Johns Hopkins University Press.

Sears, Robert R. (1977). Sources of life satisfactions of the Terman gifted men. *American Psychologist, 32,* 119–128.

Segal, Julius (1986). *Winning life's toughest battles.* New York: McGraw-Hill.

Segall, Marshall H.; Campbell, Donald T.; & Herskovits, Melville J. (1966). *The influence of culture on visual perception.* Indianapolis: Bobbs-Merrill.

Seiden, Richard (1978). Where are they now? A follow-up study of suicide attempters from the Golden Gate Bridge. *Suicide and Life-Threatening Behavior, 8,* 203–216.

Seidenberg, Mark S., & Petitto, Laura A. (1979). Signing behavior in apes: A critical review. *Cognition, 7,* 177–215.

Sekuler, Robert, & Blake, Randolph (1985). *Perception.* New York: Knopf.

Seligman, Martin E. P. (1975). *Helplessness: On depression, development, and death.* San Francisco: Freeman.

Seligman, Martin E. P. (1986). Explanatory style: Depression, Lyndon Baines Johnson, and the Baseball Hall of Fame. Invited public lecture presented at the annual meeting of the American Psychological Association, Washington.

Seligman, Martin E. P., & Hager, Joanne L. (1972,

August). Biological boundaries of learning: The sauce-Béarnaise syndrome. *Psychology Today, 6*(3), 59–61, 84–87.

Seligman, Martin E. P., & Schulman, Peter (1986). Explanatory style as a predictor of productivity and quitting among life insurance sales agents. *Journal of Personality and Social Psychology, 50,* 832–838.

Selye, Hans (1956). *The stress of life.* New York: McGraw-Hill.

Sem-Jacobsen, C. W. (1959). Effects of electrical stimulation on the human brain. *Electroencephalography and Clinical Neurophysiology, 11,* 379.

Senden, Marius von (1960). *Space and sight: The perception of space and shape in the congenitally blind before and after operation.* (P. Heath, translator.) New York: Free Press.

Serbin, Lisa A., & Connor, Jane M. (1979). Environmental control of sex related behaviors in the preschool. Paper presented at the annual meeting of the Society for Research in Child Development, San Francisco.

Serbin, Lisa A., & O'Leary, K. Daniel (1975, December). How nursery schools teach girls to shut up. *Psychology Today, 9*(7), 56–58ff.

Shapiro, Deane H., Jr. (1980). *Meditation: Self-regulation strategy and altered state of consciousness.* New York: Aldine.

Shatz, Marilyn, & Gelman, Rochel (1973). The development of communication skills: Modifications in the speech of young children as a function of the listener. *Monographs of the Society for Research in Child Development, 38.*

Shaver, Phillip, & Buhrmester, Duane (1983). Loneliness, sex-role orientation, and group life: A social needs perspective. In P. B. Paulus (ed.), *Basic group processes.* New York: Springer-Verlag.

Shaver, Phillip, & Hazan, Cindy (1987). Romantic love conceptualized as an attachment process. *Journal of Personality and Social Psychology, 52,* 511–524.

Shaver, Phillip; Hazan, Cindy; & Bradshaw, Donna (1988). Love as attachment: The integration of three behavioral systems. In R. J. Sternberg & M. Barnes (eds.), *The psychology of love.* New Haven, CT, and London: Yale University Press.

Shaver, Phillip, & O'Connor, Cary (1986). Problems in perspective. In C. Tavris (ed.), *EveryWoman's emotional well-being.* New York: Doubleday.

Shaver, Phillip, & Rubenstein, Carin (1980). Childhood attachment experience and adult loneliness. In L. Wheeler (ed.), *Review of personality and social psychology,* Vol. 1. Beverly Hills, CA: Sage.

Shaver, Phillip, & Schwartz, Judith C. (in press). Cross-cultural similarities and differences in emotion and its representation: A prototype approach. In R. B. Zajonc & S. Moscovici (eds.), *Social psychology and the emotions.* Cambridge, England: Cambridge University Press.

Shaver, Phillip; Schwartz, Judith; Krison, Donald; & O'Connor, Cary (1987). Emotion knowledge: Further exploration of a prototype approach. *Journal of Personality and Social Psychology, 52,* 1061–1086.

Sheehan, Neil (1988). *A bright shining lie: John Paul Vann and America in Vietnam*. New York: Random House.

Sheldon, William (1942). *The varieties of temperament: A psychology of constitutional differences*. New York: Harper.

Shepard, Roger N. (1967). Recognition memory for words, sentences and pictures. *Journal of Verbal Learning and Verbal Behavior, 6*, 156–163.

Shepard, Roger N., & Metzler, Jacqueline (1971). Mental rotation of three-dimensional objects. *Science, 171*, 701–703.

Sherfey, Mary Jane (1973). *The nature and evolution of female sexuality*. New York: Vintage.

Sherif, Carolyn Wood (1979). Bias in psychology. In J. Sherman & E. T. Beck (eds.), *The prism of sex*. Madison: University of Wisconsin Press.

Sherif, Muzafer (1958). Superordinate goals in the reduction of intergroup conflicts. *American Journal of Sociology, 63*, 349–356.

Sherif, Muzaier; Harvey, O. J.; White, B. J.; Hood, William; & Sherif, Carolyn (1961). Intergroup conflict and cooperation: The Robbers Cave experiment. Norman: University of Oklahoma Institute of Intergroup Relations.

Sherman, Lawrence W., & Berk, Richard A. (1984). The specific deterrent effects of arrest for domestic assault. *American Sociological Review, 49*, 261–271.

Sherrington, Robin; Brynjolfsson, Jon; Petursson, Hannes; Potter, Mark; et al. (1988, November 10). Location of a susceptibility locus for schizophrenia on chromosome 5. *Nature, 336*(6195), 164–167.

Sherwin, Robert, & Corbett, Sherry (1985). Campus sexual norms and dating relationships: A trend analysis. *Journal of Sex Research, 21*, 258–274.

Shevrin, Howard, & Dickman, Scott (1980). The psychological unconscious: A necessary assumption for all psychological theory? *American Psychologist, 35*, 421–434.

Shields, Stephanie A. (1975). Functionalism, Darwinism, and the psychology of women: A study in social myth. *American Psychologist, 30*, 739–754.

Shields, Stephanie A. (1986). Are women "emotional"? In C. Tavris (ed.), *EveryWoman's emotional well-being*. New York: Doubleday.

Shields, Stephanie A. (1988). Gender and the social meaning of emotion. Paper presented at the annual meeting of the American Psychological Association, Atlanta.

Shiffrin, R. M., & Atkinson, Richard C. (1969). Storage and retrieval processes in long-term memory. *Psychological Review, 76*, 179–193.

Shinn, Marybeth; Lehmann, Stanley; & Wong, Nora (1984). Social interaction and social support. *Journal of Social Issues, 40*(4), 55–76.

Shotland, R. Lance, & Goodstein, Lynne (1984). The role of bystanders in crime control. *Journal of Social Issues, 40*(1), 9–26.

Shotland, R. Lance, & Straw, Margaret (1976). Bystander response to an assault: When a man attacks a woman. *Journal of Personality and Social Psychology, 34*, 990–999.

Shweder, Richard A.; Mahapatra, Manamohan; & Miller, Joan G. (1987). Culture and moral development. In J. Kagan & S. Lamb (eds.), *The emergence of morality in young children*. Chicago: University of Chicago Press.

Sibatani, Atuhiro (1980, December). The Japanese brain. *Science 80*, 22–26.

Siegal, Ronald K. (1983). Natural intoxication: Self-administration of psychoactive plants by animals in natural habitats. Invited address to the 91st annual convention of the American Psychological Association, Anaheim, CA.

Siegel, Shepard (1983). Classical conditioning, drug tolerance, and drug dependence. In R. G. Smart, F. B. Glaser, Y. Israel, et al. (eds.), *Research advances in alcohol and drug problems*, Vol. 7. New York: Plenum.

Siegel, Shepard; Hinson, Riley E.; Krank, Marvin D., & McCully, Jane (1982). Heroin "overdose" death: Contribution of drug-associated environmental cues. *Science, 216*, 436–437.

Silverman, Lloyd H., & Weinberger, Joel (1985). Mommy and I are one: Implications for psychotherapy. *American Psychologist, 40*, 1296–1308.

Silverstein, Brett; Perdue, Lauren: Peterson, Barbara; Vogel, Linda; & Fantini, Deborah A. (1986). Possible causes of the thin standard of bodily attractiveness for women. *International Journal of Eating Disorders, 5*, 135–144.

Silverstein, Brett; Peterson, Barbara; & Perdue, Lauren (1986). Some correlates of the thin standard of bodily attractiveness in women. *International Journal of Eating Disorders, 5*, 145–155.

Simon, Herbert (1973). The structure of ill-structured problems. *Artificial Intelligence, 4*, 181–202.

Simon, William, & Gagnon, John (1969, March). Psychosexual development. *Trans-action, 6*, 9–18.

Simon, William, & Gagnon, John H. (1986). Sexual scripts: Permanence and change. *Archives of Sexual Behavior, 15*, 97–120.

Simons, Anne; Lustman, Patrick; Wetzel, Richard; & Murphy, George (1985). Predicting response to cognitive therapy of depression: The role of learned resourcefulness. *Cognitive Therapy and Research, 9*, 79–89.

Sims, Ethan A. (1974). Studies in human hyperphagia. In G. Bray & J. Bethune (eds.), *Treatment and management of obesity*. New York: Harper & Row.

Singer, Barry, & Toates, Frederick (1987). Sexual motivation. *The Journal of Sex Research, 23*, 481–501.

Singer, Jerome L. (1976, July). Fantasy: The foundation of serenity. *Psychology Today, 10*(2), 32–34, 37.

Singer, Jerome L. (1984). The private personality. *Personality and Social Psychology Bulletin, 10*, 7–30.

Skinner, B. F. (1938). *The behavior of organisms: An experimental analysis*. New York: Appleton-Century-Crofts.

Skinner, B. F. (1948). Superstition in the pigeon. *Journal of Experimental Psychology, 38*, 168–172.

Skinner, B. F. (1950). Are theories of learning necessary? *Psychological Review, 57*, 193–216.

Skinner, B. F. (1956). A case history in the scientific method. *American Psychologist, 11*, 221–233.

Skinner, B. F. (1957). *Verbal behavior.* New York: Appleton-Century-Crofts.

Skinner, B. F. (1972). The operational analysis of psychological terms. In B. F. Skinner, *Cumulative record* (3rd ed.). New York: Appleton-Century-Crofts.

Skinner, B. F. (1974). *About behaviorism.* New York: Knopf.

Skinner, B. F. (1976). *Walden Two.* New York: Macmillan. (Originally published in 1948.)

Skinner, B. F. (1983). *A matter of consequences.* New York: Knopf.

Skinner, B. F. (1984). The shame of American education. *American Psychologist, 39*, 947–954.

Skodak, Marie, & Skeels, Harold M. (1949). A final follow-up study of one hundred adopted children. *Journal of Genetic Psychology, 75*, 85–125.

Skreslet, Paula (1987, November 30). The prizes of first grade. *Newsweek,* 8.

Slade, Pauline (1984). Premenstrual emotional changes in normal women: Fact or fiction. *Journal of Psychosomatic Research, 28*, 1–7.

Sloane, R. Bruce; Staples, Fred; Cristol, Allan; Yorkston, Neil; & Whipple, Katherine (1975). *Psychotherapy versus behavior therapy.* Cambridge, MA: Harvard University Press.

Slobin, Daniel I. (1979). *Psycholinguistics,* 2nd ed. Glenview, IL: Scott, Foresman.

Slovic, Paul; Fischhoff, Baruch; & Lichtenstein, Sarah (1978). Accident probabilities and seat-belt usage: A psychological perspective. *Accident Analysis and Prevention, 10*, 281–285.

Slovic, Paul; Fischhoff, Baruch; & Lichtenstein, Sarah (1982). Response mode, framing, and information-processing effects in risk assessment. In R. Hogarth (ed.), *New directions for methodology of social and behavioral science: Question framing and response consistency.* San Francisco: Jossey-Bass.

Smith, Craig A., & Ellsworth, Phoebe C. (1987). Patterns of appraisal and emotion related to taking an exam. *Journal of Personality and Social Psychology, 52*, 475–488.

Smith, M. Brewster (1984). Humanistic psychology. In R. J. Corsini (ed.), *Encyclopedia of psychology,* Vol. 2. New York: Wiley-Interscience.

Smith, Mary Lee (1980). Sex bias in counseling and psychotherapy. *Psychological Bulletin, 87*, 392–407.

Smith, Mary Lee; Glass, Gene; & Miller, Thomas I. (1980). *The benefits of psychotherapy.* Baltimore, MD: Johns Hopkins University Press.

Smith, Timothy; Snyder, C. R.; & Perkins, Suzanne C. (1983). The self-serving function of hypochondriacal complaints: Physical symptoms as self-handicapping strategies. *Journal of Personality and Social Psychology, 44*, 787–797.

Smither, Robert D. (1988). *The psychology of work and human performance.* New York: Harper & Row.

Snodgrass, Sara E. (1985a). Walking behavior as indicator of personality and mood. Paper presented at the annual meeting of the American Psychological Association, Los Angeles.

Snodgrass, Sara E. (1985b). Women's intuition: The effect of subordinate role on interpersonal sensitivity. *Journal of Personality and Social Psychology, 49*, 146–155.

Snow, Barry R; Pinter, Isaac; Gusmorino, Paul; Jimenez, Arthur; Rosenblum, Andrew; & Adelglass, Howard (1986). Sex differences in chronic pain: Incidence and causal mechanisms. Paper presented at the annual meeting of the American Psychological Association, Washington.

Snyder, C. R. (1988). Reality negotiation: From excuses to hope and beyond. Paper presented at the annual meeting of the American Psychological Association, Atlanta.

Snyder, C. R., & Fromkin, Howard (1980). *Uniqueness: The human pursuit of difference.* New York: Plenum.

Snyder, C. R.; Higgins, Raymond L.; & Stucky, Rita J. (1983). *Excuses: Masquerades in search of grace.* New York: Wiley-Interscience.

Snyder, C. R., & Shenkel, Randee J. (1975, March). The P. T. Barnum effect. *Psychology Today, 8*(10), 52–54.

Snyder, C. R.; Smith, Timothy W.; Augelli, Robert W.; & Ingram, Rick E. (1985). On the self-serving function of social anxiety: Shyness as a self-handicapping strategy. *Journal of Personality and Social Psychology, 48*, 970–980.

Snyder, Mark (1979). Self-monitoring processes. In L. Berkowitz (ed.), *Advances in experimental social psychology,* Vol. 12. New York: Academic Press.

Snyder, Mark (1982). Understanding individuals and their social worlds. Paper presented at the annual meeting of the American Psychological Association, Washington.

Snyder, Solomon H. (1980). Brain peptides as neurotransmitters. *Science, 209*, 976–983.

Snyderman, Mark, & Rothman, Stanley (1987). Survey of expert opinion on intelligence and aptitude testing. *American Psychologist, 42*, 137–144.

Solomon, George F. (1985, Winter). The emerging field of psychoneuroimmunology. *Advances, 1*, 6–19.

Solomon, Richard L. (1980). The opponent-process theory of acquired motivation. *American Psychologist, 35*, 691–712.

Sommer, Robert (1977, January). Toward a psychology of natural behavior. *APA Monitor* (Reprinted in *Readings in psychology 78/79.* Guilford, CT: Dushkin, 1978, pp. 29–32.)

Sommers, Shula, & Scioli, Anthony (1986). Emotional range and value orientation: Toward a congitive view of emotionality. *Journal of Personality and Social Psychology, 51*, 417–422.

Sontag, Susan (1978). *Illness as metaphor.* New York: Farrar, Straus & Giroux.

Sorce, James F.; Emde, Robert N.; Campos, Joseph; & Klinnert, Mary D. (1985). Maternal emotional signaling: Its effect on the visual cliff behavior of 1-year-olds. *Developmental Psychology, 21*, 195–200.

Sorenson, Susan B.; Stein, Judith A.; Siegel, Judith M.; Golding, Jacqueline M.; & Burnam, M. Audrey (1987). The prevalence of adult sexual assault. *Americal Journal of Epidemiology, 126,* 1154–1164.

Spanos, Nicholas P. (1986). Hypnotic behavior: A social-psychological interpretation of amnesia, analgesia, and "trance logic." *Behavorial and Brain Sciences, 9,* 449–467.

Spearman, Charles (1927). *The abilities of man.* London: Macmillan.

Spence, Janet T. (1985). Achievement American style. *American Psychologist, 40,* 1285–1295.

Spence, Janet T., & Helmreich, Robert L. (1978). *Masculinity and femininity: Their psychological dimensions, correlates, and antecedents.* Austin: University of Texas Press.

Sperling, George (1960). The information available in brief visual presentations. *Psychological Monographs, 74* (498).

Sperry, Roger W. [R. W.] (1964). The great cerebral commissure. *Scientific American, 210*(1), 42–52.

Sperry, Roger W. [R. W.] (1977). Bridging science and values: A unifying view of mind and brain. *American Psychologist, 32,* 237–245.

Sperry, Roger W. (1982). Some effects of disconnecting the cerebral hemispheres. *Science, 217,* 1223–1226.

Spiegel, David (1986). Painstaking reminders of forgotten trance logic. *Behavioral and Brain Sciences, 9,* 484–485.

Spielberger, Charles, & Diaz-Guerrero, Rogelio (1976). *Cross-cultural anxiety.* New York: Hemisphere.

Spilich, George J. (1987). Cigarette smoking and memory: Good news and bad news. Paper delivered at the annual meeting of the American Psychological Association, New York.

Spring, Bonnie; Chiodo, June; & Bowen, Deborah J. (1987). Carbohydrataes, tryptophan, and behavior: A methodological review. *Psychological Bulletin, 102,* 234–256.

Squire, Larry R. (1986). Mechanisms of memory. *Science, 232,* 1612–1619.

Squire, Larry R. (1987). *Memory and the brain.* New York: Oxford University Press.

Sroufe, L. Alan (1978, October). Attachment and the roots of competence. *Human Nature, 1,* 50–57.

Staats, Carolyn K., & Staats, Arthur W. (1957). Meaning established by classical conditioning. *Journal of Experimental Psychology, 54,* 74–80.

Stapp, Joy; Tucker, Anthony M.; & VandenBos, Gary R. (1985). Census of psychological personnel: 1983. *American Psychologist, 40*(12), 1317–1351.

Staub, Ervin (1985). The psychology of perpetrators and bystanders. *Political Psychology, 6,* 61–85.

Staub, Ervin (1988). The evolution of caring and nonaggressive persons and societies. *Journal of Social Issues, 44,* 81–100.

Steen, Suzanne; Oppliger, Robert; & Brownell, Kelly (1988). Metabolic effects of repeated weight loss and regain in adolescent wrestlers. *Journal of the American Medical Association, 260,* 47–50.

Stein, Judith A.; Golding, Jacqueline M.; Siegel, Judith M.; Burnam, M. Audrey; & Sorenson, Susan B. (1988). Long-term psychological sequelae of child sexual abuse: The Los Angeles epidemiologic catchment area study. In G. E. Wyatt & G. J. Powell (eds.), *The lasting effects of child sexual abuse.* Newbury Park, CA: Sage.

Stein, Marvin; Keller, Steven E.; & Schleifer, Steven J. (1985). Stress and immunomodulation: The role of depression and neuroendocrine function. *The Journal of Immunology, 135,* 827–833.

Stempel, Jennifer J.; Beckwith, Bill E.; & Petros, Thomas V. (1986). The effects of alcohol on the speed of memory retrieval. Paper presented at the annual meeting of the American Psychological Association, Washington.

Stenberg, Craig R., & Campos, Joseph (1990). The development of anger expressions in infancy. In N. Stein, B. Leventhal, & T. Trabasso (eds.), *Psychological and biological approaches to emotion.* Hillsdale, NJ: Erlbaum.

Stephan, Walter (1978). School desegregation: An evaluation of predictions made in *Brown* v. *The Board of Education. Psychological Bulletin, 85,* 217–238.

Stephan, Walter (1985). Intergroup relations. In G. Lindzey & E. Aronson (eds.), *Handbook of social psychology,* Vol. II. New York: Random House.

Stephan, Walter, & Brigham, John C. (1985). Intergroup contact: Introduction. *Journal of Social Issues, 41*(3), 1–8.

Stephens, Joseph (1978). Long-term prognosis and follow-up in schizophrenia. *Schizophrenia Bulletin, 4,* 25–47.

Sternberg, Robert J. (1985). *Beyond IQ.* New York: Cambridge University Press.

Sternberg, Robert J. (1986). *Intelligence applied: Understanding and increasing your intellectual skills.* San Diego: Harcourt Brace Jovanovich.

Sternberg, Robert J. (1988a). *The triangle of love: Intimacy, passion, commitment.* New York: Basic Books.

Sternberg, Robert J. (1988b). *The triarchic mind: A new theory of human intelligence.* New York: Viking.

Stevens, Charles (1979). The neuron. *Scientific American, 241*(3), 54–65.

Stewart, Abigail; Sokol, Michael; Healy, Joseph M., Jr.; Chester, Nia L.; & Weinstock-Savoy, Deborah (1982). Adaptation to life changes in children and adults: Cross-sectional studies. *Journal of Personality and Social Psychology, 43,* 1270–1282.

Stewart, Walter W., & Feder, Ned (1987, January 15). The integrity of the scientific literature. *Nature, 325,* 207–214.

Stoch, M. B., & Smythe, P. M. (1963). Does undernutrition during infancy inhibit brain growth and subsequent intellectual development? *Archives of Diseases in Childhood, 38,* 546–552.

Stolzy, S.; Couture, L. J., & Edmonds, H. L., Jr. (1986). Evidence of partial recall during general anesthesia. *Anesthesia and Analgesia, 65,* S154 (Abstract).

Stone, Lewis J., & Hokanson, Jack E. (1969). Arousal reduction via self-punitive behavior. *Journal of Personality and Social Psychology, 12,* 72–79.

Stoner, James (1961). A comparison of individual and group decisions involving risk. Unpublished master's thesis, MIT.

Storm, Christine, & Storm, Tom (1987). A taxonomic study of the vocabulary of emotions. *Journal of Personality and Social Psychology, 53*, 805–816.

Stouffer, Samuel; Suchman, Edward; DeVinney, Leland; Star, Shirley; & Williams, Robin, Jr. (1949). *The American soldier: Adjustment during army life.* New York: Wiley.

Strack, Fritz; Martin, Leonard L.; & Stepper, Sabine (1988). Inhibiting and facilitating conditions of the human smile: A non-obtrusive test of the facial-feedback hypothesis. *Journal of Social and Personality Psychology, 54*, 768–777.

Strasser, Susan (1982). *Never done: A history of American housework.* New York: Pantheon.

Striegel-Moore, Ruth H.; Silberstein, Lisa R.; & Rodin, Judith (1986). Toward an understanding of risk factors for bulimia. *American Psychologist, 41*, 246–263.

Strupp, Hans H. (1980). Success and failure in time-limited psychotherapy. *Archives of General Psychiatry, 37*, 595–603, 708–716, 831–841, 947–954.

Strupp, Hans H. (1982). The outcome problem in psychotherapy: Contemporary perspectives. In J. H. Harvey & M. M. Parks (eds.), *Psychotherapy research and behavior change: The APA Master Lecture Series*, Vol. 1. Washington, DC: American Psychological Association.

Strupp, Hans H., & Binder, Jeffrey (1984). *Psychotherapy in a new key.* New York: Basic Books.

Strupp, Hans H., & Hadley, Suzanne (1979). Specific versus nonspecific factors in psychotherapy: A controlled study of outcome. *Archives of General Psychiatry, 36*, 1125–1136.

Strupp, Hans H.; Hadley, Suzanne; & Gomes-Schwartz, Beverly (1977). *Psychotherapy for better or worse: An analysis of the problem of negative effects.* New York: Jason Aronson.

Stunkard, Albert J. (1976). *The pain of obesity.* Palo Alto, CA: Bull.

Stunkard, Albert J. (ed.) (1980). *Obesity.* Philadelphia: Saunders.

Sue, Stanley, & Zane, Nolan (1987). The role of culture and cultural techniques in psychotherapy: A critique and reformulation. *American Psychologist, 42*, 37–45.

Suedfeld, Peter (1975). The benefits of boredom: Sensory deprivation reconsidered. *American Scientist, 63*(1), 60–69.

Sulloway, Frank J. (1979). *Freud: Biologist of the mind.* New York: Basic Books.

Suomi, Stephen J. (1987). Genetic and maternal contributions to individual differences in rhesus monkey biobehavioral development. In N. Krasnegor, E. Blass, M. Hofer, & W. Smotherman (eds.), *Perinatal development: A psychobiological perspective.* New York: Academic Press.

Suomi, Stephen J. (1989). Primate separation models of affective disorders. In J. Madden (ed.), *Adaptation, learning, and affect.* New York: Raven Press.

Susman, Elizabeth J.; Inoff-Germain, Gale; Nottelmann, Editha D.; et al. (1987). Hormones, emotional dispositions, and aggressive attributes in young adolescents. *Child Development, 58*, 1114–1134.

Sutton-Smith, Brian (1984). Recreation as folly's parody. *TAASP Newsletter, 10*, 4–13.

Syme, S. Leonard (1982, July-August). People need people. *American Health, 1*.

Szasz, Thomas (1961/1967). *The myth of mental illness.* New York: Dell Delta.

Szasz, Thomas (1970). *The manufacture of madness.* New York: Harper Torchbooks.

Szasz, Thomas (1987). *Insanity; The idea and its consequences.* New York: Wiley.

Szymanski, Kate, & Harkins, Stephen G. (1987). Social loafing and self-evaluation with a social standard. *Journal of Personality and Social Psychology, 53*, 891–897.

Tajfel, Henri (1970). Experiments in intergroup discrimination. *Scientific American, 223*, 96–202.

Tanner, Nancy, & Zihlman, Adrienne (1976, Spring). Woman in evolution. I. Innovation and selection in human origins. *Signs, 1*, 389–403.

Task Force on Consumer Issues in Psychotherapy (n.d.). Women and psychotherapy: A consumer handbook. Washington, DC: Federation of Organizations for Professional Women.

Taub, Arthur (1984). Opioid analgesics in the treatment of chronic intractable pain of non-neoplastic origin. *Pain. Supplement 2*, 204.

Tavris, Carol (1976, September). Compensatory education: The glass is half full. *Psychology Today, 10*(4), 63–70, 73–74.

Tavris, Carol (1977, July). The sexual lives of women over 60. *Ms.*, 62–65.

Tavris, Carol (1989). *Anger: The misunderstood emotion* (2nd ed.). New York: Touchstone/Simon & Schuster.

Tavris, Carol, & Wade, Carole (1984). *The longest war: Sex differences in perspective* (2nd ed.). San Diego: Harcourt Brace Jovanovich.

Taylor, Shelley E. (1983). Adjustment to life events: A theory of cognitive adaptation. *American Psychologist, 38*, 1161–1173.

Taylor, Shelley E. (1986). *Health psychology.* New York: Random House.

Taylor, Shelley E. (1988). Social self-management: Social comparisons and affiliations under threat. Invited address presented at the annual meeting of the Western Psychological Association, San Francisco.

Taylor, Shelley E. (1989). *Positive illusions: Creative self-deception and the healthy mind.* New York: Basic Books.

Taylor, Shelley E., & Brown, Jonathon D. (1988). Illusion and well-being: A social psychological perspective on mental health. *Psychological Bulletin, 103*, 193–210.

Taylor, Shelley E.; Lichtman, Rosemary R.; & Wood, Joanne V. (1984). Attributions, beliefs about control, and adjustment to breast cancer. *Journal of Personality and Social Psychology, 46*, 489–502.

Teasdale, John (1983). Negative thinking in depression: Cause, effect, or reciprocal relationship? *Advances in Behaviour Research and Therapy, 5*, 3–25.

Tellegen, Auke; Lykken, David T.; Bouchard, Thomas J., Jr.; et al. (1988). Personality similarity in twins reared apart and together. *Journal of Personality and Social Psychology, 54*, 1031–1039.

Temerlin, Maurice, & Temerlin, Jane (1982). Psychotherapy cults: An iatrogenic perversion. *Psychotherapy: Theory, Research, and Practice, 19*, 131–141.

Terman, Lewis M., & Oden, Melita H. (1959). *Genetic studies of genius. v. the gifted group at mid-life.* Stanford, CA: Stanford University Press.

Terrace, H. S. (1979). *Nim.* New York: Knopf.

Terrace, H. S. (1985). In the beginning was the "name." *American Psychologist, 40*, 1011–1028.

Tesch, Stephanie, & Whitbourne, Susan K. (1982). Intimacy and identity status in young adults. *Journal of Personality and Social Psychology, 43*, 1041–1051.

Teyler, T. J., & DiScenna, P. (1987). Long-term potentiation. *Annual Review of Neuroscience, 10*, 131–161.

Thayer, Paul W. (1983). Industrial/organizational psychology: Science and application. In C. J. Scheirer & A. Rogers (eds.), *The G. Stanley Hall lecture series*, Vol. 3. Washington, DC: American Psychological Association.

Thoits, Peggy (1984). Coping, social support, and psychological outcomes: The central role of emotion. In P. Shaver (ed.), *Review of personality and social psychology: 5*. Beverly Hills, CA: Sage.

Thomas, Alexander, & Chess, Stella (1977). *Temperament and development.* New York: Brunner/Mazel.

Thomas, Alexander, & Chess, Stella (1980). *The dynamics of psychological development.* New York: Brunner/Mazel.

Thomas, Alexander, & Chess, Stella (1982). Temperament and follow-up to adulthood. In R. Porter & G. M. Collins (eds.), *Temperamental differences in infants and young children*. London: Pitman.

Thomas, Alexander, & Chess, Stella (1984). Genesis and evolution of behavioral disorders: From infancy to early adult life. *American Journal of Psychiatry, 141*, 1–9.

Thomas, Lewis (1983). *The youngest science: Notes of a medicine-watcher.* [Paperback edition: Toronto: Bantam.]

Thompson, James (1985). *Psychological aspects of nuclear war.* Chichester, England, and New York: The British Psychological Society and John Wiley & Sons.

Thompson, Richard F. (1983). Neuronal substrates of simple associative learning: Classical conditioning. *Trends in Neurosciences, 6*, 270–275.

Thompson, Richard F. (1986). The neurobiology of learning and memory. *Science, 233*, 941–947.

Thompson, Suzanne C. (1981). Will it hurt less if I can control it? A complex answer to a simple question. *Psychological Bulletin, 90*, 89–101.

Thorndike, E. L. (1898). Animal intelligence. An experimental study of the associative processes in animals. *Psychological Review Monograph Supplement, 2*(Whole No. 8).

Thorndike, E. L. (1903). *Educational psychology.* New York: Columbia University Teachers College.

Thornton, E. M. (1984). *The Freudian fallacy: An alternative view of Freudian theory.* Garden City, NY: Dial Press (Doubleday).

Thurstone, Louis L. (1938). Primary mental abilities. *Psychometric Monographs*, No. 1.

Tiefer, Leonore (1978). The kiss. *Human Nature, 1*, July, 28–37.

Tiffany, Phyllis G., & Tiffany, Donald W. (1983). Sex reversal of experienced control during the mid-life crisis. Paper presented at the annual meeting of the American Psychological Association, Anaheim, CA.

Tollison, C. David, & Adams, Henry E. (1979). *Sexual disorders: Treatment, theory, research.* New York: Garden Press.

Tolman, Edward C. (1948). Cognitive maps in rats and men. *Psychological Review, 55*, 189–208.

Tolman, E. C., & Honzik, C. H. (1930). Introduction and removal of reward and maze performance in rats. *University of California Publications in Psychology, 4*, 257–275.

Toman, Walter (1976). *Family constellation* (3rd ed.). New York: Springer.

Tomkins, Silvan S. (1981). The quest for primary motives: Biography and autobiography of an idea. *Journal of Personality and Social Psychology, 41*, 306–329.

Torrey, E. Fuller (1983). *Surviving schizophrenia.* New York: Harper & Row/Harper Colophon.

Tranel, Daniel, & Damasio, Antonio (1985). Knowledge without awareness: An autonomic index of facial recognition by prosopagnosics. *Science, 228*, 1453–1454.

Tranel, Daniel; Damasio, Antonio; & Damasio, Hanna (1988). Intact recognition of facial expression, gender, and age in patients with impaired recognition of face identity. *Neurology, 38*, 690–696.

Troll, Lillian (1986). Old age. In C. Travis (ed.), *EveryWoman's emotional well-being.* New York: Doubleday.

Tronick, Edward Z. (1989). Emotions and emotional communication in infants. *American Psychologist, 44*, 112–119.

Truax, Charles B. (1966). Reinforcement and nonreinforcement in Rogerian psychotherapy. *Journal of Abnormal Psychology, 71*, 1–9.

Tsunoda, Tadanobu (1985). *The Japanese brain: Uniqueness and universality.* [Yoshinori Oiwa trans.] Tokyo: Taishukan.

Tucker, Don M. (1989). Asymmetries of neural architecture and the structure of emotional experience. In R. Johnson & W. Roth (eds.), *Eighth event-related potentials international conference.* New York: Oxford University Press.

Tucker, Don M., & Williamson, Peter A. (1984). Asymmetric neural control systems in human self-regulation. *Psychological Review, 91*, 185–215.

Tulving, Endel (1985). How many memory systems are there? *American Psychologist, 40*, 385–398.

Turner, Barbara F., & Adams, Catherine G. (1988).

Reported change in preferred sexual activity over the adult years. *The Journal of Sex Research, 25,* 289–303.

Turner, Judith A., & Chapman, C. Richard (1982a). Psychological interventions for chronic pain: A critical review. I. Relaxation training and biofeedback. *Pain, 12,* 1–21.

Turner, Judith A., & Chapman, C. Richard (1982b). Psychological interventions for chronic pain: A critical review. II. Operant conditioning, hypnosis, and cognitive-behavioral therapy. *Pain, 12,* 23–46.

Tversky, Amos, & Kahneman, Daniel (1973). Availability: A heuristic for judging frequency and probability. *Cognitive Psychology, 5,* 207–232.

Tversky, Amos, & Kahneman, Daniel (1981). The framing of decisions and the psychology of choice. *Science, 211,* 453–458.

Tversky, Amos, & Kahneman, Daniel (1986). Rational choice and the framing of decisions. *Journal of Business, 59,* S251–S278.

Tyler, Leona E. (1981). More stately mansions—psychology extends its boundaries. *Annual Review of Psychology, 32,* 1–20.

Vaillant, George E. (1977). *Adaptation to life.* Boston: Little, Brown.

Vaillant, George E. (1978). A 10-year follow-up of remitting schizophrenics. *Schizophrenia Bulletin, 4,* 78–85.

Vaillant, George E. (1983). *The natural history of alcoholism: Causes, patterns, and paths to recovery.* Cambridge, MA: Harvard University Press.

Vaillant, George E., & Milofsky, Eva S. (1982). The etiology of alcoholism. *American Psychologist, 37,* 494–503.

Valenstein, Elliot (1986). *Great and desperate cures: The rise and decline of psychosurgery and other radical treatments for mental illness.* New York: Basic Books.

Van Cantfort, Thomas E., & Rimpau, James B. (1982). Sign language studies with children and chimpanzees. *Sign Language Studies, 34,* 15–72.

Vance, Ellen B., & Wagner, Nathaniel N. (1977). Written descriptions of orgasm: A study of sex differences. In D. Byrne & L. A. Byrne (eds.), *Exploring human sexuality.* New York: Crowell.

Vandenberg, Brian (1985). Beyond the ethology of play. In A. Gottfried & C. C. Brown (eds.), *Play interactions: The contribution of play materials & parental involvement to children's development.* Lexington, MA: Lexington Books.

Van Lancker, Diana R., & Kempler, Daniel (1987). Comprehension of familiar phrases by left- but not by right-hemisphere damaged patients. *Brain & Language, 32,* 265–277.

Varela, Jacobo A. (1978, October). Solving human problems with human science. *Human Nature, 1,* 84–90.

Veroff, Joseph (1983). Contextual determinants of personality. *Personality and Social Psychology Bulletin, 9,* 331–343.

Veroff, Joseph; Douvan, Elizabeth; & Kulka, Richard A. (1981). *The inner American.* New York: Basic Books.

Vila, J., & Beech, H. R. (1980). Premenstrual symptomatology: An interaction hypothesis. *British Journal of Social and Clinical Psychology, 19*(1), 73–80.

Visintainer, Madelon; Volpicelli, Joseph; & Seligman, Martin E. P. (1982). Tumor rejection in rats after inescapable or escapable shock. *Science, 216,* 437–439.

Vogel, Gerald W. (1978). Alternative view of neurobiology of dreaming. *American Journal of Psychiatry, 135,* 1531–1535.

Vokey, John R., & Read, J. Don (1985). Subliminal messages: Between the devil and the media. *American Psychologist, 40,* 1231–1239.

Von Lang, Jochen, & Sibyll, Claus (eds.) (1984). *Eichmann interrogated: Transcripts from the archives of the Israeli police.* New York: Random House.

Voss, Hans-Georg, & Keller, Heidi (1983). *Curiosity and exploration: Theories and results.* New York: Academic Press.

Wachtel, Paul (1977). *Psychoanalysis and behavior therapy: Toward an integration.* New York: Basic Books.

Wade, Carole (1986). Humor. In C. Tavris (ed.), *EveryWoman's emotional well-being.* New York: Doubleday.

Wade, Carole, & Cerise, Sarah (in press). *Human sexuality* (2nd ed.). San Diego: Harcourt Brace Jovanovich.

Wagemaker, Herbert, Jr., & Cade, Robert (1978). Hemodialysis in chronic schizophrenic patients. *Southern Medical Journal, 71,* 1463–1465.

Wagenaar, Willem A. (1986). My memory: A study of autobiographical memory over six years. *Cognitive Psychology, 18,* 225–252.

Wagner, Richard K., & Sternberg, Robert J. (1986). Tacit knowledge and intelligence in the everyday world. In R. J. Sternberg & R. K. Wagner (eds.), *Practical intelligence. Nature and origins of competence in the everyday world.* New York: Cambridge University Press.

Wagner, Richard V. (1985). Psychology and the threat of nuclear war. *American Psychologist, 40,* 531–535.

Walker, Edward L. (1970). Relevant psychology is a snark. *American Psychologist, 25,* 1081–1086.

Walker, Lenore (1984). Sex differences in the development of moral reasoning: A critical review. *Child Development, 55,* 677–691.

Walker, Lenore (1986). Diagnosis and politics: Abuse disorders. Paper presented at the annual meeting of the American Psychological Association, Washington.

Walker, Stephen (1982). *Animal thought.* London and Boston: Routledge Chapman & Hall.

Wallach, Michael A., & Wallach, Lise (1983). *Psychology's sanction for selfishness: The error of egoism in theory and therapy.* New York: Freeman.

Waller, Willard (1938). *The family: A dynamic interpretation.* New York: Dryden.

Wallerstein, Judith (1984). Children of divorce: Preliminary report of a ten-year follow-up of young children. *American Journal of Orthopsychiatry, 54,* 444–458.

Wallerstein, Judith, & Blakeslee, Sandra (1989). *Second chances: Men, women and children a decade after divorce.* New York: Ticknor & Fields.

Walster, Elaine, & Festinger, Leon (1962). The effectiveness of "overheard" persuasive communications. *Journal of Abnormal and Social Psychology, 65,* 395–402.

Warren, Gayle H., & Raynes, Anthony E. (1972). Mood changes during three conditions of alcohol intake. *Quarterly Journal of Studies on Alcohol, 33,* 979–989.

Watson, David, & Clark, Lee Anna (1984). Negative affectivity: The disposition to experience aversive emotional states. *Psychological Bulletin, 96,* 465–490.

Watson, David; Clark, Lee Anna; & Tellegen, Auke (1984). Cross-cultural convergence in the structure of mood: A Japanese replication and a comparison with U.S. findings. *Journal of Personality and Social Psychology, 47,* 127–144.

Watson, David, & Pennebaker, James W. (1989). Health complaints, stress, and distress: Exploring the central role of negative affectivity. *Psychological Review, 96,* 234–254.

Watson, John B. (1913). Psychology as the behaviorist views it. *Psychological Review, 20,* 158–177.

Watson, John B. (1925). *Behaviorism.* New York: Norton.

Watson, John B., & Rayner, Rosalie (1920). Conditioned emotional reactions. *Journal of Experimental Psychology, 3,* 1–14.

Watson, Peter (1981). *Twins: An uncanny relationship?* Chicago: Contemporary Books.

Webb, Wilse B. (1974). Sleep as an adaptive response. *Perceptual and Motor Skills, 38,* 1023–1027.

Webb, Wilse B., & Agnew, H. W., Jr. (1974). Sleep and waking in a time-free environment. *Aerospace Medicine, 45,* 617–622.

Webb, Wilse B., & Cartwright, Rosalind D. (1978). Sleep and dreams. In M. Rosenzweig & L. Porter (eds.), *Annual Review of Psychology, 29,* 223–252.

Wechsler, David (1955). *Manual for the Wechsler Adult Intelligence Scale.* New York: Psychological Corporation.

Wechsler, David (1958). *The measurement and appraisal of adult intelligence* (4th ed.). Baltimore: Williams & Wilkins.

Wegner, Daniel M.; Schneider, David J.; Carter, Samuel R., III; & White, Teri L. (1987). Paradoxical effects of thought suppression. *Journal of Personality and Social Psychology, 53,* 5–13.

Wehr, Thomas A.; Sack, David A.; & Rosenthal, Norman E. (1987). Seasonal affective disorder with summer depression and winter hypomania. *American Journal of Psychiatry, 144,* 1602–1603.

Weick, Karl E. (1984). Small wins: Redefining the scale of social problems. *American Psychologist, 39,* 40–49.

Weil, Andrew (1974a, June). Parapsychology: Andrew Weil's search for the true Geller. *Psychology Today, 8*(1), 45–50.

Weil, Andrew (1974b, July). Parapsychology: Andrew Weil's search for the true Geller—Part II. The letdown. *Psychology Today, 8*(2), 74–78, 82.

Weil, Andrew T. (1986). *The natural mind: A new way of looking at drugs and the higher consciousness.* Boston: Houghton Mifflin. [Originally published in 1972.]

Weiner, Bernard (1972). *Theories of motivation: From mechanism to cognition.* Chicago: Markham.

Weiner, Bernard (ed.) (1974). *Achievement motivation and attribution theory.* Morristown, NJ: General Learning Press.

Weiner, Bernard (1982). The emotional consequences of causal attributions. In M. S. Clark & S. T. Fiske (eds.), *Affect and cognition: The 17th annual Carnegie symposium on cognition.* Hillsdale, NJ: Erlbaum.

Weiner, Bernard (1985). Social psychology of emotions with some classroom implications. Paper presented at the annual meeting of the American Psychological Association, Los Angeles.

Weiner, Bernard, & Graham, Sandra (1984). An attributional approach to emotional development. In C. E. Izard, J. Kagan, & R. B. Zajonc (eds.), *Emotions, cognition, and behavior.* Cambridge, England: Cambridge University Press.

Weiner, Bernard; Russell, Dan; & Lerman, David (1978). Affective consequences of causal ascriptions. In J. H. Harvey, W. J. Ickes, & R. F. Kidd (eds.), *New directions in attribution research,* Vol. 2. Hillsdale, NJ: Erlbaum.

Weiner, Bernard; Russell, Dan; & Lerman, David (1979). The cognition-emotion process in achievement-related contexts. *Journal of Personality and Social Psychology, 37,* 1211–1220.

Weisburd, Stefi (1984, April 7). Food for mind and mood. *Science News, 125*(14), 216–219.

Weiss, Bernard; Williams, J. Hicks; Margen, Sheldon; Abrams, Barbara; et al. (1980, March 28). Behavioral responses to artifical food colors. *Science, 207,* 1487–1489.

Weiss, Robert (ed.) (1973). *Loneliness: The experience of emotional and social isolation.* Cambridge, MA: MIT Press.

Weiss, Robert (1975). *Marital separation.* New York: Basic Books.

Weisz, John R.; Rothbaum, Fred M.; & Blackburn, Thomas C. (1984). Standing out and standing in: The psychology of control in America and Japan. *American Psychologist, 39,* 955–969.

Welfel, Elizabeth R., & Davison, Mark L. (1986). The development of reflective judgment during the college years: A four-year longitudinal study. *Journal of College Student Personnel, 27,* 209–216.

Welwood, John (ed.) (1983). *Awakening the heart: East-west approaches to psychotherapy and the healing relationship.* Boulder, CO: Shambhala.

Wender, Paul H., & Klein, Donald F. (1981). *Mind, mood, and medicine: A guide to the new biopsychiatry.* New York: Farrar, Straus & Giroux.

Wenger, M. A., & Bagchi, B. K. (1961). Studies of autonomic functions in practitioners of Yoga in India. *Behavioral Science, 6,* 312–323.

Werner, Emmy, & Smith, Ruth S. (1982). *Vulnerable but invincible: A longitudinal study of resilient children and youth.* New York: McGraw-Hill.

Wessells, Michael G. (1982). *Cognitive psychology*. New York: Harper & Row.

West, Melissa O., & Prinz, Ronald J. (1987). Parental alcoholism and childhood psychopathology. *Psychological Bulletin, 102,* 204–218.

West, Robin L. (1984). Analysis of prospective everyday memory. Paper presented at the annual meeting of the American Psychological Association, Toronto.

White, Robert W. (1959). Motivation reconsidered: The concept of competence. *Psychological Review, 66,* 297–333.

White, Sheldon H., & Pillemer, David B. (1979). Childhood amnesia and the development of a socially accessible memory system. In J. F. Kihlstrom & F. J. Evans (eds.), *Functional disorders of memory*. Hillsdale, NJ: Erlbaum.

Whiting, Beatrice B., & Edwards, Carolyn P. (1988). *Children of different worlds: The formation of social behavior*. Cambridge, MA: Harvard University Press.

Whiting, Beatrice, & Whiting, John (1975). *Children of six cultures*. Cambridge, MA: Harvard University Press.

Whorf, Benjamin L. (1941). The relation of habitual thought and behavior to language. In L. Spier (ed.), *Language, culture, and personality*. Menasha, WI: Sapir Memorial Publication Fund.

Whorf, Benjamin L. (1956). Science and linguistics. In J. B. Carroll (ed.), *Language, thought and reality: Selected writings of Benjamin Lee Whorf*. Cambridge, MA: MIT Press.

Wicklund, Robert A. (1974). *Freedom and reactance*. Potomac, MD: Erlbaum.

Wicklund, Robert A., & Brehm, Jack W. (1976). *Perspectives on cognitive dissonance*. Hillsdale, NJ: Erlbaum.

Wilen, J. (1979). Changing relationships among grandparents, parents, and their young-adult children. Paper presented at the annual meeting of the Gerontological Society of America, Washington.

Wiley, James, & Camacho, Terry (1980). Life-style and future health: Evidence from the Alameda County Study. *Preventive Medicine, 9,* 1–21.

Williams, Redford (1989). *The trusting heart: Great news about Type A behavior*. New York: Random House.

Williams, Redford B., Jr.; Barefoot, John C.; & Shekelle, Richard B. (1985). The health consequences of hostility. In M. A. Chesney & R. H. Rosenman (eds.), *Anger and hostility in cardiovascular and behavioral disorders*. New York: Hemisphere.

Wilner, Daniel; Walkley, Rosabelle; & Cook, Stuart (1955). *Human relations in interracial housing*. Minneapolis: University of Minnesota Press.

Wilson, Edward O. (1975). *Sociobiology: The new synthesis*. Cambridge, MA: Belknap/Harvard University Press.

Windholz, George, & Lamal, P. A. (1985). Kohler's insight revisited. *Teaching of Psychology, 12*(3). 165–167.

Wing, C. W., Jr., & Wallach, M. A. (1971). College admissions and the psychology of talent. New York: Holt, Rinehart and Winston.

Winick, Myron; Meyer, Knarig Katchadurian; & Harris, Ruth C. (1975). Malnutrition and environmental enrichment by early adoption. *Science, 190,* 1173–1175.

Winn, Rhonda L., & Newton, Niles (1982). Sexuality in aging. A study of 106 cultures. *Archives of Sexual Behavior, 11,* 283–298.

Winter, David G. (1988). The power motive in women—and men. *Journal of Personality and Social Psychology, 54,* 510–519.

Wispé, Lauren G., & Drambarean, Nicholas C. (1953). Physiological need, word frequency, and visual duration thresholds. *Journal of Experimental Psychology, 46,* 25–31.

Wolff, Wirt M., & Morris, Larry A. (1971). Intellectual and personality characteristics of parents of autistic children. *Journal of Abnormal Psychology, 77,* 155–161.

Wolpe, Joseph (1981). Behavior therapy versus psychoanalysis: Therapeutic and social implications. *American Psychologist, 36,* 159–164.

Wood, Gordon (1984). Research methodology: A decision-making perspective. In A. M. Rogers & C. J. Scheirer (eds.), *The G. Stanley Hall lecture series,* Vol. 4. Washington, DC: American Psychological Association.

Wooley, O. Wayne, & Wooley, Susan C. (1985). Color-A-Person: A new body image test. Paper delivered at the annual convention of the American Psychological Association, Los Angeles.

Wooley, Susan; Wooley, O. Wayne; & Dyrenforth, Susan (1979). Theoretical, practical, and social issues in behavioral treatments of obesity. *Journal of Applied Behavior Analysis, 12,* 3–25.

Woolfolk, Robert L., & Lehrer, Paul M. (1984). Are stress reduction techniques interchangeable or do they have specific effects?: A review of the comparative empirical literature. In R. L. Woolfolk & P. M. Lehrer (eds.) *Principles and practice of stress management*. New York: Guilford Press.

Woolfolk, Robert L., & Lehrer, Paul M. (eds.) (1984). *Principles and practice of stress management*. New York: Guilford Press.

Woolfolk, Robert L., & Richardson, Frank C. (1984). Behavior therapy and the ideology of modernity. *American Psychologist, 39,* 777–786.

Wright, R. L. D. (1976). *Understanding statistics: An informal introduction for the behavioral sciences*. New York: Harcourt Brace Jovanovich.

Wu, T-C; Tashkin, Donald P.; Djahed, B.; & Rose, J. E. (1988). Respiratory hazards of smoking marijuana as compared with tobacco. *New England Journal of Medicine, 318,* 347–351.

Wurtman, Richard J. (1982). Nutrients that modify brain function. *Scientific American, 264*(4), 50–59.

Wurtman, Richard J., & Lieberman, Harris R. (eds.) (1982–1983). *Research strategies for assessing the behavioral effects of foods and nutrients. Journal of Psychiatric Research, 17*(2), whole issue.

Wyatt, Gail Elizabeth (1988). The prevalence and sociocultural context of Afro-American and white American women's sexual abuse. Paper presented at the annual meeting of the American Psychological Association, Atlanta.

Wyatt, Gail E., & Mickey, M. Ray (1985). The support by parents and others as it mediates the effects of child sexual abuse: An exploratory study. Paper presented at the annual meeting of the American Psychological Association, Los Angeles.

Yoken, Carol, & Berman, Jeffrey S. (1984). Does paying a fee for psychotherapy alter the effectiveness of treatment? *Journal of Consulting and Clinical Psychology, 52*, 254–260.

Yuwiler, A.; Geller, E.; & Ritvo, E. (1985). Biochemical studies on autism. In A. Lajtha (ed.), *Handbook for neurobiochemistry*, Vol. 10. New York: Plenum.

Zahn-Waxler, Carolyn; Radke-Yarrow, Marian; & King, Robert (1979). Child-rearing and children's pro-social initiations toward victims of distress. *Child Development, 50*, 319–330.

Zajonc, Robert B. (1968). Attitudinal effects of mere exposure. *Journal of Personality and Social Psychology, 9, Monograph Supplement 2*, 1–27.

Zajonc, Robert B. (1980). Feeling and thinking: Preferences need no inferences. *American Psychologist, 35*, 151–175.

Zajonc, Robert B. (1984). On the primary of affect. *American Psychologist, 39*, 117–124.

Zajonc, Robert B. [R. B.] (1986). The decline and rise of scholastic aptitude scores: A prediction derived from the confluence model. *American Psychologist, 41*, 862–867.

Zajonc, Robert B., & Markus, Gregory B. (1975). Birth order and intellectual development. *Psychological Review, 82*, 74–88.

Zellman, Gail, & Goodchilds, Jacqueline (1983). Becoming sexual in adolescence. In E. R. Allgeier & N. B. McCormick (eds.). *Changing boundaries: Gender roles and sexual behavior*. Palo Alto, CA: Mayfield.

Zigler, Edward, & Berman, Winnie (1983). Discerning the future of early childhood intervention. *American Psychologist, 38*, 894–906.

Zilbergeld, Bernie (1983). *The shrinking of America: Myths of psychological change*. Boston: Little, Brown.

Zillmann, Dolf (1979). *Hostility and aggression*. Hillsdale, NJ: Erlbaum.

Zimbardo, Philip (1970). The human choice: Individuation, reason, and order versus deindividuation, impulse, and chaos. In W. J. Arnold & D. Levine (eds.), *Nebraska symposium on motivation, 1969*. Lincoln: University of Nebraska Press.

Zimbardo, Philip (1984). Mind control in Orwell's 1984 and ours. Paper presented at the annual meeting of the American Psychological Association, Toronto.

Zimbardo, Philip; Ebbesen, Ebbe; & Maslach, Christina (1977). *Influencing attitudes and changing behavior* (2nd ed.). Reading, MA: Addison-Wesley.

Zinberg, Norman (1974). The search for rational approaches to heroin use. In P. G. Bourne (ed.), *Addiction*. New York: Academic Press.

Zinberg, Norman (1984). *Drug, set, and setting: The basis for controlled intoxicant use*. New Haven, CT: Yale University Press.

Zinberg, Norman, & Harding, Wayne (1982). Control and intoxicant use: A theoretical and practical overview. In N. E. Zinberg & W. M. Harding (eds.), *Control over intoxicant use*. New York: Human Sciences Press.

Zivian, Marilyn, & Darjes, Richard (1983). Free recall by in-school and out-of-school adults: Performance and metamemory. *Developmental Psychology, 19*, 513–520.

Zubin, Joseph, & Spring, Bonnie (1977). Vulnerability: A new view of schizophrenia. *Journal of Abnormal Psychology, 86*, 103–126.

Zuckerman, Marvin (ed.) (1979). *Sensation seeking: Beyond the optimal level of arousal*. Hillsdale. NJ: Erlbaum.

Zuckerman, Marvin (ed.) (1983). *Biological bases of sensation seeking, impulsivity, and anxiety*. Hillsdale, NJ: Erlbaum.

Zuckerman, Marvin; Kuhlman, D. Michael; & Camac, Curt (1988). What lies beyond E and N? Factor analyses of scales believed to measure basic dimensions of personality. *Journal of Personality and Social Psychology, 54*, 96–107.

CREDITS

TEXT AND TABLES

CHAPTER 1 Page 30, George Miller in Jonathan Miller, *States of Mind*, pp. 15–16, © 1983 by Pantheon Books, a division of Random House, Inc. / p. 80, from Oliver Sacks, *The Man Who Mistook His Wife for a Hat*, © 1985 by Summit Books, a division of Simon & Schuster.
CHAPTER 3 Page 108, from Richard Restak, "Is free will a fraud?" *Science Digest, 91*(10), October 1983.
CHAPTER 4 Pages 131–132, from Ernest R. Hilgard, "Hypnosis and consciousness," *Human Nature* Magazine, January 1978, © 1977 by Human Nature, Inc.; reprinted by permission of the publisher / p. 132, from Peretz Lavie and Daniel F. Kripke, "Ultradian rhythms: The 90-minute clock inside us," *Psychology Today,* April 1975, p. 65, © 1975 PT Partners, L. P.; reprinted with permission from *Psychology Today* Magazine / p. 135, from J. Allan Hobson, *The Dreaming Brain,* © 1988 by Basic Books, Inc.
CHAPTER 5 Page 160, Table 5.1, from Eugene Galanter, "Contemporary psychophysics," in R. Brown, E. Galanter, E. H. Hess, and G. Mandler (eds.), *New Directions in Psychology,* Holt, Rinehart and Winston, 1962, p. 97 / p. 162, Table 5.2, from F. A. Geldard, *Fundamentals of Psychology,* p. 93, © 1962 by John Wiley & Sons, Inc. / p. 180, from Oliver Sacks, *The Man Who Mistook His Wife for a Hat,* © 1985 by Summit Books, a division of Simon & Schuster.
CHAPTER 6 Page 227, from Paul Chance, "Knock wood," *Psychology Today,* October 1988, pp. 68–69, © 1988 PT Partners, L. P.; reprinted with permission from *Psychology Today* Magazine / pp. 240–241, from Robert A. Rescorla, "Pavlovian conditioning: It's not what you think it is," *American Psychologist 43,* © 1988 by the American Psychological Association; reprinted by permission of the publisher.
CHAPTER 8 Page 288, from Sylvia Scribner, "Modes of thinking and ways of speaking: Culture and logic reconsidered," in P. N. Johnson-Laird and P. C. Wason (eds.), *Thinking: Read-*

ings in Cognitive Science, 1977, Cambridge University Press, New York / pp. 307–308, Albert Einstein in John Briggs, "The genius mind," *Science Digest, 92*(12), December 1984, p. 103.
CHAPTER 10 Page 346, from Robert A. Emmons and Laura A. King, "Conflict among personal strivings: Immediate and long-term implications for psychological and physical well-being," *Journal of Personality & Social Psychology, 54,* © 1988 by the American Psychological Association; reprinted by permission of the publisher / p. 365, reprinted with permission from *Los Angeles* Magazine, October 1988, © *Los Angeles* Magazine; all rights reserved.
CHAPTER 11 Page 388, from Sigmund Freud, *The Ego and the Id,* translated by James Strachey, © 1960 by James Strachey; used by permission of W. W. Norton & Co., Inc. / p. 397, from Sigmund Freud, "The psychogenesis of a case of homosexuality in a woman," in S. Freud, *Sexuality and the Psychology of Love,* 1920/1963, Collier Books / p. 415, from C. R. Snyder and Randee J. Shenkel, "The P. T. Barnum effect," *Psychology Today,* March 1975, © 1975 PT Partners, L. P.; reprinted with permission from *Psychology Today* Magazine.
CHAPTER 12 Page 435, John B. Watson, *Behaviorism,* 1925, W. W. Norton & Co., Inc., p. 104 / p. 444, Alan Sroufe, "Attachment and the roots of competence," *Human Nature* Magazine, October 1978, © 1978 by Human Nature, Inc.; reprinted by permission of the publisher / p. 452, from Richard C. Lewontin, Steve Rose, and Leon J. Kamin, *Not in Our Genes: Biology, Ideology, and Human Nature,* p. 11, © 1984 by Pantheon Books, a division of Random House, Inc.
CHAPTER 13 Page 459, from Jerome Kagan, *The Nature of the Child,* © 1984 by Basic Books, Inc. / p. 462, from Helen Bee, *The Developing Child,* 1989, Harper & Row, Publishers, Inc. / p. 466, Table 13.2, from Paul H. Mussen et al., *Child Development and Personality,* 1984, Harper & Row, Publishers, Inc. / p. 472, from Daniel Slobin, *Psycholinguistics,* 1979, Scott, Foresman and Co. / p. 474, from Helen Bee, *The Developing Child,* 1989, Harper

& Row, Publishers, Inc. / p. 482, Table 13.3, from Teresa L. Jump and Linda Haas, "Fathers in transition: Dual-career fathers participating in child care," in M. S. Kimmel (ed.), *Changing Men: New Directions in Research on Men and Masculinity,* © 1987 by Sage Publications, Inc.; reprinted by permission of the publisher.
CHAPTER 15 Page 545, from James W. Pennebaker, Janice Kiecolt-Glaser, and Ronald Glaser, "Disclosure of traumas and immune function: Health implications for psychotherapy," *Journal of Consulting and Clinical Psychology, 56,* © 1988 by the American Psychological Association; reprinted by permission of the publisher / p. 550, from Shelley Taylor, "Adjustment to life events: A theory of cognitive adaptation," *American Psychologist, 38,* © 1983 by the American Psychological Association; reprinted by permission of the publisher.
CHAPTER 16 Page 585, from Leslie Farber, "Merchandising depression," *Psychology Today,* April 1979, © 1979 PT Partners, L. P.; reprinted with permission from *Psychology Today* Magazine / p. 590, from Elton McNeil, *The Quiet Furies, Man and Disorder,* p. 81, © 1967 by Prentice-Hall, Inc., Englewood Cliffs, NJ; reprinted by permission of the publisher / p. 602, from Henry Rollin (ed.), *Coping with Schizophrenia,* 1980, Burnett, London / p. 603, from Eugen Bleuler, *Dementia Praecox or the Group of Schizophrenias,* 1950, International Universities Press, Madison CT / p. 606, from E. Fuller Torrey, *Surviving Schizophrenia,* © 1983 by E. Fuller Torrey; reprinted by permission of Harper & Row, Publishers, Inc.
CHAPTER 17 Page 619, from Berton Rouché, "The hoofbeats of a zebra," *The Medical Detectives,* vol. 2, 1984, E. P. Dutton (story first appeared in *The New Yorker*), © 1984 by Berton Rouché; reprinted by permission of Harold Ober Associates.
CHAPTER 18 Page 662, from Dean Peabody, *National Characteristics,* 1985, Cambridge University Press, New York / pp. 663–664, from Robert Abelson, "Conviction," *American Psychologist, 43,* © 1988 by the American Psychological Association; reprinted by permission of

AUTHOR INDEX

SUBJECT INDEX

ABOUT THE AUTHORS

Carole Wade earned her Ph.D. in cognitive psychology at Stanford University. She began her academic career at the University of New Mexico, was professor of psychology for ten years at San Diego Mesa College, and currently teaches undergraduate courses, including introductory psychology, at the College of Marin. She is author of *Human Sexuality* (2nd edition forthcoming) and coauthor (with Carol Tavris) of *The Longest War: Sex Differences in Perspective,* which is going into its third edition. A former associate editor of *Psychology Today,* she has a longstanding interest in making psychology accessible to the public; she lectures widely and has written numerous general-interest articles. She is a member of Divisions 1, 2, and 35 of the American Psychological Association; a charter member of the American Psychological Society; past chair of the APA's Public Information Committee; and a current member of the APA's Committee on Undergraduate Education.

Carol Tavris earned her Ph.D. in the interdisciplinary social psychology program at the University of Michigan. After taking her degree, she served as an editor at *Psychology Today* (until 1976), and she continues to contribute to many magazines. Highly regarded as a national and international lecturer, she has given keynote addresses and workshops on, among other topics, critical thinking, anger, gender, and psychology and the media. She is author of the acclaimed *Anger: The Misunderstood Emotion,* published in a second edition in 1989; coauthor (with Carole Wade) of *The Longest War: Sex Differences in Perspective;* and editor of *EveryWoman's Emotional Well-Being* (being published in paperback in 1990). She has taught at the Human Relations Center of the New School for Social Research in New York, and she now teaches psychology courses at UCLA. She is a Fellow of Divisions 9 and 35 of the American Psychological Association and a member of Divisions 1 and 8; a charter member of the American Psychological Society; and a member of The International Society for Research on Emotion.